1000
LOW

FAT

SALT

SUGAR

CHOLESTEROL

HEALTHY

RECIPES

1000
LOW

FAT

SALT

SUGAR

CHOLESTEROL

HEALTHY

RECIPES

p

This is a Parragon Publishing Book
This edition published in 2001

Parragon Publishing
Queen Street House
4 Queen Street
Bath BA1 1HE, UK

ISBN: 0-75255-804-8

Printed in China

NOTE

Cup measurements in this book are for American cups.
This book also uses imperial and metric measurements. Follow the same units
of measurement throughout; do not mix imperial and metric.
All spoon measurements are level: teaspoons are assumed to be 5 ml and
tablespoons are assumed to be 15 ml.
Unless otherwise stated, milk is assumed to be whole milk,
eggs and individual vegetables such as potatoes are medium,
and pepper is freshly ground black pepper.

The nutritional information provided for each recipe is per serving or per person.
Optional ingredients, variations, or serving suggestions have
not been included in the calculations. The times given for each recipe are an approximate
guide only because the preparation times may differ according to the techniques used by
different people and the cooking times may vary as a result of the type of oven used.

Recipes using raw or very lightly cooked eggs should be
avoided by infants, the elderly, pregnant women, convalescents,
and anyone suffering from an illness.

contents

INTRODUCTION

This book contains 1,000 recipes selected to help you improve your health by reducing your intake of saturated fats, salt, and sugar. Each recipe contains the following information: nutritional calculations, preparation and cooking times, and level of difficulty (one chef's hat for an easy recipe, rising to five chef's hats for a difficult recipe).

basic recipes

Many recipes can be adapted by choosing lowfat alternatives to the basic ingredients.

Cornstarch Paste

Cornstarch paste is made by mixing 1 part cornstarch with about 1½ parts of cold water. Stir the mixture until smooth. This paste can be used to thicken sauces.

Basic Pasta Dough

1 lb/450 g durum wheat flour

4 eggs, lightly beaten

1 tbsp olive oil

pinch of lowsodium salt

1 Lightly flour a clean counter. Sift the flour with a pinch of salt into a mound. Make a well in the center and add the eggs and olive oil. Bring the mixture together using a fork or your fingertips, until the ingredients are thoroughly combined. Knead the dough vigorously for 10–15 minutes.

2 Let the dough rest for about 25 minutes, before rolling it out as thinly and evenly as possible.

Béchamel Sauce

generous 1 cup skim milk

4 cloves

1 bay leaf

pinch of freshly grated nutmeg

2 tbsp polyunsaturated margarine

2 tbsp plain flour

pepper and lowsodium salt

1 Put the milk in a pan and add the cloves, bay leaf, and nutmeg. Gradually bring to a boil. Remove from the heat and let stand for 15 minutes.

2 Melt the margarine in another pan and stir in the flour to make a roux. Cook gently, stirring, for 1 minute. Remove the pan from the heat.

3 Strain the milk and gradually blend into the roux. Return the pan to the heat and gently bring to a boil, stirring, until the sauce thickens. Season with pepper and a pinch of salt.

Variations

All sorts of ingredients can be added to the basic Béchamel recipe to make interesting, lowfat sauces which go particularly well with vegetables and fish.

Watercress Sauce

Add 1 small bunch of watercress, finely chopped, to the basic sauce. If you can't find watercress, you can use 1 small bunch of baby spinach instead.

Green Herb Sauce

Add 1–2 tablespoon chopped fresh mixed herbs to the sauce just before serving.

Parsley Sauce

Add 2 tablespoons finely chopped fresh parsley to the basic sauce.

Mushroom Sauce

Wash and finely slice 125 g/4 oz button mushrooms, and add them to the basic sauce with 1 tablespoon of finely chopped fresh tarragon.

Lemon Sauce

Add some finely grated lemon zest and lemon juice to the basic sauce.

Mustard Sauce

Add 1 tablespoon French mustard and a squeeze of lemon juice to the basic sauce.

Basic Tomato Sauce

1 tbsp olive oil

1 small onion, chopped

1 garlic clove, chopped

14 oz/400 g canned chopped tomatoes

2 tbsp chopped fresh parsley

1 tsp dried oregano

2 bay leaves

2 tbsp tomato paste

1 tsp sugar

pepper and lowsodium salt

1 Heat the oil in a pan over a medium heat and fry the onion for 2–3 minutes or until translucent. Add the garlic and fry for 1 minute. Stir in the chopped tomatoes, parsley, oregano, bay leaves, tomato paste, and sugar, and season with pepper and a pinch of salt.

2 Bring the sauce to a boil, then lower the heat and simmer, uncovered, for 15–20 minutes, or until the sauce has reduced by half. Discard the bay leaves just before serving.

Red Wine Sauce

generous 1¾ cups Vegetable Stock (see page 8)

generous 1¾ cups red wine

small piece of onion, peeled

1 garlic clove, peeled and sliced

1 bay leaf

1 sprig fresh thyme

2–3 sprigs fresh parsley

½ tsp black peppercorns

1 tbsp redcurrant jelly

3 tbsp polyunsaturated margarine

1½ tbsp plain flour

pepper and lowsodium salt

1 Put the stock and red wine in a pan with the onion, garlic, bay leaf, thyme and parsley sprigs, and peppercorns. Bring to a boil and boil for 10–15 minutes to reduce the liquid by half.

2 Strain the liquid into a clean pan and mix in the redcurrant jelly, some pepper, and a pinch of salt.

3 Mix half the margarine with the flour to make a paste and add to the warm sauce in small pieces. Mix well after each addition.

4 Return the sauce to the heat and stir gently until it thickens slightly. Simmer gently for a few minutes to cook the flour. Beat in the remaining margarine just before serving.

Cheese Sauce

2 tbsp polyunsaturated margarine

4 tbsp plain flour

1 bay leaf

generous 1¾ cups skim milk

⅔ cup grated mature half-fat
   Cheddar cheese

1 tsp English mustard powder

pinch of cayenne pepper

black pepper

1 Melt the margarine in a pan and stir in the flour. Cook, stirring, over a low heat until the roux is light in color and crumbly in texture. Add the bay leaf. Stir in one-third of the milk, beat until the sauce is thick, then repeat twice to use all the milk.

2 Remove the sauce from the heat, remove the bay leaf, and beat in the grated cheese, mustard, a small pinch of cayenne pepper, and the black pepper. There is no need to add extra salt because the cheese will be salty.

Sweet and Sour Sauce

1 onion

1 tbsp oil

2 tsp cornstarch

generous 1¾ cups water

¼ tsp mustard powder

1 tbsp wine vinegar

1 tsp sugar

1 tsp soy sauce

8 oz/225 g pineapple, canned in its
   own juice

½ very small green bell pepper

1 tomato, skinned

black pepper and salt

1 Finely chop the onion and cook it gently in the oil until tender, then add the cornstarch. Remove from the heat and add the water, stirring constantly.

2 Simmer gently for 5 minutes. Add the mustard, vinegar, sugar, and soy sauce. Drain and chop the pineapple, then add it to the mixture with the chopped green bell pepper and tomato. Season with pepper and a pinch of salt and simmer for another 2–3 minutes.

Yogurt and Cucumber Sauce

Mix together 1¼ cups lowfat natural yogurt with 3–4 tablespoons finely chopped cucumber and 1 tablespoon chopped fresh herbs such as fennel, dill, and mint.

Yogurt and Fresh Herb Sauce

Mix 1¼ cups lowfat natural yogurt with 2 tablespoons chopped fresh herbs—parsley, chives, thyme, or mint—and season with pepper and a little lowsodium salt.

Lemon Lentil Sauce

Use this sauce to add lowfat protein to vegetables.

Soak 4½ oz/125 g lentils overnight in water, then simmer until tender. Chop 1 onion and fry it gently in 1 tablespoon of oil with 2 teaspoons of curry power for 10 minutes. Add the juice and grated zest of one lemon, then puree the sauce in a food processor. Season with pepper and a pinch of salt.

Fresh Fish Stock

1 lb/450 g fish trimmings

2½ cups water

1 onion, quartered

2 celery stalks, chopped

3–4 sprigs fresh parsley

1 bay leaf

pinch of dried thyme

⅔ cup white wine

pepper and lowsodium salt

1 Place the fish trimmings in a large pan, add the rest of the ingredients, and season with pepper and a pinch of salt.

2 Bring the stock to simmering point, and simmer, uncovered, for about 20 minutes.

3 Strain the stock and cool. Store in the refrigerator and use within 2 days.

Chinese Stock

Use this delicious stock to add an authentic flavor to Chinese soups and other recipes where cooking liquid is required.
Makes 5¼ pints/2.5 liters.

1 lb 10 oz/750 g chicken pieces

1 lb 10 oz/750 g pork spare ribs

7¾ pints/3.75 liters cold water

3–4 pieces ginger root, crushed

3–4 scallions, each tied into a knot

3–4 tbsp Chinese rice wine or dry sherry

1 Trim off any excess fat from the chicken and spare ribs; chop them into large pieces.

2 Place the chicken and pork in a large pan with the water, and add the ginger and scallion knots.

3 Bring to a boil, and skim off any scum. Reduce the heat and simmer, uncovered, for at least 2–3 hours.

4 Strain the stock, discarding the chicken, pork, ginger, and scallions. Add the wine and return to the boil. Simmer for 2–3 minutes.

5 Cool the stock and store in the refrigerator—it will keep for up to 4–5 days. Alternatively, freeze in small containers and use as required.

Fresh Vegetable Stock

Keep this stock refrigerated for up to 3 days, or frozen for up to 3 months. Makes 6 cups.

9 oz/250 g shallots

1 large carrot, diced

1 celery stalk, chopped

½ fennel bulb

1 garlic clove

1 bay leaf

4–6 sprigs of fresh parsley and tarragon

8 cups water

pepper

1 Put all the ingredients in a large pan and bring to a boil.

2 Skim off the surface scum with a flat spoon and reduce to a gentle simmer. Partially cover and cook for 45 minutes. Let cool.

3 Line a sieve with clean cheesecloth and put it over a large pitcher or

bowl. Pour the stock through the sieve. Discard the herbs and vegetables.

4 Cover with plastic wrap and store in the refrigerator or freezer until ready to use.

Fresh Beef Stock

Makes 7 cups.

2 lb 4 oz/1 kg bones from a cooked joint or raw chopped beef

2 onions, studded with 6 cloves, or sliced or roughly chopped

2 carrots, sliced

1 leek, sliced

1–2 celery stalks, sliced

1 bouquet garni

about 5 pints/2.25 liters water

1 Use chopped marrow bones with a few strips of shin of beef if possible. If uncooked, roast in a preheated oven at 450°F/230°C for 30–50 minutes, until browned.

2 Transfer to a large pan with the other ingredients. Bring to a boil and remove any scum from the surface with a perforated spoon.

3 Cover and simmer gently for 3–4 hours. Strain the stock and let cool. Remove any fat from the surface, cover with plastic wrap, and chill in the refrigerator. Use within 24 hours.

4 The stock may be frozen for up to 2 months. Place in a large plastic bag and seal, leaving at least 1 inch/2.5 cm of headspace to allow for expansion.

Fresh Chicken Stock

Makes 7 cups.

2 lb 4 oz/1 kg chicken, skinned

2 celery stalks, roughly chopped

1 onion, sliced

2 carrots, sliced

1 garlic clove

3 sprigs of fresh parsley

8 cups water

pepper and lowsodium salt

1 Put all the ingredients into a large pan.

2 Bring to the boil. Skim away surface scum using a large flat spoon. Reduce the heat to a gentle simmer, partially cover, and cook for 2 hours. Let cool.

3 Line a sieve with clean cheesecloth and place over a large pitcher or bowl. Pour the stock through the sieve. Use the cooked chicken in another recipe. Discard the other solids. Cover the stock with plastic wrap and chill.

4 Skim away any fat that forms before using the stock. Store in the refrigerator for 3–4 days, until required, or freeze in small batches.

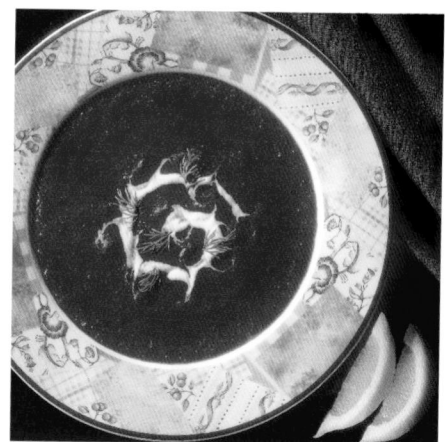

Salads and Appetizers

Salads are among the most versatile of dishes, and can serve a multitude of purposes. Some, such as Spicy Chicken Salad and Lentil & Shiitake Salad, are substantial enough for a main course. Others, such as Mozzarella & Tomato Salad, make superb accompaniments— especially to grilled meat and fish. Still others, such as Lobster & Avocado Salad, are perfect appetizers for a dinner party.

This chapter also includes a wide range of hot and cold appetizers, from familiar favorites, such as Taramasalata and Guacamole, to more exotic dishes, such as Asian Lettuce Cups and Salpicon of Crab. There is something special here for everyone and for every occasion.

Spicy Chicken Salad

This is an excellent recipe for leftover roast chicken. Add the dressing just before serving, so that the spinach retains its crispness.

NUTRITIONAL INFORMATION

Calories	225	Sugars	.........4g
Protein	........25g	Fat	..........12g
Carbohydrate	....4g	Saturates	......2g

 10 mins   0 mins

SERVES 4

INGREDIENTS

8 oz/225 g young spinach leaves

3 celery stalks, thinly sliced

½ cucumber, thinly sliced

2 scallions, thinly sliced

3 tbsp chopped fresh parsley

12 oz/350 g boneless, lean roast chicken, thinly sliced

smoked almonds, to garnish (optional)

DRESSING

1 inch/2.5 cm piece fresh ginger root, finely grated

3 tbsp olive oil

1 tbsp white wine vinegar

1 tbsp honey

½ teaspoon ground cinnamon

salt and pepper

1 Thoroughly wash and dry the spinach leaves on paper towels.

2 Toss the celery, cucumber, and scallions with the spinach and parsley in a large bowl.

3 Transfer the salad ingredients to serving plates and arrange the chicken on top.

4 To make the dressing, combine the grated ginger, olive oil, wine vinegar, honey, and cinnamon in a screw-topped jar and shake well to mix. Season with salt and pepper to taste.

5 Pour the dressing over the salad. Scatter a few smoked almonds over the salad to garnish, if using.

COOK'S TIP

For extra color, add some cherry tomatoes and some thin strips of red and yellow bell peppers and garnish with a little grated carrot.

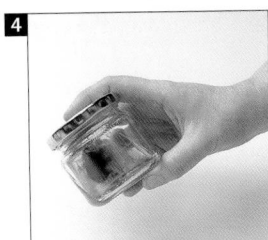

Asian Chicken Salad

Mirin—Japanese sweet rice wine—soy sauce, and sesame oil give an Asian flavor to this delicious salad.

NUTRITIONAL INFORMATION

Calories	361	Sugars	2g
Protein	34g	Fat	16g
Carbohydrate	17g	Saturates	3g

 5 mins   35 mins

SERVES 4

I N G R E D I E N T S

4 skinless, boneless chicken breasts

5 tbsp mirin or sweet sherry

5 tbsp light soy sauce

1 tbsp sesame oil

3 tbsp olive oil

1 tbsp red wine vinegar

1 tbsp Dijon mustard

9 oz/250 g egg noodles

4½ cups bean sprouts

9 oz/250 g Napa cabbage, shredded

2 scallions, sliced

1⅔ cups sliced mushrooms

1 fresh red chile, finely sliced, to garnish

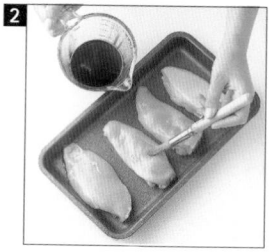  

1 Pound the chicken breasts out to an even thickness between two sheets of plastic wrap with a rolling pin or cleaver.

2 Put the chicken breasts in a roasting pan. Combine the mirin and soy sauce and brush over the chicken.

3 Cook the chicken in a preheated oven, 400°F/200°C, for 20–30 minutes, basting it frequently.

4 Remove the chicken from the oven and let cool slightly.

5 Combine the sesame oil, olive oil, and red wine vinegar with the mustard in a small bowl.

6 Cook the noodles according to the instructions on the packet. Rinse under cold running water to prevent any further cooking, then drain.

7 Toss the noodles in the dressing until the noodles are completely coated.

8 Lightly toss the bean sprouts, Napa cabbage, scallions, and mushrooms with the noodles.

9 Slice the cooked chicken very thinly and stir it into the noodles. Garnish the salad with the chile slices and serve.

Chicken & Papaya Salad

Try this recipe with a selection of different tropical fruits for an equally tasty and refreshing salad.

NUTRITIONAL INFORMATION

Calories	408	Sugars	.........8g
Protein	........30g	Fat	..........28g
Carbohydrate	...10g	Saturates	.......5g

5 mins   15 mins

SERVES 4

INGREDIENTS

4 skinless, boneless chicken breasts

1 red chile, deseeded and chopped

2 tbsp red wine vinegar

5 tbsp olive oil

1 papaya, peeled

1 avocado, peeled

2 cups alfalfa sprouts

2 cups bean sprouts

salt and pepper

TO GARNISH

diced red bell pepper

diced cucumber

1 Poach the chicken breasts in boiling water for about 15 minutes or until cooked through.

2 Remove the chicken with a slotted spoon and set aside to cool.

3 To make the dressing, combine the chile, red wine vinegar, and olive oil, season well with salt and pepper, and set aside.

4 Place the chicken breasts on a cutting board. Using a very sharp knife, cut the chicken breasts across the grain into thin diagonal slices. Set aside.

5 Slice the papaya and avocado to the same thickness as the chicken.

6 Arrange the slices of papaya and avocado, together with the chicken, in an alternating pattern on four serving plates.

7 Arrange the alfalfa sprouts and bean sprouts on the serving plates and garnish with the diced red bell pepper and cucumber. Serve the salad with the dressing.

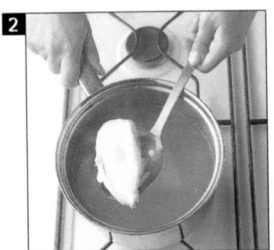

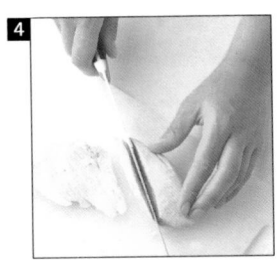

VARIATION

Try this recipe with peaches or nectarines instead of sliced papaya.

Mango Salad

This is an unusual combination but works well as long as the mango is very unripe. Papaya can be used instead, if you prefer.

NUTRITIONAL INFORMATION

Calories 26   Sugars 3g
Protein . . . . .1g   Fat 0.2g
Carbohydrate . . . .6g   Saturates 0g

 10 mins   ⏱ 0 mins

SERVES 4

I N G R E D I E N T S

1 large unripe mango, peeled and cut into long thin shreds

1 small fresh red chile, deseeded and finely chopped

2 shallots, finely chopped

2 tbsp lemon juice

1 tbsp light soy sauce

6 roasted canned chestnuts, quartered

1 watermelon, to serve

1 lollo biondo lettuce, or any crunchy lettuce

½ cup cilantro leaves

1 Soak the mango briefly in cold water, in order to remove any syrup. Meanwhile, combine the chile, shallots, lemon juice, and soy sauce. Drain the mango and combine with the chestnuts.

2 To make the melon basket, stand the watermelon on one end on a level surface. Holding a knife level and in one place, turn the watermelon on its axis so that the knife marks an even line all around the middle. Mark a 1 inch/2.5 cm wide handle across the top and through the center stem, joining the middle line at either end. (If you prefer a zigzag finish, mark the shape to be cut at this point

before any cuts are made, to ensure an even zigzag line.)

3 Take a sharp knife and, following the marks made for the handle, make the first vertical cut. Then cut down the other side of the handle. Now follow the middle line and make your straight or zigzag cut, taking care that the knife is always pointing towards the center of the

watermelon and is level with the counter, as this ensures that when you reach the handle cuts, the cut out piece of melon will pull away cleanly.

4 Hollow out the flesh with a spoon, leaving a clean edge. Line the melon basket with the lettuce and cilantro. Fill with the salad, pour over the dressing, and serve immediately.

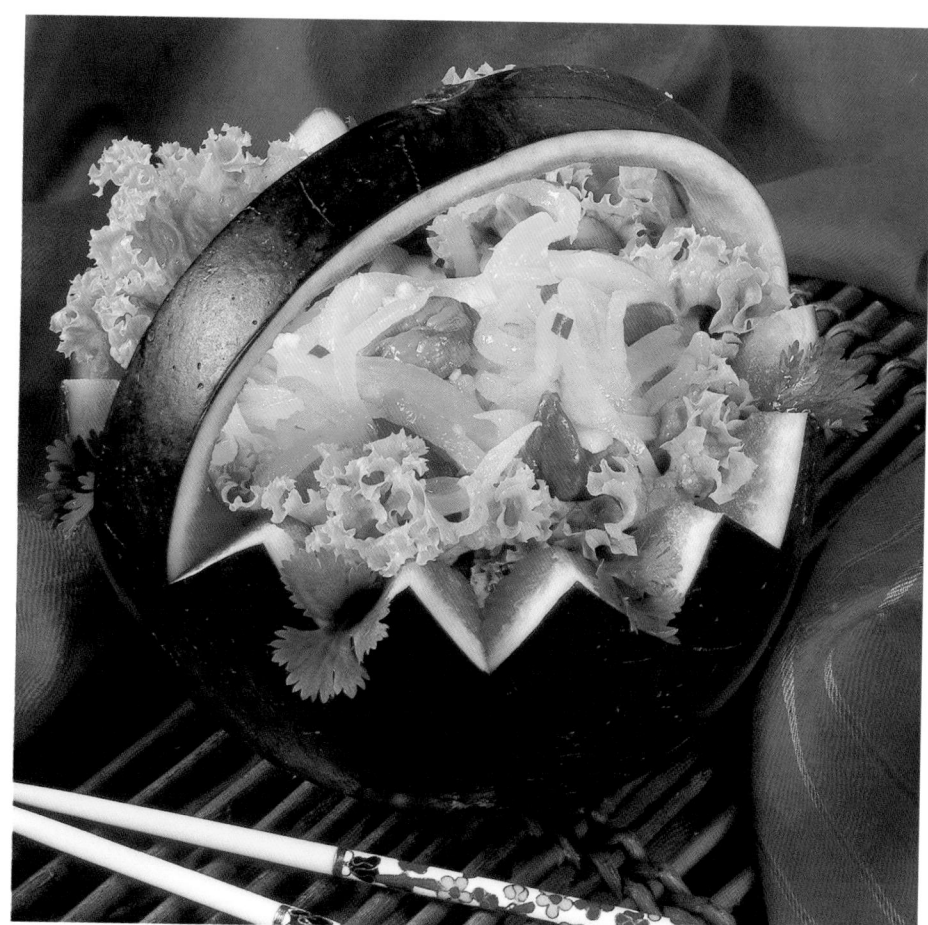

Grapefruit & Cheese Salad

Fresh pink grapefruit segments, ripe avocados, and sliced Italian dolcelatte cheese make a deliciously different salad combination.

NUTRITIONAL INFORMATION

Calories	390	Sugars	.........3g
Protein	........13g	Fat	..........36g
Carbohydrate	....4g	Saturates	......13g

25 mins · 0 mins

SERVES 4

INGREDIENTS

½ Romaine lettuce

½ oak leaf lettuce

2 pink grapefruit

2 ripe avocados

6 oz/175 g dolcelatte cheese, thinly sliced

fresh basil sprigs, to garnish

DRESSING

4 tbsp olive oil

1 tbsp white wine vinegar

salt and pepper

1 Arrange the lettuce leaves on 4 serving plates or in a salad bowl.

2 Remove the peel and pith from the grapefruit with a sharp serrated knife, catching the grapefruit juice in a bowl.

3 Segment the grapefruit by cutting down each side of the membrane. Remove all the membrane. Arrange the segments on the serving plates.

4 Peel, pit, and slice the avocados, dipping them in the grapefruit juice to prevent discoloration. Arrange the slices on the salad with the dolcelatte cheese.

5 To make the dressing, combine any remaining grapefruit juice with the olive oil and wine vinegar. Season with salt and pepper to taste, mixing thoroughly to combine.

6 Drizzle the dressing over the salads. Garnish with fresh basil leaves and serve immediately.

COOK'S TIP

Pink grapefruit segments make a very attractive color combination with the avocados, but ordinary grapefruit will work just as well. To help avocados to ripen, keep them at room temperature in a brown paper bag.

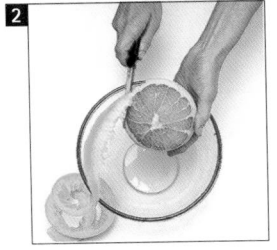

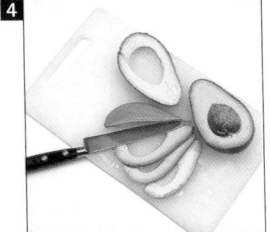

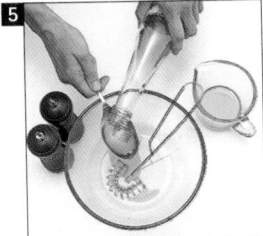

Tomato & Pasta Salad

Pasta tastes perfect in this lively salad, combined with onion and cherry tomatoes and dressed with wine vinegar, lemon juice, basil, and olive oil.

NUTRITIONAL INFORMATION

Calories 228	Sugars 4g
Protein 5g	Fat 12g
Carbohydrate ...27g	Saturates 2g

 50 mins   20 mins

SERVES 4

I N G R E D I E N T S

1½ cups dried pasta shapes

1 yellow bell pepper, halved, and deseeded

2 small zucchini, sliced

1 red onion, thinly sliced

4½ oz/125 g cherry tomatoes, halved

salt

fresh basil sprigs, to garnish

D R E S S I N G

4 tbsp olive oil

2 tbsp red wine vinegar

2 tsp lemon juice

1 tsp mustard

½ tsp superfine sugar

a handful of fresh basil leaves, torn into small pieces

salt and pepper

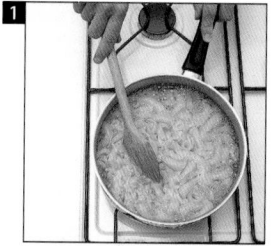
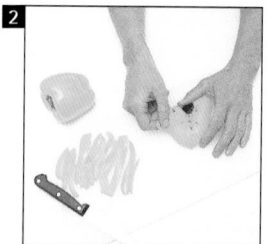

1 Cook the pasta shapes in a large pan of lightly salted boiling water for 8–10 minutes or until tender, but still firm to the bite.

2 Meanwhile, place the bell pepper halves, skin side up, under a preheated broiler until they begin to char. Remove, place in a plastic bag and tie the top. When cool enough to handle, peel off the skins and slice the flesh into strips.

3 Cook the zucchini in a small amount of lightly salted boiling water for 3–4 minutes, until cooked, yet still crunchy. Drain and refresh under cold running water to cool quickly and prevent any further cooking.

4 To make the dressing, mix together the olive oil, red wine vinegar, lemon juice, mustard, and sugar. Season well with salt and pepper. Add the basil leaves.

5 Drain the pasta well and tip it into a large serving bowl. Add the dressing and toss thoroughly to combine. Add the bell pepper strips, zucchini, onion, and cherry tomatoes, stirring to combine. Cover and set aside at room temperature for about 30 minutes to allow the flavors to develop.

6 Serve the salad, garnished with a few sprigs of fresh basil.

Bell Peppers & Rosemary

The flavor of broiled or roasted bell peppers is very different from when they are eaten raw, so do try them cooked in this way.

NUTRITIONAL INFORMATION

Calories 201	Sugars 6g
Protein 2g	Fat 19g
Carbohydrate 6g	Saturates 2g

  20 mins   10 mins

SERVES 4

I N G R E D I E N T S

4 tbsp olive oil

finely grated rind of 1 lemon

4 tbsp lemon juice

1 tbsp balsamic vinegar

1 tbsp crushed fresh rosemary, or
   1 tsp dried rosemary

2 garlic cloves, crushed

2 red bell peppers, halved and deseeded

2 yellow bell peppers, halved and deseeded

2 tbsp pine nuts

salt and pepper

fresh rosemary sprigs, to garnish

1 Mix together the olive oil, lemon rind, lemon juice, balsamic vinegar, rosemary, and garlic. Season with salt and pepper to taste.

2 Place the red and yellow bell peppers, skin side up, on the rack of a broiler pan, and then brush the olive oil mixture over them.

3 Broil the bell peppers for 3–4 minutes or until the skin begins to char, basting frequently with the olive oil mixture. Remove from the heat, cover with foil, and set aside for 5 minutes.

4 Meanwhile, sprinkle the pine nuts onto the broiler rack and toast them lightly for 2–3 minutes. Keep a close eye on them, as they tend to burn very quickly.

5 Peel the bell peppers, slice into strips and place in a warmed serving dish. Sprinkle with pine nuts and drizzle over any remaining olive oil mixture. Garnish with fresh rosemary and serve immediately.

COOK'S TIP

A combination of red and yellow bell peppers looks attractive, but you could use all one color or substitute an orange bell pepper. However, do not use green bell peppers, which are not really sweet enough for this dish.

Lentil & Tuna Salad

In this recipe, lentils, combined with spices, lemon juice, and tuna, make a wonderfully tasty and filling salad.

NUTRITIONAL INFORMATION

Calories 227   Sugars 2g
Protein ....19g   Fat 9g
Carbohydrate ...19g   Saturates 1g

25 mins   0 mins

SERVES 4

INGREDIENTS

2 ripe tomatoes

1 small red onion

3 tbsp virgin olive oil

1 tbsp lemon juice

1 tsp whole-grain mustard

1 garlic clove, crushed

½ tsp ground cumin

½ tsp ground coriander

14 oz/400 g can lentils, drained

6½ oz/185 g can tuna, drained

2 tbsp chopped fresh cilantro

pepper

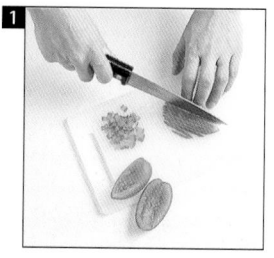

1 Using a sharp knife, deseed the tomatoes and then chop them into fine dice. Finely chop the red onion.

2 To make the dressing, whisk together the virgin olive oil, lemon juice, mustard, garlic, cumin, and ground coriander in a small bowl until thoroughly combined. Set aside until required.

3 Mix together the chopped onion, diced tomatoes, and drained lentils in a large bowl.

4 Flake the tuna with a fork and stir it into the onion, tomato, and lentil mixture. Stir in the chopped fresh cilantro and mix well.

5 Pour the dressing over the lentil and tuna salad and season with pepper to taste. Serve immediately.

COOK'S TIP

Lentils are an excellent source of protein and contain several important vitamins and minerals. Buy them dried for soaking and cooking yourself, or buy canned varieties for speed and convenience.

Mixed Bean & Apple Salad

Use any mixture of beans you have at hand in this recipe, but the wider the variety, the more colorful the salad.

NUTRITIONAL INFORMATION

Calories	183	Sugars	.........8g
Protein	.........6g	Fat	...........7g
Carbohydrate	...26g	Saturates	.......1g

 20 mins 20 mins

SERVES 4

INGREDIENTS

8 oz/225 g new potatoes, scrubbed and quartered

8 oz/225 g mixed canned beans, such as red kidney beans, small cannellini beans, and borlotti beans, drained and rinsed

1 red eating apple, diced and tossed in 1 tbsp lemon juice

1 yellow bell pepper, deseeded and diced

1 shallot, sliced

½ fennel bulb, sliced

oakleaf lettuce leaves

DRESSING

1 tbsp red wine vinegar

2 tbsp olive oil

1½ tsp mild yellow mustard

1 garlic clove, crushed

2 tsp chopped fresh thyme

1 Cook the quartered potatoes in a pan of boiling water for 15 minutes until tender. Drain and transfer to a large bowl.

2 Add the mixed beans to the potatoes, with the diced apple, yellow bell pepper, shallot, and fennel. Mix thoroughly, taking care not to break up the cooked potatoes.

3 To make the dressing, whisk all the dressing ingredients together until thoroughly combined, then pour it over the potato salad.

4 Line a serving plate or salad bowl with the oakleaf lettuce leaves and spoon the potato mixture into the center. Serve the salad immediately.

VARIATION

Use Dijon or whole-grain mustard in place of mild yellow mustard for a different flavor.

Radish & Cucumber Salad

The radishes and the herb and mustard dressing give this colorful salad a mildly pungent flavor that complements the potatoes perfectly.

NUTRITIONAL INFORMATION

Calories ....140 Sugars 3g
Protein ....3g Fat 6g
Carbohydrate ...20g Saturates 1g

50 mins   20 mins

SERVES 4

I N G R E D I E N T S

1 lb 2 oz/500 g new potatoes, scrubbed and halved

½ cucumber, thinly sliced

2 tsp salt

1 bunch of radishes, thinly sliced

D R E S S I N G

1 tbsp Dijon mustard

2 tbsp olive oil

1 tbsp white wine vinegar

2 tbsp chopped fresh mixed herbs

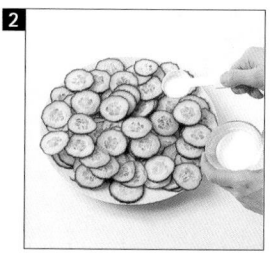 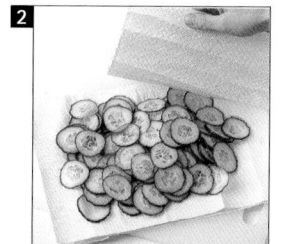 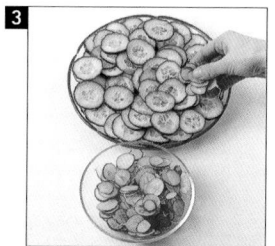

1 Cook the potatoes in a large pan of boiling water for 10–15 minutes or until tender. Drain and set aside to cool.

2 Meanwhile, spread out the cucumber slices on a plate and sprinkle with the salt. Set aside for 30 minutes, then rinse under cold running water, and pat dry with paper towels.

3 Arrange the cucumber and radish slices on a serving plate in a decorative pattern and pile the cooked potatoes in the center.

4 To make the dressing, put the mustard, olive oil, vinegar, and mixed herbs into a small bowl and whisk well. Alternatively, put the ingredients in a screw-top jar and shake vigorously until combined. Pour the dressing over the salad. Chill before serving.

COOK'S TIP

Cucumber adds not only color but also a real freshness to the salad. It is salted and left to stand to remove the excess water, which would make the salad soggy. Wash the cucumber well to remove all of the salt before adding to the salad.

Potato & Arugula Salad

This green and white salad is made with creamy, salty-flavored goat cheese—its distinctive flavor is perfect with salad greens.

NUTRITIONAL INFORMATION

Calories 104	Sugars 3.1g	
Protein 3.1g	Fat 5.3g	
Carbohydrate ..11.8g	Saturates 1.5g	

20 mins   15 mins

SERVES 4

INGREDIENTS

1 lb 5 oz/600 g potatoes, unpeeled and sliced

2 green dessert apples, diced

1 tsp lemon juice

¼ cup walnut pieces

4 oz/115 g goat cheese, cubed

5 oz arugula leaves

salt and pepper

DRESSING

2 tbsp olive oil

1 tbsp red wine vinegar

1 tsp honey

1 tsp fennel seeds

1 Cook the potatoes in a pan of boiling water for 15 minutes until tender. Drain and let cool. Transfer the cooled potatoes to a serving bowl.

2 Toss the diced apples in the lemon juice, then drain and stir them into the cold potatoes.

3 Add the walnut pieces, cheese cubes, and arugula leaves, then toss the ingredients together to mix.

4 In a small bowl, whisk all of the dressing ingredients together and then pour the dressing over the salad. Season to taste and serve immediately.

COOK'S TIP

Serve this salad immediately to prevent the apple from discoloring. Alternatively, prepare all of the other ingredients in advance and add the apple at the last minute.

  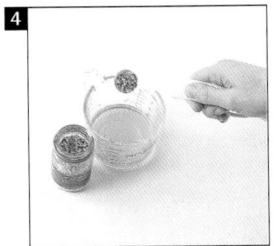

Root Vegetable Salad

This salad of grated vegetables is perfect for a light appetizer.
The peppery flavors of the daikon and radishes are refreshingly pungent.

NUTRITIONAL INFORMATION

Calories 132   Sugars 9g
Protein ....4g   Fat 8g
Carbohydrate ...12g   Saturates 1g

20 mins   0 mins

SERVES 4

INGREDIENTS

12 oz/350 g carrots

8 oz/225 g daikon

4 oz/115 g radishes

12 oz/350 g celery root

1 tbsp orange juice

2 celery stalks with leaves, washed
   and trimmed

3½ oz/100 g assorted salad greens

¼ cup chopped walnuts

DRESSING

1 tbsp walnut oil

1 tbsp white wine vinegar

1 tsp whole-grain mustard

½ tsp finely grated orange rind

1 tsp celery seeds

salt and pepper

1 Peel and coarsely grate or very finely shred the carrots, daikon, and radishes. Set them aside in separate bowls.

2 Peel and coarsely grate or finely shred the celery root and mix it immediately with the orange juice to prevent it from turning brown.

3 Remove the celery leaves and reserve. Finely chop the celery stalks.

4 Divide the salad greens among 4 serving plates and arrange the vegetables in small piles on top.

5 Mix all of the dressing ingredients together and season well. Drizzle a little over each salad.

6 Shred the reserved celery leaves and sprinkle over the salad with the chopped walnuts.

COOK'S TIP
Also known as Chinese white radish and mooli, daikon resembles a large white parsnip. It has crisp, slightly pungent flesh, which can be eaten raw or cooked. It is a useful ingredient in stir-fries.

Beet & Orange Salad

Use freshly cooked beet in this unusual combination of colors and flavors, because beet soaked in vinegar will spoil the delicate balance.

NUTRITIONAL INFORMATION

Calories	240	Sugars	........29g
Protein	........10g	Fat	...........2g
Carbohydrate	...49g	Saturates	.....0.3g

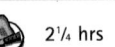 2¼ hrs   1 hr

SERVES 4

INGREDIENTS

generous 1 cup mixed long grain and wild rice

4 large oranges

1 lb/450 g cooked beet, peeled and drained (if necessary)

2 heads of endive

salt and pepper

chopped fresh chives, to garnish

DRESSING

4 tbsp low-fat cream cheese

1 garlic clove, crushed

1 tbsp whole-grain mustard

½ tsp finely grated orange rind

2 tsp honey

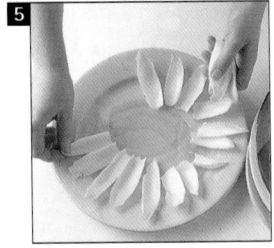

1 Cook the mixed rice according to the packet instructions. Drain and set aside to cool.

2 Meanwhile, slice the top and bottom off each orange. Using a sharp knife, remove the skin and pith. Holding the orange over a bowl to catch the juice, carefully slice between each segment. Place the segments in a separate bowl. Cover with plastic wrap and chill.

3 Dice the beet into small cubes. Mix with the orange segments, cover the bowl again, and chill.

4 When the rice has cooled completely, mix in the reserved orange juice until thoroughly incorporated and season with salt and pepper to taste.

5 Line 4 individual bowls or plates with the endive leaves. Spoon the rice over them and top with the beet and orange mixture.

6 Mix all the dressing ingredients together and spoon the dressing over the salad or serve separately in a bowl, if preferred. Garnish with chopped fresh chives and serve.

Red Hot Slaw

As well as being an exciting side dish, this colorful salad makes an unusual filling for jacket potatoes.

NUTRITIONAL INFORMATION

Calories 169	Sugars 16g	
Protein 11g	Fat 7g	
Carbohydrate ...17g	Saturates 3g	

🥘 1 hr   🕐 0 mins

SERVES 4

I N G R E D I E N T S

½ small red cabbage

1 large carrot

2 red-skinned apples

1 tbsp lemon juice

1 medium red onion

scant 1 cup grated reduced-fat Cheddar cheese

TO GARNISH

fresh red chile strips

carrot strips

DRESSING

3 tbsp reduced-calorie mayonnaise

3 tbsp low-fat plain yogurt

1 garlic clove, crushed

1 tsp paprika

1–2 tsp chili powder

pinch of cayenne pepper (optional)

salt and pepper

1 Cut the red cabbage in half and remove the central core. Finely shred the leaves and place in a large bowl. Peel and coarsely grate or finely shred the carrot and mix it into the cabbage.

2 Core the apples and finely dice, leaving on the skins. Place in another bowl and toss in the lemon juice to help prevent the apple from browning. Mix the apple into the cabbage and carrot.

3 Peel and finely shred or grate the onion. Stir into the other vegetables with the cheese and mix together.

4 To make the dressing, mix together the mayonnaise, yogurt, garlic, and paprika in a small bowl. Add chili powder according to taste and the cayenne pepper (if using)—remember this will add more spice to the dressing. Season to taste with salt and pepper.

5 Add the dressing to the vegetables and toss well to mix. Cover and chill in the refrigerator for 1 hour to allow the flavors to develop.

6 Serve garnished with strips of fresh red chile and carrot.

Chicken & Spinach Salad

Slices of lean chicken with young spinach leaves and a few fresh raspberries are served with a refreshing yogurt and honey dressing.

NUTRITIONAL INFORMATION

Calories	235	Sugars	.........9g
Protein	........37g	Fat	...........6g
Carbohydrate	....9g	Saturates	......2g

3½ hrs   25 mins

SERVES 4

INGREDIENTS

4 boneless, skinless chicken breasts, 5½ oz/150 g each

2 cups chicken stock

1 bay leaf

8 oz/225 g fresh young spinach leaves

1 small red onion, shredded

¾ cup fresh raspberries

salt and freshly ground pink peppercorns

fresh toasted croûtons, to garnish

DRESSING

4 tbsp low-fat natural yogurt

1 tbsp raspberry vinegar

2 tsp honey

 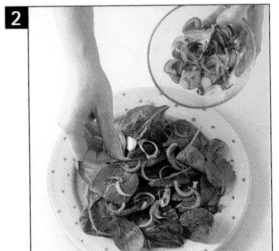 

1 Place the chicken breasts in a skillet. Pour over the stock and add the bay leaf. Bring to a boil, cover, and simmer for 15–20 minutes, turning half-way through, until the chicken is cooked through. Let cool in the liquid.

2 Arrange the spinach on 4 serving plates and top with the onion. Cover and chill.

3 Drain the cooked chicken and pat dry on absorbent paper towels. Slice the chicken breasts thinly and arrange, fanned out, on top of the spinach and onion. Sprinkle the salad with the raspberries.

4 To make the dressing, mix all the ingredients together in a small bowl. Drizzle a spoonful of dressing over each chicken breast and season with salt and ground pink peppercorns to taste. Serve the salad with freshly toasted croûtons.

VARIATION

This recipe is delicious with smoked chicken, but it will be more expensive and richer, so use slightly less. It would make an impressive appetizer for a dinner party.

Caesar Salad

This salad was the invention of a chef at Caesar's, a restaurant in Tijuana, Mexico. It has rightly earned an international reputation.

NUTRITIONAL INFORMATION

Calories .... 589 Sugars 3g
Protein .... 11g Fat 50g
Carbohydrate ... 24g Saturates 9g

  25 mins   15–20 mins

SERVES 4

INGREDIENTS

1 large Romaine lettuce or 2 Boston or Bibb lettuces

4 canned anchovies in oil, drained and halved lengthwise

Parmesan shavings, to garnish

DRESSING

2 garlic cloves, crushed

1½ tsp Dijon mustard

1 tsp Worcestershire sauce

4 canned anchovies in olive oil, drained and chopped

1 egg yolk

1 tbsp lemon juice

⅔ cup olive oil

¼ cup freshly grated Parmesan cheese

salt and pepper

CROÛTONS

4 thick slices day-old bread

2 tbsp olive oil

1 garlic clove, crushed

1 First, make the dressing. Put the garlic, mustard, Worcestershire sauce, anchovies, egg yolk, lemon juice, and seasoning into a food processor or blender and process for 30 seconds until foaming. Add the olive oil, drop by drop, until the mixture begins to thicken, then in a steady stream until all the oil is incorporated. Scrape out of the food processor or blender. Add a little hot water if the dressing is too thick. Stir in the grated Parmesan cheese. Taste for seasoning and set aside in the refrigerator until required.

2 For the croûtons, cut the bread into ½ inch/1 cm cubes. Toss with the olive oil and garlic in a bowl. Spread out on a cookie sheet in a single layer. Bake in a preheated oven, 350°F/180°C, for 15–20 minutes, stirring occasionally, until the croûtons are browned and crisp. Remove from the oven and set aside to cool.

3 Separate the lettuce into individual leaves and wash and spin dry in a salad spinner or pat dry on paper towels. (Excess moisture will dilute the dressing.) Transfer to a plastic bag and place in the refrigerator until needed.

4 To assemble the salad, tear the lettuce into pieces and place a large serving bowl. Add the dressing and toss well. Top with the halved anchovies, croûtons, and Parmesan shavings. Serve immediately.

Tuna Niçoise Salad

This is a classic version of the French Salade Niçoise. It is a substantial salad, suitable for a lunch or light summer supper.

NUTRITIONAL INFORMATION

Calories	109	Sugars	1.1g
Protein	7.2g	Fat	7.0g
Carbohydrate	4.8g	Saturates	1.2g

 10 mins   20 mins

SERVES 4

INGREDIENTS

4 eggs

1 lb/450 g new potatoes

4 oz/115 g small green beans, trimmed and halved

2 x 6 oz/175 g tuna steaks

6 tbsp olive oil, plus extra for brushing

1 garlic clove, crushed

1½ tsp Dijon mustard

2 tsp lemon juice

2 tbsp chopped fresh basil

2 Boston or Bibb lettuces

7 oz/200 g cherry tomatoes, halved

6 oz/175 g cucumber, peeled, cut in half and sliced

½ cup pitted black olives

2 oz/55 g canned anchovies in olive oil, drained

salt and pepper

1 Bring a small pan of water to a boil. Add the eggs and cook for 7–9 minutes from when the water returns to a boil—7 minutes for a slightly soft center or 9 minutes for a firm center. Drain and refresh under cold running water. Set aside.

2 Cook the potatoes in lightly salted boiling water for 10–12 minutes until tender. Add the beans 3 minutes before the end of the cooking time. Drain both vegetables well and refresh under cold water. Drain well again.

3 Wash and dry the tuna steaks. Brush with a little olive oil and season to taste. Cook on a preheated ridged griddle for 2–3 minutes each side, until just tender but still slightly pink in the center. Set aside to rest.

4 Whisk together the garlic, mustard, lemon juice, basil, and seasoning. Whisk in the olive oil.

5 To assemble the salad, break apart the lettuces and tear into large pieces. Divide among individual serving plates. Next, add the potatoes and beans, tomatoes, cucumber, and olives. Toss lightly together. Shell the eggs and cut into quarters lengthwise. Arrange these on top of the salad. Scatter the anchovies over the top.

6 Flake the tuna steaks and arrange on the salad. Pour over the dressing and serve.

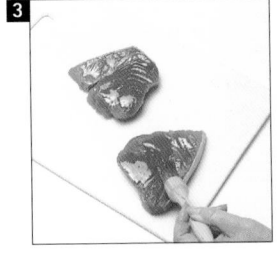

Moroccan Couscous Salad

Couscous is a type of fine semolina made from wheat. You can buy couscous pre-cooked so that it needs only the addition of boiling water.

NUTRITIONAL INFORMATION

Calories 329   Sugars 12g
Protein . . . . .19g   Fat 11g
Carbohydrate . . .42g   Saturates 2g

 40 mins   20 mins

SERVES 4

INGREDIENTS

1⅓ cups couscous

1 cinnamon stick, about 2 inches/5 cm

2 tsp coriander seeds

1 tsp cumin seeds

2 tbsp olive oil

1 small onion, finely chopped

2 garlic cloves, finely chopped

½ tsp ground turmeric

pinch of cayenne pepper

1 tbsp lemon juice

⅓ cup golden raisins

3 ripe plum tomatoes, chopped

3 oz/85 g cucumber, chopped

4 scallions, sliced

7 oz/200 g can tuna in olive oil, drained and flaked

3 tbsp chopped fresh cilantro

salt and pepper

1 Cook the couscous according to the packet instructions, omitting any butter recommended. Transfer to a large bowl and set aside.

2 Heat a small skillet and add the cinnamon stick, coriander seeds, and cumin seeds. Cook over high heat until the seeds begin to pop and smell fragrant.

Remove from the heat and grind to a fine powder with a pestle and mortar or in a spice grinder. Set aside.

3 Heat the oil in a clean skillet and add the onion. Cook over low heat for 7–8 minutes until softened and lightly browned. Add the garlic and cook for a further minute. Stir in the roasted and ground spices, turmeric, and cayenne and cook for a further minute. Remove from

the heat and stir in the lemon juice. Add this mixture to the couscous and mix well together, ensuring that all of the grains are well coated.

4 Add the golden raisins, tomatoes, cucumber, scallions, tuna, and chopped cilantro. Season with salt and pepper to taste and mix together well. Allow the salad to cool completely and serve at room temperature.

Tuna Bean Salad

Tuna is rich in omega-3 fatty acids which help to reduce cholesterol levels—and it tastes wonderful in this classic salad.

NUTRITIONAL INFORMATION

Calories 529   Sugars 3g
Protein . . . . .54g   Fat 23g
Carbohydrate . . .29g   Saturates 4g

 8¼ hrs   1½ hrs

SERVES 4

INGREDIENTS

1¼ cups navy beans

1 tbsp lemon juice

5 tbsp extra virgin olive oil, plus extra for brushing

1 garlic clove, finely chopped

1 small red onion, very thinly sliced (optional)

1 tbsp chopped fresh parsley

4 x 6 oz/175 g tuna steaks

salt and pepper

TO GARNISH

fresh parsley sprigs

lemon wedges

1 Soak the navy beans for 8 hours or overnight in at least twice their volume of cold water.

2 Drain the beans and place in a saucepan with twice their volume of fresh water. Bring to a boil over low heat, skimming off any scum that rises to the surface. Boil the beans rapidly for 10 minutes, then reduce the heat, and simmer for a further 1¼–1½ hours until the beans are tender.

3 Meanwhile, mix together the lemon juice, olive oil, garlic, and seasoning. Drain the beans thoroughly and mix together with the olive oil mixture, onion, and parsley. Season to taste and set aside.

4 Brush the tuna steaks lightly with olive oil and season. Cook on a preheated ridged griddle for 2 minutes on each side until just pink in the center.

5 Divide the bean salad among 4 serving plates. Top each with a tuna steak. Garnish with parsley sprigs and lemon wedges and serve immediately.

COOK'S TIP

You could use canned navy beans instead of dried. Reheat according to the instructions on the can, drain, and toss with the dressing as above.

Thai Seafood Salad

This colorful mixture of vegetables, topped with succulent seafood and tossed in a piquant dressing, is best served chilled.

NUTRITIONAL INFORMATION

Calories 310   Sugars 4g
Protein . . . . .30g   Fat 18g
Carbohydrate . . . .7g   Saturates 3g

1¼ hrs   10 mins

SERVES 4

INGREDIENTS

1 lb/450 g live mussels, scrubbed

8 jumbo shrimp

12 oz/350 g prepared squid sliced into rings

4 oz/115 g peeled cooked shrimp

½ red onion, thinly sliced

2 cups bean sprouts

½ red bell pepper, deseeded and sliced

4 oz/115 g bok choy, shredded

DRESSING

1 garlic clove, crushed

1 tsp grated fresh ginger root

1 red chile, deseeded and finely chopped

2 tbsp chopped fresh cilantro

1 tbsp lime juice

1 tsp finely grated lime rind

1 tbsp light soy sauce

5 tbsp sunflower or peanut oil

2 tsp sesame oil

salt and pepper

 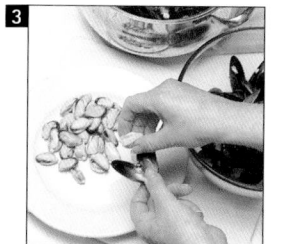 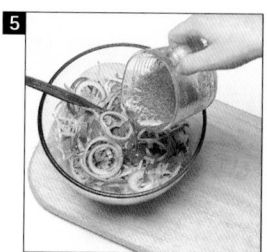

1 Place the mussels in a large pan with just the water that clings to the shells. Cook over high heat for 3–4 minutes, shaking the pan occasionally, until they have opened. Discard any that remain closed. Strain, reserving the liquid, and refresh under cold water. Drain again.

2 Bring the reserved liquid to a boil and simmer the jumbo shrimp for 5 minutes. Add the squid and cook for a further 2 minutes. Remove them with a slotted spoon and plunge into a large bowl of cold water. Reserve the poaching liquid. Drain the shrimp and squid again.

3 Remove the mussels from their shells and mix with the jumbo shrimp, squid, and peeled shrimp. Chill for 1 hour.

4 Put all the dressing ingredients, except the oils, into a blender and blend to a smooth paste. Add the oils, reserved poaching liquid, seasoning, and 4 tbsp cold water. Blend again.

5 Combine all the vegetables and toss with 2–3 tbsp of the dressing. Transfer to a large serving plate. Toss the seafood with the remaining dressing and add to the vegetables. Serve immediately.

Skate & Spinach Salad

Packed with flavor and contrasting textures, this salad makes
a filling entrée for four people or would serve six as an appetizer.

NUTRITIONAL INFORMATION

Calories 316	Sugars 18g
Protein 32g	Fat 13g
Carbohydrate . . .18g	Saturates 1g

 30 mins   15 mins

SERVES 4

INGREDIENTS

1 lb 9 oz/700 g skate wings, trimmed

2 fresh rosemary sprigs

1 fresh bay leaf

1 tbsp black peppercorns

1 lemon, quartered

1 lb/450 g baby spinach leaves

1 tbsp olive oil

1 small red onion, thinly sliced

2 garlic cloves, crushed

½ tsp chili flakes

½ cup pine nuts, lightly toasted

⅓ cup raisins

1 tbsp light molasses sugar

2 tbsp chopped fresh parsley

1 Put the skate into a large saucepan with the herbs, peppercorns, and lemon. Cover with water and bring to a boil. Cover and simmer for 4–5 minutes until the flesh begins to come away from the cartilage. Remove from the heat and set aside for 15 minutes. Lift the fish from the water and remove the flesh in shreds.

2 Meanwhile, put the spinach into a pan with just the water that clings to the leaves. Cook over high heat for 30 seconds until wilted. Drain, refresh

under cold water and drain again. Squeeze out any excess water and set aside.

3 Heat the oil in a large skillet. Cook the onion for 3–4 minutes until softened, but not browned. Add the garlic, chili flakes, pine nuts, raisins, and sugar.

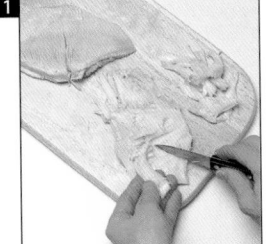

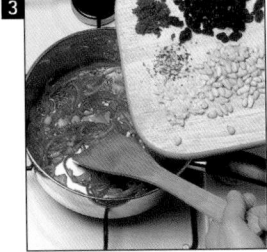

Cook for 1–2 minutes, then add the spinach and toss for 1 minute until heated through. Gently fold in the skate and cook for a further minute. Season well.

4 Divide the salad among 4 serving plates and sprinkle with the parsley.

Lobster & Avocado Salad

This isn't really an entrée but would serve very well as a light lunch with some bread or as part of a buffet.

NUTRITIONAL INFORMATION

Calories	313	Sugars	.........3g
Protein	........19g	Fat	..........25g
Carbohydrate	....4g	Saturates	.......4g

 25 mins   3 mins

SERVES 4

I N G R E D I E N T S

2 x 14 oz/400 g cooked lobsters

1 large avocado

1 tbsp lemon juice

8 oz/225 g green beans

4 scallions, thinly sliced

2 tbsp chopped fresh chervil

1 tbsp chopped fresh chives

D R E S S I N G

1 garlic clove, crushed

1 tsp Dijon mustard

pinch of sugar

1 tbsp balsamic vinegar

5 tbsp olive oil

salt and pepper

1 To prepare the lobsters, cut them in half lengthwise. Remove the intestinal vein which runs down the tail, the stomach sac, and any gray beards from the body cavity at the head end of the lobster. Crack the claws and remove the meat—in one piece if possible. Remove the meat from the tail of the lobster. Coarsely chop all the meat and set aside.

2 Split the avocado lengthwise and remove the pit. Cut each half in half again and peel off the skin. Cut the avocado flesh into chunks and toss with the lemon juice to prevent it from discoloring. Add to the lobster meat.

3 Bring a large pan of lightly salted water to a boil and add the green beans. Cook for 3 minutes, then drain, and immediately refresh under cold water. Drain again and set aside to cool completely. Cut the beans in half, then add them to the avocado and lobster.

4 Meanwhile, make the dressing by whisking together the garlic, mustard, sugar, vinegar, and seasoning. Gradually add the oil, whisking, until thickened.

5 Add the scallions, chervil, and chives to the lobster and avocado mixture and toss gently together. Drizzle over the dressing and serve immediately.

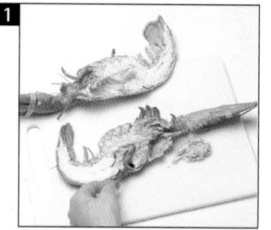  

Spicy Tropical Salad

This colorful salad, with its sweet and spicy flavors, is the perfect foil to a meaty main dish, and is wonderful with grilled food.

NUTRITIONAL INFORMATION

Calories	194	Sugars	.........7g
Protein	.........4g	Fat	..........16g
Carbohydrate	....9g	Saturates	.......3g

🖐 20 mins   🕐 0 mins

SERVES 4–6

INGREDIENTS

7 oz/200 g mixed salad greens

2–3 scallions, chopped

3–4 tbsp chopped fresh cilantro

1 small papaya

2 red bell peppers

1 avocado

1 tbsp lime juice

3–4 tbsp pumpkin seeds, toasted (optional)

DRESSING

juice of 1 lime

pinch of paprika

pinch of ground cumin

pinch of sugar

1 garlic clove, finely chopped

4 tbsp extra virgin olive oil

dash of white wine vinegar (optional)

salt

1 Combine the mixed salad greens with the scallions and cilantro. Mix well, then transfer to a large serving dish.

2 Cut the papaya in half, scoop out the seeds with a spoon, and discard. Cut the papaya into quarters, remove the peel, and slice the flesh. Arrange the slices on top of the salad greens.

3 Cut the red bell peppers in half lengthwise, remove the cores and seeds, then slice thinly. Add the bell peppers to the salad greens.

4 Cut the avocado in half around the pit. Twist apart, then remove the pit with a knife. Carefully peel off the skin, dice the flesh, and toss in lime juice to prevent it from discoloring. Add to the other salad ingredients.

5 To make the dressing, whisk together the lime juice, paprika, ground cumin, sugar, garlic, and olive oil. Season with salt to taste.

6 Pour the dressing over the salad and toss lightly to coat, adding a dash of wine vinegar if a flavor with a little more "bite" is preferred. Sprinkle the toasted pumpkin seeds, if using, over the salad and serve immediately.

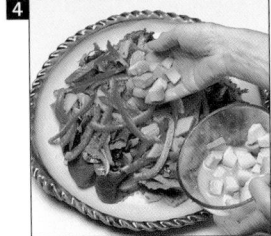

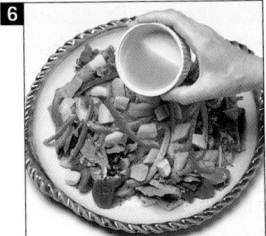

Green Bean Salad with Feta

This fresh-tasting salad is flavored with fresh cilantro, an herb that resembles flat leaf parsley in appearance, but tastes quite different.

NUTRITIONAL INFORMATION

Calories ....275 Sugars 7g
Protein ....6g Fat 25g
Carbohydrate ....8g Saturates 6g

10 mins   5 mins

SERVES 4

I N G R E D I E N T S

12 oz/350 g green beans, trimmed

1 red onion, chopped

3–4 tbsp chopped fresh cilantro

2 radishes, thinly sliced

¾ cup crumbled feta cheese

1 tsp chopped fresh oregano or
½ tsp dried oregano

2 tbsp red wine or fruit vinegar

5 tbsp extra virgin olive oil

3 ripe tomatoes, cut into wedges

pepper

1 Bring about 2 inches/5 cm water to a boil in the base of a steamer or in a medium saucepan. Add the green beans to the top of the steamer or place them in a metal colander set over the pan of water. Cover and steam for about 5 minutes until just tender.

2 Transfer the beans to a bowl and add the onion, cilantro, radishes, and crumbled feta cheese.

3 Sprinkle the oregano over the salad, then grind pepper over to taste. Whisk the vinegar and olive oil together and then pour over the salad. Toss gently to mix well.

4 Transfer to a serving platter, surround with the tomato wedges, and serve at once or chill until ready to serve.

VARIATION

This recipe is also delicious made with nopales, or edible cactus, which is available in specialist stores in cans or jars. Drain, then slice, and use instead of the green beans, missing out Step 1. Replace the feta with 1–2 chopped hard-cooked eggs.

Mexican Citrus Salad

A salad like this reminds one of how much Mexico and the Mediterranean share in terms of sunny flavors and ingredients.

NUTRITIONAL INFORMATION

Calories	267	Sugars	........15g
Protein	.........3g	Fat	..........21g
Carbohydrate	...16g	Saturates	.......4g

 20 mins   0 mins

SERVES 4

I N G R E D I E N T S

1 large pomegranate

1 grapefruit

2 sweet oranges

finely grated rind of ½ lime

1–2 garlic cloves, finely chopped

3 tbsp red wine vinegar

juice of 2 limes

½ tsp sugar

¼ tsp mustard powder

4–5 tbsp extra virgin olive oil

1 head red leafy lettuce, such as oakleaf, washed and dried

1 avocado, pitted, peeled, diced, and tossed with a little lime juice

salt and pepper

½ red onion, thinly sliced, to garnish

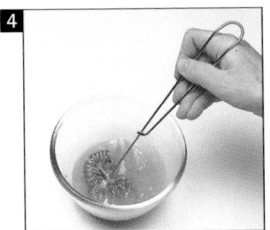

1 Cut the pomegranate into quarters, then press back the outer skin to push out the seeds into a bowl.

2 Using a sharp knife, cut a slice off the top and bottom of the grapefruit, then remove the peel and pith, cutting downward. Cut out the segments from between the membranes, then add to the pomegranate seeds.

3 Finely grate the rind of half an orange and set aside. Using a sharp knife, cut a slice off the top and bottom of both oranges, then remove the peel and pith, cutting downward and taking care to retain the shape of the oranges. Slice horizontally into slices, then cut into quarters. Add the oranges to the pomegranate and grapefruit and stir to mix well.

4 Combine the reserved orange rind with the lime rind, garlic, vinegar, lime juice, sugar, and mustard. Season to taste, then whisk in the olive oil.

5 Place the lettuce leaves in a serving bowl, then top with the citrus mixture and the avocado. Pour over the dressing and toss gently. Garnish with the onion rings and serve immediately.

Celery Root Remoulade

Finely shredded celery root in a mustard mayonnaise is a popular dish throughout France and here it is given a distinctly Provencal touch.

NUTRITIONAL INFORMATION

Calories	492	Sugars 2g
Protein	........20g	Fat 45g
Carbohydrate	....3g	Saturates 6g

  45 mins   0 mins

SERVES 4

I N G R E D I E N T S

1½ tsp lemon juice

1 tsp salt

1 lb/450 g celery root

4½ tsp Dijon mustard

1 large egg yolk

⅔ cup extra virgin olive oil

2 tsp white wine vinegar

2 tbsp capers in brine, rinsed

10½ oz/300 g fresh crab meat

radicchio leaves, rinsed and dried

fresh dill or parsley sprigs, to garnish

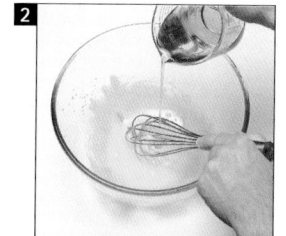

1 Put the lemon juice and salt into a large bowl of cold water. Using the shredding disc of a food processor or a hand grater, shred the celery root. Put it into the bowl of acidulated water as it is grated, to prevent discoloration.

2 To make the sauce, beat the mustard and egg yolk together in a bowl. Gradually whisk in the olive oil, drop by drop, until a mayonnaise forms (see Cook's Tip). Stir in the vinegar.

3 Drain the celery root and pat dry with paper towels. Add to the mayonnaise, stirring to coat well. Cover with plastic wrap and chill.

4 About 20 minutes before serving, remove the remoulade from the refrigerator to allow it to come to room temperature. Gently stir in the capers and crab meat.

5 Line a platter or serving bowl with radicchio leaves and spoon the celery root remoulade mixture on top. Garnish with fresh dill or parsley sprigs and serve immediately.

COOK'S TIP
If the sauce begins to curdle, beat another egg yolk in a bowl, then slowly beat into the sauce to rectify. Continue to add the remaining oil.

Greek Salad

The combination of juicy, ripe tomatoes and black olives is a classic partnership, but Greek cooks also add feta cheese for a salty flavor.

NUTRITIONAL INFORMATION

Calories	347	Sugars	.........6g
Protein	........12g	Fat	..........31g
Carbohydrate	....6g	Saturates	......11g

15 mins   0 mins

SERVES 4

I N G R E D I E N T S

9 oz/250 g feta cheese

9 oz/250 g cucumber

9 oz/250 g Greek kalamata olives

1 red onion or 4 scallions

2 large juicy tomatoes

1 tsp honey

4 tbsp extra virgin olive oil

½ lemon

salt and pepper

fresh or dried oregano, to garnish

pita bread, to serve

1 Drain the feta cheese if it is packed in brine. Place it on a cutting board and cut into ½ inch/1 cm dice. Transfer the cheese to a salad bowl.

2 Cut the cucumber in half lengthwise and use a tsp to scoop out the seeds.

Cut the flesh into ½ inch/1 cm slices and add to the bowl.

3 Pit the olives, if liked, and add them to the salad bowl. Slice the red onion or finely chop the the scallions and add to the salad bowl. Cut each tomato into quarters and scoop out the seeds with a tsp. Cut the flesh into bite-size pieces and add to the bowl.

4 Using your hands, gently toss all the ingredients together. Stir the honey into the olive oil (see Cook's Tip), add to the salad, and squeeze in lemon juice to taste. Season with pepper and a little salt, if wished. Cover with plastic wrap and chill until required.

5 Garnish the salad with the oregano and serve with pita bread.

COOK'S TIP
The small amount of honey helps to bring out the full flavor of the tomatoes.

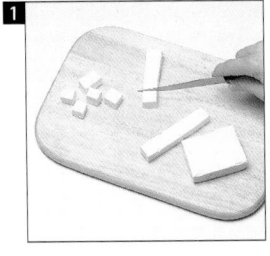

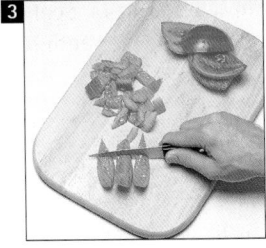

Baked Goat-Cheese Salad

Scrumptious hot goat-cheese and herb croûtes are served with a tossed leafy salad to make an excellent light snack, capturing Provençal flavors.

NUTRITIONAL INFORMATION

Calories	509	Sugars	.........3g
Protein	........18g	Fat	..........33g
Carbohydrate	...35g	Saturates	......10g

  10 mins   10 mins

SERVES 4

INGREDIENTS

9 oz/225 g mixed salad greens, such as arugula, mâche, and endive

12 slices French bread, plus extra to serve

extra virgin olive oil, for brushing

12 thin slices of Provençal goat cheese, such as Picodon

fresh herbs, such as rosemary, thyme, or oregano, finely chopped

DRESSING

6 tbsp extra virgin olive oil

3 tbsp red wine vinegar

½ tsp sugar

½ tsp Dijon mustard

salt and pepper

1 To prepare the salad, rinse the leaves under cold water and pat dry with a dish towel. Wrap in paper towels and put in a plastic bag. Seal tightly and store in the refrigerator until required.

2 To make the dressing, place all the ingredients in a screw-top jar and shake until well blended. Season with salt and pepper to taste and shake again. Set aside while preparing the croûtes.

3 Under a preheated broiler, toast the slices of French bread on both sides until they are crisp. Brush a little olive oil on one side of each slice while they are still hot, so the oil is absorbed.

4 Place the croûtes on a cookie sheet and top each with a slice of cheese. Sprinkle the herbs over the cheese and drizzle with olive oil. Bake in a preheated oven, 350°F/180°C, for 5 minutes.

5 While the croûtes are in the oven, place the salad greens in a bowl. Shake the dressing again, pour it over the salad greens and toss together. Divide the salad between 4 plates.

6 Transfer the hot croûtes to the salads. Serve immediately with extra slices of French bread.

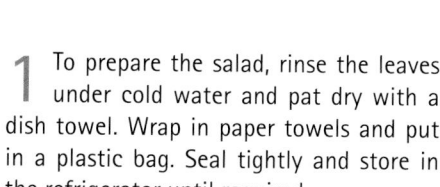

Orange & Fennel Salad

Fresh, juicy oranges and the sharp anise flavor of fennel combine to make this refreshing Spanish salad.

NUTRITIONAL INFORMATION

Calories	136	Sugars	........19g
Protein	.........3g	Fat	...........6g
Carbohydrate	...19g	Saturates	.......1g

 30 mins   0 mins

SERVES 4

I N G R E D I E N T S

4 large oranges

1 large bulb fennel

2 tsp fennel seeds

2 tbsp extra virgin olive oil

freshly squeezed orange juice, to taste

finely chopped fresh parsley, to garnish

1 Using a small serrated knife, remove the rind and pith from 1 orange, cutting carefully from the top to the bottom of the orange so it retains its shape. Work over a small bowl to catch the juices.

2 Peel the remaining oranges the same way, reserving all the juices. Cut the oranges horizontally into ¼ inch/5 mm slices and arrange in an attractive serving bowl; reserve the juices.

VARIATION

Replace the fennel with a finely sliced onion or a large bunch of scallions, finely chopped. This version is from Spain, where orange-colored oranges would be used, but in Sicily the dish is made with blood-red oranges.

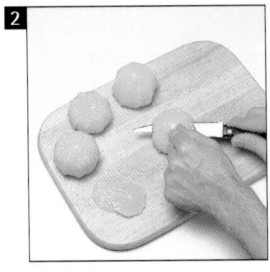

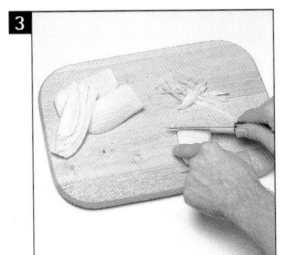

3 Cut the fronds from the fennel bulb, cut the bulb in half lengthwise and then into quarters. Cut crosswise into the very thin slices. Immediately place in the bowl of oranges and toss with a little of the reserved juice to prevent browning.

4 Sprinkle the fennel seeds over the oranges and fennel.

5 Whisk the olive oil with the remaining reserved orange juice, plus extra fresh orange juice to taste. Pour over the oranges and fennel and toss gently. Cover with plastic wrap and chill until ready to serve.

6 Just before serving, remove from the refrigerator and sprinkle with parsley. Serve chilled.

Salade Niçoise

This classic salad from Nice is often made with canned tuna,
but using seared fresh tuna steaks instead gives it a sophisticated twist.

NUTRITIONAL INFORMATION

Calories 356   Sugars 3g
Protein . . . . .22g   Fat 26g
Carbohydrate . . .10g   Saturates 4g

45 mins   20 mins

SERVES 4

I N G R E D I E N T S

9 oz/250 g green beans, trimmed

9 oz/250 g small waxy potatoes, scrubbed
  and halved

1 large tomato, cut into 8 wedges

1 large tuna steak, about 12 oz/350 g and
  ¾ inch/2 cm thick, seared (see page 30)

3 large eggs, hard-cooked

½ cup black olives

1¾ oz/50 g can anchovy fillets in oil, drained

1 tbsp chopped fresh flat leaf parsley

G A R L I C   V I N A I G R E T T E

scant ½ cup extra virgin olive oil

3 tbsp red or white wine vinegar

½ tsp sugar

½ tsp Dijon mustard

2 garlic cloves, crushed

salt and pepper

1 Put all the vinaigrette ingredients in a
  screw-top jar and shake well. Season
with salt and pepper to taste. Set aside.

2 Blanch the beans in boiling water for
  3 minutes, then drain, and place in a
large bowl. Pour over the vinaigrette.

3 Cook the potatoes in boiling water for
  about 15 minutes until tender, then

drain and add to the beans and dressing
while still hot. Toss gently and set the
vegetables aside to cool.

4 Add the sun-dried tomato pieces to
  the vegetables and toss together.
Break the seared tuna into large chunks,
add to the vegetables, and toss gently.

5 Shell the hard-cooked eggs and cut
  each into quarters lengthwise.

6 Mound the tuna and vegetables on a
  large serving platter. Arrange the
hard-cooked egg quarters around the side.
Sprinkle the olives over the salad, then
arrange the anchovies in a lattice on top.
Cover and chill.

7 About 15 minutes before serving,
  remove the salad from the refrigerator
and let come to room temperature.
Sprinkle with parsley and serve.

Lobster Salad

Lobsters are best prepared simply to ensure that none of the rich, sweet flavor is lost amid a mass of other ingredients.

NUTRITIONAL INFORMATION

Calories	487	Sugars	.........2g
Protein	........24g	Fat	..........42g
Carbohydrate	....2g	Saturates	.......6g

 15 mins   🕐 6 mins

SERVES 2

INGREDIENTS

2 raw lobster tails

salt and pepper

LEMON-DILL MAYONNAISE

1 large lemon

1 large egg yolk

½ tsp Dijon mustard

⅔ cup olive oil

1 tbsp chopped fresh dill

TO GARNISH

radicchio leaves

lemon wedges

fresh dill sprigs

1 To make the lemon-dill mayonnaise, finely grate the lemon rind and squeeze the juice. Beat the egg yolk in a small bowl and beat in the mustard and 1 tsp of the lemon juice.

2 Using a balloon whisk or electric mixer, beat in the olive oil, drop by drop, until a thick mayonnaise forms. Stir in half the lemon rind and 1 tablespoon of the lemon juice.

3 Season with salt and pepper, and add more lemon juice if desired. Stir in the dill and cover with plastic wrap. Chill in the refrigerator until required.

4 Bring a large saucepan of lightly salted water to a boil. Add the lobster tails, bring back to a boil, and cook for 6 minutes until the flesh is opaque and the shells are red. Drain immediately and set aside to cool.

5 Remove the lobster flesh from the shells and cut into bite-size pieces. Arrange the radicchio leaves on individual plates and top with the lobster flesh. Place a spoonful of the lemon-dill mayonnaise on the side. Garnish with lemon wedges and fresh dill sprigs and serve.

Mozzarella & Tomato Salad

Take advantage of the delicious varieties of cherry tomatoes that are available to make a refreshing Italian-style salad with lots of eye-appeal.

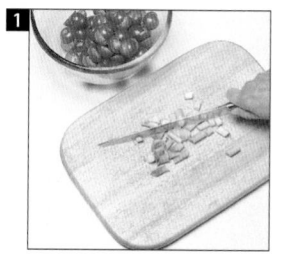
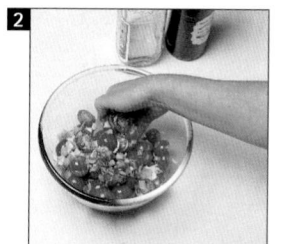

NUTRITIONAL INFORMATION

Calories 295	Sugars 3g
Protein 9g	Fat 27g
Carbohydrate 3g	Saturates 7g

4¼ hrs   0 mins

SERVES 4–6

INGREDIENTS

1 lb/450 g cherry tomatoes

4 scallions

½ cup extra virgin olive oil

2 tbsp balsamic vinegar

7 oz/200 g buffalo mozzarella (see Cook's Tip), cut into cubes

½ cup fresh flat leaf parsley

1 cup fresh basil leaves

salt and pepper

1 Using a sharp knife, cut the tomatoes in half and place them in a large bowl. Trim the scallions and finely chop both the green and white parts, then add to the bowl.

2 Pour in the olive oil and balsamic vinegar and use your hands to toss together. Season with salt and pepper to taste, add the mozzarella, and toss again. Cover with plastic wrap and chill in the refrigerator for 4 hours.

3 Remove the salad from the refrigerator 10 minutes before serving. Finely chop the parsley and add to the salad. Tear the basil leaves and sprinkle them over the salad. Toss all the ingredients together again. Adjust the seasoning and serve.

COOK'S TIP

For the best flavor, buy buffalo mozzarella—mozzarella di bufala—rather than the factory-made cow's milk version. This salad would also look good made with bocconcini which are small balls of mozzarella. Look out for these in Italian delicatessens.

Roasted Bell Pepper Salad

This is a classic way of serving the large, intensely flavored sweet bell peppers that are so abundant throughout the summer months.

NUTRITIONAL INFORMATION

Calories	144	Sugars	.........9g
Protein	.........2g	Fat	...........11g
Carbohydrate	....9g	Saturates	.......2g

 30 mins   10 mins

SERVES 4–6

I N G R E D I E N T S

4–6 large red, yellow and/or orange
   bell peppers

2 scallions, trimmed

crusty bread, to serve

LEMON-PARSLEY VINAIGRETTE

6 tbsp extra virgin olive oil

4½ tsp freshly squeezed lemon juice

2 tbsp chopped fresh flat leaf parsley

salt and pepper

1 To make the dressing, put the oil, lemon juice, and parsley in a screw-top jar and shake until well blended. Add salt and pepper to taste. Set aside.

2 Slice the tops off the bell peppers, then cut each into quarters or thirds, depending on the size. Remove the cores and seeds—the flatter the pieces are, the easier they are to cook.

VARIATIONS

For a party, marinate small, cooked shrimp in the dressing and sprinkle them over the salad. Other Mediterranean ingredients you can add to the salad include capers, anchovies, pitted and sliced green or black olives, and finely grated lemon rind.

3 Thinly slice the scallions on the diagonal and set aside.

4 Place the bell pepper pieces on a broiler rack under a preheated broiler and broil for about 10 minutes or until the skins are charred and the flesh is softened.

5 Using tongs, remove each piece as it is ready. Immediately place in a bowl and cover with plastic wrap. Set aside for about 20 minutes to cool.

6 When cool enough to handle, peel the skins off the bell peppers, then slice the flesh into long, thin strips.

7 Arrange the bell pepper strips on a serving platter. Shake the dressing again, then pour it over the salad. Sprinkle the scallions over the top. Serve with crusty bread, or cover with plastic wrap and chill until required.

Green Tabbouleh

Tomatoes are sometimes included in this refreshing bulgur salad
from Turkey, but this version relies on herbs and vegetables for its flavor.

NUTRITIONAL INFORMATION

Calories . . . . . . .333 Sugars 2g
Protein . . . . .9g Fat 7g
Carbohydrate . . .59g Saturates 1g

 30 mins   0 mins

SERVES 4

I N G R E D I E N T S

1¾ cups bulgur

7 oz/200 g cucumber

6 scallions

½ cup fresh flat leaf parsley

1 lemon

about 2 tbsp garlic-flavored
  olive oil

salt and pepper

1 Place the bulgur in a heatproof bowl, pour over 2½ cups boiling water and cover with an upturned plate. Set aside for at least 20 minutes until the bulgur has absorbed the water and become tender.

2 Meanwhile, cut the cucumber in half lengthwise and then cut each half into 3 strips lengthwise. Using a tsp, scoop out and discard the seeds. Chop the cucumber strips into bite-size pieces. Put the cucumber pieces in a serving bowl.

3 Trim the top of the green parts of each of the scallions, then cut each in half lengthwise. Finely chop and add to the cucumber.

4 Place the parsley on a cutting board and sprinkle with a little salt. Using a cook's knife or a mezzaluna, very finely chop both the leaves and stems. Add the parsley to the bowl with the cucumber and scallions. Finely grate the lemon rind into the bowl.

5 When the bulgur is cool enough to handle, either squeeze out any excess water with your hands or press out the water through a strainer with the back of a spoon, then add the bulgur to the bowl, and mix with the other ingredients.

6 Cut the lemon in half and squeeze the juice of 1 half over the salad. Add 2 tbsp of the garlic-flavored oil and stir all the ingredients together. Adjust the seasoning with salt and pepper to taste and extra lemon juice or oil if needed. Cover the bowl with plastic wrap and chill until required.

Warm Rice Salad

This easy-to-make rice salad has all the flavors of the Aegean—olive oil, lemon, feta cheese, capers, and tomatoes.

NUTRITIONAL INFORMATION

Calories	374	Sugars	.........4g
Protein	.........9g	Fat	..........24g
Carbohydrate	...33g	Saturates	.......8g

 10 mins   20 mins

SERVES 4–6

INGREDIENTS

1 cup long grain white rice

5 tbsp extra virgin olive oil

2–3 tbsp lemon juice

1 tbsp chopped fresh oregano or
  1 tsp dried oregano

½ tsp Dijon mustard

2 large ripe tomatoes, deseeded and chopped

1 red or green bell pepper, deseeded
  and chopped

¾ cup Kalamata or other brine-cured black
  olives, pitted and halved

2 cups crumbled feta cheese, plus extra
  cubes, to garnish

1 tbsp capers, rinsed and drained

2–4 tbsp chopped fresh flat leaf parsley
  or cilantro

salt and pepper

diced cucumber, to garnish

1 Bring a pan of lightly salted water to a boil. Add the rice, return to a boil, stirring once or twice, and simmer for 15–20 minutes until tender. Drain, rinse with hot water, and drain again.

2 Meanwhile, whisk the olive oil with the lemon juice, oregano, mustard, and salt and pepper in a bowl. Add the tomatoes, bell pepper, olives, feta, capers, and parsley and stir to coat in the dressing. Set aside to marinate.

3 Turn the rice into a large bowl, then add to the vegetable mixture, and toss to mix well. Season the salad with salt and pepper to taste, then divide among 4–6 individual dishes, and garnish with extra feta cheese cubes and diced cucumber. Serve just warm.

VARIATION

This salad is also delicious made with brown rice—just increase the cooking time to 25–30 minutes.

Wild Rice & Bacon Salad

Wild rice has a nutty texture, which is great in salads, and bacon and scallops make a perfect combination.

NUTRITIONAL INFORMATION

Calories	580	Sugars	.........1g
Protein	........19g	Fat	..........41g
Carbohydrate	...35g	Saturates	.......6g

 15 mins   🕐 1 hr

SERVES 4

I N G R E D I E N T S

generous ¾ cup wild rice

2½ cups water or more, if necessary

½ cup pecans or walnuts

2 tbsp vegetable oil

4 slices smoked bacon, diced or sliced

3–4 shallots, finely chopped

5 tbsp walnut oil

2–3 tbsp sherry or apple vinegar

2 tbsp chopped fresh dill

8–12 large scallops, cut in half lengthwise

salt and pepper

lemon and lime slices, to serve

1 Put the wild rice in a saucepan with the water and bring to a boil, stirring once or twice. Reduce the heat, cover, and simmer gently for 30–50 minutes, depending on whether you prefer a chewy or tender texture. Using a fork, fluff the rice into a large bowl and set aside to cool slightly.

2 Meanwhile, dry-fry the nuts in a skillet, stirring frequently, for 2–3 minutes until just beginning to color. Cool and chop coarsely, then set aside.

3 Heat 1 tbsp of the vegetable oil in the pan. Stir in the bacon and cook, stirring occasionally, until crisp and brown. Transfer to paper towels to drain. Remove some of the oil from the pan and stir in the shallots. Cook, stirring occasionally, for 3–4 minutes, until soft.

4 Stir the toasted nuts, bacon, and shallots into the rice. Add the walnut oil, vinegar, half the chopped dill, and salt and pepper to taste. Toss well to combine the ingredients, then set aside.

5 Brush a large nonstick skillet with the remaining oil. Heat until very hot, add the scallops and cook for 1 minute on each side until golden (do not overcook). Remove them from the skillet.

6 Divide the wild rice salad among 4 plates. Top with the scallops and sprinkle with the remaining dill. Garnish with a sprig of dill, if desired, and serve immediately with the lemon and lime slices.

Rice, Bean & Corn Salad

This hearty rice salad was inspired by the famous, traditional dish called succotash. It is incredibly easy to put together and tastes wonderful.

NUTRITIONAL INFORMATION

Calories 218
Sugars 3g
Protein 11g
Fat 5g
Carbohydrate . . .34g
Saturates 1g

 20 mins   30 mins

SERVES 4–6

INGREDIENTS

½ cup long grain white or brown rice

3 corn cobs

3–4 tbsp peanut oil

1 small red onion, finely chopped

1 fresh red or green chile, deseeded and finely chopped

1 tbsp lemon juice

1 tbsp lime juice

½ tsp cayenne pepper

2 tbsp chopped fresh cilantro

14 oz/400 g can lima beans, drained

¾ cup diced cooked ham

salt and pepper

1 Bring a a large saucepan of lightly salted water to a boil. Add the rice and return to a boil, stirring once or twice. Reduce the heat and simmer for 15–20 minutes until the rice is tender. (Brown rice will take 25–30 minutes.) Drain and rinse under cold running water; drain again, and set aside.

2 Scrape down each corn cob with a knife to remove the kernels. Place in a bowl and set aside. Scrape along each cob to remove the milky residue and transfer to another small bowl.

3 Heat 1 tbsp of the oil in a pan. Add the corn kernels and cook gently, stirring frequently, for about 5 minutes until tender. Add the red onion and chile and stir over low heat for about 1 minute until blended. Transfer to a plate and set aside to cool slightly.

4 Place the lemon and lime juices in a large bowl and whisk in the cayenne pepper, 2–3 tbsp of the remaining oil, and the milky corn liquid. Whisk in the chopped cilantro until well combined.

5 Using a fork, fluff in the cooked rice and corn and onion mixture. Add the beans and ham and season with salt and pepper to taste. Transfer to a serving bowl and serve immediately.

Gazpacho Rice Salad

All the flavors of a zesty Spanish gazpacho—garlic, tomatoes, bell peppers, and cucumber combined with rice—make a great summer salad.

NUTRITIONAL INFORMATION

Calories 253   Sugars 15g
Protein ....7g   Fat 5g
Carbohydrate ...46g   Saturates 1g

 30 mins   35 mins

SERVES 4

INGREDIENTS

7 tbsp extra virgin olive oil

1 onion, finely chopped

4 garlic cloves, finely chopped

1 cup long grain white rice

1½ cups vegetable stock or water

1½ tsp dried thyme

3 tbsp sherry vinegar

1 tsp Dijon mustard

1 tsp honey

1 red bell pepper, deseeded and chopped

½ yellow bell pepper, deseeded and chopped

½ green bell pepper, deseeded and chopped

1 red onion, finely chopped

½ cucumber, peeled, deseeded and chopped (optional)

3 tomatoes, deseeded and chopped

2–3 tbsp chopped flat leaf parsley

salt and pepper

TO SERVE

12 cherry tomatoes, halved

12 black olives, pitted and coarsely chopped

1 tbsp sliced almonds, toasted

1 Heat 2 tbsp of the oil in a large saucepan. Add the onion and cook, stirring frequently, for 2 minutes until beginning to soften. Stir in half the garlic and cook for a further minute.

2 Add the rice, stir to coat, and cook for about 2 minutes until translucent. Stir in the stock and half the thyme and bring to a boil. Season to taste. Cover and simmer gently for about 20 minutes until tender. Stand, still covered, for about 15 minutes; uncover and cool completely.

3 Whisk the vinegar with the remaining garlic and thyme, the mustard, honey, and salt and pepper in a large bowl. Gradually whisk in the remaining olive oil. Using a fork, gently fluff the rice into the vinaigrette.

4 Add the bell peppers, red onion, cucumber, tomatoes, and parsley; toss and adjust the seasoning. Transfer the salad to a serving bowl and garnish with the tomatoes, black olives, and toasted almonds. Serve warm.

Lentil & Shiitake Salad

Fresh shiitakes, which are now widely available, give this substantial salad a good mushroomy flavor.

NUTRITIONAL INFORMATION

Calories	469	Sugars	3g
Protein	14g	Fat	30g
Carbohydrate	37g	Saturates	4g

15 mins   1¼ hrs

SERVES 6–8

INGREDIENTS

1 cup Puy lentils, rinsed

4 tbsp olive oil

1 onion, finely chopped

1 cup long grain brown rice

½ tsp dried thyme

2 cups chicken stock

4¾ cups sliced shiitake mushrooms

2 garlic cloves, finely chopped

¾ cup diced smoked bacon, fried crisp

2 small zucchini, diced

1–2 celery stalks, thinly sliced

6 scallions, thinly sliced

2–3 tbsp chopped fresh parsley

2 tbsp chopped walnuts, toasted

salt and pepper

DRESSING

2 tbsp red or white wine vinegar

1 tbsp balsamic vinegar

1 tsp Dijon mustard

1 tsp sugar

5 tbsp extra virgin olive oil

2–3 tbsp walnut oil

1 Bring a pan of water to a boil. Add the lentils and simmer for 30 minutes. Drain and rinse under cold running water.

2 Heat 2 tbsp of the oil in a large saucepan. Cook the onion until softened. Stir in the rice and add the thyme, stock, and salt and pepper. Bring to a boil, cover, and simmer gently for 40 minutes until the rice is tender.

3 Heat the remaining oil in a skillet and stir-fry the mushrooms for about 5 minutes until golden. Stir in the garlic and cook for a further 30 seconds. Season.

4 To make the dressing, whisk together the wine and balsamic vinegars, mustard, and sugar in a large bowl. Gradually whisk in the oils. Season with salt and pepper. Add the lentils and toss gently. Fork in the rice and toss again.

5 Stir in the bacon and mushrooms, then the zucchini, celery, scallions, and parsley, and season to taste. Serve sprinkled with walnuts.

Moroccan Mixed Rice Salad

The combination of spices gives this rice salad a slightly exotic scent. Toasting the spices mellows the harshness and brings out their flavors.

NUTRITIONAL INFORMATION

Calories	469	Sugars	.......24g
Protein	........11g	Fat	.........22g
Carbohydrate	...60g	Saturates	.......3g

 15 mins   1½ hrs

SERVES 4–6

I N G R E D I E N T S

1 tbsp soy sauce

1 tbsp molasses

⅓ cup wild rice

2 tbsp olive oil

½ cup long grain rice

15 oz/425 g can garbanzo beans, drained

½ red onion, finely chopped

1 small red bell pepper, deseeded and diced

⅓ cup dried apricots, sliced

½ cup raisins

2 tbsp chopped fresh mint
   or cilantro

½ cup sliced almonds, toasted

lettuce leaves, to garnish

lemon wedges, to serve

S P I C E D   D R E S S I N G

1 tsp hot curry powder

1 tsp ground coriander

1 tsp ground turmeric

1 tsp freshly ground nutmeg

½ tsp cayenne pepper

¼ cup rice vinegar

2 tbsp honey

1 tbsp lemon juice

5 tbsp extra virgin olive oil

1 Bring 1½ cups water, the soy sauce, and molasses to a boil in a large pan. Add the wild rice and bring back to a boil. Cover and simmer gently for 30–50 minutes. Remove from the heat.

2 Heat the oil in a pan, add the brown rice, and stir for 2 minutes to coat. Add 2 cups water and bring to a boil. Cover and simmer for 40 minutes until tender. Remove from the heat.

3 Meanwhile, make the dressing. Dry-fry the spices in a small skillet, stirring, for 4–5 minutes. Cool on a plate. Whisk the vinegar with the honey and lemon juice in a large bowl, then whisk in the oil. Whisk in the cooled spice mixture.

4 Fork the rices into the dressing. Stir in the garbanzo beans, onion, bell pepper, apricots, raisins, and mint. Sprinkle with the almonds, garnish, and serve.

Pesto Risotto-Rice Salad

This is a cross between a risotto and a rice salad—using
Italian risotto rice produces a slightly heavier, stickier result.

NUTRITIONAL INFORMATION

Calories 406	Sugars 5g
Protein 7g	Fat 28g
Carbohydrate ...34g	Saturates 5g

45 mins   30 mins

SERVES 4–6

INGREDIENTS

3 tbsp extra virgin olive oil, plus extra
for drizzling

1 onion, finely chopped

1½ cups risotto rice

1 cup boiling water

6 sun-dried tomatoes in oil, drained and cut
into thin slivers

½ small red onion, very thinly sliced

3 tbsp lemon juice

PESTO

2 cups fresh basil leaves

2 garlic cloves, finely chopped

2 tbsp pine nuts, lightly toasted

½ cup extra virgin olive oil

⅔ cup freshly grated Parmesan cheese

salt and pepper

TO GARNISH

fresh basil leaves

Parmesan shavings

1 To make the pesto, put the basil, garlic, and pine nuts in a food processor and process for 30 seconds. With the motor running, gradually add the olive oil through the feeder tube until a smooth paste forms. Add the cheese and pulse until blended, but still with texture. Scrape into a small bowl and season to taste.

2 Heat 1 tablespoon of the oil in a saucepan and cook the onion until softened. Stir in the rice and cook, stirring occasionally, for 2 minutes. Stir in the water and season. Cover and simmer for 20 minutes until the rice is tender and the water absorbed. Cool slightly.

3 Put the sun-dried tomatoes and sliced onion in a bowl, add the lemon juice and 2 tablespoons of oil. Fork in the hot rice and stir in the pesto. Toss to combine. Adjust the seasoning if necessary. Cover and cool to room temperature.

4 Fork the rice mixture into a shallow serving bowl. Drizzle with some olive oil and garnish with basil leaves and Parmesan shavings. Serve the salad at room temperature, not chilled.

Red Rice Salad

This hearty salad is made with red rice, originally from France. It has an earthy flavor, which goes well with the other robust ingredients.

 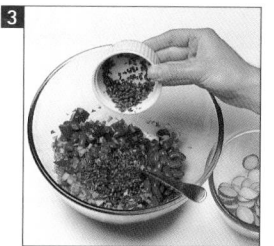 

NUTRITIONAL INFORMATION

Calories 192   Sugars 5g
Protein ....6g   Fat 5g
Carbohydrate ...33g   Saturates 1g

 1½ hrs   30 mins

SERVES 6–8

INGREDIENTS

1 tbsp olive oil

1 cup red rice

1 cup water

14 oz/400 g can red kidney beans, drained and rinsed

1 small red bell pepper, deseeded and diced

1 small red onion, finely chopped

2 small cooked beets (not in vinegar), peeled and diced

6–8 red radishes, thinly sliced

2–3 tbsp chopped fresh chives

salt and pepper

fresh chives, to garnish

HOT DRESSING

2 tbsp horseradish

1 tbsp Dijon mustard

1 tsp sugar

¼ cup red wine vinegar

½ cup extra virgin olive oil

1 Put the olive oil and red rice in a heavy pan and place over a medium heat. Add the water and 1 teaspoon of salt. Bring to a boil, reduce the heat, cover, and simmer gently until the rice is tender and all the water has been absorbed. (There are several varieties of red rice, which differ in cooking times, so follow the packet instructions.) Remove the pan from the heat and set aside to cool to room temperature.

2 To make the dressing, put the horseradish, Dijon mustard, and sugar into a small bowl and whisk thoroughly to combine. Whisk in the red wine vinegar, then gradually whisk in the oil to form a smooth dressing.

3 In a large bowl, combine the kidney beans, red bell pepper, onion, beet, radishes, and chives and toss together. Season with salt and pepper to taste.

4 Using a fork, fluff the rice into the bowl with the vegetables. Pour over the dressing and toss well. Cover and let the salad stand for about 1 hour. Spoon into a large shallow serving bowl, garnish with fresh chives, and serve immediately.

Fruity Wild Rice Salsa

Wild rice has a nutty flavor and a good texture, ideal for salsas and salads, and goes well with the black beans in this dish.

NUTRITIONAL INFORMATION

Calories 467	Sugars 15g	
Protein 10g	Fat 20g	
Carbohydrate ...49g	Saturates 4g	

 2¼ hrs   1 hr

SERVES 4–6

INGREDIENTS

scant 1 cup small black beans, soaked
    overnight in cold water

1 onion, studded with 4 cloves

¾ cup wild rice

2 garlic cloves

2 cups boiling water

1 red onion, finely chopped

2 fresh red chiles, deseeded and
    thinly sliced

1 red bell pepper, deseeded and chopped

1 small mango or papaya, peeled and diced

2 oranges, segments removed and
    juice reserved

4 passion fruits, pulp and juice

juice of 3–4 limes

½ tsp ground cumin

1 tbsp maple syrup or brown sugar

⅔ cup extra virgin olive oil

1 small bunch fresh cilantro, leaves
    stripped from stems and chopped

lime slices, to garnish

1 Drain the beans and put in a large pan with the clove-studded onion. Cover with cold water by at least 2 inches/5 cm. Bring to a boil, lower the heat, and simmer for 1 hour until the beans are tender.

Discard the onion, rinse the beans under cold running water, and drain.

2 Meanwhile, put the wild rice and garlic in a pan and pour in the boiling water. Cover and simmer over low heat for 30–50 minutes. Cool slightly and discard the garlic cloves.

3 Put the beans in a large bowl and fork in the wild rice. Add the onion, chiles, bell pepper, mango, orange segments and their juice, and the passion fruit pulp and juice. Toss well together.

4 Combine the lime juice, cumin, and maple syrup or sugar. Whisk in the olive oil and half the cilantro, then pour over the rice mixture, and toss well. Cover and set aside for up to 2 hours.

5 Spoon into a serving bowl, sprinkle with the remaining cilantro, and serve garnished with lime slices.

Shrimp Salad & Toasted Rice

This simple salad is tossed with an unusual Vietnamese-style dressing and sprinkled with dry toasted rice, which gives an interesting texture.

NUTRITIONAL INFORMATION

Calories	156	Sugars	.........4g
Protein	........12g	Fat	...........7g
Carbohydrate	....11g	Saturates	.......1g

45 mins　　5 mins

SERVES 4

INGREDIENTS

8 oz/225 g peeled cooked shrimp, with tail shells left on

cayenne pepper

1 tbsp long grain rice

2 tbsp sunflower oil

1 large head Romaine lettuce with outer leaves removed or 2 hearts

½ small cucumber, peeled, deseeded and thinly sliced

1 small bunch chives, sliced into 1 inch/2.5 cm pieces

handful of fresh mint leaves

salt and pepper

DRESSING

¼ cup rice vinegar

1 fresh red chile, deseeded and thinly sliced

3 inch/7.5 cm piece of lemongrass stalk, crushed

juice of 1 lime

2 tbsp Thai fish sauce

1 tsp sugar

1 Split each shrimp in half lengthwise, leaving the tail attached to one half. Remove the dark intestinal veins and pat dry on paper towels. Sprinkle with a little salt and cayenne pepper.

2 To make the dressing, combine the vinegar with the chile and lemongrass. Set aside to marinate.

3 Heat a wok or heavy skillet over high heat. Add the rice and stir until brown and fragrant. Turn into a mortar and cool completely. Crush gently with a pestle until coarse crumbs form.

4 Heat the oil in a clean pan and stir-fry the shrimp for 1 minute. Transfer to a plate and season with pepper.

5 Tear or shred the lettuce into bite-size pieces and transfer to a shallow salad bowl. Add the cucumber, chives, and mint leaves and toss to combine.

6 Remove the lemongrass and most of the chile slices from the rice vinegar and whisk in the lime juice, fish sauce, and sugar. Pour most of the dressing over the salad and toss well to mix. Top with the shrimp and drizzle with the remaining dressing. Sprinkle with the toasted rice and serve immediately.

Shrimp & Noodle Salad

This delicious combination of rice noodles and shrimp, lightly dressed with typical Thai flavors, makes an impressive first course or light lunch.

NUTRITIONAL INFORMATION

Calories	204	Sugars	.........8g
Protein	........15g	Fat	...........3g
Carbohydrate	...29g	Saturates	.......1g

 15 mins   2 mins

SERVES 4

INGREDIENTS

3 oz/85 g rice vermicelli or rice sticks

6 oz/175 g snow peas, cut crosswise in half, if large

5 tbsp lime juice

4 tbsp Thai fish sauce

1 tbsp sugar

1 inch/2.5 cm piece of fresh ginger root, finely chopped

1 fresh red chile, deseeded and thinly sliced on the diagonal

4 tbsp chopped fresh cilantro or mint, plus extra to garnish

4 inch/10 cm piece of cucumber, peeled, deseeded and diced

2 scallions, thinly sliced on the diagonal

16–20 large peeled cooked shrimp

2 tbsp chopped unsalted peanuts or cashews (optional)

4 whole cooked shrimp and lemon slices, to garnish

2 Bring a saucepan of water to a boil. Add the snow peas and return to a boil. Lower the heat and simmer for 1 minute. Drain, rinse under cold running water until cold, then drain, and set aside.

3 Whisk together the lime juice, fish sauce, sugar, ginger, chile, and cilantro in a large bowl. Stir in the cucumber and scallions. Add the drained noodles, snow peas, and the shrimp. Toss the salad gently together.

4 Divide the noodle salad among 4 large plates. Sprinkle with chopped cilantro and the peanuts, if using, then garnish each plate with a whole shrimp and a lemon slice. Serve immediately.

1 Put the rice noodles in a large bowl and pour over enough hot water to cover. Set aside for about 4 minutes until soft. Drain and rinse under cold running water; drain again and set aside.

Sweet & Sour Fruit

This mixture of fresh and canned fruit, which has a sweet and sour flavor, is very cooling, especially in the summer.

 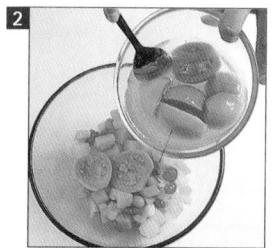 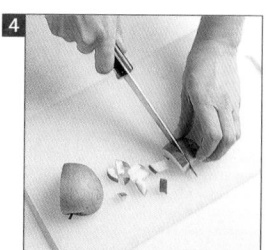

NUTRITIONAL INFORMATION

Calories 240   Sugars 58g
Protein . . . . .2g   Fat 0.4g
Carbohydrate . . .60g   Saturates 0g

 5 mins   0 mins

SERVES 4

INGREDIENTS

14 oz/400 g can mixed fruit cocktail

14 oz/400 g can guavas

2 large bananas

3 apples (optional)

1 tsp ground black pepper

1 tsp salt

½ tsp ground ginger

2 tbsp lemon juice

fresh mint leaves, to garnish

1 Drain the can of mixed fruit cocktail and place the fruit in a large, deep mixing bowl.

2 Mix the the drained fruit cocktail with the guavas and their syrup so that the fruit is well coated.

3 Peel the bananas and cut them into thick slices.

4 Peel and core the apples, if using, and cut them into dice.

5 Add the fresh fruit to the bowl containing the canned fruit and mix thoroughly together.

6 Add the ground black pepper, salt, and ginger and stir to mix. Add the

lemon juice to prevent the banana and apple from turning brown and mix again.

7 Serve the sweet and sour fruit as a snack, garnished with a few fresh mint leaves.

COOK'S TIP

Guavas are tropical fruits with a powerful, exotic smell. You may find fresh guavas in specialist shops and large supermarkets, but the canned variety is more widely available. Surprisingly, they have a higher vitamin C content than many citrus fruits.

Mussel Salad

A colorful combination of cooked mussels tossed together with chargrilled red bell peppers and salad greens in a lemon dressing.

NUTRITIONAL INFORMATION

Calories 124	Sugars 5g	
Protein 16g	Fat 5g	
Carbohydrate 5g	Saturates 1g	

40 mins | 10 mins

SERVES 4

INGREDIENTS

2 red bell peppers, halved and deseeded

12 oz/350 g cooked shelled mussels, thawed if frozen

1 head of radicchio

1 oz/25 g arugula leaves

8 cooked green-lipped mussels in their shells

TO SERVE

lemon wedges

crusty bread

DRESSING

1 tbsp olive oil

1 tbsp lemon juice

1 tsp finely grated lemon rind

2 tsp honey

1 tsp French mustard

1 tbsp chopped fresh chives

salt and pepper

1 Preheat the broiler to hot. Place the bell peppers, skin side up, on the rack. Broil for 8–10 minutes until the skin is charred and blistered and the flesh is soft. Remove from the broiler with tongs, place in a bowl, and cover with plastic wrap. Set aside for 10 minutes until cool enough to handle, then peel off the skins.

2 Slice the bell pepper flesh into thin strips and place in a bowl. Gently stir in the shelled mussels.

3 To make the dressing, whisk together the oil, lemon juice and rind, honey, mustard, and chives. until well blended. Season to taste with salt and pepper. Add the bell pepper and mussel mixture and toss gently until coated.

4 Remove the central core of the radicchio and shred the leaves. Place in a serving bowl with the arugula leaves and toss together.

5 Pile the mussel mixture into the center of the leaves and arrange the green-lipped mussels in their shells around the edge of the bowl. Serve with lemon wedges and crusty bread.

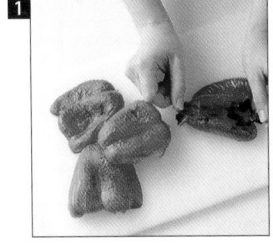

Hot & Spicy Rice Salad

Serve this spicy Indian-style dish with a low-fat plain yogurt raita for a delightfully refreshing contrast.

NUTRITIONAL INFORMATION

Calories	329	Sugars	.......27g
Protein	.........8g	Fat	..........8g
Carbohydrate	...59g	Saturates	......1g

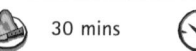 30 mins   25 mins

SERVES 4

INGREDIENTS

2 tsp vegetable oil

1 onion, finely chopped

1 fresh red chile, deseeded and finely chopped

8 cardamom pods

1 tsp ground turmeric

1 tsp garam masala

1¾ cups basmati rice, rinsed

3 cups boiling water

1 orange bell pepper, chopped

8 oz/225 g cauliflower florets, divided into small sprigs

4 ripe tomatoes, peeled, deseeded and chopped

scant 1 cup seedless raisins

¼ cup toasted sliced almonds

salt and pepper

raita of low-fat plain yogurt, onion, cucumber, and mint, to serve

1 Heat the oil in a large nonstick pan. Add the onion, chile, cardamom pods, turmeric, and garam masala and cook over a low heat for 2–3 minutes until the vegetables are just softened.

2 Stir in the rice, boiling water, orange bell pepper, and cauliflower. Season to taste with salt and pepper.

3 Cover with a tight-fitting lid and bring to a boil. Lower the heat and simmer for 15 minutes without lifting the lid.

4 Uncover the pan and fork through the rice. Stir in the tomatoes and raisins.

5 Cover the pan again, turn off the heat, and leave for 15 minutes. Discard the cardamom pods.

6 Pile onto a warmed serving platter and sprinkle over the toasted sliced almonds.

7 Serve the rice salad with the yogurt raita.

Layered Chicken Salad

This layered entrée salad has lively tastes and textures.
For an interesting variation, substitute canned tuna for the chicken.

NUTRITIONAL INFORMATION

Calories	352	Sugars	.........9g
Protein	........29g	Fat	...........9g
Carbohydrate	...43g	Saturates	......2g

 1 hr 40 mins

SERVES 4

I N G R E D I E N T S

1 lb 10 oz/750 g new potatoes, scrubbed

1 red bell pepper, halved and deseeded

1 green bell pepper, halved and deseeded

2 small zucchini, sliced

1 small onion, thinly sliced

3 tomatoes, sliced

12 oz/350 g cooked chicken, sliced

chopped fresh chives, to garnish

Y O G U R T   D R E S S I N G

⅔ cup low-fat plain yogurt

3 tbsp low-fat mayonnaise

1 tbsp chopped fresh chives

salt and pepper

1 Put the potatoes into a large pan, add just enough cold water to cover, and bring to a boil. Lower the heat, cover, and simmer for 15–20 minutes until tender.

2 Meanwhile, place the bell pepper halves, skin side up, under a preheated hot broiler and broil until the skins blacken and begin to char.

3 Remove the bell peppers with tongs, place in a bowl, and cover with plastic wrap. Set aside until cool enough to handle, then peel off the skins, and slice the flesh.

4 Bring a small pan of lightly salted water to a boil. Add the zucchini, bring back to a boil, and simmer for 3 minutes. Drain, rinse under cold running water to prevent any further cooking, and drain again. Set aside.

5 To make the dressing, whisk the yogurt, low-fat mayonnaise, and chopped chives together in a small bowl until well blended. Season to taste with salt and pepper.

6 When the potatoes are tender, drain, cool, and slice them. Add them to the dressing and mix gently to coat evenly. Spoon the potatoes onto 4 serving plates, dividing them equally.

7 Top each plate with one quarter of the bell pepper slices and zucchini. Layer one quarter of the onion and tomato slices, then the sliced chicken, on top of each serving. Garnish with chopped chives and serve immediately.

 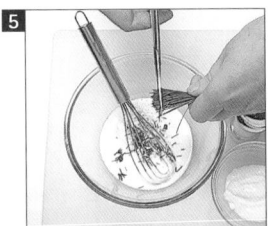 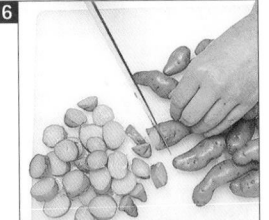

Melon and Mango Salad

A little freshly grated ginger root mixed with creamy yogurt and honey makes a perfect dressing for this refreshing salad.

NUTRITIONAL INFORMATION

Calories 189   Sugars 30g
Protein ....5g   Fat 7g
Carbohydrate ...30g   Saturates 1g

  15 mins   0 mins

SERVES 4

INGREDIENTS

1 cantaloupe melon

2 oz/55 g black grapes, halved and seeded

2 oz/55 g green grapes

1 large mango

1 bunch of watercress, trimmed

iceberg lettuce leaves, shredded

2 tbsp olive oil

1 tbsp apple vinegar

1 passion fruit

salt and pepper

DRESSING

⅔ cup low-fat plain yogurt

1 tbsp honey

1 tsp grated fresh ginger root

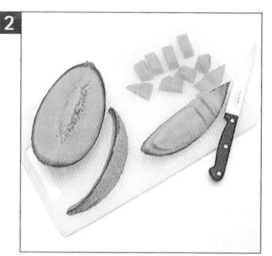

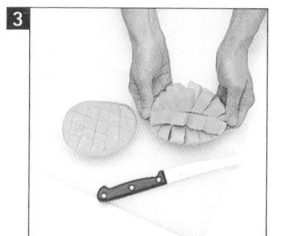

1 To make the dressing, for the melon, whisk together the yogurt, honey, and ginger in a small bowl.

2 Halve the melon, scoop out the seeds with a spoon, and discard. Slice, peel, and dice the flesh. Place in a bowl with the grapes.

3 Slice the mango on each side of its large flat pit. On each mango half, slash the flesh into a criss-cross pattern down to, but not through the skin. Push the skin from underneath to turn the mango halves inside out. Now remove the flesh and add to the melon mixture.

4 Arrange the watercress and lettuce leaves on 4 serving plates.

5 Make the dressing for the salad leaves by whisking together the olive oil and vinegar with a little salt and pepper. Drizzle over the salad greens.

6 Divide the melon mixture among the 4 plates and spoon the yogurt dressing over it.

7 Scoop the seeds out of the passion fruit and sprinkle them over the salads. Serve immediately or chill in the refrigerator until required.

Mango & Wild Rice Salad

The very slight edge that counteracts the sweetness of the fruit makes a juicy ripe mango the perfect choice for a summery salad.

NUTRITIONAL INFORMATION

Calories	320	Sugars	........10g
Protein	.........6g	Fat	..........20g
Carbohydrate	...30g	Saturates	......2g

15 mins   1¼ hrs

SERVES 4

INGREDIENTS

generous ½ cup wild rice

¾ cup basmati rice

3 tbsp hazelnut oil

1 tbsp sherry vinegar

1 ripe mango

3 celery stalks

¾ cup dried apricots, chopped

½ cup sliced almonds, toasted

2 tbsp chopped, fresh cilantro or mint

salt and pepper

fresh cilantro or mint sprigs, to garnish

1 Cook the wild rice and basmati rice in separate pans of lightly salted boiling water. Cook the wild rice for 45–50 minutes and the basmati rice for 10–12 minutes. Drain, rinse, and drain again. Place both rices in a large bowl.

2 Whisk together the oil and vinegar and season to taste with salt and pepper. Pour over the rice and toss well.

3 Cut the mango in half lengthwise, as close to the pit as possible. Remove and discard the pit.

4 Peel the skin from the mango and cut the flesh into slices.

5 Thinly slice the celery and add to the cooled rice with the mango, apricots, almonds, and chopped herbs. Toss together and transfer to a serving dish.

6 Garnish the salad with cilantro or mint sprigs and serve.

COOK'S TIP

To toast almonds, place them on a cookie sheet in a preheated oven, 350°F/180°C, for 5–10 minutes. Alternatively, toast them under the broiler, turning frequently and keeping a close eye on them because they will quickly burn.

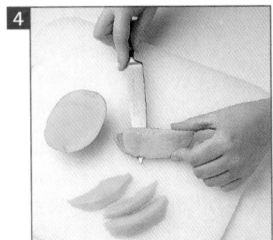

Parsley, Chicken & Ham Pâté

Pâté is easy to make at home, and this combination of lean chicken and ham mixed with herbs is especially straightforward.

NUTRITIONAL INFORMATION

Calories	119	Sugars	.........2g
Protein	........20g	Fat	...........3g
Carbohydrate	....2g	Saturates	......1g

 40 mins   0 mins

SERVES 4

I N G R E D I E N T S

8 oz/225 g skinless, boneless lean chicken, cooked

3½ oz/100 g lean ham

small bunch of fresh parsley

1 tsp grated lime rind, plus extra to garnish

2 tbsp lime juice

1 garlic clove, peeled

½ cup low-fat cream cheese

salt and pepper

T O S E R V E

lime wedges

crispbread or Melba toast

salad greens

1 Roughly dice the chicken. Trim off and discard any fat from the ham and dice the meat. Place the chicken and ham in a blender or food processor.

2 Add the parsley, lime rind and juice, and garlic and process until finely ground. Alternatively, finely chop the chicken, ham, parsley, and garlic and place in a bowl. Gently stir in the lime rind and lime juice.

3 Transfer the mixture to a bowl and stir in the cream cheese. Season with salt and pepper to taste, cover with plastic wrap, and chill in the refrigerator for about 30 minutes.

4 Spoon the pâté into individual serving dishes and garnish with extra grated lime rind. Serve the pâté with lime wedges, crispbread or Melba toast, and fresh salad greens.

VARIATION

This pâté can be made successfully with other kinds of ground, lean, cooked meat, such as turkey, beef, and pork. Alternatively, replace the meat with peeled shrimp and/or white crab meat, or with canned tuna in brine, drained.

Fragrant Asparagus Risotto

Soft, creamy rice combines with the flavors of citrus and light anise to make this a substantial appetizer for six hungry people.

NUTRITIONAL INFORMATION

Calories	223	Sugars	.........9g
Protein	.........6g	Fat	...........6g
Carbohydrate	...40g	Saturates	......1g

🍲 10 mins   🕐 45 mins

SERVES 6

I N G R E D I E N T S

4 oz/115 g fine asparagus spears, trimmed

5 cups vegetable stock

2 fennel bulbs

2 tbsp low-fat spread

1 tsp olive oil

2 celery stalks, chopped

2 medium leeks, shredded

3 cups risotto rice

3 medium oranges

salt and pepper

1 Bring a small pan of water to a boil and cook the asparagus for 1 minute. Drain and set aside.

2 Pour the stock into a pan and bring to a boil. Reduce the heat to maintain a gentle simmer.

3 Meanwhile, trim the fennel, reserving the fronds. Use a sharp knife to cut into thin slices.

4 Carefully melt the low-fat spread with the oil in a large saucepan, taking care that the water in the low-fat spread does not evaporate, and gently cook the fennel, celery, and leeks for 3–4 minutes until just softened. Add the rice and cook, stirring, for a further 2 minutes until mixed.

5 Add a ladleful of stock to the pan and cook gently, stirring, until absorbed.

6 Continue adding the stock to the rice, a ladleful at a time, until the rice becomes creamy, thick, and tender. This process will take about 25 minutes and should not be hurried.

7 Finely grate the rind and extract the juice from 1 orange and mix into the rice. Carefully remove the peel and pith from the remaining oranges. Holding the fruit over the saucepan, cut out the orange segments and add to the rice, along with any juice that falls.

8 Stir the orange into the rice along with the asparagus spears. Season to taste with salt and pepper and garnish with the fennel fronds. Serve immediately.

Chargrilled Chicken Salad

This is a quick appetizer to serve at a barbecue—if the bread is bent in half, the chicken salad can be put in the middle and eaten as finger food.

NUTRITIONAL INFORMATION

Calories . . . . . . .225 Sugars 5g
Protein . . . . .16g Fat 12g
Carbohydrate . . .15g Saturates 2g

 10 mins    15 mins

SERVES 4

I N G R E D I E N T S

2 skinless, boneless chicken breasts

1 red onion

sunflower oil for brushing

1 avocado, peeled and pitted

1 tbsp lemon juice

½ cup low-fat mayonnaise

¼ tsp chili powder

¼ tsp salt

½ tsp pepper

4 tomatoes, quartered

½ loaf sun-dried tomato focaccia bread

salad greens, to serve

1 Using a sharp knife, cut the chicken breasts into ½ inch/1 cm strips.

2 Cut the onion into 8 pieces, held together at the root. Rinse under cold running water and then brush with oil.

3 Purée or mash the avocado and lemon juice together. Whisk in the mayonnaise. Add the chili powder and season with the salt and pepper.

4 Put the chicken and onion over a hot barbecue and grill for 3–4 minutes on each side. Combine the chicken, onion, tomatoes, and avocado mixture.

5 Cut the bread in half twice, so that you have quarter-circle-shaped pieces, then in half horizontally. Toast on the hot barbecue grill for about 2 minutes on each side.

6 Spoon the chicken mixture onto the focaccia toasts and serve immediately with salad greens.

VARIATION
Instead of focaccia, serve the salad in pita breads which have been warmed through on the side of the barbecue grill.

Kachumbers

Kachumbers can be made with fruit as well as vegetables. They are served at Indian tables as an appetizer or a garnish for the main meal.

NUTRITIONAL INFORMATION

Calories	55	Sugars	.........4g
Protein	.........1g	Fat	..........4g
Carbohydrate	....4g	Saturates	.....0.5g

 15 mins 0 mins

EACH SERVES 6

INGREDIENTS

TOMATO, ONION & CUCUMBER KACHUMBER

3 ripe tomatoes

¼ cucumber, peeled

1 small onion, quartered

1 tsp lime juice

2 green chiles, deseeded and chopped (optional)

MANGO KACHUMBER

½ mango, peeled and chopped

1 small onion, chopped

1 tbsp chopped fresh cilantro

2 tomatoes, chopped

RADISH KACHUMBER

8 large radishes, sliced

½ cucumber, peeled and chopped

1 small onion, chopped

1 tbsp chopped fresh cilantro

1 tbsp oil

1 tbsp vinegar

1 To make the tomato, onion, and cucumber kachumber, peel the tomatoes. Make a small cross in the top of each one with a pointed knife, place in a bowl, and cover with boiling water. Leave for 1 minute before draining. The skins will slip off easily. Cut the tomatoes into quarters and cut each quarter in half. The seeds can be removed at this stage, if you prefer. Cut the cucumber lengthwise into quarters. Remove the seeds and cut the flesh into cubes. Cut each onion quarter into slices. Combine all the ingredients in a bowl and sprinkle with the lime juice. Add the chiles, if using, and serve.

2 To make the mango kachumber, mix all the ingredients together and serve.

3 To make the radish kachumber, combine all the ingredients in a bowl and serve.

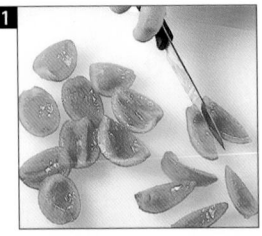
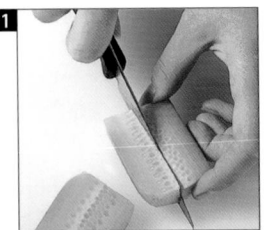

Figs & Prosciutto

This colorful fresh salad is delicious at any time of the year.
Prosciutto di Parma is thought to be the best ham in the world.

NUTRITIONAL INFORMATION

Calories 121	Sugars 6g
Protein 1g	Fat 11g
Carbohydrate 6g	Saturates 2g

 15 mins 5 mins

SERVES 4

I N G R E D I E N T S

1½ oz/40 g arugula

4 fresh figs

4 slices prosciutto

4 tbsp olive oil

1 tbsp fresh orange juice

1 tbsp honey

1 small fresh red chile

1 Tear the arugula into manageable pieces and arrange on 4 individual serving plates.

2 Using a sharp knife, cut each of the figs into quarters and place them on top of the arugula leaves.

3 Using a sharp knife, cut the prosciutto into strips and scatter over the rocket and figs.

4 Place the oil, orange juice, and honey in a screw-top jar. Shake the jar vigorously until the mixture emulsifies and forms a thick dressing. Transfer the dressing to a bowl.

5 Using a sharp knife, dice the chile. (You can remove the seeds first if you prefer a milder flavor.) Add the chopped chile to the dressing and mix well.

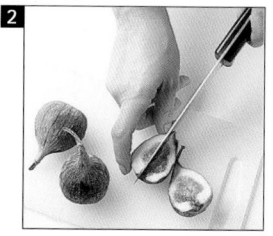

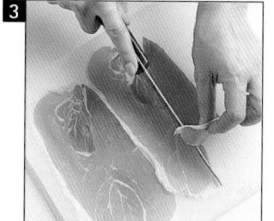

6 Drizzle the dressing over the prosciutto, arugula, and figs, tossing to mix well. Serve immediately.

COOK'S TIP

Chiles can burn the skin for several hours after chopping, so it is advisable to wear gloves when you are handling any very hot varieties and to wash your hands.

Capri Salad

This tomato, olive, and mozzarella salad, dressed with balsamic vinegar and extra virgin olive oil, makes a delicious appetizer on its own.

NUTRITIONAL INFORMATION

Calories 95	Sugars 3g
Protein 3g	Fat 8g
Carbohydrate 3g	Saturates 3g

20 mins

3–5 mins

SERVES 4

INGREDIENTS

2 beefsteak tomatoes

4½ oz/125 g mozzarella cheese

12 black olives

8 fresh basil leaves

1 tbsp balsamic vinegar

1 tbsp extra virgin olive oil

salt and pepper

fresh basil leaves, to garnish

1 Using a sharp knife, cut the tomatoes into thin slices.

2 Drain the mozzarella, if necessary, and cut into slices.

3 Pit the black olives and slice them into rings.

4 Layer the tomatoes, mozzarella slices, olives, and basil leaves in a stack, finishing with a layer of cheese on top.

5 Place each stack under a preheated hot broiler for 2–3 minutes or just long enough to melt the mozzarella.

6 Drizzle over the balsamic vinegar and olive oil, and season to taste with a little salt and pepper.

7 Transfer to individual serving plates and garnish with fresh basil leaves. Serve immediately.

COOK'S TIP

Buffalo mozzarella cheese, although it is usually more expensive because of the comparative rarity of buffalo, does have a better flavor than the cow's milk variety. It is popular in salads, but also provides a tangy layer in baked dishes.

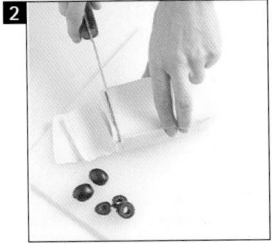

Mushroom Salad

In Italy, raw mushrooms are a great favorite in salad dishes—they have a fresh, almost creamy flavor.

 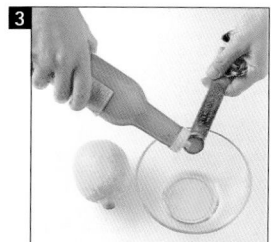 

NUTRITIONAL INFORMATION

Calories	121	Sugars	.......0.1g
Protein	.........2g	Fat	.........13g
Carbohydrate	...0.1g	Saturates	.......2g

 20 mins   0 mins

SERVES 4

INGREDIENTS

5½ oz/150 g firm white mushrooms

4 tbsp virgin olive oil

1 tbsp lemon juice

5 canned anchovy fillets, drained and chopped

1 tbsp fresh marjoram

salt and pepper

1 Gently wipe each mushroom with a damp cloth or damp paper towels in order to remove any dirt.

2 Slice the mushrooms thinly, using a sharp knife and place in a bowl.

3 To make the dressing, whisk together the olive oil and lemon juice.

4 Pour the dressing mixture over the mushrooms. Toss together so that the mushrooms are completely coated with the lemon juice and oil.

5 Stir the chopped anchovy fillets into the mushrooms. Season the mixture with pepper to taste and garnish with the fresh marjoram.

6 Set the mushroom salad aside at room temperature for about 5 minutes before serving to allow all the flavors to be absorbed.

7 Season the mushroom salad with a little salt (see Cook's Tip) and then serve immediately.

COOK'S TIP
Do not season the mushroom salad with salt until the very last minute as it will cause the mushrooms to blacken and the juices to leak. The result will not be so tasty, as the full flavors won't be absorbed and it will also look very unattractive.

Spinach Salad

Fresh baby spinach is tasty and light, and it makes an excellent and nutritious salad to go with the chicken and creamy dressing.

NUTRITIONAL INFORMATION

Calories 145	Sugars 3g
Protein 10g	Fat 10g
Carbohydrate 4g	Saturates 1g

 30 mins   0 mins

SERVES 4

I N G R E D I E N T S

½ cup mushrooms

3½ oz/100 g baby spinach, washed

3 oz/85 g radicchio leaves, shredded

3½ oz/100 g cooked skinless chicken breast fillet

2 oz/55 g prosciutto

2 tbsp olive oil

finely grated rind of ½ orange and juice of 1 orange

1 tbsp plain yogurt

salt and pepper

1 Wipe the mushrooms with a damp cloth or damp paper towels to remove any dirt.

2 Mix together the spinach and radicchio in a large salad bowl.

3 Using a sharp knife, thinly slice the mushrooms and add them to the salad bowl.

4 Shred the cooked chicken breast with your fingers and tear the prosciutto into strips. Mix them into the salad.

5 To make the dressing, place the olive oil, grated orange rind, orange juice, and yogurt into a screw-top jar. Shake the jar vigorously until the mixture is thoroughly combined. Season to taste with salt and pepper.

6 Drizzle the dressing over the spinach salad and toss to mix well. Serve.

VARIATION

Spinach is delicious when served raw. Try raw spinach in a salad garnished with bacon or garlicky croûtons. The young leaves have a wonderfully sharp flavor.

Tortelloni

These tasty little squares of pasta stuffed with mushrooms and cheese are surprisingly filling. This recipe makes 36 tortelloni.

NUTRITIONAL INFORMATION

Calories 360   Sugars 1g
Protein ....9g   Fat 21g
Carbohydrate ...36g   Saturates 12g

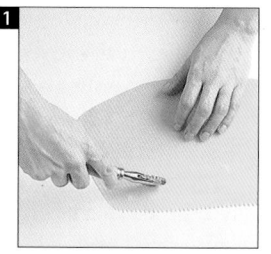

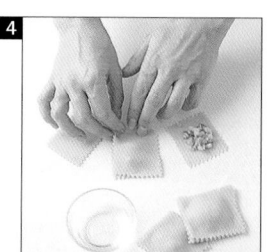

1¼ hrs   25 mins

SERVES 4

INGREDIENTS

about 10½ oz/300 g Pasta Dough (see page 6), rolled out to thin sheets

5 tbsp butter

2 oz shallots, finely chopped

3 garlic cloves, crushed

1 cup mushrooms, wiped and finely chopped

½ celery stalk, finely chopped

5 tbsp grated romano cheese, plus extra to garnish

1 tbsp vegetable oil

salt and pepper

1 Using a serrated pasta cutter, cut 2 inch/5 cm squares from the sheets of fresh pasta. To make 36 tortelloni you will need 72 squares. Once the pasta is cut, cover the squares with plastic wrap to prevent them from drying out.

2 Heat 3 tablespoons of the butter in a skillet. Add the shallots, 1 crushed garlic clove, the mushrooms, and celery and cook for 4–5 minutes.

3 Remove the skillet from the heat, stir in the cheese, and season with salt and pepper to taste.

4 Spoon ½ teaspoon of the mixture onto the middle of 36 pasta squares. Brush the edges of the squares with water and top with the remaining 36 squares. Press the edges together to seal. Set aside to rest for 5 minutes.

5 Bring a large pan of water to a boil, add the oil, and cook the tortelloni, in batches, for 2–3 minutes. The tortelloni will rise to the surface when cooked and the pasta should be tender, but still firm to the bite. Remove from the pan with a slotted spoon and drain thoroughly.

6 Meanwhile, melt the remaining butter in a pan over low heat. Add the remaining garlic and plenty of pepper and cook for 1–2 minutes. Transfer the tortelloni to serving plates and pour the garlic butter over them. Garnish with grated romano and serve immediately.

Eggplant & Linguine

Prepare the marinated eggplants well in advance so—when you are ready to eat—all you have to do is cook the pasta.

NUTRITIONAL INFORMATION

Calories 378	Sugars 3g
Protein 12g	Fat 30g
Carbohydrate . . .16g	Saturates 3g

 12¼ hrs   15 mins

SERVES 4

I N G R E D I E N T S

⅔ cup vegetable stock

⅔ cup white wine vinegar

2 tsp balsamic vinegar

3 tbsp olive oil

fresh oregano sprig

1 lb/450 g eggplants, peeled and thinly
  sliced

14 oz/400 g dried linguine

M A R I N A D E

2 tbsp extra virgin olive oil

2 garlic cloves, crushed

2 tbsp chopped fresh oregano

2 tbsp finely chopped
  roasted almonds

2 tbsp diced red bell pepper

2 tbsp lime juice

grated rind and juice of 1 orange

salt and pepper

1 Put the vegetable stock, wine vinegar, and balsamic vinegar into a pan and bring to a boil over low heat. Add 2 teaspoons of the olive oil and the sprig of oregano and simmer gently for about 1 minute.

2 Add the eggplant slices to the pan, remove from the heat, and set aside for 10 minutes.

3 Meanwhile, make the marinade. Combine the oil, garlic, fresh oregano, almonds, red bell pepper, lime juice, orange rind and juice in a large bowl and season to taste with salt and pepper.

4 Carefully remove the eggplant slices from the pan with a slotted spoon, and drain well. Add the eggplant slices to the marinade, mixing well to coat. Cover with plastic wrap and set aside in the refrigerator for about 12 hours.

5 Bring a large pan of lightly salted water to a boil. Add half of the remaining oil and the linguine. Bring back to a boil and cook for 8–10 minutes until just tender, but still firm to the bite.

6 Drain the pasta thoroughly and toss with the remaining oil while it is still warm. Arrange the pasta on a serving plate with the eggplant slices and the marinade and serve immediately.

Tricolor Timballini

An unusual way of serving pasta, these cheese molds make a charming appetizer and are excellent with a crunchy salad for a light lunch.

NUTRITIONAL INFORMATION

Calories	529	Sugars	.........7g
Protein	........18g	Fat	..........29g
Carbohydrate	...46g	Saturates	......12g

 30 mins   1 hr

SERVES 4

I N G R E D I E N T S

1 tbsp butter, softened

1 cup dry white bread crumbs

6 oz/175 g dried tricolor spaghetti, broken into 2 inch/5 cm lengths

3 tbsp olive oil

1 egg yolk

1 cup grated Swiss cheese

1¼ cups Béchamel Sauce (see page 6)

1 onion, finely chopped

1 bay leaf

⅔ cup dry white wine

⅔ cup sieved tomatoes

1 tbsp tomato paste

salt and pepper

fresh basil leaves, to garnish

1 Grease four ¾ cup molds or ramekins with the butter. Evenly coat the insides with half of the bread crumbs.

2 Bring a pan of lightly salted water to a boil. Add the spaghetti and 1 tablespoon of the oil. Bring back to a boil and cook for 8–10 minutes until just tender, but still firm to the bite. Drain and transfer to a mixing bowl. Add the egg yolk and cheese to the pasta and season.

3 Stir the Béchamel sauce into the pasta and mix well. Spoon the pasta mixture into the prepared molds or ramekins and sprinkle the remaining bread crumbs over the top.

4 Stand the ramekins on a cookie sheet and bake in a preheated oven, 425°F/220°C, for 20 minutes. Remove the cookie sheet from the oven and set the molds aside for 10 minutes.

5 Meanwhile, make the sauce. Heat the remaining oil in a pan and gently cook the onion and bay leaf for 2-3 minutes. Stir in the wine, sieved tomatoes, and tomato paste and season to taste. Simmer for 20 minutes until thickened. Remove and discard the bay leaf.

6 Turn the timballini out onto serving plates, garnish with the basil leaves, and serve with the tomato sauce.

Pasta with Pesto Vinaigrette

Sun-dried tomatoes and olives enhance this delicious pesto-inspired salad, which tastes superb served warm or cold.

NUTRITIONAL INFORMATION

Calories . . . . . . .275 Sugars 2g
Protein . . . . .9g Fat 19g
Carbohydrate . . .17g Saturates 4g

35–40 mins · 15 mins

SERVES 6

INGREDIENTS

2 cups dried pasta spirals

4 tomatoes, peeled

½ cup black olives

1 oz/25 g sun-dried tomatoes in oil, drained

2 tbsp pine nuts, toasted

2 tbsp Parmesan shavings

fresh basil sprig, to garnish

PESTO VINAIGRETTE

4 tbsp chopped fresh basil

1 garlic clove, crushed

2 tbsp freshly grated
   Parmesan cheese

4 tbsp olive oil

2 tbsp lemon juice

pepper

1 Bring a large pan of lightly salted water to a boil. Add the pasta, return to a boil, and cook for 8–10 minutes until tender, but still firm to the bite. Drain the pasta, rinse well in hot water, then drain again.

2 To make the vinaigrette, whisk together the basil, garlic, Parmesan, olive oil, and lemon juice until well blended. Season to taste with pepper.

3 Put the pasta into a bowl, pour the pesto vinaigrette over it, and toss thoroughly.

4 Cut the tomatoes into wedges. Halve and pit the olives and slice the sun-dried tomatoes. Add the tomatoes, olives, and sun-dried tomatoes to the pasta and toss well to mix.

5 Transfer the pasta mixture to a salad bowl and sprinkle the pine nuts and Parmesan shavings over the top. Serve warm, garnished with a sprig of basil.

Pasta-Stuffed Tomatoes

This unusual and inexpensive dish would make a good appetizer for eight people, or a delicious light and summery lunch for four.

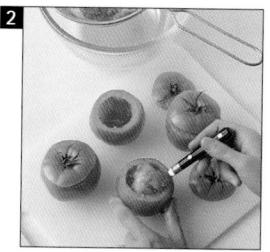

NUTRITIONAL INFORMATION

Calories 298   Sugars 4g
Protein ....10g   Fat 20g
Carbohydrate ...20g   Saturates 5g

15 mins   35 mins

SERVES 4

INGREDIENTS

4 tbsp extra virgin olive oil, plus extra for greasing

8 beefsteak tomatoes or large tomatoes

1 cup dried ditalini or other very small pasta shapes

8 black olives, pitted and finely chopped

2 tbsp finely chopped fresh basil

1 tbsp finely chopped fresh parsley

⅔ cup freshly grated Parmesan cheese

salt and pepper

fresh basil sprigs, to garnish

1 Brush a cookie sheet with olive oil. Slice the tops off the tomatoes and reserve to use as lids. If the tomatoes will not stand up, cut a thin slice off the bottom of each tomato.

2 Using a teaspoon, scoop out the tomato pulp into a strainer, but do not pierce the tomato shells. Invert the tomato shells onto paper towels, pat dry, and then set aside to drain.

3 Bring a large pan of lightly salted water to a boil. Add the pasta, bring back to a boil, and cook for 8–10 minutes or until the pasta is tender, but still firm to the bite. Drain the pasta and set aside.

4 Put the olives, basil, parsley, and Parmesan cheese into a large mixing bowl and stir in the drained tomato pulp. Add the pasta to the bowl. Stir in the olive oil, mix together well, and season to taste with salt and pepper.

5 Spoon the pasta mixture into the tomato shells and replace the lids. Arrange the stuffed tomatoes on the prepared cookie sheet and bake in a preheated oven, 375°F/190°C, for about 15–20 minutes.

6 Remove the tomatoes from the oven and set aside to cool until they are just warm.

7 Arrange the pasta-stuffed tomatoes on a serving dish, garnish with the basil sprigs, and serve.

Beet Cannolicchi

Quick and simple, this colorful, warm salad works equally well as a tasty appetizer or as a main dish for a light lunch.

NUTRITIONAL INFORMATION

Calories	449	Sugars	.......13g
Protein	.......13g	Fat	........16g
Carbohydrate	...70g	Saturates	......2g

 10 mins   25 mins

SERVES 4

INGREDIENTS

2¾ cups dried ditalini rigati

5 tbsp olive oil

2 garlic cloves chopped

14 oz/400 g can chopped tomatoes

14 oz/400 g cooked beets, diced

2 tbsp chopped fresh basil leaves

1 tsp mustard seeds

salt and pepper

TO SERVE

mixed salad greens, tossed in olive oil

4 Italian plum tomatoes, sliced

1 Bring a large pan of lightly salted water to a boil. Add the pasta and 1 tablespoon of the oil. Bring back to a boil and cook for 8–10 minutes until tender, but still firm to the bite. Drain and set aside.

2 Heat the remaining olive oil in a large pan. Add the garlic and cook over low heat for 3 minutes. Add the chopped tomatoes and cook for 10 minutes.

3 Remove the pan from the heat and carefully add the beets, basil, mustard seeds, and pasta. and season to taste with salt and pepper.

4 Serve while still warm on a bed of mixed salad greens, tossed in olive oil, and sliced plum tomatoes.

COOK'S TIP

To cook raw beets, trim off the leaves about 2 inches above the roots and ensure that the skin is not broken. Boil in very lightly salted water for 30–40 minutes until tender. Set aside to cool and then rub off the skin.

Salmon Pancakes

These pancakes are based on the latke, which is a thin, crisp pancake, and are served with smoked salmon and sour cream for a taste of luxury.

NUTRITIONAL INFORMATION

Calories 142	Sugars 1g
Protein 6.8g	Fat 7.8g
Carbohydrate . .11.9g	Saturates 2.8g

 5 mins 25 mins

SERVES 4

I N G R E D I E N T S

1 lb/450 g mealy potatoes, grated

2 scallions, chopped

2 tbsp self-rising flour

2 eggs, beaten

2 tbsp vegetable oil

salt and pepper

fresh chives, to garnish

T O P P I N G

⅔ cup sour cream

4½ oz/125 g smoked salmon

1 Rinse the grated potatoes under cold running water, drain, and pat dry on paper towels. Transfer to a mixing bowl.

2 Mix the scallions, flour, and eggs into the potatoes and season well with salt and pepper.

3 Heat 1 tablespoon of the vegetable oil in a heavy skillet. Drop about 4 tablespoons of the mixture into the skillet and spread each one with the back of a spoon to form a round (the mixture should make 16 pancakes). Cook for about 5–7 minutes, turning once, until golden. Drain well.

4 Heat the remaining oil and cook the remaining mixture in batches.

5 Top the pancakes with the sour cream and smoked salmon, garnish with fresh chives, and serve hot.

VARIATION
These pancakes are equally delicious topped with prosciutto or any other dry-cured ham instead of the smoked salmon.

Carrot & Potato Soufflé

Hot soufflés have a reputation for being difficult to make, but this one is both simple and impressive. Make sure you serve it as soon as it is ready.

NUTRITIONAL INFORMATION

Calories 294
Sugars 6g
Protein 10g
Fat 9g
Carbohydrate . . .46g
Saturates 4g

 15 mins 40 mins

SERVES 4

I N G R E D I E N T S

2 tbsp butter, melted

4 tbsp fresh whole-wheat
    bread crumbs

3 mealy potatoes, baked in their skins

2 carrots, grated

2 eggs, separated

2 tbsp orange juice

¼ tsp grated nutmeg

salt and pepper

carrot curls, to garnish

1 Brush the inside of an 3¾ cup soufflé dish with the butter. Sprinkle about three-quarters of the bread crumbs over the base and sides.

2 Cut the baked potatoes in half and scoop the flesh into a mixing bowl.

3 Add the carrots, egg yolks, orange juice, and nutmeg to the potato flesh. Season to taste with salt and pepper.

4 In a separate bowl, whisk the egg whites until soft peaks form, then gently fold into the potato mixture with a metal spoon until well incorporated.

5 Gently spoon the potato and carrot mixture into the prepared soufflé dish. Sprinkle the remaining bread crumbs over the top of the mixture.

6 Cook in a preheated oven, 400°F/200°C, for 40 minutes, until risen and golden. Do not open the oven door during the cooking time, otherwise the soufflé will sink. Serve the soufflé immediately, garnished with carrot curls.

COOK'S TIP

To bake the potatoes, prick the skins and cook in a preheated oven, 375°F/ 190°C, for about 1 hour.

 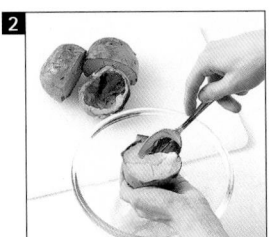 

Endive Salad

The contrast of the pink grapefruit, creamy endive, and bright green mâche makes this dish look simply stunning.

NUTRITIONAL INFORMATION

Calories	137	Sugars	........4g
Protein	........1g	Fat	.........13g
Carbohydrate	....4g	Saturates	......2g

 10 mins   0 mins

SERVES 4

I N G R E D I E N T S

1 pink grapefruit

1 avocado

2 oz/55 g mâche

2 heads endive, sliced diagonally

1 tbsp chopped fresh mint

F R E N C H   D R E S S I N G

3 tbsp olive oil

1 tbsp wine vinegar

1 small garlic clove, crushed

½ tsp Dijon or Meaux mustard

1 tsp honey

salt and pepper

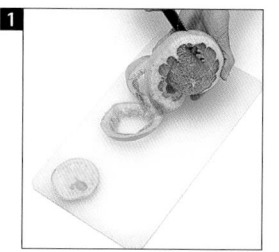
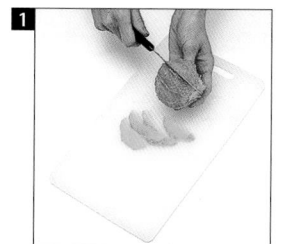
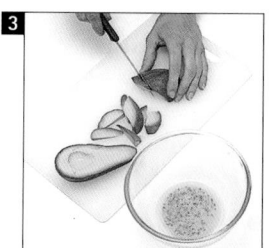

1 Peel the grapefruit with a serrated knife. Cut the grapefruit into segments by cutting between the membranes. Set aside.

2 To make the French dressing, put the oil, vinegar, garlic, mustard, and honey into a screw-top jar and shake vigorously. Season to taste with salt and pepper. Pour the dressing into a bowl.

3 Halve and pit the avocado and cut it into thin slices. Peel off the skin, put the sliced flesh into the bowl of French dressing and toss gently to coat.

4 Remove any stems from the mâche and put into a bowl with the grapefruit, endive, and chopped mint.

5 Add the avocado slices and 2 tablespoons of the French dressing. Toss well and transfer to individual serving plates. Serve immediately.

COOK'S TIP

Mâche is also known as lamb's lettuce because the shape of its dark green leaves resembles a lamb's tongue. It is also known as corn salad. It is easy to grow in the garden and will withstand the frost.

Eggplant & Rice Rolls

Slices of eggplant are blanched and stuffed with a savory rice and nut mixture, then baked in a piquant tomato and wine sauce.

NUTRITIONAL INFORMATION

Calories	142	Sugars	.........3g
Protein	.........6g	Fat	...........9g
Carbohydrate	....9g	Saturates	.......3g

🐻 🐻 🐻

🥘 30 mins   🕐 1hr 5 mins

SERVES 8

INGREDIENTS

3 eggplants (total weight about 1 lb 10 oz/750 g)

¼ cup mixed long grain and wild rice

4 scallions, thinly sliced

3 tbsp chopped cashew nuts or toasted chopped hazelnuts

2 tbsp capers, rinsed

1 garlic clove, crushed

2 tbsp grated Parmesan cheese

1 egg, beaten

1 tbsp olive oil

1 tbsp balsamic vinegar

2 tbsp tomato paste

⅔ cup water

⅔ cup white wine

salt and pepper

fresh cilantro sprigs, to garnish

1 Using a sharp knife, cut off the stem end of each eggplant, then cut off and discard a strip of skin from alternate sides of each one. Cut each eggplant into thin slices to give a total of 16 slices.

2 Blanch the eggplant slices in boiling water for 5 minutes, then drain on paper towels.

3 Cook the rice in lightly salted boiling water for about 12 minutes or until just tender. Drain and place in a bowl. Add the scallions, nuts, capers, garlic, cheese, and egg, season with salt and pepper to taste and mix well.

4 Spread a thin layer of the savory rice mixture over each slice of eggplant and then roll up the eggplant carefully, securing with a wooden toothpick. Place the rolls in a single layer in a lightly greased casserole and brush them with the olive oil.

5 Combine the vinegar, tomato paste, and water and pour over the eggplant rolls. Cook in a preheated oven, 350°/180°C, for 40 minutes or until tender and most of the liquid has been absorbed. Transfer the rolls to a serving dish.

6 Add the wine to the pan juices and heat, stirring, until the sediment loosens. Simmer for 2–3 minutes. Adjust the seasoning and strain the sauce over the eggplant rolls. Cool and then chill well in the refrigerator. Garnish with sprigs of cilantro and serve.

Garden Salad

This chunky salad includes tiny new potatoes tossed in a minty dressing, and is served with a wonderfully piquant mustard dip.

NUTRITIONAL INFORMATION

Calories 227	Sugars 6g	
Protein 4g	Fat 17g	
Carbohydrate . . .16g	Saturates 4g	

 15–20 mins · 20 mins

SERVES 8

INGREDIENTS

1 lb 2 oz/500 g tiny new potatoes

8 oz/225 g broccoli florets

4½ oz/125 g sugar snap peas

2 large carrots

4 celery stalks

1 yellow or orange bell pepper, deseeded

1 bunch scallions

1 head endive

DRESSING

3 tbsp olive oil

1 tbsp white wine vinegar

1 tsp Dijon mustard

2 tbsp chopped fresh mint

MUSTARD DIP

6 tbsp sour cream

3 tbsp thick mayonnaise

2 tsp balsamic vinegar

1½ tsp coarse-grain mustard

½ tsp horseradish

pinch of brown sugar

salt and pepper

1 Cook the potatoes in lightly salted boiling water for about 10 minutes until just tender. Meanwhile, whisk together the dressing ingredients.

2 Drain the potatoes, add to the dressing while still hot, toss well, and set aside until cold, stirring occasionally.

3 To make the dip, combine the sour cream, mayonnaise, vinegar, mustard, horseradish, and sugar and season to taste with salt and pepper. Transfer to a small bowl, cover, and chill until required.

4 Cut the broccoli into bite-size sprigs and blanch for 2 minutes in boiling water. Drain and plunge immediately into cold water. When cold, drain thoroughly.

5 Blanch the sugar snap peas in boiling water for 1 minute. Drain, rinse in cold water, and drain again.

6 Cut the carrots and celery into batons. Slice the bell pepper or cut it into small cubes. Cut off some of the green parts of the scallions and separate the endive leaves.

7 Arrange the vegetables attractively in a fairly shallow bowl with the potatoes piled up in the center. Serve with the mustard dip.

Mini Kabobs

Cubes of smoked bean curd are speared on bamboo satay sticks with crisp vegetables and marinated with lemon juice and olive oil.

NUTRITIONAL INFORMATION

Calories	322	Sugars 9g
Protein	........13g	Fat 24g
Carbohydrate	...13g	Saturates 7g

🍲 25 mins   🕐 15–20 mins

SERVES 6

INGREDIENTS

10½ oz/300 g smoked bean curd, cut into cubes

1 large red bell pepper, deseeded and diced

1 large yellow bell pepper, deseeded and diced

6 oz/175 g white mushrooms

1 small zucchini, sliced

finely grated rind and juice of 1 lemon

3 tbsp olive oil

1 tbsp chopped parsley

1 tsp superfine sugar

salt and pepper

fresh parsley sprigs, to garnish

SAUCE

1 cup cashew nuts

1 tbsp butter

1 garlic clove, crushed

1 shallot, finely chopped

1 tsp ground coriander

1 tsp ground cumin

1 tbsp superfine sugar

1 tbsp dry, unsweetened shredded coconut

⅔ cup plain yogurt

1 Thread the bean curd cubes, red and yellow bell peppers, mushrooms, and zucchini onto bamboo satay sticks. Arrange them in a shallow dish.

2 Combine the lemon rind and juice, olive oil, parsley, and sugar. Season to taste with salt and pepper. Pour over the kabobs and brush them with the mixture. Set aside for 10 minutes.

3 To make the sauce, sprinkle the cashew nuts onto a cookie sheet and toast them under a hot broiler until lightly browned.

4 Melt the butter in a pan and cook the garlic and shallot over low heat until softened. Transfer to a blender or food processor and add the nuts, coriander, cumin, sugar, coconut, and yogurt. Process for about 15 seconds or until combined. Alternatively, chop the nuts very finely and mix with the remaining ingredients.

5 Place the kabobs under a preheated broiler and cook, turning and basting with the lemon juice mixture, until lightly browned. Garnish with sprigs of parsley and serve with the cashew nut sauce.

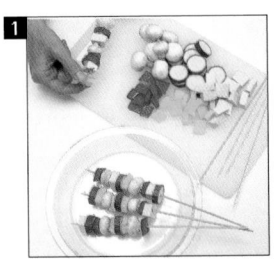

Avocado Cream Terrine

The smooth, rich taste of ripe avocados combines well with thick, creamy yogurt and light cream to make this impressive terrine.

NUTRITIONAL INFORMATION

Calories 327   Sugars 3g
Protein ....6g   Fat 32g
Carbohydrate ....4g   Saturates 8g

 2¼ hrs   0 mins

SERVES 6

INGREDIENTS

2 ripe avocados

¼ cup cold water

2 tsp gelatin

1 tbsp lemon juice

4 tbsp low-fat mayonnaise

⅔ cup plain yogurt

⅔ cup light cream

salt and pepper

mixed salad greens, to serve

TO GARNISH

cucumber slices

nasturtium flowers

1 Peel the avocados and remove and discard the pits. Put the flesh in a blender or food processor or a large bowl with the water, gelatin, lemon juice, mayonnaise, yogurt, and cream. Season to taste with salt and pepper.

2 Process for about 10–15 seconds or beat by hand, using a fork or whisk, until smooth.

3 Transfer the mixture to a small, heavy pan and heat very gently, stirring constantly, until it is just beginning to boil.

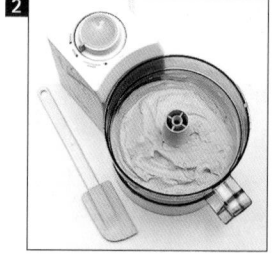  

4 Pour the mixture into a 3¾ cup terrine, nonstick loaf pan, or plastic food storage box and smooth the surface. Allow the mixture to cool and set and then chill in the refrigerator for about 1½–2 hours.

5 Turn the terrine out of its container and cut into neat slices. Arrange a bed of salad greens on 6 serving plates.

Place a slice of avocado terrine on top and garnish with cucumber slices and nasturtium flowers.

Stuffed Napa Cabbage

Mushrooms, scallions, celery, and rice are flavored with five-spice powder and wrapped in Napa cabbage leaves.

NUTRITIONAL INFORMATION

Calories 166   Sugars 3g
Protein . . . . .3g   Fat 13g
Carbohydrate . . .10g   Saturates 8g

 25 mins   45 mins

SERVES 4

INGREDIENTS

8 large Napa cabbage leaves

½ vegetable bouillon cube

generous ¼ cup long grain rice

¼ cup butter

1 bunch of scallions, trimmed and finely chopped

1 celery stalk, finely chopped

4½ oz/125 g white mushrooms, sliced

1 tsp Chinese five-spice powder

1¼ cups sieved tomatoes

salt and pepper

fresh chives, to garnish

1 Blanch the Napa cabbage leaves in boiling water for 1 minute. Refresh under cold running water and drain well. Be careful not to tear them.

2 Bring a large pan of water to a boil and stir in the bouillon cube. Add the rice, bring back to a boil, and simmer for 10–12 minutes until just tender. Drain well and set aside until required.

3 Meanwhile, melt the butter in a skillet and fry the scallions and celery over low heat for 3–4 minutes until softened, but not browned.

4 Add the mushrooms to the skillet and cook for a further 3–4 minutes, stirring frequently.

5 Add the cooked rice to the pan with the five-spice powder. Season to taste with salt and pepper and stir well.

6 Spread out the Napa cabbage leaves on a counter and divide the rice mixture among them. Roll each leaf into a neat packet, tucking in the sides to enclose the stuffing completely. Place the stuffed leaves, seam side down, in a greased casserole. Pour the sieved tomatoes over them and cover with foil. Bake in a preheated oven, 375°F/190°C, for 25–30 minutes.

7 Garnish the stuffed Napa cabbage leaves with fresh chives and serve immediately straight from the casserole.

Marinated Vegetable Salad

Lightly steamed vegetables taste superb served slightly warm
in a marinade of olive oil, white wine, vinegar, and fresh herbs.

NUTRITIONAL INFORMATION

Calories 114	Sugars 4g
Protein 3g	Fat 9g
Carbohydrate 5g	Saturates 1g

10 mins   10 mins

SERVES 6

INGREDIENTS

6 oz/175 g baby carrots

2 celery hearts, cut into 4 pieces

4 oz/115 g sugar snap peas or snow peas

1 fennel bulb, sliced

6 oz/175 g small asparagus spears

4½ tsp sunflower seeds

fresh dill sprigs, to garnish

DRESSING

¼ cup extra virgin olive oil

¼ cup dry white wine

2 tbsp white wine vinegar

1 tbsp chopped fresh dill

1 tbsp chopped fresh parsley

salt and pepper

1 Put the carrots, celery, sugar snap peas or snow peas, fennel, and asparagus into a steamer and cook over gently simmering water for 3–5 minutes until just tender. It is important that they retain a little bite.

2 Meanwhile, make the dressing. Combine the olive oil, wine, vinegar, and chopped herbs, whisking until thoroughly mixed. Season to taste with salt and pepper.

3 When the vegetables are cooked, transfer them to a serving dish and immediately pour the dressing over them. The hot vegetables will absorb the flavor of the dressing as they cool.

4 Spread out the sunflower seeds on a cookie sheet and toast them under a preheated broiler for 3–4 minutes or until lightly browned and are beginning to smell fragrant. Sprinkle the toasted sunflower seeds over the vegetables.

5 Serve the salad while the vegetables are still slightly warm, garnished with sprigs of fresh dill.

Mozzarella with Radicchio

Sliced mozzarella is served with tomatoes and radicchio, which is singed over hot coals and drizzled with pesto dressing.

NUTRITIONAL INFORMATION

Calories 413	Sugars 6g
Protein 12g	Fat 38g
Carbohydrate 6g	Saturates 14g

 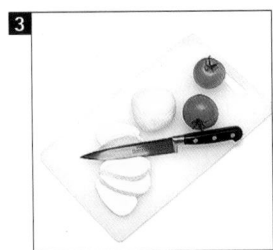 

 15 mins   2–3 mins

SERVES 4

INGREDIENTS

1 lb 2 oz/500 g mozzarella cheese

4 large tomatoes, sliced

2 heads of radicchio

fresh basil leaves, to garnish

DRESSING

1 tbsp red or green pesto

6 tbsp extra virgin olive oil

3 tbsp red wine vinegar

handful of fresh basil leaves

salt and pepper

1 First make the dressing. Whisk together the pesto, olive oil, and red wine vinegar in a small bowl until thoroughly combined.

2 Tear the basil leaves into tiny pieces and add them to the dressing. Season to taste with salt and pepper.

3 Thinly slice the mozzarella and arrange it on 4 serving plates with the tomatoes, overlapping the slices.

4 Leaving the root end on the heads of radicchio, slice each one into quarters. Grill them quickly on the barbecue grill, so that the leaves just singe on the outside. Place 2 quarters on each serving plate.

5 Drizzle the dressing over the radicchio, cheese, and tomatoes. Garnish with fresh basil leaves and serve immediately.

Warm Goat-Cheese Salad

This delicious salad combines soft goat-cheese with walnut halves, served on a bed of mixed salad leaves.

NUTRITIONAL INFORMATION

Calories 408
Sugars 8g
Protein 9g
Fat 38g
Carbohydrate 8g
Saturates 8g

 5 mins   5 mins

SERVES 4

INGREDIENTS

3 oz/85 g walnut halves

mixed salad leaves

4½ oz/125 g soft goat-cheese

snipped fresh chives, to garnish

DRESSING

6 tbsp walnut oil

3 tbsp white wine vinegar

1 tbsp clear honey

1 tsp Dijon mustard

pinch of ground ginger

salt and pepper

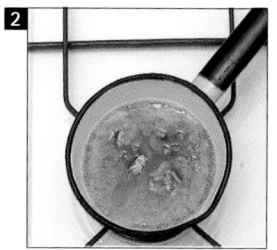

1 To make the dressing, whisk together the walnut oil, wine vinegar, honey, mustard, and ginger in a small pan. Season to taste with salt and pepper.

2 Heat the dressing gently, stirring occasionally, until warm. Add the walnut halves and continue to heat for 3–4 minutes.

3 Arrange the salad leaves on 4 serving plates and place spoonfuls of goat cheese on top. Lift the walnut halves from the dressing with a draining spoon and scatter them over the salads.

4 Transfer the warm dressing to a small pitcher. Sprinkle chives over the salads and serve with the dressing.

VARIATION

You could also use a ewe's milk cheese, such as feta, in this recipe for a sharper flavor.

Potato Skins & Two Fillings

Potato skins are always a favorite. Prepare the skins in advance and warm them through before serving with the salad fillings.

NUTRITIONAL INFORMATION

Calories ....279 Sugars 2g
Protein ....5g Fats 11g
Carbohydrate ...44g Saturates 7g

 30 mins 1¼ hrs

SERVES 4

INGREDIENTS

4 large baking potatoes

2 tbsp vegetable oil

4 tsp salt

chopped fresh chives, to garnish

TO SERVE

⅔ cup sour cream

2 tbsp chopped fresh chives

BEAN SPROUT SALAD

1 cup bean sprouts

1 celery stalk, sliced

1 orange, peeled and segmented

1 red eating apple, chopped

½ red bell pepper, deseeded and chopped

1 tbsp chopped fresh parsley

1 tbsp light soy sauce

1 tbsp honey

1 small garlic clove, crushed

BEAN FILLING

3½ oz/100 g canned, mixed beans, drained

1 onion, halved and sliced

1 tomato, chopped

2 scallions, chopped

2 tsp lemon juice

salt and pepper

1 Scrub the potatoes and put on a cookie sheet. Prick the potatoes all over with a fork and rub the oil and salt into the skin.

2 Cook in a preheated oven, 400°F/200°C, for about 1 hour or until soft.

3 Cut the potatoes in half lengthwise and scoop out the flesh, leaving a ½ inch/1 cm thick shell. Reserve the flesh for another dish, if desired. Return the shells, skin side uppermost, to the oven for 10 minutes until crisp.

4 Mix the ingredients for the bean sprout salad in a bowl, tossing well in the soy sauce, honey, and garlic to coat.

5 Combine all the ingredients for the bean filling in a separate bowl.

6 In another bowl, combine the sour cream and chopped chives until well mixed.

7 Serve the potato skins hot, with the two salad fillings, garnished with chopped chives and the sour cream and chive sauce.

Tomato & Cheese Bruschetta

These simple toasts are filled with color and flavor. They are great as a speedy appetizer and delicious as a light meal or snack.

NUTRITIONAL INFORMATION

Calories 232   Sugars 4g
Protein ....4g   Fat 15g
Carbohydrate ...20g   Saturates 8g

5–10 mins   10 mins

SERVES 4

INGREDIENTS

4 muffins

4 garlic cloves, crushed

2 tbsp butter

1 tbsp chopped basil

4 large, ripe tomatoes

1 tbsp tomato paste

8 pitted black olives, halved

2 oz/55 g mozzarella cheese, sliced

salt and pepper

fresh basil leaves, to garnish

DRESSING

1 tbsp extra virgin olive oil

2 tsp lemon juice

1 tsp honey

  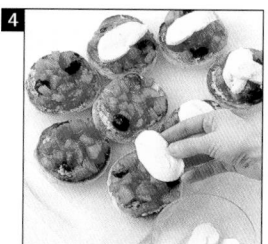

1 Cut the muffins in half to give 8 thick pieces. Toast the muffin halves under a hot broiler for 2–3 minutes until golden.

2 Beat the garlic, butter, and basil together and spread evenly onto each muffin half.

3 Cut a cross shape at the top of each tomato. Plunge the tomatoes into a bowl of boiling water—this will make the skin easier to peel. After a few minutes, pick each tomato up with a fork and peel off the skin. Chop the tomato flesh and mix with the tomato paste and olives. Divide the mixture among the muffins.

4 Mix the dressing ingredients and drizzle over each muffin. Arrange the mozzarella on top and season to taste with salt and pepper.

5 Return the muffins to the broiler for 1–2 minutes until the cheese has melted. Serve, garnished with basil leaves.

VARIATION
Use balsamic vinegar instead of the lemon juice for an authentic Italian flavor.

Vegetable-Topped Muffins

Roasted vegetables are delicious and attractive. Served on warm muffins with a herb sauce, they are unbeatable.

NUTRITIONAL INFORMATION

Calories	740	Sugars	........27g
Protein	........20g	Fat	..........45g
Carbohydrate	...67g	Saturates	......17g

1¼ hrs   35 mins

SERVES 4

1 red onion, cut into 8 wedges

1 eggplant, halved and sliced

1 yellow bell pepper, deseeded and sliced

1 zucchini, sliced

¼ cup olive oil

1 tbsp garlic vinegar

2 tbsp vermouth

2 garlic cloves, crushed

1 tbsp chopped fresh thyme

2 tsp light brown sugar

4 muffins, halved

SAUCE

2 tbsp butter

1 tbsp all-purpose flour

⅔ cup milk

5 tbsp vegetable stock

¾ cup grated Cheddar cheese

1 tsp whole-grain mustard

3 tbsp chopped fresh mixed herbs

salt and pepper

1 Arrange the onion, eggplant, yellow bell pepper and zucchini in a shallow nonmetallic dish. Combine the olive oil, garlic vinegar, vermouth, garlic, thyme, and sugar and pour over the vegetables, turning to coat well. Set aside to marinate for 1 hour.

2 Transfer the vegetables to a cookie sheet. Roast in a preheated oven, 400°F/200°C, for about 20–25 minutes or until the vegetables have softened.

3 Meanwhile, make the sauce. Melt the butter in a small pan and stir in the flour. Cook for 1 minute over a low heat, stirring constantly, then remove the pan from the heat. Gradually stir in the milk and vegetable stock and return the pan to

the heat. Bring to a boil, stirring constantly until thickened. Stir in the cheese, mustard, and mixed herbs and season well.

4 Cut the muffins in half and toast under a preheated broiler for 2–3 minutes until golden brown, then transfer a serving plate. Spoon the roasted vegetables onto the muffins and pour the sauce over the top. Serve immediately.

Carrot & Potato Medley

This is a colorful dish of shredded vegetables in a fresh garlic and honey dressing. It is delicious served with crusty bread to mop up the dressing.

NUTRITIONAL INFORMATION

Calories . . . . .81 Sugars 4.1g
Protein . . . . .1g Fat 5.6g
Carbohydrate . . . .7g Saturates 0.8g

 5 mins   5 mins

SERVES 4

I N G R E D I E N T S

2 tbsp olive oil

8 oz/225 g potatoes, cut into thin strips

1 fennel bulb, cut into thin strips

2 carrots, grated

1 red onion, cut into thin strips

chopped chives and fennel fronds
   to garnish

crusty bread, to serve

D R E S S I N G

3 tbsp olive oil

1 tbsp garlic wine vinegar

1 garlic clove, crushed

1 tsp Dijon mustard

2 tsp honey

salt and pepper

1 Heat the olive oil in a large, heavy skillet, add the potato and fennel slices, and cook over low heat, stirring occasionally, for about 2–3 minutes until just beginning to brown. Remove the vegetables from the skillet with a slotted spoon and drain thoroughly on paper towels.

2 Arrange the grated carrots, red onion strips, and potato and fennel mixture in separate piles on a serving plate.

3 To make the dressing, whisk together the oil, vinegar, garlic, mustard, and honey and season to taste with salt and pepper. Pour the dressing over the vegetables. Toss well and sprinkle with chopped chives and fennel fronds. Serve immediately or cool and store in the refrigerator until required. Serve with crusty bread.

VARIATION

Use mixed, broiled bell peppers or shredded leeks in this dish for variety, or add bean sprouts and a segmented orange, if you prefer.

Eggplant Timbale

This is a great way to serve pasta as an appetizer, wrapped in an eggplant mold. It looks really impressive, yet it is so easy to make.

NUTRITIONAL INFORMATION

Calories 291	Sugars 11g
Protein 8g	Fat 18g
Carbohydrate . . .25g	Saturates 4g

🥘 25 mins 🕐 40 mins

SERVES 4

1 large eggplant

½ cup dried macaroni

1 tbsp vegetable oil

1 onion, chopped

2 garlic cloves, crushed

2 tbsp drained canned corn

2 tbsp frozen peas, thawed

3½ oz/100 g spinach

¼ cup grated Cheddar cheese

1 egg, beaten

8 oz/225 g canned, chopped tomatoes

1 tbsp chopped fresh basil

salt and pepper

SAUCE

4 tbsp olive oil

2 tbsp white wine vinegar

2 garlic cloves, crushed

3 tbsp chopped basil

1 tbsp superfine sugar

1 Cut the eggplant lengthwise into thin strips, using a potato peeler. Place in a bowl of salted boiling water and let stand for 3–4 minutes. Drain well.

2 Grease 4 x ⅔ cup ramekin dishes and line with the eggplant strips, leaving 1 inch/2.5 cm overlapping.

3 Bring a pan of lightly salted water to a boil. Add the pasta, bring back to a boil, and cook for 8–10 minutes until tender, but still firm to the bite. Drain.

4 Heat the oil in a pan and cook the onion and garlic for 2–3 minutes. Stir in the corn and peas and remove the pan from the heat.

5 Blanch the spinach, drain well, chop, and reserve. Add the pasta to the onion mixture with the cheese, egg, tomatoes, and basil. Season to taste and mix well. Half-fill each ramekin with some of the pasta. Place the spinach on top and then the remaining pasta mixture. Fold the eggplant over the pasta filling to cover. Put the ramekins in a roasting pan half-filled with boiling water, cover, and cook in a preheated oven, 350°F/180°C, for 20–25 minutes or until set.

6 Meanwhile, heat all the sauce ingredients in a pan. Turn out the ramekins and serve with the sauce.

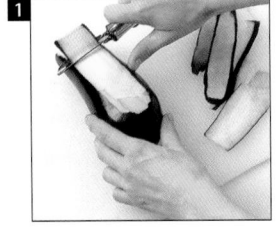

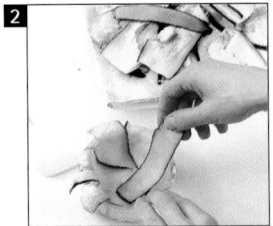

Walnut, Egg & Cheese Pâté

This unusual pâté, flavored with parsley and dill, can be served with crackers, crusty bread, or toast. The pâté requires chilling until set.

NUTRITIONAL INFORMATION

Calories	438	Sugars	.........2g
Protein	........21g	Fat	..........38g
Carbohydrate	....2g	Saturates	......18g

20 mins | 2 mins

SERVES 2

INGREDIENTS

1 celery stalk

1–2 scallions

¼ cup shelled walnuts

1 tbsp chopped fresh parsley

1 tsp chopped fresh dill or ½ tsp dried dill

1 garlic clove, crushed

dash of Worcestershire sauce

½ cup cottage cheese

2 oz/55 g blue cheese

1 hard-cooked egg

2 tbsp butter

salt and pepper

fresh herbs, to garnish

crackers, toast, or crusty bread and crudités, to serve

1 Finely chop the celery, slice the scallions very thinly, and chop the walnuts evenly. Place in a bowl.

2 Add the chopped herbs and garlic and Worcestershire sauce to taste and mix well, then stir the cottage cheese evenly through the mixture.

3 Grate the blue cheese finely into the pâté mixture. Finely chop the hard-cooked egg and stir it into the mixture. Season to taste with salt and pepper.

4 Melt the butter and stir it into the pâté, then spoon into 1 serving dish or 2 individual dishes. Smooth the top, but do not press down firmly. Chill until set.

5 Garnish with fresh herbs and serve with crackers, toast, or fresh, crusty bread and a few crudités, if liked.

COOK'S TIP
You can also use this as a stuffing for vegetables. Cut the tops off extra-large tomatoes, scoop out the seeds and fill with the pâté, piling it well up, or spoon into the hollows of celery stalks cut into 2 inch/5 cm pieces.

Thai Fish Cakes

These little fish cakes are very popular as street food in Thailand and also make a perfect appetizer with a spicy peanut dip.

NUTRITIONAL INFORMATION

Calories 205	Sugars 6g
Protein 17g	Fat 12g
Carbohydrate 7g	Saturates 2g

 15 mins 15 mins

SERVES 4–5

12 oz/350 g white fish fillet, such as cod or haddock, skinned

1 tbsp Thai fish sauce

2 tsp Thai red curry paste

1 tbsp lime juice

1 garlic clove, crushed

4 dried kaffir lime leaves, crumbled

1 egg white

3 tbsp chopped fresh cilantro

vegetable oil, for frying

salad greens, to serve

P E A N U T D I P

1 small fresh red chile

1 tbsp light soy sauce

1 tbsp lime juice

1 tbsp light brown sugar

3 tbsp chunky peanut butter

4 tbsp coconut milk

salt and pepper

between the palms of your hands, then flatten to make small round patties and set aside.

3 For the dip, halve and deseed the chile, then chop finely. Place in a small pan with the soy sauce, lime juice, sugar, peanut butter, and coconut milk and heat gently, stirring constantly, until thoroughly blended. Adjust the seasoning, adding more lime juice or sugar to taste.

4 Heat the oil in a skillet and fry the fish cakes in batches for 3–4 minutes on each side until golden brown. Drain on paper towels and serve them hot on a bed of salad greens with the chile-flavored peanut dip.

1 Put the fish fillet in a food processor with the fish sauce, curry paste, lime juice, garlic, lime leaves, and egg white, and process until a smooth paste forms.

2 Add the chopped cilantro and quickly process again until mixed. Divide the mixture into 8–10 pieces and roll into balls

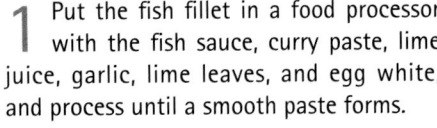

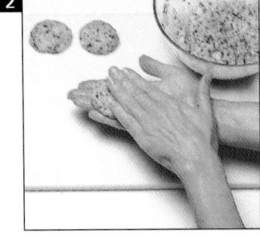

Steamed Crab Cakes

These pretty little steamed and fried crab cakes are usually served as a snack, but you can serve them as an appetizer instead.

NUTRITIONAL INFORMATION

Calories	156	Sugars 1g
Protein	........13g	Fat 11g
Carbohydrate	....2g	Saturates 4g

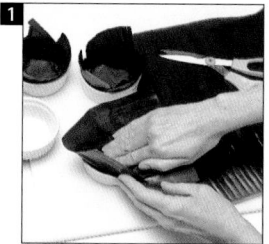

25 mins   20 mins

SERVES 4

INGREDIENTS

1–2 banana leaves

2 garlic cloves, crushed

1 tsp finely chopped lemongrass

½ tsp ground black pepper

2 tbsp chopped fresh cilantro

3 tbsp creamed coconut

1 tbsp lime juice

7 oz/200 g cooked crab meat, flaked

1 tbsp Thai fish sauce

2 egg whites

1 egg yolk, lightly beaten

8 fresh cilantro leaves

sunflower oil, for deep-frying

chili sauce, to serve

1 Line 8 x ½ cup ramekins or foil containers with the banana leaves, cutting them to shape.

2 Combine the garlic, lemongrass, pepper, and cilantro. Mash the creamed coconut with the lime juice until smooth. Stir it into the other ingredients with the crab meat and fish sauce.

3 In a clean, dry bowl, whisk the egg whites until stiff, then lightly and evenly fold them into the crab mixture.

4 Spoon the mixture into the ramekins or foil containers lined with banana leaves and press down lightly. Brush the tops with egg yolk and top each with a cilantro leaf.

5 Place in a steamer half-filled with boiling water, then cover with a close-fitting lid and steam for 15 minutes,

or until firm to the touch. Pour off the excess liquid and remove from the ramekins or foil containers.

6 Heat the oil to 350°F/180°C or until a cube of bread browns in 30 seconds. Add the crab cakes and deep-fry for about 1 minute, turning them over once, until golden brown. Serve with hot chili sauce.

Crispy Pork & Peanut Baskets

These tasty little appetite-teasers are an adaptation of a traditional recipe made with a light batter, but phyllo pastry is just as good.

NUTRITIONAL INFORMATION

Calories 243	Sugars 1g
Protein 12g	Fat 16g
Carbohydrate ...12g	Saturates 3g

 10 mins   15 mins

SERVES 4

INGREDIENTS

2 sheets phyllo pastry, each about
  16½ x 11 inches/42 x 28 cm

2 tbsp vegetable oil

1 garlic clove, crushed

4½ oz/125 g ground pork

1 tsp Thai red curry paste

2 scallions, finely chopped

3 tbsp crunchy peanut butter

1 tbsp light soy sauce

1 tbsp chopped fresh cilantro

salt and pepper

fresh cilantro sprigs, to garnish

1 Cut each sheet of phyllo pastry into 24 squares, 2¾ inches/7cm across, to make a total of 48 squares. Brush each square lightly with oil, and arrange the squares in stacks of 4 in 12 small patty pans, pointing outward. Press the pastry down into the patty pans.

2 Bake the pastry shells in a preheated oven, 400°F/ 200°C, for 6–8 minutes until golden brown.

3 Meanwhile, heat 1 tablespoon of the oil in a wok. Add the garlic and stir-fry for 30 seconds, then stir in the pork and stir-fry over high heat for 4–5 minutes until the meat is golden brown.

4 Add the curry paste and scallions and continue to stir-fry for a further minute, then stir in the peanut butter, soy sauce, and chopped cilantro. Season to taste with salt and pepper.

5 Spoon the pork mixture into the phyllo baskets and serve hot, garnished with cilantro sprigs.

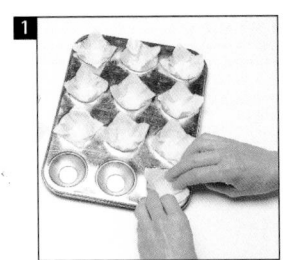

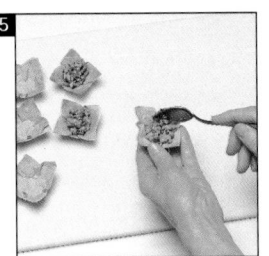

COOK'S TIP

When using phyllo pastry, remember that it dries out very quickly and becomes brittle and difficult to handle. Work quickly and keep any sheets of pastry you're not using covered with plastic wrap and a dampened cloth.

Chicken Balls with Sauce

Serve these bite-size chicken appetizers warm as a snack, with drinks, or packed cold for a picnic or lunchtime treat.

NUTRITIONAL INFORMATION

Calories 214   Sugars 29g
Protein . . . . .20g   Fat 13g
Carbohydrate . . . .5g   Saturates 2g

10 mins   25 mins

SERVES 4

INGREDIENTS

2 large skinless, boneless chicken breasts

3 tbsp vegetable oil

2 shallots, finely chopped

½ celery stalk, finely chopped

1 garlic clove, crushed

2 tbsp light soy sauce

1 small egg

1 bunch of scallions

salt and pepper

scallion tassels, to garnish

DIPPING SAUCE

3 tbsp dark soy sauce

1 tbsp rice wine

1 tsp sesame seeds

1 Cut the chicken into ¾ inch/2cm pieces. Heat half of the oil in a skillet or wok and stir-fry the chicken over high heat for 2–3 minutes until golden. Remove from the skillet or wok with a slotted spoon and set aside.

2 Add the shallots, celery, and garlic to the skillet or wok and stir-fry for 1–2 minutes until softened.

3 Place the chicken, shallots, celery, and garlic in a food processor and process until finely ground. Add 1 tablespoon of the light soy sauce and just enough egg to make a fairly firm mixture. Season to taste with salt and pepper.

4 Trim the scallions and cut into 2 inch/ 5 cm lengths. Make the dipping sauce by mixing together the dark soy sauce, rice wine, and sesame seeds in a small serving bowl and set aside.

5 Shape the chicken mixture into 16–18 walnut-size balls. Heat the remaining oil in the skillet or wok and stir-fry the chicken balls in small batches for 4–5 minutes until golden brown. As each batch is cooked drain on paper towels and keep hot.

6 Add the scallions to the skillet or wok and stir-fry for 1–2 minutes until they begin to soften, then stir in the remaining light soy sauce. Serve immediately with the chicken balls and the bowl of dipping sauce on a platter, garnished with the scallion tassels.

Warm Tuna Salad

This colorful, refreshing first course is perfect for a special occasion. The dressing can be made in advance and spooned over just before serving.

NUTRITIONAL INFORMATION

Calories 177   Sugars 4g
Protein . . . . .13g   Fat 6g
Carbohydrate . . . .6g   Saturates 1g

 15 mins   8 mins

SERVES 4

INGREDIENTS

2 oz/55 g Napa cabbage, shredded

3 tbsp rice wine

2 tbsp Thai fish sauce

1 tbsp finely shredded fresh
  ginger root

1 garlic clove, finely chopped

½ small fresh red bird-eye chile,
  finely chopped

2 tsp soft light brown sugar

2 tbsp lime juice

14 oz/400 g fresh tuna steak

sunflower oil, for brushing

4½ oz/125 g cherry tomatoes

chopped fresh mint leaves and fresh mint
  sprigs, to garnish

COOK'S TIP
You can make a quick version of
this dish using canned tuna. Just
drain and flake the tuna, omit steps
2 and 3 and continue as in the recipe.

1 Place a small pile of shredded Napa cabbage on a serving plate. Place the rice wine, fish sauce, ginger, garlic, chile, brown sugar, and 1 tablespoon of the lime juice in a screw-top jar and shake well to combine evenly.

2 Cut the tuna into strips of an even thickness. Sprinkle with the remaining lime juice.

3 Brush a wide skillet or ridged griddle with the oil and heat until very hot.

Arrange the tuna strips in the pan and cook until just firm and light golden, turning them over once. Remove and set aside.

4 Add the tomatoes to the pan and cook over high heat until lightly browned. Spoon the tuna and tomatoes over the Napa cabbage and spoon over the dressing. Garnish with chopped fresh mint and mint sprigs and serve warm.

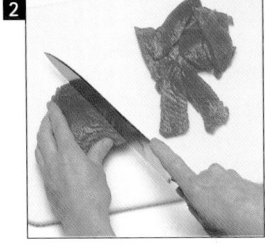

Thai-Style Corn Fritters

These quick, little fritters make a really appetizing first course, served with a spoonful of spicy chili relish and a squeeze of lime juice.

NUTRITIONAL INFORMATION

Calories	203	Sugars 3g
Protein	.........7g	Fat ...:........7g
Carbohydrate	...29g	Saturates 1g

15 mins   30 mins

SERVES 4

I N G R E D I E N T S

½ cup all-purpose flour

1 large egg

2 tsp Thai green curry paste

5 tbsp coconut milk

14 oz/400 g canned or frozen corn kernels

4 scallions

1 tbsp chopped fresh cilantro

1 tbsp chopped fresh basil

salt and pepper

vegetable oil, for frying

TO SERVE

lime wedges

chili relish

1 Place the flour, egg, curry paste, coconut milk, and about half the corn kernels in a food processor and process until a smooth, thick batter forms. Pour into a bowl.

2 Finely chop the scallions and stir into the batter with the remaining corn, chopped cilantro, and basil. Season to taste with salt and pepper.

3 Heat a small amount of oil in a wide, heavy skillet. Drop in tablespoonfuls of the batter and cook for 2–3 minutes until golden brown.

4 Turn them over and cook for a further 2–3 minutes until golden. Fry in batches, making about 12–16 fritters, keeping the cooked fritters hot while you cook the remaining batter.

5 Serve the fritters hot with lime wedges and a chili relish.

COOK'S TIP
If you prefer to use fresh corn, strip the kernels from the cobs with a sharp knife, then cook in boiling water for about 4–5 minutes until just tender. Drain well before using as instructed.

Steamed Chicken Packets

A healthy recipe with a delicate Asian flavor. Use large spinach leaves to wrap around the chicken, but make sure they are young leaves.

NUTRITIONAL INFORMATION

Calories	.216	Sugars	.7g
Protein	.31g	Fat	.7g
Carbohydrate	.7g	Saturates	.2g

 20 mins   30 mins

SERVES 4

INGREDIENTS

4 lean skinless boneless chicken breasts

1 tsp ground lemongrass

2 scallions, finely chopped

9 oz/250 g young carrots

9 oz/250 g young zucchini

2 celery stalks

1 tsp light soy sauce

9 oz/250 g spinach leaves

2 tsp sesame oil

salt and pepper

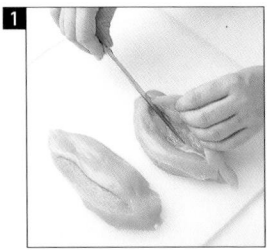

1 With a sharp knife, make a slit through 1 side of each chicken breast to open out a large pocket.

2 Sprinkle the inside of the pocket with lemongrass and season with salt and pepper to taste. Tuck the scallions into the chicken pockets.

3 Trim the carrots, zucchini, and celery, then cut into small batons. Plunge them into a pan of boiling water for 1 minute, drain, and then toss in the soy sauce.

4 Pack the pockets in each chicken breast with the vegetable mixture, but do not overfill. Fold over firmly to enclose. Reserve the remaining vegetables. Wash and dry the spinach leaves, then wrap the chicken breasts firmly in the leaves to enclose completely. If the leaves are too firm, steam them gently for a few seconds until they are softened and become flexible.

5 Place the wrapped chicken in a steamer and steam over rapidly boiling water for 20–25 minutes until tender and cooked through.

6 Stir-fry any leftover vegetable batons and spinach for 1–2 minutes in the sesame oil and serve with the chicken.

Toasted Nibbles

These tiny cheese balls are rolled in fresh herbs, toasted nuts, or paprika to make tasty nibbles for parties, buffets, or pre-dinner drinks.

NUTRITIONAL INFORMATION

Calories	310	Sugars	. . . . .1g
Protein	. . . . .15g	Fat	. . . . .27g
Carbohydrate	. . . .1g	Saturates	. . . . . .12g

 40 mins   🕐 5 mins

SERVES 4

I N G R E D I E N T S

½ cup ricotta cheese

1 cup finely grated Double Gloucester or brick cheese

2 tsp chopped fresh parsley

½ cup chopped mixed nuts

3 tbsp chopped mixed fresh herbs, such as parsley, chives, marjoram, lovage, and chervil

2 tbsp mild paprika

pepper

fresh herb sprigs, to garnish

1 Combine the ricotta and Double Gloucester or brick cheeses. Add the parsley and pepper and work together until thoroughly combined.

2 Form the mixture into small balls and place on a plate. Cover and chill in the refrigerator for about 20 minutes until they are firm.

3 Sprinkle the chopped nuts onto a cookie sheet and place them under a preheated broiler until lightly browned. Take care as they can easily burn. Remove from the broiler and set aside to cool.

4 Place the nuts, mixed herbs, and paprika into 3 separate small bowls. Remove the cheese balls from the refrigerator and divide into 3 equal piles. Roll 1 quantity of the cheese balls in the nuts, 1 quantity in the herbs, and 1 quantity in the paprika.

5 Arrange the coated cheese balls alternately on a large serving platter. Cover and chill in the refrigerator until ready to serve, and then garnish with sprigs of fresh herbs.

Fiery Salsa

Make this Mexican-style salsa to perk up jaded palates. Its lively flavors really get the tastebuds going. Serve with hot tortilla chips.

NUTRITIONAL INFORMATION

Calories ...... .328   Sugars 2g
Protein .... .4g   Fat .... .26g
Carbohydrate ...21g   Saturates 5g

30 mins   0 mins

SERVES 4

I N G R E D I E N T S

2 small fresh red chiles

1 tbsp lime or lemon juice

2 large ripe avocados

2 inch/5 cm piece of cucumber

2 tomatoes, peeled

1 small garlic clove, crushed

dash of Tabasco sauce

salt and pepper

lime or lemon slices, to garnish

tortilla chips, to serve

1 Remove and discard the stem and seeds from 1 fresh red chile. Chop the flesh very finely and place in a large mixing bowl.

2 Use the other red chile make a "flower" for the garnish. Using a small, sharp knife, slice the remaining chile from the stem to the tip several times without removing the stem, so the slices remain attached. Place in a bowl of ice water so that the "petals" open out.

3 Add the lime or lemon juice to the mixing bowl. Halve, pit, and peel the avocados. Add the flesh to the mixing bowl and mash thoroughly with a fork. The salsa should be slightly chunky. (The lime or lemon juice prevents the avocado from turning brown.)

4 Chop the cucumber and tomatoes finely and add to the avocado mixture with the crushed garlic.

5 Stir in the Tabasco sauce and season with salt and pepper. Transfer the salsa to a serving bowl. Garnish with slices of lime or lemon and the chile flower.

6 Put the bowl on a large plate, surround with tortilla chips, and serve. Do not keep this dip standing for long or it will discolor.

 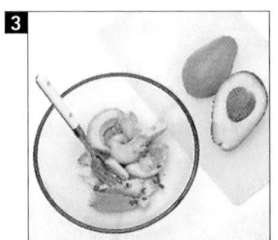 

Mint & Cannellini Bean Dip

This dip is ideal for pre-dinner drinks or for handing around at a party. The cannellini beans require soaking overnight, so prepare in advance.

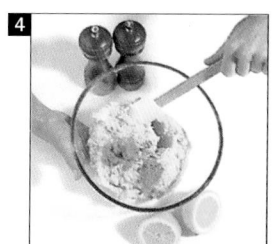

NUTRITIONAL INFORMATION

Calories 208	Sugars 1g
Protein 10g	Fat 12g
Carbohydrate ...16g	Saturates 2g

 40 mins   30 mins

SERVES 6

INGREDIENTS

scant 1 cup dried cannellini beans

1 small garlic clove, crushed

1 bunch of scallions, coarsely chopped

handful of fresh mint leaves

2 tbsp tahini

2 tbsp olive oil

1 tsp ground cumin

1 tsp ground coriander

lemon juice

salt and pepper

fresh mint sprigs, to garnish

TO SERVE

fresh vegetable crudités, such as cauliflower florets, carrots, cucumber, radishes, and bell peppers

1 Put the cannellini beans into a bowl and add sufficient cold water to cover. Set aside to soak for at least 4 hours or overnight.

2 Rinse and drain the beans, put them into a large pan, and cover them with cold water. Bring to a boil and boil rapidly for 10 minutes. Reduce the heat, cover, and simmer until tender.

3 Drain the beans thoroughly and transfer them to a bowl or food processor. Add the garlic, scallions, mint, tahini, and olive oil. Process the mixture for about 15 seconds or mash well by hand until smooth.

4 Scrape the mixture into a bowl, if necessary, and stir in the cumin, coriander, and lemon juice. Season to taste with salt and pepper. Mix thoroughly, cover with plastic wrap, and set aside in a cool place, but not the refrigerator, for 30 minutes to allow the flavors to develop.

5 Spoon the dip into individual serving bowls and garnish with sprigs of fresh mint. Place the bowls on plates and surround them with vegetable crudités. Serve at room temperature.

Fat Horses

A mixture of meats is flavored with coconut milk, Thai fish sauce, and fresh cilantro in this curious sounding dish.

NUTRITIONAL INFORMATION

Calories	195	Sugars	.........1g
Protein	........23g	Fat	...........11g
Carbohydrate	....1g	Saturates	.......6g

 10 mins 30 mins

SERVES 4

INGREDIENTS

2 tbsp creamed coconut

4 oz/115 g lean pork

4 oz/115 g skinless, boneless chicken breast

4 oz/115 g canned crab meat, drained

2 eggs

2 garlic cloves, crushed

4 scallions, chopped

1 tbsp Thai fish sauce

1 tbsp chopped fresh cilantro leaves and stems

1 tbsp molasses sugar

salt and pepper

TO GARNISH

finely sliced daikon or turnip

fresh chives

fresh red chile

fresh cilantro sprigs

3 Add the coconut mixture to the food processor or blender with the eggs, garlic, scallions, fish sauce, cilantro, and sugar. Season to taste and process for a few more seconds. Alternatively, mix these ingredients into the chopped pork, chicken, and crab meat.

4 Grease 6 ramekin dishes with a little butter. Spoon in the ground mixture, leveling the surface. Place them in a steamer, then set the steamer over a pan of gently simmering water. Cook for about 30 minutes until set.

5 Lift out the dishes and set aside to cool for a few minutes. Run a knife around the edge of each dish, then invert onto warmed plates. Serve immediately garnished with finely sliced daikon or turnip, fresh chives, red chile, and sprigs of fresh cilantro.

1 Mix the coconut with 3 tablespoons hot water. Stir to dissolve the coconut.

2 Put the pork, chicken, and crab meat into a food processor or blender and process for 10–15 seconds until ground, or chop them finely by hand, and put in a mixing bowl.

Eggplant Dipping Platter

Dipping platters are very sociable dishes, bringing together all the diners at the table. They are easy to prepare, too.

NUTRITIONAL INFORMATION

Calories 81	Sugars 4g	
Protein 4g	Fat 5g	
Carbohydrate 5g	Saturates 1g	

 15 mins   10 mins

SERVES 4

I N G R E D I E N T S

1 eggplant, peeled and cut into 1 inch/ 2.5 cm cubes

3 tbsp sesame seeds, roasted in a dry pan over low heat

1 tsp sesame oil

grated rind and juice of ½ lime

1 small shallot, diced

1 tsp sugar

1 fresh red chile, deseeded and sliced

4 oz/115 g broccoli florets

2 carrots, cut into batons

8 baby corn cobs, cut in half lengthwise

2 celery stalks, cut into batons

1 baby red cabbage, cut into 8 wedges, the leaves of each wedge held together by the core

salt and pepper

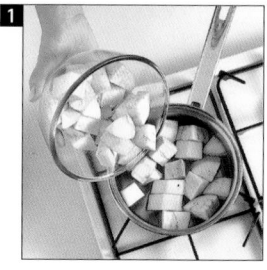  

1 Cook the diced eggplant in a pan of boiling water for 7–8 minutes. Drain well and set aside to cool slightly.

2 Meanwhile, grind the sesame seeds with the oil in a food processor or in a mortar with a pestle.

3 Add the eggplant, lime rind and juice, shallot, sugar, and chile to the sesame seeds. Season to taste with salt and pepper, then process or chop and mash by hand, until smooth.

4 Adjust the seasoning to taste, then spoon the dip into a bowl.

5 Serve the eggplant dipping platter surrounded by the broccoli, carrots, baby corn, celery, and red cabbage.

VARIATION
You can vary the selection of vegetables depending on your preference or whatever you have to hand. Other vegetables you could use are cauliflower florets and cucumber batons.

Garbanzo Beans & Prosciutto

Prosciutto is a cured ham, which is air- and salt-dried for up to 1 year.
Parma ham is said to be the best of the many different varieties available.

NUTRITIONAL INFORMATION

Calories 180	Sugars 2g
Protein 12g	Fat 7g
Carbohydrate ...18g	Saturates 1g

 10 mins   15 mins

SERVES 4

I N G R E D I E N T S

1 tbsp olive oil

1 medium onion, thinly sliced

1 garlic clove, chopped

1 small red bell pepper, deseeded and cut into thin strips

7 oz/200 g prosciutto, diced

400g/14 oz canned garbanzo beans, drained and rinsed

1 tbsp chopped fresh parsley, to garnish

crusty bread, to serve

COOK'S TIP

Whenever possible, use fresh herbs. They are becoming more readily available, and you can now buy small pots of herbs from the supermarket or grocery store and grow them at home. This ensures the herbs are fresh and also provides a continuous supply.

1 Heat the oil in a skillet. Add the onion, garlic, and bell pepper and cook over medium heat, stirring occasionally, for 3–4 minutes or until the vegetables have softened. Add the prosciutto and cook for 5 minutes or until the ham is just beginning to brown.

2 Add the garbanzo beans to the skillet and cook, stirring constantly, for 2–3 minutes until warmed through.

3 Sprinkle with chopped parsley and transfer to warm serving plates. Serve with lots of fresh crusty bread.

Mixed Bean Pâté

This is a really quick appetizer to prepare if canned beans are used.
Choose a wide variety of beans for color and flavor.

NUTRITIONAL INFORMATION

Calories	126	Sugars	.........3g
Protein	.........5g	Fat	..........6g
Carbohydrate	...13g	Saturates	.......1g

 45 mins 0 mins

SERVES 4

INGREDIENTS

400 g/14 oz can mixed beans, drained

2 tbsp olive oil

juice of 1 lemon

2 garlic cloves, crushed

1 tbsp chopped fresh cilantro

2 scallions, chopped

salt and pepper

shredded scallions, to garnish

1 Rinse the beans thoroughly under cold running water and drain well.

2 Transfer the beans to a food processor or blender and process until smooth. Alternatively, place the beans in a bowl and mash thoroughly by hand with a fork or potato masher.

3 Add the olive oil, lemon juice, garlic, cilantro, and scallions and blend until fairly smooth. Season with salt and pepper to taste.

4 Transfer the pâté to a serving bowl, cover, and chill in the refrigerator for at least 30 minutes.

5 Garnish the pâté with shredded scallions and serve.

Giant Garlic Shrimp

In Spain, giant garlic shrimp are cooked in small half-glazed earthenware dishes called "cazuelas." The shrimp arrive at your table sizzling.

NUTRITIONAL INFORMATION

Calories 385	Sugars 0g
Protein 26g	Fat 31g
Carbohydrate 1g	Saturates 5g

5 mins   5–8 mins

SERVES 4

I N G R E D I E N T S

½ cup olive oil

4 garlic cloves, finely chopped

2 hot fresh red chiles, deseeded and finely chopped

1 lb/450 g cooked jumbo shrimp

2 tbsp chopped fresh flat leaf parsley

salt and pepper

lemon wedges, to garnish

crusty bread, to serve

1 Heat the olive oil in a large, heavy skillet over low heat. Add the garlic and chiles and cook, stirring occasionally, for 1–2 minutes until softened, but not colored.

2 Add the shrimp and stir-fry for 2–3 minutes until heated through and coated in the oil and garlic mixture.

COOK'S TIP

If you can get hold of raw shrimp, cook them as above but increase the cooking time to 5–6 minutes until the shrimp are cooked through and turn bright pink. If using frozen shrimp, make sure they are thoroughly thawed before cooking.

3 Turn off the heat and add the chopped fresh flat leaf parsley, stirring well to mix. Season to taste with salt and pepper.

4 Divide the shrimp and garlic-flavored oil among warmed serving dishes and serve with lots of crusty bread. Garnish with lemon wedges.

Mussels with Pesto

These delicious morsels make an impressive, yet quick appetizer.
Serve them with some crusty bread to mop up any juices.

NUTRITIONAL INFORMATION

Calories	399	Sugars	.........1g
Protein	........14g	Fat	..........31g
Carbohydrate	...17g	Saturates	.......5g

20 mins | 12 mins

SERVES 4

INGREDIENTS

2 lb/900g live mussels

6 tbsp chopped fresh basil

2 garlic cloves, crushed

1 tbsp pine nuts, toasted

2 tbsp freshly grated Parmesan cheese

scant ½ cup olive oil

2 cups fresh white bread crumbs

salt and pepper

TO GARNISH

tomato slices

fresh basil leaves

1 Clean the mussels by scrubbing or scraping the shells and pulling out any beards that are attached to them. Discard any with broken shells or any that refuse to close when tapped. Put the mussels into a large pan with just the water on their shells, cover, and cook over high heat for 3–4 minutes, shaking the pan occasionally, until all the mussels have opened. Discard any mussels that remain closed. Drain, reserving the cooking liquid, and set aside until cool enough to handle.

2 Strain the cooking liquid into a clean pan and simmer until reduced to about 1 tablespoon. Put the liquid into a food processor with the basil, garlic, pine nuts, and Parmesan and process until finely chopped. Add the olive oil and bread crumbs and process until well mixed.

3 Open the mussels and loosen from their shells, discarding the empty half of the shell. Divide the pesto bread crumbs among the mussels.

4 Cook under a preheated broiler until the bread crumbs are crisp and golden and the mussels are heated through. Serve immediately, garnished with slices of tomato and basil leaves.

VARIATION

If you want an alternative to pine nuts, add 3 oz/85 g coarsely chopped, drained sun-dried tomatoes in oil to the pesto instead.

Stuffed Squid

This is a very typical Greek recipe for stuffing squid. Most large supermarkets with fish counters sell baby squid already cleaned.

NUTRITIONAL INFORMATION

Calories 300   Sugars 9g
Protein ....12g   Fat 18g
Carbohydrate ...19g   Saturates 2g

25 mins   1 hr

SERVES 4

INGREDIENTS

12 baby squid, cleaned

4 tbsp olive oil

1 small onion, finely chopped

1 garlic clove, finely chopped

3 tbsp basmati rice

1 tbsp seedless raisins

1 tbsp pine nuts, toasted

1 tbsp chopped fresh flat leaf parsley

14 oz/400 g canned chopped tomatoes

1 oz/25 g sun-dried tomatoes in oil, drained and finely chopped

½ cup dry white wine

salt and pepper

crusty bread, to serve

1 Chop off the tentacles from the squid. Chop the tentacles and set aside. Rub the squid tubes inside and out with 1 teaspoon salt and set aside.

2 Heat 1 tablespoon of the olive oil in a skillet and add the onion and garlic. Cook, stirring occasionally, for 4–5 minutes until softened and lightly browned. Add the tentacles and cook for 2–3 minutes. Add the rice, raisins, pine nuts, and parsley and season to taste. Remove the skillet from the heat.

3 Let the rice mixture cool slightly, then spoon it into the squid tubes, so they are about three-quarters full. Secure each filled squid with a toothpick.

4 Heat the remaining oil in a large flameproof casserole. Add the squid and fry for a few minutes on all sides until lightly browned. Add the tomatoes, sun-dried tomatoes, wine, and seasoning. Bake in a preheated oven, 350°F/180°C, for 45 minutes. Serve hot or cold with plenty of crusty bread.

  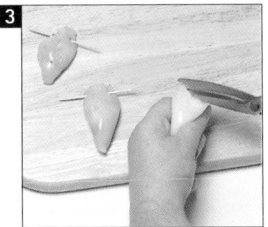

COOK'S TIP

You may need to open the squid tubes a little when stuffing them. Make a small cut with a sharp knife or kitchen scissors. Do not fill the tubes more than three-quarters full to allow the rice to expand.

Smoked Mackerel Pâté

This is a quick and easy pâté with plenty of flavor. It originates from Goa, on the west coast of India, an area famous for its seafood.

NUTRITIONAL INFORMATION

Calories 316	Sugars 3g
Protein 13g	Fat 23g
Carbohydrate . . .14g	Saturates 8g

 4 hrs   5 mins

SERVES 4

I N G R E D I E N T S

7 oz/200g smoked mackerel fillet

1 small, hot fresh green chile, deseeded and chopped

1 garlic clove, chopped

3 tbsp fresh cilantro leaves

⅔ cup sour cream

1 small red onion, chopped

2 tbsp lime juice

salt and pepper

4 slices white bread, crusts removed

1 Skin and flake the mackerel fillet, removing any small bones. Put the flesh in the bowl of a food processor with the chile, garlic, cilantro, and sour cream. Process until smooth.

2 Transfer the mixture to a bowl and mix in the onion and lime juice. Season to taste with salt and pepper. The pâté will seem very soft at this stage, but will firm up in the refrigerator. Cover with plastic wrap and chill for several hours or overnight if possible.

3 To make the Melba toasts, place the trimmed bread slices under a preheated medium broiler and toast lightly on both sides. Using a long, sharp knife, split the toasts in half horizontally, then

  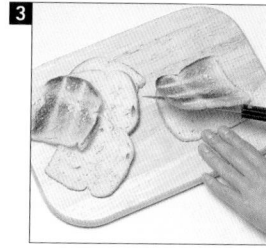

cut each across diagonally to form 4 triangles per slice.

4 Put the triangles, untoasted side up, under the broiler and toast until golden and curled at the edges. Serve the Melba toast warm or cold with the smoked mackerel pâté.

COOK'S TIP
This pâté is also very good served with crudités.

Smoked Haddock Salad

Smoked haddock has an affinity for eggs. Here it is teamed with hard-cooked quail eggs and topped with a creamy chive dressing.

NUTRITIONAL INFORMATION

Calories 366	Sugars 3g	
Protein 26g	Fat 20g	
Carbohydrate ...21g	Saturates 5g	

🥘 40 mins   🕐 15 mins

SERVES 4

INGREDIENTS

12 oz/350 g smoked haddock fillet

4 tbsp olive oil

1 tbsp lemon juice

2 tbsp sour cream

1 tbsp hot water

2 tbsp chopped fresh chives, plus extra
to garnish

1 plum tomato, skinned, deseeded, and diced

8 quail eggs

4 thick slices whole-wheat or
multigrain bread

4 oz/115 g mixed salad greens

salt and pepper

1 Fill a large skillet with water and bring to a boil. Add the fish, cover, and remove from the heat. Set aside for 10 minutes until the fish is tender. Lift out the fish, drain, and set aside until cool enough to handle. Flake the flesh, removing any small bones. Discard the poaching water.

2 Whisk together the olive oil, lemon juice, sour cream, hot water, and chives and season to taste with salt and pepper. Stir in the tomato. Set aside.

3 Bring a small pan of water to a boil. Carefully lower the quail eggs into the water. Bring back to a boil and cook the eggs for 3–4 minutes (3 minutes for a slightly soft center, 4 minutes for a firm center). Drain immediately and refresh under cold running water until cold. Carefully shell the eggs, cut in half lengthwise, and set aside.

4 Toast the bread and cut each slice diagonally to form 4 triangles. Arrange 2 halves on each of 4 serving plates. Top with the salad greens, then the flaked fish, and finally the quail eggs. Spoon over the dressing and garnish with a few extra chives.

COOK'S TIP

When buying smoked haddock, and smoked fish in general, look for undyed fish, which is always superior in quality.

Fish Cakes with Chili Sauce

If you can find them, use small chiles, called "bird-eye," for the dipping sauce. They are very hot, however, so remove the seeds if you prefer.

NUTRITIONAL INFORMATION

Calories	223	Sugars	........23g
Protein	........21g	Fat	...........4g
Carbohydrate	...25g	Saturates	.......1g

 15 mins   10 mins

SERVES 4

INGREDIENTS

1 lb/450 g firm white fish, such as hake, haddock, or cod, skinned and coarsely chopped

1 tbsp Thai fish sauce

1 tbsp red curry paste

1 kaffir lime leaf, finely shredded

2 tbsp chopped fresh cilantro

1 egg

1 tsp brown sugar

1½ oz/40 g green beans, thinly sliced crosswise

vegetable oil, for frying

salt

SWEET AND SOUR DIPPING SAUCE

4 tbsp sugar

1 tbsp cold water

3 tbsp white rice vinegar

2 small, hot fresh red chiles, finely chopped

1 tbsp Thai fish sauce

1 For the fish cakes, put the fish, fish sauce, curry paste, lime leaf, cilantro, egg, sugar, and salt into the bowl of a food processor. Process until smooth. Scrape into a bowl and stir in the green beans. Set aside.

2 To make the sauce, put the sugar, water, and vinegar into a small pan and heat gently until the sugar has dissolved. Bring to a boil and simmer for 2 minutes. Remove from the heat, stir in the chiles and fish sauce, and set aside.

3 Heat a skillet with enough oil to cover the bottom generously. Divide the fish mixture into 16 little balls. Flatten the balls into little patties and fry in the hot oil for 1–2 minutes on each side until golden. Drain on paper towels. Serve hot with the dipping sauce.

COOK'S TIP

It isn't necessary to use the most expensive cut of white fish in this recipe as the other flavors are very strong. Use whatever is cheapest.

Lime & Basil Cured Salmon

It is very important to use fresh salmon for this dish. The salt and sugar draw the moisture from the fish, leaving it raw but cured.

NUTRITIONAL INFORMATION

Calories	.382	Sugars	.27g
Protein	.31g	Fat	.17g
Carbohydrate	.27g	Saturates	.3g

 24–48 hrs 8 mins

SERVES 4

INGREDIENTS

2lb/900 g very fresh salmon fillet, from the head end, skinned

¼ cup sugar

¼ cup sea salt

5 tbsp chopped fresh basil

finely grated rind of 2 limes

1 tsp white peppercorns, lightly crushed

DRESSING

scant 1 cup rice vinegar

5 tbsp sugar

finely grated rind of 1 lime

½ tsp hot mustard

3 tbsp chopped fresh basil

1 tbsp Japanese pickled ginger, finely shredded

5½ oz/150 g mixed salad greens, to serve

TO GARNISH

lime wedges

fresh basil leaves

1 Remove any small pin bones that remain in the salmon fillet with tweezers. Wash and pat the fish dry with paper towels. Place the salmon in a large nonmetallic dish and sprinkle evenly with the sugar, sea salt, basil, lime rind, and peppercorns. Cover and chill for 24–48 hours, turning the fish occasionally.

2 For the dressing, put the rice vinegar and sugar in a small pan and stir gently over low heat until the sugar has dissolved. Bring to a boil and simmer for 5–6 minutes until the liquid is reduced by about one-third. Remove the pan from the heat and stir in the lime rind and mustard. Set aside.

3 Remove the salmon fillet from the marinade, wiping off any excess with paper towels. Using a long, sharp knife, slice very thinly.

4 To serve, stir the chopped basil and ginger into the dressing. Toss the salad greens with a little of the dressing and arrange on 6 serving plates. Divide the salmon slices among the plates and drizzle a little dressing over each. Garnish with lime wedges and basil leaves.

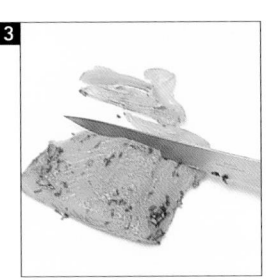

Griddled Smoked Salmon

It is best to buy packets of smoked salmon strips for this recipe because they lend themselves to folding more easily than freshly sliced salmon.

NUTRITIONAL INFORMATION

Calories . . . . . . .232 Sugars 1g
Protein . . . . .23g Fat 15g
Carbohydrate . . . .1g Saturates 2g

10 mins   6–9 mins

SERVES 4

INGREDIENTS

12 oz/350 g sliced smoked salmon

4 oz/115 g mixed salad greens

fresh dill sprigs, to garnish

VINAIGRETTE

1 tsp Dijon mustard

1 garlic clove, crushed

2 tsp chopped fresh dill

2 tsp sherry vinegar

4 tbsp olive oil

salt and pepper

1 Make 2 folds "accordion style" in each slice of salmon so that the slices form little packets.

2 To make the vinaigrette, whisk the mustard, garlic, dill, and sherry vinegar together. Season to taste with salt and pepper. Gradually whisk in the olive oil until thoroughly combined.

3 Heat a ridged griddle pan until smoking. Cook the salmon packets on 1 side only for 2–3 minutes until heated through and marked from the pan. Cook in batches, if necessary.

4 Meanwhile, toss the salad greens with some of the vinaigrette and divide them equally among 4 serving

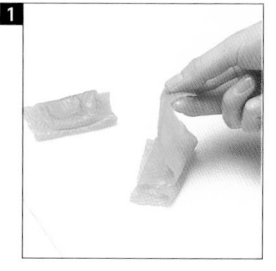

plates. Top with the cooked smoked salmon, cooked side up. Drizzle with the remaining dressing, garnish with fresh dill sprigs, and serve immediately.

COOK'S TIP
Smoked salmon is very expensive. This recipe would also work well with smoked trout.

Salmon Tartare

This would make a stunning appetizer for a dinner party, yet it is incredibly easy and speedy to prepare.

NUTRITIONAL INFORMATION

Calories 315	Sugars 2g	
Protein 31g	Fat 20g	
Carbohydrate 2g	Saturates 3g	

  30 mins   0 mins

SERVES 4

INGREDIENTS

2lb/900 g very fresh salmon fillet, skinned

3 tbsp lemon juice

3 tbsp lime juice

2 tsp sugar

1 tsp Dijon mustard

1 tbsp chopped fresh dill

1 tbsp chopped fresh basil

2 tbsp olive oil

2 oz/55 g arugula

handful of fresh basil leaves

2 oz/55 g mixed salad greens

salt and pepper

TO GARNISH

fresh dill sprigs

fresh basil leaves

1 Cut the salmon into very tiny dice and season to taste with salt and pepper. Put into a large bowl.

2 Combine the lemon juice, lime juice, sugar, mustard, dill, chopped basil, and olive oil. Pour the mixture over the salmon and mix well. Set aside for 15–20 minutes until the fish becomes opaque.

3 Meanwhile, combine the arugula, basil leaves, and salad greens. Divide among 4 serving plates.

4 To serve the salmon, fill a small ramekin or mini bowl with the mixture and turn out onto the center of the salad greens. Garnish with dill sprigs and basil leaves.

VARIATION

Haddock also responds very well to this treatment. Use half the quantity of salmon and an equal weight of very fresh haddock.

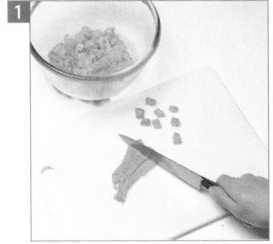

Gravlax

You need two salmon fillets for this dish, approximately the same size. Ask your fish dealer to remove all the bones and scale the fish.

NUTRITIONAL INFORMATION

Calories 608   Sugars 11g
Protein . . . . .37g   Fat 34g
Carbohydrate . . .41g   Saturates 14g

 48 hrs   0 mins

SERVES 6

I N G R E D I E N T S

2 x 1 lb/450 g salmon fillets,
    with skin on

6 tbsp coarsely chopped fresh dill

½ cup sea salt

⅓ cup sugar

1 tbsp white peppercorns, roughly crushed

12 slices brown bread, buttered,
    to serve

G A R N I S H

lemon slices

fresh dill sprigs

1 Wash the salmon fillets and dry with paper towels. Put 1 fillet, skin side down, in a nonmetallic dish.

2 Combine the dill, sea salt, sugar, and peppercorns. Spread this mixture over the first fillet of fish and place the second fillet, skin side up, on top. Put a plate, the same size as the fish, on top and put a weight on the plate (3 or 4 cans of tomatoes or similar will do).

3 Chill in the refrigerator for 2 days, turning the fish about every 12 hours and basting with any juices which have come out of the fish.

4 Remove the salmon from the brine and slice thinly, without slicing the skin, as you would smoked salmon. Cut the brown bread into triangles and serve with the salmon. Garnish with lemon wedges and sprigs of fresh dill.

COOK'S TIP
You can brush the marinade off the salmon before slicing, but the line of green along the edge of the salmon is quite attractive and, of course, full of flavor.

Thai Crab Omelet

Don't be put off by the long list of ingredients. The omelet is served cold and so can be made entirely ahead of time.

NUTRITIONAL INFORMATION

Calories	262	Sugars	.........5g
Protein	........18g	Fat	..........19g
Carbohydrate	....5g	Saturates	.......7g

2½ hrs   10 mins

SERVES 4

INGREDIENTS

8 oz/225 g white crab meat, thawed if frozen

3 scallions, finely chopped

1 tbsp chopped fresh cilantro

1 tbsp chopped fresh chives

pinch of cayenne pepper

2 tbsp vegetable oil

2 garlic cloves, crushed

1 tsp freshly grated fresh ginger root

1 fresh red chile, deseeded and finely chopped

2 tbsp lime juice

2 lime leaves, shredded

2 tsp sugar

2 tsp Thai fish sauce

3 eggs

4 tbsp coconut cream

1 tsp salt

finely chopped scallion, to garnish

1 Put the crab meat into a bowl and check for any small pieces of shell. Add the scallions, cilantro, chives, and cayenne and set aside.

2 Heat 1 tablespoon of the vegetable oil in a small pan and stir-fry the garlic, ginger, and chile for 30 seconds. Add the lime juice, lime leaves, sugar, and fish sauce. Simmer for 3–4 minutes until reduced. Remove from the heat and set aside to cool, then add to the crab mixture.

3 Lightly beat the eggs with the coconut cream and salt. Heat the remaining oil in a skillet over medium heat. Add the egg mixture and as it sets on the bottom, carefully pull the edges in toward the center, allowing unset egg to run underneath.

4 When the egg is nearly set, spoon the crab mixture down the center. Cook for a further 1–2 minutes to finish cooking the egg, then turn the omelet out of the skillet onto a serving dish. Set aside to cool, then chill in the refrigerator for 2–3 hours or overnight. Cut into 4 pieces and garnish with chopped scallion.

A Modern Kedgeree

This is a modern version of the classic dish, using smoked salmon as well as fresh salmon and lots of fresh herbs—perfect for a dinner party.

NUTRITIONAL INFORMATION

Calories	.370	Sugars	.3g
Protein	.10g	Fat	.19g
Carbohydrate	.39g	Saturates	.9g

 10 mins   35 mins

SERVES 6

INGREDIENTS

2 tbsp butter

1 tbsp olive oil

1 onion, finely chopped

1 garlic clove, finely chopped

scant 1 cup long grain rice

1¾ cups fish stock

6 oz/175 g salmon fillet, skinned and chopped

3 oz/85 g smoked salmon, chopped

2 tbsp heavy cream

2 tbsp chopped fresh dill

3 scallions, finely chopped

salt and pepper

fresh dill sprigs and lemon slices, to garnish

1 Melt the butter with the oil in a large pan. Add the onion and cook over low heat for 10 minutes until softened, but not colored. Add the garlic and cook for a further 30 seconds.

2 Add the rice and cook for 2–3 minutes, stirring constantly, until transparent. Add the fish stock and stir well. Bring to a boil, cover, and simmer very gently for 10 minutes.

3 Add the salmon fillet and the smoked salmon and stir well, adding a little more stock or water if the mixture seems dry. Cook for a further 6–8 minutes until the fish and rice are tender and all the stock is absorbed.

4 Turn off the heat and stir in the cream, chopped fresh dill, and the scallions. Season to taste with salt and pepper and serve immediately, garnished with sprigs of fresh dill and slices of lemon.

COOK'S TIP
Use smoked salmon trimmings for a budget dish.

Taramasalata with Pitas

Forget the artificially dyed, bright pink taramasalata sold in supermarkets. This is the version you will find in Greek homes.

NUTRITIONAL INFORMATION

Calories 279   Sugars 4g
Protein ....9g   Fat 21g
Carbohydrate ...14g   Saturates 3g

20 mins   20 mins

SERVES 6

INGREDIENTS

8 oz/225 g smoked cod's roe

1 small onion, finely chopped

1 garlic clove

2 oz/55 g fresh white bread, (about 2 thick slices) crusts removed

finely grated rind of 1 lemon

4 tbsp lemon juice

⅔ cup extra virgin olive oil

6 tbsp hot water

salt and pepper

hollowed-out tomatoes, to serve

fresh flat leaf parsley sprigs, to garnish

PITA WEDGES

2 pitas

olive oil, for brushing

1 Remove the skin from the smoked cod's roe. Put the roe and onion in a food processor and process until well blended and smooth. Add the garlic and process again.

2 Break the bread into the food processor, then add the lemon rind and the lemon juice. Process again until the bread is well incorporated.

3 With the motor running, gradually add the olive oil through the feeder tube, as if making a mayonnaise. When all the oil is incorporated, add the hot water and process again. Add salt and pepper to taste, plus extra lemon juice if wished. Spoon into a bowl, cover with plastic wrap, and chill until ready to serve.

4 To make the pita wedges, using a serrated knife, cut the pitas in half through the center. Cut each half into 6–8 wedges, depending on the size. Place on a cookie sheet and brush the inside surfaces of the wedges with olive oil.

5 Bake in a preheated oven, 350°F/180°C, for 20 minutes. Place on wire racks to cool.

6 Spoon the taramasalata into the tomato shells, garnish with parsley, and serve with the pita wedges for dipping.

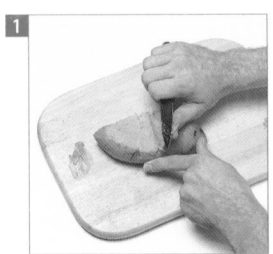

COOK'S TIP

If you see imported smoked gray mullet roe, buy it for this dish. It is more authentic—and finer tasting—than smoked cod's roe.

Hummus

Quick and easy to make, this dip features regularly on Mediterranean menus. Serve it with fingers of pita or vegetable sticks for dipping.

NUTRITIONAL INFORMATION

Calories . . . . . . .204 Sugars 1g
Protein . . . . .7g Fat 14g
Carbohydrate . . .13g Saturates 2g

13 hrs   1–2 hrs

SERVES 8

I N G R E D I E N T S

scant 1 cup dried garbanzo beans

2 large garlic cloves

7 tbsp extra virgin olive oil

2½ tbsp tahini

1 tbsp lemon juice

salt and pepper

fresh cilantro

T O   S E R V E

extra virgin olive oil

paprika

1 Place the garbanzo beans in a large bowl. Pour in at least twice their volume of cold water and set aside to soak for at least 12 hours until they have doubled in size.

2 Drain the garbanzo beans. Put them in a large flameproof casserole or pan and add twice their volume of cold water. Bring to a boil over medium heat and boil vigorously for 10 minutes, skimming the surface frequently.

3 Lower the heat and simmer gently, skimming the surface, if necessary, for about 1–2 hours until tender.

4 Meanwhile, cut the garlic cloves in half, remove and discard the pale

green or white cores, and coarsely chop the cloves. Set aside.

5 Drain the garbanzo beans, reserving 4 tablespoons of the cooking liquid. Put the olive oil, garlic, tahini, and lemon juice in a food processor and blend to a smooth paste.

6 Add the garbanzo beans and pulse until they are finely ground, but the

hummus is still lightly textured. Add a little of the reserved cooking liquid if the mixture is too thick. Season with salt and pepper to taste.

7 Scrape the hummus into a bowl, cover with plastic wrap, and chill in the refrigerator until ready to serve. To serve, drizzle with some extra virgin olive oil, sprinkle a little paprika on top, and garnish with fresh cilantro.

Tzatziki

Simple to make, this creamy Greek dip is very refreshing on a hot day and is particularly good for parties.

NUTRITIONAL INFORMATION

Calories	75	Sugars	.........2g
Protein	.........4g	Fat	...........6g
Carbohydrate	....2g	Saturates	.......3g

 3½ hrs   3–5 mins

SERVES 12

INGREDIENTS

2 large cucumbers

2½ cups Plain Strained Yogurt (see page 432) or plain thick yogurt

3 garlic cloves, crushed

1 tbsp finely chopped fresh dill

1 tbsp extra virgin olive oil

salt and pepper

TO GARNISH

1 tbsp sesame seeds

cayenne pepper

fresh dill sprigs (optional)

1 Using the coarse side of a grater, grate the cucumbers into a bowl lined with an absorbent, perforated kitchen cloth. Pull up the corners of the cloth to make a tight bundle and squeeze very hard to extract all the moisture (see Cook's Tip).

2 Put the cucumbers in a bowl and stir in the yogurt, garlic, dill, and olive oil, and season with salt and pepper to taste. Cover with plastic wrap and chill for at least 3 hours for the flavors to blend.

3 When ready to serve, remove the dip from the refrigerator and stir. Taste and adjust the seasoning if necessary.

4 Put the sesame seeds in a small, ungreased skillet and dry-fry them over medium heat until they turn golden and start to give off their aroma. Immediately pour them out of the pan onto the tzatziki—they will sizzle.

5 Sprinkle some cayenne pepper onto a plate. Lightly dip the tip of a dry pastry brush into the cayenne, then tap a light sprinkling of cayenne all over the tzatziki. Garnish with fresh dill, if wished, and serve. (Ungarnished tzatziki will keep for up to 3 days in the refrigerator.)

COOK'S TIP

It is essential to squeeze all the moisture out of the cucumbers in Step 1, or the dip will be unpleasantly watery and will separate.

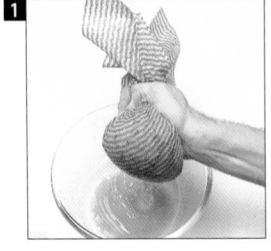  

Eggplant Spread

This simple, quick dip is so good that it is often called "poor man's caviar." It is found throughout the Mediterranean.

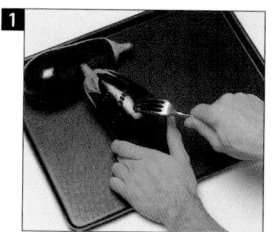

NUTRITIONAL INFORMATION

Calories	90	Sugars	.........2g
Protein	.........1g	Fat	...........8g
Carbohydrate	....2g	Saturates	.......1g

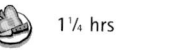

🍲 1¼ hrs   🕐 20–25 mins

SERVES 6–8

INGREDIENTS

2 large eggplants

1 tomato

1 garlic clove, chopped

4 tbsp extra virgin olive oil

2 tbsp lemon juice

2 tbsp pine nuts, lightly toasted

2 scallions, finely chopped

salt and pepper

TO GARNISH

ground cumin

2 tbsp finely chopped fresh flat
leaf parsley

1 Using a fork or metal skewer, pierce the eggplants all over. Place them on a cookie sheet in a preheated oven, 450°F/230°C, and roast for 20–25 minutes until they are very soft.

2 Use a folded dish cloth to remove the eggplants from the cookie sheet and set them aside to cool.

3 Place the tomato in a heatproof bowl, pour boiling water over to cover, and let stand for 30 seconds. Drain, then plunge into cold water to prevent it from cooking. Peel the tomato, then cut in half, and scoop out the seeds with a teaspoon. Finely dice the flesh and set aside.

4 Cut the cooled eggplants in half lengthwise. Scoop out the flesh with a spoon and transfer to a food processor. Add the garlic, olive oil, lemon juice, and pine nuts and season with salt and pepper to taste. Process until smooth. Alternatively, mash by hand.

5 Scrape the mixture into a bowl and stir in the scallions and diced tomato. Cover with plastic wrap and chill for 30 minutes before serving.

6 Garnish the dip with a pinch of ground cumin and the finely chopped parsley, then serve.

Tapenade

These robust olive and anchovy spreads can be as thick or as thin as you like. They make flavorful appetizers spread on toast.

NUTRITIONAL INFORMATION

Calories	227	Sugars	.........0g
Protein	.........5g	Fat	..........23g
Carbohydrate	....0g	Saturates	.......3g

10–15 mins   5 mins

SERVES 6

INGREDIENTS

thin slices of day-old baguette (optional)

olive oil (optional)

finely chopped fresh flat leaf parsley sprigs, to garnish

BLACK OLIVE TAPENADE

2¼ cups black Niçoise olives in brine, rinsed and pitted

1 large garlic clove

2 tbsp walnut pieces

4 canned anchovy fillets, drained

about ½ cup extra virgin olive oil

lemon juice, to taste

pepper

GREEN OLIVE TAPENADE

2¼ cups green olives in brine, rinsed and pitted

4 canned anchovy fillets, rinsed

4 tbsp blanched almonds

1 tbsp capers in brine or vinegar, rinsed

about ½ cup extra virgin olive oil

1½–3 tsp finely grated orange rind

pepper

1 To make the black olive tapenade, put the olives, garlic, walnut pieces, and anchovies in a food processor and process until blended.

2 With the motor running, slowly add the olive oil through the feeder tube, as if making mayonnaise. Add lemon juice and pepper to taste. Transfer to a bowl, cover with plastic wrap, and chill until required.

3 To make the green olive tapenade, put the olives, anchovies, almonds, and capers in a food processor and process until blended. With the motor running, slowly add the olive oil through the feeder tube, as if making mayonnaise. Add orange rind and pepper to taste. Transfer to a bowl, cover with plastic wrap, and chill until required.

4 To serve on croûtes, if wished, toast the slices of bread on both sides until crisp. Brush 1 side of each slice with a little olive oil while they are still hot, so the oil is absorbed by the toast.

5 Spread the croûtes with the tapenade of your choice and garnish with parsley.

Ceviche

This no-cook seafood salad is popular throughout the Mediterranean where freshly caught fish and shellfish are plentiful.

NUTRITIONAL INFORMATION

Calories . . . . .201 Sugars 3g
Protein . . . . .23g Fat 11g
Carbohydrate . . . .4g Saturates 2g

 2½ hrs   0 mins

SERVES 4

I N G R E D I E N T S

8 fresh scallops

16 large shrimp in shells

2 sea bass fillets, about 5½ oz/150 g each, skinned

1 large lemon

1 lime

1 red onion, thinly sliced

½ fresh red chile, deseeded and finely chopped

2–4 tbsp extra virgin olive oil

TO SERVE

salad greens

lemon or lime wedges

pepper

  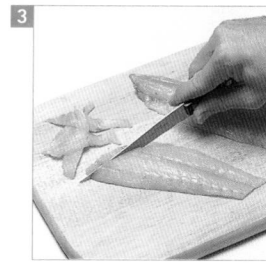

1 If the scallops are in shells, use an oyster knife or small knife to prize the shells open, then rinse under running cold water. Cut the scallops and coral free from the shells. Slice the scallop flesh into 2–3 horizontal slices each. Place in a nonmetallic bowl with the corals.

2 Remove the heads and peel the shrimp. Using a small sharp knife, devein them. Add to the scallops.

3 Cut the sea bass fillet into thin slices across the grain and add to the bowl of seafood.

4 Firmly roll the lemon and lime backward and forward on a counter to help release the juice. Cut the lemon in half and squeeze the juice over the fish. Repeat with the lime.

5 Gently stir to coat the seafood well in the citrus juices, then cover with plastic wrap, and chill in the refrigerator for 2 hours or until the seafood becomes opaque, but do not leave for longer otherwise the seafood will be too soft.

6 Using a slotted spoon, transfer the seafood to another bowl. Add the onion, chile, and olive oil and stir gently. Set aside at room temperature for about 5 minutes.

7 Spoon the seafood onto individual serving plates and serve immediately with salad greens, lemon or lime wedges, and black pepper.

Lemon Risotto

This is a stylish first course, with an aroma and fresh
taste that stimulate the tastebuds for the meal to follow.

NUTRITIONAL INFORMATION

Calories	442	Sugars	.........3g
Protein	.........6g	Fat	..........15g
Carbohydrate	...68g	Saturates	.......6g

 10 mins   35 mins

SERVES 4

INGREDIENTS

2–3 lemons

2 tbsp olive oil

2 shallots, finely chopped

2⅔ cups risotto rice

½ cup dry white vermouth

4 cups vegetable or chicken
stock, simmering

1 tbsp very finely chopped fresh flat
leaf parsley

2 tbsp butter

TO GARNISH

thin strips of pared lemon rind

fresh parsley sprigs

TO SERVE

Parmesan cheese shavings, to serve

avocado slices

1 Finely grate the rind from 2 lemons.
Roll the rindless lemons backward and
forward on a board, then squeeze
scant ½ cup juice. If you don't have
enough, squeeze another lemon. Set the
rind and juice aside.

2 Heat the olive oil in a heavy pan. Add
the shallots and cook, stirring , for
about 3 minutes until soft. Add the rice
and stir until all the grains are well coated.

3 Stir in the vermouth and cook until it
evaporates. Lower the heat to
medium–low. Add the lemon juice and a
ladleful of simmering stock. Stir, then
simmer, stirring occasionally, until all the
liquid is absorbed.

4 Add another ladleful of stock and stir,
then simmer until absorbed. Continue
adding stock in this way, letting it be
absorbed after each addition, until all the
stock has been incorporated and the
risotto is creamy in texture.

5 Stir in the lemon rind and parsley.
Add the butter, cover, remove from
the heat, and set aside for 5 minutes. Stir
well and then garnish with lemon strips
and parsley. Serve with Parmesan cheese
and avocado slices.

Fava Beans with Feta

This simple dish captures the heady flavors of the Greek islands and can be served as a salad or as a hot or cold appetizer.

NUTRITIONAL INFORMATION

Calories	140	Sugars	.........1g
Protein	.........6g	Fat	..........10g
Carbohydrate	....6g	Saturates	.......3g

 15–90 mins 5 mins

SERVES 4–6

I N G R E D I E N T S

1 lb 2 oz/500 g shelled broad beans

4 tbsp extra virgin olive oil

1 tbsp lemon juice

1 tbsp finely chopped fresh dill, plus extra to garnish

2 oz/55 g feta cheese, drained and diced

salt and pepper

lemon wedges, to serve

1 Bring a pan of water to a boil. Add the fava beans and cook for about 2 minutes until tender. Drain thoroughly and set aside.

2 When the beans are cool enough to handle, remove and discard the outer skins to reveal the bright green beans underneath. (See Cook's Tip). Put the peeled beans in a serving bowl.

3 Combine the olive oil and lemon juice, then season to taste with salt and pepper. Pour the dressing over the warm beans, add the dill, and stir gently. Adjust the seasoning, if necessary.

4 If serving hot, add the feta cheese, toss gently, and sprinkle with extra

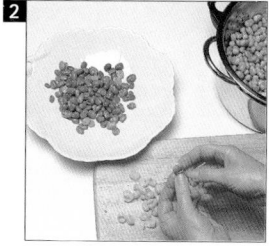

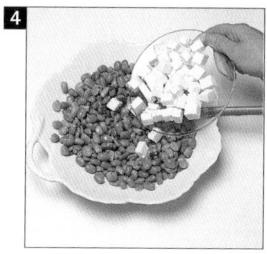

dill, then serve immediately. Alternatively, set aside the beans in their dressing to cool and then chill until required.

5 To serve cold, remove from the refrigerator 10 minutes before serving to bring to room temperature. Taste and adjust the seasoning, if necessary, then sprinkle with the feta and extra dill. Serve with lemon wedges.

COOK'S TIP
If you are lucky enough to have very young fava beans at the start of the season, it isn't necessary to remove the outer skin.

Aïoli

This garlic mayonnaise features in many traditional Provençal recipes, but also makes a delicious dip, surrounded by a selection of vegetables.

NUTRITIONAL INFORMATION

Calories	239	Sugars	.........0g
Protein	.........1g	Fat	..........26g
Carbohydrate	....1g	Saturates	.......4g

15 mins   0 mins

SERVES 6

INGREDIENTS

4 large garlic cloves or to taste

2 large egg yolks

1¼ cups extra virgin olive oil

1–2 tbsp lemon juice

1 tbsp fresh white bread crumbs

sea salt and pepper

TO SERVE (OPTIONAL)

a selection of raw vegetables, such as sliced red bell peppers, zucchini slices, whole scallions, and tomato wedges

a selection of blanched and cooled vegetables, such as baby artichoke hearts, cauliflower or broccoli florets, or green beans

COOK'S TIP

The amount of garlic in a traditional Provençal aïoli is a matter of personal taste. Local cooks use 2 cloves per person as a rule of thumb, but this version is slightly milder, although still bursting with flavor.

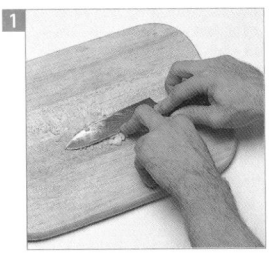

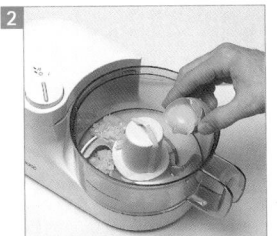

1 Finely chop the garlic on a cutting board. Add a pinch of sea salt to the garlic and use the tip and broad side of a knife to work the garlic and salt into a smooth paste.

2 Transfer the garlic paste to a food processor. Add the egg yolks and process until well blended, scraping down the side of the bowl with a rubber spatula, if necessary.

3 With the motor running, slowly pour in the olive oil in a steady stream through the feeder tube, processing until a thick mayonnaise forms.

4 Add 1 tablespoon of the lemon juice and the bread crumbs and process again. Taste and add more lemon juice if necessary. Season to taste with sea salt and pepper.

5 Place the aïoli in a bowl, cover, and chill until ready to serve. To serve, place the bowl of aïoli on a large platter and surround with a selection of raw and lightly blanched vegetables.

Skordalia

This thick Greek almond and garlic sauce makes an ideal dip
to serve with crudités, grissini, or Sesame Breadsticks, as here.

NUTRITIONAL INFORMATION

Calories 304	Sugars 1g
Protein 5g	Fat 29g
Carbohydrate 5g	Saturates 4g

30 mins   0 mins

SERVES 6

INGREDIENTS

2 oz/55 g day-old bread, about 2 slices

scant 1½ cups almonds

4–6 large garlic cloves, coarsely chopped

⅔ cup extra virgin olive oil

2 tbsp white wine vinegar

salt and pepper

fresh cilantro or flat leaf parsley sprigs,
   to garnish

Sesame Breadsticks (see page 473),
   to serve

1 Cut the crusts off the bread and tear the bread into small pieces. Put in a bowl, pour over enough water to cover, and set aside to soak for 10–15 minutes. Squeeze the bread dry, then set aside.

2 To blanch the almonds, put them in a heatproof bowl and pour over just enough boiling water to cover. Let stand for 30 seconds, then drain. The skins should slide off easily.

3 Transfer the almonds and garlic to a food processor and process until finely chopped. Add the squeezed bread and process again until well blended.

4 With the motor running, gradually add the olive oil through the feeder

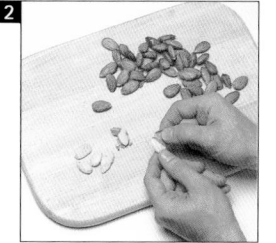
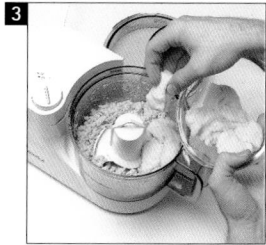

tube in a thin, steady stream until a thick paste forms. Add the vinegar and process again. Season with salt and pepper to taste.

5 Scrape the mixture into a bowl, cover, and chill until required. It will keep in the refrigerator for up to 4 days. To serve, garnish with herbs sprigs. Serve with sesame breadsticks.

VARIATIONS
Many versions of this rustic sauce exist. For variety, replace the bread with 4 tablespoons well-drained canned cannellini or fava beans. You can replace the white wine vinegar with freshly squeezed lemon juice.

Wild Rice Blinis

Blinis are small Russian pancakes made with white and buckwheat flours. Wild rice adds more texture and a nutty flavor to a real classic.

NUTRITIONAL INFORMATION

Calories	37	Sugars	.........1g
Protein	.........1g	Fat	...........2g
Carbohydrate	....4g	Saturates	.......1g

 40 mins   30 mins

SERVES 4–6

INGREDIENTS

butter or vegetable oil, for frying

4 scallions, thinly sliced diagonally

4 oz/115 g smoked salmon, thinly sliced into strips or shredded

½ cup sour cream

chopped fresh chives, to garnish

BLINIS

5 tbsp lukewarm water

1½ tsp dried yeast

½ cup all-purpose flour

9 tbsp buckwheat flour

2 tbsp sugar

½ tsp salt

1 cup milk

2 eggs, separated

2 tbsp butter, melted

⅓ cup cooked wild rice

1 To make the blinis, pour the water into a small bowl and sprinkle the yeast over it. Set aside until the yeast has dissolved and the mixture is beginning to froth.

2 Sift the flours into a large bowl and stir in the sugar and salt. Make a well in the center. Warm ¾ cup of the milk and add to the well with the yeast mixture. Gradually whisk the flour into the liquid to form a smooth batter. Cover the bowl with plastic wrap and set aside in a warm place until light and bubbly.

3 Beat the remaining milk with the egg yolks and the melted butter and then beat into the batter.

4 Using an electric mixer, whisk the egg whites until soft peaks form. Fold a spoonful into the batter, then fold in the remaining egg whites and the wild rice alternately. Be careful not to overmix.

5 Heat just enough butter or oil in a large, heavy skillet to coat lightly. Drop tablespoonfuls of the batter into the skillet and cook for 1–2 minutes until tiny bubbles form on the surface. Turn and cook for 30 seconds. Remove and keep warm in a low oven while cooking the remaining batter. Add a little more butter or oil if necessary.

6 To serve, top with the scallions, smoked salmon strips, a spoon of sour cream, and a sprinkling of chopped fresh chives.

Vietnamese Rice Wraps

A great idea for a party—just lay out the fillings, with the two dipping sauces, and let guests assemble their own "wraps."

NUTRITIONAL INFORMATION

Calories 78	Sugars 4g
Protein 6g	Fat 3g
Carbohydrate 6g	Saturates 1g

30 mins   0 mins

MAKES 20–30 WRAPS

INGREDIENTS

8 oz/225 g salmon fillet, seared

8 oz/225 g tuna steak, seared

2 cups cooked peeled shrimp

2 avocados, pitted, peeled, sliced, and sprinkled with lime juice

6–8 asparagus tips, blanched

1 small red onion, thinly sliced

16 scallions, sliced

12 black Niçoise olives, sliced

14 cherry tomatoes, halved

1–2 cups fresh cilantro leaves

20–30 x 7 inch/18 cm rice paper wrappers

lime wedges

VINEGAR SAUCE

5 tbsp rice vinegar

2 tbsp Thai fish sauce

2 tbsp superfine sugar

1 garlic clove, finely chopped

2 fresh red chiles, deseeded and sliced

2 tbsp chopped fresh cilantro

SOY DIPPING SAUCE

½ cup Thai fish sauce

4–6 tbsp lime juice

2 tbsp Japanese soy sauce

2–3 tbsp brown sugar

1 tbsp finely chopped fresh ginger root

2–4 garlic cloves, ground

1 To make the dipping sauces, put the ingredients for each into separate bowls and stir together to blend.

2 Cut the salmon and tuna into ¼ inch/ 5 mm pieces. Arrange them with the shrimp, avocados, asparagus, onion, scallions, olives, tomatoes, and cilantro on a large serving platter in groups, ready to use as different fillings. Cover loosely with plastic wrap and chill until ready to serve.

3 Dip each wrapper very briefly into a bowl of warm water to soften. Lay on clean dish cloths to absorb any excess water, then pile onto a serving plate, and cover with a damp dish cloth.

4 Let your guests fill their own wrappers. Squeeze lime wedges over the fillings and pass the dipping sauces separately.

Orange-Scented Risotto

This fragrant risotto makes a delicate first course for a special meal.
Serve with a sprinkling of grated Parmesan, if desired.

NUTRITIONAL INFORMATION

Calories	599	Sugars	.........9g
Protein	........18g	Fat	..........22g
Carbohydrate	...95g	Saturates	.......9g

 10 mins   35 mins

SERVES 4

INGREDIENTS

2 tbsp pine nuts

4 tbsp sweet butter

2 shallots, finely chopped

1 leek, finely shredded

3½ cups risotto rice

2 tbsp orange-flavored liqueur or dry
  white vermouth

6¼ cups chicken or vegetable
  stock, simmering

grated rind of 1 orange

juice of 2 oranges, strained

3 tbsp chopped fresh chives

salt and pepper

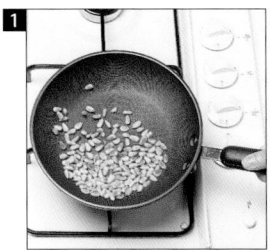

1 Toast the pine nuts in a skillet over medium heat for about 3 minutes, stirring and shaking frequently, until golden brown. Set aside.

2 Heat half the butter in a large, heavy pan over medium heat. Add the shallots and leek and cook for about 2 minutes until they begin to soften. Add the rice and cook, stirring frequently, for about 2 minutes until the rice is translucent and well coated.

3 Pour in the liqueur or vermouth; it will evaporate almost immediately.

Add a ladleful (about 1 cup) of the stock and cook, stirring, until absorbed. Continue adding the stock, about half a ladleful at a time, allowing each addition to be absorbed before adding the next—never allow the rice to cook "dry."

4 After about 15 minutes, add the orange rind and juice and continue to cook, adding more stock, until the rice is

tender, but firm to the bite, and all the liquid has been absorbed. The risotto should have a creamy consistency.

5 Remove from the heat and stir in the remaining butter and 2 tablespoons of the chives. Season to taste with salt and pepper. Spoon into serving dishes and sprinkle with the toasted pine nuts and the remaining chives.

Black Risotto

This classic recipe gets its name from the squid ink which turns the risotto "black." A sophisticated dish, sure to impress.

NUTRITIONAL INFORMATION

Calories 377   Sugars 0g
Protein . . . . .16g   Fat 12g
Carbohydrate . . .52g   Saturates 4g

 10 mins   35 mins

SERVES 6

INGREDIENTS

2–3 tbsp olive oil

1 lb/450 g cleaned squid or cuttlefish, cut crosswise into thin strips, rinsed and patted dry

2 tbsp lemon juice

2 tbsp sweet butter

3–4 garlic cloves, finely chopped

1 tsp crushed dried chile, or to taste

3 cups risotto rice

½ cup dry white wine

4 cups fish stock, simmering

2 envelopes squid or cuttlefish ink

2 tbsp chopped fresh flat leaf parsley

salt and pepper

1 Heat half the olive oil in a large heavy skillet over medium-high heat. When the oil is very hot, add the squid strips and stir-fry for 2–3 minutes until just cooked. Transfer to a plate and sprinkle with the lemon juice.

2 Heat the remaining olive oil and butter in a large heavy pan over medium heat. Add the garlic and chile and cook gently for 1 minute. Add the rice and cook, stirring frequently, for 2 minutes until translucent and well coated.

3 Pour in the white wine; it will bubble and steam rapidly. Cook, stirring frequently, until the wine is completely absorbed by the rice. Add a ladleful (about 1 cup) of the simmering fish stock and cook, stirring constantly, until it is completely absorbed.

4 Continue adding the stock, about half a ladleful at a time, allowing each addition to be absorbed before adding the next—never allow the rice to cook "dry."

This should take 20–25 minutes. The risotto should have a creamy consistency and the rice should be tender, but still firm to the bite.

5 Just before adding the last ladleful of stock, add the squid ink to the stock and stir to blend completely. Stir into the risotto with the reserved squid pieces and the chopped flat leaf parsley. Season the risotto with salt and pepper to taste and serve immediately.

Dolmades

These stuffed grape leaves are popular all over the Middle East, where they are served as part of a meze—a selection of appetizers.

NUTRITIONAL INFORMATION

Calories	111	Sugars	2g
Protein	2g	Fat	4g
Carbohydrate	17g	Saturates	2g

🥘 1 hr   🕐 1hr 20 mins

SERVES 10–12

INGREDIENTS

about 24 large grape leaves, packed in
  brine, drained

5 tbsp olive oil

1 onion, finely chopped

2 garlic cloves, finely chopped

¾ tsp dried thyme

¾ tsp dried oregano

½ tsp ground cinnamon

1 cup long grain white rice

1½ cups water

2 tsp raisins

2 tbsp pine nuts, lightly toasted

2 tbsp chopped fresh mint

1 tbsp chopped fresh flat leaf parsley

4 tbsp lemon juice

1½ cups chicken stock

salt and pepper

1 Put the grape leaves in a dish, cover with boiling water, and set aside for 2 minutes. Drain, rinse, and pat dry. Cut off any thick stems. Place the leaves shiny side down on paper towels.

2 Heat 2 tablespoons of the olive oil in a heavy pan. Cook the onion for about 3 minutes until soft. Stir in the garlic, dried herbs, and cinnamon, then add the rice, and cook for about 2 minutes, stirring, until translucent and well coated.

3 Stir in the water and raisins and bring to a boil, stirring twice. Cover and simmer for 15 minutes until the liquid is absorbed and the rice just tender.

4 Fork the rice into a bowl and add the pine nuts, mint, parsley, and half the lemon juice. Stir and season with salt and pepper and 1 tablespoon olive oil.

5 Place about 1 tablespoon of the rice mixture on a grape leaf near the stem end and roll the leaf once over the filling.

Fold in each side of the leaf, then finish rolling. Repeat with the remaining leaves.

6 Brush a large casserole with 2 tablespoons oil. Arrange the dolmades in rows, making a second layer if necessary. Sprinkle with the remaining oil and lemon juice. Add the stock to cover the rolls; add extra water if necessary.

7 Weigh down the rolls with a heatproof plate, cover tightly, and cook over very low heat for 1 hour. Remove from the heat and let cool to room temperature. Drain and serve with a little of the cooking juices, if wished.

Mujadarah

This delicious combination of rice, lentils, and caramelized onions is often served as part of a Lebanese meze.

NUTRITIONAL INFORMATION

Calories	458	Sugars	.........7g
Protein	........13g	Fat	..........21g
Carbohydrate	...54g	Saturates	.......3g

🍲 10 mins   🕐 45 mins

SERVES 6

I N G R E D I E N T S

1 cup green or brown
   lentils, rinsed

½ cup olive oil

3 large onions, thinly sliced

1 cup basmati or long grain white rice

3 cups chicken or vegetable stock

1 tsp ground allspice

salt and pepper

T O   S E R V E

lemon wedges

scallions, thinly sliced diagonally

plain yogurt

1 Bring a large pan of water to a boil. Gradually pour in the lentils (so the water remains boiling). Reduce the heat to medium-low and simmer, skimming off any foam that rises to the surface, for about 25 minutes until just tender. Drain the lentils and set aside.

2 Meanwhile, heat the oil in a large, deep skillet over medium heat until very hot. Add the onions and cook for 4–5 minutes until soft. Using a slotted spoon, transfer about two-thirds of the onions to a bowl. Continue cooking the remaining onions until brown and crisp, then drain on paper towels.

3 Add the rice to the pan and cook, stirring frequently, for 2 minutes until translucent and well coated. Add the less-cooked onions with the lentils and stock and stir gently, scraping the base of the pan to release any crispy bits. Add the allspice and season with salt and pepper.

4 Cover the pan and cook over very low heat for about 20 minutes until the rice is tender and all the stock is absorbed.

5 Fork the rice mixture into a warmed serving bowl. Top with the crispy onions. Serve immediately with lemon wedges, scallions, and yogurt.

Mediterranean Bell Peppers

Serve the bell peppers with their tops for an attractive finish—blanch the tops with the bell peppers, then bake separately for the last 10 minutes.

NUTRITIONAL INFORMATION

Calories	366	Sugars	........24g
Protein	........12g	Fat	..........12g
Carbohydrate	...54g	Saturates	.......4g

 20 mins 1¼ hrs

SERVES 6

6 large bell peppers, red, yellow and orange

1 cup long grain white rice

2–3 tbsp olive oil, plus extra for greasing and drizzling

1 large onion

2 celery stalks, chopped

2 garlic cloves, finely chopped

½ tsp ground cinnamon or allspice

⅔ cup raisins

4 tbsp pine nuts, lightly toasted

4 ripe plum tomatoes, deseeded and chopped

¼ cup white wine

4 anchovy fillets, chopped

½ bunch of chopped fresh parsley

½ bunch of chopped fresh mint

6 tbsp freshly grated Parmesan cheese

salt and pepper

fresh tomato sauce, to serve (optional)

1 Slice off the tops of the bell peppers, then remove the cores and seeds. Blanch the bell peppers in boiling water for 2–3 minutes. Remove and drain upside down.

2 Bring a pan of lightly salted water to a boil. Gradually pour in the rice and return to a boil. Simmer for about 15–20 minutes until tender, but firm to the bite. Drain and rinse under cold running water. Set aside.

3 Heat the oil in a large skillet. Add the onion and celery and cook for 2 minutes. Stir in the garlic, cinnamon, and raisins and cook for 1 minute. Fork in the rice, then stir in the pine nuts, tomatoes, wine, anchovies, parsley, and mint and cook for 4 minutes. Remove from the heat, season with salt and pepper, and stir in half the Parmesan.

4 Brush the bottom of a casserole with a little oil. Arrange the bell peppers in the dish. Divide the rice mixture equally among them and sprinkle with the remaining Parmesan. Drizzle with a little more oil and pour in enough water to come ½ inch/1 cm up the sides of the bell peppers. Loosely cover the casserole with kitchen foil. Bake in a preheated oven, 350°F/180°C, for about 40 minutes. Uncover and cook for a further 10 minutes. Serve hot with tomato sauce, if liked.

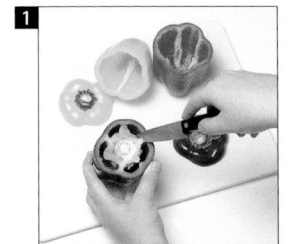

Japanese Sushi

These little snacks are made with special seasoned rice and a variety of toppings. Sushi rice is available from Japanese foodstores.

NUTRITIONAL INFORMATION

Calories 403	Sugars 6g	
Protein 24g	Fat 8g	
Carbohydrate ...56g	Saturates 1g	

 1 hr   30 mins

SERVES 4–6

I N G R E D I E N T S

14 oz/400 g sushi rice

generous 2 cups water

4 tbsp Japanese rice vinegar

1½ tbsp superfine sugar

1½ tsp salt

1½ tbsp mirin (Japanese rice wine)

N O R I M A K I   S U S H I

2 eggs

pinch of ground turmeric

1–2 tbsp vegetable oil

4 sheets dried nori seaweed

4 oz/115 g smoked salmon slices, cut into 3 inch/7.5 cm pieces

½ cucumber, lightly peeled, quartered, deseeded, then thinly sliced lengthwise

fresh chives

N I G I R I   S U S H I

16 cooked peeled shrimp

wasabi paste (Japanese horseradish)

3 oz/85 g smoked salmon fillet, cut into ¼ inch/5 mm slices

sesame seeds, lightly toasted

T O   S E R V E

pickled ginger

Japanese soy sauce

  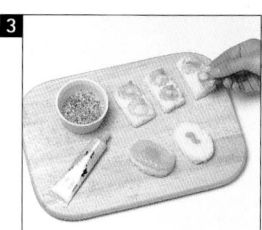

1 Put the rice and water in a pan and bring to a boil. Cover and simmer, for 20 minutes. Set aside for 10 minutes. Bring the vinegar, sugar, salt, and mirin to a boil. Pour the mixture evenly over the surface of the rice and blend in, fanning the rice at the same time.

2 For the norimaki sushi, beat the eggs with the turmeric and 1 teaspoon of the oil, then make 2 omelets, cooking in the remaining oil. Cut in half. Pass the sheets of nori over a flame for a few minutes to toast. Lay a piece of nori, toasted side down, on a sushi mat. Lay an omelet half on top, leaving a border. Spread a thin layer of sushi rice over. Place a piece of smoked salmon on the bottom third of the rice, trimming to fit, and top with cucumber and chives. Moisten the border of the nori with water and roll up. Repeat with the rest and leave to set.. Cut into 1 inch/2.5 cm slices, cover, and chill.

3 For the nigiri sushi, using wet hands, shape 2 tablespoons of the rice at a time into ovals. Top with 2 shrimp or a dab of wasabi and some smoked salmon. Sprinkle with the sesame seeds. Serve the sushi with the ginger and soy sauce.

Authentic Guacamole

Guacamole is at its best when freshly made, with enough texture to really taste the avocado. Serve with vegetable sticks or tortilla chips.

NUTRITIONAL INFORMATION

Calories	212	Sugars	.........1g
Protein	.........2g	Fat	..........21g
Carbohydrate	....3g	Saturates	.......4g

 15 mins   0 mins

SERVES 4

I N G R E D I E N T S

1 ripe tomato

2 limes

2–3 ripe small to medium avocados, or 1–2 large ones

¼–½ onion, finely chopped

pinch of ground cumin

pinch of mild chili powder

½–1 fresh green chile, such as jalapeño or serrano, deseeded and finely chopped

1 tbsp finely chopped fresh cilantro leaves, plus extra for garnishing

salt (optional)

tortilla chips, to serve (optional)

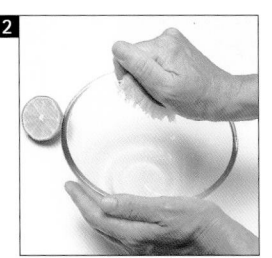  

1 Place the tomatoes in a heatproof bowl, pour boiling water over to cover, and let stand for 30 seconds. Drain and plunge into cold water. Peel off the skins. Cut the tomatoes in half, deseed, and chop the flesh.

COOK'S TIP

Try spooning guacamole into soups, especially chicken or seafood, or spreading it into sandwiches on thick crusty rolls. Spoon guacamole over refried beans and melted cheese, then dig into it with salsa and crisp tortilla chips.

2 Squeeze the juice from the limes into a small bowl. Cut 1 avocado in half around the pit. Twist the 2 halves apart in opposite directions, then remove the pit with a knife. Carefully peel off the skin, dice the flesh, and toss in the bowl of lime juice to prevent the flesh from discoloring. Repeat with the remaining avocados. Mash the avocado flesh fairly coarsely with a fork.

3 Add the onion, tomato, cumin, chili powder, chiles, and fresh cilantro to the avocados. If using as a dip for tortilla chips, do not add salt. If using as a dip for vegetable sticks, add salt to taste.

4 To serve the guacamole, transfer to a serving dish, garnish with finely chopped fresh cilantro, and serve with tortilla chips.

Veracruz Cocktail

This is a typically colourful Mexican salad dish,
full of spicy flavors and wonderfully succulent seafood.

NUTRITIONAL INFORMATION

Calories 183   Sugars 10g
Protein ....18g   Fat 7g
Carbohydrate ...13g   Saturates 1g

 50 mins   15 mins

SERVES 6

INGREDIENTS

4 cups fish stock or water mixed with 1 fish bouillon cube

2 bay leaves

1 onion, chopped

3–5 garlic cloves, cut into large chunks

1 lb 7 oz/650 g mixed seafood, such as shrimp in their shells, scallops, squid rings, pieces of squid tentacles, etc

¾ cup tomato ketchup

¼ cup Mexican hot sauce

generous pinch of ground cumin

6–8 tbsp chopped fresh cilantro

4 tbsp lime juice, plus extra for tossing

salt

1 avocado, to garnish

1 Pour the stock in a pan and add the bay leaves, half the onion, and all of the garlic. Bring to a boil, then simmer gently for about 10 minutes or until the onion and garlic are soft and the stock tastes flavorful.

2 Add the seafood in the order of the amount of cooking time required. Most small pieces of shellfish take a very short time to cook and can be added together. Cook for 1 minute, then remove the pan from the heat, and set aside so that the seafood finishes cooking by standing in the cooling stock.

3 When the stock has cooled, remove the seafood from it with a slotted spoon. Shell the shrimp and any other shellfish. Reserve the stock.

4 Combine the ketchup, hot sauce, and cumin in a bowl, reserve a quarter of the sauce mixture for serving. Add the seafood to the bowl with the remaining onion, fresh cilantro, lime juice, and about 1 cup of the reserved cooled fish stock. Stir carefully to mix and season with salt to taste.

5 Peel and pit the avocado, then dice or slice the flesh. Toss gently in lime juice to prevent discoloration.

6 Serve the seafood cocktail in individual bowls, garnished with the avocado and topped with a spoonful of the reserved sauce.

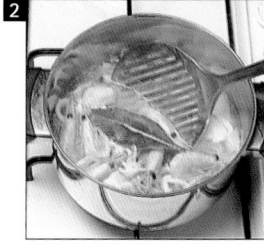

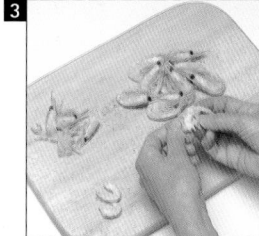

Citrus-Marinated Fish

This is one of Mexico's classic dishes: raw fish, cured in a bath of citrus juices, chiles, and aromatics. It must be made with the freshest fish.

NUTRITIONAL INFORMATION

Calories	292	Sugars	.........4g
Protein	.........2g	Fat	..........21g
Carbohydrate	....4g	Saturates	.......3g

5½ hrs | 0 mins

SERVES 4

INGREDIENTS

1 lb/450 g white fish fillets, cut into bite-size chunks

juice of 6–8 limes

2–3 tomatoes, diced

3 fresh green chiles, such as jalapeño or serrano, deseeded and thinly sliced

½ tsp dried oregano

5 tbsp extra virgin olive oil

1 small onion, finely chopped

salt and pepper

2 tbsp chopped fresh cilantro

1 Place the fish in a nonmetallic dish, add the lime juice, and mix well. Marinate in the refrigerator for 5 hours or until the mixture looks opaque. Turn from time to time so that the lime juice permeates the fish.

2 An hour before serving, add the tomatoes, chiles, oregano, olive oil, and onion and then season with salt and pepper to taste.

3 Approximately 15 minutes before serving, remove the dish from the refrigerator so that the olive oil can come to room temperature. Serve the dish immediately, sprinkled with the chopped fresh cilantro.

COOK'S TIP

This dish makes an elegant appetizer served layered with rounds of crisp tortillas, like a stacked tostada.

Salpicon of Crab

This lightly spiced crab salad is a cooling treat for a hot day. Eat it with crisp tortilla chips or wrapped in a tender warm corn tortilla.

NUTRITIONAL INFORMATION

Calories	186	Sugars	........2g
Protein	........13g	Fat	..........13g
Carbohydrate	....3g	Saturates	.......2g

 15 mins   0 mins

SERVES 4

INGREDIENTS

¼ red onion, chopped

½–1 fresh green chile, deseeded and chopped

juice of ½ lime

1 tbsp apple or other fruit vinegar, such as raspberry

1 tbsp chopped fresh cilantro

1 tbsp extra virgin olive oil

8–12 oz/225–350 g fresh crab meat

lettuce leaves, to serve

TO GARNISH

1 avocado

lime juice, for tossing

1–2 ripe tomatoes

3–5 radishes

1 Combine the onion, chile, lime juice, vinegar, fresh cilantro, and olive oil. Add the crab meat and toss the ingredients lightly together.

2 To make the garnish, cut each avocado in half around the pit. Twist the halves apart in opposite directions, then remove the pit with a knife. Carefully peel off the skin and slice the flesh. Toss the avocado gently in lime juice to prevent discoloration.

3 Halve the tomatoes, then remove the cores and seeds. Dice the flesh. Slice the radishes thinly.

4 Arrange the crab salad on a bed of lettuce leaves, garnish with the avocado, tomatoes, and radishes, and serve the salpicon immediately.

VARIATION

For a toasted crab salad sandwich, split open a baguette and heap on crab salad. Top generously with cheese. Place the open roll under the broiler to melt the cheese. Spread the toasted plain side with mayonnaise and close the sandwich. Cut and serve with salsa.

Mexican Pickles

In Mexican cantinas, these pickled vegetables are munched alongside a stack of warm buttered tortillas and washed down with glasses of beer.

NUTRITIONAL INFORMATION

Calories	101	Sugars	.........7g
Protein	.........3g	Fat	...........6g
Carbohydrate	....8g	Saturates	.......1g

 30 mins 8–12 mins

SERVES 6

INGREDIENTS

3 tbsp vegetable oil

1 onion, thinly sliced

5 garlic cloves, cut into slivers

3 carrots, thinly sliced

2 fresh green chiles, such as jalapeño or serrano, deseeded and cut into strips

1 small cauliflower, broken into florets or cut into bite-size chunks

½ red bell pepper, deseeded and diced or cut into strips

1 celery stalk, cut into bite-size pieces

½ tsp oregano leaves

1 bay leaf

¼ tsp ground cumin

5 tbsp apple vinegar

salt and pepper

COOK'S TIP

Wear rubber gloves when slicing and deseeding fresh chiles and do not touch your eyes during preparation.

1 Heat the oil in a heavy skillet and add the onion, garlic, carrots, chiles, cauliflower, red bell pepper, and celery. Cook over low heat, stirring occasionally, for about 1 minute until just softened, but not browned.

2 Add the oregano, bay leaf, cumin, and apple vinegar and season with salt and pepper to taste. Add just enough water to cover the vegetables. Cook for a further 5–10 minutes or just long enough for the vegetables to be tender, but still firm to the bite.

3 Adjust the seasoning, adding more vinegar if needed. Remove the pan from the heat and set aside to cool. Serve as a relish or with buttered tortillas Mexican style. The Mexican pickles will keep for up to 2 weeks, if stored in a sealed container in the refrigerator.

Cheese & Bean Quesadillas

These bite-size rolls are made from flour tortillas filled with a delicious mixture of refried beans, melted cheese, cilantro, and salsa.

NUTRITIONAL INFORMATION

Calories 452	Sugars 11g
Protein 18g	Fat 16g
Carbohydrate ...62g	Saturates 7g

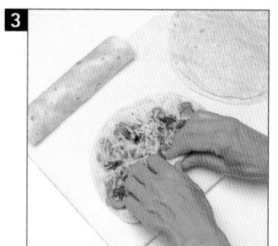

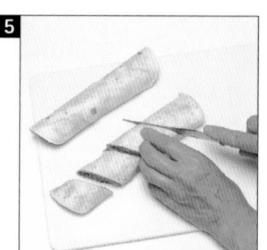

 10 mins   10 mins

SERVES 4–6

I N G R E D I E N T S

14 oz/400g canned refried beans

8 flour tortillas

1¾ cups grated Cheddar cheese, grated

1 onion, chopped

½ bunch of fresh cilantro leaves, chopped

1 quantity Salsa Cruda (see page 447)

1 Place the beans in a small pan and set over low heat to warm through.

2 Meanwhile, make the tortillas pliable, by warming them gently in a lightly greased nonstick skillet.

3 Remove the tortillas from the skillet and quickly spread with a layer of warm beans. Top each tortilla with grated cheese, onion, fresh cilantro, and a spoonful of salsa. Roll up tightly.

4 Just before serving, heat the nonstick skillet over medium heat, sprinkling lightly with a couple of drops of water. Add the tortilla rolls, cover the skillet, and heat through until the cheese melts. Allow to brown lightly, if wished.

5 Remove the tortilla rolls from the skillet and slice each roll, on the diagonal, into about 4 bite-size pieces. Serve the quesadillas at once.

COOK'S TIP
Flour tortillas can also be warmed in the microwave, but take care not to heat them for too long because they can become leathery.

Spicy Shrimp Wedges

A winning combination of textures and flavors, spiced shrimp and creamy avocado are served on crisply fried tortilla wedges.

NUTRITIONAL INFORMATION

Calories	255	Sugars	.........2g
Protein	........15g	Fat	..........13g
Carbohydrate	...22g	Saturates	.......4g

 4¼ hrs   12–15 mins

SERVES 8–10

INGREDIENTS

1 lb 2 oz/500 g cooked shrimp

4 garlic cloves, finely chopped

½ tsp mild chili powder

½ tsp ground cumin

juice of 1 lime

1 ripe tomato, diced

salt

6 corn tortillas

vegetable oil, for frying

2 avocados

scant 1 cup sour cream

mild chili powder, to garnish

1 Place the shrimp in a bowl with the garlic, chili powder, cumin, lime juice, and tomato. Add salt to taste and stir gently to mix. Chill for at least 4 hours or overnight to allow the flavors to mingle.

2 Cut the tortillas into wedges. Heat a little oil in a nonstick skillet, add a batch of tortilla wedges, and fry over medium heat until crisp. Repeat with the remaining wedges and transfer to a serving platter.

3 Cut each avocado in half around the pit. Twist the halves apart in opposite directions, then remove the pit with a knife. Carefully peel off the skin, and dice the flesh. Gently stir the avocado into the shrimp mixture.

4 Top each tortilla wedge with a small mound of the shrimp and avocado mixture. Finish with a dab of sour cream, garnish with a light sprinkling of chili powder, and serve immediately while hot and crisp.

COOK'S TIP

For speed, you can use crisp corn tortillas or nacho chips (not too salty) instead of the corn tortillas.

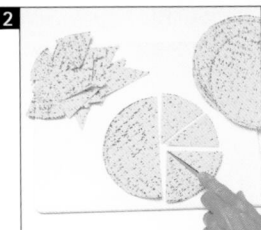

Black Bean Nachos

Packed with authentic Mexican flavors, this tasty black bean
and cheese dip is fun to eat and will get any meal off to a good start!

NUTRITIONAL INFORMATION

Calories ....429 Sugars 2g
Protein ....28g Fat 24g
Carbohydrate ...25g Saturates 15g

8¼ hrs   1¾ hrs

SERVES 4

I N G R E D I E N T S

1¼ cups dried black beans, or 1⅔ cups
  canned black beans, drained and rinsed

1½–2 cups grated cheese, such
  as Cheddar, Fontina, pecorino, asiago,
  or a combination

about ¼ tsp cumin seeds or ground cumin

about 4 tbsp sour cream

thinly sliced pickled jalapeños (optional)

1 tbsp chopped fresh cilantro

handful of shredded lettuce

tortilla chips, to serve

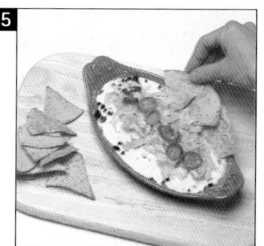

1 If using dried black beans, place them in a bowl and add water to cover. Set aside to soak overnight, then drain. Put in a pan, cover with water, and bring to a boil. Boil for 10 minutes, then reduce the heat, and simmer for about 1½ hours until tender. Drain well.

2 Spread the cooked or canned beans in the base of a shallow casserole, then sprinkle the cheese over the top. Sprinkle with cumin to taste.

3 Bake in a preheated oven, 375°F/ 190°C, for 10–15 minutes or until the beans are cooked through and the cheese is bubbling and melted.

4 Remove the beans and cheese from the oven and spoon the sour cream on top. Add the jalapeños, if using, and sprinkle with fresh cilantro and lettuce.

5 Arrange the tortilla chips around the beans, sticking them into the mixture. Serve the nachos at once.

VARIATION
To add a meaty flavor, spoon chopped and browned chorizo on top of the beans, before sprinkling over the cheese, and cook as in Step 3—the combination is excellent. Finely chopped leftover cooked meat can also be added in this way.

Refried Bean Nachos

A Mexican classic, refried beans and tortilla crisps are topped with luscious melted cheese, salsa, and assorted toppings.

NUTRITIONAL INFORMATION

Calories	287	Sugars	.........2g
Protein	........15g	Fat	..........15g
Carbohydrate	...22g	Saturates	.......7g

 15 mins   15 mins

SERVES 6–8

I N G R E D I E N T S

14 oz/400 g can refried beans

14 oz/400 g can pinto beans, drained

large pinch of ground cumin

large pinch of mild chili powder

6 oz/175 g tortilla chips

2 cups grated cheese, such as Cheddar

salsa of your choice

1 avocado, pitted, diced, and tossed with lime juice

½ small onion or 3–5 scallions, chopped

2 ripe tomatoes, diced

handful of shredded lettuce

3–4 tbsp chopped fresh cilantro

sour cream, to serve

VARIATION

Replace the sour cream with strained plain yogurt as an alternative.

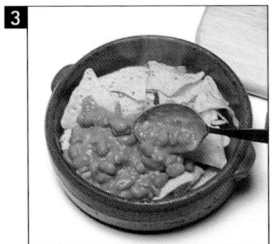

1 Place the refried beans in a pan with the pinto beans, cumin, and chili powder. Add enough water to make a thick soup-like consistency, stirring gently so that the beans do not lose their texture.

2 Heat the bean mixture over medium heat until hot, then reduce the heat, and keep the mixture warm while you prepare the rest of the dish.

3 Arrange half the tortilla chips in the bottom of a flameproof casserole or gratin dish, and cover with the bean mixture. Sprinkle with the cheese and bake in a preheated oven, 400°F/200°C, until the cheese melts.

4 Alternatively, place the casserole under a preheated broiler and broil for 5–7 minutes or until the cheese melts and lightly sizzles in places.

5 Arrange the salsa, avocado, onion, tomato, lettuce, and fresh cilantro on top of the melted cheese. Surround with the remaining tortilla chips and serve immediately with sour cream.

Masa Tartlets

Packed with Mexican flavors, these little
golden tartlets make a colorful start to a meal.

NUTRITIONAL INFORMATION

Calories ...... .474	Sugars 4g	
Protein 11g	Fat .... .23g	
Carbohydrate ...58g	Saturates 8g	

 35 mins 30 mins

SERVES 4

INGREDIENTS

8–10 tbsp masa harina

3 tbsp all-purpose flour

pinch of baking powder

about 1 cup warm water

vegetable oil, for frying

1⅔ cups pinto beans or refried beans,
   heated through

1 avocado, pitted, sliced, and tossed with
   lime juice

3 oz/85 g queso fresco or fresh cream
   cheese or crumbled feta

salsa of your choice

2 scallions, thinly sliced

TO GARNISH

fresh flat leaf parsley sprigs

lemon wedges

1 Mix the masa harina with the all-purpose flour and baking powder in a bowl, then mix in enough warm water to make a firm yet moist dough.

2 Pinch off about a walnut-size piece of dough and, using your fingers, shape into a tiny tartlet shape, pressing and pinching to make it as thin as possible without falling apart. Repeat with the remaining dough.

3 Heat a layer of oil in a deep skillet until it is smoking. Add a batch of tartlets to the hot oil and fry, spooning the hot fat into the center of the tartlets and turning once, until golden on all sides.

4 Using a slotted spoon, remove the tartlets from the hot oil and drain on paper towels. Place on a cookie sheet and keep warm in the oven on a low temperature, while cooking the remaining tartlets.

5 To serve, fill each tartlet shell with the warmed beans, avocado, cheese, salsa, and scallions. Garnish with parsley and lemon wedges and serve immediately.

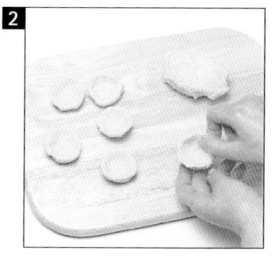

Mexican Salad

This is a colorful salad with a Mexican theme, using beans, tomatoes, and avocado. The chili dressing adds a little kick.

NUTRITIONAL INFORMATION

Calories 307   Sugars 7g
Protein . . . . .5g   Fat 26g
Carbohydrate . . .13g   Saturates 5g

10–15 mins   0 mins

SERVES 4

INGREDIENTS

lollo rosso lettuce

2 ripe avocados

2 tsp lemon juice

4 medium tomatoes

1 onion

¾ cup mixed canned beans, drained

DRESSING

4 tbsp olive oil

dash of chili oil

2 tbsp garlic wine vinegar

pinch of superfine sugar

pinch of chili powder

1 tbsp chopped fresh parsley

COOK'S TIP

The lemon juice is sprinkled on to the avocados to prevent discoloration when in contact with the air. For this reason, the salad should be prepared, assembled, and served quite quickly.

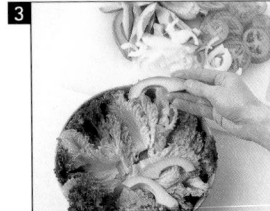

1 Line a large serving bowl with the lettuce leaves.

2 Using a sharp knife, cut the avocados in half and remove the pits. Thinly slice the flesh and immediately sprinkle with the lemon juice.

3 Thinly slice the tomatoes and onion and push the onion out into rings. Arrange the avocado, tomatoes, and onion around the salad bowl, leaving a space in the center.

4 Spoon the beans into the center of the salad and whisk the dressing ingredients together. Pour the dressing over the salad and serve.

Tuna & Anchovy Pâté

An excellent tangy combination which can be used for a sandwich filling or as a dip. The pâté will keep well in the refrigerator for up to a week.

NUTRITIONAL INFORMATION

Calories 183   Sugars 3g
Protein ....25g   Fat 6g
Carbohydrate ....9g   Saturates 2g

1¼ hrs   25 mins

SERVES 6

INGREDIENTS

PATE

1¾ oz/50 g can anchovy fillets, drained

about 14 oz/400 g canned tuna in brine, drained

¾ cup low-fat cottage cheese

generous ½ cup skim milk soft cheese

1 tbsp horseradish relish

½ tsp grated orange rind

white pepper

MELBA CROUTONS

4 slices, thick sliced whole-wheat bread

TO GARNISH

orange slices

fresh dill sprigs

1 To make the pâté, separate the anchovy fillets and pat well with paper towels to remove all traces of oil.

2 Place the anchovy fillets and all the remaining pâté ingredients into a blender or food processor. Process for a few seconds until smooth. Alternatively, finely chop the anchovy fillets and flake the tuna, then beat together with the remaining ingredients; this will make a more textured pâté.

3 Transfer to a mixing bowl, cover, and chill for 1 hour.

4 To make the Melba croûtons, place the bread slices under a preheated medium broiler for 2–3 minutes on each side until lightly browned.

5 Using a serrated knife, slice off the crusts and slide the knife between the toasted edges of the bread.

6 Stamp out circles using a 2 inch/5 cm round cutter and place on a cookie sheet. Alternatively, cut each piece of toast in half diagonally. Bake in a preheated oven,300°F/150°C, for 15–20 minutes until curled and dry.

7 Spoon the pâté onto serving plates and garnish with orange slices and fresh dill sprigs. Serve with the freshly baked Melba croûtons.

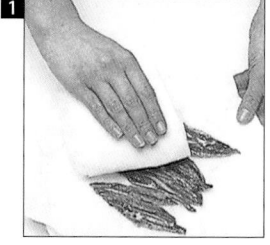

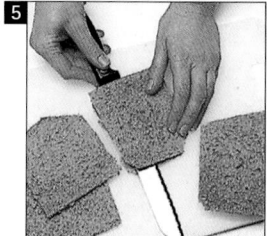

Spinach Cheese Molds

These flavor-packed little molds make a perfect appetizer or a tasty light lunch. Serve them with warm pitas.

NUTRITIONAL INFORMATION

Calories 119	Sugars 2g
Protein 6g	Fat 9g
Carbohydrate 2g	Saturates 6g

1¼ hrs   50 mins

SERVES 4

I N G R E D I E N T S

3½ oz/100 g fresh spinach leaves

10½ oz/300 g skim milk soft cheese

2 garlic cloves, crushed

fresh parsley, tarragon, and chive sprigs, finely chopped

salt and pepper

TO SERVE

mixed salad greens and fresh herbs

warm pitas

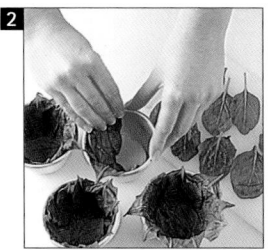  

1 Trim the stalks from the spinach leaves and rinse the leaves under cold running water. Pack the leaves into a pan while they are still wet, cover, and cook over medium heat for about 3–4 minutes until wilted—they will cook in the steam from the wet leaves (do not overcook). Drain well and pat dry with absorbent paper towels.

2 Line the bases of 4 small heatproof bowls or individual ramekin dishes with baking parchment. Line the bowls or ramekins with the spinach leaves so that the leaves overhang the edges.

3 Place the cheese in a bowl and add the garlic and herbs. Mix together thoroughly and season to taste.

4 Spoon the cheese and herb mixture into the bowls or ramekins and pull over the overlapping spinach to cover the cheese or lay extra leaves to cover the top. Place a waxed paper disc on top of each dish and weigh them down with a 3½ oz/100 g weight. Cover with plastic wrap and refrigerate for 1 hour.

5 Remove the weights and peel off the waxed paper. Loosen the molds gently by running a small metal spatula around the edges of each dish and turn them out onto individual serving plates. Serve the molds immediately with a mixture of salad greens and fresh herbs, and warm pitas.

Eggplant Salad

This tasty Middle Eastern-style salad, with tomatoes and garbanzo beans, is perfect to serve with lamb or chicken dishes.

NUTRITIONAL INFORMATION

Calories	206	Sugars	........11g
Protein	........10g	Fat	...........7g
Carbohydrate	...28g	Saturates	......1g

 2½ hrs   25 mins

SERVES 4

I N G R E D I E N T S

1 lb 2 oz/500 g eggplants

4 tbsp salt

1 tbsp olive oil

1 large onion, chopped

1 garlic clove, crushed

⅔ cup vegetable stock

14 oz/400 g can chopped tomatoes

2 tbsp tomato paste

1 tsp ground cinnamon

2 tsp superfine sugar

1 tbsp chopped fresh cilantro

1 tbsp lemon juice

15 oz/425 g can garbanzo beans, drained

pepper

fresh cilantro sprigs to garnish

T O   S E R V E

warm pitas

lemon wedges

1 Cut the eggplants into ½ inch/1 cm thick slices and then dice. Layer them in a bowl, sprinkling well with salt as you go. Set aside for 30 minutes for the bitter juices to drain out.

2 Transfer to a colander and rinse well under cold running water to remove the salt. Drain thoroughly and pat dry with paper towels.

3 Heat the oil in a large nonstick skillet, add the onion and garlic, and cook over low heat, stirring occasionally, for 2–3 minutes until slightly softened.

4 Pour in the stock and bring to a boil. Add the eggplants, canned tomatoes, tomato paste, cinnamon, sugar, and pepper. Mix well and simmer gently, uncovered, for 20 minutes until softened. Remove from the heat and set aside to cool completely.

5 Stir in the fresh cilantro, lemon juice, and garbanzo beans, cover, and chill for 1 hour.

6 Garnish with cilantro sprigs and serve with warmed pitas and lemon wedges.

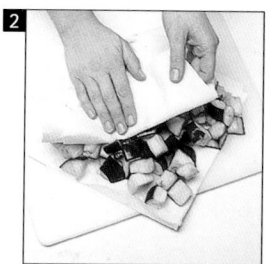

Green Bean & Carrot Salad

This colorful, summery salad of crisp vegetables is tossed in a delicious sun-dried tomato dressing.

NUTRITIONAL INFORMATION

Calories 104   Sugars 9g
Protein . . . . .2g   Fat 6g
Carbohydrate . . .10g   Saturates 1g

 10 mins   5 mins

SERVES 4

INGREDIENTS

12 oz/350 g green beans

8 oz/225 g carrots

1 red onion

1 red bell pepper

DRESSING

2 tbsp extra virgin olive oil

1 tbsp red wine vinegar

2 tsp sun-dried tomato paste

¼ tsp superfine sugar

salt and pepper

1 Trim the green beans and blanch them in boiling water for 4 minutes until just tender. Drain the beans and rinse them under cold water until they are cool. Drain again thoroughly.

2 Transfer the drained beans to a large salad bowl.

3 Peel the carrots and cut them into thin batons, using a mandoline if you have one.

4 Peel the red onion and cut it into thin slices.

5 Halve and deseed the red bell pepper and cut the flesh into thin strips.

6 Add the carrot, bell pepper, and onion to the beans and toss to mix.

7 To make the dressing, place the oil, wine vinegar, sun-dried tomato paste, and sugar in a small screw-top jar and season to taste with salt and pepper. Shake vigorously to mix.

8 Pour the dressing over the vegetables and serve immediately, or chill in the refrigerator until required.

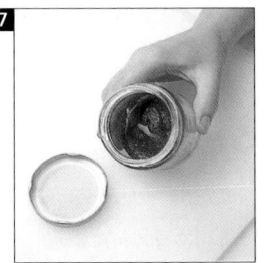

COOK'S TIP

Use canned beans if fresh ones are unavailable. Rinse off the salty canning liquid and drain well. There is no need to blanch canned beans.

Mixed Salad Greens

Make this green leafy salad with as many varieties of salad greens and edible flowers as you can find to give an unusual effect.

NUTRITIONAL INFORMATION

Calories 51	Sugars 0.1g	
Protein 0.1g	Fat 6g	
Carbohydrate 1g	Saturates 1g	

5 mins   0 mins

SERVES 4

INGREDIENTS

½ head frisée

½ head oakleaf lettuce or quattro stagione

few leaves of radicchio

1 head endive

1 oz/25 g arugula leaves

few fresh basil or flat leaf parsley sprigs

edible flowers, to garnish (optional)

FRENCH DRESSING

1 tbsp white wine vinegar

pinch of sugar

½ tsp Dijon mustard

3 tbsp extra virgin olive oil

salt and pepper

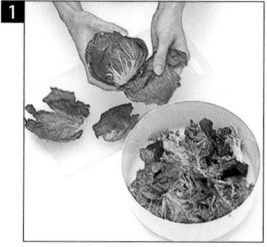 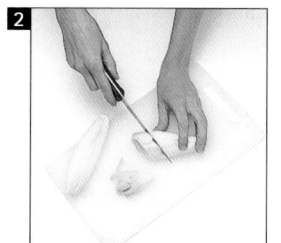 

1 Tear the frisée, oakleaf lettuce, and radicchio into pieces. Place the salad greens in a large serving bowl or individual bowls if you prefer.

2 Cut the endive into diagonal slices and add to the bowl with the arugula leaves, basil, or parsley.

3 To make the dressing, beat the vinegar, sugar, and mustard in a small bowl until the sugar has dissolved. Gradually beat in the olive oil until creamy and thoroughly mixed. Season to taste with salt and pepper.

4 Pour the dressing over the salad and toss thoroughly. Sprinkle a mixture of edible flowers over the top and serve.

COOK'S TIP

Violas, rock geraniums, nasturtiums, chive flowers, and pot marigolds add vibrant colors and a sweet flavor to any salad. Use it as a centerpiece at a dinner party, or to liven up a simple everyday meal.

Spinach & Orange Salad

This is a refreshing and very nutritious salad. Add the dressing just before serving so that the leaves do not become soggy.

NUTRITIONAL INFORMATION

Calories 126	Sugars 10g
Protein 3g	Fat 9g
Carbohydrate ...10g	Saturates 1g

 10 mins   0 mins

SERVES 4

INGREDIENTS

8 oz/225 g baby spinach leaves

2 large oranges

½ red onion, chopped

DRESSING

3 tbsp extra virgin olive oil

2 tbsp freshly squeezed orange juice

2 tsp lemon juice

1 tsp honey

½ tsp wholegrain mustard

salt and pepper

1 Wash the spinach leaves under cold running water and then dry them thoroughly on absorbent paper towels. Remove any tough stalks and tear the larger leaves into smaller pieces.

2 Slice the top and bottom off each orange with a sharp knife, then remove the peel and pith. Carefully slice between the membranes of the orange to remove the segments. Reserve any juices for the salad dressing. (Working over a small bowl may be the easiest way of doing this.)

3 Mix together the spinach leaves and orange segments and arrange them in a serving dish. Sprinkle the chopped onion over the salad.

4 To make the dressing, whisk together the olive oil, orange juice, lemon juice, honey, and mustard in a small bowl. Season to taste with salt and pepper.

5 Pour the dressing over the salad just before serving. Toss the salad well to coat the leaves with the dressing.

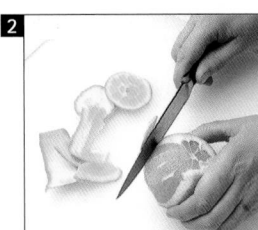

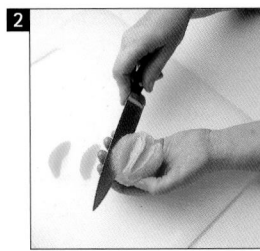

VARIATION

Use a mixture of spinach and watercress leaves, if you prefer a slightly more peppery flavor.

Three-Bean Salad

Fresh thin green beans are combined with soybeans and red kidney beans in a chive and tomato dressing to make a tasty salad.

NUTRITIONAL INFORMATION

Calories ....276 Sugars 7g
Protein ....18g Fat 15g
Carbohydrate ...18g Saturates 4g

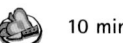 10 mins   5 mins

SERVES 6

I N G R E D I E N T S

3 tbsp olive oil

1 tbsp lemon juice

1 tbsp tomato paste

1 tbsp light malt vinegar

1 tbsp chopped fresh chives, plus extra
   to garnish

6 oz/175g thin green beans

14 oz/400 g can soybeans, rinsed
   and drained

14 oz/400 g can red kidney beans, rinsed
   and drained

2 tomatoes, chopped

4 scallions, trimmed and chopped

4½ oz/125 g feta cheese, cut into cubes

salt and pepper

mixed salad greens, to serve

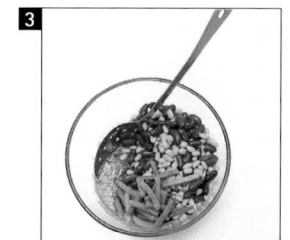

1 Put the olive oil, lemon juice, tomato paste, light malt vinegar, and chopped fresh chives into a large bowl and mix thoroughly. Set aside until required.

2 Cook the thin green beans in a small pan of lightly salted boiling water for 4–5 minutes. Drain, refresh under cold water to prevent any further cooking, and drain well again. Pat dry with absorbent paper towels.

3 Add all the beans to the dressing, stirring well to mix.

4 Add the tomatoes, scallions, and feta cheese to the bean mixture, tossing gently to coat in the dressing. Season to taste with salt and pepper.

5 Arrange the salad greens on serving plates. Pile the bean salad on top, garnish with extra chives, and serve.

COOK'S TIP

For a more substantial light meal, top the salad with 2–3 sliced hard-cooked eggs and serve with crusty bread to mop up the juices.

Smoked Trout & Apple Salad

Smoked trout and horseradish are natural partners, but with apple and watercress this makes a wonderful first course.

NUTRITIONAL INFORMATION

Calories	133	Sugars	........11g
Protein	........12g	Fat	...........5g
Carbohydrate	....11g	Saturates	......1g

 10 mins   🕐 0 mins

SERVES 4

INGREDIENTS

2 orange-red eating apples

2 tbsp French Dressing (see page 309)

½ bunch watercress

1 smoked trout, about 6 oz/175 g

melba toast, to serve

HORSERADISH DRESSING

½ cup low-fat plain yogurt

½–1 tsp lemon juice

1 tbsp horseradish sauce

milk (optional)

salt and pepper

TO GARNISH

1 tbsp chopped fresh chives

chive flowers (optional)

1 Leaving the skin on, cut the apples into quarters and remove the cores. Slice the apples into a bowl and toss in the French dressing to prevent them from turning brown.

2 Break the watercress into sprigs and arrange on 4 serving plates.

3 Skin the trout and take out the bone. Carefully remove any fine bones that remain, with your fingers or using tweezers. Flake the trout into fairly large pieces and arrange between the watercress with the apple.

4 To make the horseradish dressing, whisk all the ingredients together, adding a little milk if too thick, then drizzle over the trout. Sprinkle the chopped chives and flowers (if using) over the trout and serve with melba toast.

COOK'S TIP

To make Melba toast, toast thinly sliced bread, then cut off the crusts, and carefully slice in half horizontally using a sharp knife. Cut in half diagonally and place toasted side down in a warm oven for 15–20 minutes until the edges start to curl and the toast is crisp.

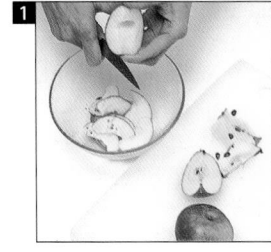
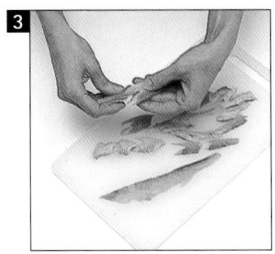

Potato Salad

You can use leftover cold potatoes, cut into bite-size pieces, for this salad, but tiny new potatoes are best for maximum flavor.

NUTRITIONAL INFORMATION

Calories 275   Sugars 8g
Protein . . . . .5g   Fat 13g
Carbohydrate . . .38g   Saturates 2g

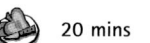 20 mins   20 mins

SERVES 4

INGREDIENTS

1 lb 9 oz/700 g tiny new potatoes

8 scallions

1 hard-cooked egg (optional)

generous 1 cup low-fat mayonnaise

1 tsp paprika

salt and pepper

TO GARNISH

2 tbsp chopped fresh chives

pinch of paprika

1 Bring a large pan of lightly salted water to a boil. Add the potatoes and cook for 10–15 minutes or until they are just tender.

2 Drain the potatoes in a colander and rinse them under cold running water until they are completely cold. Drain them again thoroughly. Transfer to a mixing bowl and set aside until required.

3 Trim and slice the scallions thinly on the diagonal.

4 Shell and chop the hard-cooked egg (if using).

5 Mix together the mayonnaise, paprika, and salt and pepper to taste in a bowl until well blended. Pour the mixture over the potatoes.

6 Add the sliced scallions and chopped egg, if using, and then toss them together gently.

7 Transfer the potato salad to a serving bowl, sprinkle with chopped chives, and a pinch of paprika. Cover and chill in the refrigerator until required.

COOK'S TIP

To make a lighter dressing, use a mixture of half mayonnaise and half plain yogurt.

Hot Potato & Ham Salad

With potatoes as a base you can vary the other ingredients, using egg, pickled herring, or beet in place of the smoked ham.

NUTRITIONAL INFORMATION

Calories	224	Sugars	.........6g
Protein	........14g	Fat	...........7g
Carbohydrate	...28g	Saturates	......2g

 10 mins   10 mins

SERVES 4

INGREDIENTS

6 oz/175 g lean smoked ham

1 lb 2 oz/500 g salad potatoes

6 scallions, white and green parts, sliced

3 pickled dill cucumbers, halved and sliced

4 tbsp low-fat mayonnaise

4 tbsp low-fat thick plain yogurt

2 tbsp chopped fresh dill

salt and pepper

1 Cut the ham into 1½ inch/3.5 cm long strips. Cut the potatoes into ½ inch/1 cm pieces. Cook the potatoes in lightly salted boiling water for about 8 minutes until tender.

2 Drain the potatoes well and return to the pan. Add the scallions, ham, and cucumber.

3 To make the dressing, combine the mayonnaise, yogurt, and chopped fresh dill in a small bowl, beating well until thoroughly mixed. Season to taste with salt and pepper.

4 Add the dressing to the pan and stir gently until the potatoes are coated with the dressing.

5 Transfer the salad into a warm dish and serve.

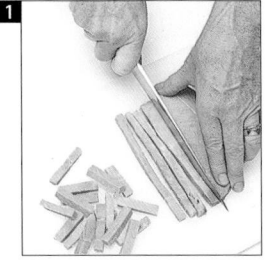
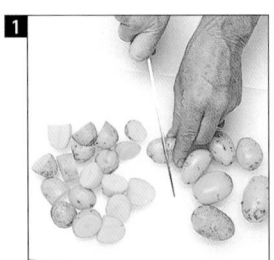

COOK'S TIP

The feathery green leaves of fresh dill are used to flavor many dishes—salads, soups, sauces, and vegetables. The distinctive flavor of fresh dill is far superior to the dried form which should, therefore, not be substituted.

Chicken & Grape Salad

Tender chicken breast, sweet grapes, and crisp celery coated in a mild curry mayonnaise make a wonderful al fresco lunch.

NUTRITIONAL INFORMATION

Calories 413   Sugars 20g
Protein . . . . .39g   Fat 20g
Carbohydrate . . .20g   Saturates 3g

15 mins   0 mins

SERVES 4

I N G R E D I E N T S

1 lb 2 oz/500 g cooked skinless, boneless
   chicken breasts

2 celery stalks, thinly sliced

2 cups black grapes

½ cup sliced almonds, toasted

pinch of paprika

fresh cilantro or flat leaf parsley sprigs,
   to garnish

C U R R Y   S A U C E

⅔ cup low-fat mayonnaise

½ cup low-fat plain yogurt

1 tbsp honey

1 tbsp curry paste

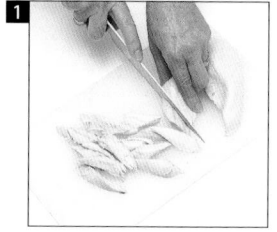

1 Cut the chicken into fairly large pieces and transfer to a bowl with the sliced celery.

2 Halve the grapes, remove the seeds, and add the fruit to the bowl.

3 To make the curry sauce, mix the mayonnaise with the yogurt, honey, and curry paste until blended.

4 Pour the curry sauce over the salad and mix together carefully until thoroughly coated.

5 Transfer to a shallow serving dish and sprinkle with the toasted almonds and paprika.

6 Garnish the salad with the cilantro or parsley and serve.

COOK'S TIP

To save time, use seedless grapes, now widely available in supermarkets, and add them whole to the salad.

Carrot & Orange Salad

A crunchy and colorful, sweet and savory dish which makes
a refreshing accompaniment or an excellent appetizer.

NUTRITIONAL INFORMATION

Calories	194	Sugars	........25g
Protein	.........6g	Fat	...........8g
Carbohydrate	...26g	Saturates	......1g

20 mins   0 mins

SERVES 4

INGREDIENTS

1 lb 2 oz/500 g celery root

2 tbsp orange juice

12 oz/350 g carrots, thinly sliced

2 celery stalks, finely chopped

1 cup celery leaves

4 oranges

4 tbsp walnut pieces

DRESSING

1 tbsp walnut oil

½ tsp grated orange rind

3 tbsp orange juice

1 tbsp white wine vinegar

1 tsp honey

salt and pepper

1 Trim and peel the celery root and slice or grate finely into a bowl. Add the orange juice and toss together to prevent it from turning brown.

2 Stir in the carrots, celery, and celery leaves. Cover with plastic wrap and chill in the refrigerator while you are preparing the oranges.

3 Slice off the tops and bottoms from the oranges. Using a sharp knife, slice off the skin, removing the pith at the same time. Cut out the orange flesh by slicing along the side of the membranes dividing the segments. reserve any juice for the dressing. Gently mix the orange segments into the celery root mixture.

4 To make the dressing, place all the ingredients in a small screw-top jar. Shake well to mix.

5 Pile the vegetable mixture onto a plate. Sprinkle over the walnut pieces and serve with the dressing.

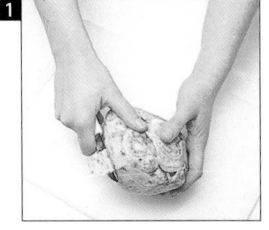

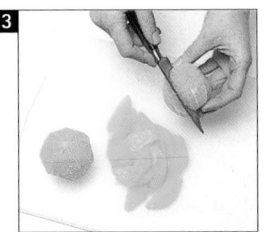

COOK'S TIP

Celery root is a variety of celery with a bulbous, knobby root. It has a rough, brown skin and creamy white flesh, and is delicious raw or cooked.

Sweet & Sour Tuna Salad

Small cannellini beans, zucchini, and tomatoes are briefly cooked in a sweet and sour sauce, before being mixed with tuna.

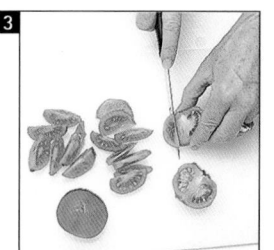

NUTRITIONAL INFORMATION

Calories ....245 Sugars 5g
Protein ....22g Fat 8g
Carbohydrate ...24g Saturates 1g

 15 mins   10 mins

SERVES 4

INGREDIENTS

2 tbsp olive oil

1 onion, chopped

2 garlic cloves, chopped

2 zucchini, sliced

4 tomatoes, peeled

14 oz/400 g can small cannellini beans, drained and rinsed

10 black olives, halved and pitted

1 tbsp capers

1 tsp superfine sugar

1 tbsp wholegrain mustard

1 tbsp white wine vinegar

7 oz/200 g canned tuna, drained

2 tbsp chopped fresh parsley, plus extra to garnish

crusty bread, to serve

1 Heat the olive oil in a large, heavy skillet. Add the chopped onion and garlic and cook over low heat, stirring occasionally, for 5 minutes until softened, but not browned.

2 Add the zucchini slices and cook, stirring occasionally, for another 3 minutes.

3 Cut the tomatoes in half, then into thin wedges.

4 Add the tomatoes to the pan with the beans, olives, capers, sugar, mustard, and vinegar.

5 Simmer for 2 minutes, stirring gently, then set aside to cool slightly.

6 Flake the tuna and stir it into the bean mixture with the parsley. Transfer to a serving dish, garnish with the extra chopped parsley, and serve lukewarm with crusty bread.

COOK'S TIP

Capers are the flowerbuds of the caper bush, which is native to the Mediterranean region. Capers are preserved in vinegar and salt and give a distinctive flavor to this salad. They are much used in Italian and Provençal cooking.

Cool Bean Salad

This is ideal for serving at a barbecue, for accompanying one of the hotter Indian curries, or for serving as part of a salad buffet at parties.

NUTRITIONAL INFORMATION

Calories 98   Sugars 5g
Protein . . . . .9g   Fat 1g
Carbohydrate . . .14g   Saturates 0.3g

 15 mins   15 mins

SERVES 4

I N G R E D I E N T S

1 red onion, thinly sliced

12 oz/350 g fava beans, fresh or frozen

⅔ cup plain yogurt

1 tbsp chopped fresh mint

1½ tsp lemon juice

1 garlic clove, halved

½ cucumber, peeled, halved, and sliced

salt and ground white pepper

1 Rinse the red onion slices briefly under cold running water and drain well.

2 Cook the fava beans in a small pan of boiling water and until tender: 8–10 minutes for fresh beans, 5–6 minutes for frozen.

3 Drain, rinse under cold running water, and drain again.

4 If you wish, shell the beans from their white outer shells to leave the sweet green bean.

5 Combine the yogurt, mint, lemon juice, garlic, and seasoning in a bowl.

6 Combine the onion, cucumber, and fava beans. Toss them in the yogurt dressing until well coated. Remove and discard the garlic halves.

7 Spoon the salad onto a serving plate and serve immediately.

COOK'S TIP

Rinsing the onion under the cold running water takes the edge off the raw taste, as it washes away some of the juices. The same technique can be used on other pungent vegetables and salads, such as scallions, bitter cucumbers, and chiles.

Chile & Bell Pepper Pasta

This roasted bell pepper and chile sauce is sweet and spicy—the perfect combination for those who like to add just a little spice to life!

NUTRITIONAL INFORMATION

Calories	423	Sugars	.........5g
Protein	.........9g	Fat	.........27g
Carbohydrate	...38g	Saturates	.......4g

25 mins | 30 mins

SERVES 4

INGREDIENTS

2 red bell peppers, halved and deseeded

1 small fresh red chile

4 tomatoes, halved

2 garlic cloves

½ cup ground almonds

7 tbsp olive oil

1 lb 8 oz/675 g fresh pasta or 12 oz/350 g dried pasta

fresh oregano leaves, to garnish

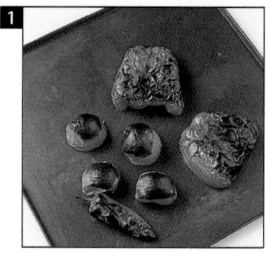 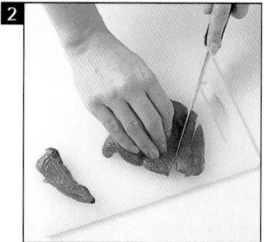 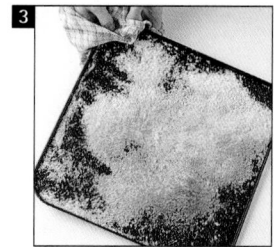

1 Place the bell peppers, skin side up, on a cookie sheet with the chile and tomatoes. Cook under a preheated broiler for 15 minutes or until charred. After 10 minutes, turn the tomatoes skin side up. Place the bell peppers and chiles in a plastic bag and set aside for 10 minutes.

2 Peel the skins from the bell peppers and chile and slice the flesh into strips. Peel the garlic, and peel and deseed the tomato halves.

3 Place the ground almonds on a cookie sheet and place under the broiler for 2–3 minutes until golden.

4 In a food processor, process the bell peppers, chile, garlic, and tomatoes to make a purée. With the motor still running, slowly add the olive oil through the feeder tube to form a thick sauce. Alternatively, mash the mixture with a fork and beat in the olive oil, drop by drop.

5 Stir the toasted ground almonds into the mixture. Warm the sauce in a pan until it is heated through.

6 Bring a large pan of lightly salted water to a boil. Add the pasta, bring back to a boil, and cook for 3–5 minutes if using fresh, or 8–10 minutes if using dried. Drain the pasta thoroughly and transfer to a serving dish. Pour over the sauce and toss to mix. Garnish with the fresh oregano leaves and serve.

VARIATION

Add 2 tablespoons of red wine vinegar to the sauce and use as a dressing for a cold pasta salad, if you wish.

Pasta & Herring Salad

This salad, which many countries claim as their own, is generally considered to be a typically Dutch dish.

NUTRITIONAL INFORMATION

Calories	774	Sugars	........21g
Protein	........33g	Fat	..........31g
Carbohydrate	...97g	Saturates	.......4g

15 mins   12 mins

SERVES 4

INGREDIENTS

2¼ cups dried pasta shells

14 oz/400 g rollmop herrings in brine

6 small potatoes, boiled and cooled

2 large tart apples

2 baby frisée lettuces

2 baby beets

4 hard-cooked eggs

6 pickled onions

6 dill pickles

2 tbsp capers, rinsed

4 tbsp olive oil

3 tbsp tarragon vinegar

salt and pepper

1 Bring a large pan of lightly salted water to a boil. Add the pasta, bring back to a boil, and cook for 8–10 minutes until tender, but still firm to the bite. Drain the pasta thoroughly and then refresh in cold water. Drain well again and set aside.

2 Cut the rollmop herrings, cooled potatoes, apples, frisée lettuces, and baby beets into small pieces. Put all of these ingredients into a large salad bowl. Add the pasta and toss lightly to mix.

3 Carefully shell and slice the eggs. Garnish the salad with the slices of egg, pickled onions, dill pickles, and capers, sprinkle with the olive oil and the tarragon vinegar, and serve immediately.

COOK'S TIP

Tarragon vinegar is available from most supermarkets, but you can easily make your own. Add a bunch of fresh tarragon to a bottle of white or red wine vinegar and set aside to steep for 48 hours.

Goat Cheese & Penne Salad

This superb and substantial salad is delicious when served with strongly flavored meat dishes, such as venison.

NUTRITIONAL INFORMATION

Calories 634	Sugars 13g
Protein 18g	Fat 51g
Carbohydrate ...27g	Saturates 13g

 1½ hrs   15 mins

SERVES 4

INGREDIENTS

2¼ cups dried penne

1 head radicchio, torn into pieces

1 lettuce, torn into pieces

7 tbsp chopped walnuts

2 ripe pears, cored and diced

1 fresh basil sprig

1 bunch of watercress, trimmed

2 tbsp lemon juice

4 tbsp olive oil

3 tbsp garlic vinegar

4 tomatoes, quartered

1 small onion, sliced

1 large carrot, grated

9 oz/250 g goat cheese, diced

salt

1 Bring a large pan of lightly salted water to a boil. Add the pasta, bring back to a boil, and cook for 8–10 minutes or until tender, but still firm to the bite. Drain the pasta, refresh under cold running water, drain thoroughly again, and set aside to cool.

2 Place the radicchio and lettuce in a large salad bowl and mix together well. Top with the pasta, walnuts, pears, basil, and watercress.

3 Combine the lemon juice, olive oil, and the vinegar in a measuring cup. Pour the dressing over the salad ingredients and toss to coat the salad greens well.

4 Add the tomato quarters, onion slices, grated carrot, and diced goat cheese and toss together, using 2 forks, until well mixed. Cover the salad with plastic wrap and chill in the refrigerator for about 1 hour before serving.

COOK'S TIP
Radicchio is a variety of endive originating in Italy. It has a slightly bitter flavor.

Italian Pasta Salad

Tomatoes and mozzarella cheese are a classic Italian combination.
Here they are joined with pasta and avocado for an extra touch of luxury.

NUTRITIONAL INFORMATION

Calories 541   Sugars 5g
Protein . . . . .12g   Fat 43g
Carbohydrate . . .29g   Saturates 10g

 15 mins   🕐 15 mins

SERVES 4

INGREDIENTS

2 tbsp pine nuts

1½ cups dried fusilli

1 tbsp olive oil

6 tomatoes

8 oz/225 g mozzarella cheese

1 large avocado

2 tbsp lemon juice

3 tbsp chopped fresh basil

salt and pepper

fresh basil sprigs, to garnish

DRESSING

6 tbsp extra virgin olive oil

2 tbsp white wine vinegar

1 tsp wholegrain mustard

pinch of sugar

1 Spread the pine nuts out on a cookie sheet and toast them under a preheated broiler for 1–2 minutes. Remove and set aside to cool.

2 Bring a large pan of lightly salted water to a boil. Add the pasta, bring back to a boil, and cook for 8–10 minutes or until tender, but still firm to the bite. Drain the pasta and refresh in cold water. Drain again and set aside to cool.

3 Thinly slice the tomatoes and the mozzarella cheese.

4 Cut the avocado in half lengthwise, carefully remove the pit, then peel. Cut the flesh into thin slices lengthwise and sprinkle with lemon juice to prevent it from turning brown.

5 To make the dressing, whisk together the oil, vinegar, mustard, and sugar in a small bowl and season to taste with salt and pepper.

6 Arrange the tomatoes, mozzarella cheese, and avocado pear alternately in overlapping slices on a large serving platter, leaving room in the center.

7 Toss the pasta with half of the dressing and the chopped basil and season to taste with salt and pepper. Spoon the pasta into the center of the platter and pour over the remaining dressing. Sprinkle over the pine nuts, garnish with fresh sprigs of basil, and serve immediately.

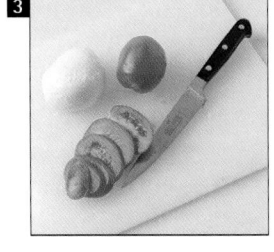

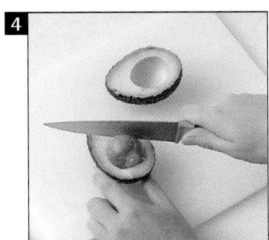

Rare Beef Pasta Salad

This mouthwatering salad is a meal in itself and would be perfect for an al fresco lunch, perhaps with a bottle of red wine.

NUTRITIONAL INFORMATION

Calories 575   Sugars 4g
Protein . . . . .31g   Fat 33g
Carbohydrate . . .44g   Saturates 9g

 15 mins   30 mins

SERVES 4

INGREDIENTS

1 lb/450 g round or sirloin steak in a
    single piece

4 cups dried fusilli

4 tbsp olive oil

2 tbsp lime juice

2 tbsp Thai fish sauce (see Cook's Tip)

2 tsp honey

4 scallions, sliced

1 cucumber, peeled and cut into 1 inch/
    2.5 cm chunks

3 tomatoes, cut into wedges

1 tbsp finely chopped fresh mint

salt and pepper

1 Season the steak with salt and pepper. Broil or pan-fry it for 4 minutes on each side. Let rest for 5 minutes, then slice thinly across the grain.

2 Meanwhile, bring a large pan of lightly salted water to a boil. Add the pasta, bring back to a boil, and cook for 8–10 minutes or until tender, but still firm to the bite. Drain the fusilli, refresh in cold water, and drain again thoroughly. Toss the fusilli in the olive oil and set aside until required.

3 Combine the lime juice, fish sauce, and honey in a small pan and cook over medium heat for 2 minutes.

4 Add the scallions, cucumber, tomatoes, and mint to the pan, then add the steak and mix well. Season to taste with salt.

5 Transfer the fusilli to a large, warm serving dish and top with the steak and salad mixture. Serve just warm or let cool completely.

COOK'S TIP

Thai fish sauce, also known as *nam pla*, is made from salted anchovies and has quite a strong flavor, so it should be used with discretion. It is available from some supermarkets and from Asian food stores.

Tuna, Bean & Anchovy Salad

Serve as part of a selection of antipasti, or for a summer lunch with hot garlic bread. Tuna and beans make a classic combination.

NUTRITIONAL INFORMATION

Calories	397	Sugars	.........8g
Protein	........23g	Fat	..........30g
Carbohydrate	...10g	Saturates	.......4g

 20 mins   0 mins

SERVES 4

INGREDIENTS

1 lb 2 oz/500 g tomatoes

7 oz/200 g canned tuna fish, drained

2 tbsp chopped fresh parsley

½ cucumber

1 small red onion, sliced

8 oz/225 g cooked green beans

1 small red bell pepper, deseeded

1 small crisp lettuce

6 tbsp Italian-style dressing

3 hard-cooked eggs

2 oz/55 g canned anchovies, drained

12 black olives, pitted

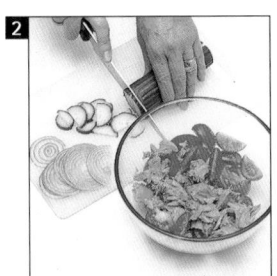

1 Cut the tomatoes into wedges, flake the tuna and put both into a bowl with the parsley.

2 Cut the cucumber into slices. Slice the onion. Add the cucumber and onion to the bowl.

3 Cut the beans in half, chop the bell pepper, and add both to the bowl with the lettuce leaves. Pour over the dressing and toss to mix, then spoon into a salad bowl. Shell the eggs and cut into quarters, arrange over the top with the anchovies, and sprinkle with the olives.

Vegetable & Pasta Salad

Roasted vegetables and pasta make a delicious, colorful salad, ideal as an appetizer or to serve with a platter of cold meats.

NUTRITIONAL INFORMATION

Calories 462   Sugars 9g
Protein . . . . .11g   Fat 32g
Carbohydrate . . .33g   Saturates 7g

 1½ hrs   1 hr

SERVES 4

INGREDIENTS

2 small eggplants, thinly sliced

1 large onion, sliced

2 large beefsteak tomatoes, peeled and cut into wedges

1 red bell pepper, deseeded and sliced

1 fennel bulb, thinly sliced

2 garlic cloves, sliced

3 tbsp olive oil

1½ cups small pasta shapes

¾ cup crumbled feta cheese

a few fresh basil leaves, torn

salt and pepper

salad greens, to serve

DRESSING

5 tbsp olive oil

juice of 1 orange

1 tsp grated orange rind

¼ tsp paprika

4 canned anchovies, finely chopped

1 Place the sliced eggplants in a colander, sprinkle with salt, and set them aside for about 1 hour to draw out some of the bitter juices. Rinse under cold, running water to remove the salt, then drain. Toss on paper towels to dry.

2 Arrange the eggplants, onion, tomatoes, bell pepper, fennel, and garlic in a single layer in a casserole, sprinkle with the oil, and season. Bake in a preheated oven, 450°F/220°C, for 45 minutes until the vegetables begin to turn brown. Remove from the oven and set aside to cool.

3 Bring a large pan of lightly salted water to a boil. Add the pasta, bring back to a boil, and cook for 10 minutes until tender, but still firm to the bite. Drain and turn into a bowl.

4 To make the dressing, mix together the olive oil, orange juice, orange rind, and paprika. Stir in the finely chopped anchovies and season with pepper to taste. Pour the dressing over the pasta while it is still hot and toss well. Set the pasta aside to cool.

5 To assemble the salad, line a shallow serving dish with the salad greens and arrange the cold roasted vegetables in the center. Spoon the pasta in a ring around the vegetables and sprinkle over the feta cheese and basil leaves.

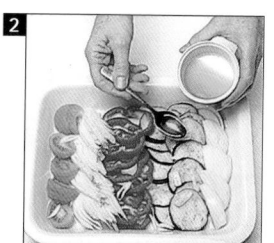

Cheese, Nut & Pasta Salad

Use colorful salad greens to provide a visual feast to match the wonderful contrasts of taste and texture.

NUTRITIONAL INFORMATION

Calories 694	Sugars 1g	
Protein 22g	Fat 57g	
Carbohydrate ...24g	Saturates 15g	

15 mins   15–20 mins

SERVES 4

INGREDIENTS

2 cups dried pasta shells

1 cup shelled and halved walnuts

mixed salad greens, such as radicchio, escarole, arugula, mâche, and frisée

2 cups crumbled dolcelatte cheese

salt

DRESSING

2 tbsp walnut oil

4 tbsp extra virgin olive oil

2 tbsp red wine vinegar

salt and pepper

1 Bring a large pan of lightly salted water to a boil. Add the pasta shells, bring back to a boil, and cook for 8–10 minutes or until just tender, but still firm to the bite. Drain the pasta, refresh under cold running water, drain thoroughly again, and set aside.

2 Spread out the shelled walnut halves on a cookie sheet and toast under a preheated broiler for 2–3 minutes. Remove from the broiler and set aside to cool while you make the dressing.

3 To make the dressing, whisk together the walnut oil, olive oil, and vinegar in a small bowl and season to taste with salt and pepper.

4 Arrange the salad greens in a large serving bowl. Pile the cooled pasta in the middle of the salad greens and sprinkle the dolcelatte cheese over them. Pour the dressing over the pasta salad, then scatter over the walnut halves, and toss together until thoroughly combined. Serve immediately.

COOK'S TIP

Dolcelatte is a semisoft, blue-veined cheese from Italy. Its texture is creamy and smooth and the flavor is delicate, but piquant. You could use Roquefort instead. It is essential that whatever cheese you choose, it is of the best quality and in peak condition.

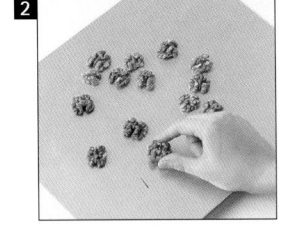  

Pasta Niçoise Salad

Based on the classic French salad niçoise, this recipe has a light olive oil dressing with the tang of capers and the fragrance of fresh basil.

NUTRITIONAL INFORMATION

Calories	214	Sugars	. . . . .2g
Protein	. . . . .26g	Fat	. . . . .7g
Carbohydrate	. . .14g	Saturates	. . . . . .1g

 15 mins 35 mins

SERVES 4

INGREDIENTS

2 cups dried farfalle

6 oz/175 g green beans

12 oz/350 g fresh tuna steaks

4 oz/115 g baby plum tomatoes, halved

8 anchovy fillets, drained

2 tbsp capers in brine, rinsed and drained

¼ cup pitted black olives in
    brine, drained

fresh basil leaves, to garnish

salt and pepper

DRESSING

1 tbsp olive oil

1 garlic clove, crushed

1 tbsp lemon juice

½ tsp finely grated lemon rind

1 tbsp shredded fresh basil leaves

  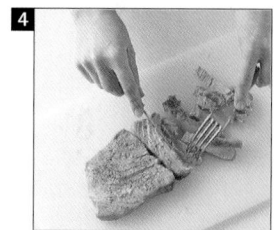

1 Bring a pan of lightly salted water to a boil. Add the pasta, bring back to a boil, and cook for 8–10 minutes until tender, but still firm to the bite. Drain well, set aside, and keep warm.

2 Bring a small pan of lightly salted water to a boil and cook the beans for 5–6 minutes until tender. Drain well and toss into the pasta.

3 Rinse and pat the tuna steaks dry on absorbent paper towels. Place the tuna steaks on the broiler rack and then season on both sides with pepper. Cook under a preheated broiler for 4–5 minutes on each side until cooked through.

4 Drain the tuna on absorbent paper towels and flake into bite-size pieces. Toss the tuna into the pasta with the tomatoes, anchovies, capers, and olives. Set aside and keep warm.

5 Meanwhile, prepare the dressing. Mix all the ingredients together and season well. Pour the dressing over the pasta mixture and mix carefully. Transfer to a warmed serving bowl and serve sprinkled with fresh basil leaves.

VARIATION
Any pasta shape is suitable for this salad—to make it even more colorful, use tricolor pasta.

Italian Mozzarella Salad

This colorful and nutritious salad is packed full of delicious flavors, but is simplicity itself to make.

NUTRITIONAL INFORMATION

Calories	79	Sugars	. . . . .2g
Protein	. . . . .4g	Fat	. . . . .6g
Carbohydrate	. . . .2g	Saturates	. . . . . . .2g

 20 mins   0 mins

SERVES 6

I N G R E D I E N T S

7 oz/200 g baby spinach

4½ oz/125 g watercress

4½ oz/125 g mozzarella cheese

8 oz/225 g cherry tomatoes

2 tsp balsamic vinegar

4½ tsp extra virgin olive oil

salt and pepper

1 Wash the spinach and watercress and drain thoroughly on absorbent paper towels. Remove any tough stalks. Place the spinach and watercress leaves in a large serving dish.

2 Cut the mozzarella into small pieces and sprinkle them over the spinach and watercress leaves.

3 Cut the cherry tomatoes in half and sprinkle them over the salad.

4 Sprinkle over the balsamic vinegar and olive oil and season with salt and pepper to taste. Toss the mixture together to coat the leaves. Serve at once or chill in the refrigerator until required.

Sesame Seed Salad

This salad uses tahini paste—sesame seed paste—as a flavoring for the dressing, which complements the eggplant.

NUTRITIONAL INFORMATION

Calories . . . . .89 Sugars 1g
Protein . . . . .3g Fat 8g
Carbohydrate . . . .1g Saturates 1g

🥗 45 mins   🕐 15 mins

SERVES 4

I N G R E D I E N T S

1 large eggplant

3 tbsp tahini paste

juice and rind of 1 lemon

1 garlic clove, crushed

pinch of paprika

1 tbsp chopped fresh cilantro

Boston or Bibb lettuce leaves

salt and pepper

G A R N I S H

strips of pimiento

lemon wedges

toasted sesame seeds

1 Cut the eggplant in half, place in a colander, and sprinkle with salt. Set aside for 30 minutes to allow the juices to drain. Rinse thoroughly under cold running water and drain well. Pat dry with paper towels.

2 Place the eggplant halves, skin side uppermost, on an oiled cookie sheet. Cook in a preheated oven, 450°F/230°C, for 10–15 minutes. Remove from the oven and set aside to cool.

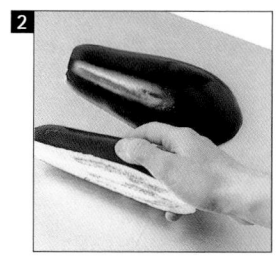

3 When the eggplant is cool enough to handle, cut it into cubes and set aside until required.

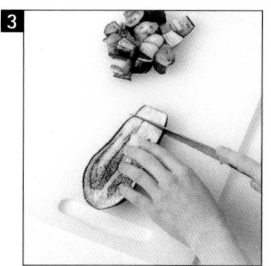

4 Combine the tahini paste, lemon juice, lemon rind, garlic, paprika, and chopped cilantro in a medium-size bowl. Season with salt and pepper to taste and stir in the eggplant cubes.

5 Line a serving dish with lettuce leaves and spoon the eggplant cubes into the center. Garnish the salad with pimiento slices, lemon wedges, and toasted sesame seeds and serve immediately.

Lobster Salad & Lime Dressing

The lobster makes this a special-occasion salad, both in cost and flavor. The richness of the lobster meat is offset by the tangy lime dressing.

NUTRITIONAL INFORMATION

Calories 181   Sugars 0.8g
Protein . . . . .6.8g   Fat 13.9g
Carbohydrate . . .7.6g   Saturates 2.2g

 5 mins   10–15 mins

SERVES 4

INGREDIENTS

1 lb/450 g waxy potatoes, scrubbed and sliced

8 oz/225 g cooked lobster meat

⅔ cup mayonnaise

2 tbsp lime juice

finely grated rind of 1 lime

1 tbsp chopped fresh parsley

2 tbsp olive oil

2 tomatoes, deseeded and diced

2 hard-cooked eggs, quartered

1 tbsp quartered pitted green olives

salt and pepper

COOK'S TIP

As seafood is used in this salad, serve it immediately or keep covered and chilled for up to 1 hour before serving.

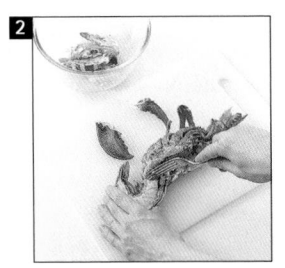

1 Cook the potatoes in a pan of boiling water for 10–15 minutes or until cooked through. Drain and reserve.

2 Remove the lobster meat from the shell and then separate it into large pieces.

3 In a bowl, combine the mayonnaise, 1 tablespoon of the lime juice, half the grated lime rind, and half the chopped parsley, then set aside.

4 In a separate bowl, whisk the remaining lime juice with the olive oil and pour the dressing over the potatoes. Arrange the potatoes on a serving plate.

5 Top with the lobster meat, tomatoes, eggs, and olives. Season to taste and sprinkle with the reserved parsley.

6 Spoon the mayonnaise onto the center of the salad, top with the reserved rind, and serve.

Mexican Potato Salad

The flavors of Mexico are echoed in this dish where potato slices are topped with tomatoes and chiles and served with guacamole.

NUTRITIONAL INFORMATION

Calories 260   Sugars 6g
Protein . . . . .6g   Fat 9g
Carbohydrate . . .41g   Saturates 2g

 20 mins   20 mins

SERVES 4

I N G R E D I E N T S

4 large waxy potatoes, sliced

1 ripe avocado

1 tsp olive oil

1 tsp lemon juice

1 garlic clove, crushed

1 onion, chopped

2 large tomatoes, sliced

1 fresh green chile, deseeded and chopped

1 yellow bell pepper, deseeded and sliced

2 tbsp chopped fresh cilantro

salt and pepper

lemon or lime wedges, to garnish

1 Bring a large pan of water to a boil. Add the potato slices, bring back to a boil, and cook for 10–15 minutes or until tender. Drain and set aside to cool.

2 Meanwhile, cut the avocado in half and remove the pit. Scoop the flesh into a bowl and mash with a fork. Guacamole is best with a slightly chunky, rather than completely smooth texture.

3 Add the olive oil, lemon juice, garlic, and chopped onion to the avocado flesh and stir to mix. Cover the bowl tightly with plastic wrap to minimize discoloration and set aside.

4 Combine the tomatoes, chopped chile, and yellow bell pepper and transfer to a salad bowl or serving platter. Add the potato slices and mix gently.

5 Arrange the avocado mixture on top of the salad and sprinkle with the chopped cilantro. Season to taste with salt and pepper and serve immediately garnished with lemon or lime wedges.

VARIATION
You can omit the green chile from this salad if you do not like hot dishes.

Pear & Roquefort Salad

The sweetness of the pear is a perfect partner to the peppery "bite" of the radicchio and the piquancy of the cheese.

NUTRITIONAL INFORMATION

Calories	94	Sugars	.......10g
Protein	.........5g	Fat	...........4g
Carbohydrate	...10g	Saturates	......3g

 10 mins   0 mins

SERVES 4

INGREDIENTS

2 oz/55 g Roquefort cheese

⅔ cup low-fat plain yogurt

2 tbsp chopped fresh chives

few leaves of lollo rosso

few leaves of radicchio

few leaves of mâche

2 ripe pears

pepper

whole fresh chives, to garnish

COOK'S TIP

Look out for bags of mixed salad greens, as these are generally more economical than buying lots of different greens separately.

1 Place the cheese in a bowl and mash with a fork. Gradually blend the yogurt into the cheese to make a smooth dressing. Add the chives and season with pepper to taste.

2 Tear the lollo rosso, radicchio, and mâche leaves into manageable pieces. Arrange the salad greens on a large serving platter or divide them between individual serving plates.

3 Cut the pears into quarters and remove the cores. Cut the quarters into slices. Arrange the pear slices over the salad leaves.

4 Drizzle the Roquefort dressing over the pears and garnish with a few whole chives.

Carrot & Nut Coleslaw

This simple salad has a dressing made from poppy seeds pan-fried in sesame oil to bring out their flavor and aroma.

NUTRITIONAL INFORMATION

Calories ....220 Sugars 7g
Protein ....4g Fat 19g
Carbohydrate ...10g Saturates 3g

 15 mins   5–10 mins

SERVES 4

I N G R E D I E N T S

1 large carrot, grated

1 small onion, finely chopped

2 celery stalks, chopped

¼ small hard white cabbage, shredded

1 tbsp chopped fresh parsley

4 tbsp sesame oil

½ tsp poppy seeds

½ cup cashew nuts

2 tbsp white wine vinegar or apple vinegar

salt and pepper

fresh parsley sprigs, to garnish

1 In a large salad bowl, combine the carrot, onion, celery, and cabbage. Stir in the chopped parsley and season to taste with salt and pepper.

2 Heat the sesame oil in a pan with a lid. Add the poppy seeds and cover the pan. Cook over medium-high heat until the seeds start to make a popping sound. Remove the pan from the heat and set aside to cool.

3 Spread out the cashew nuts on a cookie sheet. Place them under a preheated medium-hot broiler and toast

until lightly browned, being careful not to burn them. Remove from the heat and set aside to cool.

4 Add the vinegar to the oil and poppy seed mixture, then pour the poppy seed dressing over the vegetable mixture.

Add the cooled cashew nuts. Toss together to coat well.

5 Garnish the salad with sprigs of fresh parsley and serve immediately.

Melon & Strawberry Salad

This refreshing fruit-based salad is perfect for a hot summer's day and would be perfect served with grilled chicken or fish.

NUTRITIONAL INFORMATION

Calories	112	Sugars	22g
Protein	5g	Fat	1g
Carbohydrate	22g	Saturates	0.3g

 15 mins   0 mins

SERVES 4

INGREDIENTS

½ iceberg lettuce, shredded

1 small honeydew melon

2 cups strawberries, sliced

2 inch/5 cm piece of cucumber, thinly sliced

fresh mint sprigs to garnish

DRESSING

scant 1 cup plain yogurt

2 inch/5 cm piece of cucumber, peeled

a few fresh mint leaves

½ tsp finely grated lime or lemon rind

pinch of superfine sugar

3–4 ice cubes

1 Arrange the shredded lettuce on 4 serving plates.

2 Cut the melon lengthwise into quarters. Scoop out the seeds and cut through the flesh down to the skin at 1 inch/2.5 cm intervals. Cut the melon close to the skin and detach the flesh.

3 Place the chunks of melon on the beds of lettuce with the strawberries and cucumber slices.

4 To make the dressing, put the yogurt, cucumber, mint leaves, lime or lemon rind, superfine sugar, and ice cubes into a blender or food processor. Blend together for about 15 seconds until smooth. Alternatively, chop the cucumber and mint finely, crush the ice cubes, and combine with the other ingredients.

5 Serve the salad with a little dressing poured over it. Garnish with sprigs of fresh mint.

VARIATION

Omit the ice cubes from the dressing if you prefer, but make sure that the ingredients are well-chilled. This will ensure that the finished dressing is really cool.

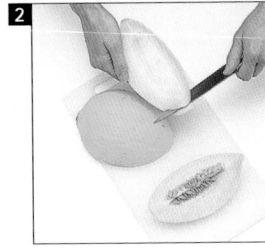

Salad with Garlic Dressing

This is a very quick and refreshing salad using a whole range of colorful ingredients, which make it look as good as it tastes.

NUTRITIONAL INFORMATION

Calories	82	Sugars	.........5g
Protein	.........2g	Fat	...........6g
Carbohydrate	....5g	Saturates	......1g

10 mins   0 mins

SERVES 4

INGREDIENTS

3 oz/85 g cucumber, cut into batons

6 scallions, halved

2 tomatoes, deseeded and cut into 8 wedges

1 yellow bell pepper, deseeded and cut into strips

2 celery stalks, cut into strips

4 radishes, quartered

3 oz/85 g arugula

1 tbsp chopped fresh mint, to garnish

DRESSING

2 tbsp lemon juice

1 garlic clove, crushed

⅔ cup low-fat natural yogurt

2 tbsp olive oil

salt and pepper

1 To make the salad, gently mix the cucumber batons, scallions, tomato wedges, yellow bell pepper strips, celery strips, radishes, and arugula in a large serving bowl.

2 To make the dressing, stir the lemon juice, garlic, natural yogurt, and olive oil together in a small bowl they are until thoroughly combined. Season with salt and pepper to taste.

3 Spoon the dressing over the salad and toss to mix. Sprinkle the salad with chopped mint and serve.

COOK'S TIP

Arugula has a distinctive warm, peppery flavor which is ideal in green salads. If arugula is unavailable, mâche makes a good substitute.

Zucchini & Mint Salad

This salad uses lots of green-colored ingredients which look and taste wonderful with the minty yogurt dressing.

NUTRITIONAL INFORMATION

Calories	49	Sugars	........5g
Protein	........4g	Fat	..........1g
Carbohydrate	....6g	Saturates	.......0g

30 mins

7–8 mins

SERVES 4

INGREDIENTS

2 zucchini, cut into batons

3½ oz/100 g green beans, cut into thirds

1 green bell pepper, deseeded and cut into strips

2 celery stalks, sliced

1 bunch of watercress

DRESSING

scant 1 cup natural yogurt

1 garlic clove, crushed

2 tbsp chopped fresh mint

pepper

1 Cook the zucchini batons and beans in a pan of lightly salted boiling water for 7–8 minutes. Drain, rinse under cold running water, and drain again. Set aside to cool completely.

2 Mix the zucchini and beans with the green bell pepper strips, celery, and watercress in a large serving bowl.

3 To make the dressing, combine the natural yogurt, garlic, and chopped fresh mint in a small bowl. Season with pepper to taste.

4 Spoon the dressing onto the salad and serve immediately.

COOK'S TIP

The salad must be served as soon as the yogurt dressing has been added—the dressing will start to separate if it is kept for any length of time.

Bean & Tomato Salad

This is a colorful salad with a Mexican theme, using beans, tomatoes, and avocado. The chili dressing adds a little kick.

NUTRITIONAL INFORMATION

Calories	347	Sugars 7g
Protein	.........9g	Fat 26g
Carbohydrate	...21g	Saturates 5g

 10 mins 0 mins

SERVES 4

INGREDIENTS

lollo rosso lettuce

2 ripe avocados

2 tsp lemon juice

4 medium tomatoes

1 onion

6 oz/175 g canned mixed beans, rinsed and drained

DRESSING

4 tbsp olive oil

dash of chili oil

2 tbsp garlic wine vinegar

pinch of superfine sugar

pinch of chili powder

1 tbsp chopped fresh parsley

 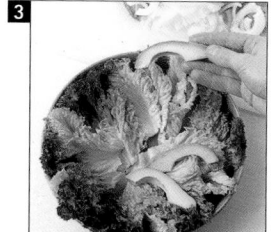 

1 Line a serving bowl with the lollo rosso lettuce leaves.

2 Cut the avocados in half and remove and discard the pits. Peel and thinly slice the flesh, then sprinkle with the lemon juice to prevent the flesh from turning brown.

3 Thinly slice the tomatoes and onion. Arrange the avocado, tomato, and onion slices around the salad bowl, leaving a space in the center. Spoon the beans into the center of the salad.

4 Whisk all the dressing ingredients together in a small bowl until thoroughly combined. Pour the dressing over the salad and serve immediately.

COOK'S TIP

Instead of whisking the dressing, place all the ingredients in a screw-top jar and shake vigorously. Any leftover dressing can then be kept and stored in the same jar.

Broiled Vegetable Salad

The vegetables for this dish are best prepared well in advance and chilled for at least an hour before serving.

NUTRITIONAL INFORMATION

Calories	230	Sugars	........10g
Protein	.........2g	Fat	..........20g
Carbohydrate	....11g	Saturates	.......3g

 1¼ hrs   10 mins

SERVES 4

INGREDIENTS

1 zucchini, sliced

1 yellow bell pepper, deseeded and sliced

1 eggplant, sliced

1 fennel bulb, cut into 8 wedges

1 red onion, cut into 8 wedges

16 cherry tomatoes

3 tbsp olive oil

1 garlic clove, crushed

fresh rosemary sprigs, to garnish

DRESSING

4 tbsp olive oil

2 tbsp balsamic vinegar

2 tsp chopped fresh rosemary

1 tsp Dijon mustard

1 tsp honey

2 tsp lemon juice

1 Spread out all of the vegetables, except for the cherry tomatoes, on a cookie sheet.

2 Mix the oil and garlic and brush over the vegetables. Cook under a medium-hot broiler for 10 minutes until tender and beginning to char. Set aside to cool. Spoon the vegetables into a serving bowl with the cherry tomatoes.

3 Mix the dressing ingredients and pour over the vegetables. Cover and chill for 1 hour. Garnish and serve.

VARIATION

This salad can also be served warm. Prepare the vegetables as above, but do not let them cool completely. Heat the dressing in a small pan over low heat, then pour it over the vegetables, and toss to mix.

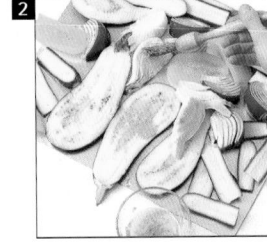

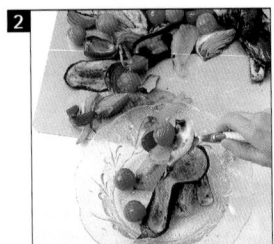

Red Cabbage & Pear Salad

Red cabbage is much underused—it is a colorful and tasty ingredient, which is perfect with fruits, such as pears or apples.

NUTRITIONAL INFORMATION

Calories	143	Sugars	14g
Protein	2g	Fat	9g
Carbohydrate	15g	Saturates	1g

15 mins   0 mins

SERVES 4

INGREDIENTS

12 oz/350 g red cabbage, finely shredded

2 Conference pears, cored and thinly sliced

4 scallions, sliced

lollo biondo leaves

1 carrot, grated

fresh chives, to garnish

DRESSING

4 tbsp pear juice

1 tsp wholegrain mustard

3 tbsp olive oil

1 tbsp garlic wine vinegar

1 tbsp chopped chives

 1 Put the red cabbage, pears, and scallions into a bowl and toss gently together to mix.

 2 Line a serving dish with lollo biondo lettuce leaves and spoon the cabbage and pear mixture into the center.

3 Sprinkle the grated carrot into the center of the cabbage to form a domed pile.

4 To make the dressing, combine the pear juice, wholegrain mustard, olive oil, garlic wine vinegar, and chives, stirring until well mixed.

5 Pour the dressing over the salad, garnish, and serve immediately. (Do not make the salad much in advance of serving because the color from the red cabbage will bleed into the other ingredients, spoiling the appearance.)

VARIATION

Experiment with different types of salad greens. The s lightly bitter flavor of endive or radicchio would work well with the sweetness of the pears.

Alfalfa & Beet Salad

This refreshing salad must be assembled just before serving
to prevent all of the ingredients being colored pink by the beet.

NUTRITIONAL INFORMATION

Calories	139	Sugars	.........7g
Protein	.........2g	Fat	...........11g
Carbohydrate	....8g	Saturates	.......2g

 10 mins   0 mins

SERVES 4

INGREDIENTS

3½ oz/100 g baby spinach

3 oz/85 g alfalfa sprouts

2 celery stalks, sliced

4 cooked beets, cut into 8 wedges

DRESSING

4 tbsp olive oil

4½ tsp garlic wine vinegar

1 garlic clove, crushed

2 tsp honey

1 tbsp chopped fresh chives

VARIATION

Add the segments of 1 large
orange to the salad to make it
even more colorful and refreshing.
Replace the garlic wine vinegar with
plain and use a different flavored oil
such as chili or herb, if you prefer.

1 If the spinach leaves are large, tear
them into smaller pieces. (Cutting
them would bruise them.) Place the
spinach and alfalfa sprouts in a large bowl
and mix together.

2 Add the celery and mix well. Toss in
the beets and mix again.

3 To make the dressing, mix the oil,
wine vinegar, garlic, honey, and
chopped chives in a small bowl.

4 Pour the dressing over the salad, toss
well, and serve immediately.

Egg Noodle Salad

A good dish for summer eating, this is light and refreshing in flavor and easy to cook. The turkey can be replaced with cooked chicken.

NUTRITIONAL INFORMATION

Calories . . . . . . .355 Sugars 6g
Protein . . . . .22g Fat 10g
Carbohydrate . . .46g Saturates 2g

20 mins   4–5 mins

SERVES 4

I N G R E D I E N T S

8 oz/225 g dried egg noodles

2 tsp sesame oil

1 carrot

2 cups bean sprouts

½ cucumber

2 scallions, finely shredded

5½ oz/150 g cooked turkey breast meat, shredded into thin slivers

D R E S S I N G

5 tbsp coconut milk

3 tbsp lime juice

1 tbsp light soy sauce

2 tsp Thai fish sauce

1 tsp chili oil

1 tsp sugar

2 tbsp chopped fresh cilantro

2 tbsp chopped fresh sweet basil

T O   G A R N I S H

peanuts

chopped fresh basil

1 Cook the noodles in boiling water for 4 minutes, or according to the packet instructions. Plunge them into a bowl of cold water to prevent any further cooking, then drain, and toss in sesame oil.

2 Use a vegetable peeler to shave off thin ribbons from the carrot. Blanch the ribbons and bean sprouts in boiling water for 30 seconds, then plunge into cold water for 30 seconds. Drain well. Shave thin ribbons of cucumber with the vegetable peeler.

3 Place the carrots, bean sprouts, cucumber, scallions, and turkey in a large bowl. Add the noodles and toss thoroughly to mix.

4 Place all the dressing ingredients in a screw-top jar and shake vigorously to mix evenly.

5 Add the dressing to the noodle mixture and toss. Pile the salad onto a serving dish. Sprinkle with peanuts and basil. Serve cold.

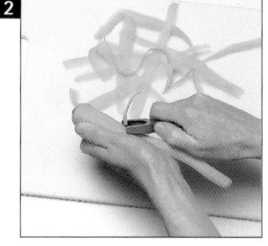  

Cucumber Salad

This refreshing spicy salad makes an excellent accompaniment for spicy broiled fish, meat, and poultry dishes.

NUTRITIONAL INFORMATION

Calories 32   Sugars 3g
Protein ....1g   Fat 1g
Carbohydrate ....5g   Saturates 0g

1 hr   0 mins

SERVES 4

INGREDIENTS

1 cucumber

1 tsp salt

1 small red onion

1 garlic clove, crushed

½ tsp chili paste

2 tsp Thai fish sauce

1 tbsp lime juice

1 tsp sesame oil

1 Trim the cucumber and coarsely grate the flesh. Place it in a strainer over a bowl, sprinkle with the salt, and set aside to drain for about 20 minutes. Discard the liquid and rinse the cucumber.

2 Peel the onion and chop finely, then add it to the cucumber. Toss to mix. Spoon the mixture into 4 individual bowls or a large serving bowl.

3 Combine the garlic, chili paste, fish sauce, lime juice, and sesame oil, then spoon the dressing over the salad. Cover the salad tightly with plastic wrap and chill in the refrigerator before serving.

COOK'S TIP

Once the salad is made, it can be chilled with the dressing for about 1–2 hours, but is best eaten on the day of making.

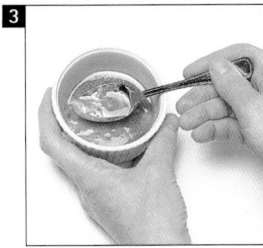

Thai Green Salad

An unusual side salad that is a good accompaniment to any simple Thai entrée, especially broiled meats and fish.

NUTRITIONAL INFORMATION

Calories 42   Sugars 3g
Protein ....2g   Fat 2g
Carbohydrate ....4g   Saturates 2g

12 mins   0 mins

SERVES 4–6

INGREDIENTS

1 small head Romaine lettuce

1 bunch of scallions

½ cucumber

4 tbsp fresh coconut, coarsely shredded and toasted

DRESSING

4 tbsp lime juice

2 tbsp Thai fish sauce

1 small fresh red bird-eye chile, seeded and finely chopped

1 tsp sugar

1 garlic clove, crushed

2 tbsp chopped fresh cilantro

1 tbsp chopped fresh mint

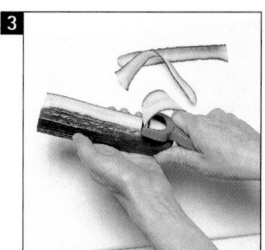

1 Tear or coarsely shred the lettuce leaves and place them in a large salad bowl. (Do not cut or you will bruise them.)

2 Trim and thinly slice the scallions diagonally, then add them to the salad bowl.

3 Use a vegetable peeler to shave thin slices along the length of the cucumber and add to the salad bowl.

4 Place all the ingredients for the dressing in a screw-top jar, close the lid tightly, and shake vigorously until thoroughly mixed.

5 Pour the dressing over the salad and toss well to coat the leaves evenly.

6 Sprinkle the coconut over the salad and toss in lightly just before serving.

COOK'S TIP

This salad is good for picnics. Pack the leaves into a plastic container and nestle the jar of dressing in the center. Cover with plastic wrap. Packed this way, the salad stays crisp and if the dressing leaks during transit, there's no mess.

Eggplant & Sesame Salad

Eggplants are a popular vegetable in Thailand, and they grow easily throughout the Far East. This dish works very well as an appetizer.

NUTRITIONAL INFORMATION

Calories 106	Sugars 6g
Protein 3g	Fat 8g
Carbohydrate 7g	Saturates 1g

 1¼ hrs   10 mins

SERVES 4

INGREDIENTS

8 baby eggplants

2 tsp chili oil

1 tbsp soy sauce

1 tbsp Thai fish sauce

1 garlic clove, thinly sliced

1 fresh red bird-eye chile, deseeded and sliced

1 tbsp sunflower oil

1 tsp sesame oil

1 tbsp lime juice

1 tsp soft light brown sugar

1 tbsp chopped fresh mint

1 tbsp sesame seeds, toasted

salt

fresh mint leaves, to garnish

   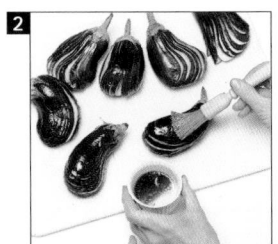 

1 Cut the eggplants lengthwise into thin slices to within 1 inch/2.5 cm of the stem end. Place in a colander, sprinkling with salt between the slices and set aside to drain for about 30 minutes. Rinse under cold running water and pat dry with paper towels.

2 Combine the chili oil, soy sauce, and fish sauce and then brush over the eggplants. Cook under a preheated hot broiler or grill over hot coals, turning them over occasionally and brushing with more chili oil glaze, for 6–8 minutes until golden brown and softened. Arrange them on a serving platter.

3 Fry the garlic and chile in the sunflower oil for 1–2 minutes until just beginning to brown. Remove from the heat and add the sesame oil, lime juice, brown sugar, and any spare chili oil glaze.

4 Add the chopped mint and spoon the warm dressing over the eggplants.

5 Set aside to marinate for about 20 minutes, then sprinkle with toasted sesame seeds. Serve garnished with fresh mint leaves.

Asian Lettuce Cups

A crisp and tasty salad with a rich and warmly spiced coconut and peanut dressing is served in pretty lettuce cups.

NUTRITIONAL INFORMATION

Calories ....136 Sugars 7g
Protein ....5g Fat 9g
Carbohydrate ....9g Saturates 2g

 15 mins 🕐 0 mins

SERVES 4

I N G R E D I E N T S

8 leaves Romaine lettuce or other firm
lettuce leaves

2 carrots

2 celery stalks

1 cup baby corn

2 scallions

2 cups bean sprouts

2 tbsp chopped roasted peanuts

D R E S S I N G

2 tbsp smooth peanut butter

3 tbsp lime juice

3 tbsp coconut milk

2 tsp Thai fish sauce

1 tsp superfine sugar

1 tsp fresh ginger root, grated

¼ tsp Thai red curry paste

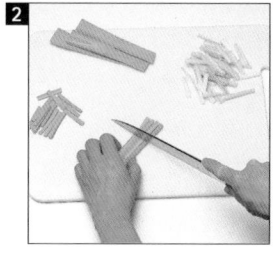  

1 Wash and trim the lettuce leaves, leaving them whole. Arrange on a serving plate or on individual plates.

2 Trim the carrots and celery and cut into fine batons. Trim the baby corn and onions and slice both diagonally into thick slices.

3 Toss together all the prepared vegetables with the bean sprouts.

Divide the salad mixture equally between the individual lettuce cups.

4 To make the dressing, place all the ingredients in a screw-top jar and shake vigorously until thoroughly mixed.

5 Divide the dressing equally among the salad cups, spooning it over the vegetables, then sprinkle with chopped peanuts. Serve immediately.

COOK'S TIP

Choose leaves with a deep cup shape to hold the salad neatly. If you prefer, Napa cabbage leaves may be used in place of lettuce. To remove the leaves from the head without tearing them, cut a thick slice from the base, then gently ease away the leafy parts.

Carrot & Mango Salad

A wonderfully refreshing, simple salad to serve as a side dish with hot and spicy meat or fish dishes. It can be prepared in advance and chilled.

NUTRITIONAL INFORMATION

Calories	109	Sugars 14g
Protein	. . . . .5g	Fat 4g
Carbohydrate	14	Saturates 1g

 10 mins   0 mins

SERVES 4

I N G R E D I E N T S

4 carrots

1 small, ripe mango

7 oz/200 g firm beancurd

1 tbsp chopped fresh chives

D R E S S I N G

2 tbsp orange juice

1 tbsp lime juice

1 tsp honey

½ tsp orange-flower water

1 tsp sesame oil

1 tsp sesame seeds, toasted

1 Peel and coarsely grate the carrots. Peel, pit, and thinly slice the mango.

2 Cut the beancurd into ½ inch/1 cm dice and toss together with the carrots and mango in a wide salad bowl.

3 For the dressing, place all the ingredients in a screw-top jar and shake vigorously to mix evenly.

4 Pour the dressing over the salad and toss well to coat the salad evenly.

5 Chill the salad for 1–2 hours, if desired. Just before serving, toss the salad lightly and sprinkle with chives. Serve immediately.

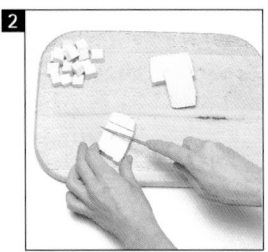

COOK'S TIP

A food processor will grate the carrots in seconds, and is especially useful for time-saving if you're catering for a crowd.

Bamboo Shoot Salad

In Thailand, fresh bamboo would always be used for this salad, but canned bamboo shoots make a very good alternative.

NUTRITIONAL INFORMATION

Calories 54	Sugars 3g	
Protein 3g	Fat 2g	
Carbohydrate 7g	Saturates 0g	

15 mins   8–10 mins

SERVES 4

INGREDIENTS

2 shallots

2 garlic cloves

2 tbsp Thai fish sauce

3 tbsp lime juice

½ tsp dried chili flakes

1 tsp granulated sugar

1 tbsp round grain rice

2 tsp sesame seeds

12 oz/350 g canned bamboo shoots, rinsed and drained

2 scallions, chopped

fresh mint leaves, to garnish

Napa cabbage leaves or lettuce, shredded, to serve

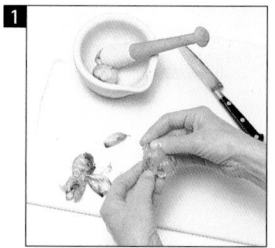  

1 Place the whole shallots and garlic under a preheated medium-hot broiler and broil until charred on the outside and tender inside. Remove the skins and place the flesh in a mortar. Grind to a smooth paste with a pestle.

2 Mix the paste with the fish sauce, lime juice, chili flakes, and sugar.

3 Place the rice and sesame seeds in a heavy skillet set over low heat and cook to a rich golden brown, shaking the pan frequently to brown evenly.

Remove from the heat and crush lightly in a mortar with a pestle.

4 Use a sharp knife to slice the bamboo shoots into fine shreds. Stir in the shallot and garlic dressing, tossing well to coat the mixture evenly.

Stir in the toasted rice and sesame seeds, then the scallions.

5 Pile the salad onto a serving dish and surround it with shredded Napa cabbage leaves. Garnish with fresh mint leaves and serve immediately.

Hot & Sour Beef Salad

Thais are primarily fish-eaters, so beef usually appears on the menu only on feast days, but, as in this dish, a little can go a long way.

NUTRITIONAL INFORMATION

Calories	207	Sugars	.........7g
Protein	........15g	Fat	..........13g
Carbohydrate	....9g	Saturates	.......3g

40 mins

8 mins

SERVES 4

INGREDIENTS

1 tsp black peppercorns

1 tsp coriander seeds

1 dried red bird-eye chile

¼ tsp Chinese five-spice powder

9 oz/250 g beef tenderloin

1 tbsp dark soy sauce

6 scallions

1 carrot

¼ cucumber

8 radishes

1 red onion

¼ head Napa cabbage

2 tbsp peanut oil

1 garlic clove, crushed

1 tsp finely chopped lemongrass

1 tbsp chopped fresh mint

1 tbsp chopped fresh cilantro

DRESSING

3 tbsp lime juice

1 tbsp light soy sauce

2 tsp soft light brown sugar

1 tsp sesame oil

1 Crush the peppercorns, coriander seeds, and chile in a mortar with a pestle, then mix with the five-spice powder, and sprinkle on a plate. Brush the beef all over with soy sauce, then roll it in the spices to coat evenly.

2 Cut the scallions into 2½ inch/ 6 cm lengths, then shred finely lengthwise. Place in ice water until curled. Drain well.

3 Trim the carrot and cut into very thin diagonal slices. Halve the cucumber, scoop out and discard the seeds, then slice the flesh thinly. Trim the radishes and cut into flower shapes.

4 Slice the onion thinly. Roughly shred the Napa cabbage leaves. Toss all the vegetables together in a large salad bowl.

5 Heat the oil in a skillet and fry the garlic and lemongrass until golden. Add the beef and cook for 3–4 minutes, turning once. Remove from the heat.

6 Slice the beef thinly and toss into the salad with the mint and cilantro. Mix together the dressing ingredients and stir into the skillet, then spoon over the salad. Serve immediately.

Chinese Chicken Salad

This is a refreshing dish, full of contrasting flavors and textures, that is ideal for a light lunch or an al fresco supper on a hot summer's evening.

NUTRITIONAL INFORMATION

Calories 162   Sugars 3g
Protein ....15g   Fat 10g
Carbohydrate ....5g   Saturates 2g

25 mins   25 mins

SERVES 4

I N G R E D I E N T S

8 oz/225 g skinless, boneless chicken breast portions

2 tsp light soy sauce

1 tsp sesame oil

1 tsp sesame seeds

2 tbsp vegetable oil

2 cups bean sprouts

1 red bell pepper, deseeded and thinly sliced

1 carrot, cut into batons

3 baby corn cobs, sliced

S A U C E

2 tsp rice wine vinegar

1 tbsp light soy sauce

dash of chili oil

T O G A R N I S H

chopped chives

carrot batons

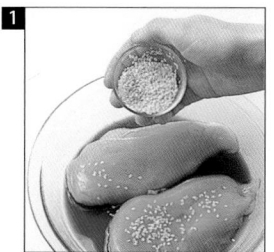 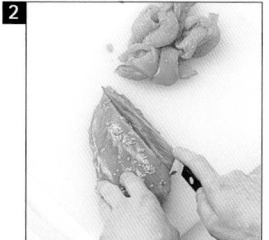 

1 Place the chicken breasts in a shallow glass dish. Combine the soy sauce and sesame oil and pour over the chicken. Sprinkle with the sesame seeds and set aside for 20 minutes, turning occasionally.

2 Remove the chicken from the marinade and cut the meat into thin slices.

3 Heat the vegetable oil in a preheated wok or large skillet. Add the chicken and cook for 4–5 minutes until cooked through and golden brown on both sides. Remove the chicken from the wok with a slotted spoon, set aside, and let cool.

4 Add the bean sprouts, sliced bell pepper, carrot batons, and baby corn cobs to the wok and stir-fry over medium heat for 2–3 minutes. Remove the

vegetables from the wok with a slotted spoon, set aside, and let cool.

5 To make the sauce, combine the rice wine vinegar, light soy sauce, and chili oil.

6 Arrange the chicken and vegetables together on a serving plate. Spoon the sauce over the salad, garnish with chives and carrot batons, and serve.

Soups and Light Meals

There is nothing to compare with homemade soup—even the aroma as it is cooking is appetizing. Light, delicately flavored soups, served hot or chilled, are a wonderful way to start a meal and stimulate the appetite, while hearty soups, brimming with vegetables, chicken, or seafood, are warming and  satisfying. Serve them with some fresh crusty bread and you have a meal in a bowl. This chapter also features other good ideas for light lunches and suppers, from Mexican tacos to Italian risottos. Recipes for all tastes include new variations on stir-fries, omelets, hash, crêpes, and even the humble baked potato.

Spinach Soup

This soup has a rich brilliant color and an intense pure flavor.
Ready-washed spinach makes it especially quick to make.

NUTRITIONAL INFORMATION

Calories	98	Sugars	.........4g
Protein	.........4g	Fat	...........4g
Carbohydrate	...12g	Saturates	.......1g

 10 mins   40 mins

SERVES 4

INGREDIENTS

1 tbsp olive oil

1 onion, halved and thinly sliced

1 leek, split lengthwise and thinly sliced

1 potato, finely diced

4 cups water

2 sprigs fresh marjoram sprigs or ¼ tsp dried marjoram

2 fresh thyme sprigs of ¼ tsp dried thyme

1 bay leaf

14 oz/400 g young spinach

freshly grated nutmeg

salt and pepper

4 tbsp light cream, to serve

1 Heat the oil in a heavy pan over medium heat. Add the onion and leek and cook, stirring occasionally, for about 3 minutes until they are just beginning to soften.

2 Add the potato, water, marjoram, thyme, and bay leaf and season with a pinch of salt. Bring to a boil, reduce the heat, cover, and cook gently for about 25 minutes until the vegetables are tender. Remove the bay leaf and the herb stems.

3 Add the spinach and continue cooking for 3–4 minutes, stirring frequently, just until it is completely wilted. Remove the pan from the heat and set aside to cool slightly.

4 Transfer the soup to a blender or food processor and process to a smooth smooth purée, working in batches if necessary. (If using a food processor, strain off the cooking liquid and reserve. Process the soup solids with enough cooking liquid to moisten them, then combine with the remaining liquid.)

5 Return the soup to the pan and thin with a little more water, if wished. Season to taste with salt, pepper, and nutmeg. Place over low heat and simmer until reheated. Ladle the soup into warmed bowls and swirl a tablespoonful of cream into each serving.

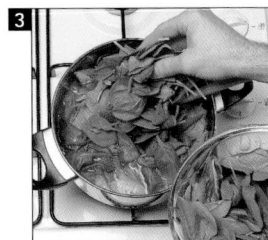

Green Vegetable Soup

This soup takes advantage of summer vegetables bursting with flavor.
If you find fresh small cannellini or other fresh beans, be sure to use them.

NUTRITIONAL INFORMATION

Calories ....260 Sugars 7g
Protein ....12g Fat 15g
Carbohydrate ...21g Saturates 4g

 15 mins   45 mins

SERVES 6

INGREDIENTS

1 tbsp olive oil

1 onion, finely chopped

1 large leek, split and thinly sliced

1 celery stalk, thinly sliced

1 carrot, quartered and thinly sliced

1 garlic clove, finely chopped

6¼ cups water

1 potato, diced

1 parsnip, finely diced

1 small kohlrabi or turnip, diced

150 g/5½ oz green beans, cut in
small pieces

5½ oz/150 g fresh or frozen peas

2 small zucchini, quartered lengthwise
and sliced

14 oz/400 g can small cannellini beans,
drained and rinsed

3½ oz/100 g spinach leaves, cut into
thin ribbons

salt and pepper

PESTO

1 large garlic clove, very finely chopped

½ cup fresh basil leaves

1 cup freshly grated Parmesan cheese

4 tbsp extra virgin olive oil

1 Heat the oil in a large pan. Cook the onion and leek over low heat, stirring occasionally, for 5 minutes. Add the celery, carrot, and garlic, cover, and cook for a further 5 minutes.

2 Add the water, potato, parsnip, kohlrabi or turnip, and green beans. Bring to a boil, reduce the heat, cover, and simmer for 5 minutes.

3 Add the peas, zucchini, and small cannellini beans and season to taste.

Cover and simmer for about 25 minutes until all the vegetables are tender.

4 Meanwhile, make the pesto. Put all the ingredients in a food processor and process until smooth, scraping down the sides as necessary. Alternatively, pound together using a pestle and mortar.

5 Add the spinach to the soup and simmer for 5 minutes. Stir a spoon of the pesto into the soup. Ladle into bowls and pass the remaining pesto separately.

Celery Root & Potato Soup

It is hard to imagine that celery root, a coarse, knobby vegetable, can taste so sweet. It makes a wonderfully flavorsome soup.

NUTRITIONAL INFORMATION

Calories 20   Sugars 1.3g
Protein ....0.8g   Fat 0.7g
Carbohydrate ...2.7g   Saturates 0.4g

 10 mins   35 mins

SERVES 4

INGREDIENTS

1 tbsp butter

1 onion, chopped

2 large leeks, halved lengthwise and sliced

1 lb 10 oz/750 g celery root, peeled and cubed

8 oz/225 g potatoes, cubed

1 carrot, quartered and thinly sliced

5 cups water

pinch of dried marjoram

1 bay leaf

freshly grated nutmeg

salt and pepper

celery leaves, to garnish

1 Melt the butter in a large pan over medium–low heat. Add the onion and leeks and cook, stirring frequently, until just softened; do not let color.

2 Add the celery root, potatoes, carrot, water, marjoram, and bay leaf with a pinch of salt. Bring to a boil, reduce the heat, cover, and simmer for about 25 minutes until the vegetables are tender. Remove and discard the bay leaf.

3 Let the soup cool slightly. Transfer to a blender or food processor and process until smooth. (If using a food processor, strain off the cooking liquid and reserve. Purée the soup solids with enough cooking liquid to moisten them, then combine with the remaining liquid.)

4 Return the puréed soup to the pan. Stir to blend the ingredients thoroughly.

Season the soup with nutmeg, salt, and pepper to taste, then simmer over medium–low heat until it is reheated.

5 Ladle the soup into warm bowls, garnish with celery leaves, and then serve immediately.

Tarragon Pea Soup

This soup is simple and quick to make using frozen peas and stock made from a bouillon cube, ingredients you are likely to have at hand.

NUTRITIONAL INFORMATION

Calories 129   Sugars 6g
Protein ....9g   Fat 4g
Carbohydrate ...16g   Saturates 2g

 10 mins   55 mins

SERVES 4

I N G R E D I E N T S

2 tsp butter

1 onion, finely chopped

2 leeks, finely chopped

1½ tbsp white rice

4½ cups frozen peas

4 cups water

1 chicken or vegetable bouillon cube

½ tsp dried tarragon

salt and pepper

chopped hard-cooked egg or croûtons,
  to garnish

1 Melt the butter in a large pan over medium-low heat. Add the onion, leeks, and rice. Cover and cook, stirring occasionally, for about 10 minutes until the vegetables are softened.

2 Add the peas, water, bouillon cube, and tarragon and bring just to a boil. Season with a little pepper. Cover and simmer gently, stirring occasionally, for about 35 minutes until the vegetables are very tender.

3 Let the soup cool slightly, then transfer to a blender or food processor, and process to a smooth purée, in batches if necessary. (If using a food processor, strain off the cooking liquid and reserve. Purée the soup solids with enough cooking liquid to moisten them, then combine with the remaining liquid.)

4 Return the soup to the pan. Taste and adjust the seasoning. Gently reheat the soup over low heat for about 10 minutes until hot.

5 Ladle into warm bowls and garnish with hard-cooked egg or croûtons.

VARIATION
Substitute frozen green beans for the peas and omit the tarragon, replacing it with a little dried thyme and/or marjoram.

Sweet & Sour Cabbage Soup

This healthy soup is made with an unusual combination of fruits and vegetables, creating a tantalizing flavor that will keep people guessing.

NUTRITIONAL INFORMATION

Calories 103	Sugars 24g
Protein 2g	Fat 0g
Carbohydrate . . .25g	Saturates 0g

 25 mins   1½ hrs

SERVES 4–6

INGREDIENTS

½ cup golden raisins

½ cup orange juice

1 tbsp olive oil

1 large onion, chopped

9 oz/250 g cabbage, shredded

2 apples, peeled and diced

½ cup apple juice

14 oz/400 g can peeled tomatoes

1 cup tomato or vegetable juice

3½ oz/100 g pineapple flesh, finely chopped

5 cups water

2 tsp wine vinegar

salt and pepper

fresh mint leaves, to garnish

1 Put the golden raisins in a bowl, pour the orange juice over them, and set aside to soak for 15 minutes.

2 Heat the oil in a large pan over medium heat. Add the onion and cook, stirring occasionally, for 3–4 minutes until it starts to soften. Add the cabbage and cook for a further 2 minutes, but do not let it brown.

3 Add the apples and apple juice, cover, and cook for 5 minutes. Stir in the tomatoes, tomato juice, pineapple, and water. Season to taste with salt and pepper and add the vinegar. Add the golden raisins with the orange juice. Bring to a boil, lower the heat, partially cover, and simmer for 1 hour until the fruit and vegetables are tender.

4 Remove the pan from the heat and set aside to cool slightly. Transfer the soup to a blender or food processor and process to a smooth purée, working in batches if necessary. (If using a food processor, strain off the cooking liquid and reserve. Purée the soup solids with enough cooking liquid to moisten them, then combine with the remaining liquid.)

5 Return the soup to the pan and simmer gently for about 10 minutes to reheat. Ladle into warm bowls. Garnish with mint leaves and serve immediately.

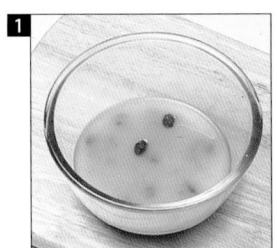

COOK'S TIP

You can use green or white cabbage to make this soup, but red cabbage would require a much longer cooking time. Savoy cabbage has too powerful a flavor.

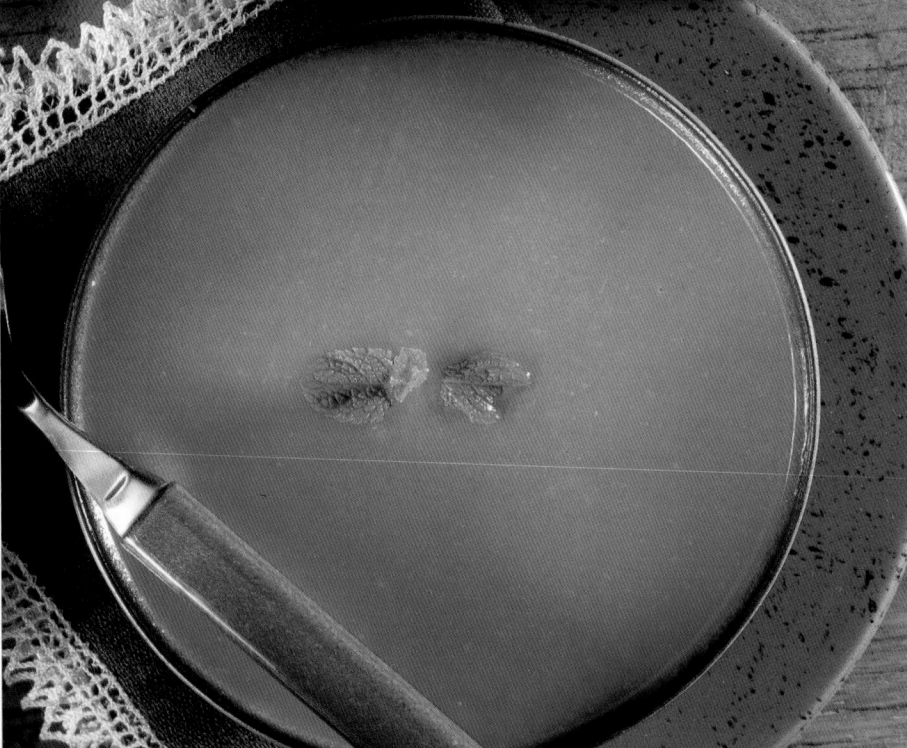

Parsnip Soup with Ginger

The exotic flavors give this simple soup a lift. If you wish, use bought ginger purée instead of grating it; add to taste as the strength varies.

NUTRITIONAL INFORMATION

Calories 151   Sugars 19g
Protein . . . . .4g   Fat 3g
Carbohydrate . . .29g   Saturates 0g

 10 mins   55 mins

SERVES 6

I N G R E D I E N T S

2 tsp olive oil

1 large onion, chopped

1 large leek, sliced

1 lb 12 oz/800 g parsnips, sliced

2 carrots, thinly sliced

4 tbsp grated fresh ginger root

2–3 garlic cloves, finely chopped

grated rind of ½ orange

6¼ cups water

1 cup orange juice

salt and pepper

chopped chives or slivers of scallion,
    to garnish

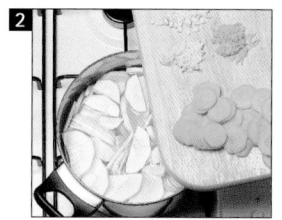

1 Heat the olive oil in a large pan over medium heat. Add the onion and leek and cook, stirring occasionally, for about 5 minutes until softened.

2 Add the parsnips, carrots, ginger, garlic, grated orange rind, water, and a pinch of salt. Reduce the heat, cover, and simmer, stirring occasionally, for about 40 minutes until the vegetables have softened.

3 Remove from the heat and set aside to cool slightly, then transfer to a blender or food processor, and process to a smooth purée, in batches if necessary.

4 Return the soup to the pan and stir in the orange juice. Add a little water or more orange juice, if you prefer a thinner consistency. Taste and adjust the seasoning with salt and pepper.

5 Simmer for about 10 minutes to heat through. Ladle into warmed bowls, garnish with chives or slivers of scallion and serve immediately.

VARIATION

You could make the soup using equal amounts (1 lb/450 g each) of carrots and parsnips.

Exotic Mushroom Soup

This soup has an intense, earthy flavor that brings to mind woodland aromas. It makes a memorable, rich-tasting appetizer.

NUTRITIONAL INFORMATION

Calories 130   Sugars 5g
Protein ....3g   Fat 9g
Carbohydrate ....6g   Saturates 5g

20 mins   1 hr

SERVES 4

INGREDIENTS

1 oz/25 g dried porcini mushrooms

1½ cups boiling water

4½ oz/125 g fresh porcini mushrooms

2 tsp olive oil

1 celery stalk, chopped

1 carrot, chopped

1 onion, chopped

3 garlic cloves, crushed

5 cups vegetable stock or water

leaves from 2 fresh thyme sprigs

1 tbsp butter

3 tbsp dry or medium sherry

2–3 tbsp sour cream

salt and pepper

chopped fresh parsley, to garnish

1 Put the dried mushrooms in a bowl and pour a boiling water over them. Set aside to soak for 10–15 minutes.

2 Brush or wash the fresh mushrooms. Trim and reserve the stems. Slice any large mushroom caps.

3 Heat the oil in a large pan over medium heat. Add the celery, carrot, onion, and mushroom stems. Cook, stirring frequently, for about 8 minutes until the onion begins to color. Stir in the garlic and continue cooking for 1 minute.

4 Add the vegetable stock or water and thyme leaves with a pinch of salt. Using a slotted spoon, transfer the soaked dried mushrooms to the pan. Strain the soaking liquid through a cheesecloth-lined strainer into the pan. Bring to a boil, reduce the heat, partially cover, and simmer gently for 30–40 minutes or until the carrots are tender.

5 Remove the pan from the heat and set aside to cool slightly, then transfer the soup solids with enough of the cooking liquid to moisten to a blender or food processor, and process to a smooth purée. Return it to the pan, combine with the remaining cooking liquid, cover, and simmer gently.

6 Meanwhile, melt the butter in a skillet over medium heat. Add the fresh mushroom caps and season to taste with salt and pepper. Cook, stirring occasionally, for about 8 minutes until they start to color, stirring more frequently as the liquid evaporates. When the skillet becomes dry, add the sherry and cook briefly.

7 Add the mushrooms and sherry to the soup. Taste and adjust the seasoning, if necessary. Ladle into warmed soup bowls, put a spoon of sour cream in each and garnish with parsley and serve.

Provençal Fish Soup

For the best results, you need to use flavorful fish, such as cod or haddock, for this recipe. Frozen fish fillets are also suitable.

NUTRITIONAL INFORMATION

Calories ....122 Sugars 6g
Protein ....12g Fat 3g
Carbohydrate ....7g Saturates 0g

 10 mins   1½ hrs

SERVES 4–6

I N G R E D I E N T S

1 tbsp olive oil

2 onions, finely chopped

1 small leek, thinly sliced

1 small carrot, finely chopped

1 celery stalk, finely chopped

1 small fennel bulb, finely chopped (optional)

3 garlic cloves, finely chopped

1 cup dry white wine

14 oz/400 g can tomatoes

1 bay leaf

pinch of fennel seeds

2 strips of orange rind

¼ tsp saffron threads

5 cups water

12 oz/350 g white fish fillets, skinned

salt and pepper

croûtons, to serve (optional)

2 Add the wine and simmer for 1 minute. Add the tomatoes, bay leaf, fennel seeds, orange rind, saffron, and water. Bring just to a boil, reduce the heat, cover, and simmer gently, stirring occasionally, for 30 minutes.

3 Add the fish and cook for a further 20–30 minutes until it flakes easily. Remove the bay leaf and orange rind.

4 Remove the pan from the heat and set aside to cool slightly, then transfer to a blender or food processor,

and process to a smooth purée, working in batches if necessary. (If using a food processor, strain off the cooking liquid and reserve. Purée the soup solids with enough cooking liquid to moisten them, then combine with the remaining liquid.)

5 Return the soup to the pan. Taste and adjust the seasoning, if necessary, and simmer for 5–10 minutes until heated through. Ladle the soup into warmed bowls and sprinkle with croûtons, if using. Serve.

1 Heat the oil in a large pan over medium heat. Add the onions and cook, stirring occasionally, for about 5 minutes until softened. Add the leek, carrot, celery, fennel, if using, and garlic and continue cooking for 4–5 minutes until the leek is wilted.

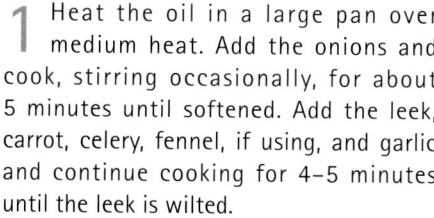   

Fennel & Tomato Soup

This light and refreshing soup is also good served cold. It is an ideal appetizer for a summer meal, served with crunchy melba toast.

NUTRITIONAL INFORMATION

Calories	110	Sugars	8g
Protein	10g	Fat	2g
Carbohydrate	13g	Saturates	0g

 30 mins 40 mins

SERVES 4

I N G R E D I E N T S

2 tsp olive oil

1 large onion, halved and sliced

2 large fennel bulbs, halved and sliced

1 small potato, diced

3¾ cups water

1⅔ cups tomato juice

1 bay leaf

1 cup peeled cooked shrimp

2 tomatoes, peeled, deseeded, and chopped

½ tsp snipped fresh dill

salt and pepper

fresh dill sprigs or fennel fronds, to garnish

1 Heat the olive oil in a large pan over medium heat. Add the sliced onion and fennel and cook, stirring occasionally, for 3–4 minutes until the onion is just softened, but not browned.

2 Add the potato, water, tomato juice, and bay leaf with a pinch of salt. Reduce the heat, cover, and simmer for about 25 minutes, stirring once or twice, until the vegetables are soft.

3 Remove the pan from the heat and set the soup aside to cool slightly, then transfer to a blender or food processor, and process until smooth, working in

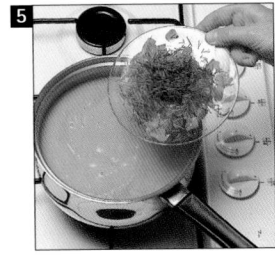

batches if necessary. (If using a food processor, strain off the cooking liquid and reserve. Purée the soup solids with enough cooking liquid to moisten them, then combine with the remaining liquid.)

4 Return the soup to the pan and add the shrimp. Simmer gently for about 10 minutes to reheat the soup and let it absorb the shrimp flavor.

5 Stir in the tomatoes and dill. Taste and adjust the seasoning, adding more salt, if needed, and pepper. Thin the soup with a little more tomato juice, if desired. Ladle into warm bowls, garnish with dill sprigs or fennel fronds, and serve.

Thai-Style Seafood Soup

As taste and tolerance for chiles varies, using chili purée, instead of fresh chiles, offers more control of the heat.

NUTRITIONAL INFORMATION

Calories	132	Sugars	.........7g
Protein	........20g	Fat	..........2g
Carbohydrate	....9g	Saturates	.......0g

 10 mins   20 mins

SERVES 4

INGREDIENTS

5 cups fish stock

1 lemongrass stalk, split lengthwise

pared rind of ½ lime or 1 lime leaf

1 inch/2.5 cm piece of fresh ginger root, sliced

¼ tsp chili purée

4–6 scallions, sliced

7 oz/200 g large of medium raw shrimp, peeled and deveined

9 oz/250 g scallops (about 16–20)

2 tbsp fresh cilantro leaves

salt

finely chopped red bell pepper or fresh red chile rings, to garnish

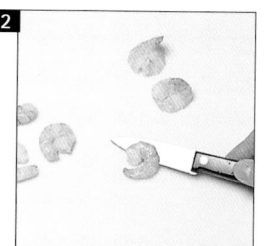

1 Put the stock in a pan with the lemongrass, lime rind or lime leaf, ginger, and chili purée. Bring just to a boil, reduce the heat, cover, and simmer for 10–15 minutes.

2 Cut the scallions in half lengthwise, then slice crosswise very thinly. Cut the shrimp almost in half lengthwise, keeping the tails intact.

3 Strain the stock, return to the pan, and bring to a simmer, with bubbles rising at the edges and the surface trembling. Add the scallions and cook for 2–3 minutes. Taste and season with salt, if needed, and stir in a little more chili purée if wished.

4 Add the scallops and shrimp and poach for about 1 minute until they turn opaque and the shrimp curl.

5 Add the cilantro leaves, ladle the soup into warmed bowls, and garnish with red bell pepper or chiles.

VARIATION
Substitute very small baby leeks, slivered or thinly sliced diagonally, for the scallions. Include the green parts.

Caribbean Seafood Soup

This pretty soup is packed with exotic flavors. It is traditionally made with local vegetables, but potato and spinach are practical alternatives.

NUTRITIONAL INFORMATION

Calories	106	Sugars	4g
Protein	14g	Fat	1g
Carbohydrate	11g	Saturates	0g

 10 mins   45 mins

SERVES 4–6

INGREDIENTS

1½ cups peeled medium shrimp

7 oz/200 g firm white fish fillets, skinned and cubed

¾ tsp ground coriander

¼ tsp ground cumin

1 tsp chili purée

3 tbsp fresh lemon juice

1 tbsp butter

1 onion, halved and thinly sliced

2 large leeks, thinly sliced

3 garlic cloves, finely chopped

1 large potato, diced

5 cups chicken or vegetable stock

9 oz/250 g spinach leaves

½ cup coconut milk

salt and pepper

1 Put the shrimp and fish in a bowl with the coriander, cumin, chili purée, and lemon juice and set aside to marinate.

2 Melt the butter in a large pan over medium heat. Add the onion and leeks, cover, and cook, stirring occasionally, for about 10 minutes until they are softened. Add the garlic and cook for a further 3–4 minutes.

3 Add the potato and stock and season to taste with salt. Bring to a boil, reduce the heat, cover, and simmer gently for about 15–20 minutes until the potato is tender.

4 Stir in the spinach and continue cooking, uncovered, for about 3 minutes until it is just wilted.

5 Remove the pan from the heat and set aside to cool slightly, then transfer to a blender or food processor, in batches if necessary. Purée the soup until smooth. (If using a food processor, strain off the cooking liquid and reserve. Purée the soup solids with enough cooking liquid to moisten them, then combine with the remaining liquid.)

6 Return the soup to the pan and stir in the coconut milk. Add the fish and shrimp with their marinade. Simmer over medium-low heat, stirring gently, but frequently, for about 8 minutes until the soup is heated through and the fish is cooked and flakes easily.

7 Taste and adjust the seasoning, if necessary, adding more chili purée and/or lemon juice if wished. Ladle into warmed bowls and serve immediately.

Beef Broth

This light, lean soup is studded with small diced vegetables and fragrant herbs. The stock may be used as a basis for other soups.

NUTRITIONAL INFORMATION

Calories	21	Sugars	. . . . .3g
Protein	. . . . .1g	Fat	. . . . .1g
Carbohydrate	. . . .4g	Saturates	. . . . . . .0g

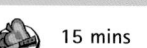 15 mins   5¼ hrs

SERVES 4–6

INGREDIENTS

7 oz/200 g celery root, finely diced

2 large carrots, finely diced

2 tsp chopped fresh marjoram

2 tsp chopped fresh parsley

2 plum tomatoes, peeled, deseeded, and diced

salt and pepper

BEEF STOCK

1 lb 4 oz/550 g boneless beef shin or stewing steak, cut into large cubes

1 lb 10 oz/750 g veal, beef, or pork bones

2 onions, quartered

5¼ pints/2.5 liters water

4 garlic cloves, sliced

2 carrots, sliced

1 large leek, sliced

1 celery stalk, cut into 2 inch/5 cm pieces

1 bay leaf

4–5 fresh thyme sprigs or ¼ tsp dried thyme

salt

  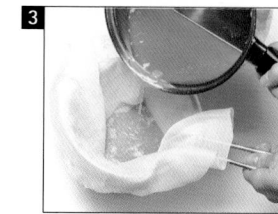

1 To make the stock, trim the fat from the beef and put the beef and the fat into a large roasting pan with the bones and onions. Roast in a preheated oven, 375°F/190°C, for 30–40 minutes until browned, turning once or twice.

Transfer the ingredients to a large flameproof casserole and then discard the beef fat.

2 Add the water (it should cover by at least 2 inches/5 cm) and bring to a boil. Skim off any foam, reduce the heat, and add the garlic, carrots, leek, celery, bay leaf, thyme, and a pinch of salt. Simmer very gently for 4 hours, skimming occasionally. If the ingredients emerge from the liquid, top up with water.

3 Strain the stock through a cheesecloth-lined strainer into a large container and remove as much fat as possible. Discard the bones and vegetables, but save the meat if wished.

4 Boil the stock very gently until it is reduced to 6½ cups. Taste and adjust the seasoning if necessary.

5 Bring a pan of salted water to a boil and add the celery root and carrots. Reduce the heat, cover, and simmer for about 15 minutes until tender. Drain.

6 Add the herbs to a boiling beef stock. Divide the cooked vegetables and tomatoes among warmed bowls, ladle over the stock, and serve.

Chicken Soup with Stars

How delicious a simple, fresh soup can be. Chicken wings are good to use for making the stock, as the meat is very sweet and doesn't dry out.

NUTRITIONAL INFORMATION

Calories 119	Sugars 2g	
Protein 14g	Fat 2g	
Carbohydrate . . .13g	Saturates 0g	

 20 mins   2¾ hrs

SERVES 5–6

I N G R E D I E N T S

¾ cup small pasta stars, or other very small shapes

chopped fresh parsley

C H I C K E N   S T O C K

2 lb 12 oz/1.25 kg chicken pieces, such as wings or legs

5¼ pints/2.5 liters water

1 celery stalk, sliced

1 large carrot, sliced

1 onion, sliced

1 leek, sliced

2 garlic cloves, crushed

8 peppercorns

4 allspice berries

3–4 parsley stems

2–3 fresh thyme sprigs

1 bay leaf

salt and pepper

2 Remove the chicken from the stock and set aside to cool. Continue simmering the stock, uncovered, for about 30 minutes. When the chicken is cool enough to handle, remove the meat from the bones and, if necessary, cut into bite-size pieces.

3 Strain the stock and remove as much fat as possible. Discard the vegetables and flavorings. (There should be about 7½ cups chicken stock.)

4 Bring the stock to a boil in a clean pan. Add the pasta and lower the heat so that the stock boils very gently. Cook for about 10 minutes or until the pasta is tender, but still firm to the bite.

5 Stir in the chicken meat. Taste the soup and adjust the seasoning if necessary. Ladle into warmed bowls and serve sprinkled with parsley.

1 Put the chicken in a large flameproof casserole with the water, celery, carrot, onion, leek, garlic, peppercorns, allspice, herbs, and ½ teaspoon salt. Bring just to a boil and skim off the foam that rises to the surface. Reduce the heat, partially cover, and simmer, for 2 hours.

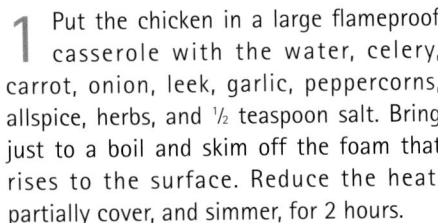  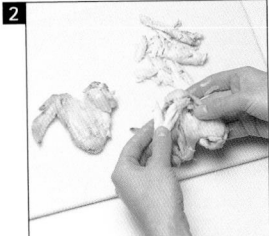 

Chicken & Rice Soup

Any kind of rice is suitable for this soup—white or brown long grain rice, or even wild rice. Leftover cooked rice is a handy addition for soups.

NUTRITIONAL INFORMATION

Calories 165	Sugars 2g	
Protein 14g	Fat 4g	
Carbohydrate ...19g	Saturates 1g	

5 mins   25 mins

SERVES 4

INGREDIENTS

6½ cups chicken stock (see Cook's Tip)

2 small carrots, very thinly sliced

1 celery stalk, finely diced

1 baby leek, halved lengthwise and
thinly sliced

1 cup baby peas, thawed if frozen

1 cup cooked rice

5½ oz/150 g cooked chicken meat, sliced

2 tsp chopped fresh tarragon

1 tbsp chopped fresh parsley

salt and pepper

fresh parsley sprigs, to garnish

crusty bread, to serve

1 Put the chicken stock in a large pan and add the carrots, celery, and leek. Bring to a boil, reduce the heat to low, partially cover, and simmer gently for 10 minutes until the vegetables are tender.

2 Stir in the peas, rice, and chicken meat and continue cooking for a further 10–15 minutes or until the vegetables are tender.

3 Add the chopped tarragon and parsley and season to taste with salt and pepper as needed.

4 Ladle the soup into warmed bowls, garnish with fresh parsley sprigs, and serve immediately with crusty bread.

COOK'S TIP

If the stock you are using is a little weak or if you have used a bouillon cube, add the herbs at the beginning, so that they can flavor the stock for a longer time.

Provençal Turkey Soup

No need to wait for Thanksgiving leftovers—pre-packed turkey, such as boneless breast or stir-fry meat, makes this a year-round favorite.

NUTRITIONAL INFORMATION

Calories	...216	Sugars	...8g
Protein	...25g	Fat	...6g
Carbohydrate	...10g	Saturates	...1g

 10 mins   50 mins

SERVES 4–5

INGREDIENTS

1 tbsp olive oil

2 red, yellow, or green bell peppers, deseeded and finely chopped

1 celery stalk, thinly sliced

1 large onion, finely chopped

½ cup dry white wine

14 oz/400 g can plum tomatoes

3–4 garlic cloves, finely chopped

4 cups turkey or chicken stock

¼ tsp dried thyme

1 bay leaf

2 zucchini, finely diced

12 oz/350 g cooked diced turkey

salt and pepper

fresh basil leaves, to garnish

1 Heat the oil in a large pan over medium heat. Add the bell peppers, celery, and onion and cook for about 8 minutes until softened and just beginning to color.

2 Add the wine and simmer for 1 minute. Add the tomatoes and garlic.

3 Stir in the stock. Add the thyme and bay leaf, season to taste with salt and pepper, and bring to a boil. Reduce the heat, cover, and simmer for about 25 minutes until the vegetables are tender.

4 Add the zucchini and turkey. Continue cooking for a further 10–15 minutes until the zucchini are completely tender.

5 Taste the soup and adjust the seasoning if necessary. Ladle into warmed bowls, garnish with basil leaves, and serve immediately.

COOK'S TIP

A large turkey leg can be used to make this soup. Put in a pan, add water to cover generously, and add 1 each carrot, celery stalk, leek, and onion, coarsely chopped, and a little salt. Poach for 3 hours. Remove the fat from the stock before making the soup.

Asian Duck Broth

This soup combines delicate flavors with a satisfying meaty taste. Although duck is notoriously fatty, the legs are leaner than the breast.

NUTRITIONAL INFORMATION

Calories	98	Sugars	........4g
Protein	.........9g	Fat	...........3g
Carbohydrate	....9g	Saturates	.......1g

10 mins   1¾ hrs

SERVES 4–6

INGREDIENTS

2 duck leg quarters, skinned

4 cups water

2½ cups chicken stock

1 inch/2.5 cm piece of fresh ginger root, sliced

1 large carrot, sliced

1 onion, sliced

1 leek, sliced

3 garlic cloves, crushed

I tsp black peppercorns

2 tbsp soy sauce

I small carrot, cut into thin strips or slivers

I small leek, cut into thin strips or slivers

1½ cups thinly sliced shiitake mushrooms

1 oz/25 g watercress leaves

salt and pepper

1 Put the duck in a large pan with the water. Bring just to a boil and skim off the foam that rises to the surface. Add the stock, ginger, carrot, onion, leek, garlic, peppercorns, and soy sauce. Reduce the heat, partially cover, and simmer gently for 1½ hours.

2 Remove the duck from the stock and set aside. When the duck is cool enough to handle, remove the meat from the bones, and slice thinly or shred into bite-size pieces, discarding any fat.

3 Strain the stock and press with the back of a spoon to extract all the liquid. Remove as much fat as possible. Discard the vegetables and flavorings.

4 Bring the stock just to a boil in a clean pan and add the strips of carrot and leek and the mushrooms with the duck meat. Reduce the heat and simmer gently for 5 minutes or until the carrot is just tender.

5 Stir in the watercress leaves and continue simmering for 1–2 minutes until they are wilted. Taste the soup and adjust the seasoning if necessary, adding a little more soy sauce if desired. Ladle the soup into warmed soup bowls and then serve immediately.

White Bean Soup

In this elegant soup, the pungent green olive purée provides a pleasant counterpoint to the natural sweetness of the beans.

NUTRITIONAL INFORMATION

Calories	 286	Sugars	.... 3g
Protein	.... 11g	Fat	.... 14g
Carbohydrate	... 30g	Saturates	.... 2g

 6¼ hrs   2 hrs

SERVES 8

INGREDIENTS

1¾ cups dried navy beans

1 tbsp olive oil

1 large onion, finely chopped

1 large leek (white part only), thinly sliced

3 garlic cloves, finely chopped

2 celery stalks finely chopped

2 small carrots, finely chopped

1 small fennel bulb, finely chopped

4¼ pints/2 liters water

¼ tsp dried thyme

¼ tsp dried marjoram

salt and pepper

TAPENADE

1 garlic clove

1 small bunch of fresh flat leaf parsley, stems removed

9 oz/250 g almond-stuffed green olives, drained

5 tbsp olive oil

1 Pick over the beans, cover generously with cold water, and set aside to soak for 6 hours or overnight. Drain the beans, put in a pan and add cold water to cover by 2 inches/5 cm. Bring to a boil and boil for 10 minutes. Drain and rinse well.

2 Heat the oil in a large heavy pan over medium heat. Add the onion and leek, cover, and cook for about 3–4 minutes, stirring occasionally, until just softened. Add the garlic, celery, carrots, and fennel and continue cooking for 2 minutes.

3 Add the water, beans, thyme, and marjoram. When the mixture begins to simmer, reduce the heat to low. Cover and simmer gently, stirring occasionally, for 1½ hours until the beans are tender.

4 Meanwhile make the tapenade. Put the garlic, parsley, and olives into a blender or food processor with the olive oil. Process to a purée and scrape into a small serving bowl.

5 Remove the pan from the heat and set aside to cool slightly, then transfer to a blender or food processor, and process to a smooth purée, in batches if necessary. (If using a food processor, strain off the cooking liquid and reserve. Purée the soup solids with enough cooking liquid to moisten them, then combine with the remaining liquid.)

6 Return the soup to the pan. Season with salt and pepper to taste and simmer until heated through. Ladle into bowls and serve, stirring a teaspoon of the tapenade into each serving.

Beans & Greens Soup

Include some pungent greens in this soup, if you can. They add a wonderful gutsy flavor and, of course, are very good for you.

NUTRITIONAL INFORMATION

Calories 282   Sugars 8g
Protein . . . . .16g   Fat 4g
Carbohydrate . . .46g   Saturates 1g

 6¼ hrs   2 hrs

SERVES 4

INGREDIENTS

1½ cups dried navy or cannellini beans

1 tbsp olive oil

2 onions, finely chopped

4 garlic cloves, finely chopped

1 celery stalk, thinly sliced

2 carrots, halved and thinly sliced

5 cups water

¼ tsp dried thyme

¼ tsp dried marjoram

1 bay leaf

4 oz/115 g leafy greens, such as Swiss chard, mustard, spinach, and kale, washed

salt and pepper

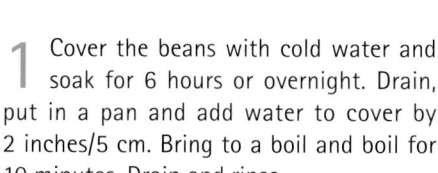

1 Cover the beans with cold water and soak for 6 hours or overnight. Drain, put in a pan and add water to cover by 2 inches/5 cm. Bring to a boil and boil for 10 minutes. Drain and rinse.

2 Heat the olive oil in a large pan over medium heat. Add the onion and cook, stirring occasionally, for about 3–4 minutes until just softened. Add the garlic, celery, and carrots and continue cooking for 2 minutes.

3 Add the water, beans, thyme, marjoram, and bay leaf. When the mixture begins to simmer, reduce the heat to low. Cover and simmer gently, stirring occasionally, for about 1¼ hours until the beans are tender. The cooking time will vary depending on the type of bean. Season to taste with salt and pepper.

4 Remove the pan from the heat and set aside to cool slightly, then transfer 2 cups to a blender or food

processor. Process to a smooth purée and recombine with the soup.

5 Cut the greens crosswise into thin ribbons, keeping tender leaves, such as spinach, separate. Add the thicker leaves and cook gently for 10 minutes. Stir in any remaining greens and cook for a further 5–10 minutes until all the greens are tender. Taste and adjust the seasoning if necessary. Ladle the soup into warmed bowls and serve immediately.

Greek Bean Soup

This is based on a simple soup typical of Greek home cooking.
The artichoke hearts make it fancier, but they are not essential.

NUTRITIONAL INFORMATION

Calories	109	Sugars	7g
Protein	6g	Fat	3g
Carbohydrate	16g	Saturates	0g

 10 mins   1¼ hrs

SERVES 6

I N G R E D I E N T S

1 tbsp olive oil

1 large onion, finely chopped

1 large carrot, finely diced

2 celery stalks, finely chopped

4 tomatoes, peeled, deseeded, and chopped, or 9 oz/250 g drained canned tomatoes

2 garlic cloves, finely chopped

2 x 14 oz/400 g cans cannellini or navy beans, drained and rinsed

5 cups water

1 zucchini, finely diced

grated rind of ½ lemon

1 tbsp chopped fresh mint or ¼ tsp dried mint

1 tsp chopped fresh thyme or ⅛ tsp dried thyme

1 bay leaf

14 oz/400 g can artichoke hearts, drained

salt and pepper

  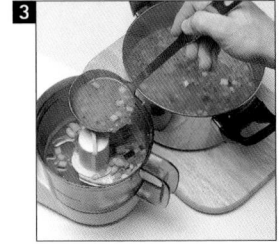

1 Heat 1 teaspoon of the olive oil in a large pan over medium heat. Add the onion and cook, stirring occasionally, for 3–4 minutes until softened. Add the carrot, celery, tomatoes, and garlic and continue cooking for a further 5 minutes, stirring frequently.

2 Add the beans and water. Bring to a boil, reduce the heat, cover, and cook gently for about 10 minutes.

3 Add the zucchini, lemon rind, mint, thyme, and bay leaf and season to taste with salt and pepper. Cover and simmer for about 40 minutes until all the vegetables are tender. Remove the pan from the heat and set aside to cool slightly. Remove the bay leaf and transfer 2 cups of the soup to a blender or food processor, process to a smooth purée, and recombine.

4 Meanwhile, heat the remaining oil in a skillet over medium heat. Fry the artichokes, cut side down, until lightly browned. Turn over and fry long enough to heat through. Ladle the soup into warmed bowls and top each with an artichoke heart. Serve immediately.

Bean & Pumpkin Soup

Pumpkin, a greatly underrated vegetable, balances the spicy heat in this soup and gives it a splash of color, too.

NUTRITIONAL INFORMATION

Calories	170	Sugars	8g
Protein	11g	Fat	3g
Carbohydrate	27g	Saturates	0g

 6¼ hrs   2½ hrs

SERVES 4–6

I N G R E D I E N T S

1½ cups dried kidney beans

1 tbsp olive oil

2 onions, finely chopped

4 garlic cloves, finely chopped

1 celery stalk, thinly sliced

1 carrot, halved and thinly sliced

2 tsp tomato paste

pinch of dried thyme

pinch of dried oregano

pinch of ground cumin

5 cups water

1 bay leaf

14 oz/400 g can chopped tomatoes

2 cups peeled diced pumpkin flesh

¼ tsp chili purée

salt and pepper

fresh cilantro leaves, to garnish

1 Pick over the beans, cover generously with cold water, and set aside to soak for 6 hours or overnight. Drain the beans, put in a pan, and add enough cold water to cover by 2 inches/5 cm. Bring to a boil and boil for 10 minutes. Drain and rinse.

2 Heat the olive oil in a large pan over medium heat. Add the onions and cook, stirring occasionally, for 3–4 minutes until they are just softened. Add the garlic, celery, and carrot and continue cooking for 2 minutes.

3 Add the kidney beans, tomato paste, thyme, oregano, cumin, water, and bay leaf. When the mixture is just beginning to simmer, reduce the heat to low. Cover and simmer gently, stirring occasionally, for 1 hour.

4 Stir in the chopped tomatoes, pumpkin, and chili purée. Continue simmering, stirring occasionally, for approximately 1 hour or until the beans and pumpkin are tender.

5 Season the soup to taste with salt and pepper and stir in a little more chili purée if liked. Ladle the soup into warmed bowls, garnish with cilantro leaves, and serve immediately.

Split Pea & Ham Soup

A hearty and heartwarming soup, this is perfect for weekend lunches—or make it ahead for a nourishing midweek supper, all ready to reheat.

NUTRITIONAL INFORMATION

Calories	300	Sugars	.........5g
Protein	........23g	Fat	...........9g
Carbohydrate	...35g	Saturates	.......2g

 10 mins   1¼–1½ hrs

SERVES 6–8

INGREDIENTS

2¼ cups split green peas

1 tbsp olive oil

1 large onion, finely chopped

1 large carrot, finely chopped

1 celery stalk, finely chopped

4 cups chicken or vegetable stock

4 cups water

8 oz/225 g lean smoked ham, finely diced

¼ tsp dried thyme

¼ tsp dried marjoram

1 bay leaf

salt and pepper

1 Rinse the peas under cold running water. Put in a pan and cover generously with water. Bring to a boil and boil for 3 minutes, skimming off the foam from the surface. Drain the peas.

2 Heat the oil in a large pan over medium heat. Add the onion and cook, stirring occasionally, for about 3–4 minutes, until just softened.

3 Add the carrot and celery and continue cooking for 2 minutes. Add the peas, pour in the stock and water, and stir to combine.

4 Bring just to a boil and stir the ham into the soup. Add the thyme, marjoram, and bay leaf. Reduce the heat, cover, and cook gently for 1–1½ hours until the ingredients are very soft. Remove and discard the bay leaf.

5 Taste and adjust the seasoning if necessary. Ladle into warm soup bowls and serve immediately.

VARIATION
You could add sliced, cooked sausages instead of or in addition to the ham.

Split Pea & Parsnip Soup

This soup is surprisingly delicate. The yellow peas give it an appealing light color, while the parsnips add an aromatic flavor.

NUTRITIONAL INFORMATION

Calories	270	Sugars	.........5g
Protein	........16g	Fat	...........7g
Carbohydrate	...39g	Saturates	.......1g

 10 mins   1 hr

SERVES 4

INGREDIENTS

generous 1 cup split yellow peas

1 tbsp olive oil

1 onion, finely chopped

1 small leek, finely chopped

3 garlic cloves, finely chopped

2 parsnips, sliced (about 8 oz/225 g)

4¼ pints/2 liters water

10 fresh sage leaves or ¼ tsp dried sage

pinch of dried thyme

¼ tsp ground coriander

1 bay leaf

salt and pepper

freshly grated nutmeg

chopped fresh cilantro leaves or parsley, to garnish

1 Rinse the peas well under cold running water. Put in a pan and cover generously with water. Bring to a boil and boil for 3 minutes, skimming off the foam from the surface. Drain the peas.

2 Heat the oil in a large pan over medium heat. Add the onion and leek and cook, stirring occasionally, for about 3 minutes until just softened. Add the garlic and parsnips and continue cooking, stirring occasionally, for 2 minutes.

3 Add the peas, water, sage, thyme, coriander, and bay leaf. Bring almost to a boil, reduce the heat, cover, and simmer gently for about 40 minutes until the vegetables are very soft. Remove the bay leaf.

4 Remove the pan from the heat and set aside to cool slightly, then transfer to a blender or food processor, and process to a smooth purée, in batches if necessary. (If using a food processor, strain off the cooking liquid and reserve. Purée the soup solids with enough cooking liquid to moisten them, then combine with the remaining liquid.)

5 Return the soup to the pan and thin with a little more water, if wished. Season generously with salt, pepper, and nutmeg. Place over low heat and simmer until reheated. Ladle into warmed soup plates and garnish with fresh cilantro leaves or parsley.

Garbanzo Soup with Chorizo

This soup is satisfying and colorful, with an appealing piquancy from the chorizo. Try to find the Iberico style, which is very meaty and lean.

NUTRITIONAL INFORMATION

Calories	394	Sugars	........11g
Protein	........24g	Fat	..........12g
Carbohydrate	...52g	Saturates	.......3g

 10 mins   1¾ hrs

SERVES 4

INGREDIENTS

generous 1 cup dried garbanzo beans, soaked overnight in cold water to cover

4 oz/115 g lean chorizo, skinned and finely diced

1 onion, finely chopped

1 shallot, finely chopped

1 carrot, thinly sliced

2 garlic cloves, finely chopped

14 oz/400 g can chopped tomatoes

5 cups water

1 bay leaf

¼ tsp dried thyme

¼ tsp dried oregano

1¾ cups diced pumpkin

8 oz/225 g potato, diced

1¼ cups finely chopped curly kale leaves

salt and pepper

1 Drain the garbanzo beans and put in a pan with enough cold water to cover generously. Bring to a boil over high heat and cook for 10 minutes. Drain.

2 Put the chorizo in a large, dry pan over medium-low heat. Cook, stirring frequently, for 5–10 minutes to render as much fat as possible. Remove with a draining spoon and drain on absorbent paper towels.

3 Pour off the excess fat from the pan and return to the heat. Add the onion, shallot, carrot, and garlic and cook, stirring occasionally, for 3–4 minutes.

4 Add the garbanzo beans, tomatoes, water, herbs, and chorizo. Bring almost to a boil, reduce the heat, cover, and simmer gently for 30 minutes.

5 Stir in the pumpkin and potato, cover, and continue cooking for about 30 minutes until the garbanzo beans are tender. Season to taste with salt and pepper.

6 Stir in the kale and continue to cook, uncovered, for 15–20 minutes or until it is tender. Taste and adjust the seasoning if necessary. Ladle the soup into warmed bowls and serve immediately.

COOK'S TIP

You can easily chop the kale in a food processor; it should be like chopped parsley. Alternatively, slice crosswise into very thin ribbons.

Hummus & Zucchini Soup

This light and elegant soup couldn't be easier. Its subtle flavor makes it a great starter for entertaining, especially when feeding vegetarians.

NUTRITIONAL INFORMATION

Calories 135	Sugars 3g
Protein 5g	Fat 9g
Carbohydrate 8g	Saturates 0g

10 mins   30 mins

SERVES 4

INGREDIENTS

1 tsp olive oil

1 small onion, sliced

3 zucchini, sliced (about 1 lb/450 g)

2 cups vegetable or chicken stock

6 oz/175 g ready-made hummus

fresh lemon juice, to taste

salt and pepper

finely chopped fresh parsley, to garnish

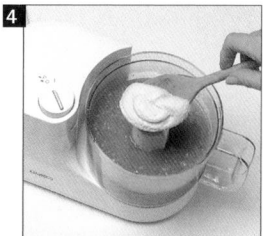

1 Heat the olive oil in a pan over medium heat. Add the onion and zucchini slices, cover, and cook, stirring occasionally, for about 3 minutes until they begin to soften.

2 Add the stock and season lightly with salt and pepper. Bring to a boil, reduce the heat, cover, and simmer gently for about 20 minutes until the vegetables are tender.

3 Remove the pan from the heat and set aside to cool slightly, then transfer to a blender or food processor, and process to a smooth purée. (If using a food processor, strain off the liquid and reserve. Purée the soup solids with enough cooking liquid to moisten them, then combine with the remaining liquid.)

4 Add the hummus to the puréed soup in the blender or processor and process to combine.

5 Return the soup to the pan and reheat gently over medium-low heat. Taste and adjust the seasoning, if necessary, adding a little lemon juice if wished. Ladle into warmed bowls, sprinkle with parsley, and serve immediately.

COOK'S TIP
If you wish, peel the zucchini. It gives the soup a nice pale color.

Tomato & Lentil Soup

This soup is simple and satisfying, with subtle flavors. It uses ingredients you are likely to have at hand, so it's ideal for a last-minute meal.

NUTRITIONAL INFORMATION

Calories 197   Sugars 9g
Protein . . . . .12g   Fat 3g
Carbohydrate . . .33g   Saturates 0g

🦪 🦪

🥘 10 mins   🕐 1 hr

SERVES 6

INGREDIENTS

1 tbsp olive oil

1 leek, thinly sliced

1 large carrot, quartered and thinly sliced

1 large onion, finely chopped

2 garlic cloves, finely chopped

generous 1 cup split red lentils

5 cups water

1½ cups tomato juice

14 oz/400 g can chopped tomatoes

¼ tsp ground cumin

¼ tsp ground coriander

1 bay leaf

salt and pepper

chopped fresh dill or parsley, to garnish

1 Heat the oil in a large pan over medium heat. Add the leek, carrot, onion, and garlic. Cover and cook, stirring occasionally, for 4–5 minutes until the vegetables are slightly softened.

2 Rinse and drain the lentils (check for any small stones). Add the lentils to the pan and stir in the water, tomato juice, and tomatoes. Add the cumin, coriander, and bay leaf with a pinch of salt. Bring to a boil, reduce the heat, and simmer gently for about 45 minutes or until the vegetables are tender. Remove the bay leaf.

3 Remove the pan from the heat and set aside to cool slightly. If you prefer a smooth soup, transfer the mixture to a blender or food processor and process to a smooth purée, working in batches if necessary. (If using a food processor, strain off the cooking liquid and reserve. Purée the soup solids with enough cooking liquid to moisten them, then combine with the remaining liquid.) Process only about half of the mixture if you prefer a soup with a chunkier texture.

4 Return the puréed soup to the pan and stir to blend. Season with salt and pepper to taste. Simmer over medium-low heat until reheated.

5 Ladle the soup into warm bowls, garnish with dill or parsley, and serve.

Golden Vegetable Soup

In this simple-to-make soup, the flavors meld after blending to create a delicious taste. It is also very healthy and looks appealing.

NUTRITIONAL INFORMATION

Calories	155	Sugars	.........5g
Protein	........10g	Fat	...........3g
Carbohydrate	...22g	Saturates	.......0g

 10 mins 1½ hrs

SERVES 6

INGREDIENTS

1 tbsp olive oil

1 onion, finely chopped

1 garlic clove, finely chopped

1 carrot, halved and thinly sliced

1 lb/450 g green cabbage, shredded

14 oz/400 g can chopped tomatoes

½ tsp dried thyme

2 bay leaves

6¾ cups vegetable stock

scant 1 cup Puy lentils

2 cups water

salt and pepper

fresh cilantro leaves or parsley, to garnish

1 Heat the oil in a large pan over medium heat. Add the onion, garlic, and carrot and cook, stirring occasionally, for 3–4 minutes. Add the cabbage and cook for a further 2 minutes.

2 Add the tomatoes, thyme, and 1 bay leaf, then pour in the stock. Bring to a boil, reduce the heat, partially cover, and simmer for about 45 minutes until the vegetables are tender.

3 Meanwhile, put the lentils in another pan with the remaining bay leaf and the water. Bring just to a boil, reduce the heat, and simmer for about 25 minutes until tender. Drain off any remaining water and set aside.

4 Remove the soup pan from the heat and set aside to cool slightly, then transfer to a blender or food processor, and process to a smooth purée, working in batches, if necessary. (If using a food processor, strain off the cooking liquid and reserve. Purée the soup solids with enough cooking liquid to moisten them, then combine with the remaining liquid.)

5 Return the soup to the pan and add the cooked lentils. Taste and adjust the seasoning, if necessary, and cook for about 10 minutes to heat through. Ladle into warm bowls and garnish with coriander leaves or parsley.

Mushroom & Barley Soup

This old-fashioned soup is nourishing and warming, with distinctive flavors and a nice chewy texture.

NUTRITIONAL INFORMATION

Calories	204	Sugars	.........7g
Protein	.........5g	Fat	...........8g
Carbohydrate	...31g	Saturates	.......3g

5 mins   1¼ hrs

SERVES 4

INGREDIENTS

¼ cup pearl barley

6¾ cups chicken or
    vegetable stock

1 bay leaf

1 tbsp butter

12 oz/350 g mushrooms, thinly sliced

1 tsp olive oil

1 onion, finely chopped

2 carrots, thinly sliced

1 tbsp chopped fresh tarragon

1 tbsp chopped fresh parsley

salt and pepper

1 tbsp chopped fresh parsley or tarragon,
    to garnish

1 Rinse and drain the barley. Bring 2 cups of the stock to a boil in a small pan. Add the bay leaf and a pinch of salt. Stir in the barley, reduce the heat, cover, and simmer for 40 minutes.

2 Melt the butter in a large skillet over medium heat. Add the mushrooms and season to taste with salt and pepper. Cook, stirring occasionally, for about 8 minutes until they are golden brown. Stir more often after the mushrooms start to color. Remove the skillet from the heat.

3 Heat the oil in a large pan over medium heat and add the onion and carrots. Cook, stirring occasionally, for about 3 minutes until the onion is softened and translucent.

4 Add the remaining stock and bring to a boil. Stir in the barley with its cooking liquid and add the mushrooms. Reduce the heat, cover, and simmer gently, stirring occasionally, for about 20 minutes.

5 Stir in the tarragon and parsley. Ladle into warmed bowls, garnish with fresh parsley or tarragon, and serve.

COOK'S TIP

The barley will continue to absorb liquid if the soup is stored, so if you are making ahead, you may need to add a little more stock or water when reheating the soup.

Rice & Black-Eye Pea Soup

This soup is satisfying and very healthy. Brown rice gives a pleasing chewy texture, but white rice could be used instead.

NUTRITIONAL INFORMATION

Calories	285	Sugars	.........7g
Protein	........18g	Fat	...........5g
Carbohydrate	...43g	Saturates	.......1g

 6¼ hrs   2 hrs

SERVES 4

INGREDIENTS

2¾ cups dried black-eye peas

1 tbsp olive oil

1 large onion, finely chopped

2 garlic cloves, finely chopped or crushed

2 carrots, finely chopped

2 celery stalks, finely chopped

1 small red bell pepper, deseeded and finely chopped

½ cup finely diced lean smoked ham

½ tsp fresh thyme leaves

1 bay leaf

5 cups chicken or vegetable stock

2½ cups water

½ cup brown rice

salt and pepper

chopped fresh parsley or chives, to garnish

1 Put the beans in a bowl, cover generously with cold water, and set aside to soak for at least 6 hours or overnight. Drain the beans, put in a pan, and add enough cold water to cover by inches/5 cm. Bring to a boil and boil for 10 minutes. Drain and rinse well.

2 Heat the oil in a large heavy pan over medium heat. Add the onion, cover, and cook, stirring frequently, for 3–4 minutes until just softened. Add the garlic, carrots, celery, and bell pepper, stir well, and cook for a further 2 minutes.

3 Transfer to a larger pan if necessary. Add the beans, ham, thyme, bay leaf, stock, and water. Bring to a boil, reduce the heat, cover, and simmer gently, stirring occasionally, for 1 hour or until the beans are just tender.

4 Stir in the rice and season the soup with salt, if needed, and pepper. Continue cooking for 30 minutes or until the rice and beans are tender.

5 Remove and discard the bay leaf. Taste the soup and adjust the seasoning if necessary. Ladle into warmed bowls and serve garnished with parsley or chives.

Piquant Oatmeal Soup

This unusual soup, of Mexican origin, is simple and comforting.
It has a hint of chili heat, but its character is more sweet than spicy.

NUTRITIONAL INFORMATION

Calories	172	Sugars	.........4g
Protein	.........4g	Fat	...........9g
Carbohydrate	...21g	Saturates	.......4g

 15 mins   40 mins

SERVES 6

INGREDIENTS

scant 1 cup rolled oats

3 tbsp butter

1 large sweet onion

2–3 garlic cloves

12 oz/350 g tomatoes, peeled, deseeded, and chopped

6¼ cups chicken stock

¼ tsp ground cumin

1 tsp harissa or ½ tsp chili purée

1–2 tbsp lime juice

salt and pepper

chopped scallions, to garnish

1 Place a heavy skillet over medium heat. Add the oats and toast, stirring frequently for about 25 minutes until lightly and evenly browned. Remove the oats from the skillet and set aside to cool completely.

2 Melt the butter in a large pan over medium heat. Add the onion and garlic and cook, stirring occasionally, until the onion is softened.

3 Add the tomatoes, stock, cumin, harissa or chili purée, and season to taste with salt.

4 Stir in the oats and bring to a boil. Lower the heat so that the soup simmers gently and cook for 6 minutes.

5 Stir in 1 tablespoon of the lime juice. Taste and adjust the seasoning. Add more lime juice if desired. Ladle the soup into warmed bowls and sprinkle with scallions to garnish.

COOK'S TIP

This soup is very quick to prepare once the oats are toasted. The oats could be prepared in advance at a convenient time.

Melon Gazpacho

Glass bowls are pretty for serving this soup, which makes a very light and refreshing appetizer for warm days.

NUTRITIONAL INFORMATION

Calories 98   Sugars 20g
Protein ....3g   Fat 1g
Carbohydrate ...21g   Saturates 0g

45 mins   6–7 mins

SERVES 4

INGREDIENTS

1 tsp oil

1 onion, finely chopped

1 large garlic clove, finely chopped

1 tsp chopped fresh chile

1 lb 9 oz/700 g seedless Cantaloupe melon flesh, cubed

½ tsp raspberry vinegar or 1 tsp lemon juice

½ ripe green melon, about 1 lb 2 oz/500 g

salt

chopped chives, to garnish

1 Heat the oil in a small pan over low heat. Add the onion, garlic, and chilli and cook, stirring occasionally, for about 6–7 minutes until the onion is softened, but not browned.

2 Put the Cantaloupe melon flesh in a blender or food processor, add the onion, garlic, and chile and process to a smooth purée, stopping to scrape down the sides as needed. You may need to work in batches. Add the vinegar or lemon juice with a pinch of salt and process briefly to combine.

3 Cover with plastic wrap and chill in the refrigerator for about 30 minutes or until the mixture is cold.

4 Remove the seeds from the green melon, then cut into balls with a melon baller. Alternatively, cut into cubes with a sharp knife.

5 Divide the soup equally among four shallow bowls and then top each one with some green melon balls. Sprinkle lightly with chopped fresh chives to garnish and then serve.

COOK'S TIP

If you are wary of using fresh chile, omit it and add a few drops of hot pepper sauce to taste at the end of Step 2 to liven up the soup.

Cold Tomato & Orange Soup

This soup is made from raw vegetables and fruit, so it is full of goodness, as well as flavor, and is wonderfully refreshing on a warm day.

NUTRITIONAL INFORMATION

Calories	98	Sugars	. . . . . . .22g
Protein	. . . . .3g	Fat	. . . . .0g
Carbohydrate	. . .22g	Saturates	. . . . . . .0g

 45 mins   🕐 0 mins

SERVES 4

I N G R E D I E N T S

3 large seedless oranges

4 ripe tomatoes

2 celery stalks, chopped

3 carrots, grated

1½ cups tomato juice

salt

Tabasco sauce (optional)

1 tbsp chopped fresh mint

fresh mint sprigs, to garnish

1 Working over a bowl to catch the juices, peel the oranges. Cut down between the membranes and drop the orange segments into the bowl.

2 Put the tomatoes in a small bowl and pour over boiling water to cover. Stand for 10 seconds, then drain. Peel off the skins and cut the tomatoes in half

crosswise. Scoop out the seeds into a strainer set over a bowl; reserve the tomato juices.

3 Put the tomatoes, celery, and carrots in a blender or food processor. Add the orange segments and their juice and the juice saved from the tomatoes. Process to a smooth purée.

4 Scrape into a bowl and stir in the tomato juice. Cover with plastic wrap and chill until cold.

5 Taste the soup and add salt, if needed, and a few drops of Tabasco sauce, if wished. Stir in the chopped mint, ladle into cold bowls, and garnish with fresh mint sprigs.

COOK'S TIP

This soup really needs to be made in a blender for the best texture. A food processor can be used, but the soup will not be completely smooth.

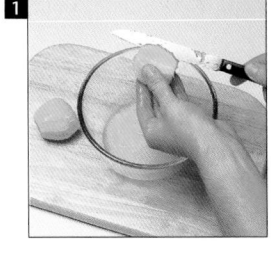

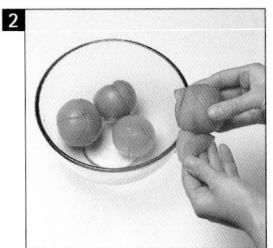

Avocado & Almond Soup

This rich-tasting chilled soup has an inviting color and would make an appetizing start to a dinner party.

NUTRITIONAL INFORMATION

Calories	392	Sugars	.........5g
Protein	.........8g	Fat	..........36g
Carbohydrate	....9g	Saturates	.......6g

 50 mins    30 mins

SERVES 4

I N G R E D I E N T S

2½ cups water

1 onion, finely chopped

1 celery stalk, finely chopped

1 carrot, grated

4 garlic cloves, chopped or crushed

1 bay leaf

scant 1 cup ground almonds

2 ripe avocados (about 1 lb/450 g)

3–4 tbsp fresh lemon juice

salt

chopped fresh chives, to garnish

1 Combine the water, onion, celery, carrot, garlic, bay leaf, and ½ teaspoon salt in a pan. Bring to a boil, reduce the heat, cover, and simmer for about 30 minutes or until the vegetables are very tender.

2 Strain the mixture, reserving the liquid and the vegetables separately. Remove and discard the bay leaf.

3 Put the vegetables into a blender or food processor. Add the almonds and a small amount of the liquid and process to a very smooth purée, scraping down the sides as necessary. Add as much of the remaining liquid as the capacity of the blender or processor permits and process to combine. Scrape into a bowl, stir in any remaining liquid, cover, and chill until cold.

4 Cut the avocados in half, discard the pits, and scoop the flesh into the blender or food processor. Add the cold soup base and process to a smooth purée, scraping down the sides as necessary. For a thinner consistency, add a few spoonfuls of cold water.

5 Add the lemon juice and season with salt to taste. Ladle into chilled small bowls and sprinkle each serving lightly with chives.

Chilled Borscht

There are innumerable versions of this soup of Eastern European origin. This refreshing vegetarian version is light and flavorful.

NUTRITIONAL INFORMATION

Calories	93	Sugars	........12g
Protein	.........4g	Fat	...........3g
Carbohydrate	...15g	Saturates	.......0g

45 mins   1½ hrs

SERVES 4–6

INGREDIENTS

¼ medium cabbage, cored and coarsely chopped

1 tbsp vegetable oil

1 onion, finely chopped

1 leek, halved lengthwise and sliced

14 oz/400 g can peeled tomatoes

5 cups water, plus extra if needed

1 carrot, thinly sliced

1 small parsnip, finely chopped

3 beets (raw or cooked), peeled and cubed

1 bay leaf

1½ cups tomato juice

2–3 tbsp chopped fresh dill

fresh lemon juice (optional)

salt and pepper

sour cream or plain yogurt, to garnish

1 Cover the cabbage generously with cold water in a pan. Bring to a boil, boil for 3 minutes, then drain.

2 Heat the oil in a large pan over medium-low heat. Add the onion and leek, cover, and cook, stirring occasionally, for about 5 minutes until the vegetables begin to soften.

3 Add the tomatoes, water, carrot, parsnip, beets, and bay leaf. Stir in the blanched cabbage and add a pinch of salt. Bring to a boil, reduce the heat, and simmer for about 1¼ hours until all the vegetables are tender. Remove and discard the bay leaf.

4 Remove the pan from the heat and set aside to cool slightly, then transfer to a blender or food processor, and process to a smooth purée, working in batches if necessary. (If using a food processor, strain off the cooking liquid and reserve. Purée the soup solids with enough cooking liquid to moisten them, then combine with the remaining liquid.)

5 Scrape the soup into a large container and stir in the tomato juice. Set aside to cool, then chill in the refrigerator.

6 Stir in the dill. Thin the soup with more tomato juice or water, if wished. Season to taste with salt and pepper and lemon juice, if wished. Ladle into chilled soup bowls, top each with a spiral of sour cream or a spoon of yogurt.

Iced Salsa Soup

A chunky mix of colorful vegetables, highlighted with Mexican flavors, this cold soup makes a lively appetizer at the start of any meal.

NUTRITIONAL INFORMATION

Calories 128	Sugars 12g	
Protein 5g	Fat 4g	
Carbohydrate ...22g	Saturates 1g	

🍲 45 mins   🕐 12–15 mins

SERVES 4

INGREDIENTS

2 large corn cobs or 1⅓ cups frozen corn kernels

1 tbsp olive oil

1 orange or red bell pepper, deseeded and finely chopped

1 green bell pepper, deseeded and finely chopped

1 sweet onion, such as Vidalia, finely chopped

3 ripe tomatoes, peeled, deseeded, and chopped

½ tsp chili powder

½ cup water

2 cups tomato juice

chili purée (optional)

salt and pepper

TO GARNISH

3–4 scallions, finely chopped

fresh cilantro leaves

1 Cut the corn kernels from the cobs, or if using frozen corn, thaw and drain.

2 Heat the oil in a pan over medium-high heat. Add the bell peppers and cook, stirring briskly, for 3 minutes. Add the onion and continue cooking for about 2 minutes or until it starts to color slightly.

3 Add the tomatoes, corn, and chili powder. Continue cooking, stirring frequently, for 1 minute. Pour in the water and when it begins to boil, reduce the heat, cover, and cook for a further 4–5 minutes or until the bell peppers are just barely tender.

4 Transfer the mixture to a large container and stir in the tomato juice. Season with salt and pepper to taste and add more chili powder if wished. Cover with plastic wrap and chill in the refrigerator until cold.

5 Taste and adjust the seasoning. For a spicier soup, stir in a little chili purée to taste. For a thinner soup, add a small amount of ice water. Ladle into chilled bowls and garnish with scallions and fresh cilantro leaves.

Spicy Red Bell Pepper Soup

This brilliantly colored soup makes a great summer starter, especially when bell peppers are abundant in farm markets—or in your garden.

NUTRITIONAL INFORMATION

Calories 90	Sugars 13g
Protein 3g	Fat 3g
Carbohydrate ...15g	Saturates 0g

45 mins   45 mins

SERVES 6

INGREDIENTS

1 tbsp olive oil

1 lb/450 g leeks, thinly sliced

1 large onion, halved and thinly sliced

2 garlic cloves, finely chopped or crushed

6 red bell peppers, deseeded and sliced

4 cups water

½ tsp ground cumin

½ tsp ground coriander

1 tsp chili purée

1–2 tsp fresh lemon juice

salt and pepper

finely chopped scallion greens or fresh chives, to garnish

3 Set aside to cool slightly, then transfer to a blender or food processor, and process to a smooth purée, in batches if necessary. (If using a food processor, strain off the cooking liquid and reserve. Purée the soup solids with enough cooking liquid to moisten them, then combine with the remaining liquid.)

4 Put the soup in a large bowl, then season with salt and pepper, and add lemon juice to taste. Allow to cool completely, cover with plastic wrap, and chill in the refrigerator until cold.

5 Before serving, taste and adjust the seasoning, if necessary. Add a little more chili purée if a spicy taste is preferred. Ladle into chilled bowls and garnish with scallion greens or chives.

1 Heat the oil in a large pan over medium heat. Add the leeks, onion, and garlic and cook, stirring occasionally, for about 5 minutes until the onion is softened.

2 Stir in the bell peppers and cook for a further 2–3 minutes. Add the water, cumin, ground coriander, and chili purée with a pinch of salt. Bring to a boil, reduce the heat, cover, and simmer gently for about 35 minutes until all the vegetables are tender.

Cucumber Soup

Parsley tames the pungent garlic flavor of this traditional Balkan soup. The cucumber and yogurt make it a refreshing summer appetizer.

NUTRITIONAL INFORMATION

Calories	208	Sugars 10g
Protein	.........8g	Fat 15g
Carbohydrate	...10g	Saturates 2g

45 mins 0 mins

SERVES 4

INGREDIENTS

1 large cucumber

½ cup walnut pieces, toasted (see Cook's Tip)

½ cup fresh parsley leaves

1 small garlic clove, very finely chopped

2 tbsp olive oil

4 tbsp water

1 tbsp fresh lemon juice

1¼ cups plain strained yogurt

salt and pepper

fresh mint leaves, to garnish

1 Peel the cucumber, slice lengthwise, and scoop out the seeds with a small, pointed spoon. Cut the flesh into 1 inch/2.5 cm pieces.

2 Put the walnuts, parsley leaves, garlic, oil, and water in a blender or food processor with half of the cucumber and process to a smooth purée, stopping to scrape down the sides as necessary.

3 Add the remaining cucumber to the blender or processor with a pinch of salt and the lemon juice. Process briefly until smooth.

4 Scrape the purée into a large bowl and stir in the yogurt. Season to taste with salt and pepper and add a little more lemon juice, if wished.

5 Cover with plastic wrap and chill in the refrigerator for about 30 minutes or until cold. Taste and adjust the seasoning if necessary. Ladle into chilled bowls and garnish with mint leaves.

COOK'S TIP
Toasting the walnuts gives them extra flavor. Just heat them in a dry skillet over medium-low heat until they begin to color and smell aromatic.

Cold Cilantro Soup

This soup brings together Thai flavors for a cool, refreshing appetizer. It highlights fresh cilantro, now much more widely available.

NUTRITIONAL INFORMATION

Calories 79	Sugars 5g
Protein 3g	Fat 3g
Carbohydrate . . .13g	Saturates 0g

 45 mins 30 mins

SERVES 4

INGREDIENTS

2 tsp olive oil

1 large onion, finely chopped

1 leek, thinly sliced

1 garlic clove, thinly sliced

4 cups water

1 zucchini, about 7 oz/200 g, peeled and chopped

4 tbsp long grain white rice

2 inch/5 cm piece of lemongrass

2 lime leaves

2 cups fresh cilantro leaves and soft stems

chili purée, optional

salt and pepper

finely chopped red bell pepper and/or fresh red chiles, to garnish

1 Heat the oil in a large pan over medium heat. Add the onion, leek, and garlic and cook, stirring occasionally, for 4–5 minutes until the onion is softened, but not browned.

2 Add the water, zucchini, and rice with a pinch of salt and some pepper. Stir in the lemongrass and lime leaves. Bring just to a boil and reduce the heat to low. Cover and simmer for 15–20 minutes until the rice is soft and tender.

3 Add the fresh cilantro leaves and stems, pushing them down into the liquid. Continue cooking over low heat for 2–3 minutes until the leaves are wilted. Remove and discard the lemongrass and lime leaves.

4 Remove from the heat and set aside to cool slightly, then transfer to a blender or food processor, and process to a smooth purée, working in batches if necessary. (If using a food processor, strain off the cooking liquid and reserve. Purée the soup solids with enough cooking liquid to moisten them, then combine with the remaining liquid.)

5 Scrape the soup into a large container. Season to taste with salt and pepper. Cover with plastic wrap and chill in the refrigerator until cold.

6 Taste and adjust the seasoning. For a spicier soup, stir in a little chili purée to taste. For a thinner soup, add a small amount of ice water. Ladle into chilled bowls and garnish with finely chopped red bell pepper and/or chiles.

Cock-a-Leekie Soup

A traditional Scottish soup in which a whole chicken is cooked with the vegetables to add extra flavor to the stock.

NUTRITIONAL INFORMATION

Calories 45   Sugars 4g
Protein ....5g   Fat 1g
Carbohydrate ....5g   Saturates 0.2g

2½ hrs   2 hrs

SERVES 4–6

INGREDIENTS

2lb 4 oz–3 lb 5 oz/1–1.5 kg oven-ready chicken plus giblets, if available

3¼–4 pints/1.75–2 liters chicken stock

1 onion, sliced

4 leeks, thinly sliced

pinch of ground allspice or ground coriander

1 bouquet garni

12 no-need-to-soak prunes, halved and pitted

salt and pepper

warm crusty bread, to serve

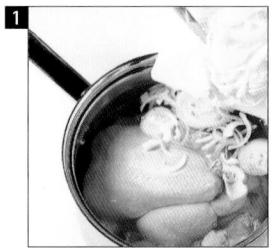

1 Put the chicken, giblets, if using, stock, and onion in a large pan. Bring to a boil and skim off any scum that rises to the surface.

2 Add the leeks, allspice or coriander, and bouquet garni to the pan, season with salt and pepper, cover, and simmer gently for about 1½ hours until the chicken flesh is falling off the bones.

3 Remove the chicken and bouquet garni from the pan and skim any fat from the surface of the soup.

4 Chop some of the chicken flesh and return to the pan. Add the prunes, bring back to a boil, and simmer, uncovered, for about 20 minutes. Taste and adjust the seasoning, if necessary, and serve with warm crusty bread.

VARIATION
You can replace the chicken stock with 3 chicken bouillon cubes dissolved in the same amount of water, if you prefer.

Hot & Sour Soup

Hot-and-sour mixtures are popular throughout the East, especially in Thailand. This soup typically has either shrimp or chicken added.

NUTRITIONAL INFORMATION

Calories 71   Sugars 0g
Protein . . . . .8g   Fat 4g
Carbohydrate . . . .1g   Saturates 0g

15 mins   30 mins

SERVES 4

INGREDIENTS

12 oz/350 g raw or cooked shrimp in shells

1 tbsp vegetable oil

1 lemongrass stalk, roughly chopped

2 kaffir lime leaves, shredded

1 fresh green chile, deseeded and chopped

5 cups chicken or fish stock

1 lime

1 tbsp Thai fish sauce

1 fresh red bird-eye chile, deseeded and thinly sliced

1 scallion, thinly sliced

salt and pepper

1 tbsp finely chopped fresh cilantro, to garnish

1 Peel the shrimp and reserve the shells. Devein the shrimp, cover with plastic wrap, and chill.

2 Heat the oil in a large pan. Add the shrimp shells and stir-fry for 3–4 minutes until they turn pink. Add the lemongrass, lime leaves, chile, and stock. Pare a thin strip of rind from the lime and grate the rest. Add the pared rind to the pan.

3 Bring to a boil, then lower the heat, cover, and simmer for about 20 minutes.

4 Strain the liquid and pour it back into the pan. Squeeze the juice from the lime and add to the pan with the fish sauce, and season with salt and pepper to taste.

5 Bring the mixture to a boil. Lower the heat, add the shrimp, and simmer for 2–3 minutes.

6 Add the thinly sliced chile and scallion. Sprinkle with the chopped fresh coriander and grated lime rind and serve immediately.

COOK'S TIP

To devein the shrimp, remove the shells. Cut a slit along the back of each shrimp and remove the fine black vein that runs along the length of the back. Wipe with paper towels.

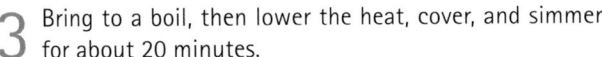

Creamy Corn Soup

This filling combination of tender corn kernels and a creamy stock is extra delicious with lean diced ham sprinkled on top.

NUTRITIONAL INFORMATION

Calories . . . . .307 Sugars 15g
Protein . . . . .19g Fat 14g
Carbohydrate . . .28g Saturates 5g

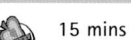 15 mins   25 mins

SERVES 4

INGREDIENTS

1 large onion, chopped

10 oz/300 g potatoes, diced

4 cups skim milk

1 bay leaf

½ tsp freshly grated nutmeg

1 lb/450 g corn kernels, canned or frozen, drained or thawed

1 tbsp cornstarch

3 tbsp cold water

4 tbsp low-fat plain yogurt

salt and pepper

TO GARNISH

generous ½ cup diced lean ham

2 tbsp chopped fresh chives

1 Place the onion and potato in a large pan and pour in the milk.

2 Add the bay leaf, nutmeg, and half the corn to the pan. Bring to a boil, cover, and simmer over low heat for 15 minutes until the potato is softened. Stir the soup occasionally and keep the heat low so that the milk does not burn on the bottom of the pan.

3 Remove and discard the bay leaf and set the liquid aside to cool for about 10 minutes. Transfer to a blender and process for a few seconds. Alternatively, rub the soup through a strainer.

4 Pour the smooth liquid into a clean pan. Blend the cornstarch with the cold water to make a paste and stir it into the soup.

5 Bring the soup back to a boil, stirring until it thickens, and add the remaining corn. Heat through gently for 2–3 minutes until hot.

6 Remove the soup from the heat and season with salt and pepper to taste. Add the yogurt and stir until it is thoroughly blended.

7 Ladle the creamy corn soup into warm bowls and serve sprinkled with the diced ham and chopped chives.

Pumpkin & Coconut Soup

This substantial soup is filling and, if served with crusty bread, is all you need for a satisfying lunch. For a first course, serve in small bowls.

NUTRITIONAL INFORMATION

Calories . . . . .105 Sugars 6g
Protein . . . . .3g Fat 7g
Carbohydrate . . . .8g Saturates 4g

 15 mins   40 mins

SERVES 6

INGREDIENTS

2 lb 4 oz/1 kg pumpkin

1 tbsp peanut oil

1 tsp yellow mustard seeds

1 garlic clove, crushed

1 large onion, chopped

1 celery stalk, chopped

1 small fresh red chile, chopped

3¾ cups stock

1 tsp shrimp paste

5 tbsp coconut cream, plus extra
   to garnish

salt and pepper

1 Cut the pumpkin in half and remove the seeds. Cut away the skin and dice the flesh.

2 Heat the oil in a large flameproof casserole and fry the mustard seeds until they begin to pop. Stir in the garlic, onion, celery, and chile and stir-fry for 1–2 minutes.

3 Add the pumpkin with the stock and shrimp paste and bring to a boil. Lower the heat, cover, and simmer gently for about 30 minutes until the ingredients are very tender.

4 Remove from the heat and set aside to cool slightly, then transfer the mixture to a food processor or blender, and process to a smooth purée. Return the mixture to the pan and stir in the coconut cream. Reheat gently.

5 Adjust the seasoning to taste with salt and pepper, ladle into bowls, and serve hot, with a little extra coconut cream swirled in each bowl.

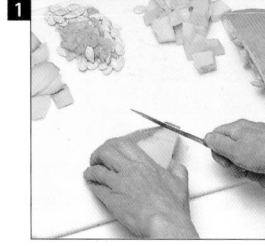  

COOK'S TIP

Made from ground shrimp that have been fermented in brine, shrimp paste is widely used throughout Southeast Asia to add a savory flavor.

Mushroom & Beancurd Broth

Dried black mushrooms are sold in Asian stores. Although they are expensive, they are worth buying because they have a distinctive flavor.

NUTRITIONAL INFORMATION

Calories	65	Sugars	.....1g
Protein	.....4g	Fat	.....5g
Carbohydrate	....2g	Saturates	.....1g

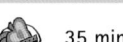 35 mins   15 mins

SERVES 4

INGREDIENTS

4 dried black mushrooms

1 tbsp sunflower oil

1 tsp sesame oil

1 garlic clove, crushed

1 fresh green chile, deseeded and finely chopped

6 scallions

1¼ cups sliced fresh oyster mushrooms

2 kaffir lime leaves, finely shredded

4 cups Fresh Beef Stock (see page 9)

2 tbsp lime juice

1 tbsp rice vinegar

1 tbsp Thai fish sauce

3 oz/85 g firm beancurd, diced

salt and pepper

1 Pour ⅔ cup boiling water over the dried black mushrooms in a heatproof bowl and set aside to soak for about 30 minutes. Drain, reserving the soaking liquid, then coarsely chop the black mushrooms.

2 Heat the sunflower and sesame oils in a large pan or wok over high heat. Add the garlic, chile, and scallions and stir-fry for 1 minute until softened, but not browned.

3 Add all of the mushrooms, the kaffir lime leaves, stock, and reserved mushroom liquid. Bring to a boil.

4 Stir in the lime juice, rice vinegar, and fish sauce, lower the heat, and simmer gently for 3–4 minutes.

5 Add the beancurd and season to taste with salt and pepper. Heat gently until boiling, then serve immediately.

COOK'S TIP

To make a vegetarian version of the broth, use a well-flavored vegetable stock and replace the fish sauce with light soy sauce.

Rice Soup with Eggs

This version of a classic Thai soup, sometimes eaten for breakfast, is a good way of using up any leftover cooked rice.

NUTRITIONAL INFORMATION

Calories 197   Sugars 1g
Protein ....11g   Fat 10g
Carbohydrate ...17g   Saturates 2g

5 mins   10 mins

SERVES 4

INGREDIENTS

1 tsp sunflower oil

1 garlic clove, crushed

½ cup ground pork

3 scallions, sliced

1 tbsp grated fresh ginger root

1 fresh red bird-eye chile, deseeded
  and chopped

4 cups chicken stock

generous 1 cup cooked long grain rice

1 tbsp Thai fish sauce

4 small eggs

salt and pepper

2 tbsp shredded fresh cilantro, to garnish

1 Heat the oil in a large pan or wok. Add the garlic and pork and cook gently, stirring constantly, for about 1 minute until the meat is broken up, but not browned.

2 Stir in the scallions, ginger, chile, and stock and bring to a boil, stirring constantly. Add the rice, lower the heat, and simmer for 2 minutes.

3 Add the fish sauce and season to taste with salt and pepper. Carefully break the eggs into the soup and then simmer over very low heat for approximately 3–4 minutes until set.

4 Ladle the soup into large, warmed bowls, allowing 1 egg per portion. Garnish with shredded fresh cilantro and serve immediately.

COOK'S TIP

If you prefer, beat the eggs together and cook like an omelet until set, then cut into ribbon-like strips and added to the soup just before serving.

Spinach & Ginger Soup

This mildly spiced, rich green soup is delicately scented with ginger and lemongrass. It makes a good light appetizer or summer lunch dish.

NUTRITIONAL INFORMATION

Calories 38   Sugars 0.8g
Protein ....3.2g   Fat 1.8g
Carbohydrate ...2.4g   Saturates 0.2g

 5–10 mins   25 mins

SERVES 4

I N G R E D I E N T S

2 tbsp sunflower oil

1 onion, chopped

2 garlic cloves, finely chopped

2 tsp chopped fresh ginger root

9 oz/250 g young spinach leaves

1 small lemongrass stalk, finely chopped

4 cups chicken or vegetable stock

8 oz/225 g potatoes, chopped

1 tbsp rice wine or dry sherry

1 tsp sesame oil

salt and pepper

1 Heat the oil in a large pan. Add the onion, garlic, and ginger and cook over low heat, stirring occasionally, for 3–4 minutes until softened.

2 Reserve 2–3 small spinach leaves. Add the remaining leaves and lemongrass to the pan, stirring until the spinach is wilted. Add the stock and potatoes to the pan and bring to a boil. Lower the heat, cover, and simmer for about 10 minutes.

3 Remove the pan from the heat and set aside to cool slightly. Then tip the soup into a blender or food processor and process until completely smooth.

4 Return the soup to the pan and add the rice wine, then adjust the seasoning to taste with salt and pepper. Heat until just about to boil.

5 Finely shred the reserved spinach leaves and sprinkle some over the top. Drizzle a few drops of sesame oil into the soup. Ladle into warmed soup bowls, sprinkle the remaining shredded spinach on each, and serve the soup immediately.

COOK'S TIP

To make a creamy-textured spinach and coconut soup, s tir in about 4 tablespoons creamed coconut or replace about 1¼ cups of the stock with coconut milk. Serve the soup with shavings of fresh coconut scattered over the surface.

Avocado & Lime Soup

A delightfully simple soup with a blend of typical Thai flavors, which needs no cooking and can be served at any time of day.

NUTRITIONAL INFORMATION

Calories	188	Sugars	.........2g
Protein	.........3g	Fat	..........18g
Carbohydrate	....4g	Saturates	.......5g

 15 mins 0 mins

SERVES 4

INGREDIENTS

2 ripe avocados

1 small mild onion, chopped

1 garlic clove, crushed

2 tbsp chopped fresh cilantro

1 tbsp chopped fresh mint

2 tbsp lime juice

3 cups vegetable stock

1 tbsp rice vinegar

1 tbsp light soy sauce

salt and pepper

GARNISH

2 tbsp sour cream or crème fraîche

1 tbsp finely chopped fresh cilantro

2 tsp lime juice

finely shredded lime rind

1 Halve and pit the avocados and scoop out the flesh. Place in a blender or food processor with the onion, garlic, cilantro, mint, lime juice, and about half the vegetable stock, and process until completely smooth.

2 Transfer to a bowl. Add the remaining stock, rice vinegar, and soy sauce and process again to mix well. Taste and season, if necessary, with salt and pepper or with a little extra lime juice if required. Cover and refrigerate until needed.

3 To make the lime and cilantro cream garnish, combine the sour cream, cilantro, and lime juice in a bowl. Ladle the soup into chilled bowls, spoon the lime and cilantro cream into them, and sprinkle with lime rind.

COOK'S TIP

The top surface of the soup may darken slightly if the soup is stored for longer than about an hour, but don't worry—just give it a quick stir before serving. If you plan to keep the soup for several hours, lay a piece of plastic wrap over the surface to seal it from the air.

Spinach & Beancurd Soup

This is a very colorful and delicious soup. If spinach is not in season, watercress or lettuce can be used instead.

NUTRITIONAL INFORMATION

Calories	33	Sugar	.........1g
Protein	.........4g	Fat	...........2g
Carbohydrate	....1g	Saturates	.....0.2g

15 mins 10 mins

SERVES 4

INGREDIENTS

1 block firm beancurd

4½ oz/125 g spinach leaves without stems

3 cups Chinese Stock (see page 8) or water

1 tbsp light soy sauce

salt and pepper

1 Using a sharp knife to avoid squashing it, cut the beancurd into small pieces about ¼ inch/5 mm thick.

2 Wash the spinach leaves under cold, running water and drain well.

3 Cut the spinach leaves into small pieces or shreds, discarding any discolored leaves and tough stalks. (If possible, use fresh young spinach leaves, which have not yet developed tough ribs. Otherwise, it is important to cut out all the ribs and stems for this soup.) Set the spinach aside until required.

4 In a preheated wok or large skillet, bring the Chinese stock or water to a rolling boil.

5 Add the beancurd cubes and light soy sauce, bring back to a boil, and simmer gently for about 2 minutes over medium heat.

6 Add the spinach and simmer for 1 more minute, stirring gently. Skim the surface of the soup to make it clear and season to taste.

7 Transfer the soup to a warm soup tureen or individual serving bowls and serve with chopsticks to pick up the pieces of food and a broad, shallow spoon for drinking the soup.

COOK'S TIP

Soup is an integral part of a Chinese meal; it is usually presented in a large bowl placed in the center of the table, and consumed as the meal progresses. It serves as a refresher between different dishes and as a beverage throughout the meal.

Green Soup

This fresh-tasting soup with green beans, cucumber, and watercress can be served warm, or chilled on a hot summer day.

NUTRITIONAL INFORMATION

Calories 121	Sugars 2g	
Protein 2g	Fat 8g	
Carbohydrate . . .10g	Saturates 1g	

 15–45 mins 25 mins

SERVES 4

INGREDIENTS

1 tbsp olive oil

1 onion, chopped

1 garlic clove, chopped

7 oz/200 g potato, cut into 1 inch/
2.5 cm cubes

3 cups vegetable or chicken stock

1 small cucumber or ½ large cucumber, cut
into chunks

3 oz/85 g watercress

4½ oz/125 g green beans, trimmed and
halved lengthwise

salt and pepper

1 Heat the oil in a large pan and cook the onion and garlic over medium heat for 3–4 minutes or until softened.

2 Add the cubed potato and cook for a further 2–3 minutes. Stir in the stock and bring to a boil. Lower the heat and simmer for 5 minutes.

3 Add the cucumber to the pan and cook for a further 3 minutes or until the potatoes are tender. Test by inserting the tip of a knife into the potato cubes—it should pass through easily.

4 Add the watercress and cook until just wilted. Remove from heat and set aside to cool slightly, then transfer to a food processor, and process to a smooth purée. Alternatively, before adding the watercress, mash the vegetables with a potato masher and push through a strainer, then chop the watercress finely and stir into the soup.

5 Bring a small pan of water to a boil and steam the beans for 3–4 minutes or until tender. Add the beans to the soup, season to taste with salt and pepper, and warm through. Ladle into warmed soup bowls and serve immediately or set aside to cool and then chill.

VARIATION

Try using 4½ oz/125 g snow peas instead of the beans. You can also use spinach if watercress is unavailable.

Pumpkin Soup

This thick, creamy soup has a wonderful, warming golden color. It is flavored with orange and thyme.

NUTRITIONAL INFORMATION

Calories 111	Sugars 4g	
Protein 2g	Fat 6g	
Carbohydrate 5g	Saturates 2g	

10 mins   35–40 mins

SERVES 4

INGREDIENTS

2 tbsp olive oil

2 medium onions, chopped

2 garlic cloves, chopped

2 lb/900 g pumpkin, peeled and cut into 1 inch/2.5 cm chunks

6¾ cups boiling vegetable or chicken stock

finely grated rind and juice of 1 orange

3 tbsp fresh thyme leaves

⅔ cup milk

salt and pepper

crusty bread, to serve

1 Heat the olive oil in a large pan. Add the onions and cook over medium heat, stirring occasionally, for 3–4 minutes or until softened. Add the garlic and pumpkin and cook, stirring frequently, for a further 2 minutes.

2 Add the boiling vegetable or chicken stock, orange rind and juice, and 2 tablespoons of the thyme to the pan. Cover and simmer for 20 minutes or until the pumpkin is tender.

3 Transfer to a food processor and process until smooth. Alternatively, mash the mixture with a potato masher until smooth. Season to taste.

4 Return the soup to the pan and add the milk. Reheat for 3–4 minutes or until it is piping hot, but not boiling.

5 Sprinkle with the remaining fresh thyme just before serving.

6 Divide the soup among 4 warmed soup bowls and serve with lots of fresh crusty bread.

COOK'S TIP
Pumpkins are usually large vegetables. To make things a little easier, ask the grocer to cut a chunk off for you. Alternatively, make double the quantity and freeze the soup for up to 3 months.

Curried Chicken Soup

Tender cooked chicken strips and baby corn cobs are the main flavors in this delicious clear soup, with just a hint of ginger.

NUTRITIONAL INFORMATION

Calories 206	Sugars 5g
Protein 29g	Fat 5g
Carbohydrate ...13g	Saturates 1g

 5 mins   30 mins

SERVES 4

INGREDIENTS

1 cup canned corn, drained

3¾ cups chicken stock

12 oz/350 g cooked, lean chicken, cut into strips

16 baby corn cobs

1 tsp Chinese curry powder

½ inch/1 cm piece of fresh ginger root, grated

3 tbsp light soy sauce

2 tbsp chopped fresh chives

1 Place the canned corn in a food processor, with ⅔ cup of the chicken stock and process until the mixture forms a smooth purée.

2 Pass the corn purée through a fine strainer, pressing with the back of a spoon to remove any husks.

3 Pour the remaining chicken stock into a large pan and add the strips of cooked chicken. Stir in the corn purée to combine well.

4 Add the baby corn cobs and bring the soup to a boil. Boil over medium heat for 10 minutes.

5 Add the Chinese curry powder, grated fresh ginger root, and light soy sauce and stir well to combine. Cook for a further 10–15 minutes.

6 Stir in the chopped chives. Transfer the soup to warmed soup bowls and serve immediately.

COOK'S TIP

Prepare the soup up to 24 hours in advance without adding the chicken. Cool, cover, and store in the refrigerator. Add the chicken and heat the soup through thoroughly before serving.

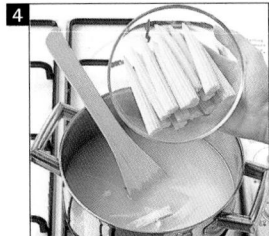
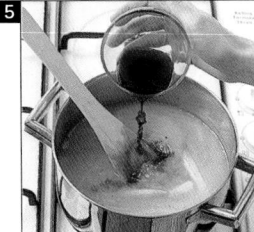

Beef Noodle Soup

Thin strips of beef are marinated in soy sauce and garlic to form the basis of this delicious soup. Served with noodles, it is both filling and delicious.

NUTRITIONAL INFORMATION

Calories 186   Sugars 1g
Protein ....17g   Fat 5g
Carbohydrate ...20g   Saturates 1g

 35 mins   20 mins

SERVES 4

INGREDIENTS

8 oz/225 g lean beef

1 garlic clove, crushed

2 scallions, chopped

3 tbsp soy sauce

1 tsp sesame oil

8 oz/225 g egg noodles

3¾ cups beef stock

3 baby corn cobs, sliced

½ leek, shredded

4½ oz/125 g broccoli, cut into florets

pinch of chili powder

1 Using a sharp knife, cut the beef into thin strips and place in a large bowl with the garlic, scallions, soy sauce, and sesame oil.

2 Combine the ingredients in the bowl, turning the beef to coat. Cover and set aside to marinate in the refrigerator for 30 minutes.

3 Cook the noodles in a pan of boiling water for 3–4 minutes. Drain thoroughly and set aside.

4 Put the beef stock in a large pan and bring to a boil. Add the beef, with the marinade, the baby corn, shredded leek, and broccoli florets. Cover and simmer over low heat for 7–10 minutes or until the beef and vegetables are tender and cooked through.

5 Stir in the noodles and chili powder and cook for a further 2–3 minutes.

6 Transfer the soup to warmed bowls and serve immediately.

VARIATION

Vary the vegetables used or use those to hand. If preferred, use a few drops of chili sauce instead of chili powder, but remember it is very hot!

Sweet Potato & Onion Soup

This simple recipe uses the sweet potato with its distinctive flavor and color, combined with a hint of orange and cilantro.

NUTRITIONAL INFORMATION

Calories	320	Sugars	........26g
Protein	.........7g	Fat	...........7g
Carbohydrate	...62g	Saturates	......1g

 15 mins   30 mins

SERVES 4

INGREDIENTS

2 tbsp vegetable oil

2 lb/900 g sweet potatoes, diced

1 carrot, diced

2 onions, sliced

2 garlic cloves, crushed

2½ cups vegetable stock

1¼ cups unsweetened orange juice

1 cup low-fat plain yogurt

2 tbsp chopped fresh cilantro

salt and pepper

TO GARNISH

fresh cilantro sprigs

orange rind

1 Heat the vegetable oil in a large, heavy pan and add the sweet potatoes, carrot, onions, and garlic. Sauté the vegetables over low heat, stirring constantly for 5 minutes until softened.

2 Pour in the vegetable stock and orange juice and bring to a boil.

3 Reduce the heat to a simmer, cover the pan, and cook the vegetables for 20 minutes or until the sweet potatoes and carrot are tender.

4 Transfer the mixture to a food processor or blender, in batches, and process for 1 minute until puréed. Return the purée to the rinsed-out pan.

5 Stir in the yogurt and chopped cilantro and season to taste with salt and pepper.

6 Serve the soup in warm bowls and garnish with cilantro sprigs and orange rind.

VARIATION

This soup can be chilled before serving, if preferred. If chilling, stir the yogurt into the dish just before serving. Serve in chilled bowls.

Red Bell Pepper Soup

This soup has a real Mediterranean flavor, using sweet red bell peppers, tomato, chile, and basil. It is great served with a warm olive bread.

NUTRITIONAL INFORMATION

Calories ....55 Sugar 10g
Protein ....2g Fats 0.5g
Carbohydrates ...11g Saturates 0.1g

 5 mins   25 mins

SERVES 4

I N G R E D I E N T S

8 oz/225 g red bell peppers, deseeded
  and sliced

1 onion, sliced

2 garlic cloves, crushed

1 fresh green chile, chopped

1¼ cups sieved tomatoes

2½ cups vegetable stock

2 tbsp chopped fresh basil

fresh basil sprigs, to garnish

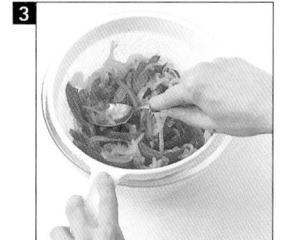

1 Put the red bell peppers in a large, heavy pan with the onion, garlic, and chile. Add the sieved tomatoes and vegetable stock and bring to a boil over medium heat, stirring constantly.

2 Reduce the heat to low and simmer for 20 minutes or until the bell peppers have softened. Drain, reserving the liquid and vegetables separately.

3 Purée the vegetables by pressing through a strainer with the back of a spoon. Alternatively, process in a food processor to a smooth purée.

4 Return the vegetable purée to a clean pan and add the reserved cooking liquid. Add the basil and heat through until hot. Garnish the soup with fresh basil sprigs and serve.

VARIATION
This soup is also delicious served cold with ⅔ cup plain yogurt swirled into it.

Avgolemono

The hallmarks of this traditional Greek lemon and egg soup are its fresh flavor and its lightness. Serve with Olive Rolls (see page 474).

NUTRITIONAL INFORMATION

Calories ....138 Sugars 1g
Protein ....8g Fat 6g
Carbohydrate ...15g Saturates 1g

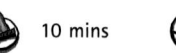 10 mins   🕐 12 mins

SERVES 4–6

I N G R E D I E N T S

5 cups chicken stock

3½ oz/100 g dried orzo, or other small pasta shapes

2 large eggs

4 tbsp lemon juice

salt and pepper

T O   G A R N I S H

finely chopped fresh flat leaf parsley

1 Pour the stock into a flameproof casserole or heavy pan and bring to a boil. Sprinkle in the orzo, return to a boil, and cook for 8–10 minutes until the pasta is tender, but still firm to the bite.

2 Whisk the eggs in a bowl for at least 30 seconds. Add the lemon juice and continue whisking for a further 30 seconds.

3 Reduce the heat under the pan of stock and orzo until the stock is not boiling.

4 Very gradually add 4–5 tablespoons of the hot (not boiling) stock to the lemon and egg mixture, whisking constantly. Gradually add another 1 cup of the stock, whisking to prevent the eggs from curdling.

5 Gradually pour the lemon and egg mixture into the pan, whisking until the soup thickens slightly. Do not allow it to boil. Season to taste with salt and pepper.

6 Spoon the soup into warmed soup bowls and sprinkle with chopped flat leaf parsley. Serve immediately.

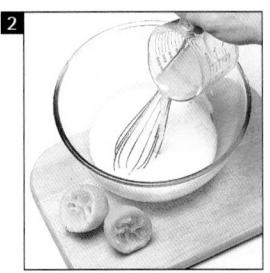

VARIATION

To make a more substantial soup, add 10½ oz/300 g finely chopped cooked, skinless chicken meat. This version uses orzo, a small pasta shape that looks like barley grains, but you can substitute long grain rice.

Bell Pepper & Tomato Soup

Juicy tomatoes and sweet red bell peppers are roasted and then combined with fresh dill and orange to make a fantastic soup.

NUTRITIONAL INFORMATION

Calories 54   Sugars 9g
Protein ....2g   Fat 1g
Carbohydrate ...10g   Saturates 0g

10 mins   1 hr

SERVES 6–8

INGREDIENTS

2 lb 4 oz/1 kg plum tomatoes, halved

2 large red bell peppers, deseeded and halved

1 onion, quartered

3 fresh dill sprigs, tied together, plus extra to garnish

1 thin piece of orange rind

juice of 1 orange

2½ cups vegetable stock

1–1½ tbsp red wine vinegar

salt and pepper

Mediterranean Bread (see page 472), to serve

1 Place the tomatoes and bell peppers on a cookie sheet, cut sides up to catch the juices. Add the onion quarters. Place in a preheated oven, 450°F/230°C, and roast for 20–25 minutes until the vegetables just start to blacken and char on the edges.

2 As the vegetables become charred, transfer them to a large flameproof casserole or stockpot. Add the dill, orange rind and juice, stock, and salt and pepper to taste. Bring to a boil.

3 Lower the heat, partially cover, and simmer for 25 minutes. Remove the bundle of dill and transfer the rest of the ingredients to a food mill (see Cook's Tip) and purée. Alternatively, process in a food processor and press though a fine strainer.

4 Return the soup to the rinsed casserole or stockpot and reheat. Stir in the vinegar and adjust the seasoning with salt and pepper, if necessary. Ladle into warmed bowls and garnish with extra dill sprigs. Serve hot with slices of Mediterranean bread.

COOK'S TIP

A food mill, or mouli-legume as it is called in France, is ideal for puréeing vegetable soups and sauces because it removes the skin and seeds in the process.

Pistou

This hearty soup of beans and vegetables is from Nice and gets its name from the fresh basil sauce stirred in at the last minute.

NUTRITIONAL INFORMATION

Calories	55	Sugars	.......1.2g
Protein	........3.8g	Fat	..........2.6g
Carbohydrate	...4.2g	Saturates	.....0.6g

 10 mins   25 mins

SERVES 6

INGREDIENTS

2 young carrots

1 lb/450 g potatoes

7 oz/200 g fresh peas in their pods

7 oz/200 g thin green beans

5½ oz/150 g young zucchini

2 tbsp olive oil

1 garlic clove, crushed

1 large onion, finely chopped

11¼ cups vegetable stock or water

1 bouquet garni of 2 fresh parsley sprigs and 1 bay leaf tied in a 3 inch/7.5 cm piece of celery

¾ cup dried small soup pasta

1 large tomato, peeled, deseeded, and chopped or diced

Parmesan cheese shavings, to serve

PISTOU SAUCE

3 cups fresh basil leaves

1 garlic clove

5 tbsp extra virgin olive oil

salt and pepper

1 To make the pistou sauce, put the basil leaves, garlic, and olive oil in a food processor and process until thoroughly blended. Season with salt and pepper to taste. Scrape the sauce into a bowl, cover with plastic wrap, and store in the refrigerator until required.

2 Cut the carrots in half lengthwise, then slice. Cut the potatoes into quarters lengthwise, then slice. Set aside in a bowl of water until ready to use to prevent them from discoloring.

3 Shell the peas. Trim the beans and cut them into 1 inch/2.5 cm pieces. Cut the zucchini in half lengthwise, then slice.

4 Heat the oil in a large pan or flameproof casserole. Add the garlic and cook for 2 minutes, stirring. Add the onion and cook for for a further 2 minutes until soft. Add the carrots and potatoes and stir for about 30 seconds.

5 Pour in the stock and bring to a boil. Lower the heat, partially cover, and simmer for 8 minutes until the vegetables are starting to become tender.

6 Stir in the peas, beans, zucchini, bouquet garni, and pasta. Season and cook for 4 minutes until the vegetables and pasta are tender. Stir in the pistou sauce and serve with Parmesan shavings.

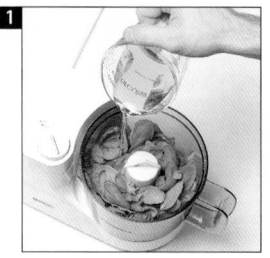  

Tomato & Red Rice Soup

The firm texture and nutty flavor of red rice is particularly good in this soup, but if you have difficulty in finding it, use long grain brown rice.

NUTRITIONAL INFORMATION

Calories . . . . . . .150 Sugars 8g
Protein . . . . .3g Fat 5g
Carbohydrate . . .24g Saturates 1g

10 mins   50 mins

SERVES 4–6

I N G R E D I E N T S

2 tbsp olive oil

1 onion, finely chopped

1 carrot, finely chopped

1 celery stalk, finely chopped

3–4 garlic cloves, finely chopped

2 lb/900 g fresh ripe tomatoes, peeled, deseeded, and finely chopped

1 bay leaf

½ cinnamon stick (optional)

1 tsp fresh thyme leaves or ½ tsp dried thyme

1 tsp dried oregano

1 tbsp brown sugar

½ tsp cayenne pepper6¼ cups chicken stock or water

½ cup red rice or long grain brown rice

1 tbsp chopped fresh oregano leaves

salt and pepper

freshly grated Parmesan cheese, to serve

1 Heat the oil in a large pan over medium heat. Add the onion, carrot, and celery and cook, stirring occasionally, for about 10 minutes until very soft and beginning to color. Stir in the garlic and cook for a further minute.

2 Add the tomatoes, bay leaf, cinnamon stick, if using, thyme, dried oregano, sugar, and cayenne and cook, stirring occasionally, for about 5 minutes until the tomatoes begin to disintegrate.

3 Add the stock and the rice and bring to a boil, skimming off any foam that rises to the surface. Reduce the heat, cover, and simmer for about 30 minutes until the rice is tender, adding more stock if necessary.

4 Stir in the fresh oregano leaves and season to taste with salt and pepper. Remove and discard the bay leaf and cinnamon stick. Serve immediately with Parmesan cheese for sprinkling.

Barley & Rice Soup

This hearty winter soup makes a warming lunch
or supper when served with a crusty loaf of ciabatta.

NUTRITIONAL INFORMATION

Calories 260   Sugars 8g
Protein ....9g   Fat 6g
Carbohydrate ...46g   Saturates 1g

 15 mins   1½ hrs

SERVES 4–6

INGREDIENTS

½ cup pearl barley

½ cup long grain brown rice

1 lb/450 g Swiss chard, trimmed and
   soaked for 10 minutes

2 tbsp olive oil

1 large onion, finely chopped

2 carrots, finely chopped

2 celery stalks, finely chopped

2 garlic cloves, finely chopped

14 oz/400 g can chopped plum tomatoes

1 bay leaf

1 tsp dried thyme

1 tsp herbes de Provence or dried oregano

4 cups chicken or vegetable stock

1 lb/450 g can cannellini beans, drained

2 tbsp chopped fresh parsley

salt and pepper

freshly grated Parmesan cheese, to serve

1 Bring a large pan of water to a boil. Add the barley and the brown rice and return to a boil. Reduce the heat and simmer gently for 30–35 minutes until just tender. Drain and set aside.

2 Drain the Swiss chard. Cut out the hard white stems. Slice the stems crosswise into very thin strips and set aside. Roll the leaves into a long cigar shape, shred thinly, and set aside.

3 Heat the oil in a large, heavy pan. Add the onion, carrots, and celery and cook, stirring frequently, for about 5 minutes until soft and beginning to color. Add the garlic and cook for a minute longer. Add the tomatoes with their juice, the bay leaf, thyme, and herbes de Provence. Reduce the heat, partially cover, and simmer for about 7 minutes until all the vegetables are soft.

4 Stir in the sliced white chard stems and the stock. Simmer gently for about 20 minutes. Add the shredded green chard and simmer for a further 15 minutes.

5 Stir in the beans and parsley with the cooked barley and brown rice. Season with salt and pepper. Bring back to a boil and simmer for a further 8–10 minutes. Remove the bay leaf and serve with Parmesan.

Italian Escarole & Rice Soup

This is a simple Italian soup made with the slightly bitter green scarola, or escarole, a member of the endive family.

NUTRITIONAL INFORMATION

Calories 183   Sugars 2g
Protein ....4g   Fat 11g
Carbohydrate ...19g   Saturates 7g

15 mins   1¼ hrs

SERVES 4–6

INGREDIENTS

1 lb/450 g escarole or endive

4 tbsp butter

1 onion, finely chopped

4 cups chicken stock

1 cup risotto rice

freshly grated nutmeg

2–4 tbsp freshly grated Parmesan cheese

salt and pepper

fresh herbs, to garnish

1 Separate the leaves from the escarole or endive. Wash under cold running water and drain. Stack several leaves in a pile and roll tightly, then shred the leaves into ½ inch/1 cm ribbons. Continue with the remaining leaves.

2 Melt the butter in a large heavy pan over medium heat. Add the onion and cook, stirring occasionally, for about 4 minutes until soft and just beginning to color. Stir in the shredded escarole or endive and cook, stirring frequently, for 2 minutes until the leaves wilt.

3 Add half the stock and season to taste with salt and pepper. Reduce the heat, cover the pan, and simmer gently over very low heat for about 25–35 minutes until tender.

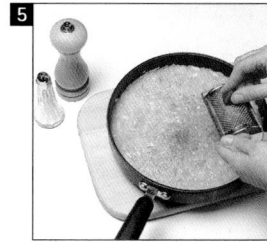

4 Add the remaining stock and bring to a boil. Sprinkle in the rice, partially cover, and simmer over medium heat, stirring occasionally, for 15–20 minutes until the rice is just tender, but still slightly firm to the bite.

5 Remove from the heat and season with more salt and pepper, if necessary, and nutmeg. Ladle into bowls and sprinkle with a little Parmesan. Serve immediately, garnished with herbs.

COOK'S TIP

You can substitute ½ cup long grain white rice for the risotto rice, but the round, risotto rice is slightly more starchy.

Turkey & Rice Soup

You can always use the leftover turkey from Thanksgiving to make the stock for this rich and satisfying soup.

NUTRITIONAL INFORMATION

Calories ....189 Sugars 4g
Protein ....18g Fat 3g
Carbohydrate ...23g Saturates 1g

20 mins
2¾–3¾ hrs

SERVES 8–10

INGREDIENTS

1 onion, finely chopped

2 carrots, diced

1 cup long grain white rice

2 leeks, thinly sliced

2 cups frozen peas

4 oz/115 g fresh or thawed frozen snow peas, thinly sliced

4 oz/115 g fresh spinach or watercress, washed and shredded

1 lb/450 g cooked turkey meat, diced

1 tbsp finely chopped fresh parsley

salt and pepper

STOCK

1 bunch of fresh parsley

2 turkey legs

1 bay leaf

1 tsp dried thyme

2 onions, unpeeled, cut into quarters

2 carrots, cut into chunks

2 celery stalks, cut into chunks

1 parsnip, cut into chunks (optional)

1 eating apple or pear (optional)

1 tbsp black peppercorns

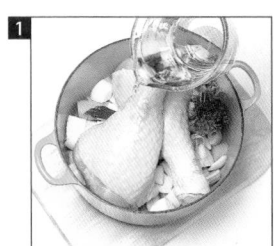

1 To make the stock, first tie the parsley sprigs into a bundle, then put in a large pan with the remaining stock ingredients and enough cold water to cover by 1 inch/2.5 cm.

2 Bring to a boil, skimming off any foam. Boil for 2 minutes, then reduce the heat to low, and simmer very gently for 2–3 hours. Cool the stock slightly, then strain into a large bowl. Skim off any fat from the surface, then wipe paper towels across the surface.

3 Measure 6½ pints/3 liters of the turkey stock into a large pan. Add the onion and carrots and bring to a boil.

4 Add the rice, reduce the heat, and simmer, stirring once or twice, for 15–20 minutes until the rice is tender.

5 Stir the remaining vegetables into the soup and simmer for 10 minutes. Add the cooked turkey meat, heat through, and season to taste with salt and pepper. Stir in the parsley and serve.

Yucatecan Citrus Soup

Roasted onion and garlic are combined with tangy citrus flavors to create a soup full of tantalizing tastes.

NUTRITIONAL INFORMATION

Calories 119	Sugars 14g	
Protein 4g	Fat 4g	
Carbohydrate . . .17g	Saturates 0g	

10 mins   45 mins

SERVES 4

INGREDIENTS

2 onions

15 large garlic cloves, unpeeled

1 tbsp extra virgin olive oil

5⅔ cups vegetable, chicken or fish stock

1 cup water

8 ripe tomatoes, diced

pinch of dried oregano

1 fresh green chile, such as jalapeño or serrano, deseeded and chopped

pinch of ground cumin

½ tsp finely grated grapefruit rind

½ tsp finely grated lime rind

½ tsp finely grated orange rind

juice and diced flesh of 2 limes

juice of 1 orange

juice of 1 grapefruit

salt and pepper

TO GARNISH

tortilla chips, or sliced tortilla strips fried until crisp

2 tbsp chopped fresh cilantro

1 Cut 1 unpeeled onion in half. Peel and finely chop the other onion.

2 Heat a large heavy skillet, add the unpeeled onion halves and garlic, and cook over medium-high heat until the skins char and the onions are caramelized on their cut sides; the garlic should be soft on the inside. Remove from the skillet and set aside to cool slightly.

3 Meanwhile, heat the oil in a pan and lightly cook the remaining onion until softened. Add the stock and water and bring to a boil. Reduce the heat and simmer for a few minutes.

4 Peel the charred onion and garlic, then chop coarsely, and add to the simmering soup, with the tomatoes, oregano, chile, and cumin. Cook, stirring occasionally, for about 15 minutes.

5 Add the citrus rind, season to taste with salt and pepper, then simmer for a further 2 minutes. Remove from the heat and stir in the lime flesh and citrus juices.

6 Ladle into warmed soup bowls, garnish with tortilla chips and fresh cilantro, and serve immediately.

Spicy Gazpacho

This classic Spanish cold soup is given a Mexican twist by adding chiles and fresh cilantro. Serve with chunks of crusty bread.

NUTRITIONAL INFORMATION

Calories ....125 Sugars 10g
Protein ....3g Fat 8g
Carbohydrate ....11g Saturates 1g

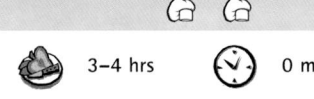

3–4 hrs   0 mins

SERVES 4–6

INGREDIENTS

1 cucumber

2 green bell peppers

6 ripe tomatoes

½ fresh hot chile

½–1 onion, finely chopped

3–4 garlic cloves, chopped

4 tbsp extra virgin olive oil

¼ –½ tsp ground cumin

2–4 tsp sherry vinegar or a combination of balsamic vinegar and wine vinegar

4 tbsp chopped fresh cilantro

2 tbsp chopped fresh parsley

1¼ cups vegetable or chicken stock

2½ cups tomato juice or canned crushed tomatoes

salt and pepper

ice cubes, to serve

1 Cut the cucumber in half lengthwise, then cut into quarters. Remove the seeds with a teaspoon and dice the flesh. Cut the bell peppers in half, remove the cores and seeds, then dice the flesh.

2 If you prefer to peel the tomatoes, place in a heatproof bowl, pour boiling water over to cover, and stand for 30 seconds. Drain and plunge into cold water. The skins will then slide off easily. Cut the tomatoes in half, deseed if wished, then chop the flesh. Deseed and chop the fresh chile.

3 Combine half the cucumber, green bell pepper, tomatoes, and onion in a blender or food processor with all the chile, garlic, olive oil, cumin, vinegar, cilantro, and parsley. Process with enough stock for a smooth purée.

4 Pour the puréed soup into a bowl and stir in the remaining stock and tomato juice or crushed tomatoes. Add the remaining green bell pepper, cucumber, tomatoes, and onion, stirring well. Season with salt and pepper to taste, then cover with plastic wrap, and chill in the refrigerator for a few hours.

5 Ladle the chilled soup into bowls and serve with ice cubes in each bowl.

VARIATION

Freeze tomato juice ice cubes as a delicious alternative.

Spicy Zucchini Soup

Mild red chili powder and pan-browned garlic give flavor to this simple, vegetable soup. Quick to make, it's ideal for a light lunch.

NUTRITIONAL INFORMATION

Calories 98	Sugars 1g
Protein 2g	Fat 7g
Carbohydrate 8g	Saturates 1g

 5 mins   15 mins

SERVES 4

INGREDIENTS

2 tbsp vegetable oil

4 garlic cloves, thinly sliced

1–2 tbsp mild red chili powder

¼–½ tsp ground cumin

6¾ cups chicken, vegetable or beef stock

2 zucchini, cut into bite-size chunks

4 tbsp long grain rice

salt and pepper

fresh oregano sprigs, to garnish

lime wedges, to serve (optional)

1 Heat the oil in a heavy pan, add the garlic, and cook, stirring frequently, for about 2 minutes until softened and just beginning to change color. Stir in the chili powder and cumin and cook over medium-low heat, stirring constantly, for a minute.

2 Stir in the stock, zucchini, and rice, then cook over medium-high heat for about 10 minutes until the zucchini are just tender and the rice is cooked through. Season the soup to taste with salt and pepper.

3 Ladle into warmed soup bowls, garnish with oregano, and serve with lime wedges.

VARIATION
Instead of rice, use rice-shaped pasta, such as orzo or semone de melone, or very thin pasta known as fideo. Use yellow summer squash instead of the zucchini and add cooked pinto beans in place of the rice. Diced tomatoes also make a tasty addition.

Mexican Vegetable Soup

Crisp tortilla chips act as croûtons in this hearty vegetable soup which is found throughout Mexico. Add cheese to melt in, if you wish.

NUTRITIONAL INFORMATION

Calories 201   Sugars 9g
Protein . . . . .6g   Fat 9g
Carbohydrate . . .27g   Saturates 1g

10 mins   40 mins

SERVES 4

INGREDIENTS

2 tbsp vegetable or extra virgin olive oil

1 onion, finely chopped

4 garlic cloves, finely chopped

¼–½ tsp ground cumin

2–3 tsp mild chili powder

1 carrot, sliced

1 waxy potato, diced

12 oz/350 g diced fresh or canned tomatoes

1 zucchini, diced

¼ small cabbage, shredded

4 cups vegetable or chicken stock or water

1 corn cob, the kernels cut off the cob or 1 cup canned corn

about 10 green beans, cut into bite-size lengths

salt and pepper

TO SERVE

4–6 tbsp chopped fresh cilantro

salsa of your choice or chopped fresh chile, to taste

tortilla chips

1 Heat the oil in a heavy pan. Add the onion and garlic and cook for a few minutes until softened, then sprinkle in the cumin and chili powder. Stir in the carrot, potato, tomatoes, zucchini, and cabbage and cook, stirring occasionally, for 2 minutes.

2 Pour in the stock. Cover and cook over medium heat for about 20 minutes until the vegetables are tender.

3 Add extra water if necessary, then stir in the corn and green beans, and cook for a further 5–10 minutes or until the beans are tender. Season with salt and pepper to taste, bearing in mind that the tortilla chips may be salty.

4 Ladle the soup into soup bowls and sprinkle each portion with fresh cilantro. Top with a spoon of salsa, then add a handful of tortilla chips.

Crab & Cabbage Soup

From the Vera Cruz region of Mexico, this delicious soup uses fresh crab meat to add a rich flavor to a mildly spicy vegetable and fish broth.

NUTRITIONAL INFORMATION

Calories 131   Sugars 10g
Protein . . . . .13g   Fat 4g
Carbohydrate . . .12g   Saturates 0g

25 mins   35 mins

SERVES 4

INGREDIENTS

¼ cabbage

1 lb/450 g ripe tomatoes

4 cups fish stock or water mixed with
   1–2 fish bouillon cubes

1 onion, thinly sliced

1 small carrot, diced

4 garlic cloves, finely chopped

6 tbsp chopped fresh cilantro

1 tsp mild chili powder

1 whole cooked crab or 6–8 oz/175–225 g
   crab meat

1 tbsp torn fresh oregano leaves

salt and pepper

TO SERVE

1–2 limes, cut into wedges

salsa of your choice

1 Cut out and discard any thick stalk from the cabbage, then shred the leaves finely using a large knife.

2 To peel the tomatoes, place in a heatproof bowl, pour boiling water over to cover, and stand for 30 seconds. Drain and plunge into cold water. The skins will then slide off easily. Roughly chop the peeled tomatoes.

3 Place the tomatoes and stock in a pan with the onion, carrot, cabbage, garlic, fresh cilantro, and chili powder. Bring to a boil, then reduce the heat, and simmer for about 20 minutes until the vegetables are just tender.

4 Remove the crab meat from the whole crab, if using. Twist off the legs and claws and crack with a heavy knife. Remove the flesh from the legs with a skewer; leave the cracked claws intact, if wished. Remove the body section from the main crab shell and remove the meat, discarding the stomach sac and feathery gills that lie along each side of the body.

5 Add the oregano leaves and crab meat to the pan and simmer for 10–15 minutes to combine the flavors. Season to taste with salt and pepper.

6 Ladle into deep soup bowls and serve immediately with 1–2 wedges of lime, per serving. Hand around a bowl of your chosen salsa separately.

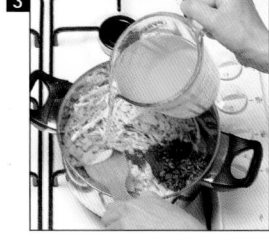 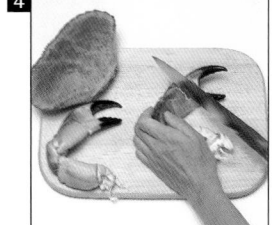 

Fish & Roasted Tomato Soup

Mexico's long shoreline yields an abundance of fish and shellfish, which are often turned into spicy, satisfying soups—just like this one.

NUTRITIONAL INFORMATION

Calories 220	Sugars 6g	
Protein 27g	Fat 10g	
Carbohydrate 7g	Saturates 1g	

 20 mins   30–60 mins

SERVES 4

INGREDIENTS

5 ripe tomatoes

5 garlic cloves, unpeeled

1 lb 2 oz/500 g red snapper, cut into chunks

4 cups fish stock, or water plus
  1–2 fish bouillon cubes

2–3 tbsp olive oil

1 onion, chopped

2 fresh chiles, such as serrano, deseeded
  and thinly sliced

lime wedges, to serve

1 Heat an ungreased heavy skillet, add the whole tomatoes and garlic, and cook over high heat until charred. Alternatively, place under a preheated broiler until the skins of the vegetables blacken and char and the flesh inside is tender. As another alternative, place the tomatoes and garlic cloves in a roasting pan and bake in a preheated oven, 375–400°F/190–200°C, for about about 40 minutes.

2 Set the tomatoes and garlic aside to cool, then remove the skins, and chop coarsely, combining them with any juices from the skillet or roasting pan. Set aside.

3 Poach the snapper in the stock over medium heat for about 5 minutes just until it is opaque and firm. Remove the pan from the heat and set aside.

4 Heat the oil in another pan and cook the chopped onion until softened. Strain in the cooking liquid from the fish, then add the coarsely chopped tomatoes and garlic, and stir.

5 Bring to a boil, then reduce the heat, and simmer gently for about 5 minutes to combine the flavors. Add the sliced chiles.

6 Divide chunks of the poached red snapper among warmed soup bowls, ladle over the hot soup, and serve immediately with lime wedges for squeezing over the top.

Chicken & Chipotle Soup

This soup evolved from the foodstalls that line the streets of Tlalpan, a suburb of Mexico City: avocado, chicken, and chiles make it special.

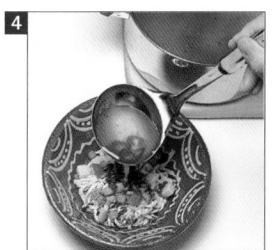

NUTRITIONAL INFORMATION

Calories 216	Sugars 1g
Protein 28g	Fat 11g
Carbohydrate 2g	Saturates 2g

 10 mins   5 mins

SERVES 4

INGREDIENTS

6¾ cups chicken stock

2–3 garlic cloves, finely chopped

1–2 chipotle chiles, cut into very thin strips (see Cook's Tip)

1 avocado

lime or lemon juice, for tossing

3–5 scallions, thinly sliced

12–14 oz/350–400 g skinless boneless cooked chicken breast portions, torn or cut into shreds or thin strips

2 tbsp chopped fresh cilantro

TO SERVE

1 lime, cut into wedges

handful of tortilla chips (optional)

1 Place the stock in a pan with the garlic and chipotle chiles and bring to a boil.

2 Meanwhile, cut the avocado in half around the pit. Twist apart, then remove the pit with a knife. Carefully peel off the skin, dice the flesh, and toss in lime or lemon juice to prevent the flesh from turning brown.

3 Arrange the scallions, chicken, avocado, and fresh cilantro in the base of 4 individual soup bowls or in a large tureen.

4 Ladle the hot stock into the bowls and serve with lime wedges and a handful of tortilla chips if using.

COOK'S TIP

Chipotle chiles are smoked and dried jalapeño chiles and are available canned or dried. They add a distinctive smoky flavor to dishes and are very hot. Drain canned chipotles before using. Dried chipotles need to be reconstituted before using.

Chicken & Asparagus Soup

This light, clear soup has a delicate flavor of asparagus and herbs.
Use a good quality stock for best results.

NUTRITIONAL INFORMATION

Calories	224	Sugars	.........2g
Protein	........27g	Fat	...........5g
Carbohydrate	...12g	Saturates	......1g

 10 mins   15 mins

SERVES 4

INGREDIENTS

8 oz/225 g fresh asparagus

3¾ cups chicken stock

⅔ cup dry white wine

fresh parsley sprig

fresh dill sprig

fresh tarragon sprig

1 garlic clove

2 oz/55 g vermicelli rice noodles

12 oz/350 g lean cooked chicken,
   finely shredded

1 small leek

salt and white pepper

1 Wash the asparagus and trim away the woody ends. Cut each spear into pieces 1½ inches/4 cm long.

2 Pour the stock and wine into a large pan and bring to a boil over medium heat.

3 Wash the herbs and tie them together with clean string. Peel the garlic clove and add, with the herbs, to the pan. Add the asparagus and noodles. Lower the heat, cover, and simmer for 5 minutes.

4 Stir in the chicken and season to taste with salt and pepper. Simmer gently for a further 3-4 minutes until heated through.

5 Trim the leek, slice it down the center, and wash under running water to remove any dirt. Shake dry and shred very finely.

6 Remove the herbs and garlic from the pan and discard. Ladle the soup into warmed bowls, sprinkle with shredded leek, and serve immediately.

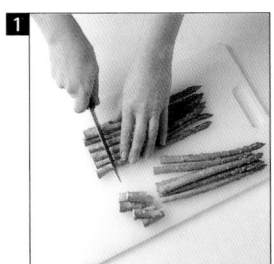

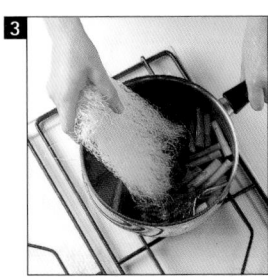

VARIATION

You can use any of your favorite herbs in this recipe, but choose those with a subtle flavor so that they do not overpower the asparagus. Small, tender asparagus spears give the best results and flavor.

Beet & Potato Soup

A deep red soup makes a stunning first course—and it's easy in the microwave. A swirl of sour cream gives a very pretty effect.

NUTRITIONAL INFORMATION

Calories ....120 Sugars 11g
Protein ....4g Fat 2g
Carbohydrate ...22g Saturates 1g

20 mins 30 mins

SERVES 6

INGREDIENTS

1 onion, chopped

12 oz/350 g potatoes, diced

1 small cooking apple, peeled, cored, and grated

3 tbsp water

1 tsp cumin seeds

1 lb 2 oz/500 g cooked beet, peeled and diced

1 bay leaf

pinch of dried thyme

1 tsp lemon juice

2½ cups hot vegetable stock

4 tbsp sour cream

salt and pepper

fresh dill sprigs, to garnish

1 Place the onion, potatoes, apple, and water in a large bowl. Cover and cook on HIGH power for 10 minutes.

2 Stir in the cumin seeds and cook on HIGH power for 1 minute.

3 Stir in the beet, bay leaf, thyme, lemon juice, and stock. Cover and cook on HIGH power for 12 minutes, stirring halfway through. Set aside, uncovered, for 5 minutes.

4 Remove and discard the bay leaf. Strain the vegetables and reserve the liquid in a pitcher.

5 Place the vegetables with a little of the reserved liquid in a food processor or blender and process to a smooth and creamy purée. Alternatively, either mash the vegetable with a potato masher or press through a strainer.

6 Pour the vegetable purée into a clean bowl with the reserved liquid and mix well. Season with salt and pepper to taste. Cover and cook on HIGH power for 4–5 minutes until piping hot.

7 Serve the soup in warmed bowls. Swirl 1 tablespoon of sour cream into each serving and garnish with a few sprigs of fresh dill.

Spiced Fruit Soup

This delicately flavored apple and apricot soup is gently spiced with ginger and allspice and finished with a swirl of sour cream.

NUTRITIONAL INFORMATION

Calories	147	Sugar	........28g
Protein	.........3g	Fats	.........0.4g
Carbohydrates	...29g	Saturates	......0g

 7¾ hrs   25 mins

SERVES 4–6

I N G R E D I E N T S

generous 1 cup dried apricots, soaked overnight or no-need-to-soak dried apricots

1 lb 2 oz/500 g eating apples, peeled, cored, and chopped

1 small onion, chopped

1 tbsp lemon or lime juice

3 cups chicken stock

⅔ cup dry white wine

¼ tsp ground ginger

pinch of ground allspice

salt and pepper

TO GARNISH

4–6 tbsp sour cream

ground ginger or ground allspice

1 Drain the apricots, if necessary, and chop coarsely.

2 Put the apricots in a pan and add the apples, onion, lemon or lime juice, and stock. Bring to a boil, cover, and simmer gently for about 20 minutes.

3 Set the soup aside to cool a little, then press through a strainer or process in a food processor or blender until a smooth purée. Pour the fruit soup into a clean pan.

4 Add the wine and spices and season to taste. Bring back to a boil, then set aside to cool. If it is too thick, add a little more stock or water and then chill in the refrigerator for several hours.

5 Garnish with sour cream and dust lightly with ginger or allspice.

VARIATION

Other fruits can be combined with apples to make fruit soups — try raspberries, blackberries, black currants, or cherries. If the fruits have a lot of seeds or pits, the soup should be strained after puréeing.

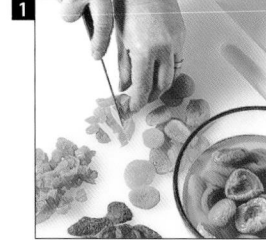

Beef Soup with Rice

Strips of tender lean beef are combined with crisp water chestnuts and cooked rice in a tasty beef broth with a tang of orange.

NUTRITIONAL INFORMATION

Calories	.210	Sugar	.4g
Protein	.20g	Fats	.5g
Carbohydrates	.21g	Saturates	.2g

 25 mins   25 mins

SERVES 4

INGREDIENTS

12 oz/350 g lean beef, such as round or sirloin

4 cups beef stock

1 cinnamon stick, broken

2 star anise

2 tbsp dark soy sauce

2 tbsp dry sherry

3 tbsp tomato paste

4 oz/115 g can water chestnuts, drained and sliced

1 cup cooked white rice

1 tsp finely grated orange rind

6 tbsp orange juice

salt and pepper

TO GARNISH

strips of orange rind

2 tbsp chopped fresh chives

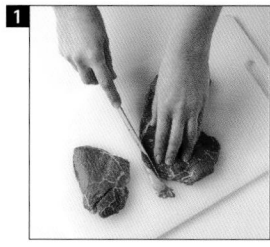  

1 Carefully trim away any fat from the beef. Cut the beef into thin strips and then place in a large pan.

2 Pour in the beef stock and add the cinnamon, star anise, soy sauce, sherry, tomato paste, and water chestnuts. Bring to a boil over medium heat, skimming off any scum that rises to the surface with a flat ladle or skimmer. Cover the pan, lower the heat, and simmer gently for about 20 minutes or until the beef strips are tender.

3 Skim the soup with a flat ladle again to remove any more scum. Remove and discard the 2 pieces of cinnamon stick and the star anise and blot the surface of the soup with absorbent paper towels to remove as much fat as possible.

4 Stir in the rice, grated orange rind, and orange juice. Season to taste with salt and pepper. Heat through for 2–3 minutes before ladling into warmed bowls. Serve garnished with strips of orange rind and chopped chives.

Mixed Bean Soup

This is a really hearty soup, filled with color, flavor, and goodness, which may be adapted to any vegetables that you have at hand.

NUTRITIONAL INFORMATION

Calories	190	Sugars	.........9g
Protein	........10g	Fat	...........4g
Carbohydrate	...30g	Saturates	.....0.5g

 5 mins 40 mins

SERVES 4

INGREDIENTS

1 tbsp vegetable oil

1 red onion, halved and sliced

3½ oz/100 g potato, diced

1 carrot, diced

1 leek, sliced

1 fresh green chile, sliced

3 garlic cloves, crushed

1 tsp ground coriander

1 tsp chili powder

4 cups vegetable stock

1 lb/450 g mixed canned beans, such as red kidney, borlotti, or small cannellini, drained and rinsed

salt and pepper

2 tbsp chopped fresh cilantro, to garnish

1 Heat the oil in a large pan and add the onion, potato, carrot, and leek. Cook, stirring occasionally, for 2 minutes until the vegetables are slightly softened.

2 Add the chile and garlic and cook for 1 further minute.

3 Stir in the ground coriander, chili powder, and the vegetable stock.

4 Bring the soup to a boil, reduce the heat, and cook for 20 minutes or until the vegetables are tender.

5 Stir in the beans, season to taste, and cook, stirring occasionally, for a further 10 minutes.

6 Ladle the soup into bowls, garnish with chopped cilantro, and serve.

COOK'S TIP

Serve this soup with slices of warm corn bread or a cheese loaf.

Yogurt & Spinach Soup

Whole young spinach leaves add vibrant color to this unusual soup.
Serve with hot, crusty bread for a nutritious light meal.

NUTRITIONAL INFORMATION

Calories 227   Sugars 13g
Protein . . . . .14g   Fat 7g
Carbohydrate . . .29g   Saturates 2g

15 mins   30 mins

SERVES 4

I N G R E D I E N T S

2½ cups chicken stock

4 tbsp long grain rice, rinsed and drained

4 tbsp water

1 tbsp cornstarch

2½ cups low-fat plain yogurt

3 egg yolks, lightly beaten

juice of 1 lemon

12 oz/350 g young spinach leaves, washed
  and drained

salt and pepper

1 Pour the stock into a large pan, season, and bring to a boil. Add the rice and simmer for 10 minutes until barely cooked. Remove from the heat.

2 Combine the water and cornstarch to a smooth paste. Pour the yogurt into a second pan and stir in the cornstarch mixture. Set the pan over low heat and bring the yogurt to a boil, stirring with a wooden spoon in one direction only. This will stabilize the yogurt and prevent it from separating or curdling on contact with the hot stock. When the yogurt has reached boiling point, stand the pan on a heat diffuser and simmer gently for 10 minutes. Remove the pan from the heat and set the mixture aside to cool slightly before stirring in the beaten egg yolks.

3 Pour the yogurt mixture into the stock, stir in the lemon juice, and stir to blend thoroughly. Keep the soup warm, but do not allow it to boil.

4 Blanch the washed and drained spinach leaves in a large pan of boiling, salted water for 2–3 minutes until they begin to soften, but have not wilted. Tip the spinach into a colander, drain well, and stir it into the soup. Warm through. Taste the soup and adjust the seasoning if necessary. Serve immediately in wide shallow soup plates, with hot, fresh crusty bread.

Coconut & Crab Soup

Thai red curry paste is quite fiery, but adds a superb flavor to this dish. It is available in jars or packets from supermarkets.

NUTRITIONAL INFORMATION

Calories 122	Sugar 9g	
Protein 11g	Fats 4g	
Carbohydrates ...11g	Saturates 1g	

 5 mins   8–10 mins

SERVES 4

INGREDIENTS

1 tbsp peanut oil

2 tbsp Thai red curry paste

1 red bell pepper, deseeded and sliced

2½ cups coconut milk

2½ cups fish stock

2 tbsp Thai fish sauce

8 oz/225 g canned or fresh white crab meat

8 oz/225 g fresh or frozen crab claws

2 tbsp chopped fresh cilantro

3 scallions, sliced

1 Heat the oil in a large preheated wok, swirling it around to coat. Add the red curry paste and red bell pepper and stir-fry over medium heat for 1 minute.

2 Add the coconut milk, fish stock, and fish sauce and bring to a boil.

3 Add the crab meat, crab claws, cilantro, and scallions.

4 Stir the mixture well and heat thoroughly for 2–3 minutes or until all the ingredients are warmed through.

5 Transfer the soup to 4 warmed bowls and serve hot.

COOK'S TIP

Clean the wok after use by washing it with water, using a mild detergent if necessary, and a soft cloth or brush. Do not scrub or use any abrasive cleaner as this will scratch the surface. Dry thoroughly then wipe the surface all over with a little oil to protect it.

Red Lentil Soup with Yogurt

Tasty red lentil soup flavored with chopped cilantro is an easy microwave dish. The yogurt adds a light piquancy to the soup.

NUTRITIONAL INFORMATION

Calories . . . . . . .280 Sugars 6g
Protein . . . . .17g Fat 7g
Carbohydrate . . .40g Saturates 4g

5 mins   30 mins

SERVES 4

I N G R E D I E N T S

2 tbsp butter

1 onion, finely chopped

1 celery stalk, finely chopped

1 large carrot, grated

1 bay leaf

1 cup red lentils

5 cups hot vegetable or
  chicken stock

2 tbsp chopped fresh cilantro

4 tbsp low-fat plain yogurt

salt and pepper

fresh cilantro sprigs, to garnish

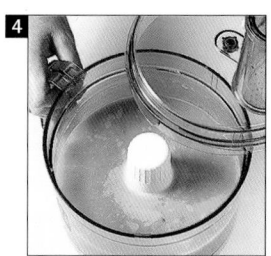

1 Place the butter, onion, and celery in a large bowl. Cover and cook on HIGH power for 3 minutes.

2 Add the carrot, bay leaf, and lentils. Pour in the stock. Cover and cook on HIGH power for 15 minutes, stirring halfway through.

3 Remove the bowl from the microwave oven, cover, and stand for 5 minutes.

4 Remove and discard the bay leaf, then process, in batches, in a food processor, until smooth. Alternatively, press the soup through a strainer.

5 Pour the soup into a clean bowl. Season with salt and pepper to taste and stir in the cilantro. Cover and cook on HIGH power for 4–5 minutes until the soup is piping hot.

6 Serve in warmed soup bowls. Stir 1 tablespoon of yogurt into each serving and garnish with small sprigs of fresh cilantro.

COOK'S TIP

For an extra creamy soup try adding low-fat crème fraîche or sour cream instead of yogurt.

Spicy Lentil Soup

For a warming, satisfying meal on a cold day,
this lentil dish is packed full of flavor and goodness.

NUTRITIONAL INFORMATION

Calories 155	Sugars 4g	
Protein 11g	Fat 3g	
Carbohydrate ...22g	Saturates 0.4g	

 1 hr 1¼ hrs

SERVES 4

INGREDIENTS

½ cup red lentils

2 tsp vegetable oil

1 large onion, finely chopped

2 garlic cloves, crushed

1 tsp ground cumin

1 tsp ground coriander

1 tsp garam masala

2 tbsp tomato paste

4 cups vegetable stock

12 oz/350 g can corn, drained

salt and pepper

TO SERVE

low-fat plain yogurt

chopped fresh parsley

warmed pitas

1 Rinse the red lentils thoroughly under cold running water. Drain well and set side.

2 Heat the oil in a large nonstick pan and fry the onion and garlic gently until softened but not browned.

3 Stir in the cumin, coriander, garam masala, tomato paste, and 4 tablespoons of the stock. Mix well and simmer gently for 2 minutes.

4 Add the lentils and pour in the remaining stock. Bring to a boil, reduce the heat, cover, and simmer for 1 hour until the lentils are tender and the soup thickened. Stir in the corn and heat through for 5 minutes. Season to taste with salt and pepper.

5 Ladle into warmed soup bowls and top each with a spoonful of yogurt and a sprinkling of parsley. Serve with warmed pitas.

COOK'S TIP

Many of the ready-prepared ethnic breads available today either contain fat or are brushed with oil before baking. Always check the ingredients list for fat content.

Lentil & Ham Soup

This is a good hearty soup, based on a stock made from a ham knuckle, with plenty of vegetables and red lentils to thicken it and add flavor.

NUTRITIONAL INFORMATION

Calories . . . . .219 Sugars 4g
Protein . . . . .17g Fat 3g
Carbohydrate . . .33g Saturates 1g

 2¼ hrs   1¾ hrs

SERVES 4–6

I N G R E D I E N T S

1 cup red lentils

6¼ cups stock or water

2 onions, chopped

1 garlic clove, crushed

2 large carrots, chopped

1 lean ham knuckle or 6 oz/175 g lean
  bacon, chopped

4 large tomatoes, peeled and chopped

2 bay leaves

9 oz/250 g potatoes, chopped

1 tbsp white wine vinegar

¼ tsp ground allspice

salt and pepper

chopped scallions or chopped fresh parsley,
  to garnish

1 Put the lentils and stock or water in a pan and set aside to soak for 1–2 hours.

2 Add the onions, garlic, carrots, ham knuckle or chopped bacon, tomatoes, and bay leaves. Season to taste with salt and pepper.

3 Bring the mixture to a boil over medium heat, then lower the heat, cover, and simmer for about 1 hour until the lentils are tender, stirring occasionally to prevent the lentils from sticking to the bottom of the pan.

4 Add the potatoes and continue to simmer for about 20 minutes until the potatoes and the meat on the ham knuckle are tender.

5 Remove and discard the bay leaves. Remove the knuckle and chop 14½ oz/125 g of the meat and reserve. If liked, press half the soup through a strainer or process in a food processor or blender until smooth. Return to the pan with the rest of the soup.

6 Adjust the seasoning, add the vinegar and allspice, and the reserved chopped ham. Simmer gently for a further 5–10 minutes. Serve sprinkled liberally with scallions or chopped parsley.

Smoked Haddock Soup

Smoked haddock gives this soup a wonderfully rich flavor, while the mashed potatoes and cream thicken and enrich the stock.

NUTRITIONAL INFORMATION

Calories	169	Sugars	...........8g
Protein	...........16g	Fat	...........5g
Carbohydrate	...16g	Saturates	......3g

 25 mins 40 mins

SERVES 4–6

I N G R E D I E N T S

8 oz/225 g smoked haddock fillet

1 onion, finely chopped

1 garlic clove, crushed

2½ cups water

2½ cups skim milk

2⅔–4 cups hot mashed potatoes

2 tbsp butter

about 1 tbsp lemon juice

6 tbsp low-fat plain yogurt

4 tbsp fresh parsley, chopped

salt and pepper

1 Put the fish, onion, garlic, and water into a pan. Bring to a boil, cover, and simmer over low heat for 15–20 minutes.

2 Remove the fish from the pan. Strip off the skin and remove all the bones, and reserve both. Flake the flesh finely with a fork.

3 Return the skin and bones to the cooking liquid and simmer for 10 minutes. Strain, discarding the skin and bones. Pour the cooking liquid into a clean pan.

4 Add the milk and flaked fish and season to taste with salt and pepper. Bring to a boil and simmer for about 3 minutes.

5 Gradually whisk in sufficient mashed potato to give a fairly thick soup, then stir in the butter, and sharpen to taste with lemon juice.

6 Add the yogurt and 3 tablespoons of the chopped parsley. Reheat gently and adjust the seasoning if necessary. Sprinkle with the remaining parsley and serve the soup immediately.

COOK'S TIP

Undyed smoked haddock may be used in place of the bright yellow fish; it will give a paler color, but just as much flavor. Alternatively, use smoked cod or smoked whiting.

Carrot & Cumin Soup

Carrot soups are very popular and and here cumin, tomato, potato, and celery give the soup both richness and depth.

NUTRITIONAL INFORMATION

Calories 114   Sugars 8g
Protein . . . . .3g   Fat 6g
Carbohydrate . . .12g   Saturates 4g

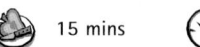 15 mins    45 mins

SERVES 4–6

INGREDIENTS

3 tbsp butter or margarine

1 large onion, chopped

1–2 garlic cloves, crushed

12 oz/350 g carrots, sliced

3¾ cups chicken or vegetable stock

¾ tsp ground cumin

2 celery stalks, thinly sliced

4 oz/115 g potato, diced

2 tsp tomato paste

2 tsp lemon juice

2 fresh or dried bay leaves

about 1¼ cups skim milk

salt and pepper

celery leaves, to garnish

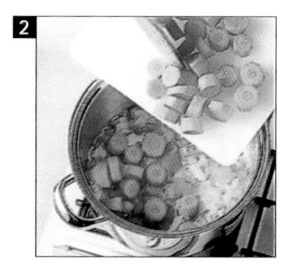  

1 Melt the butter or margarine in a large pan. Add the onion and garlic and cook very gently until softened.

2 Add the carrots and cook gently for a further 5 minutes, stirring frequently and taking care they do not brown.

3 Add the stock, cumin, seasoning, celery, potato, tomato paste, lemon juice, and bay leaves and bring to a boil. Cover and simmer for about 30 minutes until the vegetables are tender.

4 Remove and discard the bay leaves, cool the soup a little, and then press it through a strainer or process in a food processor or blender until smooth.

5 Pour the soup into a clean pan, add the milk, and bring to a boil over low heat. Taste and adjust the seasoning if necessary.

6 Ladle into warmed bowls, garnish each serving with a small celery leaf and serve.

COOK'S TIP

This soup can be frozen for up to 3 months. Add the milk when reheating.

Spiced Cauliflower Soup

This thick puréed soup flavored with Indian spices and yogurt is a good choice for the microwave. Serve with hot nan bread.

NUTRITIONAL INFORMATION

Calories	123	Sugars	........13g
Protein	.........8g	Fat	...........4g
Carbohydrate	...14g	Saturates	......1g

 10 mins   25 mins

SERVES 4

INGREDIENTS

12 oz/350 g cauliflower, divided into
  small florets

12 oz/350 g rutabaga, diced

1 onion, chopped

1 tbsp vegetable oil

3 tbsp water

1 garlic clove, crushed

2 tsp grated fresh ginger root

1 tsp cumin seeds

1 tsp black mustard seeds

2 tsp ground coriander

2 tsp ground turmeric

3¾ cups hot vegetable stock

1¼ cups low-fat plain yogurt

salt and pepper

chopped fresh cilantro,
  to garnish

1 Place the cauliflower, rutabaga, onion, oil, and water in a large bowl. Cover and cook on HIGH power for 10 minutes, stirring halfway through.

2 Add the garlic, ginger, cumin, mustard seeds, ground coriander, and turmeric. Stir well, cover, and cook on HIGH power for 2 minutes.

3 Pour in the stock, cover, and cook on HIGH power for 10 minutes. Stand, covered, for 5 minutes.

4 Strain the vegetables and reserve the liquid. Process the vegetables with a little of the reserved liquid in a food processor or blender until smooth and creamy. Alternatively, either mash the soup or press it through a strainer.

5 Pour the vegetable purée and remaining reserved liquid into a clean bowl and mix well. Season to taste with salt and pepper.

6 Stir in the yogurt and cook on HIGH power for 3–4 minutes until hot, but not boiling, otherwise the yogurt will curdle. Ladle into warmed bowls and serve garnished with chopped fresh cilantro.

Cucumber & Tomato Soup

Although this chilled soup is not an authentic Indian dish, it is wonderful served as a "cooler" between hot, spicy courses.

NUTRITIONAL INFORMATION

Calories 73   Sugar 16g
Protein . . . . .2g   Fats 1g
Carbohydrates . . .16g   Saturates 0.2g

12 hrs   0 mins

SERVES 6

I N G R E D I E N T S

4 tomatoes, peeled and deseeded

3 lb 5 oz/1.5 kg watermelon, seedless if available

4 inch/10 cm piece of cucumber, peeled and deseeded

2 scallions, green parts only, chopped

1 tbsp chopped fresh mint

salt and pepper

fresh mint sprigs, to garnish

1 Using a sharp knife, cut 1 tomato into ½ inch/1 cm dice.

2 Remove the rind from the melon, and remove the seeds if it is not seedless.

3 Put the 3 remaining tomatoes into a blender or food processor and, with the motor running, add the cucumber, scallions, and watermelon. Process until smooth.

4 If not using a food processor, push the deseeded watermelon through a strainer. Stir the diced tomatoes and mint into the melon purée. Adjust the seasoning to taste. Chop the cucumber, scallions and the 3 remaining tomatoes finely and add to the melon.

5 Cover and chill the cucumber and tomato soup overnight in the refrigerator. Check the seasoning and transfer to a serving bowl. Garnish with mint sprigs.

COOK'S TIP

Although this soup does improve if chilled overnight, it is also delicious as a quick appetizer if whipped up just before a meal, and served immediately.

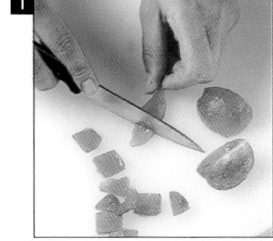

Chunky Potato & Beef Soup

This is a real winter warmer—pieces of tender beef and chunky mixed vegetables are cooked in a stock flavored with sherry.

NUTRITIONAL INFORMATION

Calories	187	Sugars	.........3g
Protein	........14g	Fat	...........9g
Carbohydrate	...12g	Saturates	......2g

 5 mins   35 mins

SERVES 4

INGREDIENTS

2 tbsp vegetable oil

8 oz/225 g lean braising or frying steak, cut into strips

8 oz/225 g new potatoes, halved

1 carrot, diced

2 celery stalks, sliced

2 leeks, sliced

3¾ cups beef stock

8 baby corn cobs, sliced

1 bouquet garni

2 tbsp dry sherry

salt and pepper

chopped fresh parsley, to garnish

crusty bread, to serve

COOK'S TIP

Make double the quantity of soup and freeze the remainder in a rigid container for later use. When ready to use, place in the refrigerator to thaw thoroughly, then heat until piping hot.

1 Heat the vegetable oil in a large pan. Add the strips of steak to the pan and cook for 3 minutes, turning constantly.

2 Add the halved potatoes, diced carrot, and sliced celery and leeks. Cook, stirring constantly, for a further 5 minutes.

3 Pour in the beef stock and bring to a boil over medium heat. Reduce the heat until the liquid is simmering gently, then add the sliced baby corn cobs and the bouquet garni.

4 Cook the soup for a further 20 minutes or until the meat and all the vegetables are tender.

5 Remove the bouquet garni from the pan and discard. Stir the dry sherry into the soup and then season to taste with salt and pepper.

6 Pour the soup into warmed soup bowls and garnish with the chopped fresh parsley. Serve immediately with crusty bread.

Carrot, Apple & Celery Soup

For this fresh-tasting soup, use your favorite variety of eating apple rather than a cooking variety, which will give too tart a flavor.

NUTRITIONAL INFORMATION

Calories ......153 Sugars 34g
Protein ....2g Fat 1g
Carbohydrate ...36g Saturates 0.2g

1¼ hrs   40 mins

SERVES 4

INGREDIENTS

2 lb/900 g carrots, finely diced

1 medium onion, chopped

3 celery stalks, diced

4 cups vegetable stock

3 medium-size eating apples

2 tbsp tomato paste

1 bay leaf

2 tsp superfine sugar

¼ large lemon

salt and pepper

celery leaves, shredded, to garnish

3 Meanwhile, wash, core, and cut the remaining apple into thin slices, without peeling.

4 Place the apple slices in a small pan and squeeze over the lemon juice. Heat the apple slices gently and simmer for 1–2 minutes until tender.

5 Drain the apple slices and set aside until required.

6 Place the carrot and apple mixture in a blender or food processor and process until smooth. Alternatively, press the mixture through a strainer with the back of a wooden spoon.

7 Gently re-heat the soup if necessary and season with salt and pepper to taste. Ladle the soup into warmed bowls and serve topped with the reserved apple slices and shredded celery leaves.

1 Place the carrots, onion, and celery in a large, heavy pan and add the stock. Bring to a boil, lower the heat, cover, and simmer for 10 minutes.

2 Meanwhile, peel, core, and dice 2 of the apples. Add the pieces of apple, the tomato paste, bay leaf, and superfine sugar to the pan and bring to a boil over medium heat. Reduce the heat, half cover, and simmer for 20 minutes. Remove and discard the bay leaf.

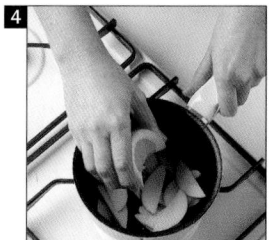

Peking Duck Soup

This is a hearty and robustly flavored soup, containing pieces of duck and vegetables cooked in a rich stock.

NUTRITIONAL INFORMATION

Calories	92	Sugars	.........3g
Protein	.........8g	Fat	...........5g
Carbohydrate	....3g	Saturates	.......1g

5 mins   35 mins

SERVES 4

INGREDIENTS

4 oz/115 g lean duck breast meat

8 oz/225 g Napa cabbage

3¾ cups chicken or duck stock

1 tbsp dry sherry or Chinese rice wine

1 tbsp light soy sauce

2 garlic cloves, crushed

pinch of ground star anise

1 tbsp sesame seeds

1 tsp sesame oil

1 tbsp chopped fresh parsley

1 Remove the skin from the duck breast and finely dice the flesh. Using a sharp knife, shred the Napa cabbage.

2 Put the stock in a large pan and bring to a boil over medium heat. Add the sherry or rice wine, soy sauce, diced duck meat, and shredded Napa cabbage and stir thoroughly. Reduce the heat and simmer gently for 15 minutes.

3 Stir in the garlic and star anise and cook over a low heat for a further 10–15 minutes or until the duck is tender.

4 Meanwhile, dry-fry the sesame seeds in a preheated, heavy skillet or wok, stirring constantly, until they give off their fragrance.

5 Remove the sesame seeds from the skillet or wok and stir them into the soup, with the sesame oil and the chopped fresh parsley.

6 Ladle the Peking duck soup into warmed bowls and serve immediately.

VARIATION

If Napa cabbage is unavailable, use leafy green cabbage instead. You may wish to adjust the quantity to taste, as ordinary green cabbage has a stronger flavor and odor than Napa cabbage.

Shrimp Gumbo

This soup is packed with onions, red bell peppers, rice, shrimp, and okra, a vegetable which adds flavor and acts as a thickening agent.

NUTRITIONAL INFORMATION

Calories	177	Sugar	.........5g
Protein	........12g	Fats	...........8g
Carbohydrates	...15g	Saturates	......1g

1 hr   45 mins

SERVES 4–6

INGREDIENTS

2 tbsp olive oil

1 large onion, finely chopped

2 slices lean bacon, finely chopped (optional)

1–2 garlic cloves, crushed

1 large or 2 small red bell peppers, finely chopped or coarsely ground

3¾ cups fish or vegetable stock

1 bay leaf

1 mace blade

pinch of ground allspice

3 tbsp long grain rice

1 tbsp white wine vinegar

4½–6 oz/125–175 g okra, trimmed and very thinly sliced

1 cup peeled shrimp

1 tbsp anchovy extract

2 tsp tomato paste

1–2 tbsp chopped fresh parsley

salt and pepper

TO GARNISH

whole shrimp

fresh parsley sprigs

1 Heat the oil in a large pan and cook the onion, bacon, if using, and garlic over low heat for 4–5 minutes until soft. Add the bell peppers and cook gently for a further 2 minutes.

2 Add the stock, bay leaf, mace, allspice, rice, vinegar, and seasoning and bring to a boil. Cover and simmer gently for about 20 minutes, stirring occasionally, until the rice is just tender.

3 Add the okra, shrimp, anchovy extract, and tomato paste, cover, and simmer gently for about 15 minutes until the okra is tender and the mixture has thickened slightly.

4 Remove and discard the bay leaf and mace and adjust the seasoning if necessary. Stir in the parsley, ladle into warmed bowls, and serve garnished with a whole shrimp and parsley sprigs.

Pork Chili Soup

This meaty chili tastes lighter than one made with beef.
Good for informal entertaining, the recipe is easily doubled.

NUTRITIONAL INFORMATION

Calories	308	Sugars	........13g
Protein	........40g	Fat	..........10g
Carbohydrate	...15g	Saturates	.......3g

10 mins   50–60 mins

SERVES 3

INGREDIENTS

2 tsp olive oil

1 lb 2 oz/500 g lean ground pork

1 onion, finely chopped

1 celery stalk, finely chopped

1 bell pepper, deseeded and finely chopped

2–3 garlic cloves, finely chopped

14 oz/400 g can chopped tomatoes in juice

3 tbsp tomato paste

2 cups chicken or meat stock

¼ tsp ground coriander

¼ tsp ground cumin

¼ tsp dried oregano

1 tsp mild chili powder

salt and pepper

chopped fresh cilantro leaves or parsley,
    to garnish

sour cream, to serve

2 Add the tomatoes, tomato paste, and the stock. Stir in the coriander, cumin, oregano, and chili powder. Season with salt and pepper to taste.

3 Bring just to a boil, then reduce the heat to low, cover, and simmer for about 30–40 minutes until all the vegetables are very tender. Taste and adjust the seasoning, adding more chili powder if you like it hotter.

4 Ladle the chili into warm bowls and sprinkle with chopped cilantro or parsley. You can either hand the sour cream separately or top each serving with a spoonful.

1 Heat the oil in a pan over medium-high heat. Add the pork, season with salt and pepper, and cook, stirring frequently, until no longer pink. Reduce the heat to medium and add the onion, celery, bell pepper, and garlic. Cover and cook, stirring occasionally, for a further 5 minutes until the onion is softened.

Asian Pork Balls in Broth

Steaming the meatballs over the soup gives added flavor to the broth.
A bamboo steamer that rests on the top of a pan is useful for this recipe.

NUTRITIONAL INFORMATION

Calories 67   Sugars 1g
Protein ....9g   Fat 2g
Carbohydrate ....3g   Saturates 1g

 15 mins   18 mins

SERVES 6

I N G R E D I E N T S

4 cups chicken stock

1¼ cups thinly sliced shiitake mushrooms

6 oz/175 g bok choy or other Napa
cabbage, sliced into thin ribbons

6 scallions, thinly sliced

salt and pepper

PORK BALLS

8 oz/225 g lean ground pork

1 oz/25 g fresh spinach leaves,
finely chopped

2 scallions, finely chopped

1 garlic clove, very finely chopped

pinch of Chinese five-spice powder

1 tsp soy sauce

1 To make the pork balls, put the pork, spinach, scallions, and garlic in a bowl. Add the five-spice powder and soy sauce and mix until thoroughly combined.

2 Shape the pork mixture into 24 balls. Place them in a single layer in a steamer that will fit over the top of a pan or in a wok.

3 Bring the stock just to a boil in a pan or wok that will accommodate the steamer. Lower the heat so that the liquid just bubbles gently. Add the mushrooms to the stock and place the steamer, covered, on top of the pan or wok. Steam for 10 minutes. Remove the steamer and set aside on a plate.

4 Add the bok choy or Napa cabbage and scallions to the pan or wok and cook gently in the stock for 3-4 minutes or until the greens are wilted. Season the broth to taste with salt and pepper.

5 Divide the pork balls evenly among 6 warmed bowls and ladle the soup over them. Serve immediately.

Spicy Lamb Soup

Packed with tomatoes, garbanzo beans, and vegetables, this thick and hearty entrée soup is bursting with exotic flavors and aromas.

NUTRITIONAL INFORMATION

Calories	...323	Sugars	...6g
Protein	...27g	Fat	...13g
Carbohydrate	...25g	Saturates	...4g

 10 mins 1¾ hrs

SERVES 4–5

INGREDIENTS

1–2 tbsp olive oil

1 lb/450 g lean boneless lamb, such as shoulder fillet, trimmed of fat and cut into ½ inch/1 cm cubes

1 onion, finely chopped

2–3 garlic cloves, crushed

5 cups water

14 oz/400 g can chopped tomatoes

1 bay leaf

½ tsp dried thyme

½ tsp dried oregano

pinch of ground cinnamon

¼ tsp ground cumin

¼ tsp ground turmeric

1 tsp harissa

14 oz/400 g can garbanzo beans, rinsed and drained

1 carrot, diced

1 potato, diced

1 zucchini, quartered lengthwise and sliced

1 cup fresh or thawed frozen green peas

salt and pepper

chopped fresh mint or cilantro leaves, to garnish

1 Heat the oil in a large pan or flameproof casserole over medium-high heat. Add the lamb, in batches if necessary, and cook, stirring occasionally, until evenly browned on all sides, adding a little more oil if needed. Remove the meat, with a slotted spoon.

2 Reduce the heat and add the onion and garlic to the pan. Cook, stirring frequently, for 1–2 minutes.

3 Add the water and return all the meat to the pan. Bring just to a boil and skim off any foam that rises to the surface. Reduce the heat and stir in the tomatoes, bay leaf, thyme, oregano, cinnamon, cumin, turmeric, and harissa. Simmer for about 1 hour or until the meat is very tender. Discard the bay leaf.

4 Stir in the garbanzo beans, carrot, and potato and simmer for about 15 minutes. Add the zucchini and peas and simmer for a further 15–20 minutes or until all the vegetables are tender.

5 Season to taste with salt and pepper and add more harissa if desired. Ladle the soup into warmed bowls, garnish with chopped fresh mint or cilantro, and serve immediately.

Scotch Broth

This traditional winter soup is full of goodness, with lots
of tasty golden vegetables along with tender barley and lamb.

NUTRITIONAL INFORMATION

Calories 186   Sugars 6g
Protein ....13g   Fat 5g
Carbohydrate ...23g   Saturates 2g

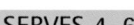

10–15 mins   1½ hrs

SERVES 4–6

INGREDIENTS

¼ cup pearl barley

10½ oz/300 g lean boneless lamb, such as
shoulder fillet, trimmed of fat and cut into
½ inch/1 cm cubes

3 cups water

2 garlic cloves, finely chopped or crushed

4 cups chicken or meat stock

1 onion, finely chopped

1 bay leaf

1 large leek, quartered lengthwise
and sliced

2 large carrots, finely diced

1 parsnip, finely diced

4½ oz/125 g rutabaga, diced

2 tbsp chopped fresh parsley

salt and pepper

1 Rinse the barley under cold running
water. Put in a pan and add water to
cover generously. Bring to a boil over
medium heat and boil for 3 minutes,
skimming off the foam from the surface.
Remove the pan from the heat, cover, and
set aside.

2 Put the lamb in another large pan
with the measured water and bring
to a boil. Skim off the foam that rises to
the surface.

3 Stir in the garlic, stock, onion, and
bay leaf. Reduce the heat, partially
cover, and simmer for 15 minutes.

4 Drain the barley and add to the soup.
Add the leek, carrots, parsnip, and
rutabaga. Simmer, stirring occasionally, for
about 1 hour or until the lamb and
vegetables are tender.

5 Season to taste with salt and pepper,
stir in the parsley, and serve.

COOK'S TIP

This soup is lean when the
lamb is trimmed. By making it
beforehand, you can remove any
hardened fat before reheating.

Hunter's Soup

This soup is perfect for the sweet meat of rabbit, which is traditionally paired with tomatoes and mushrooms.

NUTRITIONAL INFORMATION

Calories	377	Sugars	........13g
Protein	........36g	Fat	..........17g
Carbohydrate	...16g	Saturates	.......6g

20 mins | 2½ hrs

SERVES 4

INGREDIENTS

1–2 tbsp olive oil

2 lb/900 g rabbit portions

1 onion, finely chopped

2–3 garlic cloves, finely chopped or crushed

generous ½ cup finely chopped lean smoked bacon

½ cup white wine

5 cups chicken stock

2 cups tomato juice

2 tbsp tomato paste

2 carrots, halved lengthwise and sliced

1 bay leaf

¼ tsp dried thyme

¼ tsp dried oregano

1 tbsp butter

10½ oz/300 g mushrooms, sliced or quartered if small

salt and pepper

chopped fresh parsley, to garnish

1 Heat the oil in a large pan over medium heat. Add the rabbit, in batches if necessary, and cook until lightly browned on all sides, adding a little more oil if needed. Remove from the pan.

2 Reduce the heat slightly and add the onion, garlic, and bacon to the pan. Cook, stirring frequently, for a further 2 minutes until the onion has softened.

3 Add the wine and simmer for 1 minute. Add the stock and return the rabbit to the pan with any juices. Bring to a boil and skim off any foam that rises to the surface.

4 Reduce the heat and stir in the tomato juice, tomato paste, carrots, bay leaf, thyme, and oregano. Season with salt and pepper. Cover and simmer gently for 1 hour or until very tender.

5 Remove the rabbit pieces with a draining spoon and, when cool enough to handle, remove the meat from the bones. Discard any fat or gristle, along with the bones. Cut the meat into bite-size pieces and return to the soup.

6 Melt the butter in a skillet over medium-high heat. Add the mushrooms and season with salt and pepper. Fry gently until lightly golden, then add to the soup. Simmer for 10-15 minutes to blend. Season to taste and serve sprinkled with parsley.

Potato & Garbanzo Soup

This spicy and substantial soup uses ingredients you are likely to have to hand and makes a delicious meal-in-a-bowl.

NUTRITIONAL INFORMATION

Calories 40   Sugars 1.6g
Protein . . . . .1.8g   Fat 1g
Carbohydrate . . .6.5g   Saturates 0.1g

 5 mins   50 mins

SERVES 4

INGREDIENTS

1 tbsp olive oil

1 large onion, finely chopped

2–3 garlic cloves, finely chopped or crushed

1 carrot, quartered and thinly sliced

12 oz/350 g potatoes, diced

¼ tsp ground turmeric

¼ tsp garam masala

¼ tsp mild curry powder

14 oz/400 g canned chopped tomatoes

3¾ cups water

¼ tsp chili purée or to taste

14 oz/400 g canned garbanzo beans, rinsed
    and drained

¾ cup fresh or frozen peas

salt and pepper

chopped fresh cilantro, to garnish

1 Heat the olive oil in a large pan over medium heat. Add the onion and garlic and cook for 3–4 minutes, stirring occasionally, until the onion is beginning to soften.

2 Add the carrot, potatoes, turmeric, garam masala, and curry powder and continue cooking for 1–2 minutes.

3 Add the tomatoes, water, and chili purée with a pinch of salt. Reduce the heat, cover, and simmer for 30 minutes, stirring occasionally.

4 Add the garbanzo beans and peas to the pan, then simmer for a further 15 minutes or until all the vegetables are tender.

5 Taste the soup and adjust the seasoning, if necessary, adding a little more chili if desired. Ladle into warm soup bowls and sprinkle with cilantro.

Lentil, Potato & Ham Soup

A comforting and satisfying cold-weather soup, this is good served with bread as an entrée, but it is not too filling to serve as an appetizer.

NUTRITIONAL INFORMATION

Calories	61	Sugars	.......1.4g
Protein	........5.4g	Fat	..........0.8g
Carbohydrate	...8.6g	Saturates	.....0.3g

 5 mins   45 mins

SERVES 5

INGREDIENTS

1¼ cups Puy lentils

2 tsp butter

1 large onion, finely chopped

2 carrots, finely chopped

1 garlic clove, finely chopped

2 cups water

1 bay leaf

¼ tsp dried sage or rosemary

4 cups chicken stock

8 oz/225 g potatoes, diced (see Cook's Tip)

1 tbsp tomato paste

¾ cup finely diced smoked ham

salt and pepper

chopped fresh parsley, to garnish

1 Rinse and drain the lentils and remove any small stones if necessary.

2 Melt the butter in a large pan or flameproof casserole over medium heat. Add the onion, carrots, and garlic, cover and cook, stirring occasionally, for about 4–5 minutes until the onion is slightly softened.

3 Add the lentils with the water, bay leaf, and sage or rosemary. Bring to a boil, reduce the heat, cover, and simmer for 10 minutes.

4 Add the stock, potatoes, tomato paste, and ham. Bring back to a simmer. Cover and continue simmering for 25–30 minutes or until the vegetables are tender.

5 Season to taste with salt and pepper and remove and discard the bay leaf. Ladle into warm bowls, garnish with parsley, and serve immediately.

COOK'S TIP

Cut the potatoes into small cubes, about ¼ inch/5 mm, so that they will be in proportion with the lentils.

Fennel & Broccoli Soup

This rustic vegetable soup is appealing in its simplicity.
Served with ciabatta, focaccia, or garlic bread, it makes a good light lunch.

NUTRITIONAL INFORMATION

Calories 108	Sugars 3g
Protein 6g	Fat 3g
Carbohydrate . . .15g	Saturates 0g

 15 mins 1¼ hrs

SERVES 4

INGREDIENTS

¼ cup pearl barley

6¼ cups chicken or
    vegetable stock

1 bay leaf

½ tsp chopped fresh thyme leaves, or ⅛ tsp
    dried thyme

9 oz/250 g broccoli

2 tsp olive oil

1 large leek, halved lengthwise and
    finely chopped

2 garlic cloves, finely chopped

1 celery stalk, thinly sliced

1 large fennel bulb, thinly sliced

1 tbsp chopped fresh basil

salt and pepper

freshly grated Parmesan cheese, to serve

1 Rinse the barley and drain. Bring 2 cups of the stock to a boil in a small pan. Add the bay leaf and thyme. Add a pinch of salt. Stir in the barley, reduce the heat, partially cover, and simmer for about 30–40 minutes until tender.

2 Cut the broccoli into florets and peel the stems. Cut the stems into very thin batons, about 1 inch/2.5 cm long. Cut the florets into small slivers and reserve them separately.

3 Heat the oil in a large pan over medium-low heat and add the leek and garlic. Cook, stirring frequently, for about 5 minutes until softened. Add the celery, fennel, and broccoli stems and cook for 2 minutes.

4 Stir in the remaining stock and bring to a boil. Add the barley with its cooking liquid. Season to taste with salt and pepper. Reduce the heat, cover the pan, and simmer gently, stirring occasionally, for 10 minutes.

5 Uncover the pan and adjust the heat so the soup bubbles gently. Stir in the broccoli florets and cook for a further 10–12 minutes or until the broccoli is tender. Stir in the basil. Taste and adjust the seasoning if necessary. Ladle into warmed bowls and serve with plenty of Parmesan cheese to sprinkle over.

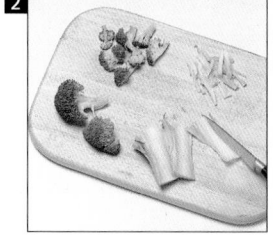  

Vegetable Soup with Bulgur

This healthy and colorful soup makes good use of your herb garden.
The fresh herbs give it a vibrant flavor.

NUTRITIONAL INFORMATION

Calories 93   Sugars 8g
Protein ....5g   Fat 3g
Carbohydrate ...13g   Saturates 0g

 10 mins   1 hr

SERVES 5–6

INGREDIENTS

1 tbsp olive oil

2 onions, chopped

3 garlic cloves, finely chopped or crushed

⅓ cup bulgur

5 tomatoes, peeled and sliced or 14 oz/
    400 g can plum tomatoes in juice

1¾ cups peeled diced pumpkin or acorn
    squash

1 large zucchini, quartered lengthwise
    and sliced

4 cups boiling water

2 tbsp tomato paste

¼ tsp chili purée

1½ oz/40 g chopped mixed fresh oregano,
    basil, and flat leaf parsley

1 oz/25 g arugula leaves, coarsely chopped

1½ cups shelled fresh or frozen peas

salt and pepper

freshly grated Parmesan cheese, to serve

1 Heat the oil in a large pan over medium-low heat and add the onions and garlic. Cook for 5–8 minutes, stirring occasionally, until the onions soften.

2 Stir in the bulgur and continue cooking, stirring constantly, for 1 minute.

3 Layer the tomatoes, pumpkin or squash, and zucchini in the pan.

4 Combine half the water with the tomato paste, chili purée, and a pinch of salt. Pour over the vegetables. Cover and simmer for 15 minutes.

5 Uncover the pan and stir. Put all the herbs and the arugula on top of the soup and layer the peas over them. Pour in the remaining water and gradually bring to a boil. Reduce the heat and simmer for about 20–25 minutes or until all the vegetables are tender.

6 Stir the soup. Taste and adjust the seasoning, adding salt and pepper, if necessary, and a little more chili purée if you wish. Ladle into warmed bowls and serve with Parmesan cheese.

Bouillabaisse

This world-famous French soup makes a festive seafood extravaganza worthy of any special occasion or celebration.

NUTRITIONAL INFORMATION

Calories . . . . .55 Sugars 1.1g
Protein . . . . .7.2g Fat 1.8g
Carbohydrate . . .2.6g Saturates 0.3g

10 mins   1 hr

SERVES 6

INGREDIENTS

1 lb/450 g jumbo shrimp

1 lb 10 oz/750 g firm white fish fillets, such as sea bass, snapper, and monkfish

4 tbsp olive oil

grated rind of 1 orange

1 large garlic clove, finely chopped

½ tsp chili paste or harissa

1 large leek, sliced

1 onion, halved and sliced

1 red bell pepper, deseeded and sliced

3–4 tomatoes, cored and cut into 8 wedges

4 garlic cloves, sliced

1 bay leaf

pinch of saffron threads

½ tsp fennel seeds

2½ cups water

5 cups fish stock

1 fennel bulb, finely chopped

1 large onion, finely chopped

8 oz/225 g potatoes, halved and thinly sliced

9 oz/250 g scallops

salt and pepper

toasted French bread slices, to serve

ready-prepared aïoli, to serve

1 Peel the shrimp and reserve the shells. Cut the fish fillets into serving pieces about 2 inches/5 cm square. Trim off any ragged edges and reserve. Put the fish in a bowl with 2 tablespoons of the olive oil, the orange rind, garlic, and chili paste or harissa. Turn to coat well, cover, and chill the shrimp and fish separately.

2 Heat 1 tablespoon of the olive oil in a large pan over medium heat. Add the leek, sliced onion, and red bell pepper. Cover and cook for 5 minutes, stirring, until the onion softens. Stir in the tomatoes, sliced garlic, bay leaf, saffron, fennel seeds, shrimp shells, fish trimmings, water, and fish stock. Bring to a boil, then simmer, covered, for 30 minutes. Strain the stock.

3 Heat the remaining oil in a large pan. Add the fennel and chopped onion and cook for 5 minutes, stirring, until softened.

Add the stock and potatoes and bring to a boil. Reduce the heat slightly, cover, and cook for 12–15 minutes until just tender.

4 Lower the heat and add the fish, thick pieces first and thinner ones after 2–3 minutes. Add the shrimp and scallops and simmer until all the seafood is cooked and opaque throughout.

5 Taste the soup and adjust the seasoning. Ladle into warm bowls. Spread the aïoli sauce on the toasted bread slices and arrange on top of the soup.

Beef & Spring Vegetable Soup

This lean, pretty soup makes an elegant light entrée for 4 or it will serve 6 as an appetizer. Last-minute assembly is needed, but it's worth it.

NUTRITIONAL INFORMATION

Calories 166	Sugars 3g	
Protein 16g	Fat 4g	
Carbohydrate ...17g	Saturates 1g	

 15–20 mins   35 mins

SERVES 4–6

INGREDIENTS

12 small new potatoes, quartered

4 slim carrots, quartered lengthwise and cut into 1½ inch/4 cm lengths

5½ oz/150 g tiny green beans, cut into 1½ inch/4 cm lengths

6¾ cups rich beef or meat stock

2 tbsp soy sauce

3 tbsp dry sherry

12 oz/350 g beef tenderloin, about 2 inches/5 cm thick

2¼ cups sliced shiitake mushrooms

1 tbsp chopped fresh parsley

1 tbsp chopped fresh chives

salt and pepper

1 Bring a pan of lightly salted water to a boil and add the potatoes and carrots. Reduce the heat, cover, and boil gently for about 15 minutes until tender. Bring another pan of lightly salted water to a boil, add the beans, and boil for about 5 minutes until just tender. Drain the vegetables and reserve.

2 Bring the stock to a boil in a pan and add the soy sauce and sherry. Season with salt and pepper. Reduce the heat, add the beef, and simmer gently for 10 minutes. (The beef should be very rare, as it will continue cooking in the bowls.)

3 Add the mushrooms and simmer for a further 3 minutes. Warm the bowls in a low oven.

4 Remove the meat and set aside to rest on a carving board. Taste the stock and adjust the seasoning, if necessary. Bring the stock back to a boil.

5 Cut the meat in half lengthwise and slice each half into pieces about ⅛ inch/3 mm thick. Season the meat lightly with salt and pepper and divide among the warm bowls.

6 Drop the reserved vegetables into the stock and heat through for about 1 minute. Ladle the stock over the meat, dividing the vegetables as evenly as possible. Sprinkle over the parsley and chives and serve immediately.

Chicken & Garbanzo Soup

This entrée soup is Mexican in origin. Its appeal comes from an unusual combination of fruits and vegetables.

NUTRITIONAL INFORMATION

Calories	304	Sugars	........17g
Protein	........18g	Fat	...........7g
Carbohydrate	...45g	Saturates	.......1g

 45 mins 1½ hrs

SERVES 8

I N G R E D I E N T S

1 lb 12 oz/800 g skinless chicken legs
  or thighs

1 celery stalk, sliced

1 large carrot, halved and sliced

1 large onion, finely chopped

2 garlic cloves, finely chopped

5¾ pints/2.5 liters chicken stock

4–5 fresh parsley stems

1 bay leaf

¾ cup diced lean smoked ham

14 oz/400 g can garbanzo beans, drained
  and rinsed

1 large turnip, diced

2 zucchini, halved and sliced

1 large potato, diced

1 sweet potato, diced

1 cup corn kernels

3 large pears, peeled, cored, and cut into
  bite-size pieces

3 tbsp fresh lime juice

2 tbsp olive oil

2 very green, unripe bananas, cut into
  ¼ inch/5 mm slices

salt and pepper

chopped fresh parsley, to garnish

1 Put the chicken into a large pan or flameproof casserole with the celery, carrot, onion, garlic, stock, parsley stems, and bay leaf. Bring just to a boil over medium-high heat and skim off any foam that rises to the surface. Reduce the heat, partially cover, and simmer for about 45 minutes or until the chicken is tender.

2 Remove the chicken from the stock and set aside to cool. Reserve the stock, but discard the parsley stems and bay leaf. Remove the chicken meat from the bones and cut into bite-size pieces. Skim the fat from the stock.

3 Bring the stock just to a boil. Add the ham, garbanzo beans, turnip, zucchini, potato, sweet potato, and corn. Return the meat to the stock. Lower the heat, partially cover, and simmer for about 30 minutes or until all the vegetables are tender.

4 Add the pears and lime juice to the soup and cook for about 5 minutes until they are just poached. Season to taste and add more lime juice if wished.

5 Heat the oil in a skillet over medium-high heat. Fry the bananas until golden. Drain on paper towels and keep warm. Ladle the soup into bowls and top with fried banana slices. Garnish with parsley and serve.

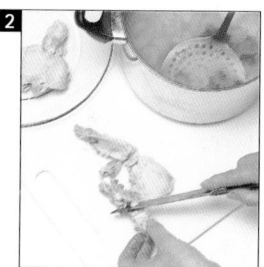

Beef & Vegetable Soup

A wonderful meal-in-a-bowl, this soup is ideal for a winter supper or lunch. The beefy flavor, enhanced with spices, is very warming.

NUTRITIONAL INFORMATION

Calories	167	Sugars	.........7g
Protein	........16g	Fat	...........5g
Carbohydrate	...17g	Saturates	.......2g

🍲 15 mins   🕐 20 mins

SERVES 4–6

INGREDIENTS

8 oz/225 g tomatoes

2 corn cobs

4 cups beef soup

1 carrot, thinly sliced

1 onion, chopped

1–2 small waxy potatoes, diced

¼ cabbage, thinly sliced

¼ tsp ground cumin

¼ tsp mild chili powder

¼ tsp paprika

8 oz/225 g cooked beef, cut into
  bite-size pieces

3–4 tbsp chopped fresh cilantro (optional)

hot salsa of your choice, to serve

1 To peel the tomatoes, place them in a heatproof bowl, pour in enough boiling water to cover, and stand for 30 seconds. Drain and plunge into cold water. The skins will then slide off easily. Chop the tomatoes.

2 Using a large knife, cut the corn cobs into 1 inch/2.5 cm pieces.

3 Place the stock in a pan with the tomatoes, carrot, onion, potatoes, and cabbage. Bring to a boil, then reduce the heat and simmer for 10–15 minutes or until the vegetables are tender.

4 Add the corn cob pieces, the cumin, chili powder, paprika, and beef pieces. Bring back to a boil over medium heat and cook until heated through.

5 Ladle into warmed soup bowls and serve sprinkled with fresh cilantro, if using, with a salsa of your choice handed around separately.

COOK'S TIP

To thicken the soup and give it a flavor of the popular Mexican steamed dumplings, known as a tamale, add a few tablespoons of masa harina, mixed into a thinnish paste with a little water, at Step 4. Stir well, then continue cooking until thickened.

 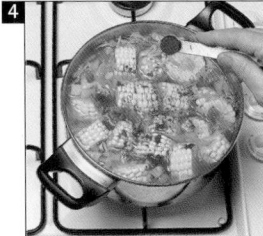 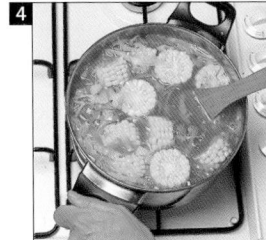

Pozole

The dish of hulled corn kernels—hominy—simmered in rich stock is eaten all over Mexico, and is served with lots of fresh garnishes.

NUTRITIONAL INFORMATION

Calories	300	Sugars	. . . . .3g
Protein	. . . . .39g	Fat	. . . . .8g
Carbohydrate	. . .19g	Saturates	. . . . . . .2g

 45 mins   1 hr

SERVES 4

I N G R E D I E N T S

1 lb/450 g stewing pork, such as lean belly

½ small chicken

about 4¼ pints/2 liters water

1 chicken bouillon cube

1 garlic bulb, divided into cloves but not peeled

1 onion, chopped

2 bay leaves

1 lb/450 g canned or cooked hominy or garbanzo beans

¼–½ tsp ground cumin

salt and pepper

T O   S E R V E

½ small cabbage, thinly shredded

fried pork skin

dried oregano leaves

dried chili flakes

tortilla chips

lime wedges

1 Place the pork and chicken in a large pan. Add enough water to fill the pan. (Do not worry about having too much stock—it is wonderful for the rest of the week and freezes well.)

2 Bring to a boil, then skim off the scum that rises to the surface. Reduce the heat and add the bouillon cube, garlic, onion, and bay leaves. Cover and simmer over medium-low heat until the pork and chicken are both tender and cooked through.

3 Using a slotted spoon, remove the pork and chicken from the soup and set aside to cool. When cool enough to handle, remove the chicken flesh from the bones and cut into small pieces. Then, cut the pork into bite-size pieces. Set aside.

4 Skim the fat off the soup and discard the bay leaves. Add the hominy or garbanzo beans and cumin. Season with salt and pepper to taste. Bring to a boil.

5 To serve, place a little pork and chicken in soup bowls. Top with cabbage, fried pork skin, oregano, and chili flakes, then ladle in the hot soup. Serve with tortilla chips and lime wedges.

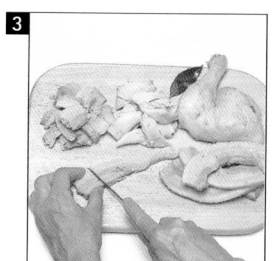

Crab & Avocado Soft Tacos

Crab and avocado make an elegant yet authentic filling for tacos. Taste and you will be transported to a beach somewhere south of Acapulco!

NUTRITIONAL INFORMATION

Calories	522	Sugars 4g
Protein	........22g	Fat 19g
Carbohydrate	...69g	Saturates 7g

   10–15 mins   10 mins

SERVES 4

INGREDIENTS

8 corn tortillas

1 avocado

lime or lemon juice, for tossing

4–6 tbsp sour cream

9–10 oz/250–275 g cooked crab meat

½ lime

½ fresh green chile, such as jalapeño or serrano, deseeded and chopped or thinly sliced

1 ripe tomato, deseeded and diced

½ small onion, finely chopped

2 tbsp chopped fresh cilantro

salsa of your choice, to serve (optional)

VARIATION

For tostadas, fry the tortillas in a little oil in a nonstick pan until crisp. Top one crisp tortilla with the filling. Prepare a second tortilla with the filling and place on top of the first. Repeat once more, to make a small tower, top with shredded lettuce, and serve.

1 Heat the tortillas in an ungreased nonstick skillet, sprinkling them with a few drops of water as they heat; wrap in a clean dish cloth as you work to keep them warm.

2 Cut the avocado in half around the pit. Twist apart, then remove the pit with a knife. Carefully peel off the skin from the avocado, slice the flesh, and toss in lime or lemon juice to prevent it from turning brown.

3 Spread 1 tortilla with sour cream. Top with crab meat, a squeeze of lime juice, and a sprinkling of chile, tomato, onion, cilantro, and avocado, adding a splash of salsa if desired. Repeat the procedure with the remaining tortillas and serve immediately.

Fish Tacos Ensenada Style

These tacos of fried fish chunks and red cabbage salad are served up in the cantinas and fondas of the coastal town of Ensenada in Mexico.

NUTRITIONAL INFORMATION

Calories 491	Sugars 5g
Protein 32g	Fat 5g
Carbohydrate . . .84g	Saturates 0g

10–15 mins   25 mins

SERVES 4

INGREDIENTS

about 1 lb/450 g firm-fleshed white fish filets, such as red snapper or cod

¼ tsp dried oregano

¼ tsp ground cumin

1 tsp mild chili powder

2 garlic cloves, finely chopped

3 tbsp all-purpose flour

vegetable oil, for frying

¼ red cabbage, thinly sliced or shredded

juice of 2 limes

hot pepper sauce or salsa to taste

8 corn tortillas

1 tbsp chopped fresh cilantro

½ onion, chopped (optional)

salt and pepper

salsa of your choice

1 Place the fish on a plate and sprinkle with half the oregano, cumin, chili powder, and garlic. Season with salt and pepper, then dust with the flour.

2 Heat the oil in a heavy skillet until it is smoking, then fry the fish, in several batches, until it is golden on the outside, and just tender in the middle. Remove from the pan and place on paper towels to drain.

3 Combine the cabbage with the remaining oregano, cumin, chili, and garlic, then stir in the lime juice, salt, and hot pepper sauce to taste. Set aside.

4 Heat the tortillas in an ungreased nonstick skillet, sprinkling with a few drops of water as they heat. Wrap the tortillas in a clean dish cloth as you work to keep them warm. Alternatively, heat through in a stack in the pan, alternating the tortillas from the top to the bottom so that they warm evenly.

5 Place some of the warm fried fish in each tortilla, along with a large spoonful of the hot cabbage salad. Sprinkle with chopped fresh cilantro and onion, if desired. Add the salsa to taste and serve immediately.

Fish & Bean Tostadas

Crisp tostadas are topped with spiced fish, refried beans, and crunchy lettuce—perfect for a well-balanced lunch.

NUTRITIONAL INFORMATION

Calories	.519	Sugars	.2g
Protein	.35g	Fat	.6g
Carbohydrate	.82g	Saturates	.0g

 45 mins 10–15 mins

SERVES 4

INGREDIENTS

about 1lb/450 g firm-fleshed white fish, such as red snapper or cod

½ cup fish stock, or water mixed with a fish bouillon cube

¼ tsp ground cumin

¼ tsp mild chili powder

pinch of dried oregano

4 garlic cloves, finely chopped

juice of ½ lemon or lime

8 soft corn tortillas

vegetable oil, for frying

14 oz/400g can refried beans, warmed with 2 tbsp water

salsa of your choice

2–3 leaves Romaine lettuce, shredded

3 tbsp chopped fresh cilantro

2 tbsp chopped onion

salt and pepper

TO GARNISH

sour cream

chopped fresh herbs

1 Put the fish in a pan with the fish stock, cumin, chili, oregano, and garlic. Season with salt and pepper to taste. Bring to a boil over low heat, then immediately remove the pan from the heat, and set the fish aside to cool in the cooking liquid.

2 When cool enough to handle, remove the fish from the liquid with a slotted spoon; reserve the cooking liquid. Break the fish up into bite-size pieces, put in a bowl, sprinkle with the lemon or lime juice and set aside.

3 To make tostadas, fry the tortillas in a small amount of oil in a nonstick skillet until crisp. Spread the tostadas evenly with the warm refried beans.

4 Gently reheat the fish with a little of the reserved cooking liquid, then spoon the fish on top of the beans. Top each tostada with some of the salsa, lettuce, chopped fresh cilantro, and onion. Garnish each one with a spoon of sour cream and a sprinkling of chopped fresh herbs. Serve immediately.

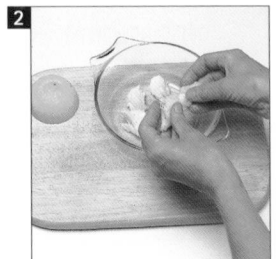

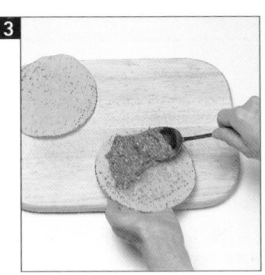

Fish Burritos

You can use any fish you like in this tasty Mexican snack.
Tacos are eaten in the hand, rather like sandwiches.

NUTRITIONAL INFORMATION

Calories ....269 Sugars 3g
Protein ....20g Fat 2g
Carbohydrate ...46g Saturates 0g

45 mins   10–15 mins

SERVES 4–6

INGREDIENTS

about 1 lb/450 g firm-fleshed white fish, such as red snapper or cod

¼ tsp ground cumin

pinch of dried oregano

4 garlic finely cloves, chopped

½ cup fish stock, or water mixed with a fish bouillon cube

juice of ½ lemon or lime

8 flour tortillas

2–3 leaves Romaine lettuce, shredded

2 ripe tomatoes, diced

Salsa Cruda (see page 447)

salt and pepper

lemon slices, to garnish

1 Season the fish to taste with salt and pepper, then put in a pan with the cumin, oregano, garlic, and enough fish stock to cover.

2 Bring to a boil and cook for about a minute. Remove the pan from the heat and set the fish aside to cool in the cooking liquid for about 30 minutes.

3 Remove the fish from the stock and break up into bite-size pieces. Sprinkle with the lemon or lime juice and set aside.

4 Heat the tortillas in an ungreased nonstick skillet, sprinkling them with a few drops of water as they heat. Wrap in a clean dish cloth as you work to keep them warm.

5 Arrange shredded lettuce in the middle of a tortilla, spoon on a few chunks of the fish, then sprinkle with the tomato. Add a little salsa cruda. Repeat with the other tortillas and serve immediately garnished with lemon slices.

VARIATION

Cook several peeled waxy potatoes in the fish stock, then dice, and serve wrapped up in the warm tortillas with the lettuce, fish, tomato. and salsa. Alternatively, add sliced lime-dressed avocado with the filling.

Chicken Tacos from Puebla

Seasoned chicken fills these soft tacos, along with creamy refried beans, avocado, smoky chipotle, and sour cream. A feast of tastes!

NUTRITIONAL INFORMATION

Calories	674	Sugars	.........6g
Protein	........34g	Fat	..........25g
Carbohydrate	...80g	Saturates	.......9g

10 mins   15 mins

SERVES 4

I N G R E D I E N T S

8 corn tortillas

2 tsp vegetable oil

8–12 oz/225–350 g cooked chicken, diced or shredded

8 oz/225 g can refried beans, warmed with 2 tbsp water

¼ tsp ground cumin

¼ tsp dried oregano

1 avocado, pitted, peeled, sliced, and tossed with lime juice

Salsa Verde (see page 448)

1 canned chipotle chile in adobo marinade, chopped, or bottled chipotle salsa

¾ cup sour cream

½ onion, chopped

handful of lettuce leaves

5 radishes, diced

salt and pepper

VARIATION

Replace the chicken with 1 lb/450 g ground beef browned with a seasoning of chopped onion, mild chili powder, and ground cumin to taste.

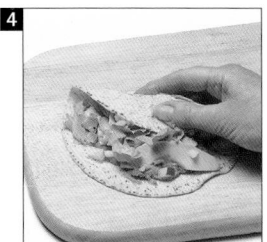

1 Heat the tortillas in an ungreased nonstick skillet in a stack, alternating the top and bottom tortillas so that they all heat evenly. Wrap in kitchen foil or a clean dish cloth to keep warm.

2 Heat the oil in a skillet, add the chicken, and heat through. Season with salt and pepper to taste.

3 Combine the refried beans with the cumin and oregano.

4 Spread a tortilla with warm refried beans, then top with a spoonful of the chicken, 1–2 slices of avocado, a dab of salsa, chipotle to taste, a spoon of sour cream, and a sprinkling of onion, lettuce, and radishes. Season with salt and pepper to taste, then roll up as tightly as you can. Repeat with the remaining tortillas and serve immediately.

Chicken Tostadas

Chicken makes a delicate, yet satisfying topping for crisp tostadas. Leftover cooked chicken can also be used and tastes delicious.

NUTRITIONAL INFORMATION

Calories ....663 Sugars 3g
Protein ....45g Fat 32g
Carbohydrate ...49g Saturates 11g

20 mins   10–15 mins

SERVES 4–6

INGREDIENTS

6 corn tortillas

vegetable oil, for frying

1lb/450 g skinless, boneless chicken breast or thigh, cut into strips or diced

1 cup chicken stock

2 garlic cloves, finely chopped

14 oz/400g can refried beans

2 tbsp water

large pinch of ground cumin

2 cups grated cheese

1 tbsp chopped fresh cilantro

2 ripe tomatoes, diced

crisp lettuce leaves, such as Romaine or iceberg, shredded

4–6 radishes, diced

3 scallions, thinly sliced

1 ripe avocado, pitted, peeled, diced or sliced, and tossed with lime juice

sour cream to taste

1–2 canned chipotle chiles in adobo marinade, cut into thin strips

1 To make tostadas, heat a small amount of oil in a heavy, nonstick skillet and fry the tortillas, in batches, until crisp.

2 Put the chicken in a pan with the stock and garlic. Bring to a boil, then reduce the heat, and simmer for 1–2 minutes until the chicken begins to turn opaque.

3 Remove the chicken from the heat and set aside to steep in the hot liquid to cook through.

4 Gently heat the beans with the water. Stir in the cumin and keep warm.

5 Reheat the tostadas under a preheated broiler, if necessary. Spread the hot beans on the tostadas, then sprinkle with the grated cheese. Lift the cooked chicken from the cooking liquid with a slotted spoon and divide among the tostadas. Top with the chopped fresh cilantro, diced tomatoes, lettuce leaves, diced radishes, scallions, avocado, sour cream, and a few strips of chipotle chile. Serve immediately.

 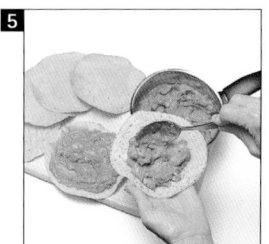 

Santa Fe Enchiladas

These enchiladas are served stacked, in the traditional New Mexican style, but you can always roll them up with the filling if you prefer.

NUTRITIONAL INFORMATION

Calories	645	Sugars	.........2g
Protein	........47g	Fat	..........22g
Carbohydrate	...75g	Saturates	.......7g

15 mins   30–35 mins

SERVES 4

INGREDIENTS

2–3 tbsp masa harina or 1 corn tortilla, crushed or crumbled

4 tbsp mild chili powder

2 tbsp paprika

2 garlic cloves, finely chopped

¼ tsp ground cumin

pinch of ground cinnamon

pinch of ground allspice

pinch of dried oregano

4 cups vegetable, chicken, or beef stock, simmering

1 tbsp lime juice

8 flour tortillas

about 1lb/450 g cooked chicken or pork, cut into pieces

¾ cup grated cheese

1 tbsp extra virgin olive oil

4–6 eggs

TO SERVE

½ onion, finely chopped

1 tbsp finely chopped fresh cilantro

salsa of your choice

1 Mix the masa harina or crushed tortilla with the chili powder, paprika, garlic, cumin, cinnamon, allspice, oregano, and enough water to make a thin paste. Process in a blender or food processor until smooth.

2 Stir the paste into the simmering stock, reduce the heat, and cook until it thickens slightly, then remove the sauce from the heat, and stir in the lime juice.

3 Dip the tortillas into the warm sauce. Cover 1 tortilla with some of the cooked meat. Top with a second dipped tortilla and more meat filling. Make 3 more towers in this way.

4 Transfer the tortilla towers to a shallow casserole, pour the remaining sauce over them, then sprinkle with the grated cheese. Bake the enchiladas in a preheated oven, 350°F/180°C, for 15-20 minutes or until the cheese has melted and is bubbling.

5 Meanwhile, heat the olive oil in a nonstick skillet and cook the eggs until the whites are set and the yolks are still soft.

6 To serve the enchiladas, top each with a fried egg. Serve with the chopped onion mixed with fresh cilantro and a salsa of your choice.

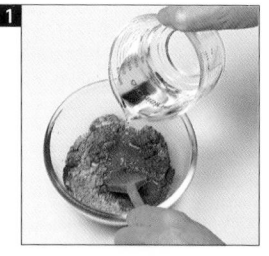 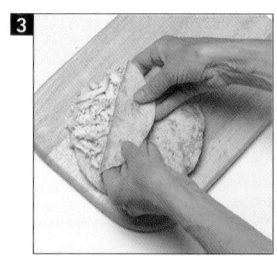 

Chicken Tortilla Flutes

These crisply fried, rolled tortillas are known as *flautas*, meaning "flutes" in Spanish, because of their delicate, long shape.

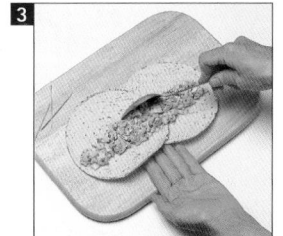

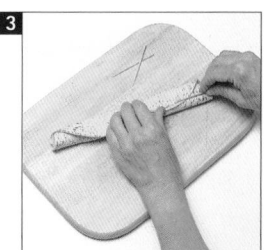

NUTRITIONAL INFORMATION

Calories	.551	Sugars	.5g
Protein	.37g	Fat	.17g
Carbohydrate	.71g	Saturates	.4g

 15 mins   10–15 mins

SERVES 4

INGREDIENTS

8 corn tortillas

12 oz/350 g cooked chicken, diced

1 tsp mild chili powder

1 onion, chopped

2 tbsp finely chopped fresh cilantro

1–2 tbsp crème fraîche

vegetable oil, for frying

1 quantity of Guacamole (see page 138)

salsa of your choice

salt

1 Heat the tortillas in an ungreased, heavy, nonstick skillet in a stack, alternating the top and bottom tortillas so that all of them warm evenly. Wrap in kitchen foil or a clean dish cloth to keep them warm.

2 Place the chicken in a bowl with the chili powder, half the onion, and half the cilantro. Season to taste with salt. Stir in enough crème fraîche to hold the mixture together.

3 Arrange 2 corn tortillas on a counter so that they are overlapping, then spoon some of the filling along the center. Roll up very tightly and secure in place with 1–2 toothpicks. Repeat with the remaining tortillas and filling.

4 Heat the oil in a deep skillet and fry the rolls until golden and crisp. Carefully remove from the oil with a slotted spoon and drain on paper towels.

5 Place the rolls on warmed individual plates and garnish with the guacamole, salsa, diced tomato, the remaining onion, and remaining fresh cilantro. Serve immediately.

VARIATION
Replace the chicken with seafood, such as cooked shrimp or crab meat, and serve the rolls with lemon wedges.

Tortilla & Chorizo Casserole

Called *chilaquiles* in Mexico, this dish turns everyday leftovers into something quite special. Excellent served for brunch, topped with an egg.

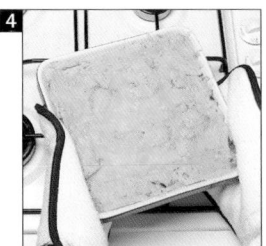

NUTRITIONAL INFORMATION

Calories 402	Sugars 4g
Protein 17g	Fat 15g
Carbohydrate . . .53g	Saturates 8g

 10 mins   1¼ hrs

SERVES 6–8

INGREDIENTS

12 stale tortillas, cut into strips

1 tbsp vegetable oil

2–3 chorizo sausages, thinly sliced or diced

2 garlic cloves, finely chopped

8 oz/225 g chopped canned tomatoes

3 tbsp chopped fresh cilantro

2 cups chicken or vegetable stock

2 cups grated cheese

1 onion, finely chopped

salt and pepper

1 Place the tortilla strips in a roasting pan, toss with the oil, and bake in a preheated oven, 375°F/190°C, for about 30 minutes until they are crisp and golden.

VARIATION

Serve with a fried egg or two alongside. The soft yolk tastes wonderful with the spicy casserole—offer a bowl of spicy salsa for those who want it hotter.

2 Brown the chorizo sausages with the garlic in a heavy skillet over low heat until the meat is cooked. Pour away any excess fat. Add the tomatoes and chopped cilantro and season with salt and pepper to taste.

3 In a shallow casserole, approximately 12 inches/30 cm square, layer the tortilla strips and chorizo mixture, finishing with the tortilla strips.

4 Pour the stock over the top of the dish, then sprinkle with the grated cheese. Bake in a preheated oven, 375°F/190°C, for about 40 minutes until the tortilla strips are fairly soft.

5 Serve immediately, sprinkled with the chopped onion.

Tamales

Traditional Mexican fare, *tamales* are large dumplings of cornmeal, stuffed with a moist filling. They make attractive party food.

NUTRITIONAL INFORMATION

Calories	264	Sugars	.........2g
Protein	.........5g	Fat	..........13g
Carbohydrate	...34g	Saturates	.......6g

 3½ hrs   40–60 mins

SERVES 4–6

INGREDIENTS

8–10 corn husks or several banana leaves, cut into 12 inch/30 cm squares

6 tbsp vegetable shortening

½ tsp salt

pinch of sugar

pinch of ground cumin

2 cups masa harina

½ tsp baking powder

about 1 cup beef, chicken or vegetable stock

TO SERVE

shredded lettuce

salsa of your choice

FILLING

⅔ cup cooked corn, mixed with a little grated cheese and chopped fresh green chile, or simmered pork in a mild chili sauce

1 If using corn husks, soak in hot water to cover for at least 3 hours or overnight. If using banana leaves, warm them by placing over an open flame for just a few seconds to make them pliable.

2 To make the tamale dough, beat the shortening until it is fluffy, then beat in the salt, sugar, cumin, masa harina, and baking powder until the mixture resembles tiny bread crumbs.

3 Add the stock very gradually, in several batches, beating until the mixture becomes fluffy and resembles whipped cream.

4 Spread 1–2 tablespoons of the tamale mixture on either a soaked and drained corn husk or a piece of pliable heated banana leaf.

5 Spoon in the filling. Fold the sides of the husks or leaves over the filling to enclose. Wrap each packet in a square of kitchen foil and arrange in a steamer.

6 Pour hot water in the base of the steamer, cover, and steam. Cook for 40–60 minutes, topping up the water in the base of the steamer when needed. Remove the tamales and serve with lettuce and salsa.

Jalisco-Style Eggs

This hearty breakfast dish from Jalisco is a classic Mexican way of serving eggs—a feast of flavors.

NUTRITIONAL INFORMATION

Calories	410	Sugars	. . . . .3g
Protein	. . . . .19g	Fat	. . . . .32g
Carbohydrate	. . .12g	Saturates	. . . . . .13g

 15 mins 20 mins

SERVES 4

INGREDIENTS

4 corn tortillas

1 avocado

lime or lemon juice, for tossing

6 oz/175g chorizo sausage, sliced or diced

2 tbsp butter or water, for cooking

4 eggs

4 tbsp crumbled feta or
   Wensleydale cheese

salsa of your choice

1 tbsp chopped fresh cilantro

1 tbsp finely chopped scallions

1 Heat the tortillas in an ungreased, heavy, nonstick skillet, sprinkling them with a few drops of water as they heat. Wrap the tortillas in a clean dish cloth or kitchen foil as you work to keep them warm. Alternatively, heat through in a stack in the pan, alternating the top and bottom tortillas so that they warm evenly. Wrap in a dish cloth or kitchen foil to keep them warm.

2 Cut the avocado in half around the pit. Twist the halves apart, then remove the pit with a knife. Carefully peel off the skin, dice the flesh, and then toss it in lime or lemon juice to prevent it from turning brown.

3 Brown the chorizo sausage in a pan, then arrange on each warmed tortilla. Keep warm.

4 Meanwhile, heat the butter or water in a nonstick skillet, break in an egg, and cook until the white is just set but the yolk still soft. Remove from the pan and place on top of 1 tortilla. Keep warm while you cook the remaining eggs.

5 Arrange the avocado, cheese, and a spoonful of salsa on each tortilla. Add the fresh cilantro and scallions and serve immediately.

Fish & Crab Chowder

Packed full of flavor, this delicious fish dish is really a meal in itself, but it is ideal accompanied by a crisp side salad.

NUTRITIONAL INFORMATION

Calories	440	Sugars	........10g
Protein	........49g	Fat	...........7g
Carbohydrate	...43g	Saturates	......1g

 40 mins   25 mins

SERVES 4

INGREDIENTS

1 large onion, finely chopped

2 celery stalks, finely chopped

⅔ cup dry white wine

2½ cups fish stock

2½ cups skim milk

1 bay leaf

8 oz/225 g smoked cod fillet, skinned and cut into 1 inch/2.5 cm cubes

8 oz/225 g smoked haddock fillets, skinned and cut into 1 inch/2.5 cm cubes

2 x 6 oz/175 g cans crab meat, drained

8 oz/225 g blanched green beans, sliced into 1 inch/2.5 cm pieces

1⅓ cups cooked brown rice

4 tsp cornstarch mixed with 4 tbsp water

salt and pepper

chopped fresh parsley to garnish

mixed salad greens, to serve

  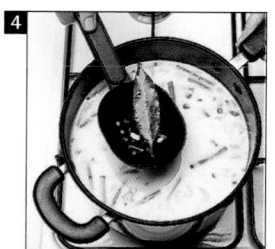

1 Place the onion, celery, and wine in a large nonstick pan. Bring to a boil, cover, and cook over low heat for 5 minutes.

2 Uncover the pan and cook for a further 5 minutes until almost all the liquid has evaporated.

3 Pour in the stock and milk and add the bay leaf. Bring to a simmer and stir in the cod and haddock. Simmer over low heat, uncovered, for 5 minutes.

4 Add the crab meat, beans, and cooked brown rice and simmer gently for 2–3 minutes until just heated through.

Remove the bay leaf with a slotted spoon and discard.

5 Stir in the cornstarch mixture until thickened slightly. Season to taste with salt and pepper and ladle into warmed soup bowls. Garnish with chopped parsley and serve with a mixed salad.

Pad Thai

All over Thailand and Southeast Asia, street stalls (even floating ones) sell these simple delicious rice noodles, stir-fried to order.

NUTRITIONAL INFORMATION

Calories 527   Sugars 8g
Protein ....34g   Fat 17g
Carbohydrate ...58g   Saturates 3g

 30 mins   10 mins

SERVES 4

INGREDIENTS

8 oz/225 g flat rice noodles

2 tbsp peanut or vegetable oil

8 oz/225 g skinless, boneless chicken breasts, thinly sliced

4 shallots, finely chopped

2 garlic cloves, finely chopped

4 scallions, cut on the diagonal into 2 inch/5 cm pieces

12 oz/350 g fresh white crab meat

1½ cups fresh bean sprouts, rinsed

1 tbsp preserved radish or fresh radish, finely diced

2–4 tbsp roasted peanuts, chopped

fresh cilantro sprigs, to garnish

SAUCE

3 tbsp Thai fish sauce

2–3 tbsp rice vinegar or apple vinegar

1 tbsp chili bean sauce or oyster sauce

1 tbsp toasted sesame oil

1 tbsp palm sugar or light brown sugar

½ tsp cayenne pepper or fresh red chile, thinly sliced

1 To make the sauce, whisk together all the sauce ingredients in a small bowl and set aside.

2 Put the rice noodles in a large bowl and pour over enough hot water to cover; set aside for 15 minutes until softened. Drain, rinse, and drain again.

3 Heat the oil in a heavy wok over high heat until very hot, but not smoking. Add the chicken strips and stir-fry for 1–2 minutes until they just begin to color. Using a slotted spoon, transfer to a plate. Reduce the heat to medium-high.

4 Stir the shallots, garlic, and scallions into the wok and stir-fry for about 1 minute. Stir in the drained noodles, then the prepared sauce.

5 Return the reserved chicken to the pan with the crab meat, bean sprouts, and radish. Toss well and cook for about 5 minutes until heated through, tossing frequently. If the noodles begin to stick, add a little water.

6 Turn into a warmed serving dish and sprinkle with the chopped peanuts. Garnish with coriander sprigs and serve immediately.

Chicken & Cheese Jackets

Use the breasts from a roasted chicken to make these delicious potatoes and serve as a light lunch or supper dish.

NUTRITIONAL INFORMATION

Calories 417	Sugars 4g
Protein 28g	Fat 10g
Carbohydrate . . .57g	Saturates 5g

 10 mins   50 mins

SERVES 4

I N G R E D I E N T S

4 large baking potatoes

8 oz/225 g cooked, skinless, boneless chicken breasts

4 scallions

generous 1 cup low-fat soft cheese

pepper

coleslaw, salad greens or mixed salad, to serve

1 Scrub the potatoes and pat dry with absorbent paper towels.

2 Prick the potatoes all over with a fork. Bake in a preheated oven, 400°F/200°C, for about 50 minutes until tender.

3 Meanwhile, using a sharp knife, dice the chicken breasts and trim and thickly slice the scallions. Place the chicken and scallions in a bowl.

4 Add the low-fat soft cheese to the bowl and stir well to combine and coat the chicken.

5 Cut a cross through the top of each potato and pull slightly apart. Spoon the chicken filling into the potatoes and sprinkle with pepper.

6 Serve the chicken and cheese jackets immediately with coleslaw, salad greens, or a mixed salad.

COOK'S TIP

Look for Quark in the chilled section of the supermarket. It is a low-fat, white, fresh curd cheese made from cow's milk and has a delicate, slightly sour flavor.

Teppanyaki

This simple, Japanese style of cooking is ideal for thinly sliced breast of chicken. You can use thin turkey scallops, if you prefer.

NUTRITIONAL INFORMATION

Calories 206	Sugars 4g
Protein 30g	Fat 7g
Carbohydrate 6g	Saturates 2g

5 mins   10 mins

SERVES 4

INGREDIENTS

4 boneless chicken breasts

1 red bell pepper

1 green bell pepper

4 scallions

8 baby corn cobs

scant 2 cups bean sprouts

1 tbsp sesame or sunflower oil

4 tbsp shoyu or soy sauce

4 tbsp mirin

1 tbsp grated fresh ginger root

COOK'S TIP

Mirin is a rich, sweet rice wine from Japan. You can buy it in Asian supermarkets, but if it is not available, add 1 tablespoon soft light brown sugar to the sauce instead.

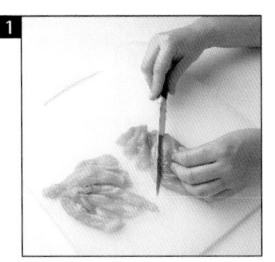

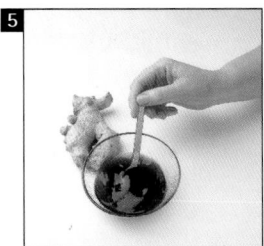

1 Remove the skin from the chicken and slice at a slight angle, to a thickness of about ¼ inch/5 mm.

2 Deseed and thinly slice the red and green bell peppers and trim and slice the scallions and corn cobs.

3 Arrange the peppers, scallions, corn cobs, and bean sprouts on a plate with the sliced chicken.

4 Heat a large griddle or heavy skillet, then lightly brush with sesame or sunflower oil. Add the vegetables and chicken slices, in small batches, allowing space between them so that they cook thoroughly.

5 Combine the shoyu or soy sauce, mirin, and ginger in a small serving bowl and serve as a dip with the chicken and vegetables.

Pasta & Chicken Medley

Strips of cooked chicken are tossed with colored pasta, grapes, and carrot sticks in a pesto-flavored dressing.

NUTRITIONAL INFORMATION

Calories	.609	Sugars	.11g
Protein	.26g	Fat	.38g
Carbohydrate	.45g	Saturates	.6g

 30 mins 10 mins

SERVES 2

INGREDIENTS

generous 1–1⅓ cups dried pasta shapes, such as twists or bows

2 tbsp mayonnaise

2 tsp bottled pesto sauce

1 tbsp sour cream

6 oz/175g cooked skinless, boneless chicken meat

1–2 celery stalks

4½ oz/125 g black grapes (preferably seedless)

1 large carrot

salt and pepper

celery leaves, to garnish

FRENCH DRESSING

1 tsp wine vinegar

1 tbsp extra virgin olive oil

salt and pepper

1 To make the French dressing, whisk all the ingredients together until smooth.

2 Bring a large pan of lightly salted water to a boil. Add the pasta, bring back to a boil, and cook for 8–10 minutes until tender, but still firm to the bite. Drain thoroughly, rinse, and drain again. Transfer to a bowl and mix in the French dressing while still hot, then set aside until cold.

3 Combine the mayonnaise, pesto sauce, and sour cream in a bowl and season to taste with salt and pepper.

4 Cut the chicken into thin strips. Cut the celery diagonally into thin slices. Reserve a few grapes for garnish, halve the rest, and remove any seeds. Cut the carrot into narrow julienne strips.

5 Add the chicken, celery, halved grapes, carrot, and mayonnaise mixture to the pasta and toss thoroughly. Taste and adjust the seasoning, adding more salt and pepper if necessary.

6 Arrange the pasta mixture on 2 plates and garnish with the reserved black grapes and the celery leaves.

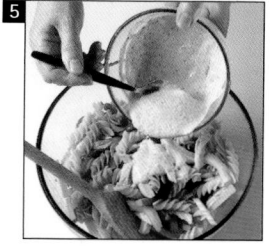

Vegetable Frittata

A frittata is a type of Italian omelet—you can add almost anything to the eggs. It is also delicious eaten cold and makes an ideal picnic dish.

NUTRITIONAL INFORMATION

Calories 310	Sugars 4g	
Protein 18g	Fat 17g	
Carbohydrate . . .24g	Saturates 4g	

 15 mins   20 mins

SERVES 4

I N G R E D I E N T S

3 tbsp olive oil

1 onion, chopped

2 garlic cloves, chopped

8 oz/225 g zucchini, thinly sliced

4 eggs

14 oz/400g can borlotti beans, rinsed and drained

3 tomatoes, peeled and chopped

2 tbsp chopped fresh parsley

1 tbsp chopped fresh basil

½ cup grated Swiss cheese

salt and pepper

1 Heat 2 tablespoons of the oil in a skillet. Add the onion and garlic and cook over medium heat, stirring occasionally, for 2–3 minutes or until softened. Add the zucchini and cook, stirring occasionally, for 3–4 minutes or until softened.

2 Break the eggs into a bowl and season with salt and pepper to taste. Beat lightly and stir in the onion and zucchini mixture, the beans, tomatoes, parsley, and basil.

3 Heat the remaining oil in a 9½ inch/ 24 cm omelet pan, add the egg mixture, and cook over low heat for approximately 5 minutes until the eggs have almost set and the underside of the frittata is golden brown.

4 Sprinkle the cheese over the top and place the pan under a preheated moderate broiler for 3–4 minutes or until set on the top, but still moist in the middle. Cut into wedges and serve warm or at room temperature.

COOK'S TIP

Swiss cheese is made from unpasteurized cow's milk and has a sweet, nutty flavor, which enhances the taste of this frittata. It is firm and close textured, and has small holes interspersed throughout.

Mediterranean Chicken

This recipe uses ingredients found in the Languedoc area of France, where cooking over hot embers is a way of life.

NUTRITIONAL INFORMATION

Calories 143   Sugars 4g
Protein ....13g   Fat 8g
Carbohydrate ....4g   Saturates 2g

2¾ hrs   40 mins

SERVES 4

INGREDIENTS

4 chicken quarters

salad greens, to serve

MARINADE

4 tbsp low-fat plain yogurt

3 tbsp sun-dried tomato paste

1 tbsp olive oil

½ cup fresh basil leaves, lightly crushed

2 garlic cloves, coarsely chopped

1 First, make the marinade. Combine the yogurt, sun-dried tomato paste, olive oil, crushed basil leaves, and garlic in a small bowl and stir well to mix.

2 Transfer the marinade to a dish large enough to hold the chicken quarters in a single layer. Add the chicken quarters and turn them to ensure that all the chicken pieces are thoroughly coated in the marinade.

3 Cover with plastic wrap and set aside to marinate in the refrigerator for at least 2 hours. Remove the dish from the refrigerator and set aside, still covered, at room temperature for 30 minutes.

4 Place the chicken over a medium barbecue and cook for about 30–40 minutes, turning frequently. Test for readiness by piercing the flesh at the thickest part—usually at the top of the drumstick—with the point of a sharp knife. If the juices that run out are clear, it is cooked through. If there is any sign of pink, cook for a further 5–10 minutes, then test again.

5 Serve immediately with salad greens. This dish is also delicious eaten cold.

VARIATION

For a marinade with an extra zingy flavor combine 2 coarsely chopped garlic cloves, the juice of 2 lemons, and 3 tbsp olive oil. Prepare and cook the chicken in the same way.

Pasta & Shrimp Packets

This is the ideal dish when you have guests because the packets can be prepared in advance, then put in the oven when you are ready to eat.

NUTRITIONAL INFORMATION

Calories 640	Sugars 1g	
Protein 50g	Fat 29g	
Carbohydrate . . .42g	Saturates 4g	

 15 mins   30 mins

SERVES 4

I N G R E D I E N T S

1lb/450 g dried fettuccine

⅔ cup ready made pesto sauce

4 tsp extra virgin olive oil

1 lb 10 oz/750 g large raw shrimp, peeled and deveined

2 garlic cloves, crushed

½ cup dry white wine

salt and pepper

1 Cut out 4 x 12 inch/30 cm squares of waxed paper.

2 Bring a pan of lightly salted water to a boil. Add the pasta, bring back to a boil, and cook for 2–3 minutes until just softened. Drain and set aside.

3 Combine the fettuccine and half of the pesto sauce. Spread out the paper

squares and put 1 teaspoon of the olive oil in the middle of each. Divide the fettuccine among the squares, then divide the shrimp, and place on top of the fettuccine.

4 Combine the remaining pesto sauce and the garlic and spoon it over the shrimp. Season each packet with salt and pepper to taste and then sprinkle with the white wine.

5 Dampen the edges of the waxed paper and wrap the packets loosely, twisting the edges to seal.

6 Place the packets on a cookie sheet and bake in a preheated oven, 400°F/200°C, for 10–15 minutes until piping hot and the shrimp have changed color. Transfer the packets to 4 individual serving plates and serve.

COOK'S TIP

Traditionally, these packets are designed to look like moneybags. The resemblance is more effective with waxed paper than with foil.

Citrus Fish Kabobs

Use your favorite fish for this dish as long as it is firm enough to thread onto skewers. The tang of orange makes this a refreshing meal.

NUTRITIONAL INFORMATION

Calories 333   Sugar 0g
Protein . . . . .18g   Fats 3g
Carbohydrates . . .18g   Saturates 4g

 2½ hrs   10 mins

SERVES 4

INGREDIENTS

1lb/450 g firm white fish fillet, such as cod or monkfish

1lb/450 g thick salmon fillet

2 large oranges

1 pink grapefruit

1 bunch of fresh bay leaves

1 tsp finely grated lemon rind

3 tbsp lemon juice

2 tsp honey

2 garlic cloves, crushed

salt and pepper

TO SERVE

crusty bread

mixed salad

1 Skin the white fish fillet and the salmon, then rinse and pat dry on paper towels. Cut each fillet into 16 pieces.

2 Using a sharp knife, remove the skin and pith from the oranges and grapefruit. Cut out the segments of flesh, removing all remaining traces of the pith and dividing membranes.

3 Thread the pieces of fish alternately with the orange and grapefruit segments and the bay leaves onto

8 skewers. Place the fish kabobs in a shallow dish.

4 In a small bowl, combine the lemon rind, lemon juice, honey, and crushed garlic. Pour the mixture over the fish kabobs and season to taste with salt and pepper. Cover with plastic wrap and set aside in the refrigerator to marinate for 2 hours, turning occasionally.

5 Remove the fish kabobs from the marinade and place on a broiler rack. Cook under a preheated medium broiler, turning once, for 7–8 minutes until cooked through and the fish is opaque.

6 Transfer the kabobs to warmed individual serving plates and serve immediately with crusty bread and a fresh mixed salad.

 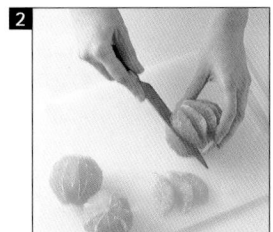 

Crab with Napa Cabbage

The delicate flavors of Napa cabbage and crab meat are enhanced by the coconut milk in this recipe.

NUTRITIONAL INFORMATION

Calories	109	Sugars	.........1g
Protein	.........11g	Fat	...........6g
Carbohydrate	....2g	Saturates	.......1g

 5 mins   10 mins

SERVES 4

INGREDIENTS

8 oz/225 g shiitake mushrooms

2 tbsp vegetable oil

2 garlic cloves, crushed

6 scallions, sliced

1 head Napa cabbage, shredded

1 tbsp mild curry paste

6 tbsp coconut milk

7 oz/200 g canned white crab
    meat, drained

1 tsp chili flakes

1 Using a sharp knife, cut the mushrooms into slices.

2 Heat the vegetable oil in a large preheated wok or a skillet with a heavy base.

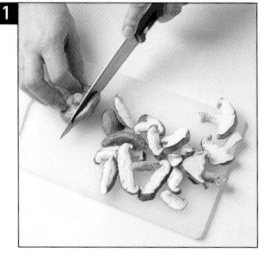  

3 Add the mushrooms and garlic to the wok or skillet and stir-fry over medium heat for 3 minutes or until the mushrooms have softened.

4 Add the scallions and shredded Napa cabbage to the wok and stir-fry for about 10 minutes until the leaves have just wilted.

5 Mix together the mild curry paste and coconut milk in a small bowl.

6 Add the curry paste and coconut milk mixture to the wok or skillet, with the crab meat and chili flakes. Mix together until thoroughly combined. Continue to heat the mixture in the wok until the juices start to bubble.

7 Transfer the crab and vegetable stir-fry to warm individual serving bowls and serve immediately.

COOK'S TIP

Shiitake mushrooms are now readily available in the fresh vegetable section of most large supermarkets.

Basque Tuna Stew

Although versions of this stew are eaten throughout Spain, it originated in the Basque region to satisfy the hearty appetites of local fishermen.

NUTRITIONAL INFORMATION

Calories 718   Sugars 9g
Protein . . . . .63g   Fat 26g
Carbohydrate . . .62g   Saturates 5g

 10 mins   1 hr

SERVES 4

INGREDIENTS

5 tbsp olive oil

1 large onion, chopped

2 garlic cloves, chopped

7 oz/200 g can chopped tomatoes

1 lb 9 oz/700 g potatoes, cut into 2 inch/
5 cm chunks

3 green bell peppers, deseeded and
roughly chopped

1¼ cups cold water

2 lb/900 g tuna fillet, cut into chunks

4 slices crusty white bread

salt and pepper

1 Heat 2 tablespoons of the oil in a pan and add the onion. Cook over low heat, stirring occasionally, for 8–10 minutes until softened and brown. Add the garlic and cook a further minute. Add the tomatoes, cover, and simmer for 30 minutes until thickened.

2 Meanwhile, place the potatoes and green bell peppers in another pan. Add the water, which should just cover the vegetables. If necessary, add a little more or pour a little away. Bring to a boil, cover, and simmer gently over medium heat for about 15 minutes until the potatoes are almost tender.

3 Add the tuna and the tomato mixture to the potatoes and bell peppers and season to taste with salt and pepper. Cover and simmer for 6–8 minutes until the tuna is tender.

4 Meanwhile, heat the remaining oil in a large skillet over medium heat and add the bread slices. Fry on both sides until golden. Drain on paper towels. Serve the fried bread with the stew.

VARIATION

Substitute any very firm-fleshed fish, such as shark or swordfish, for the tuna used in this recipe.

Sardines with Pesto

This is a very quick and tasty midweek supper dish. Use a good quality ready-made pesto for an even speedier supper.

NUTRITIONAL INFORMATION

Calories 617   Sugars 0g
Protein . . . . .27g   Fat 56g
Carbohydrate . . . .1g   Saturates 11g

 25 mins   6 mins

SERVES 4

INGREDIENTS

16 large sardines, scaled and gutted

2 cups fresh basil leaves

2 garlic cloves, crushed

2 tbsp pine nuts, toasted

⅔ cup freshly grated Parmesan cheese

⅔ cup olive oil

salt and pepper

lemon wedges, to garnish

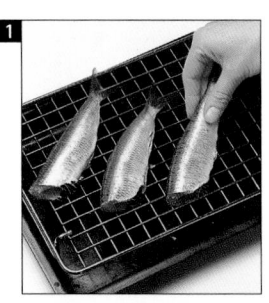

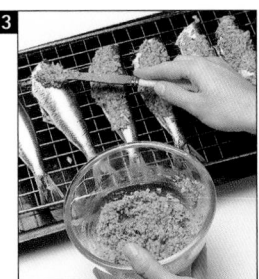

1 Wash and the sardines and pat dry with paper towels. Arrange them on a broiler pan.

2 Put the basil leaves, garlic, and pine nuts in a food processor. Process until finely chopped. Scrape out of the food processor and stir in the Parmesan and oil. Season to taste.

3 Spread a little of the pesto over 1 side of the sardines and place under a preheated hot broiler for 3 minutes. Turn the fish, spread with more pesto, and broil for a further 3 minutes until the sardines are cooked through.

4 Serve immediately with extra pesto and garnished with lemon wedges.

VARIATION

This treatment will also work well with other small oily fish, such as herrings and sprats.

Shrimp Rostis

These crisp little vegetable and shrimp patties make an ideal light lunch or supper, accompanied by a mixed leaf salad.

NUTRITIONAL INFORMATION

Calories 445	Sugars 9g	
Protein 19g	Fat 29g	
Carbohydrate ...29g	Saturates 4g	

10 mins   1 hr

SERVES 4

INGREDIENTS

12 oz/350 g potatoes

12 oz/350 g celery root

1 carrot

½ small onion

2 cups peeled cooked shrimp, thawed if frozen and well-drained on paper towels

2½ tbsp all-purpose flour

1 egg, lightly beaten

vegetable oil, for frying

salt and pepper

CHERRY TOMATO SALSA

8 oz/225 g mixed cherry tomatoes, quartered

½ small mango, finely diced

1 fresh red chile, deseeded and finely chopped

½ small red onion, finely chopped

1 tbsp chopped fresh cilantro

1 tbsp chopped fresh chives

2 tbsp olive oil

2 tsp lemon juice

salt and pepper

1 For the salsa, mix the tomatoes, mango, chile, onion, cilantro, chives, olive oil, lemon juice, and seasoning. Set aside for the flavors to steep.

2 Using a food processor or the fine blade of a box grater, finely grate the potatoes, celery root, carrot, and onion. Combine with the shrimp, flour, and egg. Season well and set aside.

3 Divide the shrimp mixture into 8 equal pieces. Press each into a greased 4 inch/10 cm metal pastry cutter (if you have only 1 cutter, you can simply shape the rostis individually).

4 Heat a shallow layer of oil in a large skillet. When hot, transfer the rostis, still in the cutters, to the skillet, in 4 batches if necessary. When the oil sizzles underneath, remove the cutter. Cook gently, pressing down with a spatula, for 6–8 minutes on each side, until crisp and browned and the vegetables are tender. Drain on paper towels and keep warm while you cook the remainder. Serve hot with the tomato salsa.

Provençal Mussels

This recipe conjures up the flavors of southern France—tomatoes, wine, herbs, and garlic combine to make a tasty mussel stew.

NUTRITIONAL INFORMATION

Calories	194	Sugars	.........5g
Protein	........12g	Fat	..........10g
Carbohydrate	....9g	Saturates	.......2g

10 mins   1¼ hrs

SERVES 4

INGREDIENTS

2 lb/900 g live mussels

3 tbsp olive oil

1 onion, finely chopped

3 garlic cloves, finely chopped

2 tsp fresh thyme leaves

⅔ cup red wine

2 x 14 oz/400g cans chopped tomatoes

2 tbsp chopped fresh parsley

salt and pepper

crusty bread, to serve

1 Clean the mussels by scrubbing or scraping the shells and pulling out any beards. Discard any mussels with broken shells or that do not close when tapped sharply. Put the mussels in a large pan with just the water that clings to their shells. Cover and cook over high heat, vigorously shaking the pan occasionally, for 3–4 minutes until all the mussels have opened. Discard any mussels that remain closed. Drain, reserving the cooking liquid. Set aside.

2 Heat the oil in a large pan and add the onion. Cook over low heat for 8–10 minutes until softened, but not colored. Add the garlic and thyme and cook for a further minute. Add the wine and simmer rapidly until reduced and syrupy. Add the tomatoes and strain in the mussel cooking liquid. Bring to a boil, cover, and simmer for 30 minutes. Uncover the pan and cook for a further 15 minutes.

3 Add the mussels and cook for a further 5 minutes until heated through. Stir in the parsley, season to taste with salt and pepper, and serve with plenty of fresh crusty bread.

VARIATION

Replace the mussels with an equal quantity of clams.

Sicilian Pasta

This is based on a traditional dish combining broccoli and anchovies, but here lemon and garlic have been added for more flavor.

NUTRITIONAL INFORMATION

Calories 529	Sugars 4g
Protein 17g	Fat 20g
Carbohydrate ...75g	Saturates 3g

10 mins   30 mins

SERVES 4

INGREDIENTS

6 tbsp olive oil

1 cup fresh white bread crumbs

1 lb/450 g broccoli, cut into small florets

12 oz/350 g dried tagliatelle

4 canned anchovy fillets, drained and chopped

2 garlic cloves, sliced

grated rind 1 lemon

large pinch of chili flakes

salt and pepper

freshly grated Parmesan cheese, to serve

1 Heat 2 tablespoons of the olive oil in a skillet and add the bread crumbs. Stir-fry over medium heat for 4–5 minutes until golden and crisp. Drain thoroughly on paper towels.

2 Bring a large pan of lightly salted water to a boil and add the broccoli. Blanch for 3 minutes, then drain, reserving the water. Refresh the broccoli under cold water and drain again. Pat dry on paper towels and set aside.

3 Bring the water back to a boil and add the tagliatelle. Bring back to a boil and cook for 8–10 minutes until tender, but still firm to the bite.

4 Meanwhile, heat 2 tablespoons of the remaining oil in a large, heavy skillet or wok and add the anchovies. Cook over low heat for 1 minute, then mash with a wooden spoon to a paste. Add the garlic, lemon rind, and chili flakes and cook gently for 2 minutes. Add the broccoli and cook for a further 3–4 minutes until heated through.

5 Drain the cooked pasta and add to the broccoli mixture with the remaining olive oil. Season to taste with salt and pepper. Toss together well.

6 Divide the tagliatelle among warmed serving plates. Top with the fried bread crumbs and Parmesan cheese and serve immediately.

Pasta Puttanesca

The story goes that this was a dish made and eaten by Italian prostitutes who needed a quick and simple meal to keep them going.

NUTRITIONAL INFORMATION

Calories 359	Sugars 10g
Protein 10g	Fat 14g
Carbohydrate ...51g	Saturates 2g

 5 mins   25 mins

SERVES 4

INGREDIENTS

3 tbsp extra virgin olive oil

1 large red onion, finely chopped

4 canned anchovy fillets, drained

pinch of chili flakes

2 garlic cloves, finely chopped

14 oz/400g can chopped tomatoes

2 tbsp tomato paste

8 oz/225 g dried spaghetti

¼ cup pitted black olives,
    roughly chopped

¼ cup pitted green olives,
    roughly chopped

1 tbsp capers, rinsed and drained

4 sun-dried tomatoes in oil, drained and
    coarsely chopped

salt and pepper

1 Heat the oil in a pan and cook the onion, anchovies, and chili flakes. for 10 minutes until softened. Add the garlic and cook for 30 seconds. Stir in the tomatoes and tomato paste and bring to a boil. Simmer gently for 10 minutes.

2 Meanwhile, bring a pan of lightly salted water to a boil. Add the pasta, bring back to a boil, and cook for about 8–10 minutes until tender, but still firm to the bite.

3 Add the olives, capers, and sun-dried tomatoes to the sauce. Simmer for a further 2–3 minutes. Season to taste.

4 Drain the pasta well and stir in the sauce. Toss thoroughly to mix. Transfer to a serving dish and serve hot.

Linguine with Sardines

This is a very quick dish that is ideal for midweek suppers because it is so simple to prepare, but is packed full of flavor.

NUTRITIONAL INFORMATION

Calories 547   Sugars 5g
Protein ....23g   Fat 23g
Carbohydrate ...68g   Saturates 3g

 10 mins   12 mins

SERVES 4

INGREDIENTS

8 sardines, filleted

1 fennel bulb

4 tbsp olive oil

3 garlic cloves, sliced

1 tsp chili flakes

12 oz/350 g dried linguine

½ tsp finely grated lemon rind

1 tbsp lemon juice

2 tbsp pine nuts, toasted

2 tbsp chopped fresh parsley

salt and pepper

1 Wash the sardine fillets and pat dry on paper towels. Roughly chop them into large pieces and set aside. Trim the fennel bulb and slice very thinly.

2 Heat 2 tablespoons of the olive oil in a large, heavy skillet and add the garlic and chili flakes. Cook for 1 minute, then add the fennel slices. Cook over medium-high heat, stirring occasionally, for 4–5 minutes until softened. Lower the heat, add the sardine pieces, and cook for a further 3–4 minutes until just cooked.

3 Meanwhile, bring a pan of lightly salted water to a boil. Add the pasta, bring back to a boil, and cook for about 8–10 minutes until tender, but still firm to the bite. Drain well and return to the pan.

4 Add the lemon rind, lemon juice, pine nuts, and parsley to the sardines and toss together. Season to taste with salt and pepper. Add to the pasta with the remaining olive oil and toss together gently. Transfer to a warmed serving dish and serve immediately.

COOK'S TIP
Reserve a couple of tablespoons of the pasta cooking water and add to the pasta with the sauce if the mixture seems a little dry.

Crab Ravioli

These small packets are made from wonton wrappers, filled with mixed vegetables and crab meat for a melt-in-the-mouth appetizer.

NUTRITIONAL INFORMATION

Calories	292	Sugars	.........1g
Protein	........25g	Fat	..........17g
Carbohydrate	....11g	Saturates	.......5g

 20 mins   25 mins

SERVES 4

INGREDIENTS

1 lb/450 g fresh or canned crab meat, drained

½ red bell pepper, deseeded and finely diced

4 oz/115 g Napa cabbage, shredded

½ cup bean sprouts, roughly chopped

1 tbsp light soy sauce

1 tsp lime juice

16 wonton wrappers

1 small egg, beaten

2 tbsp peanut oil

1 tsp sesame oil

salt and pepper

1 Combine the crab meat, red bell pepper, Napa cabbage, bean sprouts, soy sauce, and lime juice. Season and set aside for 15 minutes.

2 Spread out the wonton wrappers on a counter. Spoon a little of the crab meat mixture into the center of each wrapper. Brush the edges with egg and fold in half, pushing out any air. Press the edges together to seal.

3 Heat the peanut oil in a preheated wok or skillet. Fry the ravioli, in batches for 3–4 minutes, turning frequently, until browned. Remove with a slotted spoon and drain on paper towels.

4 Heat any remaining filling in the wok or skillet over gentle heat until hot. Sprinkle the ravioli with the sesame oil, transfer to a warmed serving platter, and serve immediately.

COOK'S TIP

Make sure that the edges of the ravioli are sealed well and that all of the air is pressed out to prevent them from opening during cooking.

Spaghettini with Crab

This dish is probably one of the simplest in the book, yet the flavor is as impressive as a recipe over which you have slaved for hours.

NUTRITIONAL INFORMATION

Calories	488	Sugars	.........3g
Protein	........13g	Fat	..........19g
Carbohydrate	...65g	Saturates	.......3g

10 mins   10 mins

SERVES 4

I N G R E D I E N T S

1 dressed crab, about 1lb/450 g including the shell

12 oz/350 g dried spaghettini

6 tbsp extra virgin olive oil

1 fresh red chile, deseeded and finely chopped

2 garlic cloves, finely chopped

3 tbsp chopped fresh parsley

2 tbsp lemon juice

1 tsp finely grated lemon rind

salt and pepper

lemon wedges, to garnish

1 Scoop the meat from the crab shell into a bowl. Mix the white and brown meat lightly together and set aside.

2 Bring a large pan of lightly salted water to a boil. Add the pasta, bring back to a boil, and cook for 8–10 minutes until tender, but still firm to the bite. Drain well and return to the pan.

3 Meanwhile, heat 2 tablespoons of the olive oil in a skillet. Add the chile and garlic. Cook for 30 seconds, then add the crab meat, parsley, lemon juice, and lemon rind. Stir-fry over low heat for a further minute until the crab meat is just heated through.

4 Add the crab mixture to the pasta with the remaining olive oil and season to taste with salt and pepper. Toss together thoroughly, transfer to a warmed serving dish, and serve immediately, garnished with lemon wedges.

COOK'S TIP
If you prefer to buy your own fresh crab you will need a large crab weighing about 2 lb 4 oz/1 kg.

Fish & Bread Soup

Good fish to choose for this soup might include eel, skate, or cod. Avoid oily fish, such as mackerel, herring, and salmon.

NUTRITIONAL INFORMATION

Calories	755	Sugars	.........9g
Protein	........46g	Fat	..........54g
Carbohydrate	...23g	Saturates	.......9g

 40 mins 1¼ hrs

SERVES 6–8

INGREDIENTS

4 lb/1.8 kg mixed whole fish

8 oz/225 g raw shrimp, shell on

5 pints/2.25 liters water

⅔ cup olive oil

2 large onions, coarsely chopped

2 celery stalks, coarsely chopped

1 leek, coarsely chopped

1 small fennel bulb, coarsely chopped

5 garlic cloves, chopped

1 strip of orange peel

3 tbsp orange juice

14 oz/400g can chopped tomatoes

1 red bell pepper, deseeded and sliced

1 bay leaf

1 fresh thyme sprig

pinch of saffron

pinch of cayenne pepper

6–8 thick slices sourdough bread

salt and pepper

RED BELL PEPPER SAUCE

1 red bell pepper, deseeded and quartered

⅔ cup olive oil

1 egg yolk

pinch of saffron

pinch of chili flakes

1 Fillet the fish, reserving all the bones. Coarsely chop the flesh. Peel the shrimp. Place the fish bones and shrimp shells in a large pan with the water and bring to a boil. Lower the heat and simmer for 20 minutes, then strain.

2 Heat the oil in a large pan and add the onions, celery, leek, fennel, and garlic. Cook over low heat, stirring occasionally, for 20 minutes without coloring. Add the orange peel and juice, tomatoes, red bell pepper, bay leaf, thyme, saffron, shrimp, fish, and stock, bring to a boil, then simmer for 40 minutes.

3 To prepare the sauce. Brush the red bell pepper quarters with some of the olive oil. Place under a preheated broiler for 8–10 minutes, turning once, until the skins have blackened and the flesh is tender. Transfer to a plastic bag.

4 When cool enough to handle, peel off the skin. Roughly chop the flesh and place it in a food processor with the egg yolk, saffron, and chili flakes. Process until smooth. With the motor running, add the olive oil, in a slow stream until the sauce begins to thicken. Continue adding in a steady stream. Transfer to a serving bowl and season to taste with salt and pepper.

5 When the soup is cooked, pour it into a food processor or blender. Process until smooth and then push it through a strainer with a wooden spoon into a clean pan. Return to the heat and season with cayenne, salt, and pepper to taste.

6 Toast the bread on both sides under a preheated broiler and place a slice in the bottom of each individual soup plate. Ladle over the soup and serve immediately, handing the sauce separately.

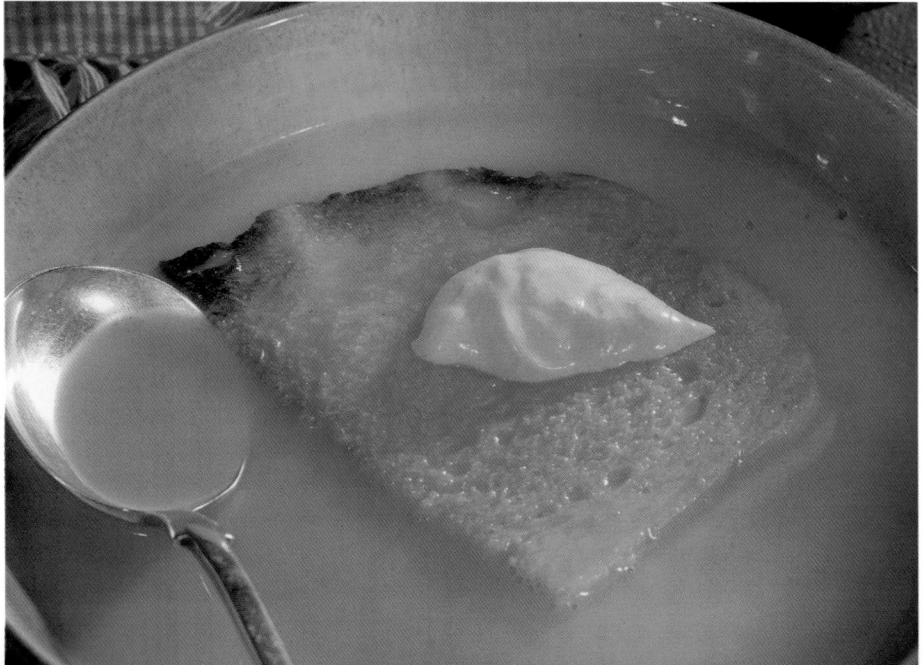

Salt Cod Hash

As well as being a simple supper dish, this would make a delicious addition to a brunch menu.

NUTRITIONAL INFORMATION

Calories 857   Sugars 5g
Protein . . . . .58g   Fat 36g
Carbohydrate . . .82g   Saturates 10g

5 mins, plus 50 hrs soaking/salting   30 mins

SERVES 4

INGREDIENTS

2 tbsp sea salt

1 lb 10 oz/750 g fresh boneless cod fillet

4 eggs

3 tbsp olive oil, plus extra
    for drizzling

8 strips smoked lean bacon, chopped

1 lb 9 oz/700g old potatoes, diced

8 garlic cloves

8 thick slices white bread

2 plum tomatoes, peeled and chopped

2 tsp red wine vinegar

2 tbsp chopped fresh parsley, plus extra
    to garnish

salt and pepper

lemon wedges, to garnish

1 Sprinkle the salt over both sides of the cod fillet. Place in a shallow dish, cover, and chill for 48 hours. When ready to cook, remove the cod from the refrigerator and rinse under cold water. Set aside to soak in cold water for 2 hours, then drain well.

2 Bring a large pan of water to a boil and add the fish. Remove from the heat and set aside for 10 minutes. Drain the fish on paper towels and flake the flesh. Discard the soaking water.

3 Bring a pan of water to a boil. Add the eggs and simmer for 7–9 minutes from when the water returns to a boil—7 minutes for a slightly soft center, 9 for a firm center. Drain, then plunge the eggs into cold water. Shell the eggs and coarsely chop. Set aside.

4 Heat the oil in a large skillet and add the bacon. Cook over medium heat for 4–5 minutes until crisp and brown. Remove with a slotted spoon and drain on paper towels. Put the potatoes and garlic in the skillet and cook over medium heat for 8–10 minutes until crisp and golden. Meanwhile, toast the bread on both sides. Drizzle the bread with olive oil and set aside.

5 Add the tomatoes, bacon, fish, vinegar, and chopped egg to the potatoes and garlic. Cook for 2 minutes. Stir in the parsley and season to taste with salt and pepper. Put the toast onto serving plates, top with the hash, and garnish with parsley and lemon wedges.

Onion & Tuna Tart

This is a variation of Pissaladière, the classic French tart
of slow-cooked onions on a bread base, very like a pizza.

NUTRITIONAL INFORMATION

Calories 541	Sugars 14g
Protein 22g	Fat 25g
Carbohydrate . . .61g	Saturates 9g

1½ hrs 1¾ hrs

SERVES 4

INGREDIENTS

8 oz/225 g white bread flour, plus extra
    for dusting

1 tsp salt

1 envelope active dry yeast (about 2½ tsp)

2 tbsp olive oil, plus extra for greasing

⅔ cup lukewarm water

TOPPING

¼ cup butter

2 tbsp olive oil

2 lb/900 g onions, thinly sliced

1 tsp sugar

1 tsp salt

1 tsp fresh thyme leaves

7 oz/200 g can tuna, drained

¾ cup pitted black olives

pepper

salad greens, to serve

1 To make the topping, heat the butter
and oil in a large pan and add the
onions. Stir well, cover, and cook over very
low heat for 20 minutes. Add the sugar
and salt. Cook over the lowest heat for a
further 30–40 minutes, stirring until
collapsed and beginning to brown. Cook
for a further 15–20 minutes until evenly
golden. Remove from the heat, stir in the
thyme, and season to taste.

2 Meanwhile, make the base. Combine
the flour, salt, and yeast in a large
bowl. Add the oil and enough water to
make a soft dough that leaves the sides of
the bowl clean. Tip the dough onto a
lightly floured counter and knead for
5 minutes until smooth and elastic.
Alternatively, use a food mixer with a
dough hook and knead for 5 minutes.

3 Form the dough into a neat ball and
place in a lightly oiled bowl. Lightly
oil the top of the dough, cover with a
clean dish cloth, and set aside to rise in a
warm place for about 1 hour or until
doubled in bulk.

4 Preheat the oven to 450°F/220°C with
a cookie sheet on the top shelf. Punch

down the risen dough by punching the
center with your fist. Tip out the dough
onto the counter and knead briefly. Roll
out the dough, using a rolling pin, to fit a
lightly oiled jelly roll pan measuring
13 x 9 inches/32.5 x 23 cm, leaving a rim.
You may have to stretch the dough to fit
the pan as it is very springy.

5 Spread the onions over the dough.
Flake the tuna with a fork and sprinkle
it over the top of the onions. Arrange the
olives over the tuna and season to taste
with pepper. Transfer the pan to the
preheated cookie sheet and bake for about
20 minutes until the dough is golden.
Serve immediately with salad greens.

 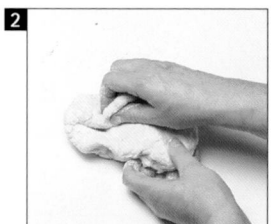 

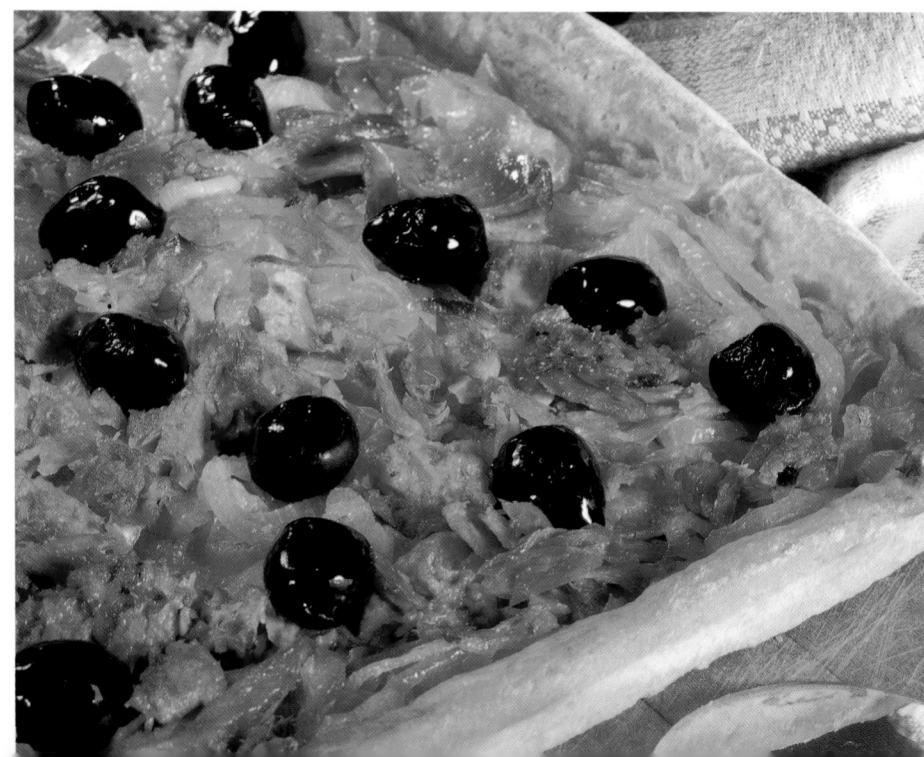

Smoked Salmon Crêpes

Buckwheat flour is traditionally used for the crêpes in this Breton recipe. It is available from large supermarkets and healthfood stores.

NUTRITIONAL INFORMATION

Calories	385	Sugars 4g
Protein	........24g	Fat 21g
Carbohydrate	...27g	Saturates 9g

 25 mins   25 mins

SERVES 4

I N G R E D I E N T S

½ cup all-purpose flour

½ cup buckwheat flour

pinch of salt

2 large eggs

scant 1 cup milk

5 tbsp water

2 tbsp butter, melted

vegetable oil, for frying

FILLING

½ cup crème fraîche

1 tbsp capers, rinsed, drained and
  roughly chopped

3 scallions, finely chopped

1 fresh red chile, deseeded and
  finely chopped

1 tbsp chopped fresh dill

1 tbsp chopped fresh chives

1 tsp lemon rind

8 oz/225 g sliced smoked salmon

salt and pepper

1 For the filling, combine the crème fraîche, capers, scallions, chile, dill, chives, lemon rind, and seasoning.

2 To make the buckwheat crêpes, sift together the flours and salt into a large bowl. Make a well in the center and add the eggs. Combine the milk and water and add half this mixture to the flour and eggs. Mix together until smooth. Gradually add the remaining milk mixture to make a smooth batter. Stir in the melted butter.

3 Heat an 8 inch/20 cm crêpe pan or skillet over medium heat. Dip a piece of wadded paper towels into a little vegetable oil and rub this over the surface of the pan to give a thin coating. Ladle about 2 tablespoons of the crêpe batter into the pan, tilting and shaking the pan to coat the base evenly. Cook for 1 minute until the edges start to lift away from the

pan. Using a large spatula, carefully lift the crêpe and turn it over. It should be pale golden. Cook for 30 seconds on the second side. Remove from the pan and place on a warmed plate. Re-grease and reheat the pan and repeat with the remaining mixture to make 12–14 crêpes, depending on their thickness. Stack the cooked crêpes, interleaved with waxed paper or baking parchment.

4 Place a slice of smoked salmon on each crêpe and top with about 2 teaspoons of the crème fraîche mixture. Fold the crêpe in half, then in half again to form a triangle, and serve.

Crab Soufflé

Soufflés are always impressive and this one is no exception. Serve straight from the oven, but don't worry if it sinks en route to the table.

NUTRITIONAL INFORMATION

Calories	214	Sugars	.........1g
Protein	........15g	Fat	..........14g
Carbohydrate	....8g	Saturates	.......7g

 15 mins   35 mins

SERVES 4–6

INGREDIENTS

3 tbsp butter, plus extra for greasing

generous ⅓ cup dried bread crumbs

1 small onion, finely chopped

1 garlic clove, crushed

2 tsp mustard powder

¼ cup all-purpose flour

1 cup milk

½ cup grated Swiss cheese

3 eggs, separated

8 oz/225 g crab meat, thawed if frozen

2 tbsp chopped fresh chives

pinch of cayenne pepper

salt and pepper

1 Generously butter a 6¼ cup soufflé dish. Add the bread crumbs, then shake and turn the dish to coat the base and sides completely. Shake out any excess. Set aside on a cookie sheet.

2 Melt the butter in a large pan. Add onion and cook over low heat, stirring occasionally, for 5 minutes until softened, but not colored. Add the garlic and cook for a further minute. Stir in the mustard powder and flour and cook, stirring constantly, for 1 minute. Gradually add the milk, stirring constantly, until smooth. Increase the heat slightly and gradually bring to a boil, stirring constantly. Simmer gently for 2 minutes. Remove from the heat and stir in the cheese. Set aside to cool slightly.

3 Lightly beat in the egg yolks, then gently fold in the crab meat, chives, and cayenne, and season to taste with salt and pepper.

4 In a clean bowl, whisk the egg whites until they form stiff peaks. Add a large spoonful of the egg whites to the crab mixture and fold together to slacken. Add the remaining egg whites and fold together carefully, but thoroughly. Spoon into the prepared dish.

5 Cook in a preheated oven, 400°F/ 200°C, for 25 minutes until risen and golden. Serve immediately.

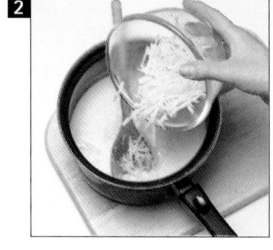

Chorizo & Garbanzo Tapas

A glass of chilled sherry and a selection of Spanish tapas is a great way to unwind at the end of the day.

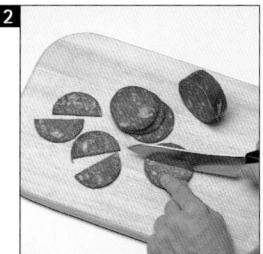

NUTRITIONAL INFORMATION

Calories 462	Sugars 3g
Protein 18g	Fat 36g
Carbohydrate ...17g	Saturates 9g

  10 mins 8 mins

SERVES 4

INGREDIENTS

7 tbsp olive oil

about 2 tbsp sherry vinegar

9 oz/250 g fresh chorizo sausage, in 1 piece

1 small Bermuda onion, finely chopped

14 oz/400g can garbanzo beans

salt and pepper

finely chopped fresh oregano or flat leaf parsley, to garnish

chunks of fresh bread, to serve

1 Place 6 tablespoons of the olive oil and 2 tablespoons of the vinegar in a bowl and whisk together. Taste and add a little more sherry vinegar, if desired. Season with salt and pepper to taste and set aside.

2 Using a small, sharp knife, remove the casing from the chorizo sausage. Cut the meat into ¼ inch/5 mm thick slices, then cut each slice into half-moon shapes.

3 Heat the remaining olive oil in a small, heavy skillet over medium–high heat. Add the onion and cook, stirring occasionally, for 2–3 minutes. Add the chorizo sausage and cook for about 3 minutes or until the chorizo sausage is cooked through.

4 Using a slotted spoon, remove the sausage and onion and drain on crumpled paper towels. Transfer to the bowl with the dressing while they are still hot and stir together.

5 Empty the garbanzo beans into a strainer and rinse well under cold running water; shake off the excess water. Add to the bowl with the other ingredients and stir together. Set aside to cool.

6 Just before serving, adjust the seasoning, then spoon the salad into a serving bowl, and sprinkle with chopped herbs. Serve with chunks of fresh bread.

Broiled Sardines

If you drive along the Mediterranean coast, you'll come across small harbor-side restaurants broiling the day's catch of sardines.

NUTRITIONAL INFORMATION

Calories . . . . .399 Sugars 1g
Protein . . . . .21g Fat 34g
Carbohydrate . . . .2g Saturates 6g

 2½ hrs   3 mins

SERVES 4–6

I N G R E D I E N T S

12 sardines

olive oil

fresh flat leaf parsley sprigs, to garnish

lemon wedges, to serve

D R E S S I N G

⅔ cup extra virgin olive oil

finely grated rind of 1 large lemon

4 tbsp lemon juice

4 shallots, thinly sliced

1 small fresh red chile, deseeded and
    finely chopped

1 large garlic clove, finely chopped

salt and pepper

1 To make the dressing, place all the ingredients in a screw-top jar, season with salt and pepper, then shake until blended. Pour into a nonmetallic dish that is large enough to hold the sardines in a single layer. Set aside.

2 To prepare the sardines, chop off the heads and make a slit all along the length of each belly. Pull out the insides, rinse the fish inside and out with cold water, and pat dry with paper towels.

3 Line the broiler pan with foil, shiny side up. Brush the foil with a little olive oil to prevent the sardines from sticking. Arrange the sardines on the foil in a single layer and brush with a little of the dressing. Broil under a preheated broiler for about 90 seconds.

4 Turn the fish over, brush with a little more dressing, and continue broiling for a further 90 seconds or until they are cooked through and flake easily.

5 Transfer the fish to the dish with the dressing. Spoon the dressing over the fish and set aside to cool . Cover with plastic wrap and chill in the refrigerator for at least 2 hours to allow the flavours to blend.

6 Transfer the sardines to a serving platter and garnish with parsley sprigs. Serve with lemon wedges for squeezing over the fish.

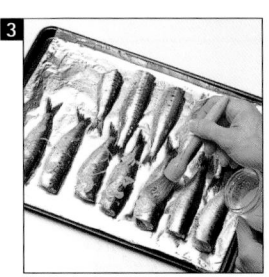

Spanish Tortilla

This classic Spanish dish is often served as part of a tapas selection. A variety of cooked vegetables can be added to this recipe.

NUTRITIONAL INFORMATION

Calories 430	Sugars 6g	
Protein 16g	Fat 20g	
Carbohydrate ...50g	Saturates 4g	

 10 mins   35 mins

SERVES 4

INGREDIENTS

2 lb 4 oz/1 kg waxy potatoes, thinly sliced

4 tbsp vegetable oil

1 onion, sliced

2 garlic cloves, crushed

1 green bell pepper, deseeded and diced

2 tomatoes, deseeded and chopped

2½ tbsp canned corn, drained

6 large eggs, beaten

2 tbsp chopped fresh parsley

salt and pepper

1 Parboil the potatoes in a pan of lightly salted boiling water for 5 minutes. Drain well.

2 Heat the oil in a large skillet, add the potatoes and onion and

then sauté over low heat, stirring constantly, for 5 minutes until the potatoes have browned.

3 Add the garlic, green bell pepper, tomatoes, and corn, mixing well.

4 Pour in the eggs and add the parsley. Season to taste with salt and pepper. Cook for 10–12 minutes until the underside is cooked through.

5 Remove the skillet from the heat and continue to cook the tortilla under a preheated medium broiler for 5–7 minutes or until the tortilla is set and the top is golden brown.

6 Cut the tortilla into wedges or cubes, depending on your preference, and transfer to serving dishes. Serve with salad. In Spain tortillas are served hot, cold or warm.

COOK'S TIP

Ensure that the handle of your pan is heatproof before placing it under the broiler and be sure to use an oven mitt when removing it because it will be very hot.

Piperade

Serve this rustic egg and bell pepper dish to add a Mediterranean flavor to a light lunch. It's particularly good with prosciutto.

NUTRITIONAL INFORMATION

Calories 316	Sugars 8g	
Protein 17g	Fat 15g	
Carbohydrate . . .31g	Saturates 4g	

 10 mins   25 mins

SERVES 4–6

INGREDIENTS

2 tbsp olive oil

1 large onion, finely chopped

1 large red bell pepper, deseeded and sliced

1 large yellow bell pepper, deseeded and sliced

1 large green bell pepper, deseeded and sliced

8 large eggs

2 tomatoes, deseeded and chopped

2 tbsp finely chopped fresh flat leaf parsley

salt and pepper

fresh flat leaf parsley sprigs, to garnish

4–6 slices thick country-style bread, toasted, to serve

1 Heat the olive oil in a heavy skillet over medium–high heat. Add the onion and bell peppers, reduce the heat, and cook, stirring occasionally, for 15–20 minutes until softened.

2 Place the eggs in a mixing bowl and whisk until well blended. Season with salt and pepper to taste. Set aside.

3 When the bell peppers are soft, pour the eggs into the pan and cook, stirring constantly, over very low heat until they are almost set, but still creamy. Remove the pan from the heat.

4 Stir in the tomatoes and parsley. Taste and adjust the seasoning, if necessary. Place the slices of toast on individual serving plates and spoon the eggs and vegetables on top. Garnish with sprigs of flat leaf parsley and serve immediately.

COOK'S TIP

To make this dish more substantial, serve with thickly cut slices of Serrano ham from Spain or prosciutto from Italy. The salty taste of both contrasts well with the sweetness of the bell peppers.

Corsican Clam Spaghetti

Fresh mussels can also be used to make this simple but delicious pasta sauce. Serve with a glass of chilled white wine.

NUTRITIONAL INFORMATION

Calories 550   Sugars 10g
Protein ....25g   Fat 16g
Carbohydrate ...82g   Saturates 2g

50 mins   25 mins

SERVES 4

I N G R E D I E N T S

14 oz/400g dried or fresh spaghetti

salt and pepper

C O R S I C A N   C L A M   S A U C E

2 lb/900 g live clams

4 tbsp olive oil

3 large garlic cloves, crushed

pinch of dried chili flakes (optional)

2 lb/900 g tomatoes, peeled and chopped, with juice reserved

½ cup green or black olives, pitted and chopped

1 tbsp chopped fresh oregano or ½ tsp dried oregano

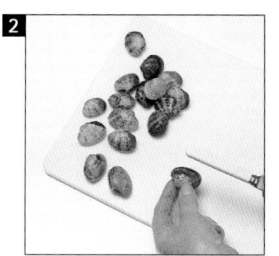

1 Place the clams in a bowl of lightly salted water and set aside to soak for 30 minutes. Rinse them under cold, running water and scrub lightly to remove any sand from the shells.

2 Discard any broken clams or open clams that do not shut when firmly tapped with the back of a knife. This indicates they are dead and could cause food poisoning if eaten. Set the clams aside to soak in a large bowl of water. Meanwhile, bring a large pan of lightly salted water to a boil.

3 Heat the oil in a large skillet over medium heat. Add the garlic and chili flakes, if using, and fry, stirring constantly, for about 2 minutes.

4 Stir in the tomatoes, olives, and oregano. Lower the heat and simmer, stirring frequently, until the tomatoes soften and start to break up. Cover and simmer for 10 minutes.

5 Meanwhile, add the spaghetti to the pan of boiling water, bring back to a boil, and cook until tender, but still firm to

the bite—8–10 minutes for dried spaghetti and 2–3 minutes for fresh. Drain well, reserving about ½ cup of the cooking water. Keep the pasta warm.

6 Add the clams and reserved cooking liquid to the sauce and stir. Bring to a boil, stirring constantly. Discard any clams that have not opened and transfer the sauce to a larger pan.

7 Add the pasta to the sauce and toss until well coated. Transfer the pasta to individual dishes. Serve immediately.

Pasta with Broccoli

Orecchiette, the cupped-shape pasta from southern Italy, is excellent for this filling dish because it scoops up the robust, chunky sauce.

NUTRITIONAL INFORMATION

Calories 685	Sugars 4g
Protein 33g	Fat 29g
Carbohydrate ...78g	Saturates 9g

 10 mins   15 mins

SERVES 4

INGREDIENTS

1 lb 2 oz/500 g broccoli

3½ cups dried orecchiette

5 tbsp olive oil

2 large garlic cloves, crushed

1¾ oz/50 g can anchovy fillets in oil, drained and finely chopped

⅔ cup freshly grated Parmesan cheese

⅔ cup freshly grated romano cheese

salt and pepper

1 Bring 2 pans of lightly salted water to a boil. Chop the broccoli florets and stems into bite-size pieces. Add them to 1 pan and cook for 10 minutes. Drain well.

2 Add the pasta to the other pan of boiling water, bring back to a boil, and cook for 8–10 minutes until tender, but still firm to the bite.

VARIATIONS

You could add dried chili flakes to taste with the garlic in Step 3, if you wish to. If you have difficulty in finding orecchiette, try using pasta bows instead.

3 Meanwhile, heat the oil in a large pan over medium heat. Add the garlic and fry, stirring constantly, for 3 minutes. Add the chopped anchovies to the pan and cook for 3 minutes, stirring and mashing with a wooden spoon to break them up.

4 Drain the pasta, add it to the anchovy mixture, and stir. Add the broccoli and stir gently to mix.

5 Add the grated cheeses to the pasta and stir constantly over medium–high heat until the cheeses melt and the pasta and broccoli are coated.

6 Adjust the seasoning to taste—the anchovies and cheeses are salty, so you will need to add pepper, if anything. Spoon into bowls or onto warmed plates and serve immediately.

Panzanella

This traditional, refreshing Italian salad of day-old bread is ideal to serve for lunch or as a simple supper on a hot day.

NUTRITIONAL INFORMATION

Calories 213   Sugars 11g
Protein . . . . .7g   Fat 6g
Carbohydrate . . .33g   Saturates 1g

45 mins   10 mins

SERVES 4–6

I N G R E D I E N T S

9 oz/250 g day-old Herb Focaccia (see page 476) or ciabatta bread or French bread

4 large, vine-ripened tomatoes

extra virgin olive oil

4 red, yellow and/or orange bell peppers

3½ oz/100 g cucumber

1 large red onion, finely chopped

8 canned anchovy fillets, drained and chopped

2 tbsp capers in brine, rinsed and patted dry

about 4 tbsp red wine vinegar

about 2 tbsp balsamic vinegar

salt and pepper

fresh basil leaves, to garnish

1 Cut the bread into 1 inch/2.5 cm cubes and place in a large bowl. Working over a plate to catch any juices, quarter the tomatoes, reserving the juices. Using a teaspoon, scoop out the cores and seeds, then finely chop the flesh. Add to the bread cubes.

2 Drizzle 5 tablespoons olive oil over the mixture and toss with your hands until well coated. Pour in the reserved tomato juice and toss again. Set aside for about 30 minutes.

3 Meanwhile, halve and deseed the peppers. Place on a broiler rack, skin side up, and cook under a preheated broiler for 10 minutes or until the skins are charred and the flesh softened. Place in a plastic bag, seal, and set aside for 20 minutes. Peel off the skins and finely chop the flesh.

4 Cut the cucumber in half lengthwise, then cut each half into 3 strips lengthwise. Using a teaspoon, scoop out and discard the seeds. Dice the cucumber.

5 Add the onion, bell peppers, cucumber, anchovy fillets, and capers to the bread and toss together. Sprinkle with the red wine and balsamic vinegars and season to taste with salt and pepper.

6 Drizzle with extra olive oil or vinegar if necessary, but be careful not to let the salad become too oily or soggy. Sprinkle the fresh basil leaves over the salad to garnish and serve immediately.

 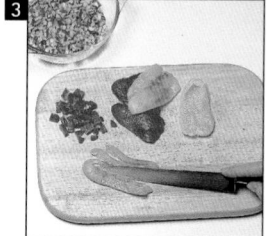 

Rice & Chicken Chowder

Wild rice gives soups a wonderful texture as well as flavor—and it looks good too. Smoked chicken complements the nuttiness of the rice.

NUTRITIONAL INFORMATION

Calories 322	Sugars 4g
Protein 14g	Fat 19g
Carbohydrate . . .25g	Saturates 9g

 15 mins   1¾ hrs

SERVES 6–8

INGREDIENTS

scant ½ cup wild rice

3 fresh corn cobs, husks and silks removed

2 tbsp vegetable oil

1 large onion, finely chopped

1 celery stalk, thinly sliced

1 leek, trimmed and thinly sliced

½ tsp dried thyme

2 tbsp all-purpose flour

4 cups chicken stock

9 oz/250 g skinless, boneless smoked chicken, diced or shredded

1 cup heavy or whipping cream

1 tbsp chopped fresh dill

salt and pepper

fresh dill sprigs, to garnish

1 Bring a large pan of water to a boil. Add a tablespoon of salt and sprinkle in the wild rice. Return to a boil, then reduce the heat, cover, and simmer for about 40 minutes until just tender, but still firm to the bite. Do not overcook the rice, as it will continue to cook in the soup. Drain and rinse; then set aside.

2 Hold the corn cobs vertical to a cutting board and, using a sharp, heavy knife, cut down along the cobs to remove the kernels. Set aside the kernels. Scrape the cob to remove the milky juices and reserve for the soup.

3 Heat the vegetable oil in a large pan over medium heat. Add the onion, celery, leek, and dried thyme. Cook, stirring frequently, for about 8 minutes until the vegetables are very soft.

4 Sprinkle over the flour and stir until blended. Gradually whisk in the stock, add the corn with any juices, and bring to a boil. Skim off any foam. Reduce the heat and simmer for about 25 minutes until the vegetables are very soft and tender.

5 Stir in the smoked chicken, wild rice, cream, and dill. Season with salt and pepper to taste. Simmer for about 10 minutes until the chicken and rice are heated through. Garnish with dill sprigs and serve immediately.

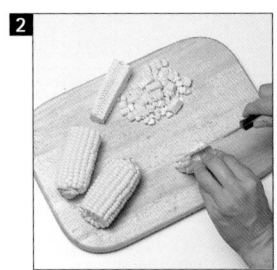

Baked Tomato Rice

A good quick supper for the family, this dish is incredibly simple to put together, yet is truly delicious.

NUTRITIONAL INFORMATION

Calories 708   Sugars 7g
Protein . . . . .27g   Fat 35g
Carbohydrate . . .76g   Saturates 16g

 5 mins   45 mins

SERVES 4

I N G R E D I E N T S

2 tbsp vegetable oil

1 onion, coarsely chopped

1 red bell pepper, deseeded and chopped

2 garlic cloves, finely chopped

½ tsp dried thyme

1½ cups long grain rice

4 cups chicken or vegetable stock

8 oz/225 g canned chopped tomatoes

1 bay leaf

2 tbsp shredded fresh basil

1½ cups grated sharp Cheddar cheese

2 tbsp chopped fresh chives

4 herbed pork sausages, cooked and cut into ½ inch/1 cm pieces

2–3 tbsp freshly grated Parmesan cheese

1 Heat the vegetable oil in a large flameproof casserole over medium heat. Add the onion and red bell pepper and cook, stirring frequently, for about 5 minutes until soft and lightly colored. Stir in the garlic and thyme and cook for 1 further minute.

2 Add the rice and cook, stirring frequently, for about 2 minutes until the rice is well coated and translucent. Stir in the stock, tomatoes, and bay leaf. Bring to a boil and simmer vigorously for 5 minutes until the stock is almost completely absorbed.

3 Stir in the basil, Cheddar cheese, chives, and pork sausages and bake, covered, in a preheated oven, 350°F/180°C, for about 25 minutes.

4 Sprinkle with the Parmesan cheese and return to the oven, uncovered, for 5 minutes until the top is golden.

VARIATION

For a vegetarian version, replace the pork sausages with a 14 oz/400g can of drained lima beans, kidney beans, or corn. Alternatively, try a mixture of sautéed mushrooms and zucchini.

Mexican Tomato Rice

The tomatoes in this recipe give the rice its distinctive pinkish color. The texture of the rice will be slightly "wet."

NUTRITIONAL INFORMATION

Calories . . . . .311 Sugars 4g
Protein . . . . .7g Fat 11g
Carbohydrate . . .50g Saturates 2g

   30 mins   40 mins

SERVES 6–8

INGREDIENTS

2 cups long grain rice

1 large onion, chopped

2–3 garlic cloves, crushed

12 oz/350 g canned Italian plum tomatoes

3–4 tbsp olive oil

4 cups chicken stock

1 tbsp tomato paste

1 habañero or other hot chile

1½ cups frozen peas, thawed

4 tbsp chopped fresh cilantro

salt and pepper

TO SERVE

1 large avocado, peeled, pitted, sliced, and sprinkled with lime juice

lime wedges

4 scallions, chopped

1 tbsp chopped fresh cilantro

1 Cover the rice with hot water and set aside to stand for 15 minutes. Drain, then rinse under cold running water.

2 Place the onion and garlic in a food processor and process until a smooth purée forms. Scrape the purée into a small bowl and set aside. Put the tomatoes in the food processor and process until smooth, then strain into another bowl, pushing through any solids with the back of a wooden spoon.

3 Heat the oil in a flameproof casserole over medium heat. Add the rice and cook, stirring frequently, for 4 minutes until golden and translucent. Add the onion purée and cook, stirring frequently, for a further 2 minutes. Add the stock, processed canned tomatoes, and tomato paste and bring to a boil.

4 Using a pin or long needle, carefully pierce the chile in 2–3 places. Add to the rice, season to taste with salt and pepper, and reduce the heat to low. Cover and simmer for about 25 minutes until the rice is tender and the liquid just absorbed. Discard the chile, stir in the peas and cilantro, and cook for about 5 minutes to heat through.

5 To serve, gently fork the rice mixture into a warmed, large, shallow serving bowl. Arrange the avocado slices and lime wedges on top. Sprinkle the chopped scallions and chopped cilantro over and serve immediately.

Curried Rice Patties

Substantial and flavorful, these patties are a delicious alternative
to beef burgers. Leave the rice with a little bite to give extra texture.

NUTRITIONAL INFORMATION

Calories 311	Sugars 4g	
Protein 7g	Fat 11g	
Carbohydrate . . .50g	Saturates 2g	

1¼ hrs   55 mins

SERVES 4–6

I N G R E D I E N T S

⅓ cup basmati rice

2 tbsp olive oil, plus extra for drizzling

1 red onion, finely chopped

2 garlic cloves

2 tsp curry powder

½ tsp crushed dried chili flakes

1 small red bell pepper, deseeded and diced

1 cup frozen peas, thawed

1 small leek, finely chopped

1 tomato, peeled, deseeded, and chopped

11 oz/310 g can garbanzo beans, rinsed
    and drained

1½ cups fresh white bread crumbs

1–2 tbsp chopped fresh cilantro or mint

1 egg, lightly beaten

vegetable oil, for frying

salt and pepper

cucumber slices, to garnish

lime wedges, to serve

D R E S S I N G

½ cup tahini

2 garlic cloves, crushed

½ tsp ground cumin

pinch of cayenne pepper

5 tbsp lemon juice

1 To make the dressing, process the tahini, garlic, cumin, cayenne, and lemon juice in a food processor until creamy. Slowly pour in the oil, then gradually add enough water to make a creamy dressing (about ½ cup).

2 Bring a pan of water to a boil. Add ½ teaspoon of the salt and sprinkle in the rice; simmer for 15–20 minutes until the rice is just tender. Drain, rinse, and set aside.

3 Heat the olive oil in a large pan. Add the onion and garlic and cook until beginning to soften. Stir in the curry powder and chili flakes and cook for 2 minutes. Add the red bell pepper, peas, leek, and tomato and cook gently for about 7 minutes until tender. Set aside.

4 Process the garbanzo beans in a food processor until smooth. Add half the vegetables and process again. Transfer to a large bowl and add the remaining vegetable mixture, bread crumbs, cilantro, and egg. Mix well. Stir in the rice and season to taste with salt and pepper. Chill for 1 hour in the refrigerator, then shape into 4–6 patties.

5 Fry the patties in oil for 6–8 minutes until golden. Garnish with cucumber slices and serve with the dressing and lime wedges.

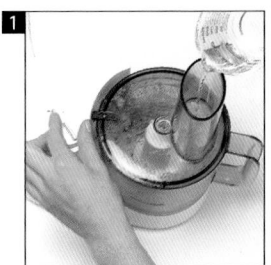

Easy Cheese Risotto

Although this is the easiest, most basic risotto, it is one of the most delicious. Because there are few ingredients, use the best of each.

NUTRITIONAL INFORMATION

Calories 353	Sugars 2g
Protein 10g	Fat 15g
Carbohydrate ...40g	Saturates 9g

 5 mins   30 mins

SERVES 4–6

INGREDIENTS

4–6 tbsp sweet butter

1 onion, finely chopped

2⅔ cups risotto rice

½ cup dry white vermouth or white wine

5 cups chicken or vegetable stock, simmering

1 cup freshly grated Parmesan cheese, plus extra for sprinkling

salt and pepper

1 Heat about 2 tablespoons of the butter in a large heavy pan over medium heat. Add the onion and cook for about 2 minutes until just beginning to soften. Add the rice and cook, stirring frequently, for about 2 minutes until translucent and well coated with the butter.

COOK'S TIP

If you prefer not to use butter, soften the onion in 2 tablespoons olive oil and stir in about 2 tablespoons extra virgin olive oil with the Parmesan at the end.

2 Pour in the vermouth: it will bubble and steam rapidly and evaporate almost immediately. Add a ladleful (about 1 cup) of the simmering stock and cook, stirring constantly, until the stock is completely absorbed.

3 Continue adding the stock, about half a ladleful at a time, allowing each addition to be absorbed before adding the next—never allow the rice to cook "dry."

This should take 20–25 minutes. The risotto should have a creamy consistency and the rice grains should be tender, but still firm to the bite.

4 Switch off the heat and stir in the remaining butter and the grated Parmesan cheese. Season with salt and pepper to taste. Cover the pan, let stand for about 1 minute, then serve with extra Parmesan for sprinkling.

Minted Green Risotto

This tasty risotto gets its vibrant green color from the spinach and mint. Serve with Italian-style rustic bread and salad for an informal supper.

NUTRITIONAL INFORMATION

Calories	512	Sugars	.........7g
Protein	........20g	Fat	..........24g
Carbohydrate	...51g	Saturates	......12g

 10 mins   35 mins

SERVES 6

I N G R E D I E N T S

2 tbsp sweet butter

4 cups fresh shelled peas or thawed frozen peas

2 lb 4 oz/1 kg young spinach leaves, washed and drained

1 bunch of fresh mint, leaves stripped from stalks

2 tbsp chopped fresh basil

2 tbsp chopped fresh oregano

pinch of freshly grated nutmeg

4 tbsp mascarpone cheese or heavy cream

2 tbsp vegetable oil

1 onion, finely chopped

4 celery stalks, including leaves, finely chopped

2 garlic cloves, finely chopped

½ tsp dried thyme

2⅔ cups risotto rice

¼ cup dry white vermouth

4 cups chicken or vegetable stock, simmering

1 cup freshly grated Parmesan cheese

1 Heat half the butter in a deep skillet over medium-high heat until sizzling. Add the peas, spinach, mint leaves, basil, and oregano and season with the nutmeg. Cook, stirring frequently, for about 3 minutes until the spinach and mint leaves are wilted. Cool slightly.

2 Pour the spinach mixture into a food processor and process for 15 seconds. Add the mascarpone or cream and process again for about 1 minute. Transfer to a bowl and set aside.

3 Heat the oil and remaining butter in a large, heavy pan over medium heat. Add the onion, celery, garlic, and thyme and cook for about 2 minutes until the vegetables are softened. Add the rice and cook, stirring frequently, for about 2 minutes until the rice is translucent and well coated.

4 Add the vermouth to the rice; it will bubble and steam rapidly. When it is almost absorbed, add a ladleful (about 1 cup) of the simmering stock. Cook, stirring constantly, until the stock is completely absorbed.

5 Continue adding the stock, about half a ladleful at a time, allowing each addition to be absorbed before adding the next. This should take 20–25 minutes. The risotto should have a creamy consistency and the rice should be just tender. Stir in the spinach-cream mixture and the Parmesan. Serve immediately.

Cannellini Bean Risotto

The Italians, particularly the Tuscans, love dishes made with beans.
This recipe combines beans and rice to make a rich and creamy risotto.

NUTRITIONAL INFORMATION

Calories	424	Sugars	.....2g
Protein	.....15g	Fat	.....19g
Carbohydrate	...50g	Saturates	.....9g

10 mins   35 mins

SERVES 6–8

I N G R E D I E N T S

1⅓ cups cannellini or white kidney beans, soaked and cooked according to packet instructions

2–3 tbsp olive oil

1 large red or sweet white onion, finely chopped

3–4 celery stalks, finely chopped

4 oz/115 g pancetta or thick-cut smoked bacon

2–3 garlic cloves, ground chopped fresh oregano

3½ cups risotto rice

4 cups chicken stock, simmering

4 tbsp sweet butter at room temperature

1⅓ cups freshly grated Parmesan cheese

salt and pepper

1 Mash half of the cannellini beans and set aside. Alternatively, press them through a food mill.

2 Heat the olive oil in a large heavy pan over medium heat. Add the onion and celery and cook, stirring occasionally, for about 2 minutes until softened. Add the pancetta or bacon, garlic, and oregano and cook, stirring occasionally, for a further 1–2 minutes. Add the rice and cook, stirring frequently, for about 2 minutes until it is translucent and well coated with the oil.

3 Add a ladleful (about 1 cup) of the simmering stock; it will bubble and steam rapidly. Cook, stirring constantly, until the stock is absorbed.

4 Continue adding the stock, about half a ladleful at a time, allowing each addition to be absorbed before adding the next. This should take 20–25 minutes. The risotto should have a creamy consistency and the rice should be tender, but still firm to the bite.

5 Stir in the beans and the bean purée, season with salt and pepper to taste, and heat through. Add a little more stock if necessary.

6 Remove from the heat and stir in the butter and half the Parmesan. Cover and let stand for about 1 minute. Serve sprinkled with the remaining Parmesan.

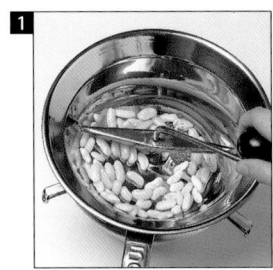

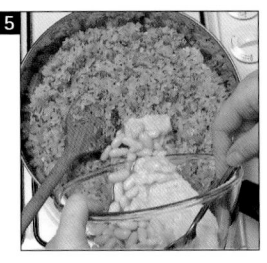

Exotic Mushroom Risotto

Distinctive-tasting exotic mushrooms, so popular in Italy, give this aromatic risotto a wonderful, robust flavor.

NUTRITIONAL INFORMATION

Calories 425	Sugars 2g
Protein 16g	Fat 17g
Carbohydrate ...54g	Saturates 6g

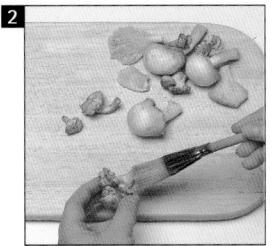

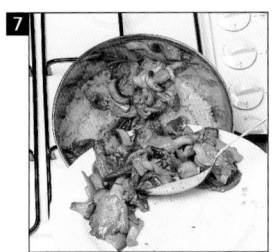

 35 mins   35 mins

SERVES 6

I N G R E D I E N T S

2 oz/55 g dried porcini or morel mushrooms

about 1 lb 2 oz/500 g mixed fresh exotic mushrooms, such as porcini, girolles, horse mushrooms, and chanterelles, halved if large

4 tbsp olive oil

3–4 garlic cloves, finely chopped

4 tbsp sweet butter

1 onion, finely chopped

3 cups risotto rice

¼ cup dry white vermouth

5 cups chicken stock, simmering

1⅓ cups freshly grated Parmesan cheese

4 tbsp chopped fresh flat leaf parsley

salt and pepper

1 Place the dried mushrooms in a bowl and add boiling water to cover. Set aside to soak for 30 minutes, then carefully lift out and pat dry. Strain the soaking liquid through a strainer lined with paper towels and set aside.

2 Trim the wild mushrooms and gently brush clean.

3 Heat 3 tablespoons of the olive oil in a large skillet. Add the mixed fresh mushrooms and stir-fry for 1–2 minutes.

Add the garlic and the soaked mushrooms and cook, stirring frequently, for 2 minutes. Transfer to a plate.

4 Heat the remaining oil and half the butter in a large, heavy pan. Add the onion and cook, stirring occasionally, for about 2 minutes until softened. Add the rice and cook, stirring frequently, for about 2 minutes until it is translucent and well coated.

5 Add the vermouth. When almost absorbed, add a ladleful (about 1 cup) of the stock. Cook, stirring constantly, until the liquid is absorbed.

6 Continue adding the stock, about half a ladleful at a time, allowing each addition to be completely absorbed before adding the next. This should take 20–25 minutes. The risotto should have a creamy consistency and the rice should be tender, but firm to the bite.

7 Add half the reserved mushroom soaking liquid to the risotto and stir in the mushrooms. Season with salt and pepper to taste and add more mushroom liquid if necessary. Remove the pan from the heat and stir in the remaining butter, the grated Parmesan, and chopped parsley. Serve immediately.

Roasted Pumpkin Risotto

The combination of sweet creamy pumpkin with the slight saltiness of dolcelatte cheese and the pungency of sage is delicious.

NUTRITIONAL INFORMATION

Calories 615	Sugars 2g	
Protein 19g	Fat 37g	
Carbohydrate . . .53g	Saturates 18g	

 10 mins   40 mins

SERVES 6

INGREDIENTS

4 tbsp olive oil

4 tbsp sweet butter, diced

1lb/450 g pumpkin flesh, cut into ½ inch/ 1 cm dice

¾ tsp dried sage

2 garlic cloves, finely chopped

2 tbsp lemon juice

2 large shallots, finely chopped

3 cups risotto rice

¼ cup dry white vermouth

5 cups chicken stock, simmering

⅔ cup freshly grated Parmesan cheese

10½ oz/300 g dolcelatte cheese, diced

salt and pepper

celery leaves, to garnish

1 Put half the olive oil and about 1 tablespoon of the butter in a roasting pan and heat in a preheated oven, 400°F/200°C.

2 When the butter has melted, arrange the pumpkin in the pan and sprinkle with the sage, half the garlic, and salt and pepper to taste. Toss together and roast for about 10 minutes until just softened and beginning to caramelize. Transfer the pumpkin to a plate.

3 Roughly mash about half the cooked pumpkin with the lemon juice and reserve with the remaining diced pumpkin.

4 Heat the remaining oil and 1 tablespoon of the remaining butter in a large, heavy pan over medium heat. Add the shallots and remaining garlic and cook, stirring occasionally, for about 1 minute. Add the rice and cook, stirring constantly, for about 2 minutes until it is well coated.

5 Pour in the vermouth; it will bubble and steam rapidly. Add a ladleful (about 1 cup) of the simmering stock and cook, stirring constantly, until the stock is absorbed.

6 Continue adding the stock, about half a ladleful at a time, allowing each addition to be absorbed before adding the next—never allow the rice to cook "dry." This should take 20–25 minutes. The risotto should have a creamy consistency and the rice should be tender, but still firm to the bite.

7 Stir all the pumpkin—mashed and diced—into the risotto with the remaining butter and the grated Parmesan. Remove from the heat and fold in the diced dolcelatte. Serve immediately, garnished with celery leaves.

Hot Pink Risotto

The beet and red wine give this risotto its stunning color and also impart a rich sweet flavor, which is unusual but surprisingly delicious.

NUTRITIONAL INFORMATION

Calories	397	Sugars	.........9g
Protein	........11g	Fat	...........11g
Carbohydrate	...61g	Saturates	.......3g

10 mins   40 mins

SERVES 4–6

INGREDIENTS

1½ cups dried sour cherries or
   dried cranberries

1 cup fruity red wine, such
   as Valpolicella

3 tbsp olive oil

1 large red onion, finely chopped

2 celery stalks, finely chopped

½ tsp dried thyme

1 garlic clove, finely chopped

3 cups risotto rice

5 cups chicken or vegetable stock,
   simmering

4 cooked beet (not in vinegar), diced

2 tbsp chopped fresh dill

2 tbsp chopped fresh chives

salt and pepper

⅔ cup freshly grated Parmesan cheese, to
   serve (optional)

1 Put the cherries or cranberries in a pan with the wine and bring to a boil. Simmer for 2–3 minutes until slightly reduced. Remove from the heat and set aside.

2 Heat the oil in a large heavy pan over medium heat. Add the onion, celery, and thyme and cook, stirring occasionally, for about 2 minutes until just beginning to soften. Add the garlic and rice and cook, stirring constantly, until the rice is well coated.

3 Add a ladleful (about 1 cup) of the simmering stock; it will bubble and steam rapidly. Cook, stirring constantly, until the stock is absorbed.

4 Continue adding the stock, about half a ladleful at a time, allowing each addition to be absorbed before adding the next. This should take 20–25 minutes. The risotto should have a creamy consistency and the rice should be tender, but firm to the bite. Halfway through the cooking time, remove the cherries or cranberries from the wine with a slotted spoon and add to the risotto with the beet and half the wine. Continue adding the stock or remaining wine.

5 Stir in the dill and chives and season to taste with salt and pepper. Serve with the Parmesan, if wished.

Arugula & Tomato Risotto

It's worth searching around for wild arugula because its robust peppery flavor makes all the difference to this dish.

NUTRITIONAL INFORMATION

Calories	546	Sugars	.........6g
Protein	........23g	Fat	..........24g
Carbohydrate	...57g	Saturates	......12g

10 mins   30 mins

SERVES 4–6

INGREDIENTS

2 tbsp olive oil

2 tbsp sweet butter

1 large onion, finely chopped

2 garlic cloves, finely chopped

3 cups risotto rice

½ cup dry white vermouth

3½ pints/1.5 liters chicken or vegetable stock, simmering

6 vine-ripened or Italian plum tomatoes, deseeded and chopped

4½ oz/126 g wild arugula

handful of fresh basil leaves

1⅓ cups freshly grated Parmesan cheese

2 cups coarsely grated or diced fresh Italian buffalo mozzarella

salt and pepper

1 Heat the oil and half the butter in a large skillet. Add the onion and cook for about 2 minutes until just beginning to soften. Stir in the garlic and rice and cook, stirring frequently, until the rice is translucent and well coated.

2 Pour in the vermouth; it will evaporate almost immediately. Add a ladleful (about 1 cup) of the stock and cook, stirring, until it is absorbed.

3 Continue adding the stock, about half a ladleful at a time, allowing each addition to be absorbed before adding the next. Just before the rice is tender, stir in the chopped tomatoes and arugula. Shred the basil leaves and immediately stir into the risotto. Continue to cook, adding more stock, until the risotto is creamy and the rice is tender, but firm to the bite.

4 Remove from the heat and stir in the remaining butter, the grated Parmesan, and mozzarella. Season to taste with salt and pepper. Remove the pan from the heat, cover, and let stand for about 1 minute. Serve immediately, before the mozzarella melts completely.

Sunshine Risotto

Romano is an Italian cheese made from sheep's milk. Although it is made all over Italy, the aged romano from Sardinia is particularly fine.

NUTRITIONAL INFORMATION

Calories 436   Sugars 8g
Protein . . . . .15g   Fat 14g
Carbohydrate . . .66g   Saturates 5g

 35 mins   35 mins

SERVES 6

I N G R E D I E N T S

about 12 sun-dried tomatoes

2 tbsp olive oil

1 large onion, finely chopped

4–6 garlic cloves, finely chopped

3½ cups risotto rice

3½ pints/1.5 liters chicken or vegetable stock, simmering

2 tbsp chopped fresh flat leaf parsley

1⅛ cups grated aged romano cheese

extra virgin olive oil, for drizzling

1 Place the sun-dried tomatoes in a bowl and pour over enough boiling water to cover. Set aside to soak for about 30 minutes until soft and supple. Drain and pat dry, then shred thinly, and set aside.

2 Heat the oil in a heavy pan over medium heat. Add the onion and cook for about 2 minutes until beginning to soften. Add the garlic and cook for 15 seconds. Add the rice and cook, stirring frequently, for 2 minutes until the rice is translucent and well coated with oil.

3 Add a ladleful (about 1 cup) of the simmering stock; the stock will bubble and steam rapidly. Cook, stirring constantly, until the liquid is absorbed.

4 Continue adding the stock, about half a ladleful at a time, allowing each addition to be absorbed before adding the next—never allow the rice to cook "dry."

5 After about 15 minutes, stir in the sun-dried tomatoes. Continue to cook, adding the stock, until the rice is tender, but firm to the bite. The risotto should have a creamy consistency.

6 Remove the pan from the heat and stir in the chopped parsley and half the romano. Remove the pan from the heat, cover, let stand for about 1 minute, then spoon into serving dishes. Drizzle with extra virgin olive oil and sprinkle the remaining romano over the top. Serve immediately.

Radicchio Risotto

The slightly bitter flavor of radicchio is balanced by the addition of sweet heavy cream, while pancetta provides a smoky contrast.

NUTRITIONAL INFORMATION

Calories 358   Sugars 2g
Protein ....11g   Fat 16g
Carbohydrate ...46g   Saturates 7g

 10 mins   30 mins

SERVES 6–8

INGREDIENTS

1 large head radicchio, outer damaged leaves removed

2 tbsp sunflower or other vegetable oil

2 tbsp sweet butter

4 oz/115 g pancetta or thick-cut smoked bacon, diced

1 large onion, finely chopped

1 garlic clove, finely chopped

3½ cups risotto rice

3½ pints/1.5 liters chicken or vegetable stock, simmering

¼ cup heavy cream

⅔ cup freshly grated Parmesan cheese

3–4 tbsp chopped fresh flat leaf parsley

salt and pepper

fresh flat leaf parsley sprigs, to garnish

1 Cut the radicchio head in half lengthwise; remove the triangular core. Place the halves cut side down and shred finely. Set aside.

2 Heat the oil and butter in a heavy pan over medium heat. Add the pancetta or bacon and cook for 3–4 minutes, stirring occasionally, until it begins to color. Add the onion and garlic and cook for 1 minute.

3 Add the rice and cook, stirring frequently, for 2 minutes until translucent and well coated. Stir in the radicchio for 1 minute until just beginning to wilt. Reduce the heat to medium.

4 Add a ladleful (about 1 cup) of the simmering stock; the stock will bubble and steam rapidly. Cook, stirring constantly, until all the stock has been completely absorbed.

5 Continue adding the stock, about half a ladleful at a time, allowing each addition to be absorbed before adding the next. This should take 20–25 minutes. The risotto should have a creamy consistency and the rice should be tender.

6 Stir in the cream, Parmesan, and parsley. Season with salt and pepper. Remove from the heat. Cover and stand for 1 minute. Garnish with parsley and serve.

Frittata Risotto

An excellent way of using up leftover risotto, this fried risotto "cake" makes a great light lunch or evening snack.

NUTRITIONAL INFORMATION

Calories 567   Sugars 14g
Protein . . . . .14g   Fat 34g
Carbohydrate . . .50g   Saturates 14g

 10 mins   15 mins

SERVES 4–6

I N G R E D I E N T S

5 tbsp olive oil

1 large red onion, finely chopped

1 red bell pepper, deseeded and chopped

1 garlic clove, finely chopped

3–4 sun-dried tomatoes, finely shredded

2 tbsp chopped fresh flat leaf parsley
    or basil

1 quantity Easy Cheese Risotto with
    Parmesan (see page 340) or other
    risotto, cooled

about ⅔ cup freshly grated
    Parmesan cheese

1 Heat 2 tablespoons of the oil in a large, heavy skillet over medium-high heat. Add the onion and red bell pepper and cook for 3–4 minutes until the vegetables are soft.

2 Add the garlic and sun-dried tomatoes and cook for 2 minutes. Remove from the heat. Stir in the parsley and set aside to cool slightly.

3 Put the risotto in a bowl and break it up with a fork. Stir in the vegetable mixture with half the Parmesan.

4 Reserve 1 tablespoon of the remaining oil and heat the rest in the cleaned skillet over medium heat. Remove from the heat and spoon in the risotto mixture, pressing it into an even cake-like layer, about ¾–1 inch/2–2.5 cm thick. Return the skillet to the heat and cook for about 4 minutes until brown on the underside.

5 With a spatula, loosen the edges and give the skillet a shake. Slide the frittata onto a large plate. Protecting your hands, invert the skillet over the frittata and, holding both firmly together, flip them over. Return to the heat and drizzle the remaining oil around the edge of the frittata, gently pulling the edges toward the center with the spatula. Cook for 1–2 minutes to seal the bottom, then slide onto a serving plate.

6 Sprinkle the top with some of the remaining Parmesan. Cut into wedges and serve with the rest of the Parmesan.

Oven-Baked Risotto

This easy-to-make risotto is a good choice for entertaining, because it eliminates the need for constant stirring.

NUTRITIONAL INFORMATION

Calories	428	Sugars	.........2g
Protein	........15g	Fat	..........18g
Carbohydrate	...14g	Saturates	.......6g

 10 mins   50 mins

SERVES 4

I N G R E D I E N T S

4 tbsp olive oil

14 oz/400 g portobello or large field mushrooms, thickly sliced

4 oz/115 g pancetta or thick-cut smoked bacon, diced

1 large onion, finely chopped

2 garlic cloves, finely chopped

3 cups risotto rice

5 cups chicken stock, simmering

2 tbsp chopped fresh tarragon or flat leaf parsley

1 cup freshly grated Parmesan cheese, plus extra for sprinkling

salt and pepper

1 Heat 2 tablespoons of the oil in a large, heavy skillet over high heat. Add the mushrooms and stir-fry for 2–3 minutes until golden and tender-crisp. Transfer to a plate.

2 Add the pancetta or bacon to the skillet and cook for about 2 minutes, stirring frequently, until crisp and golden. Remove with a slotted spoon and add to the mushrooms on the plate.

3 Heat the remaining oil in a heavy pan over medium heat. Add the onion and cook for about 2 minutes. Add the garlic and rice and cook, stirring, for approximately 2 minutes until the rice is well coated with the oil.

4 Gradually stir the stock into the rice, then add the mushroom and pancetta or bacon mixture and the tarragon. Season with salt and pepper. Bring to a boil.

5 Remove from the heat and transfer to a casserole.

6 Cover and bake in a preheated oven, 350°F/180°C, for about 20 minutes until the rice is almost tender and most of the liquid is absorbed. Uncover and stir in the Parmesan. Continue to bake for about 15 minutes longer until the rice is tender, but still firm to the bite. Serve immediately with extra Parmesan for sprinkling.

Jamaican Rice and Peas

A favorite Caribbean dish, this was probably originally made with pigeon peas, but you can use any dried bean you like.

NUTRITIONAL INFORMATION

Calories 482   Sugars 11g
Protein . . . . .19g   Fat 8g
Carbohydrate . . .89g   Saturates 2g

 8 hrs   2–3 hrs

SERVES 6–8

I N G R E D I E N T S

1 lb/450 g dried beans, such as black-eye peas, black beans, or small red kidney beans, soaked in cold water overnight

2 tbsp vegetable oil

1 large onion, chopped

2–3 garlic cloves, finely chopped

2 fresh red chiles, deseeded and chopped

2¼ cups long grain white rice

1¾ cups canned coconut milk

¾ tsp dried thyme

salt

T O M A T O   S A L S A

4 ripe tomatoes, deseeded and cut into
  ¼ inch/5 mm dice

1 red onion, finely chopped

4 tbsp chopped fresh cilantro

2 garlic cloves, finely chopped

1–2 jalapeño chiles, deseeded and
  thinly sliced

1–2 tbsp extra virgin olive oil

1 tbsp fresh lime juice

1 tsp brown sugar

salt and pepper

---

1 Drain the peas and/or beans and put in a large pan. Cover with cold water by about 2 inches/5 cm and bring to a boil over high heat, skimming off any foam.

2 Boil vigorously for about 10 minutes, then drain, and rinse. Return to the pan, cover with cold water, and bring to a boil over high heat.

3 Reduce the heat, partially cover, and simmer for 1¼–1½ hours for black-eye peas, 1½–2 hours for black beans, or 50–60 minutes for kidney beans, until tender. Drain, reserving the cooking liquid.

4 Heat the oil in another pan. Cook the onion for about 2 minutes. Stir in the garlic and chiles and cook for a further minute. Add the rice and stir until coated.

5 Stir in the coconut milk, thyme, and 1 teaspoon salt. Add the cooked peas/beans and 2 cups of the reserved cooking liquid to cover. Bring the mixture to a boil, then reduce the heat to low, cover tightly, and cook for 20–25 minutes.

6 Meanwhile, make the tomato salsa. Combine all the ingredients in a bowl, cover, and set aside at room temperature.

7 Remove the rice from the heat and stand, covered, for 5 minutes, then fork into a warmed serving bowl. Serve hot with the tomato salsa.

Creole Jambalaya

This rich, rice-based stew combines a fabulous mix of meat and seafood with exciting peppery flavorings of Creole cuisine.

NUTRITIONAL INFORMATION

Calories	424	Sugars	........8g
Protein	........31g	Fat	..........11g
Carbohydrate	...54g	Saturates	.......2g

 15 mins   45 mins

SERVES 6–8

INGREDIENTS

2 tbsp vegetable oil

3 oz/85 g smoked ham, cut into bite-size pieces

3 oz/85 g andouille or other smoked pork sausage, cut into chunks

2 large onions, finely chopped

3–4 celery stalks, finely chopped

2 green bell peppers, deseeded and diced

2 garlic cloves, finely chopped

8 oz/225 g skinless boneless chicken breast or thighs, cut into pieces

4 ripe tomatoes, peeled and chopped

¾ cup sieved tomatoes

2 cups fish stock

2 cups long grain white rice

4 scallions, thickly sliced

2¼ cups peeled raw shrimp

9 oz/250 g cooked white crab meat

12 oysters, shelled, with their liquor

SEASONING MIX

2 dried bay leaves

1 tsp salt

1½–2 tsp cayenne pepper

1½ tsp dried oregano

1 tsp ground white pepper

1 tsp black pepper

1 To make the seasoning mix, combine all the ingredients in a bowl.

2 Heat the oil in a flameproof casserole over medium heat. Add the ham and sausage and cook for 8 minutes, stirring frequently, until golden. Using a slotted spoon, transfer to a large plate.

3 Add the onions, celery, and bell peppers to the casserole and cook for about 4 minutes until just softened. Stir in the garlic, then remove, and set aside.

4 Add the chicken to the casserole and cook for 3–4 minutes until beginning to color. Stir in the seasoning mix to coat. Return the ham, sausage, and vegetables to the casserole and stir to combine. Add the tomatoes and sieved tomatoes, then pour in the stock. Bring to a boil.

5 Stir in the rice, reduce the heat, and simmer for about 12 minutes. Stir in the scallions and shrimp, cover again, and cook for 4 minutes.

6 Gently stir in the crab meat and oysters with their liquor. Cook until the rice is just tender. Remove from the heat and leave to stand, covered, for about 3 minutes before serving.

Murgh Pullau

In India, the meat and rice are cooked together for ease of preparation, but here they are cooked separately to ensure perfect timing.

NUTRITIONAL INFORMATION

Calories	850	Sugars	.......14g
Protein	........44g	Fat	..........47g
Carbohydrate	...63g	Saturates	......20g

 15 mins   50 mins

SERVES 4–6

I N G R E D I E N T S

1¾ cups basmati rice

4 tbsp ghee or butter

1 cup sliced almonds

¾ cups unsalted, shelled pistachio nuts

4–6 skinless boneless chicken breasts, each cut into 4 pieces

2 onions, thinly sliced

2 garlic cloves, finely chopped

2 bay leaves

1 inch/2.5 cm piece fresh ginger root, chopped

6 green cardamom pods, lightly crushed

4–6 cloves

1 tsp ground coriander

½ tsp cayenne pepper

1 cup plain yogurt

1 cup heavy cream

2–4 tbsp chopped fresh cilantro or mint

8 oz/225 g seedless green grapes, halved if large

salt and pepper

1 Bring a pan of salted water to a boil. Gradually pour in the rice, return to a boil, then simmer until the rice is just tender. Drain and rinse under cold running water. Set aside.

2 Meanwhile, heat the ghee in a deep skillet over medium heat. Add the nuts and cook, stirring constantly, for 3 minutes until golden. Remove from the skillet and set aside.

3 Add the chicken to the skillet and cook for about 5 minutes, turning, until golden. Remove from the skillet. Add the onions to the skillet. Cook for 10 minutes. Stir in the garlic, bay leaf, and spices and cook for 3 minutes.

4 Add 2–3 tablespoons of the yogurt and cook, stirring constantly, until all the moisture evaporates. Continue adding the remaining yogurt in the same way until it is all incorporated.

5 Return the chicken and nuts to the skillet and stir to coat. Stir in ½ cup boiling water. Season with salt and pepper, cover, and cook over low heat for about 10 minutes until the chicken is cooked through. Stir in the cream, cilantro, and grapes and remove the skillet from the heat.

6 Fork the rice into a bowl, then gently fold in the chicken and sauce. Stand for 5 minutes before serving.

Singapore Noodles

This is a special and well-known dish, which is a delicious meal in itself, packed with chicken, shrimp, and vegetables.

NUTRITIONAL INFORMATION

Calories	627	Sugars	.........3g
Protein	........44g	Fat	..........32g
Carbohydrate	...44g	Saturates	.......4g

 5 mins   20 mins

SERVES 4

I N G R E D I E N T S

8 oz/225 g dried egg noodles

6 tbsp vegetable oil

4 eggs, beaten

3 garlic cloves, crushed

1½ tsp chili powder

8 oz/225 g skinless, boneless chicken, cut into thin strips

3 celery stalks, sliced

1 green bell pepper, deseeded and sliced

4 scallions, sliced

1 oz/25 g water chestnuts, quartered

2 fresh red chiles, sliced

2½ cups peeled, cooked shrimp

3 cups bean sprouts

2 tsp sesame oil

1 Soak the noodles in boiling water for 4 minutes or until soft. Set aside to drain on paper towels.

2 Heat 2 tablespoons of the oil in a preheated wok. Add the eggs and stir until set. Remove the cooked eggs from the wok, set aside, and keep warm.

3 Add the remaining oil to the wok. Add the garlic and chili powder and stir-fry for 30 seconds.

4 Add the chicken and stir-fry for 4–5 minutes until beginning to brown.

5 Stir in the celery, green bell pepper, scallions, water chestnuts, and chiles and cook for a further 8 minutes or until the chicken is cooked through.

6 Add the shrimp and the reserved noodles to the wok, together with the bean sprouts, and toss to mix well.

7 Break the cooked egg with a fork and sprinkle it over the noodles, then sprinkle the sesame oil over the noodles. Serve immediately.

COOK'S TIP

When mixing precooked ingredients into the dish, such as the egg and noodles, ensure that they are heated right through and are hot when ready to serve.

Steak & Bean Salad

The Californian influence on Mexican food is evident in this big, hearty salad. Packed with delicious ingredients, it is a meal in itself.

NUTRITIONAL INFORMATION

Calories 498	Sugars 12g
Protein 29g	Fat 27g
Carbohydrate . . .38g	Saturates 6g

 25 mins   4–6 mins

SERVES 4

I N G R E D I E N T S

12 oz/350 g tender steak, such as short loin or tenderloin

4 garlic cloves, chopped

juice of 1 lime

4 tbsp extra virgin olive oil

1 tbsp white or red wine vinegar

¼ tsp mild chili powder

¼ tsp ground cumin

½ tsp paprika

pinch of sugar (optional)

5 scallions, thinly sliced

about 7 oz/200 g crisp lettuce leaves, such as Romaine, or mixed herb leaves

8 oz/225 g can corn, drained

14 oz/400 g can pinto, black or red kidney beans, rinsed and drained

1 avocado, pitted, sliced, and tossed with a little lime juice

2 ripe tomatoes, diced

¼ fresh green or red chile, chopped

3 tbsp chopped fresh cilantro

generous handful of crisp tortilla chips, broken into pieces

salt and pepper

1 Place the steak in a nonmetallic dish with the garlic, half the lime juice, and half the olive oil. Season with salt and pepper, cover with plastic wrap, then set aside to marinate for at least 15 minutes, preferably longer.

2 To make the dressing, combine the remaining lime juice with the rest of the olive oil, the vinegar, chili powder, cumin, and paprika. Add sugar to taste, if wished. Set aside.

3 Pan fry the steak or cook under a preheated broiler until browned on the outside and cooked to your liking in the middle. Remove from the pan, cut into strips, and set aside. Keep warm or allow to cool, according to taste.

4 Toss the scallions with the lettuce and arrange on a serving platter. Pour about half the dressing over the leaves, then arrange the corn, beans, avocado, and tomatoes over the top. Sprinkle with the chile and chopped fresh cilantro.

5 Arrange the steak and the tortilla chips on top, pour over the rest of the dressing, and serve immediately.

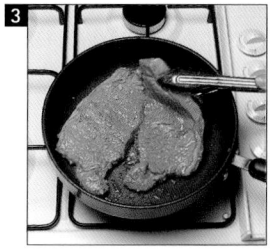

Thai Potato Crab Cakes

These crab cakes are based on a traditional Thai recipe. They make a delicious snack when served with this sweet and sour cucumber sauce.

NUTRITIONAL INFORMATION

Calories 254   Sugars 9g
Protein . . . . .12g   Fat 6g
Carbohydrate . . .40g   Saturates 1g

 10 min   🕐 30 mins

SERVES 4

INGREDIENTS

1 lb/450 g mealy potatoes, diced

6 oz/175 g white crab meat, drained if canned

4 scallions, chopped

1 tsp light soy sauce

½ tsp sesame oil

1 tsp chopped lemongrass

1 tsp lime juice

3 tbsp all-purpose flour

2 tbsp vegetable oil

salt and pepper

SAUCE

4 tbsp finely chopped cucumber

2 tbsp honey

1 tbsp garlic wine vinegar

½ tsp light soy sauce

1 chopped fresh red chile

TO GARNISH

1 fresh red chili, sliced

cucumber slices

1 Cook the diced potatoes in a pan of boiling water for 10 minutes until cooked through. Drain well and mash.

2 Mix the crab meat into the potato with the scallions, soy sauce, sesame oil, lemongrass, lime juice, and flour. Season with salt and pepper.

3 Divide the crab and potato mixture into 8 equal portions and shape them into small rounds, using floured hands.

4 Heat the oil in a wok or skillet and cook the cakes, in batches of 4 at a time, for 5–7 minutes, turning once.

Remove from the pan with a spatula and keep warm.

5 Meanwhile, make the sauce. In a small serving bowl, mix the cucumber, honey, vinegar, soy sauce, and chile.

6 Garnish the cakes with the sliced red chile and cucumber slices and serve with the sauce.

Red Snapper & Coconut Loaf

This fish and coconut loaf is ideal to take along on picnics, because it can be served cold as well as hot.

NUTRITIONAL INFORMATION

Calories ....138 Sugars 12g
Protein ....11g Fat 1g
Carbohydrate ...23g Saturates 0g

15 mins   1¼ hrs

SERVES 4–6

INGREDIENTS

8 oz/225 g red snapper fillets, skinned

2 tomatoes, deseeded and finely chopped

2 green bell peppers, finely chopped

1 onion, finely chopped

1 fresh red chile, finely chopped

2¾ cups bread crumbs

2½ cups coconut liquid

salt and pepper

HOT PEPPER SAUCE

½ cup tomato ketchup

1 tsp West Indian hot pepper sauce

¼ tsp hot mustard

TO GARNISH

lemon twists

fresh chervil sprigs

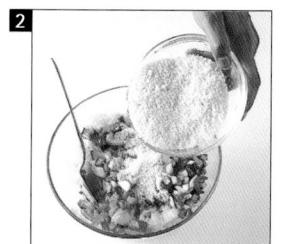

1 Finely chop the fish and mix with the tomatoes, bell peppers, onion, and fresh chile.

2 Stir in the bread crumbs, coconut liquid, and seasoning. If using fresh coconut, use a hammer and the tip of a sturdy knife to poke out the "eyes" in the top and pour out the liquid.

3 Grease and base line a 1 lb 2 oz/500 g loaf pan and add the fish mixture.

4 Bake in a preheated oven, 400°F/200°C, for 1–1¼ hours until set.

5 To make the hot pepper sauce, combine the tomato ketchup, West Indian hot pepper sauce, and mustard until smooth and creamy.

6 To serve, cut the loaf into slices, arrange on a serving platter, garnish with lemon twists and chervil, and serve hot or cold with the sauce.

COOK'S TIP

Be careful when preparing chiles because the juices can irritate the skin, especially the face. Wash your hands after handling them or wear clean rubber gloves to prepare them if preferred.

Migas

A wonderful brunch or late-night supper dish, this is made by scrambling eggs with chiles, tomatoes, and crisp tortilla chips.

NUTRITIONAL INFORMATION

Calories 441	Sugars 5g
Protein 22g	Fat 20g
Carbohydrate . . .46g	Saturates 8g

 10 mins   10–12 mins

SERVES 4

I N G R E D I E N T S

2 tbsp butter

6 garlic cloves, finely chopped

1 fresh green chile, such as jalapeño or serrano, deseeded and diced

1½ tsp ground cumin

6 ripe tomatoes, coarsely chopped

8 eggs, lightly beaten

8–10 corn tortillas, cut into strips and fried until crisp, or an equal quantity of tortilla chips

4 tbsp chopped fresh cilantro

3–4 scallions, thinly sliced

mild chili powder, to garnish

VARIATION

Add browned ground beef or pork to the softly scrambling egg mixture at Step 3. A bunch of cooked, chopped, spinach or Swiss chard can be stirred in as well, to add fresh color.

1 Melt half the butter in a pan. Add the garlic and chile and cook until softened, but not browned. Add the cumin and cook for 30 seconds, stirring constantly, then add the tomatoes and cook over medium heat for a further 3–4 minutes or until the tomato juices have evaporated. Remove from the pan and set aside.

2 Melt the remaining butter in a skillet over low heat and pour in the beaten eggs. Cook, stirring constantly, until the eggs begin to set.

3 Add the chile and tomato mixture, stirring gently to mix into the eggs.

4 Carefully add the tortilla strips or chips and continue cooking, stirring once or twice, until the eggs are the consistency you wish. The tortillas should be pliable and chewy.

5 Transfer to a warmed serving plate and surround with the chopped fresh cilantro and sliced scallions. Garnish with a sprinkling of mild chili powder and serve immediately.

Eggs Oaxaca Style

Cooking an omelet, then cutting it into strips and simmering them in a spicy sauce makes an unusual dish for brunch or dinner.

NUTRITIONAL INFORMATION

Calories 260   Sugars 9g
Protein . . . . .19g   Fat 16g
Carbohydrate . . .10g   Saturates 4g

15 mins   15 mins

SERVES 4

I N G R E D I E N T S

2 lb 4 oz/1 kg ripe tomatoes

about 12 small pearl onions, halved

8 garlic cloves, unpeeled

2 fresh mild green chiles

pinch of ground cumin

pinch of dried oregano,

pinch of sugar (optional)

2–3 tsp vegetable oil

8 eggs, lightly beaten

1–2 tbsp tomato paste

salt and pepper

1–2 tbsp chopped fresh cilantro,
    to garnish

1 Heat an ungreased, heavy skillet, add the tomatoes, and char lightly, turning them once or twice. Remove from the skillet and set aside to cool.

2 Meanwhile lightly char the onions, garlic, and chiles in the pan. Remove from the pan and set aside to cool slightly.

3 Cut the cooled tomatoes into pieces and place in a blender or food processor, with their charred skins.

4 Remove the stems and seeds from the chiles, then peel, and chop. Remove the skins from the garlic, then chop. Roughly chop the onions. Add the chiles, garlic, and onions to the tomatoes.

5 Process to make a coarse purée, then add the cumin and oregano. Season with salt and pepper to taste and add sugar if necessary.

6 Heat the oil in a nonstick skillet, add a ladleful of beaten eggs, and cook to make a thin omelet. Continue to make omelets, stacking them on a plate as they are cooked. Slice the omelets into noodle-like ribbons.

7 Bring the sauce to a boil, adjust the seasoning, and add tomato paste to taste. Add the omelet strips, warm through, and serve immediately, garnished with a sprinkling of fresh cilantro.

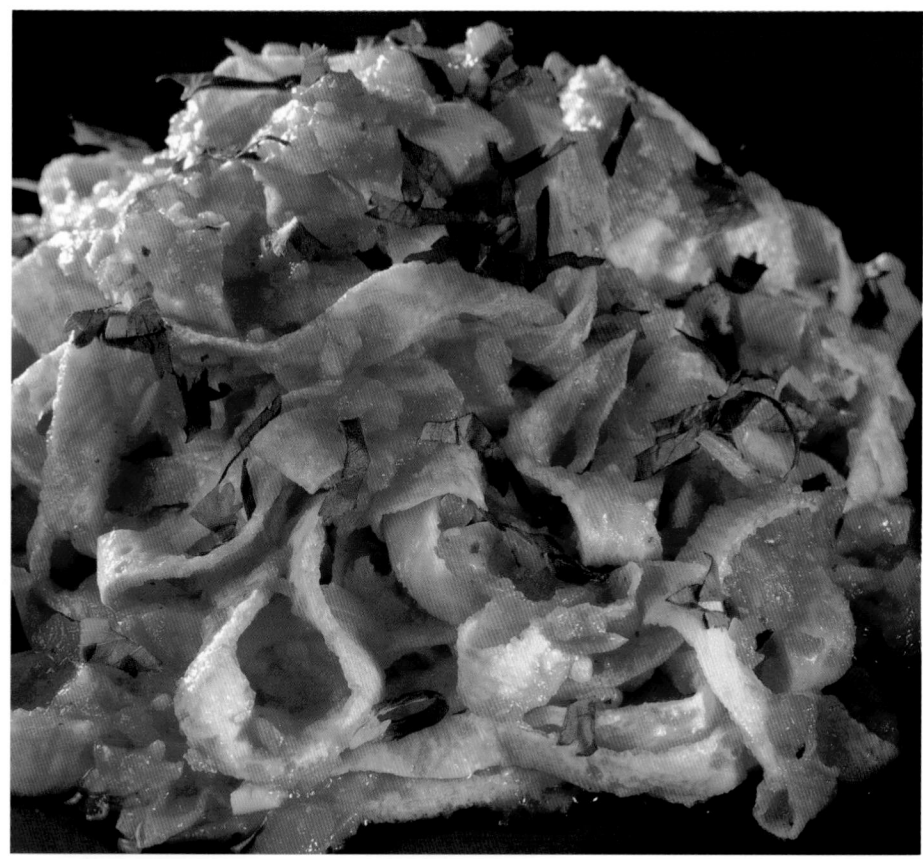

Eggs with Refried Beans

In the Yucatan, this classic dish would be sandwiched between two crisp tortillas, but layering it all on top of one tortilla looks much more festive.

NUTRITIONAL INFORMATION

Calories 661	Sugars 13g
Protein 35g	Fat 29g
Carbohydrate . . .66g	Saturates 10g

 15 mins 25 mins

SERVES 4

INGREDIENTS

14 oz/400 g tomatoes, peeled and chopped

1 onion, chopped

1 garlic clove, finely chopped

½ fresh green chile, such as jalapeño or serrano, deseeded and chopped

¼ tsp ground cumin

2 tbsp extra virgin olive oil

1 tbsp butter

1 plantain, peeled and diced

4 corn tortillas, warmed or fried crisply into a tostada

about 14 oz/400 g can refried beans, warmed with 2 tbsp of water

2 tbsp water

4 eggs

1 red bell pepper, broiled, peeled, deseeded, and cut into strips

3–4 tbsp cooked green peas, cooled

4–6 tbsp diced cooked or smoked ham

½–⅔ cup crumbled feta cheese

3 scallions, thinly sliced

salt and pepper

1 Put the tomatoes in a blender or food processor with the onion, garlic, chile, cumin, salt, and pepper and process to a purée.

2 Heat the oil in a heavy skillet , then ladle in a little of the tomato mixture, and cook until it reduces in volume and becomes almost paste-like. Continue adding and reducing the tomato mixture in this way. Keep warm.

3 Melt the butter in a heavy, nonstick skillet. Add the plantain and cook over medium heat, stirring frequently, until browned. Remove and set aside. Spread the tortillas with the refried beans and keep warm in a low oven.

4 Add the water to the nonstick skillet, break in an egg, and cook until the white is set but the yolk is still soft. Remove from the skillet and place on top of 1 tortilla. Cook the remaining eggs in the same way, adding them to the remaining tortillas.

5 To serve, spoon the warm sauce around the eggs on each tortilla. Sprinkle the diced plantain, bell pepper, peas, ham, feta cheese, and scallions over the top. Season with salt and pepper to taste and serve immediately.

Spicy Meat & Chipotle Hash

This specialty from the Puebla in Mexico makes divine soft tacos: simply serve with a stack of warm corn tortillas and let everyone roll their own.

NUTRITIONAL INFORMATION

Calories	210	Sugars	....3g
Protein	....26g	Fat	....10g
Carbohydrate	....4g	Saturates	....4g

10 mins

15–20 mins

SERVES 6

INGREDIENTS

1 tbsp vegetable oil

1 onion, finely chopped

1 lb/450 g leftover cooked meat, cooled and cut into thin strips

1 tbsp mild chili powder

2 ripe tomatoes, deseeded and diced

about 1 cup meat stock

½–1 canned chipotle chili, mashed, plus a little of the adobo sauce, or a dash of chipotle salsa

½ cup sour cream

4–6 tbsp chopped fresh cilantro

4–6 tbsp chopped radishes

3–4 leaves crisp lettuce, shredded

1 Heat the oil in a skillet , add the onion, and cook over low heat, stirring occasionally, for 5 minutes until softened. Add the meat and sauté, stirring frequently, for about 3 minutes, until lightly browned.

2 Add the chili powder, tomatoes, and stock and cook, mashing the meat gently, until the tomatoes have disintegrated and reduced to a sauce.

3 Add the chipotle chili or salsa and continue to cook and mash until the sauce and meat are nearly blended.

4 Serve the dish with a stack of warmed corn tortillas so that people can fill them with the meaty mixture to make tacos. Also serve sour cream, chopped fresh cilantro, radishes, and shredded lettuce for each person to add to the meat.

COOK'S TIP

Avocados add an interesting texture contrast to the spicy meat—serve with 2 sliced avocados, tossed with lime juice. Try serving on top of tostada, crisply fried tortillas, instead of wrapping taco-style.

Pad Thai Noodles

The combination of ingredients in this classic noodle dish varies,
but it commonly contains a mixture of pork and shrimp or other seafood.

NUTRITIONAL INFORMATION

Calories 477   Sugars 6g
Protein ....26g   Fat 14g
Carbohydrate ...60g   Saturates 3g

    10 mins   5 mins

SERVES 4

INGREDIENTS

9 oz/250 g rice stick noodles

3 tbsp peanut oil

3 garlic cloves, finely chopped

4 oz/115 g pork tenderloin, chopped into
  ¼ inch/5 mm pieces

1¾ cups peeled, cooked shrimp

1 tbsp sugar

3 tbsp Thai fish sauce

1 tbsp tomato ketchup

1 tbsp lime juice

2 eggs, beaten

2 cups bean sprouts

TO GARNISH

1 tsp dried red chili flakes

2 scallions, thickly sliced

2 tbsp chopped fresh cilantro

1 Soak the rice noodles in hot water for about 10 minutes or according to the packet instructions. Drain thoroughly and set aside.

2 Heat the groundnut oil in a large skillet or wok, add the garlic, and stir-fry over high heat for 30 seconds. Add the pork and stir-fry for 2–3 minutes until browned all over.

3 Stir in the shrimp, then add the sugar, fish sauce, ketchup, and lime juice, and continue stir-frying for a further 30 seconds.

4 Stir in the eggs and stir-fry until lightly set. Stir in the noodles, then add the bean sprouts, and stir-fry for a further 30 seconds to cook lightly.

5 Turn out onto a warm serving dish and sprinkle with the chili flakes, scallions, and cilantro. Serve hot.

COOK'S TIP
Drain the rice noodles before adding them to the pan, as excess moisture will spoil the texture of the dish.

Noodles with Mushrooms

An alternative to classic dishes such as Pad Thai Noodles (see page 362), this quick and easy dish is very filling.

NUTRITIONAL INFORMATION

Calories . . . . .361 Sugars 3g
Protein . . . . .9g Fat 12g
Carbohydrate . . .53g Saturates 2g

  20 mins   8–10 mins

SERVES 4

I N G R E D I E N T S

8 oz/225 g rice stick noodles

2 tbsp peanut oil

1 garlic clove, finely chopped

¾ inch/2 cm piece fresh ginger root, finely chopped

4 shallots, thinly sliced

1 cup sliced shiitake mushrooms

3½ oz/100 g firm beancurd, cut into ⅝ inch/ 1.5 cm dice

2 tbsp light soy sauce

1 tbsp rice wine

1 tbsp Thai fish sauce

1 tbsp smooth peanut butter

1 tsp chili sauce

2 tbsp toasted peanuts, chopped

shredded fresh basil leaves, to serve

1 Soak the rice stick noodles in hot water for 15 minutes or according to the package directions. Drain well.

2 Heat the peanut oil in a pan. Add the garlic, ginger, and shallots and stir-fry for 1–2 minutes until softened and lightly browned.

3 Add the mushrooms and stir-fry over medium heat for another 2–3 minutes.

Stir in the beancurd and toss gently to brown lightly.

4 Combine the soy sauce, rice wine, fish sauce, peanut butter, and chili sauce, then stir into the pan.

5 Stir in the rice noodles and toss to coat evenly in the sauce. Sprinkle with peanuts and shredded basil leaves and serve hot.

COOK'S TIP

For an easy pantry dish, replace the shiitake mushrooms with a can of Chinese straw mushrooms. Alternatively, use dried shiitake mushrooms, soaked and drained before use.

Drunken Noodles

Perhaps this would be more correctly named "drunkards' noodles," because it's a dish that is supposedly often eaten as a hangover cure.

NUTRITIONAL INFORMATION

Calories . . . . . . .278 Sugars 3g
Protein . . . . .12g Fat 7g
Carbohydrate . . .40g Saturates 1g

 20 mins   8–10 mins

SERVES 4

I N G R E D I E N T S

6 oz/175 g rice stick noodles

2 tbsp vegetable oil

1 garlic clove, crushed

2 small fresh green chiles, chopped

1 small onion, thinly sliced

5½ oz/150 g lean ground pork or chicken

1 small green bell pepper, deseeded and finely chopped

4 kaffir lime leaves, finely shredded

1 tbsp dark soy sauce

1 tbsp light soy sauce

½ tsp sugar

1 tomato, cut into thin wedges

2 tbsp fresh sweet basil leaves, finely shredded, to garnish

1 Soak the rice stick noodles in hot water for 15 minutes or according to the package directions. Drain well.

2 Heat the oil in a wok and stir-fry the garlic, chiles and onion for 1 minute.

3 Stir in the pork or chicken and stir-fry over high heat for a further minute, then add the bell pepper and continue stir-frying for a further 2 minutes.

4 Stir in the lime leaves, soy sauces, and sugar. Add the noodles and tomato and toss well to heat thoroughly.

5 Sprinkle with the sliced basil leaves and serve hot.

COOK'S TIP

Fresh kaffir lime leaves freeze well, so if you buy more than you need, simply tie them in a tightly sealed plastic freezer bag and freeze for up to a month. They can be used straight from the freezer.

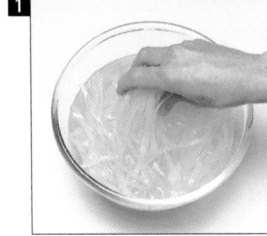

Rice Noodles with Spinach

This quick stir-fried noodle dish is simple to prepare, and makes a delicious light lunch in minutes.

NUTRITIONAL INFORMATION

Calories 159	Sugars 3g	
Protein 8g	Fat 2g	
Carbohydrate ...27g	Saturates 0g	

 20 mins   6–8 mins

SERVES 4

I N G R E D I E N T S

4 oz/115 g thin rice stick noodles

2 tbsp dried shrimp, (optional)

9 oz/250 g baby spinach

1 tbsp peanut oil

2 garlic cloves, finely chopped

2 tsp Thai green curry paste

1 tsp sugar

1 tbsp light soy sauce

1 Soak the noodles in hot water for 15 minutes or according to the package directions, then drain well.

2 Put the dried shrimp, If using, in a bowl and add hot water to cover. Set aside to soak for 10 minutes, then drain.

3 Wash the baby spinach thoroughly, drain well, and pat dry. Remove any tough stalks.

4 Heat the oil in a skillet or wok and stir-fry the garlic for 1 minute. Stir in the curry paste and stir-fry for 30 seconds. Stir in the soaked shrimp, if using, and stir-fry for 30 seconds.

5 Add the spinach and stir-fry for 1–2 minutes until the leaves are just wilted.

6 Stir in the sugar and soy sauce, then add the noodles, and toss thoroughly to mix evenly. Serve immediately.

COOK'S TIP

It is best to choose young spinach leaves for this dish, as they are beautifully tender and cook within a matter of seconds. If you can only get older spinach, however, shred the leaves before adding to the dish so they cook more quickly.

Stir-Fried Rice with Egg

Many Thai rice dishes are made from leftover rice that has been cooked for an earlier meal. Any leftover vegetables or meat can be used too.

NUTRITIONAL INFORMATION

Calories ....334 Sugars 49g
Protein ....7g Fat 9g
Carbohydrate ...60g Saturates 1g

5–10 mins   5 mins

SERVES 4

INGREDIENTS

2 tbsp groundnut oil

1 egg, beaten with 1 tsp water

1 garlic clove, finely chopped

1 small onion, finely chopped

1 tbsp Thai red curry paste

1¼ cups long grain rice, cooked

½ cup cooked peas

1 tbsp Thai fish sauce

2 tbsp tomato ketchup

2 tbsp chopped fresh cilantro

TO GARNISH

fresh red chiles

cucumber slices

1 To make chile flowers for the garnish, hold the stem of each chile with your fingertips and use a small sharp, pointed knife to cut a slit down the length from near the stem end to the tip. Turn the chile about a quarter turn and make another cut. Repeat to make a total of 4 cuts, then scrape out the seeds. Cut each "petal" again, in half or into quarters, to make 8–16 petals. Place the chile in ice water.

2 Heat about 1 teaspoon of the oil in a wok. Pour in the egg mixture, swirling it to coat the pan evenly and make a thin layer. When set and golden, remove the egg from the pan and roll up. Set aside.

3 Add the remaining oil to the wok and stir-fry the garlic and onion for 1 minute. Add the curry paste, then stir in the rice and peas. Stir until heated through.

4 Stir in the fish sauce, ketchup, and cilantro. Remove the wok from the heat and pile the rice on to a warm serving dish.

5 Slice the egg roll into spiral strips, without unrolling, and use to garnish the rice. Add the cucumber slices and chile flowers. Serve hot.

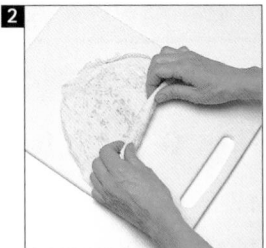

Crêpes with Curried Crab

Homemade crêpes are delicious—here, white crab meat is lightly flavored with curry spices and tossed in a low-fat dressing.

NUTRITIONAL INFORMATION

Calories 279	Sugars 9g
Protein 25g	Fat 7g
Carbohydrate ...31g	Saturates 1g

40 mins · 25 mins

SERVES 4

INGREDIENTS

1 cup buckwheat flour

1 large egg, beaten

1¼ cups skim milk

4½ oz/125 g frozen spinach, thawed, well drained, and chopped

2 tsp vegetable oil

FILLING

12 oz/350 g white crab meat

1 tsp mild curry powder

1 tbsp mango chutney

1 tbsp reduced-calorie mayonnaise

2 tbsp low-fat plain yogurt

2 tbsp chopped fresh cilantro

TO SERVE

salad greens

lemon wedges

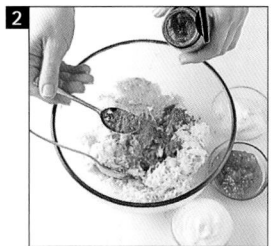

1 Sift the flour into a bowl. Make a well in the center of the flour and add the egg. Whisk in the milk, then blend in the spinach. Transfer to a pitcher and set aside for 30 minutes.

2 To make the filling, combine all the ingredients, except the cilantro, in a bowl, cover, and chill until required. Whisk the batter. Brush a small crêpe pan with a little oil, heat until hot, and pour in enough batter to cover the base thinly. Cook for 1–2 minutes, flip over, and cook for 1 minute until golden. Make 7 more crêpes, layering them on a plate with baking parchment.

3 Stir the cilantro into the crab mixture. Fold each crêpe into quarters. Open 1 fold and fill with the crab mixture. Serve warm, with salad greens and lemon wedges.

VARIATION

Try lean diced chicken in a light white sauce or peeled shrimp instead of the crab.

Spicy Garbanzo Snack

You can use dried garbanzo beans, soaked overnight, for this popular Indian snack, but the canned variety is just as flavorsome.

NUTRITIONAL INFORMATION

Calories	 190	Sugars	.... 4g
Protein	.... 9g	Fat	.... 3g
Carbohydrate	... 34g	Saturates	..... 0.3g

 5 mins   🕐 5 mins

SERVES 4

INGREDIENTS

2 medium potatoes

1 medium onion

14 oz/400 g can garbanzo beans, drained

2 tbsp tamarind paste

6 tbsp water

1 tsp chili powder

2 tsp sugar

salt and pepper

TO GARNISH

1 tomato, sliced

2 fresh green chiles, chopped

fresh cilantro leaves

1 Using a sharp knife, cut the potatoes into dice. Place them in a pan, add water just to cover, and bring to a boil. Cover and simmer over medium heat for 10 minutes until cooked through. Test by inserting the tip of a knife into the potatoes—they should feel soft and tender. Drain and set aside.

2 Using a sharp knife, finely chop the onion. Set aside until required. Put the garbanzo beans into a bowl.

3 Combine the tamarind paste and water. Add the chili powder, sugar, and 1 teaspoon salt and mix again. Pour the mixture over the garbanzo beans.

4 Add the onion and the diced potatoes to the garbanzo beans and stir to mix. Season to taste with pepper.

5 Transfer to a serving bowl and garnish with tomatoes, chiles and cilantro leaves.

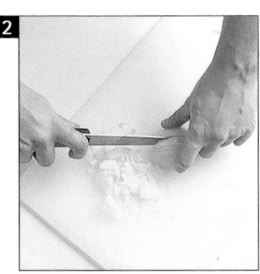

COOK'S TIP

Garbanzo beans have a nutty flavor and slightly crunchy texture. Indian cooks also grind these to make a flour called gram or besan, which is used to make breads, thicken sauces, and to make batters for deep-fried dishes.

Potato & Mushroom Bake

Use any mixture of mushrooms at hand for this creamy layered bake. It can be served straight from the dish in which it is cooked.

NUTRITIONAL INFORMATION

Calories 304	Sugars 2g
Protein 4g	Fat 24g
Carbohydrate . . .20g	Saturates 15g

15 mins   1 hr

SERVES 4

INGREDIENTS

2 tbsp butter

1 lb 2 oz/500 g waxy potatoes, thinly sliced

2 cups sliced mixed mushrooms

1 tbsp chopped rosemary

4 tbsp chopped chives

2 garlic cloves, crushed

⅔ cup heavy cream

salt and pepper

snipped chives, to garnish

1 Grease a shallow round ovenproof dish with butter.

2 Parboil the sliced potatoes in a pan of boiling water for 10 minutes. Drain well. Layer a quarter of the potatoes in the base of the dish.

3 Arrange one-quarter of the mushrooms on top of the potatoes and sprinkle with one-quarter of the rosemary, chives, and garlic. Continue making layers in the same order, finishing with a layer of potatoes on top.

4 Pour the cream over the top of the potatoes. Season to taste with salt and pepper.

5 Cook in a preheated oven, 375°F/ 190°C, for about 45 minutes, or until the bake is golden brown and piping hot.

6 Garnish with snipped chives and serve at once straight from the dish.

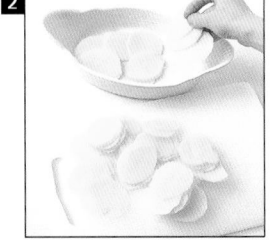

COOK'S TIP

For a special occasion, the bake may be made in a lined cake pan and then turned out to serve.

Cranberry Turkey Burgers

This recipe is bound to be popular with children and is very easy to prepare for their supper.

NUTRITIONAL INFORMATION

Calories 209   Sugars 15g
Protein . . . . .22g   Fat 5g
Carbohydrate . . .21g   Saturates 1g

 45 mins   25 mins

SERVES 4

INGREDIENTS

12 oz/350 g lean ground turkey

1 onion, finely chopped

1 tbsp chopped fresh sage

6 tbsp dry white bread crumbs

4 tbsp cranberry sauce

1 egg white, lightly beaten

2 tsp sunflower oil

salt and pepper

TO SERVE

4 toasted whole-wheat
    burger rolls

½ lettuce, shredded

4 tomatoes, sliced

4 tsp cranberry sauce

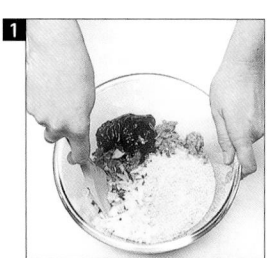

COOK'S TIP

Look out for a variety of ready ground meats at your butchers or supermarket. If unavailable, you can grind your own by choosing lean cuts and processing them in a blender or food processor.

1 Combine the turkey, onion, sage, bread crumbs, and cranberry sauce and season to taste with salt and pepper, then bind with egg white.

2 Press into 4 x 4 inch/10 cm rounds, about ¾ inch/2 cm thick. Chill the burgers for 30 minutes.

3 Line a broiler rack with baking parchment, making sure the ends are secured underneath the rack to ensure they don't catch fire. Place the burgers on top and brush lightly with oil. Put under a preheated moderate broiler and cook for 10 minutes. Turn the burgers over, brush again with oil. Cook for a further 12–15 minutes until cooked through.

4 Fill the burger rolls with lettuce, tomato, and a burger and top with cranberry sauce.

Rice & Tuna Bell Peppers

Broiled mixed sweet bell peppers are filled with tender tuna, corn, nutty brown and wild rice, and grated, reduced-fat cheese.

NUTRITIONAL INFORMATION

Calories 332   Sugars 13g
Protein ....27g   Fat 8g
Carbohydrate ...42g   Saturates 4g

 10 mins   50–60 mins

SERVES 4

I N G R E D I E N T S

¼ cup wild rice

¼ cup brown rice

4 assorted medium bell peppers

7 oz/200 g can tuna fish in brine, drained and flaked

11½ oz/325 g can corn kernels, drained

scant 1 cup grated reduced-fat sharp Cheddar cheese

1 bunch fresh basil leaves, shredded

2 tbsp dry white bread crumbs

1 tbsp freshly grated Parmesan cheese

salt and pepper

fresh basil leaves, to garnish

crisp salad greens, to serve

1 Place the wild rice and brown rice in different pans, cover with boiling water, and bring back to a boil. Cook for about 40–50 minutes or according to the instructions on the packet. Drain the rice well.

2 Meanwhile, preheat the broiler to medium. Halve the bell peppers, remove the seeds and stalks, and arrange the bell peppers on the broiler rack, cut side down. Cook for 5 minutes, turn over, and cook for a further 4–5 minutes.

3 Transfer the cooked rice to a large bowl and add the flaked tuna and drained corn. Gently fold in the grated cheese. Stir the basil leaves into the rice mixture and season with salt and pepper to taste.

4 Divide the tuna and rice mixture into 8 equal portions. Pile each portion into each cooked bell pepper half. Combine the bread crumbs and Parmesan cheese and sprinkle over each bell pepper.

5 Place the bell peppers back under the broiler again for 4–5 minutes until hot and golden brown.

6 Serve the bell peppers immediately, garnished with basil and accompanied with fresh, crisp salad greens.

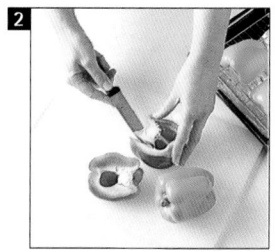

Cheese & Ham Savory

Lean ham wrapped around crisp celery, topped with a light crust of cheese and scallions, makes a delicious light lunch.

NUTRITIONAL INFORMATION

Calories	188	Sugars	.........5g
Protein	........15g	Fat	..........12g
Carbohydrate	....5g	Saturates	......7g

 10 mins 10 mins

SERVES 4

INGREDIENTS

4 celery stalks, with leaves

12 thin slices of lean ham

1 bunch of scallions

¾ cup low-fat soft cheese with garlic and herbs

6 tbsp low-fat plain yogurt

4 tbsp freshly grated Parmesan cheese

celery salt and pepper

TO SERVE

tomato salad

crusty bread

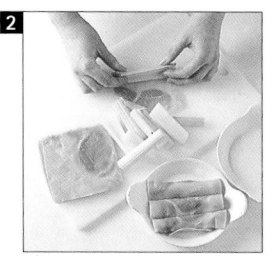

COOK'S TIP

Parmesan is useful in low-fat recipes because its intense flavor means you need to use only a small amount.

1 Wash the celery, remove the leaves, and reserve for the garnish. Slice each stalk into 3 equal portions.

2 Cut any visible fat off the ham and lay the slices on a cutting board. Place a piece of celery on each piece of ham and roll up. Place 3 ham and celery rolls in each of 4 small, heatproof dishes.

3 Trim the scallions, then finely shred both the white and green parts. Sprinkle the scallions over the ham and celery rolls and season with celery salt and pepper.

4 Combine the soft cheese and yogurt and spoon the mixture over the ham and celery rolls.

5 Preheat the broiler to medium. Sprinkle each portion with 1 tablespoon grated Parmesan cheese and broil for 6–7 minutes until hot and the cheese has formed a crust. If the cheese starts to brown too quickly, lower the broiler setting slightly.

6 Garnish the ham and celery rolls with celery leaves and serve with a tomato salad and crusty bread.

Soufflé Omelet

Sweet cherry tomatoes, mushrooms, and peppery arugula leaves make a mouthwatering filling for these light, fluffy omelets.

NUTRITIONAL INFORMATION

Calories 146   Sugars 2g
Protein ....10g   Fat 11g
Carbohydrate ....2g   Saturates 2g

   1¼ hrs   45 mins

SERVES 4

INGREDIENTS

6 oz/175 g cherry tomatoes

8 oz/225 g mixed mushrooms, such as white, crimini, shiitake, and oyster

4 tbsp vegetable stock

small bunch of fresh thyme

4 eggs, separated

½ cup water

4 egg whites

4 tsp olive oil

1 oz/25 g arugula leaves

salt and pepper

fresh thyme sprigs, to garnish

1 Halve the tomatoes and place them in a pan. Wipe the mushrooms with paper towels, trim if necessary, and slice if large. Place the mushrooms in the pan with the tomatoes.

2 Add the stock and thyme, still tied together, to the pan. Bring to a boil, cover, and simmer for 5–6 minutes until tender. Drain, remove the thyme, and discard. Keep the mixture warm.

3 Meanwhile, separate the eggs and whisk the egg yolks with the water until frothy. In a clean, grease-free bowl, whisk the 8 egg whites until stiff and dry.

4 Spoon the egg yolk mixture into the egg whites and, using a metal spoon, fold together until well mixed. Take care not to knock out too much of the air.

5 For each omelet, brush a small omelet pan with 1 teaspoon of the oil and heat until hot. Pour in a quarter of the egg mixture and cook for 4–5 minutes until the mixture has set.

6 Finish cooking the omelet under a preheated medium broiler for 2–3 minutes.

7 Transfer the omelet to a warm serving plate. Fill the omelet with a few arugula leaves and a quarter of the mushroom and tomato mixture. Flip over the top of the omelet, garnish with sprigs of thyme, and serve.

Potatoes with a Spicy Filling

These twice-baked potatoes have an unusual filling made from the Middle Eastern flavors of garbanzo beans, cumin, and cilantro.

NUTRITIONAL INFORMATION

Calories 335   Sugars 7g
Protein . . . . .15g   Fat 7g
Carbohydrate . . .57g   Saturates 1g

 20 mins   1½ hrs

SERVES 4

I N G R E D I E N T S

4 large baking potatoes

1 tbsp vegetable oil, optional

15½ oz/425 g canned garbanzo beans, drained

1 tsp ground coriander

1 tsp ground cumin

4 tbsp chopped fresh cilantro

⅔ cup low-fat plain yogurt

salt and pepper

S A L A D

2 tomatoes

½ cucumber

½ red onion

4 tbsp chopped fresh cilantro

1 Preheat the oven to 400°F/200°C. Scrub the potatoes and pat them dry with paper towels. Prick the potatoes all over with a fork. Brush with oil (if using) and season with salt and pepper.

2 Place the potatoes on a baking sheet and bake for 1–1¼ hours or until cooked through. Cool for 10 minutes.

3 Mash the garbanzo beans in a large mixing bowl. Stir in the ground coriander, cumin, and half the cilantro. Cover with plastic wrap and set aside.

4 Halve the cooked potatoes and scoop the flesh into a bowl, keeping the shells intact. Mash the flesh until smooth and gently mix into the garbanzo mixture with the plain yogurt. Season well with salt and pepper to taste.

5 Place the potato shells on a baking sheet and fill with the potato and garbanzo mixture. Return the potatoes to the oven and bake for 10–15 minutes until heated through.

6 Meanwhile, make the salad. Using a sharp knife, chop the tomatoes. Slice the cucumber and cut the red onion into thin slices. Toss all the ingredients together with the cilantro in a serving dish.

7 Serve the potatoes sprinkled with the remaining chopped cilantro and the prepared salad.

COOK'S TIP

For an even lower fat version of this recipe, bake the potatoes without oiling them first.

Vegetable Curry

This vegetable curry is quick and easy to prepare and it tastes superb.
A colorful Indian salad and a mint raita make perfect accompaniments.

NUTRITIONAL INFORMATION

Calories . . . . . . .473 Sugars 18g
Protein . . . . .19g Fat 9g
Carbohydrate . . .84g Saturates 1g

 10 mins   50 mins

SERVES 4

I N G R E D I E N T S

1 tbsp vegetable oil

2 garlic cloves, crushed

1 onion, chopped

3 celery stalks, sliced

1 apple, chopped

1 tbsp medium curry powder

1 tsp ground ginger

14 oz/400 g can garbanzo beans, rinsed
   and drained

4 oz/115 g thin green beans, sliced

8 oz/225 g cauliflower, broken into florets

8 oz/225 g potatoes, cut into cubes

2⅓ cups sliced mushrooms

2½ cups vegetable stock

1 tbsp tomato paste

2 tbsp golden raisins

scant 1 cup basmati rice

1 tbsp garam masala

salad, to serve

M I N T   R A I T A

scant 1 cup low-fat plain yogurt

2 cups fresh mint leaves, chopped

1 Heat the oil in a large pan. Add the garlic, onion, celery, and apple and cook over low heat, stirring occasionally, for 3–4 minutes. Add the curry powder and ginger and cook, stirring constantly, for 1 minute.

2 Add the garbanzo beans, green beans, cauliflower florets, potatoes, mushrooms, vegetable stock, tomato paste, and golden raisins and stir well to mix. Bring to a boil, then reduce the heat, cover, and simmer for 35–40 minutes.

3 Meanwhile, make the mint raita. Combine the yogurt and mint in a small bowl. Cover with plastic wrap and chill in the refrigerator until ready to serve.

4 Cook the rice in boiling, lightly salted water for 20 minutes or according to the instructions on the packet. Drain thoroughly.

5 Just before serving, stir the garam masala into the curry. Divide among 4 warmed serving plates and serve immediately with the rice, mint raita, and salad.

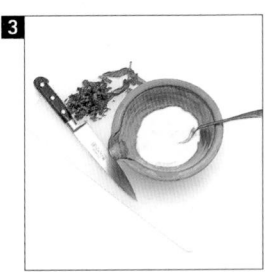

Vermicelli with Clam Sauce

This is another cook-in-a-hurry recipe that transforms pantry ingredients into a dish with style.

NUTRITIONAL INFORMATION

Calories .... 392 Sugars 2g
Protein .... 23g Fat 15g
Carbohydrate ... 37g Saturates 6g

5 mins   20 mins

SERVES 4

INGREDIENTS

14 oz/400 g vermicelli, spaghetti, or other long pasta

2 tbsp butter

salt

fresh basil sprigs, to garnish

2 tbsp flaked Parmesan, to serve

SAUCE

1 tbsp olive oil

2 onions, chopped

2 garlic cloves, chopped

2 x 7 oz/200 g jars clams in brine

½ cup white wine

4 tbsp chopped parsley

½ tsp dried oregano

pinch of grated nutmeg

pepper

1 Bring a large pan of lightly salted water to a boil. Add the pasta, bring back to a boil, and cook for 8–10 minutes until tender, but still firm to the bite. Drain well, return to the pan, and add the butter. Cover and shake. Set the pan aside and keep warm.

2 To make the clam sauce, heat the oil in a pan. Add the onion and cook over low heat, stirring occasionally, for 5 minutes until softened. Stir in the garlic and cook for 1 further minute.

3 Strain the liquid from 1 jar of clams and pour it into the pan. Strain the liquid from the other jar of clams and discard. Reserve the clams.

4 Add the wine to the pan. Bring to simmering point, stirring constantly, and simmer for 3 minutes.

5 Add the clams and herbs to the pan and season to taste with pepper and nutmeg. Lower the heat and cook until the sauce is heated through.

6 Transfer the pasta to a warmed serving platter and pour the clam sauce over it.

7 Garnish with the basil and sprinkle on the Parmesan. Serve hot.

Mushroom Cannelloni

Thick pasta tubes are filled with a mixture of seasoned, chopped mushrooms, and baked in a rich, fragrant tomato sauce.

NUTRITIONAL INFORMATION

Calories	156	Sugar	.........8g
Protein	.........6g	Fats	...........1g
Carbohydrates	...21g	Saturates	.....0.2g

35 mins   1½ hrs

SERVES 4

INGREDIENTS

12 oz/350 g crimini mushrooms

1 onion, finely chopped

1 garlic clove, crushed

1 tbsp chopped fresh thyme

½ tsp ground nutmeg

4 tbsp dry white wine

scant 1 cup fresh white bread crumbs

12 dried quick-cook cannelloni

salt and pepper

Parmesan shavings, to garnish (optional)

TOMATO SAUCE

1 large red bell pepper

¾ cup dry white wine

scant 2 cups passata (strained tomatoes)

2 tbsp tomato paste

2 bay leaves

1 tsp superfine sugar

1 Finely chop the mushrooms; put in a pan with the onion and garlic. Stir in the thyme, nutmeg, and 4 tablespoons of wine. Bring to a boil, cover, and simmer for 10 minutes.

2 Stir in the bread crumbs to bind the mixture together and season to taste with salt and pepper. Remove the pan from the heat and let cool for 10 minutes.

3 To make the sauce, halve and seed the bell pepper, place on the broiler rack, and cook under a preheated broiler for 8–10 minutes until charred. Let cool for 10 minutes.

4 Once the bell pepper has cooled, peel off the charred skin. Chop the flesh and place in a food processor with the wine. Blend until smooth, then pour into a pan.

5 Mix the remaining sauce ingredients with the bell pepper and wine. Bring to a boil and simmer for 10 minutes. Discard the bay leaves.

6 Cover the base of an ovenproof dish with a thin layer of sauce. Fill the cannelloni with the mushroom mixture and place in the dish. Spoon over the remaining sauce, cover with foil, and bake in a preheated oven, 400°F/200°C for 35–40 minutes. Garnish with Parmesan shavings, if desired, and serve immediately.

COOK'S TIP

Crimini mushrooms, also known as champignons de Paris, are common cultivated mushrooms that may have brown or white caps.

Vegetable Stir-Fry

A range of delicious flavors are captured in this simple recipe, which is ideal if you are in a hurry.

NUTRITIONAL INFORMATION

Calories	138	Sugars	.........5g
Protein	.........3g	Fat	..........12g
Carbohydrate	....5g	Saturates	.......2g

 5 mins   25 mins

SERVES 4

INGREDIENTS

3 tbsp vegetable oil

8 pearl onions, halved

1 eggplant, cubed

8 oz/225 g zucchini, sliced

8 oz/225 g open-cap mushrooms, halved

2 cloves garlic, crushed

14 oz/400 g canned chopped tomatoes

2 tbsp sundried tomato paste

2 tbsp soy sauce

1 tsp sesame oil

1 tbsp Chinese rice wine or dry sherry

freshly ground black pepper

fresh basil leaves, to garnish

1 Heat the vegetable oil in a large preheated wok or skillet.

2 Add the pearl onions and eggplant to the wok or skillet and cook for 5 minutes, or until the vegetables are golden and just beginning to soften.

3 Add the sliced zucchini, mushrooms, garlic, chopped tomatoes, and sundried tomato paste to the wok and cook for about 5 minutes. Reduce the heat and simmer for 10 minutes, or until the vegetables are tender, but not soft.

4 Add the soy sauce, sesame oil, and rice wine or sherry to the wok, bring back to a boil and cook for 1 minute.

5 Season the vegetable stir-fry with freshly ground black pepper and scatter with fresh basil leaves. Serve immediately on warm serving plates.

COOK'S TIP

Basil has a very strong flavor which is perfect with vegetables and Chinese flavorings. Instead of using basil simply as a garnish in this dish, try adding a handful of fresh basil leaves to the stir-fry in step 4.

Barbecue Mushrooms

Large mushrooms have more flavor than the smaller white mushrooms. Serve these mushrooms as part of a vegetarian barbecue.

NUTRITIONAL INFORMATION

Calories 148	Sugars 1g
Protein 11g	Fat 7g
Carbohydrate 11g	Saturates 3g

 10 mins   15 mins

SERVES 4

I N G R E D I E N T S

12 open cap mushrooms

4 tsp olive oil

4 scallions, chopped

1¾ cups fresh brown bread crumbs

1 tsp chopped fresh oregano

3½ oz/100 g low-fat mature
   Cheddar cheese

1 Remove the stems from the mushrooms, reserving the caps. Chop the stems finely.

2 Heat half the oil in a skillet. Add the mushroom stems and scallions and cook over low heat, stirring occasionally, for 5 minutes.

3 Transfer the mushroom stems and scallions to a large bowl with a slotted spoon and add the bread crumbs and oregano. Mix well.

4 Crumble the cheese into small pieces in a small bowl. Add the cheese to the breadcrumb mixture and mix well. Carefully spoon the stuffing mixture into the mushroom caps.

5 Drizzle the remaining oil over the stuffed mushrooms. Cook the mushrooms on an oiled rack over medium hot coals for 10 minutes or until cooked through. Alternatively, arrange on a cookie sheet and bake in a preheated oven, 350°F/180°C for about 20 minutes or until cooked through.

6 Transfer the mushrooms to serving plates and serve hot.

VARIATION

For a change, replace the cheese with finely-chopped chorizo sausage (remove the skin first), chopped hard-cooked eggs, chopped olives, or chopped anchovy fillets. Mop up the juices with some crusty bread.

Lime Chicken Kabobs

These succulent chicken kabobs are coated in a sweet
lime dressing and are served with a lime and mango relish.

NUTRITIONAL INFORMATION

Calories 199   Sugars 14g
Protein ....28g   Fat 4g
Carbohydrate ...14g   Saturates 1g

🍴 15 mins   🕐 10 mins

SERVES 4

I N G R E D I E N T S

4 lean skinless boneless chicken breasts,
   about 4½ oz/125 g each

3 tbsp lime marmalade

1 tsp white wine vinegar

½ tsp lime rind, finely grated

1 tbsp lime juice

salt and pepper

TO SERVE

lime wedges

boiled white rice, sprinkled with
   chili powder

SALSA

1 small mango

1 small red onion

1 tbsp lime juice

1 tbsp chopped fresh cilantro

COOK'S TIP

To prevent sticking, lightly oil
metal skewers or dip bamboo
skewers in water before threading
the chicken onto them.

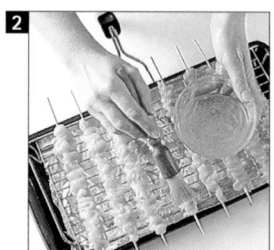

1 Slice the chicken breasts into thin pieces and thread onto 8 skewers so that the meat forms an S-shape along each skewer.

2 Arrange the chicken kabobs on a broiler rack. Combine the lime marmalade, vinegar, lime rind, and juice. Season with salt and pepper. Brush the dressing over the chicken and cook under a preheated broiler for 5 minutes. Turn the kabobs over, brush with the dressing again, and broil for a further 4–5 minutes.

3 Meanwhile, prepare the salsa. Peel the mango and slice the flesh off the smooth, central pit. Dice the flesh into small pieces and place in a small bowl.

4 Peel and finely chop the onion and mix into the mango, with the lime juice and chopped cilantro. Season to taste, cover, and chill until required.

5 Serve the chicken kabobs with the salsa, accompanied with wedges of lime and boiled rice.

Shrimp Pasta Bake

This dish is ideal for an easy family supper. You can use whatever pasta you like, but the tricolor varieties will give the most colorful results.

NUTRITIONAL INFORMATION

Calories ....723 Sugars 9g
Protein ....56g Fat 8g
Carbohydrate ...114g Saturates 2g

10 mins   50 mins

SERVES 4

INGREDIENTS

2 cups tricolor pasta shapes

1 tbsp vegetable oil

2⅓ cups sliced white mushrooms

1 bunch of scallions, trimmed
   and chopped

14 oz/400 g canned tuna in brine, drained
   and flaked

6 oz/175 g peeled shrimp, thawed
   if frozen

2 tbsp cornstarch

scant 2 cups skim milk

4 medium tomatoes, thinly sliced

½ cup fresh bread crumbs

¼ cup reduced-fat grated Cheddar cheese

salt and pepper

TO SERVE

whole-wheat bread

fresh salad

1 Bring a large pan of lightly salted water to a boil. Add the pasta, bring back to a boil, and cook for 8–10 minutes until tender, but still firm to the bite. Drain well.

2 Meanwhile, heat the oil in a large skillet. Add the mushrooms and all but a handful of the scallions and cook over low heat, stirring occasionally, for 4–5 minutes until softened.

3 Place the cooked pasta in a bowl and stir in the mushroom mixture, tuna, and shrimp.

4 Blend the cornstarch with a little milk to make a paste. Pour the remaining milk into a pan and stir in the paste. Heat, stirring, until the sauce begins to thicken. Season to taste. Stir the sauce into the pasta mixture. Transfer to a casserole and place on a cookie sheet.

5 Arrange the tomato slices over the pasta and sprinkle with the bread crumbs and cheese. Bake in a preheated oven, 375°F/190°C, for 25–30 minutes until golden. Serve sprinkled with the reserved scallions and accompanied with bread and salad.

Italian Omelet

A baked omelet of substantial proportions with potatoes, onions, artichokes, and sun-dried tomatoes.

NUTRITIONAL INFORMATION

Calories 481   Sugars 4g
Protein . . . . .22g   Fat 26g
Carbohydrate . . .42g   Saturates 10g

 10 mins   🕐 45 mins

SERVES 4

I N G R E D I E N T S

2 lb/900 g potatoes

1 tbsp vegetable oil

1 large onion, sliced

2 garlic cloves, chopped

6 sun-dried tomatoes in oil, drained and cut into strips

14 oz/400 g can artichoke hearts, drained and halved

generous 1 cup ricotta cheese

4 large eggs, beaten

2 tbsp milk

⅔ cup grated Parmesan cheese

3 tbsp chopped fresh thyme

salt and pepper

1 Peel the potatoes and place them in a bowl of cold water (see Cook's Tip). Cut the potatoes into thin slices.

2 Bring a large pan of water to a boil and add the potato slices. Bring back to a boil, then simmer for 5–6 minutes or until just tender.

3 Heat the oil in a large, heavy skillet. Add the onions and garlic and cook over low heat, stirring occasionally, for about 3–4 minutes until they are softened, but not browned.

4 Add the sun-dried tomatoes and cook for a further 2 minutes.

5 Arrange a third of the potatoes in the bottom of a deep, casserole. Cover with half the onion mixture, then half the artichokes, followed by half the ricotta. Repeat the layers in the same order, finishing with a layer of potato slices on the top of the casserole.

6 Combine the eggs, milk, half of the grated Parmesan, and the thyme and season with salt and pepper to taste. Pour the mixture over the potatoes. Sprinkle the remaining Parmesan on top and bake in a preheated oven, 375°F/190°C, for 20–25 minutes or until golden brown. Cut the omelet into slices and serve it immediately.

COOK'S TIP

Placing the potatoes in a bowl of cold water will prevent them from turning brown while you are cutting the rest into slices.

Omelet in Tomato Sauce

These omelet strips are delicious smothered in a succulent and aromatic tomato and rosemary flavored sauce.

NUTRITIONAL INFORMATION

Calories	198	Sugars	.........6g
Protein	........10g	Fat	..........15g
Carbohydrate	....6g	Saturates	.......8g

10 mins   35 mins

SERVES 4

I N G R E D I E N T S

2 tbsp butter

1 onion, finely chopped

2 garlic cloves, chopped

4 eggs, beaten

⅔ cup milk

¾ cup diced Swiss cheese

14 oz/400 g can tomatoes, chopped

1 tbsp rosemary, stalks removed

⅔ cup vegetable stock

freshly grated Parmesan cheese,
   for sprinkling

fresh crusty bread, to serve

1 Melt the butter in a large skillet . Add the onion and garlic and cook over low heat, stirring occasionally, for 4–5 minutes until softened.

2 Beat together the eggs and milk and add the mixture to the pan.

3 Using a spatula, raise the cooked edges of the omelet and tip any uncooked egg around the edge of the pan.

4 Sprinkle over the cheese. Cook for 5 minutes, turning once, until golden on both sides. Remove the omelet from the pan and roll up.

5 Add the tomatoes, rosemary, and vegetable stock to the skillet and bring to a boil, stirring constantly. Lower the heat and simmer for about 10 minutes until reduced and thickened.

6 Slice the omelet into strips and add to the tomato sauce. Cook for about 3–4 minutes or until piping hot.

7 Sprinkle the Parmesan cheese over the omelet strips and serve with fresh, crusty bread.

VARIATION
Try adding 3½ oz/100 g diced pancetta or unsmoked bacon in step 1 and cooking the meat with the onions.

Chicken Liver Crostini

Crostini are small pieces of toast with a savoury topping—in this case, chicken livers. This is a popular Italian antipasto dish.

NUTRITIONAL INFORMATION

Calories	250	Sugars	.........1g
Protein	........15g	Fat	...........9g
Carbohydrate	...28g	Saturates	.......2g

10 mins   7–8 mins

SERVES 4

INGREDIENTS

2 tbsp olive oil

1 garlic clove, finely chopped

8 oz/225 g fresh or thawed frozen
   chicken livers

2 tbsp white wine

2 tbsp lemon juice

4 fresh sage leaves, finely chopped or 1 tsp
   dried, crumbled sage

4 slices ciabatta or other Italian bread

salt and pepper

lemon wedges, to garnish

1 Heat the olive oil in a heavy-bottomed skillet and cook the garlic over a low heat, stirring constantly, for 1 minute. Remove the pan from the heat.

2 Rinse and roughly chop the chicken livers, using a sharp knife.

3 Return the pan to a medium heat. Add the chicken livers with the white wine and lemon juice. Cook, stirring frequently, for 3–4 minutes or until the juices from the chicken livers run clear. Stir in the sage and season to taste.

4 Toast the bread under a preheated broiler for 2 minutes on both sides or until golden brown.

5 Spoon the hot chicken liver mixture on top of the toasted bread and serve garnished with wedges of lemon.

COOK'S TIP

Overcooked liver is dry and tasteless. Cook the chopped liver for only 3–4 minutes— it should be soft and tender.

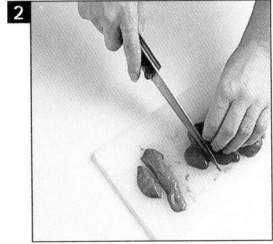

Spaghetti alla Carbonara

Ensure that all of the cooked ingredients are as hot as possible before adding the eggs, so that they cook on contact.

NUTRITIONAL INFORMATION

Calories	1092	Sugars	9g
Protein	37g	Fat	69g
Carbohydrate	86g	Saturates	36g

🍲 10 mins   🕐 15 mins

SERVES 4

I N G R E D I E N T S

15 oz/425 g dried spaghetti

1 tbsp olive oil

1 large onion, thinly sliced

2 garlic cloves, chopped

6 oz/175 g rindless bacon, cut into thin strips

2 tbsp butter

2½ cups sliced mushrooms, thinly sliced

1¼ cups heavy cream

3 eggs, beaten

generous 1 cup freshly grated Parmesan cheese, plus extra to serve (optional)

salt and pepper

fresh sage sprigs, to garnish

1 Warm a large serving dish or bowl. Bring a large pan of lightly salted water to a boil. Add the spaghetti, bring back to a boil, and cook for 8–10 minutes until tender, but still firm to the bite. Drain well, return to the pan and keep warm.

2 Meanwhile, heat the olive oil in a skillet over medium heat. Add the onion and fry, stirring occasionally, for 2–3 minutes until translucent. Add the garlic and bacon and fry until the bacon is crisp. Transfer to the warm dish or bowl.

3 Melt the butter in the skillet. Add the mushrooms and cook over medium heat, stirring occasionally, for 3–4 minutes until tender. Return the bacon mixture to the skillet. Cover and keep warm.

4 Combine the cream, eggs, and cheese in a large bowl and season to taste with salt and pepper.

5 Working very quickly, tip the spaghetti into the bacon and mushroom mixture and pour over the eggs. Toss the spaghetti quickly into the egg and cream mixture, using 2 forks, and serve immediately. If you wish, serve with extra grated Parmesan cheese.

COOK'S TIP

The key to success with this recipe is not to overcook the egg. That is why it is important to keep all the ingredients hot enough just to cook the egg and to work rapidly to avoid scrambling it.

Smoked Ham Linguine

Served with freshly made Italian bread or tossed with pesto, this makes a mouthwatering light lunch.

NUTRITIONAL INFORMATION

Calories	537	Sugars	.........4g
Protein	........22g	Fat	..........29g
Carbohydrate	....71g	Saturates	.......8g

 8–10 mins   20 mins

SERVES 4

I N G R E D I E N T S

1 lb/450 g dried linguine

1 lb/450 g green broccoli florets

8 oz/225 g Italian smoked ham

salt and pepper

Italian bread, such as ciabatta or focaccia, to serve

ITALIAN CHEESE SAUCE

1 tbsp butter

1½ tsp all-purpose flour

½ cup milk

1 tbsp light cream

pinch of freshly grated nutmeg

¼ cup grated Cheddar cheese

1 tbsp freshly grated Parmesan cheese

salt and pepper

COOK'S TIP

There are many types of Italian bread which would be suitable to serve with this dish. Ciabatta is made with olive oil and is available plain and with different additional ingredients, such as olives or sun-dried tomatoes.

1 First, make the Italian cheese sauce. Melt the butter in a pan, stir in the flour, and cook for 1 minute. Remove from the heat and gradually whisk in the milk. Stir in the cream and nutmeg and season to taste with salt and pepper. Return to the heat, bring to a boil, stirring constantly, then simmer for 5 minutes. Remove from the heat and stir in the cheeses until melted and thoroughly blended. Set aside.

2 Bring a large pan of lightly salted water to a boil. Add the pasta and broccoli, bring back to a boil, and cook for 8–10 minutes until the pasta is tender, but still firm to the bite. Drain well.

3 Cut the Italian smoked ham into thin strips. Toss the linguine, broccoli, and ham into the cheese sauce and gently warm through. Season with pepper and serve with Italian bread.

Spinach & Anchovy Pasta

This colorful light meal can be made with a variety of different pasta, including spaghetti and linguine.

NUTRITIONAL INFORMATION

Calories	.619	Sugars	.5g
Protein	.21g	Fat	.31g
Carbohydrate	.67g	Saturates	.3g

10 mins   25 mins

SERVES 4

INGREDIENTS

2 lb/900 g fresh, young spinach leaves

14 oz/400 g dried fettuccine

5 tbsp olive oil

3 tbsp pine nuts

3 garlic cloves, crushed

8 canned anchovy fillets, drained and chopped

salt

1 Trim off any tough spinach stalks. Rinse the spinach leaves and place them in a large pan with only the water that is clinging to them after washing. Cover and cook over high heat, shaking the pan from time, until the spinach has wilted, but retains its color. Drain well, set aside, and keep warm.

2 Bring a large pan of lightly salted water to a boil. Add the fettuccine, bring back to a boil, and cook for 8–10 minutes until it is just tender, but still firm to the bite.

3 Meanwhile, heat 4 tablespoons of the olive oil in a pan. Add the pine nuts and fry until golden. Remove the pine nuts from the pan with a slotted spoon and set aside until required.

4 Add the garlic to the pan and fry until golden. Add the anchovies and stir in the spinach. Cook, stirring constantly, for 2–3 minutes until heated through. Return the pine nuts to the pan.

5 Drain the fettuccine, toss in the remaining olive oil, and transfer to a warm serving dish. Spoon the anchovy and spinach sauce over the fettuccine, toss lightly, and serve immediately.

COOK'S TIP

If you are in a hurry, you can use frozen spinach. Thaw and drain it thoroughly, pressing out as much moisture as possible. Cut the leaves into strips and add to the dish with the anchovies in step 4.

Braised Fennel & Linguine

This anise-flavored vegetable gives that little extra punch
to this delicious creamy pasta dish.

NUTRITIONAL INFORMATION

Calories 650	Sugars 6g
Protein 14g	Fat 39g
Carbohydrate ...62g	Saturates 22g

20 mins   50 mins

SERVES 4

INGREDIENTS

6 fennel bulbs

⅔ cup vegetable stock

2 tbsp butter

6 slices rindless smoked bacon, diced

6 shallots, quartered

2½ tbsp all-purpose flour

7 tbsp heavy cream

1 tbsp Madeira

1lb/450 g dried linguine pasta

1 tbsp olive oil

salt and pepper

1 Trim the fennel bulbs, then peel off and reserve the outer layer of each. Cut the bulbs into quarters and put them in a large pan with the stock and the reserved outer layers. Bring to a boil, lower the heat, and simmer for 5 minutes.

COOK'S TIP

Fennel will keep in the salad drawer of the refrigerator for 2–3 days, but it is best eaten as fresh as possible. Cut surfaces turn brown quickly, so do not prepare it too much in advance of cooking.

2 Using a slotted spoon, transfer the fennel to a large dish. Discard the outer layers of the fennel bulbs. Bring the vegetable stock to a boil and reduce by half. Set aside.

3 Melt the butter in a skillet. Add the bacon and shallots and cook over medium heat, stirring frequently, for 4 minutes. Add the flour, reduced stock, cream, and Madeira and cook, stirring constantly, for 3 minutes or until the sauce is smooth. Season to taste with salt and pepper and pour over the fennel.

4 Bring a large pan of lightly salted water to a boil. Add the pasta and oil, bring back to a boil, and cook for 8–10 minutes until tender, but still firm to the bite. Drain and transfer to a deep casserole.

5 Add the fennel and sauce and braise in a preheated oven, 350°F/180°C, for 20 minutes. Serve immediately.

Baked Fennel Gratinati

Fennel is a common ingredient in Italian cooking. In this dish its distinctive flavor is offset by the smooth Béchamel Sauce.

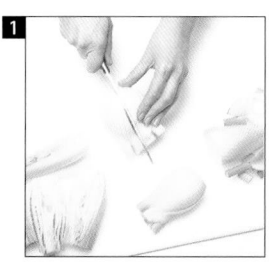
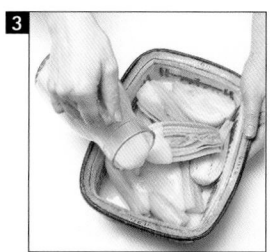

NUTRITIONAL INFORMATION

Calories	426	Sugars	.........9g
Protein	........13g	Fat	..........35g
Carbohydrate	...16g	Saturates	......19g

 5–10 mins   45 mins

SERVES 4

I N G R E D I E N T S

4 fennel bulbs

2 tbsp butter

⅔ cup dry white wine

Béchamel Sauce (see page 6), enriched with 2 egg yolks

½ cup fresh white bread crumbs

3 tbsp freshly grated Parmesan cheese

salt and pepper

fennel fronds, to garnish

1 Remove any bruised or tough outer stalks of fennel and cut each bulb in half. Put into a pan of lightly salted boiling water and simmer for 20 minutes until tender, then drain.

2 Butter a casserole liberally and arrange the drained fennel in it.

3 Stir the wine into the Béchamel sauce and season with salt and pepper to taste. Pour over the fennel.

4 Sprinkle evenly with the bread crumbs and then the Parmesan.

5 Bake in a preheated oven, 400°F/ 200°C, for 20 minutes until the top is golden. Serve immediately, garnished with fennel fronds.

Rice & Peas

If you can get fresh peas—and willing helpers to shell them—do use them: you will need 2 lb 4 oz/1 kg. Add them to the pan with the stock.

NUTRITIONAL INFORMATION

Calories	....	.409
Protein	....	15g
Carbohydrate	...	38g

Sugars	....	.2g
Fat	....	.23g
Saturates	......	.12g

 10 mins   50 mins

SERVES 4

INGREDIENTS

1 tbsp olive oil

4 tbsp butter

2 oz/55 g pancetta or fatty
    bacon, chopped

1 small onion, chopped

6¼ cups hot chicken stock

1¾ cups risotto rice

3 tbsp chopped fresh parsley

2 cups fresh, frozen or canned
    baby peas

⅔ cup freshly grated Parmesan cheese

pepper

1 Heat the olive oil and half of the butter in a heavy pan. Add the pancetta or bacon and onion and cook over low heat, stirring occasionally, for 5 minutes until the onion is softened and translucent, but not browned.

2 Add the stock and fresh peas, if using, to the pan and bring to a boil. Stir in the rice and season to taste with pepper. Bring to a boil, lower the heat, and simmer, stirring occasionally, for about 20–30 minutes until the rice is tender.

3 Add the parsley and frozen or canned baby peas, if using, and cook for about 8 minutes until the peas are heated through. Stir in the remaining butter and the Parmesan.

4 Transfer to a warmed serving dish and serve immediately with freshly ground black pepper.

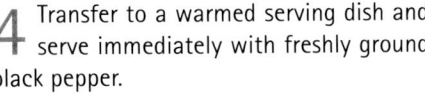

Filled Eggplants

Combined with tomatoes and melting mozzarella cheese, pasta makes a tasty filling for baked eggplant shells.

NUTRITIONAL INFORMATION

Calories . . . . . . .342 Sugars 6g
Protein . . . . .11g Fat 16g
Carbohydrate . . .40g Saturates 4g

 25 mins   55 mins

SERVES 4

I N G R E D I E N T S

2 cups dried penne or other short
  pasta shapes

4 tbsp olive oil, plus extra for brushing

2 eggplants

1 large onion, chopped

2 garlic cloves, crushed

14 oz/400 g canned chopped tomatoes

2 tsp dried oregano

2 oz/55 g mozzarella cheese, thinly sliced

⅓ cup freshly grated Parmesan cheese

5 tbsp dry bread crumbs

salt and pepper

salad greens, to serve

1 Bring a large pan of lightly salted water to a boil. Add the pasta and 1 tablespoon of the olive oil, bring back to a boil, and cook for 8–10 minutes or until the pasta is just tender, but still firm to the bite. Drain, return to the pan, cover, and keep warm.

2 Cut the eggplants in half lengthwise and score around the inside with a sharp knife, being careful not to pierce the shells. Scoop out the flesh with a spoon. Brush the insides of the shells with olive oil. Chop the flesh and set aside.

3 Heat the remaining oil in a skillet. Fry the onion over low heat for 5 minutes, until softened. Add the garlic and fry for 1 minute. Add the chopped eggplant and cook, stirring frequently, for 5 minutes. Add the tomatoes and oregano and season to taste with salt and pepper. Bring to a boil and simmer for 10 minutes until thickened. Remove the skillet from the heat and stir in the pasta.

4 Brush a cookie sheet with oil and arrange the eggplant shells in a single layer. Divide half of the tomato and pasta mixture among them. Sprinkle over the slices of mozzarella, then pile the remaining tomato and pasta mixture on top. Mix the Parmesan cheese and bread crumbs and sprinkle over the top, patting it lightly into the mixture.

5 Bake in a preheated oven, 400°C/ 200°C, for approximately 25 minutes or until the topping is golden brown. Serve hot with a selection of mixed fresh salad greens.

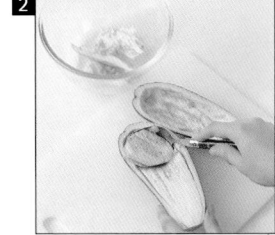

Ciabatta Rolls

Sandwiches are always a welcome snack, but can be mundane.
These crisp rolls filled with roasted bell peppers and cheese are irresistible.

NUTRITIONAL INFORMATION

Calories 328	Sugars 6g	
Protein 8g	Fat 19g	
Carbohydrate ...34g	Saturates 9g	

 15 mins   10 mins

SERVES 4

INGREDIENTS

4 ciabatta rolls

2 tbsp olive oil

1 garlic clove, crushed

FILLING

1 red bell pepper

1 green bell pepper

1 yellow bell pepper

4 radishes, sliced

1 bunch of watercress

½ cup cream cheese

1 Slice the ciabatta rolls in half. Heat the olive oil and garlic in a pan. Pour the garlic and oil mixture over the cut surfaces of the rolls and set aside.

2 Halve and deseed the bell peppers and place, skin side up, on a broiler rack. Cook under a preheated hot broiler for 8–10 minutes until just beginning to char. Remove the bell peppers from the broiler and place in a plastic bag. When cool enough to handle, peel and slice thinly.

3 Arrange the radish slices on 1 half of each roll with a few watercress leaves. Spoon the cream cheese on top. Pile the roasted bell peppers on top of the cream cheese and top with the other half of the roll. Serve immediately.

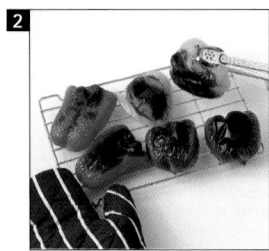

Pasta with Garlic & Broccoli

Broccoli coated in a garlic-flavored cream sauce, served on herb tagliatelle. Try sprinkling with toasted pine nuts to add extra crunch.

NUTRITIONAL INFORMATION

Calories	538	Sugars 4g
Protein	........23g	Fat 29g
Carbohydrate	...50g	Saturates 17g

 5 mins   5 mins

SERVES 4

INGREDIENTS

1 lb 2 oz/500 g broccoli

1⅓ cups garlic and herb
   cream cheese

4 tbsp milk

12 oz/350 g fresh herb tagliatelle

⅓ cup freshly grated
   Parmesan cheese

chopped fresh chives, to garnish

1 Cut the broccoli into even-size florets. Bring a pan of lightly salted water to a boil. Add the broccoli, bring back to a boil, and cook for 3 minutes, then drain thoroughly.

2 Put the soft cheese into a pan and heat gently, stirring constantly, until melted. Add the milk and stir over low heat until well combined.

3 Add the broccoli to the cheese mixture and stir to coat.

4 Meanwhile, bring a large pan of lightly salted water to a boil. Add the tagliatelle and bring back to a boil. Cook for 3–4 minutes until tender, but still firm to the bite.

5 Drain the tagliatelle thoroughly and divide among 4 warmed serving

plates. Spoon the broccoli and cheese sauce on top. Sprinkle with grated Parmesan cheese, garnish with chopped chives, and serve immediately.

COOK'S TIP

A herb flavored pasta goes particularly well with the broccoli sauce, but failing this, a tagliatelle verde or "paglia e fieno" (literally "straw and hay"—thin green and yellow noodles) will fill the bill.

Mixed Mushroom Patties

These patties are packed with creamy potato and a variety of mushrooms and will be loved by vegetarians and meat-eaters alike.

NUTRITIONAL INFORMATION

Calories	298	Sugars	.......0.8g
Protein	.........5g	Fat	..........22g
Carbohydrate	...22g	Saturates	.......5g

 20 mins   25 mins

SERVES 4

INGREDIENTS

1 lb 2 oz/500 g mealy potatoes, diced

2 tbsp butter

2 cups chopped mixed mushrooms

2 garlic cloves, crushed

1 small egg, beaten

1 tbsp chopped fresh chives, plus extra to garnish

flour, for dusting

vegetable oil, for frying

salt and pepper

salad, to serve

1 Cook the potatoes in a pan of lightly salted boiling water for 10 minutes or until cooked through.

2 Drain the potatoes well, mash with a potato masher or fork, and set aside.

3 Meanwhile, melt the butter in a skillet. Add the mushrooms and garlic and cook over medium heat, stirring constantly, for 5 minutes. Drain well.

4 Stir the mushrooms and garlic into the potatoes, together with the beaten egg and chives.

5 Divide the mixture equally into 4 portions and shape them into round patties. Toss them in the flour until the outsides of the patties are completely coated, shaking off any excess.

6 Heat the oil in a skillet. Add the mushroom patties and fry over medium heat for 10 minutes until they are golden brown, turning them over halfway through. Serve the cakes immediately, with a simple crisp salad.

COOK'S TIP

Prepare the patties in advance, cover, and set aside to chill in the refrigerator for up to 24 hours, if you wish.

Hash Browns

Hash Browns are a popular recipe of fried potato squares, often served as brunch. This recipe includes extra vegetables.

NUTRITIONAL INFORMATION

Calories	339	Sugars	........9g
Protein	........10g	Fat	..........21g
Carbohydrate	...29g	Saturates	.......7g

 20 mins 45 mins

SERVES 4

INGREDIENTS

1 lb 2 oz/500 g waxy potatoes

1 carrot, diced

1 celery stalk, diced

¾ cup diced white mushrooms

1 onion, diced

2 garlic cloves, crushed

¼ cup frozen peas, thawed

⅔ cup freshly grated Parmesan cheese

4 tbsp vegetable oil

2 tbsp butter

salt and pepper

SAUCE

1¼ cups sieved tomatoes

2 tbsp chopped fresh cilantro

1 tbsp Worcestershire sauce

½ tsp chili powder

2 tsp brown sugar

2 tsp mild mustard

5 tbsp vegetable stock

1 Cook the potatoes in a pan of lightly salted boiling water for 10 minutes. Drain and set aside to cool. Meanwhile, cook the carrot in lightly salted boiling water for 5 minutes.

2 When the potatoes are cool enough to handle, grate them with a coarse grater.

3 Drain the carrot and add it to the grated potatoes, with the celery, mushrooms, onion, garlic, peas, and cheese. Season to taste with salt and pepper.

4 Put all of the sauce ingredients in a small pan and bring to a boil. Reduce the heat to low and simmer for 15 minutes.

5 Divide the potato mixture into 8 portions of equal size and shape into flattened rectangles with your hands.

6 Heat the oil and butter in a skillet and cook the hash browns in batches over low heat for 4–5 minutes on each side, until crisp and golden brown.

7 Transfer the hash browns to a serving plate and serve immediately with the tomato sauce.

Spanish Potato Bake

In this variation of a traditional Spanish dish, *huevos* (eggs) are cooked on top of a spicy sausage, tomato, and potato mixture.

NUTRITIONAL INFORMATION

Calories 443	Sugars 7g	
Protein 21g	Fat 25g	
Carbohydrate ...36g	Saturates 8g	

 5 mins   🕐 35 mins

SERVES 4

INGREDIENTS

1 lb 8 oz/675 g waxy potatoes, diced

3 tbsp olive oil

1 onion, halved and sliced

2 garlic cloves, crushed

14 oz/400 g canned plum
  tomatoes, chopped

3 oz/85 g chorizo sausage, sliced

1 green bell pepper, deseeded and cut
  into strips

½ tsp paprika

¼ cup pitted black olives, halved

8 eggs

1 tbsp chopped fresh parsley

salt and pepper

crusty bread, to serve

1 Cook the diced potatoes in a pan of boiling water for 10 minutes or until softened. Drain and set aside.

2 Heat the olive oil in a large, heavy skillet, add the onion and garlic, and cook over low heat, stirring occasionally, for 2–3 minutes until the onion has softened.

3 Add the tomatoes and cook over low heat for about 10 minutes until the mixture has reduced slightly.

4 Stir the potatoes into the skillet with the chorizo, green bell pepper, paprika, and olives. Cook for 5 minutes, stirring constantly. Transfer the mixture to a shallow casserole.

5 Make 8 small hollows in the top of the mixture and break an egg into each hollow.

6 Cook in a preheated oven, 425°F, for 5–6 minutes or until the eggs are just cooked. Sprinkle with parsley and serve with crusty bread.

VARIATION

Add a little extra spice to the dish by incorporating 1 teaspoon chili powder in step 4, if desired.

  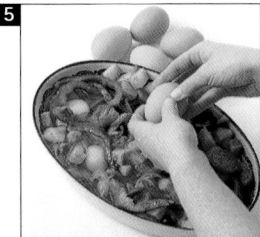

Tomato & Sausage Pan-Fry

This simple dish is delicious as a main meal. Choose good sausages flavored with herbs or use flavored sausages, such as mustard or leek.

NUTRITIONAL INFORMATION

Calories ....458 Sugars 11g
Protein ....21g Fat 25g
Carbohydrate ...34g Saturates 8g

 5 mins   30 mins

SERVES 4

INGREDIENTS

1 lb 5 oz/600 g potatoes, sliced

1 tbsp vegetable oil

8 flavored sausages

1 red onion, cut into 8 wedges

1 tbsp tomato paste

⅔ cup red wine

⅔ cup sieved tomatoes

2 large tomatoes, each cut into 8 wedges

6 oz/175 g broccoli florets, blanched

2 tbsp chopped fresh basil

salt and pepper

shredded fresh basil, to garnish

1 Cook the sliced potatoes in a pan of boiling water for 7 minutes. Drain thoroughly and set aside.

2 Meanwhile, heat the vegetable oil in a large, heavy skillet. Add the sausages and cook over medium-low heat for about 5 minutes, turning them frequently to ensure that they are browned on all sides.

3 Add the onion wedges to the skillet and cook, stirring occasionally, for a further 5 minutes.

4 Stir in the tomato paste, red wine, and passata and mix well. Add the tomato wedges, broccoli florets, and chopped basil and mix gently.

5 Add the parboiled potato slices to the pan. Cook the mixture for about 10 minutes or until the sausages are completely cooked through. Season to taste with salt and pepper.

6 Transfer to a warmed serving dish, garnish the pan-fry with fresh shredded basil, and serve hot.

COOK'S TIP
Omit the sieved tomatoes from this recipe and use canned plum tomatoes or chopped tomatoes instead.

Chicken & Banana Patties

Even plain potato patties are a great favorite. In this recipe, the potatoes are combined with ground chicken and mashed banana.

NUTRITIONAL INFORMATION

Calories	439	Sugars	........11g
Protein	........22g	Fat	..........23g
Carbohydrate	...39g	Saturates	......10g

5–10 mins   25–30 mins

SERVES 4

INGREDIENTS

1 lb/450 g mealy potatoes, diced

8 oz/225 g ground chicken

1 large banana

2 tbsp all-purpose flour

1 tsp lemon juice

1 onion, finely chopped

2 tbsp chopped fresh sage

2 tbsp butter

2 tbsp vegetable oil

⅔ cup light cream

⅔ cup chicken stock

salt and pepper

fresh sage leaves, to garnish

1 Cook the diced potatoes in a pan of boiling water for about 10 minutes until tender. Drain well and mash until smooth. Stir in the ground chicken.

2 Mash the banana and add it to the potato with the flour, lemon juice, onion, and half of the chopped sage. Season to taste with salt and pepper and stir the mixture together.

3 Divide the mixture into 8 equal portions. With lightly floured hands, shape each portion into a round patty.

4 Heat the butter and oil in a skillet, add the chicken and banana patties and cook for 12–15 minutes or until cooked through, turning once. Remove from the skillet and keep warm.

5 Stir the cream and stock into the skillet with the remaining chopped sage. Cook over low heat for 2–3 minutes.

6 Arrange the patties on a warmed serving plate, garnish with fresh sage leaves, and serve immediately with the cream and sage sauce.

COOK'S TIP

Do not boil the sauce once the cream has been added, as it will curdle. Cook it gently over very low heat.

Penne & Butternut Squash

The creamy, nutty flavor of squash complements the "al dente" texture of the pasta. This recipe has been adapted for the microwave oven.

NUTRITIONAL INFORMATION

Calories 499   Sugars 4g
Protein . . . . .20g   Fat 26g
Carbohydrate . . .49g   Saturates 13g

 15 mins   30 mins

SERVES 4

INGREDIENTS

2 tbsp olive oil

1 garlic clove, crushed

1 cup fresh white bread crumbs

1 lb 2 oz/500 g peeled and deseeded
   butternut squash

8 tbsp water

1 lb 2 oz/500 g fresh penne, or other
   pasta shapes

1 tbsp butter

1 onion, sliced

4 oz/115 g ham, cut into strips

scant 1 cup light cream

½ cup grated Cheddar cheese

2 tbsp chopped fresh parsley

salt and pepper

1 Combine the olive oil, garlic, and bread crumbs and spread out on a large plate. Cook on HIGH power for 4–5 minutes, stirring every minute, until crisp and beginning to brown. Remove from the microwave and set aside.

2 Dice the squash. Place in a large bowl with half of the water. Cover and cook on HIGH power for 8–9 minutes, stirring occasionally. Stand for 2 minutes.

3 Place the pasta in a large bowl, add a little salt, and pour over boiling water to cover by 1 inch/2.5 cm. Cover and cook on HIGH power for 5 minutes, stirring once, until the pasta is just tender, but still firm to the bite. Stand, covered, for 1 minute before draining.

4 Place the butter and onion in a large bowl. Cover and cook on HIGH power for 3 minutes.

5 Coarsely mash the squash, using a fork. Add to the onion with the pasta, ham, cream, cheese, parsley and remaining water. Season generously and mix well.

Cover and cook on HIGH power for 4 minutes until heated through.

6 Serve the pasta sprinkled with the crisp garlic crumbs.

COOK'S TIP

If the squash weighs more than is needed for this recipe, blanch the excess for 3–4 minutes on HIGH power in a covered bowl with a little water. Drain, cool, and place in a freezer bag. Store in the freezer for up to 3 months.

Pasta & Chili Tomatoes

The pappardelle and vegetables are tossed in a delicious chili and tomato sauce for a quick and economical meal.

NUTRITIONAL INFORMATION

Calories	353	Sugars	.........7g
Protein	........10g	Fat	..........24g
Carbohydrate	...26g	Saturates	.......4g

 15 mins   20 mins

SERVES 4

INGREDIENTS

10 oz/280 g dried pappardelle

3 tbsp peanut oil

2 garlic cloves, crushed

2 shallots, sliced

8 oz/225 g green beans, sliced

3½ oz/100 g cherry tomatoes, halved

1 tsp chili flakes

4 tbsp crunchy peanut butter

⅔ cup coconut milk

1 tbsp tomato paste

sliced scallions, to garnish

1 Bring a large pan of lightly salted water to a boil. Add the pappardelle, bring back to a boil, and cook for 8–10 minutes until tender, but still firm to the bite. Drain thoroughly and set aside.

2 Meanwhile, heat the peanut oil in a large, heavy skillet or preheated wok. Add the garlic and shallots and stir-fry for 1 minute.

3 Add the green beans and drained pasta to the skillet or wok and stir-fry for 5 minutes. Add the cherry tomatoes and mix well.

4 Combine the chili flakes, peanut butter, coconut milk, and tomato paste. Pour the chili mixture into the skillet or wok, toss well to combine, and heat through.

5 Transfer to warm serving dishes and garnish with scallion slices. Serve immediately.

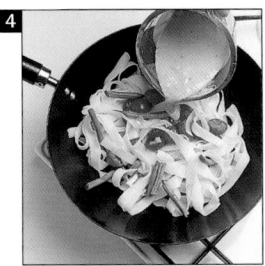

VARIATION

Add slices of chicken or beef to the recipe and stir-fry with the beans and pasta in step 3 for a more substantial main meal.

Filled Pitas

Pita breads are warmed over hot coals, then split and filled with a Greek salad tossed in a fragrant rosemary dressing.

NUTRITIONAL INFORMATION

Calories	456	Sugars	........4g
Protein	........13g	Fat	..........25g
Carbohydrate	...49g	Saturates	.......7g

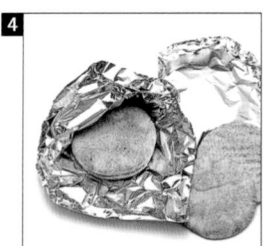

 15 mins   10 mins

SERVES 4

I N G R E D I E N T S

½ iceberg lettuce, roughly chopped

2 large tomatoes, cut into wedges

3 inch/7.5 cm piece of cucumber, cut into chunks

¼ cup pitted black olives

4 oz/115 g feta cheese

4 pitas

D R E S S I N G

6 tbsp olive oil

3 tbsp red wine vinegar

1 tbsp crushed rosemary

½ tsp superfine sugar

salt and pepper

1 To make the salad, combine the lettuce, tomatoes, cucumber, and black olives.

2 Cut the feta cheese into chunks and add to the salad. Toss gently.

3 To make the dressing, whisk together the olive oil, red wine vinegar, rosemary, and sugar. Season to taste with salt and pepper. Place in a small pan or heatproof bowl and heat very gently or place on the side of a barbecue to warm through gently.

4 Wrap the individual pitas tightly in foil and place on a hot barbecue for 2–3 minutes, turning once, to warm through.

5 Unwrap the pitas and split them open. Fill with the Greek salad mixture and drizzle over the warm dressing. Serve immediately.

COOK'S TIP
Substitute different herbs for the rosemary—either oregano or basil would make a delicious alternative. Pack plenty of the salad into the pitas—they taste much better when they are full to bursting.

Thai-Style Crab Sandwich

A hearty, open sandwich, topped with a classic flavor combination—
crab with avocado and ginger. Perfect for a light summer lunch.

NUTRITIONAL INFORMATION

Calories 768	Sugars 3g	
Protein 26g	Fat 49g	
Carbohydrate ...58g	Saturates 8g	

 8 mins   0 mins

SERVES 2

INGREDIENTS

2 tbsp lime juice

¾ inch/2 cm piece fresh ginger root, grated

¾ inch/2 cm piece of lemongrass,
   finely chopped

5 tbsp mayonnaise

2 large slices crusty bread

1 ripe avocado

5½ oz/150 g cooked crab meat

pepper

fresh cilantro sprigs, to garnish

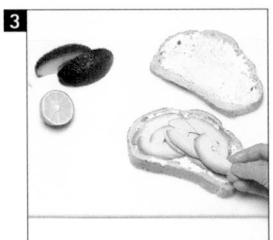

COOK'S TIP

To make lime-and-ginger
mayonnaise, process 2 egg yolks,
1 tbsp lime juice and ½ tsp grated
ginger root in a blender. With the
motor running, gradually add 1¼ cups
olive oil, drop by drop, until the
mixture is thick and smooth. Season
to taste with salt and pepper.

1 Mix half the lime juice with the
ginger and lemongrass. Add the
mayonnaise and mix well.

2 Spread 1 tablespoon of mayonnaise
smoothly over each slice of bread.

3 Halve the avocado and remove the
pit. Peel and slice the flesh thinly,
then arrange the slices on the bread.
Sprinkle with lime juice.

4 Spoon the crab meat over the
avocado, then add any remaining lime
juice. Spoon over the remaining
mayonnaise, season with freshly ground
black pepper, top with a cilantro sprig, and
serve immediately.

Stuffed Eggs

These savory stuffed eggs make a good picnic dish or they can be popped into a lunch bag for an unusual treat.

NUTRITIONAL INFORMATION

Calories 337	Sugars 2g	
Protein 24g	Fat 28g	
Carbohydrate ...22g	Saturates 5g	

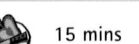 15 mins   15 mins

SERVES 4

I N G R E D I E N T S

4 large eggs

3½ oz/100 g ground pork

6 oz175 g can white crab meat, drained

1 garlic clove, crushed

1 tsp Thai fish sauce

½ tsp lemongrass, ground

1 tbsp chopped fresh cilantro

1 tbsp dry shredded coconut

generous ¾ cup all-purpose flour

about ⅔ cup coconut milk

sunflower oil, for deep-frying

salt and pepper

salad greens, to serve

cucumber flower, to garnish

1 Place the eggs in a pan of simmering water and bring to a boil, then simmer for 10 minutes. Drain the eggs, crack the shells, and cool under cold running water. Peel off the shells.

2 Cut the eggs lengthwise down the middle and scoop out the yolks. Place the yolks in a bowl with the pork, crab meat, garlic, fish sauce, lemongrass, cilantro, and coconut. Season with salt and pepper and mix the ingredients together thoroughly.

3 Divide the mixture into 8 equal portions, then fill each of the egg whites with the mixture, pressing together with your hands to form the shape of a whole egg.

4 Whisk together the flour and enough coconut milk to make a thick coating batter, then season with salt and pepper. Heat a 2 inch/5 cm depth of oil in a large pan to 375°F/190°C or until a cube of day-old bread browns in 30 seconds. Dip each egg into the coconut batter, then shake off the excess.

5 Fry the eggs, in 2 batches, for about 5 minutes, turning occasionally, until golden brown. Remove with a slotted spoon and drain on paper towels. Serve warm or cold with salad greens garnished with cucumber flowers.

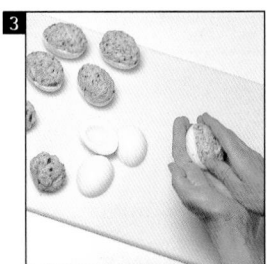

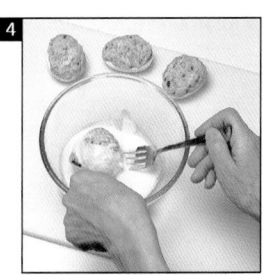

Thai Stuffed Omelet

Served with a colorful, crisp salad, this makes a tasty light lunch or supper dish and, on its own, could be served as a substantial appetizer.

NUTRITIONAL INFORMATION

Calories 250	Sugars 1g	
Protein 21g	Fat 18g	
Carbohydrate 2g	Saturates 4g	

5–10 mins   25 mins

SERVES 4

INGREDIENTS

2 garlic cloves, chopped

4 black peppercorns

4 fresh cilantro sprigs

2 tbsp vegetable oil

7 oz/200 g ground pork

2 scallions, chopped

1 large, firm tomato, chopped

6 large eggs

1 tbsp Thai fish sauce

½ tsp ground turmeric

mixed salad greens, to serve

1 Place the garlic, peppercorns, and cilantro in a mortar and crush with a pestle to a smooth paste.

COOK'S TIP

If you prefer, spread half the pork mixture evenly over one omelette, then place a second omelette on top, without folding. Cut into slim wedges to serve.

2 Heat 1 tablespoon of the vegetable oil in a wok over medium heat. Add the paste and fry for 1–2 minutes until it just changes color.

3 Stir in the pork and stir-fry until it is lightly browned. Add the scallions and tomato and stir-fry for a further minute, then remove the wok from the heat.

4 Heat the remaining oil in a small, heavy skillet. Beat the eggs with the fish sauce and turmeric, then pour a quarter of the egg mixture into the pan.

As the mixture begins to set, stir lightly to ensure that all the egg is cooked.

5 Spoon a quarter of the pork mixture down the center of the omelet, then fold the sides inward, enclosing the filling. Make and fill 3 more omelets with the remaining eggs and pork mixture.

6 Slide the omelets onto a warm serving plate and serve immediately with the mixed salad greens.

Sesame Noodles with Shrimp

Delicately scented with sesame oil and seeds and fresh cilantro, these noodles make an unusual lunch or supper dish.

NUTRITIONAL INFORMATION

Calories ....430 Sugars 2g
Protein ....23g Fat 15g
Carbohydrate ...56g Saturates 3g

5 mins   10 mins

SERVES 4

INGREDIENTS

1 garlic clove, chopped

1 scallion, chopped

1 small fresh red chile, deseeded and sliced

1 tbsp chopped fresh cilantro

10½ oz/300 g fine egg noodles

2 tbsp vegetable oil

2 tsp sesame oil

1 tsp shrimp paste

2 cups peeled raw shrimp

2 tbsp lime juice

2 tbsp Thai fish sauce

1 tsp sesame seeds, toasted

1 Place the garlic, onion, chile, and cilantro into a mortar and grind with a pestle to a smooth paste.

2 Drop the noodles into a pan of boiling water and bring back to a boil, then simmer for 4 minutes or according to the packet instructions.

3 Meanwhile, heat the vegetable and sesame oils in a skillet or wok and stir in the shrimp paste and ground cilantro mixture. Stir over medium heat for about 1 minute.

4 Stir in the shrimp and stir-fry for 2 minutes. Stir in the lime juice and fish sauce and cook for a further minute.

5 Drain the noodles and toss them into the skillet or wok. Sprinkle with the sesame seeds and serve immediately.

COOK'S TIP

The roots of cilantro are widely used in Thai cooking, so if you can buy fresh cilantro with the root attached, the whole plant can be used in this dish for maximum flavor. If not, just use the stalks and leaves.

Hot & Sour Noodles

This simple, fast-food dish is sold from street food stalls in Thailand, with many and varied additions of meat and vegetables.

NUTRITIONAL INFORMATION

Calories	337	Sugars	.........1g
Protein	........10g	Fat	...........11g
Carbohydrate	...53g	Saturates	.......1g

 5 mins ⊘ 8 mins

SERVES 4

INGREDIENTS

9 oz/250 g dried medium egg noodles

1 tbsp sesame oil

1 tbsp chili oil

1 garlic clove, crushed

2 scallions, finely chopped

scant 1 cup sliced white mushrooms

1½ oz/40 g dried Chinese black mushrooms, soaked, drained, and sliced

2 tbsp lime juice

3 tbsp light soy sauce

1 tsp sugar

shredded Napa cabbage, to serve

TO GARNISH

2 tbsp chopped fresh cilantro

2 tbsp chopped, toasted peanuts

COOK'S TIP

Thai chili oil is very hot, so if you want a milder flavor, use vegetable oil for the initial cooking instead, then add a final drizzle of chili oil just for seasoning.

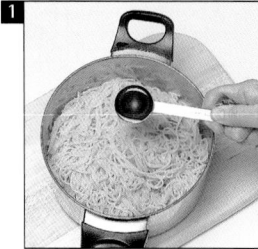

1 Cook the noodles in a large pan of boiling water for 3–4 minutes or according to the package instructions. Drain well, return to the pan, toss with the sesame oil, and set aside.

2 Heat the chili oil in a large skillet or wok and quickly stir-fry the garlic, onions, and white mushrooms for 2 minutes until just softened.

3 Add the black mushrooms, lime juice, soy sauce, and sugar and continue stir-frying until boiling. Add the noodles and toss to mix.

4 Make a bed of shredded Napa cabbage on a serving platter and spoon the noodle mixture on top. Garnish with the fresh cilantro and chopped peanuts and serve immediately.

Beancurd with Chili Sauce

Tempting golden cubes of fried beancurd, with colorful fresh carrot and bell peppers, combine with a warm ginger sauce to make an unusual dish.

NUTRITIONAL INFORMATION

Calories	149	Sugars	.........9g
Protein	.........8g	Fat	...........9g
Carbohydrate	...10g	Saturates	.......1g

 10 mins 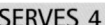 5 mins

SERVES 4

I N G R E D I E N T S

10½ oz/300 g firm beancurd

2 tbsp vegetable oil

1 garlic clove, sliced

1 carrot, cut into batons

½ green bell pepper, deseeded and cut into batons

1 fresh red bird-eye chile, deseeded and finely chopped

2 tbsp soy sauce

1 tbsp lime juice

1 tbsp Thai fish sauce

1 tbsp soft light brown sugar

pickled garlic slices, to serve (optional)

1 Drain the beancurd and pat dry with paper towels. Using a sharp knife, cut into ¾ inch/2 cm cubes.

2 Heat the oil in a wok. Add the garlic and stir-fry over medium heat for 1 minute. Remove the garlic with a slotted spoon and add the beancurd, then fry quickly until well-browned, turning gently to brown on all sides.

3 Lift out the beancurd with a slotted spoon, drain well, and keep hot. Stir the carrot and green bell pepper batons into the wok and stir-fry for 1 minute.

4 Spoon the carrot and bell peppers onto a warmed serving dish and pile the beancurd on top.

5 Mix together the chili, soy sauce, lime juice, fish sauce, and sugar, stirring until the sugar is dissolved.

6 Spoon the sauce over the beancurd and serve immediately topped with slices of pickled garlic, if you like.

COOK'S TIP

Make sure to buy firm fresh beancurd for this dish—the softer "silken" type is more like junket in texture and not firm enough to hold its shape well during frying. It is better for adding to soups.

Side Dishes

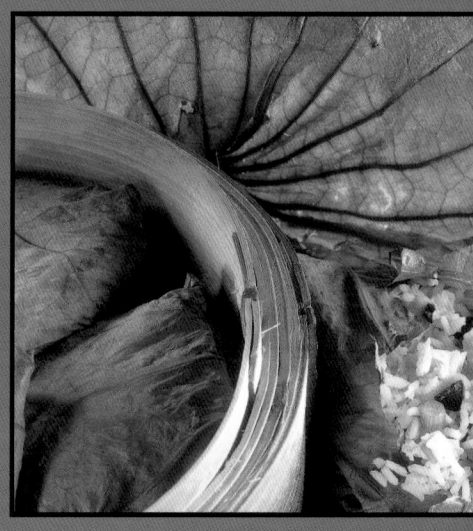

A clever choice of side dishes can turn an ordinary meal into a special occasion. Many of the recipes in this chapter, such as Thai Fragrant Coconut Rice and Vegetables with Vermouth, are quick and easy to prepare, yet will add a note of distinction to any meal. There can be few things more appetizing than homemade bread and rolls. This chapter includes recipes from around the world—Herb Focaccia from Italy, Peshwari Nan from India, and Irish Soda Bread.

Salsas, chutneys, dhals, and raitas also feature to add that important finishing touch to family suppers and dinner parties alike.

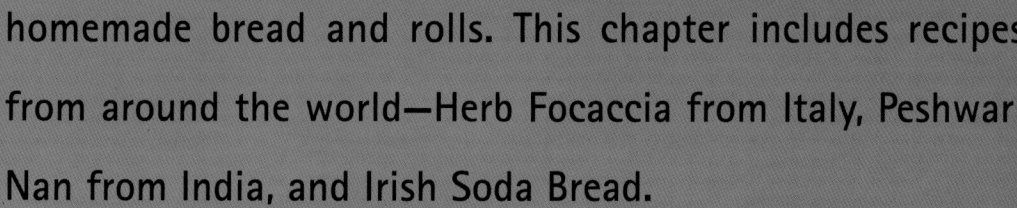

Baked Fennel

Fennel is a very versatile vegetable, which is good cooked or used raw in salads. It is an especially popular ingredient in many Italian dishes.

NUTRITIONAL INFORMATION

Calories 111	Sugars 6g
Protein 7g	Fat 7g
Carbohydrate 7g	Saturates 3g

10 mins   35 mins

SERVES 4

INGREDIENTS

2 fennel bulbs

2 celery stalks, cut into 3 inch/
   7.5 cm pieces

6 sun-dried tomatoes, halved

scant 1 cup sieved tomatoes

2 tsp dried oregano

⅔ cup freshly grated Parmesan cheese

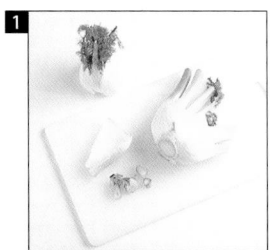  

1 Using a sharp knife, trim the fennel, discarding any tough outer leaves, and cut the bulb into quarters.

2 Bring a large pan of water to the boil, add the fennel and celery and cook for 8–10 minutes or until just tender. Remove with a draining spoon and drain.

3 Place the fennel pieces, celery and sun-dried tomatoes in a large ovenproof dish.

4 Mix the passata and oregano and pour the mixture over the fennel.

5 Sprinkle the surface evenly with the Parmesan cheese and bake in a preheated oven, 375°F/190°C, for 20 minutes or until hot. Serve as a starter with fresh crusty bread or as a vegetable side dish.

Potatoes, Olives & Anchovies

This side dish makes a delicious accompaniment for broiled fish or for lamb chops. The fennel adds a subtle anise flavor.

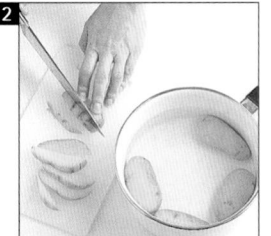

NUTRITIONAL INFORMATION

Calories	202	Sugars 2g
Protein	. . . . .7g	Fat 12g
Carbohydrate	. . .19g	Saturates 1g

 10 mins   30 mins

SERVES 4

I N G R E D I E N T S

1 lb/450 g baby new potatoes, scrubbed

¾ cup mixed olives

8 canned anchovy fillets, drained and chopped

2 tbsp olive oil

2 fennel bulbs, trimmed and sliced

2 fresh rosemary sprigs, stalks removed

salt

1 Bring a large pan of lightly salted water to a boil. Add the potatoes, bring back to a boil, and simmer over medium heat for 8–10 minutes or until tender. Remove the potatoes from the pan using a slotted spoon and set aside to cool slightly.

2 Once the potatoes are cool enough to handle, cut them into wedges, using a sharp knife.

3 Pit the mixed olives with a cherry pitter or small, sharp knife and cut them in half.

4 Using a sharp knife, chop the anchovy fillets into thinner strips.

5 Heat the olive oil in a large, heavy skillet. Add the potato wedges, sliced fennel, and rosemary. Cook over medium heat, stirring occasionally, for 7–8 minutes or until the potatoes are golden.

6 Stir in the olives and anchovies and cook for 1 minute or until completely warmed through.

7 Transfer the potato mixture to warmed serving plates and serve.

COOK'S TIP

Fresh rosemary is a particular favorite with Italians, but you can experiment with your favorite herbs in this recipe, if you prefer.

Coconut Rice with Lentils

Rice and green lentils are cooked with coconut, lemongrass, and curry leaves. This recipe will also serve two people as an entrée.

NUTRITIONAL INFORMATION

Calories 511	Sugars 3g	
Protein 12g	Fat 24g	
Carbohydrate . . .67g	Saturates 15g	

5 mins

50 mins

SERVES 4

INGREDIENTS

⅓ cup green lentils

1¼ cups long grain rice

2 tbsp vegetable oil

1 onion, sliced

2 garlic cloves, crushed

3 curry leaves

1 lemon grass stalk, chopped or grated rind of ½ lemon

1 fresh green chile, deseeded and chopped

½ tsp cumin seeds

1½ tsp salt

3 oz/85 g creamed coconut

2½ cups hot water

2 tbsp chopped fresh cilantro

TO GARNISH

shredded radishes

shredded cucumber

1 Wash the lentils and place in a pan. Cover with cold water, bring to a boil and boil rapidly for 10 minutes.

2 Wash the rice thoroughly and drain well. Set aside until required.

3 Heat the vegetable oil in a large pan with a tight-fitting lid. Add the onion and cook over medium heat, stirring occasionally, for 3–4 minutes. Stir in the garlic, curry leaves, lemongrass or lemon rind, chile, cumin seeds, and salt.

4 Drain the lentils and rinse them. Add to the onion and spices with the rice and mix well.

5 Combine the creamed coconut with the hot water and stir until dissolved. Stir the coconut liquid into the rice mixture and bring to a boil. Lower the heat, cover, and simmer gently, undisturbed, for 15 minutes.

6 Without removing the lid, remove the pan from the heat and set aside for 10 minutes to allow the rice and lentils to finish cooking in their own steam.

7 Stir in the cilantro and remove and discard the curry leaves. Transfer to a warmed serving dish and serve garnished with the radishes and cucumber.

Vegetables in Coconut Milk

This is a deliciously crunchy way to prepare a mixture of raw vegetables and would be ideal as a buffet dish for a party.

NUTRITIONAL INFORMATION

Calories 201   Sugars 10g
Protein . . . . .9g   Fat 13g
Carbohydrate . . .13g   Saturates 3g

5 mins   5 mins

SERVES 4

I N G R E D I E N T S

1 fresh red chile, deseeded and chopped

1 tsp coriander seeds

1 tsp cumin seeds

2 garlic cloves, crushed

juice of 1 lime

generous 1 cup coconut milk

2 cups bean sprouts

4 oz/115 g white cabbage, shredded

1½ cups snow peas, trimmed

4 oz/115 g carrots, thinly sliced

4 oz/115 g cauliflower florets

3 tbsp peanut butter

grated or shaved coconut, to serve

1 Grind the chile, coriander and cumin seeds, garlic, and lime juice in a mortar with a pestle or in a food processor until a smooth paste.

2 Put the spice paste into a medium pan and heat gently for about 1 minute or until fragrant. Add the coconut milk and stir constantly until just about to boil.

3 Combine the bean sprouts, shredded white cabbage, snow peas, sliced carrots, and cauliflower florets in a large mixing bowl.

4 Stir the peanut butter into the coconut mixture until well blended and then pour into the bowl, stirring to coat the vegetables. Serve garnished with grated or shaved coconut.

COOK'S TIP
If you prefer, the cauliflower, carrots, and snow peas may be blanched first for less bite.

Steamed Lotus Rice

The fragrance of the lotus leaves penetrates the rice, giving it a unique taste. Lotus leaves can be bought from specialty Chinese stores.

NUTRITIONAL INFORMATION

Calories 163   Sugars 0.1g
Protein . . . . .5g   Fat 6g
Carbohydrate . . .2.1g   Saturates 1g

35 mins   40 mins

SERVES 4

INGREDIENTS

2 lotus leaves

4 Chinese dried mushrooms

scant 1 cup long grain rice

1 cinnamon stick

6 cardamom pods

4 cloves

1 tsp salt

2 eggs

1 tbsp vegetable oil

2 scallions, chopped

1 tbsp soy sauce

2 tbsp sherry

1 tsp sugar

1 tsp sesame oil

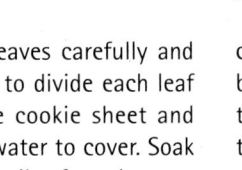

1 Unfold the lotus leaves carefully and cut along the fold to divide each leaf in half. Lay on a large cookie sheet and pour over enough hot water to cover. Soak for about 30 minutes until softened.

2 Meanwhile, place the mushrooms in a bowl, cover with warm water, and set aside to soak for 20–25 minutes.

3 Bring a pan of water to a boil. Add the rice with the cinnamon stick, cardamom pods, cloves, and salt, bring back to a boil, and cook for 10 minutes—the rice should be partially cooked. Drain thoroughly and remove the cinnamon stick. Place the rice in a bowl.

4 Beat the eggs lightly. Heat the oil in a wok and cook the eggs quickly, stirring until set. Remove and set aside.

5 Drain the mushrooms, squeezing out the excess water. Remove the tough stems and chop the mushrooms. Stir into the rice with the cooked egg, scallions, soy sauce, sherry or rice wine, sugar, and sesame oil.

6 Drain the lotus leaves and divide the rice into 4 portions. Place a portion in the center of each leaf and fold up to form a packet. Place in a steamer, cover, and steam over simmering water for 20 minutes. To serve, cut the tops of the lotus leaves open to expose the rice inside.

Chinese Fried Rice

It is essential that the rice is both cold and dry, with separate grains, in order to make this recipe properly.

NUTRITIONAL INFORMATION

Calories ....475 Sugars 3g
Protein ....16g Fat 16g
Carbohydrate ...72g Saturates 3g

5 mins   30 mins

SERVES 4

INGREDIENTS

3 cups water

½ tsp salt

1½ cups long grain rice

2 eggs

4 tsp cold water

3 tbsp sunflower oil

4 scallions, sliced diagonally

1 red, green or yellow bell pepper, deseeded and thinly sliced

3–4 lean bacon strips, rinded and cut into strips

3½ cups fresh bean sprouts

¼ cup frozen peas, thawed

2 tbsp soy sauce (optional)

salt and pepper

1 Pour the water into a wok with the salt and bring to a boil. Rinse the rice in a strainer under cold water until the water runs clear, drain well, and add to a boiling water. Stir well, then cover the wok tightly with the lid, and simmer gently for 12–13 minutes. (Don't remove the lid during cooking or the steam will escape and the rice will not be cooked.)

2 Remove the lid, stir the rice and spread out on a large plate or cookie sheet to cool and dry.

3 Beat each egg separately with salt and pepper and 2 teaspoons of cold water. Heat 1 tablespoon of the oil in the wok, pour in the first egg, swirl it around, and cook, undisturbed, until set. Remove to a board and cook the second egg. Cut the omelets into thin slices.

4 Add the remaining oil to the wok, add the scallions and bell pepper and stir-fry for 1–2 minutes. Add the bacon and continue to stir-fry for a further 1–2 minutes. Add the bean sprouts and peas and toss together thoroughly. Stir in the soy sauce, if using.

5 Add the rice and seasoning and stir-fry for about 1 minute, then add the strips of omelet, and continue to stir for about 2 minutes or until the rice is piping hot. Transfer to a warmed serving dish and serve immediately.

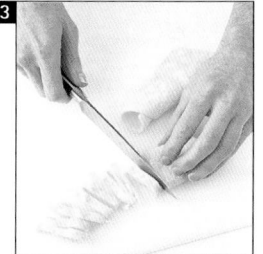

Curried Rice with Beancurd

Cooked rice is combined with marinated beancurd, vegetables and peanuts to make this deliciously rich curry. Serve as part of a Thai meal.

NUTRITIONAL INFORMATION

Calories 598	Sugars 2g
Protein 16g	Fat 25
Carbohydrate . . .81g	Saturates 4g

15 mins   15 mins

SERVES 4

INGREDIENTS

1 tsp coriander seeds

1 tsp cumin seeds

1 tsp ground cinnamon

1 tsp cloves

1 star anise

1 tsp cardamom seeds

1 tsp white peppercorns

4 tbsp sunflower oil

6 shallots, coarsely chopped

6 garlic cloves, coarsely chopped

2 inch/5 cm piece of lemongrass, sliced

4 fresh red chiles, deseeded and chopped

grated rind of 1 lime

1 tsp salt

9 oz/250 g marinated tofu, cut into 1 inch/ 2.5 cm cubes

4 oz/115 g green beans, cut into 1 inch/ 2.5 cm lengths

6 cups cooked rice

3 shallots, finely diced and deep-fried

1 scallion, finely chopped

2 tbsp chopped roasted peanuts

1 tbsp lime juice

1 To make the curry paste, grind the coriander and cumin seeds, cinnamon, cloves, star anise, cardamom seeds, and peppercorns in a mortar with a pestle or in a spice grinder or coffee grinder kept for the purpose.

2 Heat 1 tablespoon of the sunflower oil in a preheated wok until it is really hot. Add the chopped shallots, garlic, and lemongrass and cook over low heat for about 5 minutes until softened. Add the chiles and stir together with the dry spices. Stir in the lime rind and salt.

3 To make the curry, heat the remaining oil in a wok or large, heavy skillet. Add the beancurd and stir-fry gently over high heat for 2 minutes to seal. Stir in the curry paste and beans. Add the rice and stir over high heat for about 3 minutes.

4 Transfer to a warmed serving dish. Sprinkle with the deep-fried shallots, scallion, and peanuts. Squeeze over the lime juice and serve.

Toovar Dhal

Dried pulses and lentils can be cooked in similar ways, but the soaking and cooking times do vary, so check the pack for instructions.

NUTRITIONAL INFORMATION

Calories 195   Sugars 4g
Protein ....11g   Fat 5g
Carbohydrate ...28g   Saturates 3g

10 mins   50 mins

SERVES 6

INGREDIENTS

2 tbsp vegetable ghee

1 large onion, finely chopped

1 garlic clove, crushed

1 tbsp grated fresh ginger root

1 tbsp cumin seeds, ground

2 tsp coriander seeds, ground

1 dried red chile

1 inch/2.5 cm piece of cinnamon stick

1 tsp salt

½ tsp ground turmeric

1 cup split yellow peas, soaked in cold water for 1 hour and drained

14 oz/400 g can plum tomatoes

1¼ cups water

2 tsp garam masala

1 Heat the ghee in a large pan, add the onion, garlic, and ginger and fry for 3–4 minutes until the onion has softened slightly.

2 Add the cumin, coriander, chile, cinnamon, salt, and turmeric, then stir in the split peas until well mixed.

3 Add the tomatoes, with their can juices, breaking up the tomatoes slightly with the back of a spoon.

4 Add the water and bring to a boil. Reduce the heat to very low and simmer, uncovered, stirring occasionally, for about 40 minutes until most of the liquid has been absorbed and the split peas are tender. Skim the surface occasionally with a slotted spoon to remove any scum.

5 Gradually stir in the garam masala, tasting after each addition, until it is to your taste. Serve hot.

COOK'S TIP

Use a nonstick pan if you have one, because the mixture is quite dense and does stick to the base of the pan occasionally. If the dhal is overstirred, the split peas will break up and the dish will not have much texture or bite.

Brindil Bhaji

This is one of the most delicious—and easiest—of the
Indian bhaji dishes and has a wonderful sweet spicy flavor.

NUTRITIONAL INFORMATION

Calories . . . . .117 Sugars 8g
Protein . . . . .3g Fat 8g
Carbohydrate . . . .9g Saturates 5g

20 mins   20 mins

SERVES 4

INGREDIENTS

1 lb 2oz/500 g eggplants, sliced

2 tbsp vegetable ghee

1 onion, thinly sliced

2 garlic cloves, sliced

1 inch/2.5 cm piece of fresh root
ginger, grated

½ tsp ground turmeric

1 dried red chile

½ tsp salt

14 oz/400 g can tomatoes

1 tsp garam masala

fresh cilantro sprigs, to garnish

VARIATION
Other vegetables can be used instead
of the eggplants. Try zucchini,
potatoes, or bell peppers, or any
combination of these vegetables,
using the same sauce.

 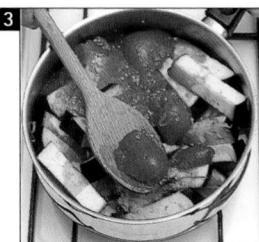

1 Cut the eggplant slices into finger-
width strips.

2 Heat the vegetable ghee in a heavy
pan. Add the onion and cook over
medium heat, stirring constantly, for 7–8
minutes, until very soft and just beginning
to color.

3 Add the garlic and eggplant strips,
increase the heat, and cook, stirring
constantly, for 2 minutes. Stir in the
ginger, turmeric, chile, salt, and tomatoes,
with their can juices. Use the back of a
wooden spoon to break up the tomatoes.
Lower the heat and simmer, uncovered, for
15–20 minutes, until the eggplants are
very soft.

4 Stir in the garam masala and simmer
for a further 4–5 minutes.

5 Transfer the brindil bhaji to a warmed
serving plate, garnish with fresh
cilantro sprigs, and serve immediately.

Beans in Tomato Sauce

Nothing could be simpler, quicker, or tastier than a delicious mix of beans cooked in a high-speed fresh tomato sauce.

NUTRITIONAL INFORMATION

Calories . . . . .221 Sugars 8g
Protein . . . . .12g Fat 7g
Carbohydrate . . .30g Saturates 1g

10 mins   15 mins

SERVES 4

INGREDIENTS

14 oz/400g canned cannellini beans

14 oz/400g canned borlotti beans

2 tbsp olive oil

1 celery stalk, thinly sliced

2 garlic cloves, chopped

6 oz/175 g baby onions, halved

1 lb /450 g tomatoes

3 oz/85 g arugula

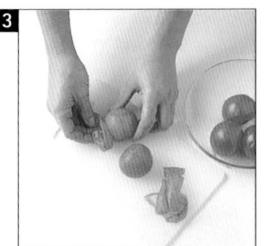

1 Drain both cans of beans and reserve 6 tablespoons of the liquid.

2 Heat the oil in a large pan. Add the celery, garlic, and onions and sauté for 5 minutes or until the onions are golden.

3 Cut a cross in the base of each tomato and plunge them into boiling water for 30 seconds until the skins split. Remove them with a draining spoon and set aside until cool enough to handle. Peel off the skins and chop the flesh. Add the tomatoes and the reserved bean liquid to the pan and cook for 5 minutes.

4 Add the beans to the pan and cook for another 3–4 minutes or until the beans are hot.

5 Stir in the arugula and allow to wilt slightly before serving.

COOK'S TIP

Another way to peel a tomato is to cut a cross in the base, push it onto a fork, and hold it over a gas flame, turning it slowly so that the skin heats evenly all over. The skin will start to bubble and split and should then slide off easily.

Chinese Omelet

This omelet contains chicken and shrimp. It is cooked as a whole omelet and then sliced for serving as part of a Chinese meal.

NUTRITIONAL INFORMATION

Calories	309	Sugars	.........0g
Protein	........34g	Fat	..........19g
Carbohydrate	...0.2g	Saturates	.......5g

 5 mins   5 mins

SERVES 4

INGREDIENTS

8 eggs

8 oz/225 g cooked chicken, shredded

12 jumbo shrimp, peeled and deveined

2 tbsp chopped fresh chives

2 tsp light soy sauce

dash of chili sauce

2 tbsp vegetable oil

1 Lightly beat the eggs in a large mixing bowl. Add the shredded chicken and jumbo shrimps, mixing well.

2 Stir in the chopped chives, light soy sauce, and chili sauce, mixing well to combine all the ingredients.

3 Heat the vegetable oil in a large heavy skillet over medium heat. Pour in the egg mixture, tilting the pan to coat the bottom evenly and completely.

4 Cook the eggs over medium heat, gently stirring the omelet with a fork to let the raw egg run underneath the set egg, until the surface is just set and the underside is a golden brown color.

5 When the omelet is set, slide it out of the pan with the aid of a spatula. Cut the Chinese omelet into squares or slices and serve immediately.

VARIATION

You could add extra flavor to the omelet by stirring in 3 tablespoons of finely chopped fresh cilantro or 1 teaspoon of sesame seeds with the chives in step 2.

Caraway Cabbage

This makes a delicious vegetable accompaniment to all types of food: it can also be served as a vegetarian main dish.

NUTRITIONAL INFORMATION

Calories	223	Sugars	........17g
Protein	.........6g	Fat	..........14g
Carbohydrate	...18g	Saturates	.......1g

5 mins

10 mins

SERVES 4

INGREDIENTS

1 lb 2oz/500 g white cabbage

1 tbsp sunflower oil

4 scallions, thinly sliced diagonally

6 tbsp raisins

½ cup walnut pieces or pecan nuts, coarsely chopped

5 tbsp milk or vegetable stock

1 tbsp caraway seeds

1–2 tbsp chopped fresh mint

salt and pepper

fresh mint sprigs, to garnish

1 Remove any tough outer leaves from the cabbage and cut out the stem, then shred the leaves very finely, either by hand or using the fine slicing blade on a food processor.

2 Heat the sunflower oil in a wok, swirling it around until it is really hot.

3 Add the scallions to the wok and stir-fry for 1–2 minutes.

4 Add the shredded cabbage and stir-fry for 3–4 minutes, keeping the cabbage moving all the time and stirring from the outside to the center of the wok to prevent it from going brown.

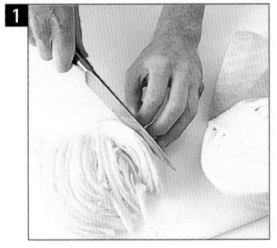

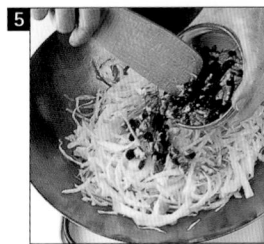

5 Add the raisins, walnuts or pecans, and milk or vegetable stock and cook, stirring constantly, for 3–4 minutes until the cabbage begins to soften slightly, but is still crisp.

6 Season to taste with salt and pepper, add the caraway seeds and 1 tablespoon of the chopped mint, and cook for a further 1 minute. Transfer to a warm serving dish and serve sprinkled with the remaining chopped mint and garnished with sprigs of fresh mint.

VARIATION

Red cabbage may be cooked in the same way in the wok, but substitute 2 tablespoons red or white wine vinegar and 3 tablespoons water for the milk and add 1 tablespoon brown sugar. Add a finely chopped dessert apple if liked.

Ginger & Orange Broccoli

Thinly sliced broccoli florets are lightly stir-fried and served in a delightful ginger and orange sauce.

NUTRITIONAL INFORMATION

Calories ....133 Sugars 6g
Protein ....9g Fat 7g
Carbohydrate ...10g Saturates 1g

5 mins   10 mins

SERVES 4

INGREDIENTS

1 lb 10 oz/750 g broccoli

2 thin slices fresh ginger root

2 garlic cloves

1 orange

2 tsp cornstarch

1 tbsp light soy sauce

½ tsp sugar

2 tbsp vegetable oil

1 Divide the broccoli into small florets. Peel the stems, using a vegetable peeler, and then cut the stems into thin slices, using a sharp knife.

2 Cut the ginger root into thin sticks and slice the garlic.

3 Peel 2 long strips of rind from the orange and cut into thin strips. Place the strips in a bowl, cover with cold water and set aside.

4 Squeeze the juice from the orange and mix with the cornstarch, light soy sauce, sugar, and 4 tablespoons water.

5 Heat the vegetable oil in a wok or large skillet. Add the sliced broccoli stem and stir-fry for 2 minutes.

6 Add the ginger slices, garlic, and broccoli florets and stir-fry for a further 3 minutes.

7 Stir the orange and soy sauce sauce mixture into the wok and cook, stirring constantly, until the sauce has thickened and coated the broccoli.

8 Drain the reserved orange rind and stir into the wok. Transfer to a serving dish and serve immediately.

VARIATION

This dish could be made with cauliflower, if you prefer, or a mixture of cauliflower and broccoli.

Marinated Fennel

Fennel has a wonderful anise flavor which is ideal for broiling or cooking on a barbecue. This marinated recipe is really delicious.

NUTRITIONAL INFORMATION

Calories 117   Sugars 3g
Protein . . . . 1g   Fat 11g
Carbohydrate . . . . 3g   Saturates 2g

1¼ hrs   10 mins

SERVES 4

I N G R E D I E N T S

2 fennel bulbs

1 red bell pepper, seeded and cut into
    large dice

1 lime, cut into 8 wedges

M A R I N A D E

2 tbsp lime juice

4 tbsp olive oil

2 garlic cloves, crushed

1 tsp wholegrain mustard

1 tbsp chopped thyme

fennel fronds, to garnish

crisp salad, to serve

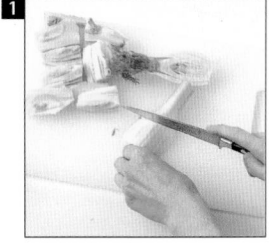  

1 Cut off and reserve the fennel fronds for the garnish. Cut each of the bulbs into 8 pieces and place in a shallow dish. Add the bell pepper and mix well.

2 To make the marinade, combine the lime juice, olive oil, garlic, mustard, and thyme. Pour the marinade over the fennel and bell pepper and toss to coat thoroughly. Cover with plastic wrap and set aside to marinate for 1 hour.

3 Thread the fennel and bell pepper onto wooden skewers with the lime wedges. Cook the kabobs under a preheated medium broiler, turning and basting frequently with the marinade, for about 10 minutes. Alternatively, cook on a medium hot barbecue, turning and basting frequently, for about 10 minutes.

4 Transfer the kabobs to serving plates, garnish with fennel fronds, and serve immediately with a crisp salad.

COOK'S TIP

Soak the skewers in cold water for 20 minutes before using to prevent them from burning during broiling or grilling. You could substitute 2 tablespoons orange juice for the lime juice and add 1 tbsp honey, if you prefer.

Ratatouille

A slow-cooked Provençal vegetable stew, this goes particularly well with roast lamb, but is also excellent with any broiled meat or poultry.

NUTRITIONAL INFORMATION

Calories	157	Sugars	........11g
Protein	.........4g	Fat	...........9g
Carbohydrate	...14g	Saturates	.......1g

40 mins   45 mins

SERVES 4–6

INGREDIENTS

1 large eggplant, about 10½ oz/300 g

5 tbsp olive oil

2 large onions, thinly sliced

2 large garlic cloves, crushed

4 zucchini, sliced

2 x 14 oz/400 g cans chopped tomatoes

1 tsp sugar

1 bouquet garni of 2 fresh thyme sprigs,
    2 large fresh parsley sprigs, 1 fresh basil
    sprig, and 1 bay leaf, tied in a 3 inch/
    7.5 cm piece of celery

salt and pepper

fresh basil leaves, to garnish

1 Coarsely chop the eggplant, then place in a colander. Sprinkle with salt and set aside for 30 minutes to drain. Rinse well under cold running water to remove all traces of the salt and pat dry with paper towels.

2 Heat the olive oil in a large heavy flameproof casserole over medium heat. Add the onions, lower the heat, and cook, stirring occasionally, for 10 minutes until softened and light golden brown.

3 Add the garlic and continue to fry for 2 minutes until the onions are very tender and lightly browned.

4 Add the eggplant, zucchini, tomatoes, with their can juices, sugar, and bouquet garni. Season with salt and pepper to taste. Bring to a boil, then lower the heat to very low, cover, and simmer for 30 minutes.

5 Taste and adjust the seasoning if necessary. Remove and discard the bouquet garni. Garnish the vegetable stew with basil leaves and serve immediately.

COOK'S TIP

This is equally good served hot, at room temperature or chilled. To make a vegetarian meal, serve it over cooked couscous or with tabbouleh.

Sweet & Sour Zucchini

This versatile dish has a distinctly Middle Eastern flavor and, like many Mediterranean dishes, is well balanced and healthy.

NUTRITIONAL INFORMATION

Calories	90	Sugars	.........5g
Protein	.........3g	Fat	..........4g
Carbohydrate	....5g	Saturates	.......1g

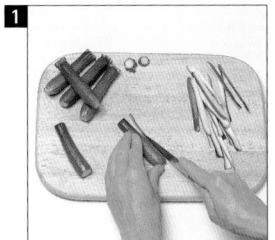

15 mins   25–30 mins

SERVES 4–6

INGREDIENTS

1 lb 2oz/500 g zucchini

3 tbsp olive oil

1 large garlic clove, finely chopped

3 tbsp white wine vinegar

3 tbsp water

6–8 anchovy fillets, canned or salted

3 tbsp pine nuts

3 tbsp raisins

salt and pepper

fresh flat leaf parsley sprigs, to garnish

1 Cut the zucchini into long, thin strips. Heat the olive oil in a large, heavy skillet over medium heat. Add the garlic and then cook, stirring constantly, for about 2 minutes.

2 Add the zucchini and cook, stirring frequently, until they just start to turn brown. Add the vinegar and water. Lower the heat and simmer, stirring frequently, for 10 minutes.

3 Meanwhile, drain the anchovies, if canned, or rinse if they are salted. Coarsely chop, then use the back of a wooden spoon to mash them to a paste.

4 Stir the anchovies, pine nuts, and raisins into the pan. Increase the heat and stir until the zucchini are coated in a thin sauce and are tender. Taste and adjust the seasoning, remembering that the anchovies are very salty.

5 Either serve immediately or set aside to cool completely and then serve at room temperature. To serve, garnish with fresh parsley sprigs.

VARIATION
Replace the raisins with golden raisins. Add a little grated lemon or orange rind for added zing.

Braised Fennel

So important in Mediterranean cooking, fennel is often braised and served as a vegetable accompaniment to meat, poultry, or fish dishes.

NUTRITIONAL INFORMATION

Calories ....149 Sugars 2g
Protein ....6g Fat 13g
Carbohydrate ....2g Saturates 7g

 10 mins   45 mins

SERVES 4–6

I N G R E D I E N T S

2 lemon slices

3 fennel bulbs

4½ tsp olive oil

3 tbsp butter

4 fresh thyme sprigs or ½ tbsp dried thyme

¾ cup chicken or vegetable stock

1 cup freshly grated Parmesan cheese

pepper

COOK'S TIP

This is an ideal way to serve older fennel bulbs, but will not improve any that have been stored too long and dried out.

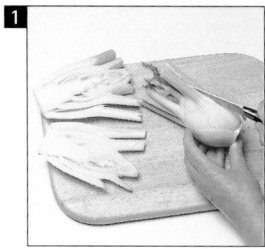  

1 Bring a large pan of water to a boil and add the lemon slices. Trim the fennel bulbs and slice each of them lengthwise. Add them to the pan, bring the water back to a boil, and simmer the fennel for about 8 minutes until almost tender. Drain well.

2 Put the oil and butter in a flameproof casserole and melt over medium heat. Swirl the melted mixture around so that the bottom and sides of the casserole are well coated.

3 Add the fennel slices and stir until coated. Add the thyme and season with pepper to taste. Pour in the stock and sprinkle the cheese over the top.

4 Bake in a preheated oven, 400°F/ 200°C for 25–30 minutes until the fennel has absorbed the stock and is tender and the cheese has melted and become golden brown. Serve immediately.

Vegetables à la Grecque

"A la Grecque" is the French term for cooked vegetables left to cool in their highly flavored cooking liquid and then served cold.

NUTRITIONAL INFORMATION

Calories 67	Sugars 4g	
Protein 2g	Fat 4g	
Carbohydrate 6g	Saturates 1g	

 12¼ hrs   35–40 mins

SERVES 4–6

I N G R E D I E N T S

9 oz/250 g small pickling onions

9 oz/250 g mushrooms

9 oz/250 g zucchini

2 cups water

5 tbsp olive oil

2 tbsp lemon juice

2 strips lemon rind

2 large garlic cloves, thinly sliced

½ Spanish onion, finely chopped

1 bay leaf

15 black peppercorns, lightly crushed

10 coriander seeds, lightly crushed

pinch of dried oregano

finely chopped fresh flat leaf parsley or
    coriander, to garnish

focaccia, to serve

1 Put the small pickling onions in a heatproof bowl and pour over boiling water to cover. Set aside for 2 minutes, then drain. Peel and set aside.

2 Trim the mushroom stems. Cut the mushrooms into halves or quarters, if they are large, or leave whole if small. Trim the zucchini, cut off strips of the peel for a decorative finish, then cut into ¼ inch/5 mm slices. Set both the mushrooms and zucchini aside.

3 Put the water, olive oil, lemon juice and rind, garlic, Spanish onion, bay leaf, peppercorns, coriander seeds, and oregano in a pan over high heat and bring to a boil. Lower the heat and simmer for 15 minutes.

4 Add the small onions and continue to simmer for 5 minutes. Add the mushrooms and zucchini and simmer for a further 2 minutes. Using a slotted spoon, transfer all the vegetables to a heatproof dish or casserole.

5 Return the liquid to a boil and boil until reduced to about 6 tablespoons. Pour the liquid over the vegetables and set aside to cool completely.

6 Cover with plastic wrap and chill for at least 12 hours.

7 To serve, put the vegetables and cooking liquid in a serving dish and sprinkle the fresh herbs over them. Serve with chunks of focaccia.

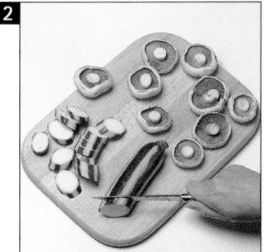

Glazed Baby Onions

These onions are bathed in a rich, intensely flavored glaze,
making them a good accompaniment to any broiled or roasted meat.

NUTRITIONAL INFORMATION

Calories . . . . .81 Sugars 8g
Protein . . . . .1g Fat 4g
Carbohydrate . . . .11g Saturates 1g

10 mins   25 mins

SERVES 4–6

I N G R E D I E N T S

1 lb 2oz/500 g baby onions

2 tbsp olive oil

2 large garlic cloves, crushed

1¼ cups vegetable or chicken stock

1 tbsp fresh thyme leaves

1 tbsp brown sugar

2 tbsp red wine vinegar

about 1½ tsp balsamic vinegar

salt and pepper

fresh thyme sprigs, to garnish

2 Using a small knife and your fingers, peel off the skins, which should slip off easily.

3 Heat the olive oil in a large skillet over medium heat. Add the onions and cook, stirring constantly, for about 8 minutes until they are golden all over.

4 Add the garlic and cook, stirring, for 2 minutes. Add the stock, thyme leaves, sugar, and wine vinegar, stirring until the sugar has dissolved.

5 Bring to a boil, then lower the heat, and simmer gently for 10 minutes or until the onions are tender when you pierce them with the tip of a sharp knife and the cooking liquid is reduced to a syrupy glaze.

6 Stir in the balsamic vinegar. Season to taste with salt and pepper and add extra balsamic vinegar, if desired. Transfer to a serving dish and serve the onions either hot or cold, garnished with fresh thyme sprigs.

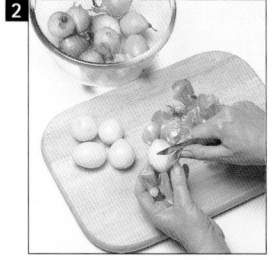

1 Put the baby onions in a large heatproof bowl, pour over enough boiling water to cover, and set aside for 2 minutes. Drain well.

VARIATION

For extra texture, stir in 2 tablespoons toasted pine nuts just before serving. Do not add them earlier or they will become soft.

Spiced Lentils with Spinach

This dish is a good accompaniment to broiled lamb and veal dishes.
Serve with a tomato and onion salad for a vegetarian meal.

NUTRITIONAL INFORMATION

Calories 179   Sugars 3g
Protein . . . . .11g   Fat 5g
Carbohydrate . . .24g   Saturates 1g

15 mins   35 mins

SERVES 4–6

INGREDIENTS

2 tbsp olive oil

1 large onion, finely chopped

1 large garlic clove, crushed

½ tbsp ground cumin

½ tsp ground ginger

generous 1 cup Puy lentils

about 2½ cups vegetable or
chicken stock

3½ oz/100 g baby spinach leaves

2 tbsp fresh mint leaves

1 tbsp fresh cilantro leaves

1 tbsp fresh flat leaf parsley leaves

freshly squeezed lemon juice

salt and pepper

strips of lemon rind, to garnish

1 Heat the oil in a large skillet over medium heat. Add the onion and cook, stirring occasionally, for about 6 minutes. Stir in the garlic, cumin, and ginger and cook, stirring occasionally, until the onion starts to brown.

2 Stir in the lentils. Pour in enough stock to cover the lentils by 1 inch/ 2.5 cm and bring to a boil. Lower the heat and simmer for 20–30 minutes until the lentils are tender.

3 Meanwhile, rinse the spinach leaves in several changes of cold water and shake dry. Finely chop the mint, coriander and parsley leaves.

4 If there isn't any stock left in the pan, add a little extra. Add the spinach and stir through until it just wilts. Stir in the mint, cilantro, and parsley. Adjust the seasoning, adding lemon juice and salt and pepper. Transfer to a serving bowl and serve, garnished with lemon rind.

COOK'S TIP

This recipe uses green lentils from Puy in France because they are good at keeping their shape even after long cooking. You can, however, also use orange or brown lentils, but it is necessary to watch them while they cook or they will quickly turn to a mush.

Saucy Borlotti Beans

Fresh sage, a herb used frequently in Mediterranean cooking, adds a subtle flavor to these pink and white speckled beans.

NUTRITIONAL INFORMATION

Calories	.84	Sugars	.6g
Protein	.4g	Fat	.3g
Carbohydrate	.10g	Saturates	.0g

20 mins · 30 mins

SERVES 4–6

I N G R E D I E N T S

1 lb 5 oz/600 g fresh borlotti beans

4 large leaves fresh sage, torn

1 tbsp olive oil

1 large onion, thinly sliced

1¼ cups good-quality bottled or homemade (see page 828) tomato sauce for pasta

salt and pepper

shredded fresh sage leaves, to garnish

1 Shell the borlotti beans. Bring a pan of water to a boil, add the beans and torn sage leaves, bring back to a boil, and simmer for about 12 minutes or until tender. Drain and set aside.

VARIATION

If fresh borlotti beans are unavailable, use 2 x 10½ oz/300 g cans instead. Drain and rinse, then add with the sage and tomato sauce in Step 2.

2 Heat the olive oil in a large, heavy skillet over medium heat. Add the onion and cook, stirring occasionally, for about 5 minutes until softened and translucent, but not browned. Stir the tomato sauce into the pan with the cooked borlotti beans and the torn fresh sage leaves.

3 Increase the heat and bring to a boil, stirring. Lower the heat, partially cover, and simmer for about 10 minutes or until the the sauce has slightly reduced.

4 Adjust the seasoning, transfer to a serving bowl, and serve hot, garnished with fresh sage leaves.

Flavored Olives

You are sure to find Mediterranean stalls selling all kinds of flavored olives. This nutritional analysis is based on a portion of 3 Provençal olives.

NUTRITIONAL INFORMATION

Calories 53	Sugars 0g
Protein 0g	Fat 6g
Carbohydrate 0g	Saturates 1g

🍽 10–15 mins 🕐 0 mins

MAKES 1 X 2¼ CUPS

INGREDIENTS

fresh herb sprigs, to serve

PROVENCAL OLIVES

3 dried red chiles

1 tsp black peppercorns

2⅔ cups black Niçoise olives in brine

2 lemon slices

1 tsp black mustard seeds

1 tbsp garlic-flavored olive oil

fruity extra virgin olive oil

CATALAN OLIVES

½ broiled red or orange pepper

1⅓ cups black olives in brine

1⅓ cups pimento-stuffed olives in brine

1 tbsp capers in brine, rinsed

pinch of dried chili flakes

4 tbsp chopped fresh cilantro leaves

1 bay leaf

fruity extra virgin olive oil

GREEK OLIVES

½ large lemon

2⅔ cups kalamata olives in brine

4 fresh thyme sprigs

1 shallot, very finely chopped

1 tbsp fennel seeds, lightly crushed

1 tsp dried dill

fruity extra virgin olive oil

1 To make the Provencal olives, place the dried red chiles and black peppercorns in a mortar, and lightly crush. Drain and rinse the olives, then pat dry with paper towels. Put all the ingredients in a 2¼ cup preserving jar, pouring in enough olive oil to cover.

2 Seal the jar and leave for at least 10 days before serving, shaking the jar daily.

3 To make the Catalan olives, finely chop the bell pepper. Drain and rinse both types of olives, then pat dry with paper towels. Put all the ingredients into a 2¼ cup preserving jar, pouring in enough olive oil to cover. Seal and marinate as in Step 2.

4 To make the Greek olives, cut the lemon into 4 slices, then cut each slice into wedges. Drain and rinse the olives, then pat dry with paper towels.

5 Slice each olive lengthwise on 1 side down to the pit. Put all the ingredients in a 2¼ cup preserving jar, pouring in olive oil to cover. Seal and marinate as in Step 2.

6 To serve, spoon the olives into a bowl and garnish with fresh herbs.

Plain Strained Yogurt

Smooth and creamy, this yogurt makes a refreshing start to hot days, spread on pitas for breakfast, or as a dip for an afternoon snack.

NUTRITIONAL INFORMATION*

Calories	32	Sugars	.........3g
Protein	.........2g	Fat	...........1g
Carbohydrate	....3g	Saturates	.......1g

 36½ hrs   0 mins

MAKES ABOUT 2¼ CUPS

I N G R E D I E N T S

4 cups plain yogurt

½ tsp salt

O P T I O N A L   T O P P I N G S

fruity extra virgin olive oil

orange blossom or lavender honey

coriander seeds, crushed

paprika

very finely chopped fresh mint or cilantro

finely grated lemon rind

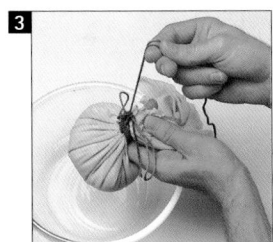

1 Place a 50 x 30 inch/125 x 75 cm piece of cheesecloth in a pan, cover with water and bring to a boil. Remove the pan from the heat and, using a wooden spoon, lift out the cheesecloth. Wearing rubber gloves to protect your hands, wring the cheesecloth dry.

2 Fold the cheesecloth into a double layer and line a colander or strainer set over a large bowl. Put the yogurt in a bowl and stir in the salt. Spoon the yogurt into the center of the cheesecloth.

3 Tie the cheesecloth so it is suspended above the bowl. If your sink is deep enough, gather up the corners of the cheesecloth and tie it to the faucet. If not, lay a broom handle across 2 chairs and put the bowl between the chairs. Tie the cheesecloth to the broom handle. Remove the colander or strainer and let the yogurt drain into the bowl for at least 12 hours.

4 Transfer the yogurt to a nylon strainer placed in a bowl. Cover lightly with plastic wrap and refrigerate for 24 hours until soft and creamy. The yogurt will keep in the refrigerator for up to 5 days.

5 To serve, taste and add extra salt if needed. Spoon the yogurt into a bowl and sprinkle with the topping of your choice or a combination of toppings.

* Nutritional information per 1 tablespoon of yogurt.

Spiced Pilau with Saffron

A Middle Eastern influence is evident in this fragrant pilau, studded with nuts, fruit, and spices. Serve with roast lamb or a chicken dish.

NUTRITIONAL INFORMATION

Calories	347	Sugars	.........9g
Protein	.........5g	Fat	...........11g
Carbohydrate	...60g	Saturates	.......3g

🍲 40 mins   ⏱ 30 mins

SERVES 4–6

I N G R E D I E N T S

pinch of saffron threads

2 cups boiling water

1 tsp salt

2 tbsp butter

2 tbsp olive oil

1 large onion, very finely chopped

3 tbsp pine nuts

1¾ cups long grain rice

scant ½ cup golden raisins or raisins

6 green cardamom pods, lightly crushed

6 cloves

pepper

very finely chopped fresh cilantro or flat leaf
    parsley, to garnish

1 Toast the saffron threads in dry skillet over medium heat, stirring for 2 minutes or until they give off their aroma. Immediately tip them onto a plate.

2 Pour the boiling water into a measuring cup, stir in the saffron and 1 teaspoon salt, and set aside for at least 30 minutes to steep.

3 Melt the butter with the oil in a skillet over medium heat. Add the onion and cook, stirring occasionally, for about 5 minutes until softened.

4 Lower the heat, stir in the pine nuts and continue cooking for 2 minutes, stirring constantly, until they just start to turn golden. Take care that they do not burn.

5 Stir in the rice, ensuring that all the grains are coated with oil. Stir for 1 minute, then add the golden raisins or raisins, cardamom pods, and cloves. Pour in the saffron-flavored water and bring to a boil. Lower the heat, cover, and simmer gently for 15 minutes without removing the lid.

6 Remove the pan from the heat and set aside for 5 minutes without uncovering. Remove the lid and check that the rice is tender, all the liquid has been absorbed, and the surface has small indentations all over.

7 Fluff up the rice with a fork. Taste and adjust the seasoning, if necessary, and stir the chopped herbs through. Serve the pilau immediately.

Spinach & Herb Orzo

Serve this quick and easy, vibrant green pasta dish with any broiled meat or seafood. Orzo is a kind of pasta shaped like long grains of barley.

NUTRITIONAL INFORMATION

Calories	304	Sugars	.........8g
Protein	........12g	Fat	...........6g
Carbohydrate	...54g	Saturates	.......1g

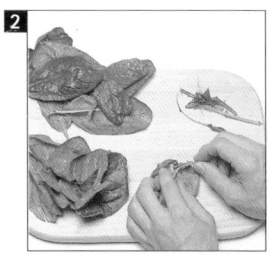

  15–20 mins   10 mins

SERVES 4

INGREDIENTS

1 tsp salt

2¼ cups dried orzo

7 oz/200 g baby spinach leaves

5½ oz/150 g arugula

1 cup fresh flat leaf parsley leaves

1 cup fresh cilantro leaves

4 scallions

2 tbsp extra virgin olive oil

1 tbsp garlic-flavored olive oil

pepper

TO SERVE

radicchio or other salad greens

½ cup well-drained, crumbled feta cheese (optional)

lemon slices

1 Bring 2 pans of water to a boil, and put 12 ice cubes in a bowl of cold water. Add the salt and orzo to 1 of the pans, bring back to a boil, and cook for 8–10 minutes until the pasta is tender, but still firm to the bite.

2 Meanwhile, remove the spinach stems if they are tough. Rinse the leaves in several changes of water to remove any grit. Coarsely chop the arugula, parsley, cilantro, and the green parts of the scallions.

3 Add the spinach, arugula, parsley, cilantro, and scallions to the second pan of boiling water and blanch for 15 seconds. Drain and transfer to the ice water to preserve the color.

4 When the spinach, arugula, parsley, cilantro, and scallions are cool, drain well and squeeze out all the excess water. Transfer to a small food processor and process. Add the olive oil and garlic-flavored oil and process again until thoroughly blended.

5 Drain the orzo well and stir in the spinach mixture. Toss well and adjust the seasoning.

6 Line a serving platter with radicchio or other salad greens and pile the orzo on top. Sprinkle with crumbled feta cheese, if using, and garnish with lemon slices. Serve hot or let cool to room temperature.

Thai Fragrant Coconut Rice

Basmati rice is cooked with creamed coconut, lemongrass, fresh ginger, and spices to make a wonderfully aromatic, fluffy rice.

NUTRITIONAL INFORMATION

Calories 258	Sugars 0.4g
Protein 5g	Fat 6g
Carbohydrate ...51g	Saturates 4g

🍲 5 mins   🕐 20 mins

SERVES 4–6

I N G R E D I E N T S

1 inch/2.5 cm piece of fresh ginger
  root, sliced

2 cloves

1 piece of lemongrass, bruised
  and halved

2 tsp ground nutmeg

1 cinnamon stick

1 bay leaf

2 small thin strips lime rind

1 tsp salt

1 oz/25 g creamed coconut, chopped

2½ cups water

1¾ cups basmati rice

pepper

1 Place the ginger, cloves, lemongrass, nutmeg, cinnamon stick, bay leaf, lime rind, salt, creamed coconut, and water in a large, heavy pan and bring to a boil over low heat.

2 Add the rice, stir well, then cover, and simmer over very gentle heat for about 15 minutes or until all the liquid has been absorbed and the rice is tender, but still has a bite to it.

3 Alternatively, bring the mixture to a boil, then cover tightly, and turn off the heat. Set aside for 20–25 minutes before removing the lid—the rice will be perfectly cooked.

4 Remove the pan from the heat, add pepper to taste, then fluff up the rice with a fork.

5 Remove the large pieces of spices and the lemon rind before serving.

COOK'S TIP

When using a whole stem of lemongrass, rather than chopped lemongrass, beat it well to bruise it so that the flavor is fully released. Grated lemon rind or a pared piece of lemon rind can be used instead.

Tomato Rice

Rice cooked with tomatoes and onions will add color to your table, especially when garnished with green chiles and cilantro.

NUTRITIONAL INFORMATION

Calories	866	Sugars	.........7g
Protein	........15g	Fat	..........46g
Carbohydrate	..106g	Saturates	.......6g

10 mins   35 mins

SERVES 4

INGREDIENTS

⅔ cup vegetable oil

2 medium onions, sliced

1 tsp onion seeds

1 tsp finely chopped fresh ginger root

1 tsp crushed garlic

½ tsp ground turmeric

1 tsp chili powder

1½ tsp salt

14 oz/400 g can tomatoes

2½ cups basmati rice

2½ cups water

TO GARNISH

3 fresh green chiles, finely chopped

fresh cilantro leaves, chopped

3 hard-cooked eggs

COOK'S TIP

Onion seeds are always used whole in Indian cooking. They are often used in pickles and often sprinkled over the top of nan breads. Onion seeds don't have anything to do with the vegetable, but they look similar to the plant's seed, hence the name.

1 Heat the oil in a heavy pan. Add the onions and fry over a moderate heat, stirring frequently, for 5 minutes until golden brown.

2 Add the onion seeds, ginger, garlic, turmeric, chili powder, and salt, stirring to combine.

3 Reduce the heat, add the tomatoes, and stir-fry for 10 minutes, breaking them up.

4 Add the rice to the tomato mixture, stirring gently to coat the rice completely. Stir in the water. Cover the pan and cook over low heat until the water has been absorbed and the rice is tender, but still has some bite.

5 Transfer the tomato rice to a warmed serving dish. Garnish with the finely chopped green chiles, cilantro leaves, and hard-cooked eggs. Serve the tomato rice immediately.

Fidellos Tostados

The Sephardic Jews from Spain have been eating a
very thin vermicelli-like pasta called *fidellos* for centuries.

NUTRITIONAL INFORMATION

Calories 327	Sugars 3g	
Protein 9g	Fat 7g	
Carbohydrate ...59g	Saturates 1g	

5 mins   30 mins

SERVES 6

I N G R E D I E N T S

12 oz/350 g vermicelli or angel hair pasta in coils, coarsely broken

½ cup long grain white rice

3 tbsp extra virgin olive oil

7 oz/200 g canned chopped tomatoes, drained

2½ cups chicken stock or water, plus extra if necessary

1 bay leaf

1–2 tsp chopped fresh oregano or 1 tsp dried oregano

½ tsp dried thyme leaves

salt and pepper

T O   G A R N I S H

fresh oregano or thyme sprigs

chopped fresh oregano or thyme

1 Put the pasta and rice in a dry, large, heavy pan or flameproof casserole over medium heat and cook for 5–7 minutes, stirring frequently, until light golden. (The pasta will break unevenly, but this does not matter.)

2 Stir in 2 tablespoons of the olive oil, with the chopped tomatoes, stock, bay leaf, oregano, and thyme, then season with about 1 teaspoon of salt and pepper to taste.

3 Bring to a boil, reduce the heat to medium, and simmer for about 8 minutes, stirring frequently, to help unwind and separate the pasta coils.

4 Reduce the heat to low, cover, and cook for about 10 minutes until the rice and pasta are tender and all the liquid has been absorbed. If the rice and pasta are too firm, add about ½ cup more stock or water and continue to cook, covered, for a further 5 minutes. Remove the pan from the heat.

5 Using a fork, fluff the rice and pasta into a warmed, deep serving bowl and drizzle with the remaining oil. Sprinkle with the chopped oregano or thyme, garnish with fresh herb sprigs, and serve immediately.

Spicy Potato-Rice Pilaf

This spicy blend of potatoes, rice, and peas can be served as part of an Indian meal, but is also rich enough to serve on its own.

NUTRITIONAL INFORMATION

Calories 217   Sugars 3g
Protein . . . . .6g   Fat 4g
Carbohydrate . . .39g   Saturates 0g

 35 mins   30 mins

SERVES 4–6

INGREDIENTS

1 cup basmati rice, soaked in cold water for 20 minutes

2 tbsp vegetable oil

½–¾ tsp cumin seeds

8 oz/225 g potatoes, cut into ½ inch/ 1 cm pieces

2 cups frozen peas, thawed

1 fresh green chile, deseeded and thinly sliced (optional)

½ tsp salt

1 tsp garam masala

½ tsp ground turmeric

¼ tsp cayenne pepper

2½ cups water

2 tbsp chopped fresh cilantro

1 red onion, finely chopped

plain yogurt, to serve

1 Rinse the soaked rice under cold running water until the water runs clear, drain, and set aside.

2 Heat the oil in a large heavy pan over medium heat. Add the cumin seeds and stir for about 10 seconds until the seeds pop and color.

3 Add the potatoes, peas, and green chile, if using, and stir-fry for about 3 minutes until the potatoes are just beginning to soften.

4 Add the rice and cook, stirring frequently, until well coated and beginning to turn translucent.

5 Stir in the salt, garam masala, turmeric, and cayenne pepper, then add the water. Bring to a boil, stirring once or twice, then reduce the heat, cover, and simmer until most of the water is absorbed and the surface is filled with little steam-holes. Do not stir.

6 Reduce the heat to very low and, if possible, raise the pan about 1 inch/ 2.5 cm above the heat source by resting on a ring. Cover and steam for about 10 minutes longer. Remove from the heat, uncover, and put a clean dish cloth or paper towels over the rice. Re-cover and set aside for 5 minutes.

7 Gently fork the rice and potato mixture into a warmed serving bowl and sprinkle with the cilantro and chopped red onion. Serve hot with the yogurt handed separately.

Coconut-Scented Rice

Cooked slowly to produce a tender, creamy rice with lots of flavor, this makes an excellent accompaniment to broiled chicken, pork, or even fish.

NUTRITIONAL INFORMATION

Calories 127   Sugars 2g
Protein . . . . .2g   Fat 1g
Carbohydrate . . .29g   Saturates 0g

 5 mins   50 mins

SERVES 4–6

INGREDIENTS

1½ cups water

1 cup coconut milk

1 tsp salt

1 cup long grain brown rice

2–3 strips of lemon rind

1 cinnamon stick

about 15 cloves

1 tbsp chopped fresh parsley

fresh coconut shavings (optional)

1 Bring the water to a boil in a heavy pan over medium heat and whisk in the coconut milk. Return the liquid to a boil, add the salt, and sprinkle in the rice. Add the strips of lemon rind, the cinnamon stick, and cloves.

2 Reduce the heat to low, cover, and simmer gently for about 45 minutes until the rice is tender and the liquid is completely absorbed. Uncover and leave the rice over high heat for about 1 minute, to allow any steam to escape and the rice to dry out a little.

3 Remove and discard the cloves, then sprinkle with the chopped parsley and coconut, if using. Fluff up the grains, fork the rice into a warmed serving bowl, and serve immediately.

VARIATION

For a more Southeast Asian flavor, use 1 fresh red chile, pierced in 2–3 places with a pin, a bruised lime leaf, and a 3 inch/7.5 cm piece of lemongrass, lightly crushed, instead of the lemon rind and cloves.

Fragrant Orange Rice

This delicious rice, scented with star anise for a slightly exotic effect, is excellent served with Mediterranean and Middle Eastern meat stews.

NUTRITIONAL INFORMATION

Calories	177	Sugars	.........6g
Protein	.........3g	Fat	...........3g
Carbohydrate	...34g	Saturates	.......2g

 10–25 mins 20–25 mins

SERVES 4–6

INGREDIENTS

1–2 tbsp butter

3–4 shallots, finely chopped

1 cup basmati rice

1 inch/2.5 cm piece of fresh ginger root

1–2 fresh bay leaves, lightly bruised

2 star anise

1 small cinnamon stick

grated rind and juice of 1 orange

1 tbsp raisins, finely chopped

1¼ cups chicken stock or water

salt and pepper

fresh cilantro leaves, to garnish (optional)

1 Melt the butter in a heavy pan placed over medium heat. Add the shallots and cook, stirring occasionally, for 2–3 minutes until translucent and beginning to soften.

2 Add the rice and cook, stirring frequently, for 3 minutes until the rice is well coated with the butter and is translucent. Using a large, heavy knife, lightly crush the piece of ginger root. Add to the pan with the bay leaves, star anise, and cinnamon stick. Stir in the grated orange rind, orange juice, and raisins and mix thoroughly.

3 Add the stock and bring to a boil. Season with salt and pepper to taste and reduce the heat. Cover and cook over low heat for 15–18 minutes until the rice is tender and the liquid completely absorbed. Remove from the heat, uncover, and place a clean dish cloth over the rice. Re-cover and set aside for up to 20 minutes.

4 Fork the rice into a serving bowl and remove the bay leaves, star anise. and cinnamon stick—or keep them in for decoration. Sprinkle the top with a few cilantro leaves, if wished, and serve hot.

COOK'S TIP

Washing and soaking the rice removes any starch. Cover the rice with water and soak for about 20 minutes, stirring occasionally. Drain, then rinse under cold running water until the water runs clear. Drain and proceed with the recipe.

Lemon-Scented Rice

The fresh clean flavors of this pilaf make it an ideal accompaniment for a wide variety of dishes from plain roasted meats to exotic curries.

NUTRITIONAL INFORMATION

Calories	173	Sugars	.........0g
Protein	.........3g	Fat	...........4g
Carbohydrate	...33g	Saturates	.......1g

10–15 mins   30 mins

SERVES 6–8

INGREDIENTS

2 tbsp olive oil or butter

2–4 scallions, finely chopped

3–4 tbsp chopped fresh mint

1½ cups long grain white rice

2¼ cups chicken stock

1 lemon

salt and pepper

TO GARNISH

2–3 fresh mint sprigs

thin lemon slices

thin lime slices

1 Heat the oil or butter in a medium heavy pan over medium heat. Add the scallions and mint and cook, stirring constantly, for about 1 minute until the mint is brightly colored and giving off its aroma.

2 Add the rice and cook, stirring frequently, for about 2 minutes until well coated with the oil or butter and just translucent. Add the chicken stock and bring to a boil, stirring once or twice. Season with salt and pepper to taste.

3 Pare 3–4 strips of lemon rind and add to the pan. Squeeze the juice from the lemon and stir into the rice and stock.

4 When the stock comes to a boil, reduce the heat to low and simmer gently, tightly covered, for about 20 minutes until the rice is tender and the stock absorbed. Remove the pan from the heat and set aside for 5–10 minutes.

5 Fork the rice into a warmed serving bowl, garnish with mint sprigs and slices of lemon and lime. Serve hot.

COOK'S TIP

This basic technique for pilaf rice can be used with other flavor combinations and herbs. The important thing is to fry the rice until well coated and add just enough water to be absorbed by the rice.

Stuffed Cabbage

Hailing from Eastern Europe, this recipe is a delicious way to stretch a small amount of meat.

NUTRITIONAL INFORMATION

Calories 424	Sugars 25g
Protein 29g	Fat 16g
Carbohydrate ...42g	Saturates 5g

 20 mins   1 hr 50 mins

SERVES 6–8

INGREDIENTS

1 cup fresh white bread crumbs

½ cup milk

1 tbsp vegetable oil

1 onion, finely chopped

2 garlic cloves, finely chopped

1 lb/450 g ground beef

1 lb/450 g ground pork or veal

2 tbsp tomato ketchup

3 tbsp chopped fresh dill

1 tsp chopped fresh thyme leaves

½ cup long grain white rice

salt and pepper

1 large cabbage, such as Savoy, leaves separated and blanched

TOMATO SAUCE

2 tbsp olive oil

2 large onions, thinly sliced

2 x 14 oz/400 g cans chopped tomatoes

2 cups sieved tomatoes

¼ cup tomato catsup

grated rind and juice of 1 large lemon

2 tbsp brown sugar

⅔ cup raisins

1 Combine the bread crumbs and the milk and set aside to soak. Heat the oil in a pan and cook the onion and garlic for about 2 minutes until soft.

2 Place the beef and pork or veal in a bowl. Mix in the catsup, herbs, rice, and seasoning. Add the bread crumbs and cooked onion and garlic.

3 To make the tomato sauce, heat the oil and cook the onions for 3 minutes until soft. Stir in the tomatoes and the remaining ingredients and bring to a boil, then simmer for about 15 minutes, stirring occasionally. Set aside.

4 Spoon 1–2 tablespoons of the meat mixture onto a cabbage leaf above the stem end. Fold the stem end over the filling, then fold over the sides. Roll up to enclose. Repeat with the remaining leaves until the meat mixture is used up.

5 Spoon enough tomato sauce to cover the bottom of a large casserole. Arrange the filled cabbage rolls, seam side down, in the casserole. Spoon the remaining sauce over the rolls to cover—add a little water if necessary. Cover tightly and bake in a preheated oven, 325°F/160°C, for about 1½ hours, basting once or twice.

6 Transfer the cabbage rolls to a warmed serving plate and keep warm. Heat the sauce to thicken, if necessary, then pour over the rolls, and serve.

Iranian Steamed Crusty Rice

The trick is to achieve a light fragrant rice with a crunchy golden brown crust; it may take several attempts, but it's worth the effort.

NUTRITIONAL INFORMATION

Calories	330	Sugars	.........0g
Protein	.........5g	Fat	...........9g
Carbohydrate	...57g	Saturates	.......5g

 5 mins 45 mins

SERVES 6

INGREDIENTS

generous 2 cups basmati or long grain white rice

2 tbsp salt

4 tbsp butter or ghee

¼ cup water

1 Bring at least 4¼ pints/2 liters water to a boil. Add the salt. Gradually add the rice, then simmer for 7–10 minutes until almost tender, gently stirring occasionally. Drain and rinse under warm running water to remove any starch.

2 Heat the butter or ghee with the water in a large, heavy pan over medium heat until the butter melts and the water is steaming. Remove half of this mixture and reserve. Spoon enough rice into the pan to cover the bottom, smoothing lightly and evenly.

3 Spoon the remaining rice into the pan. Cover the rice with a thin dish cloth, then cover the pan tightly, and reduce the heat to very low. Cook for 15 minutes.

4 Remove the covers and, with the handle of a wooden spoon, gently poke several holes into the rice to allow the steam to escape.

5 Pour the remaining butter and water mixture over the rice, re-cover as before, and cook for 10–15 minutes. Uncover and transfer the pan to a chilled surface (see Cook's Tip). This helps to loosen the crust from the bottom.

6 Using a fork, fluff the loose rice into a serving bowl. Break up the crusty brown layer into pieces and arrange around the serving dish.

COOK'S TIP
To chill the counter for cooling down the pan of hot rice, place 2 trays of ice-cubes on it ahead of time.

Zucchini & Tomatoes

Lightly cooked zucchini are mixed with ripe, juicy tomatoes and dressed with a chili vinaigrette to create a perfect side salad.

NUTRITIONAL INFORMATION

Calories	92	Sugars	.........3g
Protein	.........2g	Fat	...........8g
Carbohydrate	....4g	Saturates	.......1g

30 mins   10 mins

SERVES 4–6

I N G R E D I E N T S

1 large fresh mild green chile, or a combination of 1 green bell pepper and ½–1 fresh green chile

4 zucchini, sliced

2–3 garlic cloves, finely chopped

pinch of sugar

¼ tsp ground cumin

2 tbsp white wine vinegar

4 tbsp extra virgin olive oil

2–3 tbsp chopped fresh cilantro

4 ripe tomatoes, diced or sliced

salt and pepper

1 Roast the mild chile or the combination of the green bell pepper and chile, in a heavy ungreased skillet or under a preheated broiler until the skin is charred. Place in a plastic bag, twist to seal well, and set aside for 20 minutes.

2 Peel the skin from the chile and bell pepper, if using, then remove the seeds, and slice the flesh. Set aside.

3 Bring about 2 inches/5 cm water to a boil in the bottom of a steamer. Add the zucchini to the top part of the steamer, cover, and steam for about 5 minutes until just tender.

4 Meanwhile, combine the garlic, sugar, cumin, white wine vinegar, olive oil, and cilantro in a bowl. Stir in the chile and bell pepper, if using, then season with salt and pepper to taste.

5 Arrange the zucchini and tomatoes in a serving bowl or on a platter and spoon over the chili dressing. Toss gently, if wished, and serve.

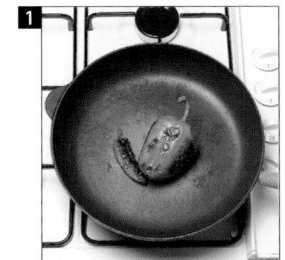

VARIATION

Add 2 cups cooked peeled shrimp to the zucchini and tomatoes, then coat with the dressing as in Step 5.

Summer Squash Medley

Garlic butter and a hint of chile flavor this summertime vegetable pot of squash and corn. Serve with almost any meaty entrée.

NUTRITIONAL INFORMATION

Calories	140	Sugars	.........5g
Protein	.........4g	Fat	...........6g
Carbohydrate	...20g	Saturates	.......3g

 10 mins   10 mins

SERVES 4–6

INGREDIENTS

2 corn cobs

2 small zucchini or other green summer squash, such as pattypan, cubed or sliced

2 small yellow summer squash, cubed or sliced

2 tbsp butter

3 garlic cloves, finely chopped

3–4 large, ripe tomatoes, diced

pinch of mild chili powder

pinch of ground cumin

½ fresh green chile, such as jalapeño, deseeded and chopped

pinch of sugar

salt and pepper

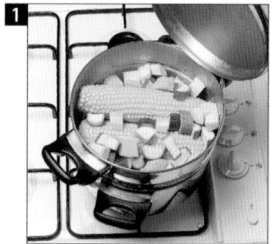

1 Pour about 2 inches/5 cm water into the bottom of a steamer and bring to a boil. Add the corn cobs, zucchini or green squash, and summer squash to the top part of the steamer, cover, and steam for about 3 minutes until tender, depending on their maturity and freshness. Alternatively, blanch in boiling salted water for about 3 minutes, then drain. Set aside until they are cool enough to handle.

2 Using a large knife, slice the kernels off the corn cobs and set aside.

3 Melt the butter in a heavy skillet. Add the garlic and cook for 1 minute to soften. Add the tomatoes, chili powder, ground cumin, green chile, and sugar to taste. Season with salt and pepper to taste and cook over low heat for a few minutes or until the flavors have mingled.

4 Add the corn kernels, zucchini, and squash. Cook for 2 minutes, stirring, to warm through. Transfer to a warmed serving dish and serve immediately.

VARIATION
Any leftovers will make a good base for a lovely summer soup. Simply thin with lots of stock and freshen up with chopped herbs.

Potatoes in Green Sauce

Earthy potatoes, served in a tangy spicy tomatillo sauce and topped with scallions and sour cream, are delicious.

NUTRITIONAL INFORMATION

Calories 61   Sugars 1.4g
Protein . . . . .2g   Fat 1.4g
Carbohydrate . .10.6g   Saturates 0.2g

 5 mins   25 mins

SERVES 4

I N G R E D I E N T S

2 lb 4 oz/1 kg small waxy potatoes

1 onion, halved and unpeeled

8 garlic cloves, unpeeled

1 fresh green chile

8 tomatillos, outer husks removed, or small tart tomatoes

1 cup chicken, meat, or vegetable stock, preferably homemade

1 tsp ground cumin

1 fresh thyme sprig or generous pinch of dried thyme

1 fresh oregano sprig or generous pinch of dried oregano

2 tbsp vegetable or extra virgin olive oil

1 zucchini, coarsely chopped

1 bunch of fresh cilantro, chopped

salt

1 Put the potatoes in a pan of lightly salted water. Bring to a boil and cook for about 15 minutes or until almost tender. Do not overcook them. Drain and set aside.

2 Meanwhile lightly char the onion, garlic, chile, and tomatillos or tomatoes in a heavy, ungreased skillet. Set aside, and when cool enough to handle, peel, and chop the onion, garlic, and chile. Chop the tomatillos or tomatoes. Put in a blender or food processor with half the stock and process to form a purée. Add the cumin, thyme, and oregano.

3 Heat the oil in the heavy skillet. Add the purée and cook over medium heat, stirring constantly, for 5 minutes to reduce slightly and concentrate the flavors.

4 Add the potatoes and zucchini to the purée and pour in the remaining stock. Add about half of the chopped cilantro and cook for a further 5 minutes or until the zucchini is tender.

5 Transfer to a serving bowl and serve sprinkled with the remaining chopped cilantro to garnish.

Two Classic Salsas

A Mexican meal is not complete without an accompanying salsa.
These two salsas are ideal for seasoning any traditional dish.

NUTRITIONAL INFORMATION

Calories 21   Sugars 3g
Protein . . . . .1g   Fat 0g
Carbohydrate . . . .4g   Saturates 0g

  5 mins   0 mins

SERVES 4–6

I N G R E D I E N T S

JALAPEÑO SALSA

1 onion, finely chopped

2–3 garlic cloves, finely chopped

4–6 tbsp coarsely chopped pickled
jalapeño chiles

juice of ½ lemon

about ¼ tsp ground cumin

salt

SALSA CRUDA

6–8 ripe tomatoes, finely chopped

about ½ cup tomato juice

3–4 garlic cloves, finely chopped

½–1 bunch fresh cilantro leaves,
coarsely chopped

pinch of sugar

3–4 fresh green chiles, such as jalapeño or
serrano, deseeded and finely chopped

½–1 tsp ground cumin

3–4 scallions, finely chopped

salt

1 To make the jalapeño salsa, put the onion in a bowl with the garlic, jalapeños, lemon juice, and cumin. Season to taste with salt and stir together. Cover with plastic wrap and chill in the refrigerator until required.

2 To make a chunky-textured salsa cruda, stir all the ingredients together in a bowl and season with salt to taste. Cover with plastic wrap and chill in the refrigerator until required.

3 To make a smoother-textured salsa, process the ingredients in a blender or food processor. Scrape into a bowl, cover, and chill as above.

COOK'S TIP

You can vary the amount of garlic, chiles, and ground spices according to taste, but make sure the salsa has quite a "kick," otherwise it will not be effective.

Hot Mexican Salsas

These salsas capture the inimitable tangy, spicy flavor of Mexico. Choose from a fresh minty fruit salsa, charred chile salsa, or a spicy "green" salsa.

NUTRITIONAL INFORMATION

Calories	59	Sugars	........12g
Protein	.........1g	Fat	...........0g
Carbohydrate	...12g	Saturates	.......0g

🍞 10 mins   🕐 5 mins

SERVES 4–6

I N G R E D I E N T S

TROPICAL FRUIT SALSA

½–1 fresh green chile

½–1 fresh red chile

½ pineapple, peeled, cored, and diced

1 mango, peeled, pitted, and diced

½ red onion, chopped

1 tbsp sugar

juice of 1 lime

3 tbsp chopped fresh mint

salt

CHARRED CHILE SALSA

2–3 fresh green chiles

1 green bell pepper

2 garlic cloves, finely chopped

juice of ½ lime

1 tsp salt

2–3 tbsp extra virgin olive oil

pinch each dried oregano and ground cumin

SALSA VERDE

1 lb/450 g oz canned tomatillos, drained

1–2 fresh green chiles

1 green bell pepper, deseeded and chopped

1 small onion, chopped

1 bunch fresh cilantro, finely chopped

½ tsp ground cumin

salt

1 To make the tropical fruit salsa, deseed the green chile and chop both chiles. Combine all the ingredients in a large bowl and season with salt to taste. Cover the bowl with plastic wrap and chill in the refrigerator until required.

2 For the charred chile salsa, char the chiles and green bell pepper in an ungreased skillet. Cool, deseed, peel, and chop. Combine the chiles and green bell pepper with the garlic, lime juice, salt, and oil in a bowl. Top with oregano and cumin.

3 For the salsa verde, drain and chop the tomatillos. Deseed and finely chop the chiles and deseed and chop the green bell pepper. Combine all the ingredients in a bowl and season with salt to taste. If a smoother sauce is preferred, blend the ingredients in a food processor, then spoon into a bowl to serve.

Fresh Pineapple Salsa

This sweet fruity salsa is fresh and fragrant, a wonderful foil to spicy dishes and perfect with food cooked on the barbecue.

NUTRITIONAL INFORMATION

Calories	37	Sugars	........8g
Protein	.........1g	Fat	..........0.5g
Carbohydrate	....8g	Saturates	.......0g

 15 mins   0 mins

SERVES 4

INGREDIENTS

½ ripe pineapple

juice of 1 lime or lemon

1 garlic clove, finely chopped

1 scallion, thinly sliced

½–1 fresh green or red chile, deseeded and finely chopped

½ red bell pepper, deseeded and chopped

3 tbsp chopped fresh mint

3 tbsp chopped fresh cilantro

pinch of salt

pinch of sugar

1 Using a long, sharp knife, cut off the top and bottom of the pineapple. Place the pineapple upright on a board, then slice off the skin, cutting downward. If any "eyes" still remain, cut them out with a small, pointed knife.

2 Cut the pineapple flesh into slices about ½ inch/1 cm thick, halve the slices, and remove the cores. Dice the flesh. Reserve any juice that accumulates as you cut the pineapple.

3 Place the pineapple and any juice in a bowl and stir in the lime juice, garlic, scallion, chile, and red bell pepper. Stir in the chopped fresh mint and cilantro. Add the salt and sugar and stir well to combine all the ingredients. Cover with plastic wrap and chill until ready to serve.

COOK'S TIP

A fresh pineapple is ripe if it has a sweet aroma. The flesh will still be fairly firm to touch. Fresh-looking leaves are a sign of good condition.

Mexican Beans

A pot of beans, bubbling away on the stove, is the basic everyday food of Mexico—delicious and healthy.

NUTRITIONAL INFORMATION

Calories 282	Sugars 1g
Protein 18g	Fat 1g
Carbohydrate ...50g	Saturates 0g

 8¼ hrs   2½ hrs

SERVES 4–6

INGREDIENTS

1 lb 2oz/500 g dried pinto or borlotti beans

fresh mint sprig

fresh thyme sprig

fresh flat leaf parsley sprig

1 onion, cut into chunks

salt

TO SERVE

warmed flour or corn tortillas

shreds of scallion

1 Pick through the beans and remove any pieces of grit or stones. Put the beans in a bowl, cover with cold water, and set aside to soak overnight. If you want to cut down on soaking time, bring the beans to a boil, boil for 5 minutes, then remove from the heat, cover, and set aside for 2 hours.

2 Drain the beans, place in a pan, and cover with fresh water. Add the mint, thyme, and parsley sprigs. Bring to a boil, then reduce the heat to very low, cover, and simmer gently for about 2 hours until the beans are tender. The best way to check that they are done is to sample a bean every so often after 1¾ hours cooking time.

3 Add the onion chunks and continue to cook until the onion and beans are very tender.

4 To serve as a side dish, drain, season with salt, and serve in a bowl lined with warmed corn or flour tortillas, garnished with scallion shreds.

COOK'S TIP

If using the beans for refried beans, do not drain because the liquid is required for the recipe.

Rice with Lime

The tangy citrus taste of lime is marvelous with all sorts of rice dishes. You could add wild rice to this dish, if desired.

NUTRITIONAL INFORMATION

Calories 227   Sugars 1g
Protein . . . . .4g   Fat 7g
Carbohydrate . . .39g   Saturates 1g

5 mins   15 mins

SERVES 4

I N G R E D I E N T S

2 tbsp vegetable oil

1 small onion, finely chopped

3 garlic cloves, finely chopped

scant 1 cup long grain rice

2 cups chicken or vegetable stock

juice of 1 lime

1 tbsp chopped fresh cilantro

1 Heat the oil in a heavy pan or flameproof casserole. Add the onion and garlic and cook gently, stirring occasionally, for 2 minutes.

2 Add the rice and cook for a further minute, stirring constantly. Pour in the stock, increase the heat, and bring the rice to a boil. Reduce the heat to a very low simmer.

3 Cover and cook the rice for about 10 minutes or until it is just tender and the liquid is absorbed.

4 Sprinkle in the lime juice and fork the rice to fluff up and to mix the juice in. Sprinkle with the chopped cilantro and serve immediately.

COOK'S TIP

Garnish the rice with sautéed plantains: slice a ripe peeled plantain on the diagonal, then fry in a heavy pan in a small amount of oil until browned in spots and tender. Arrange in the bowl of rice.

Cumin Rice

Cumin seeds add a distinctive flavor to this colorful rice dish. Serve as a side dish for any roasted or broiled meat.

NUTRITIONAL INFORMATION

Calories 258	Sugars 4g
Protein 5g	Fat 9g
Carbohydrate ...49g	Saturates 5g

20 mins   20 mins

SERVES 4

INGREDIENTS

2 tbsp butter

1 tbsp vegetable oil

1 green bell pepper, deseeded and sliced

1 red bell pepper, deseeded and sliced

3 scallions, thinly sliced

3–4 garlic cloves, finely chopped

scant 1 cup long grain rice

1½ tsp cumin seeds

½ tsp dried oregano or marjoram, crushed

2 cups chicken or vegetable stock

1 Heat the butter and oil in a heavy pan or flameproof casserole. Add the green and red bell peppers and cook, stirring occasionally, until softened.

2 Add the scallions, garlic, rice, and cumin seeds. Cook, stirring constantly, for about 5 minutes or until the rice turns slightly golden.

3 Add the oregano and stock to the pan or casserole, bring to a boil, then reduce the heat, and simmer gently for 5–10 minutes until the rice is tender.

4 Cover with a clean dish cloth and remove from the heat. Set aside for about 10 minutes. Fluff up the rice with a fork and serve.

VARIATION

Fold through a portion or two of black beans, and serve as a side dish with hearty roasted meat or poultry.

Green Rice

A paste of roasted onions, garlic, and chiles, puréed with lots of green cilantro leaves, gives this rice a lovely fresh color and stunning taste.

NUTRITIONAL INFORMATION

Calories ....386 Sugars 4g
Protein ....5g Fat 22g
Carbohydrate ...45g Saturates 2g

20 mins | 20–25 mins

SERVES 4

INGREDIENTS

1–2 onions, halved and unpeeled

6–8 large garlic cloves, unpeeled

1 large mild chile, or 1 green bell pepper
  and 1 small green chile

1 bunch of fresh cilantro leaves, chopped

1 cup chicken or vegetable stock

6 tbsp vegetable or olive oil

scant 1 cup long grain rice

salt and pepper

fresh cilantro sprig, to garnish

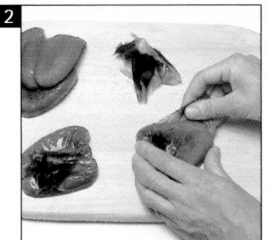

1 Heat a heavy ungreased skillet and cook the onion, garlic, chile, and green bell pepper, if using, until lightly charred on all sides, including the cut sides of the onions. Cover and then set aside to cool.

2 When the vegetables are cool enough to handle, remove the seeds and skins from the chile and green bell pepper, if using. Chop the flesh.

3 Remove the skins from the onions and garlic and chop the flesh finely.

4 Place the chile, green bell pepper, if using, onions, and garlic in a food processor with the cilantro leaves and stock, then process to a smooth purée.

5 Heat the oil in a heavy pan and fry the rice until it is glistening and lightly browned in places, stirring to prevent it from burning. Add the vegetable purée, cover, and cook over low heat for 10–15 minutes until the rice is just tender.

6 Fluff up the rice with a fork, then cover, and set for about 5 minutes. Adjust the seasoning, garnish with a sprig of cilantro, and serve.

COOK'S TIP
Leftover green rice is delicious mixed with ground beef and/or pork for savory meatballs, or as a filling for bell peppers.

Rice with Black Beans

Any kind of bean cooking liquid is delicious for cooking rice—black beans are particularly good for their startling gray color and earthy flavor.

NUTRITIONAL INFORMATION

Calories	252	Sugars	.........2g
Protein	.........5g	Fat	...........8g
Carbohydrate	...43g	Saturates	.......1g

15 mins   15 mins

SERVES 4

INGREDIENTS

1 onion, chopped

5 garlic cloves, chopped

1 cup chicken or vegetable stock

2 tbsp vegetable oil

scant 1 cup long grain rice

1 cup liquid from cooking black beans
(including some black beans, too)

½ tsp ground cumin

salt and pepper

TO GARNISH

3–5 scallions, thinly sliced

2 tbsp chopped fresh cilantro leaves

1 Put the onion in a blender or food processor with the garlic and stock and process to a chunky sauce.

2 Heat the oil in a heavy pan. Add the rice and cook over low heat, stirring constantly, until it is golden. Add the onion mixture, with the cooking liquid from the black beans (and any beans, too). Add the cumin and season with salt and pepper to taste.

3 Cover the pan and cook over low heat for about 10 minutes or until the rice is just tender. The rice should be a grayish color and taste delicious.

4 Fluff up the rice with a fork, re-cover, and set aside to rest for about 5 minutes. Serve sprinkled with thinly sliced scallions and the chopped fresh cilantro leaves.

VARIATION

Instead of black beans, use pinto beans or garbanzo beans. Proceed as above and serve with any savory spicy sauce or as an accompaniment to roasted meat.

Lentils Simmered with Fruit

Although this might seem an unusual combination, when you taste this traditional Mexican dish you will discover just how delicious it is.

NUTRITIONAL INFORMATION

Calories	23	Sugars 18g
Protein	........10g	Fat 7g
Carbohydrate	...36g	Saturates 1g

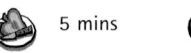 5 mins    45 mins

SERVES 4

INGREDIENTS

⅔ cup brown or green lentils

about 4 cups water

2 tbsp vegetable oil

3 small to medium onions, chopped

4 garlic cloves, coarsely chopped

1 large tart apple, coarsely chopped

about ¼ ripe pineapple, peeled and coarsely chopped

2 tomatoes, deseeded and diced

1 almost ripe banana, cut into bite-size pieces

cayenne pepper

salt

fresh parsley sprig, to garnish

1 Put the lentils in a pan and add the water. Bring to a boil, then reduce the heat, and simmer gently for about 40 minutes until the lentils are tender. Do not let them become mushy.

2 Meanwhile, heat the oil in a skillet and cook the onions and garlic, over low heat for 10 minutes until lightly browned. Add the apple and continue to cook until golden. Add the pineapple, heat through, stirring, then add the tomatoes. Cook over medium heat until thickened, stirring occasionally.

3 Drain the lentils, reserving ½ cup of the cooking liquid. Add the drained lentils to the sauce, stirring in the reserved liquid if necessary. Heat through for a minute to mingle the flavors.

4 Add the banana to the skillet, then season to taste with cayenne pepper and salt. Garnish with the parsley sprig and serve immediately.

VARIATION
Instead of lentils, prepare the dish using cooked pinto or borlotti beans.

Balti Dhal

This dish uses chana dhal, a husked, split, black garbanzo bean, which is yellow on the inside and has a nutty taste.

NUTRITIONAL INFORMATION

Calories	132	Sugars	.........2g
Protein	.........6g	Fat	...........6g
Carbohydrate	...15g	Saturates	......1g

5 mins   1¼ hrs

SERVES 4

INGREDIENTS

1 cup chana dhal or yellow split peas, washed

½ tsp ground turmeric

1 tsp ground coriander

1 tsp salt

4 curry leaves

2 tbsp oil

½ tsp asafetida powder (optional)

1 tsp cumin seeds

2 onions, chopped

2 garlic cloves, crushed

½ inch/1 cm piece of fresh ginger root, grated

½ tsp garam masala

1 Put the chana dhal or yellow split peas in a large pan and pour in enough water to cover by 1 inch/2.5 cm. Bring to a boil and use a spoon to remove the scum that has formed.

2 Add the turmeric, ground coriander, salt, and curry leaves. Lower the heat and simmer for 1 hour, until the chana dhal or yellow split peas are tender, but not mushy. Drain well.

3 Heat the oil in a karahi (Balti pan) or wok. Add the asafetida, if using, and stir-fry for 30 seconds.

4 Add the cumin seeds and stir-fry until they start popping.

5 Add the onions and stir-fry for 5 minutes until golden brown.

6 Add the garlic, ginger, garam masala, and chana dhal or yellow split peas and stir-fry for 2 minutes. Serve the Balti dhal immediately as a side dish with a curry meal or set aside to cool, then store in the refrigerator for later use.

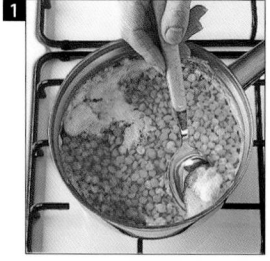  

COOK'S TIP

Dhal keeps well so it is a good idea to make a large amount and store it in the refrigerator or freezer in small portions. Reheat before serving.

Corn-on-the-Cob

Corn cobs are available nearly all the year round and can be barbecued with the husks on or off. Cook them as soon as possible after purchase.

NUTRITIONAL INFORMATION

Calories	79	Sugars 2g
Protein	.........3g	Fat 2g
Carbohydrate	...14g	Saturates 0.2g

 25 mins   30–40 mins

SERVES 6

I N G R E D I E N T S

4–6 corn cobs

vegetable oil, for brushing

T O   S E R V E

butter (optional)

salt (optional)

1 Soak the cobs in lukewarm water for 20 minutes. Drain them thoroughly and pat dry with paper towels.

2 If the cobs have no husks, brush with oil and cook on a hot barbecue for 30 minutes, brushing occasionally with the oil and turning often.

3 If the cobs have husks, tear off all but the last 2 layers and brush with oil.

4 Cook on a hot barbecue for 40 minutes, brushing with oil once or twice and turning occasionally.

5 Serve the corn cobs hot, without the husks. If you like, add a pat of butter and season with salt to taste.

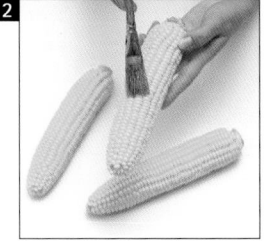

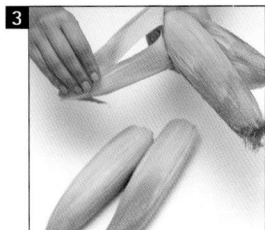

Eggplant Curry

This is a rich vegetable dish, ideal served with a tandoori chicken and nan bread. It is also delicious served as a vegetarian dish with rice.

NUTRITIONAL INFORMATION

Calories 73   Sugars 6g
Protein ....3g   Fat 4g
Carbohydrate ....6g   Saturates 1g

15 mins   15 mins

SERVES 4

INGREDIENTS

2 eggplants

1 cup low-fat plain yogurt

2 cardamom pods

½ tsp ground turmeric

1 dried red chile

½ tsp coriander seeds

½ tsp ground black pepper

1 tsp garam masala

1 clove

2 tbsp sunflower oil

1 onion, sliced lengthwise

2 garlic cloves, crushed

1 tbsp grated fresh ginger root

6 ripe tomatoes, peeled, deseeded, and quartered

fresh cilantro, to garnish

1 Roast the eggplants over a naked flame or place under a preheated broiler, turning frequently, for about 5 minutes until charred and black all over. Peel under cold running water. Cut off the stem ends and discard.

2 Put the peeled eggplants into a large bowl and mash lightly with a fork. Stir in the yogurt.

3 Grind the cardamom pods, turmeric, red chile, coriander seeds, black pepper, garam masala, and clove in a large mortar with a pestle or in a spice grinder.

4 Heat the oil in a wok or heavy skillet over a moderate heat and cook the onion, garlic, and ginger until softened. Add the tomatoes and ground spices and stir well.

5 Add the eggplant mixture to the skillet and stir well. Cook for 5 minutes over low heat, stirring constantly, until all the flavors are combined and some of the liquid has evaporated.

6 Serve the eggplant immediately, garnished with cilantro.

Casseroled Potatoes

This potato dish is cooked in the oven with leeks and wine. It is very quick and simple to make.

NUTRITIONAL INFORMATION

Calories ....187 Sugars 2g
Protein ....4g Fat 3g
Carbohydrate ...31g Saturates 2g

 10 mins   50 mins

SERVES 4

INGREDIENTS

1½ lb/675 g waxy potatoes, cut into chunks

1 tbsp butter

2 leeks, sliced

⅔ cup dry white wine

⅔ cup vegetable bouillon

1 tbsp lemon juice

2 tbsp chopped mixed fresh herbs

salt and pepper

TO GARNISH

grated lemon zest

mixed fresh herbs, optional

1 Cook the potato chunks in a pan of boiling water for 5 minutes. Drain them thoroughly.

2 Meanwhile, melt the butter in a skillet and sauté the leeks for 5 minutes or until they have softened.

3 Spoon the partly cooked potatoes and leeks into an ovenproof dish.

4 In a measuring pitcher, mix together the wine, vegetable bouillon, lemon juice, and chopped mixed herbs. Season to taste with salt and pepper, then pour the mixture over the potatoes.

5 Cook in a preheated oven, 375°F/190°C, for 35 minutes or until the potatoes are tender.

6 Garnish the potato casserole with lemon zest and fresh herbs (if using) and serve as an accompaniment to meat casseroles or roasted meat.

COOK'S TIP

Cover the ovenproof dish halfway through cooking if the leeks start to brown on the top.

Vegetables with Vermouth

Serve these vegetables in their paper packets to retain all the juices. The result is truly delicious.

NUTRITIONAL INFORMATION

Calories 62   Sugars 9g
Protein ....2g   Fat 0.5g
Carbohydrate ...12g   Saturates 0.1g

10 mins   20 mins

SERVES 4

INGREDIENTS

1 carrot, cut into batons

1 fennel bulb, sliced

3½ oz/100 g zucchini, sliced

1 red bell pepper, sliced

4 small onions, halved

½ cup vermouth

4 tbsp lime juice

grated rind of 1 lime

pinch of paprika

4 fresh tarragon sprigs

salt and pepper

fresh tarragon sprigs, to garnish

1 Place all of the vegetables in a large bowl and mix well.

2 Cut 4 large squares of baking parchment and place a quarter of the vegetables in the center of each. Bring the sides of the paper up and pinch together to make an open packet.

3 Mix together the vermouth, lime juice, lime rind, and paprika and pour a quarter of the mixture into each packet. Season with salt and pepper and add a tarragon sprig to each. Pinch the tops of the packets together to seal.

4 Place the packets in a steamer, cover, and cook for 15–20 minutes or until the vegetables are tender. Garnish with tarragon sprigs and serve immediately.

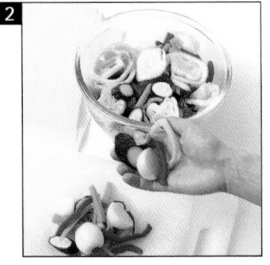  

COOK'S TIP

Vermouth is a fortified white wine flavored with various herbs and spices. It is available in both sweet and dry forms.

Raitas

Raitas are easy to prepare, very versatile, and have a cooling effect which will be appreciated if you are serving hot, spicy dishes.

NUTRITIONAL INFORMATION

Calories 33   Sugars 5g
Protein . . . . .3g   Fat 0.4g
Carbohydrate . . . .5g   Saturates 0.3g

 10 mins   🕐 5 mins

SERVES 4

I N G R E D I E N T S

MINT RAITA

scant 1 cup low-fat plain yogurt

¼ cup water

1 small onion, finely chopped

½ tsp mint sauce

½ tsp salt

3 fresh mint leaves, to garnish

CUCUMBER RAITA

8 oz/225 g cucumber

1 medium onion

½ tsp salt

½ tsp mint sauce

1¼ cups low-fat plain yogurt

⅔ cup water

fresh mint leaves, to garnish

EGGPLANT RAITA

1 medium eggplant

1 tsp salt

1 small onion, finely chopped

2 fresh green chiles, deseeded and finely chopped

scant 1 cup low-fat plain yogurt

3 tbsp water

1 To make the mint raita, place the yogurt in a bowl and whisk with a fork. Gradually whisk in the water. Add the onion, mint sauce, and salt and blend together. Garnish with mint leaves.

2 To make the cucumber raita, peel and slice the cucumber. Chop the onion finely. Place the cucumber and onion in a large bowl, then add the salt and the mint sauce. Add the yogurt and the water, place the mixture in a blender, and blend well. Serve garnished with mint leaves.

3 To make the eggplant raita, remove the top end of the eggplant and chop the rest into small pieces. Boil in a pan of water until softened, then drain, and mash. Add the salt, onion, and green chiles, mixing well. Whisk the yogurt with the water, add to the mixture, and mix thoroughly.

Sesame Seed Chutney

This chutney is delicious served with spiced rice dishes
and also makes an unusual filling to spread in sandwiches.

NUTRITIONAL INFORMATION

Calories 120	Sugars 0g	
Protein 4g	Fat 12g	
Carbohydrate ...0.2g	Saturates 2g	

 10 mins   5 mins

SERVES 4

INGREDIENTS

8 tbsp sesame seeds

2 tbsp water

½ bunch of fresh cilantro

3 fresh green chiles, chopped

1 tsp salt

2 tsp lemon juice

chopped fresh red chili, to garnish

1 Place the sesame seeds in a large, heavy pan and dry roast them, stirring constantly. Set the sesame seeds aside to cool.

2 Once cooled, place the sesame seeds in a food processor or mortar and grind well to form a fine powder.

3 Add the water to the ground sesame seeds and mix thoroughly to form a smooth paste.

4 Finely chop the cilantro. Add the chiles and cilantro to the sesame seed paste and grind again.

5 Add the salt and lemon juice to the mixture and grind once again.

6 Remove the mixture from the food processor or mortar and transfer to a serving dish. Garnish with chopped red chile and serve.

COOK'S TIP

Dry roasting brings out the flavor of spices and takes just a few minutes. You will be able to tell when the spices are ready because of the wonderful fragrance that develops. Stir the spices constantly to ensure that they do not burn.

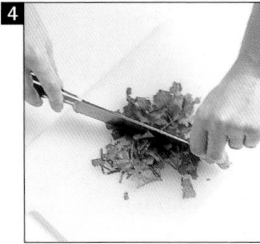

Gram Flour Bread

This filling bread goes well with any vegetarian curry and lime pickle. Store the gram flour in a cool, dark place in an airtight container.

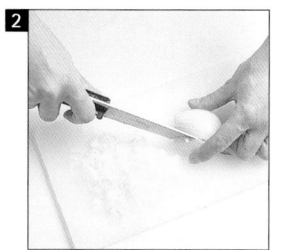

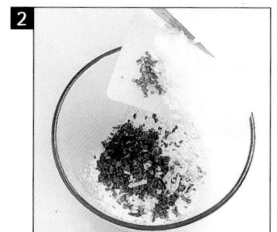

NUTRITIONAL INFORMATION

Calories	112	Sugars	1g
Protein	3g	Fat	2g
Carbohydrate	21g	Saturates	0g

 30 mins 15 mins

SERVES 4–6

I N G R E D I E N T S

generous ¾ cup whole-wheat flour (ata or chapati flour), plus extra for dusting

⅔ cup gram flour

½ tsp salt

1 small onion

fresh cilantro leaves, very finely chopped

2 fresh green chiles, deseeded and very finely chopped

⅔ cup water

2 tsp ghee

1 Sift the whole-wheat and gram flours together into a large mixing bowl. Add the salt to the flours and mix together thoroughly.

2 Chop the onion very finely. Blend the onion, cilantro, and chiles into the flour mixture.

3 Add the water and mix to form a soft dough. Cover the dough with a clean dish cloth or plastic wrap and set aside for about 15 minutes.

4 Turn out the dough and knead thoroughly for 5–7 minutes. Divide the dough into 8 equal portions.

5 Roll out the dough portions to rounds about 7 inches/18 cm in diameter on a lightly floured surface.

6 Place the dough portions individually in a skillet and cook over medium heat, turning three times and lightly greasing each side with the ghee each time. Transfer the gram flour bread to serving plates and serve hot.

COOK'S TIP
In Indian kitchens, gram flour is used to make breads, bhajis, and batters and to thicken sauces and stabilize yogurt when it is added to hot dishes.

Spicy Cauliflower

This is a perfectly delicious way to serve cauliflower. It can be enjoyed as a salad or at a picnic, or as a side dish to a main meal.

NUTRITIONAL INFORMATION

Calories	.68	Sugars	.3g
Protein	.5g	Fat	.4g
Carbohydrate	.4g	Saturates	.1g

 5 mins   15 mins

SERVES 4

INGREDIENTS

1 lb 2oz/500 g cauliflower, cut into florets

1 tbsp sunflower oil

1 garlic clove

½ tsp ground turmeric

1 tsp cumin seeds, ground

1 tsp coriander seeds, ground

1 tsp yellow mustard seeds

12 scallions, thinly sliced

salt and pepper,

1 Blanch the cauliflower in boiling water, drain and set aside. Cauliflower holds a lot of water, which tends to make it too soft, so turn the florets upside down at this stage and you will end up with a crisper result.

2 Heat the oil gently in a large, heavy skillet or wok. Add the garlic clove, turmeric, ground cumin, ground coriander, and mustard seeds. Stir well and cover the skillet or wok.

3 When you hear the mustard seeds popping, add the scallions and stir well. Cook, stirring constantly, for 2 minutes until softened. Season to taste with salt and pepper.

4 Add the cauliflower and stir for 3–4 minutes until coated completely with the spices and thoroughly heated.

5 Remove and discard the garlic clove and serve immediately.

COOK'S TIP

For a special occasion, this dish looks great made with baby cauliflowers instead of florets. Peel off most of the outer leaves, leaving a few for decoration, and blanch the baby cauliflowers whole for 4 minutes, and drain. Continue as in step 2.

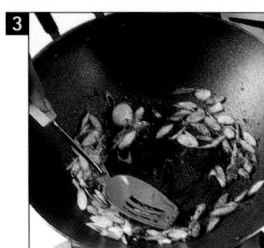

Trio of Potato Purées

These small molds filled with layers of flavored potato look very impressive. They are ideal with fish or roast meats.

 15 mins   1¼ hrs

SERVES 4

I N G R E D I E N T S

1 tbsp butter, plus extra for greasing

10½ oz /300 g mealy potatoes, chopped

4½ oz/125 g rutabaga, chopped

1 carrot, chopped

1 lb/450 g spinach

1 tbsp skim milk

¼ cup all-purpose flour

1 egg

½ tsp ground cinnamon

1 tbsp orange juice

¼ tsp grated nutmeg

salt and pepper

carrot thin sticks, to garnish

1 Lightly grease four ⅔ cup/150 ml ramekins with butter.

2 Cook the potatoes in a pan of boiling water for 10 minutes. In separate pans cook the rutabaga and carrot in boiling water for 10 minutes. Blanch the spinach in boiling water for 5 minutes. Drain the vegetables. Add the milk and butter to the potatoes and mash until smooth. Stir in the flour and egg.

3 Divide the potato mixture into 3 bowls. Spoon the rutabaga into one bowl and mix well. Spoon the carrot into the second bowl and mix well. Spoon the spinach into the third bowl and mix well.

4 Add the cinnamon to the rutabaga and potato mixture and season to taste. Stir the orange juice into the carrot and potato mixture. Stir the nutmeg into the spinach and potato mixture.

5 Spoon a layer of the rutabaga and potato mixture into each of the ramekins and smooth over the top. Cover each with a layer of spinach and potato mixture, then top with the carrot and potato mixture. Cover the ramekins with foil and place in a roasting pan. Half-fill the pan with boiling water and cook in a preheated oven, 350°F/180°C, for 40 minutes or until set.

6 Turn out on to serving plates. Garnish with the carrot sticks and serve immediately.

Italian Potato Wedges

These oven-cooked potato wedges use classic pizza ingredients and are delicious served with plain meats, such as pork or lamb.

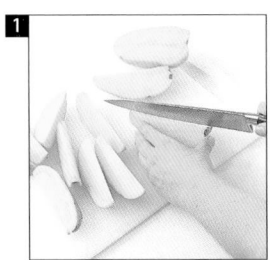

NUTRITIONAL INFORMATION

Calories	115	Sugars	.........4g
Protein	.........6g	Fat	...........5g
Carbohydrate	...13g	Saturates	.......3g

 15 mins   35 mins

SERVES 4

INGREDIENTS

2 large waxy potatoes, unpeeled

4 large ripe tomatoes, peeled and seeded

⅔ cup vegetable bouillon

2 tbsp tomato paste

1 small yellow bell pepper, cut into strips

4½ oz/125 g white mushrooms, quartered

1 tbsp chopped fresh basil

½ cup grated cheese

salt and pepper

1 Cut each of the potatoes into 8 equal wedges. Parboil the potatoes in a pan of boiling water for 15 minutes. Drain well and place in a shallow ovenproof dish.

2 Chop the tomatoes and add to the dish. Mix together the vegetable bouillon and tomato paste, then pour the mixture over the potatoes and tomatoes.

3 Add the yellow bell pepper strips, quartered mushrooms, and chopped basil. Season well with salt and pepper.

4 Sprinkle the grated cheese over the top and cook in a preheated oven, 375°F/190°C, for 15–20 minutes until the topping is golden brown. Serve at once.

Roasted Vegetables

Rosemary branches can be used as brushes for basting and as skewers. Soak the rosemary skewers overnight to prevent them from charring.

NUTRITIONAL INFORMATION

Calories . . . . .16 Sugars 3g
Protein . . . . .1g Fat 0.3g
Carbohydrate . . . .3g Saturates 0g

 15 mins   15 mins

SERVES 6

I N G R E D I E N T S

1 small red cabbage

1 fennel bulb

1 orange bell pepper, cut into 1½ inch/
    4 cm dice

1 eggplant, halved and sliced into ½ inch/
    1 cm pieces

2 zucchini, thickly sliced diagonally

olive oil, for brushing

6 rosemary twigs, about 6 inches/15 cm
    long, soaked in cold water

salt and pepper

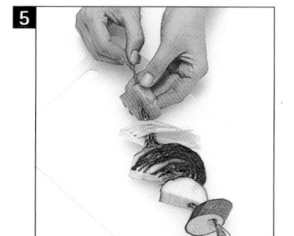

1 Put the red cabbage on its side on a cutting board and cut through the middle of its stem and heart. Divide each piece into 4, each time including a section of the stem in the slice to hold it together.

2 Prepare the fennel in the same way as the red cabbage.

3 Blanch the red cabbage and fennel in boiling water for 3 minutes, then drain well.

4 With a wooden skewer, carefully pierce a hole through the middle of each piece of vegetable.

5 Thread a piece of orange bell pepper, fennel, red cabbage, eggplant, and zucchini onto each rosemary twig, gently pushing the rosemary through the skewer holes.

6 Brush liberally with olive oil and season with plenty of salt and pepper.

7 Cook over a hot barbecue or under a preheated broiler for 8–10 minutes, turning occasionally. Serve immediately.

VARIATION

Fruit skewers are a deliciously quick and easy dessert. Thread pieces of banana, mango, peach, strawberry, apple, and pear onto soaked wooden skewers and cook over the dying embers. Brush with sugar syrup toward the end of cooking.

Potato & Vegetable Curry

Meat is very expensive in India and much of the population is vegetarian, so the cuisine is typified by tasty ways of cooking with vegetables.

NUTRITIONAL INFORMATION

Calories 301	Sugars 10g
Protein 9g	Fat 12g
Carbohydrate . . .41g	Saturates 1g

5 mins   45 mins

SERVES 4

INGREDIENTS

4 tbsp vegetable oil

1 lb 8 oz/675 g waxy potatoes, cut into large chunks

2 onions, quartered

3 garlic cloves, crushed

1 tsp garam masala

½ tsp ground turmeric

½ tsp ground cumin

½ tsp ground coriander

2 tsp grated fresh ginger root

1 fresh red chile, chopped

8 oz/225 g cauliflower florets

4 tomatoes, peeled and quartered

¾ cup frozen peas

2 tbsp chopped fresh cilantro

1¼ cups vegetable stock

shredded fresh cilantro, to garnish

boiled rice or warm Indian bread, to serve

COOK'S TIP

Use a large heavy-based saucepan or frying pan for this recipe to ensure that the potatoes are cooked thoroughly.

1 Heat the vegetable oil in a large heavy pan or skillet. Add the potato chunks, onions, and garlic and fry over low heat, stirring frequently, for 2–3 minutes until the onions are beginning to soften.

2 Add the garam masala, turmeric, ground cumin, ground coriander, ginger, and chile to the pan, mixing the spices into the vegetables until they are well coated. Cook over low heat, stirring constantly, for 1 minute.

3 Add the cauliflower, tomatoes, peas, chopped fresh cilantro, and vegetable stock to the curry mixture.

4 Cook the potato curry over low heat for 30–40 minutes or until the potatoes are tender and completely cooked through.

5 Garnish the potato curry with fresh cilantro and serve with plain boiled rice or warm Indian bread.

Cheese Crisp-Topped Mash

Liven up mashed potato by topping it with a crisp mixture flavored with herbs, mustard, and onion, which turns crunchy on baking.

NUTRITIONAL INFORMATION

Calories	131	Sugars	.......1.4g
Protein	........3.8g	Fat	.........5.7g
Carbohydrate	..17.3g	Saturates	.....3.4g

10 mins   20–25 mins

SERVES 4

INGREDIENTS

2 lb/900 g mealy potatoes, diced

2 tbsp butter

2 tbsp milk

½ cup grated sharp cheese or blue cheese

CRUMBLE TOPPING

3 tbsp butter

1 onion, cut into chunks

1 garlic clove, crushed

1 tbsp whole-grain mustard

3 cups fresh whole-wheat bread crumbs

2 tbsp chopped fresh parsley

salt and pepper

1 Cook the potatoes in a pan of lightly salted boiling water for 10 minutes or until cooked through.

2 Meanwhile, make the crisp topping. Melt the butter in a skillet. Add the onion, garlic, and whole-grain mustard and cook gently for 5 minutes, stirring constantly, until the onion chunks have softened.

3 Put the bread crumbs and parsley in a mixing bowl and stir in the onion. Season to taste with salt and pepper.

4 Drain the potatoes thoroughly and place them in a mixing bowl. Add the butter and milk, then mash until smooth. Stir in the grated cheese while the potato is still hot.

5 Spoon the mashed potato into a shallow casserole and sprinkle with the crisp topping.

6 Cook in a preheated oven, 400°F, for 10–15 minutes until the crisp topping is golden brown and crunchy. Serve immediately.

COOK'S TIP

For extra crunch, add freshly cooked vegetables, such as celery and peppers, to the mashed potato in step 4.

Cheese & Potato Strudel

This bread has a delicious cheese and garlic flavor and is best eaten straight from the oven, as soon as it is the right temperature.

NUTRITIONAL INFORMATION

Calories	387	Sugars	.........1g
Protein	........13g	Fat	...........8g
Carbohydrate	...70g	Saturates	.......4g

2½ hrs   55 mins

SERVES 8

INGREDIENTS

butter, for greasing

6 cups white bread flour, plus extra for dusting

6 oz/175 g mealy potatoes, diced

2 envelopes (5 tsp) active dry yeast

2 cups vegetable stock

2 garlic cloves, crushed

2 tbsp chopped fresh rosemary

1 cup grated Swiss cheese

1 tbsp vegetable oil

1 tbsp salt

1 Lightly grease and flour a cookie sheet. Cook the potatoes in a pan of boiling water for 10 minutes or until soft. Drain well and mash.

2 Transfer the mashed potatoes to a large mixing bowl, stir in the yeast, flour, and stock, and mix to form a smooth dough. Add the garlic, rosemary, and ¾ cup of the cheese and knead the dough for 5 minutes. Make a hollow in the dough, pour in the oil, and knead the dough again.

3 Cover the dough and set it aside in a warm place for 1½ hours or until doubled in size.

4 Knead the dough again and divide it into 3 equal portions. Roll each portion into a sausage shape about 14 inches/35 cm long.

5 Press one end of each of the sausage shapes firmly together, then carefully braid the dough, without breaking it, and fold the remaining ends under, sealing them firmly.

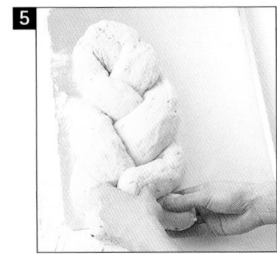

6 Place the strudel on the cookie sheet, cover, and set aside to rise for 30 minutes.

7 Sprinkle the remaining cheese over the top of the strudel and cook in a preheated oven, 375°F/190°C, for 40 minutes or until the base of the loaf sounds hollow when tapped. Serve while it is warm.

Mini Focaccia

This is a delicious Italian bread made with olive oil.
The topping of red onions and thyme is particularly flavorsome.

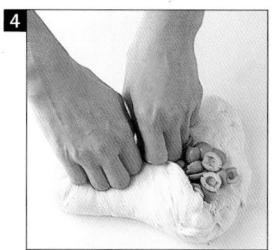

NUTRITIONAL INFORMATION

Calories	439	Sugars	.........3g
Protein	.........9g	Fat	..........15g
Carbohydrate	....71g	Saturates	.......2g

 2¼ hrs 25 mins

SERVES 4

INGREDIENTS

2 tbsp olive oil, plus extra for greasing

2 cups white bread flour

½ tsp salt

1 envelope active dry yeast

generous 1 cup lukewarm water

1 cup pitted green or black
olives, halved

TOPPING

2 red onions, sliced

2 tbsp olive oil

1 tsp sea salt

1 tbsp fresh thyme leaves

1 Lightly oil several cookie sheets. Sift the flour and salt into a large mixing bowl, then stir in the yeast. Pour in the olive oil and lukewarm water and mix everything together to form a dough.

2 Turn the dough out onto a lightly floured counter and knead it for about 5 minutes. Alternatively, use an electric mixer with a dough hook.

3 Place the dough in a greased bowl, cover, and set aside in a warm place for about 1–1½ hours or until it has doubled in size. Punch down the dough by kneading it again for 1–2 minutes.

4 Knead half of the olives into the dough. Divide the dough into quarters and then shape the quarters into rounds. Place them on the cookie sheets and push your fingers into the dough to create a dimpled effect.

5 To make the topping, sprinkle the red onions and remaining olives over the rounds. Drizzle the oil over the top and sprinkle with the sea salt and thyme leaves. Cover and set aside to rise for 30 minutes.

6 Bake in a preheated oven, 375°F/ 190°C, for 20–25 minutes or until the focaccia are golden.

7 Transfer to a wire rack to cool completely before serving.

VARIATION
Use this quantity of dough to make 1 large focaccia, if you prefer.

Mediterranean Bread

Many of the flavors of the Mediterranean are captured in this rustic loaf. It is a perfect accompaniment for pasta dishes, stews, and casseroles.

NUTRITIONAL INFORMATION

Calories . . . . .222 Sugars 1g
Protein . . . . .5g Fat 12g
Carbohydrate . . .26g Saturates 2g

🥖 🥖 🥖

🧈 2 hrs   🕐 40 mins

MAKES 1 LOAF

I N G R E D I E N T S

3½ cups all-purpose flour, plus extra
   for dusting

1 envelope active dry yeast

1 tsp salt

1 tbsp coriander seeds, lightly crushed

2 tsp dried oregano

scant 1 cup lukewarm water

3 tbsp olive oil, plus extra for greasing

5½ oz/150 g sun-dried tomatoes in oil,
   drained, patted dry and chopped

3 oz/85 g feta cheese, drained, patted dry
   and cubed

1 cup black olives, patted dry, pitted
   and sliced

1 Combine the flour, yeast, salt, coriander seeds, and oregano and make a well in the center. Gradually add most of the water and the oil to make a dough. Gradually add the remaining water, if needed, drawing in all the flour.

2 Turn out onto a lightly floured counter and knead for 10 minutes, gradually kneading in the tomatoes, cheese, and olives. Wash the bowl and lightly coat it with oil.

3 Shape the dough into a ball, put it in the bowl, and turn the dough over.

Cover tightly and set the dough aside until it doubles in volume.

4 Turn the dough out onto a lightly floured counter. Knead lightly, then shape into a ball. Place on a lightly floured cookie sheet. Cover and set aside to rise until it doubles in volume again.

5 Lightly sprinkle the top of the loaf with flour. Using a sharp knife, cut 3 shallow slashes in the top. Bake in a preheated oven, 450°F/230°C, for 20 minutes. Lower the temperature to 400°F/200°C and bake for a further 20 minutes or until the loaf sounds hollow when you tap it on the bottom. Transfer to a wire rack to cool completely. This loaf keeps well for up to 3 days stored in an airtight container.

Sesame Breadsticks

The irregular shape of these Greek-style breadsticks adds to their appeal. They are crisp and crunchy on the outside with a soft, chewy interior.

NUTRITIONAL INFORMATION

Calories	61	Sugars	.........0g
Protein	.........2g	Fat	...........2g
Carbohydrate	...10g	Saturates	.......0g

1¾ hrs   10 mins

MAKES 32 STICKS

I N G R E D I E N T S

2 cups unbleached white bread flour, plus extra for dusting

2 cups strong whole-wheat flour

1 envelope active dry yeast

2 tsp salt

½ tsp sugar

2 cups lukewarm water

4 tbsp olive oil, plus extra for greasing

1 egg white, lightly beaten

sesame seeds, for sprinkling

1 Combine the flours, yeast, salt, and sugar in a bowl and make a well in the center. Gradually stir in most of the water and the olive oil to make a dough. Gradually add the remaining water, if necessary, drawing in all the flour.

2 Turn out onto a lightly floured counter and knead for about 10 minutes until smooth and elastic. Wash the bowl and lightly coat with olive oil.

3 Shape the dough into a ball, put it in the bowl, and turn over so it is coated. Cover tightly with a dish cloth or lightly oiled plastic wrap and set aside in a warm place until the dough has doubled in volume. Meanwhile, line a cookie sheet with baking parchment.

4 Turn out the dough onto a lightly floured counter and knead lightly. Divide the dough into 2 equal pieces. Roll each piece into a 16 inch/40 cm rope and then cut each rope into 8 equal pieces. Cut each piece in half again to make a total of 32 pieces.

5 Cover the dough you are not working with a dish cloth or plastic wrap to prevent it from drying out. Roll each piece of dough into a thin 10 inch/25 cm rope on a very lightly floured counter. Carefully transfer the cookie sheet.

6 Cover and set aside to rise for 10 minutes. Brush with the egg white, then sprinkle evenly and thickly with sesame seeds. Bake in a preheated oven, 450°F/230°C, for 10 minutes.

7 Brush again with egg white, and bake for a further 5 minutes or until golden brown and crisp. Transfer the breadsticks to wire racks to cool.

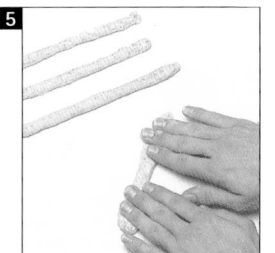

Olive Rolls

These rustic-style bread rolls depend on fruity olive oil and good-quality olives. You could use any of the Flavored Olives (see page 431).

NUTRITIONAL INFORMATION

Calories 181	Sugars 1g
Protein 6g	Fat 3g
Carbohydrate . . .35g	Saturates 0.5g

1¾ hrs   30 mins

MAKES 16 ROLLS

I N G R E D I E N T S

1 cup olives in brine or
oil, drained

6½ cups unbleached white bread flour, plus
extra for dusting

1½ tsp salt

1 envelope active dry yeast

2 cups lukewarm water

2 tbsp extra virgin olive oil, plus extra
for brushing

4 tbsp finely chopped fresh oregano,
parsley, or thyme leaves or 1 tbsp dried
mixed herbs

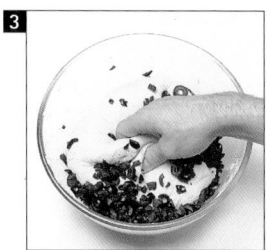

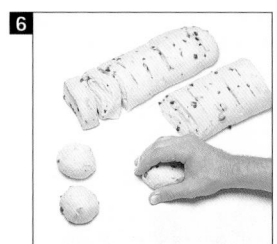

1 Pit the olives with an olive or cherry pitter and finely chop. Pat off the excess brine or olive oil with paper towels. Set aside.

2 Combine the flour, salt, and yeast in a bowl and make a well in the center. Gradually stir in most of the water and the olive oil to make a dough. Gradually add the remaining water, if necessary, drawing in all the flour.

3 Lightly knead in the chopped olives and herbs. Turn out the dough onto a lightly floured counter and knead for 10 minutes until smooth and elastic. Wash the bowl and lightly coat with oil.

4 Shape the dough into a ball, put it in the bowl, and turn over so it is coated. Cover tightly with a dish cloth or lightly oiled plastic wrap and set aside to rise until it has doubled in volume. Dust a cookie sheet with flour.

5 Turn out the dough onto a lightly floured counter and knead lightly. Roll the dough into 8 inch/20 cm ropes on a very lightly floured counter.

6 Cut the dough into 16 even pieces. Shape each piece into a ball and place on the prepared cookie sheet. Cover and set aside to rise for 15 minutes.

7 Lightly brush the top of each roll with olive oil. Bake in a preheated oven, 425°F/220°C, for about 25–30 minutes or until the rolls are golden brown. Transfer to a wire rack and set aside to cool completely before serving.

Fougasse

This distinctive-looking bread, with its herringbone slits, is baked daily throughout Provence. It is best eaten on the day it is baked.

NUTRITIONAL INFORMATION

Calories 161	Sugars 1g
Protein 5g	Fat 0g
Carbohydrate . . .36g	Saturates 0g

1¾ hrs   25 mins

MAKES 2 LARGE LOAVES

I N G R E D I E N T S

6½ cups unbleached white bread flour, plus extra for dusting

1 envelope active dry yeast

2 tsp salt

1 tsp sugar

2 cups lukewarm water

olive oil, for greasing

1 Combine the flour, yeast, salt, and sugar in a bowl and make a well in the center. Gradually stir in most of the water to make a dough. Gradually add the remaining water, if necessary, drawing in all the flour.

2 Turn out onto a lightly floured counter and knead for 10 minutes until smooth and elastic. Wash the bowl and lightly coat with olive oil.

3 Shape the dough into a ball, put it in the bowl, and turn the dough over. Cover the bowl tightly with a dish cloth or lightly oiled plastic wrap and set aside in a warm place to rise until the dough has doubled in volume.

4 Punch down the dough and turn out onto a lightly floured counter. Knead lightly, then cover with the upturned bowl, and let stand for 10 minutes.

5 Put a roasting pan of water in the bottom of the oven while it preheats to 450°F/230°C, then lightly flour a cookie sheet.

6 Divide the dough into 2 pieces and roll each one into a 12 inch/30 cm oval, ½ inch/1 cm thick. Using a sharp knife, cut 5 x 3 inch/7.5 cm slices on an angle in a herringbone pattern on each of the dough ovals. Cut all the way through the dough, using the tip of the knife to open the slits.

7 Spray the loaves with cold water. Bake for 20 minutes, turn upside down, and continue baking for 5 minutes until the loaves sound hollow when tapped on the bottom. Transfer to wire racks to cool.

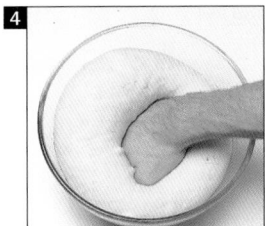

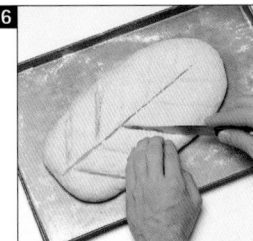

Herb Focaccia

Rich with olive oil, this bread is so delicious it would turn a simple salad or bowl of soup into a positive feast.

NUTRITIONAL INFORMATION

Calories 210   Sugars 1g
Protein . . . . .6g   Fat 5g
Carbohydrate . . . .5g   Saturates 1g

 2 hrs   15 mins

MAKES 1 LOAF

INGREDIENTS

3½ cups unbleached white bread flour, plus extra for dusting

1 envelope active dry yeast

1½ tsp salt

½ tsp sugar

1¼ cups lukewarm water

3 tbsp extra virgin olive oil, plus extra for greasing

4 tbsp finely chopped fresh herbs

polenta or cornmeal, for sprinkling

coarse sea salt, for sprinkling

1 Combine the flour, yeast, salt, and sugar in a bowl and make a well in the center. Gradually stir in most of the water and 2 tablespoons of the olive oil to make a dough. Gradually add the remaining water, if necessary, drawing in all the flour.

2 Turn out onto a lightly floured counter and knead. Transfer to a bowl and lightly knead in the herbs for 10 minutes until soft but not sticky. Wash the bowl and lightly coat with olive oil.

3 Shape the dough into a ball, put it in the bowl, and turn the dough over. Cover tightly with a dish cloth or lightly greased plastic wrap and set aside in a warm place to rise until the dough has doubled in volume. Meanwhile, sprinkle polenta over a cookie sheet.

4 Turn the dough out onto a lightly floured counter and knead lightly. Cover with the upturned bowl and let stand for 10 minutes.

5 Roll out and pat the dough into a 10 inch/25 cm circle, about ½ inch/1 cm thick and carefully transfer it to the prepared cookie sheet. Cover with a dish cloth and set aside to rise again for 15 minutes.

6 Using a lightly oiled finger, poke indentations all over the surface of the loaf. Drizzle the remaining olive oil over and sprinkle lightly with sea salt. Bake in a preheated oven, 450°F/230°C, for 15 minutes or until golden brown and the loaf sounds hollow when rapped on the bottom. Transfer to a wire rack to cool completely.

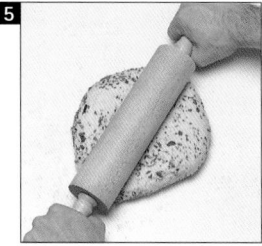

Yellow Split Pea Casserole

If ever there was a winter warmer, this is it—an intensely satisfying dish, ideal for serving with rice or fresh nan bread.

NUTRITIONAL INFORMATION

Calories	358	Sugars	........10g
Protein	........19g	Fat	..........12g
Carbohydrate	...45g	Saturates	......1g

2¼ hrs   1½ hrs

SERVES 4

INGREDIENTS

2 tbsp ghee

1 tsp black mustard seeds

1 onion, finely chopped

2 garlic cloves, crushed

1 carrot, grated

1 inch/2.5 cm piece of fresh
  ginger root, grated

1 fresh green chile, deseeded and
  finely chopped

1 tbsp tomato paste

generous 1 cup yellow split peas, soaked in
  water for 2 hours and drained

14 oz/400 g can chopped tomatoes

2¼ cups vegetable stock

1¾ cups diced pumpkin

8 oz/225 g cauliflower, cut into florets

2 tbsp vegetable oil

1 large eggplant, diced

1 tbsp chopped fresh cilantro

1 tsp garam masala

salt and pepper

1 Melt the ghee in a large pan over medium heat. Add the mustard seeds and when they start to splutter, add the onion, garlic, carrot, and ginger.

2 Cook, stirring occasionally, for about 5 minutes until the vegetables have softened. Add the green chile and stir in the tomato paste. Stir in the split peas.

3 Add the tomatoes and stock and bring to a boil. Season to taste with salt and pepper.

4 Lower the heat and simmer gently, stirring occasionally, for 40 minutes. Add the pumpkin and cauliflower florets, cover, and simmer for a further 30 minutes until the split peas are soft.

5 Meanwhile, heat the oil in a large, heavy skillet over high heat. Add the eggplant and stir until sealed on all sides. Remove from the pan with a slotted spoon and drain on paper towels.

6 Stir the eggplant into the split pea mixture with the cilantro and garam masala. Check and adjust the seasoning if necessary. Transfer to a warmed serving dish and serve immediately.

Sauté of Summer Vegetables

The freshness of lightly cooked summer vegetables is enhanced by the aromatic flavor of a tarragon and white wine dressing.

NUTRITIONAL INFORMATION

Calories 217   Sugars 8g
Protein . . . . .2g   Fat 18g
Carbohydrate . . . .9g   Saturates 9g

 10 mins   10–15 mins

SERVES 4

INGREDIENTS

8 oz/225 g baby carrots, scrubbed

4½ oz/125 g string beans

2 zucchini, trimmed

1 bunch of large scallions

1 bunch of radishes

4 tbsp butter

2 tbsp light olive oil

2 tbsp white wine vinegar

4 tbsp dry white wine

1 tsp superfine sugar

1 tbsp chopped fresh tarragon

salt and pepper

fresh tarragon sprigs, to garnish

1 Cut the carrots in half lengthwise, slice the beans and zucchini, and halve the scallions and radishes, so that all the vegetables are cut to even-size pieces.

2 Melt the butter in a large, heavy skillet or wok. Add all the vegetables and fry them over medium heat, stirring frequently, until they are tender, but still crisp and firm to the bite.

3 Meanwhile, pour the olive oil, vinegar, and white wine into a small pan and add the sugar. Place over low heat, stirring until the sugar has dissolved. Remove the pan from the heat and then add the chopped tarragon.

4 When the vegetables are just cooked, pour over the "dressing." Stir through, tossing the vegetables well to coat.

Season to taste with salt and pepper and then transfer to a warmed serving dish. Garnish with sprigs of fresh tarragon and serve the sauté immediately.

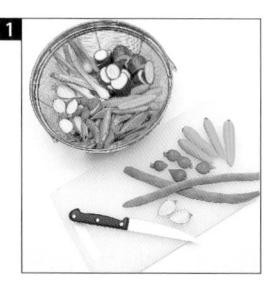

Seasonal Stir-Fry

When selecting different fresh vegetables for this dish, bear in mind that there should always be a contrast in color as well as in texture.

NUTRITIONAL INFORMATION

Calories . . . . .108　Sugars 3g
Protein . . . . .3g　Fat 9g
Carbohydrate . . . .4g　Saturates 1g

🍳 10 mins　⏲ 10 mins

SERVES 4

I N G R E D I E N T S

1 medium red bell pepper, deseeded

4 oz/115 g zucchini

4 oz/115 g cauliflower

115 g/4 oz green beans

3 tbsp vegetable oil

a few small slices of fresh ginger root

½ tsp salt

½ tsp sugar

1–2 tbsp vegetable stock or
　water (optional)

1 tbsp light soy sauce

a few drops of sesame oil (optional)

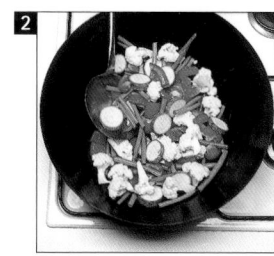

1 Using a sharp knife or Chinese cleaver, cut the red bell pepper into small squares. Thinly slice the zucchini. Trim the cauliflower and divide into small florets, discarding any thick stems. Make sure the vegetables are cut into roughly similar shapes and sizes to ensure that they cook evenly. Trim the green beans, then cut them in half.

2 Heat the vegetable oil in a preheated wok or large, heavy skillet. Add the prepared vegetables with the ginger and stir-fry for about 2 minutes.

3 Add the salt and sugar to the wok or skillet and continue to stir-fry for 1–2 minutes, adding a little vegetable stock or water if the mixture appears to be too dry. Do not add any liquid unless necessary.

4 Add the light soy sauce and sesame oil, if using, and stir well to coat the vegetables lightly.

5 Transfer the stir-fried vegetables to a warmed serving dish or bowl and serve immediately.

VARIATION

Almost any vegetables could be used in this dish, but make sure there is a good variety of color, and always include several crisp vegetables such as carrots or snow peas.

Sidekick Vegetables

Colorful vegetables are grilled over hot coals to make this unusual hot salad, which is served with a spicy chili sauce on the side.

NUTRITIONAL INFORMATION

Calories	224	Sugars	........14g
Protein	.........4g	Fat	..........15g
Carbohydrate	...21g	Saturates	.......2g

15 mins   30 mins

SERVES 4

INGREDIENTS

1 red bell pepper, deseeded

1 orange or yellow bell pepper, deseeded

2 zucchini

2 corn cobs

1 eggplant

olive oil, for brushing

chopped fresh thyme, rosemary, and parsley

salt and pepper

lime or lemon wedges, to serve

DRESSING

2 tbsp olive oil

1 tbsp sesame oil

1 garlic clove, crushed

1 small onion, finely chopped

1 celery stalk, finely chopped

1 small fresh green chile, deseeded and chopped

4 tomatoes, chopped

2 inch/5 cm piece of cucumber, chopped

1 tbsp tomato paste

1 tbsp lime or lemon juice

1 To make the dressing, heat the olive and sesame oils together in a pan or skillet. Add the garlic and onion, and cook over low heat, stirring occasionally, for about 3 minutes until softened.

2 Add the celery, chile, and tomatoes to the pan and cook, stirring frequently, for 5 minutes.

3 Stir in the chopped cucumber, tomato paste, and lime or lemon juice, and simmer over low heat for 8–10 minutes until thick and pulpy. Season to taste with salt and pepper.

4 Cut the vegetables into thick slices and brush with a little olive oil.

5 Cook the vegetables over the hot coals of the barbecue for about 5–8 minutes, sprinkling them with salt and pepper and fresh herbs as they cook, and turning once.

6 Divide the vegetables among 4 serving plates and spoon some of the dressing onto the side. Serve immediately, sprinkled with a few more chopped herbs and accompanied by the lime or lemon wedges.

Spicy Peas & Spinach

This is quite a filling accompaniment and so should be served with a fairly light entrée—it goes well with egg dishes.

NUTRITIONAL INFORMATION

Calories	340	Sugars	.........6g
Protein	........21g	Fat	..........14g
Carbohydrate	...34g	Saturates	.......2g

2¼ hrs   25 mins

SERVES 4

INGREDIENTS

1 cup green split peas

2 lb/900 g spinach

4 tbsp vegetable oil

1 onion, halved and sliced

1 tsp grated fresh ginger root

1 tsp ground cumin

½ tsp chili powder

½ tsp ground coriander

2 garlic cloves, crushed

1¼ cups vegetable stock

salt and pepper

fresh cilantro sprigs and lime wedges, to garnish

1 Rinse the peas under cold running water. Transfer to a mixing bowl, cover with cold water, and set aside to soak for 2 hours. Drain well.

2 Place the spinach in a large pan with just the water clinging to its leaves after washing. Cook over medium heat for 5 minutes until just wilted. Drain well, squeeze out any excess moisture, and coarsely chop.

3 Heat the vegetable oil in a large pan and add the onion, ginger, cumin, chili powder, ground coriander, and garlic.

Cook over low heat, stirring constantly, for 2–3 minutes.

4 Add the peas and spinach and stir in the stock. Cover and simmer for 10–15 minutes or until the peas are cooked and the liquid has been absorbed. Season with salt and pepper to taste. Transfer to a warmed serving dish, garnish with fresh cilantro sprigs and lime wedges and serve immediately.

COOK'S TIP
Once the split peas have been added, stir occasionally to prevent them from sticking to the base of the pan.

Cauliflower & Spinach Curry

The contrast in color in this recipe makes it very appealing to the eye, especially as the cauliflower is lightly colored with yellow turmeric.

NUTRITIONAL INFORMATION

Calories 228	Sugars 6g
Protein 8g	Fat 18g
Carbohydrate 8g	Saturates 2g

 10 mins   25 mins

SERVES 4

INGREDIENTS

1 medium cauliflower

6 tbsp vegetable oil

1 tsp mustard seeds

1 tsp ground cumin

1 tsp garam masala

1 tsp ground turmeric

2 garlic cloves, crushed

1 onion, halved and sliced

1 fresh green chile, sliced

1 lb 2 oz/500 g spinach

5 tbsp vegetable stock

1 tbsp chopped fresh cilantro

salt and pepper

fresh cilantro sprigs, to garnish

1 Break the cauliflower into small florets.

2 Heat the oil in a deep flameproof casserole. Add the mustard seeds and cook until they begin to pop.

3 Stir in the remaining spices, the garlic, onion, and chile and cook, stirring constantly, for 2–3 minutes.

4 Add the cauliflower, spinach, stock and chopped cilantro and season to taste with salt and pepper. Cook over low heat for 15 minutes or until the cauliflower is tender. Uncover and boil for 1 minute to thicken the juices.

5 Transfer the curry to a warmed serving dish, garnish with cilantro sprigs and serve.

COOK'S TIP

Mustard seeds are used throughout India and are particularly popular in southern Indian vegetarian cooking. They are fried in oil first to bring out their flavor before the other ingredients are added.

Baked Celery with Cream

This dish is sprinkled with bread crumbs for a crunchy topping, underneath which is hidden a creamy celery and pecan mixture.

NUTRITIONAL INFORMATION

Calories . . . . . . .237 Sugars 5g
Protein . . . . .7g Fat 19g
Carbohydrate . . . .11g Saturates 7g

 15 mins   40 mins

SERVES 4

INGREDIENTS

1 head of celery

½ tsp ground cumin

½ tsp ground coriander

1 garlic clove, crushed

1 red onion, thinly sliced

½ cup pecan halves

⅔ cup vegetable stock

⅔ cup light cream

1 cup fresh whole-wheat bread crumbs

5 tbsp grated Parmesan cheese

salt and pepper

celery leaves, to garnish

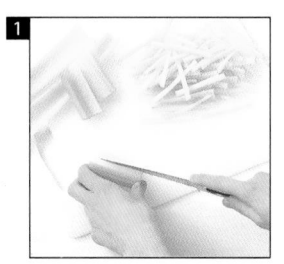

1 Trim the celery and cut it into fine batons. Place the celery in a casserole with the cumin, ground coriander, crushed garlic, red onion, and pecan halves. Toss well to mix and to coat the vegetables in the spices.

2 Combine the stock and cream in a pitcher, stirring well to mix. Pour the cream mixture over the vegetables. Season with salt and pepper to taste.

3 Combine the bread crumbs and cheese in a small bowl and sprinkle over the top to cover the vegetables.

4 Cook in a preheated oven, 400°F/ 200°C, for 40 minutes or until the vegetables are tender and the topping is crispy. Garnish with celery leaves and serve immediately.

COOK'S TIP
Once grated, Parmesan cheese quickly loses its "bite" so it is best to grate only the amount you need for the recipe. Wrap the rest tightly in foil and it will keep for several months in the refrigerator.

Bulgur Pilau

Bulgur is very easy to use and, as well as being full of nutrients,
it is a delicious alternative to rice, having a distinctive nutty flavor.

NUTRITIONAL INFORMATION

Calories	637	Sugars	........25g
Protein	........16g	Fat	..........26g
Carbohydrate	...90g	Saturates	......11g

  15 mins   35–40 mins

SERVES 4

I N G R E D I E N T S

6 tbsp butter or margarine

1 red onion, halved and sliced

2 garlic cloves, crushed

2 cups bulgur

6 oz/175 g tomatoes, deseeded
  and chopped

½ cup baby corn cobs, halved lengthwise

3 oz/85 g small broccoli florets

3¾ cups vegetable stock

2 tbsp honey

scant ½ cup golden raisins

½ cup pine nuts

½ tsp ground cinnamon

½ tsp ground cumin

salt and pepper

sliced scallions, to garnish

1 Melt the butter or margarine in a large flameproof casserole over medium heat. Add the onion and garlic and cook, stirring occasionally, for 2–3 minutes until softened, but not browned.

2 Add the bulgur, tomatoes, corn cobs, broccoli florets, and vegetable stock and bring to a boil. Reduce the heat, cover, and simmer gently, stirring occasionally, for 15–20 minutes.

3 Stir in the honey, golden raisins, pine nuts, ground cinnamon, and cumin and season with salt and pepper to taste, mixing well. Remove the casserole from the heat, and set aside, covered, for 10 minutes.

4 Spoon the bulgur pilau into a warmed serving dish. Garnish with thinly sliced scallions and serve the pilau immediately.

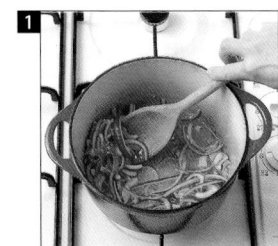

COOK'S TIP

The dish is left to stand for 10 minutes so that the bulgur can finish cooking and the flavors of the ingredients will mingle.

Soda Bread

This variation of traditional Irish soda bread is best eaten on the day it has been baked, when it is deliciously fresh.

NUTRITIONAL INFORMATION

Calories 203	Sugars 7g
Protein 8g	Fat 2g
Carbohydrate . . .42g	Saturates 0g

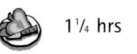 1¼ hrs   40 mins

SERVES 4

I N G R E D I E N T S

butter, for greasing

2½ cups all-purpose white flour, plus extra for dusting

2½ cups all-purpose whole-wheat flour

2 tsp baking powder

1 tsp baking soda

2 tbsp superfine sugar

1 tsp salt

1 egg, beaten

scant 1 cup plain yogurt

1. Grease a cookie sheet with butter and dust with flour.

2. Sift the white and whole-wheat flours, baking powder, baking soda, sugar, and salt into a large bowl and add any bran remaining in the strainer.

3. In a pitcher, beat together the egg and yogurt and pour the mixture into the dry ingredients. Mix everything together to make a soft and sticky dough.

4. On a lightly floured counter, knead the dough for a few minutes until it is smooth, then shape the dough into a round about 2 inches/5 cm deep.

5. Transfer the dough to the cookie sheet. Mark a cross shape in the top of the loaf.

6. Bake in a preheated oven, 375°F/190°C, for about 40 minutes or until the bread is golden brown all over.

7. Transfer the loaf to a wire rack and let cool completely. Cut into slices to serve.

VARIATION

For a fruity version of this soda bread, add scant 1 cup raisins to the dry ingredients in step 2.

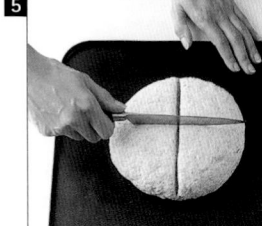

Cheese & Chive Bread

This is a quick bread to make. It is full of a wonderful cheese flavor and, to enjoy it at its best, it should be eaten as fresh as possible.

NUTRITIONAL INFORMATION

Calories 190   Sugars 1g
Protein . . . . .7g   Fat 9g
Carbohydrate . . .22g   Saturates 5g

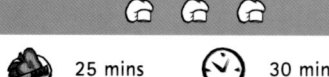

🍳 25 mins   🕐 30 mins

SERVES 8

INGREDIENTS

butter, for greasing

2 cups self-rising flour

1 tsp salt

1 tsp mustard powder

1 cup grated sharp cheese

2 tbsp chopped fresh chives

1 egg, beaten

2 tbsp butter, melted

⅔ cup milk

1 Grease a 9 inch/23 cm square cake pan with a little butter and line the base with baking parchment.

2 Sift the flour, salt, and mustard powder into a large mixing bowl.

3 Reserve 3 tablespoons of the grated cheese for sprinkling over the top of the loaf before baking in the oven.

4 Stir the remaining grated cheese into the bowl, together with the chopped fresh chives. Mix well together.

5 Add the beaten egg, melted butter, and milk to the dry ingredients and stir the mixture thoroughly to combine.

6 Pour the mixture into the prepared pan and spread evenly with a spatula. Sprinkle over the reserved grated cheese.

7 Bake the loaf in a preheated oven, 375°F/190°C, for about 30 minutes.

8 Let the bread cool slightly in the pan. Turn out onto a wire rack to cool completely. Cut into triangles to serve.

COOK'S TIP

You can use any hard sharp cheese of your choice—from Cheddar to pecorino—for this recipe.

Garlic Bread Rolls

This bread is not at all like the store-bought, ready-made garlic bread. Instead it has a subtle flavor and a soft texture.

NUTRITIONAL INFORMATION

Calories 265	Sugars 3g	
Protein 10g	Fat 6g	
Carbohydrate ...46g	Saturates 2g	

 1¾ hrs   35 mins

SERVES 8

INGREDIENTS

butter, for greasing

12 garlic cloves, peeled

1½ cups milk

1lb/450 g white bread flour

1 tsp salt

1 envelope active dry yeast

1 tbsp dried mixed herbs

2 tbsp sunflower oil

1 egg, beaten

milk, for brushing

rock salt, for sprinkling

1 Lightly grease a cookie sheet with a little butter.

2 Place the garlic cloves and milk in a pan, bring to a boil, and simmer gently for 15 minutes. Let cool slightly, then process in a blender or food processor to purée the garlic.

3 Sift the flour and salt into a large mixing bowl and stir in the active dry yeast and mixed herbs.

4 Add the garlic-flavored milk, sunflower oil, and beaten egg to the dry ingredients and mix everything thoroughly to form a dough.

5 Place the dough on a lightly floured counter and knead lightly for a few minutes until smooth and soft.

6 Place the dough in a lightly greased bowl, cover, and set aside to rise in a warm place for about 1 hour or until doubled in size.

7 Punch down the dough by kneading it for 2 minutes. Shape into 8 rolls and place on the cookie sheet. Score the top of each roll with a knife, cover, and set aside for 15 minutes.

8 Brush the rolls with milk and sprinkle rock salt over the top.

9 Bake in a preheated oven, 425°F/ 220°C, for 15–20 minutes. Transfer the rolls to a wire rack and set aside to cool before serving.

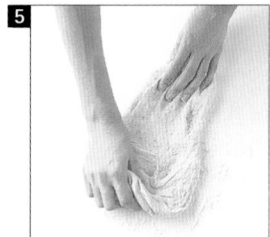

Sun-Dried Tomato Rolls

These white rolls have the addition of finely chopped sun-dried tomatoes. The tomatoes are sold in jars and are available at most supermarkets.

NUTRITIONAL INFORMATION

Calories . . . . .214 Sugars 1g
Protein . . . . .5g Fat 12g
Carbohydrate . . .22g Saturates 7g

2¼ mins   15 mins

SERVES 4

I N G R E D I E N T S

butter, for greasing

2 cups white bread flour

½ tsp salt

1 envelope active dry yeast

7 tbsp butter, melted and
   cooled slightly

3 tbsp milk, warmed

2 eggs, beaten

2 oz/55 g sun-dried tomatoes in oil, well
   drained and finely chopped

milk, for brushing

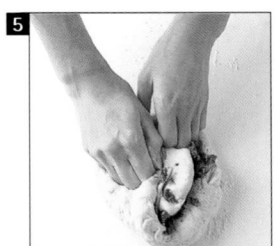

1 Lightly grease a cookie sheet with a little butter.

2 Sift the flour and salt into a large mixing bowl. Stir in the yeast, then pour in the butter, milk, and eggs. Mix together to form a dough.

3 Turn the dough onto a lightly floured counter and knead for about 5 minutes. Alternatively, use an electric mixer with a dough hook.

4 Place the dough in a greased bowl, cover, and set aside to rise in a warm place for 1–1½ hours or until the dough has doubled in size. Punch down the dough for 2–3 minutes.

5 Knead the sun-dried tomatoes into the dough, sprinkling the counter with a little extra flour because the tomatoes are quite oily.

6 Divide the dough into 8 equal-size balls and place them on the prepared cookie sheet. Cover and set aside to rise for about 30 minutes or until the rolls have doubled in size.

7 Brush the rolls with milk and bake in a preheated oven, 450°F/230°C, for 10–15 minutes or until the rolls are golden brown all over.

8 Transfer the rolls to a wire rack and let cool slightly before serving.

VARIATION

Add some finely chopped anchovies or olives to the dough in step 5 for extra flavor, if wished.

Garlic & Sage Bread

This freshly made herb bread is an ideal accompaniment to salads and soups and is suitable for vegans.

NUTRITIONAL INFORMATION

Calories 207	Sugars 3g
Protein 9g	Fat 2g
Carbohydrate . . .42g	Saturates 0g

1¼ hrs   30 mins

MAKES 6

I N G R E D I E N T S

vegetable oil, for greasing

2¼ cups strong brown bread flour

1 envelope active dry yeast

3 tbsp chopped fresh sage

2 tsp sea salt

3 garlic cloves, finely chopped

1 tsp honey

⅔ cup lukewarm water

1 Grease a cookie sheet. Sift the flour into a large mixing bowl and stir in the bran remaining in the strainer.

2 Stir in the active dry yeast, chopped sage and half of the sea salt. Reserve 1 teaspoon of the chopped garlic for sprinkling and stir the remainder into the bowl. Add the honey and lukewarm water and mix together thoroughly to form a dough.

3 Turn the dough out onto a lightly floured counter and knead it for about 5 minutes until smooth and elastic (alternatively, use an electric mixer with a dough hook).

4 Place the dough in a greased bowl, cover with lightly oiled plastic wrap, and set aside to rise in a warm place until doubled in size.

5 Knead the dough again for a few minutes. Roll it into a long sausage and then shape it into a ring. Place on the cookie sheet. Cover and set aside to rise for 30 minutes or until springy to the touch. Sprinkle with the remaining sea salt and garlic.

6 Bake the loaf in a preheated oven, 400°F/200°C, for 25–30 minutes. Transfer to a wire rack to cool completely before serving.

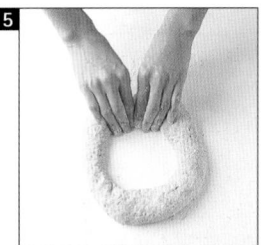

COOK'S TIP

Roll the dough into a long sausage and then curve it into a circular shape. You can omit the sea salt for sprinkling, if you prefer.

Peshwari Nan

A tandoor oven throws out a ferocious heat; this bread is traditionally cooked on its side wall, where the heat is slightly less intense.

NUTRITIONAL INFORMATION

Calories	420	Sugars	........13g
Protein	........11g	Fat	...........9g
Carbohydrate	...77g	Saturates	.......3g

  3¾ hrs   30 mins

SERVES 6

INGREDIENTS

¼ cup lukewarm water

pinch of sugar

½ tsp active dry yeast

4½ cups white bread flour, plus extra for dusting

½ tsp salt

¼ cup plain yogurt

2 tart eating apples, peeled, cored, and diced

vegetable oil, for brushing

scant ½ cup golden raisins

½ cup sliced almonds

1 tbsp fresh cilantro leaves

2 tbsp grated coconut

1 Combine the water and sugar in a bowl and sprinkle over the yeast. Set aside for 5–10 minutes, until the yeast has dissolved and the mixture is foamy.

2 Put the flour and salt into a bowl and make a well in the center. Add the yeast mixture and yogurt. Draw in the flour until it is all absorbed. Mix thoroughly, adding enough lukewarm water to form a soft dough. Turn out onto a floured board and knead for 10 minutes until smooth. Put into an oiled bowl, cover, and set aside for 3 hours in a warm place.

3 Meanwhile, line the broiler pan with foil, shiny side up.

4 Put the apples into a pan with a little water. Bring to a boil, mash them down, reduce the heat, and simmer for 20 minutes, mashing occasionally.

5 Divide the dough into 4 pieces and roll each piece out to an 8 inch/20 cm oval. Pull one end out into a teardrop shape, about ¼ inch/5 mm thick. Lay on a floured surface and prick the dough all over with a fork.

6 Brush both sides of the bread with oil. Place 1 oval under a preheated broiler at the highest setting. Cook for 3 minutes, turn the bread over, using tongs, and cook for a further 3 minutes. It should have dark brown spots all over.

7 Spread a teaspoonful of the apple purée all over the bread, then sprinkle over a quarter of the golden raisins, sliced almonds, cilantro leaves, and the coconut. Broil the remaining 3 ovals of dough and spread with the apple purée and flavorings in the same way.

Green Stir-Fry

The basis of this recipe is bok choy, also known as pak choi or Chinese greens. If unavailable, use Swiss chard or Savoy cabbage instead.

NUTRITIONAL INFORMATION

Calories 107   Sugars 6g
Protein . . . . .4g   Fat 8g
Carbohydrate . . . .6g   Saturates 1g

5 mins   10 mins

SERVES 4

I N G R E D I E N T S

2 tbsp peanut oil

2 garlic cloves, crushed

½ tsp ground star anise

1 tsp salt

12 oz/350 g bok choy, shredded

8 oz/225 g baby spinach

1 oz/25 g snow peas

1 celery stalk, sliced

1 green bell pepper, deseeded and sliced

¼ cup vegetable stock

1 tsp sesame oil

1 Heat the peanut oil in a preheated wok or large skillet, swirling the it around the base until it is really hot.

2 Add the crushed garlic and stir-fry over medium heat for about 30 seconds. Stir in the ground star anise, salt, shredded bok choy, spinach, snow peas, celery, and green bell pepper and stir-fry for 3–4 minutes.

3 Add the vegetable stock, lower the heat, cover the wok or skillet, and cook for 3–4 minutes. Remove the lid and stir in the sesame oil. Mix thoroughly to combine all the ingredients.

4 Transfer the green vegetable stir-fry to a warmed serving dish and serve immediately.

COOK'S TIP

Star anise is an important ingredient in Chinese cuisine. The attractive star-shaped pods are often used whole to add a decorative garnish to dishes. The flavor is similar to licorice, but with spicy undertones and is quite strong.

Lemon Dhal

This dhal is eaten almost every day in most households in Hyderabad in India. Traditionally it is cooked with tamarind, but lemon juice is easier.

NUTRITIONAL INFORMATION

Calories 386   Sugars 0.7g
Protein . . . . .5g   Fat 35g
Carbohydrate . . .12g   Saturates 4g

10 mins   30 mins

SERVES 4

INGREDIENTS

scant ½ cup masoor dhal

1 tsp finely chopped fresh ginger root

1 tsp crushed garlic

1 tsp chili powder

½ tsp ground turmeric

scant 2 cups water

1 tsp salt

3 tbsp lemon juice

2 fresh green chiles

fresh cilantro leaves

BAGHAAR

⅔ cup vegetable oil

4 garlic cloves

6 dried red chiles

1 tsp white cumin seeds

3 Deseed the green chiles, if wished, and chop or slice. Add the chiles and cilantro leaves to the dhal and set aside.

4 To make the baghaar, heat the oil in a heavy pan. Add the garlic, red chiles, and white cumin seeds and fry for about 1 minute. Turn off the heat.

5 When the baghaar has cooled slightly, pour it over the dhal. If the dhal is too runny, set it, uncovered, over medium heat for 3–5 minutes until it has thickened slightly.

6 Transfer the dhal to a warmed serving dish and serve hot.

1 Rinse the masoor dhal and place in a large pan. Add the ginger, garlic, chili powder, and turmeric. Stir in 1¼ cups of the water and bring to a boil over medium heat. Half cover the pan and simmer until the dhal is soft enough to be mashed.

2 Mash the dhal. Add the salt, lemon juice, and the remaining water, stirring to mix thoroughly. It should be of a fairly smooth consistency.

Black-Eye Peas

This Indian dish is very good served with chapatis and a vegetable curry. The beans need to be soaked overnight so prepare well in advance.

NUTRITIONAL INFORMATION

Calories 757   Sugars 5g
Protein . . . . .10g   Fat 69g
Carbohydrate . . .26g   Saturates 7g

 8¼ hrs   1 hr

SERVES 4

INGREDIENTS

¾ cup black-eye peas

1¼ cups vegetable oil

2 medium onions, sliced

1 tsp finely chopped fresh ginger root

1 tsp crushed garlic

1 tsp chili powder

1½ tsp salt

1½ tsp ground coriander

1½ tsp ground cumin

⅔ cup water

2 fresh green chiles, finely chopped

fresh cilantro leaves

1 tbsp lemon juice

1 Rinse the black-eye peas, place them in a bowl, cover with cold water, and set aside to soak overnight.

2 Drain the peas, place in a pan, and add water to cover. Bring to a boil over low heat, then simmer gently for about 30 minutes. Drain the peas thoroughly and set aside.

3 Heat the oil in a heavy pan. Add the onions and cook, stirring frequently, for 5–8 minutes, until golden brown. Add the ginger, garlic, chili powder, salt, ground coriander, and ground cumin and

stir-fry the mixture over low heat for about 3–5 minutes.

4 Add the water to the pan, cover, and simmer until all of the water has completely evaporated.

5 Add the black-eye peas, green chiles, and cilantro leaves to the onions and stir-fry for 3–5 minutes.

6 Transfer the black-eye peas to a serving dish, sprinkle over the lemon

juice, and serve immediately. Alternatively, allow the beans to cool and serve cold.

COOK'S TIP
Black-eye peas are oval-shaped, gray or beige beans with a dark dot in the center. They have a slightly smoky flavor. They are sold canned, as well as dried.

Kabli Chana Sag

Pulses such as garbanzo beans are widely used in India.
They need to be soaked overnight so prepare well in advance.

NUTRITIONAL INFORMATION

Calories 217	Sugars 5g	
Protein 12g	Fat 9g	
Carbohydrate . . .25g	Saturates 1g	

🥄 10 mins   🕐 1–2 hrs

SERVES 6

I N G R E D I E N T S

1 cup garbanzo beans, soaked overnight
  and drained

5 cloves

1 inch/2.5 cm piece of cinnamon stick

2 garlic cloves

3 tbsp sunflower oil

1 small onion, sliced

3 tbsp lemon juice

1 tsp coriander seeds

2 tomatoes, peeled, deseeded, and chopped

1 lb 2 oz/500g spinach, rinsed and any
  tough stems removed

1 tbsp chopped fresh cilantro

TO GARNISH

fresh cilantro sprigs

lemon slices

1 Put the garbanzo beans into a pan
with enough water to cover. Add the
cloves, cinnamon, and 1 whole unpeeled
garlic clove that has been lightly crushed
with the back of a knife to release the
juices. Bring to a boil, reduce the heat, and
simmer for 1–2 hours or until the garbanzo
beans are tender when tested with a
toothpick. Skim off any foam that comes
to the surface.

2 Meanwhile, heat 1 tablespoon of the
oil in a heavy pan. Crush the
remaining garlic clove. Put it into the pan
with the onion and cook over a moderate
heat, stirring occasionally, for about
5 minutes.

3 Remove the cloves, cinnamon, and
garlic from the pan of garbanzo beans
and discard. Drain the garbanzo beans.
Place ⅓ cup of the garbanzo beans in a
food processor with the onion and garlic,
the lemon juice, and 1 tablespoon of the
oil and process until smooth. Alternatively,
blend together with a fork in a bowl. Stir
this purée into the remaining beans.

4 Heat the remaining oil in a large
skillet, add the coriander seeds, and
stir for 1 minute until they give off their
aroma. Add the tomatoes, stir, and add the
spinach. Cover and cook over a moderate
heat for 1 minute. The spinach should be
wilted, but not soggy. Stir in the chopped
cilantro and remove from the heat.

5 Transfer the garbanzo beans to a
warmed serving dish and spoon over
the spinach mixture. Garnish with the
cilantro sprigs and slices of lemon and
serve immediately.

White Lentils

This dhal is dry when cooked, so give it a baghaar (seasoned oil dressing). It makes an excellent accompaniment to any meal of kormas.

NUTRITIONAL INFORMATION

Calories 129   Sugars 1g
Protein ....6g   Fat 6g
Carbohydrate ...14g   Saturates 1g

5 mins   45 mins

SERVES 4

INGREDIENTS

scant ½ cup urid dhal

1 tsp finely chopped fresh ginger root

2½ cups water

1 tsp salt

1 tsp pepper

fresh mint leaves, to garnish

chapatis, to serve

BAGHAAR

2 tbsp vegetable ghee

2 garlic cloves

2 fresh red chiles, finely chopped

1 Rinse the lentils thoroughly and put them in a large pan with the ginger. Add the water and bring to a boil. Cover and simmer over medium heat for about 30 minutes. Check to see whether the lentils are cooked by rubbing them between your finger and thumb. If they are still a little hard in the middle, cook for a further 5–7 minutes. If necessary, remove the lid and cook until any remaining water has evaporated.

2 Add the salt and pepper to the lentils, mix well, and set aside.

3 To make the baghaar, heat the ghee in a separate pan. Add the garlic and

chopped red chiles and stir well to mix thoroughly.

4 Pour the garlic and chile mixture over the lentils.

5 Transfer the white lentils to warmed individual serving dishes, garnish with mint leaves, and serve hot with chapatis.

COOK'S TIP
Ghee was traditionally made from clarified butter, which can withstand higher temperatures than ordinary butter. Vegetable ghee has largely replaced it now because it is lower in saturated fats.

Split Peas with Vegetables

Here is a simple, yet nourishing and flavorful way of cooking yellow split peas. Vary the choice of vegetables and spices according to taste.

NUTRITIONAL INFORMATION

Calories 490	Sugars 8g	
Protein 21g	Fat 19g	
Carbohydrate ...63g	Saturates 3g	

 4¼ hrs 1 hr

SERVES 4

INGREDIENTS

1 cup dried yellow split peas

5 cups water

½ tsp ground turmeric (optional)

1 lb 2 oz/500 g new potatoes

5 tbsp vegetable oil

2 onions, coarsely chopped

6 oz/175 g white mushrooms

1 tsp ground coriander

1 tsp ground cumin

1 tsp chili powder

1 tsp garam masala

scant 1 cup vegetable stock

½ cauliflower, broken into florets

¾ cup frozen peas

6 oz/175 g cherry tomatoes, halved

salt and pepper

fresh mint sprigs, to garnish

VARIATION

Chana dhal (popular with vegetarians because of its high protein content) may be used instead of yellow split peas, if preferred. Chana dhal is similar to yellow split peas, although the grains are smaller and the flavor sweeter.

1 Place the split peas in a bowl, add the water, and set aside to soak for at least 4 hours or overnight.

2 Place the peas and the soaking liquid in a large pan, stir in the turmeric, if using, and bring to a boil. Skim off any scum that rises to the surface, half-cover the pan, and simmer gently for 20 minutes or until the peas are tender and almost dry. Remove the pan from the heat and set aside.

3 Meanwhile, cut the potatoes into ¼ inch/5 mm thick slices. Heat the oil in a flameproof casserole, add the onions, potatoes, and mushrooms, and cook over low heat, stirring frequently, for 5 minutes. Stir in the spices and fry, stirring frequently, for 1 minute, then season with salt and pepper to taste, and add the stock and cauliflower florets.

4 Cover the pan and simmer, stirring occasionally, for 25 minutes or until the potatoes are tender. Add the split peas (and any of the cooking liquid) and the frozen peas. Bring to a boil, cover, and continue cooking for 5 minutes.

5 Stir in the halved cherry tomatoes and cook for 2 minutes. Taste and adjust the seasoning, if necessary. Serve hot, garnished with mint sprigs.

Tarka Dhal

This is just one version of many dhals that are served throughout India; as many people are vegetarian, dhals form a staple part of the diet.

NUTRITIONAL INFORMATION

Calories	183	Sugars	.........4g
Protein	.........8g	Fat	...........8g
Carbohydrate	...22g	Saturates	.......5g

10 mins   25 mins

SERVES 4

INGREDIENTS

2 tbsp ghee

2 shallots, sliced

1 tsp yellow mustard seeds

2 garlic cloves, crushed

8 fenugreek seeds

1 tsp grated fresh ginger root

½ tsp salt

generous ½ cup red lentils

1 tbsp tomato paste

2½ cups water

2 tomatoes, peeled and chopped

1 tbsp lemon juice

4 tbsp chopped fresh cilantro

½ tsp garam masala

½ tsp chili powder

1 Heat half of the ghee in a large pan and add the shallots. Cook for 2–3 minutes over high heat, then add the mustard seeds. Cover the pan until the seeds begin to pop.

2 Immediately remove the lid from the pan and add the garlic, fenugreek, ginger, and salt.

3 Stir once and add the lentils, tomato paste, and water. Bring to a boil, then lower the heat and simmer gently for 10 minutes.

4 Stir in the tomatoes, lemon juice, and chopped cilantro and simmer for 4–5 minutes until the lentils are tender.

5 Transfer to a serving dish. Heat the remaining ghee in a pan. Remove from the heat and stir in the garam masala and chili powder. Pour over the tarka dhal and serve.

COOK'S TIP

The flavors in a dhal can be altered to suit your particular taste; for example, for extra heat, add more chili powder or chiles, or add fennel seeds for a pleasant anise flavor.

Green Pumpkin Curry

The Indian pumpkin used in this curry is long and green and sold by weight. It can easily be bought from any Asian stores.

NUTRITIONAL INFORMATION

Calories	347	Sugars 6g
Protein	........2g	Fat 34g
Carbohydrate	....8g	Saturates 4g

10 mins   30 mins

SERVES 4

I N G R E D I E N T S

⅔ cup vegetable oil

2 medium onions, sliced

½ tsp white cumin seeds

scant 4 cups chopped green pumpkin

1 tsp dried mango powder

1 tsp finely chopped fresh ginger root

1 tsp crushed garlic

1 tsp crushed dried red chile

½ tsp salt

1¼ cups water

chapatis or nan bread, to serve

1 Heat the vegetable oil in a large heavy skillet. Add the onions and cumin seeds and fry over medium heat, stirring occasionally, for about 5 minutes until the onions are softened and a light golden brown and the seeds are giving off their aroma.

2 Add the cubed pumpkin to the skillet and stir-fry over low heat for 3–5 minutes.

3 Combine the dried mango powder, ginger, garlic, chile, and salt. Add the spice mixture to the pan, stirring well to combine with the vegetables.

4 Add the water, cover, and cook over low heat, stirring occasionally, for 10–15 minutes.

5 Transfer to serving plates and serve with chapatis or nan bread.

COOK'S TIP

Cumin seeds are popular with Indian cooks because of their warm, pungent flavor and aroma. The seeds are sold whole or ground and are usually included as one of the flavorings in garam masala.

Okra Curry

This is a delicious dry bhujia (vegetarian curry) which should be served hot with chapatis. Okra is a tasty vegetable and needs few spices.

NUTRITIONAL INFORMATION

Calories 371   Sugars 8g
Protein . . . . .4g   Fat 35g
Carbohydrate . . .10g   Saturates 4g

10 mins   30 mins

SERVES 4

I N G R E D I E N T S

1 lb/450 g okra

⅔ cup vegetable oil

2 medium onions, sliced

3 fresh green chiles, finely chopped

2 curry leaves

1 tsp salt

1 tomato, sliced

2 tbsp lemon juice

fresh cilantro leaves

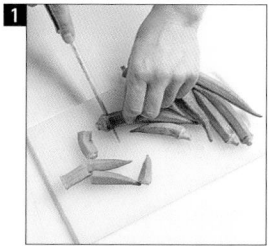  

1 Rinse the okra and drain thoroughly. Using a sharp knife, chop off and discard the ends of the okra. Cut the okra into 1 inch/2.5 cm long pieces.

2 Heat the vegetable oil in a large, heavy skillet. Add the onions, green chiles, curry leaves, and salt and mix together. Stir-fry the vegetables over low heat for 5 minutes.

3 Gradually add the okra, mixing in gently with a slotted spoon. Stir-fry the vegetable mixture over medium heat for 12–15 minutes.

4 Add the sliced tomato to the skillet and sprinkle over half the lemon juice. Taste and add more if required.

5 Sprinkle the cilantro leaves into the skillet, cover, and simmer for a further 3–5 minutes.

6 Transfer the curry to warmed serving plates and serve hot.

COOK'S TIP

Okra has a remarkable glutinous quality which naturally thickens curries and casseroles.

Sweet Hot Carrots & Beans

Take care not to overcook the vegetables in this tasty dish—they are definitely at their best served tender-crisp.

NUTRITIONAL INFORMATION

Calories	268	Sugars	........16g
Protein	.........5g	Fat	..........19g
Carbohydrate	...19g	Saturates	.......3g

🍲 10 mins   🕐 15 mins

SERVES 4

INGREDIENTS

1 lb 2 oz/500 g young carrots

8 oz/225 g green beans

1 bunch of scallions

4 tbsp vegetable ghee or vegetable oil

1 tsp ground cumin

1 tsp ground coriander

3 cardamom pods, split and seeds removed

2 dried red chiles

2 garlic cloves, crushed

1–2 tsp honey

1 tsp lemon or lime juice

½ cup unsalted, toasted cashews

1 tbsp chopped fresh cilantro or parsley

salt and pepper

TO GARNISH

slices of lime or lemon

fresh cilantro sprigs

1 Cut the carrots lengthwise into quarters and then in half crosswise if very long. Trim the beans. Cut the scallions into 2 inch/5 cm pieces.

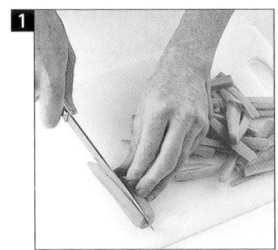

2 Cook the carrots and beans in a pan of lightly salted boiling water for 5–6 minutes until tender-crisp. Drain well.

3 Heat the ghee or oil in a large skillet, add the scallions, carrots, beans, cumin, ground coriander, cardamom seeds, and whole dried chiles. Cook over low heat, stirring frequently, for 2 minutes.

4 Stir in the garlic, honey, and lemon or lime juice and continue cooking, stirring occasionally, for a further 2 minutes. Season to taste with salt and pepper. Remove and discard the chiles.

5 Sprinkle the vegetables with the cashews and chopped cilantro and mix together lightly. Serve immediately, garnished with lime or lemon slices and cilantro sprigs.

Long Beans with Tomatoes

Indian meals often need some green vegetables to complement the spicy dishes and to set off the richly flavored sauces.

NUTRITIONAL INFORMATION

Calories 76	Sugars 3g	
Protein 2g	Fat 6g	
Carbohydrate 4g	Saturates 3g	

15 mins   25 mins

SERVES 6

INGREDIENTS

1 lb 2 oz/500 g green beans, cut into 2 inch/5 cm lengths

2 tbsp vegetable ghee

1 inch/2.5 cm piece of fresh ginger root, grated

1 garlic clove, crushed

1 tsp ground turmeric

½ tsp cayenne pepper

1 tsp ground coriander

4 tomatoes, peeled, seeded, and diced

⅔ cup vegetable stock

1 Blanch the beans briefly in boiling water, drain, refresh under cold running water, and drain again.

2 Melt the ghee in a large pan over a moderate heat. Add the grated ginger and crushed garlic, stir, and add the turmeric, cayenne, and ground coriander. Stir over low heat for about 1 minute until fragrant.

3 Add the diced tomatoes, tossing them until they are thoroughly coated in the spice mix.

4 Add the vegetable stock to the pan, bring to a boil, and simmer over medium-high heat, stirring occasionally, for about 10 minutes until the sauce has reduced and thickened.

5 Add the beans, reduce the heat to moderate, and heat through, stirring constantly, for 5 minutes.

6 Transfer to a warmed serving dish and serve immediately.

COOK'S TIP

Ginger graters are an invaluable piece of equipment to have when cooking Indian food. These small, flat graters, made of either bamboo or china, can be held directly over the pan while you grate.

Spicy Corn

This dish is an ideal accompaniment to a wide range of Indian dishes and would also go well with a Western-style casserole.

NUTRITIONAL INFORMATION

Calories 162   Sugars 6g
Protein ....2g   Fat 11g
Carbohydrate ...15g   Saturates 7g

 10 mins   10 mins

SERVES 4

INGREDIENTS

1 cup frozen or canned corn

1 tsp ground cumin

1 tsp crushed garlic

1 tsp ground coriander

1 tsp salt

2 fresh green chiles

1 medium onion, finely chopped

3 tbsp sweet butter

4 red chiles, crushed

½ tsp lemon juice

1 tbsp fresh cilantro leaves, plus extra to garnish

1 Thaw frozen corn, if using, or drain canned corn, and set aside.

2 Place the ground cumin, garlic, ground coriander, salt, 1 fresh green chile, and the onion in a mortar or a food processor and grind to form a smooth paste.

3 Heat the butter in a large skillet. Add the onion and spice mixture to the pan and fry over medium heat, stirring occasionally, for about 5–7 minutes.

4 Add the crushed red chiles to the mixture in the skillet and stir to combine.

5 Add the corn to the skillet and stir-fry for another 2 minutes.

6 Add the remaining green chile, lemon juice, and the fresh cilantro leaves to the skillet, stirring to combine.

7 Transfer the spicy corn mixture to a warmed serving dish. Garnish with extra fresh cilantro leaves and serve hot.

COOK'S TIP

Coriander is available ground or as seeds and is one of the essential ingredients in Indian cooking. Coriander seeds are often dry roasted before use to develop their flavor.

Fragrant Jasmine Rice

Jasmine rice has a delicate flavor and it can be served completely plain. This simple dish just has the light tang of lemon and soft scent of basil.

NUTRITIONAL INFORMATION

Calories	384	Sugars	.........0g
Protein	.........7g	Fat	...........4g
Carbohydrate	...86g	Saturates	.......1g

 15 mins   15 mins

SERVES 4

I N G R E D I E N T S

2 cups jasmine rice

3½ cups water

rind of ½ lemon, finely grated

2 tbsp fresh sweet basil, chopped

1 Wash the rice in several changes of cold water until the water runs clear. Bring the water to a boil in a large pan, then add the rice.

2 Bring back to a rolling boil. Turn the heat to a low simmer, cover the pan, and simmer for a further 12 minutes.

3 Remove the pan from the heat and set aside, covered, for 10 minutes. It is important to leave the pan tightly covered while the rice steams inside, so that the grains cook evenly and become fluffy and separate.

4 Fluff up the rice with a fork, then stir in the lemon rind. Serve sprinkled with basil leaves.

Coconut Rice with Pineapple

Cooking rice in coconut milk makes it very satisfying and nutritious, and this is often used as a base with meat, fish, vegetables, or eggs.

NUTRITIONAL INFORMATION

Calories 278   Sugars 11g
Protein ....5g   Fat 7g
Carbohydrate ...54g   Saturates 5g

 5 mins   20 mins

SERVES 4

INGREDIENTS

1 cup long grain rice

2¼ cups coconut milk

2 lemongrass stalks

scant 1 cup water

2 fresh pineapple slices, peeled and diced

2 tbsp toasted coconut

chili sauce, to serve

1 Wash the rice in several changes of cold water until the water runs clear. Place in a large pan with the coconut milk.

2 Place the lemongrass on a firm counter and bruise it by hitting firmly with a rolling pin or meat mallet. Add the stalks to the pan.

3 Add the water and bring to a boil. Lower the heat, cover the pan tightly, and simmer gently for 15 minutes. Remove the pan from the heat and fluff up the rice with a fork.

4 Remove and discard the lemongrass and stir in the pineapple. Sprinkle with toasted coconut and serve immediately with chili sauce.

VARIATION

A sweet version of this dish can be made by simply omitting the lemongrass and stirring in palm sugar or superfine sugar to taste during cooking. Serve as a dessert, with extra pineapple slices.

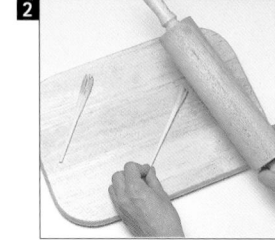

Chile & Coconut Sambal

A sweet-sour sambal that goes well with broiled or grilled fish. It can also be stirred into rice or noodles or curry dishes as extra flavoring.

NUTRITIONAL INFORMATION

Calories	118	Sugars	.........3g
Protein	.........1g	Fat	..........11g
Carbohydrate	....3g	Saturates	......10g

10 mins   0 mins

SERVES 6–8

INGREDIENTS

1 small coconut

1 fresh pineapple slice, peeled and finely diced

1 small onion, finely chopped

2 small fresh green chiles, deseeded and chopped

2 inch/5 cm piece of lemongrass

½ tsp salt

1 tsp shrimp paste

1 tbsp lime juice

2 tbsp chopped fresh cilantro

fresh cilantro sprigs, to garnish

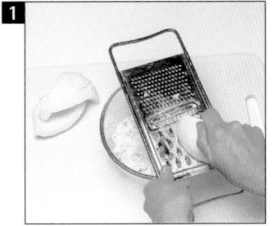

1 Puncture 2 of the coconut eyes with a screwdriver and pour the milk out from the shell. Crack the coconut shell, prize away the flesh, and coarsely grate it into a bowl. Alternatively, grate the coconut using the grating blade in a food processor and then scrape into a bowl.

2 Mix the coconut with the pineapple, onion, chiles, and lemongrass.

3 Blend together the salt, shrimp paste, and lime juice, then stir into the coconut mixture.

4 Stir in the cilantro. Spoon into a small dish to serve and garnish with fresh cilantro sprigs.

VARIATION

To make a quicker version of this sambal, stir a teaspoon of Thai green curry paste into freshly grated coconut and add finely diced pineapple and lime juice to taste.

Vegetables in Peanut Sauce

This colorful mix of vegetables in a rich, spicy peanut sauce can be served either as a side dish or as a vegetarian entrée.

NUTRITIONAL INFORMATION

Calories	249	Sugars	........10g
Protein	........10g	Fat	..........17g
Carbohydrate	...12g	Saturates	03

 10 mins   8–10 mins

SERVES 4

INGREDIENTS

2 carrots

1 small cauliflower, trimmed

2 small heads bok choy

5½ oz/150 g green beans

2 tbsp vegetable oil

1 garlic clove, finely chopped

6 scallions, sliced

1 tsp chili paste

2 tbsp soy sauce

2 tbsp Chinese rice wine

4 tbsp smooth peanut butter

3 tbsp coconut milk

COOK'S TIP

It's important to cut the vegetables thinly into pieces of a similar size so that they cook quickly and evenly. Prepare all the vegetables before you start to cook.

1 Cut the carrots diagonally into thin slices. Cut the cauliflower into small florets, then slice the stalk thinly. Thickly slice the bok choy. Cut the beans into 1¼ inch/3 cm lengths.

2 Heat the oil in a large skillet or wok. Add the garlic and scallions and stir-fry over medium heat for about 1 minute. Stir in the chili paste and cook for a few seconds.

3 Add the carrots and cauliflower and stir-fry for 2–3 minutes.

4 Add the bok choy and beans and stir-fry for a further 2 minutes. Stir in the soy sauce and rice wine.

5 Mix the peanut butter with the coconut milk and stir into the pan, then cook, stirring constantly, for a further minute. Serve immediately.

Thai Red Bean Curry

The "red" in the title refers not to the beans, but to the sauce, which has a warm, rusty red color. This is a good way to serve fresh or frozen beans.

NUTRITIONAL INFORMATION

Calories ....89 Sugars 4g
Protein ....2g Fat 7g
Carbohydrate ....5g Saturates 1g

8 mins 10 mins

SERVES 4

INGREDIENTS

14 oz/400 g green beans

1 garlic clove, finely sliced

1 fresh red bird-eye chile, deseeded and chopped

½ tsp paprika

1 piece of lemongrass stalk, finely chopped

2 tsp Thai fish sauce

½ cup coconut milk

1 tbsp sunflower oil

2 scallions, sliced

1 Cut the beans into 2 inch/5 cm pieces and cook in a small pan of boiling water for about 2 minutes. Drain well and set aside.

2 Place the garlic, chile, paprika, lemongrass, fish sauce, and coconut milk in a blender and process to a smooth paste. Alternatively, place in a mortar and pound to a smooth paste with a pestle.

3 Heat the oil in a heavy skillet. Stir-fry the scallions over high heat for about 1 minute. Add the paste and bring the mixture to a boil.

4 Lower the heat and simmer gently for 3–4 minutes to reduce the liquid by about half. Add the beans and simmer for a further 1–2 minutes until tender and cooked through. Serve hot.

COOK'S TIP
Young string beans can be used instead of green beans. Remove any strings from the beans, then cut at a diagonal angle into short lengths. Cook as in the recipe until tender.

Stir-Fried Ginger Mushrooms

This quick vegetarian stir-fry is actually more like a rich curry,
with lots of warm spice and garlic, balanced with creamy coconut milk.

NUTRITIONAL INFORMATION

Calories 174   Sugars 7g
Protein . . . . .8g   Fat 9g
Carbohydrate . . .15g   Saturates 1g

 10 mins   8 mins

SERVES 4

I N G R E D I E N T S

2 tbsp vegetable oil

3 garlic cloves, crushed

1 tbsp Thai red curry paste

½ tsp ground turmeric

15 oz/425 g canned Chinese straw
mushrooms, drained and halved

¾ inch/2 cm piece of fresh ginger root,
finely shredded

scant ½ cup coconut milk

1½ oz/40 g dried Chinese black
mushrooms, soaked, drained, and sliced

1 tbsp lemon juice

1 tbsp light soy sauce

2 tsp sugar

½ tsp salt

8 cherry tomatoes, halved

7 oz/200 g firm beancurd, diced

fresh cilantro leaves, to garnish

boiled fragrant rice, to serve

1 Heat the oil in a skillet and stir-fry the garlic for about 1 minute. Stir in the curry paste and turmeric and cook for about a further 30 seconds.

2 Stir in the straw mushrooms and ginger and stir-fry for about 2 minutes. Stir in the coconut milk and bring to a boil.

3 Stir in the Chinese dried black mushrooms, lemon juice, soy sauce, sugar, and salt and heat thoroughly. Add the tomatoes and beancurd and toss gently to heat through.

4 Sprinkle the cilantro leaves over the mixture and serve immediately with fragrant rice.

Potatoes in Creamed Coconut

A colorful way to serve potatoes that is quick and easy to make.
Serve it with spicy meat curries with a salad on the side.

NUTRITIONAL INFORMATION

Calories	93	Sugars	.......1.5g
Protein	........2.8g	Fat	..........4.8g
Carbohydrate	..10.3g	Saturates	.....4.0g

 10 mins   15 mins

SERVES 4

I N G R E D I E N T S

1 lb 5 oz/600 g potatoes

1 onion, thinly sliced

2 fresh red bird-eye chiles, finely chopped

½ tsp salt

½ tsp ground black pepper

3 oz/85 g creamed coconut

1½ cups vegetable or chicken stock

fresh cilantro or basil, chopped, to garnish

1 Peel the potatoes thinly. Use a sharp knife to cut into ¾ inch/2 cm chunks.

2 Place the potatoes in a pan with the onion, chiles, salt, pepper, and creamed coconut. Stir in the stock.

3 Bring to a boil, stirring, then lower the heat, cover the pan, and simmer gently, stirring occasionally, until the potatoes are tender.

4 Adjust the seasoning to taste, then sprinkle with chopped cilantro or basil. Serve immediately while hot.

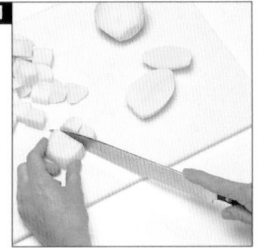  

COOK'S TIP

If the potatoes are thin-skinned, or a new variety, simply wash or scrub to remove any dirt and cook with the skins on. This adds extra dietary fiber and nutrients to the finished dish and cuts down on the preparation time. Baby new potatoes can be cooked whole.

Stir-Fried Broccoli

Chinese oyster sauce has a sweet-salty flavor, ideal for adding a richly Asian flavor to plain vegetables.

NUTRITIONAL INFORMATION

Calories . . . . .81 Sugars 2g
Protein . . . . .5g Fat 4g
Carbohydrate . . . .6g Saturates 1g

 5 mins   6–8 mins

SERVES 4

I N G R E D I E N T S

14 oz/400 g broccoli

1 tbsp peanut oil

2 shallots, finely chopped

1 garlic clove, finely chopped

1 tbsp Chinese rice wine or dry sherry

5 tbsp oyster sauce

¼ tsp ground black pepper

1 tsp chili oil

1 Trim the broccoli and cut into small florets. Blanch in a small pan of boiling water for about 30 seconds, then drain well.

2 Heat the oil in a large skillet or wok and stir-fry the shallots and garlic for 1–2 minutes until golden brown.

3 Add the broccoli and stir-fry for 2 minutes. Add the wine and oyster sauce and stir for a further 1 minute.

4 Stir in the pepper and drizzle with a little chili oil just before serving. Serve the stir-fry hot.

COOK'S TIP

To make chili oil, tuck fresh red or green chiles into a jar and top up with olive oil or a light vegetable oil. Cover with a lid and let the flavor steep for at least 3 weeks before using.

Roasted Thai Bell Peppers

A colorful side dish that also makes a good buffet party salad.
This is best made in advance to give time for the flavors to mingle.

NUTRITIONAL INFORMATION

Calories 83	Sugars 17g	
Protein 2g	Fat 1g	
Carbohydrate ...17g	Saturates 0g	

  1¼ hrs   5–10 mins

SERVES 4

INGREDIENTS

2 red bell peppers

2 yellow bell peppers

2 green bell peppers

2 fresh red bird-eye chiles, deseeded and finely chopped

1 lemongrass stalk, finely shredded

4 tbsp lime juice

2 tbsp palm sugar

1 tbsp Thai fish sauce

 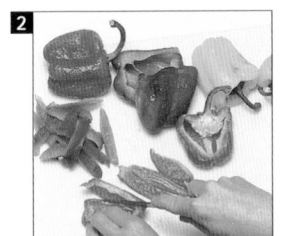 

1 Roast the bell peppers under a hot broiler, grill over hot coals, or roast in a hot oven, turning them over occasionally, until the skins are blackened and charred. Set aside to cool slightly, then remove the skins. Cut each bell pepper in half and remove the seeds.

2 Thickly slice the bell peppers and transfer to a large mixing bowl.

3 Place the chiles, lemongrass, lime juice, sugar, and fish sauce in a screw-top jar and shake vigorously until thoroughly mixed.

4 Pour the dressing over the bell peppers. Set aside to cool completely, cover with plastic wrap, and chill in the refrigerator for at least an hour before serving. Transfer to a serving dish to serve.

COOK'S TIP

The flavors will mingle best if the bell peppers are still slightly warm when you pour the dressing over. Prepare the dressing while the bell peppers are cooking, so it's ready to pour over when they are done.

Bok Choy with Crab Meat

Bok choy has a delicate, fresh flavor and crisp texture, which is best retained by quick cooking, making it an ideal choice for stir-frying.

NUTRITIONAL INFORMATION

Calories	101	Sugars	....2g
Protein	....9g	Fat	....6g
Carbohydrate	...3g	Saturates	....1g

 5 mins   8 mins

SERVES 4

INGREDIENTS

2 heads bok choy, about 9 oz/ 250 g total weight

2 tbsp vegetable oil

1 garlic clove, thinly sliced

2 tbsp oyster sauce

3½ oz/100 g cherry tomatoes, halved

6 oz/170 g can white crab meat, drained

salt and pepper

1 Trim the bok choy and cut into 1 inch/2.5 cm thick slices.

2 Heat the oil in a large skillet or wok and stir-fry the garlic over high heat for 1 minute.

3 Add the bok choy and stir-fry for 2–3 minutes until the leaves wilt, but the stalks are still crisp.

4 Add the oyster sauce and tomatoes and stir-fry for a further minute.

5 Add the crab meat and season to taste with salt and pepper. Stir to heat thoroughly and break up the distribution of crab meat before serving.

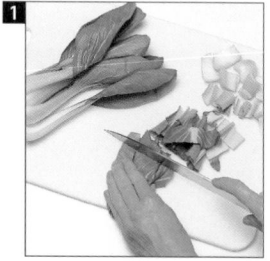

VARIATION

If bok choy is not available, Napa cabbage makes a good alternative for this dish.

Zucchini Curry

This delicious curry is spiced with fenugreek seeds, which have a beautiful aroma and a distinctive taste.

NUTRITIONAL INFORMATION

Calories 188	Sugars 5g
Protein 3g	Fat 17g
Carbohydrate 6g	Saturates 2g

20 mins   15 mins

SERVES 4

I N G R E D I E N T S

6 tbsp vegetable oil

1 medium onion, finely chopped

3 fresh green chiles, finely chopped

1 tsp finely chopped fresh ginger root

1 tsp crushed garlic

1 tsp chili powder

1 lb 2 oz/500 g zucchini, thinly sliced

2 tomatoes, sliced

1 tbsp fresh cilantro leaves, plus extra to garnish

2 tsp fenugreek seeds

chapatis, to serve

1 Heat the oil in a large, heavy skillet or wok. Add the onion, chiles, chopped fresh ginger, garlic, and chili powder and stir-fry over low heat for about 2–3 minutes until the onion is just beginning to soften.

2 Add the zucchini and the tomatoes and stir-fry over medium heat for 5–7 minutes.

3 Add the cilantro leaves and fenugreek seeds to the skillet or wok and stir-fry over medium heat for 5 minutes, until the vegetables are tender.

4 Remove the skillet from the heat and transfer the zucchini and fenugreek seed mixture to warmed serving dishes. Garnish with cilantro leaves and serve hot with chapatis.

VARIATION
You could use coriander seeds instead of the fenugreek seeds, if you prefer.

Spinach & Chana Dhal

An attractive-looking dish, this makes a good accompaniment to almost any recipe. For a contrast in color and taste, serve with a tomato curry.

NUTRITIONAL INFORMATION

Calories 175	Sugars 1g
Protein 6g	Fat 12g
Carbohydrate ...12g	Saturates 1g

3 hrs 5 mins   45 mins

SERVES 6

INGREDIENTS

4 tbsp chana dhal

6 tbsp vegetable oil

1 tsp mixed onion and mustard seeds

4 dried red chiles

14–15 oz/400–425 g can spinach, drained

1 tsp finely chopped fresh ginger root

1 tsp ground coriander

1 tsp ground cumin

1 tsp salt

1 tsp chili powder

2 tbsp lemon juice

1 fresh green chile, deseeded and finely chopped, to garnish

1 Soak the chana dhal in a bowl of warm water for at least 3 hours, preferably overnight.

2 Place the dhal in a pan, cover with water, and bring to a boil. Lower the heat and simmer gently for 30 minutes. Drain well.

3 Heat the oil in another pan. Add the mixed onion and mustard seeds and dried red chiles and fry, stirring constantly, until they turn a shade darker.

4 Add the drained spinach to the pan, mixing gently. Add the ginger, ground coriander, ground cumin, salt, and chili powder. Reduce the heat and gently stir-fry the mixture for 7-10 minutes.

5 Add the drained dhal to the pan and blend into the spinach mixture well, stirring gently so that it does not break up.

6 Transfer the mixture to a warmed serving dish. Sprinkle over the lemon juice and garnish with the chopped green chile. Serve immediately.

COOK'S TIP

Very similar in appearance to moong dhal—the yellow split peas—chana dhal have slightly less shiny grains.

Bok Choy with Cashew Nuts

Plum sauce is readily available in jars and has a terrific, sweet flavor which superbly complements the vegetables.

NUTRITIONAL INFORMATION

Calories 241	Sugars 7g	
Protein 7g	Fat 19g	
Carbohydrate 11g	Saturates 4g	

 5 mins   15 mins

SERVES 4

INGREDIENTS

2 red onions

6 oz/175 g red cabbage

2 tbsp peanut oil

8 oz/225 g bok choy

2 tbsp plum sauce

scant 1 cup roasted cashew nuts

1 Using a sharp knife, cut the red onions into thin wedges and thinly shred the red cabbage.

2 Heat the peanut oil in a large preheated wok or heavy skillet until it is really hot.

3 Add the onion wedges to the wok or skillet and stir-fry for about 5 minutes or until the onions are just beginning to brown.

4 Add the red cabbage to the wok and stir-fry for a further 2–3 minutes.

5 Add the bok choy leaves to the wok or skillet and stir-fry for about 5 minutes or until the leaves have just wilted.

6 Drizzle the plum sauce over the vegetables, toss together until well combined, and heat until the liquid is beginning to bubble.

7 Sprinkle the roasted cashew nuts over the stir-fry and transfer to warm serving bowls. Serve immediately.

VARIATION

Use unsalted peanuts instead of the cashew nuts if you prefer.

Honey-Fried Spinach

This stir-fry is the perfect accompaniment to beancurd dishes and it is wonderfully quick and simple to make.

NUTRITIONAL INFORMATION

Calories	146	Sugars	.........9g
Protein	.........4g	Fat	...........9g
Carbohydrate	...10g	Saturates	.......2g

 5 mins   15 mins

SERVES 4

I N G R E D I E N T S

4 scallions

3 tbsp peanut oil

12 oz/350 g shiitake mushrooms, sliced

2 garlic cloves, crushed

12 oz/350 g baby leaf spinach

2 tbsp dry sherry

2 tbsp honey

1 Using a sharp knife, thickly slice the scallions on the diagonal.

2 Heat the peanut oil in a large preheated wok or in a skillet with a heavy base.

3 Add the shiitake mushrooms to the wok or skillet and stir-fry for about 5 minutes or until they have softened.

COOK'S TIP

Single-flower honey has a better, more individual flavor than blended honey. Acacia honey is typically Chinese, but you could also try clover, lemon blossom, lime flower, or orange blossom.

4 Stir the crushed garlic into the wok or skillet. Add the baby leaf spinach and stir-fry for a further 2–3 minutes or until the spinach leaves have just begun to wilt.

5 Combine the dry sherry and honey in a small bowl, stirring until thoroughly mixed. Drizzle the sherry and honey mixture over the spinach and heat through over low heat, stirring gently to coat the spinach leaves thoroughly in the mixture.

6 Transfer the stir-fry to warm serving dishes, scatter with the sliced scallions, and serve immediately.

Broccoli & Black Bean Sauce

Broccoli works well with the black bean sauce and Napa cabbage in this recipe, while the almonds add extra crunch and flavor.

NUTRITIONAL INFORMATION

Calories ....139 Sugars 3g
Protein ....7g Fat 10g
Carbohydrate ....5g Saturates 1g

 5 mins   15 mins

SERVES 4

INGREDIENTS

1 lb/450 g broccoli florets

2 tbsp sunflower oil

1 onion, sliced

2 garlic cloves, thinly sliced

¼ cup sliced almonds

1 head Napa cabbage, shredded

4 tbsp black bean sauce

1 Bring a large pan of water to a boil. Add the broccoli florets to the pan and cook for 1 minute. Drain, rinse in cold water to prevent any further cooking, and drain thoroughly again.

2 Meanwhile, heat the sunflower oil in a large preheated wok.

3 Add the onion and garlic slices to the wok and stir-fry until just beginning to brown.

4 Add the drained broccoli florets and the sliced almonds and stir-fry for a further 2–3 minutes.

5 Add the shredded Napa cabbage to the wok and stir-fry for a further 2 minutes.

6 Stir the black bean sauce into the vegetables, tossing to coat them thoroughly, and cook until the juices are just beginning to bubble.

7 Transfer the vegetables to warm serving bowls and serve immediately.

VARIATION

Use unsalted cashew nuts instead of the almonds, if preferred.

Poultry, Meat, Game, and Fish

You don't have to make sacrifices to enjoy a healthy diet, but it does pay to be sensible. Ring the changes with occasional meat-free days, because red meat, in particular, is often quite high in fat. Poultry and game are both leaner and you can—and should—eat fish two or three times a week. Some countries are renowned for their healthy diets and many of the mouthwatering dishes in this chapter have been inspired by their cuisines—sizzling Chinese stir-fries, flavorful Italian pasta sauces, and succulent Mediterranean stews—while the range of fabulous fish and seafood dishes is virtually endless.

Oat-Crusted Chicken Pieces

A very low-fat chicken recipe with a refreshingly light, mustard-spiced sauce, which is ideal for a healthy lunch bag or a light meal with salad.

NUTRITIONAL INFORMATION

Calories	120	Sugars	........3g
Protein	........15g	Fat	..........3g
Carbohydrate	....8g	Saturates	......1g

 5 mins   40 mins

SERVES 4

INGREDIENTS

¼ cups rolled oats

1 tbsp chopped fresh rosemary

4 skinless chicken quarters

1 egg white, lightly beaten

⅔ cup low-fat plain yogurt

2 tsp wholegrain mustard

salt and pepper

grated carrot salad, to serve

1 Combine the rolled oats, chopped fresh rosemary, and salt and pepper.

2 Brush each piece of chicken evenly with a little egg white, then coat in the oat mixture.

3 Place the chicken pieces on a baking sheet and bake in a preheated oven, 400°F/200°C, for about 40 minutes. Test to see if the chicken is cooked by inserted a skewer into the thickest part—the juices should run clear without a trace of pink.

4 Combine the yogurt and mustard and season with salt and pepper to taste.

5 Serve the chicken, hot or cold, with the sauce and a grated carrot salad.

Chicken with Two Sauces

With its red and yellow bell pepper sauces, this quick and simple dish is colorful, healthy, and perfect for an impromptu lunch or supper.

NUTRITIONAL INFORMATION

Calories 257	Sugars 7g	
Protein 29g	Fat 10g	
Carbohydrate 8g	Saturates 2g	

  10 mins   1½ hrs

SERVES 4

I N G R E D I E N T S

2 tbsp olive oil

2 medium onions, finely chopped

2 garlic cloves, crushed

2 red bell peppers, chopped

pinch of cayenne pepper

2 tsp tomato paste

2 yellow bell peppers, chopped

pinch of dried basil

4 lean skinless, boneless chicken
    breast portions

⅔ cup dry white wine

⅔ cup chicken stock

bouquet garni

salt and pepper

fresh herbs, to garnish

1 Heat 1 tablespoon of olive oil in each of 2 medium pans. Place half the chopped onions, 1 of the garlic cloves, the red bell peppers, cayenne pepper, and tomato paste in 1 of the pans. Place the remaining onion and garlic, the yellow bell peppers, and basil in the other pan.

2 Cover each pan and cook over very low heat for 1 hour until the bell peppers are very soft. If either mixture becomes dry, add a little water. Transfer the contents of the first pan to a food processor and process, then strain. Repeat with the contents of the other pan.

3 Return to the pans and season with salt and pepper. Gently reheat the sauces while the chicken is cooking.

4 Put the chicken portions into a skillet and add the wine and stock. Add the bouquet garni and bring the liquid to a simmer over medium-low heat. Cook the chicken for about 20 minutes until tender and cooked through.

5 To serve, put a pool of each sauce onto 4 individual serving plates, slice the chicken breast portions and arrange them on the plates. Garnish with fresh herbs and serve immediately.

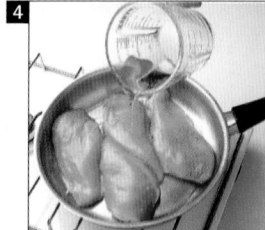

Golden Glazed Chicken

A glossy glaze with sweet and fruity flavors coats lean chicken breast portions in this quick and tasty recipe.

NUTRITIONAL INFORMATION

Calories 427
Protein 39g
Carbohydrate . . .42g
Sugars 11g
Fat 12g
Saturates 3g

5 mins

35 mins

SERVES 4

INGREDIENTS

6 skinless boneless chicken
   breast portions

1 tsp ground turmeric

1 tbsp wholegrain mustard

1¼ cups orange juice

2 tbsp honey

2 tbsp sunflower oil

1¾ cups long grain rice

1 orange

3 tbsp chopped fresh mint

salt and pepper

fresh mint sprigs, to garnish

1 With a sharp knife, mark the surface of the chicken breast portions in a diamond pattern and place in a single layer a shallow dish.

2 Combine the turmeric, mustard, orange juice, and honey and pour the mixture over the chicken. Season with salt and pepper to taste. Chill until required.

3 Lift the chicken from the marinade and pat dry on paper towels. Reserve the marinade.

4 Heat the oil in a wide pan, add the chicken, and sauté until golden, turning once. Drain off any excess oil. Pour the marinade into the pan, cover, and simmer for 10–15 minutes until the chicken is tender.

5 Cook the rice in lightly salted boiling water for 15–20 minutes until tender, then drain well. Finely grate the orange rind and stir it into the rice with the mint.

6 Remove the white pith from the orange and cut the flesh into segments.

7 Serve the chicken with the orange and mint rice, garnished with orange segments and mint sprigs.

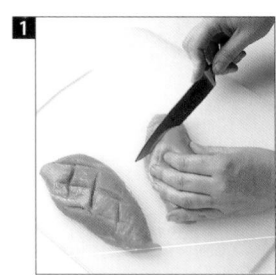

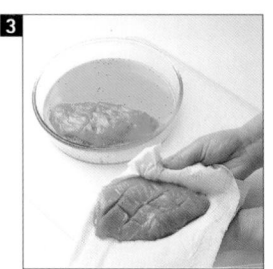

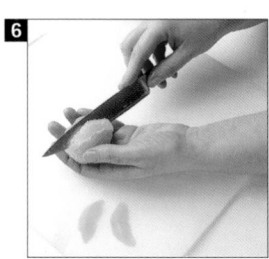

COOK'S TIP

To make a slightly sharper sauce, use small grapefruit instead of the oranges.

Spiced Chicken Casserole

Spices, herbs, fruit, nuts, and vegetables are combined to make an appealing casserole with lots of flavor.

NUTRITIONAL INFORMATION

Calories	385	Sugars	........14g
Protein	........37g	Fat	..........15g
Carbohydrate	...19g	Saturates	.......2g

🍲 10 mins   🕐 2¼ hrs

SERVES 4

INGREDIENTS

3 tbsp olive oil

2 lb/900 g skinless, boneless chicken, sliced

10 shallots or pickling onions

3 carrots, chopped

2 oz/55 g chestnuts, sliced

2 oz/55 g flaked almonds, toasted

1 tsp freshly grated nutmeg

3 tsp ground cinnamon

1¼ cups white wine

1¼ cups chicken stock

¾ cup white wine vinegar

1 tbsp chopped fresh tarragon

1 tbsp chopped fresh flat-leaf parsley

1 tbsp chopped fresh thyme

grated rind of 1 orange

1 tbsp dark muscovado sugar

4½ oz/125 g seedless black grapes, halved

sea salt and pepper

fresh herbs, to garnish

wild rice or puréed potato, to serve

1 Heat the olive oil in a large, heavy-bottomed pan and add the chicken, shallots or pickling onions, and carrots. Cook, stirring frequently, over a medium heat for about 6 minutes or until the chicken is browned.

2 Add the nuts, nutmeg, cinnamon, wine, stock, wine vinegar, herbs, orange rind, and sugar and season to taste with salt and pepper. Simmer over low heat for 2 hours until the meat is very tender. Stir the casserole occasionally.

3 Add the grapes just before serving and serve with wild rice or puréed potato. Garnish with herbs.

Chicken with Shallots

This recipe has an Asian flavor, which can be enhanced with chopped scallions, cinnamon, and lemon grass.

NUTRITIONAL INFORMATION

Calories	277	Sugars	.........6g
Protein	........28g	Fat	...........11g
Carbohydrate	...17g	Saturates	.......2g

15 mins   1 hr 50 mins

SERVES 4-8

INGREDIENTS

6 tbsp sesame oil

1¾ lb/900 g chicken meat

2 oz/60 g all-purpose flour, seasoned

32 shallots, sliced

1 lb 2 oz/500 g exotic mushrooms, roughly chopped

1¼ cups chicken stock

2 tbsp Worcestershire sauce

1 tbsp honey

2 tbsp grated fresh root ginger

⅔ cup yogurt

salt and pepper

flat-leaf parsley, to garnish

wild rice and white rice, to serve

COOK'S TIP

Mushrooms can be stored in the refrigerator for 24–36 hours. Keep them in paper bags because they "sweat" in plastic. You do not need to peel mushrooms but exotic mushrooms must be washed thoroughly.

1 Heat the oil in a large skillet. Coat the chicken in the seasoned flour and cook for about 4 minutes, until browned all over. Transfer to a large, deep casserole and keep warm until required.

2 Slowly cook the shallots and mushrooms in the juices.

3 Add the chicken stock, Worcestershire sauce, honey, and fresh ginger, then season to taste with salt and pepper.

4 Pour the mixture over the chicken, and cover the casserole with a lid or aluminum foil.

5 Cook in the center of a preheated oven, 300°F/150°C, for about 1½ hours, until the meat is very tender. Add the yogurt and cook for another 10 minutes. Serve the casserole with a mixture of wild rice and white rice, and garnish with fresh parsley.

Spicy Tomato Chicken

These low-fat, spicy skewers are cooked in a matter of minutes—assemble them ahead of time and store in the refrigerator until you need them.

NUTRITIONAL INFORMATION

Calories ....195 Sugars 11g
Protein ....28g Fat 4g
Carbohydrate ...12g Saturates 1g

  10 mins 🕐 10 mins

SERVES 4

INGREDIENTS

1 lb 2 oz/500 g skinless, boneless
  chicken breast portions

3 tbsp tomato paste

2 tbsp honey

2 tbsp Worcestershire sauce

1 tbsp chopped fresh rosemary

9 oz/250 g cherry tomatoes

fresh rosemary sprigs, to garnish

couscous or rice, to serve

1 Cut the chicken into 1 inch/2.5 cm chunks and place in a bowl.

2 Combine the tomato paste, honey, Worcestershire sauce, and chopped rosemary in a small bowl. Add to the chicken, stirring to coat evenly.

3 Alternating the chicken pieces and cherry tomatoes, thread them onto 8 wooden skewers. (If the skewers have been soaked in water they will not char.)

4 Spoon over any remaining glaze. Cook under a preheated hot broiler for about 8–10 minutes, turning occasionally, until the chicken is thoroughly cooked.

5 Serve on a bed of couscous or rice and garnish with sprigs of rosemary.

COOK'S TIP
Couscous is made from semolina that has been made into separate grains. It usually just needs moistening or steaming before serving.

Chicken with Bramble Sauce

This fall recipe can be made with freshly picked wild blackberries from the hedges if you're lucky enough to live near a good supply.

NUTRITIONAL INFORMATION

Calories	174	Sugars	.........5g
Protein	........27g	Fat	..........4g
Carbohydrate	....5g	Saturates	......1g

1¼ hrs   20 mins

SERVES 4

INGREDIENTS

4 chicken breast portions or 8 thighs

4 tbsp dry white wine or hard cider

2 tbsp chopped fresh rosemary

pepper

fresh rosemary sprigs and blackberries,
   to garnish

SAUCE

1¾ cups blackberries

1 tbsp apple vinegar

2 tbsp red currant jelly

¼ tsp freshly grated nutmeg

1 Cut the chicken into 1 inch/2.5 cm pieces and place in a bowl. Sprinkle over the wine or hard cider and chopped rosemary and season to taste with pepper. Cover and set aside to marinate for at least an hour.

2 Drain the marinade from the chicken and thread the meat onto 8 metal or wooden skewers. Reserve the marinade for the sauce.

3 Cook under a preheated moderately hot broiler for 8–10 minutes, turning occasionally, until golden.

4 To make the sauce, place the marinade in a pan with the blackberries and simmer gently until soft. Press though a strainer.

5 Return the blackberry purée to the pan, add the apple vinegar and red currant jelly, and bring to a boil. Boil the sauce, uncovered, until it is reduced by about one-third.

6 Spoon a little bramble sauce onto each of 4 individual serving plates and place a chicken skewer on top. Sprinkle with nutmeg. Garnish each skewer with rosemary and blackberries. Serve immediately.

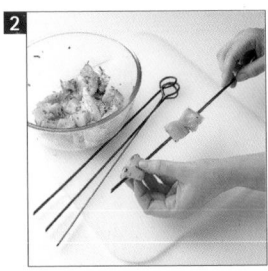

COOK'S TIP

If you use canned fruit,
omit the red currant jelly.

Thai Stir-Fried Chicken

Coconut adds a creamy texture and delicious flavor to this Thai-style stir-fry, which is spiked with green chile.

NUTRITIONAL INFORMATION

Calories	184	Sugars	.........6g
Protein	........24g	Fat	...........5g
Carbohydrate	....8g	Saturates	.......2g

15 mins   10 mins

SERVES 4

I N G R E D I E N T S

3 tbsp sesame oil

12 oz/350 g skinless, boneless chicken breast, thinly sliced

8 shallots, sliced

2 garlic cloves, finely chopped

2 tsp grated fresh ginger root

1 fresh green chile, deseeded and finely chopped

1 red bell pepper, deseeded and thinly sliced

1 green bell pepper, deseeded and thinly sliced

3 zucchini, thinly sliced

2 tbsp ground almonds

1 tsp ground cinnamon

1 tbsp oyster sauce

¾ oz/20 g creamed coconut, grated

salt and pepper

1 Heat the sesame oil in a preheated wok or heavy skillet. Add the chicken, season with salt and pepper to taste, and stir fry over medium heat for about 4 minutes.

2 Add the shallots, garlic, ginger, and fresh green chile and stir-fry for a further 2 minutes.

3 Add the red and green bell peppers and zucchini and stir-fry for about 1 minute.

4 Stir in the almonds, cinnamon, oyster sauce, and creamed coconut and season to taste with salt and pepper. Stir-fry for 1 minute to heat through and then serve immediately.

COOK'S TIP

Creamed coconut is sold in blocks by supermarkets and Asian stores. It is a useful pantry standby because it adds richness and depth of flavor.

Chicken & Noodle One-Pot

Flavorsome chicken and vegetables are cooked with Chinese egg noodles in a coconut sauce. Serve in deep soup bowls.

NUTRITIONAL INFORMATION

Calories	256	Sugars	.........7g
Protein	........30g	Fat	...........8g
Carbohydrate	...18g	Saturates	.......2g

5 mins   20 mins

SERVES 4

INGREDIENTS

1 tbsp sunflower oil

1 onion, sliced

1 garlic clove, crushed

1 inch/2.5 cm piece of fresh
ginger root, grated

1 bunch of scallions, sliced diagonally

1 lb 2 oz/500 g skinless chicken breast
fillet, cut into bite-size pieces

2 tbsp mild curry paste

2 cups coconut milk

1¼ cups chicken stock

9 oz/250 g Chinese egg noodles

2 tsp lime juice

salt and pepper

fresh basil sprigs, to garnish

1 Heat the sunflower oil in a wok or large, heavy skillet.

2 Add the onion, garlic, ginger, and scallions and stir-fry over medium heat for 2 minutes until softened.

3 Add the chicken and curry paste and stir-fry for 4 minutes or until the vegetables and chicken are golden brown. Stir in the coconut milk, stock, and salt and pepper to taste and mix well.

4 Bring to a boil, break the noodles into large pieces, if necessary, add to the wok or pan, cover, and simmer, stirring occasionally, for about 6–8 minutes until the noodles are just tender.

5 Add the lime juice and adjust the seasoning if necessary.

6 Serve the chicken and noodle one-pot immediately in deep soup bowls, garnished with basil sprigs.

 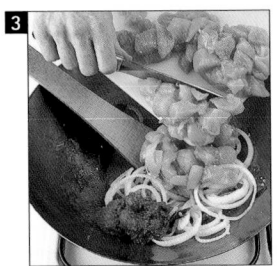 

COOK'S TIP

If you enjoy hot flavors, substitute the mild curry paste in the above recipe with hot curry paste (found in most supermarkets) but reduce the quantity to 1 tablespoon.

Chicken Pepperonata

All the sunshine colors and flavors of Italy are combined in this easy and economical dish.

NUTRITIONAL INFORMATION

Calories 328   Sugars 7g
Protein ....35g   Fat 15g
Carbohydrate ...13g   Saturates 4g

 15 mins   40 mins

SERVES 4

INGREDIENTS

8 chicken thighs

2 tbsp whole-wheat flour

2 tbsp olive oil

1 small onion, thinly sliced

1 garlic clove, crushed

1 large red bell pepper, deseeded and thinly sliced

1 large yellow bell pepper, deseeded and thinly sliced

1 large green bell pepper. deseeded and thinly sliced

14 oz/400 g can chopped tomatoes

1 tbsp chopped fresh oregano

salt and pepper

fresh oregano, to garnish

crusty whole-wheat bread, to serve

1 Remove the skin from the chicken thighs and toss the meat in the flour.

2 Heat the oil in a wide skillet and fry the chicken over medium heat until sealed and lightly browned, then remove from the skillet.

3 Add the onion to the skillet, lower the heat, and cook, stirring occasionally, for about 5 minutes until softened, but not browned. Add the garlic, bell pepper slices, tomatoes, and oregano, then bring to a boil, stirring constantly.

4 Arrange the chicken on top of the vegetables, season to taste with salt and pepper, then cover the pan tightly, and simmer for 20–25 minutes or until the chicken is completely cooked and tender.

5 Taste and adjust the seasoning, if necessary. Transfer the chicken to a plate. Spoon the vegetables onto a warmed serving platter and top with the chicken. Garnish with fresh oregano and serve immediately with fresh, crusty whole-wheat bread.

Gardener's Chicken

Any combination of small, young vegetables, such as zucchini, leeks, and onions, can be roasted with this delicious stuffed chicken.

NUTRITIONAL INFORMATION

Calories 674	Sugars 18g	
Protein 35g	Fat 40g	
Carbohydrate ...45g	Saturates 12g	

 10 mins 1¾ hrs

SERVES 4

I N G R E D I E N T S

9 oz/250 g parsnips, chopped

2 small carrots, chopped

½ cup fresh bread crumbs

¼ tsp freshly grated nutmeg

1 tbsp chopped fresh parsley

1 x 3 lb/1/5 kg chicken

1 bunch of fresh parsley

½ onion

2 tbsp butter, softened

4 tbsp olive oil

1 lb 2 oz/500 g new potatoes, scrubbed

1 lb 2 oz/500 g baby carrots, trimmed

salt and pepper

 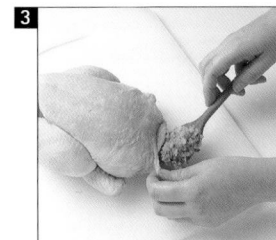 

1 To make the stuffing, put the parsnips and chopped carrots into a pan, half cover with water, and bring to a boil. Lower the heat, cover, and simmer until tender. Drain well, then process in a blender or food processor to a smooth purée. Transfer the purée to a bowl and set aside to cool.

2 Mix the bread crumbs, nutmeg, and parsley into the purée and season to taste with salt and pepper.

3 Put the stuffing into the neck end of the chicken and push a little under the skin over the breast meat. Secure the flap of skin with a small metal skewer or toothpick.

4 Place the bunch of parsley and onion inside the cavity of the chicken, then place the chicken in a large roasting pan.

5 Spread the butter over the skin and season with salt and pepper, cover with foil, and place in a preheated oven, 375°F/190°C, for 30 minutes.

6 Meanwhile, heat the oil in a skillet, and lightly brown the potatoes.

7 Transfer the potatoes to the roasting pan and add the baby carrots. Baste the chicken and continue to cook for a further hour, basting the chicken and vegetables after 30 minutes. Remove the foil for the last 20 minutes to let the skin crisp. Garnish the vegetables with chopped parsley and serve immediately.

Chicken & Almond Rissoles

Cooked potatoes and cooked chicken are combined to make tasty rissoles rolled in chopped almonds, then served with stir-fried vegetables.

NUTRITIONAL INFORMATION

Calories . . . . .161 Sugars 3g
Protein . . . . .12g Fat 9g
Carbohydrate . . . .8g Saturates 1g

35 mins   20 mins

SERVES 4

INGREDIENTS

4 oz/115 g parboiled potatoes

1 carrot

4 oz/115 g cooked chicken

1 garlic clove, crushed

½ tsp dried tarragon or thyme

pinch of ground allspice or
   ground coriander

1 egg yolk or ½ egg, beaten

¼ cup sliced almonds

salt and pepper

STIR-FRIED VEGETABLES

1 celery stalk

2 scallions, trimmed

1 tbsp peanut oil

8 baby corn cobs

1½ oz/40 g snow peas or sugar snap
   peas, trimmed

2 tsp balsamic vinegar

salt and pepper

2 Add the egg and bind the ingredients together. Divide the mixture in half and shape into "sausages." Chop the almonds and then evenly coat each rissole in the nuts. Place the rissoles in a greased casserole and cook in a preheated oven, 400°F/200°C, for about 20 minutes until well browned.

3 To prepare the stir-fried vegetables, cut the celery and scallions on the diagonal into thin slices. Heat the peanut oil in a skillet and toss in the vegetables. Cook over high heat for 1–2 minutes, then add the corn cobs and snow peas or sugar snap peas, and cook for a further 2–3 minutes. Finally, add the balsamic vinegar and season to taste with salt and pepper.

4 Place the rissoles on serving plates and add the stir-fried vegetables.

1 Grate the parboiled potatoes and raw carrots coarsely into a bowl. Finely chop or mince the chicken. Add to the vegetables with the garlic, herbs and spices and salt and pepper to taste.

Chicken & Corn Sauté

This quick and healthy dish is stir-fried, which means you need use only the minimum of oil for cooking.

NUTRITIONAL INFORMATION

Calories	280	Sugars	.........7g
Protein	........31g	Fat	...........11g
Carbohydrate	....9g	Saturates	.......2g

 5 mins   10 mins

SERVES 4

INGREDIENTS

4 skinless, boneless chicken breast portions

9 oz/250 g baby corn cobs

9 oz/250 g snow peas

2 tbsp sunflower oil

1 tbsp sherry vinegar

1 tbsp honey

1 tbsp light soy sauce

1 tbsp sunflower seeds

pepper

rice or Chinese egg noodles, to serve

1 Using a sharp knife, slice the chicken breast portions into long, thin strips.

2 Cut the baby corn cobs in half lengthwise and trim the mangetouts.

3 Heat the sunflower oil in a preheated wok or a wide skillet.

4 Add the chicken and stir-fry over fairly high heat for 1 minute.

5 Add the baby corn cobs and snow peas and stir-fry over moderate heat for 5–8 minutes, until evenly cooked. The vegetables should be tender, but still slightly crunchy.

6 Combine the sherry vinegar, honey, and soy sauce in a small bowl.

7 Stir the vinegar mixture into the wok or skillet with the sunflower seeds.

8 Season to taste with pepper. Cook, stirring constantly, for 1 minute.

9 Serve the chicken and corn sauté hot with rice or Chinese egg noodles.

VARIATION

Rice vinegar or balsamic vinegar make good substitutes for the sherry vinegar.

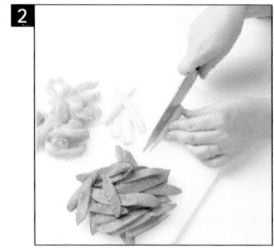

Chicken Tikka

Traditionally, chicken tikka is cooked in a fiery-hot clay tandoori oven, but it works well on the barbecue, too.

NUTRITIONAL INFORMATION

Calories ....173 Sugars 6g
Protein ....28g Fat 4g
Carbohydrate ....6g Saturates 2g

2¼ hrs   15 mins

SERVES 4

INGREDIENTS

4 skinless, boneless chicken breast portions

½ tsp salt

4 tbsp lemon or lime juice

vegetable oil, for brushing

MARINADE

⅔ cup low-fat natural yogurt

2 garlic cloves, crushed

1 inch/2.5 cm piece of fresh
  ginger root grated

1 tsp ground cumin

1 tsp chili powder

½ tsp ground coriander

½ tsp ground turmeric

SAUCE

⅔ cup low-fat natural yogurt

1 tsp mint sauce

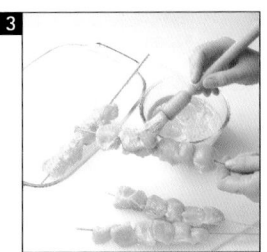

1 Cut the chicken into 1 inch/2.5 cm cubes. Sprinkle with the salt and the citrus juice. Set aside for 10 minutes.

2 To make the marinade, combine all the ingredients in a small bowl until well mixed.

3 Thread the cubes of chicken onto skewers. Brush the marinade over the chicken. Cover and set aside to marinate in the refrigerator for at least 2 hours, preferably overnight. Cook the chicken skewers over hot coals, brushing with oil and turning frequently, for 15 minutes or until cooked through.

4 Meanwhile, combine the yogurt and mint sauce to make the sauce and serve with the chicken.

COOK'S TIP

Use the marinade to coat other chicken portions, such as drumsticks, if you prefer. Cook over medium hot coals for 30–40 minutes, until the juices run clear when the chicken is pierced with a skewer.

Karahi Chicken

A karahi is an extremely versatile two-handled metal pan,
similar to a wok. Food is always cooked over high heat in a karahi.

NUTRITIONAL INFORMATION

Calories . . . . .270 Sugars 1g
Protein . . . . .41g Fat 11g
Carbohydrate . . . .1g Saturates 2g

5 mins 20 mins

SERVES 4

I N G R E D I E N T S

2 tbsp ghee

3 garlic cloves, crushed

1 onion, finely chopped

2 tbsp garam masala

1 tsp coriander seeds, ground

½ tsp dried mint

1 bay leaf

1 lb 10 oz/750 g lean boneless
    chicken, diced

scant 1 cup chicken stock

1 tbsp chopped fresh cilantro

salt

warm nan bread or chapatis, to serve

1 Heat the ghee in a karahi, wok, or a large, heavy skillet. Add the garlic and onion. Stir-fry for about 4 minutes until the onion is golden.

2 Stir in the garam masala, ground coriander, mint, and bay leaf.

3 Add the chicken and cook over high heat, stirring occasionally, for about 5 minutes. Add the stock, lower the heat, and simmer for 10 minutes until the sauce has thickened and the chicken juices run clear when the meat is tested with the point of a sharp knife.

4 Stir in the chopped fresh cilantro and season with salt to taste, mix well, and serve immediately with warm nan bread or chapatis.

COOK'S TIP

Always heat a karahi or wok
before you add the oil to help
maintain the high temperature.

  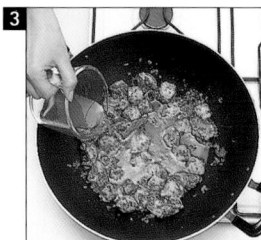

Spicy Sesame Chicken

This is a quick and easy recipe for the broiler or barbecue grill, perfect for lunch or to eat outdoors on a picnic.

NUTRITIONAL INFORMATION

Calories 110   Sugars 3g
Protein . . . . .15g   Fat 4g
Carbohydrate . . . .3g   Saturates 1g

5 mins   15 mins

SERVES 4

I N G R E D I E N T S

4 chicken quarters

⅔ cup low-fat natural yogurt

finely grated rind and juice of 1 small lemon

2 tsp medium-hot curry paste

1 tbsp sesame seeds

T O S E R V E

salad

nan bread

lemon wedges

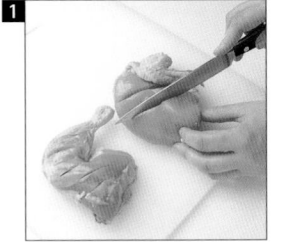

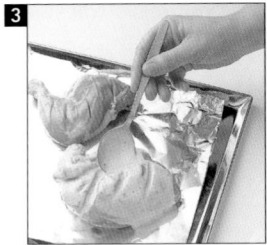

1 Remove the skin from the chicken and slash the flesh at intervals with a sharp knife.

2 Combine the yogurt, lemon rind, lemon juice, and curry paste.

3 Spread the mixture over the chicken and arrange on a foil-lined broiler pan or cookie sheet.

4 Place under a preheated broiler and cook, turning once, for 12–15 minutes until golden brown and cooked. Test by piercing the thickest part with a skewer; the juices should run clear. Just before the end of the cooking time, sprinkle with the sesame seeds.

5 Serve with a salad, nan bread, and lemon wedges.

VARIATION
Poppy seeds, fennel seeds, or cumin seeds, or a mixture of all three, can also be used to sprinkle over the chicken.

Springtime Chicken Pot Pie

Fresh spring vegetables are the basis of this colorful casserole, which is topped with hearty whole-wheat dumplings.

NUTRITIONAL INFORMATION

Calories 560   Sugars 10g
Protein . . . . .39g   Fat 18g
Carbohydrate . . .64g   Saturates 4g

15 mins   1½ hrs

SERVES 4

INGREDIENTS

1 tbsp vegetable oil

8 skinless chicken drumsticks

1 small onion, sliced

12 oz/350 g baby carrots

2 baby turnips

4½ oz/125 g fava beans or peas

1 tsp cornstarch

1¼ cups chicken stock

2 bay leaves

salt and pepper

BISCUIT TOPPING

2¼ cups whole-wheat flour

2 tsp baking powder

2 tbsp soft sunflower margarine

2 tsp dry wholegrain mustard

½ cup grated low-fat sharp
   Cheddar cheese

skim milk, to mix, plus extra
   for brushing

sesame seeds, for sprinkling

1 Heat the oil in a large, heavy pan and fry the chicken, turning occasionally, until golden brown. Drain well and place in a casserole. Add the onion to the pan and cook, stirring occasionally, for 2–3 minutes until softened.

2 Cut the carrots and turnips into equal-size pieces. Add to the casserole with the onions and beans or peas.

3 Blend the cornstarch with a little of the stock, then stir in the rest, and heat gently, stirring until boiling. Pour into the casserole and add the bay leaves. Season to taste with salt and pepper.

4 Cover tightly and bake in a preheated oven, 400°F/200°C, for 50–60 minutes or until the chicken juices run clear when pierced with a skewer.

5 For the topping, sift the flour and baking powder. Mix in the margarine with a fork. Stir in the mustard, cheese, and enough milk to mix to a fairly soft dough.

6 Roll out and cut 16 rounds with a 1½ inch/4 cm cutter. Uncover the casserole, arrange the biscuit rounds on top of the chicken, then brush with milk, and sprinkle with sesame seeds. Return to the oven and bake for 20 minutes or until the topping is golden and firm.

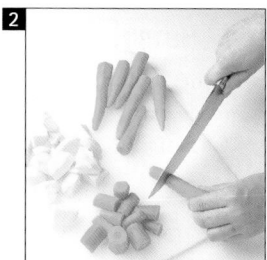

Skewered Chicken Spirals

These unusual chicken kabobs have a wonderful Italian flavor, and the bacon helps keep them moist during cooking.

NUTRITIONAL INFORMATION

Calories 231   Sugars 1g
Protein . . . . .29g   Fat 13g
Carbohydrate . . . .1g   Saturates 5g

15 mins   10 mins

SERVES 4

INGREDIENTS

4 skinless, boneless chicken breast portions

1 garlic clove, crushed

2 tbsp tomato paste

4 slices smoked lean bacon

large handful of fresh basil leaves

vegetable oil, for brushing

salt and pepper

salad greens, to serve

1 Spread out a piece of chicken between two sheets of plastic wrap and beat firmly with a rolling pin or meat mallet to flatten the chicken to an even thickness. Repeat with the remaining chicken.

2 Combine the garlic and tomato paste and spread the mixture over the chicken. Lay a bacon slice over each, then sprinkle with the basil. Season with salt and pepper to taste.

3 Roll up each piece of chicken firmly, then cut into thick slices. Thread the slices onto 4 skewers, making sure the skewer holds the chicken in a spiral shape.

4 Brush lightly with oil and cook on a hot barbecue or under a preheated broiler for about 10 minutes, turning once. Serve hot with salad greens.

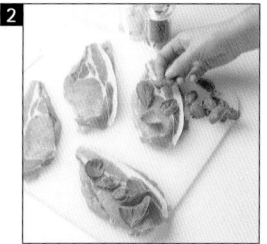

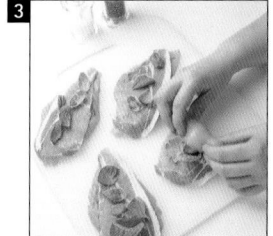

Chicken Tikka Kabobs

Chicken tikka is a low-fat Indian dish. Recipes vary, but you can try your own combination of spices to suit your personal taste.

NUTRITIONAL INFORMATION

Calories 191	Sugars 8g	
Protein 30g	Fat 4g	
Carbohydrate 8g	Saturates 2g	

2¼ hrs   15 mins

SERVES 4

INGREDIENTS

4 x 4½ oz/125 g boneless, skinless chicken breast portions

1 garlic clove, crushed

1 tsp grated fresh ginger root

1 fresh green chile, deseeded and finely chopped

6 tbsp low-fat plain yogurt

1 tbsp tomato paste

1 tsp ground cumin

1 tsp ground coriander

1 tsp ground turmeric

1 large ripe mango

1 tbsp lime juice

salt and pepper

fresh cilantro leaves, to garnish

TO SERVE

boiled white rice

lime wedges

mixed salad greens

warmed nan bread

1 Cut the chicken into 1 inch/2.5 cm cubes and place in a shallow dish.

2 Combine the garlic, ginger, chile, yogurt, tomato paste, spices, and seasoning. Spoon over the chicken, cover, and chill for 2 hours.

3 Using a vegetable peeler, peel the skin from the mango. Slice down either side of the pit and cut the mango flesh into cubes. Toss in lime juice, cover, and chill until required.

4 Thread the chicken and mango pieces alternately onto 8 skewers. Place the skewers on a broiler rack and brush the chicken with the yogurt marinade and the lime juice left from the mango.

5 Place under a preheated moderate broiler for 6–7 minutes. Turn over, brush again with the marinade and lime juice, and cook for a further 6–7 minutes until the juices run clear when the chicken is pierced with a sharp knife.

6 Serve the kabobs immediately on a bed of rice on a warmed platter, garnished with fresh cilantro leaves and accompanied by lime wedges, mixed salad greens, and nan bread.

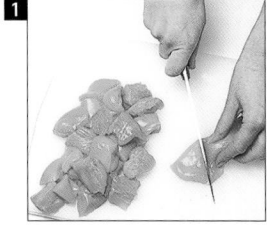

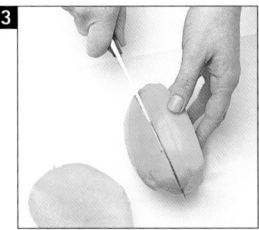

Sweet & Sour Drumsticks

Chicken drumsticks are marinated to impart a tangy, sweet-and-sour flavor and a shiny glaze before being cooked on a barbecue grill.

NUTRITIONAL INFORMATION

Calories 171   Sugars 9g
Protein . . . . .23g   Fat 5g
Carbohydrate . . .10g   Saturates 1g

 1¼ hrs   20 mins

SERVES 4

INGREDIENTS

8 chicken drumsticks

4 tbsp red wine vinegar

2 tbsp tomato paste

2 tbsp soy sauce

2 tbsp honey

1 tbsp Worcestershire sauce

1 garlic clove

pinch of cayenne pepper

salt and pepper

crisp salad greens, to serve

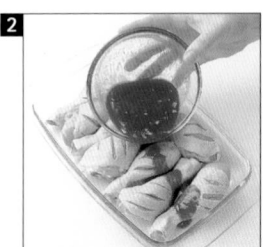

1 Skin the chicken drumsticks, if desired, and slash 2–3 times with a sharp knife. Put the chicken drumsticks into a non-metallic shallow dish, arranging them in a single layer.

2 Combine the vinegar, tomato paste, soy sauce, honey, Worcestershire sauce, and garlic in a bowl. Season to taste with cayenne, salt, and pepper. Pour the mixture over the chicken, turning to coat. Cover and set aside in the refrigerator to marinate for 1 hour.

3 Cook the drumsticks on a hot barbecue or under a preheated broiler for about 20 minutes, brushing with the glaze several times during cooking, until the chicken is well browned and the juices run clear when the thickest part is pierced with a skewer.

4 Transfer the drumsticks to a warmed serving dish and serve immediately with crisp salad greens.

COOK'S TIP

For a tangy flavor, add the juice of 1 lime to the marinade. While the drumsticks are cooking, check regularly to ensure that they are not burning on the outside.

Orange Chicken Stir-Fry

Chicken thighs are inexpensive, meaty, and readily available. Although not so tender as breast portions, they are perfect for stir-frying.

NUTRITIONAL INFORMATION

Calories ....267 Sugars 11g
Protein ....23g Fat 11g
Carbohydrate ...15g Saturates 2g

 10 mins   15 mins

SERVES 4

INGREDIENTS

3 tbsp sunflower oil

12 oz/350 g skinless boneless chicken thighs, cut into thin strips

1 onion, sliced

1 garlic clove, crushed

1 red bell pepper, deseeded and sliced

3 oz/85 g snow peas

4 tbsp light soy sauce

4 tbsp sherry

1 tbsp tomato paste

finely grated rind and juice of 1 orange

1 tsp cornstarch

2 oranges

2 cups bean sprouts

cooked rice or noodles, to serve

1 Heat the oil in a large preheated wok. Add the chicken and stir-fry for 2–3 minutes or until sealed on all sides.

2 Add the onion, garlic, red bell pepper, and snow peas to the wok. Stir-fry for a further 5 minutes or until the vegetables are just tender and the chicken is completely cooked through.

3 Combine the soy sauce, sherry, tomato paste, orange rind and juice, and the cornstarch. Add to the wok and cook, stirring constantly, until the juices start to thicken.

4 Using a sharp knife, peel and segment the oranges. Add the segments to the wok with the bean sprouts and heat through for a further 2 minutes.

5 Transfer the stir-fry to warmed serving plates and serve immediately with cooked rice or noodles.

COOK'S TIP

Bean sprouts are sprouting mung beans and are a regular ingredient in Chinese cooking. They require very little cooking and may even be eaten raw, if wished.

Green Salsa Chicken

Chicken breast fillets bathed in a fragrant sauce make a delicate dish, perfect for dinner parties. Serve with rice to complete the meal.

NUTRITIONAL INFORMATION

Calories	349	Sugars 7g
Protein	........34g	Fat 20g
Carbohydrate	...10g	Saturates 12g

🥟 10 mins   🕐 20–25 mins

SERVES 4

INGREDIENTS

4 skinless chicken breast fillets

all-purpose flour, for dusting

2–3 tbsp butter or a mixture of butter and vegetable oil

1 lb/450 g mild green salsa or puréed tomatillos

1 cup chicken stock

1–2 garlic cloves, finely chopped

3–5 tbsp chopped fresh cilantro

½ fresh green chile, deseeded and chopped

½ tsp ground cumin

salt and pepper

TO SERVE

1 cup sour cream

several leaves Romaine lettuce, shredded

3–5 scallions, thinly sliced

coarsely chopped fresh cilantro

1 Sprinkle the chicken with salt and pepper,, then dredge in flour. Shake off the excess.

2 Melt the butter or heat the butter and oil mixture in a large, heavy skillet. Add the chicken and cook over medium-high heat, turning once, until the fillets are golden all over, but not quite cooked through—they will continue to cook slightly in the sauce. Remove from the skillet and set aside.

3 Place the salsa, stock, garlic, cilantro, chile, and cumin in a pan and bring to a boil. Reduce the heat to a low simmer. Add the chicken to the sauce, spooning the sauce over it. Continue to cook until the chicken is cooked through and tender.

4 Remove the chicken from the pan and season with salt and pepper to taste. Serve immediately with the sour cream, shredded lettuce, sliced scallions, and chopped fresh cilantro leaves.

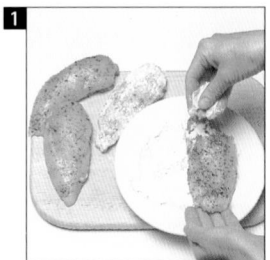

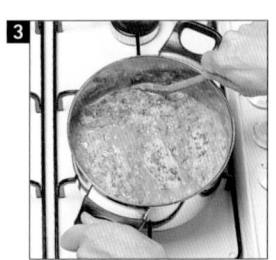

Citrus-Marinated Chicken

This is a great dish for a summer meal. The marinade gives the chicken an appetizing flavor and helps keep it succulent and moist.

NUTRITIONAL INFORMATION

Calories 315	Sugars 2g
Protein 42g	Fat 41g
Carbohydrate 4g	Saturates 6g

 1¼ hrs   20–25 mins

SERVES 4

INGREDIENTS

1 chicken, cut into 4 pieces

1 tbsp mild chili powder

1 tbsp paprika

2 tsp ground cumin

juice and rind of 1 orange

juice of 3 limes

pinch of sugar

8–10 garlic cloves, finely chopped

1 bunch of fresh cilantro, coarsely chopped

2–3 tbsp extra virgin olive oil

¼ cup beer, tequila, or pineapple juice (optional)

salt and pepper

fresh cilantro sprigs, to garnish

TO SERVE

lime wedges

tomato, bell pepper, and scallion salad

1 Place the chicken pieces in a large nonmetallic dish. Combine the chili powder, paprika, cumin, orange juice and rind, lime juice, sugar, garlic, chopped cilantro, and olive oil in a bowl. Stir in the beer, tequila, or pineapple juice, if using, and season to taste with salt and pepper.

2 Pour the marinade over the chicken, turn to coat well, then cover, and set aside to marinate for at least an hour at room temperature. If possible, marinate in the refrigerator for 24 hours.

3 Remove the chicken from the marinade and pat dry with paper towels. Reserve the marinade.

4 Put the chicken on a broiler pan and cook under a preheated broiler for 20–25 minutes, turning once, until the chicken is cooked through. Alternatively, cook in a ridged griddle pan. Brush with the marinade occasionally. To test whether it is cooked, pierce a thick part with a skewer—the juices should run clear.

5 Transfer the chicken to warmed serving plates, garnish with cilantro, and serve immediately with lime wedges and a refreshing side salad.

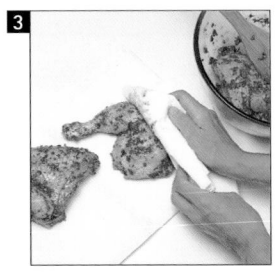

Squabs in Green Marinade

Flavored with a green herb marinade, these elegant squabs are packed with lively Mexican flavors.

NUTRITIONAL INFORMATION

Calories 614	Sugars 6g
Protein 44g	Fat 49g
Carbohydrate 8g	Saturates 19g

3¼ hrs   15–20 mins

SERVES 4

INGREDIENTS

10 garlic cloves, chopped

juice of 1 lime

1 bunch of fresh cilantro, finely chopped

½ fresh green chile, deseeded and chopped

1 tsp ground cumin

4 squabs

1½ cups plain yogurt

1 red bell pepper, roasted, peeled, deseeded, and diced

¼–1 tsp marinade from chipotle canned in adobo or chipotle salsa

3–5 scallions, thinly sliced

handful of toasted pumpkin seeds

salt and pepper

1 Combine 9 garlic cloves with the lime juice, about three-quarters of the fresh cilantro, the green chile, and half the cumin in a bowl. Press the mixture onto the squabs and set aside to marinate for at least 3 hours in the refrigerator.

2 Place the squabs in a roasting pan and cook in a preheated oven, 400°F/ 200°C, for 15 minutes. Pierce the thigh of 1 squab with a knife and if the juices run clear, it is cooked. If necessary, return to the oven and continue to roast until cooked through.

3 Meanwhile, combine the yogurt with the red bell pepper, chipotle marinade or salsa, and remaining garlic and cumin. Season with salt and pepper.

4 Serve each squab with a spoonful of the bell pepper sauce, and a sprinkling of the remaining cilantro, the scallions, and pumpkin seeds.

VARIATION
For grilled lamb, skewer lamb chunks, such as shoulder or leg, onto metal or soaked bamboo skewers. Marinate in the green herbed marinade as in Step 1, then cook over the hot coals of a barbecue until the lamb is cooked to your liking.

Chicken with Purslane

Purslane has become fashionable, owing to its unique flavor and healthy dose of omega-3 fatty acids. It has always been popular in Mexico.

NUTRITIONAL INFORMATION

Calories	.414	Sugars	.7g
Protein	.43g	Fat	.22g
Carbohydrate	.11g	Saturates	.5g

 1¾ hrs   50–60 mins

SERVES 4

INGREDIENTS

juice of 1 lime

6 garlic cloves, finely chopped

¼ tsp dried oregano

¼ tsp dried marjoram

¼ tsp dried thyme

½ tsp ground cumin

1 chicken, cut into 4 pieces

about 10 large dried mild chiles, such as pasilla, toasted

2 cups boiling water

2 cups chicken stock

3 tbsp extra virgin olive oil

1 lb 9 oz/700 g tomatoes, charred under the broiler, peeled, and deseeded

handful of corn tortilla chips, crushed

several large handfuls of fresh purslane, cut into bite-size lengths

½ lime

salt and pepper

lime wedges, to serve

1 Combine the lime juice, half the garlic, the oregano, marjoram, thyme, cumin, and salt to taste. Rub the mixture over the chicken and set aside to marinate for at least an hour at room temperature or overnight in the refrigerator.

2 Place the chiles in a pan and pour the boiling water over them. Cover and set aside for 30 minutes until softened. Remove the stems and seeds. Purée the chiles in a food processor or blender, adding just enough of the stock to make a smooth paste. Add the rest of the stock and mix well.

3 Heat 1 tablespoon of oil in a heavy skillet. Add the chile purée with the tomatoes and remaining garlic. Cook over medium heat, stirring, until it has thickened and reduced by about half.

4 Remove the chicken from the marinade, reserving any marinade juices. Brown the chicken in the remaining oil, then place in flameproof casserole. Add any reserved juices and the reduced chile sauce. Cover and simmer over low heat for about 30 minutes until the chicken is tender and cooked through.

5 Stir the crushed tortillas into the sauce and cook for a few minutes, then add the purslane. Season with salt, pepper, and a squeeze of lime. Heat through and serve with lime wedges.

Spanish Chicken with Garlic

The slow cooking takes all the harsh flavoring out of the garlic cloves and makes them meltingly tender in this simple dish.

NUTRITIONAL INFORMATION

Calories 496   Sugars 1g
Protein . . . . .41g   Fat 22g
Carbohydrate . . .15g   Saturates 5g

 15 mins    50 mins

SERVES 4

INGREDIENTS

2–3 tbsp all-purpose flour

cayenne pepper

4 chicken quarters, patted dry

about 4 tbsp olive oil

20 large garlic cloves, each halved and green core removed

1 large bay leaf

2 cups chicken stock

4 tbsp dry white wine

chopped fresh parsley, to garnish

salt and pepper

1 Put about 2 tablespoons of the flour in a bag and season to taste with cayenne, salt, and pepper. Add a chicken piece and shake until it is lightly coated with the flour, shaking off the excess. Repeat with the remaining pieces, adding more flour and seasoning, if necessary.

2 Heat 3 tablespoons of the olive oil in a large skillet. Add the garlic cloves and fry for about 2 minutes, stirring, to flavor the oil. Remove with a slotted spoon and set aside.

3 Add the chicken pieces to the skillet, skin side down, and fry for 5 minutes or until the skin is golden brown. Turn and

fry for a further 5 minutes, adding an extra 1–2 tablespoons of oil if necessary.

4 Return the garlic to the skillet. Add the bay leaf, chicken stock, and wine and bring to a boil. Lower the heat, cover, and simmer for 25 minutes or until the chicken is tender and the garlic cloves are very soft.

5 Transfer the chicken to a serving platter and keep warm. Bring the cooking liquid to a boil and boil until reduced to about 1 cup. Adjust the seasoning if necessary.

6 Spoon the sauce over the chicken pieces and sprinkle the garlic cloves around it. Garnish with parsley and serve.

Moroccan Chicken Couscous

"Couscous" is the name of both the small grains that are a staple of Moroccan kitchens and the fragrant stew traditionally served with them.

NUTRITIONAL INFORMATION

Calories 610   Sugars 24g
Protein . . . . .38g   Fat 13g
Carbohydrate . . .90g   Saturates 3g

 25 mins   1¼ hrs

SERVES 4–6

INGREDIENTS

3–4 tbsp olive oil

8 chicken pieces with bones, such as quarters, breast portions, and legs

2 large onions, chopped

2 large garlic cloves, crushed

1 inch/2.5 cm piece of fresh ginger root, finely chopped

¾ cup dried garbanzo beans, soaked overnight and drained

4 large carrots, cut into thick chunks

pinch of saffron threads, dissolved in 2 tbsp boiling water

finely grated rind of 2 lemons

2 red bell peppers, deseeded and sliced

2 large zucchini, cut into chunks

2 tomatoes, cored, deseeded, and chopped

½ cup dried apricots, chopped

½ tsp ground cumin

½ tsp ground coriander

½ tsp cayenne pepper

2½ cups water

1 tbsp butter

1 lb 5 oz/600 g instant couscous

salt and pepper

harissa, to serve (optional)

1 Heat 3 tablespoons of the oil in a large flameproof casserole. Pat the chicken pieces dry with paper towels, add to the oil, skin side down, and cook for 5 minutes until crisp and brown. Remove from the casserole and set aside.

2 Add the onions to the casserole, adding a little extra oil if necessary. Cook the onions for 5 minutes, then add the garlic and ginger, and cook, stirring occasionally, for a further 2 minutes.

3 Return the chicken pieces to the casserole. Add the garbanzo beans, carrots, saffron, and lemon rind. Pour in enough water to cover by 1 inch/2.5 cm and bring to a boil.

4 Lower the heat, cover, and simmer for 45 minutes or until the garbanzo

beans are tender. Add the bell peppers, zucchini, tomatoes, dried apricots, cumin, coriander, and cayenne pepper and season with salt and pepper to taste. Re-cover and simmer for a further 15 minutes.

5 Meanwhile, bring the water to a boil. Stir in ½ teaspoon salt and the butter. Sprinkle in the couscous. Cover the pan tightly, remove from the heat, and set aside for 10 minutes or until the grains are tender.

6 Fluff the couscous with a fork. Taste and adjust the seasoning of the stew if necessary. Spoon the couscous into individual bowls and serve the stew and a bowl of harissa, if using, separately.

Chicken Basquaise

Sweet bell peppers are typical of dishes from the Basque region in France.
In this recipe, Bayonne ham, from the Pyrenees, adds a delicious flavor.

NUTRITIONAL INFORMATION

Calories	559	Sugars	.........8g
Protein	........50g	Fat	..........21g
Carbohydrate	...44g	Saturates	.......6g

 15 mins   1½ hrs

SERVES 4–5

I N G R E D I E N T S

3 lb/1.35 kg chicken, cut into 8 pieces

all-purpose flour, for dusting

2–3 tbsp olive oil

1 Bermuda onion, thickly sliced

2 red or yellow bell peppers, deseeded and
cut lengthwise into thick strips

2 garlic cloves

5½ oz/150 g spicy chorizo sausage, peeled
and cut into ½ inch/1 cm pieces

1 tbsp tomato paste

1 cup long grain white rice

2 cups chicken stock

1 tsp crushed dried chiles

½ tsp dried thyme

¾ cup diced Bayonne or other air-dried ham

12 dry-cured black olives

2 tbsp chopped fresh flat leaf parsley

salt and pepper

 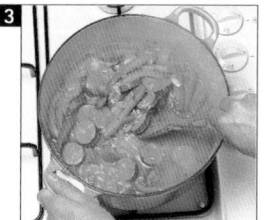 

1 Pat the chicken pieces dry with paper
towels. Put 2 tablespoons flour in a
plastic bag, season with salt and pepper,
and add the chicken pieces. Seal the bag
and shake to coat the chicken.

2 Heat 2 tablespoons of the oil in a
large flameproof casserole over
medium-high heat. Add the chicken and
cook, turning frequently, for about
15 minutes until well browned all over.
Transfer to a plate.

3 Heat the remaining oil in the
casserole and add the onion and red
bell peppers. Reduce the heat to medium
and stir-fry until beginning to color and
soften. Add the garlic, chorizo, and tomato
paste and cook, stirring constantly, for
about 3 minutes. Add the rice and cook,
stirring to coat, for about 2 minutes until
the rice is translucent.

4 Add the stock, crushed chiles, and
thyme, season to taste with salt and
pepper, and stir well. Bring to a boil.
Return the chicken to the casserole,
pressing it gently into the rice. Cover and
cook over very low heat for about
45 minutes until the chicken is cooked
through and the rice is tender.

5 Gently stir the ham, black olives, and
half the parsley into the rice mixture.
Re-cover and heat through for a further
5 minutes. Sprinkle with the remaining
parsley and serve immediately.

Fruity Squabs

This rich fruit-filled stuffing, inspired by a Turkish pilaf, is a wonderful way to use leftover rice. It would be equally delicious with lamb.

NUTRITIONAL INFORMATION

Calories 1052   Sugars 47g
Protein . . . . .34g   Fat 51g
Carbohydrate . .106g   Saturates 17g

45 mins   1 hr

SERVES 4

INGREDIENTS

4 fresh squabs

4–6 tbsp butter, melted

STUFFING

1 cup port

¾ cup raisins

½ cup dried no-soak apricots, sliced

2–3 tbsp extra virgin olive oil

1 onion, finely chopped

1 celery stalk, thinly sliced

2 garlic cloves, finely chopped

1 tsp ground cinnamon

½ tsp allspice or ¼ tsp ground cloves

1 tsp dried oregano

1 tsp dried mint or basil

8 oz/225 g unsweetened chestnuts, canned or vacuum-packed

1 cup long grain white rice, cooked

grated rind and juice of 2 oranges

1½ cups chicken stock

½ cup walnut halves, lightly toasted and chopped

2 tbsp chopped fresh mint

2 tbsp chopped fresh flat leaf parsley

salt and pepper

1 To make the stuffing, combine the port, raisins, and apricots in a small bowl, cover, and set aside for about 15 minutes.

2 Meanwhile, heat the oil in a large heavy pan. Add the onion and celery and cook for 3–4 minutes. Add the garlic, the spices and dried herbs, and the chestnuts and cook, stirring occasionally, for about 4 minutes. Add the rice and half the orange rind and juice, then pour in the stock. Simmer gently for 5 minutes until most of the liquid is absorbed.

3 Drain the raisins and apricots, reserving the port, and stir into the rice mixture with the walnuts, mint, and parsley. Cook for a further 2 minutes. Season with salt and pepper to taste, then remove from the heat, and cool.

4 Rub the squabs inside and out with salt and pepper. Lightly fill the cavity of each bird with the stuffing; do not pack too tightly. Tie the legs of each bird together, tucking in the tail. Form extra stuffing into balls.

5 Arrange the birds in a roasting pan with any stuffing balls and brush with melted butter. Drizzle any remaining butter around the pan. Pour over the remaining orange rind and juice and the reserved port.

6 Roast in a preheated oven, 350°F/180°C, basting frequently, for about 45 minutes until cooked. Transfer to a platter, cover with foil, and set aside to rest for 5 minutes. Serve with any roasting juices.

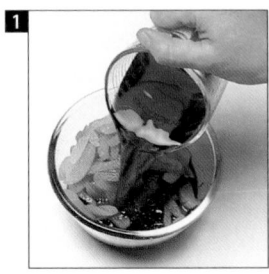

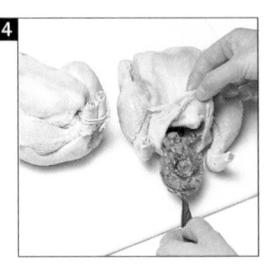

Ginger Chicken & Corn

Chicken wings and corn in a sticky ginger marinade are designed to be eaten with the fingers—there's no other way!

NUTRITIONAL INFORMATION

Calories	123	Sugars	.........3g
Protein	........14g	Fat	...........6g
Carbohydrate	....3g	Saturates	......1g

🍖 10 mins   🕐 20 mins

SERVES 4

INGREDIENTS

3 corn cobs

12 chicken wings

1 inch/2.5 cm piece of fresh ginger root

6 tbsp lemon juice

4 tsp sunflower oil

1 tbsp golden superfine sugar

baked potatoes or salad, to serve

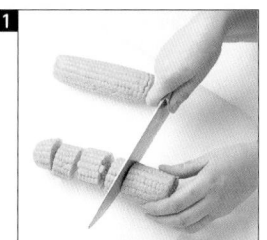
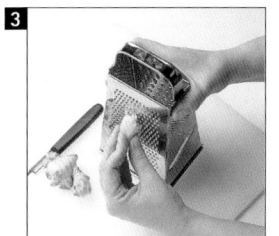
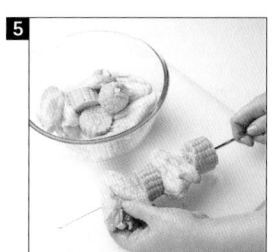

1 Remove the husks and silks from the corn. Using a sharp knife, cut each cob into 6 slices.

2 Place the corn in a large bowl with the chicken wings.

3 Peel and grate the ginger root or chop very finely. Place in a bowl and add the lemon juice, sunflower oil, and golden superfine sugar. Mix together until thoroughly combined.

4 Toss the corn and chicken in the ginger mixture to coat evenly.

5 Thread the corn and chicken wings alternately onto metal or pre-soaked wooden skewers to make turning easier.

6 Cook under a preheated moderately hot broiler or on a barbecue grill for about 15–20 minutes, basting with the gingery glaze and turning frequently until the corn is golden brown and tender and the chicken is cooked. Serve immediately with baked potatoes or salad.

COOK'S TIP
Cut off the wing tips before cooking because they burn very easily. Alternatively, you can cover them with small pieces of foil.

Thai-Style Chicken Skewers

The chicken is marinated in an aromatic sauce before being cooked on the barbecue grill. Use bay leaves if kaffir lime leaves are unavailable.

NUTRITIONAL INFORMATION

Calories 218   Sugars 4g
Protein . . . . .28g   Fat 10g
Carbohydrate . . . .5g   Saturates 2g

2¼ hrs   20 mins

SERVES 4

INGREDIENTS

4 skinless boneless chicken breast portions

1 onion, cut into wedges

1 large red bell pepper, deseeded

1 large yellow bell pepper deseeded

12 kaffir lime leaves

2 tbsp sunflower oil

2 tbsp lime juice

tomato halves, to serve

MARINADE

1 tbsp Thai red curry paste

⅔ cup canned coconut milk

1 To make the marinade, place the red curry paste in a small pan over medium heat and cook for 1 minute. Add half of the coconut milk to the pan and bring the mixture to a boil. Boil for 2–3 minutes until the liquid has reduced by about two-thirds.

2 Remove the pan from the heat and stir in the remaining coconut milk. Set aside to cool.

3 Cut the chicken into 1 inch/2.5 cm pieces. Stir the chicken into the cold marinade, cover, and chill in the refrigerator for at least 2 hours.

4 Cut the onion into wedges and cut the bell peppers into 1 inch/2.5 cm pieces.

5 Remove the chicken pieces from the marinade and thread them onto skewers, alternating the chicken with the vegetables and lime leaves.

6 Combine the oil and lime juice in a small bowl and brush the mixture over the kabobs. Grill the skewers over hot coals, turning and basting frequently, for 10–15 minutes until the chicken is cooked through. Grill the tomato halves for the last few minutes of the cooking time and serve with the chicken skewers.

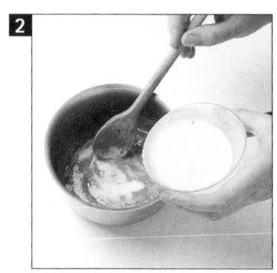

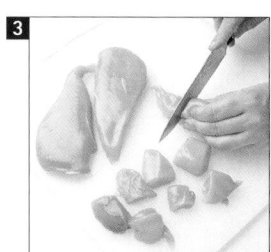

COOK'S TIP

Cooking the marinade first intensifies the flavor. It is important to let the marinade cool before adding the chicken because bacteria may breed in the warm temperature.

Whisky Roast Chicken

An unusual change from a plain roast, with a distinctly warming Scottish flavor and a delicious oatmeal stuffing.

NUTRITIONAL INFORMATION

Calories	254	Sugars	.........6g
Protein	........27g	Fat	...........8g
Carbohydrate	....11g	Saturates	......2g

5 mins   1½ hrs

SERVES 6

I N G R E D I E N T S

1 chicken, weighing 4 lb 8 oz/2 kg

vegetable oil, for brushing

1 tbsp heather honey

2 tbsp Scotch whisky

2 tbsp all-purpose flour

1¼ cups chicken stock

vegetables and sauté potatoes, to serve

S T U F F I N G

1 tbsp sunflower oil

1 medium onion, finely chopped

1 celery stalk, thinly sliced

1 tsp dried thyme

4 tbsp rolled oats

4 tbsp chicken stock

salt and pepper

1 To make the stuffing, heat the oil in a pan and cook the onion and celery over moderate heat, stirring occasionally, until softened and lightly browned.

2 Remove from the heat and stir in the thyme, oats, and stock, and season with salt and pepper to taste.

3 Stuff the neck end of the chicken with the mixture and tuck the neck flap under. Place in a roasting pan, brush lightly with oil, and roast in a preheated oven, 375°F/190°C, for about 1 hour.

4 Mix the honey with 1 tablespoon whisky and brush the mixture over the chicken. Return to the oven for a further 20 minutes or until the chicken is golden brown and the juices run clear when pierced through the thickest part with a skewer.

5 Lift the chicken onto a serving plate. Skim the fat from the juices, then stir in the flour. Stir over moderate heat until the mixture bubbles, then gradually add the stock and remaining whisky to the pan.

6 Bring to a boil, stirring constantly, then simmer for 1 minute, and serve the chicken with the sauce, vegetables, and sauté potatoes.

Chicken & Lemon Skewers

A tangy lemon yogurt is served with these tasty chicken skewers flavored with lemon and cilantro.

NUTRITIONAL INFORMATION

Calories	181	Sugars	6g
Protein	30g	Fat	4g
Carbohydrate	6g	Saturates	2g

2¼ hrs   15 mins

SERVES 4

INGREDIENTS

4 skinless boneless chicken breast portions

1 tsp ground coriander

2 tsp lemon juice

1¼ cups low-fat plain yogurt

1 lemon

2 tbsp chopped fresh cilantro

vegetable oil, for brushing

salt and pepper

fresh cilantro sprigs, to garnish

TO SERVE

lemon wedges

salad greens

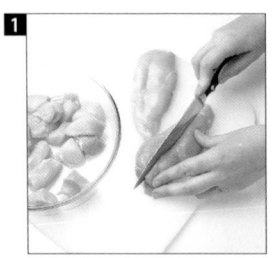

1 Cut the chicken into 1 inch/2.5 cm pieces and place them in a shallow, nonmetallic dish.

2 Add the ground coriander, lemon juice, and 4 tablespoons of the yogurt to the chicken and season to taste with salt and pepper. Mix together until thoroughly combined. Cover with plastic wrap and set aside to marinate in the refrigerator for at least 2 hours.

3 To make the lemon yogurt, put the remaining yogurt in a bowl. Peel and finely chop the lemon, discarding any seeds and all traces of pith. Stir the lemon into the yogurt with the chopped fresh cilantro. Cover with plastic wrap and chill in the refrigerator until required.

4 Thread the chicken pieces onto metal or soaked bamboo skewers. Brush the barbecue rack with oil and cook the chicken over hot coals for about 15 minutes, brushing occasionally with the oil and turning frequently.

5 Transfer the chicken kabobs to warm serving plates and garnish with sprigs of fresh cilantro. Serve with the lemon yogurt, lemon wedges, and salad greens.

Marmalade Chicken

Marmalade lovers will enjoy this festive recipe. You can use any favorite marmalade, such as lemon or grapefruit.

NUTRITIONAL INFORMATION

Calories	304	Sugars	. . . . .20g
Protein	. . . . .29g	Fat	. . . . .7g
Carbohydrate	. . .30g	Saturates	. . . . . .2g

🕐 10 mins   🕐 2 hrs

SERVES 6

I N G R E D I E N T S

1 chicken, weighing about 5 lb/2.25 kg

bay leaves

vegetable oil, for brushing

2 tbsp marmalade

S T U F F I N G

1 tbsp sunflower oil

1 celery stalk, finely chopped

1 small onion, finely chopped

2¼ cups fresh whole-wheat breadcrumbs

4 tbsp marmalade

2 tbsp chopped fresh parsley

1 egg, beaten

salt and pepper

S A U C E

2 tsp cornstarch

2 tbsp orange juice

3 tbsp marmalade

⅔ cup chicken stock

1 medium orange

2 tbsp brandy

1 Lift the neck flap of the chicken and remove the wishbone. Place a sprig of bay leaves inside the body cavity.

2 To make the stuffing, heat the oil in a pan and cook the celery and onion until softened. Add the other ingredients. Season with salt and pepper to taste. Stuff the neck cavity of the chicken.

3 Place the chicken in a roasting pan and brush lightly with oil. Roast in a preheated oven, 375°F/190°C, for about 1 hour 50 minutes or until the juices run clear when the chicken is pierced with the point of a knife. Glaze the chicken with the marmalade.

4 For the sauce, blend the cornstarch in a pan with the orange juice, then add the marmalade and stock. Heat gently, stirring constantly, until thickened. Remove from the heat.

5 Cut the segments from the orange, discarding all white pith and membrane, add to the sauce with the brandy, and bring to a boil. Serve with the roast chicken.

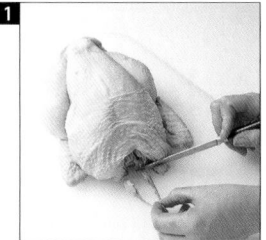

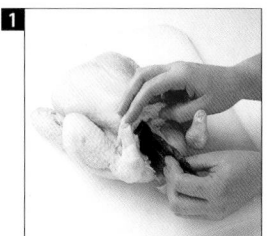

Garlic Chicken Cushions

Stuffed with creamy ricotta, spinach, and garlic, then gently cooked in a rich tomato sauce, this chicken dish can be made ahead of time.

NUTRITIONAL INFORMATION

Calories 316   Sugars 6g
Protein . . . . .40g   Fat 13g
Carbohydrate . . . .6g   Saturates 5g

10 mins   40 mins

SERVES 4

I N G R E D I E N T S

4 part-boned chicken breasts

4 oz/115 g frozen spinach, thawed

¾ cup low-fat ricotta cheese

2 garlic cloves, crushed

1 tbsp olive oil

1 onion, chopped

1 red bell pepper, deseeded and sliced

15 oz/425 g canned chopped tomatoes

6 tbsp wine or chicken stock

10 stuffed olives, sliced

salt and pepper

fresh flat-leaf parsley sprigs, to garnish

pasta, to serve

1 Make a slit between the skin and meat on one side of each chicken breast. Lift the skin to form a pocket, being careful to leave the skin attached to the other side.

2 Put the spinach into a strainer and press out the water with a spoon. Mix with the ricotta, half the garlic, and the seasoning.

3 Spoon the spinach mixture under the skin of each chicken breast, then secure the edge of the skin with toothpicks.

4 Heat the oil in a skillet, add the onion, and cook for a minute, stirring. Add the remaining garlic and the red bell pepper and cook for 2 minutes. Stir in the tomatoes, wine or stock, olives, and seasoning. Set the sauce aside and chill the chicken if preparing in advance.

5 Bring the sauce to a boil, pour into an ovenproof dish, and arrange the chicken breasts on top in a single layer.

6 Cook, uncovered, in a preheated oven, 400°F/200°C, for about 35 minutes, until the chicken is golden and cooked through. Test by making a slit in one of the chicken breasts with a skewer to make sure the juices run clear.

7 Spoon a little of the sauce over the chicken breasts, then transfer to serving plates, and garnish with parsley. Serve with pasta.

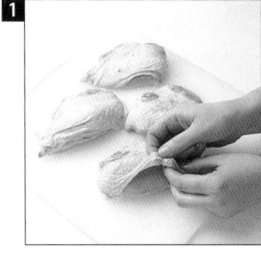

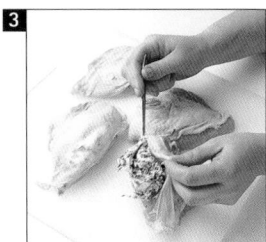

Rustic Chicken & Orange Pot

Low in fat and high in fiber, this colorful casserole makes a healthy, hearty, and utterly delicious one-pot meal.

NUTRITIONAL INFORMATION

Calories	345	Sugars	.........6g
Protein	........29g	Fat	..........10g
Carbohydrate	...39g	Saturates	......2g

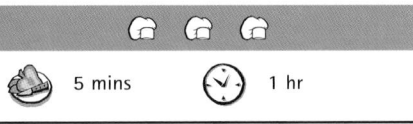

🥪 5 mins   🕐 1 hr

SERVES 4

I N G R E D I E N T S

8 skinless chicken drumsticks

1 tbsp whole-wheat flour

1 tbsp olive oil

2 medium red onions

1 garlic clove, crushed

1 tsp fennel seeds

1 bay leaf

finely grated rind and juice of
   1 small orange

14 oz/400 g can chopped tomatoes

14 oz/400 g can cannellini or small navy
   beans, drained

salt and black pepper

T O P P I N G

3 thick slices whole-wheat bread,
   crusts removed

2 tsp olive oil

1 Toss the chicken in the flour to coat evenly. Heat the oil in a nonstick pan. Add the chicken and cook over fairly high heat, turning frequently, until golden brown. Transfer to a large casserole.

2 Slice the red onions into thin wedges. Add to the pan and cook over medium heat for a few minutes until lightly browned. Stir in the garlic, then add the onions and garlic to the casserole.

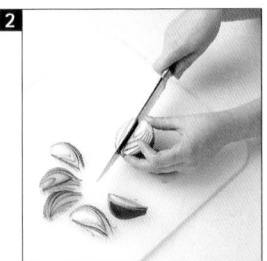

3 Add the fennel seeds, bay leaf, orange rind and juice, tomatoes, and cannellini or small navy beans and season to taste with salt and pepper.

4 Cover tightly and cook in a preheated oven, 375°F/ 190°C, for 30–35 minutes until the chicken juices are clear and not pink when pierced through the thickest part with a skewer.

5 To make the topping, cut the bread into small dice and toss in the oil. Remove the lid from the casserole and sprinkle the bread cubes on top of the chicken. Bake for a further 15–20 minutes until the bread is golden and crisp. Serve immediately straight from the casserole.

Chicken & Beans

Beans are a valuable source of nourishment. You could use any variety of beans in this recipe, but adjust the cooking times accordingly.

NUTRITIONAL INFORMATION

Calories . . . . .291 Sugars 3g
Protein . . . . .33g Fat 10g
Carbohydrate . . .18g Saturates 2g

 12 hrs   1 hr

SERVES 4

I N G R E D I E N T S

1 cup dried black-eye peas, soaked overnight and drained

1 tsp salt

2 onions, chopped

2 garlic cloves, crushed

1 tsp ground turmeric

1 tsp ground cumin

2 lb 12 oz/1.25 kg chicken, cut into 8 pieces

1 green bell pepper, deseeded and chopped

2 tbsp vegetable oil

1 inch/2.5 cm piece of fresh ginger root, grated

2 tsp coriander seeds

½ tsp fennel seeds

2 tsp garam masala

1 tbsp chopped fresh cilantro, to garnish

COOK'S TIP

For convenience, you can use a 15 oz/425 g can of black-eye peas instead of dried peas. Add them at step 2.

1 Put the dried black-eye peas into a Balti pan or wok with the salt, onions, garlic, turmeric, and cumin. Cover the beans with water, bring to a boil, and cook for 15 minutes.

2 Add the chicken and green bell pepper to the pan and bring to a boil. Lower the heat and simmer gently for 30 minutes until the beans are tender and the chicken juices run clear when the thickest parts of the pieces are pierced with a sharp knife or skewer.

3 Heat the oil in a Balti pan or wok and cook the ginger, coriander seeds, and fennel seeds for 30 seconds.

4 Stir the spices into the chicken and add the garam masala. Simmer for a further 5 minutes, garnish with chopped cilantro, and serve immediately.

Chicken & Spinach Lasagna

A delicious pasta dish with all the colors of the Italian flag—red tomatoes, green spinach and pasta, and white chicken and sauce.

NUTRITIONAL INFORMATION

Calories 358   Sugars 12g
Protein . . . . .42g   Fat 9g
Carbohydrate . . .22g   Saturates 4g

25 mins   50 mins

SERVES 4

INGREDIENTS

12 oz/350 g frozen chopped spinach, thawed and drained

½ tsp ground nutmeg

1 lb/450 g lean, cooked chicken, diced

4 sheets no pre-cook lasagna verde

1½ tbsp cornstarch

scant 2 cups skim milk

4 tbsp freshly grated Parmesan cheese

salt and pepper

salad greens, to serve

TOMATO SAUCE

14 oz/400 g can chopped tomatoes

1 medium onion, finely chopped

1 garlic clove, crushed

⅔ cup white wine

3 tbsp tomato paste

1 tsp dried oregano

1 To make the tomato sauce, place the tomatoes in a pan and stir in the onion, garlic, wine, tomato paste, and oregano. Bring to a boil and simmer for 20 minutes until thick. Season to taste with salt and pepper.

2 Drain the spinach again and pat dry on paper towels. Arrange the spinach in the base of a casserole. Sprinkle with nutmeg and season to taste.

3 Arrange the diced chicken over the spinach and spoon the tomato sauce over it. Arrange the sheets of lasagna over the tomato sauce.

4 Blend the cornstarch with a little of the milk to make a paste. Pour the remaining milk into a pan and stir in the cornstarch paste. Heat gently for 2–3 minutes, stirring constantly, until the sauce thickens. Season to taste with salt and pepper.

5 Spoon the sauce over the lasagna to cover it completely and transfer the dish to a cookie sheet. Sprinkle the grated cheese over the sauce and bake in a preheated oven, 400°F/200°C, for 25 minutes until golden brown and bubbling. Serve immediately with fresh salad greens.

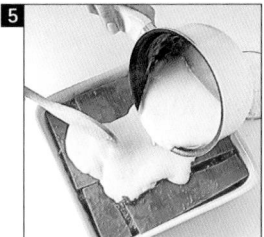

Chicken & Chili Bean Pot

This aromatic chicken dish has a spicy Mexican kick. Chicken thighs have a wonderful flavor when cooked in this way.

NUTRITIONAL INFORMATION

Calories	333	Sugars	........10g
Protein	........25g	Fat	..........13g
Carbohydrate	...32g	Saturates	......2g

🐖 🐖

🍲 10 mins   🕐 40 mins

SERVES 4

INGREDIENTS

2 tbsp all-purpose flour

1 tsp chili powder

8 chicken thighs or 4 chicken legs

3 tbsp vegetable oil

2 garlic cloves, crushed

1 large onion, chopped

1 green or red bell pepper, deseeded
   and chopped

1¼ cups chicken stock

12 oz/350 g tomatoes, chopped

14 oz/400 g can red kidney beans, rinsed
   and drained

2 tbsp tomato paste

salt and pepper

1 Combine the flour and chili powder in a shallow dish and add salt and pepper to taste. Rinse the chicken, but do not dry. Dip the chicken into the seasoned flour, turning to coat it on all sides.

2 Heat the oil in a large, deep skillet or flameproof casserole and add the chicken. Cook over high heat, turning the pieces frequently, for 3–4 minutes until browned all over.

3 Lift the chicken out of the skillet or casserole with a slotted spoon and drain on paper towels.

4 Add the garlic, onion, and bell pepper to the skillet or casserole and cook over medium heat, stirring occasionally, for 2–3 minutes until softened.

5 Add the stock, tomatoes, kidney beans, and tomato paste, stirring well. Bring to a boil, then return the chicken to the pan. Reduce the heat, cover, and simmer for about 30 minutes until the chicken is tender. Taste and adjust the seasoning, if necessary, and serve.

COOK'S TIP

For extra intensity of flavor,
use sun-dried tomato paste
instead of ordinary tomato paste.

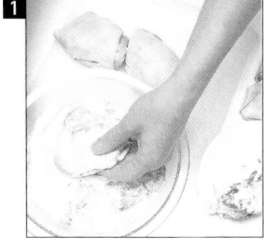

Sweet & Sour Chicken

This sweet-citrus chicken is delicious hot or cold. Sesame-flavored noodles are the ideal accompaniment for the hot version.

NUTRITIONAL INFORMATION

Calories ....248 Sugars 8g

Protein ....30g Fat 8g

Carbohydrate ...16g Saturates 2g

5 mins   25 mins

SERVES 4

INGREDIENTS

4 boneless chicken breast portions, about
4½ oz/125 g each

2 tbsp honey

1 tbsp dark soy sauce

1 tsp finely grated lemon rind

1 tbsp lemon juice

salt and pepper

TO GARNISH

1 tbsp chopped fresh chives

grated lemon rind

TO SERVE

8 oz/225 g rice noodles

2 tsp sesame oil

1 tbsp sesame seeds

1 tsp finely grated lemon rind

 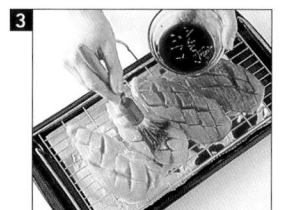 

1 Skin and trim the chicken breast portions to remove any excess fat, then wash, and pat them dry with absorbent paper towels. Using a sharp knife, score the chicken breast portions with a criss-cross pattern on both sides (making sure that you do not cut all the way through the meat.)

2 Combine the honey, soy sauce, lemon rind, and juice in a small bowl and season with black pepper.

3 Arrange the chicken on the broiler rack and brush with half the honey mixture. Cook under a preheated broiler for 10 minutes, then turn over and brush with the remaining mixture. Cook for a further 8–10 minutes or until cooked through and tender. The juices should run clear when pierced with a skewer.

4 Meanwhile, prepare the noodles according to the instructions on the packet. Drain well and transfer to a warmed serving bowl. Add the sesame oil, sesame seeds, and lemon rind and toss well to mix. Season to taste with salt and pepper and keep warm.

5 Drain the chicken and serve immediately with a small mound of noodles, garnished with chopped fresh chives and grated lemon rind.

Crispy Stuffed Chicken

An attractive entrée of chicken breast portions filled with mixed bell peppers and set on a delicious tomato sauce.

NUTRITIONAL INFORMATION

Calories	196	Sugars	.........4g
Protein	........29g	Fat	...........6g
Carbohydrate	....6g	Saturates	......2g

 20 mins   🕐 50 mins

SERVES 4

I N G R E D I E N T S

4 skinless boneless chicken breast portions, 5½ oz/150 g each

4 fresh tarragon sprigs

½ orange bell pepper, deseeded and sliced

½ green bell pepper, deseeded and sliced

½ cup whole-wheat bread crumbs

1 tbsp sesame seeds

4 tbsp lemon juice

1 small red bell pepper, halved and deseeded

7 oz/200 g canned chopped tomatoes

1 small red chile, deseeded and chopped

¼ tsp celery salt

salt and pepper

fresh tarragon, to garnish

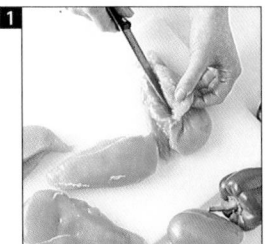

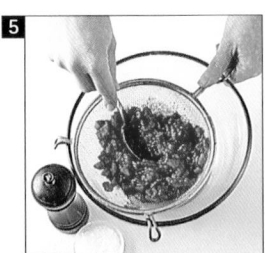

1 Make a slit in each of the chicken portions with a small, sharp knife to create a pocket. Season inside each pocket with salt and pepper.

2 Place a sprig of tarragon and a few slices of orange and green bell pepper in each pocket. Place the chicken on a nonstick cookie sheet and sprinkle with the bread crumbs and sesame seeds.

3 Spoon 1 tablespoon of lemon juice over each chicken portion and bake in a preheated oven, 375°F/ 190°C, for 35–40 minutes until the chicken is tender and cooked through.

4 Meanwhile, preheat the broiler to hot. Arrange the red bell pepper halves, skin side up, on the rack and cook for 5–6 minutes until the skin begins to char and blister. Set the broiled bell peppers aside to cool for about 10 minutes, then peel off the skins.

5 Put the red bell pepper in a blender, add the tomatoes, chile, and celery salt and process for a few seconds. Season to taste. Alternatively, finely chop the red bell pepper and press through a strainer with the tomatoes and chile.

6 When the chicken is cooked, heat the sauce, spoon a little onto a warm plate, and arrange a chicken in the center. Garnish with tarragon and serve.

Chicken & Ham Lasagna

You can use your favorite mushrooms, such as chanterelles or oyster mushrooms, for this delicately flavored dish.

NUTRITIONAL INFORMATION

Calories	708	Sugars	. . . . .17g
Protein	. . . . .35g	Fat	. . . . .35g
Carbohydrate	. . .57g	Saturates	. . . . . .14g

  40 mins   1¾ hrs

SERVES 4

I N G R E D I E N T S

butter, for greasing

14 sheets pre-cooked lasagna

3¾ cups Béchamel Sauce (see page 6)

1 cup freshly grated Parmesan cheese

CHICKEN AND EXOTIC MUSHROOM SAUCE

2 tbsp olive oil

2 garlic cloves, crushed

1 large onion, finely chopped

3½ cups sliced exotic mushrooms

10½ oz/300 g ground chicken

3 oz/85 g chicken livers, finely chopped

4 oz/115 g prosciutto, diced

⅔ cup Marsala wine

10 oz/280 g canned chopped tomatoes

1 tbsp chopped fresh basil leaves

2 tbsp tomato paste

salt and pepper

1 To make the chicken and exotic mushroom sauce, heat the olive oil in a large pan. Add the garlic, onion, and mushrooms and cook, stirring frequently, for 6 minutes.

2 Add the ground chicken, chicken livers, and prosciutto and cook over low heat, stirring frequently, for about 12 minutes or until the meat has browned.

3 Stir the Marsala, tomatoes, basil, and tomato paste into the mixture in the pan and cook for 4 minutes. Season with salt and pepper to taste, cover, and simmer gently for 30 minutes. Uncover the pan, stir thoroughly, and simmer for a further 15 minutes.

4 Lightly grease a casserole with butter. Arrange sheets of lasagna over the bottom of the dish, spoon a layer of the chicken and exotic mushroom sauce over them, then spoon over a layer of Béchamel sauce. Place another layer of lasagna on top and repeat the process twice, finishing with a layer of Béchamel sauce. Sprinkle over the grated cheese and bake in a preheated oven, 375°F/190°C, for 35 minutes until golden brown and bubbling. Serve immediately.

Chicken Risotto Milanese

This famous dish is known throughout the world—it is perhaps the best known of all Italian risottos, although there are many variations.

NUTRITIONAL INFORMATION

Calories	.857	Sugars	1g
Protein	57g	Fat	38g
Carbohydrate	72g	Saturates	21g

5 mins   55 mins

SERVES 4

INGREDIENTS

½ cup butter

2 lb/900 g skinless boneless chicken, thinly sliced

1 large onion, chopped

1 lb 2 oz/500 g risotto rice

2½ cups chicken stock

⅔ cup white wine

1 tsp crumbled saffron

salt and pepper

⅔ cup grated Parmesan cheese, to serve

1 Heat 4 tablespoons of the butter in a deep skillet and cook the chicken and onion until golden brown.

2 Add the rice, stir well, and cook over low heat for 15 minutes.

3 Heat the stock until boiling and gradually add to the rice. Add the white wine, saffron, salt and pepper to taste and mix well. Simmer gently for 20 minutes, stirring occasionally, and adding more stock if necessary.

4 Set aside for 2–3 minutes and just before serving, add a little more stock and simmer for 10 minutes. Serve the risotto, sprinkled with the grated Parmesan cheese and the remaining butter.

Chicken with Orange Sauce

The refreshing combination of chicken and orange sauce makes this a perfect dish for a warm summer evening.

NUTRITIONAL INFORMATION

Calories ....797 Sugars 28g
Protein ....59g Fat 25g
Carbohydrate ...77g Saturates 6g

🍲 15 mins   🕐 25 mins

SERVES 4

INGREDIENTS

2 tbsp canola oil

2 tbsp olive oil

4 x 8 oz/225 g chicken suprêmes

⅔ cup orange brandy

2 tbsp all-purpose flour

⅔ cup freshly squeezed
   orange juice

1 oz/25 g zucchini, cut into thin batons

1 oz/25 g red bell pepper, cut into
   thin batons

1 oz/25 g leek, finely shredded

14 oz/400 g dried whole-wheat spaghetti

3 large oranges, peeled and cut
   into segments

rind of 1 orange, cut into very fine strips

2 tbsp chopped fresh tarragon

⅔ cup ricotta cheese

salt and pepper

fresh tarragon leaves, to garnish

1 Heat the canola oil and 1 tablespoon of the olive oil in a skillet. Add the chicken and cook over fairly high heat until golden brown. Add the orange brandy and cook for 3 minutes. Sprinkle in the flour and cook, stirring constantly, for 2 minutes.

2 Lower the heat and add the orange juice, zucchini, red bell pepper, and leek and season to taste. Simmer for 5 minutes until the sauce has thickened.

3 Meanwhile, bring a pan of lightly salted water to a boil. Add the spaghetti, bring back to a boil, and cook for 10 minutes until tender, but still firm to the bite. Drain the spaghetti, transfer to a warmed serving dish, and drizzle over the remaining oil.

4 Add half of the orange segments, half of the orange rind, the tarragon, and ricotta cheese to the sauce in the pan and cook for 3 minutes.

5 Place the chicken on top of the pasta, pour over a little sauce, and garnish with orange segments, rind, and tarragon. Serve immediately with any extra sauce.

Tagliatelle & Chicken Sauce

Spinach ribbon noodles covered with a rich tomato sauce and topped with creamy chicken make a very appetizing dish.

NUTRITIONAL INFORMATION

Calories 853   Sugars 6g
Protein . . . . .32g   Fat 71g
Carbohydrate . . .23g   Saturates 34g

30 mins   25 mins

SERVES 4

INGREDIENTS

Basic Tomato Sauce (see page 7)

8 oz/225 g fresh or dried green tagliatelle

salt

fresh basil leaves, to garnish

CHICKEN SAUCE

4 tbsp sweet butter

14 oz/400 g skinless boneless chicken breast portions, thinly sliced

¾ cup blanched almonds

1¼ cups heavy cream

salt and pepper

1 Make the tomato sauce, set aside, and keep warm.

2 To make the chicken sauce, melt the butter in a large, heavy skillet over medium heat. Add the chicken strips and almonds and cook, stirring frequently, for about 5–6 minutes until the chicken is cooked through.

3 Meanwhile, pour the cream into a small pan, set over low heat, and bring to a boil. Boil for about 10 minutes until reduced by almost half. Pour the cream over the chicken and almonds, stir well, and season with salt and pepper to taste. Remove the pan from the heat, set aside, and keep warm.

4 Bring a large pan of lightly salted water to a boil. Add the pasta, bring back to a boil, and cook until tender, but still firm to the bite. Fresh tagliatelle will take 2–3 minutes and dried pasta will take 8–10 minutes, timed from when the water returns to a boil. Drain, then return to the pan, cover, and keep warm.

5 When ready to serve, turn the pasta into a warmed serving dish and spoon the tomato sauce over it. Spoon the chicken and cream into the center, sprinkle with the basil leaves, and serve.

Potato, Leek & Chicken Pie

This pie has an attractive phyllo pastry case that has a "ruffled" top made with strips of the pastry brushed with melted butter.

NUTRITIONAL INFORMATION

Calories	543	Sugars	.........7g
Protein	........21g	Fat	..........27g
Carbohydrate	...56g	Saturates	......16g

 10 mins 1¼ hrs

SERVES 4

I N G R E D I E N T S

8 oz/225 g waxy potatoes, cubed

5 tbsp butter

1 skinless chicken breast fillet, about 6 oz/175 g, cubed

1 leek, sliced

2 cups sliced crimini mushrooms

2½ tbsp all-purpose flour

1¼ cups milk

1 tbsp Dijon mustard

2 tbsp chopped fresh sage

8 oz/225 g phyllo pastry, thawed if frozen

3 tbsp butter, melted

salt and pepper

  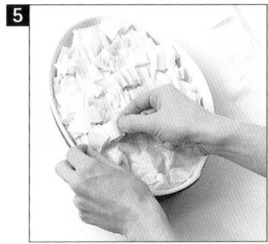

1 Cook the potato cubes in a pan of boiling water for 5 minutes. Drain and set aside.

2 Melt the butter in a skillet and cook the chicken cubes for 5 minutes or until browned all over.

3 Add the leek and mushrooms and cook for 3 minutes, stirring. Stir in the flour and cook for 1 minute stirring constantly. Gradually stir in the milk and bring to a boil. Add the mustard, sage, and potato cubes and simmer for 10 minutes.

4 Meanwhile, line a deep pie dish with half of the sheets of phyllo pastry. Spoon the sauce into the dish and cover with 1 sheet of pastry. Brush the pastry with butter and lay another sheet on top. Brush this sheet with butter.

5 Cut the remaining phyllo pastry into strips and fold them onto the top of the pie to create a ruffled effect. Brush the strips with the melted butter and cook in a preheated oven, 350°F, for 45 minutes or until golden brown and crisp. Serve hot.

COOK'S TIP

If the top of the pie starts to brown too quickly, cover it with foil halfway through the cooking time to allow the pastry base to cook through without the top burning.

Potato Crisp Pie

This is a layered pie of potatoes, broccoli, tomatoes, and chicken slices in a creamy sauce, topped with a crisp oat layer.

NUTRITIONAL INFORMATION

Calories . . . . .630 Sugars 12g
Protein . . . . .25g Fat 40g
Carbohydrate . . .38g Saturates 24g

 10 mins   55 mins

SERVES 4

INGREDIENTS

1 lb 5 oz/600 g waxy potatoes, sliced

5 tbsp butter

1 skinless chicken breast fillet, about 6 oz/175 g

2 garlic cloves, crushed

4 scallions, sliced

2½ tbsp all-purpose flour

⅔ cup dry white wine

⅔ cup heavy cream

8 oz/225 g broccoli florets

4 large tomatoes, sliced

3 oz/85 g Swiss cheese, sliced

1 cup plain yogurt

4 tbsp rolled oats, toasted

1 Cook the potatoes in a pan of boiling water for 10 minutes. Drain and set aside.

2 Meanwhile, melt the butter in a large, heavy skillet. Cut the chicken into strips and cook over medium heat for 5 minutes, turning. Add the garlic and scallions and cook for a further 2 minutes.

3 Stir in the flour and cook for 1 minute. Gradually stir in the wine and cream. Bring to a boil, stirring constantly, then reduce the heat until the sauce is simmering, and cook for 5 minutes.

4 Meanwhile, blanch the broccoli in boiling water, drain, and refresh in cold water.

5 Place half of the potatoes in the base of a pie dish and top with half of the tomatoes and half of the broccoli.

6 Spoon the chicken sauce on top and repeat the layers in the same order once more.

7 Arrange the Swiss cheese on top and spoon the yogurt over the top. Sprinkle with the oats and cook in a preheated oven, 400°F/200°C, for 25 minutes until the top is golden brown. Serve the pie immediately.

COOK'S TIP

Add chopped nuts, such as pine nuts, to the topping for extra crunch, if you prefer.

Chicken & Potato Casserole

Small new potatoes are ideal for this recipe because they can be cooked whole. If larger potatoes are used, cut them in half or into chunks.

NUTRITIONAL INFORMATION

Calories 856   Sugars 7g
Protein . . . . .35g   Fat 58g
Carbohydrate . . .40g   Saturates 26g

5 mins   1½ hrs

SERVES 4

INGREDIENTS

2 tbsp vegetable oil

5 tbsp butter

4 chicken portions, about 8 oz/225 g each

2 leeks, sliced

1 garlic clove, crushed

4 tbsp all-purpose flour

3¾ cups chicken stock

1¼ cups dry white wine

4 oz/115 g baby carrots, halved lengthwise

4 oz/115 g baby corn cobs, halved lengthwise

1 lb/450 g small new potatoes

1 bouquet garni

⅔ cup heavy cream

salt and pepper

plain rice or fresh vegetables, to serve

1 Heat the oil and butter in a large skillet. Cook the chicken for 10 minutes, turning until browned all over. Transfer the chicken to a casserole.

2 Add the leek and garlic to the skillet and cook for 2–3 minutes, stirring constantly. Stir in the flour and cook for a further 1 minute, stirring constantly. Remove the skillet from the heat and stir in the stock and wine. Season well.

3 Return the skillet to the heat and bring the mixture to a boil. Stir in the carrots, baby corn cobs, new potatoes, and bouquet garni.

4 Transfer the mixture to the casserole. Cover and cook in a preheated oven, 350°F/180°C, for about 1 hour.

5 Remove the casserole from the oven and stir in the cream. Return the casserole to the oven, uncovered, and cook for a further 15 minutes. Remove the bouquet garni and discard. Taste and adjust the seasoning, if necessary. Serve the casserole with plain rice or fresh vegetables, such as broccoli.

COOK'S TIP

Use turkey fillets instead of the chicken, if preferred, and vary the vegetables according to those you have at hand.

Lemongrass Chicken

An unusual recipe in which fresh lemongrass stalks are used as skewers, which impart their delicate lemony flavor to the chicken mixture.

NUTRITIONAL INFORMATION

Calories	140	Sugars	.........2g
Protein	........19g	Fat	...........7g
Carbohydrate	....2g	Saturates	.......1g

 30 mins   4–6 mins

SERVES 4

INGREDIENTS

2 long or 4 short lemongrass stalks

2 large skinless boneless chicken breast portions, about 14 oz/400 g in total

1 small egg white

1 carrot, finely grated

1 small fresh red chile, deseeded and chopped

2 tbsp chopped fresh garlic chives

2 tbsp chopped fresh cilantro

1 tbsp sunflower oil

salt and pepper

fresh cilantro and lime slices, to garnish

1 If the lemon grass stalks are long, cut them in half across the middle to make 4 short lengths. Cut each stalk in half lengthwise, so you have 8 sticks.

2 Roughly chop the chicken pieces and place them in a food processor with the egg white. Process to a smooth paste, then add the carrot, chile, chives, cilantro, and salt and pepper. Process for a few seconds to mix well.

3 Chill the mixture in the refrigerator for about 15 minutes. Divide the mixture into 8 equal portions and use your hands to shape the mixture around the lemongrass "skewers."

4 Brush the skewers with oil and broil under a preheated medium-hot broiler for 4–6 minutes, turning them occasionally, until golden brown and thoroughly cooked. Alternatively, grill over medium-hot coals.

5 Serve hot, garnished with fresh cilantro and slices of lime.

COOK'S TIP

If you can't find whole lemongrass stalks, use wooden or bamboo skewers instead, and add ½ teaspoon ground lemongrass to the mixture with the other flavorings.

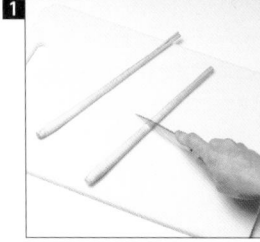
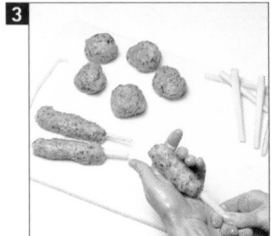

Chicken in Banana Leaves

Large leaves, such as banana, are often used in Thai cooking as a natural wrapping for all kinds of ingredients.

NUTRITIONAL INFORMATION

Calories 185	Sugars 0g
Protein 18g	Fat 12g
Carbohydrate ...0.5g	Saturates 1g

🦐 🦐 🦐

1¼ hrs   10–12 mins

SERVES 4–6

I N G R E D I E N T S

1 garlic clove, chopped

1 tsp finely chopped fresh ginger root

¼ tsp ground black pepper

2 fresh cilantro sprigs

1 tbsp Thai fish sauce

1 tbsp whiskey

3 boneless skinless chicken breast portions

2–3 banana leaves, cut into 3 inch/
  7.5 cm squares

sunflower oil, for frying

sweet chili dipping sauce (see Cook's Tip),
  to serve

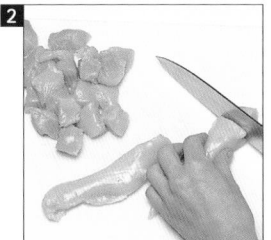

1 Place the garlic, ginger, pepper, cilantro, Thai fish sauce, and whiskey in a mortar and grind to a smooth paste with a pestle.

2 Cut the chicken into 1 inch/2.5 cm chunks and toss in the paste to coat evenly. Cover and set aside in the refrigerator to marinate for about 1 hour.

3 Place a piece of chicken on a square of banana leaf and wrap it up like a parcel to enclose the chicken completely. Secure with wooden toothpicks or tie with a piece of bamboo string.

4 Heat an ⅛ inch/3 mm depth of oil in a heavy skillet until hot.

5 Fry the parcels for 8–10 minutes, turning them over occasionally until golden brown and the chicken is thoroughly cooked. Serve immediately with a sweet chili dipping sauce.

COOK'S TIP

To make a sweet chili dip to serve with the chicken pieces, combine equal amounts of chili sauce and tomato ketchup, then stir in a dash of rice wine to taste.

Roast Chicken with Ginger

This is a version of a sweet-and-sour chicken dish often sold by street traders in the East—they grill the chickens whole or cut in half.

NUTRITIONAL INFORMATION

Calories	260	Sugars	.........9g
Protein	........42g	Fat	...........5g
Carbohydrate	....11g	Saturates	.......2g

8¼ hrs   1¼ hrs

SERVES 4

INGREDIENTS

1¼ inch/3 cm piece fresh ginger root, finely chopped

2 garlic cloves, finely chopped

1 small onion, finely chopped

1 lemongrass stalk, finely chopped

½ tsp salt

1 tsp black peppercorns

3 lb 5 oz/1.5 kg chicken

1 tbsp coconut cream

2 tbsp lime juice

2 tbsp honey

1 tsp cornstarch

2 tsp water

stir-fried vegetables, to serve

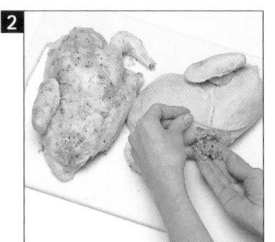

1 Put the ginger, garlic, onion, lemongrass, salt, and peppercorns in a mortar and crush with a pestle to form a smooth paste.

2 Cut the chicken in half lengthwise, using poultry shears or strong kitchen scissors. Spread the paste all over the chicken, both inside and out. Loosen the breast skin and gently spread the paste underneath. Transfer the chicken to a large plate, cover with plastic wrap, and set aside in the refrigerator to marinate overnight or at least for several hours.

3 Heat the coconut cream, lime juice, and honey in a small pan, stirring until smooth. Brush a little of the mixture evenly over the chicken.

4 Place the chicken halves on a rack over a roasting pan half-filled with boiling water. Roast in a preheated oven, 350°F/180°C, basting occasionally with the lime and honey mixture, for about 1 hour or until the chicken is a rich golden brown and the juices run clear when the thickest part is pierced with a skewer.

5 Boil the water from the roasting pan to reduce it to about ½ cup. Blend the cornstarch and water and stir into the reduced liquid. Heat to a boil, then stir until thickened and clear. Serve the chicken with the sauce and vegetables.

Chicken & Mango Stir-Fry

A colorful, exotic mix of flavors that works surprisingly well, this dish is easy and quick to cook—ideal for a midweek family meal.

NUTRITIONAL INFORMATION

Calories	200	Sugars	. . . . .5g
Protein	. . . . .23g	Fat	. . . . .6g
Carbohydrate	. . . .7g	Saturates	. . . . . . .1g

5 mins   12 mins

SERVES 4

INGREDIENTS

6 skinless, boneless chicken thighs

2 tsp grated fresh ginger root

1 garlic clove, crushed

1 small fresh red chile, deseeded

1 large red bell pepper, deseeded

4 scallions, thickly sliced diagonally

7 oz/200 g snow peas

scant 1 cup baby corn cobs

1 large ripe mango

2 tbsp sunflower oil

1 tbsp light soy sauce

3 tbsp rice wine or sherry

1 tsp sesame oil

salt and pepper

chopped fresh chives, to garnish

1 Cut the chicken into long, thin strips and place in a bowl. Combine the ginger, garlic, and chile, then stir the mixture into the chicken strips to coat them evenly.

2 Slice the bell pepper thinly, cutting diagonally. Trim and diagonally slice the scallions. Cut the snow peas and corn cobs in half diagonally. Peel the mango, remove the pit, and slice thinly.

3 Heat the sunflower oil in a large, preheated heavy skillet or wok over high heat. Add the chicken and stir-fry for 4–5 minutes until just turning golden brown. Add the bell pepper slices and stir-fry over medium heat for 4–5 minutes until softened.

4 Add the sliced scallions, snow peas, and baby corn cobs and stir-fry for a further minute.

5 Combine the soy sauce, rice wine or sherry, and sesame oil and stir the mixture into the wok. Add the mango slices and stir gently for 1 minute until heated through.

6 Season with salt and pepper to taste, garnish with chopped fresh chives, and serve immediately.

Spicy Cilantro Chicken

These simple marinated chicken portions are packed with powerful, zesty flavors, best accompanied by plain boiled rice and a cucumber salad.

NUTRITIONAL INFORMATION

Calories	.171	Sugars	.8g
Protein	.31g	Fat	.2g
Carbohydrate	.9g	Saturates	.0.5g

1¼ hrs   15–20 mins

SERVES 4

INGREDIENTS

4 skinless boneless chicken breast portions

2 garlic cloves, peeled

1 fresh green chile, deseeded

¾ inch/2 cm piece of fresh ginger root

4 tbsp chopped fresh cilantro

rind of 1 lime, finely grated

3 tbsp lime juice

2 tbsp light soy sauce

1 tbsp superfine sugar

¾ cup coconut milk

TO SERVE

plain boiled rice

cucumber and radish salad

1 Using a sharp knife, cut 3 deep slashes into the skinned side of each chicken breast portion. Place them in a single layer in a wide, nonmetallic dish.

2 Put the garlic, chile, ginger, cilantro, lime rind and juice, soy sauce, superfine sugar, and coconut milk in a food processor and process to a smooth purée.

3 Spread the purée over both sides of the chicken portions, coating them evenly. Cover the dish with plastic wrap and set aside to marinate in the refrigerator for about 1 hour.

4 Lift the chicken from the marinade, drain off the excess, and place in a broiler pan. Cook under a preheated broiler for 12–15 minutes until thoroughly and evenly cooked.

5 Meanwhile, place the remaining marinade in a pan and bring to a boil. Lower the heat and simmer for several minutes to heat thoroughly. Remove the pan from the heat.

6 Place the chicken breast portions on warmed individual serving plates and pour over the sauce. Serve immediately accompanied with boiled rice and cucumber and radish salad.

Green Chicken Curry

Thai curries are traditionally very hot and designed to make a little go a long way—the thin, highly spiced juices are eaten with lots of rice.

NUTRITIONAL INFORMATION

Calories 193   Sugars 9g
Protein . . . . .22g   Fat 8g
Carbohydrate . . . .9g   Saturates 1g

10 mins   50 mins

SERVES 4

INGREDIENTS

6 skinless boneless chicken thighs

1¾ cups coconut milk

2 garlic cloves, crushed

2 tbsp Thai fish sauce

2 tbsp Thai green curry paste

12 baby eggplants

3 fresh green chiles, finely chopped

3 kaffir lime leaves, shredded

4 tbsp chopped fresh cilantro

boiled rice, to serve

1 Cut the chicken thighs into bite-size pieces. Pour the coconut milk into a large pan or wok and bring to a boil over high heat.

2 Add the chicken, garlic, and fish sauce to the pan or wok and bring back to a boil. Lower the heat and simmer gently for about 30 minutes or until the chicken is just tender.

3 Remove the chicken from the mixture with a slotted spoon. Set aside and keep warm.

4 Stir the green curry paste into the pan until fully incorporated, then add the eggplants, chiles, and lime leaves and simmer for 5 minutes.

5 Return the chicken to the pan or wok and bring to a boil. Season with salt and pepper to taste, then stir in the chopped cilantro. Serve the curry immediately with boiled rice.

COOK'S TIP
Baby eggplants, or "pea eggplants" as they are called in Thailand, are traditionally used in this curry. If you can't find them in an Asian food store, use chopped ordinary eggplant or substitute a few green peas.

Braised Garlic Chicken

The intense flavors of this dish are helped by the slow, gentle cooking. The meat should be almost falling off the bone.

NUTRITIONAL INFORMATION

Calories	282	Sugars	.........3g
Protein	........29g	Fat	..........16g
Carbohydrate	....5g	Saturates	.......3g

15 mins   1 hr

SERVES 4

INGREDIENTS

4 garlic cloves, chopped

4 shallots, chopped

2 small fresh red chiles, deseeded and chopped

1 lemongrass stalk, finely chopped

1 tbsp chopped fresh cilantro

1 tsp shrimp paste

½ tsp ground cinnamon

1 tbsp tamarind paste

2 tbsp vegetable oil

8 chicken pieces, such as drumsticks or thighs

1¼ cups chicken stock

1 tbsp Thai fish sauce

1 tbsp smooth peanut butter

4 tbsp toasted peanuts, chopped

salt and pepper

stir-fried vegetables and boiled noodles, to serve

1 Place the garlic, shallots, chiles, lemongrass, cilantro, and shrimp paste in a mortar and grind with a pestle to an almost smooth paste. Stir in the cinnamon and tamarind paste.

2 Heat the oil in a wide skillet or wok. Add the chicken pieces, turning frequently, until they are golden brown on all sides. Remove them from the wok with a slotted spoon and keep hot. Tip away any excess fat.

3 Add the garlic paste to the skillet or wok and cook over medium heat, stirring constantly, until lightly browned.

Stir in the stock and return the chicken to the skillet or wok.

4 Bring to a boil, then cover tightly, lower the heat, and simmer, stirring occasionally, for 25–30 minutes until the chicken is tender and thoroughly cooked. Stir in the fish sauce and peanut butter and simmer the mixture gently for a further 10 minutes.

5 Season with salt and pepper to taste and sprinkle the toasted peanuts over the chicken. Serve immediately, with a colorful selection of stir-fry vegetables and boiled noodles.

Rice Noodles with Chicken

The great thing about stir-fries is you can cook with very little fat and still get lots of flavor, as in this light, healthy lunch dish.

NUTRITIONAL INFORMATION

Calories	329	Sugars	.........3g
Protein	........25g	Fat	...........4g
Carbohydrate	...46g	Saturates	.......1g

 25 mins   10 mins

SERVES 4

INGREDIENTS

7 oz/200 g rice stick noodles

1 tbsp sunflower oil

1 garlic clove, finely chopped

¾ inch/2 cm piece of fresh ginger root, finely chopped

4 scallions, chopped

1 fresh red bird-eye chile, deseeded and sliced

10½ oz/300 g skinless boneless, chicken, finely chopped

2 chicken livers, finely chopped

1 celery stalk, thinly sliced

1 carrot, cut into fine batons

10½ oz/300 g shredded Napa cabbage

4 tbsp lime juice

2 tbsp Thai fish sauce

1 tbsp soy sauce

2 tbsp shredded fresh mint

slices of pickled garlic

fresh mint sprig, to garnish

1 Soak the rice noodles in hot water for 15 minutes or according to the package instructions. Drain well.

2 Heat the oil in a wok or large skillet and stir-fry the garlic, ginger, scallions, and chile for about 1 minute. Stir in the chicken and chicken livers, then stir-fry over high heat for 2–3 minutes until beginning to brown.

3 Stir in the celery and carrot and stir-fry for 2 minutes to soften. Add the Napa cabbage, then stir in the lime juice, fish sauce, and soy sauce.

4 Add the noodles and stir to heat thoroughly. Sprinkle with shredded mint and pickled garlic. Serve immediately, garnished with a mint sprig.

Sweet Maple Chicken

You can use any chicken portions for this recipe. Thighs are economical for large barbecue parties, but you could also use wings or drumsticks.

NUTRITIONAL INFORMATION

Calories ....122 Sugars 16g
Protein ....11g Fat 1g
Carbohydrate ...17g Saturates 1g

35 mins   20 mins

SERVES 6

I N G R E D I E N T S

12 boneless chicken thighs

5 tbsp maple syrup

1 tbsp superfine sugar

grated rind and juice of ½ orange

2 tbsp catsup

2 tsp Worcestershire sauce

TO GARNISH

orange slices

fresh parsley sprigs

TO SERVE

Italian bread, such as focaccia

salad greens

cherry tomatoes, quartered

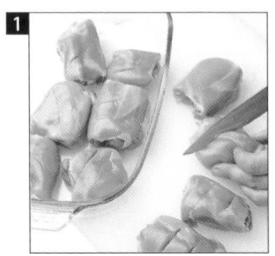

1 Using a long sharp knife, make 2–3 diagonal slashes in the flesh of the chicken to allow the flavors to permeate. Arrange the chicken thighs in a single layer in a shallow, nonmetallic dish.

2 To make the marinade, combine the maple syrup, sugar, orange rind and juice, catsup, and Worcestershire sauce in a small bowl.

3 Pour the marinade over the chicken, turning the chicken well to coat thoroughly. Cover with plastic wrap and chill in the refrigerator until required.

4 Remove the chicken from the marinade, reserving the marinade.

5 Transfer the chicken to the barbecue and cook over hot coals for 20 minutes, turning the chicken and basting with the marinade frequently. Alternatively, cook under a preheated broiler for 20 minutes, turning and basting.

6 Transfer the chicken to warmed serving plates and garnish with slices of orange and a sprig of parsley. Serve immediately with Italian bread, fresh salad greens, and cherry tomatoes.

Kabobs with Bell Peppers

These chicken skewers are rather special and are well worth the extra effort needed to prepare them.

NUTRITIONAL INFORMATION

Calories	398	Sugars	........12g
Protein	........27g	Fat	..........22g
Carbohydrate	...25g	Saturates	.......4g

🕐 1½ hrs   🕐 20 mins

SERVES 4

INGREDIENTS

3 skinless boneless chicken breasts

6 tbsp olive oil

4 tbsp lemon juice

½ small onion, grated

1 tbsp chopped fresh sage

8 tbsp sage and onion stuffing mix

6 tbsp boiling water

2 green bell peppers, deseeded

SAUCE

1 tbsp olive oil

1 red bell pepper, deseeded and
  finely chopped

1 small onion, finely chopped

pinch of sugar

7½ oz/210 g can chopped tomatoes

1 Cut the chicken into even-size pieces. Mix the oil, lemon juice, grated onion, and sage and pour the mixture into a plastic bag. Add the chicken, seal the bag, and shake to coat the chicken. Set aside in the refrigerator to marinate for at least 30 minutes, shaking the bag occasionally.

2 Place the stuffing mix in a heatproof bowl and add the boiling water, stirring well until fully incorporated. Set aside until required.

3 Cut each green bell pepper into 6 strips, then blanch the strips in boiling water for 3–4 minutes until softened. Drain, refresh under cold running water, then drain well again.

4 Form about 1 teaspoon of the stuffing mixture into a ball and roll it up in a strip of green bell pepper. Repeat for the remaining stuffing mixture and bell pepper strips. Thread 3 bell pepper rolls onto each skewer alternately with pieces of chicken. Chill in the refrigerator.

5 To make the sauce, heat the oil in a small pan. Add the red bell pepper

and onion and cook over low heat, stirring occasionally, for 5 minutes. Stir in the sugar and tomatoes and simmer for about 5 minutes. Set aside and keep warm.

6 Grill the skewers on an oiled rack over hot coals, basting frequently with the remaining marinade, for about 15 minutes until the chicken is cooked. Serve with the red bell pepper sauce.

Maryland Chicken Kabobs

This is a barbecue variation of the traditional dish, Chicken Maryland.
Serve with corn-on-the-cob (see page 457).

NUTRITIONAL INFORMATION

Calories 443   Sugars 14g
Protein ....37g   Fat 26g
Carbohydrate ...16g   Saturates 6g

  1¼–2¼ hrs   8–10 mins

SERVES 4

INGREDIENTS

8 skinless boneless chicken thighs

1 tbsp white wine vinegar

1 tbsp lemon juice

1 tbsp light corn syrup or honey

6 tbsp olive oil

1 garlic clove, crushed

4 strips rindless, smoked bacon

2 bananas

salt and pepper

TO SERVE

4 cooked corn-on-the-cob (see page 457)

mango chutney

1 Cut the chicken into bite-size pieces. Combine the vinegar, lemon juice, syrup or honey, oil, garlic, and salt and pepper to taste in a large bowl. Add the chicken to the marinade and toss until the chicken is well coated. Cover and set aside to marinate for 1-2 hours.

2 Stretch the bacon strips with the back of a knife and then cut each bacon strip in half. Cut the bananas into 1 inch/2.5 cm lengths and brush them with lemon juice to prevent them from turning brown.

3 Wrap a piece of bacon around each piece of banana.

4 Remove the chicken from the marinade, reserving the marinade for basting. Thread the chicken pieces and the bacon and banana rolls alternately onto metal or bamboo skewers.

5 Grill the kabobs over hot coals for 8-10 minutes until the chicken is completely cooked through. Baste the kabobs with the marinade and turn the skewers frequently.

6 Serve with corn-on-the-cob and mango chutney.

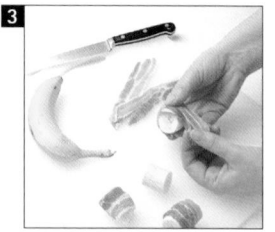

VARIATION

For a quick Maryland-style dish, omit the marinating and cook the chicken thighs over hot coals for about 20 minutes, basting with the marinade. Grill the bananas in their skins beside the chicken. Serve the bananas split open with a teaspoon of mango chutney.

Sherried Liver Brochettes

Economical and flavorsome, these tasty chicken liver skewers make an ideal light lunch or a perfect addition to a summer brunch party.

NUTRITIONAL INFORMATION

Calories 767   Sugars 3g
Protein ....31g   Fat 43g
Carbohydrate ...51g   Saturates 8g

3½–4½ hrs   15 mins

SERVES 4

INGREDIENTS

14 oz/400 g chicken livers, trimmed
  and cleaned

3 strips rindless bacon

1 ciabatta loaf or small French stick

8 oz/225 g baby spinach

MARINADE

⅔ cup dry sherry

4 tbsp olive oil

1 tsp wholegrain mustard

salt and pepper

MUSTARD MAYONNAISE

8 tbsp mayonnaise

1 tsp wholegrain mustard

1 Cut the chicken livers into 2 inch/5 cm pieces. To make the marinade, combine the sherry, oil, mustard, and salt and pepper to taste in a shallow dish. Add the chicken livers to the marinade and toss until well coated. Set aside to marinate for 3–4 hours.

2 To make the mayonnaise, stir the mustard into the mayonnaise and chill in the refrigerator.

3 Stretch the bacon with the back of a knife and cut each strip in half. Remove the chicken livers from the marinade, reserving the marinade for basting. Wrap the bacon around half of the chicken liver pieces. Thread the bacon and chicken liver rolls and the plain chicken liver pieces alternately onto 6 pre-soaked wooden skewers.

4 Grill the skewers over hot coals for about 10-12 minutes, turning and basting with the reserved marinade frequently.

5 Meanwhile, cut the bread into 6 pieces and toast the cut sides on the barbecue until golden brown.

6 To serve, top the toasted bread with spinach leaves and place the brochettes on top. Spoon over the mustard mayonnaise and serve immediately.

Yellow Bean Chicken

Ready-made yellow bean sauce is available from large supermarkets and Chinese foodstores. It is made from yellow soybeans and is quite salty.

NUTRITIONAL INFORMATION

Calories ....234 Sugars 1g
Protein ....26g Fat 12g
Carbohydrate ....6g Saturates 2g

25 mins   10 mins

SERVES 4

INGREDIENTS

1 lb/450 g skinless, boneless
    chicken breast portions

1 egg white, beaten

1 tbsp cornstarch

1 tbsp rice wine vinegar

1 tbsp light soy sauce

1 tsp superfine sugar

3 tbsp vegetable oil

1 garlic clove, crushed

½ inch/1 cm piece of fresh
    ginger root, grated

1 green bell pepper, deseeded and diced

2 large mushrooms, sliced

3 tbsp yellow bean sauce

yellow or green bell pepper strips,
    to garnish

1 Trim any fat from the chicken and cut the meat into 1 inch/2.5 cm cubes.

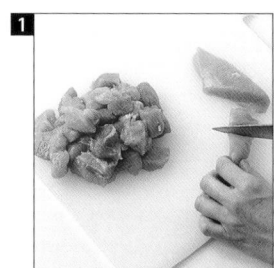

2 Mix the egg white and cornstarch in a shallow bowl. Add the chicken and turn in the mixture to coat. Set aside for 20 minutes.

3 Mix the rice wine vinegar, soy sauce, and superfine sugar in a bowl.

4 Remove the chicken from the egg white mixture.

5 Heat the oil in a preheated wok, add the chicken, and stir-fry for 3–4 minutes until golden brown. Remove the chicken from the wok with a slotted spoon, set aside, and keep warm.

6 Add the garlic, ginger, bell pepper, and mushrooms to the wok and stir-fry for 1–2 minutes.

7 Add the yellow bean sauce and cook for 1 minute. Stir in the vinegar mixture and return the chicken to the wok. Cook for 1–2 minutes and serve hot, garnished with bell pepper strips.

VARIATION

Black bean sauce would work equally well with this recipe. Although this would affect the appearance of the dish, because black bean sauce is much darker, the flavors would be compatible.

Chicken Biryani

This biryani recipe may look rather complicated, but is not difficult to follow. You can substitute lamb, marinated overnight, for chicken.

NUTRITIONAL INFORMATION

Calories ....382 Sugars 8g
Protein ....42g Fat 20g
Carbohydrate ...10g Saturates 11g

3¼ mins   1½–1¾ hrs

SERVES 4

INGREDIENTS

1½ tsp fresh ginger root, finely chopped

1½ tsp garlic, crushed

1 tbsp garam masala

1 tsp chili powder

½ tsp ground turmeric

2 tsp salt

20 green/white cardamom seeds, crushed

1¼ cups plain yogurt

3 lb 5 oz/1.5 kg chicken, skinned and
    cut into 8 pieces

⅔ cup milk

saffron strands

6 tbsp ghee

2 medium onions, sliced

2¼ cups basmati rice

2 cinnamon sticks

4 black peppercorns

1 tsp black cumin seeds

4 fresh green chiles

fresh cilantro leaves, finely chopped

4 tbsp lemon juice

1 Blend together the ginger, garlic, garam masala, chili powder, turmeric, 1 tsp salt, and cardamom seeds and mix with the yogurt and chicken pieces. Set aside to marinate for 3 hours.

2 Pour the milk into a pan and bring to a boil. Pour it over the saffron and set aside.

3 Heat the ghee in a pan and cook the onions until golden brown. Remove half of the onions and ghee from the pan and set aside.

4 Place the rice, cinnamon sticks, 4 peppercorns, and the black cumin seeds in a pan of water. Bring the rice to a boil and remove from the heat when half-cooked. Drain and place in a bowl. Mix with the remaining salt.

5 Add the chicken mixture to the pan with the onions and ghee. Deseed the chiles, if wished, and finely chop. Add half each of the chiles, cilantro, lemon juice, and saffron. Add the rice and then the rest of the ingredients, including the fried onions and ghee. Cover tightly so no steam escapes. Cook on low heat for 1 hour. Check that the meat is cooked through before serving. If the meat is not cooked, return to the heat, and cook for a further 15 minutes. Mix thoroughly before serving hot.

Glazed Turkey Steaks

Prepare these steaks the day before they are needed and serve in toasted ciabatta bread, accompanied by crisp salad greens.

NUTRITIONAL INFORMATION

Calories 219	Sugars 4g	
Protein 28g	Fat 10g	
Carbohydrate 4g	Saturates 1g	

12 hrs   15 mins

SERVES 4

INGREDIENTS

⅓ cup red currant jelly

2 tbsp lime juice

3 tbsp olive oil

2 tbsp dry white wine

¼ tsp ground ginger

pinch of grated nutmeg

4 turkey breast steaks

salt and pepper

TO SERVE

mixed salad greens

vinaigrette dressing

1 ciabatta loaf

cherry tomatoes

1 Place the red currant jelly and lime juice in a pan and heat gently until the jelly melts. Add the oil, wine, ginger, and nutmeg.

2 Place the turkey steaks in a shallow, nonmetallic dish and season with salt and pepper. Pour over the marinade, turning the meat so that it is well coated. Cover and chill overnight.

3 Remove the turkey from the marinade, reserving the marinade for basting, and grill on an oiled rack over hot coals for about 4 minutes on each side. Baste the turkey steaks frequently with the reserved marinade.

4 Meanwhile, toss the salad greens in the vinaigrette dressing. Cut the ciabatta loaf in half lengthwise and place, cut side down, at the side of the barbecue. Grill until golden. Place each steak on top of salad greens, sandwich between 2 pieces of bread, and serve immediately with cherry tomatoes.

COOK'S TIP

Turkey and chicken scallops are also ideal for cooking on the barbecue. Because they are thin, they cook through without burning on the outside. Leave them overnight in a marinade of your choice and cook, basting with a little lemon juice and oil.

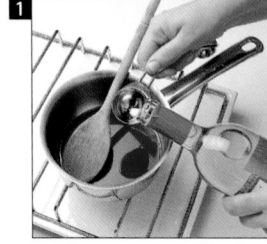
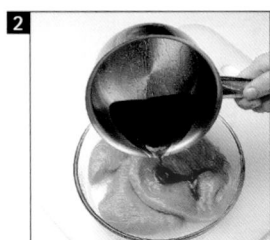

Turkey with Cheese Pockets

Wrapping strips of bacon around the turkey helps to keep the cheese filling enclosed in the pocket—and adds extra flavor.

NUTRITIONAL INFORMATION

Calories	.518	Sugars	.0g
Protein	.66g	Fat	.28g
Carbohydrate	.0g	Saturates	.9g

15 mins   20 mins

SERVES 4

INGREDIENTS

4 turkey breast portions, each about 225 g/8 oz

4 portions full-fat cheese (such as Bel Paese), ½ oz/15 g each

4 sage leaves or ½ tsp dried sage

8 strips rindless bacon

4 tbsp olive oil

2 tbsp lemon juice

salt and pepper

TO SERVE

garlic bread

salad greens

cherry tomatoes

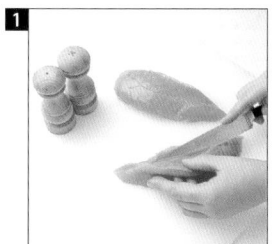 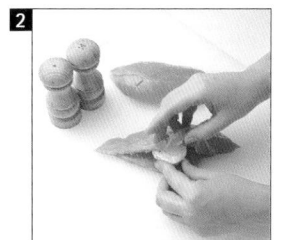 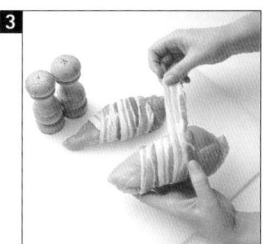

1 Carefully cut a pocket into the side of each turkey breast portion. Open out each pocket a little and season inside with salt and pepper to taste.

2 Place a portion of cheese into each pocket, spreading it a little with a knife. Tuck a sage leaf into each pocket or sprinkle with a little dried sage.

3 Stretch the bacon out with the back of a knife. Wrap 2 pieces of bacon around each turkey portion, so that the pocket opening is completely covered.

4 Combine the oil and lemon juice in a small bowl.

5 Grill the turkey over medium hot coals for about 10 minutes on each side, basting with the oil and lemon mixture frequently.

6 Place the garlic bread at the side of the barbecue and toast lightly.

7 Transfer the turkey to warm serving plates. Serve with the toasted garlic bread, salad greens, and cherry tomatoes.

VARIATION
You can vary the cheese you use to stuff the turkey—try grated mozzarella or slices of Brie or Camembert. Also try placing 1 teaspoon of red currant jelly or cranberry sauce into each pocket instead of the sage.

Turkey & Sausage Kabobs

Serve these chile-spiced and flavorsome kabobs with fresh bread, such as ciabatta, focaccia, or a French stick.

NUTRITIONAL INFORMATION

Calories ....238 Sugars 3g
Protein ....18g Fat 17g
Carbohydrate ....3g Saturates 5g

1 hr   15 mins

SERVES 8

INGREDIENTS

12 oz/350 g turkey breast fillet

10½ oz/300 g chorizo sausage

1 eating apple

1 tbsp lemon juice

8 bay leaves

BASTE

6 tbsp olive oil

2 garlic cloves, crushed

1 fresh red chile, deseeded and chopped

salt and pepper

1 To make the baste, place the oil, garlic, and chile in a small screw-top jar and season to taste with salt and pepper. Shake well to combine. Set aside for 1 hour for the garlic and chile to flavor the oil.

COOK'S TIP

The flavored oil used in this recipe can be used to baste any broiled meat, fish, or vegetables. It will give plain foods a subtle chili flavor and will keep in the refrigerator for about 2 weeks.

2 Cut the turkey into 1 inch/2.5 cm pieces. Cut the sausage into 1 inch/2.5 cm lengths. Cut the apple into chunks and remove the core. Toss the apple in lemon juice to prevent discoloration.

3 Thread the turkey and sausage pieces onto 8 metal or soaked bamboo skewers, alternating with the apple chunks and bay leaves.

4 Grill the kabobs over hot coals for about 15 minutes or until the turkey is cooked. Turn and baste the kabobs frequently with the flavored oil. Alternatively, cook under a preheated broiler, turning and basting frequently with the oil, for 15 minutes.

5 Transfer the kabobs to warmed serving plates and serve immediately.

Turkey & Vegetable Loaf

This impressive-looking turkey loaf is flavored with herbs and a layer of juicy tomatoes and covered with zucchini ribbons.

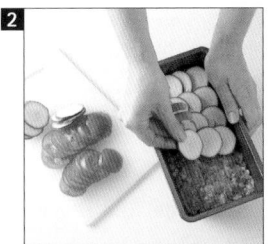

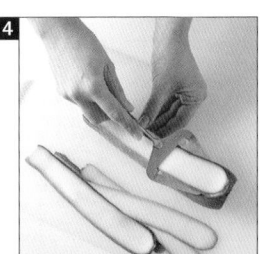

NUTRITIONAL INFORMATION

Calories	165	Sugars	.........1g
Protein	........36g	Fat	..........2g
Carbohydrate	....1g	Saturates	.....0.5g

 10 mins 1¼ hrs

SERVES 4

INGREDIENTS

1 onion, finely chopped

1 garlic clove, crushed

2 lb/900 g lean ground turkey

1 tbsp chopped fresh parsley

1 tbsp chopped fresh chives

1 tbsp chopped fresh tarragon

1 egg white, lightly beaten

2 zucchini, 1 medium, 1 large

2 tomatoes

salt and pepper

tomato and herb sauce, to serve (optional)

1 Line a nonstick loaf pan with baking parchment. Place the onion, garlic, and turkey in a bowl, add the herbs, and season to taste with salt and pepper. Mix together with your hands, then add the egg white to bind.

2 Press half of the turkey mixture into the bottom of the pan. Trim and thinly slice the medium zucchini and the tomatoes and arrange the slices over the meat. Top with the rest of the turkey mixture and press down firmly.

3 Cover with a layer of kitchen foil and place in a roasting pan. Pour in enough boiling water to come halfway up the sides of the loaf pan. Bake in a preheated oven, 375°F/190°C, for about 1–1¼ hours, removing the foil for the last 20 minutes of cooking. Test that the loaf is cooked by inserting a toothpick into the center—the juices should run clear. The loaf will also shrink away from the sides of the pan.

4 Meanwhile, trim the ends from the large zucchini. Using a vegetable peeler or hand-held metal cheese slice, cut the zucchini lengthwise into thin slices. Bring a pan of water to a boil and blanch the zucchini ribbons for 1–2 minutes until just tender. Drain them and and keep them warm.

5 Remove the turkey loaf from the pan and transfer to a warm serving platter. Drape the zucchini ribbons over it and then serve with a tomato and herb sauce, if desired.

Beef Teriyaki

This Japanese-style teriyaki sauce complements grilled beef, but it can also be used to accompany chicken or salmon.

NUTRITIONAL INFORMATION

Calories	184	Sugars	.........6g
Protein	........24g	Fat	...........5g
Carbohydrate	....8g	Saturates	......2g

2¼ hrs   15 mins

SERVES 4

INGREDIENTS

1 lb/450 g extra thin lean beef steaks

8 scallions, cut into short lengths

1 yellow bell pepper, deseeded and cut into chunks

salad greens, to serve

SAUCE

1 tsp cornstarch

2 tbsp dry sherry

2 tbsp white wine vinegar

3 tbsp soy sauce

1 tbsp molasses sugar

1 garlic clove, crushed

½ tsp ground cinnamon

½ tsp ground ginger

1 Place the meat in a shallow, nonmetallic dish. To make the sauce, combine the cornstarch with the sherry to a smooth paste, then stir in the vinegar, soy sauce, sugar, garlic, cinnamon, and ginger. Pour the sauce over the meat, turn to coat, and set aside to marinate for at least 2 hours.

2 Remove the meat from the sauce, draining well. Pour the sauce into a small pan.

3 Cut the meat into thin strips and thread these, concertina-style, onto pre-soaked wooden skewers, alternating each strip of meat with pieces of scallion and yellow bell pepper.

4 Gently heat the sauce until it is just simmering, stirring occasionally.

5 Grill the kabobs over hot coals for 5–8 minutes, turning and basting the beef and vegetables occasionally with the reserved teriyaki sauce.

6 Arrange the skewers on serving plates and pour the remaining sauce over the kabobs. Serve immediately with salad greens.

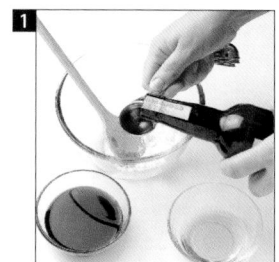

Sweet Lamb Fillet

Lamb fillet, enhanced by a sweet and spicy glaze, is cooked on the barbecue in a kitchen foil packet for deliciously moist results.

NUTRITIONAL INFORMATION

Calories 258	Sugars 13g	
Protein 24g	Fat 13g	
Carbohydrate ...13g	Saturates 5g	

5 mins | 1 hr

SERVES 4

INGREDIENTS

2 fillets of neck of lean lamb,
  each 8 oz/225 g

1 tbsp olive oil

½ onion, finely chopped

1 garlic clove, crushed

1 inch/2.5 cm piece of fresh
  ginger root, grated

5 tbsp apple juice

3 tbsp smooth apple sauce

1 tbsp molasses sugar

1 tbsp tomato ketchup

½ tsp mild mustard

salt and pepper

TO SERVE

salad greens

croûtons

crusty bread

1 Place the lamb fillet on a large piece of double thickness kitchen foil. Season with salt and pepper to taste.

2 Heat the oil in a small pan and cook the onion and garlic for 2–3 minutes until softened, but not browned. Stir in the grated ginger and cook for 1 minute, stirring occasionally. Stir in the apple juice, apple sauce, sugar, ketchup, and mustard and bring to a boil. Boil rapidly for about 10 minutes until reduced by half. Stir the mixture occasionally so that it does not burn and stick to the pan.

3 Brush half of the sauce over the lamb fillets, then wrap up the lamb in the kitchen foil to enclose it completely. Grill the lamb packet over hot coals for about 25 minutes, turning the foil packet over occasionally.

4 Open out the kitchen foil and brush the lamb with some of the remaining sauce. Continue to grill for a further 15–20 minutes or until cooked through.

5 Place the lamb on a cutting board, remove the foil, and cut the meat into thick slices. Transfer to serving plates and spoon over the remaining sauce. Serve with salad greens, croûtons, and fresh crusty bread.

Ginger Rice with Duck

For the best result, buy a 5 lb/2.25 kg duck, remove the breasts and use the carcass to make a flavorful stock.

NUTRITIONAL INFORMATION

Calories 432   Sugars 4g
Protein ....27g   Fat 16g
Carbohydrate ...48g   Saturates 4g

 15 mins   30 mins

SERVES 4–6

INGREDIENTS

2 duck breasts, cut diagonally into thin slices

2–3 tbsp Japanese soy sauce

1 tbsp mirin or medium sherry

2 tsp brown sugar

2 inch/5 cm piece of fresh ginger root, finely chopped or grated

4 tbsp peanut oil

2 garlic cloves, crushed

1½ cups long grain white or brown rice

4 cups chicken stock

4 oz/115 g cooked lean ham, thinly sliced

6 oz/175 g snow peas, cut diagonally in half

¾ cup fresh bean sprouts, rinsed

8 scallions, thinly sliced diagonally

2–3 tbsp chopped fresh cilantro

sweet or hot chili sauce (optional)

1 Put the duck in a shallow bowl with a tablespoon of soy sauce, the mirin, half the brown sugar, and one-third of the ginger. Stir to coat and set aside to marinate at room temperature.

2 Heat 2–3 tablespoons peanut oil in a large heavy pan over medium-high heat. Add the garlic and half the remaining ginger and stir-fry for about 1 minute until fragrant. Add the rice and cook, stirring, for about 3 minutes until translucent and beginning to color.

3 Add 3 cups stock and a teaspoon of soy sauce and bring to a boil. Reduce the heat to very low, cover, and simmer for 20 minutes until the rice is tender and the liquid is absorbed. Do not uncover the pan, but remove from the heat and set aside.

4 Heat the remaining peanut oil in a large wok. Drain the duck breast and gently stir-fry for about 3 minutes until just colored. Add 1 tablespoon soy sauce and the remaining sugar and cook for 1 minute. Remove from the wok, set aside, and keep warm.

5 Stir in the ham, snow peas, bean sprouts, scallions, the remaining ginger, and half the cilantro. Add about ½ cup of the stock and stir-fry for 1 minute or until the stock is almost reduced. Fork in the rice and toss together. Add a dash of chili sauce.

6 To serve, turn into a warmed serving dish, arrange the duck on top and sprinkle with the remaining cilantro. Serve immediately.

Duck with Lime & Kiwi Fruit

Tender breasts of duck served in thin slices, with a sweet, but very tangy lime and wine sauce, full of pieces of kiwi fruit—sheer bliss.

NUTRITIONAL INFORMATION

Calories	264	Sugars	........20g
Protein	........20g	Fat	..........10g
Carbohydrate	...21g	Saturates	.......2g

1¼ hrs   15 mins

SERVES 4

INGREDIENTS

4 boneless or part-boned duck breasts

grated rind and juice of 2 large limes

2 tbsp sunflower oil

4 scallions, thinly sliced diagonally

4½ oz/125 g carrots, cut into thin batons

6 tbsp dry white wine

¼ cup sugar

2 kiwi fruit, peeled, halved, and sliced

salt and pepper

fresh parsley sprigs and lime halves tied in knots (see Cook's Tip), to garnish

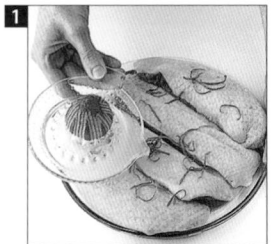

1 Trim any fat from the duck, then prick the skin all over with a fork, and place in a shallow dish. Add half the grated lime and half the juice to the duck breasts, rubbing in thoroughly. Set aside in a cool place for at least 1 hour, turning the breasts at least once.

2 Drain the duck breasts, reserving the marinade. Heat 1 tbsp of oil in a wok. Add the duck and fry quickly to seal all over, then lower the heat, and continue to cook for about 5 minutes, turning several times until just cooked through and well browned all over. Remove and keep warm.

3 Wipe the wok clean with paper towels and heat the remaining oil.

Add the scallions and carrots and stir-fry for 1 minute, then add the remaining lime marinade, wine, and sugar. Bring to a boil and simmer for 2–3 minutes until the mixture is slightly syrupy.

4 Add the duck breasts to the sauce, season to taste, and add the kiwi fruit. Stir-fry for 1 minute or until really hot and both the duck and kiwi fruit are well coated in the sauce.

5 Cut each duck breast into slices, leaving a "hinge" at one end, open out into a fan shape, and arrange on

plates. Spoon the sauce over the duck, sprinkle with the remaining pieces of lime peel, garnish, and serve immediately.

COOK'S TIP

To make the garnish, trim a piece off the base of each lime half so they stand upright. Pare off a thin strip of rind from the top of the lime halves, about ¼ inch/5 mm thick, but do not detach it. Tie the strip into a knot with the end bending over the cut surface of the lime.

Duck with Berry Sauce

Duck is a rich meat and is best accompanied by piquant fruit, as in this sophisticated dinner party dish.

NUTRITIONAL INFORMATION

Calories 293	Sugars 10g
Protein 28g	Fat 8g
Carbohydrate . . .13g	Saturates 2g

1¼ hrs   30 mins

SERVES 4

INGREDIENTS

1 lb/450 g boneless duck breasts

2 tbsp raspberry vinegar

2 tbsp brandy

1 tbsp honey

1 tsp sunflower oil, for brushing

salt and pepper

TO SERVE

2 kiwi fruit, peeled and thinly sliced

assorted vegetables

SAUCE

1⅓ cups raspberries, thawed if frozen

1¼ cups rosé wine

2 tsp cornstarch blended with 4 tsp cold water

1 Skin and trim the duck breasts to remove any excess fat. Using a sharp knife, score the flesh in diagonal lines and pound it with a meat mallet or a covered rolling pin until it is ¾ inch/1.5 cm thick.

2 Place the duck breasts in a shallow dish. Combine the vinegar, brandy, and honey in a small bowl and spoon it over the duck. Cover and chill in the refrigerator for about 1 hour.

3 Drain the duck breasts, reserving the marinade, and place on the broiler

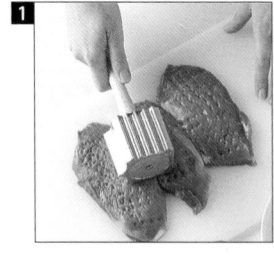

rack. Season and brush with a little oil. Cook for 10 minutes under a preheated broiler, turn over, season, and brush with oil again. Cook for a further 8–10 minutes until the meat is cooked through.

4 Meanwhile, make the sauce. Reserve about ⅓ cup raspberries and place the rest in a pan. Add the reserved marinade and the wine. Bring to a boil and simmer for 5 minutes until slightly reduced. Strain

the sauce through a fine strainer, pressing the raspberries with the back of a spoon. Return the liquid to the pan and add the cornstarch paste. Heat through, stirring, until thickened. Add the reserved raspberries and season to taste.

5 Thinly slice the duck breasts and alternate with slices of kiwi fruit on warm serving plates. Spoon over the sauce and serve with a selection of vegetables.

Slices of Duckling with Pasta

A wonderful raspberry and honey sauce superbly counterbalances the richness of the duckling—served on a bed of linguine.

NUTRITIONAL INFORMATION

Calories 686   Sugars 15g
Protein ....62g   Fat 20g
Carbohydrate ...70g   Saturates 7g

15 mins   25 mins

SERVES 4

INGREDIENTS

4 x 9 oz/250 g boneless duckling breasts

2 tbsp butter

⅓ cup finely chopped carrots

4 tbsp finely chopped shallots

1 tbsp lemon juice

⅔ cup meat stock

4 tbsp honey

⅔ cup fresh or thawed
    frozen raspberries

¼ cup plain flour

1 tbsp Worcestershire sauce

14 oz/400 g dried linguine

salt and pepper

TO GARNISH

fresh raspberries

fresh flat leaf parsley sprigs

1 Trim and score the duck breasts with a sharp knife and season to taste with salt and pepper. Melt the butter in a skillet, add the duck breasts, and fry all over until lightly colored.

2 Add the carrots, shallots, lemon juice, and half the meat stock and simmer over low heat for 1 minute. Stir in half of the honey and half of the raspberries.

Sprinkle over half of the flour and cook, stirring constantly for 3 minutes. Season with pepper to taste and add the Worcestershire sauce.

3 Stir in the remaining stock and cook for 1 minute. Stir in the remaining honey and remaining raspberries and sprinkle over the remaining flour. Cook for a further 3 minutes.

4 Remove the duck breasts from the pan, but leave the sauce to continue simmering over very low heat.

5 Meanwhile, bring a large pan of lightly salted water to a boil. Add the linguine, bring back to a boil, and cook for 8–10 minutes or until tender, but still firm to the bite. Drain and divide between 4 individual plates.

6 Slice the duck breast lengthwise into ¼ inch/5 mm thick pieces. Pour a little sauce over the pasta and arrange the sliced duck in a fan shape on top of it. Garnish with raspberries and flat leaf parsley and serve immediately.

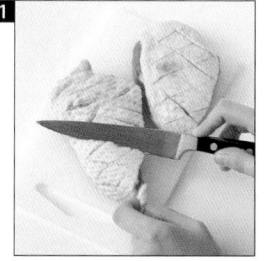  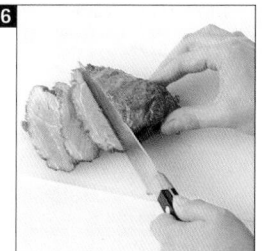

Duck with Chili & Lime

Duck is excellent cooked with strong flavors, and when it is marinated and coated in this rich, dark, sticky glaze, it's irresistible.

NUTRITIONAL INFORMATION

Calories	.264	Sugars	.1g
Protein	.30g	Fat	.11g
Carbohydrate	.13g	Saturates	.3g

3¼ hrs 10 mins

SERVES 4

INGREDIENTS

4 boneless duck breast portions

2 garlic cloves, crushed

4 tsp light brown sugar

3 tbsp lime juice

1 tbsp soy sauce

1 tsp chili sauce

1 tsp vegetable oil

2 tbsp plum preserve

½ cup chicken stock

salt and pepper

1 Using a small, sharp knife, cut deep slashes in the skin of the duck to make a diamond pattern. Place the duck portions in a wide, nonmetallic dish.

2 Combine the garlic, sugar, lime juice, soy sauce, and chili sauce, then spoon over the duck, turning well to coat them evenly. Cover the dish with plastic wrap and set aside to marinate in the refrigerator for at least 3 hours or, preferably, overnight.

3 Drain the duck, reserving the marinade. Heat a large, heavy pan until very hot and brush with the oil. Add the duck breast portions, skin side down, and cook for about 5 minutes or until the skin is browned and crisp. Tip away the excess fat. Turn the duck breasts over.

4 Continue cooking on the other side for 2–3 minutes to brown. Add the reserved marinade, plum preserve, and stock and simmer for 2 minutes. Season to taste and with salt and pepper. Serve hot, with the juices spooned over.

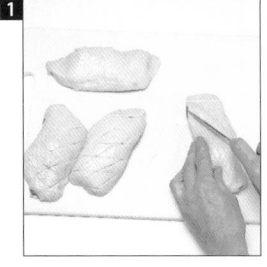

COOK'S TIP

To reduce the overall fat content of this dish, remove the skin from the duck breast portions before cooking and reduce the cooking time slightly.

Curried Roasted Duck

In this recipe, the duck is "roasted" under a hot broiler until golden and crisp, so much of the fat drains off before adding it to the curry.

NUTRITIONAL INFORMATION

Calories 412   Sugars 18g
Protein . . . . .41g   Fat 20g
Carbohydrate . . .19g   Saturates 5g

40 mins   40 mins

SERVES 4

INGREDIENTS

3 lb 8 oz/1.6 kg duckling

2 tbsp peanut oil

1 small pineapple

1 large onion, chopped

1 garlic clove, finely chopped

1 tsp finely chopped fresh ginger root

½ tsp ground coriander

1 tbsp Thai green curry paste

1 tsp soft light brown sugar

2 cups coconut milk

1 tbsp chopped fresh cilantro

salt and pepper

fresh red chile strips, to garnish

boiled jasmine rice, to serve

1 Using a large knife or poultry shears, cut the duck in half lengthwise, cutting through the line of the breastbone. Wipe inside and out with paper towels. Sprinkle with salt and pepper, prick the skin with a fork, and brush with oil.

2 Place the duck, cut side down, on a broiler pan and cook under a preheated hot broiler for 25–30 minutes, turning occasionally, until golden brown. Tip away the fat in the pan at frequent intervals, as it may catch fire.

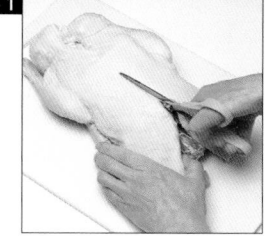 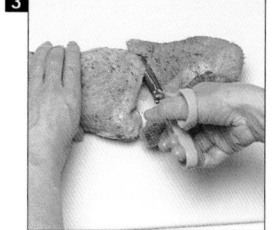 

3 Set the duck aside to cool, then cut each half into 2 portions. Peel and core the pineapple and cut out the "eyes." Cut the flesh into dice.

4 Heat the remaining oil in a large pan. Add the onion and garlic and cook over low heat, stirring occasionally, for 3–4 minutes until softened. Stir in the ginger, ground coriander, curry paste, and brown sugar and stir-fry for 1 minute.

5 Stir in the coconut milk and bring to a boil. Add the duck pieces and the pineapple. Reduce the heat and simmer gently for 5 minutes. Sprinkle with cilantro and serve on a bed of boiled jasmine rice, garnished with chile strips.

Crispy Duck with Noodles

A robustly flavored dish that makes a substantial entrée.
Serve it with a refreshing cucumber salad or a light vegetable stir-fry.

NUTRITIONAL INFORMATION

Calories	433	Sugars	.........7g
Protein	........25g	Fat	..........18g
Carbohydrate	...59g	Saturates	.......2g

 1¼ hrs   20 mins

SERVES 4

INGREDIENTS

3 duck breasts, total weight about 14 oz/400 g

2 garlic cloves, crushed

1½ tsp chili paste

1 tbsp honey

3 tbsp dark soy sauce

½ tsp five-spice powder

9 oz/250 g rice stick noodles

1 tsp vegetable oil

1 tsp sesame oil

2 scallions, sliced

3½ oz/100 g snow peas

2 tbsp tamarind juice

sesame seeds, to garnish

1 Prick the duck breast skin all over with a fork and place in a deep dish.

2 Combine the garlic, chili paste, honey, soy sauce, and five-spice powder, then pour over the duck. Turn the breasts over to coat them evenly, then cover, and set aside to marinate in the refrigerator for at least 1 hour.

3 Meanwhile, soak the rice noodles in hot water for 15 minutes or according to the packet instructions. Drain well.

4 Drain the duck breasts from the marinade and broil on a rack under high heat for about 10 minutes, turning them over occasionally, until they become a rich golden brown. Remove and slice thinly.

5 Heat the vegetable and sesame oils in a pan and stir-fry the scallions and snow peas for 2 minutes. Stir in the reserved marinade and the tamarind juice and bring to a boil.

6 Add the sliced duck and noodles and toss to heat thoroughly. Transfer to warmed serving plates and serve immediately, sprinkled with sesame seeds.

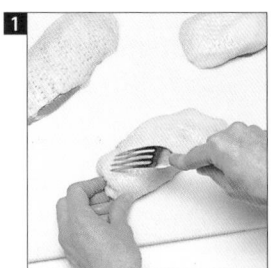

Citrus Duckling Skewers

The tartness of citrus fruit goes well with the rich meat of duckling.
Duckling makes a delightful change from chicken for the barbecue.

NUTRITIONAL INFORMATION

Calories	205	Sugars	.........5g
Protein	........24g	Fat	..........10g
Carbohydrate	....5g	Saturates	......2g

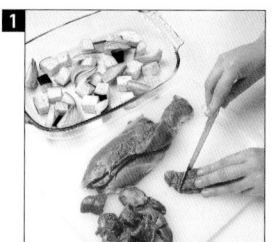

🕐 45 mins 🕐 20 mins

SERVES 12

INGREDIENTS

3 skinless boneless duckling breasts

1 small red onion, cut into wedges

1 small eggplant, cut into cubes

lime and lemon wedges, to
   garnish (optional)

MARINADE

grated rind and juice of 1 lemon

grated rind and juice of 1 lime

grated rind and juice of 1 orange

1 garlic clove, crushed

1 tsp dried oregano

2 tbsp olive oil

dash of Tabasco sauce

1 Cut the duckling into bite-size pieces. Place in a nonmetallic bowl with the prepared vegetables.

2 To make the marinade, place the lemon, lime and orange rinds and juices, garlic, oregano, oil, and Tabasco sauce in a screw-top jar and shake until well combined. Pour the marinade over the duckling and vegetables and toss to coat. Set aside to marinate for 30 minutes.

3 Remove the duckling and vegetables from the marinade and thread them onto skewers, reserving the marinade.

4 Grill the skewers on an oiled rack over medium hot coals, turning and basting frequently with the reserved marinade, for 15-20 minutes until the meat is cooked through. Alternatively, cook under a preheated broiler.

5 Serve the kabobs immediately, garnished with lime and lemon wedges for squeezing, if using.

COOK'S TIP

For more zing, add 1 teaspoon of chili sauce to the marinade. The meat can be marinated for several hours, but it is best to marinate the vegetables separately for only about 30 minutes.

Sesame Orange Duckling

Moist and flavorful, this dish is reminiscent of traditional duck à la orange, but the flavor is even better.

NUTRITIONAL INFORMATION

Calories 510	Sugars 16g	
Protein 51g	Fat 26g	
Carbohydrate . . .18g	Saturates 7g	

2¼ hrs   40 mins

SERVES 4

INGREDIENTS

4 tbsp soy sauce

2 tbsp fine-cut marmalade

2 tbsp orange juice

2 garlic cloves, crushed

½ inch/1 cm piece of fresh
   ginger root, grated

1 tbsp sherry vinegar

4 duckling portions

2 oranges, sliced

4 tbsp sesame seeds

TO SERVE

salad greens

fresh herbs

1 Combine the soy sauce, marmalade, orange juice, garlic, ginger, and sherry vinegar in a small bowl.

2 Trim away any excess fat from the duckling portions.

3 Place the duckling portions in a shallow, nonmetallic dish and pour over the orange mixture. Cover and set aside to marinate for at least 2 hours.

4 Divide most of the orange slices between 4 double-thickness pieces of kitchen foil, reserving some orange slices to serve. Place a duckling portion on top of the oranges and pour some of the marinade over each portion. Fold over the foil to enclose the duckling completely.

5 Grill over hot coals, turning occasionally, for about 40 minutes or until the meat is just cooked. Alternatively, cook under a preheated broiler.

6 Remove the foil packets from the heat and sprinkle the skin of the duckling with the sesame seeds. Place the duckling, skin side down, directly on the oiled rack over the hot coals and grill for a further 5 minutes until the skin is crisp. Alternatively, cook, skin side up, under the broiler. Serve with the orange slices, salad greens, and fresh herbs.

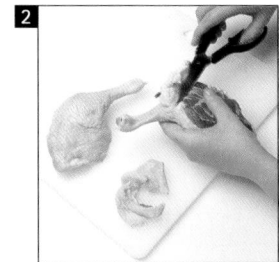

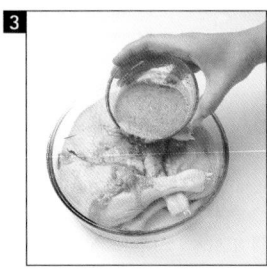

COOK'S TIP

Cooking the duckling in foil packets keeps the meat moist and preserves the flavor of the marinade. If you prefer, omit the foil and cook them directly on the rack. Turn and baste frequently until cooked. Sprinkle with sesame seeds for the last few minutes of cooking.

Glazed Duckling

A salsa is a cross between a sauce and a relish. Salsas are easy to prepare and will liven up all kinds of simple broiled meats—like this one.

NUTRITIONAL INFORMATION

Calories 483	Sugars 28g
Protein 48g	Fat 20g
Carbohydrate ...29g	Saturates 6g

 1¼ hrs   🕐 40–45 mins

SERVES 4

INGREDIENTS

2 tbsp Dijon mustard

1 tsp paprika

½ tsp ground ginger

½ tsp ground nutmeg

2 tbsp molasses sugar

2 duckling halves

salad greens, to serve

SALSA

8 oz/225 g can pineapple in
    natural juice

2 tbsp molasses sugar

1 small red onion, finely chopped

1 fresh red chile, deseeded and chopped

 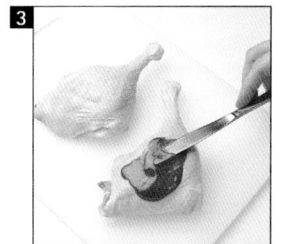 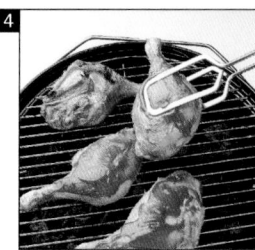

1 First, make the salsa. Drain the canned pineapple, reserving 2 tablespoons of the juice. Finely chop the pineapple flesh.

2 Place the pineapple, reserved juice, sugar, onion, and chile in a bowl and mix well. Cover with plastic wrap and set aside for at least 1 hour for the flavors to develop fully.

3 Meanwhile, combine the mustard, paprika, ginger, nutmeg, and sugar in a small bowl. Spoon the mixture onto the skin of the duckling halves and spread evenly over them.

4 Grill the duckling, skin side up, over hot coals for about 30 minutes. Turn the duckling over and grill for about 10–15 minutes or until the duckling is cooked through.

5 Serve immediately with fresh salad greens and the salsa.

VARIATION
Use canned apricots or peaches to make the salsa for a tasty alternative. The salsa is also delicious served with pork, lamb, or chicken.

Duck with Mangoes

Use fresh mangoes in this recipe for a terrific flavor and color. If they are unavailable, use canned mangoes and rinse them before using.

NUTRITIONAL INFORMATION

Calories 235   Sugars 6g
Protein . . . . .23g   Fat 14g
Carbohydrate . . . .6g   Saturates 2g

5 mins   35 mins

SERVES 4

I N G R E D I E N T S

2 ripe mangoes

1¼ cups chicken stock

2 garlic cloves, crushed

1 tsp grated fresh ginger root

2 large skinless duck breasts,
    about 8 oz/225 g each

3 tbsp vegetable oil

1 tsp wine vinegar

1 tsp light soy sauce

1 leek, sliced

chopped fresh parsley, to garnish

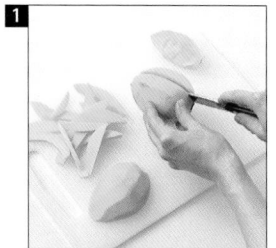

1 Peel the mangoes and cut the flesh from each side of the pits. Cut the flesh into strips.

2 Put half of the mango pieces and the chicken stock in a food processor and process until smooth. Alternatively, press half of the mangoes through a fine strainer and mix with the stock.

3 Rub the garlic and ginger over the duck breasts. Heat the oil in a preheated wok and cook the duck breasts, turning frequently, until sealed. Reserve the oil in the wok and remove the duck.

4 Place the duck breasts on a rack set over a roasting pan and cook in a preheated oven, 425°F/220°C, for about 20 minutes, until the duck is cooked through and tender.

5 Meanwhile, place the mango and stock mixture in a saucepan and add the wine vinegar and light soy sauce.

6 Bring the mixture to a boil and cook over high heat, stirring constantly, until reduced by half.

7 Heat the oil reserved in the wok and stir-fry the sliced leek and remaining mango for 1 minute. Remove from the wok, transfer to a serving dish, and keep warm until required.

8 Slice the cooked duck breasts and arrange the slices on top of the leek and mango mixture. Pour the sauce over the duck slices, garnish with chopped parsley, and serve immediately.

Red Spiced Beef

A spicy stir-fry flavored with paprika, chili and tomato, with a crisp bite to it from the celery strips, makes this a wonderful midweek supper.

NUTRITIONAL INFORMATION

Calories	431	Sugars	....0g
Protein	....32g	Fat	....28g
Carbohydrate	...14g	Saturates	....10g

40 mins   10 mins

SERVES 4

INGREDIENTS

1 lb 6 oz/625 g short loin or loin end steak

2 tbsp paprika

2–3 tsp mild chili powder

½ tsp salt

6 celery stalks

4 tomatoes, peeled, seeded and sliced

6 tbsp stock or water

2 tbsp tomato paste

2 tbsp honey

3 tbsp wine vinegar

1 tbsp Worcestershire sauce

2 tbsp sunflower oil

4 scallions, thinly sliced diagonally

1–2 garlic cloves, crushed

celery leaves, to garnish (optional)

Chinese noodles, to serve

3 Cut the celery into 2 inch/ 5 cm lengths, then cut the lengths into strips about ¼ inch/5 mm thick.

4 Combine the stock, tomato paste, honey, vinegar, and Worcestershire sauce and set aside.

5 Heat the oil in the wok until really hot. Add the scallion, celery, tomatoes, and garlic and stir-fry for about 1 minute until the vegetables are beginning to soften, then add the steak strips. Stir-fry over high heat for 3-4 minutes until the meat is well sealed.

6 Add the sauce to the wok and continue to stir-fry briskly until thoroughly coated and sizzling.

7 Garnish with celery leaves, if liked and serve with noodles.

1 Using a sharp knife or meat cleaver, cut the steak across the grain into narrow strips about ½ inch/1 cm thick and place in a bowl.

2 Combine the paprika, chili powder, and salt, add to the beef and mix until the meat strips are evenly coated with the spices. Set the beef aside to marinate in a cool place for at least 30 minutes.

Beef & Orange Curry

A spicy blend of tender chunks of succulent beef with the tang of orange and the warmth of Indian spices.

NUTRITIONAL INFORMATION

Calories	345	Sugars	........24g
Protein	........28g	Fat	..........13g
Carbohydrate	...31g	Saturates	......3g

15 mins   1¼ hrs

SERVES 4

INGREDIENTS

1 tbsp vegetable oil

8 oz/225 g shallots, halved

2 garlic cloves, crushed

1 lb/450 g lean round steak or short loin beef, trimmed and cut into ¾ inch/2 cm cubes

3 tbsp curry paste

2 cups Fresh Beef Stock (see page 9)

4 medium oranges

2 tsp cornstarch

salt and pepper

2 tbsp chopped fresh cilantro, to garnish

boiled basmati rice, to serve

RAITA

½ cucumber, finely diced

3 tbsp chopped fresh mint

⅔ cup low-fat plain yogurt

1 Heat the oil in a large pan. Add the shallots, garlic, and beef cubes and cook over low heat, stirring occasionally, for 5 minutes until the beef is evenly browned all over.

2 Blend together the curry paste and stock. Add the mixture to the beef and stir to mix thoroughly. Bring to a boil, cover, and simmer for about 1 hour.

3 Grate the rind of 1 orange. Squeeze the juice from the orange and from 1 other. Peel the other 2 oranges, removing the pith. Slice between each segment and remove the flesh.

4 Blend the cornstarch with the orange juice. At the end of the cooking time, stir the orange rind into the beef with the orange and cornstarch mixture. Bring to a boil and simmer, stirring constantly, for 3-4 minutes until the sauce thickens. Season to taste with salt and pepper and stir in the orange segments.

5 To make the raita, mix the cucumber with the mint and stir in the yogurt. Season with salt and pepper to taste.

6 Serve the curry with rice and the cucumber raita, garnished with chopped cilantro.

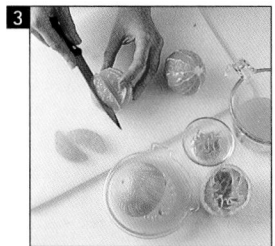

Tagliatelle with Meatballs

There is an appetizing contrast of textures and flavors in this satisfying family dish, which has now become known the world over.

NUTRITIONAL INFORMATION

Calories . . . . .910 Sugars 13g
Protein . . . . .40g Fat 54g
Carbohydrate . . .65g Saturates 19g

 45 mins   1 hr 5 mins

SERVES 4

INGREDIENTS

1 lb 2 oz/500 g ground lean beef

1 cup soft white bread crumbs

1 garlic clove, crushed

2 tbsp chopped fresh parsley

1 tsp dried oregano

pinch of freshly grated nutmeg

¼ tsp ground coriander

⅔ cup freshly grated Parmesan cheese

2–3 tbsp milk

all-purpose flour, for dusting

3 tbsp olive oil

14 oz/400 g dried tagliatelle

2 tbsp butter, diced

salt and pepper

SAUCE

3 tbsp olive oil

2 large onions, sliced

2 celery stalks, thinly sliced

2 garlic cloves, chopped

14 oz/400 g can chopped tomatoes

4½ oz/125 g sun-dried tomatoes in oil, drained and chopped

2 tbsp tomato paste

1 tbsp molasses sugar

⅔ cup white wine or water

1 To make the sauce, heat the oil in a skillet. Add the onions and celery and cook until translucent. Add the garlic and cook for 1 minute. Stir in the tomatoes, tomato paste, sugar, and wine, and season to taste with salt and pepper. Bring to a boil and simmer for 10 minutes.

2 Meanwhile, break up the meat in a bowl with a wooden spoon until it becomes a sticky paste. Stir in the bread crumbs, garlic, herbs, and spices. Stir in the cheese and enough milk to make a firm paste. Flour your hands, take large spoonfuls of the mixture, and shape it into 12 balls. Heat the oil in a skillet and fry the meatballs for 5–6 minutes until browned.

3 Pour the tomato sauce over the meatballs. Lower the heat, cover the pan, and simmer for 30 minutes, turning once or twice. Add a little extra water if the sauce is beginning to become dry.

4 Bring a large pan of lightly salted water to a boil. Add the pasta, bring back to a boil, and cook for 8–10 minutes, until tender, but still firm to the bite. Drain the pasta, then turn into a warmed serving dish, dot with the butter, and toss with 2 forks. Spoon the meatballs and sauce over the pasta and serve immediately.

Lamb Biriyani

For an authentic finishing touch, garnish with crisply fried onion rings, toasted sliced almonds, and chopped pistachio nuts.

NUTRITIONAL INFORMATION

Calories 668   Sugars 16g
Protein . . . . .41g   Fat 35g
Carbohydrate . . .78g   Saturates 15g

3½ hrs   50 mins

SERVES 6–8

INGREDIENTS

2 lb/900 g boned lean leg or shoulder of lamb, cut into 1 inch/2.5 cm cubes

6 garlic cloves, finely chopped

1½ inch/4 cm piece of fresh ginger root, finely chopped

1 tbsp ground cinnamon

1 tbsp green cardamom pods, crushed

1 tsp whole cloves

2 tsp coriander seeds, crushed

2 tsp cumin seeds, crushed

½ tsp ground turmeric (optional)

2 fresh green chiles, chopped

grated rind and juice of 1 lime

1 bunch of fresh cilantro, finely chopped

1 bunch of fresh mint, finely chopped

½ cup plain yogurt

8 tbsp ghee, butter or vegetable oil

4 onions, 3 thinly sliced and 1 chopped

1 lb 5 oz/600 g basmati rice

2 cinnamon sticks, broken

½ tsp freshly grated nutmeg

3–4 tbsp raisins

5 cups chicken stock

1 cup hot milk

1 tsp saffron threads, lightly crushed

salt and pepper

1 Combine the lamb, garlic, spices, lime rind and juice, and 2 tablespoons each of cilantro and mint, and yogurt. Set aside to marinate for 2–3 hours.

2 Heat half the fat in a large skillet. Cook the sliced onions for 8 minutes until lightly browned. Add the meat and any juices. Season to taste. Stir in 1 cup water and simmer for 18–20 minutes until the lamb is cooked.

3 Meanwhile, heat the remaining fat in a flameproof casserole. Add the chopped onion and cook for 2 minutes until soft. Add the rice and cook, stirring, for 3–4 minutes until well coated. Add the cinnamon, nutmeg, raisins, and stock. Bring to a boil, stirring once or twice, and season with salt and pepper. Simmer, covered, over low heat for 12 minutes until the liquid is reduced, but the rice is still a little firm.

4 Pour the hot milk over the saffron; stand for 10 minutes. Remove the rice from the heat and stir in the saffron-milk. Fold in the lamb mixture. Cover and bake in a preheated oven, 350°F/180°C, until the rice is cooked.

Pork Stroganoff

Tender, lean pork, cooked in a tasty, rich tomato
sauce, is flavored with the extra tang of plain yogurt.

NUTRITIONAL INFORMATION

Calories	223	Sugars	.........7g
Protein	........22g	Fat	..........10g
Carbohydrate	...12g	Saturates	......3g

2¼ hrs   30 mins

SERVES 4

I N G R E D I E N T S

12 oz/350 g lean pork tenderloin

1 tbsp vegetable oil

1 medium onion, chopped

2 garlic cloves, crushed

¼ cup all-purpose flour

2 tbsp tomato paste

2 cups Fresh Chicken or Fresh Vegetable
   Stock (see pages 8 and 9)

1¾ cups sliced white mushrooms

1 large green bell pepper, deseeded
   and diced

½ tsp ground nutmeg, plus extra to garnish

4 tbsp low-fat plain yogurt, plus extra
   to serve

salt and pepper

white rice, freshly boiled, to serve

1 Trim away any excess fat and silver skin from the pork,
then cut the meat into slices ½ inch/1 cm thick.

2 Heat the oil in a large pan. Add the pork, onion, and
garlic and cook over low heat, stirring occasionally, for
4–5 minutes until lightly browned.

3 Stir in the flour and tomato paste, pour in the stock,
and stir to mix.

4 Add the mushrooms, green bell pepper and nutmeg
and season to taste with salt and pepper. Bring to a
boil, cover, and simmer for 20 minutes until the pork is
tender and cooked through.

5 Remove the pan from the heat, set aside to cool
slightly, then stir in the yogurt.

6 Serve the pork and sauce on a bed of rice, with an
extra spoonful of yogurt, and garnish with a dusting of
ground nutmeg.

COOK'S TIP

You can buy ready-made
stock from leading supermarkets.
Although more expensive, they
are more nutritious than bouillon
cubes, which are high in salt
and artificial flavorings.

Caribbean Pork

Serve these tasty marinated pork chops with a coconut-flavored savory rice and accompanied by sweet potatoes.

NUTRITIONAL INFORMATION

Calories 740	Sugars 33g	
Protein 39g	Fat 27g	
Carbohydrate ...78g	Saturates 12g	

 2¼ hrs   20 mins

SERVES 4

INGREDIENTS

4 pork tenderloin chops

4 tbsp molasses sugar

4 tbsp orange or pineapple juice

2 tbsp Jamaican rum

1 tbsp dry shredded coconut

½ tsp ground cinnamon

mixed salad greens, to serve

COCONUT RICE

generous 1 cup basmati rice

2 cups water

⅔ cup coconut milk

4 tbsp raisins

4 tbsp roasted peanuts or cashew nuts

salt and pepper

2 tbsp dry shredded coconut, toasted

VARIATION

These pork chops are delicious served with grilled pineapple slices. Sprinkle the pineapple with molasses sugar and cinnamon. Grill over hot coals for about 5 minutes, turning once, until piping hot.

1 Trim any excess fat from the pork and place it in a nonmetallic dish.

2 Combine the sugar, fruit juice, rum, coconut, and cinnamon in a bowl, stirring until the sugar dissolves. Pour the mixture over the pork and set aside to marinate in the refrigerator for at least 2 hours or preferably overnight.

3 Remove the pork, reserving the marinade for basting. Grill over hot coals for 15–20 minutes, basting frequently with the marinade.

4 Meanwhile, make the coconut rice. Rinse the rice under cold water, place it in a pan with the water and coconut milk, and gradually bring to a boil. Stir, cover, and reduce the heat. Simmer gently for 12 minutes or until the rice is tender and the liquid has been absorbed. Fluff up with a fork.

5 Stir the raisins and nuts into the rice, season with salt and pepper to taste, and sprinkle with the coconut. Transfer the pork and rice to warm serving plates and serve with the mixed salad greens.

Ham & Pineapple Kabobs

This traditional and much-loved combination of flavors always works well on the barbecue.

NUTRITIONAL INFORMATION

Calories	426	Sugars	........11g
Protein	........31g	Fat	..........29g
Carbohydrate	....11g	Saturates	......13g

15 mins   8 mins

SERVES 4

INGREDIENTS

1 lb/450 g thick ham steak

15 oz/425 g can pineapple pieces in natural juice

8 oz/225 g firm Brie, chilled

2 tbsp sunflower oil

1 garlic clove, crushed

1 tbsp lemon juice

½ tsp ground nutmeg

¼ tsp ground cloves

pepper

cooked rice, to serve

1 Cut the ham into even-size chunks. Place the chunks in a pan of boiling water and simmer for 5 minutes.

2 Drain the pineapple pieces and reserve 3 tablespoons of the juice. Cut the chilled cheese into large chunks.

3 To make the baste, combine the pineapple juice, oil, garlic, lemon juice, nutmeg, cloves, and pepper to taste in a small screw-top jar and shake until well combined. Set aside until required.

4 Remove the ham from the pan with a slotted spoon. Thread the ham onto skewers, alternating with the pineapple and cheese pieces.

5 Grill the kabobs over warm coals, turning and basting frequently with the oil and pineapple juice mixture, for 2–4 minutes on each side until the pineapple and ham are hot and the cheese is just beginning to melt. Do not overcook, otherwise the cheese will become runny and the kabobs will become a mess; allow enough time to reheat the ham and for the pineapple to warm through.

6 Serve the kabobs on a bed of cooked rice.

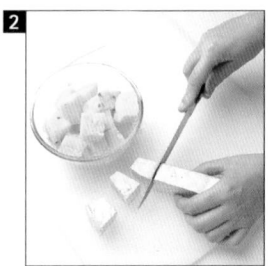

Saucy Sausages

Although there is much more to barbecues than sausages, they can make a welcome appearance from time to time.

NUTRITIONAL INFORMATION

Calories 369	Sugars 18g
Protein 15g	Fat 24g
Carbohydrate ...25g	Saturates 7g

10 mins | 35 mins

SERVES 4

INGREDIENTS

2 tbsp sunflower oil

1 large onion, chopped

2 garlic cloves, chopped

8 oz/225 g can chopped tomatoes

1 tbsp Worcestershire sauce

2 tbsp brown fruity sauce

2 tbsp molasses sugar

4 tbsp white wine vinegar

½ tsp mild chili powder

¼ tsp mustard powder

dash of Tabasco sauce

1 lb/450 g sausages

salt and pepper

bread finger rolls, to serve

COOK'S TIP

Choose any well-flavored sausages for this recipe. Bratwurst is a good choice, as are uncooked Kielbasa sausages. Venison sausages have a good, gamey flavor and taste wonderful cooked on the barbecue.

1 To make the sauce, heat the oil in a small pan and cook the onion and garlic for 4–5 minutes until softened and just beginning to brown.

2 Add the tomatoes, Worcestershire sauce, brown fruity sauce, sugar, wine vinegar, chili powder, mustard powder, Tabasco sauce, and salt and pepper to taste to the pan and bring to a boil.

3 Reduce the heat and simmer gently for 10–15 minutes until the sauce

begins to thicken slightly. Stir occasionally so that the sauce does not burn and stick to the bottom of the pan. Set aside and keep warm until required.

4 Grill the sausages over hot coals for 10–15 minutes, turning frequently. Do not prick them with a fork or the fat will run out and cause a fire.

5 Insert the sausages into the bread rolls and serve immediately with the barbecue sauce.

Pork & Sage Kabobs

The ground pork mixture is shaped into meatballs and threaded onto skewers. It has a slightly sweet flavor that is popular with children.

NUTRITIONAL INFORMATION

Calories 96   Sugars 0g
Protein ....8g   Fat 7g
Carbohydrate ....2g   Saturates 2g

🌀 🌀 🌀

🍲 50 mins   🕐 8–10 mins

SERVES 12

INGREDIENTS

1 lb/450 g ground pork

½ cup fresh bread crumbs

1 small onion, very finely chopped

1 tbsp chopped fresh sage

2 tbsp apple sauce

¼ tsp ground nutmeg

salt and pepper

BASTE

3 tbsp olive oil

1 tbsp lemon juice

TO SERVE

6 small pitas

mixed salad greens

6 tbsp thick, plain yogurt

1 Place the ground pork in a mixing bowl with the bread crumbs, onion, sage, apple sauce, and nutmeg. Season with salt and pepper to taste. Mix until the ingredients are well combined.

2 Using your hands, shape the mixture into small balls about the size of large marbles. Place on a plate, cover with plastic wrap, and chill in the refrigerator for at least 30 minutes.

3 Meanwhile, soak 12 small wooden skewers in cold water for at least 30 minutes. Thread the pork meatballs onto the skewers. Cover with plastic wrap and set aside in the refrigerator until you are ready to cook.

4 To make the baste, combine the olive oil and lemon juice in a small bowl, whisking with a fork until the mixture is well blended.

5 Grill the kabobs over hot coals for 8–10 minutes, turning and basting frequently with the lemon and oil mixture, until the meat is golden brown and cooked through.

6 Line the pitas with the salad greens and spoon over some of the yogurt. Serve with the kabobs.

Pork Balls with Mint Sauce

Made with lean ground pork, the balls are first stir-fried, then braised in the wok with stock and pickled walnuts to give a tangy flavor.

NUTRITIONAL INFORMATION

Calories 318	Sugars 2g
Protein 30g	Fat 20g
Carbohydrate 6g	Saturates 5g

  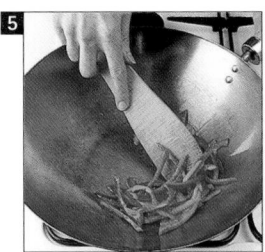

5 mins   25 mins

SERVES 4

INGREDIENTS

1 lb 2 oz/500 g lean ground pork

¾ cup fine fresh white bread crumbs

½ tsp ground allspice

1 garlic clove, crushed

2 tbsp chopped fresh mint

1 egg, beaten

2 tbsp sunflower oil

1 red bell pepper, deseeded

generous 1 cup chicken stock

4 pickled walnuts, sliced

salt and pepper

fresh mint, to garnish

rice or Chinese noodles, to serve

1 Combine the ground pork, bread crumbs, allspice, garlic, and half the chopped mint in a mixing bowl. Season to taste with salt and pepper, then bind together with the beaten egg.

2 Shape the meat mixture into 20 small balls with your hands, damping your hands if it is easier for shaping.

3 Heat the sunflower oil in a wok or heavy skillet, swirling the oil around until really hot, then add the pork balls and stir-fry for about 4-5 minutes or until browned all over.

4 Remove the pork balls from the wok using a slotted spoon as they are ready and drain thoroughly on absorbent paper towels.

5 Pour off all but 1 tablespoon of fat and oil from the wok or skillet. Thinly slice the red bell pepper, then add to the pan, and stir-fry for 2–3 minutes or until the slices begin to soften, but not color.

6 Add the chicken stock and bring to a boil. Season well with salt and pepper and return the pork balls to the wok, stirring well to coat in the sauce. Simmer for 7-10 minutes, turning the pork balls from time to time.

7 Add the remaining chopped mint and the pickled walnuts to the wok and continue to simmer for 2-3 minutes, turning the pork balls regularly to coat them in the sauce.

8 Adjust the seasoning and serve the pork balls with rice or Chinese noodles or with a stir-fried vegetable dish, and garnished with sprigs of fresh mint.

Pork Fry with Vegetables

This is a very simple dish which lends itself to almost any combination of vegetables that you have to hand.

NUTRITIONAL INFORMATION

Calories 216	Sugars 3g	
Protein 19g	Fat 12g	
Carbohydrate 5g	Saturates 3g	

  5 mins   15 mins

SERVES 4

I N G R E D I E N T S

12 oz/350 g lean pork tenderloin, thinly sliced

2 tbsp vegetable oil

2 garlic cloves, crushed

½ inch/1 cm piece of fresh ginger root, cut into slivers

1 carrot, cut into thin strips

1 red bell pepper, deseeded and diced

1 fennel bulb, sliced

1 oz/25 g water chestnuts, halved

1½ cups bean sprouts

2 tbsp Chinese rice wine

1¼ cups pork or chicken stock

pinch of dark brown sugar

1 tsp cornstarch

2 tsp water

1 Heat the oil in a preheated wok. Add the garlic, ginger, and pork. Stir-fry for 1–2 minutes until the meat is sealed.

2 Add the carrot, bell pepper, fennel, and water chestnuts and stir-fry for about 2-3 minutes.

3 Add the bean sprouts and stir-fry for 1 minute. Remove the pork and vegetables, set aside, and keep warm.

4 Add the Chinese rice wine, pork or chicken stock, and sugar to the wok. Blend the cornstarch to a smooth paste with the water and stir it into the sauce. Bring to a boil, stirring constantly until thickened and clear.

5 Return the meat and vegetables to the wok and cook for 1–2 minutes until heated through and coated with the sauce. Serve immediately.

VARIATION

Use dry sherry instead of the Chinese rice wine if you have difficulty obtaining it.

Stir-Fried Pork with Pasta

This delicious dish, with its hint of Thai cooking, will certainly get the tastebuds tingling—and it's ready in next to no time.

NUTRITIONAL INFORMATION

Calories	.751	Sugars	.10g
Protein	.37g	Fat	.27g
Carbohydrate	.96g	Saturates	.8g

10 mins   15 mins

SERVES 4

INGREDIENTS

3 tbsp sesame oil

12 oz/350 g pork tenderloin, cut into thin strips

1 lb/450 g dried taglioni

8 shallots, sliced

2 garlic cloves, finely chopped

1 inch/2.5 cm piece of fresh ginger root, grated

1 fresh green chile, finely chopped

1 red bell pepper, deseeded and thinly sliced

1 green bell pepper, deseeded and thinly sliced

3 zucchini, thinly sliced

2 tbsp ground almonds

1 tsp ground cinnamon

1 tbsp oyster sauce

2 oz/55 g creamed coconut, grated

salt and pepper

COOK'S TIP

Creamed coconut is available from Chinese and Asian food stores and some large supermarkets. It is sold in the form of compressed blocks and adds a concentrated coconut flavor to the dish.

1 Heat the sesame oil in a preheated wok. Season the pork with salt and pepper to taste, add to the wok, and stir-fry for 5 minutes.

2 Meanwhile, bring a large pan of lightly salted water to a boil. Add the taglioni, bring back to a boil, and cook for about 10 minutes until just tender, but still firm to the bite. Drain, set the pasta aside, and keep warm.

3 Add the shallots, garlic, ginger, and chile to the wok and stir-fry for

2 minutes. Add the bell peppers and zucchini and stir-fry for 1 minute.

4 Finally, add the ground almonds, cinnamon, oyster sauce, and creamed coconut to the wok and stir-fry for about 1 minute.

5 Transfer the taglioni to a warmed serving dish. Top with the stir-fry and serve immediately.

Pasta & Pork in Cream

This unusual and attractive dish is extremely delicious. Make the Red Wine Sauce well in advance to reduce the preparation time.

NUTRITIONAL INFORMATION

Calories 735	Sugars 4g	
Protein 31g	Fat 52g	
Carbohydrate ...37g	Saturates 19g	

8¾ hrs

35 mins

SERVES 4

INGREDIENTS

1 lb/450 g pork tenderloin, thinly sliced

4 tbsp olive oil

8 oz/225 g white mushrooms, sliced

scant 1 cup Red Wine Sauce (see page 7)

1 tbsp lemon juice

pinch of saffron

3 cups dried orecchioni

4 tbsp heavy cream

12 quail eggs (see Cook's Tip)

salt

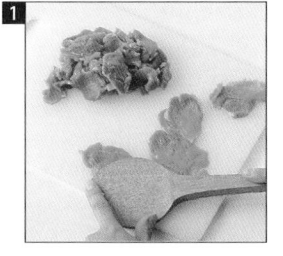

1 Place the slices of pork between 2 sheets of plastic wrap and pound with a meat mallet or rolling pin until wafer thin, then cut into strips.

2 Heat the olive oil in a large, heavy skillet over medium heat. Add the pork slices and stir-fry for 5 minutes. Add the mushrooms to the skillet and stir-fry for a further 2 minutes.

3 Pour over the Red Wine Sauce, lower the heat, and simmer very gently for 20 minutes.

4 Meanwhile, bring a large pan of lightly salted water to a boil. Add the lemon juice, saffron, and orecchioni and cook for 8–10 minutes until the pasta is tender, but still firm to the bite. Drain the pasta and keep warm.

5 Stir the heavy cream into the skillet with the pork and heat gently for a few minutes.

6 Boil the quail eggs for 3 minutes, cool them in cold water, and then remove the shells.

7 Transfer the pasta to a large, warm serving plate, top with the pork and the sauce, and garnish with the eggs. Serve immediately.

COOK'S TIP

In this recipe, the quail eggs are soft-cooked. As they are extremely difficult to shell when warm, it is important that they are thoroughly cooled first. Otherwise, they will break up unattractively.

Potato, Sausage & Onion Pie

This is a delicious supper dish for all of the family. Use good-quality, preferably low-fat, herb sausages for a really tasty pie.

NUTRITIONAL INFORMATION

Calories	399	Sugars	.........6g
Protein	........14g	Fat	..........22g
Carbohydrate	...39g	Saturates	......11g

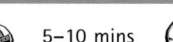

5–10 mins   40 mins

SERVES 4

INGREDIENTS

2 large waxy potatoes, unpeeled and sliced

2 tbsp butter

4 thick pork and herb sausages

1 leek, sliced

2 garlic cloves, crushed

⅔ cup vegetable stock

⅔ cup hard cider or apple juice

2 tbsp chopped fresh sage

2 tbsp cornstarch

4 tbsp water

¾ cup grated sharp cheese

salt and pepper

1 Cook the sliced potatoes in a pan of boiling water for about 10 minutes. Drain and set aside.

2 Meanwhile, melt the butter in a large, heavy skillet and cook the sausages over medium heat for about 8–10 minutes, turning them frequently so that they brown on all sides. Remove the sausages from the skillet and cut them into thick slices.

3 Add the leek, garlic, and sausage slices to the skillet and cook for 2–3 minutes.

4 Add the vegetable stock, hard cider or apple juice, and sage. Season with salt and pepper to taste.

5 Blend the cornstarch with the water to a smooth paste. Stir it into the skillet and bring to a boil, stirring constantly until the sauce is thick and clear. Spoon the mixture evenly into the base of a deep pie dish.

6 Arrange the potato slices on top of the sausage mixture to cover it completely. Season with salt and pepper to taste and sprinkle the grated cheese over the top.

7 Cook in a preheated oven, 375°F, for 25–30 minutes or until the potatoes are cooked and the cheese is golden brown. Serve hot.

Nasi Goreng

A meal in itself, this mouthwatering fried rice dish is bursting with the exotic flavors of Indonesia. The perfect supper dish!

NUTRITIONAL INFORMATION

Calories 504	Sugars 8g	
Protein 49g	Fat 15g	
Carbohydrate ...47g	Saturates 4g	

15 mins   20 mins

SERVES 4

INGREDIENTS

1 large onion, chopped

2–3 garlic cloves

1 tsp shrimp paste

2 fresh red chiles, deseeded and chopped

about ½ cup vegetable oil

3 eggs, lightly beaten

1 lb/450 g beef round steak, about ½ inch/
   1cm thick

2 carrots, cut into thin batons

6 oz/175 g Chinese long beans or green
   beans, cut into 1 inch/2.5 cm pieces

6 small scallions, cut into ½ inch/
   1 cm pieces

9 oz/250 g raw shelled shrimp

4⅓ cups cooked long grain white rice, at
   room temperature

6 tbsp dark soy sauce

TO GARNISH

4 tbsp ready-fried onion flakes

4 inch/10 cm piece cucumber, deseeded
   and cut into thin sticks

2 tbsp chopped fresh cilantro

1 Put the onion, garlic, shrimp paste, and chiles into a food processor and process until a paste forms. Add a little oil and process until smooth. Set aside.

2 Heat 1–2 tablespoons oil in a large, nonstick skillet. Pour in the egg to form a thin layer and cook for 1 minute until just set. Turn and cook for 5 seconds on the other side. Slide out and cut in half. Roll up each half, then slice into ¼ inch/5 mm wide strips. Set aside.

3 Heat 2 tablespoons oil in the same skillet over high heat and add the steak. Cook for 2 minutes on each side to brown and seal, but do not cook completely. Cool, then cut into thin strips, and reserve.

4 Heat 2 tablespoons oil in a large wok over medium-high heat. Add the reserved chili paste and cook, stirring frequently, for about 3 minutes. Add 2 tablespoons oil, the carrots, and long or green beans. Stir-fry for about 2 minutes. Add the sliced scallions, shrimp, and beef strips and stir-fry until the shrimp have turned pink.

5 Stir in the rice, half the sliced omelet, 2 tablespoons soy sauce, and ¼ cup water. Cover and steam for 1 minute. Spoon into a warmed serving dish, top with the remaining omelet, and drizzle with the remaining soy sauce. Sprinkle with the onion flakes, cucumber, and cilantro and serve immediately.

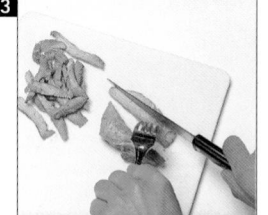  

Honey-Glazed Duck

Chinese-style duck is incredibly easy to prepare, but makes an impressive and truly delicious entrée for a dinner party.

NUTRITIONAL INFORMATION

Calories 230	Sugars 9g	
Protein 23g	Fat 9g	
Carbohydrate ...14g	Saturates 3g	

2¼ hrs   30 mins

SERVES 4

INGREDIENTS

1 tsp dark soy sauce

2 tbsp honey

1 tsp garlic vinegar

2 garlic cloves, crushed

1 tsp ground star anise

2 tsp cornstarch

2 tsp water

2 large boneless duck breasts, about 8 oz/225 g each

TO GARNISH

celery leaves

cucumber wedges

chopped fresh chives

1 Combine the soy sauce, honey, garlic vinegar, garlic, and star anise. Blend the cornstarch with the water to form a smooth paste and stir it into the mixture.

COOK'S TIP

If the duck begins to burn slightly while it is cooking in the oven, cover with foil. Check that the duck breasts are cooked through by inserting the point of a sharp knife into the thickest part of the flesh— the juices should run clear.

2 Place the duck breasts in a shallow casserole. Brush with the soy marinade, turning them to coat completely. Cover and set aside to marinate in the refrigerator for at least 2 hours or overnight.

3 Remove the duck from the marinade and cook in a preheated oven, 425°F/ 220°C, for 20-25 minutes, basting frequently with the glaze.

4 Remove the duck from the oven and transfer to a preheated broiler. Broil for about 3-4 minutes to caramelize the top, without charring.

5 Remove the duck from the broiler pan and cut it into thin slices. Arrange the duck slices on a warmed serving dish, garnish with celery leaves, cucumber wedges, and chopped fresh chives and serve immediately.

Broiled Ground Lamb

This tasty dish with a hint of spice is a good way to perk up a dreary week, and it is quick enough to prepare after a busy day at work.

NUTRITIONAL INFORMATION

Calories 341	Sugars 5g
Protein 25g	Fat 24g
Carbohydrate 8g	Saturates 6g

 10 mins   40 mins

SERVES 4

I N G R E D I E N T S

5 tbsp oil

2 onions, sliced

1 lb/450 g ground lamb

2 tbsp yogurt

1 tsp chili powder

1 tsp finely chopped fresh ginger root

1 tsp fresh garlic, crushed

1 tsp salt

1½ tsp garam masala

½ tsp ground allspice

2 fresh green chiles

fresh cilantro leaves

salad greens, to serve

TO GARNISH

fresh cilantro leaves, chopped

1 lemon, cut into wedges

1 Heat the oil in a pan. Add the sliced onions and cook over low heat until golden brown.

2 Place the ground lamb in a large bowl. Add the yogurt, chili powder, ginger, garlic, salt, garam masala, and ground allspice and mix to combine. Add the lamb mixture to the fried onions and stir-fry for 10–15 minutes. Remove the mixture from the heat and set aside.

3 Meanwhile, place the chiles and half of the cilantro leaves in a food processor and process. Alternatively, finely chop the chiles and cilantro with a sharp knife. Set aside until required.

4 Put the ground lamb mixture in a food processor and process. Alternatively, place in a large bowl and mash with a fork. Mix the lamb mixture with the chiles and cilantro and blend well.

5 Transfer the mixture to a shallow heatproof dish. Cook under a preheated medium-hot broiler for about 10–15 minutes, moving the mixture about with a fork. Watch it carefully to prevent it from burning.

6 Garnish with cilantro leaves and lemon wedges and serve with salad greens.

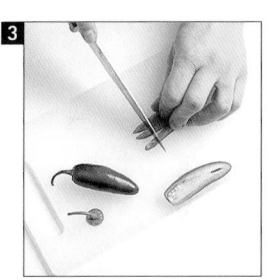

Ground Lamb with Peas

This version of a useful stand-by is livened up with chiles and ginger and flavored with garlic and cilantro.

NUTRITIONAL INFORMATION

Calories	357	Sugars 3g
Protein	........25g	Fat 26g
Carbohydrate	....6g	Saturates 6g

5 mins   25 mins

SERVES 4

INGREDIENTS

6 tbsp oil

1 medium onion, sliced

3 fresh green chiles

1 bunch of fresh cilantro

2 tomatoes, chopped

1 tsp salt

1 tsp finely chopped fresh ginger root

1 tsp fresh garlic, crushed

1 tsp chili powder

1 lb/450 g lean ground lamb

1 cup peas

1 Heat the oil in a medium-sized pan. Add the onion slices and cook, stirring constantly, until golden brown.

2 Add 2 of the green chiles, half of the fresh cilantro leaves, and the chopped tomatoes to the pan and reduce the heat to a gentle simmer.

3 Add the salt, ginger, garlic, and chili powder to the pan and stir thoroughly to combine.

4 Add the ground lamb to the pan and stir-fry the mixture for 7–10 minutes until the meat turns brown.

5 Stir in the peas and cook, stirring occasionally, for 3–4 minutes.

6 Transfer the lamb and pea mixture to warmed serving plates and garnish with the remaining chopped green chile and the fresh cilantro leaves.

COOK'S TIP

It is usually said that most of the heat of chiles is in the seeds. In fact, it is in the flesh surrounding the seeds. Deseeding the chile removes most of this fiery flesh.

Lamb Cooked in Spinach

This succulent lamb dish shows the influence of southern Indian cooking and is both quick and easy to prepare.

NUTRITIONAL INFORMATION

Calories ....944 Sugars 8g
Protein ....31g Fat 87g
Carbohydrate ....11g Saturates 12g

   5 mins   🕐 1¼ hrs

SERVES 4

I N G R E D I E N T S

1¼ cups vegetable oil

2 medium onions, sliced

¼ bunch of fresh cilantro

3 fresh green chiles, chopped

1½ tsp finely chopped fresh ginger root

1½ tsp crushed fresh garlic

1 tsp chili powder

½ tsp ground turmeric

1 lb/450 g lean lamb, with or
    without the bone

1 tsp salt

2 lb 4 oz/1 kg fresh spinach, trimmed,
    washed, and chopped or 15 oz/
    425 g can spinach

3 cups pints water

TO GARNISH

fresh red chiles, finely chopped

4 Add the lamb and stir-fry for a further 5 minutes. Add the salt and the fresh or canned spinach and cook, stirring occasionally, for a further 3–5 minutes.

5 Stir in the water, cover, and cook over low heat for about 45 minutes. Remove the lid and check the meat. If it is not tender, turn the meat over, increase the heat, and cook, uncovered, until the surplus water has been absorbed. Stir-fry the mixture for a further 5–7 minutes.

6 Transfer the lamb and spinach mixture to a warmed serving dish and garnish with finely chopped red chiles and the remaining chopped green chile. Serve immediately.

1 Heat the oil in a pan and cook the onions until they turn pale gold.

2 Add the fresh cilantro and 2 of the chopped green chiles to the pan and stir-fry for 3–5 minutes.

3 Reduce the heat and stir in the ginger, garlic, chili powder, and turmeric.

Shish Kabobs

Grilled lean lamb, vegetables, and salad are
tucked inside toasted pitas for an irresistible light meal.

NUTRITIONAL INFORMATION

Calories	296	Sugars	.........3g
Protein	........24g	Fat	..........21g
Carbohydrate	....4g	Saturates	.......6g

2½ hrs   8–10 mins

SERVES 4

INGREDIENTS

1 lb/450 g lean lamb

1 red onion, cut into wedges

1 green bell pepper, deseeded

MARINADE

1 onion

4 tbsp olive oil

grated rind and juice of ½ lemon

1 garlic clove, crushed

½ tsp dried oregano

½ tsp dried thyme

TO SERVE

4 pitas

crisp lettuce leaves, shredded

2 tomatoes, sliced

chili sauce (optional)

1 Trim any fat from the lamb and cut into large, even-size chunks.

2 To make the marinade, grate the onion or chop it very finely in a food processor. Remove the juice by squeezing the onion between 2 plates set over a small bowl. Combine the onion juice with the remaining marinade ingredients in a nonmetallic dish and add the meat. Toss the meat in the marinade to coat, cover with plastic wrap, and set aside to marinate in the refrigerator for at least 2 hours or overnight.

3 Divide the onion wedges in half. Cut the green bell pepper into chunks.

4 Remove the meat from the marinade, reserving the marinade for basting. Thread the meat onto skewers, alternating with the onion and pieces of green bell pepper. Grill for 8–10 minutes, turning and basting with the reserved marinade frequently.

5 Meanwhile, toast the pitas on the side of the barbecue until warmed through. To serve, split open the pitas and fill with a little shredded lettuce and the meat and vegetables. Top with tomatoes and chili sauce, if using, and serve immediately.

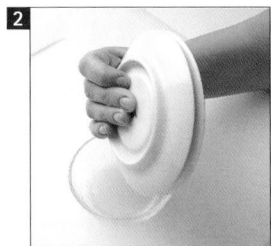

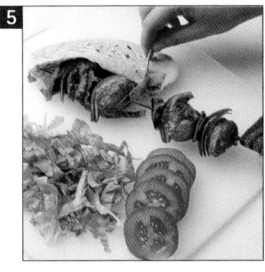

VARIATION

These kabobs are delicious served
with saffron-flavored rice. For easy
saffron rice, simply use saffron
bouillon cubes when cooking the rice.

Pot Roasted Leg of Lamb

This dish from the Abruzzi region of Italy uses a slow cooking method. The meat absorbs the flavorings and becomes very tender.

NUTRITIONAL INFORMATION

Calories 734   Sugars 6g
Protein . . . . .71g   Fat 42g
Carbohydrate . . . .7g   Saturates 15g

🕒 35 mins   🕐 3 hrs

SERVES 4

I N G R E D I E N T S

3 lb 8 oz/1.6 kg leg of lamb

3–4 fresh rosemary sprigs

4 oz/115 g bacon strips

4 tbsp olive oil

2–3 garlic cloves, crushed

2 onions, sliced

2 carrots, sliced

2 celery stalks, sliced

1¼ cups dry white wine

1 tbsp tomato paste

1¼ cups stock

12 oz/350 g tomatoes, peeled, quartered, and deseeded

1 tbsp chopped fresh parsley

1 tbsp chopped fresh oregano or marjoram

salt and pepper

fresh rosemary sprigs, to garnish

1 Wipe the joint of lamb all over, trimming off any excess fat, then season with salt and pepper, rubbing well in. Lay the sprigs of rosemary over the lamb, cover evenly with the bacon strips, and tie in place with string.

2 Heat the oil in a skillet and fry the lamb for about 10 minutes, turning several times. Remove from the skillet.

3 Transfer the oil from the skillet to a large flameproof casserole and cook the garlic and onion for 3–4 minutes until beginning to soften. Add the carrots and celery and cook for a few minutes longer.

4 Lay the lamb on top of the vegetables and press down to partly submerge. Pour the wine over the lamb, add the tomato paste, and simmer for about 3–4 minutes. Add the stock, tomatoes, and herbs and season to taste with salt and pepper. Bring back to a boil for a further 3–4 minutes.

5 Cover the casserole tightly and cook in a moderate oven, 350°F/180°C, for 2–2½ hours until very tender.

6 Remove the lamb from the casserole and if preferred, take off the bacon and herbs along with the string. Keep warm. Strain the juices, skimming off any excess fat, and serve in a pitcher. The vegetables may be arranged around the pot roast or in a serving dish. Garnish with fresh sprigs of rosemary.

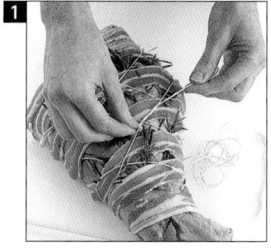

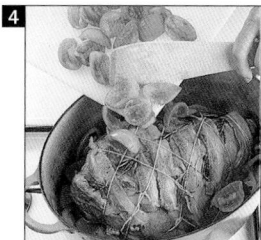

Veal Chops with Salsa Verde

This vibrant green Italian sauce adds a touch of Mediterranean flavor to any simply cooked meat or shellfish.

NUTRITIONAL INFORMATION

Calories 481	Sugars 1g
Protein 41g	Fat 34g
Carbohydrate 2g	Saturates 5g

10 mins   5 mins

SERVES 4

I N G R E D I E N T S

4 veal chops, such as loin chops, about 8 oz/225 g each and ¾ inch/2 cm thick

garlic-flavored olive oil, for brushing

salt and pepper

fresh oregano or basil leaves, to garnish

S A L S A   V E R D E

2 cups fresh flat leaf parsley leaves

3 canned anchovy fillets in oil, drained

1½ tsp capers in brine, rinsed and drained

1 shallot, finely chopped

1 garlic clove, halved, green core removed, and chopped

1 tbsp lemon juice

6 large fresh basil leaves or ¾ tsp freeze-dried basil

2 fresh oregano sprigs or ½ tsp dried oregano

½ cup extra virgin olive oil

COOK'S TIP

The salsa verde will keep for up to 2 days in a covered container in the refrigerator. It is also fantastic served with broiled red snapper. Or use it to replace the pesto sauce in Mediterranean Monkfish (see page 748).

1 To make the salsa verde, put the parsley, anchovies, capers, shallot, garlic, lemon juice, basil, and oregano in a blender or food processor and process until they are thoroughly chopped and blended.

2 With the motor running, add the oil through the top or feeder tube and process until thickened. Season with pepper to taste. Scrape to a bowl, cover with plastic wrap and chill in the refrigerator.

3 Lightly brush the veal chops with olive oil and season to taste with salt and pepper. Place under a preheated broiler and cook for about 3 minutes. Turn over, brush with more oil and broil for a further 2 minutes until cooked when tested with the tip of a knife.

4 Transfer the chops to warmed individual plates and spoon a little of the chilled salsa verde beside them. Garnish the chops with fresh oregano or basil and serve with the remaining salsa verde handed separately.

Citrus Osso Bucco

The orange and lemon rinds, together with fresh basil, give this traditional Italian dish a real southern flavor.

NUTRITIONAL INFORMATION

Calories 310   Sugars 4g
Protein . . . . .42g   Fat 6g
Carbohydrate . . .16g   Saturates 2g

 15 mins   🕐 1½ hrs

SERVES 6

I N G R E D I E N T S

1–2 tbsp all-purpose flour

6 meaty slices osso bucco

2 lb 4 oz/1 kg fresh tomatoes, peeled, deseeded and diced or 2 x 14 oz/400 g cans chopped tomatoes

1–2 tbsp olive oil

9 oz/250 g very finely chopped onions

9 oz/250 g finely diced carrots

1 cup dry white wine

1 cup veal stock

6 large fresh basil leaves, torn

1 large garlic clove, very finely chopped

finely grated rind of 1 large lemon

finely grated rind of 1 orange

2 tbsp finely chopped fresh flat leaf parsley

salt and pepper

1 Put the flour in a plastic bag and season with salt and pepper. Add the osso bucco, a few pieces at a time, and shake until well coated. Remove and shake off the excess flour.

2 If using canned tomatoes, put them in a strainer and leave to drain.

3 Heat 1 tablespoon of the oil in a large flameproof casserole. Add the osso bucco and fry for 10 minutes on each slide until well browned. Remove from the pan.

4 Add 1–2 teaspoons more oil to the casserole if necessary. Add the onions and cook, stirring constantly, for about 5 minutes until soft. Stir in the carrots and cook until softened.

5 Add the tomatoes, wine, stock, and basil and return the osso bucco to the pan. Bring to a boil, then lower the heat., cover, and simmer for 1 hour. Check that the meat is tender with the tip of a knife. If not, continue cooking for 10 minutes and test again.

6 When the meat is tender, sprinkle with the garlic and lemon and orange rinds, re-cover, and cook over low heat for a further 10 minutes.

7 Taste and adjust the seasoning if necessary. Sprinkle with the parsley and serve immediately.

Basque Pork & Beans

Dried cannellini beans feature in many Italian, Spanish, French, and Greek stews and casseroles, especially during the winter.

NUTRITIONAL INFORMATION

Calories 240	Sugars 6g	
Protein 30g	Fat 4g	
Carbohydrate ...23g	Saturates 1g	

   15 mins   1½ hrs

SERVES 4–6

INGREDIENTS

7 oz/200 g dried cannellini beans, soaked in cold water overnight

olive oil, for frying

1 lb 5 oz/600 g boneless leg of pork, cut into 5 cm/2 inch chunks

1 large onion, sliced

3 large garlic cloves, crushed

14 oz/400 g can chopped tomatoes

2 green bell peppers, deseeded and sliced

finely grated rind of 1 large orange

salt and pepper

finely chopped fresh parsley, to garnish

1 Drain the cannellini beans and put in a large pan with fresh water to cover. Bring to a boil and boil rapidly for 10 minutes. Lower the heat and simmer for 20 minutes. Drain and set aside.

VARIATIONS

Any leftover beans and bell peppers can be used as a pasta sauce. Add sliced and fried chorizo sausage for a spicier dish.

2 Add enough oil to cover the base of a skillet in a very thin layer. Heat the oil over medium heat, add a few pieces of the pork, and fry on all sides until brown. Remove from the skillet and set aside. Repeat with the remaining pork.

3 Add 1 tablespoon oil to the skillet, if necessary, then add the onion and cook for 3 minutes. Stir in the garlic and cook for a further 2 minutes. Return the pork to the skillet.

4 Add the tomatoes and bring to a boil. Lower the heat, stir in the bell pepper slices, orange rind, and the drained beans. Season with salt and pepper to taste.

5 Transfer the contents of the pan to a casserole. Cover the casserole and cook in a preheated oven, 350°F/180°c, for 45 minutes until the beans and pork are both tender. Sprinkle with chopped fresh parsley and serve immediately straight from the casserole.

Country Pork with Onions

This rustic Mediterranean stew makes the most of inexpensive cuts that require slow cooking and robust flavoring.

NUTRITIONAL INFORMATION

Calories	335	Sugars	........10g
Protein	........35g	Fat	..........12g
Carbohydrate	...13g	Saturates	.......2g

15 mins   3¾–4¼ hrs

SERVES 4

INGREDIENTS

2 large pork shoulder

2 large garlic cloves, sliced

3 tbsp olive oil

2 carrots, finely chopped

2 celery stalks, finely chopped

1 large onion, finely chopped

2 fresh thyme sprigs, broken into pieces

2 fresh rosemary sprigs, broken into pieces

1 large bay leaf

1 cup dry white wine

1 cup water

20 pickling onions

salt and pepper

roughly chopped fresh flat leaf parsley, to garnish

1 Using the tip of a sharp knife, make slits all over the pork and insert the garlic slices.

2 Heat 1 tablespoon of the oil in a flameproof casserole over medium heat. Add the carrots, celery, and onion and cook, stirring occasionally, for about 10 minutes until softened.

3 Place the pork on top of the vegetables. Sprinkle the thyme and rosemary over the meat. Add the bay leaf, wine, and water and season with pepper.

4 Bring to a boil, then remove the casserole from the heat. Cover tightly and cook in a preheated oven, 325°F/160°C, for 3½ hours or until the meat is very tender.

5 Meanwhile, put the onions in a bowl, pour over boiling water to cover, and set aside for 1 minute. Drain, then slip off all the skins. Heat the remaining oil in a large, heavy skillet. Add the onions, partially cover, and cook over low heat for 15 minutes, shaking the pan occasionally, until the onions are just starting to turn golden in color.

6 When the pork is tender, add the onions to the casserole and return to the oven for a further 15 minutes. Remove the pork and onions from the casserole and keep warm.

7 Using a large metal spoon, skim off as much fat as possible from the surface of the cooking liquid. Strain the cooking liquid into a bowl, pressing down lightly to extract the flavor; reserve the strained vegetables. Adjust the seasoning.

8 Cut the pork from the bones, if wished, then arrange on a serving platter with the onions and strained vegetables. Spoon the sauce over the meat and vegetables. Garnish with parsley.

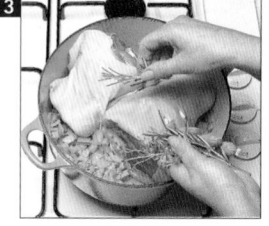  

Maltese Rabbit with Fennel

Rabbit is a popular ingredient in Malta. In some restaurants it features as the house specialty, rather than seafood as one might expect.

NUTRITIONAL INFORMATION

Calories	454	Sugars	.........3g
Protein	........36g	Fat	..........23g
Carbohydrate	...19g	Saturates	.......5g

🥘 15 mins   🕐 1¾ hrs

SERVES 4

INGREDIENTS

5 tbsp olive oil

2 large fennel bulbs, sliced

2 carrots, diced

1 large garlic clove, crushed

1 tbsp fennel seeds

about 4 tbsp all-purpose flour

2 wild rabbits, cut into pieces

1 cup dry white wine

1 cup water

bouquet garni of 2 fresh flat leaf parsley sprigs, 1 fresh rosemary sprig, and 1 bay leaf, tied in a 3 inch/7.5 cm piece of celery

salt and pepper

thick crusty bread, to serve

TO GARNISH

finely chopped fresh flat leaf parsley or cilantro

fresh rosemary sprigs

1 Heat 3 tablespoons of the olive oil in a large, flameproof casserole over medium heat. Add the fennel and carrots and cook, stirring occasionally, for 5 minutes. Stir in the garlic and fennel seeds and cook for a further 2 minutes or until the fennel is tender. Remove the fennel and carrots from the casserole with a slotted spoon and set aside.

2 Put the flour in a plastic bag and season with salt and pepper. Add 2 rabbit pieces and shake to lightly coat, then shake off any excess flour. Continue until all the pieces of rabbit are coated, adding more flour if necessary.

3 Add the remaining oil to the casserole. Fry the rabbit pieces for about 5 minutes on each side until golden brown, working in batches. Remove the rabbit from the casserole as it is cooked.

4 Pour in the wine and bring to a boil, stirring to scrape up all the sediment from the bottom. Return the rabbit pieces, fennel, and carrots to the casserole and pour in the water. Add the bouquet garni and season with salt and pepper to taste.

5 Bring to a boil. Lower the heat, cover, and simmer for about 1¼ hours until the rabbit is tender.

6 Discard the bouquet garni. Garnish with herbs and serve straight from the casserole with lots of bread to mop up the juices.

Azerbaijani Lamb Pilaf

This type of dish is popular in the Balkans, through Russia, to the Middle East. The saffron and pomegranate juice give it an exotic air.

NUTRITIONAL INFORMATION

Calories	399	Sugars	........19g
Protein	........25g	Fat	..........13g
Carbohydrate	...45g	Saturates	.......4g

 10 mins   50 mins

SERVES 4–6

I N G R E D I E N T S

2–3 tbsp vegetable oil

1 lb 7 oz/650 g boneless lamb shoulder, cut into 1 inch/2.5 cm cubes

2 onions, coarsely chopped

1 tsp ground cumin

1 cup risotto, long grain, or basmati rice

1 tbsp tomato paste

1 tsp saffron threads

scant ½ cup pomegranate juice (see Cook's Tip)

1½ pints/850 ml lamb or chicken stock or water

½ cup dried apricots or prunes, ready soaked and halved

2 tbsp raisins

salt and pepper

TO SERVE

2 tbsp chopped fresh mint

2 tbsp chopped fresh watercress

1 Heat the oil in a large flameproof casserole or wide pan over high heat. Add the lamb, in batches, and cook stirring and turning frequently, for about 7 minutes until lightly browned.

2 Add the onions, reduce the heat to medium-high, and cook for about 2 minutes until beginning to soften. Add the cumin and rice and cook, stirring to coat, for about 2 minutes until the rice is translucent. Stir in the tomato paste and the saffron threads.

3 Add the pomegranate juice and stock and bring to a boil, stirring. Stir in the apricots or prunes and raisins. Reduce the heat to low, cover, and simmer for 20–25 minutes until the lamb and rice are tender and the liquid is absorbed.

4 To serve, season to taste, sprinkle the chopped mint and watercress over the pilaf, and serve from the casserole.

COOK'S TIP

Pomegranate juice is available from Middle Eastern grocery stores. If you cannot find it, substitute unsweetened grape or apple juice.

Mumbar

This Middle Eastern dish is basically a long sausage coiled into a skillet to simmer. The baharat, or spice mix, is a typical flavoring.

NUTRITIONAL INFORMATION

Calories . . . . . . .256 Sugars 3g
Protein . . . . .25g Fat 12g
Carbohydrate . . .14g Saturates 5g

25 mins   40 mins

SERVES 6–8

INGREDIENTS

½ cup basmati rice

2lb/900 g finely ground lamb

1 small onion, finely chopped

3–4 garlic cloves, crushed

1 bunch of fresh flat leaf parsley, finely chopped

1 bunch of fresh cilantro finely chopped

2–3 tbsp tomato catsup

1 tbsp vegetable oil

pared rind and juice of 1 lime

3 cups hot lamb stock

salt and pepper

BAHARAT

2 tbsp black peppercorns

1 tbsp coriander seeds

2 tsp cloves

1½ tsp cumin seeds

1 tsp cardamom seeds

1 cinnamon stick, broken into small pieces

1 nutmeg

2 tbsp hot paprika

1 To make the baharat, grind the first 6 ingredients into a fine powder. Grate the whole nutmeg into the mix and stir in the paprika. Store in an airtight jar.

2 Bring a pan of salted water to a boil. Pour in the rice, return to a boil, then simmer until the rice is tender, but firm to the bite. Drain and rinse.

3 Place the lamb in a large bowl and break up with a fork. Add the onion, garlic, parsley, cilantro, catsup, and 1 teaspoon of the baharat. Stir in the cooked rice and season to taste. Squeeze the mixture to make it paste-like.

4 Divide into 4–6 pieces and roll each into a sausage 1 inch/2.5cm thick. Brush a 9–10 inch/23–25 cm skillet with the oil. Starting in the center of the skillet, coil the sausage pieces, joining each piece, to form 1 long coiled sausage.

5 Press lightly to make an even layer, then tuck the lime rind between the spaces of the coil. Add the lime juice, pour in the hot stock, and cover with a heatproof plate to keep in place.

6 Bring to a boil, then simmer for about 10 minutes. Cover and cook for a further 15 minutes. Drain and slide the sausage onto a serving plate. Sprinkle with a little more of the baharat to serve.

Red Pork Curry

Thai food has become so popular in recent years that most ingredients can be found in your local supermarket.

NUTRITIONAL INFORMATION

Calories	398	Sugars	........12g
Protein	........38g	Fat	...........9g
Carbohydrate	...47g	Saturates	.......3g

 15 mins   45 mins

SERVES 4–6

I N G R E D I E N T S

2 lb/900 g boned pork shoulder, sliced

3 cups coconut milk

2 fresh red chiles, deseeded and sliced

2 tbsp Thai fish sauce

2 tsp brown sugar

1 large red bell pepper, deseeded and sliced

6 kaffir lime leaves, shredded

½ bunch fresh mint leaves, shredded

½ bunch Thai basil leaves or Italian-style basil, shredded

cooked jasmine-scented or Thai fragrant rice, cooked and kept warm

RED CURRY PASTE

1 tbsp coriander seeds

2 tsp cumin seeds

2 tsp black or white peppercorns

1 tsp salt

5–8 dried hot red chiles

3–4 shallots, chopped

6–8 garlic cloves

2 inch/5 cm piece fresh galangal or ginger root, coarsely chopped

2 tsp kaffir lime rind or 2 kaffir lime leaves

1 tbsp ground red chili powder

1 tbsp shrimp paste

2 lemongrass stalks, thinly sliced

1 To make the red curry paste, grind the coriander seeds, cumin seeds, peppercorns, and salt to a fine powder in a mortar with a pestle. Add the chiles, 1 at a time, according to taste, until ground.

2 Put the shallots, garlic, galangal or ginger, kaffir lime rind or leaves, chili powder, and shrimp paste in a food processor. Process for about 1 minute. Add the ground spices and process again. Adding water, a few drops at a time, continue to process until a thick paste forms. Scrape into a bowl and stir in the lemongrass.

3 Put about half the red curry paste in a large deep heavy skillet with the pork. Cook over medium heat, stirring gently, for 2–3 minutes until the pork is evenly coated and begins to brown.

4 Stir in the coconut milk and bring to a boil. Cook, stirring frequently, for about 10 minutes. Reduce the heat, stir in the chiles, Thai fish sauce, and brown sugar, and simmer for about 20 minutes. Add the red bell pepper and simmer for a further 10 minutes.

5 Chop the lime leaves and add to the curry with half the mint and basil. Transfer to a serving dish, sprinkle with the remaining mint and basil, and serve with the rice.

Classic Beef Fajitas

Sizzling marinated strips of meat rolled up in soft flour tortillas with a tangy salsa are a real Mexican treat, perfect for relaxed entertaining.

NUTRITIONAL INFORMATION

Calories 623   Sugars 6g
Protein . . . . .36g   Fat 23g
Carbohydrate . . .72g   Saturates 7g

 45 mins   15–20mins

SERVES 4–6

I N G R E D I E N T S

1 lb 9 oz/700 g steak, cut into strips

6 garlic cloves, chopped

juice of 1 lime

pinch of mild chili powder

pinch of paprika

pinch of ground cumin

1–2 tbsp extra virgin olive oil

12 flour tortillas

vegetable oil, for frying

1–2 avocados, pitted, peeled, sliced, and tossed with lime juice

½ cup sour cream

salt and pepper

PICO DE GALLO SALSA

8 ripe tomatoes, diced

3 scallions, sliced

1–2 fresh green chiles, such as jalapeño or serrano, deseeded and chopped

3–4 tbsp chopped fresh cilantro

5–8 radishes, diced

ground cumin

1 Combine the beef with half the garlic, half the lime juice, the chili powder, paprika, cumin, and olive oil. Add salt and pepper, mix well, and marinate for at least 30 minutes at room temperature or up to overnight in the refrigerator.

2 To make the pico de gallo salsa, put the tomatoes in a bowl with the scallions, green chiles cilantro, and radishes. Season to taste with cumin, salt, and pepper. Set aside.

3 Heat the tortillas in a lightly greased nonstick skillet. Wrap in kitchen foil, as you work, to keep them warm.

4 Stir-fry the meat in a little oil over high heat until browned and just cooked through.

5 Serve the sizzling hot meat with the warm tortillas, the pico de gallo salsa, avocado, and sour cream for each person to make his or her own rolled up fajitas.

Ropa Vieja

Fill warmed tortillas with this tender, browned beef and a selection of crisp vegetables to make wonderful tacos.

NUTRITIONAL INFORMATION

Calories 495	Sugars 3g	
Protein 58g	Fat 27g	
Carbohydrate 5g	Saturates 10g	

 45 mins   2¼ hrs

SERVES 6

INGREDIENTS

3 lb 5 oz/1.5 kg stewing beef

beef stock

1 carrot, sliced

10 garlic cloves, sliced

2 tbsp vegetable oil

2 onions, thinly sliced

3–4 mild fresh green chiles, such as
  anaheim or poblano, deseeded and sliced

warmed flour tortillas, to serve

SALAD GARNISHES

3 ripe tomatoes, diced

8–10 radishes, diced

3–4 tbsp chopped fresh cilantro

4–5 scallions, chopped

1–2 limes, cut into wedges

2 Remove the pan from the heat and set the meat aside to cool in the liquid. When cool enough to handle, remove from the liquid and shred with your fingers and a fork.

3 Heat the oil in a large skillet. Add the remaining garlic, onions, and chiles and cook over low heat, stirring occasionally, until lightly colored. Remove from the skillet and set aside.

4 Increase the heat. Add the meat to the skillet and cook over medium-high heat until browned and crisp. Transfer to a warmed serving dish. Top with the onion mixture and surround with the tomatoes, radishes, cilantro, scallions, and lime wedges. Serve with warmed flour tortillas.

1 Put the meat in a large pan and cover with a mixture of stock and water. Add the carrot and half the garlic with salt and pepper to taste. Cover and bring to a boil, then reduce the heat to low. Skim the scum from the surface, then re-cover the pan, and cook the meat gently for about 2 hours until very tender.

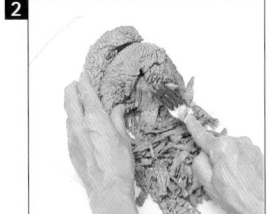

Michoacan Beef

This rich, smoky-flavored Mexican stew is delicious; leftovers make a great filling for tacos, too.

NUTRITIONAL INFORMATION

Calories 315	Sugars 6g	
Protein 41g	Fat 10g	
Carbohydrate . . .16g	Saturates 3g	

10 mins   2 hrs

SERVES 4–6

INGREDIENTS

about 3 tbsp all-purpose flour

2 lb 4 oz/1 kg stewing beef, cut into large bite-size pieces

2 tbsp vegetable oil

2 onions, chopped

5 garlic cloves, chopped

14 oz/400 g tomatoes, diced

1½ dried chipotle chiles, reconstituted, deseeded, and cut into thin strips, or a few shakes of bottled chipotle salsa

6¼ cups beef stock

12 oz/350 g green beans

pinch of sugar

salt and pepper

TO SERVE

simmered beans

cooked rice

COOK'S TIP

This is traditionally made with nopales, edible cacti, which give the dish a distinctive flavor. Look for them in specialist stores. For this recipe you need 12–14 oz/350–400 g canned or fresh nopales.

1 Place the flour in a large bowl and season with salt and pepper. Add the beef and toss to coat well. Remove from the bowl, shaking off the excess flour.

2 Heat the oil in a skillet and brown the meat briefly over high heat. Reduce the heat to medium, add the onions and garlic, and cook for 2 minutes.

3 Add the tomatoes, chiles, and stock, cover, and simmer over low heat for 1½ hours or until the meat is very tender, adding the green beans 15 minutes before the end of the cooking time. Skim off any fat that rises to the surface.

4 Transfer to individual bowls and serve with simmered beans and rice.

Spicy Pork with Prunes

Prunes add an earthy, wine flavor to this spicy stew.
Serve with tortillas or crusty bread to dip into the rich sauce.

NUTRITIONAL INFORMATION

Calories 352	Sugars 1g
Protein 39g	Fat 12g
Carbohydrate ...24g	Saturates 2g

8¼ hrs   3–4 hrs

SERVES 4–6

I N G R E D I E N T S

3 lb 5 oz/1.5 kg pork joint, such as leg
  or shoulder

juice of 2–3 limes

10 garlic cloves, chopped

3–4 tbsp mild chili powder

4 tbsp vegetable oil

2 onions, chopped

2¼ cups chicken stock

25 small tart tomatoes, roughly chopped

25 prunes, pitted

1–2 tsp sugar

pinch of ground cinnamon

pinch of ground allspice

pinch of ground cumin

salt

warmed corn tortillas, to serve

1 Combine the pork with the lime juice, garlic, chili powder, 2 tablespoons of oil, and salt. Set aside to marinate in the refrigerator overnight.

2 Remove the pork from the marinade. Wipe the pork dry with paper towels and reserve the marinade. Heat the remaining oil in a flameproof casserole and brown the pork evenly until just golden. Add the onions, the reserved marinade, and stock. Cover and cook in a preheated oven, 350°F/180°C, for about 2–3 hours until tender.

3 Spoon off fat from the surface of the cooking liquid and add the tomatoes. Continue to cook for about 20 minutes until the tomatoes are tender. Mash the tomatoes into a coarse purée. Add the prunes and sugar, then adjust the seasoning, adding cinnamon, allspice, and cumin to taste, as well as extra chili powder, if wished.

4 Increase the oven temperature to 400°F/200°C and return the meat and sauce to the oven for a further 20–30 minutes or until the meat has browned on top and the juices have thickened.

5 Remove the meat and set aside for a few minutes. Carefully carve it into thin slices and spoon the sauce over the top. Serve warm with corn tortillas.

Red Mole of Pork & Chiles

Plantain and sesame seeds add a delicious hint of sweetness to this fragrant stew of pork and mild chiles.

NUTRITIONAL INFORMATION

Calories 432   Sugars 9g
Protein . . . . .42g   Fat 21g
Carbohydrate . . .20g   Saturates 4g

15 mins   4 hrs

SERVES 6

INGREDIENTS

2 lb 12 oz/1.25 kg pork shoulder or lean side, cut into bite-size pieces

1 onion, chopped

1 garlic bulb

2 bay leaves

1–2 bouillon cubes

6 dried ancho chiles

6 guajillo chiles

3–5 ripe large flavorful tomatoes

¼ tsp ground cloves

¼ tsp ground allspice

6 tbsp sesame seeds, toasted

1 large ripe plantain or banana, peeled and diced

3 tbsp vegetable oil

6–8 waxy potatoes, cut into chunks

3 tbsp yerba santa, or a combination of chopped fresh mint, oregano, and cilantro

1 cinnamon stick

salt and pepper

1 Place the pork in a large pan with the onion, garlic, bay leaves, and salt and pepper. Fill with cold water to the top.

2 Bring to a boil, then reduce the heat to a slow simmer. Skim off the scum, then stir in the bouillon cubes. Cover and cook for about 3 hours until the meat is very tender.

3 Meanwhile, lightly roast the chiles in an ungreased heavy skillet until they just change color. Put them in a bowl and cover with boiling water. Cover and set aside for about 20–30 minutes until softened.

4 Roast the tomatoes in the skillet, to brown the bases, then char the tops under a hot broiler. Set aside to cool.

5 When the chiles are softened, remove the stems and seeds, then process them in a food processor or blender with enough liquid to make a paste. Add the roasted tomatoes, cloves, and allspice, with two-thirds of the sesame seeds and the plantain. Purée until smooth.

6 Remove the meat from the pan and reserve. Skim the fat from the surface of the stock.

7 Heat the oil in a pan, add the tomato paste mixture, and cook for about 10 minutes until thickened. Do not let it burn. Add the potatoes and the herbs with enough of the stock to keep the potatoes covered in sauce. Add the cinnamon stick.

8 Cover and cook until the potatoes are tender, then add the reserved meat, and heat through. Serve in bowls, sprinkled with the reserved sesame seeds.

Chile Verde

If tomatillos are not available, use fresh tomatoes and bottled green salsa instead, and add a good hit of lime juice at the end.

NUTRITIONAL INFORMATION

Calories ....433 Sugars 6g
Protein ....56g Fat 19g
Carbohydrate ....9g Saturates 4g

10 mins   1½ hrs

SERVES 4

INGREDIENTS

2 lb 4 oz/1 kg pork, cut into bite-
   size chunks

1 onion, chopped

2 bay leaves

1 garlic bulb, cut in half

1 bouillon cube

2 garlic cloves, chopped

1 lb/450 g oz fresh tomatillos, husks
   removed, cooked in a small amount of
   water until just tender, then chopped, or
   1 lb/450 g canned tomatillos

2 large fresh mild green chiles, such as
   anaheim, or a combination of 1 green bell
   pepper and 2 jalapeño chiles, deseeded
   and chopped

3 tbsp vegetable oil

1 cup pork or chicken stock

½ tsp mild chili powder

½ tsp cumin

4–6 tbsp chopped fresh cilantro,
   to garnish

TO SERVE

warmed flour tortillas

lime wedges

1 Place the pork in a large pan with the onion, bay leaves, and garlic bulb. Add water to cover and bring to a boil. Skim off the scum from the surface and add the bouillon cube, stirring well to mix and dissolve. Reduce the heat to very low and simmer gently for about 1½ hours or until the meat is very tender.

2 Meanwhile, put the chopped garlic in a blender or food processor with the tomatillos and green chiles and bell pepper, if using. Process to a purée.

3 Heat the oil in a pan, add the tomatillo mixture, and cook over medium-high heat for about 10 minutes or until thickened. Add the stock, chili powder, and cumin.

4 When the meat is tender, remove from the pan, and add to the sauce. Simmer gently to combine the flavors.

5 Garnish with the chopped cilantro and serve with warmed tortillas and lime wedges.

Meatballs in a Spicy Sauce

Called *albondigas* in Mexico, these tasty meatballs are set off brilliantly against the rich sauce and golden sweet potatoes.

NUTRITIONAL INFORMATION

Calories	.540	Sugars	.29g
Protein	.31g	Fat	.20g
Carbohydrate	.64g	Saturates	.6g

20 mins · 20 mins

SERVES 4

INGREDIENTS

8 oz/225 g ground pork

8 oz/225 g ground beef or lamb

6 tbsp cooked rice or finely crushed tortilla chips

1 egg, lightly beaten

1½ onions, finely chopped

5 garlic cloves, finely chopped

½ tsp ground cumin

pinch of ground cinnamon

2 tbsp raisins

2 tbsp vegetable oil, plus extra for frying

1 tbsp molasses sugar

1–2 tbsp apple or wine vinegar

14 oz/400 g can tomatoes, drained and chopped

1½ cups beef stock

1–2 tbsp mild chili or ancho chili powder

1 tbsp paprika

1 tbsp chopped fresh cilantro

1 tbsp chopped fresh parsley or mint

2 sweet potatoes, peeled and cut into small bite-size chunks

salt and pepper

grated cheese, to serve

1 Combine the meat with the rice or crushed tortilla chips, the egg, half the onion, half the garlic, the cumin, cinnamon, and raisins.

2 Divide the mixture into even-size pieces and roll into balls. Fry the balls in a nonstick skillet over medium heat, adding a tiny amount of oil, if necessary, to help them brown. Remove the balls from the pan and set aside. Wipe the skillet clean.

3 Place the molasses sugar in a blender or food processor with the vinegar, tomatoes, stock, chili powder, paprika, and remaining onion and garlic. Process together until blended, then stir in the chopped fresh herbs. Set aside.

4 Heat the oil in the cleaned skillet, add the sweet potatoes, and cook until tender and golden brown. Pour in the blended sauce and add the meatballs to the pan. Cook for about 10 minutes until the meatballs are heated through and the flavors have completely combined. Season with salt and pepper to taste. Serve immediately accompanied with freshly grated cheese.

Chili con Carne

Probably the best-known Mexican dish and one that is a great
favorite with all. The chili content can be increased to suit your taste.

NUTRITIONAL INFORMATION

Calories 443	Sugars 11g
Protein 48g	Fat 15g
Carbohydrate . . .30g	Saturates 4g

🥔 5 mins   🕐 2½ hrs

SERVES 4

INGREDIENTS

1 lb 10 oz/750 g lean braising or
  stewing steak

2 tbsp vegetable oil

1 large onion, sliced

2–4 garlic cloves, crushed

1 tbsp all-purpose flour

scant 2 cups tomato juice

14 oz/400 g can tomatoes

1–2 tbsp sweet chili sauce

1 tsp ground cumin

15 oz/425 g can red kidney beans, drained

½ teaspoon dried oregano

1–2 tbsp chopped fresh parsley

salt and pepper

chopped fresh herbs, to garnish

boiled rice and tortillas, to serve

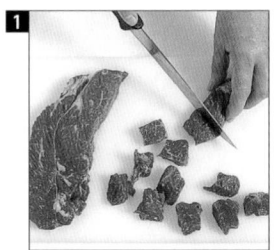 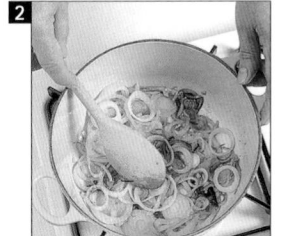 

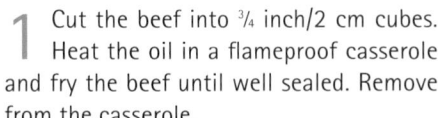

1 Cut the beef into ¾ inch/2 cm cubes. Heat the oil in a flameproof casserole and fry the beef until well sealed. Remove from the casserole.

2 Add the onion and garlic to the casserole and cook until lightly browned. Stir in the flour and cook for 1–2 minutes. Stir in the tomato juice and tomatoes and bring to a boil. Replace the beef and add the chili sauce, cumin, and seasoning. Cover and place in a preheated oven, 1325°F/160°C, for 1½ hours or until almost tender.

3 Stir in the beans, oregano, and parsley and adjust the seasoning. Cover the casserole and return to the oven for 45 minutes. Serve sprinkled with herbs and with boiled rice and tortillas.

COOK'S TIP

Because chili con carne requires quite a lengthy cooking time, it saves time and fuel to prepare double the quantity you need and freeze half of it to serve on another occasion. Thaw and use within 3–4 weeks.

Baked Ham with Sauce

A joint of cured ham or collar bacon is first par-boiled, then baked with a mustard topping. Serve hot or cold with this tangy Cumberland sauce.

NUTRITIONAL INFORMATION

Calories . . . . .414 Sugars 4g
Protein . . . . .70g Fat 13g
Carbohydrate . . . .4g Saturates 5g

  10 mins   5¾ hrs

SERVES 4–6

INGREDIENTS

4–6 lb/2–3 kg lean cured ham or prime collar joint of bacon

2 bay leaves

1–2 onions, quartered

2 carrots, thickly sliced

6 cloves

GLAZE

1 tbsp red currant jelly

1 tbsp wholegrain mustard

CUMBERLAND SAUCE

1 orange

3 tbsp red currant jelly

2 tbsp lemon or lime juice

2 tbsp orange juice

2–4 tbsp port

1 tbsp wholegrain mustard

TO GARNISH

salad greens

orange slices

 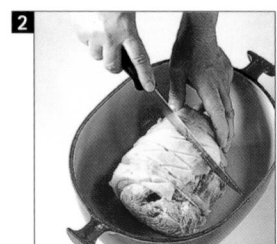 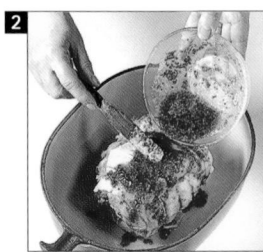

1 Put the meat in a large pan. Add the bay leaves, onion, carrots, and cloves and cover with cold water. Bring to a boil over low heat, cover, and simmer for half the cooking time. To calculate the cooking, time, allow 30 minutes per 1 lb 2 oz/500 g plus 30 minutes.

2 Drain the meat and remove the skin. Put the meat in a roasting pan and score the fat. To make the glaze, combine the ingredients and spread over the fat. Cook in a preheated oven, 350°F/ 180°C, for the remainder of the cooking time. Baste at least once.

3 To make the sauce, pare the rind from half the orange and cut into strips. Cook in boiling water for 3 minutes. Drain.

4 Place all the remaining sauce ingredients in a small pan and heat gently, stirring occasionally, until the red currant jelly dissolves. Add the orange rind strips and simmer gently for a further 3–4 minutes.

5 Slice the ham or bacon and place on a warmed serving platter. Garnish with salad greens and orange slices and serve with the Cumberland sauce.

Meatball Brochettes

Children will love these tasty meatballs on a skewer, which are economical and easy to make for the barbecue.

NUTRITIONAL INFORMATION

Calories 120   Sugars 2g
Protein ....17g   Fat 5g
Carbohydrate ....2g   Saturates 2g

1 hr   10 mins

SERVES 4

INGREDIENTS

1 oz/25 g cracked wheat

12 oz/350 g lean ground beef

1 onion, very finely chopped (optional)

1 tbsp tomato catsup

1 tbsp brown fruity sauce

1 tbsp chopped, fresh parsley

beaten egg, to bind

8 cherry tomatoes

8 white mushrooms

vegetable oil, to baste

8 bread finger rolls, to serve

1 Place the cracked wheat in a bowl and cover with boiling water. Set aside to soak for 20 minutes or until softened. Drain thoroughly and set aside to cool.

2 Place the soaked wheat, ground beef, onion, if using, catsup, brown fruity sauce, and chopped fresh parsley together in a mixing bowl and mix well until all the ingredients are well combined. Add a little beaten egg if necessary to bind the mixture together.

3 Using your hands, shape the meat mixture into 18 even-size balls. Set aside to chill in the refrigerator for 30 minutes.

4 Thread the meatballs onto 8 pre-soaked wooden skewers, alternating them with the cherry tomatoes and white mushrooms.

5 Brush the brochettes with a little oil and grill over hot coals, turning occasionally and brushing with a little more oil if the meat starts to dry out, for about 10 minutes until cooked through.

6 Transfer the brochettes to warm serving plates. Cut open the bread finger rolls and push the meat and vegetables off the skewer into the open rolls, using a fork.

Savory Hotpot

This hearty lamb stew is full of vegetables and herbs, and is topped with a layer of crisp, golden potato slices—a satisfying family meal.

NUTRITIONAL INFORMATION

Calories 365   Sugars 5g
Protein ....23g   Fat 11g
Carbohydrate ...48g   Saturates 4g

 15 mins   2 hrs

SERVES 4

INGREDIENTS

8 lean lamb shoulder chops or any lean
   stewing lamb

1–2 garlic cloves, crushed

2 lamb's kidneys (optional)

1 large onion, thinly sliced

1 leek, sliced

2–3 carrots, sliced

1 tsp chopped fresh tarragon or sage, or
   ½ tsp dried tarragon or sage

2 lb 4 oz/1 kg potatoes, thinly sliced

1¼ cups stock

2 tbsp margarine, melted, or
   1 tbsp vegetable oil

salt and pepper

chopped fresh parsley, to garnish

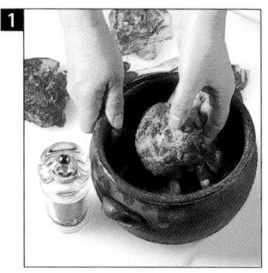 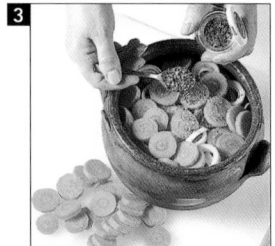 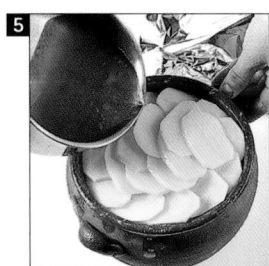

1 Trim any excess fat from the lamb, season well with salt and pepper, and arrange in a large casserole. Sprinkle with the garlic.

2 If using kidneys, remove the skin, halve, and cut out the cores. Chop into small pieces and sprinkle them over the lamb.

3 Place the vegetables over the lamb, allowing the pieces to slip in between the meat, then sprinkle with the herbs.

4 Arrange the potato slices on top of the meat and vegetables, in an overlapping pattern.

5 Bring the stock to a boil, season with salt and pepper to taste, then pour over the casserole.

6 Brush the potatoes with the melted margarine or vegetable oil, cover with greased foil or a lid, and cook in a preheated oven, 350°F/180°C, for 1½ hours.

7 Remove the foil or lid from the casserole, increase the temperature to 425°F/220°C and return the casserole to the oven for about 30 minutes until the potatoes are browned.

8 Garnish the hotpot with the chopped fresh parsley and serve immediately.

Steak in a Wine Marinade

Tenderloin, short loin, and round steak are all suitable cuts for this dish, although round steak retains the most flavor.

NUTRITIONAL INFORMATION

Calories 356   Sugars 2g
Protein ....41g   Fat 9g
Carbohydrate ....2g   Saturates 4g

🍲 3 hrs   🕐 15 mins

SERVES 4

INGREDIENTS

4 round steaks, about 9 oz/250 g each

2½ cups red wine

1 onion, quartered

2 tbsp Dijon mustard

2 garlic cloves, crushed

salt and pepper

4 large portobello mushrooms

olive oil for brushing

branch of fresh rosemary (optional)

1 Snip through the fat strip on the steaks in 3 places, so that the steak retains its shape when grilled.

2 Combine the red wine, onion, mustard, garlic, salt, and pepper. Lay the steaks in a shallow non-porous dish and pour over the marinade. Cover and chill in the refrigerator for 2–3 hours.

3 Remove the steaks from the refrigerator 30 minutes before you intend to cook them to let them come to room temperature. This is especially important if the steak is thick, so that it cooks more evenly and is not well done on the outside and raw in the middle.

4 Sear both sides of the steak—about 1 minute on each side—over a hot barbecue. If it is about 1 inch/2.5 cm thick, keep it over a hot barbecue and cook for about 4 minutes on each side. This will give a medium-rare steak—cook it more or less, to suit your taste. If the steak is a thicker cut, move it to a less hot part of the barbecue or further away from the coals. To test the readiness of the meat while cooking, simply press it with your finger—the more the meat yields, the less it is cooked.

5 Brush the mushrooms with the olive oil and cook them alongside the steak for 5 minutes, turning once. When you put the mushrooms on the grill put the rosemary branch, if using, in the fire to flavor the meat slightly.

6 Remove the steak and set aside to rest for 1–2 minutes before serving. Slice the mushrooms and serve immediately with the meat.

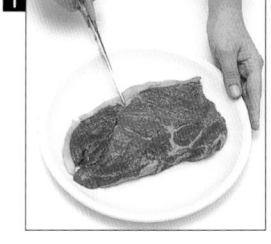

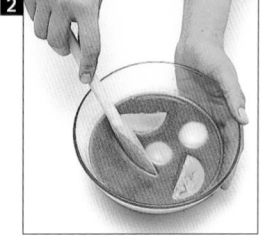

Beef & Potato Goulash

In this recipe, the potatoes are actually cooked in the goulash. For a change, you may prefer to substitute small, scrubbed new potatoes.

NUTRITIONAL INFORMATION

Calories	477	Sugars	........11g
Protein	........47g	Fat	..........16g
Carbohydrate	...39g	Saturates	......5g

 15 mins 2¼ mins

SERVES 4

INGREDIENTS

2 tbsp vegetable oil

1 large onion, sliced

2 garlic cloves, crushed

1 lb 10 oz/750 g lean stewing steak

2 tbsp paprika

14 oz/400 g canned chopped tomatoes

2 tbsp tomato paste

1 large red bell pepper, deseeded
  and chopped

2½ cups sliced mushrooms

2½ cups beef stock

1 lb 2 oz/500 g potatoes, cut into
  large chunks

1 tbsp cornstarch

salt and pepper

TO GARNISH

4 tbsp low-fat plain yogurt

paprika

chopped fresh parsley

1 Heat the oil in a large pan. Add the onion and garlic and cook over medium heat, stirring occasionally, for 3–4 minutes until softened.

2 Cut the steak into chunks, add to the pan, and cook over high heat for about 3 minutes until browned all over.

3 Lower the heat to medium and stir in the paprika. Add the tomatoes, tomato paste, bell pepper,. and mushrooms. Cook, stirring constantly, for 2 minutes.

4 Pour in the beef stock. Bring to a boil, stirring occasionally, then reduce the heat to low. Cover and simmer gently for about 1½ hours until the meat is cooked through and tender.

5 Add the potatoes, cover, and cook for a further 20–30 minutes until tender.

6 Blend the cornstarch with a little water and add to the pan, stirring until thickened and blended. Cook for 1 minute, then season with salt and pepper to taste. Top with the yogurt, sprinkle over the paprika and chopped fresh parsley, and serve immediately.

Ginger Beef with Chili

Serve these fruity, hot and spicy steaks with noodles.
Use a nonstick ridged skillet to cook with a minimum of fat.

NUTRITIONAL INFORMATION

Calories 179   Sugars 8g
Protein ....21g   Fat 6g
Carbohydrate ....8g   Saturates 2g

40 mins   10 mins

SERVES 4

I N G R E D I E N T S

4 lean beef steaks, such as round, short loin
  or tenderloin, 3½ oz/100 g each

2 tbsp ginger wine

1 inch/2.5 cm piece of fresh ginger root,
  finely chopped

1 garlic clove, crushed

1 tsp ground chili

1 tsp vegetable oil

salt and pepper

fresh red chile strips, to garnish

TO SERVE

freshly cooked noodles

2 scallions, shredded

RELISH

8 oz/225 g fresh pineapple

1 small red bell pepper

1 fresh red chile

2 tbsp light soy sauce

1 piece of preserved ginger in syrup,
  drained and chopped

1 Trim any excess fat from the steaks if necessary. Using a meat mallet or covered rolling pin, pound the steaks until they are ½ inch/1 cm thick. Season on both sides with salt and pepper to taste and place in a shallow dish.

2 Combine the ginger wine, fresh ginger root, garlic, and chili and pour over the meat. Cover with plastic wrap and chill for 30 minutes.

3 Meanwhile, make the relish. Peel and finely chop the pineapple and place it in a bowl. Halve, deseed, and finely chop the bell pepper and chile. Stir into the pineapple with the soy sauce and preserved ginger. Cover with plastic wrap and chill until required.

4 Brush a ridged skillet with the oil and heat until very hot. Drain the beef and add to the skillet, pressing down to seal. Lower the heat and cook for 5 minutes. Turn the steaks over and cook for a further 5 minutes.

5 Drain the steaks on paper towels and transfer to warmed serving plates. Garnish with chile strips and serve with noodles, scallions, and the relish.

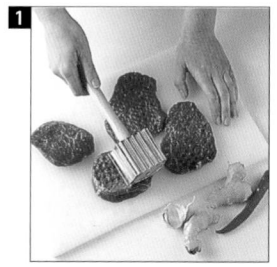

Lamb Couscous

Couscous is a dish that originated among the Berbers of North Africa. When steamed, it is a delicious plump grain, ideal for serving with stews.

NUTRITIONAL INFORMATION

Calories 537	Sugars 11g
Protein 32g	Fat 14g
Carbohydrate . . .73g	Saturates 4g

15 mins

35 mins

SERVES 4

INGREDIENTS

2 medium red onions, sliced

juice of 1 lemon

1 large red bell pepper, deseeded and thickly sliced

1 large green bell pepper, deseeded and thickly sliced

1 large orange bell pepper, deseeded and thickly sliced

pinch of saffron strands

cinnamon stick, broken

1 tbsp honey

1¼ cups vegetable stock

2 tsp olive oil

12 oz/350 g lean lamb fillet, trimmed and sliced

1 tsp harissa

7 oz/200 g can chopped tomatoes

15 oz/425 g can garbanzo beans, drained

2 cups precooked couscous

2 tsp ground cinnamon

salt and pepper

1 Toss the onions in the lemon juice and transfer to a pan. Stir in the bell peppers, saffron, cinnamon stick, and honey. Pour in the stock, bring to a boil, cover, and simmer for 5 minutes.

2 Meanwhile, heat the oil in a skillet and gently fry the lamb for 3–4 minutes until browned all over.

3 Using a slotted spoon, transfer the lamb to the pan with the onions and bell peppers. Season and stir in the harissa, tomatoes, and garbanzo beans. Mix thoroughly, bring back to a boil, and simmer, uncovered, for 20 minutes.

4 Soak the couscous, following the packet instructions. Bring a pan of water to a boil. Put the couscous in a steamer or cheesecloth-lined strainer over the pan of boiling water. Cover and steam.

5 Transfer the couscous to a serving platter and dust with ground cinnamon. Discard the cinnamon stick and spoon the stew over the couscous.

Spicy Mexican Beans

These stewed beans form the basis of many Mexican recipes. Don't add salt until the beans are tender—it prevents them from softening.

NUTRITIONAL INFORMATION

Calories	234	Sugars	.........6g
Protein	........11g	Fat	..........13g
Carbohydrate	...20g	Saturates	......2g

12 hrs   4 hrs

SERVES 4

INGREDIENTS

8 oz/225 g pinto beans or cannellini beans

1 large onion, sliced

2 garlic cloves, crushed

4 cups water

salt

chopped fresh cilantro or parsley,
   to garnish

BEAN STEW

1 large onion, sliced

2 garlic cloves, crushed

8 strips lean bacon, diced

2 tbsp oil

14 oz/400 g can chopped tomatoes

1 tsp ground cumin

1 tbsp sweet chili sauce

REFRIED BEANS

1 onion, chopped

2 garlic cloves, crushed

2 tbsp oil

1 Soak the beans in a bowl of cold water overnight. Drain the beans and put into a pan with the onion, garlic, and water, bring to a boil, cover, and simmer gently for 1½ hours. Stir well, add more boiling water, if necessary, and simmer, covered, for a further 1–1½ hours or until the beans are tender.

2 When the beans are tender, add salt to taste and continue to cook, uncovered, for about 15 minutes to let most of the liquid evaporate to form a thick sauce. Serve the basic beans hot, sprinkled with chopped cilantro or parsley. Alternatively, cool, then store in the refrigerator for up to 1 week.

3 To make a bean stew, fry the onion, garlic, and bacon for 3–4 minutes in the oil, add the other ingredients and basic beans, and bring to a boil. Cover and simmer for 30 minutes, then season.

4 To make refried beans, fry the onion and garlic in the oil until golden brown. Add a quarter of the basic beans with a little of their liquid and mash. Continue adding and mashing the beans, while simmering gently until thick. Adjust the seasoning and serve hot.

Sweet & Sour Venison Stir-Fry

Venison is super-lean and low in fat, so it's the perfect choice for a healthy diet. Cooked quickly with crisp vegetables, it's ideal in a stir-fry.

NUTRITIONAL INFORMATION

Calories	.219	Sugars	.18g
Protein	.23g	Fat	.5g
Carbohydrate	.20g	Saturates	.1g

 15 mins   15 mins

SERVES 4

I N G R E D I E N T S

1 bunch of scallions

1 red bell pepper

3½ oz/100 g snow peas

3½ oz/100 g baby corn cobs

12 oz/350 g lean venison steak

1 tbsp vegetable oil

1 garlic clove, crushed

1 inch/2.5 cm piece fresh ginger root, finely chopped

3 tbsp light soy sauce, plus extra for serving

1 tbsp white wine vinegar

2 tbsp dry sherry

2 tsp honey

8 oz/225 g can pineapple pieces in natural juice, drained

½ cup bean sprouts

freshly cooked rice, to serve

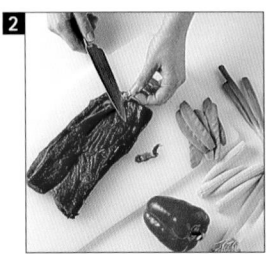

VARIATION

For a nutritious meal-in-one, cook 8 oz/225 g egg noodles in boiling water for 3–4 minutes. Drain and add to the pan in step 4, with the pineapple and bean sprouts. Add an extra 2 tablespoons soy sauce with the pineapple and bean sprouts.

1 Cut the scallions into 1 inch/2.5 cm pieces. Halve and deseed the red bell pepper and cut it into 1 inch/2.5 cm pieces. Trim the snow peas and baby corn cobs.

2 Trim any fat from the meat and cut it into thin strips. Heat the oil in a large skillet or wok until hot and stir-fry the meat, garlic, and ginger for 5 minutes.

3 Add the scallions, red bell pepper, snow peas, and baby corn cobs, then stir in the soy sauce, vinegar, sherry, and honey. Stir-fry for a further 5 minutes.

4 Carefully stir in the pineapple pieces and bean sprouts and cook for a further 1–2 minutes to heat through. Serve with freshly cooked rice and extra soy sauce for dipping.

Lasagna Verde

The sauce in this delicious baked pasta dish can also be used as an alternative sauce for Spaghetti Bolognese.

NUTRITIONAL INFORMATION

Calories 619   Sugars 7g
Protein . . . . .29g   Fat 45g
Carbohydrate . . .21g   Saturates 19g

   1¾ hrs    55 mins

SERVES 4

I N G R E D I E N T S

1 quantity Pasticcio Sauce (see page 646)

1 tbsp olive oil

8 oz/225 g lasagna verde

butter, for greasing

Béchamel Sauce (see page 6)

⅔ cup freshly grated Parmesan cheese

salt

salad greens, tomato salad, or black olives, to serve

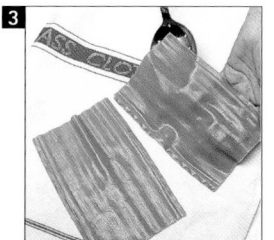

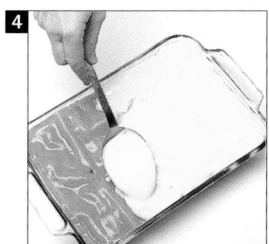

1 Make the meat sauce as described on page 646, but cook for 10–12 minutes longer than the time given, in an uncovered pan, to allow the excess liquid to evaporate. It needs to be reduced to the consistency of a thick paste.

2 Have ready a large pan of boiling, salted water and add the olive oil. Drop the pasta sheets into the boiling water, a few at a time, and return the water to a boil before adding further pasta sheets. If you are using fresh lasagna, cook the sheets for a total of 8 minutes. If you are using dried or partly pre-cooked pasta, cook it according to the the instructions on the packet.

3 Remove the pasta sheets from the pan with a slotted spoon. Spread them out in a single layer on clean, damp dish towels to prevent them from sticking.

4 Grease a rectangular casserole, about 10–11 inches/25–28 cm long. To assemble the dish, spoon a little of the meat sauce into the prepared dish, cover with a layer of lasagna, then spoon over a little Béchamel sauce, and sprinkle with some of the cheese. Continue making layers in this way, covering the final layer of lasagna sheets with the remaining Béchamel sauce.

5 Sprinkle on the remaining cheese and bake in a preheated oven, 375°F/190°C, for 40 minutes or until the sauce is golden brown and bubbling. Serve with salad greens, a tomato salad, or a bowl of black olives.

Pasticcio

A recipe that has both Italian and Greek origins, this dish
may be served hot or cold, cut into thick, satisfying squares.

NUTRITIONAL INFORMATION

Calories 590	Sugars 8g	
Protein 34g	Fat 39g	
Carbohydrate ...23g	Saturates 16g	

 35 mins 1¼ hrs

SERVES 6

INGREDIENTS

8 oz/225 g fusilli, or other short
  pasta shapes

1 tbsp olive oil

4 tbsp heavy cream

salt

fresh rosemary sprigs, to garnish

meat Sauce

2 tbsp olive oil, plus extra for brushing

1 onion, thinly sliced

1 red bell pepper, deseeded and chopped

2 garlic cloves, chopped

1 lb 6 oz/625 g lean ground beef

14 oz/400 g canned chopped tomatoes

½ cup dry white wine

2 tbsp chopped fresh parsley

1¾ oz/50 g canned anchovies, drained
  and chopped

salt and pepper

TOPPING

1¼ cups plain yogurt

3 eggs

pinch of freshly grated nutmeg

⅔ cup freshly grated Parmesan cheese

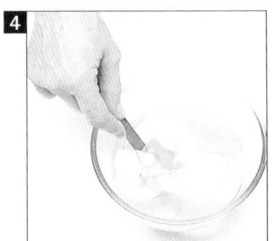

1 To make the sauce, heat the oil in a large skillet and fry the onion and bell pepper for 3 minutes. Stir in the garlic and cook for 1 minute. Add the beef and cook, stirring frequently, until browned.

2 Add the tomatoes and wine, stir well, and bring to a boil. Simmer, uncovered, for 20 minutes or until the sauce is fairly thick. Stir in the parsley and anchovies and season to taste.

3 Bring a large pan of lightly salted water to a boil. Add the oil and pasta, bring back to a boil, and cook for 8–10 minutes until tender, but still firm to the bite. Drain, then transfer to a bowl. Stir in the cream and set aside.

4 To make the topping, beat the yogurt with the eggs and nutmeg until well combined and season with salt and pepper to taste.

5 Brush a large, shallow casserole with oil. Spoon in half of the pasta mixture and cover with half of the meat sauce. Repeat these layers, then spread the topping evenly over the final layer. Sprinkle the grated Parmesan cheese evenly on top.

6 Bake in a preheated oven, 375°F/ 190°C, for 25 minutes or until the topping is golden brown and bubbling. Garnish with sprigs of fresh rosemary and serve immediately.

Meatballs in Red Wine Sauce

A different twist is given to this traditional and ever-popular pasta dish with a rich, but subtle, sauce.

NUTRITIONAL INFORMATION

Calories	811	Sugars	. . . . .7g
Protein	. . . . .30g	Fat	. . . . .43g
Carbohydrate	. . .76g	Saturates	. . . . . .12g

 45 mins   1½ hrs

SERVES 4

I N G R E D I E N T S

⅔ cup milk

2 cups fresh white bread crumbs

2 tbsp butter

generous ½ cup olive oil

3¼ cups sliced oyster mushrooms

2½ tbsp whole-wheat flour

scant 1 cup beef stock

⅔ cup red wine

4 tomatoes, peeled and chopped

1 tbsp tomato paste

1 tsp brown sugar

1 tbsp finely chopped fresh basil

12 shallots, chopped

1lb/450 g ground steak

1 tsp paprika

1lb/450 g dried egg tagliatelle

salt and pepper

fresh basil sprigs, to garnish

1 Pour the milk into a bowl, add the bread crumbs, and set aside to soak for 30 minutes.

2 Heat half the butter and 4 tablespoons of the oil in a pan. Fry the mushrooms for 4 minutes, then stir in the flour, and cook for 2 minutes. Add the stock and wine and simmer for 15 minutes. Add the tomatoes, tomato paste, sugar, and basil. Season and simmer for 30 minutes.

3 Mix the shallots, steak, and paprika with the bread crumbs and season to taste. Shape the mixture into 14 meatballs.

4 Heat 4 tablespoons of the remaining oil and the rest of the butter in a large skillet. Fry the meatballs, turning frequently, until brown all over. Transfer to a deep casserole, pour over the red wine and mushroom sauce, cover, and bake in a preheated oven, 350°F/180°C, for 30 minutes.

5 Bring a pan of lightly salted water to a boil. Add the pasta and the remaining oil, bring back to a boil, and cook for 8–10 minutes or until tender, but still firm to the bite. Drain and transfer to a serving dish. Remove the casserole from the oven and cool for 3 minutes. Pour the meatballs and sauce onto the pasta, garnish, and serve.

Polenta with Rabbit Stew

Polenta can be served fresh, as in this dish, or it can be cooled, then sliced, and broiled or fried.

NUTRITIONAL INFORMATION

Calories	726	Sugars	.........2g
Protein	........61g	Fat	..........25g
Carbohydrate	...55g	Saturates	.......6g

   20 mins   1¾ minutes

SERVES 4

I N G R E D I E N T S

butter, for greasing

2⅔ cups polenta or cornmeal

1 tbsp coarse sea salt

5 cups water

4 tbsp olive oil

4 lb 8 oz/2 kg rabbit joints

3 garlic cloves, peeled

3 shallots, sliced

⅔ cup red wine

1 carrot, sliced

1 celery stalk, sliced

2 bay leaves

1 fresh rosemary sprig

3 tomatoes, peeled and diced

¾ cup pitted black olives

salt and pepper

1 Grease a large casserole with a little butter. Mix the polenta, salt, and water in a large pan, whisking well to prevent lumps from forming. Bring to a boil over medium heat and boil for 10 minutes, stirring vigorously and constantly. Turn into the prepared casserole and bake in a preheated oven, 375°F/190°C, for 40 minutes.

2 Meanwhile, heat the oil in a large pan and add the rabbit pieces, garlic, and shallots. Fry for 10 minutes until browned.

3 Stir in the wine and cook for a further 5 minutes.

4 Add the carrot, celery, bay leaves, rosemary, tomatoes, olives, and 1¼ cups water. Cover the pan and simmer for about 45 minutes or until the rabbit is tender. Season with salt and pepper to taste.

5 To serve, spoon or cut a portion of polenta and place on each serving plate. Top with a ladleful of rabbit stew. Serve immediately.

Potato Kibbeh

Kibbeh is a Middle Eastern dish, traditionally made with cracked wheat, lamb, and spices. Serve with tahini, salad, and Middle Eastern bread.

NUTRITIONAL INFORMATION

Calories	600	Sugars	.........4g
Protein	........20g	Fat	..........35g
Carbohydrate	...53g	Saturates	.......8g

40 mins   20 mins

SERVES 4

INGREDIENTS

1 cup bulgur

12 oz/350 g mealy potatoes, diced

2 small eggs

2 tbsp butter, melted

pinch of ground cumin

pinch of ground coriander

pinch of grated nutmeg

salt and pepper

vegetable oil, for deep-frying

STUFFING

6 oz/175 g ground lamb

1 small onion, chopped

1 tbsp pine nuts

1 oz/25 g dried apricots, chopped

pinch of grated nutmeg

pinch of ground cinnamon

1 tbsp chopped fresh cilantro

2 tbsp lamb stock

1 Put the bulgur in a bowl and pour in boiling water to cover. Set aside to soak for 30 minutes until the water has been absorbed and the bulgur has swollen.

2 Meanwhile, cook the diced potatoes in a pan of boiling water for 10 minutes or until cooked through. Drain and mash until smooth.

3 Add the bulgur to the mashed potatoes with the eggs, melted butter, cumin, coriander, and nutmeg. Mix well and season with salt and pepper to taste.

4 To make the stuffing, dry-fry the lamb for 5 minutes, add the onion, and cook for a further 2–3 minutes. Add the remaining stuffing ingredients and cook for 5 minutes until the lamb stock has been absorbed. Let the mixture cool slightly, then divide into 8 portions. Roll each one into a ball.

5 Divide the potato mixture into 8 portions and flatten each into a round. Place a portion of stuffing in the center of each round. Shape the coating around the stuffing to encase it.

6 Heat the oil in deep-fryer to 350°F/180°C or until a cube of bread browns in 30 seconds. Cook the kibbeh for 5–7 minutes until golden brown. Drain well and serve immediately.

Meatballs in Spicy Sauce

These meatballs are delicious served with plenty of warm crusty bread to "mop up" the spicy sauce.

NUTRITIONAL INFORMATION

Calories 95   Sugars 2.7g
Protein . . . . .4.5g   Fat 5.8g
Carbohydrate . . .6.6g   Saturates 2.3g

 5 mins   1¼ hrs

SERVES 4

I N G R E D I E N T S

8 oz/225 g mealy potatoes, diced

8 oz/225 g ground beef or lamb

1 onion, finely chopped

1 tbsp chopped fresh cilantro

1 celery stalk, finely chopped

2 garlic cloves, crushed

2 tbsp butter

1 tbsp vegetable oil

salt and pepper

chopped fresh cilantro, to garnish

S A U C E

1 tbsp vegetable oil

1 onion, finely chopped

2 tsp brown sugar

14 oz/400 g canned chopped tomatoes

1 fresh green chile, chopped

1 tsp paprika

⅔ cup vegetable stock

2 tsp cornstarch

1 Cook the diced potatoes in a pan of boiling water for 25 minutes until cooked through. Drain well and transfer to a large mixing bowl. Mash until smooth.

2 Add the ground beef or lamb, onion, cilantro, celery, and garlic and mix together well.

3 Bring the mixture together with your hands and roll it into 20 small balls.

4 To make the sauce, heat the vegetable oil in a pan and sauté the onion for 5 minutes. Add the remaining sauce ingredients and bring to a boil, stirring constantly. Lower the heat and simmer for 20 minutes.

5 Meanwhile, heat the butter and oil for the meatballs in a heavy skillet. Add the meatballs in batches and cook, turning frequently, for 10–15 minutes until browned all over. Keep warm while cooking the remainder. Serve the meatballs in a warm, shallow casserole with the sauce poured around them and garnished with the fresh cilantro.

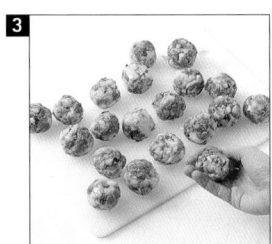

Potato, Beef & Peanut Pot

The spicy peanut sauce in this recipe will complement almost any meat; the dish is just as delicious made with chicken or pork.

NUTRITIONAL INFORMATION

Calories ....559 Sugars 5g
Protein ....35g Fat 37g
Carbohydrate ...24g Saturates 13g

 5 mins   1 hr

SERVES 4

INGREDIENTS

1 tbsp vegetable oil

5 tbsp butter

1 lb/450 g lean steak, cut into thin strips

1 onion, halved and sliced

2 garlic cloves, crushed

1 lb 5 oz/600 g waxy potatoes, cubed

½ tsp paprika

4 tbsp crunchy peanut butter

2½ cups beef stock

4 tbsp unsalted peanuts

2 tsp light soy sauce

2 oz/55 g sugar snap peas

1 red bell pepper, deseeded and sliced

fresh parsley sprigs, to garnish (optional)

1 Heat the oil and butter in a flameproof casserole.

2 Add the steak strips and cook them gently for about 3–4 minutes, stirring and turning the meat until it is sealed on all sides.

3 Add the onion and garlic and cook for a further 2 minutes, stirring constantly.

4 Add the potato cubes and cook for 3–4 minutes or until they begin to brown slightly.

5 Stir in the paprika and peanut butter, then gradually stir in in the beef stock. Bring the mixture to a boil, stirring frequently.

6 Finally, add the peanuts, soy sauce, sugar snap peas, and red bell pepper.

7 Cover and cook over low heat for 45 minutes or until the beef is cooked right through.

8 Garnish the dish with parsley sprigs, if desired, and serve immediately.

COOK'S TIP
Serve this dish with plain boiled rice or noodles, if you wish.

Potato & Meat Phyllo Packets

These small packets are perfect for special occasions. Crisp pastry encases a tasty potato and beef filling, cooked in red wine.

NUTRITIONAL INFORMATION

Calories 388	Sugars 5g
Protein 15g	Fat 12g
Carbohydrate ...53g	Saturates 5g

 10 mins   35 mins

SERVES 4

INGREDIENTS

8 oz/225 g waxy potatoes, finely diced

1 tbsp vegetable oil

4 oz/115 g ground beef

1 leek, sliced

1 small yellow bell pepper, deseeded and finely diced

1⅔ cups sliced white mushrooms

1 tbsp all-purpose flour

1 tbsp tomato paste

6 tbsp red wine

6 tbsp beef stock

1 tbsp chopped fresh rosemary

8 oz/225 g phyllo pastry, thawed if frozen

2 tbsp butter, melted

salt and pepper

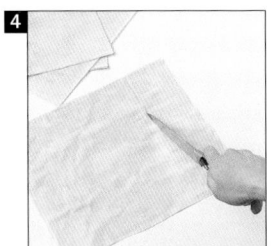

1 Cook the diced potatoes in a pan of boiling water for 5 minutes. Drain and set aside.

2 Meanwhile, heat the oil in a pan and cook the ground beef, leek, yellow bell pepper, and mushrooms over low heat for 5 minutes.

3 Stir in the flour and tomato paste and cook for 1 minute. Gradually add the red wine and beef stock, stirring to thicken. Add the chopped rosemary, season to taste with salt and pepper, and set aside to cool slightly.

4 Lay 4 sheets of phyllo pastry on a counter or board. Brush each sheet with butter and lay a second layer of phyllo on top. Trim the sheets to make four 8 inch/20 cm squares.

5 Brush the edges of the pastry with a little butter. Spoon a quarter of the beef mixture into the center of each square. Bring up the corners and the sides of the squares to form a packet, scrunching the edges together. Make sure that the packets are well sealed by pressing the pastry together, otherwise the filling will leak.

6 Place the packets on a cookie sheet and brush with butter. Bake in a preheated oven, 350°F, for 20 minutes. Serve hot.

Beef with Bean Sprouts

A quick and easy stir-fry for any day of the week, this simple beef recipe is a good one-pan main dish.

NUTRITIONAL INFORMATION

Calories	.544	Sugars	.8g
Protein	.39g	Fat	.21g
Carbohydrate	.55g	Saturates	.5g

 5 mins 15 mins

SERVES 4

INGREDIENTS

1 bunch of scallions, thinly sliced lengthwise

2 tbsp sunflower oil

1 garlic clove, crushed

1 tsp finely chopped fresh ginger root

1 lb 2 oz/500 g tender beef, cut into thin strips

1 large red bell pepper, deseeded and sliced

1 small fresh red chile, deseeded and chopped

6 cups fresh bean sprouts

1 small lemongrass stalk, finely chopped

2 tbsp smooth peanut butter

4 tbsp coconut milk

1 tbsp rice vinegar

1 tbsp soy sauce

1 tsp brown sugar

9 oz/250 g medium egg noodles

salt and pepper

1 Set aside some of the sliced scallions for the garnish. Heat the sunflower oil in a heavy skillet or wok over high heat. Add the remaining scallions, the garlic, and ginger and stir-fry for 2–3 minutes until softened. Add the beef strips and stir-fry for 4–5 minutes until they are evenly browned.

2 Add the red bell pepper and stir-fry for a further 3–4 minutes. Add the chile and bean sprouts and stir-fry for 2 minutes. Combine the lemongrass, peanut butter, coconut milk, vinegar, soy sauce, and sugar, then stir the mixture into the wok.

3 Meanwhile, cook the egg noodles in lightly salted boiling water for 4 minutes or according to the packet instructions. Drain and stir into the skillet or wok, tossing to mix evenly.

4 Season with salt and pepper to taste. Sprinkle the reserved scallion slices over the stir-fry, and serve hot.

Beef Satay

Satay recipes vary throughout the East, but these little beef skewers are a classic version of the traditional dish.

NUTRITIONAL INFORMATION

Calories 489   Sugars 14g
Protein . . . . .38g   Fat 31g
Carbohydrate . . .17g   Saturates 8g

2¼ hrs   15 mins

SERVES 4

INGREDIENTS

1 lb 2 oz/500 g beef tenderloin

2 garlic cloves, crushed

¾ inch/2 cm piece of fresh ginger root, finely grated

1 tbsp brown sugar

1 tbsp dark soy sauce

1 tbsp lime juice

2 tsp sesame oil

1 tsp ground coriander

1 tsp ground turmeric

½ tsp chili powder

chopped cucumber and red bell pepper, to serve

PEANUT SAUCE

1¼ cups coconut milk

8 tbsp crunchy peanut butter

½ small onion, grated

2 tsp brown sugar

½ tsp chili powder

1 tbsp dark soy sauce

1 Cut the beef into ½ inch/1 cm cubes and place in a large bowl.

2 Add the garlic, ginger, sugar, soy sauce, lime juice, sesame oil, ground coriander, turmeric, and chili powder. Mix well to coat the pieces of meat evenly. Cover with plastic wrap and set aside to marinate in the refrigerator for at least 2 hours, or overnight.

3 To make the peanut sauce, place all the ingredients in a heavy pan and stir over medium heat until boiling. Remove from the heat and keep warm.

4 Thread the beef cubes onto bamboo skewers. Cook the skewers under a preheated broiler for 3–5 minutes, turning often, until golden. Alternatively, grill over hot coals. It is important to cook the beef quickly, so make sure the broiler or barbecue is very hot before you begin to cook. Serve the skewers with the peanut sauce and garnish with chopped cucumber and red bell pepper pieces.

Beef with Lemongrass

Colorful bell peppers help to complete this delicately flavored stir-fry steeped in lemongrass and ginger.

NUTRITIONAL INFORMATION

Calories	230	Sugars	.........4g
Protein	........26g	Fat	..........12g
Carbohydrate	....6g	Saturates	.......3g

🧊 5 mins   🕐 8 mins

SERVES 4

INGREDIENTS

1 lb 2 oz/500 g lean beef tenderloin

2 tbsp vegetable oil

1 garlic clove, finely chopped

1 lemongrass stalk, finely shredded

2 tsp finely chopped fresh
   ginger root

1 red bell pepper, deseeded and
   thickly sliced

1 green bell pepper, deseeded and
   thickly sliced

1 onion, thickly sliced

2 tbsp lime juice

salt and pepper

boiled noodles or rice, to serve

1 If you have time, place the beef in the freezer for 30 minutes beforehand. This helps firm it up, which makes it easier to slice very thinly. Cut the beef into long, thin strips, cutting across the grain.

2 Heat the oil in a large skillet or wok over high heat. Add the garlic and stir-fry for 1 minute.

3 Add the beef and stir-fry for a further 2–3 minutes until lightly colored. Stir in the lemongrass and ginger and remove the skillet or wok from the heat.

4 Remove the beef from the skillet or wok and set aside. Add the bell peppers and onion to the skillet or wok and stir-fry over high heat for 2–3 minutes until the onions are just turning golden brown and slightly softened.

5 Return the beef to the skillet or wok, stir in the lime juice, and season to taste with salt and pepper. Serve immediately with noodles or rice.

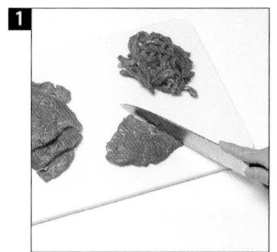

COOK'S TIP

When preparing lemongrass, take care to remove the outer layers, which can be tough and fibrous. Use only the center, tender part, which has the finest flavor.

Red-Hot Beef with Cashews

Hot and spicy, these quick-cooked beef strips are very tempting.
Serve them with lots of plain rice and cucumber slices to offset the heat.

NUTRITIONAL INFORMATION

Calories	257	Sugars 1g
Protein	........32g	Fat 13g
Carbohydrate	....3g	Saturates 4g

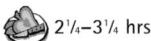 2¼–3¼ hrs   10 mins

SERVES 4

INGREDIENTS

1 lb 2 oz/500 g boneless, lean beef sirloin, thinly sliced

1 tsp vegetable oil

1 tsp sesame oil

4 tbsp unsalted cashew nuts

1 scallion, thickly sliced diagonally

cucumber slices, to garnish

MARINADE

1 tbsp sesame seeds

1 garlic clove, chopped

1 tbsp finely chopped fresh ginger root

1 fresh red bird-eye chile, chopped

2 tbsp dark soy sauce

1 tsp red curry paste

1 Cut the beef into ½ inch/1 cm wide strips. Place them in a large, nonmetallic bowl.

2 To make the marinade, dry-fry the sesame seeds in a heavy pan over medium heat for 2–3 minutes.

3 Place the seeds in a mortar with the garlic, ginger, and chile and grind to a smooth paste with a pestle. Add the soy sauce and curry paste and mix well.

4 Spoon the paste over the beef strips and toss well to coat the meat evenly. Cover and set aside to marinate in the refrigerator for 2–3 hours or overnight.

5 Heat a heavy skillet or griddle until very hot and brush with vegetable oil. Add the beef strips and cook quickly, turning frequently, until lightly browned. Remove from the heat and spoon into a pile on a warmed serving dish.

6 Heat the sesame oil in a small pan and fry the cashew nuts until golden. Add the scallions and stir-fry for 30 seconds. Sprinkle the mixture onto the beef and serve, garnished with cucumber.

Hot Beef & Coconut Curry

The heat of the chiles in this red-hot curry is balanced and softened by the coconut milk, producing a creamy-textured and lavishly spiced dish.

NUTRITIONAL INFORMATION

Calories	230	Sugars	.........6g
Protein	........29g	Fat	..........10g
Carbohydrate	....8g	Saturates	.......3g

 10 mins   45 mins

SERVES 4

I N G R E D I E N T S

1¾ cups coconut milk

2 tbsp Thai red curry paste

2 garlic cloves, crushed

1lb 2 oz/500 g braising steak

2 kaffir lime leaves, shredded

3 tbsp kaffir lime juice

2 tbsp Thai fish sauce

1 large fresh red chile, deseeded and sliced

½ tsp ground turmeric

2 tbsp chopped fresh basil leaves

2 tbsp chopped fresh cilantro leaves

salt and pepper

shredded coconut, to garnish

boiled rice, to serve

1 Place the coconut milk in a large pan and bring to a boil. Lower the heat and simmer gently over low heat for about 10 minutes until the milk has thickened. Stir in the red curry paste and garlic and simmer for a further 5 minutes.

2 Cut the beef into ¾ inch/2 cm chunks, add to the pan, and bring to a boil, stirring. Lower the heat and add the lime leaves, lime juice, fish sauce, chile,

turmeric, and ½ teaspoon salt. Cover the pan and simmer gently for a further 20–25 minutes until the meat is tender and cooked through, adding a little water if the sauce looks too dry.

3 Stir in the basil and cilantro and adjust the seasoning with salt and pepper to taste. Transfer to a warmed serving dish, sprinkle with coconut, and serve with boiled rice.

COOK'S TIP

This recipe uses one of the larger, milder red chile peppers—either fresno or Dutch—simply because they give more color to the dish. If you prefer to use small Thai, or bird-eye, chiles, you'll still need only 1 as they are much hotter.

Beef Toppers

Beef burgers need never be dull when they
are accompanied by one of these tasty toppings.

NUTRITIONAL INFORMATION

Calories	537	Sugars 13g
Protein	........60g	Fat 25g
Carbohydrate	...19g	Saturates 8g

1 hr   10–20 mins

SERVES 4

INGREDIENTS

1 lb 9 oz/700 g lean ground beef

1 onion, finely chopped

2 tbsp Worcestershire sauce

salt and pepper

sesame rolls, toasted, to serve

SAVORY MUSHROOMS

1⅔ cups sliced white mushrooms

1 tbsp soy sauce

1 tbsp Worcestershire sauce

GUACAMOLE

1 avocado

1 garlic clove

1 tbsp lemon juice

1 tbsp tomato relish

BARBECUE SAUCE

3 tbsp brown fruity sauce

3 tbsp tomato catsup

1 tsp wholegrain mustard

1 tbsp honey

1 To make the savory mushrooms, combine all the ingredients and set aside to marinate for at least 30 minutes.

2 To make the guacamole, peel, pit, and mash the avocado. Combine it with the remaining ingredients, cover, and chill in the refrigerator.

3 To make the barbecue sauce, combine all the ingredients, cover, and chill.

4 To make the beefburgers, combine the ground beef, onion, and Worcestershire sauce and season to taste with salt and pepper. Divide the mixture into 6 portions and pat each into a neat round, about ½ inch/1 cm thick. Cover and chill in the refrigerator for at least 30 minutes.

5 Grill over hot coals for 5–10 minutes on each side. Serve the burgers in the rolls, with your chosen topping spooned on top.

Boozy Beef Steaks

A simple marinade flavored with whiskey or brandy
gives plain steaks a fabulous flavor for very little effort.

NUTRITIONAL INFORMATION

Calories 371   Sugars 5g
Protein . . . . .48g   Fat 14g
Carbohydrate . . . .6g   Saturates 6g

2¼ hrs   6–12 mins

SERVES 4

INGREDIENTS

4 beef steaks

4 tbsp whiskey or brandy

2 tbsp soy sauce

1 tbsp molasses sugar

pepper

fresh parsley sprigs, to garnish

TO SERVE

slices of tomato

garlic bread

1 Make a few cuts in the edge of fat on each steak, using a sharp knife or kitchen scissors. This will prevent the meat from curling as it cooks.

2 Place the meat in a shallow, nonmetallic dish.

3 Combine the whiskey or brandy, soy sauce, sugar, and pepper to taste in a small bowl, stirring until the sugar has dissolved. Pour the marinade over the steak, turning to coat. Cover with plastic wrap and set aside to marinate in the refrigerator for at least 2 hours.

4 Drain the steak. Grill over hot coals, searing the meat over the hottest part of the barbecue for approximately 2 minutes on each side.

5 Move the steak to an area of the barbecue with slightly less intense heat (usually the sides) and cook for a further 4–10 minutes on each side, depending on how well done you like your steaks. Test the meat is cooked by inserting the tip of a knife into the meat—the juices will run from red when the meat is still rare, to clear as it becomes well cooked.

6 Meanwhile, lightly grill the slices of tomato for 1–2 minutes.

7 Transfer the meat and the tomatoes to warmed serving plates. Garnish each with a sprig of fresh parsley and serve immediately with garlic bread.

Surf & Turf Kabobs

This dish originated in Australia. The name refers to the shrimp from the sea—the "surf"—and the meat from the land—the "turf."

NUTRITIONAL INFORMATION

Calories	186	Sugars	.........0g
Protein	........20g	Fat	...........11g
Carbohydrate	....2g	Saturates	.......2g

🕒 35 mins   🕐 5–10 mins

SERVES 4

I N G R E D I E N T S

1 lb/450 g round or sirloin steak

18 raw shrimp

M A R I N A D E

5 tbsp oyster sauce

1 tbsp soy sauce

3 tbsp lemon juice

4 tbsp sunflower oil

1 With a sharp knife, cut the steaks into 24 even-size pieces and place them in a nonmetallic dish.

2 Peel and devein the shrimp, leaving the tails attached.

3 To make the marinade, combine the oyster sauce, soy sauce, lemon juice, and sunflower oil in a small bowl. Pour the mixture over the meat, turning to coat, and set aside to marinate for 15 minutes.

4 Add the shrimp to the marinade, toss to coat, and marinate for 5 minutes.

5 Remove the steak cubes and shrimp from the marinade, reserving the marinade for basting. Thread the meat onto metal or pre-soaked wooden skewers, alternating the steak with the shrimp. (Pre-soaking wooden skewers helps to prevent them from burning.)

6 Grill the kabobs over hot coals for 5–10 minutes, basting with the reserved marinade and turning frequently.

7 Transfer the kabobs to warmed serving plates and serve immediately.

VARIATION

Other shellfish, such as lobster and crab, can be added to the skewers. These kabobs are also delicious marinated in and basted with a herb, garlic, and oil marinade.

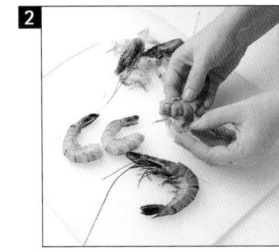

Beef with Exotic Mushrooms

Choose fairly thick steaks for this dish—it will be easier to cut a pocket in the side of each one.

NUTRITIONAL INFORMATION

Calories 414	Sugars 0g
Protein 49g	Fat 24g
Carbohydrate 1g	Saturates 13g

10 mins   6–12 mins

SERVES 4

INGREDIENTS

4 tenderloin or short loin steaks

2 tbsp butter

1–2 garlic cloves, crushed

5½ oz/150 g mixed exotic mushrooms

2 tbsp chopped fresh parsley

TO SERVE

salad greens

cherry tomatoes, halved

1 Place the steaks on a cutting board and using a sharp knife, cut a pocket in the side of each steak.

2 To make the stuffing, heat the butter in a skillet, add the garlic, and cook gently for about 1 minute.

3 Add the mushrooms to the skillet and cook gently for 4–6 minutes until tender. Stir in the parsley.

4 Divide the mushroom mixture into 4 and insert a portion into the pocket of each steak. Seal the pocket closed with a toothpick. If preparing ahead, let the mixture cool before stuffing the steaks.

5 Grill the steaks over hot coals, searing the meat over the hottest part of the barbecue for about 2 minutes on each side. Move the steaks to an area with slightly less intense heat (usually the sides) and grill for a further 4–10 minutes on each side, depending on how well done you like your steaks.

6 Transfer the steaks to serving plates and remove the toothpicks. Serve with salad greens and cherry tomatoes.

COOK'S TIP

Exotic mushrooms, such as shiitake, oyster, and chanterelle, are now readily available in supermarkets. Look for boxes of mixed exotic mushrooms, which are usually cheaper than buying the different types individually.

Roasted Red Pork

This red-glazed, sweet and tender pork, of Chinese origin, is a colorful addition to many stir-fries, salads, and soups.

NUTRITIONAL INFORMATION

Calories	276	Sugars	.........5g
Protein	........34g	Fat	..........13g
Carbohydrate	....7g	Saturates	.......4g

8¼ hrs   1 hrs

SERVES 4

INGREDIENTS

1 lb 5 oz/600 g pork tenderloin

red chile flower, to garnish

Napa cabbage, shredded to serve

MARINADE

2 garlic cloves, crushed

1 tbsp grated fresh ginger root

1 tbsp light soy sauce

1 tbsp Thai fish sauce

1 tbsp rice wine

1 tbsp hoisin sauce

1 tbsp sesame oil

1 tbsp palm sugar or brown sugar

½ tsp Chinese five-spice powder

a few drops red food coloring (optional)

1 Combine all the ingredients for the marinade and spread the mixture over the pork, turning to coat evenly. Place in a large dish, cover, and set aside in the refrigerator to marinate overnight.

2 Place a rack in a roasting pan, then half-fill the pan with boiling water. Lift the pork from the marinade and place on the rack. Reserve the marinade for later.

3 Roast in a preheated oven, 425°F/220°C, for about 20 minutes. Baste with the reserved marinade, then lower the heat to 350°F/180°C and continue roasting for a further 35–40 minutes, basting occasionally with the marinade, until the pork is a rich reddish brown and thoroughly cooked.

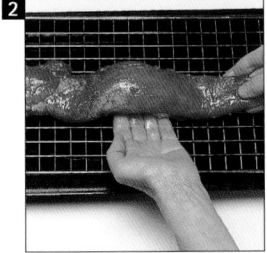

4 Transfer the pork to a cutting board and cut into even slices. Arrange the slices on a bed of shredded Napa cabbage on a serving platter, garnish with a red chile flower, and serve immediately.

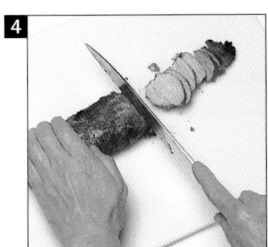

COOK'S TIP

The pork may also be broiled. Cut the meat into slices or strips and coat in the marinade, then arrange on a foil-lined broiler pan and broil under high heat, turning occasionally and basting with marinade.

Pork with Soy & Sesame

Thai cooks are fond of adding sweet flavors to meat, as in this unusual pork dish, with soy and garlic to balance the sweetness of the honey.

NUTRITIONAL INFORMATION

Calories ....322 Sugars 8g
Protein ....35g Fat 14g
Carbohydrate ...13g Saturates 14g

40 mins   35 mins

SERVES 4

I N G R E D I E N T S

2 pork tenderloins, about 9½ oz/275 g each

2 tbsp dark soy sauce

2 tbsp honey

2 garlic cloves, crushed

1 tbsp sesame seeds

1 onion, thinly sliced and pushed out
   into rings

1 tbsp seasoned all-purpose flour

sunflower oil, for frying

crisp salad, to serve

1 Trim the pork tenderloins and place them in a wide nonmetallic dish.

2 Combine the soy sauce, honey, and garlic. Spread this mixture over the pork, turning the meat to coat it evenly. Set aside to marinate for 30 minutes.

3 Lift the pork into a roasting pan or shallow ovenproof dish. Sprinkle evenly with sesame seeds.

4 Roast the pork in a preheated oven, 400°F/200°C, for about 20 minutes, spooning over any juices. Cover loosely with foil to prevent over-browning and roast for a further 10–15 minutes until the meat is thoroughly cooked.

5 Meanwhile, dip the onion rings in the flour and shake off the excess. Heat the oil and fry the onion rings until golden and crisp, turning occasionally.

6 Remove the pork from the oven and set aside for 5 minutes, then cut into slices. Serve the slices on a bed of crisp salad, garnished with fried onion rings.

COOK'S TIP

This pork is also excellent served cold, and it's a good choice for picnics, especially served with a spicy sambal or chili relish.

Spicy Fried Ground Pork

A warmly spiced dish, this is ideal for a quick family meal. Just cook fine egg noodles for an accompaniment while the meat sizzles.

NUTRITIONAL INFORMATION

Calories 278	Sugars 4g
Protein 28g	Fat 16g
Carbohydrate 7g	Saturates 4g

 5 mins   15 mins

SERVES 4

I N G R E D I E N T S

2 garlic cloves

3 shallots

2 tbsp sunflower oil

2 tsp finely chopped fresh
  ginger root

1 lb 2 oz/500 g lean ground pork

2 tbsp Thai fish sauce

1 tbsp dark soy sauce

1 tbsp red curry paste

4 dried kaffir lime leaves, crumbled

4 plum tomatoes, chopped

3 tbsp chopped fresh cilantro

salt and pepper

boiled fine egg noodles, to serve

TO GARNISH

fresh cilantro sprigs

COOK'S TIP

Dried kaffir lime leaves are a useful pantry ingredient as they can be crumbled easily straight into quick dishes such as this. If you prefer to use fresh kaffir lime leaves, shred them finely and add to the dish.

1 Peel and finely chop the garlic and shallots. Heat the oil in a wok over a medium heat. Add the garlic, shallots, and ginger and stir-fry for about 2 minutes. Stir in the pork and continue stir-frying until golden brown.

2 Stir in the fish sauce, soy sauce, curry paste, and lime leaves and stir-fry for a further 1–2 minutes over high heat.

3 Add the chopped tomatoes and cook, stirring occasionally, for a further 5–6 minutes.

4 Stir in the chopped cilantro and season to taste with salt and pepper. Serve hot, spooned onto boiled fine egg noodles, garnished with cilantro sprigs.

Thai-Spiced Sausages

These mildly spiced little sausages are a good choice for a buffet meal.
They can be made a day in advance, and are equally good hot or cold.

NUTRITIONAL INFORMATION

Calories 206   Sugars 0g
Protein ....22g   Fat 11g
Carbohydrate ....4g   Saturates 2g

15 mins   8–10 mins

SERVES 4

INGREDIENTS

14 oz/400 g lean ground pork

4 tbsp cooked rice

1 garlic clove, crushed

1 tsp Thai red curry paste

1 tsp ground black pepper

1 tsp ground coriander

½ tsp salt

3 tbsp lime juice

2 tbsp chopped fresh cilantro

3 tbsp peanut oil

coconut sambal or soy sauce, to serve

1 Place the pork, rice, garlic, curry paste, pepper, ground coriander, salt, lime juice, and chopped cilantro in a bowl and knead together with your hands to mix evenly.

2 Use your hands to shape the mixture into 12 small sausage shapes. If you can buy sausage casings, fill the casings and twist at intervals.

3 Heat the oil in a large skillet over medium heat. Add the sausages, in batches if necessary, and fry for 8–10 minutes, turning them over occasionally, until they are evenly golden brown. Serve hot with a coconut sambal or soy sauce.

COOK'S TIP

These sausages can also be served as an appetizer— shape the mixture into slightly smaller shapes to make about 16 bite-size sausages. Serve them with a soy dip.

Thai-Style Burgers

If your family likes to eat burgers, try these—they have a much more interesting flavor than conventional hamburgers.

NUTRITIONAL INFORMATION

Calories	358	Sugars	.........1g
Protein	........23g	Fat	..........29g
Carbohydrate	....2g	Saturates	.......5g

15 mins   6–8 mins

SERVES 4

INGREDIENTS

1 small lemongrass stalk

1 small fresh red chile, deseeded

2 garlic cloves, peeled

2 scallions

7 oz/200 g closed-cup mushrooms

14 oz/400 g ground pork

1 tbsp Thai fish sauce

3 tbsp chopped fresh cilantro

sunflower oil, for frying

2 tbsp mayonnaise

1 tbsp lime juice

salt and pepper

TO SERVE

4 sesame hamburger rolls

shredded Napa cabbage

1 Place the lemongrass, chile, garlic, and scallions in a food processor and process to a smooth paste. Add the mushrooms and process until very finely chopped.

2 Add the ground pork, fish sauce, and cilantro. Season to taste with salt and pepper, then divide the mixture into 4 equal portions, and shape with lightly floured hands into flat burger shapes.

3 Heat the oil in a heavy skillet over medium heat. Add the burgers and fry for 6–8 minutes until well cooked or as you like them.

4 Meanwhile, mix the mayonnaise with the lime juice. Split the hamburger rolls and spread the lime-flavored mayonnaise on the cut surfaces. Add a few shredded Napa cabbage greens, top with a burger, and sandwich together. Serve immediately, while still hot.

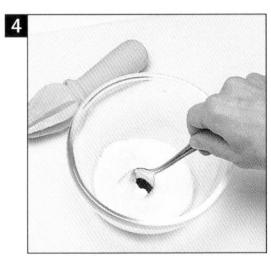

COOK'S TIP

You can add a spoonful of your favourite relish to each burger, or alternatively, add a few pieces of crisp pickled vegetables for a change of texture.

Red Lamb Curry

This curry uses the typically red-hot chili flavor of Thai red curry paste, made with dried red chilies, to give it a warm, russet-red color.

NUTRITIONAL INFORMATION

Calories	363	Sugars	........11g
Protein	........29g	Fat	..........19g
Carbohydrate	...21g	Saturates	.......6g

5 mins

35–40 mins

SERVES 4

INGREDIENTS

1 lb 2 oz/500 g boneless lean
    leg of lamb

2 tbsp vegetable oil

1 large onion, sliced

2 garlic cloves, crushed

2 tbsp red curry paste

⅔ cup coconut milk

1 tbsp brown sugar

1 large red bell pepper, deseeded and
    thickly sliced

½ cup lamb or beef stock

1 tbsp Thai fish sauce

2 tbsp lime juice

8 oz/225 g can water chestnuts, drained

2 tbsp fresh cilantro, chopped

2 tbsp fresh basil, chopped

salt and pepper

boiled jasmine rice, to serve

fresh basil leaves, to garnish

 1 Trim the meat and cut it into 1¼ inch/3 cm cubes. Heat the oil in a large skillet or wok over high heat and stir-fry the onion and garlic for 2–3 minutes to soften. Add the meat and stir-fry until lightly browned.

2 Stir in the curry paste and cook for a few seconds, then add the coconut milk and sugar and bring to a boil. Reduce the heat and simmer for 15 minutes, stirring occasionally.

3 Stir in the red bell pepper, stock, fish sauce, and lime juice, cover, and continue simmering for a further 15 minutes or until the meat is tender.

4 Add the water chestnuts, cilantro, and basil, adjust the seasoning to taste. Serve with jasmine rice garnished with fresh basil leaves.

COOK'S TIP

This curry can also be made with other lean red meats. Try replacing the lamb with trimmed duck breasts or pieces of lean braising beef.

Red Wine Lamb Skewers

Use the best quality red wine you can afford. Instead of using fresh herbs, you can add a bouquet garni to the marinade.

NUTRITIONAL INFORMATION

Calories	353	Sugars	.........5g
Protein	........24g	Fat	..........21g
Carbohydrate	....7g	Saturates	.......6g

2½ hrs   8–10 mins

SERVES 4

INGREDIENTS

1 lb/450 g lean lamb

12 pearl onions or shallots

12 white mushrooms

MARINADE

⅔ cup red wine

4 tbsp olive oil

2 tbsp brandy (optional)

1 onion, sliced

1 bay leaf

fresh thyme sprig

2 fresh parsley sprigs

TO SERVE

salad greens

cherry tomatoes

1 Carefully trim away any excess fat from the lamb. Cut the lamb into large pieces.

2 To make the marinade, combine the wine, oil, brandy, onion, bay leaf, and thyme and parsley sprigs in a nonmetallic dish.

3 Add the meat and toss to coat. Cover the dish with plastic wrap and set aside to marinate in the refrigerator for at least 2 hours or preferably overnight.

4 Bring a pan of water to a rolling boil, drop in the unpeeled pearl onions, and blanch them for 3 minutes. Drain and refresh under cold water, and then drain again. Trim the onions and remove their skins.

5 Remove the meat from the marinade, reserving the liquid for basting. Thread the meat onto skewers, alternating with the pearl onions and mushrooms.

6 Grill the kabobs over hot coals for 8–10 minutes, turning and basting the meat and vegetables with the reserved marinade a few times.

7 Transfer the kabobs to warmed serving plates and serve with fresh salad greens and cherry tomatoes.

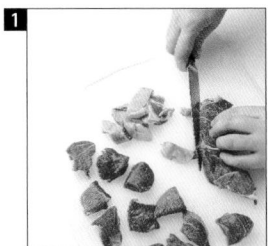

VARIATION

This recipe also works well with beef. Bacon rolls can also be added to the skewers, if you like.

Lamb & Black Bean Burritos

Stir-fried marinated lamb strips are paired with earthy black beans in these tasty filled tortillas.

NUTRITIONAL INFORMATION

Calories 551   Sugars 4g
Protein . . . . .45g   Fat 19g
Carbohydrate . . .52g   Saturates 7g

4¼ hrs   15–20 mins

SERVES 4

INGREDIENTS

1 lb 5 oz/650 g lean lamb

3 garlic cloves, finely chopped

juice of ½ lime

½ tsp mild chili powder

½ tsp ground cumin

pinch of dried oregano

1–2 tbsp extra virgin olive oil

14 oz/400 g cooked or canned black beans, seasoned with cumin, salt and pepper

4 large flour tortillas

2–3 tbsp chopped fresh cilantro

salsa of your choice

salt and pepper

1 Slice the lamb into thin strips, then combine with the garlic, lime juice, chili powder, cumin, oregano, and olive oil. Season with salt and pepper. Set aside to marinate in the refrigerator for 4 hours.

2 Warm the black beans with a little water in a pan.

3 Heat the tortillas in an ungreased nonstick skillet, sprinkling them with a few drops of water as they heat; wrap the tortillas in a clean dish cloth as you work to keep them warm. Alternatively, heat through in a stack in the skillet, alternating the top and bottom tortillas so that they warm evenly.

4 Stir-fry the lamb in a heavy nonstick skillet over high heat until browned on all sides. Remove from the heat.

5 Spoon some of the beans and browned meat into a tortilla, sprinkle with cilantro, then top with salsa, and roll up. Repeat with the remaining tortillas and serve immediately.

VARIATION
Add a spoonful or two of cooked rice to each burrito.

Carnitas

In this classic Mexican dish, pieces of pork are first simmered to make them meltingly tender, then browned until irresistibly crisp.

NUTRITIONAL INFORMATION

Calories 236   Sugars 1g
Protein . . . . .36g   Fat 9g
Carbohydrate . . . .3g   Saturates 3g

 45 mins   2½ hrs

SERVES 4–6

I N G R E D I E N T S

2 lb 4 oz/1 kg pork, such as lean side

1 onion, chopped

1 garlic bulb, cut in half

½ tsp ground cumin

2 meat bouillon cubes

2 bay leaves

vegetable oil, for frying

salt and pepper

fresh chile strips, to garnish

TO SERVE

cooked rice

refried beans (see page 643)

salsa of your choice

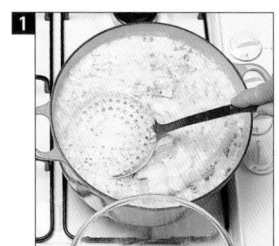
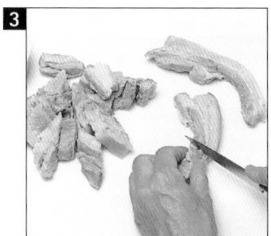

1 Place the pork in a heavy pan with the onion, garlic, cumin, bouillon cubes, and bay leaves. Add just enough water to cover. Bring to a boil, then reduce the heat to very low. Skim off the foam and scum that forms on the surface of the liquid.

2 Simmer very gently for about 2 hours or until the meat is cooked through and tender. Remove the pan from the heat and set the meat aside to cool in the cooking liquid.

3 Remove the meat from the pan with a slotted spoon. Cut off any rind (roast separately to make cracklings). Cut the meat into bite-size pieces and sprinkle with salt and pepper to taste. Reserve 1¼ cups of the cooking liquid.

4 Brown the meat in a heavy skillet for about 15 minutes to cook out the fat. Add the reserved cooking liquid and reduce. Cover and cook the meat for a further 15 minutes, turning the meat occasionally.

5 Transfer the meat to a serving dish, garnish with chile strips, and serve with rice, refried beans, and salsa.

Simmered Medley

A big pot of "cocido" is warming on a cold day, great for a family meal.
Serve with a selection of several salsas and a stack of corn tortillas.

NUTRITIONAL INFORMATION

Calories	555	Sugars	........17g
Protein	........47g	Fat	..........33g
Carbohydrate	...19g	Saturates	......12g

🧊 10 mins   🕐 2¼ hrs

SERVES 6–8

I N G R E D I E N T S

2 lb/900 g boneless pork

2 bay leaves

1 onion, chopped

8 garlic cloves, finely chopped

2 tbsp chopped fresh cilantro

1 carrot, thinly sliced

2 celery stalks, diced

2 chicken bouillon cubes

½ chicken, cut into portions

4–5 ripe tomatoes, diced

½ tsp mild chili powder

grated rind of ¼ orange

¼ tsp ground cumin

juice of 3 oranges

1 zucchini, cut into bite-size pieces

¼ cabbage, thinly sliced and blanched

1 apple, cut into bite-size pieces

about 10 prunes, pitted

¼ tsp ground cinnamon

pinch of ground ginger

2 hard chorizo sausages, about 12 oz/350 g
   in total, cut into bite-size pieces

salt and pepper

rice, tortillas, and salsa, to serve

1 Combine the pork, bay leaves, onion, garlic, cilantro, carrot, and celery in a large pan and fill with cold water. Bring to a boil, skim off the scum on the surface. Reduce the heat and simmer for 1 hour.

2 Add the bouillon cubes to the pan, with the chicken, tomatoes, chili powder, orange rind, and cumin. Cook for a further 45 minutes or until the chicken is tender. Spoon off the fat that forms on the top.

3 Add the orange juice, zucchini, cabbage, apple, prunes, cinnamon, ginger, and chorizo. Simmer for a further 20 minutes or until the zucchini is soft and tender and the chorizo is completely cooked through.

4 Season the stew with salt and pepper to taste. Serve immediately with rice, tortillas, and salsa.

Traditional Provençal Daube

It isn't sunny all year round in the Mediterranean. In the winter, when the fierce winds blow, warming hearty stews are welcome.

NUTRITIONAL INFORMATION

Calories	.312	Sugars	.4g
Protein	.21g	Fat	.12g
Carbohydrate	.20g	Saturates	.3g

4½ hrs   3½–4 hrs

SERVES 4–6

INGREDIENTS

1 lb 9 oz/700 g boneless lean stewing beef, such as leg, cut into 2 inch/5 cm pieces

1¾ cups full-bodied dry red wine

2 tbsp olive oil

4 large garlic cloves, crushed

4 shallots, thinly sliced

9 oz/250 g unsmoked lardons

5–6 tbsp all-purpose flour

9 oz/250 g large crimini mushrooms, sliced

14 oz/400 g can chopped tomatoes

large bouquet garni of 1 bay leaf, 2 dried thyme sprigs, and 2 fresh parsley sprigs, tied in a 3 inch/7.5 cm piece of celery

2 inch/5 cm strip of dried orange rind (optional)

2 cups beef stock

1¾ oz/50 g can anchovy fillets in oil

2 tbsp capers in brine, drained and rinsed

2 tbsp red wine vinegar

2 tbsp finely chopped fresh parsley

salt and pepper

1 Place the stewing beef in a nonmetallic bowl with the wine, olive oil, half the garlic, and the shallots. Cover and set aside to marinate for at least 4 hours, stirring occasionally.

2 Meanwhile, place the lardons in a pan of water, bring to a boil, and simmer for 10 minutes. Drain.

3 Place 4 tablespoons of the flour in a bowl and stir in about 2 tablespoons water to make a thick paste. Cover with plastic wrap and set aside.

4 Strain the marinated beef, reserving the marinade. Pat the beef dry and toss in seasoned flour.

5 Arrange a layer of lardons, mushrooms, and tomatoes in a large flameproof casserole, then add a layer of beef. Continue layering until all the ingredients are used, tucking in the bouquet garni and orange rind, if using.

6 Pour in the beef stock and reserved marinade. Spread the flour paste around the rim of the casserole. Press on the lid to make a tight seal (make more paste if necessary).

7 Cook in a preheated oven, 325°F/ 160°C, for 2½ hours. Meanwhile, drain the anchovies, then mash with the capers and remaining garlic in a mortar with a pestle.

8 Remove the casserole, break the seal, and stir in the mashed anchovies, vinegar, and parsley. Re-cover and continue cooking for 1–1½ hours until the meat is tender. Taste and adjust the seasoning and serve immediately.

Vitello Tonnato

This classic dish of cold, thinly sliced veal with a creamy tuna sauce makes the most luxurious hot-weather meal.

NUTRITIONAL INFORMATION

Calories . . . . .205 Sugars 0g
Protein . . . . .3g Fat 8g
Carbohydrate . . . .0g Saturates 2g

 10 hrs   1¼–1½ hrs

SERVES 6–8

INGREDIENTS

1 boned and rolled piece of veal leg, about 2 lb/900 g boned weight

olive oil

salt and pepper

TUNA MAYONNAISE

5½ oz/150 g can tuna in olive oil

2 large eggs

about 3 tbsp lemon juice

olive oil

TO GARNISH

8 black olives, pitted and halved

1 tbsp capers in brine, rinsed and drained

finely chopped fresh flat leaf parsley

lemon wedges

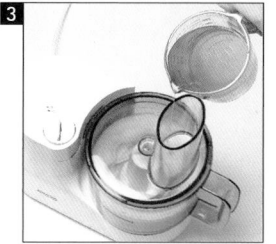

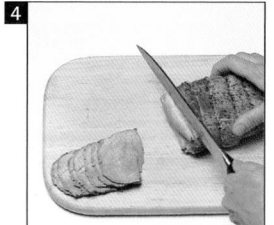

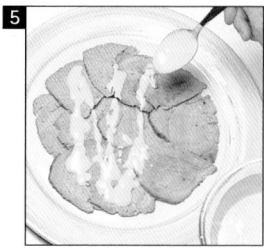

1 Rub the veal all over with olive oil and pepper and place in a roasting pan. Cover the meat with a piece of foil if there isn't any fat on it, then roast in a preheated oven, 450°F/230°C, for about 10 minutes. Lower the temperature to 350°F/180°C and continue roasting for a further 1 hour for medium or 1¼ hours for well-done. Set the veal aside to cool completely, reserving any juices in the roasting pan.

2 Drain the tuna, reserving the oil. Blend the eggs in a food processor with 1 teaspoon of the lemon juice and a pinch of salt. Add olive oil to the tuna oil to make up to 1¼ cups.

3 With the motor running, add the oil to the eggs, drop by drop, until a thin mayonnaise forms. Add the tuna and process until smooth. Blend in lemon juice to taste. Adjust the seasoning.

4 Slice the meat very thinly. Add any juices to the reserved roasting juices. Gradually pour the veal juices into the tuna mayonnaise, whisking to a thin, pouring consistency.

5 Layer the veal slices with the sauce on a platter, ending with a layer of sauce. Cover and chill overnight. Garnish with olives, capers, and parsley. Arrange lemon wedges around the edge and serve.

Lamb Skewers on Rosemary

Wild rosemary scents the air all over the Mediterranean—here, branches of the herb are used as skewers for succulent lamb cubes.

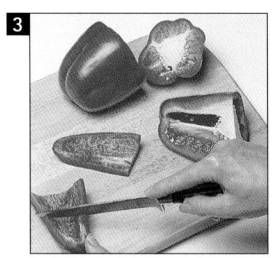

NUTRITIONAL INFORMATION

Calories	286	Sugars	.........5g
Protein	........27g	Fat	..........16g
Carbohydrate	....7g	Saturates	.......6g

🕐 4 hrs   🕐 10–12 mins

MAKES 4

I N G R E D I E N T S

1 lb 2 oz/500 g boneless leg of lamb

4 long, thick branches of fresh rosemary

1 or 2 red bell peppers, depending on the size

12 large garlic cloves, peeled

olive oil

Spiced Pilau with Saffron (see page 433), to serve

M A R I N A D E

2 tbsp olive oil

2 tbsp dry white wine

½ tsp ground cumin

1 fresh oregano sprig, chopped

1 At least 4 hours before cooking, cut the lamb into 2 inch/5 cm cubes. Combine all the marinade ingredients in a bowl. Add the lamb cubes, stir to coat, and set aside to marinate for at least 4 hours.

2 An hour before cooking, put the rosemary in a bowl of cold water and set aside to soak.

3 Slice the tops off the bell peppers. Cut the bell peppers in half, then quarters, and remove the seeds. Cut the quarters into 2 inch/5 cm pieces.

4 Bring a small pan of water to a boil, add the red bell pepper pieces and garlic cloves and blanch for 1 minute. Drain and refresh under cold running water, and drain well again. Pat dry with paper towels and set aside.

5 Remove the rosemary branches from the water and pat dry with paper towels. To make the skewers, remove the rosemary needles from about the first 1¾ inches/4 cm of the branches so you have a "handle" to turn them over with while broiling.

6 Thread alternate pieces of lamb, garlic, and red bell pepper pieces on to the 4 rosemary skewers: the meat should be tender enough to push the sprig through it, but, if not, use a metal skewer to poke a hole in the center of each cube.

7 Lightly oil the broiler rack. Place the skewers on the rack about 5 inches/ 12.5 cm under a preheated hot broiler and cook for 10–12 minutes, brushing with any leftover marinade or with olive oil and turning, until the meat is cooked. Serve with the pilau.

Cypriot Lamb with Orzo

This recipe, which uses an inexpensive cut of lamb, fills the bill when you are catering for a crowd, as it requires little attention while cooking.

NUTRITIONAL INFORMATION

Calories 447	Sugars 5g
Protein 44g	Fat 15g
Carbohydrate . . .36g	Saturates 7g

30 mins 3¾–4¼ hrs

SERVES 6

INGREDIENTS

2 large garlic cloves

1 shoulder of lamb

2 x 14 oz/400 g cans chopped tomatoes

4 fresh thyme sprigs

4 fresh parsley sprigs

1 bay leaf

½ cup water

2¼ cups orzo pasta

salt and pepper

fresh thyme sprigs, to garnish

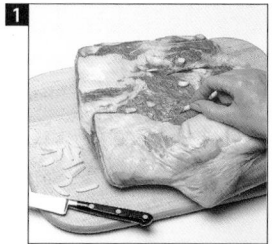

1 Cut the garlic cloves in half and remove the green cores, then thinly slice. Using the tip of a sharp knife, make slits all over the lamb shoulder, then insert the garlic slices into the slits.

2 Tip the tomatoes and their juices into a roasting pan large enough to hold the lamb shoulder. Add the thyme, parsley, and bay leaf. Place the lamb on top, skin side up, and cover the pan tightly with a sheet of foil, shiny side down. Scrunch the foil all around the edge so that none of the juices can escape during cooking.

3 Place the pan in a preheated oven, 325°F/160°C, and cook for 3½–4 hours until the lamb is cooked through and tender and the tomatoes are reduced to a thick sauce.

4 Remove the lamb from the roasting pan and set aside. Using a large metal spoon, skim off as much fat from the surface of the tomato sauce as possible.

5 Add the water and orzo to the tomatoes, stirring so the grains are submerged. Add a little extra water if the sauce seems too thick. Season to taste with salt and pepper. Return the lamb to the roasting pan.

6 Re-cover the roasting pan and return to the oven for 15 minutes or until the orzo is tender. Remove and discard the bay leaf. Set the lamb aside to rest for about 10 minutes, then slice, and serve with the orzo in tomato sauce, garnished with fresh thyme sprigs.

Beef Khorma with Almonds

This khorma, a traditional northern Indian recipe, has a thick, richly flavored and creamy textured sauce and is quite simple to cook.

NUTRITIONAL INFORMATION

Calories	735	Sugars	.........6g
Protein	........41g	Fat	..........60g
Carbohydrate	....9g	Saturates	.......9g

🍲 20 mins   🕐 1½ hrs

SERVES 4

INGREDIENTS

1¼ cups vegetable oil

3 medium onions, finely chopped

2 lb 4 oz/1 kg lean beef, cubed

1½ tsp garam masala

1½ tsp ground coriander

1½ tsp finely chopped fresh root ginger

1½ tsp crushed garlic

1 tsp salt

⅔ cup natural yogurt

2 cloves

3 green cardamoms

4 black peppercorns

2½ cups water

chapatis, to serve

TO GARNISH

6 almonds, soaked, peeled, and chopped

2 fresh green chiles, chopped

a few fresh cilantro leaves

1 Heat the oil in a pan. Add the onions and stir-fry until golden brown. Remove half of the onions from the pan, set aside, and reserve.

2 Add the meat to the remaining onions in the pan and stir-fry for about 5 minutes. Remove the pan from the heat.

3 Combine the garam masala, ground coriander, ginger, garlic, salt, and yogurt in a bowl. Gradually add the meat to the spice mixture and mix to coat well. Return the meat mixture to the pan. Cook, stirring constantly, for 5–7 minutes or until the mixture is golden.

4 Add the cloves, cardamoms, and peppercorns. Add the water, lower the heat, cover the pan, and then simmer for approximately 45–60 minutes. If necessary, add another 1¼ cups water and cook for another 10–15 minutes, stirring occasionally.

5 Just before serving, garnish with the reserved onions, chopped almonds, green chiles and the fresh cilantro leaves. Serve with chapatis.

Sliced Beef with Yogurt

Roasting the spices for this dish gives it a nice dark color and a richer flavor. Serve with chapatis and white lentils for a substantial meal.

NUTRITIONAL INFORMATION

Calories 981   Sugars 5g
Protein . . . . .33g   Fat 94g
Carbohydrate . . . .6g   Saturates 14g

20 mins

45 mins

SERVES 4

INGREDIENTS

1 lb/450 g lean beef slices, cut into 1 inch/2.5 cm slices

5 tbsp natural yogurt

1 tsp finely chopped fresh root ginger

1 tsp crushed garlic

1 tsp chili powder

pinch of ground turmeric

2 tsp garam masala

1 tsp salt

2 cardamoms

1 tsp black cumin seeds

2 oz/55 g ground almonds

1 tbsp desiccated coconut

1 tbsp poppy seeds

1 tbsp sesame seeds

1¼ cups vegetable oil

2 medium onions, finely chopped

1¼ cups water

2 fresh green chiles

a few fresh cilantro leaves, chopped

1 Place the beef in a large bowl. Combine with the yogurt, ginger, garlic, chili powder, turmeric, garam masala, salt, cardamoms, and black cumin seeds and set aside until required.

2 Dry-fry the ground almonds, desiccated coconut, poppy seeds, and sesame seeds in a heavy skillet until golden, shaking the pan occasionally.

3 Transfer the spice mixture to a food processor and process until finely ground. (Add 1 tablespoon water to blend, if necessary.) Add the ground spice mixture to the meat mixture and combine.

4 Heat a little oil in a large pan and cook the onions until golden brown. Remove the onions from the pan. Stir-fry the meat in the remaining oil for about 5 minutes, then return the onions to the pan, and stir-fry for a further 5–7 minutes. Add the water, cover, and simmer over low heat, stirring occasionally, for 25–30 minutes. Add the chiles and cilantro and serve hot.

Spaghetti & Shellfish

Frozen shelled shrimp from the freezer can become the star ingredient in this colorful and tasty dish.

NUTRITIONAL INFORMATION

Calories	.510	Sugars	.38g
Protein	.33g	Fat	.24g
Carbohydrate	.44g	Saturates	.11g

 35 mins   30 mins

SERVES 4

INGREDIENTS

8 oz/225 g dried short-cut spaghetti, or long spaghetti broken into 15 cm/ 6 inch lengths

1 tbsp olive oil

1¼ cups chicken stock

1 tsp lemon juice

1 small cauliflower, cut into florets

2 carrots, thinly sliced

4 oz/115 g snow peas

4 tbsp butter

1 onion, sliced

8 oz/225 g zucchini, thinly sliced

1 garlic clove, chopped

12 oz/350 g frozen shelled shrimp, thawed

2 tbsp chopped fresh parsley

⅓ cup grated Parmesan cheese

½ tsp paprika

salt and pepper

4 unshelled shrimp, to garnish (optional)

1 Bring a large pan of lightly salted water to a boil. Add the pasta, bring back to a boil, and cook for 8–10 minutes until tender, but still firm to the bite. Drain, then return to the pan, and stir in the oil. Keep warm.

2 Bring the stock and lemon juice to a boil. Add the cauliflower and carrots and cook for 3–4 minutes until barely tender. Remove with a slotted spoon and set aside. Add the snow peas and cook for 1–2 minutes until they begin to soften. Remove with a slotted spoon and add to the other vegetables. Reserve the stock for future use.

3 Melt half of the butter in a skillet over medium heat and cook the onion and zucchini for about 3 minutes. Add the garlic and shrimp and cook for a further 2–3 minutes until thoroughly heated through.

4 Stir in the reserved vegetables and heat through. Season to taste with salt and pepper, then stir in the remaining butter.

5 Transfer the spaghetti to a warmed serving dish. Pour on the sauce and sprinkle with parsley. Toss well, using 2 forks, until thoroughly coated. Sprinkle on the grated cheese and paprika, and garnish with unshelled shrimp, if using. Serve immediately.

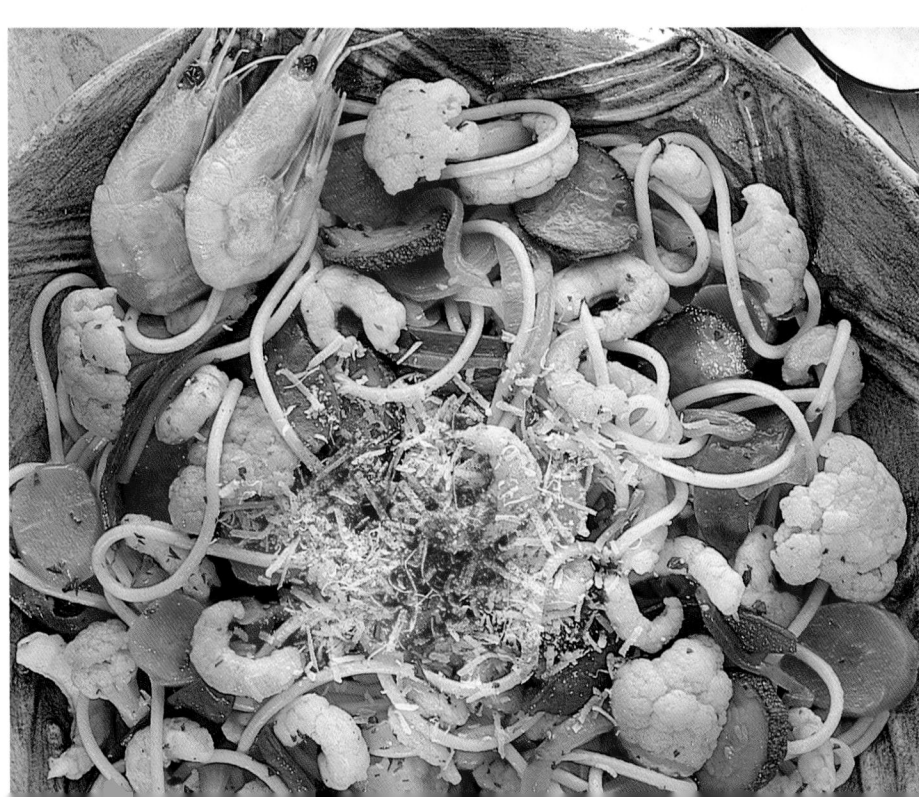

Charred Tuna Steaks

Tuna has a firm flesh, which is ideal for grilling on a barbecue, but it can be a little dry unless it is marinated first.

NUTRITIONAL INFORMATION

Calories 153   Sugars 1g
Protein ....29g   Fat 3g
Carbohydrate ....1g   Saturates 1g

 2 hrs   15 mins

SERVES 4

I N G R E D I E N T S

4 tuna steaks

3 tbsp light soy sauce

1 tbsp Worcestershire sauce

1 tsp wholegrain mustard

1 tsp superfine sugar

1 tbsp sunflower oil

salad greens, to serve

T O   G A R N I S H

flat leaf parsley

lemon wedges

1 Place the tuna steaks in a single layer a shallow dish.

2 Combine the light soy sauce, Worcestershire sauce, mustard, sugar, and oil in a small bowl. Pour the marinade over the tuna steaks. Gently turn the tuna steaks to coat well.

3 Cover with plastic wrap and set aside in the refrigerator to marinate for at least 30 minutes and up to 2 hours.

4 Remove the tuna steaks from the marinade, reserving the marinade for basting. Grill over hot coals for about 10–15 minutes, turning once and basting frequently with the reserved marinade.

5 Transfer the tuna steaks to warmed serving plates. Garnish with flat leaf parsley and lemon wedges and serve immediately with fresh salad greens.

COOK'S TIP

If a marinade contains soy sauce, the marinating time should be limited, usually to 2 hours. If it is allowed to marinate for too long, the fish will dry out and become tough.

Baked Sea Bass

Sea bass is often paired with subtle Asian flavors.
For a special occasion, you may like to bone the fish.

NUTRITIONAL INFORMATION

Calories	140	Sugars	.......0.1g
Protein	........29g	Fat	...........1g
Carbohydrate	...0.1g	Saturates	.....0.2g

10 mins   15 mins

SERVES 4–6

I N G R E D I E N T S

2 sea bass, about 2 lb 4 oz/1 kg each,
 cleaned and scaled

2 scallions, green part only, cut
 into strips

2 inch/5 cm piece of fresh ginger root, cut
 into strips

2 garlic cloves, unpeeled, lightly crushed

2 tbsp mirin or dry sherry

salt and pepper

TO SERVE

pickled sushi ginger (optional)

soy sauce

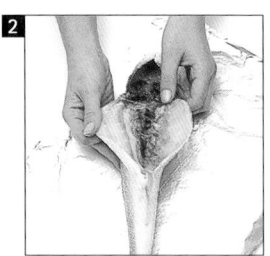 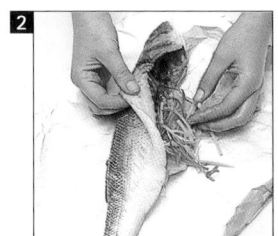 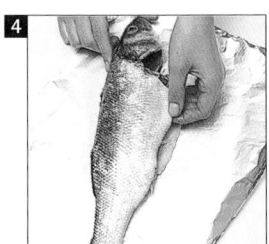

1 For each fish lay out a double thickness of foil and oil the top piece well or lay a piece of baking parchment over the foil.

2 Place the fish in the middle of the foil and expose the cavities. Divide the scallion and ginger between each cavity. Put a garlic clove in each cavity.

3 Pour the mirin or dry sherry over both fish and season them to taste with salt and pepper.

4 Close the cavities and lay each fish on its side. Bring over the foil and fold the edges together to seal securely. Fold each end neatly.

5 Cook over a medium barbecue for 15 minutes, turning once.

6 To serve, remove the foil and cut each fish into 2 or 3 pieces. Serve with the pickled ginger, if using, accompanied by soy sauce.

COOK'S TIP

Fresh sea bass is just as delicious when cooked very simply. Stuff the fish with garlic and chopped herbs, brush with olive oil, and bake in the oven.

Italian Fish Stew

This robust stew is full of Mediterranean flavors. If you do not want to prepare the fish yourself, ask your local fish store to do it for you.

NUTRITIONAL INFORMATION

Calories	236	Sugars	........4g
Protein	........20g	Fat	..........7g
Carbohydrate	...25g	Saturates	.......1g

5–10 mins   25 mins

SERVES 4

I N G R E D I E N T S

2 tbsp olive oil

2 red onions, finely chopped

1 garlic clove, crushed

2 zucchini, sliced

14 oz/400 g can chopped tomatoes

3¾ cups fish or vegetable stock

¾ cup dried pasta shapes

12 oz/350 g firm white fish, such as cod, haddock, or hake

1 tbsp chopped fresh basil or oregano or 1 tsp dried oregano

1 tsp grated lemon rind

1 tbsp cornstarch

1 tbsp water

salt and pepper

fresh basil or oregano sprigs, to garnish

1 Heat the oil in a large pan. Add the onions and garlic and cook over low heat, stirring occasionally, for about 5 minutes until softened. Add the zucchini and cook, stirring frequently, for 2–3 minutes.

2 Add the tomatoes and stock to the pan and bring to a boil. Add the pasta, bring back to a boil, reduce the heat, and cover. Simmer for 5 minutes.

3 Skin and bone the fish, then cut it into chunks. Add to the pan with the basil or oregano and lemon rind and simmer gently for 5 minutes until the fish is opaque and flakes easily (take care not to overcook it) and the pasta is tender, but still firm to the bite.

4 Blend the cornstarch with the water to a smooth paste and stir into the stew. Cook gently for 2 minutes, stirring constantly, until thickened. Season with salt and pepper to taste.

5 Ladle the stew into 4 warmed soup bowls. Garnish with basil or oregano sprigs and serve immediately.

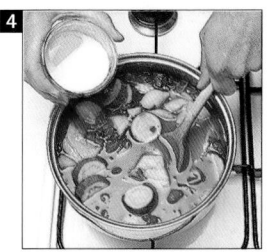

Shrimp Bhuna

This is a fiery recipe with subtle undertones. Since the flavor of the shrimp should be noticeable, the spices should not take over this dish.

NUTRITIONAL INFORMATION

Calories . . . . .141 Sugars 0.4g
Protein . . . . .19g Fat 7g
Carbohydrate . . . .1g Saturates 1g

🖐 15 mins 🕐 20 mins

SERVES 4–6

INGREDIENTS

2 dried red chiles, deseeded if desired

3 fresh green chiles, finely chopped

1 tsp ground turmeric

½ tsp pepper

1 tsp paprika

3 garlic cloves, crushed

2 tsp white wine vinegar

½ tsp salt

1 lb 2 oz/500 g uncooked, peeled jumbo shrimp

3 tbsp vegetable oil

1 onion, very finely chopped

¾ cup water

2 tbsp lemon juice

2 tsp garam masala

fresh cilantro, to garnish

1 Combine the chiles, spices, garlic, vinegar, and salt in a nonmetallic bowl. Stir in the shrimp and set aside for 10 minutes.

2 Heat the oil in a large skillet or wok, add the onion, and cook, stirring occasionally, for 3–4 minutes until soft.

3 Add the shrimp and the spice mixture to the skillet or wok and stir-fry over high heat for 2 minutes. Reduce the heat, add the water, and boil for 10 minutes, stirring occasionally, until the water has evaporated and the curry is fragrant.

4 Stir in the lemon juice and garam masala, then transfer the mixture to a warm serving dish, and garnish with fresh cilantro sprigs. Serve immediately.

COOK'S TIP

Garam masala should be used sparingly and is generally added to foods toward the end of their cooking time. It is also used sprinkled over cooked meats, vegetables, and beans as a garnish.

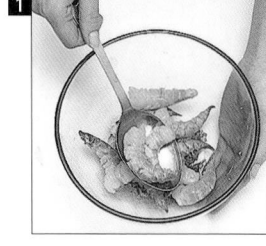

Shellfish in Red Curry Sauce

For something very quick and simple that sets your tastebuds alight, try this inspired dish of shrimp in a wonderfully spicy sauce.

NUTRITIONAL INFORMATION

Calories	175	Sugars	.........3g
Protein	........29g	Fat	...........5g
Carbohydrate	....3g	Saturates	......1g

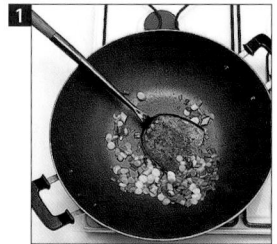
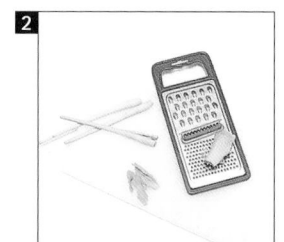

10 mins   10 mins

SERVES 4

INGREDIENTS

1 tbsp vegetable oil

6 scallions, sliced

1 lemongrass stalk

½ inch/1 cm piece of fresh ginger root

generous 1 cup coconut milk

2 tbsp Thai red curry paste

1 tbsp Thai fish sauce

1 lb 2 oz/500 g raw jumbo shrimp

1 tbsp chopped fresh cilantro

fresh chiles, to garnish

1 Heat the vegetable oil in a wok or large skillet. Add the scallions and cook over low heat for about 2 minutes until softened.

2 Bruise the stalk of lemongrass using a meat mallet or rolling pin. Peel and finely grate the fresh ginger root.

3 Add the lemongrass and ginger to the wok or skillet with the coconut milk, Thai red curry paste, and Thai fish sauce. Heat gently until the coconut milk is almost boiling.

4 Peel the shrimp, leaving the tails intact. Remove the black vein along the back of each shrimp.

5 Add the shrimp to the wok or skillet with the chopped cilantro and cook gently for 5 minutes.

6 Transfer the shrimp with the sauce to a warm serving bowl, garnish with fresh chiles, and serve immediately.

VARIATION
Try this recipe using Thai green curry sauce instead of red. Both varieties are obtainable from many supermarkets—look for them in the Asian foods section.

Baked Crab with Ginger

In Chinese restaurants, only live crabs are used, but ready-cooked ones can be used at home quite successfully.

NUTRITIONAL INFORMATION

Calories 261	Sugars 0.5g
Protein 18g	Fat 17g
Carbohydrate 5g	Saturates 2g

35 mins   10 mins

SERVES 4

INGREDIENTS

1 large or 2 medium crabs, weighing about 1 lb 10 oz/750 g in total

2 tbsp Chinese rice wine or dry sherry

1 egg, lightly beaten

1 tbsp cornstarch

3–4 tbsp vegetable oil

1 tbsp finely chopped fresh ginger root

3–4 scallions, cut into short lengths

2 tbsp light soy sauce

1 tsp sugar

about 5 tbsp Chinese Stock (see page 8) or water

½ tsp sesame oil

fresh cilantro leaves, to garnish

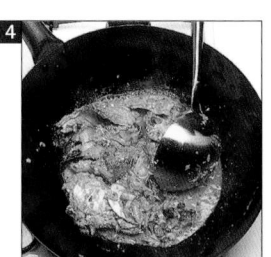

COOK'S TIP

Crabs are almost always sold ready-cooked. The crab should feel heavy for its size, and when it is shaken, there should be no sound of water inside. A good medium-size crab should yield about 1 lb 2 oz/ 500 g meat, enough for 3-4 people.

1 Cut the crab in half from the underbelly. Break off the claws and crack them with the back of a cleaver or a large kitchen knife.

2 Discard the legs and crack the shell, breaking it into several pieces. Discard the feathery gills from both sides of the body and the stomach sac. Place the crab meat in a bowl.

3 Combine the wine or sherry, egg, and cornstarch. Pour the mixture over the crab meat and set aside to marinate for 10–15 minutes.

4 Heat the vegetable oil in a preheated wok. Stir-fry the crab meat with the chopped ginger and scallions for 2–3 minutes.

5 Add the soy sauce, sugar, and stock or water, blend well, and bring to a boil. Cover and cook for 3–4 minutes, then remove the lid, sprinkle with sesame oil, and serve, garnished with cilantro leaves.

Herrings with Hot Pesto

Oily fish, such as herrings and mackerel, form a vital part of the healthy diet, because they are rich in essential omega 3 fatty acids.

NUTRITIONAL INFORMATION

Calories	382	Sugars	.........2g
Protein	........28g	Fat	..........29g
Carbohydrate	....3g	Saturates	.......5g

 10 mins   10 mins

SERVES 4

I N G R E D I E N T S

4 herrings or small mackerel, cleaned and gutted

2 tbsp olive oil

8 oz/225 g tomatoes, peeled, deseeded, and chopped

8 canned anchovy fillets in oil, drained and chopped

about 30 fresh basil leaves

2 oz/55 g pine nuts

2 garlic cloves, crushed

1 Cook the herrings or mackerel under a preheated broiler for about 8–10 minutes on each side, or until the skin is slightly charred on both sides.

2 Meanwhile, heat 1 tablespoon of the olive oil in a large pan. Add the tomatoes and anchovies and cook over medium heat for 5 minutes.

3 To make the pesto sauce, put the basil, pine nuts, garlic, and remaining oil into a food processor and process to form a smooth paste. Alternatively, pound the ingredients by hand in a mortar with a pestle.

4 Add the pesto mixture to the pan of tomato and anchovies and stir to heat through.

5 Spoon some of the pesto sauce on to warmed individual serving plates. Place the fish on top and pour the rest of the pesto sauce over the fish. Serve immediately.

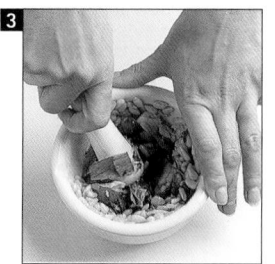

Fish with Black Bean Sauce

Steaming is one of the preferred methods of cooking whole fish in China because it maintains both the flavor and the texture.

NUTRITIONAL INFORMATION

Calories	292	Sugars	.........3g
Protein	........44g	Fat	...........7g
Carbohydrate	....6g	Saturates	.....0.4g

 10 mins   🕐 10 mins

SERVES 4

INGREDIENTS

2 lb/900 g whole snapper, cleaned and scaled

3 garlic cloves, crushed

2 tbsp black bean sauce

1 tsp cornstarch

2 tsp sesame oil

2 tbsp light soy sauce

2 tsp superfine sugar

2 tbsp dry sherry

1 small leek, shredded

1 small red bell pepper, deseeded and cut into thin strips

shredded leek and lemon wedges, to garnish

boiled rice or noodles, to serve

1 Rinse the fish inside and out with cold running water and pat dry with paper towels.

2 Make 2–3 diagonal slashes in the flesh on each side of the fish, using a sharp knife. Rub the garlic into the fish.

3 Combine the black bean sauce, cornstarch, sesame oil, light soy sauce, sugar, and dry sherry.

4 Place the fish in a shallow heatproof dish and pour the sauce mixture over the top. Sprinkle the shredded leek and bell pepper strips on top of the sauce.

5 Place the dish in the top of a steamer, cover, and steam for 10 minutes or until the fish is cooked through.

6 Transfer the fish to a serving dish, garnish with shredded leek and lemon wedges, and serve immediately with boiled rice or noodles.

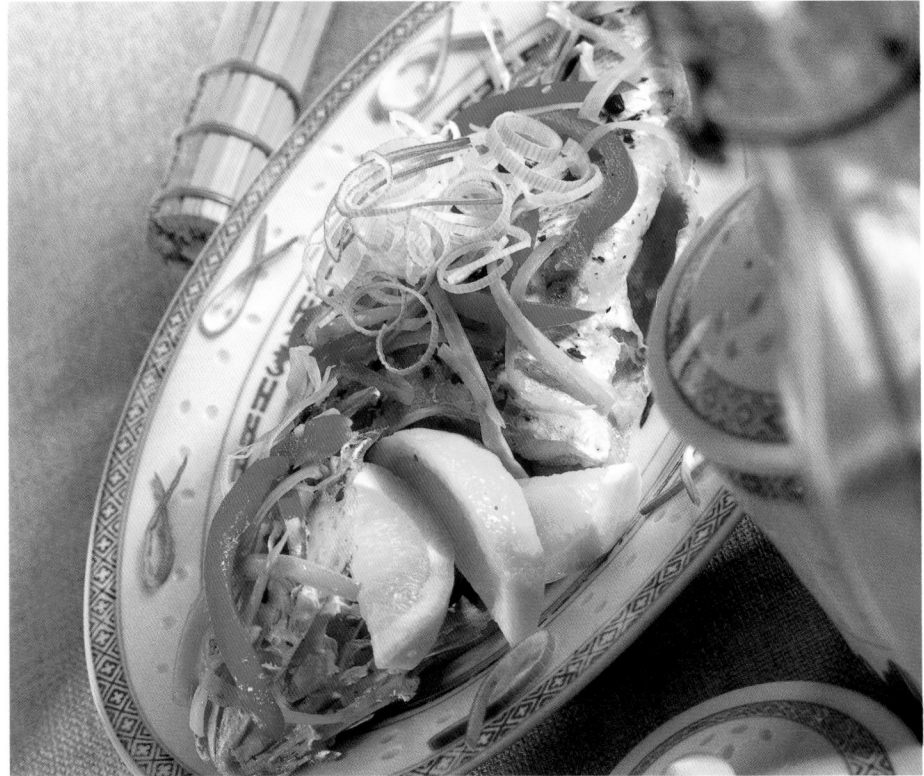

COOK'S TIP

Insert the point of a sharp knife into the fish to test if it is cooked. The fish is cooked through if the knife goes into the flesh easily.

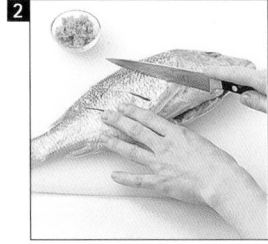

Fragrant Tuna Steaks

Fresh tuna steaks are very meaty—they have a firm texture,
yet the flesh is succulent. Tuna is rich in valuable omega 3 oils.

NUTRITIONAL INFORMATION

Calories ....239 Sugars 0.1g
Protein ....42g Fat 8g
Carbohydrate ...0.5g Saturates 2g

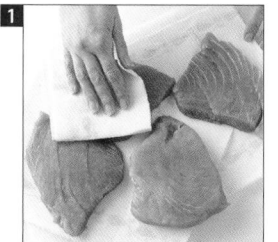  

🕐 15 mins   🕐 15 mins

SERVES 4

INGREDIENTS

4 tuna steaks, 6 oz/175 g each

½ tsp finely grated lime rind

1 garlic clove, crushed

2 tsp olive oil

1 tsp ground cumin

1 tsp ground coriander

1 tbsp lime juice

pepper

fresh cilantro, to garnish

TO SERVE

avocado relish (see Cook's Tip)

tomato wedges

lime wedges

1 Trim the skin from the tuna steaks, rinse the fish, and pat dry on absorbent paper towels.

2 In a small bowl, combine the grated lime rind, garlic, olive oil, cumin, ground coriander, and pepper, to taste, to make a paste.

3 Spread the paste thinly on both sides of the tuna. Heat a nonstick, ridged skillet until hot and press the tuna steaks into the skillet to seal them. Lower the heat and cook for 5 minutes. Turn the fish over and cook for a further 4–5 minutes until the fish is cooked through. Drain on paper towels and transfer to a warmed serving plate.

4 Sprinkle the lime juice and chopped cilantro over the fish. Serve immediately with avocado relish, and tomato and lime wedges.

COOK'S TIP

For the avocado relish, peel, pit, and chop a small ripe avocado. Mix in 1 tablespoon lime juice, 1 tablespoon chopped fresh cilantro, 1 finely chopped small red onion, and some chopped mango or tomato. Season to taste.

Salmon with Pineapple

Presentation plays a major part in Chinese cooking and this dish demonstrates this perfectly with the wonderful combination of colors.

NUTRITIONAL INFORMATION

Calories	347	Sugars	........12g
Protein	........24g	Fat	..........20g
Carbohydrate	...16g	Saturates	.......3g

 10 mins 15 mins

SERVES 4

INGREDIENTS

scant 1 cup baby corn cobs

2 tbsp sunflower oil

1 red onion, sliced

1 orange bell pepper, deseeded and sliced

1 green bell pepper, deseeded and sliced

1 lb/450 g salmon fillet, skinned

1 tbsp paprika

8 oz/225 g canned cubed pineapple in natural juice, drained

2 cups bean sprouts

2 tbsp tomato ketchup

2 tbsp soy sauce

2 tbsp medium sherry

1 tsp cornstarch

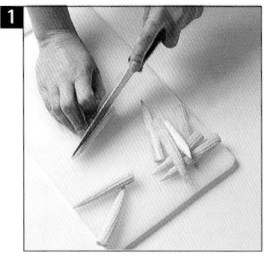

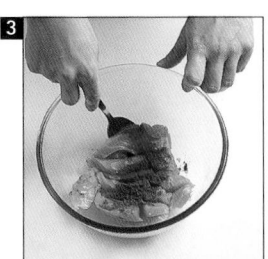

1 Cut each baby corn cob in half. Heat the oil in a large preheated wok. Add the onion, bell peppers, and baby corn cobs to the wok and stir-fry for 5 minutes.

2 Rinse the salmon fillet under cold running water and pat dry with absorbent paper towels.

3 Cut the salmon flesh into thin strips and place in a large bowl. Sprinkle with the paprika and toss well to coat.

4 Add the salmon to the wok together with the pineapple and stir-fry for a further 2–3 minutes or until the fish is tender.

5 Add the bean sprouts to the wok and toss well.

6 Mix together the tomato ketchup, soy sauce, sherry, and cornstarch. Add to the wok and cook until the juices start to thicken. Transfer to warm serving plates and serve immediately.

VARIATION

You can use trout fillets instead of the salmon as an alternative, if you prefer.

Gingered Monkfish

This dish is a real treat and is perfect for special occasions. Monkfish has a tender flavor which is ideal with asparagus, chili sauce, and ginger.

NUTRITIONAL INFORMATION

Calories ....133 Sugars 0g
Protein ....21g Fat 5g
Carbohydrate ....1g Saturates 1g

5 mins

10 mins

SERVES 4

INGREDIENTS

1 lb/450 g monkfish

1 tbsp grated fresh ginger root

2 tbsp sweet chili sauce

1 tbsp corn oil

3½ oz/100 g fine asparagus

3 scallions, sliced

1 tsp sesame oil

1 Remove any membrane from the monkfish. Using a sharp knife, slice the monkfish into thin flat rounds. Set aside until required.

2 Combine the grated ginger root and the sweet chili sauce in a small bowl until thoroughly blended. Brush the ginger and chili sauce mixture over the monkfish pieces, using a pastry brush.

COOK'S TIP

Monkfish is quite expensive, but it is well worth using, as it has a wonderful flavor and texture. Otherwise, you could use cubes of chunky cod fillet instead.

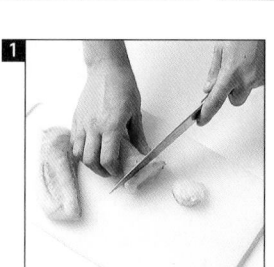

3 Heat the corn oil in a large preheated wok or heavy skillet.

4 Add the monkfish pieces, asparagus and chopped scallions to the wok or skillet and cook over medium heat for about 5 minutes, constantly stirring very gently so the fish pieces do not break up.

5 Remove the wok or skillet from the heat, drizzle the sesame oil over the stir-fry, and toss gently to combine.

6 Transfer the stir-fried gingered monkfish to warm serving plates and serve immediately.

Goan Fish Curry

Goan cuisine is famous for seafood and vindaloo dishes, which tend to be very hot. This recipe is a mild curry, but very flavorful.

NUTRITIONAL INFORMATION

Calories	302	Sugars	.........7g
Protein	........31g	Fat	..........17g
Carbohydrate	....8g	Saturates	.......7g

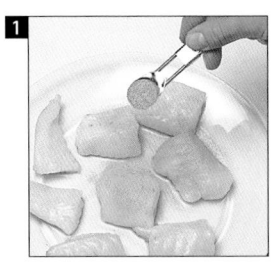

 30 mins 🕐 12 mins

SERVES 4

I N G R E D I E N T S

1 lb 10 oz/750 g monkfish fillet, cut into chunks

1 tbsp apple vinegar

1 tsp salt

1 tsp ground turmeric

3 tbsp vegetable oil

2 garlic cloves, crushed

1 small onion, finely chopped

2 tsp ground coriander

1 tsp cayenne pepper

2 tsp paprika

2 tbsp tamarind pulp plus 2 tbsp boiling water (see method)

3 oz/85 g creamed coconut, cut into pieces

1¼ cups warm water

plain boiled rice, to serve

1 Put the fish on a plate and drizzle the vinegar over it. Combine half the salt and half the turmeric and sprinkle evenly over the fish. Cover and set aside for 20 minutes.

2 Heat the oil in a heavy skillet and add the garlic. Brown slightly, then add the onion, and cook, stirring occasionally, for 3–4 minutes until soft, but not browned. Add the ground coriander and stir for 1 minute.

3 Mix the remaining turmeric, cayenne, and paprika with about 2 tablespoons water to make a paste. Add to the skillet and cook over low heat for 1–2 minutes.

4 Stir the tamarind pulp and boiling water. When thickened and the pulp has come away from the seeds, rub through a strainer. Discard the seeds.

5 Add the coconut, warm water, and tamarind paste to the skillet and stir until the coconut has dissolved. Add the fish and any juices on the plate and simmer gently for 4–5 minutes until the sauce has thickened and the fish is just tender. Serve on a bed of plain boiled rice.

Thai Green Fish Curry

This pale green curry paste can be used as the basis for all sorts of Thai dishes. It is also delicious with chicken and beef.

NUTRITIONAL INFORMATION

Calories	217	Sugars	.........3g
Protein	........12g	Fat	..........17g
Carbohydrate	....5g	Saturates	......10g

🧈 15 mins   🕐 15 mins

SERVES 4

INGREDIENTS

2 tbsp vegetable oil

1 garlic clove, chopped

1 small eggplant, diced

½ cup coconut cream

2 tbsp Thai fish sauce

1 tsp sugar

8 oz/225 g firm white fish, cut into pieces, such as cod, haddock, halibut

½ cup fish stock

2 kaffir lime leaves, finely shredded

about 15 leaves Thai basil, if available, or ordinary basil

plain boiled rice or noodles, to serve

GREEN CURRY PASTE

5 fresh green chiles, deseeded and chopped

2 tsp chopped lemongrass

1 large shallot, chopped

2 garlic cloves, chopped

1 tsp grated fresh ginger root or galangal

2 fresh cilantro roots, chopped

½ tsp ground coriander

¼ tsp ground cumin

1 kaffir lime leaf, finely chopped

1 tsp shrimp paste (optional)

½ tsp salt

1 Make the curry paste. Put all the ingredients into a blender or spice grinder and blend to a smooth paste, adding a little water if necessary. Alternatively, pound together all the ingredients, using a mortar and pestle, until smooth. Set aside.

2 Heat the oil in a skillet or wok until almost smoking. Add the garlic and fry until golden. Add the curry paste and stir-fry for a few seconds before adding the eggplant. Stir-fry for about 4–5 minutes until softened.

3 Add the coconut cream. Bring to a boil and stir until the cream thickens and curdles slightly. Add the fish sauce and sugar and stir into the mixture.

4 Add the fish pieces and stock. Simmer, stirring occasionally, for 3–4 minutes until the fish is just tender. Add the lime leaves and basil and then cook for a further minute.

5 Transfer the curry to a warmed serving dish and serve with plain boiled rice or noodles.

Mackerel Escabeche

Although the word *escabeche* is Spanish in origin, variations of this dish are cooked all over the Mediterranean.

NUTRITIONAL INFORMATION

Calories	750	Sugars	.........3g
Protein	........33g	Fat	..........63g
Carbohydrate	...12g	Saturates	......11g

40 mins   12–14 mins

SERVES 4

INGREDIENTS

⅔ cup olive oil

4 mackerel, filleted

2 tbsp seasoned flour, for dusting

4 tbsp red wine vinegar

1 onion, thinly sliced

1 strip of orange rind, removed with a vegetable peeler

1 fresh thyme sprig

1 fresh rosemary sprig

1 bay leaf

4 garlic cloves, crushed

2 fresh red chiles, bruised

1 tsp salt

3 tbsp chopped fresh flat leaf parsley

crusty bread, to serve

VARIATION

Substitute 12 whole sardines, cleaned and with heads removed. Cook in the same way. Tuna steaks are also very delicious served escabeche.

1 Heat half the olive oil in a heavy skillet. Dust the mackerel fillets with the seasoned flour. Add the fish to the skillet, in batches if necessary, and cook for about 30 seconds on each side until not quite cooked through.

2 Transfer the mackerel fillets to a shallow dish large enough to hold the fillets in a single layer and set aside.

3 Add the vinegar, onion, orange rind, thyme, rosemary, garlic, chiles, and salt to the skillet. Bring to a boil over low heat and simmer for 10 minutes.

4 Add the remaining olive oil and the chopped parsley. Remove and discard the bay leaf. Pour the mixture over the mackerel and set aside until cold. Serve with plenty of crusty bread.

Haddock Baked in Yogurt

This is a very simple, convenient, but flavorsome dish, using mainly pantry ingredients—apart from the fresh fish.

NUTRITIONAL INFORMATION

Calories ....448 Sugars 16g
Protein ....47g Fat 21g
Carbohydrate ...20g Saturates 8g

20 mins | 40 mins

SERVES 4

INGREDIENTS

2 large onions, thinly sliced

2 lb/900 g haddock fillet

scant 2 cups plain yogurt

2 tbsp lemon juice

1 tsp sugar

2 tsp ground cumin

2 tsp ground coriander

pinch of garam masala

pinch of cayenne pepper

1 tsp grated fresh ginger root

3 tbsp vegetable oil

¼ cup cold sweet butter, diced

salt and pepper

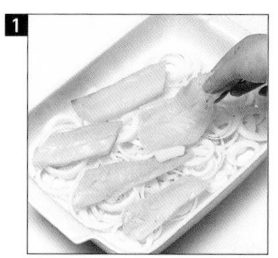  

1 Line the base of a large casserole with the onion slices. Cut the fish widthwise into strips about 2 inches/5 cm wide and lay the strips in a single layer over the onions.

2 In a bowl, combine the yogurt, lemon juice, sugar, cumin, coriander, garam masala, cayenne, ginger, and oil and season to taste with salt and pepper. Pour this sauce over the fish, tipping the dish to make sure it runs under the fish as well. Cover tightly with kitchen foil or a lid.

3 Bake in a preheated oven, 375°F/ 190°C, for 30 minutes or until the fish is just tender.

4 Carefully pour the sauce off the fish into a pan. Bring to a boil over low heat and simmer to reduce to about 1½ cups. Remove from the heat.

5 Add the cubes of butter to the sauce and whisk until melted and fully incorporated. Pour the sauce over the fish and serve immediately.

COOK'S TIP

When you pour the sauce off the fish it will look thin and separated, but reducing and stirring in the butter will help to amalgamate it.

Cod Italienne

Not strictly authentic, but this dish uses the typical Italian ingredients of tomatoes, capers, olives, and basil to make a delicious supper dish.

NUTRITIONAL INFORMATION

Calories 387	Sugars 8g
Protein 44g	Fat 16g
Carbohydrate . . .10g	Saturates 6g

 15 mins   1½ hrs

SERVES 4

I N G R E D I E N T S

2 tbsp olive oil

1 onion, finely chopped

2 garlic cloves, finely chopped

2 tsp chopped fresh thyme

⅔ cup red wine

2 x 14 oz/400 g cans chopped tomatoes

pinch of sugar

½ cup pitted black olives, roughly chopped

½ cup pitted green olives, roughly chopped

2 tbsp capers, drained, rinsed and roughly chopped

2 tbsp chopped fresh basil

4 cod steaks, each weighing about 6 oz/175 g

5½ oz/150 g buffalo Mozzarella, drained and sliced

salt and pepper

buttered noodles, to serve

1 Heat the olive oil in a large pan. Add the onion and cook over low heat, stirring occasionally, for 5 minutes until softened, but not colored.

2 Add the garlic and thyme and cook, stirring constantly, a further minute.

3 Add the red wine and increase the heat. Simmer until reduced and syrupy. Add the tomatoes and sugar and bring to a boil. Cover and simmer gently for 30 minutes. Uncover and simmer for a further 20 minutes until thick. Stir in the olives, capers, and basil. Season to taste with salt and pepper.

4 Arrange the cod steaks in a shallow casserole and spoon the tomato sauce over the top. Bake in a preheated oven, 375°F/190°C, for 20–25 minutes until the fish is just tender.

5 Remove the casserole from the oven and arrange the mozzarella slices on top of the fish.

6 Return to the oven for a further 5–10 minutes until the cheese has melted. Serve with buttered noodles.

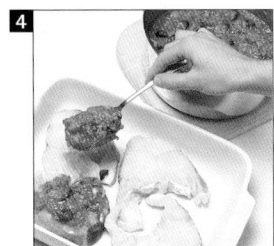

Cod Curry

Using curry paste in this recipe makes it quick
and easy to prepare. It makes an ideal family supper.

NUTRITIONAL INFORMATION

Calories 310   Sugars 4g
Protein . . . . .42g   Fat 8g
Carbohydrate . . .19g   Saturates 1g

10 mins   25 mins

SERVES 4

INGREDIENTS

1 tbsp vegetable oil

1 small onion, chopped

2 garlic cloves, chopped

1 inch/2.5 cm piece of fresh ginger root,
   roughly chopped

2 large ripe tomatoes, peeled and
   roughly chopped

⅔ cup fish stock

1 tbsp medium curry paste

1 tsp ground coriander

14 oz/400 g can garbanzo beans, drained
   and rinsed

1 lb 10 oz/750 g cod fillet, cut into
   large chunks

4 tbsp chopped fresh cilantro

4 tbsp thick yogurt

salt and pepper

steamed basmati rice, to serve

1 Heat the oil in a large pan and add the onion, garlic, and ginger. Cook over low heat for 4–5 minutes until softened. Remove from the heat. Put the onion mixture into a food processor or blender with the tomatoes and fish stock and process until smooth.

2 Return to the pan with the curry paste, ground coriander, and garbanzo beans. Mix together well, then simmer gently for 15 minutes until thickened.

3 Add the pieces of fish and return to a simmer. Cook for 5 minutes until the fish is just tender. Remove from the heat and set aside for 2–3 minutes.

4 Stir in the cilantro and yogurt. Season and serve with basmati rice.

VARIATIONS

Instead of cod, make this
curry using raw shrimp and
omit the garbanzo beans.

Home-Salted Cod

After a period of unpopularity, salt cod is now becoming fashionable.
You will need to begin preparing this dish two days ahead.

NUTRITIONAL INFORMATION

Calories 283   Sugars 0g
Protein ....39g   Fat 7g
Carbohydrate ....7g   Saturates 1g

50 hrs   2¼ hrs

SERVES 6

INGREDIENTS

¼ cup sea salt

3 lb 5 oz/1.5 kg fresh boneless cod fillet,
  from the head end, skin on

1 cup dried garbanzo beans,
  soaked overnight

1 fresh red chile

4 garlic cloves

2 bay leaves

1 tbsp olive oil

1¼ cups chicken stock

pepper

extra virgin olive oil, to drizzle

GREMOLATA

3 tbsp chopped fresh parsley

2 garlic cloves, finely chopped

finely grated rind of 1 lemon

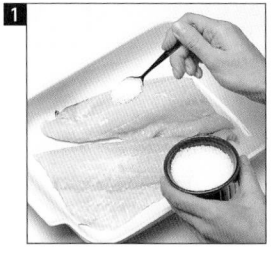
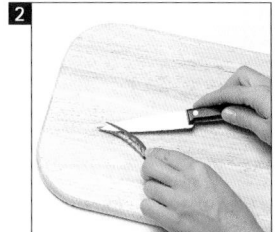

1 Sprinkle the salt over both sides of the cod. Place in a shallow dish, cover, and chill for 48 hours. Rinse the fish under cold running water, then set aside to soak in cold water for 2 hours.

2 Drain the garbanzo beans, rinse, and drain again. Put into a large pan. Add double their volume of water and bring to a boil over low heat. Remove any scum that rises to the surface. Split the chile lengthwise and add to the garbanzo beans with the garlic cloves and bay leaves. Cover and simmer for 1½–2 hours until very tender, skimming occasionally.

3 Drain the cod and pat dry with paper towels. Brush with the olive oil and season with black pepper. Cook under a preheated broiler or on a hot ridged griddle pan for 3–4 minutes on each side until tender. Meanwhile, add the stock to the garbanzo beans and bring back to a boil. Remove and keep warm.

4 For the gremolata, combine the parsley, garlic, and grated lemon rind.

5 To serve, ladle the garbanzo beans and their cooking liquid into 6 warmed soup bowls. Top with the cod and sprinkle over the gremolata. Drizzle generously with olive oil and serve immediately.

Cotriade

This is a rich French stew of fish and vegetables, flavored with saffron and herbs. The fish and vegetables, and the soup, are served separately.

NUTRITIONAL INFORMATION

Calories . . . . .81 Sugars 0.9g
Protein . . . . .7.4g Fat 3.9g
Carbohydrate . . .3.8g Saturates 1.1g

15 mins · 40 mins

SERVES 4

INGREDIENTS

pinch of saffron

2½ cups hot fish stock

1 tbsp olive oil

2 tbsp butter

1 onion, sliced

2 garlic cloves, chopped

1 leek, sliced

1 small fennel bulb, thinly sliced

1 lb/450 g potatoes, cut into chunks

⅔ cup dry white wine

1 tbsp fresh thyme leaves

2 bay leaves

4 ripe tomatoes, peeled and chopped

2 lb/900 g mixed fish fillets, such as haddock, hake, mackerel, or red mullet, coarsely chopped

2 tbsp chopped fresh parsley

salt and pepper

crusty bread, to serve

1 Using a mortar and pestle, crush the saffron and add it to the fish stock. Stir the mixture and set aside to steep for at least 10 minutes.

2 Heat the olive oil and butter together in a large, heavy pan. Add the onion and cook over low heat, stirring occasionally, for 4–5 minutes until softened, but not browned. Add the garlic, leek, fennel, and potatoes. Cover and cook for a further 10–15 minutes until the vegetables are softened.

3 Add the white wine and simmer rapidly for 3–4 minutes until it has reduced by about half. Add the thyme, bay leaves ,and tomatoes and stir well. Add the saffron-steeped fish stock. Bring to a boil, cover, and simmer over low heat for about 15 minutes until all the vegetables are tender.

4 Add the fish, return to a boil, and simmer for a further 3–4 minutes until all the fish is tender. Add the parsley and season to taste. Using a slotted spoon, remove the fish and vegetables to a warmed serving dish. Serve the soup with plenty of crusty bread.

VARIATION
Once the fish and vegetables have been cooked, you could process the soup in a food processor or blender and pass it through a strainer to give a smooth fish soup.

Squid Stew

This is a rich and flavorful stew of slowly cooked squid, in a sauce of tomatoes and red wine. The squid becomes very tender.

NUTRITIONAL INFORMATION

Calories 284	Sugars 5g
Protein 31g	Fat 12g
Carbohydrate 9g	Saturates 2g

 20 mins   2¼ hrs

SERVES 4

INGREDIENTS

1 lb 10 oz/750 g squid

3 tbsp olive oil

1 onion, chopped

3 garlic cloves, finely chopped

1 tsp fresh thyme leaves

14 oz/400 g can chopped tomatoes

⅔ cup red wine

1¼ cups water

1 tbsp chopped fresh parsley

salt and pepper

1 To prepare whole squid, hold the body firmly and grasp the tentacles just inside the body. Pull firmly to remove the innards. Find the transparent "quill" and remove. Grasp the wings on the outside of the body and pull to remove the outer skin.

VARIATIONS

This recipe can be used as the basis for a more substantial fish stew. Before adding the parsley, add extra seafood such as scallops, pieces of fish fillet, and large shrimp. Cook for a further 2 minutes.

Trim the tentacles just below the beak and reserve. Wash the body and tentacles under cold running water. Slice the body into rings. Drain well on paper towels.

2 Heat the oil in a large, flameproof casserole. Add the prepared squid and cook over medium heat, stirring occasionally, until lightly browned.

3 Reduce the heat and add the onion, garlic, and thyme. Cook for a further 5 minutes until softened.

4 Stir in the tomatoes, red wine, and water. Bring to a boil and cook in a preheated oven, 275°F/140°C, for 2 hours. Stir in the parsley and season to taste. Serve immediately.

Spanish Fish Stew

This is an impressive-looking Catalan dish using two classic Spanish cooking methods—the *sofrito* and the *picada*.

NUTRITIONAL INFORMATION

Calories	346	Sugars	.........4g
Protein	........37g	Fat	..........13g
Carbohydrate	....11g	Saturates	.......2g

🦐 🦐 🦐 🦐

🧊 30 mins   🕐 1 hr

SERVES 6

INGREDIENTS

5 tbsp olive oil

2 large onions, finely chopped

2 tomatoes, peeled, deseeded, and diced

2 slices white bread, crusts removed

4 almonds, toasted

3 garlic cloves, roughly chopped

12 oz/350 g cooked lobster

7 oz/200 g cleaned squid

7 oz/200 g monkfish fillet

7 oz/200 g cod fillet, skinned

1 tbsp all-purpose flour

6 large raw shrimp

6 langoustines

18 live mussels, scrubbed, beards removed

8 large live clams, scrubbed

1 tbsp chopped fresh parsley

½ cup brandy

salt and pepper

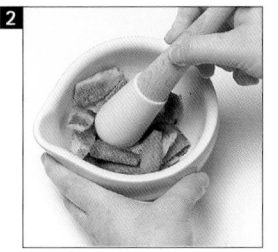
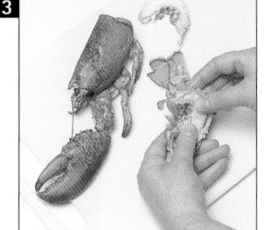

1 Heat 3 tablespoons of the oil and cook the onions gently for 10–15 minutes until lightly golden. Add the tomatoes and cook until they have softened.

2 Heat 1 tablespoon of the remaining oil and cook the slices of bread until crisp. Break into pieces and put into a mortar with the almonds and 2 garlic cloves. Pound to a fine paste. Alternatively, process in a food processor.

3 Split the lobster lengthwise. Remove and discard the intestinal vein, the stomach sac, and the spongy gills. Crack the claws and remove the meat. Take out the flesh from the tail and chop into large chunks. Slice the squid into rings.

4 Season the monkfish, cod, and lobster and dust with flour. Heat a little of the remaining oil and separately brown the monkfish, cod, lobster, squid, shrimp, and langoustines. Arrange them in a flameproof casserole as they brown.

5 Add the mussels and clams and the remaining garlic and parsley. Set the pan over low heat. Pour over the brandy and ignite. When the flames have died down, add the tomato mixture and just enough water to cover. Bring to a boil and simmer for 3–4 minutes until the mussels and clams have opened. Stir in the bread mixture and season. Simmer for a further 5 minutes and serve.

Moroccan Fish Tagine

A tagine is a Moroccan cooking vessel consisting of an earthenware dish with a domed lid that has a steam hole in the top.

NUTRITIONAL INFORMATION

Calories	188	Sugars 5g
Protein	........17g	Fat 11g
Carbohydrate	....7g	Saturates 1g

 10 mins   1¼ hrs

SERVES 4

INGREDIENTS

2 tbsp olive oil

1 large onion, finely chopped

pinch of saffron threads

½ tsp ground cinnamon

1 tsp ground coriander

½ tsp ground cumin

½ tsp ground turmeric

7 oz/200 g can chopped tomatoes

1¼ cups fish stock

4 small red snapper cleaned, boned, and heads and tails removed

½ cup pitted green olives

1 tbsp chopped preserved lemon

3 tbsp fresh chopped fresh cilantro

salt and pepper

couscous, to serve

COOK'S TIP

For preserved lemons, take enough lemons to fill a preserving jar. Quarter them lengthwise without cutting all the way through. Pack them with ¼ cup sea salt per lemon. Add the juice of 1 more lemon and top up with water to cover. Leave for 1 month.

1 Heat the olive oil in a large pan or flameproof casserole. Add the onion and cook gently, stirring occasionally, for 10 minutes without coloring until softened. Add the saffron, cinnamon, ground coriander, cumin, and turmeric and cook for a further 30 seconds, stirring.

2 Add the chopped tomatoes and fish stock and stir well. Bring to a boil, cover, and simmer for 15 minutes. Uncover and simmer for a further 20–35 minutes until thickened.

3 Cut each red snapper in half, then add the pieces to the pan, pushing them into the sauce. Simmer gently for a further 5–6 minutes until the fish is just cooked.

4 Carefully stir in the olives, preserved lemon, and the chopped cilantro. Season to taste and serve with couscous.

Stewed Sardines

This is an unusual stew of sardines cooked with baby onions, tomatoes, olives, raisins, Marsala, and pine nuts.

NUTRITIONAL INFORMATION

Calories	412	Sugars	14g
Protein	26g	Fat	27g
Carbohydrate	15g	Saturates	5g

1¼ hrs   50 mins

SERVES 4

INGREDIENTS

scant ½ cup raisins

3 tbsp Marsala

4 tbsp olive oil

8 oz/225 g baby onions, halved if large

2 garlic cloves, chopped

1 tbsp chopped fresh sage

4 large tomatoes, peeled and chopped

⅔ cup fish or vegetable stock

2 tbsp balsamic vinegar

1 lb/450 g fresh sardines, cleaned

¼ cup pitted black olives

¼ cup pine nuts, toasted

2 tbsp chopped fresh parsley

1 Put the raisins in a small bowl and pour over the Marsala. Set aside to soak for about 1 hour until the raisins are plump. Strain, reserving both the Marsala and the raisins.

2 Heat the olive oil in a large pan and fry the onions over low heat for 15 minutes until golden and tender. Add the garlic and chopped sage and cook for a further minute.

3 Add the tomatoes, cook for a further 2–3 minutes, then add the stock, vinegar, and reserved Marsala. Bring to a boil, cover, and simmer for 25 minutes.

4 Add the sardines and simmer gently for 2–3 minutes before adding the raisins, olives and pine nuts. Simmer for 2–3 minutes until the sardines are cooked. Add the parsley and serve immediately.

VARIATIONS
Substitute Home-Salted Cod (see page 696) or smoked cod for the sardines.

Red Shrimp Curry

Like all Thai curries, this one has as its base a paste
of chiles and other spices and a sauce of coconut milk.

NUTRITIONAL INFORMATION

Calories 149   Sugars 4g
Protein ....15g   Fat 7g
Carbohydrate ....6g   Saturates 1g

15 mins   10 mins

SERVES 4

INGREDIENTS

2 tbsp vegetable oil

1 garlic clove, finely chopped

1 tbsp red curry paste (see below)

scant 1 cup coconut milk

2 tbsp Thai fish sauce

1 tsp sugar

12 large raw shrimp, deveined

2 kaffir lime leaves, finely shredded

1 small fresh red chile, deseeded and
thinly sliced

10 leaves Thai basil, if available, or
ordinary basil

RED CURRY PASTE

3 dried long red chiles

½ tsp ground coriander

¼ tsp ground cumin

½ tsp ground black pepper

2 garlic cloves, chopped

2 lemongrass stalks, chopped

1 kaffir lime leaf, finely chopped

1 tsp grated fresh ginger root or galangal

1 tsp shrimp paste (optional)

½ tsp salt

1 Make the red curry paste. Put all the ingredients in a
blender or spice grinder and blend to a smooth paste,
adding a little water if necessary. Alternatively, pound the
ingredients together using a mortar and pestle until
smooth. Set aside.

2 Heat the oil in a wok or skillet until almost smoking.
Add the chopped garlic and fry until golden. Add
1 tablespoon of the curry paste and cook, stirring
constantly, for a further minute. Add half the coconut milk,
the fish sauce, and the sugar. Stir well until the mixture has
thickened slightly.

3 Add the shrimp and simmer for 3–4 minutes until they
turn color. Add the remaining coconut milk, the lime
leaves, and fresh red chile. Cook for a further 2–3 minutes
until the shrimp are just tender.

4 Add the basil leaves and stir until wilted. Transfer to a
warmed serving dish and serve immediately.

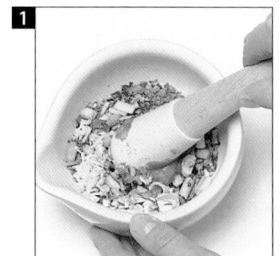

Curried Shrimp

The best way to approach this recipe is to prepare everything beforehand, including measuring out the spices. The cooking time is then very quick.

NUTRITIONAL INFORMATION

Calories ....272 Sugars 5g
Protein ....29g Fat 15g
Carbohydrate ....5g Saturates 2g

40 mins   15 mins

SERVES 4

I N G R E D I E N T S

12 oz/350 g small zucchini

1 tsp salt

1 lb/450 g cooked jumbo shrimp

5 tbsp vegetable oil

4 garlic cloves, finely chopped

5 tbsp chopped fresh cilantro

1 fresh green chile, deseeded and
  finely chopped

½ tsp ground turmeric

1½ tsp ground cumin

pinch of cayenne pepper

7 oz/200 g can chopped tomatoes

1 tsp grated fresh ginger root

1 tbsp lemon juice

lime wedges, to garnish

steamed basmati rice, to serve

1 Cut the zucchini into batons. Put into a colander, sprinkle with a little of the salt, and set aside for 30 minutes. Rinse, drain, and pat dry. Spread the shrimp on paper towels to drain.

2 Heat the oil in a wok or skillet over high heat. Add the garlic. As soon as the garlic begins to brown, add the zucchini, cilantro, chile, turmeric, cumin, cayenne, tomatoes, ginger, lemon juice, and remaining salt. Stir well and bring to a boil.

3 Cover and simmer over low heat for about 5 minutes. Uncover and add the shrimp.

4 Increase the heat to high and simmer for about 5 minutes until the liquid is reduced to a thick sauce. Serve with basmati rice, garnished with lime wedges.

VARIATION

If you can't find cooked jumbo shrimp for this recipe, use cooked peeled small shrimp instead, but these release quite a lot of liquid, so you may need to increase the final simmering time to thicken the sauce.

Broiled Red Mullet

Try to get small red mullet for this dish. If you can only get larger fish, serve one to each person and increase the cooking time accordingly.

NUTRITIONAL INFORMATION

Calories . . . . .111 Sugars 0.8g
Protein . . . . . . .10.2g Fat 5.4g
Carbohydrate . . .5.9g Saturates 0.7g

🥖 10 mins   🕐 20 mins

SERVES 4

I N G R E D I E N T S

1 lemon, thinly sliced

2 garlic cloves, crushed

4 fresh flat leaf parsley sprigs

4 fresh thyme sprigs

8 fresh sage leaves

2 large shallots, sliced

8 small red mullet, cleaned

8 slices prosciutto

salt and pepper

SAUTE POTATOES AND SHALLOTS

4 tbsp olive oil

2 lb/900 g potatoes, diced

8 whole garlic cloves, unpeeled

12 small whole shallots

FOR THE DRESSING

4 tbsp olive oil

1 tbsp lemon juice

1 tbsp chopped fresh flat leaf parsley

1 tbsp chopped fresh chives

salt and pepper

1 For the sauté potatoes and shallots, heat the olive oil in a large skillet and add the potatoes, garlic, and shallots. Cook gently, stirring frequently, for 12–15 minutes until golden, crisp, and tender.

2 Meanwhile, divide the lemon slices, halved if necessary, garlic, parsley, thyme, sage, and shallots among the cavities of the fish. Season well. Wrap a slice of prosciutto around each fish. Secure with a toothpick.

3 Arrange the fish on a broiler pan and cook under a preheated hot broiler for 5–6 minutes on each side until tender.

4 To make the dressing, combine the oil, and lemon juice with the chopped parsley and chives. Season with salt and pepper to taste.

5 Divide the potatoes and shallots among 4 serving plates and top each with the fish. Drizzle the dressing over them and serve immediately.

Poached Rainbow Trout

This colorful, flavorsome dish is served cold and therefore makes a lovely summer lunch or *al fresco* supper dish.

NUTRITIONAL INFORMATION

Calories 99   Sugars 1.1g
Protein . . . . .5.7g   Fat 6.3g
Carbohydrate . . .3.7g   Saturates 1g

 25 mins   1 hr

SERVES 4

INGREDIENTS

3 lb/1.3 kg rainbow trout fillets

1 lb 9 oz/700 g new potatoes

3 scallions, finely chopped

1 egg, hard-cooked and chopped

COURT-BOUILLON

3¾ cups cold water

3¾ cups dry white wine

3 tbsp white wine vinegar

2 large carrots, coarsely chopped

1 onion, coarsely chopped

2 celery stalks, coarsely chopped

2 leeks, coarsely chopped

2 garlic cloves, coarsely chopped

2 fresh bay leaves

4 fresh parsley sprigs

4 fresh thyme sprigs

6 black peppercorns

1 tsp salt

WATERCRESS MAYONNAISE

1 egg yolk

1 tsp Dijon mustard

1 tsp white wine vinegar

2 oz/55 g watercress leaves, chopped

1 cup light olive oil

salt and pepper

1 First make the court-bouillon. Place all the ingredients in a large pan and bring to a boil over low heat. Cover and simmer for about 30 minutes. Strain the liquid through a fine strainer into a clean pan. Bring to a boil again and simmer rapidly, uncovered, for 15–20 minutes until the court-bouillon is reduced to about 2½ cups.

2 Place the trout in a large skillet. Add the court-bouillon and bring to a boil over low heat. Remove from the heat and set the fish aside in the liquid to cool.

3 Meanwhile, make the watercress mayonnaise. Put the egg yolk, mustard, wine vinegar, watercress, and salt and pepper to taste into a food processor or blender and process for 30 seconds until foaming. Begin adding the olive oil, drop by drop, until the mixture begins to thicken. Continue adding the oil in a slow steady stream until it is all incorporated. Add a little hot water if the mixture seems too thick. Season to taste and set aside.

4 Cook the potatoes in plenty of lightly salted boiling water for about 12–15 minutes until soft and tender. Drain well and refresh them under cold running water. Set the potatoes aside until cold.

5 When the potatoes are cold, cut them in half, if they are very large, and toss thoroughly with the watercress mayonnaise, finely chopped scallions, and hard-cooked egg.

6 Carefully lift the fish from the poaching liquid and drain on paper towels. Carefully pull the skin away from each of the trout fillets and serve immediately with the potato salad.

Baked Salmon

This is a wonderful dish to serve as part of a buffet lunch or supper and can be served hot or cold.

NUTRITIONAL INFORMATION

Calories ...... .892	Sugars 2g
Protein 41g	Fat .... .79g
Carbohydrate 2g	Saturates ..... .12g

30 mins   1½ hrs

SERVES 8–10

INGREDIENTS

6 lb 8 oz/3 kg salmon, filleted

8 tbsp chopped mixed herbs

2 tbsp green peppercorns in brine, drained

1 tsp finely grated lime rind

6 tbsp dry vermouth or dry white wine

salt and pepper

fresh parsley sprigs, to garnish

RED BELL PEPPER RELISH

½ cup white wine vinegar

1¼ cups light olive oil

1–2 tsp chili sauce

6 scallions, thinly sliced

1 orange or red bell pepper, deseeded and finely diced

1 tbsp chopped fresh flat leaf parsley

2 tbsp chopped fresh chives

CAPER AND DILL PICKLE MAYONNAISE

1½ cups mayonnaise

3 tbsp chopped capers

3 tbsp finely chopped dill pickles

2 tbsp chopped fresh flat leaf parsley

1 tbsp Dijon mustard

1 Wash and dry the salmon fillets and place 1 fillet, skin side down, on a large sheet of oiled foil. Combine the herbs, peppercorns, and lime rind and spread over the top. Season to taste with salt and pepper and lay the second fillet on top, skin side up. Drizzle over the vermouth or white wine. Wrap the foil over the salmon, twisting well to make a loose, but tightly sealed parcel.

2 Transfer the foil parcel to a large cookie sheet and bake in a preheated oven, 250°F/120°C, for 1½ hours until tender. Remove from the oven and set aside to rest for 20 minutes before serving.

3 Meanwhile, make the red bell pepper relish. Whisk together the vinegar, olive oil, and chili sauce to taste. Add the scallions, red bell pepper, parsley, and chives. Season to taste with salt and pepper and set aside.

4 To make the caper and dill pickle mayonnaise, mix all the ingredients together and set aside.

5 Unwrap the cooked salmon and slice thickly. Arrange the slices on a large serving platter and serve with the red bell pepper relish and caper and dill pickle mayonnaise. Garnish with fresh parsley sprigs.

Grilled Monkfish

Monkfish cooks very well on a barbecue because it is a firm-fleshed fish. Make sure that you remove the membrane before cooking.

NUTRITIONAL INFORMATION

Calories 219   Sugars 0g
Protein . . . . .28g   Fat 12g
Carbohydrate . . . .1g   Saturates 2g

2¼ hrs   5–6 mins

SERVES 4

I N G R E D I E N T S

4 tbsp olive oil

grated rind of 1 lime

2 tsp Thai fish sauce

2 garlic cloves, crushed

1 tsp grated fresh ginger root

2 tbsp chopped fresh basil

1 lb 9 oz/700 g monkfish fillet, cut
  into chunks

2 limes, each cut into 6 wedges

salt and pepper

1 Combine the olive oil, lime rind, fish sauce, garlic, grated ginger, and basil in a nonmetallic bowl. Season to taste with salt and pepper and set aside.

2 Wash the fish chunks and pat dry with paper towels. Add them to the marinade and mix well to coat. Cover and set aside in the refrigerator to marinate for 2 hours, stirring occasionally.

3 If you are using bamboo skewers, soak them in cold water for 30 minutes to prevent them from charring.

4 Lift the monkfish pieces from the marinade with a slotted spoon and thread them onto the skewers, alternating with the lime wedges.

5 Transfer the skewers, either to a hot barbecue or to a preheated ridged griddle pan. Cook for 5–6 minutes, turning regularly, until the fish is tender. Serve the skewers immediately.

VARIATION

You could use any type of white fleshed fish for this recipe but sprinkle the pieces with salt and leave for 2 hours to firm the flesh, before rinsing, drying, and then adding to the marinade.

Swordfish Steaks

Swordfish has a firm, meaty texture, but has a
tendency to dry out during cooking unless well marinated first.

NUTRITIONAL INFORMATION

Calories	548	Sugars	.........0g
Protein	........28g	Fat	..........48g
Carbohydrate	....1g	Saturates	.......7g

2¼ hrs   4–6 mins

SERVES 4

I N G R E D I E N T S

4 x swordfish steaks, about 5½ oz/
   150 g each

4 tbsp olive oil

1 garlic clove, crushed

1 tsp lemon rind

lemon wedges, to garnish

S A L S A   V E R D E

1 cup flat leaf parsley leaves

½ cup mixed fresh herbs, such as basil,
   mint, chives

1 garlic clove, chopped

1 tbsp capers, drained and rinsed

1 tbsp green peppercorns in brine, drained

4 anchovies in oil, drained and
   roughly chopped

1 tsp Dijon mustard

½ cup extra virgin olive oil

salt and pepper

VARIATIONS

Any firm fleshed-fish will
do for this recipe. Try tuna
or even shark instead.

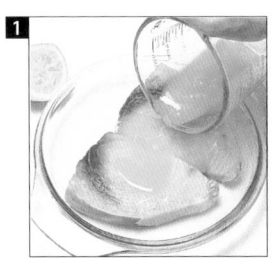  

1 Wash the dry the swordfish steaks
and place in a nonmetallic dish.
Combine the olive oil, garlic, and lemon
rind. Pour over the swordfish steaks and
set aside to marinate for 2 hours.

2 For the salsa verde, put all the
ingredients into a food processor or
blender. Process to a smooth paste, adding
a little warm water if necessary. Season to
taste with salt and pepper and set aside.

3 Remove the swordfish steaks from the
marinade. Cook on a barbecue or in a
preheated ridged griddle pan for
2–3 minutes each side until tender. Serve
immediately with the salsa verde and
garnished with lemon wedges.

Swordfish or Tuna Fajitas

Fajitas are usually made with chicken or lamb, but using a firm fish, such as swordfish or tuna, works very well too.

NUTRITIONAL INFORMATION

Calories ....766 Sugars 12g
Protein ....52g Fat 36g
Carbohydrate ...63g Saturates 10g

 1¼–2¼ hrs   7 mins

SERVES 4

INGREDIENTS

3 tbsp olive oil

2 tsp chili powder

1 tsp ground cumin

pinch of cayenne pepper

1 garlic clove, crushed

2 lb/900 g swordfish or tuna

1 red bell pepper, deseeded and
    thinly sliced

1 yellow bell pepper, deseeded and
    thinly sliced

2 zucchini, cut into batons

1 large onion, thinly sliced

12 soft flour tortillas

1 tbsp lemon juice

3 tbsp chopped fresh cilantro

salt and pepper

⅔ cup sour cream, to serve

GUACAMOLE

1 large avocado, peeled and pitted

1 tomato, peeled, deseeded, and diced

1 garlic clove, crushed

dash of Tabasco sauce

2 tbsp lemon juice

salt and pepper

1 Combine the olive oil, chili powder, cumin, cayenne, and garlic. Cut the swordfish or tuna into large chunks and mix with the marinade. Set aside for 1–2 hours.

2 Heat a large skillet until hot. Add the fish and its marinade to the skillet and cook, stirring occasionally, for 2 minutes until the fish begins to brown.

3 Add the red and yellow bell peppers, zucchini, and onion and continue cooking for a further 5 minutes until the vegetables have softened, but are still firm.

4 Meanwhile, warm the tortillas in a low oven or microwave according to the packet instructions.

5 To make the guacamole, mash the avocado flesh with a fork until fairly smooth, stir in the tomato, garlic, Tabasco, and lemon juice. Season to taste with salt and pepper.

6 Add the lemon juice, cilantro, and seasoning to the fish and vegetable mix. Spoon some of the mixture down the warmed tortilla. Top with guacamole and a spoonful of sour cream and roll up.

Smoked Fish Pie

What cookbook would be complete without a fish pie? This is a classic version with smoked fish, shrimp, and vegetables.

NUTRITIONAL INFORMATION

Calories 562	Sugars 9g
Protein 42g	Fat 29g
Carbohydrate ...35g	Saturates 16g

 10 mins   1½ hrs

SERVES 4

INGREDIENTS

2 tbsp olive oil

1 onion, finely chopped

1 leek, thinly sliced

1 carrot, diced

1 celery stalk, diced

4 oz/115 g white mushrooms, halved

grated rind of 1 lemon

12 oz/350 g skinless smoked cod or
    haddock fillets, cubed

12 oz/350 g skinless white fish fillets, such
    as haddock, hake or monkfish, cubed

2 cups peeled cooked shrimp

2 tbsp chopped fresh parsley

1 tbsp chopped fresh dill

SAUCE

4 tbsp butter

4 tbsp all-purpose flour

1 tsp mustard powder

2½ cups milk

¾ cup grated Swiss cheese

TOPPING

1 lb 8 oz/675 g potatoes, unpeeled

4 tbsp butter, melted

4 tbsp grated Swiss cheese

salt and pepper

1 For the sauce, melt the butter in a large pan, add the flour and mustard powder. Stir until smooth and cook over very low heat for 2 minutes without coloring. Gradually whisk in the milk until smooth. Simmer gently for 2 minutes, then stir in the grated cheese until melted and smooth. Remove the pan from the heat and put a piece of plastic wrap over the surface of the sauce to prevent a skin from forming. Set aside.

2 Meanwhile, for the topping, cook the whole potatoes in plenty of lightly salted boiling water for about 15 minutes until tender. Drain well and set aside until cool enough to handle.

3 Heat the olive oil in a clean pan and add the onion. Cook over low heat, stirring occasionally, for 5 minutes until softened. Add the sliced leek, the diced carrot and celery, and the mushrooms and cook for a further 10 minutes, stirring occasionally, until all the vegetables have softened. Stir in the grated lemon rind and cook briefly.

4 Add the softened vegetables with the fish, shrimp, parsley, and dill to the sauce. Season to taste and transfer to a greased 7½ cup casserole.

5 Peel the cooled potatoes and grate them coarsely. Mix with the melted butter. Cover the fish and vegetable mixture with the grated potato and sprinkle with the grated Swiss cheese.

6 Cover loosely with foil and bake in a preheated oven, 400°F/200°C, for 30 minutes. Remove the foil and bake for an additional 30 minutes until the topping is tender and golden and the filling is bubbling. Serve immediately with your favorite selection of vegetables.

Hake Steaks with Chermoula

The cooking time may seem long and indeed you could decrease it slightly if you prefer, but in Morocco they like their fish well cooked!

NUTRITIONAL INFORMATION

Calories	590	Sugars	.........1g
Protein	........42g	Fat	..........46g
Carbohydrate	....2g	Saturates	.......7g

1¼ hrs   35–40 mins

SERVES 4

I N G R E D I E N T S

4 hake steaks, about 8 oz/225 g each

1 cup pitted green olives

freshly cooked vegetables, to serve

M A R I N A D E

6 tbsp finely chopped fresh cilantro

6 tbsp finely chopped fresh parsley

6 garlic cloves, crushed

1 tbsp ground cumin

1 tsp ground coriander

1 tbsp paprika

pinch of cayenne pepper

⅔ cup fresh lemon juice

1¼ cups olive oil

1 For the marinade, combine the fresh cilantro, parsley, garlic, cumin, ground coriander, paprika, cayenne, lemon juice, and olive oil in a bowl.

2 Wash the hake steaks and pat dry with paper towels. Place them in an casserole. Pour the marinade over the fish and set aside for at least 1 hour and preferably overnight.

3 Before cooking, sprinkle the olives over the fish. Cover the dish with foil.

4 Cook in a preheated oven, 325°F/ 160°C, for 35–40 minutes until the fish is tender. Serve immediately with freshly cooked vegetables.

VARIATION
Remove the fish from the marinade and dust with seasoned flour. Fry in oil or clarified butter until golden. Warm the marinade, but do not boil, and serve as a sauce with lemon slices.

Stuffed Mackerel

This is an easier variation of a Middle Eastern recipe for stuffed mackerel which involves removing the mackerel flesh, while leaving the skin intact.

NUTRITIONAL INFORMATION

Calories	488	Sugars	........12g
Protein	........34g	Fat	..........34g
Carbohydrate	...12g	Saturates	.......6g

10 mins   20 mins

SERVES 4

INGREDIENTS

4 large mackerel, cleaned

1 tbsp olive oil

1 small onion, thinly sliced

1 tsp ground cinnamon

½ tsp ground ginger

2 tbsp raisins

2 tbsp pine nuts, toasted

8 grape leaves in brine, drained

salt and pepper

 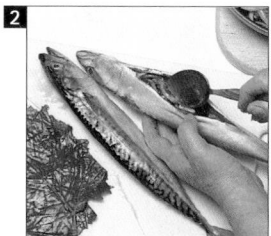 

VARIATION

This stuffing works equally well with many other fish, including sea bass and red snapper.

1 Wash the fish, pat dry with paper towels, and set aside. Heat the oil in a small skillet and add the onion. Cook gently for 5 minutes until softened. Add the cinnamon and ginger and cook for 30 seconds, then add the raisins and pine nuts. Season to taste. Remove from the heat and let cool.

2 Stuff each fish with a quarter of the stuffing mixture. Wrap each fish in 2 grape leaves, securing with toothpicks.

3 Cook on a preheated barbecue or ridged griddle pan for 5 minutes on each side until the grape leaves have scorched and the fish is tender.

Tuna Fishcakes

These fishcakes make a satisfying and quick midweek supper. The tomato sauce is flavored with a tempting combination of lemon, garlic, and basil.

NUTRITIONAL INFORMATION

Calories ....638 Sugars 5g
Protein ....35g Fat 40g
Carbohydrate ...38g Saturates 5g

5 mins   1¼ hrs

SERVES 4

INGREDIENTS

8 oz/225 g potatoes, cubed

1 tbsp olive oil

1 large shallot, finely chopped

1 garlic clove, finely chopped

1 tsp fresh thyme leaves

14 oz/400 g canned tuna in olive
    oil, drained

grated rind of ½ lemon

1 tbsp chopped fresh parsley

2–3 tbsp all-purpose flour

1 egg, lightly beaten

2 cups fresh bread crumbs

vegetable oil, for frying

salt and pepper

QUICK TOMATO SAUCE

2 tbsp olive oil

14 oz/400 g canned chopped tomatoes

1 garlic clove, crushed

½ tsp sugar

grated rind of ½ lemon

1 tbsp chopped fresh basil

salt and pepper

1 For the tuna fishcakes, cook the potatoes in plenty of boiling salted water for 12–15 minutes until tender. Mash, leaving a few lumps, and set aside.

2 Heat the oil in a small skillet and cook the shallot gently for 5 minutes until softened. Add the garlic and thyme leaves and cook for an additional minute. Let cool slightly, then add to the potatoes with the tuna, lemon rind, parsley, and seasoning. Mix together well, but leave some texture.

3 Form the mixture into 6–8 patties. Dip the cakes first in the flour, then the egg, and finally, the bread crumbs to coat. Chill for 30 minutes.

4 For the tomato sauce, put the olive oil, tomatoes, garlic, sugar, lemon rind, and basil into a pan, season to taste with salt and pepper, and bring to a boil. Cover and simmer for 30 minutes. Uncover and simmer for 15 minutes until thickened.

5 Heat enough oil in a skillet to cover the base generously. Fry the fishcakes in batches for 3–4 minutes each side until golden and crisp. Drain on paper towels while you fry the remaining fishcakes. Serve hot with the tomato sauce.

Salmon Frittata

A frittata is an Italian slow-cooked omelet, similar to the Spanish tortilla. Here it is filled with salmon, herbs, and vegetables.

NUTRITIONAL INFORMATION

Calories	300	Sugars	.........5g
Protein	........22g	Fat	..........21g
Carbohydrate	....7g	Saturates	.......8g

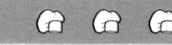

 15 mins 1 hr

SERVES 6

I N G R E D I E N T S

9 oz/250 g skinless, boneless salmon

3 fresh thyme sprigs

fresh parsley sprig

5 black peppercorns

½ small onion, sliced

½ celery stalk, sliced

½ carrot, chopped

6 oz/175 g asparagus spears, chopped

3 oz/85 g baby carrots, halved

4 tbsp butter

1 large onion, thinly sliced

1 garlic clove, finely chopped

1 cup peas, fresh or frozen

8 eggs, lightly beaten

2 tbsp chopped fresh parsley

1 tbsp chopped fresh dill

salt and pepper

lemon wedges, to garnish

TO SERVE

crème fraîche

salad

crusty bread

1 Place the salmon in a pan with 1 thyme sprig, the parsley sprig, peppercorns, onion, celery, and carrot. Add water and bring to a boil. Remove the pan from the heat and set aside for 5 minutes. Lift out the fish, flake the flesh, and set aside. Discard the poaching liquid.

2 Blanch the asparagus in boiling water for 2 minutes. Drain and refresh under cold water. Blanch the carrots for 4 minutes. Drain and refresh under cold water. Drain again and pat dry. Set aside.

3 Heat half the butter in a large skillet and add the onion. Cook gently for 8–10 minutes until softened, but not colored. Add the garlic and remaining thyme and cook for a further minute. Add the asparagus, carrots, and peas and heat through. Remove from the heat.

4 Add the vegetables to the eggs with the chopped parsley, dill, salmon, and seasoning and stir briefly. Heat the remaining butter in the skillet and return the mixture to the pan. Cover and cook over low heat for 10 minutes.

5 Cook under a preheated broiler for a further 5 minutes until set and golden. Serve hot or cold in wedges, topped with a spoon of crème fraîche, salad, and crusty bread. Garnish with lemon wedges.

Mixed Seafood Brochettes

If your fish store sells halibut steaks, you will probably need one large skinned and boned steak for this dish.

NUTRITIONAL INFORMATION

Calories 455   Sugars 0g
Protein ....32g   Fat 20g
Carbohydrate ...39g   Saturates 9g

2¼ hrs   20 mins

SERVES 4

INGREDIENTS

8 oz/225 g skinless halibut fillet

8 oz/225 g skinless salmon fillet

8 scallops

8 large jumbo shrimp or langoustines

16 fresh bay leaves

1 lemon, sliced

4 tbsp olive oil

grated rind 1 lemon

4 tbsp chopped fresh mixed herbs,
    such as thyme, parsley, chives, basil

pepper

LEMON BUTTER RICE

scant 1 cup long grain rice

grated rind and juice 1 lemon

4 tbsp butter

salt and pepper

TO GARNISH

lemon wedges

fresh dill sprigs

1 Chop the halibut and salmon into 8 pieces each. Thread onto 8 skewers, with the scallops and jumbo shrimp or langoustines, alternating with the bay leaves and lemon slices. Put the skewers into a nonmetallic dish in a single layer if possible.

2 Combine the olive oil, lemon rind, herbs, and pepper. Pour this mixture over the fish. Cover and set aside to marinate for 2 hours, turning once or twice.

3 For the lemon butter rice, bring a large pan of lightly salted water to a boil and add the rice and lemon rind. Return to a boil, then lower the heat, and simmer for 7–8 minutes until the rice is tender. Drain thoroughly and immediately stir in the lemon juice and butter. Season with salt and pepper to taste.

4 Meanwhile, lift the fish brochettes from their marinade and cook on a hot barbecue or under a preheated hot broiler for 8–10 minutes, turning frequently, until cooked through. Serve with lemon butter rice and garnish with lemon wedges and dill.

Chargrilled Scallops

Marinated scallops, chargrilled and served with couscous
studded with colorful vegetables and herbs—simply wonderful.

NUTRITIONAL INFORMATION

Calories	401	Sugars	.........3g
Protein	........20g	Fat	..........21g
Carbohydrate	...34g	Saturates	.......3g

2½ hrs   8 mins

SERVES 4

INGREDIENTS

16 king scallops

3 tbsp olive oil

grated rind of 1 lime

2 tbsp chopped fresh basil

2 tbsp chopped fresh chives

1 garlic clove, finely chopped

pepper

JEWELED COUSCOUS

1⅓ cup couscous

½ red bell pepper, deseeded and halved

½ yellow bell pepper, deseeded and halved

4 tbsp extra virgin olive oil

4 oz/115 g cucumber, chopped into ½ inch/
1 cm pieces

3 scallions, finely chopped

1 tbsp lime juice

2 tbsp shredded fresh basil

salt and pepper

TO GARNISH

fresh basil leaves

lime wedges

1 Put the scallops into a nonmetallic dish. Combine the olive oil, lime rind, basil, chives, garlic, and pepper. Pour over the scallops and cover. Set aside to marinate for 2 hours.

2 Cook the couscous according to the packet instructions, omitting any butter recommended.

3 Brush the bell pepper halves with a little oil and place under a preheated hot broiler for 5–6 minutes, turning once, until the skins are charred and the flesh is tender. Put in a plastic bag and set aside until cool enough to handle. Peel off the skins and chop the flesh into ½ inch/1 cm pieces. Add to the couscous with the remaining olive oil, cucumber, scallions, lime juice, and seasoning.

4 Lift the scallops from the marinade with a slotted spoon and thread onto 4 skewers. Cook on a hot barbecue or preheated ridged griddled pan for 1 minute on each side until charred and firm, but not quite cooked through. Remove from the heat and set aside to rest for 2 minutes.

5 Stir the shredded basil into the couscous and divide it among 4 individual serving plates. Put a skewer on each, garnish with basil leaves and lime wedges. Serve immediately.

Seafood Lasagna

You can use any fish and any sauce you like in this recipe—
try smoked haddock and whiskey sauce, or cod with cheese sauce.

NUTRITIONAL INFORMATION

Calories	790	Sugars	........23g
Protein	........55g	Fat	..........32g
Carbohydrate	...74g	Saturates	......19g

30 mins   45 mins

SERVES 4

INGREDIENTS

1lb/450 g smoked haddock fillet, skin removed and flesh flaked

4 oz/115 g shrimp

4 oz/115 g sole fillet, skin removed and flesh sliced

juice of 1 lemon

4 tbsp butter

3 leeks, very thinly sliced

6 tbsp all-purpose flour

about 2½ cups milk

2 tbsp honey

1¾ cups grated mozzarella cheese

1 lb/450 g pre-cooked lasagna

⅔ cup freshly grated Parmesan cheese

pepper

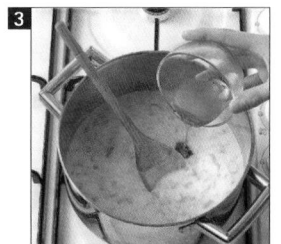

1 Put the haddock fillet, shrimp, and sole fillet into a large bowl and season with pepper and lemon juice to taste. Set aside while you make the sauce.

2 Melt the butter in a large pan. Add the leeks and cook over low heat, stirring occasionally, for 8 minutes until softened. Add the flour and cook, stirring constantly, for 1 minute. Gradually stir in enough milk to make a smooth, thick, creamy sauce.

3 Blend in the honey and mozzarella cheese and cook for a further 3 minutes. Turn off the heat and mix in the fish and shrimp.

4 Make alternate layers of fish sauce and lasagna in a casserole, finishing with a layer of fish sauce on top. Generously sprinkle over the grated Parmesan cheese and bake in a preheated oven, 350°F/180°C, for 30 minutes. Serve immediately.

VARIATION
For a cider sauce, substitute 1 finely chopped shallot for the leeks, 1¼ cups hard cider and 1¼ cups heavy cream for the milk, and 1 teaspoon mustard for the honey. For a Tuscan sauce, substitute 1 chopped fennel bulb for the leeks; omit the honey.

Spaghetti al Vongole

This is a very full-flavored and elegant looking dish, especially if you can find small clams that have richly colored shells.

NUTRITIONAL INFORMATION

Calories 471   Sugars 9g
Protein . . . . .24g   Fat 8g
Carbohydrate . . .75g   Saturates 1g

 10 mins   1 hr

SERVES 4

INGREDIENTS

2 lb/900 g live clams, scrubbed

2 tbsp olive oil

1 large onion, finely chopped

2 garlic cloves, finely chopped

1 tsp fresh thyme leaves

⅔ cup white wine

14 oz/400 g can chopped tomatoes

12 oz/350 g dried spaghetti

1 tbsp chopped fresh parsley

salt and pepper

1 Put the clams into a large pan with just the water clinging to their shells. Cook, covered, over high heat, shaking the pan occasionally, for 3–4 minutes until all the clams have opened. Remove from the heat and strain, reserving the cooking liquid. Discard any clams that remain closed. Set aside.

2 Heat the oil in a pan and add the onion. Cook for 10 minutes over low heat until softened, but not colored. Add the garlic and thyme and cook for a further 30 seconds.

3 Increase the heat and add the white wine. Simmer rapidly until reduced and syrupy. Add the tomatoes and reserved clam liquid. Cover and simmer for 15 minutes. Uncover and simmer for a further 15 minutes until thickened. Season to taste with salt and pepper.

4 Meanwhile, bring a large pan of lightly salted water to a boil. Add the pasta, bring back to a boil, and cook for 8–10 minutes until tender, but still firm to the bite. Drain well and return to the pan.

5 Add the clams to the tomato sauce and heat through for 2–3 minutes. Add the parsley and stir well. Add the tomato sauce to the pasta and toss together until the pasta is well coated in sauce. Serve immediately.

COOK'S TIP

If you are able to get only very large clams, reserve a few in their shells to garnish and shell the rest.

Squid Ink Pasta

This is a dramatic looking dish, with its jet-black pasta and rich sauce of squid. Definitely one for special occasions.

NUTRITIONAL INFORMATION

Calories 418   Sugars 2g
Protein . . . . .22g   Fat 12g
Carbohydrate . . .56g   Saturates 2g

  1½ hrs   30 mins

SERVES 6

INGREDIENTS

1 lb/450 g squid with their ink

10½ oz/300 g white bread flour

½ cup fine semolina

2 eggs

SAUCE

4 tbsp olive oil

2 garlic cloves, finely chopped

1 tsp paprika

3 plum tomatoes, peeled, deseeded, and diced

⅔ cup white wine

1 tbsp chopped fresh parsley

salt and pepper

1 To prepare the squid, grasp the head and tentacles and pull to remove the innards. The silvery ink sac lies at the furthest point from the tentacles—be careful to keep it intact. Cut the ink sac away from the innards. Cut the tentacles just below the beak and discard the remaining innards. Remove the "quill" from the body and remove the wings and skin. Wash the body and tentacles well.

2 Slice the body widthwise into rings and set aside with the tentacles. Slit open the ink sac and dilute with water to make ¼ cup. Set aside.

3 To make the pasta, sift together the flour and semolina. Make a well in the center and add the eggs. Using a wooden spoon, draw the flour and eggs together. Gradually add the squid ink—you may not need it all. Mix to a firm dough. Add a little more water if it seems too stiff and a little more flour if it seems too wet. Alternatively, put all the ingredients in the bowl of a mixer fitted with a kneading hook and mix together. Knead the dough for 10 minutes until smooth and elastic. The dough should have the feel of soft leather and be neither sticky nor should it break easily. Wrap in plastic wrap and set aside for 30 minutes.

4 Using a pasta machine, thinly roll out the dough and cut into thin ribbons. Alternatively, roll out by hand on a lightly floured counter and cut into ribbons with a sharp knife or pasta wheel. Hang to dry.

5 Meanwhile, make the sauce, heat the oil in a pan, and add the garlic and paprika. Fry over medium heat for 30 seconds. Add the squid and cook, stirring constantly, for 4–5 minutes until lightly browned and firm. Add the tomatoes and cook for 3–4 minutes until collapsed. Add the white wine and simmer gently for 15 minutes. Stir in the parsley and season to taste with salt and pepper.

6 Meanwhile, bring a large pan of lightly salted water to a boil. Add the pasta, bring back to a boil, and cook for 2–3 minutes until tender, but still firm to the bite. Drain, turn into a serving bowl, toss with the sauce, and serve immediately.

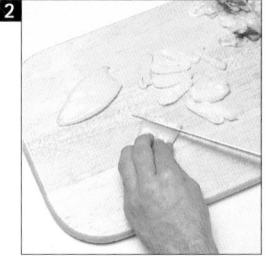  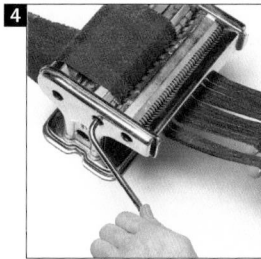

Fideua

Fideua is a pasta dish which can be found south of Valencia, in western Spain. It is very like a paella, but is made with very fine pasta.

NUTRITIONAL INFORMATION

Calories	373	Sugars	.........4g
Protein	........23g	Fat	...........8g
Carbohydrate	...52g	Saturates	.......1g

10 mins   20 mins

SERVES 6

INGREDIENTS

3 tbsp olive oil

1 large onion, chopped

2 garlic cloves, finely chopped

pinch of saffron, crushed

½ tsp paprika

3 tomatoes, peeled, deseeded, and chopped

12 oz/350 g egg vermicelli, broken roughly into 2 inch/5 cm lengths

⅔ cup white wine

1¼ cups fish stock

12 large raw shrimp

18 live mussels, scrubbed and bearded

12 oz/350 g cleaned squid, cut into rings

18 large clams, scrubbed

2 tbsp chopped fresh parsley

salt and pepper

lemon wedges, to serve

1 Heat the olive oil in a large, heavy skillet or paella pan. Add the onion and cook over low heat for 5 minutes until softened. Add the garlic and cook for a further 30 seconds. Add the saffron and paprika and stir well. Add the tomatoes and cook for a further 2–3 minutes until they have collapsed.

2 Add the vermicelli and stir well. Add the wine and boil rapidly until it has been absorbed.

3 Add the fish stock, shrimp, mussels, squid, and clams. Stir and return to a low simmer for 10 minutes until the shrimp and squid are cooked through and the mussels and clams have opened. Discard any that remain shut. The stock should be almost completely absorbed.

4 Add the parsley and season to taste with salt and pepper. Serve immediately in warmed bowls, garnished with lemon wedges.

VARIATION

Use whatever combination of shellfish you prefer. Try langoustines, shrimp, and monkfish.

Thai Noodles

This classic Thai noodle dish is flavored with the ubiquitous Thai fish sauce, roasted peanuts, and shrimp.

NUTRITIONAL INFORMATION

Calories	344	Sugars	.........2g
Protein	........21g	Fat	..........17g
Carbohydrate	...27g	Saturates	.......2g

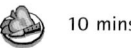

10 mins   5 mins

SERVES 4

I N G R E D I E N T S

12 oz/350 g cooked, peeled jumbo shrimp

4 oz/115 g flat rice noodles or rice vermicelli

4 tbsp vegetable oil

2 garlic cloves, finely chopped

1 egg

2 tbsp lemon juice

4½ tsp Thai fish sauce

½ tsp sugar

2 tbsp chopped, roasted peanuts

½ tsp cayenne pepper

2 scallions, cut into 1 inch/ 2.5 cm pieces

1 cup fresh bean sprouts

1 tbsp chopped fresh cilantro

lemon wedges, to serve

1 Drain the jumbo shrimp on kitchen paper to remove excess moisture. Set aside. Cook the rice noodles according to the packet instructions. Drain well and set aside until required.

2 Heat the oil in a wok or large, heavy skillet and add the garlic. Cook, stirring constantly, until just golden. Add the egg and stir quickly to break it up. Cook for a few seconds.

3 Add the shrimp and noodles, scraping down the sides of the wok or pan to ensure they mix with the egg and garlic.

4 Add the lemon juice, fish sauce, sugar, half the peanuts, the cayenne, scallions, and half the bean sprouts stirring quickly all the time. Cook over high heat for a further 2 minutes until everything is heated through.

5 Turn onto a warmed serving plate. Top with the remaining peanuts and bean sprouts and sprinkle with the cilantro. Serve with lemon wedges.

VARIATION

This is a basic dish to which lots of different cooked seafood could be added. Cooked squid rings, mussels, and langoustines would all work just as well.

Kedgeree

Originally, an Indian dish of rice and lentils, kedgeree has come to be a dish of rice, spices, and smoked fish served with hard-cooked eggs.

NUTRITIONAL INFORMATION

Calories 457   Sugars 3g
Protein . . . . .33g   Fat 18g
Carbohydrate . . .40g   Saturates 6g

15 mins   35 mins

SERVES 4

INGREDIENTS

1 lb/450 g smoked haddock fillet

2 tbsp olive oil

1 large onion, chopped

2 garlic cloves, finely chopped

½ tsp ground turmeric

½ tsp ground cumin

1 tsp ground coriander

scant 1 cup basmati rice

4 eggs

2 tbsp butter

1 tbsp chopped fresh parsley

TO SERVE

lemon wedges

mango chutney

1 Pour boiling water over the haddock fillet and set aside for 10 minutes. Lift the fish from the water, discard the skin and bones, and flake the flesh. Reserve the water.

2 Heat the oil in a large pan and add the onion. Cook for 10 minutes over medium heat until starting to brown. Add the garlic and cook for a further 30 seconds. Add the turmeric, cumin, and coriander and stir-fry for 30 seconds until the spices smell fragrant. Stir in the rice.

3 Measure 1½ cups of the haddock poaching water and add to the pan. Stir well and bring to a boil. Cover and cook over very low heat for about 12–15 minutes until the rice is tender and the stock has been completely absorbed.

4 Meanwhile, bring a small pan of water to a boil and add the eggs. When the water has returned to a boil cook the eggs for 8 minutes. Immediately drain the eggs and refresh under cold water to stop them from further cooking. Set aside.

5 Add the reserved fish pieces, the butter, and parsley to the rice. Turn onto a large serving dish. Shell and quarter the eggs and arrange on top of the rice. Serve with lemon wedges and mango chutney.

Jambalaya

Jambalaya is a dish of Cajun origin. There are as many versions of this dish as there are people who cook it. Here is a straightforward one.

NUTRITIONAL INFORMATION

Calories	283	Sugars	.........8g
Protein	........30g	Fat	..........14g
Carbohydrate	...12g	Saturates	.......3g

 10 mins 45 mins

SERVES 4

I N G R E D I E N T S

2 tbsp vegetable oil

2 onions, roughly chopped

1 green bell pepper, deseeded and roughly chopped

2 celery stalks, roughly chopped

3 garlic cloves, finely chopped

2 tsp paprika

10½ oz/300 g skinless, boneless chicken breast portions, chopped

3½ oz/100 g kabanos sausages, chopped

3 tomatoes, peeled and chopped

2¼ cups long grain rice

3¾ cups hot chicken or fish stock

1 tsp dried oregano

2 bay leaves

12 large shrimp tails

4 scallions, finely chopped

2 tbsp chopped fresh parsley

salt and pepper

salad, to serve

1 Heat the vegetable oil in a large skillet and add the onions, bell pepper, celery, and garlic. Cook over low heat, stirring occasionally, for about 8–10 minutes until all the vegetables have softened. Add the paprika and cook for a further 30 seconds. Add the chicken and sausages and cook for 8–10 minutes until lightly browned. Add the tomatoes and cook for 2–3 minutes until collapsed.

2 Add the rice to the pan and stir well. Pour in the hot stock and stir in the oregano and bay leaves. Cover and simmer for 10 minutes over a very low heat.

3 Add the shrimp and stir well. Cover again and cook for a further 6–8 minutes until the rice is tender and the shrimp are cooked through.

4 Stir in the scallions and parsley and season to taste. Serve with salad.

COOK'S TIP

Jambalaya is a versatile dish which has some basic ingredients—onions, green bell peppers, celery, rice, and seasonings—to which you can add whatever you have to hand.

Lobster Risotto

This is a special occasion dish, just for two. However, you could easily double the recipe for a dinner party if necessary.

NUTRITIONAL INFORMATION

Calories 487	Sugars 8g
Protein 10g	Fat 10g
Carbohydrate ...86g	Saturates 2g

 15 mins   35 mins

SERVES 2

INGREDIENTS

1 cooked lobster, about 14 oz–1 lb/ 400–450 g

4 tbsp butter

1 tbsp olive oil

1 onion, finely chopped

1 garlic clove, finely chopped

1 tsp fresh thyme leaves

1½ cups risotto rice

2½ cups simmering fish stock

⅔ cup sparkling wine

1 tsp green or pink peppercorns in brine, drained and roughly chopped

1 tbsp chopped fresh parsley

1 To prepare the lobster, remove the claws by twisting. Crack the claws using the back of a large knife and set aside. Split the body lengthwise. Remove and discard the intestinal vein, the stomach sac, and the spongy gills. Remove the meat from the tail and roughly chop. Set aside with the claws.

2 Heat half the butter and the oil in a large skillet. Add the onion and cook gently for 4–5 minutes until softened. Add the garlic and cook for a further 30 seconds. Add the thyme and rice. Cook, stirring for 1–2 minutes until the rice is well coated and translucent.

3 Increase the heat under the pan to medium and begin adding the stock, a ladleful at a time, stirring well between additions. Continue for 2–25 minutes until all the stock has been absorbed.

4 Add the lobster meat and claws. Stir in the wine, increasing the heat. When the wine is absorbed, remove the pan from the heat and stir in the peppercorns, remaining butter. and parsley. Set aside for 1 minute then serve immediately.

VARIATION

For a slightly cheaper version substitute 1 lb/450 g shrimp for the lobster.

Shrimp & Asparagus Risotto

An unusual and striking dish with fresh shrimp and asparagus is very simple to prepare and ideal for impromptu supper parties.

NUTRITIONAL INFORMATION

Calories ......566 Sugars 4g
Protein ....30g Fat 14g
Carbohydrate ...86g Saturates 2g

10 mins   40 mins

SERVES 4

INGREDIENTS

5 cups vegetable stock

12 oz/350 g asparagus, cut into 2 inch/ 5 cm lengths

2 tbsp olive oil

1 onion, finely chopped

1 garlic clove, finely chopped

3 cups risotto rice

1 lb/450 g raw jumbo shrimp, peeled and deveined

2 tbsp olive paste or tapenade

2 tbsp chopped fresh basil

salt and pepper

Parmesan cheese shavings, to garnish

1 Bring the vegetable stock to a boil in a large pan. Add the asparagus and cook for 3 minutes until just tender. Strain, reserving the stock, and refresh the asparagus under cold running water. Drain and set aside.

2 Heat the oil in a large, heavy skillet. Add the onion and cook over low heat, stirring occasionally, for 5 minutes until softened. Add the garlic and cook for a further 30 seconds. Add the rice and cook, stirring constantly for about 1–2 minutes until thoroughly coated with the oil and slightly translucent.

3 Keep the stock on low heat. Increase the heat under the skillet to medium and begin adding the stock, a ladleful at a time, stirring well between additions. Continue until almost all the stock has been absorbed. This should take about 20–25 minutes.

4 Add the shrimp and asparagus with the last ladleful of stock and cook for a further 5 minutes until the shrimp and rice are tender and the stock has been absorbed. Remove from the heat.

5 Stir in the olive paste, basil, and seasoning and set aside for 1 minute. Serve immediately, garnished with Parmesan shavings.

Spicy Monkfish Rice

A Thai-influenced dish of rice, cooked in coconut milk, with spicy broiled monkfish and fresh peas—what could be better?

NUTRITIONAL INFORMATION

Calories 440   Sugars 8g
Protein . . . . .22g   Fat 14g
Carbohydrate . . .60g   Saturates 2g

30 mins   30 mins

SERVES 4

INGREDIENTS

1 fresh hot red chile, deseeded and chopped

1 tsp crushed chili flakes

2 garlic cloves, chopped

pinch of saffron

3 tbsp roughly chopped fresh mint leaves

4 tbsp olive oil

2 tbsp lemon juice

12 oz/350 g monkfish fillet, cut into bite-size pieces

1 onion, finely chopped

generous 1 cup long grain rice

14 oz/400 g can chopped tomatoes

scant 1 cup coconut milk

1 cup peas

salt and pepper

2 tbsp chopped fresh cilantro, to garnish

1 Process the chile, chill flakes, garlic, saffron, mint, olive oil, and lemon juice in a food processor or blender until combined, but not smooth.

2 Put the monkfish into a nonmetallic dish and pour over the spice paste, turning to coat. Cover and set aside for 20 minutes to marinate.

3 Heat a large pan until very hot. Using a slotted spoon, lift the monkfish from the marinade and add, in batches, to the hot pan. Cook for 3–4 minutes until browned and firm. Remove with a slotted spoon and set aside.

4 Add the onion and remaining marinade to the pan and cook for 5 minutes until softened and lightly browned. Add the rice and stir until well coated. Add the tomatoes and coconut milk. Bring to a boil, cover, and simmer very gently for 15 minutes. Stir in the peas, season, and arrange the fish over the top. Cover with foil and continue to cook over a very low heat for 5 minutes. Serve garnished with the chopped cilantro.

Herring & Potato Pie

The combination of herrings, apples, and potatoes is popular throughout northern Europe. In salads, one often sees the addition of beets.

NUTRITIONAL INFORMATION

Calories 574	Sugars 10g
Protein 17g	Fat 36g
Carbohydrate . . .48g	Saturates 19g

20 mins   1 hr

SERVES 4

INGREDIENTS

1 tbsp Dijon mustard

4 oz/115 g butter, softened

1 lb/450 g herrings, filleted

1 lb 10 oz/750 g potatoes

1 large onion, sliced

2 cooking apples, thinly sliced

1 tsp chopped fresh sage

2½ cups hot fish stock

2 oz/55 g ciabatta, crusts removed and made into bread crumbs

salt and pepper

fresh parsley sprigs, to garnish

1 Mix the mustard with 2 tablespoons of the butter until smooth. Spread this mixture over the cut sides of the herring fillets. Season and roll up the fillets. Set aside. Generously grease a 10 cup pie dish with some of the remaining butter.

2 Thinly slice the potatoes, using a mandoline if possible. Blanch for 3 minutes in plenty of lightly salted boiling water until just tender. Drain well, refresh under cold water, and then pat dry.

3 Heat 2 tablespoons of the remaining butter in a skillet and add the onion. Cook gently for 8–10 minutes until soft, but not colored. Remove from the heat and set aside.

4 Put half the potato slices into the base of the pie dish with some seasoning, then add half the apple and half the onion. Put the herring fillets on top of the onion and sprinkle with the sage. Repeat the layers in reverse order, ending with potato. Season well and add enough hot stock to come halfway up the sides of the dish.

5 Melt the remaining butter and stir in the bread crumbs until well combined. Sprinkle the bread crumbs over the pie. Bake in a preheated oven, 375°F/190°C, for 40–50 minutes until the bread crumbs are golden and the herrings are cooked through. Serve garnished with parsley.

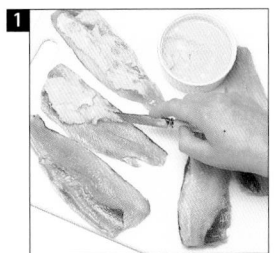

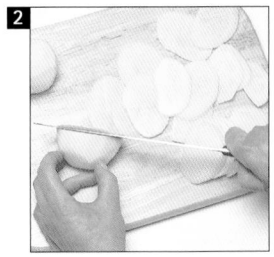

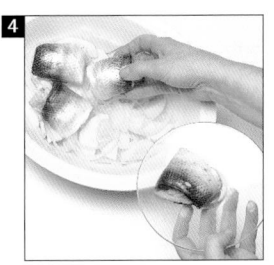

VARIATION

If herrings are unavailable, substitute mackerel or sardines.

Pizza Marinara

Traditionally, a pizza topped with mixed shellfish would have no cheese but in this case it helps to protect the fish from overcooking.

NUTRITIONAL INFORMATION

Calories ....638 Sugars 5g
Protein ....55g Fat 26g
Carbohydrate ...50g Saturates 11g

15 mins   25 mins

SERVES 4

INGREDIENTS

½ quantity Basic Pizza Dough (see page 838)

1 quantity Basic Tomato Sauce (see page 7)

handful of fresh basil leaves

MIXED SEAFOOD

16 live mussels, scrubbed and bearded

16 large live clams, scrubbed

1 tbsp olive oil

12 raw jumbo shrimp

8 oz/225 g cleaned squid, cut into rings

2 x 5½ oz/150 g mozzarella cheese, drained and sliced

olive oil, for drizzling

salt and pepper

1 To prepare the shellfish, put the mussels and clams in a pan with only the water clinging to their shells. Cover and cook over high heat, shaking occasionally, for 3–4 minutes until the shells have opened. Discard any that remain closed.

2 Strain the shellfish, discarding the cooking liquid. Set aside to cool. When cool enough to handle, remove the mussels and clams from their shells and set aside.

3 Heat the oil in a skillet and add the shrimp and squid. Cook for 2–3 minutes until the shrimp have turned pink and the squid has become firm.

4 Preheat the oven to 450°F/230°C, with cookie sheets on the top and middle shelves. Divide the pizza dough in half and shape into 10 inch/25 cm rounds. Put onto floured cookie sheets.

5 Spread half the tomato sauce on each pizza and add the mussels, clams, jumbo shrimp, and squid. Season to taste with salt and pepper and top with the sliced mozzarella. Drizzle with olive oil and place the cookie sheets on top of the preheated cookie sheets.

6 Cook for 12–15 minutes, swapping halfway through the cooking time, until golden. Serve immediately, sprinkled with the basil.

Sole Florentine

This is a classic combination of rolled sole fillets in a creamy cheese sauce cooked with spinach. You can make the cheese sauce in advance.

NUTRITIONAL INFORMATION

Calories 945   Sugars 12g
Protein . . . . .80g   Fat 59g
Carbohydrate . . .23g   Saturates 32g

45 mins   50 mins

SERVES 4

INGREDIENTS

2½ cups milk

2 strips of lemon rind

2 tsp fresh tarragon

1 bay leaf

½ onion, sliced

2 tbsp butter, plus extra for greasing

4 tbsp all-purpose flour

2 tsp mustard powder

3 tbsp freshly grated Parmesan cheese

1¼ cups heavy cream

pinch of freshly grated nutmeg

1 lb/450 g fresh spinach

4 x 1 lb 10 oz/750 g Dover sole, quarter-cut fillets (2 from each side of the fish)

salt and pepper

TO SERVE

crisp salad greens

crusty bread

Strain the steeped milk, discarding the lemon, herbs, and onion. Gradually whisk in the milk until smooth. Bring to a boil over low heat, stirring constantly until thickened. Simmer gently for 2 minutes. Remove from the heat and stir in the cheese, cream, nutmeg, and seasoning. Cover the surface with plastic wrap.

spinach and pour over the cheese sauce. Transfer to a preheated oven, 400°F/200°C, and cook for 35 minutes until bubbling and golden. Serve immediately with crisp salad greens and crusty bread.

1 Put the milk, lemon rind, tarragon, bay leaf, and onion into a pan and bring to a boil over low heat. Remove from the heat and set aside for 30 minutes for the flavours to steep.

2 Melt the butter in a clean pan and stir in the flour and mustard powder.

3 Grease a large casserole. Blanch the spinach leaves in boiling salted water for 30 seconds. Drain and refresh under cold water. Drain and pat dry. Put the spinach in the base of the casserole.

4 Wash and dry the fish fillets. Season and roll up. Arrange on top of the

VARIATION
For a budget version of this dish, use lemon sole instead of Dover sole.

Tilapia en Papillote

The beauty of this dish is that the fish cooks with a selection of vegetables, so you need cook only some boiled new potatoes to serve with it.

NUTRITIONAL INFORMATION

Calories	368	Sugars	. . . . .2g
Protein	. . . . .49g	Fat	. . . . .18g
Carbohydrate	. . . .3g	Saturates	. . . . . . .3g

10 mins   15 mins

SERVES 4

INGREDIENTS

2 tilapia, filleted

1 cup pitted black olives

12 cherry tomatoes, halved

4 oz/115 g green beans

handful of fresh basil leaves

4 fresh lemon slices

4 tsp olive oil

salt and pepper

fresh basil leaves, to garnish

boiled new potatoes, to serve

1 Wash and dry the fish fillets and set aside. Cut 4 large rectangles of baking parchment measuring about 18 x 12 inches/45 x 30 cm. Fold in half to give a 9 x 12 inch/23 x 30 cm rectangle. Cut this into a large heart shape and open out.

2 Lay 1 tilapia fillet on 1 half of the parchment heart. Top with a quarter of the olives, tomatoes, green beans, basil, and 1 lemon slice. Drizzle over 1 teaspoon of olive oil and season to taste with salt and pepper.

3 Fold over the other half of the parchment and fold the edges of the parchment together to enclose. Repeat to make 4 packets.

4 Place the packets on a cookie sheet and cook in a preheated oven, 400°F/200°C, for about 15 minutes or until the fish is tender.

5 Transfer each packet to a serving plate, unopened, letting your guests open their parcels and enjoy the wonderful aroma. Suggest that they garnish their portions with fresh basil and serve with a generous helping of boiled new potatoes.

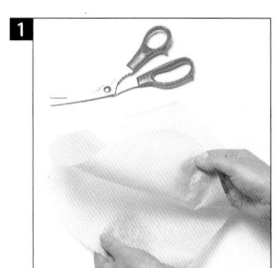

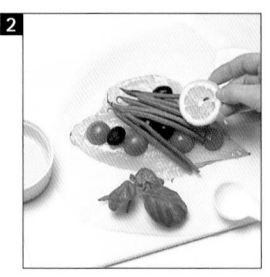

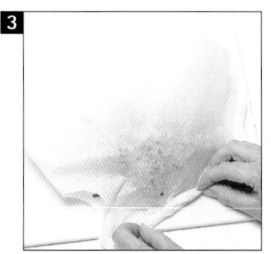

VARIATIONS

Try spreading the fish with a little olive paste, some chopped sun-dried tomatoes, a little goat cheese, and fresh basil.

Sea Bass with Artichokes

Baby artichokes are slowly cooked with olive oil, garlic, thyme, and lemon to create a soft blend of flavors that harmonize very well with the fish.

NUTRITIONAL INFORMATION

Calories	400	Sugars	.........3g
Protein	........28g	Fat	..........30g
Carbohydrate	....7g	Saturates	.......5g

20 mins   35 mins

SERVES 6

INGREDIENTS

4 lb/1.8 kg baby artichokes

2½ tbsp fresh lemon juice, plus the cut halves of the lemon

⅔ cup olive oil, plus extra for brushing

10 garlic cloves, thinly sliced

1 tbsp fresh thyme, plus extra, to garnish

6 x 4 oz/115 g sea bass fillets

1 tbsp olive oil

salt and pepper

crusty bread, to serve

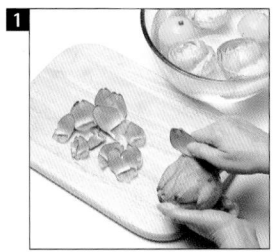
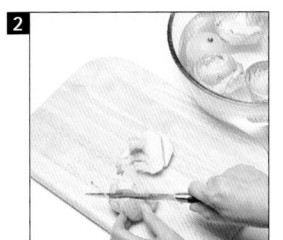

1 Peel away the tough outer leaves of each artichoke until the heart is revealed. Slice off the pointed top at about halfway between the point and the top of the stem. Cut off the stem and pare off what is left of the dark green leaves surrounding the bottom of the artichoke.

2 Submerge the prepared artichokes in water containing the cut halves of the lemon to prevent them from browning. When all the artichokes have been prepared, turn them, choke side down, and slice thinly.

3 Warm the olive oil in a large pan and add the sliced artichokes, garlic, thyme, lemon juice, and seasoning. Cover

and cook the artichokes over low heat for 20–30 minutes, without coloring, until they are tender.

4 Meanwhile, brush the sea bass fillets with olive oil and season well. Cook on a preheated ridged griddle pan or grill on a barbecue for 3–4 minutes on each side until just tender.

5 Divide the stewed artichokes between serving plates and top each with a sea bass fillet. Garnish with chopped thyme and serve with lots of crusty bread.

VARIATIONS
Artichokes cooked this way also suit cod, halibut, or salmon.

Sea Bass with Ratatouille

Sea bass is surely the king of round fish. Here it is cooked very simply and served with a highly flavored sauce of ratatouille and a basil dressing.

NUTRITIONAL INFORMATION

Calories 373   Sugars 9g
Protein . . . . .42g   Fat 18g
Carbohydrate . . .10g   Saturates 3g

45 mins   1 hr

SERVES 4

INGREDIENTS

2 large sea bass, filleted

olive oil, for brushing

salt and pepper

RATATOUILLE

1 large eggplant

2 medium zucchini

1 tbsp sea salt

4 tbsp olive oil

1 medium onion, roughly chopped

2 garlic cloves, crushed

½ red bell pepper, deseeded and roughly chopped

½ green bell pepper, deseeded and roughly chopped

2 large tomatoes, peeled and chopped

1 tbsp chopped fresh basil

DRESSING

5 tbsp roughly chopped fresh basil

2 garlic cloves, roughly chopped

4 tbsp olive oil

1 tbsp lemon juice

salt and pepper

1 To make the ratatouille, roughly chop the eggplant and zucchini. Put them in a colander with the salt and set aside to drain for 30 minutes. Rinse thoroughly and pat dry on paper towels. Set aside.

2 Heat the oil in a large pan and add the onion and garlic. Cook over low heat, stirring occasionally, for 10 minutes until softened. Add the bell peppers, eggplant, and zucchini. Season to taste and stir well. Cover and simmer very gently for 30 minutes until all the vegetables have softened. Add the tomatoes and cook for another 15 minutes.

3 Meanwhile make the dressing. Put the basil, garlic, and half the olive oil into a food processor and process until finely chopped. Add the remaining olive oil, lemon juice, and seasoning.

4 Season the sea bass fillets and brush with a little oil. Preheat a skillet until very hot and add the fish, skin side down. Cook for 2–3 minutes until the skin is browned and crispy. Turn the fish and cook for a further 2–3 minutes until it is just cooked through.

5 To serve, stir the basil into the ratatouille then divide among 4 serving plates. Top with the fresh fried fish and spoon around the dressing.

Whole Sea Bass with Ginger

This is a lovely Asian-inspired dish of sea bass, delicately flavored with scallions, ginger, and soy sauce.

NUTRITIONAL INFORMATION

Calories	185	Sugars	.........1g
Protein	........31g	Fat	..........6g
Carbohydrate	....2g	Saturates	.......1g

🕙 10 mins   🕐 15 mins

SERVES 4

INGREDIENTS

1 lb 12 oz/800 g whole sea bass, cleaned and scaled

4 tbsp light soy sauce

5 scallions, cut into long, fine shreds

2 tbsp finely shredded fresh ginger root

4 tbsp fresh cilantro leaves

5 tsp sunflower oil

1 tsp sesame oil

4 tbsp hot fish stock

lime wedges, to garnish

steamed rice, to serve

1 Wash the fish and pat dry with paper towels. Brush all over with 2 tablespoons of the soy sauce. Sprinkle half the scallions and all the ginger over a steaming tray or large plate and put the fish on top.

2 Half fill a large pan with water and fit a steamer on top. Bring the water to a boil. Put the steaming plate with the sea bass into the steamer and cover with a tight-fitting lid. Keeping the water boiling, steam the fish for 10–12 minutes until tender and cooked through.

3 Carefully remove the plate and lift the fish onto a serving platter, leaving behind the scallions and ginger. Scatter over the remaining scallions and fresh cilantro leaves.

4 Put the sunflower oil into a small pan and heat until almost smoking. Add the sesame oil and immediately pour the hot oils over the fish and scallions. Mix the remaining soy sauce with the fish stock and pour this over the fish. Serve immediately with steamed rice and garnished with lime wedges.

Cold Poached Cod Steaks

Poached cod has a very delicate flavor. Here it is teamed with a piquant relish of finely diced, colorful vegetables, both served cold.

NUTRITIONAL INFORMATION

Calories . . . . .395 Sugars 4g
Protein . . . . .3g Fat 27g
Carbohydrate . . . .5g Saturates 4g

2¼ hrs   20 mins

SERVES 4

INGREDIENTS

1 small carrot, thinly sliced

1 small onion, thinly sliced

1 celery stalk, thinly sliced

3 fresh parsley sprigs

3 fresh thyme sprigs

1 garlic clove, sliced

7½ cups water

1 tsp salt

4 x 6 oz/175 g cod steaks

PICKLED VEGETABLE RELISH

1 small carrot, finely diced

¼ red bell pepper, deseeded and finely diced

½ small red onion, finely diced

1 garlic clove, finely chopped

3 tbsp finely diced cornichon pickles

4 tbsp chopped pitted green olives

1 tbsp capers, drained and rinsed

2 salted anchovies, soaked in water for 15 minutes, chopped

1 tbsp red wine vinegar

scant ½ cup olive oil

2 tbsp chopped fresh parsley

salt and pepper

salad greens, to serve

1 Put the carrot, onion, celery, parsley, thyme, garlic, water, and salt into a large pan. Bring to a boil and simmer gently for 10 minutes. Add the fish and poach for 5–7 minutes until just firm in the center. Remove the fish with a slotted spoon and set aside to cool. Chill in the refrigerator for 2 hours.

2 Meanwhile, make the pickled vegetable relish. In a nonmetallic bowl, combine the carrot, red bell pepper, red onion, garlic, cornichons, olives, capers, anchovies, vinegar, olive oil, and parsley. Season to taste, adding a little more vinegar or olive oil to taste. Cover and chill in the refrigerator for 1 hour.

3 To serve, place a cold cod steak on each of 4 serving plates. Spoon the relish over the top. Serve immediately with dressed salad greens.

Cuttlefish in their own Ink

This is a dramatic-looking dish owing to the inclusion of the cuttlefish ink. Although typically Spanish, it is teamed with polenta here.

NUTRITIONAL INFORMATION

Calories	430	Sugars	.........2g
Protein	........24g	Fat	..........14g
Carbohydrate	...44g	Saturates	.......2g

15 mins   45 mins

SERVES 4

INGREDIENTS

1lb/450 g small cuttlefish or squid, with their ink

4 tbsp olive oil

1 small onion, finely chopped

2 garlic cloves, finely chopped

1 tsp paprika

6 oz/175 g ripe tomatoes, peeled, deseeded, and chopped

⅔ cup red wine

⅔ cup fish stock

1⅓ cups instant polenta

3 tbsp chopped fresh flat leaf parsley

salt and pepper

1 Cut off the cuttlefish tentacles in front of the eyes and remove the beak from the center of the tentacles. Cut the head from the body and discard. Cut open the body section along the dark colored back. Remove the cuttle bone and the entrails, reserving the ink sac. Skin the body. Chop the flesh roughly and set aside. Split open the ink sac and dilute the ink in a little water. Set aside.

2 Heat the oil in a large pan and add the onion. Cook gently for 8–10 minutes until softened and golden. Add the garlic and cook for a further 30 seconds. Add the cuttlefish and cook for a further 5 minutes until starting to brown. Add the paprika and stir for 30 seconds before adding the tomatoes. Cook for 2–3 minutes until collapsed.

3 Add the red wine, fish stock, and diluted ink and stir well. Bring to a boil and simmer gently, uncovered, for 25 minutes until the cuttlefish is tender and the sauce has thickened. Season to taste with salt and pepper.

4 Meanwhile, cook the polenta according to the packet instructions. When cooked, remove from the heat and stir in the parsley and seasoning.

5 Divide the polenta among serving plates and top with the cuttlefish and its sauce.

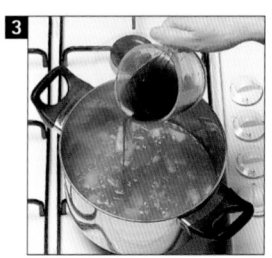

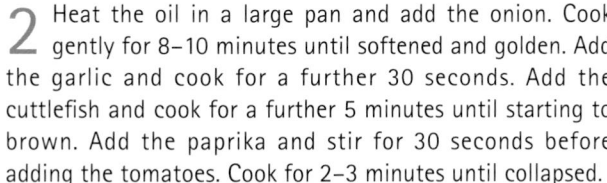

Noisettes of Salmon

This is an interesting and elegant way of presenting ordinary salmon steaks. It will taste even better if you can obtain wild salmon.

NUTRITIONAL INFORMATION

Calories 381	Sugars 3g	
Protein 36g	Fat 26g	
Carbohydrate 3g	Saturates 4g	

20 mins   25 mins

SERVES 4

I N G R E D I E N T S

4 salmon steaks

4 tbsp butter, softened

1 garlic clove, crushed

2 tsp mustard seeds

2 tbsp chopped fresh thyme

1 tbsp chopped fresh parsley

2 tbsp vegetable oil

4 tomatoes, peeled, deseeded, and chopped

salt and pepper

TO SERVE

new potatoes

green vegetables or salad

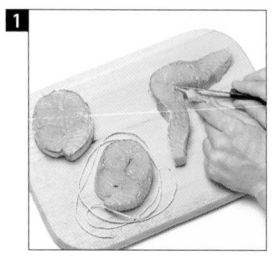  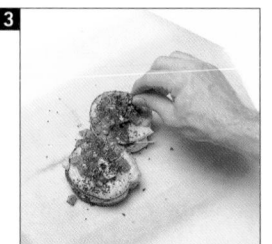

1 Carefully remove the central bone from the salmon steaks and cut the steaks in half. Curl each piece around to form a medallion and tie with string.

Blend together the butter, garlic, mustard seeds, thyme, and parsley and season to taste with salt and pepper. Set aside.

2 Heat the oil in a ridged pan or skillet and brown the salmon noisettes on both sides, in batches if necessary. Drain thoroughly on paper towels and set aside to cool.

3 Cut 4 pieces of baking parchment into 12 inch/30 cm squares. Place

2 salmon noisettes on top of each square and top with a little of the flavored butter and tomato. Draw up the edges of the parchment and fold together to enclose the fish. Place on a cookie sheet.

4 Cook the packets in a preheated oven, 400°F/200°C, for about 10–15 minutes or until the salmon is cooked through. Serve immediately with new potatoes and a green vegetable of your choice.

VARIATIONS

You can make cod steaks into noisettes in the same way. Cook them with butter flavored with fresh chives and basil.

Whole Poached Salmon

Although the fish is quite simply cooked, a whole salmon always makes a very impressive centerpiece.

NUTRITIONAL INFORMATION

Calories 661	Sugars 1g
Protein 35g	Fat 57g
Carbohydrate 1g	Saturates 9g

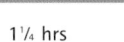

🍮 1¼ hrs   🕐 10 mins

SERVES 4–6

INGREDIENTS

3 lb 5 oz/1.5 kg salmon, cleaned and scaled

3 x quantity Fresh Fish Stock (see page 8)

½ cucumber, very thinly sliced

WATERCRESS MAYONNAISE

1 egg yolk

1 garlic clove, crushed

1 tsp Dijon mustard

1 tbsp lemon juice

2 cups watercress leaves, roughly chopped

1 tbsp chopped fresh basil

1 cup light olive oil

1 scallion, finely chopped

salt and pepper

1 Wash and dry the salmon and remove the fins. Place the salmon in a fish kettle or large, heavy roasting pan. Pour the stock over the fish. Bring to a simmer over low heat, then remove from the heat and set aside to go cold.

2 Meanwhile, make the watercress mayonnaise. Put the egg yolk, garlic, mustard, lemon juice, watercress, and basil into a food processor and process until the herbs are very finely chopped.

Begin adding the olive oil, drop by drop, until the mixture begins to thicken. Continue adding the olive oil in a steady stream until it is all incorporated. Scrape the mayonnaise into a bowl, add the scallion, and season to taste with salt and pepper. Cover and chill in the refrigerator.

3 When the salmon is cold, carefully lift it from the poaching liquid and pat dry. Carefully peel away and discard the skin from the rounder, uppermost side, then carefully turn the fish and remove the skin from the flatter, underside. Carefully slide a large knife along the backbone of the fish to remove the flesh in 1 piece.

Turn it over onto your serving platter so that the cut side is up.

4 Remove the bones from the remaining piece of fish. Finally, turn the remaining flesh on top of the first piece to reform the fish. This makes serving the salmon much easier.

5 Lay the cucumber slices on top of the fish, starting at the tail end, in a pattern resembling scales. Serve cold with the mayonnaise.

 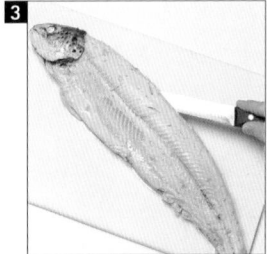 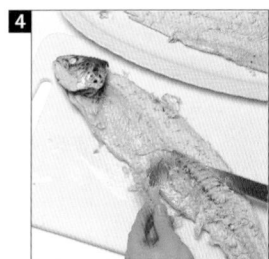

Stuffed Monkfish Tail

A very impressive-looking dish which is simple to prepare.
Although monkfish is quite expensive, there is very little wastage.

NUTRITIONAL INFORMATION

Calories	154	Sugars	.........0g
Protein	........24g	Fat	...........6g
Carbohydrate	....0g	Saturates	.......1g

30 mins   25 mins

SERVES 6

INGREDIENTS

1 lb 10 oz/750 g monkfish tail, skinned and trimmed

6 slices prosciutto

4 tbsp chopped fresh mixed herbs, such as parsley, chives, basil, sage

1 tsp finely grated lemon rind

2 tbsp olive oil

salt and pepper

TO SERVE

stir-fried vegetables

new potatoes

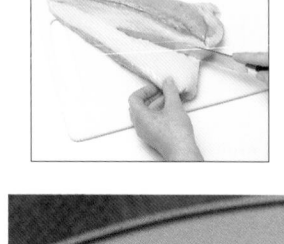
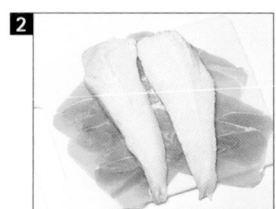

1 Using a sharp knife, carefully cut down each side of the central bone of the monkfish to leave 2 fillets. Wash the fillets and pat dry with paper towels.

COOK'S TIP

It is possible to remove the central bone from a monkfish tail without separating the 2 fillets completely. This makes it easier to stuff, but takes some practice.

2 Lay the prosciutto slices widthwise on a clean counter so that they overlap slightly. Lay the fish fillets lengthwise on top of the ham so that the 2 cut sides face each other.

3 Combine the herbs and lemon rind. Season well. Pack this mixture onto the cut surface of 1 monkfish fillet. Press the 2 fillets together and wrap tightly with the prosciutto slices. Secure with string or toothpicks.

4 Heat the olive oil in a large ovenproof skillet and place the fish in the pan, seam side down first, and brown the wrapped monkfish tail all over.

5 Cook in a preheated oven, 400°F/ 200°C, for 25 minutes until golden and the fish is tender. Remove from the oven and set aside to rest for 10 minutes before slicing thickly. Serve with shredded stir-fried vegetables and new potatoes.

Spinach Roulade

Although something of a dinner party cliché, a roulade is still an attractive and very appetizing dish.

NUTRITIONAL INFORMATION

Calories 331	Sugars 5g
Protein 27g	Fat 21g
Carbohydrate ...10g	Saturates 9g

   25 mins   40 mins

SERVES 4

INGREDIENTS

olive oil, for brushing

8 oz/225 g frozen spinach, thawed and well drained

2 tbsp butter

4 tbsp all-purpose flour

scant 1 cup milk

4 eggs, separated

1 tbsp chopped fresh tarragon

½ tsp freshly grated nutmeg

salt and pepper

FILLING

12 oz/350 g skinless smoked cod fillet

½ cup ricotta cheese

⅓ cup grated Parmesan cheese

4 scallions, finely chopped

2 tbsp freshly chopped chives

2 oz/55 g sun-dried tomatoes in olive oil, drained and finely chopped

1 Brush a 13 x 9 inch/33 x 23 cm jelly roll pan with olive oil and line with baking parchment. Squeeze the spinach to remove as much liquid as possible. Chop finely and set aside.

2 Melt the butter in a pan, add the flour, and cook for 30 seconds, stirring constantly. Gradually add the milk until smooth, stirring constantly. Bring gradually to a boil and simmer, stirring constantly, for 2 minutes. Remove from the heat and set aside to cool slightly.

3 Stir in the spinach, egg yolks, tarragon, nutmeg, and seasoning. Whisk the egg whites until they hold stiff peaks. Fold a large spoonful into the spinach mixture to slacken it, then fold in the remaining egg whites, carefully but thoroughly to avoid losing any volume. Pour the mixture into the prepared pan and smooth the surface.

4 Cook in a preheated oven, 400°F/200°C, for 15 minutes until risen and golden and firm in the center.

Turn out immediately onto a clean dish cloth, peel off the baking parchment, and roll up from a short end.

5 For the filling, cover the cod fillet with boiling water and set aside for 10 minutes until just tender. Remove the fish and flake the flesh carefully, removing any bones. Combine with the ricotta, Parmesan, scallions, chives, and sun-dried tomatoes and season to taste.

6 Unroll the roulade and spread with the cod mixture, leaving a 1 inch/ 2.5 cm border all around. Tightly re-roll the roulade and return to the oven, seam side down, for 20 minutes. Transfer to a serving plate and serve immediately.

Seafood Rice

This satisfying rice casserole, bursting with Mediterranean flavors, can be made with any combination of seafood you choose.

NUTRITIONAL INFORMATION

Calories 571	Sugars 18g
Protein 25g	Fat 16g
Carbohydrate ...81g	Saturates 3g

🕑 15 mins   🕐 1 hr

SERVES 4–6

INGREDIENTS

4 tbsp olive oil

16 large raw peeled shrimp

8 oz/225 g cleaned squid, sliced

2 green bell peppers, deseeded and cut lengthwise into ½ inch/1 cm strips

1 large onion, finely chopped

4 garlic cloves, finely chopped

2 bay leaves

1 tsp saffron threads

½ tsp dried crushed chiles

3½ cups risotto or Valencia rice

1 cup dry white wine

3¾ cups fish, chicken or vegetable stock

12–16 littleneck clams, well scrubbed

12–16 large mussels, well scrubbed

salt and pepper

2 tbsp chopped fresh flat leaf parsley

BELL PEPPER SAUCE

2–3 tbsp olive oil

2 onions, finely chopped

4–6 garlic cloves, finely chopped

4–6 roasted red bell peppers in olive oil

14 oz/400 g can chopped tomatoes

1–1½ tsp hot paprika

salt

1 To make the bell pepper sauce, heat the oil in a pan. Add the onions and cook for 6–8 minutes until golden. Stir in the garlic and cook for a minute. Add the remaining ingredients and simmer gently, stirring occasionally, for about 10 minutes. Process in a food processor to a smooth sauce. Set aside and keep warm.

2 Heat half the oil in a wide pan over a high heat. Add the shrimp and stir-fry for 2 minutes until pink. Transfer to a plate. Add the squid and stir-fry for about 2 minutes until just firm. Set aside with the shrimp.

3 Heat the remaining oil in the pan, add the green bell peppers and onion and stir-fry for about 6 minutes until just tender. Stir in the garlic, bay leaves, saffron, and chiles and cook for 30 seconds. Add the rice and cook, stirring constantly, until thoroughly coated.

4 Add the wine and stir until absorbed. Add the stock and season to taste with salt and pepper. Bring to the boil and cover. Simmer gently for about 20 minutes until the rice is just tender and the liquid is almost absorbed.

5 Add the clams and mussels. Re-cover and cook for about 10 minutes until the shells open. Discard any that remain closed. Stir in the shrimp and squid. Re-cover and heat through. Sprinkle with the chopped parsley and serve immediately with the sauce.

Crab Risotto

A different way to make the most of crab, this rich-tasting and colorful risotto is full of interesting flavors.

NUTRITIONAL INFORMATION

Calories	447	Sugars	........11g
Protein	........22g	Fat	..........13g
Carbohydrate	...62g	Saturates	.......2g

15 mins   50 mins

SERVES 4–6

I N G R E D I E N T S

2–3 large red bell peppers

3 tbsp olive oil

1 onion, finely chopped

1 small fennel bulb, finely chopped

2 celery stalks, finely chopped

¼–½ tsp cayenne pepper

3 cups risotto rice

1 lb 12 oz/800 g can Italian peeled plum
   tomatoes, drained and chopped

¼ cup dry white vermouth (optional)

6¾ cups fish or chicken
   stock, simmering

1 lb/450 g fresh cooked crab meat

¼ cup lemon juice

2–4 tbsp chopped fresh parsley or chervil

salt and pepper

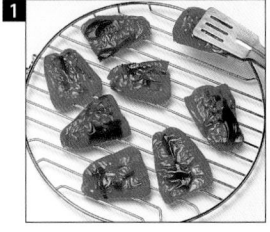

1 Broil the bell peppers until the skins are charred. Transfer to a plastic bag and twist to seal. When cool enough to handle, peel off the charred skins, working over a bowl to catch the juices. Remove the cores and seeds. Chop the flesh and set aside, reserving the juices.

2 Heat the olive oil in a large heavy pan. Add the onion, fennel, and celery and cook over low heat, stirring occasionally, for 2–3 minutes until the vegetables are softened. Add the cayenne and rice and cook, stirring frequently, for about 2 minutes until the rice is translucent and well coated.

3 Stir in the chopped tomatoes and vermouth, if using. The liquid will bubble and steam rapidly. When the liquid is almost absorbed, add a ladleful (about 1 cup) of the simmering stock. Cook, stirring constantly, until the liquid is completely absorbed.

4 Continue adding the stock, about half a ladleful at a time, allowing each addition to be absorbed before adding the next. This should take 20–25 minutes. The risotto should have a creamy consistency and the rice should be tender, but still firm to the bite.

5 Stir in the red bell peppers and reserved juices, the crab meat, lemon juice, and parsley or chervil and heat. Season with salt and pepper to taste. Serve the risotto immediately.

Risotto with Clams

This simple recipe is an excellent way of using the tiny Venus clams when they are in season. The tomatoes add a splash of color.

NUTRITIONAL INFORMATION

Calories	463	Sugars	.........4g
Protein	........25g	Fat	..........12g
Carbohydrate	...65g	Saturates	.......2g

15 mins   40 mins

SERVES 6

INGREDIENTS

¼ cup olive oil

1 large onion, finely chopped

4 lb 8 oz/2 kg tiny clams, such as Venus, well scrubbed

½ cup dry white wine

4 cups fish stock

2½ cups water

3 garlic cloves, finely chopped

½ tsp crushed dried chili

3½ cup risotto rice

3 ripe plum tomatoes, peeled and coarsely chopped

3 tbsp lemon juice

2 tbsp chopped fresh chervil or parsley

salt and pepper

1 Heat 1–2 tablespoons of the oil in a large heavy pan over medium-high heat. Add the onion and stir-fry for about 1 minute. Add the clams and wine and cover tightly. Cook for 2–3 minutes, shaking the pan frequently, until the clams begin to open. Remove from the heat and discard any clams that do not open.

2 When cool enough to handle, remove the clams from their shells. Rinse in the cooking liquid. Cover the clams and set aside. Strain the cooking liquid through a coffee filter or a strainer lined with paper towels and reserve.

3 Bring the fish stock and water to a boil in a pan, then reduce the heat, and keep at a gentle simmer.

4 Heat the remaining olive oil in a large, heavy pan over medium heat. Add the garlic and chili and cook gently for 1 minute. Add the rice and cook, stirring frequently, for about 2 minutes until translucent and well coated with oil.

5 Add a ladleful (about 1 cup) of the simmering stock mixture; it will bubble and steam rapidly. Cook, stirring constantly, until the liquid is absorbed.

6 Continue adding the stock, about half a ladleful at a time, letting each addition be absorbed before adding the next—never allow the rice to cook "dry." This should take 20–25 minutes. The risotto should have a creamy consistency and the rice should be tender, but still firm to the bite.

7 Stir in the tomatoes, reserved clams and their cooking liquid, the lemon juice, and chervil. Heat through gently. Season to taste with salt and pepper and serve immediately.

Rich Lobster Risotto

Although lobster is expensive, this dish is worth it.
Keeping it simple lets the lobster flavor come through.

NUTRITIONAL INFORMATION

Calories	688	Sugars	.........3g
Protein	........32g	Fat	..........31g
Carbohydrate	...69g	Saturates	......16g

10 mins   25 mins

SERVES 4

INGREDIENTS

1 tbsp vegetable oil

4 tbsp sweet butter

2 shallots, finely chopped

2⅔ cups risotto rice

½ tsp cayenne pepper

5 tbsp dry white vermouth

6¼ cups shellfish, fish, or chicken
    stock, simmering

8 oz/225 g cherry tomatoes, quartered
    and deseeded

2–3 tbsp heavy or whipping cream

1 lb/450 g cooked lobster meat, cut into
    coarse chunks

2 tbsp chopped fresh chervil or dill

salt and white pepper

1 Heat the oil and half the butter in a large heavy pan over medium heat. Add the shallots and cook, stirring occasionally, for about 2 minutes until just beginning to soften. Add the rice and cayenne and cook, stirring frequently, for about 2 minutes until the rice is translucent and well coated with the oil and butter.

2 Pour in the vermouth; it will bubble and steam rapidly and evaporate almost immediately. Add a ladleful (about 1 cup) of the simmering stock and cook, stirring constantly, until the stock is completely absorbed.

3 Continue adding the stock, about half a ladleful at a time, letting each addition be completely absorbed before adding the next—never allow the rice to cook "dry." This process should take about 20–25 minutes. The risotto should have a creamy consistency and the rice should be tender, but still firm to the bite.

4 Stir in the tomatoes and cream and cook for about 2 minutes.

5 Add the cooked lobster meat with the remaining butter and chervil and cook long enough to just heat the lobster meat gently. Serve immediately.

Pickled Tuna

When Mediterranean fishermen bring in a bountiful catch, some of the fish is traditionally preserved so that it can be enjoyed a few days later.

NUTRITIONAL INFORMATION

Calories	.714	Sugars	.10g
Protein	.55g	Fat	.48g
Carbohydrate	.13g	Saturates	.8g

25¾ hrs　　25 mins

SERVES 4

INGREDIENTS

4 large tuna steaks, each about 8 oz/225 g and ¾ inch/2 cm thick

1 cup olive oil

2 large red onions, thinly sliced

2 carrots, thinly sliced

2 large bay leaves, torn

1 garlic clove, very finely chopped

1 cup white wine vinegar or sherry vinegar

½ tsp dried chili flakes, crushed

1 tbsp coriander seeds, lightly crushed

salt and pepper

finely chopped fresh parsley, to garnish

1 Rinse the tuna and pat dry with paper towels. Heat 4 tablespoons of the oil in a large skillet, preferably nonstick.

2 Add the tuna steaks to the skillet and fry for 2 minutes over medium–high heat. Turn the steaks and continue to cook for 2 minutes until browned and medium cooked, or 4 minutes for well done. Remove the tuna from the skillet and drain well on paper towels. Let cool.

3 Heat the remaining oil in the skillet. Add the onions and cook for 8 minutes until soft, but not brown. Stir in

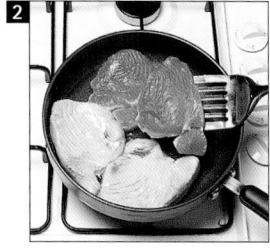

the carrots, bay leaves, garlic, vinegar, and dried chiles and season with salt and pepper to taste. Cook for a further 10 minutes or until the carrots are tender. Stir in the coriander seeds 1 minute before the end of the cooking time.

4 When the tuna has cooled completely, remove any skin and bones from it. Break each of the tuna steaks into 4 or 5 large chunks.

5 Put the fish pieces in a nonmetallic bowl and pour the hot onion mixture over. Very gently mix together, taking care not to break up the fish pieces.

6 Set aside until completely cool, then cover with plastic wrap, and chill in the refrigerator for at least 24 hours: the fish will stay fresh in the refrigerator for up to 5 days. To serve, sprinkle with parsley and serve at room temperature.

Seafood Stew

Similar to Bouillabaisse, this meal-in-a-pot should contain the best of the day's catch—even if it's from a supermarket.

NUTRITIONAL INFORMATION

Calories .... 226 Sugars 4g
Protein .... 31g Fat 9g
Carbohydrate ... .6g Saturates 1g

🕐 45 mins   🕐 30 mins

SERVES 4–6

INGREDIENTS

8 oz/225 g clams

1 lb 9 oz/700 g mixed fish, such as sea bass, skate, red snapper, rock fish, and any Mediterranean fish you can find

12–18 jumbo shrimp

about 3 tbsp olive oil

1 large onion, finely chopped

2 garlic cloves, very finely chopped

2 tomatoes, halved, deseeded, and chopped

3 cups Fresh Fish Stock (see page 8), or good-quality, ready-made chilled fish stock

1 tbsp tomato paste

1 tsp fresh thyme leaves

pinch of saffron threads

pinch of sugar

salt and pepper

finely chopped fresh parsley, to garnish

1 Soak the clams in a bowl of lightly salted water for 30 minutes. Rinse them under cold, running water and lightly scrub to remove any sand from the shells. Discard any broken clams or open clams that do not shut when firmly tapped with the back of a knife, as these will be unsafe to eat.

2 Prepare the fish as necessary, removing any skin and bones, then cut into bite-size chunks.

3 To prepare the shrimp, break off the heads. Peel off the shells, leaving the tails intact, if wished. Using a small knife, make a slit along the back of each and remove the thin black vein. Set all the seafood aside.

4 Heat the oil in a large pan. Add the onion and cook for 5 minutes, stirring. Add the garlic and cook for about another 2 minutes until the onion is soft, but not brown.

5 Add the tomatoes, stock, tomato paste, thyme leaves, saffron threads, and sugar, then bring to a boil, stirring to dissolve the tomato paste. Lower the heat, cover, and simmer for 15 minutes. Season to taste with salt and pepper.

6 Add the seafood and simmer until the clams open and the fish flakes easily. Discard any clams that do not open. Garnish and serve immediately.

Shrimp Skewers

Shrimp of all sizes are popular fare in the Mediterranean, where they are often cooked very simply by broiling—the key is not to overcook.

NUTRITIONAL INFORMATION

Calories 203   Sugars 4g
Protein . . . . .81g   Fat 17g
Carbohydrate . . . .4g   Saturates 3g

 45 mins   2–3½ mins

MAKES 8 SKEWERS

INGREDIENTS

32 large jumbo shrimp

olive oil, for brushing

skordalia (see page 129) or aïoli (see page 128), to serve

MARINADE

½ cup extra virgin olive oil

2 tbsp lemon juice

1 tsp finely chopped fresh red chile

1 tsp balsamic vinegar

pepper

TOMATO SALSA

2 large tomatoes, peeled, deseeded, and chopped

4 scallions, white parts only, very finely chopped

1 red bell pepper, peeled, deseeded, and chopped

1 orange or yellow bell pepper, peeled, deseeded, and chopped

1 tbsp extra virgin olive oil

2 tsp balsamic vinegar

4 fresh basil sprigs

salt and pepper

1. To make the marinade, place all the ingredients in a nonmetallic bowl and whisk together until thoroughly combined. Set aside.

2. To prepare the shrimp, break off the heads. Peel off the shells, leaving the tails intact. Using a small knife, make a slit along the back and remove the thin black vein. Add the shrimp to the marinade and stir until well coated. Cover and chill for 15 minutes.

3. Make the salsa. Put all the ingredients, except the basil, in a nonmetallic bowl and toss together. Season to taste with salt and pepper. Cover and chill until required.

4. Thread 4 shrimp onto a metal skewer, bending each in half. Repeat with 7 more skewers. Brush with marinade.

5. Brush a broiler rack with oil. Place the skewers on the rack, then cook under a preheated hot broiler, about 3 inches/7.5 cm from the heat; for 1 minute. Turn the skewers over, brush again, and cook for a further 1–1½ minutes until the shrimp turn pink and opaque.

6. Tear the basil leaves and toss with the salsa. Arrange each skewer on a plate with some salsa and garnish with parsley. Serve with skordalia or aïoli for dipping.

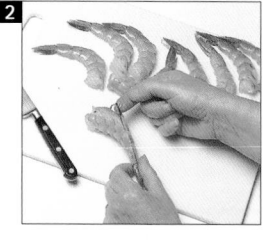

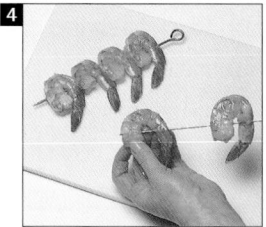

Swordfish à la Maltese

The firm texture of swordfish means it is often simply broiled, but it also lends itself to this delicate technique of cooking in a paper packet.

NUTRITIONAL INFORMATION

Calories	303	Sugars	........10g
Protein	........34g	Fat	..........13g
Carbohydrate	...13g	Saturates	.......3g

15 mins   30 mins

SERVES 4

INGREDIENTS

1 tbsp fennel seeds

2 tbsp extra virgin olive oil, plus extra for brushing and drizzling

2 large onions, thinly sliced

1 small garlic clove, crushed

4 swordfish steaks, about 6 oz/175 g each

1 large lemon, halved

2 large tomatoes, finely chopped

4 fresh thyme sprigs

salt and pepper

 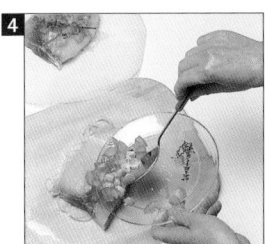 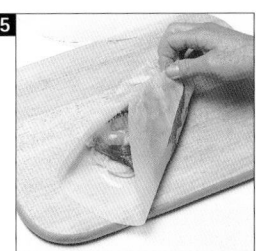

1 Place the fennel seeds in a dry skillet over medium-high heat and toast, stirring constantly, until they give off their aroma. Watch carefully, as they can easily burn. Immediately tip the seeds out of the pan onto a plate. Set aside.

2 Heat 2 tablespoons of the olive oil in the skillet. Add the onions and cook over low heat, stirring occasionally, for 5 minutes. Add the garlic and continue to cook until the onions are very soft and tender, but not brown. Remove the skillet from the heat.

3 Cut out 4 x 12 inch/30 cm circles of baking parchment. Very lightly brush the center of each paper circle with olive oil. Divide the onions equally among the paper circles, flattening them out to about the size of the fish steaks.

4 Top the onions in each packet with a swordfish steak. Squeeze lemon juice over the fish steaks and drizzle with a little olive oil. Sprinkle the tomatoes and fennel seeds over the top, add a fresh thyme sprig to each swordfish steak, and season with salt and pepper to taste.

5 Fold the edges of the parchment together, scrunching them tightly so no cooking juices escape. Place on a cookie sheet and cook in a preheated oven, 400°F/200°C, for 20 minutes.

6 To test if the fish is cooked, open 1 packet and pierce the flesh with a knife—it should flake easily. Serve straight from the paper packets.

Mediterranean Monkfish

Some of the best seafood dishes are the simplest and this recipe proves the point. This is a delicious dish to serve in the summer.

NUTRITIONAL INFORMATION

Calories 401	Sugars 5g
Protein 39g	Fat 25g
Carbohydrate 6g	Saturates 7g

15 mins   16–18 mins

SERVES 4

INGREDIENTS

1 lb 4 oz/600 g cherry tomatoes, a mixture of yellow and red, if available

2 monkfish fillets, about 12 oz/350 g each

8 tbsp pesto sauce

salt and pepper

fresh basil sprigs, to garnish

new potatoes, to serve

1 Cut the tomatoes in half and spread out, cut sides up, on the base of an ovenproof serving dish. Set aside.

2 Using your fingers, rub off the thin gray membrane that covers monkfish.

3 If the skin has not been removed, place the fish skin side down on the counter. Loosen enough skin at one end of the fillet so you can grip it. Work from the

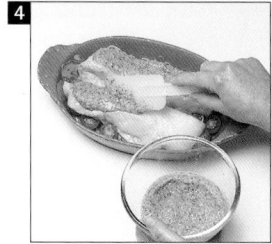

front to the back. Insert the knife, almost flat, and using a gentle sawing action, remove the skin. Rinse the fillets well and pat dry with paper towels.

4 Place the fillets on top of the tomatoes, tucking the thin end under, if necessary, (see Cook's Tip). Spread 4 tablespoons of the pesto sauce over each fillet and season with pepper.

5 Cover the dish tightly with foil, shiny side down. Place in a preheated oven, 450°F/230°C, and roast for 16–18 minutes until the fish is cooked through, the flesh flakes easily, and the tomatoes are collapsing into a thick sauce.

6 Adjust the seasoning, if necessary. Garnish with basil sprigs and serve immediately with new potatoes.

COOK'S TIP

Monkfish fillets are often cut from the tail, which means one end is much thinner than the rest and prone to over-cooking. If you can't get fillets that are the same thickness, fold the thin end under to ensure even cooking.

Wrapped Red Snapper

Fresh thyme, which grows wild throughout the Mediterranean region, flavors this rustic dish. Serve with boiled new potatoes.

NUTRITIONAL INFORMATION

Calories	329	Sugars	.........8g
Protein	........37g	Fat	..........16g
Carbohydrate	....9g	Saturates	.......5g

20 mins   35 mins

SERVES 4

INGREDIENTS

3 tbsp olive oil, plus extra for rubbing

2 large red bell peppers, deseeded and
　　thinly sliced

2 large fennel bulbs, thinly sliced

1 large garlic clove, crushed

8 fresh thyme sprigs, plus extra
　　to garnish

20–24 grape leaves in brine

1 lemon

4 red snapper, about 8 oz/225 g each,
　　scaled and gutted

salt and pepper

1 Heat the oil in a large skillet over medium–low heat. Add the bell peppers, fennel, garlic, and 4 sprigs of thyme and stir together. Cook, stirring occasionally, for about 20 minutes until the vegetables are cooked thoroughly and are very soft, but not browned.

2 Meanwhile, rinse the grape leaves under cold, running water and pat dry with paper towels. Slice 4 thin slices off the lemon, then cut each slice in half. Finely grate the rind of ½ the lemon.

3 Stuff the snapper cavities with the lemon slices and remaining thyme

sprigs. Rub a little olive oil on each fish and sprinkle with the lemon rind. Season with salt and pepper to taste.

4 Depending on the size of the snapper, wrap 5 or 6 grape leaves around each fish to enclose completely. Put the wrapped snapper on top of the fennel and bell peppers. Cover the pan and cook over medium–low heat for 12–15 minutes until

the snapper are cooked through and the flesh flakes easily when tested with the tip of a knife.

5 Transfer the cooked fish to warmed individual plates and spoon the fennel and bell peppers beside them. Garnish with thyme sprigs and serve immediately.

 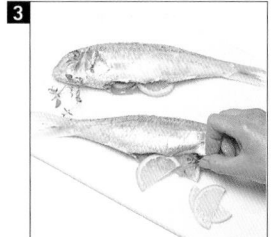 

Mussels Marinara

The Spanish, French, and Italians all serve variations
of this simple mussel recipe, which is universally popular.

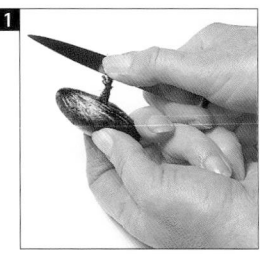

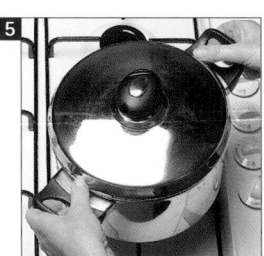

NUTRITIONAL INFORMATION

Calories	278	Sugars 6g
Protein	........18g	Fat 14g
Carbohydrate	...10g	Saturates 2g

 40 mins   20 mins

SERVES 4

INGREDIENTS

4 lb 8 oz/2 kg live mussels

4 tbsp olive oil

4–6 large garlic cloves, halved

2 x 400 g /14 oz cans chopped tomatoes

1¼ cups dry white wine

2 tbsp finely chopped fresh flat leaf parsley,
  plus extra to garnish

1 tbsp finely chopped fresh oregano

salt and pepper

French bread, to serve

1 Soak the mussels in a bowl of lightly salted water for 30 minutes. Rinse them under cold, running water and lightly scrub to remove any sand from the shells. Using a small sharp knife, remove the "beards" from the shells.

2 Discard any broken mussels or open mussels that do not shut when firmly tapped with the back of a knife. This indicates they are dead and could cause food poisoning if eaten. Rinse the mussels again, then set aside in a colander.

3 Heat the olive oil in a large pan or stockpot over medium-high heat. Add the garlic and cook, stirring, for about 3 minutes. Using a slotted spoon, remove the garlic from the pan.

4 Add the tomatoes and their juice, the wine, parsley, and oregano and bring to a boil, stirring. Lower the heat, cover, and simmer for 5 minutes to let the flavors blend.

5 Add the mussels, cover the pan, and simmer for 5–8 minutes, shaking the pan regularly, until the mussels open. Using a slotted spoon, transfer the mussels to serving bowls, discarding any that remain closed.

6 Season the sauce with salt and pepper to taste. Ladle the sauce over the mussels, sprinkle with extra chopped parsley, and serve immediately with plenty of fresh French bread.

Yucatecan Fish

Annatto seeds are rock-hard little red seeds with a lemony flavor that need to be soaked overnight before you can grind them.

NUTRITIONAL INFORMATION

Calories 179   Sugars 1g
Protein ....24g   Fat 8g
Carbohydrate ....1g   Saturates 2g

3½ hrs   15 mins

SERVES 8

INGREDIENTS

4 tbsp annatto seeds, soaked in water overnight

3 garlic cloves, finely chopped

1 tbsp mild chili powder

1 tbsp paprika

1 tsp ground cumin

½ tsp dried oregano

2 tbsp beer or tequila

juice of 1 lime and I orange or 3 tbsp pineapple juice

2 tbsp olive oil

2 tbsp chopped fresh cilantro

¼ tsp ground cinnamon

¼ tsp ground cloves

2 lb 4 oz/1 kg swordfish steaks

banana leaves, for wrapping (optional)

fresh cilantro leaves, to garnish

orange wedges, to serve

1 Drain the annatto seeds, then crush them to a paste with a pestle in a mortar. Work in the garlic, chili powder, paprika, cumin, oregano, beer or tequila, fruit juice, olive oil, fresh cilantro, cinnamon, and cloves.

2 Smear the annatto paste onto the swordfish steaks, cover, and set aside to marinate in the refrigerator for at least 3 hours or overnight.

3 Wrap the fish steaks in banana leaves, tying with string to make packets. Bring water to a boil in a steamer, then add a batch of fish packets to the top part of the steamer and cook for about 15 minutes or until the fish is cooked through and flakes easily.

4 Alternatively, cook the fish without wrapping in the banana leaves. To cook on the barbecue, place in a hinged basket or on a rack and cook over the hot coals for 5–6 minutes on each side until cooked through. Or cook the fish under a preheated broiler for 5–6 minutes on each side until cooked through.

5 Garnish with cilantro and serve immediately with orange wedges for squeezing over the fish.

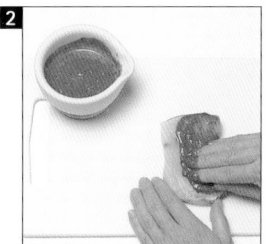

Shrimp in Green Sauce

The sweet briny flesh of shrimp is wonderful paired
with the smoky scent of chipotle chiles.

NUTRITIONAL INFORMATION

Calories	225	Sugars	........13g
Protein	........24g	Fat	..........8g
Carbohydrate	...17g	Saturates	.......1g

10 mins   15–20 mins

SERVES 4

INGREDIENTS

2 tbsp vegetable oil

3 onions, chopped

5 garlic cloves, chopped

5–7 ripe tomatoes, diced

6–8 oz/175–225 g green beans, cut into
 2 inch/5 cm pieces and blanched for
 1 minute

¼ tsp ground cumin

pinch of ground allspice

pinch of ground cinnamon

½–1 canned chipotle chile in adobo
 marinade, with some of the marinade

2 cups fish stock or water mixed with a fish
 bouillon cube

1 lb/450 g raw shrimp, peeled

fresh cilantro sprigs

1 lime, cut into wedges

1 Heat the oil in a large pan. Add the
 onions and garlic and cook over low
heat, stirring occasionally, for about
5–10 minutes until softened. Add the
tomatoes and cook for 2 minutes.

2 Add the green beans, cumin, allspice,
 cinnamon, chipotle chile and
marinade, and fish stock. Bring to a boil,
then reduce the heat, and simmer for a
few minutes to combine the flavors.

3 Add the shrimp and cook, stirring
 gently, for 1–2 minutes only, then
remove the pan from the heat and set the
shrimp aside to steep in the hot liquid to
finish cooking. They are cooked when they
have turned a bright pink color.

4 Serve the shrimp immediately,
 garnished with the fresh cilantro, and
accompanied by the lime wedges.

VARIATION

If you can find them,
use bottled nopales (edible
cacti), cut into strips, to add
an exotic touch to the dish.

Barbecued Clams

Cook with Mexican flair by serving clams
from the barbecue, topped with a spicy corn salsa.

NUTRITIONAL INFORMATION

Calories	189	Sugars	.........9g
Protein	........23g	Fat	..........2g
Carbohydrate	...21g	Saturates	.......1g

35 mins · 10 mins

SERVES 4

INGREDIENTS

4 lb 8 oz/2 kg live clams

5 ripe tomatoes

2 garlic cloves, finely chopped

8 oz/225 g can corn, drained

3 tbsp finely chopped fresh cilantro

3 scallions, thinly sliced

¼ tsp ground cumin

juice of ½ lime

½–1 fresh green chile, deseeded and
    finely chopped

salt

lime wedges, to serve

1 Place the clams in a large bowl. Cover with cold water and add a handful of salt. Set aside to soak for 30 minutes.

2 Meanwhile, peel the tomatoes. Place them in a heatproof bowl, pour boiling water over to cover, and stand for 30 seconds. Drain and plunge into cold water. The skins will then slide off easily. Cut the tomatoes in half, deseed, then chop the flesh.

3 To make the salsa, combine the tomatoes, chopped garlic, corn, cilantro, scallions, cumin, lime juice, and chile in a bowl. Season with salt to taste. Cover and set aside.

4 Drain the clams, discarding any that are open. Place the clams on the hot coals of a barbecue, allowing about 5 minutes per side. They will pop open when they are ready. Discard any that remain closed.

5 Transfer to a plate. Top with the salsa, and serve with lime wedges for squeezing over the clams.

VARIATION
Mussels can be used
in place of the clams
very successfully.

Chili-Marinated Shrimp

Avocado salsa is delicious spooned onto anything spicy
from the broiler or barbecue grill, especially seafood.

NUTRITIONAL INFORMATION

Calories	.321	Sugars	.2g
Protein	.31g	Fat	.21g
Carbohydrate	.4g	Saturates	.4g

15 mins

3–5 mins

SERVES 4

INGREDIENTS

1 lb 7 oz/650 g large shrimp, shelled

½ tsp ground cumin

½ tsp mild chili powder

½ tsp paprika

2 tbsp orange juice

grated rind of 1 orange

2 tbsp extra virgin olive oil

2 tbsp chopped fresh cilantro, plus extra
    to garnish

2 ripe avocados

½ onion, finely chopped

¼ fresh green or red chile, deseeded
    and chopped

juice of ½ lime

salt and pepper

VARIATION

For luscious sandwiches, toast crusty
rolls, cut in half and buttered, over
the hot coals and fill them with the
cooked shrimp and avocado sauce.

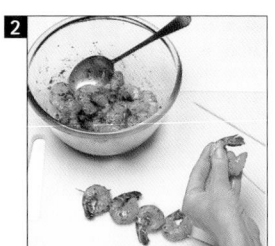

1 Combine the shrimp with the cumin,
chili powder, paprika, orange juice
and rind, olive oil, and half the cilantro.
Season to taste with salt and pepper.

2 Thread the shrimp onto metal
skewers, or bamboo skewers soaked in
cold water for 30 minutes.

3 Cut the avocados in half around the
pit. Twist apart, then remove the pit
with a knife. Carefully peel off the skin,
then dice the flesh. Immediately combine
the avocados with the remaining cilantro,
onion, chile, and lime juice. Season with
salt and pepper and set aside.

4 Place the shrimp on a hot barbecue
and cook for only a few minutes on
each side.

5 Serve the shrimp, garnished with
cilantro and accompanied by the
avocado sauce.

Simmered Squid

This flavorful squid dish from Vera Cruz in Mexico would be good with warmed flour tortillas, for do-it-yourself tacos.

NUTRITIONAL INFORMATION

Calories 307	Sugars 6g
Protein 36g	Fat 14g
Carbohydrate . . .10g	Saturates 2g

🧊 10 mins   🕐 20 mins

SERVES 4

INGREDIENTS

3 tbsp extra virgin olive oil

2 lb/900 g cleaned squid, cut into rings and tentacles

1 onion, chopped

3 garlic cloves, chopped

14 oz/400 g can chopped tomatoes

½–1 fresh mild green chile, deseeded and chopped

1 tbsp finely chopped fresh parsley

¼ tsp chopped fresh thyme

¼ tsp chopped fresh oregano

¼ tsp chopped fresh marjoram

pinch of ground cinnamon

pinch of ground allspice

pinch of sugar

15–20 pimiento-stuffed green olives, sliced

1 tbsp capers

salt and pepper

1 tbsp chopped fresh cilantro, to garnish

1 Heat the oil in a pan and lightly fry the squid until it turns opaque. Season with salt and pepper and remove from the pan with a slotted spoon.

2 Add the onion and garlic to the remaining oil in the pan and cook until softened. Stir in the tomatoes, chile, herbs, cinnamon, allspice, sugar, and olives. Cover and cook over medium-low heat for 5–10 minutes until the mixture thickens slightly. Uncover the pan and cook for a further 5 minutes to concentrate the flavors and reduce the liquid.

3 Stir in the reserved squid and any of the juices that have gathered. Add the capers and heat through.

4 Adjust the seasoning if necessary, then serve immediately, garnished with fresh cilantro.

Pan-Fried Scallops Mexicana

Scallops, with their sweet flesh, are delicious with the piquant flavors of Mexico. They are best prepared simply, served with lime.

NUTRITIONAL INFORMATION

Calories	182	Sugars	.........0g
Protein	........22g	Fat	...........9g
Carbohydrate	....4g	Saturates	.......4g

5 mins 10 mins

SERVES 4–8

INGREDIENTS

2 tbsp butter

2 tbsp extra virgin olive oil

1 lb 7 oz/650 g scallops, shelled

4–5 scallions, thinly sliced

3–4 garlic cloves, finely chopped

½ fresh green chili, deseeded and finely chopped

2 tbsp finely chopped fresh cilantro

juice of ½ lime

salt and pepper

lime wedges, to serve

VARIATION

Mix leftover scallops with a little aïoli or mayonnaise mixed with garlic and a little olive oil. Serve with roasted peppers on a bed of greens, with a handful of salty black olives.

1 Heat half the butter and olive oil in a heavy skillet until the butter foams.

2 Add the scallops and cook quickly until just turning opaque; do not overcook. Remove from the pan with a slotted spoon and keep warm.

3 Add the remaining butter and oil to the pan, then toss in the scallions and garlic and cook over medium heat until the scallions are wilted. Return the scallops to the pan.

4 Remove the pan from the heat and add the chopped chili and coriander. Squeeze in the lime juice. Season with salt and pepper to taste and stir to mix well.

5 Serve immediately with lime wedges for squeezing over the scallops.

Spicy Broiled Salmon

The woody smoked flavors of the chipotle chile are delicious brushed onto salmon for broiling.

NUTRITIONAL INFORMATION

Calories 419   Sugars 2g
Protein . . . . .41g   Fat 28g
Carbohydrate . . . .2g   Saturates 5g

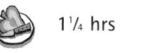

1¼ hrs   6–8 mins

SERVES 4

INGREDIENTS

4 salmon steaks, about 6–8 oz/
175–225 g each

lime slices, to garnish

MARINADE

4 garlic cloves

2 tbsp extra virgin olive oil

pinch of ground allspice

pinch of ground cinnamon

juice of 2 limes

1–2 tsp marinade from canned chipotle
chiles or bottled chipotle chili salsa

¼ tsp ground cumin

pinch of sugar

salt and pepper

TO SERVE

tomato wedges

3 scallions, finely chopped

shredded lettuce

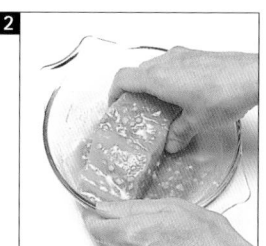

1 To make the marinade, finely chop the garlic and place in a bowl with the olive oil, allspice, cinnamon, lime juice, chipotle marinade, cumin, and sugar. Add salt and pepper and stir.

2 Coat the salmon with the marinade, then place in a nonmetallic dish. Marinate for at least 1 hour.

3 Transfer the salmon to a broiler pan and cook under a preheated broiler for 3–4 minutes on each side. Alternatively, cook the salmon over hot coals on a barbecue until cooked through.

4 To serve, mix the tomato wedges with the scallions. Place the salmon on individual serving plates and arrange the tomato salad and shredded lettuce beside it. Garnish with lime slices and serve immediately.

VARIATION
The marinade also
goes well with fresh
tuna steaks.

Fish Baked with Lime

Tangy and simple to prepare, this is excellent served with rice
and beans for an easy lunch—serve with a glass of chilled beer.

NUTRITIONAL INFORMATION

Calories	302	Sugars	.........4g
Protein	........47g	Fat	..........10g
Carbohydrate	....5g	Saturates	.......1g

 10–15 mins   15–20 mins

SERVES 4

INGREDIENTS

2 lb 4 oz/1 kg white fish fillets, such as
bass, plaice, or cod

1 lime, halved

3 tbsp extra virgin olive oil

1 large onion, finely chopped

3 garlic cloves, finely chopped

2–3 pickled jalapeño chiles (jalapeños en
escabeche), chopped

6–8 tbsp chopped fresh cilantro

salt and pepper

lemon and lime wedges, to serve

1 Place the fish fillets in a bowl and
sprinkle with salt and pepper. Squeeze
the juice from the lime over the fish.

2 Heat the olive oil in a skillet. Add the
onion and garlic and cook for about
2 minutes, stirring frequently, until
softened. Remove from the heat.

3 Place a third of the onion mixture and
a little of the chiles and cilantro in
the bottom of a shallow casserole or

roasting pan. Arrange the fish on top. Top
with the remaining onion mixture, chiles
and cilantro.

4 Bake in a preheated oven,
350°F/180°C, for 15–20 minutes or
until the fish has become slightly opaque
and firm to the touch. Serve immediately,
with lemon and lime wedges for squeezing
over the fish.

VARIATION

Add sliced flavorful fresh tomatoes,
or canned chopped tomatoes, to the
onion mixture at the end of step 2.

Mackerel with Lime

The secret of this dish lies in the simple, fresh flavors
which perfectly complement the richness of the barbecued fish.

NUTRITIONAL INFORMATION

Calories 302   Sugars 0g
Protein . . . . .21g   Fat 24g
Carbohydrate . . . .0g   Saturates 4g

10 mins   10 mins

SERVES 4

I N G R E D I E N T S

4 small mackerel

¼ tsp ground coriander

¼ tsp ground cumin

4 fresh cilantro sprigs

3 tbsp chopped, fresh cilantro

1 fresh red chile, deseeded and chopped

grated rind and juice of 1 lime

2 tbsp sunflower oil

salt and pepper

1 lime, sliced, to garnish

chile flowers (optional), to garnish

salad greens, to serve

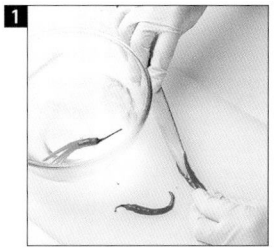 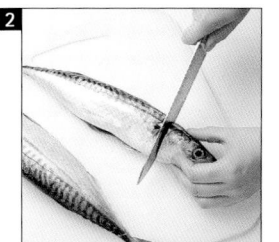 

1 To make the chile flower, if using, cut the tip of small chiles lengthwise into thin strips, leaving the chiles intact at the stem end. Remove the seeds and place the chiles in ice water.

2 Clean and gut the mackerel, if this has not been done by the fish store, removing the heads if preferred. Rinse and pat dry. Sprinkle the fish with the ground spices and salt and pepper to taste. Sprinkle 1 teaspoon of chopped cilantro inside the cavity of each fish.

3 Combine the chopped cilantro, chile, lime rind and juice, and the oil in a small bowl. Brush the mixture liberally over the fish.

4 Place the fish in a hinged rack. Grill over hot coals for 3–4 minutes on each side, turning once. Brush frequently with the remaining basting mixture. Transfer to plates and garnish with chile flowers, if using, and lime slices, and serve with salad greens.

COOK'S TIP
This recipe is suitable for other oily fish, such as trout, herring, or sardines.

Fish & Yogurt Quenelles

These quenelles, made from a thick purée of fish and yogurt, can be prepared well in advance and stored in the refrigerator before poaching.

NUTRITIONAL INFORMATION

Calories	228	Sugars	.........7g
Protein	........39g	Fat	...........2g
Carbohydrate	...14g	Saturates	......1g

🕐 45 mins   🕐 15 mins

SERVES 4

I N G R E D I E N T S

1 lb 10 oz/750 g white fish fillets, such as cod, coley, or whiting, skinned

2 small egg whites

½ tsp ground coriander

1 tsp ground mace

⅔ cup low-fat plain yogurt

1 small onion, sliced

salt and pepper

mixture of boiled basmati rice and wild rice, to serve

S A U C E

1 bunch of watercress, trimmed

1¼ cups chicken stock

2 tbsp cornstarch

⅔ cup low-fat plain yogurt

2 tbsp low-fat crème fraîche

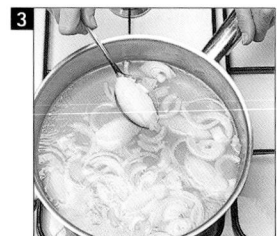
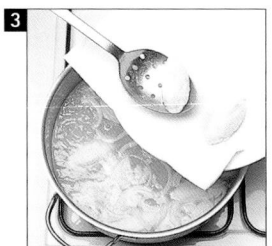

1 Cut the fish into pieces and process it in a food processor for 30 seconds. Add the egg whites and process for a further 30 seconds to a stiff paste. Add the coriander, mace, seasoning, and the yogurt and process until smooth. Cover and chill for at least 30 minutes.

2 Spoon the mixture into a pastry bag, and pipe into sausage shapes about 4 inches/10 cm long. Alternatively, take rounded dessert spoons of the mixture and shape into ovals using 2 spoons.

3 Bring about 2 inches/5 cm of water to a boil in a skillet and add the onion. Lower the quenelles into the water, using a spatula or spoon. Cover the pan, and poach for 8 minutes, turning once. Remove with a slotted spoon and drain.

4 Chop the watercress, reserving a few sprigs for garnish. Process the remainder with the stock, then pour into a small pan. Stir the cornstarch into the yogurt and pour the mixture into the pan. Bring to a boil, stirring.

5 Stir in the crème fraîche, season, and remove from the heat. Garnish with the watercress sprigs. Serve immediately.

Fish & Rice with Dark Rum

Based on a traditional Cuban recipe, this dish is similar to Spanish paella, but it has the added kick of dark rum.

NUTRITIONAL INFORMATION

Calories	547	Sugars	.........9g
Protein	........27g	Fat	...........4g
Carbohydrate	...85g	Saturates	......1g

2¼ hrs   35 mins

SERVES 4

INGREDIENTS

1 lb/450 g firm white fish fillets (such as cod or monkfish), skinned and cut into 1 inch/2.5 cm cubes

2 tsp ground cumin

2 tsp dried oregano

2 tbsp lime juice

⅔ cup dark rum

1 tbsp molasses sugar

3 garlic cloves, finely chopped

1 large onion, chopped

1 medium red bell pepper, deseeded and sliced into rings

1 medium green bell pepper, deseeded and sliced into rings

1 medium yellow bell pepper, deseeded and sliced into rings

5 cups fish stock

1¾ cups long grain rice

salt and pepper

crusty bread, to serve

TO GARNISH

fresh oregano leaves

lime wedges

1 Place the cubes of fish in a bowl and add the cumin, oregano, lime juice, rum, and sugar. Season to taste with salt and pepper. Mix thoroughly, cover with plastic wrap, and set aside to chill for 2 hours.

2 Meanwhile, place the garlic, onion, and bell peppers in a large pan. Pour in the stock and stir in the rice. Bring to a boil, lower the heat, cover, and simmer for 15 minutes.

3 Gently stir in the fish and the marinade juices. Bring back to a boil and simmer, uncovered, stirring occasionally but taking care not to break up the fish, for about 10 minutes until the fish is cooked through and the rice is tender.

4 Season to taste with salt and pepper and transfer to a warmed serving plate. Garnish with fresh oregano and lime wedges and serve with crusty bread.

Smoked Haddock Casserole

This quick, easy, and inexpensive dish would be ideal for a midweek family supper, because it is both nourishing and filling.

NUTRITIONAL INFORMATION

Calories . . . . . . .525 Sugars 8g
Protein . . . . .41g Fat 18g
Carbohydrate . . .53g Saturates 10g

20 mins   45 mins

SERVES 4

INGREDIENTS

2 tbsp butter, plus extra for greasing

1lb/450 g smoked haddock fillets,
  cut into 4 slices

2½ cups milk

2½ tbsp all-purpose flour

pinch of freshly grated nutmeg

3 tbsp heavy cream

1 tbsp chopped fresh parsley

2 eggs, hard-cooked and mashed to a pulp

1lb/450 g dried fusilli pasta

1 tbsp lemon juice

salt and pepper

boiled new potatoes and beet, to serve

1 Thoroughly grease a casserole with butter. Put the haddock in the casserole and pour in the milk. Bake in a preheated oven, 400°F/200°C, for about 15 minutes.

2 Carefully pour the cooking liquid into a jug without breaking up the fish. Set the fish aside in the casserole.

3 Melt the butter in a pan and stir in the flour. Gradually whisk in the reserved cooking liquid. Season to taste with salt, pepper, and nutmeg. Stir in the cream, parsley, and mashed hard-cooked egg and cook, stirring constantly, for 2 minutes.

4 Meanwhile, bring a large pan of lightly salted water to a boil. Add the fusilli and lemon juice, bring back to a boil, and cook for 8–10 minutes until just tender, but still firm to the bite.

5 Drain the pasta and spoon or tip it over the fish. Top with the egg sauce and return the casserole to the oven for 10 minutes.

6 Serve the casserole immediately with boiled new potatoes and beet.

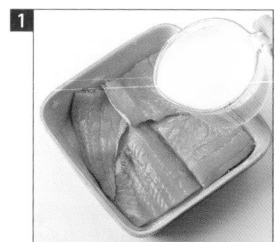

VARIATION

You can use any type of dried pasta for this casserole. Try penne, conchiglie, or rigatoni.

A Seafood Medley

You can use almost any kind of sea fish in this recipe. Red porgy is an especially good choice.

NUTRITIONAL INFORMATION

Calories	699	Sugars	.........4g
Protein	........56g	Fat	..........35g
Carbohydrate	...35g	Saturates	......20g

20 mins   30 mins

SERVES 4

INGREDIENTS

12 raw jumbo shrimp

12 raw shrimp

1 lb/450 g fillet of porgy

4 tbsp butter

12 scallops, shelled

4½ oz/125 g freshwater shrimp

juice and finely grated rind of 1 lemon

pinch of saffron powder or threads

4 cups vegetable stock

⅔ cup rose petal vinegar

4 cups dried farfalle

⅔ cup white wine

1 tbsp pink peppercorns

4 oz/115 g baby carrots

⅔ cup heavy cream or
    plain yogurt

salt and pepper

1 Peel and devein the jumbo shrimp and peel the shrimp. Thinly slice the porgy. Melt the butter in a skillet, add the porgy, scallops, jumbo shrimp, and shrimp and cook for 1–2 minutes.

2 Season with pepper to taste. Add the lemon juice and grated rind. Very carefully add a pinch of saffron powder or a few strands of saffron to the cooking juices (not to the seafood).

3 Remove the seafood from the pan, set aside, and keep warm.

4 Return the pan to the heat and add the stock. Bring to a boil and reduce by one-third. Add the rose petal vinegar and cook for about 4 minutes until reduced again.

5 Bring a pan of lightly salted water to a boil. Add the pasta, bring back to a boil, and cook for 8–10 minutes until tender, but still firm to the bite. Drain the pasta, transfer to a serving plate, and top with the seafood.

6 Add the wine, peppercorns, and carrots to the pan and reduce the sauce for 6 minutes. Add the cream or yogurt and simmer for 2 minutes.

7 Pour the sauce over the seafood and pasta and serve immediately.

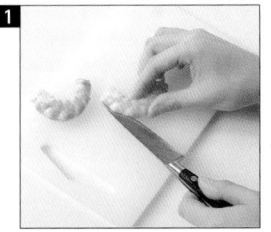

Potato-Topped Cod

This simple dish has a spicy bread crumb topping over layers of cod and potatoes. It is cooked in the oven until crisp and golden.

NUTRITIONAL INFORMATION

Calories 118   Sugars 1g
Protein . . . . .9.8g   Fat 4.4g
Carbohydrate . .10.5g   Saturates 2.6g

 5–10 mins   35 mins

SERVES 4

INGREDIENTS

5 tbsp butter

2 lb/900 g waxy potatoes, sliced

1 large onion, finely chopped

1 tsp whole-grain mustard

1 tsp garam masala

pinch of chili powder

1 tbsp chopped fresh dill

1½ cups fresh bread crumbs

1 lb 9 oz/700 g cod fillets

4 tbsp grated Swiss cheese

salt and pepper

fresh dill sprigs, to garnish

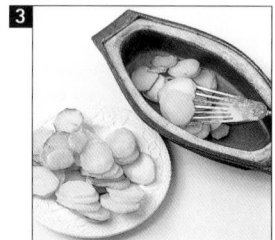

1 Melt half of the butter in a skillet. Add the potatoes and fry for 5 minutes, turning until they are browned all over. Remove the potatoes from the pan with a slotted spoon.

2 Add the remaining butter to the skillet and stir in the onion, mustard, garam masala, chili powder, dill, and bread crumbs. Cook for 1–2 minutes, stirring and mixing well.

3 Layer half of the potatoes in the bottom of a casserole and place the cod fillets on top. Cover the cod fillets with the rest of the potato slices. Season to taste with salt and pepper.

4 Spoon the spicy mixture from the skillet over the potatoes and sprinkle with the grated cheese.

5 Cook in a preheated oven, 400°F/200°C, for 20–25 minutes or until the topping is golden and crisp and the fish is cooked through. Remove from the oven, garnish with fresh dill sprigs and serve immediately.

COOK'S TIP

This dish is ideal served with baked vegetables, which can be cooked in the oven at the same time.

Smoked Fish & Potato Pâté

This smoked fish pâté is given a tart fruity flavor by the gooseberries, which complement the fish perfectly.

NUTRITIONAL INFORMATION

Calories 418   Sugars 4g
Protein . . . . .18g   Fat 25g
Carbohydrate . . .32g   Saturates 6g

 20 mins   10 mins

SERVES 4

I N G R E D I E N T S

1 lb 7 oz/650 g mealy potatoes, diced

10½ oz/300 g smoked mackerel, skinned and flaked

3 oz/85 g cooked gooseberries

2 tsp lemon juice

2 tbsp low-fat crème fraîche

1 tbsp capers, rinsed

1 gherkin, chopped

1 tbsp chopped dill pickle

1 tbsp chopped fresh dill

salt and pepper

lemon wedges, to garnish

toast or warm crusty bread, to serve

1 Cook the diced potatoes in a pan of boiling water for 10 minutes until tender, then drain well.

2 Place the cooked potatoes in a food processor or blender.

3 Add the skinned and flaked smoked mackerel and process for 30 seconds until fairly smooth. Alternatively, place the ingredients in a bowl and mash them with a fork.

4 Add the cooked gooseberries, lemon juice, and crème fraîche to the fish and potato mixture. Blend for a further 10 seconds or mash well.

5 Stir in the capers, gherkin, dill pickle, and fresh dill. Season to taste with salt and pepper.

6 Turn the fish pâté into a serving dish, garnish with lemon wedges and serve with slices of toast or warm crusty bread cut into chunks or slices.

COOK'S TIP

Use stewed, canned, or bottled cooked gooseberries for convenience and to save time, or when fresh gooseberries are out of season.

Layered Fish & Potato Pie

This is a really delicious and filling dish. Layers of potato slices and mixed fish are cooked in a creamy sauce and topped with grated cheese.

NUTRITIONAL INFORMATION

Calories 116   Sugars 1.9g
Protein . . . . .6.2g   Fat 6.1g
Carbohydrate . . .9.7g   Saturates 3.8g

 10 mins   ⏱ 55 mins

SERVES 4

INGREDIENTS

2 lb/900 g waxy potatoes, sliced

5 tbsp butter

1 red onion, halved and sliced

5 tbsp all-purpose flour

2 cups milk

⅔ cup heavy cream

8 oz/225 g smoked haddock fillet, cubed

8 oz/225 g cod fillet, cubed

1 red bell pepper, deseeded and diced

4 oz/115 g broccoli florets

⅔ cup freshly grated Parmesan cheese

salt and pepper

1 Cook the sliced potatoes in a pan of boiling water for 10 minutes. Drain and set aside.

2 Meanwhile, melt the butter in a pan, add the onion and cook gently for 3–4 minutes.

3 Add the flour and cook for 1 minute. Blend in the milk and cream and bring to a boil, stirring until the sauce has thickened.

4 Arrange half of the potato slices in the bottom of a shallow casserole.

5 Add the fish, red bell pepper, and broccoli to the sauce and cook over low heat for 10 minutes. Season with salt and pepper, then spoon the mixture over the potatoes in the dish.

6 Arrange the remaining potato slices in a layer over the fish mixture. Sprinkle the Parmesan cheese over the top.

7 Cook in a preheated oven, 350°F/180°C, for 30 minutes or until the potatoes are cooked and the topping is golden.

COOK'S TIP

Choose your favorite combination of fish, adding salmon or various shellfish for special occasions.

Thai Steamed Mussels

Thai cooks are fond of basil, and frequently sprinkle it over salads and soups. The familiar sweet basil is suitable for this dish.

NUTRITIONAL INFORMATION

Calories	252	Sugars 2g
Protein	........22g	Fat 14g
Carbohydrate	....8g	Saturates 8g

15 mins   5 mins

SERVES 2

I N G R E D I E N T S

2 lb 4 oz/1 kg fresh mussels in shells

2 shallots, finely chopped

1 lemongrass stalk, thinly sliced

1 garlic clove, finely chopped

3 tbsp Chinese rice wine or sherry

2 tbsp lime juice

1 tbsp Thai fish sauce

2 tbsp butter

4 tbsp chopped fresh basil

salt and pepper

fresh basil leaves, to garnish

crusty bread, to serve

1 Scrub the mussels, removing any beards. Rinse in and drain. Discard any that do not close when tapped or that have damaged shells.

2 Place the shallots, lemongrass, garlic, rice wine, lime juice, and fish sauce in a large pan and place over high heat.

3 Add the mussels, cover, and steam for about 2–3 minutes, shaking the pan occasionally during cooking until the mussel shells open.

4 Discard any mussels which have not opened, then stir in the chopped basil, and season with salt and pepper.

5 Lift out the mussels with a slotted spoon and divide among 2 deep bowls. Quickly whisk the butter into the pan juices until incorporated, then pour the juices over the mussels.

6 Garnish each bowl with fresh basil leaves and serve with plenty of crusty bread to mop up the juices.

COOK'S TIP

If you prefer to serve this dish as a starter, this amount will be enough for four portions. Fresh clams in shells are also very good when cooked by this method.

Sweet & Sour Seafood

This unusual seafood dish with a sweet lime dressing can be doubled up for a buffet-style main dish and is a good dish to prepare for a crowd.

NUTRITIONAL INFORMATION

Calories	97	Sugars	.........5g
Protein	........13g	Fat	...........2g
Carbohydrate	....8g	Saturates	.......0g

 20 mins   10 mins

SERVES 4

INGREDIENTS

18 live mussels

6 large scallops

7 oz/200 g baby squid, cleaned

2 shallots, finely chopped

6 raw jumbo shrimp, peeled and deveined

¼ cucumber

1 carrot, peeled

¼ head Napa cabbage, shredded

DRESSING

4 tbsp lime juice

2 garlic cloves, finely chopped

2 tbsp Thai fish sauce

1 tsp sesame oil

1 tbsp brown sugar

2 tbsp chopped fresh mint

¼ tsp ground black pepper

salt

1 Scrub the mussels and remove any "beards." Discard any damaged mussels or open ones that do not close when firmly tapped. Steam them in just the water which clings to them for 1–2 minutes until opened. Lift out with a slotted spoon, reserving the liquid in the pan. Discard any mussels that have not opened.

2 Separate the corals from the scallops and cut the whites in half horizontally. Cut the tentacles from the squid and slice the body cavities into rings.

3 Add the shallots to the liquid in the pan and simmer over high heat until the liquid is reduced to about 3 tablespoons. Add the scallops, squid, and jumbo shrimp and stir for 2–3 minutes until cooked. Remove and spoon the mixture into a wide bowl.

4 Cut the cucumber and carrot in half lengthwise, then slice thinly on a diagonal angle to make long, pointed slices. Toss with the Napa cabbage.

5 To make the dressing, place all the ingredients in a screw-top jar and shake well until evenly combined. Season with salt to taste.

6 Toss the vegetables and seafood together. Spoon the dressing over the vegetables and seafood and serve immediately.

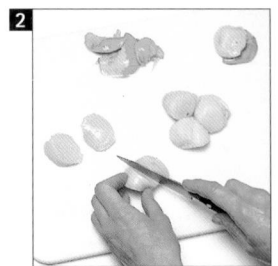

Steamed Yellow Fish Fillets

Thailand has an abundance of fresh fish, which is an important part of the local diet. Steaming is popular and suits many different types of fish.

NUTRITIONAL INFORMATION

Calories 165   Sugars 1g
Protein . . . . .23g   Fat 2g
Carbohydrate . . .13g   Saturates 1g

15 mins   12–15 mins

SERVES 4

INGREDIENTS

1 lb 2 oz/500 g firm fish fillets, such as red snapper, sole, or monkfish

1 dried red bird-eye chile

1 small onion, chopped

3 garlic cloves, chopped

2 fresh cilantro sprigs

1 tsp coriander seeds

½ tsp ground turmeric

½ tsp ground black pepper

1 tbsp Thai fish sauce

2 tbsp coconut milk

1 small egg, beaten

2 tbsp rice flour

fresh red and green chile strips, to garnish

soy sauce, to serve

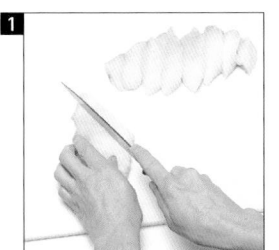

1 Remove any skin from the fish and cut the fillets diagonally into long ¾ inch/2 cm wide strips.

2 Place the dried chile, onion, garlic, cilantro, and coriander seeds in a mortar and grind with a pestle to a smooth paste.

3 Add the turmeric, pepper, fish sauce, coconut milk, and beaten egg, stirring well to mix.

4 Dip the fish strips into the paste mixture, then into the rice flour to coat lightly.

5 Bring the water in the bottom of a steamer to a boil, then arrange the fish strips in the top of the steamer. Cover and steam for about 12–15 minutes until the fish is just firm.

6 Transfer to a serving plate, garnish with chiles, and serve with soy sauce.

COOK'S TIP

If you don't have a steamer, improvize by placing a large metal colander over a large pan of boiling water and cover with an upturned plate to enclose the fish as it steams.

Thai Baked Fish

Almost any whole fish can be cooked by this method, but snapper, sea bass, or tilapia are particularly good with the Thai flavors.

NUTRITIONAL INFORMATION

Calories	..267	Sugars	..9g
Protein	..38g	Fat	..8g
Carbohydrate	..11g	Saturates	..2g

15 mins   35 mins

SERVES 4

INGREDIENTS

handful of fresh sweet basil leaves

1 lb 10 oz/750 g whole red snapper, sea bass, or tilapia, cleaned

2 tbsp peanut oil

2 tbsp Thai fish sauce

2 garlic cloves, crushed

1 tsp finely grated fresh galangal or ginger root, finely grated

2 large fresh red chiles, sliced diagonally

1 yellow bell pepper, deseeded and diced

1 tbsp palm sugar

1 tbsp rice vinegar

2 tbsp water or fish stock

2 tomatoes, deseeded and sliced into thin wedges

1 Reserve a few fresh basil leaves for garnish and tuck the rest inside the body cavity of the fish.

2 Heat 1 tablespoon oil in a wide skillet and fry the fish quickly to brown, turning once. Place the fish on a large piece of foil in a roasting pan and spoon over the fish sauce. Wrap the foil over the fish loosely and bake in a preheated oven, 375°F/190°C, for about 25–30 minutes until just cooked through.

3 Meanwhile, heat the remaining oil and fry the garlic, galangal, and chiles for 30 seconds. Add the bell pepper and stir-fry for a further 2–3 minutes until softened, but not browned.

4 Stir in the sugar, rice vinegar, and water, then add the tomatoes and bring to a boil over low heat. Remove the pan from the heat.

5 Remove the fish from the oven and transfer to a warmed serving plate. Add the fish juices to the pan, stir in, then spoon the sauce over the fish, and sprinkle with the reserved basil leaves. Serve immediately.

COOK'S TIP

Large red chiles are less hot than the tiny red bird-eye chiles, so you can use them more freely in cooked dishes such as this for a mild heat. Remove the seeds if you prefer.

Curry Crust Cod

An easy, economical main dish that transforms a plain piece
of fish into an exotic meal—try it with other white fish, too.

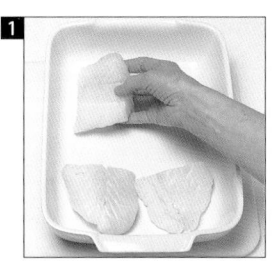

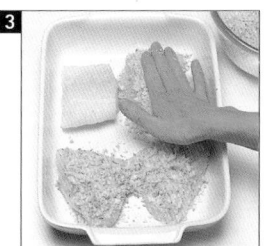

NUTRITIONAL INFORMATION

Calories	223	Sugars	.........1g
Protein	........31g	Fat	...........4g
Carbohydrate	...16g	Saturates	.......0g

 15 mins   35–40 mins

SERVES 4

I N G R E D I E N T S

½ tsp sesame oil

4 cod fillets, about 5½ oz/150 g each

1½ cups fresh white bread crumbs

2 tbsp blanched almonds, chopped

2 tsp Thai green curry paste

rind of ½ lime, finely grated

salt and pepper

lime slices and rind and mixed salad
   greens, to garnish

boiled new potatoes, to serve

1 Brush the sesame oil over the base of a wide, shallow casserole or roasting pan, then place the pieces of cod in a single layer.

2 Combine the fresh bread crumbs chopped, almonds, curry paste, and grated lime rind, stirring well to blend thoroughly and evenly. Season to taste with salt and pepper.

3 Spoon the crumb mixture over the fish, pressing down lightly. Bake in a preheated oven, 400°F/200°C, for about 35–40 minutes until the fish is cooked through and the curry crumb topping is golden brown.

4 Serve hot, garnished with lime slices, lime rind, and mixed salad greens and accompanied with boiled new potatoes.

COOK'S TIP
To test whether the
fish is cooked through, use a
fork to pierce it in the thickest
part—if the flesh is white all the
way through and flakes apart
easily, it is cooked sufficiently.

Fried Fish with Soy & Ginger

This impressive dish is worth cooking for a special dinner, as it really is a talking point. Buy a very fresh whole fish on the day you plan to cook it.

NUTRITIONAL INFORMATION

Calories	290	Sugars	.........7g
Protein	........27g	Fat	...........11g
Carbohydrate	...23g	Saturates	.......1g

20 mins

20 mins

SERVES 4–6

I N G R E D I E N T S

6 dried Chinese mushrooms

3 tbsp rice vinegar

2 tbsp brown sugar

3 tbsp dark soy sauce

3 inch/7.5 cm fresh root ginger, finely chopped

4 scallions, sliced diagonally

2 tsp cornstarch

2 tbsp lime juice

1 sea bass, about 2 lb 4 oz/1 kg, cleaned

4 tbsp all-purpose flour

sunflower oil, for deep-frying

salt and pepper

shredded Napa cabbage and radish slices, to serve

1 radish, sliced but left whole, to garnish

1 Soak the dried mushrooms in hot water for about 10 minutes, then drain well, reserving ½ cup of the liquid. Cut the mushrooms into thin slices.

2 Combine the reserved mushroom liquid with the rice vinegar, sugar, and soy sauce. Place in a pan with the mushrooms and bring to a boil. Reduce the heat and simmer for 3–4 minutes.

3 Add the ginger and scallions and simmer for 1 minute. Blend the cornstarch and lime juice to a smooth paste, stir into the pan, and cook, stirring constantly, for 1–2 minutes until the sauce thickens and clears. Set the sauce aside while you cook the fish.

4 Season the fish inside and out with salt and pepper, then dust lightly with flour, shaking off the excess.

5 Heat a 1 inch/2.5 cm depth of oil in a wide pan to 375°F/190°C or until a cube of bread browns in 30 seconds.

Carefully lower the fish into the oil and fry on 1 side for about 3–4 minutes until golden. Use 2 metal spatulas or spoons to turn the fish carefully and fry on the other side for a further 3–4 minutes until golden brown all over.

6 Lift the fish out of the pan, draining off the excess oil, and place on a serving plate. Heat the sauce until boiling, then spoon it over the fish. Serve immediately, surrounded by shredded Napa cabbage with sliced radishes and garnished with the sliced whole radish.

Sweet & Sour Tuna

Tuna is a firm, meaty-textured fish that is abundant in the seas around Thailand. You can also use shark or mackerel in this piquant dish.

NUTRITIONAL INFORMATION

Calories	303	Sugars	........12g
Protein	........31g	Fat	..........12g
Carbohydrate	...20g	Saturates	.......3g

10 mins   15 mins

SERVES 4

INGREDIENTS

4 fresh tuna steaks, about 1 lb 2 oz/500 g total weight

¼ tsp ground black pepper

2 tbsp peanut oil

1 onion, diced

1 small red bell pepper, deseeded and cut into thin batons

1 garlic clove, crushed

½ cucumber, deseeded and cut into thin batons

2 pineapple slices, diced

1 tsp finely chopped fresh ginger root

1 tbsp brown sugar

1 tbsp cornstarch

1½ tbsp lime juice

1 tbsp Thai fish sauce

generous 1 cup fish stock

lime and cucumber slices, to garnish

1 Sprinkle the tuna steaks with pepper on both sides. Heat a heavy skillet or griddle and brush with a little of the oil. Cook the tuna steaks for about 8 minutes, turning them over once.

2 Heat the remaining oil in another pan and gently cook the onion, bell pepper, and garlic for 3–4 minutes.

3 Remove the pan from the heat and stir in the cucumber, pineapple, ginger, and sugar.

4 Blend the cornstarch with the lime juice and fish sauce, then stir into the stock, and add to the pan. Stir over medium heat until boiling, then cook for 1–2 minutes until thickened and clear.

5 Spoon the sauce over the tuna and serve immediately, garnished with lime slices and cucumber.

COOK'S TIP

Tuna can be served quite lightly cooked, and can be dry if it is overcooked.

Thai-Spiced Salmon

Marinated in delicate Thai spices and quickly pan-fried to perfection, these salmon fillets are ideal for a special dinner.

NUTRITIONAL INFORMATION

Calories ....329 Sugars 0g
Protein ....30g Fat 23g
Carbohydrate ....0g Saturates 4g

40 mins   4–5 mins

SERVES 4

INGREDIENTS

1 inch/2.5 cm piece of fresh
    ginger root, grated

1 tsp coriander seeds, crushed

¼ tsp chili powder

1 tbsp lime juice

1 tsp sesame oil

4 salmon fillets with skin, about 5½ oz/
    150 g each

2 tbsp vegetable oil

boiled rice and stir-fried vegetables,
    to serve

1 Combine the grated ginger, crushed coriander, chili powder, lime juice, and sesame oil.

2 Place the salmon in a wide, nonmetallic dish or on a plate and spoon the mixture over the flesh side of the fillets, spreading it to coat each piece of salmon evenly.

3 Cover the dish with plastic wrap and chill the salmon in the refrigerator for 30 minutes.

4 Heat a wide, heavy skillet or griddle pan with the oil over high heat. Place the salmon on the hot pan or griddle, skin side down.

5 Cook the salmon for 4–5 minutes, without turning, until the salmon is crusty underneath and the flesh flakes easily. Serve immediately with boiled rice and stir-fried vegetables.

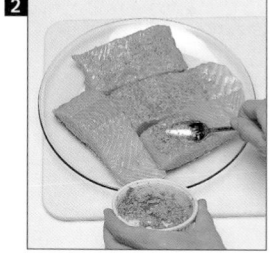  

COOK'S TIP

It's important to use a heavy-bottomed pan or solid griddle for this recipe, so the fish cooks evenly throughout without sticking. If the fish is very thick, you may prefer to turn it over carefully to cook on the other side for 2–3 minutes.

Salmon with Red Curry

If you can't find any banana leaves to wrap the fish, use foil or baking parchment, which work equally well.

NUTRITIONAL INFORMATION

Calories	.351	Sugars	.6g
Protein	.36g	Fat	.20g
Carbohydrate	.6g	Saturates	.3g

🥘 10 mins   🕐 15–20 mins

SERVES 4

INGREDIENTS

4 salmon steaks, about 6 oz/175 g each

2 banana leaves, halved

1 garlic clove, crushed

1 tsp grated fresh ginger root

1 tbsp Thai red curry paste

1 tsp brown sugar

1 tbsp Thai fish sauce

2 tbsp lime juice

TO GARNISH

lime wedges

finely chopped fresh red chile

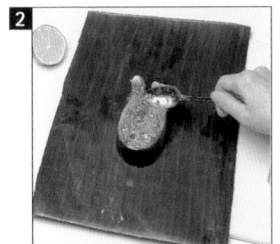
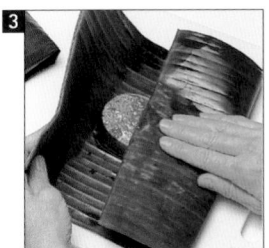

1 Place a salmon steak on the center of each half banana leaf.

2 Combine the garlic, ginger, curry paste, sugar, and fish sauce. Spread this mixture evenly over the surface of each steak and sprinkle with lime juice.

3 Wrap the banana leaves around the fish, tucking in the sides as you go to make a neat bundle. Alternatively, use baking parchment or foil.

4 Place the packets seam side down on a cookie sheet and bake in a preheated oven, 425°F/220°C, for about 15–20 minutes until the fish is cooked and the banana leaves are beginning to brown. Serve garnished with lime wedges and chopped chile.

COOK'S TIP

Fresh banana leaves are often sold in packs containing several leaves, but if you buy more than you need, they will store in the refrigerator for about a week.

Spicy Thai Seafood Stew

The fish in this fragrant, curry-like stew can be varied according to taste or availability, but do choose ones that stay firm when cooked.

NUTRITIONAL INFORMATION

Calories	267	Sugars	.........7g
Protein	........42g	Fat	...........7g
Carbohydrate	....9g	Saturates	.......1g

5 mins 10 mins

SERVES 4

INGREDIENTS

7 oz/200 g prepared squid

1 lb 2 oz/500 g firm white fish fillet, preferably monkfish or halibut

1 tbsp sunflower oil

4 shallots, finely chopped

2 garlic cloves, finely chopped

2 tbsp green Thai curry paste

2 small lemongrass stalks, finely chopped

1 tsp shrimp paste

2¼ cups coconut milk

7 oz/200 g raw jumbo shrimp, peeled and deveined

12 live clams, scrubbed

8 fresh basil leaves, finely shredded, plus extra to garnish

boiled rice, to serve

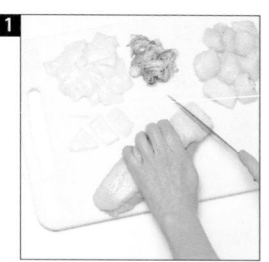

COOK'S TIP

If you prefer, fresh mussels in shells can be used instead of clams—add them in Step 4 and follow the recipe.

1 Cut the squid body cavities into thick rings and cut the fish fillet into bite-size chunks.

2 Heat the oil in a large skillet or wok and stir-fry the shallots, garlic, and curry paste for 1–2 minutes. Add the lemongrass and shrimp paste, stir in the coconut milk, and bring to a boil.

3 Reduce the heat to low. When the liquid is simmering gently, add the white fish chunks, squid rings, and jumbo shrimp to the skillet or wok. Stir and then simmer for 2 minutes.

4 Add the clams and simmer for a further minute until the clams open. Discard any clams that do not open.

5 Sprinkle the shredded basil leaves over the stew and serve immediately, garnished with whole basil leaves and spooned over boiled rice.

Squid with Black Bean Sauce

Squid really is wonderful if cooked quickly, as in this recipe, and contrary to popular belief, it is not tough and rubbery unless it is overcooked.

NUTRITIONAL INFORMATION

Calories	180	Sugars	.........2g
Protein	........19g	Fat	...........7g
Carbohydrate	...10g	Saturates	.......1g

5 mins   20 mins

SERVES 4

INGREDIENTS

1 lb/450 g squid rings

2 tbsp all-purpose flour

½ tsp salt

1 green bell pepper

2 tbsp peanut oil

1 red onion, sliced

5¾ oz/160 g jar black bean sauce

1 Rinse the squid rings under cold running water and pat thoroughly dry with paper towels.

2 Place the all-purpose flour and salt in a bowl and mix together. Add the squid rings and toss until they are evenly coated. Shake off any excess.

3 Using a sharp knife, deseed the bell pepper. Slice the flesh into thin strips.

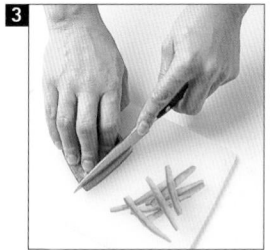

4 Heat the peanut oil in a large preheated wok or heavy skillet, swirling the oil around the base of the wok until it is really hot.

5 Add the bell pepper strips and red onion to the wok or skillet and stir-fry for about 2 minutes or until the vegetables are just beginning to soften.

6 Add the squid rings to the wok or skillet and cook for a further 5 minutes or until the squid is cooked through and tender. Be careful not to overcook the squid.

7 Add the black bean sauce to the wok and heat through until the cooking juices are just bubbling. Transfer the squid stir-fry to warm serving bowls and serve immediately.

COOK'S TIP

Serve this recipe with fried rice or noodles tossed in soy sauce, if you wish.

Spicy Lime Scallops

Really fresh scallops have a delicate flavor and texture, needing only minimal cooking, as in this simple stir-fry.

NUTRITIONAL INFORMATION

Calories 145   Sugars 1g
Protein ....17g   Fat 7g
Carbohydrate ....4g   Saturates 3g

 10 mins   8 mins

SERVES 4

INGREDIENTS

16 large scallops

1 tbsp butter

1 tbsp vegetable oil

1 tsp crushed garlic

1 tsp grated fresh ginger root

1 bunch of scallions, thinly sliced

finely grated rind of 1 kaffir lime

1 small fresh red chile, deseeded and very finely chopped

3 tbsp kaffir lime juice

lime wedges and boiled rice, to serve

COOK'S TIP

If fresh scallops are not available, frozen ones can be used, but make sure they are thoroughly thawed before you cook them.

1 Trim the scallops, then wash, and pat dry. Separate the corals from the white parts, then horizontally slice each white part in half, making 2 rounds.

2 Heat the butter and vegetable oil in a skillet or wok. Add the garlic and ginger and stir-fry for 1 minute without browning. Add the scallions and stir-fry for a further minute.

3 Add the scallops and stir-fry over high heat for 4–5 minutes. Stir in the lime rind, chile, and lime juice and cook for a further minute.

4 Serve the scallops hot, with the juices spooned over them, accompanied by lime wedges and boiled rice.

Shrimp Skewers with Chile

Whole jumbo shrimp cook very quickly on a barbecue or under a broiler, so they're ideal for summertime cooking, indoors or outside.

NUTRITIONAL INFORMATION

Calories	106	Sugars	.........8g
Protein	........11g	Fat	...........3g
Carbohydrate	....8g	Saturates	.......1g

4 Cook the skewers under a preheated hot broiler for 5–6 minutes, turning them over once, until they turn pink and begin to brown. Alternatively, grill over hot coals.

5 Thread a wedge of lime onto the end of each skewer and serve with crusty bread and salad greens.

🕐 2¼ hrs   🕐 10 mins

SERVES 4

INGREDIENTS

1 garlic clove, chopped

1 fresh red bird-eye chile, deseeded and chopped

1 tbsp tamarind paste

1 tbsp sesame oil

1 tbsp dark soy sauce

2 tbsp lime juice

1 tbsp brown sugar

16 large whole raw jumbo shrimp

crusty bread, lime wedges, and salad greens, to serve

1 Put the garlic, chile, tamarind, sesame oil, soy sauce, lime juice, and sugar in a small pan. Stir over low heat until the sugar is dissolved, then remove from the heat, and set aside to cool completely.

2 Wash and dry the shrimp, and place in a single layer in a wide, nonmetallic dish. Spoon the marinade over the shrimp and turn them over to coat evenly. Cover the dish with plastic wrap and set aside in the refrigerator to marinate for at least 2 hours, or preferably overnight.

3 Meanwhile, soak 4 bamboo or wooden skewers in water for about 30 minutes. Drain and thread 4 shrimp onto each skewer.

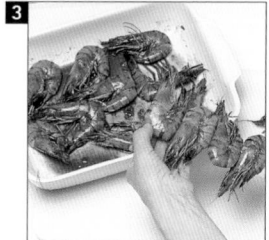

Rice with Seafood

This souplike entrée rice dish is packed with a tempting array of fresh seafood and is typically Thai in flavor.

NUTRITIONAL INFORMATION

Calories	.370	Sugars	.0g
Protein	.27g	Fat	.8g
Carbohydrate	.52g	Saturates	.1g

5–10 mins   20 mins

SERVES 4

INGREDIENTS

12 live mussels, scrubbed and bearded

8¾ cups fish stock

2 tbsp vegetable oil

1 garlic clove, crushed

1 tsp grated fresh ginger root

1 fresh red bird-eye chile, chopped

2 scallions, chopped

generous 1 cup long grain rice

2 small squid, cleaned and sliced

3½ oz/100 g firm white fish fillet, such as halibut or monkfish, cut into chunks

1 cup peeled raw shrimp

2 tbsp Thai fish sauce

3 tbsp chopped fresh cilantro

1 Discard any mussels with damaged shells or open ones that do not close when firmly tapped with a knife. Pour 4 tablespoons of the stock into a large pan. Add the mussels, cover, and cook over medium heat, shaking the pan until the mussels open. Remove from the heat and discard any which do not open.

2 Heat the oil in a large skillet or wok and stir-fry the garlic, ginger, chile, and scallions for 30 seconds. Add the remaining stock and bring to a boil.

3 Stir in the rice, then add the squid, fish chunks, and shrimp. Lower the heat and simmer gently for 15 minutes or until the rice is cooked. Add the fish sauce and mussels.

4 Ladle into wide bowls and sprinkle with cilantro before serving.

COOK'S TIP

You could use leftover cooked rice for this dish. Just simmer the seafood gently until cooked, then stir in the rice at the end.

Blackened Fish

The word "blackened" refers to the spicy, Cajun marinade that is used to coat the fish and that chars slightly as it cooks.

NUTRITIONAL INFORMATION

Calories 331   Sugars 0g
Protein . . . . .37g   Fat 20g
Carbohydrate . . . .0g   Saturates 8g

 10 mins   20 mins

SERVES 4

INGREDIENTS

4 white fish steaks, such as cod, conger
  eel, shark, or catfish

1 tbsp paprika

1 tsp dried thyme

1 tsp cayenne pepper

1 tsp freshly ground black pepper

½ tsp freshly ground white pepper

½ tsp salt

¼ tsp ground allspice

2 tbsp sweet butter

3 tbsp sunflower oil

1 Rinse the fish steaks and pat them dry with absorbent paper towels.

2 Combine the paprika, thyme, cayenne, black pepper, white pepper, salt, and allspice in a shallow dish.

3 Place the butter and oil in a small pan and heat, stirring occasionally, until the butter melts.

4 Brush the butter mixture liberally all over the fish steaks, on both sides.

5 Dip the fish into the spice mixture until well coated on both sides.

6 Grill the fish over hot coals for about 10 minutes on each side, turning once. Continue to baste the fish with the remaining butter mixture during the cooking time. Alternatively, cook under a preheated broiler, brushing frequently with the butter mixture, until cooked through and tender. Serve immediately.

VARIATION

A whole fish—red snapper, for example—rather than steaks is also delicious cooked this way. The spicy seasoning can also be used to coat chicken portions, if you like.

Chargrilled Porgy

Porgy have quite tough scales, which need to be removed before cooking. Ask the fish store to do this for you.

NUTRITIONAL INFORMATION

Calories	397	Sugars	.........1g
Protein	........35g	Fat	..........28g
Carbohydrate	....1g	Saturates	.......3g

🕑 15 mins 🕐 20–30 mins

SERVES 2

INGREDIENTS

2 small porgy, scaled, gutted, trimmed, and cleaned

2 lemon slices

2 bay leaves

salt and pepper

BASTE

4 tbsp olive oil

2 tbsp lemon juice

½ tsp chopped fresh oregano

½ tsp chopped fresh thyme

TO GARNISH

fresh bay leaves

fresh thyme sprig

lemon wedges

1 Using a sharp knife, cut 2–3 deep slashes into the bodies of both fish in order to help them fully absorb the flavor of the basting sauce.

2 Place a slice of lemon and a bay leaf inside the cavity of each fish. Season inside the cavity with salt and pepper.

3 In a small bowl, combine the ingredients for the baste using a fork. Alternatively, place the basting ingredients in a small screw-top jar and shake vigorously to combine.

4 Brush some of the baste liberally over the fish and place them on a rack over hot coals. Grill for 20-30 minutes, turning and basting frequently. Alternatively, cook under a preheated broiler, basting frequently.

5 Transfer the fish to a serving plate, garnish with fresh bay leaves, thyme, and lemon wedges, and serve.

COOK'S TIP

The flavor of the dish will be enhanced if you use good fresh ingredients in the sauce. Dried herbs can be used, but remember that the flavor is much more intense, so use only half the quantity of the fresh herbs listed here.

Salmon Brochettes

These tasty kabobs have a lovely summery flavor, perfect for the barbecue. Serve on bread croûtes with fresh tomato sauce.

NUTRITIONAL INFORMATION

Calories	535	Sugars	.........7g
Protein	........26g	Fat	..........42g
Carbohydrate	...14g	Saturates	.......7g

🍞 35 mins   🕐 15 mins

SERVES 4

INGREDIENTS

1 lb/450 g salmon, skinned and cut into large chunks

1 tbsp cornstarch

½ tsp salt

½ tsp pepper

1 small egg white, beaten

1 red bell pepper, deseeded and cut into chunks

1 green bell pepper, deseeded and cut into chunks

4 tbsp olive oil

ciabatta bread, to serve

TOMATO SAUCE

4 tomatoes, deseeded and quartered

¼ cucumber, peeled, deseeded, and chopped

8 fresh basil leaves

6 tbsp olive oil

2 tbsp lemon juice

salt and pepper

1 Place the salmon in a shallow dish and sprinkle over the cornflour and season to taste with salt and pepper. Add the beaten egg white and toss well to coat. Set aside to chill for 15 minutes.

2 Thread the pieces of salmon on to 4 skewers, alternating the fish pieces with the chunks of red and green peppers. Set the skewers aside while you make the tomato sauce.

3 To make the sauce, place all of the ingredients in a food processor and chop coarsely. Alternatively, chop the tomatoes, cucumber and basil leaves by hand and mix with the oil and lemon juice. Season to taste with salt and pepper. Cover and chill in the refrigerator until required.

4 Barbecue the salmon brochettes over hot coals for 10 minutes, brushing frequently with olive oil to prevent them from drying during cooking. Alternatively, cook under a preheated grill.

5 Slice the ciabatta bread at an angle to produce 4 long slices. Lightly toast on the barbecue or under the grill.

6 Spread the tomato sauce over each slice of bread and top with a salmon brochette. Serve immediately.

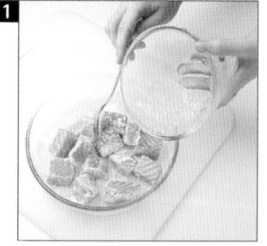

VARIATION

Serve the salmon brochettes on toasted French sticks, if preferred.

Nutty Stuffed Trout

Stuff the trout just before cooking. If you prefer, the fish can be cooked in foil packets on the barbecue or in a moderate oven.

NUTRITIONAL INFORMATION

Calories 356	Sugars 2g	
Protein 40g	Fat 17g	
Carbohydrate 11g	Saturates 3g	

 10 mins   25 mins

SERVES 4

INGREDIENTS

4 medium trout, cleaned

2 tbsp sunflower oil

1 small onion, finely chopped

½ cup toasted mixed nuts, chopped

grated rind of 1 orange

2 tbsp orange juice

1½ cups fresh whole-wheat bread crumbs

1 egg, beaten

vegetable oil, for brushing

salt and pepper

orange slices, to garnish

orange and watercress salad, to serve

1 Season the trout inside and out with salt and pepper.

COOK'S TIP

For the dressing, combine 2 tablespoons orange juice, 1 tablespoon white wine vinegar, 3 tablespoons olive oil, ½ teaspoon wholegrain mustard, and salt and pepper to taste. Pour the dressing over the salad just before serving.

2 To make the stuffing, heat the oil in a small pan and cook the onion over a low heat for 5 minutes until softened. Remove the pan from the heat and stir in the chopped nuts, grated orange rind, orange juice and bread crumbs. Add just enough of the beaten egg to bind the mixture together.

3 Divide the stuffing into 4 equal portions and spoon them into the cavity of each fish.

4 Brush the fish liberally with oil and grill over medium hot coals for 10 minutes on each side, turning once. When the fish is cooked the flesh will be white and firm and the skin will be beginning to crispen.

5 Transfer the fish to individual serving plates and garnish with orange slices.

6 Serve the fish with an orange and watercress salad and an orange and mustard dressing (see Cook's Tip).

Bacon & Scallop Skewers

Wrapping bacon around the scallops helps to protect the delicate flesh from the intense heat and allows them to cook without becoming tough.

NUTRITIONAL INFORMATION

Calories 271   Sugars 6g
Protein . . . . .17g   Fat 20g
Carbohydrate . . . .7g   Saturates 5g

 2½ hrs   🕐 5 mins

SERVES 4

I N G R E D I E N T S

grated rind and juice of ½ lemon

4 tbsp sunflower oil

½ tsp dried dill

12 scallops

1 red pepper

1 green pepper

1 yellow pepper

6 rashers smoked streaky bacon

1 Combine the lemon rind and juice, oil and dill in a non-metallic dish. Add the scallops and mix thoroughly to coat in the marinade. Set aside to marinate for 1–2 hours.

2 Cut the red, green and yellow peppers in half and deseed them. Cut the pepper halves into 1 inch/2.5 cm pieces and then set aside until required.

3 Carefully remove the rind from the bacon. Stretch the rashers with the back of a knife, then cut each one in half.

4 Remove the scallops from the reserved marinade, reserving any excess marinade. Wrap a piece of bacon around each scallop.

5 Thread the scallops on to skewers, alternating with the pepper pieces.

6 Barbecue the bacon and scallop skewers over hot coals for about 5 minutes, basting frequently with the lemon and oil marinade.

7 Transfer to warmed serving plates and serve immediately.

VARIATION

Peel 4–8 raw shrimp and add them to the marinade with the scallops. Thread them on to the skewers alternating with the scallops and peppers.

Herb & Garlic Shrimp

Shrimp cook very rapidly—and if overcooked, develop an unpleasant texture. However, there is no virtue in undercooking them.

NUTRITIONAL INFORMATION

Calories	150	Sugars	.........0g
Protein	........16g	Fat	...........9g
Carbohydrate	....1g	Saturates	.......5g

 50 mins   12 mins

SERVES 4

INGREDIENTS

12 oz/350 g raw shrimp, peeled and deveined

2 tbsp chopped fresh parsley

4 tbsp lemon juice

2 tbsp olive oil

5 tbsp butter

2 garlic cloves, chopped

salt and pepper

1 Place the shrimp in a shallow, nonmetallic dish with the parsley and lemon juice and season with salt and pepper to taste. Cover and set aside to marinate in the herb mixture for at least 30 minutes.

2 Heat the oil and butter in a small pan with the garlic until the butter melts. Stir to mix thoroughly.

3 Remove the shrimp from the marinade with a slotted spoon and add them to the pan containing the garlic butter. Stir until well coated, then thread the shrimp onto skewers.

4 Grill the kabobs over hot coals for 5–10 minutes, turning the skewers occasionally, until the shrimp turn pink and are cooked through. Brush the shrimp with the remaining garlic butter during the cooking time. Alternatively, cook under a preheated broiler, turning and brushing frequently with the garlic butter.

5 Transfer the herb and garlic shrimp kabobs to warmed serving plates. Drizzle over any of the remaining garlic butter and serve immediately.

VARIATION

If raw shrimp are unavailable, use cooked shrimp, but reduce the cooking time. Small cooked shrimp can also be cooked in a kitchen foil packet instead of on the skewers.

Steamed Stuffed Snapper

Red mullet may be used instead of the snapper, although their size makes them a little more difficult to stuff. Use one mullet per person.

NUTRITIONAL INFORMATION

Calories ....406 Sugar 4g
Protein ....68g Fat 9g
Carbohydrate ....9g Saturates 0g

   20 mins   10 mins

SERVES 4

INGREDIENTS

3 lb/1.4 kg whole snapper, cleaned and scaled

6 oz/175 g spinach

orange slices and shredded scallion, to garnish

STUFFING

⅓ cup cooked long grain rice

1 tsp grated fresh ginger root

2 scallions, finely chopped

2 tsp light soy sauce

1 tsp sesame oil

½ tsp ground star anise

1 orange, segmented and chopped

1 Rinse the fish inside and out under cold running water and pat dry with paper towels.

2 Blanch the spinach for 40 seconds, rinse in cold water, and drain well, pressing out as much moisture as possible.

3 Arrange the spinach on a heatproof plate and place the fish on top.

4 To make the stuffing, combine the cooked rice, grated ginger, scallions, soy sauce, sesame oil, star anise, and orange in a bowl.

5 Spoon the stuffing into the body cavity of the fish, pressing it in well with a spoon.

6 Cover the plate and cook in a steamer for 10 minutes or until the fish is cooked through.

7 Garnish the fish with orange slices and scallion and serve.

COOK'S TIP

The name "snapper" covers a family of tropical and subtropical fish that vary in color. They may be red, orange, pink, gray, or blue-green and almost all have a fine flavor. They range in size from 6 inches/15 cm to 3 ft/90 cm.

Braised Fish Fillets

Almost any white fish, such as lemon sole or flounder, can be used to make this delicious dish with a Chinese flavor.

NUTRITIONAL INFORMATION

Calories	107	Sugars	.........2g
Protein	........17g	Fat	...........2g
Carbohydrate	....6g	Saturates	.....0.3g

35 mins | 10 mins

SERVES 4

INGREDIENTS

3–4 small Chinese dried mushrooms

10–12 oz/280–350 g fish fillets

1 tsp salt

½ egg white, lightly beaten

1 tsp cornstarch

2½ cups vegetable oil

1 tsp finely chopped fresh ginger root

2 scallions, finely chopped

1 garlic clove, finely chopped

½ small green bell pepper, deseeded and diced

½ small carrot, thinly sliced

2 oz/55 g canned sliced bamboo shoots, drained and rinsed

½ tsp sugar

1 tbsp light soy sauce

1 tsp rice wine or dry sherry

1 tbsp chili bean sauce

2–3 tbsp vegetable stock or water

a few drops of sesame oil

1 Soak the dried mushrooms in a bowl of warm water for 30 minutes. Drain thoroughly on paper towels, reserving the soaking water for stock or soup. Squeeze the mushrooms to extract all of the moisture, cut off and discard any hard stalks, and slice the caps thinly.

2 Cut the fish into bite-size pieces, then place in a shallow dish, and mix with a pinch of salt, the egg white, and cornstarch, turning the fish to coat well.

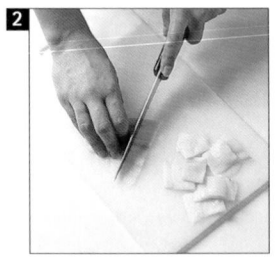

3 Heat the oil in a preheated wok. Add the fish pieces to the wok and deep-fry for about 1 minute. Remove the fish pieces with a slotted spoon and drain on paper towels.

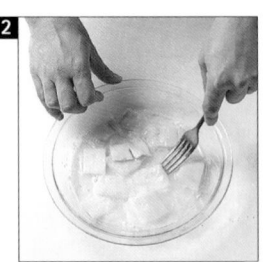

4 Carefully pour off the excess oil, leaving about 1 tablespoon in the wok. Add the ginger, scallions, and garlic and cook over medium heat for a few seconds to flavor the oil, then add the green bell pepper, carrots, and bamboo shoots, and stir-fry for about 1 minute.

5 Add the sugar, soy sauce, wine, chili bean sauce, stock or water, and the remaining salt and bring to a boil. Add the fish pieces, stirring to coat with the sauce, and braise for 1 minute. Sprinkle with sesame oil and serve.

Bengali-Style Fish

Fresh fish is eaten a great deal in Bengal and this dish is made with mustard oil, which gives the fish a good flavor.

NUTRITIONAL INFORMATION

Calories ....356 Sugars 4g
Protein ....32g Fat 23g
Carbohydrate ....5g Saturates 3g

15 mins   25–35 mins

SERVES 4

INGREDIENTS

1 tsp ground turmeric

1 tsp salt

2 lb 4 oz/1 kg cod fillet, skinned and cut into pieces

6 tbsp corn oil

4 fresh green chiles

1 tsp finely chopped fresh ginger root

1 tsp crushed garlic

2 medium onions, finely chopped

2 tomatoes, finely chopped

6 tbsp mustard oil

generous 1¾ cups water

chopped fresh cilantro leaves, to garnish

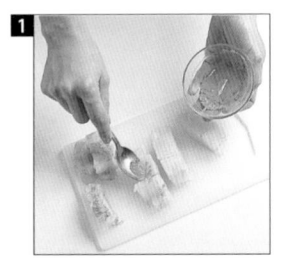

1 Combine the turmeric and salt in a small bowl. Spoon the mixture over the fish pieces.

2 Heat the oil in a skillet. Add the fish and cook over low heat until pale golden yellow. Remove the fish with a draining spoon and set aside.

3 Place the fresh chiles, ginger, garlic, onions, tomatoes, and mustard oil in a mortar and grind with a pestle to a fine paste. Alternatively, process the ingredients in a food processor.

4 Transfer the spice paste to a heavy-bottomed pan and dry-fry over a low heat, stirring occasionally, until golden brown and aromatic.

5 Remove the pan from the heat and gently place the fish pieces into the paste, without breaking them. Return the pan to the heat, add the water, and cook over medium heat, stirring occasionally, for 15–20 minutes, or until the fish is tender and cooked through.

6 Serve immediately, garnished with chopped cilantro.

Vegetables

Whether you are a vegetarian or a meat-eater, vegetable dishes are the perfect choice for a healthy diet. Most vegetables are naturally low in fats, high in fiber, and packed with essential vitamins and minerals—and they are full of flavor, too. With this chapter you are spoilt for choice with a huge range of dishes that takes full advantage of the breathtaking versatility of vegetables. Some are just perfect filled with a tasty stuffing, while others make wonderful pasta sauces and succulent curries. Vegetable kabobs are a real treat on the barbecue and don't overlook the delights of crêpes and omelets.

Vegetable Chili

This is a hearty and flavorful soup that is good on its own or spooned over cooked rice or baked potatoes for a more substantial meal.

NUTRITIONAL INFORMATION

Calories	213	Sugars	........11g
Protein	........12g	Fat	..........10g
Carbohydrate	...21g	Saturates	.......5g

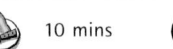 10 mins   1¼ hrs

SERVES 5–6

INGREDIENTS

1 medium eggplant, peeled if wished, cut into 1 inch/2.5 cm slices

1 tbsp olive oil, plus extra for brushing

1 large red or yellow onion, finely chopped

2 red or yellow bell peppers, deseeded and finely chopped

3–4 garlic cloves, finely chopped or crushed

2 x 14 oz/400g cans chopped tomatoes

1 tbsp mild chili powder

½ tsp ground cumin

½ tsp dried oregano

2 small zucchini, quartered lengthwise and sliced

14 oz/400g can kidney beans, drained and rinsed

2 cups water

1 tbsp tomato paste

6 scallions, finely chopped

1 cup grated Cheddar cheese

salt and pepper

1 Brush the eggplant slices on 1 side with olive oil. Heat half the oil in a large, heavy skillet over medium-high heat. Add the eggplant slices, oiled side up, and cook for 5–6 minutes until browned on 1 side. Turn the slices over, cook on the other side until browned and then transfer to a plate. Cut the slices into bite-size pieces.

2 Heat the remaining oil in a large pan over medium heat. Add the onion and bell peppers and cook, stirring occasionally, for 3–4 minutes until the onion is just softened, but not browned. Add the garlic and continue cooking for 2–3 minutes or until the onion is just beginning to color.

3 Add the tomatoes, chili powder, cumin, and oregano. Season to taste with salt and pepper. Bring just to a boil, reduce the heat, cover, and simmer gently for 15 minutes.

4 Add the zucchini, eggplant pieces, and kidney beans. Stir in the water and tomato paste. Bring back to a boil, cover, and continue simmering for about 45 minutes or until the vegetables are tender. Taste and adjust the seasoning if necessary. If you prefer a hotter dish, stir in a little more chili powder.

5 Ladle into warmed bowls and top with scallions and cheese.

Stuffed Red Bell Peppers

Stuffed bell peppers are a well known and popular dish, but this is a new version adapted for the barbecue.

NUTRITIONAL INFORMATION

Calories ....144 Sugars 4g
Protein ....1g Fat 12g
Carbohydrate ....9g Saturates 2g

40 mins   10 mins

SERVES 4

INGREDIENTS

2 red bell peppers, halved lengthwise
   and deseeded

2 tomatoes, halved

2 zucchini, thinly sliced lengthwise

1 red onion, cut into 8 sections, each
   section held together by the root

4 tbsp olive oil

2 tbsp fresh thyme leaves

¼ cup mixed basmati and wild
   rice, cooked

salt and pepper

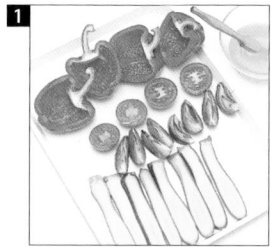

1 Put the bell peppers, tomatoes, zucchini, and onion sections onto a cookie sheet.

2 Brush the vegetables with olive oil and sprinkle with the thyme leaves.

3 Cook the pepper, onion, and zucchini over a medium barbecue for about 6 minutes, turning once.

4 When the peppers are cooked and tender, put a spoonful of the cooked rice into each of the halves.

5 Add the tomato halves to the barbecue and cook for 2–3 minutes only. Serve all the vegetables hot, seasoned with plenty of salt and pepper.

COOK'S TIP

When chargrilled, red, orange, and yellow bell peppers all take on a remarkable sweet quality.

Pasta & Bean Casserole

A satisfying winter dish, this is a slow-cooked, one-pot meal.
The navy beans need to be soaked overnight, so prepare well in advance.

NUTRITIONAL INFORMATION

Calories	323	Sugars	.........5g
Protein	........13g	Fat	..........12g
Carbohydrate	...41g	Saturates	.......2g

25 mins   3½ hrs

SERVES 4

INGREDIENTS

1¼ cups dried navy beans,
   soaked overnight and drained

2 cups dried penne, or other
   short pasta shapes

6 tbsp olive oil

3¾ cups vegetable stock

2 large onions, sliced

2 garlic cloves, chopped

2 bay leaves

1 tsp dried oregano

1 tsp dried thyme

5 tbsp red wine

2 tbsp tomato paste

2 celery stalks, sliced

1 fennel bulb, sliced

1⅔ cups sliced mushrooms

8 oz/225 g tomatoes, sliced

1 tsp molasses sugar

1 cup dry white bread crumbs

salt and pepper

TO SERVE

salad greens

crusty bread

1 Put the beans in a large pan, add water to cover, and bring to a boil. Boil the beans rapidly for 20 minutes, then drain them, and set aside.

2 Cook the pasta for only 3 minutes in a large pan of boiling salted water, adding 1 tablespoon of the oil. Drain in a colander, and set aside.

3 Put the beans in a large flameproof casserole, pour in the vegetable stock, and stir in the remaining olive oil, the onions, garlic, bay leaves, herbs, wine, and tomato paste.

4 Bring to a boil, cover the casserole, and cook in a preheated oven, 350°F/180°C, for 2 hours.

5 Remove the casserole from the oven and add the reserved pasta, the celery, fennel, mushrooms, and tomatoes, and season to taste with salt and pepper.

6 Stir in the sugar and sprinkle the bread crumbs on top. Cover the casserole again, return to the oven, and continue cooking for 1 hour. Serve straight from the casserole with salad greens and crusty bread.

Artichoke & Olive Spaghetti

The tasty flavors and delightful textures of artichoke hearts and black olives make a winning combination.

NUTRITIONAL INFORMATION

Calories	393	Sugars	........11g
Protein	........14g	Fat	...........11g
Carbohydrate	...63g	Saturates	.......2g

🥐 🥐

🍲 20 mins   🕐 35 mins

SERVES 4

INGREDIENTS

2 tbsp olive oil

1 large red onion, chopped

2 garlic cloves, crushed

1 tbsp lemon juice

4 baby eggplants, quartered

2½ cups sieved tomatoes

2 tsp superfine sugar

2 tbsp tomato paste

14 oz/400g can artichoke hearts, drained and halved

1 cup pitted black olives

12 oz/350 g whole-wheat dried spaghetti

salt and pepper

fresh basil sprigs, to garnish

olive bread, to serve

3 Gently stir in the artichoke hearts and olives and cook for 5 minutes.

4 Meanwhile, bring a large pan of lightly salted water to a boil. Ad d the pasta, bring back to a boil, and cook for 8–10 minutes or until tender, but still firm to the bite. Drain, toss in the remaining oil, and season to taste.

5 Transfer the spaghetti to a warmed serving bowl and top with the vegetable sauce. Garnish with basil sprigs and serve with olive bread.

1 Heat 1 tablespoon of the oil in a large, heavy skillet. Add the onion, garlic, lemon juice, and eggplants and cook over low heat, stirring occasionally, for 4–5 minutes or until lightly browned.

2 Pour in the sieved tomatoes, season with salt and pepper to taste, and stir in the sugar and tomato paste. Bring to a boil, reduce the heat and simmer gently for 20 minutes.

Asian-Style Millet Pilau

Millet makes an interesting alternative to rice, which is the more traditional ingredient for a pilau. Serve with a crisp Asian salad.

NUTRITIONAL INFORMATION

Calories	660	Sugars	........28g
Protein	........15g	Fat	..........27g
Carbohydrate	...94g	Saturates	.......5g

20 mins   30 mins

SERVES 4

INGREDIENTS

1½ cups millet grains

1 tbsp vegetable oil

1 bunch of scallions, white and green parts, chopped

1 garlic clove, crushed

1 tsp grated fresh ginger root

1 orange bell pepper, seeded and diced

2½ cups water

1 orange

⅔ cup chopped pitted dates

2 tsp sesame oil

1 cup roasted cashew nuts

2 tbsp pumpkin seeds

salt and pepper

Asian salad vegetables, to serve

1 Place the millet in a large pan and toast over medium heat, shaking the pan occasionally, for 4–5 minutes until the grains begin to crack and pop.

2 Heat the oil in another pan. Add the scallions, garlic, ginger, and bell pepper and cook over medium heat, stirring frequently, for 2–3 minutes until just softened, but not browned. Add the millet and pour in the water.

3 Using a vegetable peeler, pare the rind from the orange and add the rind to the pan. Squeeze the juice from the orange into the pan. Season to taste with salt and pepper.

4 Bring to a boil, reduce the heat, cover, and cook gently for 20 minutes until all the liquid has been absorbed. Remove the pan from the heat, stir in the dates and sesame oil, and set aside to stand for 10 minutes.

5 Remove and discard the orange rind and stir in the cashew nuts. Pile into a warmed serving dish, sprinkle with pumpkin seeds, and serve immediately with Asian salad vegetables.

Eggplant Bake

This dish combines layers of eggplant, tomato sauce, mozzarella, and Parmesan cheese to create a very tasty appetizer or light lunch.

NUTRITIONAL INFORMATION

Calories 232	Sugars 8g
Protein 10g	Fat 18g
Carbohydrate 8g	Saturates 6g

 5 mins    45 mins

SERVES 4

INGREDIENTS

3–4 tbsp olive oil

2 garlic cloves, crushed

2 large eggplants

3½ oz/100 g mozzarella cheese, thinly sliced

scant 1 cup sieved tomatoes

⅔ cup freshly grated Parmesan cheese

1 Heat 2 tablespoons of the olive oil in a large, heavy skillet. Add the garlic and cook, stirring constantly, for 30 seconds.

2 Slice the eggplants lengthwise. Add the slices to the pan and cook in the oil for 3–4 minutes on each side or until tender. (You will probably have to cook them in batches, so add the remaining oil as necessary.)

3 Remove the eggplants with a draining spoon and drain on absorbent paper towels.

4 Place a layer of eggplant slices in a shallow casserole. Cover with a layer of mozzarella and then pour over a third of the sieved tomatoes. Continue layering in the same order, finishing with a layer of sieved tomatoes on top.

5 Generously sprinkle the grated Parmesan cheese over the top and bake in a preheated oven, 400°F/200°C, for 25–30 minutes.

6 Transfer to serving plates and set aside to cool, then serve warm or chilled.

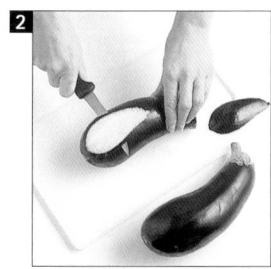

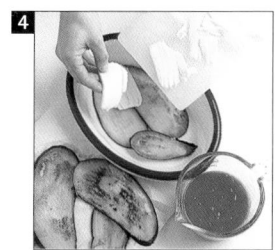

Chargrilled Vegetables

This medley of bell peppers, zucchini, eggplant, and red onion can be served on its own or as an unusual side dish.

NUTRITIONAL INFORMATION

Calories 66   Sugars 7g
Protein . . . . .2g   Fat 3g
Carbohydrate . . . .7g   Saturates 0.5g

🐾 🐾

🧊 15 mins   🕐 15 mins

SERVES 4

INGREDIENTS

1 large red bell pepper

1 large green bell pepper

1 large orange bell pepper

1 large zucchini

4 baby eggplants

2 medium red onions

2 tbsp lemon juice

1 tbsp olive oil

1 garlic clove, crushed

1 tbsp chopped fresh rosemary or 1 tsp dried rosemary

salt and pepper

TO SERVE

cracked wheat, cooked

tomato and olive relish

1 Halve and deseed the peppers and cut into even-size pieces, about 1 inch/2.5 cm wide.

2 Trim the zucchini, cut in half lengthwise, and slice into 1 inch/2.5 cm pieces. Place the bell peppers and zucchini in a large bowl.

3 Trim the eggplants and quarter them lengthwise. Peel the onions, then cut each of them into 8 even-size wedges. Add the eggplants and onions to the bell peppers and zucchini.

4 In a small bowl, whisk the lemon juice with the olive oil, garlic, and rosemary Season to taste with salt and pepper. Pour the mixture over the vegetables and stir to coat evenly.

5 Thread the vegetables onto 8 metal or pre-soaked wooden skewers. Arrange the kabobs on the broiler rack and cook under a preheated broiler, turning frequently, for about 10–12 minutes until the vegetables are lightly charred and just softened. Alternatively, cook on a barbecue over hot coals, turning frequently, for about 8–10 minutes until softened and beginning to char.

6 Drain the vegetable kabobs and serve immediately on a bed of cracked wheat, accompanied with a tomato and olive relish.

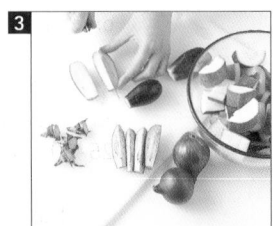

Spaghetti with Ricotta

This light pasta dish has a delicate flavor ideally suited for a summer lunch.

NUTRITIONAL INFORMATION

Calories . . . . .701 Sugars 12g

Protein . . . . .17g Fat 40g

Carbohydrate . . .73g Saturates 15g

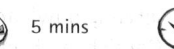

5 mins   25 mins

SERVES 4

INGREDIENTS

12 oz/350 g dried spaghetti

3 tbsp butter

2 tbsp chopped fresh flat leaf parsley

1 cup freshly ground almonds

½ cup ricotta cheese

pinch of freshly grated nutmeg

pinch of ground cinnamon

⅔ cup crème fraîche

2 tbsp olive oil

½ cup hot chicken stock

1 tbsp pine nuts

salt and pepper

fresh flat leaf parsley sprigs, to garnish

1 Bring a pan of lightly salted water to a boil. Add the spaghetti, bring back to a boil, and cook for 8–10 minutes until tender, but still firm to the bite.

2 Drain the pasta, return to the pan, and toss with the butter and chopped parsley. Set aside and keep warm.

3 To make the sauce, combine the ground almonds, ricotta cheese, nutmeg, cinnamon, and crème fraîche in a small pan and stir over low heat to a thick paste. Gradually stir in the oil. When the oil has been fully incorporated, gradually stir in the hot chicken stock, until smooth. Season to taste with pepper.

4 Transfer the spaghetti to a warm serving dish, pour the sauce over it, and toss together well (see Cook's Tip). Sprinkle over the pine nuts, garnish with the sprigs of fresh flat leaf parsley, and serve immediately.

COOK'S TIP

Use 2 large forks to toss spaghetti or other long pasta, so that it is thoroughly coated with the sauce. Special spaghetti forks are available from some cookware departments and kitchen stores.

Lemon Spaghetti

Steaming vegetables helps to preserve their nutritional content and lets them retain their bright, natural colors and crunchy texture.

NUTRITIONAL INFORMATION

Calories	133	Sugars	........8g
Protein	.........8g	Fat	...........1g
Carbohydrate	...25g	Saturates	.....0.2g

10 mins   25 mins

SERVES 4

INGREDIENTS

8 oz/225 g celery root

2 medium carrots

2 medium leeks

1 small red bell pepper

1 small yellow bell pepper

2 garlic cloves

1 tsp celery seeds

1 tbsp lemon juice

10½ oz/300 g spaghetti

salt

chopped celery leaves, to garnish

LEMON DRESSING

1 tsp finely grated lemon rind

1 tbsp lemon juice

4 tbsp low-fat plain yogurt

salt and pepper

2 tbsp chopped fresh chives

1 Peel the celery root and carrots, cut into thin batons, and place in a bowl. Trim and slice the leeks, rinse under cold running water to flush out any trapped dirt, then shred finely. Halve, deseed, and slice the bell peppers. Peel and thinly slice the garlic.

2 Add all of the vegetables to the bowl with the celery root and the carrots. Toss the vegetables with the celery seeds and lemon juice.

3 Bring a large pan of lightly salted water to a boil. Add the pasta, bring back to a boil, and cook for 8–10 minutes until tender, but still firm to the bite. Drain and keep warm.

4 Meanwhile, bring another large pan of water to a boil, put the vegetables in a steamer, and place over the boiling water. Cover and steam for 6–7 minutes or until tender.

5 Meanwhile, combine all the ingredients for the lemon dressing.

6 Transfer the spaghetti and vegetables to a warmed serving bowl and mix with the dressing. Garnish with chopped celery leaves and serve.

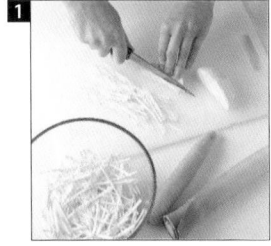

Mixed Bean Pan-Fry

Fresh green beans have a wonderful flavor that is hard to beat.
If you cannot find fresh beans, use thawed, frozen beans instead.

NUTRITIONAL INFORMATION

Calories	179	Sugars	........4g
Protein	........10g	Fat	...........11g
Carbohydrate	...10g	Saturates	.......1g

🕐 10 mins   🕐 15 mins

SERVES 4

INGREDIENTS

12 oz/350 g mixed fresh beans, such as green and fava beans, podded

2 tbsp vegetable oil

2 garlic cloves, crushed

1 red onion, halved and sliced

8 oz/225 g firm marinated beancurd, diced

1 tbsp lemon juice

½ tsp ground turmeric

1 tsp apple spice

⅔ cup vegetable stock

2 tsp sesame seeds

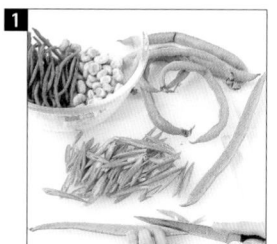

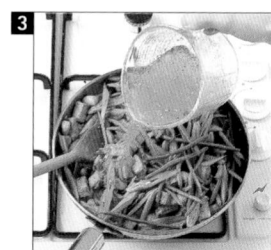

1 Trim and chop the green beans and set aside until required.

2 Heat the oil in a medium skillet. Add the garlic and onion and cook over low heat, stirring frequently, for 2 minutes. Add the beancurd and cook, stirring gently occasionally, for a further 2–3 minutes, until just beginning to turn golden brown.

3 Add the green beans and fava beans. Stir in the lemon juice, turmeric, apple spice, and vegetable stock and bring to a boil over medium heat.

4 Reduce the heat and simmer for about 5–7 minutes or until the beans are tender. Sprinkle with sesame seeds and serve immediately.

VARIATION
Use smoked tofu instead of marinated tofu for an alternative and quite distinctive flavor.

Penne & Vegetables

The sweet cherry tomatoes in this recipe add color and flavor and are complemented by the black olives and mixed bell peppers.

NUTRITIONAL INFORMATION

Calories	380	Sugars	.........6g
Protein	.........8g	Fat	..........16g
Carbohydrate	...48g	Saturates	.......7g

 10 mins   25 mins

SERVES 4

INGREDIENTS

8 oz/225 g dried penne

2 tbsp olive oil

2 tbsp butter

2 garlic cloves, crushed

1 green bell pepper, deseeded and thinly sliced

1 yellow bell pepper, deseeded and thinly sliced

16 cherry tomatoes, halved

1 tbsp chopped oregano

½ cup dry white wine

2 tbsp quartered, pitted black olives

2¾ oz/75 g arugula

salt and pepper

fresh oregano sprigs, to garnish

VARIATION

If arugula is unavailable, spinach makes a good substitute. Follow the same cooking instructions as for arugula.

1 Bring a pan of lightly salted water to a boil. Add the pasta, bring back to a boil, and cook for 8–10 minutes until tender, but still firm to the bite. Drain.

2 Heat the oil and butter in a pan. Sauté the garlic for 30 seconds. Add the bell peppers and cook, stirring occasionally, for 3–4 minutes.

3 Stir in the cherry tomatoes, oregano, wine, and olives and cook for 3–4 minutes. Season with salt and pepper and stir in the arugula until just wilted.

4 Transfer the pasta to a serving dish, spoon over the sauce, and garnish.

Beancurd Stir-Fry

This is a quick stir-fry dish, making it the perfect choice for a midweek supper after a busy day at work.

NUTRITIONAL INFORMATION

Calories ....124 Sugars 2g
Protein ....6g Fat 6g
Carbohydrate ....11g Saturates 1g

5 mins   25 mins

SERVES 4

INGREDIENTS

6 oz/175 g potatoes, cubed

1 tbsp vegetable oil

1 red onion, sliced

8 oz/225 g firm bean curd, diced

2 zucchini, diced

8 canned artichoke hearts, halved

⅔ cup sieved tomatoes

1 tbsp sweet chilli sauce

1 tbsp soy sauce

1 tsp superfine sugar

2 tbsp chopped fresh basil

salt and pepper

1 Cook the potatoes in a pan of lightly salted boiling water for 10 minutes. Drain thoroughly and set aside until required.

2 Heat the vegetable oil in a wok or large skillet and stir-fry the red onion for 2 minutes until it has softened.

3 Stir in the beancurd and zucchini and stir-fry for 3–4 minutes until they begin to brown slightly.

4 Add the cooked potatoes to the wok or skillet, stirring gently to mix.

5 Stir in the artichoke hearts, sieved tomatoes, sweet chili sauce, soy sauce, sugar, and basil.

6 Season to taste with salt and pepper and cook for a further 5 minutes, stirring constantly.

7 Transfer the beancurd and vegetable stir-fry to serving dishes and serve immediately.

COOK'S TIP
Canned artichoke hearts should be drained thoroughly and rinsed before use because they often have salt added.

Roasted Vegetable Pilaf

Red rice has an aromatic, nutty flavor which complements the robust flavors of the roasted root vegetables.

NUTRITIONAL INFORMATION

Calories	773	Sugars	........30g
Protein	........11g	Fat	..........42g
Carbohydrate	...94g	Saturates	.......9g

 15 mins   1¼ hrs

SERVES 4–6

INGREDIENTS

½ cup olive oil

grated rind and juice of 1 orange

2 tbsp balsamic vinegar

2 tsp coriander seeds, lightly crushed

1 bay leaf

½ tsp crushed dried chiles

8–10 small raw beets, trimmed, scrubbed, and halved

9oz/250 g shallots or baby onions

6–8 baby parsnips

4–6 baby carrots

1 tsp chopped fresh rosemary leaves

14 oz/400g red rice

3¼ cups hot chicken stock

1 red onion

1 small carrot, cut into thin batons

1 leek, cut into ½ inch/1 cm rounds

¾ cup pine nuts, lightly roasted

1 tsp brown sugar

1–2 tbsp chopped fresh cilantro

generous 1 cup dried cranberries or raisins, soaked in boiling water for 15 minutes

salt and pepper

TO SERVE

1 cup sour cream

2 tbsp chopped roasted walnuts

1 Put 4 tablespoons of the olive oil in a large bowl and whisk in the orange rind and juice, vinegar, coriander seeds, bay leaf, and crushed chiles. Add the beets, shallots, parsnips, and baby carrots and stir to coat.

2 Turn into a roasting pan and roast in a preheated oven, 400°F/200°C, turning occasionally, for 45–55 minutes until tender. Remove from the oven, sprinkle with the rosemary and salt and pepper, and keep warm.

3 Put the rice in a large pan with the hot stock. Place over medium-high heat and bring to a boil. Reduce the heat to low, cover, and simmer for about 40 minutes until the rice is tender and the stock absorbed. Remove from the heat, but do not uncover.

4 Heat the remaining oil in a large pan. Add the onion and carrot batons and cook for 8–10 minutes until tender. Add the leek, pine nuts, sugar, and cilantro and cook for 2–3 minutes until the vegetables are lightly caramelized. Drain the dried fruit and stir into the vegetable mixture with the rice. Season with salt and pepper.

5 Arrange the roasted vegetables and rice on a serving platter and top with the sour cream. Sprinkle with the chopped walnuts and serve.

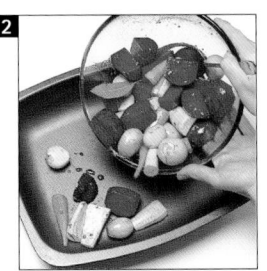

Risotto Primavera

This is a nice way to use those first green vegetables that signal the spring (*la primavera* in Italian.) Feel free to add other favorite vegetables.

NUTRITIONAL INFORMATION

Calories 381   Sugars 3g
Protein . . . . .13g   Fat 19g
Carbohydrate . . .43g   Saturates 8g

15 mins   40 mins

SERVES 6–8

INGREDIENTS

8 oz/225 g fresh thin asparagus spears

4 tbsp olive oil

6 oz/175 g young green beans, cut into
    1 inch/2.5 cm pieces

6 oz/175 g young zucchini, quartered and
    cut into 1 inch/2.5 cm lengths

2 cups shelled fresh peas

1 onion, finely chopped

1–2 garlic cloves, finely chopped

3 cups risotto rice

scant 7 cups chicken stock, simmering

4 scallions, cut into 1 inch/
    2.5 cm lengths

4 tbsp sweet butter

1⅓ cups freshly grated Parmesan cheese

2 tbsp chopped fresh chives

2 tbsp shredded fresh basil

salt and pepper

scallions, to garnish (optional)

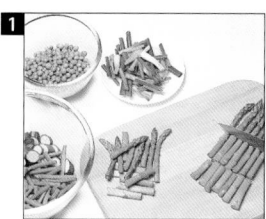

1 Trim the woody ends of the asparagus and cut off the tips. Cut the stems into 1 inch/2.5 cm pieces and set aside with the tips.

2 Heat 2 tablespoons of the olive oil in a large skillet over high heat until very hot. Add the asparagus, beans, zucchini, and peas and stir-fry for 3–4 minutes until they are bright green and just beginning to soften. Set aside.

3 Heat the remaining olive oil in a large heavy pan over medium heat. Add the onion and cook for about 1 minute until it begins to soften. Stir in the garlic and cook for 30 seconds. Add the rice and cook, stirring frequently, for 2 minutes until translucent and coated with oil.

4 Add a ladleful (about 1 cup) of the hot stock; the stock will bubble rapidly. Cook, stirring constantly, until the stock is absorbed.

5 Continue adding the stock, about half a ladleful at a time, letting each addition to be absorbed before adding the next—never allow the rice to cook "dry." This should take 20–25 minutes. The risotto should have a creamy consistency and the rice should be tender, but still firm to the bite.

6 Stir in the stir-fried vegetables and scallions with a little more stock. Cook for 2 minutes, stirring frequently, then season with salt and pepper. Stir in the butter, Parmesan, chive, and basil.

7 Remove the pan from the heat, cover, and set aside for about 1 minute. Transfer the risotto to a warmed serving dish, garnish with scallions, if wished, and serve immediately.

Zucchini & Basil Risotto

An easy way of livening up a simple risotto is to use a flavored olive oil—here a basil-flavored oil heightens the taste of the dish.

NUTRITIONAL INFORMATION

Calories 460	Sugars 5g
Protein 13g	Fat 18g
Carbohydrate ...64g	Saturates 7g

5–10 mins   35 mins

SERVES 4–6

INGREDIENTS

4 tbsp basil-flavored extra virgin olive oil, plus extra for drizzling

4 zucchini, diced

1 yellow bell pepper, deseeded and diced

2 garlic cloves, finely chopped

1 large onion, finely chopped

3½ cups risotto rice

4 tbsp dry white vermouth

scant 7 cups chicken or vegetable stock, simmering

2 tbsp sweet butter, at room temperature

large handful of fresh basil leaves, torn, plus a few leaves to garnish

1 cup freshly grated Parmesan cheese

1 Heat half the oil in a large skillet over high heat. When very hot, but not smoking, add the zucchini and yellow bell pepper and stir-fry for 3 minutes until lightly golden. Stir in the garlic and cook for about 30 seconds longer. Transfer to a plate and set aside.

2 Heat the remaining oil in a large heavy pan over medium heat. Add the onion and cook, stirring occasionally, for about 2 minutes until softened. Add the rice and cook, stirring frequently, for about 2 minutes until the rice is translucent and well coated with the olive oil.

3 Pour in the vermouth; it will bubble and steam rapidly and evaporate almost immediately. Add a ladleful (about 1 cup) of the simmering stock and cook, stirring constantly, until the stock is completely absorbed.

4 Continue adding the stock, about half a ladleful at a time, letting each addition to be absorbed before adding the next. This should take 20–25 minutes. The risotto should have a creamy consistency and the rice should be tender, but still firm to the bite.

5 Stir in the zucchini mixture with any juices, the butter, basil, and grated Parmesan. Drizzle with a little oil and garnish with basil. Serve hot.

Risotto Verde

Baby spinach and fresh herbs are the basis of this colorful, refreshing, and summery risotto.

NUTRITIONAL INFORMATION

Calories 374	Sugars 5g	
Protein 10g	Fat 9g	
Carbohydrate ...55g	Saturates 2g	

 5 mins   45 mins

SERVES 4

INGREDIENTS

7½ cups vegetable stock

2 tbsp olive oil

2 garlic cloves, crushed

2 leeks, shredded

2 cups risotto rice

1¼ cups dry white wine

4 tbsp chopped fresh mixed herbs

8 oz/225 g baby spinach

3 tbsp low-fat plain yogurt

salt and pepper

shredded leek, to garnish

1 Pour the stock into a large pan and bring to a boil. Reduce the heat to a simmer.

2 Meanwhile, heat the oil in a separate pan and cook the garlic and leeks, stirring occasionally, for 2–3 minutes until softened, but not browned.

3 Stir in the rice and cook stirring constantly, until translucent and well coated with oil.

4 Pour in half of the wine and a little of the hot stock; it will bubble and steam rapidly. Cook over gentle heat until all of the liquid has been absorbed.

5 Add the remaining stock and wine and cook over low heat for 25 minutes or until the rice is creamy.

6 Stir in the chopped mixed herbs and baby spinach, season to taste with salt and pepper, and cook for a further 2 minutes. Stir in the plain yogurt, garnish with the shredded leek, and serve the risotto immediately.

COOK'S TIP

Do not hurry the process of cooking the risotto as the rice must absorb the liquid slowly in order for it to reach the correct consistency.

Potatoes with Goat Cheese

This makes a luscious side dish to serve with meat or a satisfying vegetarian entrée. Goat cheese is a traditional food of Mexico.

NUTRITIONAL INFORMATION

Calories	725	Sugars	.........4g
Protein	........30g	Fat	..........43g
Carbohydrate	...56g	Saturates	.....28g

 2 mins   35 mins

SERVES 4

INGREDIENTS

2 lb 12 oz/1.25 kg baking potatoes, peeled and cut into chunks

pinch of salt

pinch of sugar

scant 1 cup crème fraîche

½ cup vegetable or chicken stock

3 garlic cloves, finely chopped

a few shakes of bottled chipotle salsa, or 1 dried chipotle chile, reconstituted, deseeded, and thinly sliced

8 oz/225 g goat cheese, sliced

1½ cups grated mozzarella or Cheddar cheese

⅔ cup grated Parmesan or romano cheese

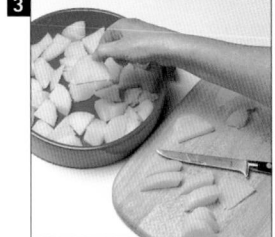

1 Put the potatoes in a pan of water with the salt and sugar. Bring to a boil and cook for about 10 minutes until they are half cooked.

2 Combine the crème fraîche with the stock, garlic, and salsa or chile.

3 Arrange half the potatoes in a casserole. Pour half the crème fraîche sauce over the potatoes and cover with the goat cheese. Top with the remaining potatoes and the sauce.

4 Sprinkle with the grated mozzarella or Cheddar cheese, then with the grated Parmesan or romano.

5 Bake in a preheated oven, 350°F/180°C, for about 25 minutes, until the potatoes are tender and the cheese topping is lightly golden and has become crisp in places. Serve immediately straight from the casserole.

Vegetable Tostadas

Top a crisp tostada—fried tortilla—with spicy vegetables and you have a vegetarian feast.

NUTRITIONAL INFORMATION

Calories 541   Sugars 10g
Protein . . . . .25g   Fat 20g
Carbohydrate . . .69g   Saturates 9g

 10 mins   20 mins

SERVES 4

INGREDIENTS

4 corn tortillas

vegetable oil, for frying

2–3 tbsp extra virgin olive oil or vegetable oil

2 potatoes, diced

1 carrot, diced

3 garlic cloves, finely chopped

1 red bell pepper, deseeded and diced

1 tsp mild chili powder

1 tsp paprika

½ tsp ground cumin

3–4 ripe tomatoes, diced

4 oz/115 g green beans, blanched and cut into bite-size lengths

pinch of dried oregano

14 oz/400g cooked black beans, drained

2 cups crumbled feta cheese

3–4 leaves Romaine lettuce, shredded

3–4 scallions, thinly sliced

1 To make the tostadas, fry the tortillas in a small amount of oil in a nonstick pan until crisp.

2 Heat the olive oil in a skillet, add the potatoes and carrot, and cook until softened. Add the garlic, red bell pepper, chili powder, paprika, and cumin. Cook for 2–3 minutes until the bell pepper has softened.

3 Add the tomatoes, green beans, and oregano. Cook for 8–10 minutes until the vegetables are tender and form a sauce-like mixture. The mixture should not be too dry; add a little water if necessary, to keep it moist.

4 Heat the black beans in a pan with a tiny quantity of water and keep warm. Reheat the tostadas under the broiler.

5 Layer the beans over the hot tostadas, then sprinkle with the cheese, and top with a few spoonfuls of the hot vegetables in sauce. Serve immediately, each tostada sprinkled with the lettuce and scallions.

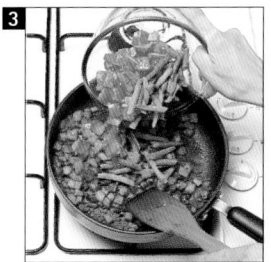

Black Bean Chili

Black beans are fragrant and flavorful; enjoy this bean stew Mexican style with soft tortillas, or Californian style with crisp tortilla chips.

NUTRITIONAL INFORMATION

Calories 428	Sugars 11g	
Protein 31g	Fat 10g	
Carbohydrate ...53g	Saturates 2g	

8¼ hrs   2¾ hrs

SERVES 4

INGREDIENTS

14 oz/400g dried black beans

2 tbsp olive oil

1 onion, chopped

5 garlic cloves, coarsely chopped

2 slices bacon, diced (optional)

½–1 tsp ground cumin

½–1 tsp mild chili powder

1 red bell pepper, deseeded and diced

1 carrot, diced

14 oz/400g fresh tomatoes, diced, or
 chopped canned tomatoes

1 bunch of fresh cilantro,
 coarsely chopped

salt and pepper

1 Soak the beans overnight in cold water to cover, then drain. Put in a pan, cover with water, and bring to a boil. Boil for 10 minutes, then reduce the heat, and simmer for about 1½ hours until tender. Drain well, reserving 1 cup of the cooking liquid.

2 Heat the oil in a skillet. Add the onion and garlic and cook over low heat, stirring occasionally, for 2 minutes. Stir in the bacon, if using, and cook, stirring occasionally, until the bacon is cooked and the onion is softened. but not browned.

3 Stir in the cumin and chili powder and continue to cook, stirring constantly, for a few seconds. Add the red bell pepper, carrot, and tomatoes. Cook over medium heat for about 5 minutes.

4 Add half the cilantro and the beans and their reserved liquid. Season to taste with salt and pepper. Simmer for 30–45 minutes or until the stew is very flavorful and has thickened.

5 Stir in the remaining cilantro, taste and adjust the seasoning, if necessary, and serve immediately.

COOK'S TIP

You can use canned beans, if wished: drain and use 1 cup water for the liquid added in step 4.

Dolmas

Start a Greek meal with these vegetarian stuffed grape leaves.
You will need a large skillet with a lid to hold all the stuffed grape leaves.

NUTRITIONAL INFORMATION

Calories . . . . .82 Sugars 2g
Protein . . . . .1g Fat 7g
Carbohydrate . . . .5g Saturates 1g

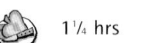 1¼ hrs   45 mins

MAKES 25–30

I N G R E D I E N T S

8 oz/225 g grape leaves preserved in brine,
about 40 in total

⅔ cup olive oil

4 tbsp lemon juice

1¼ cups water

lemon wedges, to serve

F I L L I N G

scant ⅔ cup long grain rice, not basmati

1½ cups water

¼ cup currants

½ cup pine nuts, chopped

2 scallions, very finely chopped

1 tbsp very finely chopped fresh cilantro

1 tbsp very finely chopped fresh parsley

1 tbsp very finely chopped fresh dill

finely grated rind of ½ lemon

salt and pepper

1 Rinse the grape leaves under cold running water and place them in a heatproof bowl. Pour over enough boiling water to cover and set aside to soak for 5 minutes. Drain well.

2 Meanwhile, place the rice and water in a pan with a pinch of salt and bring to a boil. Lower the heat, cover, and simmer for 10–12 minutes or until all the liquid is completely absorbed. Drain and set aside to cool.

3 Stir the currants, pine nuts, scallions, cilantro, parsley, dill, and lemon rind into the cooled rice. Season to taste with salt and pepper.

4 Line the bottom of a large skillet with 3 or 4 of the thickest grape leaves or with any that are torn.

5 Put a grape leaf on the counter, vein side upward, with the pointed end facing away from you. Put a small, compact roll of the rice stuffing at the base of the leaf. Fold up the bottom end of the leaf.

6 Fold in each side to overlap in the center. Roll up the leaf around the filling. Squeeze lightly in your hand. Continue this process with the remaining leaves and stuffing mixture.

7 Place the leaf rolls in a single layer in the pan, seam side down. Combine the olive oil, lemon juice, and water and pour into the pan.

8 Fit a heatproof plate over the rolls and cover the pan. Simmer for 30 minutes. Remove from the heat and let the stuffed grape leaves cool in the liquid. Serve chilled with lemon wedges.

Spinach & Herb Frittata

If you find the prospect of turning over a Spanish tortilla daunting, try this Italian version of a flat omelet, that finishes cooking under a broiler.

NUTRITIONAL INFORMATION

Calories ....145 Sugars 0g
Protein ....8g Fat 12g
Carbohydrate ....1g Saturates 13g

 15 mins   12 mins

SERVES 6–8

INGREDIENTS

4 tbsp olive oil

6 scallions, sliced

9 oz/250 g young spinach leaves, any coarse stems removed, rinsed

6 large eggs

3 tbsp finely chopped mixed fresh herbs, such as flat leaf parsley, thyme and cilantro

2 tbsp freshly grated Parmesan cheese, plus extra for garnishing

salt and pepper

fresh parsley sprigs, to garnish

1 Heat a 10 inch/25 cm skillet, preferably nonstick with a flameproof handle, over medium heat. Add the oil and heat. Add the scallions and cook for about 2 minutes.

2 Add the spinach and cook until it just wilts.

3 Beat the eggs in a large bowl and season to taste with salt and pepper. Using a draining spoon, transfer the spinach and onions to the bowl of eggs and stir in the herbs. Pour the excess oil left in the skillet into a heatproof pitcher, then scrape off the crusty sediment from the bottom of the skillet.

4 Reheat the skillet. Add 2 tablespoons of the reserved oil. Pour in the egg mixture, smoothing it into an even layer. Cook, shaking the skillet occasionally, for 6 minutes or until the base is set when you lift up the side with a spatula.

5 Sprinkle the top of the frittata with the Parmesan. Place the skillet under a preheated broiler and cook for about 3 minutes or until the excess liquid is set and the cheese is golden.

6 Remove the skillet from the heat and slide the frittata onto a serving plate. Set aside for at least 5 minutes before cutting and garnishing with extra Parmesan and parsley. Serve hot, warm, or at room temperature.

Spanakopittas

These Greek spinach and feta pies, encased in layers of crisp phyllo pastry, are also often made in one large pan.

NUTRITIONAL INFORMATION

Calories . . . . . . .952 Sugars 15g
Protein . . . . .18g Fat 61g
Carbohydrate . . .87g Saturates 29g

 20 mins  30 mins

SERVES 4

I N G R E D I E N T S

2 tbsp olive oil

6 scallions, chopped

9 oz/250 g fresh young spinach leaves, tough stems removed, rinsed

¼ cup long grain rice (not basmati), boiled until tender and drained

4 tbsp chopped fresh dill

4 tbsp chopped fresh parsley

4 tbsp pine nuts

2 tbsp raisins

½ cup crumbled, drained (f necessary, feta cheese

1 nutmeg

pinch of cayenne pepper (optional)

40 sheets phyllo pastry

about 9 oz/250 g melted butter

pepper

1 Heat the oil in a pan, add the scallions, and cook for about 2 minutes. Add the spinach, with just the water clinging to the leaves, and cook, stirring constantly, until the leaves wilt. Transfer to a bowl and, when cool enough to handle, squeeze dry.

2 Stir in the rice, herbs, pine nuts, raisins, and feta cheese. Grate in one-quarter of the nutmeg and add black and cayenne peppers to taste.

3 Place the phyllo sheets in a stack. Cut 40 x 6 inch/15 cm squares. Remove 8 slices and cut into 8 x 4 inch/10 cm circles. Re-wrap the unused phyllo and cover the squares and circles with a damp dish cloth.

4 Brush a loose-bottomed 4 inch/10 cm tart pan with butter. Place 1 square of phyllo in the tin and brush with more butter. Repeat with 7 more sheets. Do not push the phyllo into the edges. Repeat this process with the other tins.

5 Spoon in one-quarter of the filling into each tin and smooth the surface. Top with a phyllo circle and brush with butter. Repeat with another phyllo circle. Fold the overhanging phyllo over the top and brush with butter.

6 Put the pies on a cookie sheet and bake in a preheated oven, 350°F/180°C, for 20–25 minutes until crisp and golden. Set aside for 5 minutes before turning out.

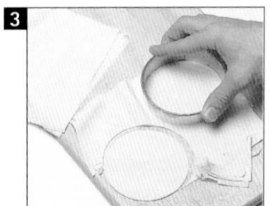

Pizza Biancas

Simple, fresh flavors are the highlight of this thin pizza.
For the best results, use buffalo mozzarella imported from Italy.

NUTRITIONAL INFORMATION

Calories	1191	Sugars	.........5g
Protein	........60g	Fat	..........40g
Carbohydrate	..158g	Saturates	......21g

1½ hrs   15 mins

MAKES TWO 9 INCH/23 CM PIZZAS

INGREDIENTS

3½ cups all-purpose flour, plus extra
　for dusting

1 envelope active dry yeast

1 tsp salt

1 tbsp extra virgin olive oil, plus extra
　for greasing

TOPPING

2 zucchini

10½ oz/300 g buffalo mozzarella

1½–2 tbsp finely chopped fresh rosemary,
　or ½ tbsp dried rosemary

1 To make the crust, heat 1 cup water in the microwave on HIGH for 1 minute or until it reads 125°F/52°C on an instant-read thermometer. Alternatively, heat the water in a pan over low heat until it is lukewarm.

2 Stir the flour, yeast, and salt together and make a well in the center. Stir in most of the water with the olive oil to make a dough. Add the remaining water, if necessary, to form a soft dough.

3 Turn out onto a lightly floured counter and knead for about 10 minutes until smooth but still soft. Wash the bowl and lightly coat with olive oil. Shape the dough into a ball, put in the bowl, and turn the dough over so it is coated. Cover and set aside until doubled in size.

4 Turn the dough out onto a lightly floured counter. Quickly knead a few times, then cover with the upturned bowl, and set aside for 10 minutes.

5 Meanwhile, using a vegetable peeler, cut long, thin strips of zucchini. Drain and dice the mozzarella.

6 Divide the dough in half and shape each half into a ball. Cover 1 ball and roll out the other into a 9 inch/23 cm round. Place the round on a lightly floured cookie sheet.

7 Scatter half the mozzarella over the base. Add half the zucchini strips and sprinkle with half the rosemary. Repeat with the remaining dough and remaining topping ingredients.

8 Bake in a preheated oven, 425°F/ 220°C, for 15 minutes or until crispy. Serve immediately.

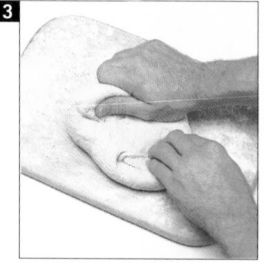

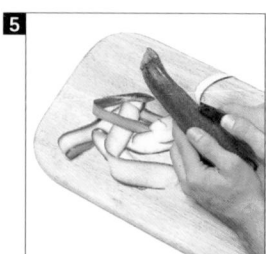

Baked Eggplant Gratin

Serve plenty of crusty French bread with this dish because it soaks up the delicious juices.

NUTRITIONAL INFORMATION

Calories	261	Sugars	. . . . .5g
Protein	. . . . .20g	Fat	. . . . .18g
Carbohydrate	. . . .6g	Saturates	. . . . . .10g

45 mins   40 mins

SERVES 4–6

I N G R E D I E N T S

1 large eggplant, about 1 lb 12 oz/800 g

10½ oz/300 g mozzarella cheese

3 oz/85 g Parmesan cheese

olive oil

generous 1 cup Tomato Sauce (see page 7), or good-quality bottled tomato sauce for pasta

salt and pepper

1 Trim the eggplant and, using a sharp knife, cut it into ¼ inch/5 mm slices crosswise. Arrange the slices on a large plate, sprinkle with salt, and set aside for 30 minutes to drain.

2 Meanwhile, drain and grate the mozzarella cheese and finely grate the Parmesan cheese. Set aside.

3 Rinse the eggplant slices thoroughly under cold running water and pat dry with paper towels. Lightly brush a cookie sheet with olive oil and arrange the eggplant slices in a single layer. Brush the tops with olive oil.

4 Roast in a preheated oven, 400°F/200°C, for 5 minutes. Using tongs, turn the slices over, then brush with a little more olive oil and bake for a further 5 minutes or until the eggplant is cooked through and tender. Remove the eggplant, but do not turn off the oven.

5 Spread about 1 tablespoon olive oil over the bottom of a gratin dish or other ovenproof serving dish. Add a layer of eggplant slices, about a quarter of the tomato sauce, and top with a quarter of the mozzarella. Season to taste with salt and pepper.

6 Continue layering until all the ingredients are used, ending with a layer of sauce. Sprinkle the Parmesan over the top. Bake for 30 minutes until bubbling. Set aside for about 5 minutes before serving.

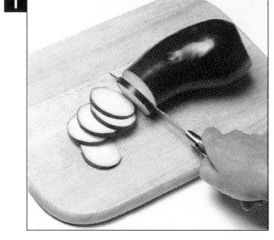

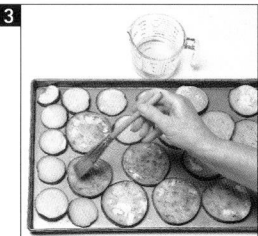

Chinese Vegetable Crêpes

Chinese crêpes are made with hardly any fat—they are simply flattened white flour dough.

NUTRITIONAL INFORMATION

Calories 312   Sugars 5g
Protein . . . . .13g   Fat 19g
Carbohydrate . . .25g   Saturates 7g

 5 mins   10 mins

SERVES 4

INGREDIENTS

1 tbsp vegetable oil

1 garlic clove, crushed

1 inch/2.5 cm piece of fresh ginger root, grated

1 bunch of scallions, trimmed and shredded lengthwise

1½ oz snow peas, shredded

8 oz/225 g beancurd, drained and cut into ½ inch/1 cm pieces

2 tbsp dark soy sauce, plus extra to serve

2 tbsp hoisin sauce, plus extra to serve

¾ cup canned bamboo shoots, drained

2 oz/55 g canned water chestnuts, drained and sliced

1¾ cups bean sprouts

1 small fresh red chile, deseeded and thinly sliced

1 small bunch of fresh chives

12 soft Chinese crêpes

TO SERVE

shredded Napa cabbage leaves

1 cucumber, sliced

strips of fresh red chile

1 Heat the oil in a nonstick wok or a large skillet and stir-fry the garlic and ginger for 1 minute.

2 Add the scallions, snow peas, beancurd, and soy and hoisin sauces. Stir-fry for 2 minutes.

3 Add the bamboo shoots, water chestnuts, bean sprouts, and chile to the pan. Stir-fry gently for 2 minutes until the vegetables are just tender.

4 Chop the chives into 1 inch/2.5 cm lengths and stir into the mixture.

5 Heat the crêpes according to the packet instructions and keep warm.

6 Divide the vegetables and beancurd equally among the crêpes. Roll up and serve with the Napa cabbage leaves, cucumber, chile strips, and extra soy and hoisin sauces for dipping.

Mixed Vegetable Balti

Any combination of vegetables or pulses can be used in this recipe. It would make a good dish for an informal vegetarian supper party.

NUTRITIONAL INFORMATION

Calories 207   Sugars 6g
Protein . . . . .8g   Fat 9g
Carbohydrate . . .24g   Saturates 1g

 10 mins   1 hr

SERVES 4

INGREDIENTS

1⅓ cups split yellow peas

3 tbsp vegetable oil

1 tsp onion seeds

2 onions, sliced

4 oz/115 g zucchini, sliced

4 oz/115 g potatoes, cut into ½ inch/ 1 cm cubes

4 oz/115 g carrots, sliced

1 small eggplant, sliced

8 oz/225 g tomatoes, chopped

1¼ cups water

3 garlic cloves, chopped

1 tsp ground cumin

1 tsp ground coriander

1 tsp salt

2 fresh green chiles, sliced

½ tsp garam masala

2 tbsp chopped fresh cilantro

3 Add the onions and stir-fry over medium heat until golden brown.

4 Add the zucchini, potatoes, carrots, and eggplant to the pan. Stir-fry the vegetables for about 2 minutes.

5 Stir in the tomatoes, water, garlic, cumin, ground coriander, salt, chiles, garam masala, and reserved split peas.

6 Bring to a boil, then lower the heat, and simmer for 15 minutes until all the vegetables are tender.

7 Stir the fresh cilantro into the vegetables. Transfer to a warmed serving dish and serve immediately.

1 Put the split peas into a pan and cover with lightly salted water. Bring to a boil and simmer for 30 minutes. Drain the peas and keep warm.

2 Heat the oil in a karahi or wok, add the onion seeds, and fry until they start popping.

 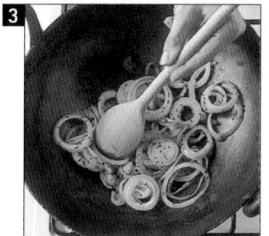 

Beancurd Skewers

Although beancurd is rather bland on its own, it develops a fabulous flavor when it is marinated in garlic and herbs.

NUTRITIONAL INFORMATION

Calories . . . . . . .149 Sugars 5g
Protein . . . . .13g Fat 9g
Carbohydrate . . . .5g Saturates 1g

🍞 40 mins   🕐 15 mins

SERVES 4

I N G R E D I E N T S

12 oz/350 g beancurd

1 red bell pepper

1 yellow bell pepper

2 zucchini

8 white mushrooms

lemon slices, to garnish

M A R I N A D E

grated rind and juice of ½ lemon

1 garlic clove, crushed

½ tsp chopped fresh rosemary

½ tsp chopped fresh thyme

1 tbsp walnut oil

1 To make the marinade, combine the lemon rind and juice, garlic, rosemary, thyme, and oil in a shallow dish.

2 Drain the beancurd, pat it dry on paper towels, and cut it into squares with a sharp knife. Add to the marinade and toss to coat. Cover and set aside to marinate for 20–30 minutes.

3 Meanwhile, deseed and cut the peppers into 1 inch/2.5 cm pieces. Blanch in boiling water for 4 minutes, refresh in cold water and drain.

4 Using a canelle knife or potato peeler, remove strips of peel from the zucchini. Cut the zucchini into 1 inch/2.5 cm chunks.

5 Remove the beancurd from the marinade, reserving the liquid. Thread it onto 8 skewers, alternating with the peppers, zucchini, and white mushrooms.

6 Grill the skewers over medium hot coals for about 6 minutes, turning and basting with the reserved marinade. Alternatively, cook under a preheated broiler. Transfer the skewers to warmed individual serving plates, garnish with slices of lemon, and serve.

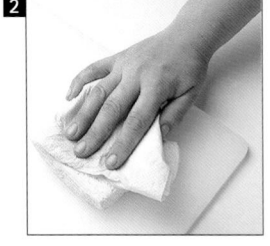

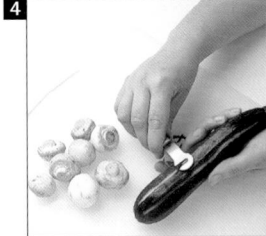

Potato & Tomato Calzone

These pizza dough Italian pasties are best served hot with a salad for a delicious lunch or supper dish.

NUTRITIONAL INFORMATION

Calories 524	Sugars 8g	
Protein 17g	Fat 8g	
Carbohydrate ..103g	Saturates 2g	

1½ hrs   35 mins

SERVES 4

INGREDIENTS

DOUGH

4 cups white bread flour

1 tsp active dry yeast

1¼ cups vegetable bouillon

1 tbsp clear honey

1 tsp caraway seeds

skim milk, for glazing

FILLING

1 tbsp vegetable oil

1⅓ cups diced waxy potatoes

1 onion, halved and sliced

2 garlic cloves, crushed

1½ oz/40 g sun-dried tomatoes

2 tbsp chopped fresh basil

2 tbsp tomato paste

2 celery stalks, sliced

½ cup grated mozzarella cheese

1 To make the dough, sift the flour into a large mixing bowl and stir in the yeast. Make a well in the center of the mixture. Stir in the vegetable bouillon, honey, and caraway seeds, and bring the mixture together to form a dough.

2 Turn the dough out on to a lightly floured counter and knead for 8 minutes until smooth. Place the dough in a lightly oiled mixing bowl, then cover and leave to rise in a warm place for 1 hour or until it has doubled in size.

3 Meanwhile, make the filling. Heat the oil in a skillet and add all the remaining ingredients except for the cheese. Cook for about 5 minutes, stirring.

4 Divide the risen dough into 4 pieces. On a lightly floured counter, roll them out to form four 7 inch/ 18 cm circles. Spoon equal amounts of the filling on to one half of each circle. Sprinkle the cheese over the filling. Brush the edge of the dough with milk and fold the dough over to form 4 semi-circles, pressing to seal the edges.

5 Place on a non-stick baking sheet and brush with milk. Cook in a preheated oven, 425°F/220°C, for 30 minutes until golden and risen.

Coconut Vegetable Curry

A mildly spiced but richly flavored Indian-style dish full of different textures and flavors. Serve with nan bread to soak up the tasty sauce.

NUTRITIONAL INFORMATION

Calories 159	Sugars 8g	
Protein 8g	Fat 6g	
Carbohydrate ...19g	Saturates 1g	

🕐 1¾ hrs   🕐 35 mins

SERVES 4

INGREDIENTS

1 large eggplant, cut into 1 inch/
  2.5 cm cubes

2 tbsp vegetable oil

2 garlic cloves, crushed

1 fresh green chile, deseeded and
  finely chopped

1 tsp grated fresh ginger root

1 onion, finely chopped

2 tsp garam masala

8 cardamom pods

1 tsp ground turmeric

1 tbsp tomato paste

3 cups Fresh Vegetable Stock (see page 8)

1 tbsp lemon juice

8 oz/225 g potatoes, diced

9 oz/250 g small cauliflower florets

8 oz/225 g okra, trimmed

2 cups frozen peas

⅔ cup coconut milk

salt and pepper

flaked coconut, to garnish

nan bread, to serve

1 Layer the eggplant in a bowl, sprinkling with salt as you go. Set aside for 30 minutes. Rinse well under running water. Drain and dry. Set aside.

2 Heat the oil in a large pan and gently cook the garlic, chile, ginger, onion, and spices for 4–5 minutes.

3 Stir in the tomato paste, stock, lemon juice, potatoes, and cauliflower and mix well. Bring to a boil, cover, and simmer for 15 minutes.

4 Stir in the eggplant, okra, peas, and coconut milk and season with salt and pepper to taste. Continue to simmer, uncovered, for a further 10 minutes until tender. Discard the cardamom pods. Pile the curry onto a warmed serving platter, garnish with flaked coconut, and serve with nan bread.

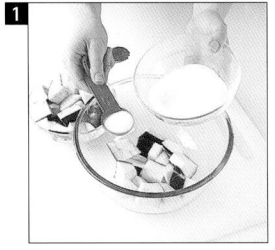

Stuffed Vegetables

You can fill your favorite vegetables with this nutty-tasting combination of cracked wheat, tomatoes, and cucumber.

NUTRITIONAL INFORMATION

Calories 194	Sugars 7g	
Protein 5g	Fat 4g	
Carbohydrate ...36g	Saturates 0.5g	

40 mins | 25 mins

SERVES 4

INGREDIENTS

4 large beefsteak tomatoes

4 medium zucchini

2 orange bell peppers

salt and pepper

FILLING

1⅓ cups cracked wheat

¼ cucumber

1 medium red onion

2 tbsp lemon juice

2 tbsp chopped fresh cilantro

2 tbsp chopped fresh mint

1 tbsp olive oil

2 tsp cumin seeds

TO SERVE

warm pitas and low-fat hummus

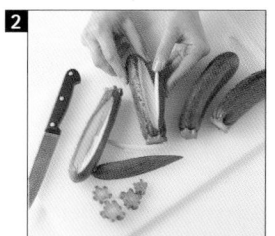
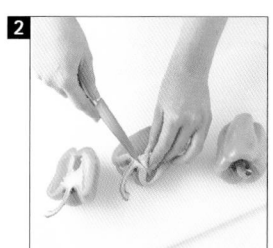

1 Cut off the tops of the tomatoes and reserve. Using a teaspoon, scoop out the tomato pulp, chop, and place in a bowl. Season the tomato shells, then turn them upside down on paper towels.

2 Trim the zucchini and cut a V-shaped groove lengthwise down each one. Finely chop the cut-out zucchini flesh and add to the tomato pulp. Season the zucchini shells and set aside. Halve the bell peppers. Leaving the stalks intact, cut out the seeds and discard. Season the bell pepper shells and set aside.

3 To make the filling, soak the cracked wheat according to the instructions on the packet. Finely chop the cucumber and add to the reserved tomato pulp and zucchini mixture. Finely chop the red onion, and add to the vegetable mixture with the lemon juice, herbs, olive oil, and cumin and mix together well. Season to taste with salt and pepper.

4 When the wheat has soaked, mix with the vegetables and stuff into the tomato, zucchini, and bell pepper shells. Place the tops on the tomatoes, transfer to a roasting pan, and bake in a preheated oven, 400°F/200°C, for 20–25 minutes until cooked through. Drain and serve with pitas and hummus.

Curried Vegetable Kabobs

Warmed Indian bread is served with grilled vegetable kabobs, which are brushed with a curry-spiced yogurt baste.

NUTRITIONAL INFORMATION

Calories .... .396 Sugars 11g
Protein ....13g Fat 13g
Carbohydrate ...60g Saturates 0.3g

 25 mins   20 mins

SERVES 4

INGREDIENTS

YOGURT BASTE

⅔ cup low-fat plain yogurt

1 tbsp chopped fresh mint or 1 tsp dried mint

1 tsp ground cumin

1 tsp ground coriander

½ tsp chili powder

pinch of ground turmeric

pinch of ground ginger

salt and pepper

KABOBS

8 small new potatoes

1 small eggplant

1 zucchini, cut into chunks

8 crimini or closed-cup mushrooms

8 small tomatoes

fresh mint sprigs, to garnish

warm nan bread, to serve

1 To make the spiced yogurt baste, combine the yogurt and the spices. Season to taste with salt and pepper. Cover and chill.

2 Boil the potatoes until just tender. Meanwhile, chop the eggplant into chunks and sprinkle them liberally with salt. Set aside for 10–15 minutes to extract the bitter juices. Rinse and drain them well. Drain the potatoes.

3 Thread the vegetables onto 4 metal or wooden skewers, alternating the different types. If using wooden skewers, soak in warm water for 10 minutes.

4 Place the skewers in a shallow dish and evenly coat with the yogurt baste. Cover with plastic wrap and chill until required. Wrap the nan bread in foil and place toward one side of the barbecue to warm through.

5 Grill the kabobs on the barbecue, basting with any remaining spiced yogurt, until they just begin to char slightly. Serve the kabobs immediately with the warmed nan bread, garnished with sprigs of fresh mint.

  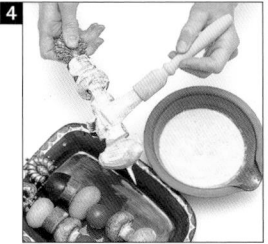

Eggplant Gratin

Similar to a simple moussaka, this recipe is made up of layers of tomatoes, eggplant, and potatoes.

NUTRITIONAL INFORMATION

Calories .... .409 Sugars .... .17g
Protein ....28g Fat .... .14g
Carbohydrate ...45g Saturates 3g

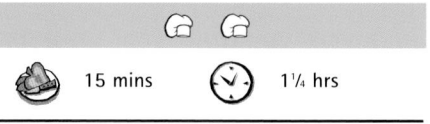

15 mins   1¼ hrs

SERVES 4

INGREDIENTS

1 lb/450 g waxy potatoes, sliced

1 tbsp vegetable oil

1 onion, chopped

2 garlic cloves, crushed

1 lb/450 g beancurd, diced

2 tbsp tomato paste

2 tbsp all-purpose flour

1¼ cups vegetable stock

2 large tomatoes, sliced

1 eggplant, sliced

2 tbsp chopped fresh thyme

2¼ cups low-fat plain yogurt

2 eggs, beaten

salt and pepper

1 Cook the sliced potatoes in a pan of boiling water for 10 minutes until just tender, but not breaking up. Drain and set aside.

2 Heat the oil in a heavy pan and cook the onion and garlic, stirring occasionally, for 2–3 minutes.

3 Add the diced beancurd, tomato paste, and flour and cook, stirring constantly, for 1 minute. Gradually stir in the vegetable stock and bring to a boil, stirring constantly. Reduce the heat and simmer for 10 minutes.

4 Arrange a layer of the potato slices in the base of a deep casserole. Spoon the beancurd mixture on top.

5 Layer the tomatoes, then the eggplant, and then the remaining potato slices on top of the beancurd mixture, so that it is completely covered.

6 Combine the yogurt and beaten eggs in a bowl and season to taste with salt and pepper. Spoon the yogurt topping over the sliced potatoes.

7 Cook the gratin in a preheated oven, 375°F/190°C, for 35–45 minutes or until the topping is browned. Serve the gratin immediately.

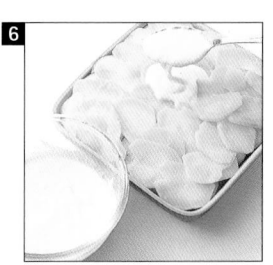

Vegetable Curry

This colorful and interesting mixture of vegetables, cooked in a spicy sauce, is excellent served with rice and nan bread.

NUTRITIONAL INFORMATION

Calories 421	Sugars 20g
Protein 12g	Fat 24g
Carbohydrate . . .42g	Saturates 3g

 10 mins   45 mins

SERVES 4

INGREDIENTS

8 oz/225 g turnips or rutabaga

1 eggplant

12 oz/350 g new potatoes

8 oz/225 g cauliflower

8 oz/225 g white mushrooms

1 large onion

3 carrots

6 tbsp vegetable ghee or vegetable oil

2 garlic cloves, crushed

4 tsp finely chopped fresh ginger root

1–2 fresh green chiles, deseeded and chopped

1 tbsp paprika

2 tsp ground coriander

1 tbsp mild or medium curry powder or paste

2 cups vegetable stock

14 oz/400g canned chopped tomatoes

1 green bell pepper, deseeded and sliced

1 tbsp cornstarch

⅔ cup coconut milk

2–3 tbsp ground almonds

salt

fresh cilantro sprigs, to garnish

1 Cut the turnips or rutabaga, eggplant, and potatoes into ½ inch/1 cm cubes. Divide the cauliflower into small florets. Leave the mushrooms whole or slice them thickly if preferred. Slice the onion and carrots.

2 Heat the ghee or oil in a large pan. Add the onion, turnip or rutabaga, potato, and cauliflower and cook over low heat, stirring frequently, for 3 minutes.

3 Add the garlic, ginger, chiles, paprika, ground coriander, and curry powder or paste and cook, stirring, for 1 minute.

4 Add the stock, tomatoes, eggplant, and mushrooms and season with salt. Cover and simmer, stirring occasionally, for about 30 minutes or until tender. Add the green bell pepper and carrots, cover, and cook for a further 5 minutes.

5 Blend the cornstarch with the coconut milk to a smooth paste and stir into the mixture. Add the ground almonds and simmer, stirring constantly, for 2 minutes. Taste and adjust the seasoning if necessary. Transfer the curry to serving plates and serve hot, garnished with sprigs of fresh cilantro.

Pesto Pasta

Italian pesto is usually laden with fat. This version has just as much flavor, but is much healthier.

NUTRITIONAL INFORMATION

Calories . . . . . . .283 Sugars 5g
Protein . . . . .14g Fat 3g
Carbohydrate . . .37g Saturates 1g

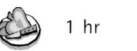 1 hr   🕐 30 mins

SERVES 4

I N G R E D I E N T S

3¼ cups sliced crimini mushrooms

⅔ cup fresh vegetable stock

6 oz/175 g asparagus, trimmed and cut into
    2 inch/5 cm lengths

10½ oz/300 g green and white tagliatelle

14 oz/400g canned artichoke hearts,
    drained and halved

grissini, to serve

P E S T O

2 large garlic cloves, crushed

½ cup fresh basil leaves

6 tbsp low-fat plain yogurt

2 tbsp freshly grated Parmesan cheese

salt and pepper

T O   G A R N I S H

shredded fresh basil leaves

Parmesan shavings

1 Place the mushrooms in a pan with the stock. Bring to a boil, cover, and simmer for 3–4 minutes until just tender. Drain and set aside, reserving the cooking liquid to use in soups if wished.

2 Bring a small pan of water to a boil and cook the asparagus for 3–4 minutes until just tender. Drain and set aside until required.

3 Bring a large pan of lightly salted water to a boil. Add the pasta, bring back to a boil, and cook until tender, but still firm to the bite: 8–10 minutes for dried pasta or 2–3 minutes for fresh tagliatelle. Drain, return to the pan, and keep warm.

4 Meanwhile, make the pesto. Place all of the ingredients in a blender or food processor and process for a few seconds until smooth. Alternatively, finely chop the basil and mix all the ingredients together.

5 Add the mushrooms, asparagus, and artichoke hearts to the pasta and cook, stirring, over low heat for 2–3 minutes. Remove from the heat and mix with the pesto.

6 Transfer to a warm bowl. Garnish with basil and Parmesan and serve.

Mixed Bean Stir-Fry

Any type of canned beans can be used, such as lima beans or black-eye peas, but rinse them under cold water and drain well before use.

NUTRITIONAL INFORMATION

Calories	326	Sugars	........16g
Protein	........18g	Fat	...........7g
Carbohydrate	...51g	Saturates	......1g

10 mins   10 mins

SERVES 4

INGREDIENTS

14 oz/400g can red kidney beans

14 oz/400g can cannellini beans

6 scallions

7 oz/200 g can pineapple rings or pieces in natural juice, chopped

2 tbsp pineapple juice

3–4 pieces of preserved ginger

2 tbsp ginger syrup from the jar

thinly pared rind of ½ lime or lemon, cut into julienne strips

2 tbsp lime or lemon juice

2 tbsp soy sauce

1 tsp cornstarch

1 tbsp sesame oil

4 oz/115 g green beans, cut into 1½ inch/ 4 cm lengths

8 oz/225 g can bamboo shoots

salt and pepper

1 Drain all the beans, rinse under cold water, and drain again very thoroughly.

2 Cut 4 scallions into narrow diagonal slices. Thinly slice the remainder and reserve for garnish.

3 Combine the pineapple and juice, ginger and syrup, lime rind and juice, soy sauce and cornstarch in a bowl.

4 Heat the oil in the wok, swirling it around until really hot. Add the diagonally sliced scallions and stir-fry for about a minute, then add the green beans. Drain and thinly slice the bamboo shoots, add to the wok, and continue to stir-fry for 2 minutes.

5 Add the pineapple and ginger mixture and bring just to a boil. Add the canned beans and stir until very hot— for about a minute.

6 Season to taste with salt and pepper, sprinkle with the reserved chopped scallions, and serve.

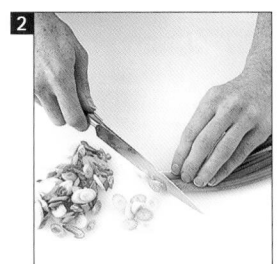

COOK'S TIP

Beans are an important source of protein for vegetarians. Combine them with rice or other cereals for a really healthy balance.

Biryani with Onions

An assortment of vegetables cooked with tender rice, flavored and colored with bright yellow turmeric and other warming Indian spices.

NUTRITIONAL INFORMATION

Calories 223	Sugars 18g	
Protein 8g	Fat 4g	
Carbohydrate . . .42g	Saturates 1g	

 1¼ hrs   🕐 25 mins

SERVES 4

I N G R E D I E N T S

scant 1 cup basmati rice, rinsed

¼ cup red lentils, rinsed

1 bay leaf

6 cardamom pods, split

1 tsp ground turmeric

6 cloves

1 tsp cumin seeds

1 cinnamon stick, broken

1 onion, chopped

8 oz/225 g cauliflower, broken into small florets

1 large carrot, diced

scant 1 cup frozen peas

⅓ cup golden raisins

2½ cups Fresh Vegetable Stock (see page 8)

salt and pepper

nan bread, to serve

C A R A M E L I Z E D   O N I O N S

2 tsp vegetable oil

1 medium red onion, shredded

1 medium onion, shredded

2 tsp superfine sugar

1 Place the rice, lentils, bay leaf, spices, onion, cauliflower, carrot, peas, and golden raisins in a large pan. Season with salt and pepper to taste and mix well.

2 Pour in the stock, bring to a boil, cover, and simmer for 15 minutes, stirring occasionally, until the rice is tender. Remove from the heat and set aside, covered, for 10 minutes to allow the stock to be absorbed. Remove and discard the bay leaf, cardamom pods, cloves, and cinnamon stick.

3 Heat the oil in a skillet and cook the onions over medium heat for 3–4 minutes until just softened. Add the superfine sugar, increase the heat, and cook, stirring constantly, for a further 2–3 minutes until the onions are golden.

4 Gently combine the rice and vegetables and transfer to warm serving plates. Spoon over the caramelized onions and serve immediately with plain, warmed nan bread.

Gnocchi with Tomato Sauce

Freshly made potato gnocchi are delicious, especially when they are topped with a fragrant tomato sauce.

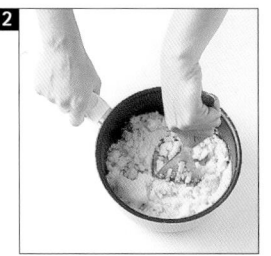

NUTRITIONAL INFORMATION

Calories 216	Sugars 5g
Protein 5g	Fat 6g
Carbohydrate . . .39g	Saturates 1g

 30 mins   45 mins

SERVES 4

INGREDIENTS

12 oz/350 g mealy potatoes, halved

⅔ cup self-rising flour, plus extra for dusting

2 tsp dried oregano

2 tbsp vegetable oil

1 large onion, chopped

2 garlic cloves, chopped

14 oz/400 g canned chopped tomatoes

½ vegetable bouillon cube dissolved in scant ½ cup boiling water

2 tbsp fresh basil, shredded, plus whole leaves to garnish

salt and pepper

Parmesan cheese, freshly grated, to serve

1 Bring a large pan of water to a boil. Add the potatoes and cook for 12–15 minutes or until tender. Drain and set aside to cool.

2 Peel and then mash the potatoes with the salt and pepper, sifted flour, and oregano. Mix together with your hands to form a dough.

3 Heat the oil in a skillet. Add the onions and garlic and cook for 3–4 minutes. Add the tomatoes and stock and cook, uncovered, for 10 minutes. Season with salt and pepper to taste.

4 Roll the potato dough into a sausage about 1 inch/2.5 cm in diameter. Cut the sausage into 1 inch/2.5 cm lengths. Flour your hands, then press a fork into each piece to create a series of ridges on one side and the indent of your index finger on the other side.

5 Bring a large pan of water to a boil, add the gnocchi, in batches, and cook for 2–3 minutes. They should rise to the surface when cooked. Remove from the pan with a slotted spoon, drain well, and keep warm while you are cooking the remaining batches.

6 Stir the basil into the tomato sauce and pour over the gnocchi. Garnish with basil leaves and season with pepper to taste. Sprinkle with grated Parmesan and serve immediately.

VARIATION

The gnocchi can also be served with a pesto sauce made from fresh basil leaves, pine nuts, garlic, olive oil, and romano or Parmesan cheese.

Green Easter Pie

This traditional Easter risotto pie is from the Piedmont region in northern Italy. Serve it warm or chilled in slices.

NUTRITIONAL INFORMATION

Calories . . . . . . .392 Sugars 3g
Protein . . . . .17g Fat 17g
Carbohydrate . . .41g Saturates 5g

🖐 🖐 🖐

🍲 25 mins   🕐 50 mins

SERVES 4

I N G R E D I E N T S

butter, for greasing

3 oz/85 g arugula leaves

2 tbsp olive oil

1 onion, chopped

2 garlic cloves, chopped

1 cup risotto rice

3 cups hot chicken or vegetable stock

½ cup white wine

⅔ cup freshly grated Parmesan cheese

1 cup frozen peas, thawed

2 tomatoes, diced

4 eggs, beaten

3 tbsp chopped fresh marjoram

1 cup fresh bread crumbs

salt and pepper

4 Add the rice to the skillet, mix well to combine, then begin adding the stock a ladleful at a time. Wait until each ladleful of stock has been absorbed before adding the next.

5 Continue to cook the mixture, adding the wine, until the rice is tender. This will take at least 15 minutes. Remove the skillet from the heat.

6 Stir in the Parmesan cheese, peas, arugula leaves, tomatoes, eggs, and 2 tablespoons of the marjoram. Season to taste with salt and pepper.

7 Spoon the risotto into the prepared pan and level the surface by pressing down with the back of a wooden spoon.

8 Top with the bread crumbs and the remaining marjoram.

9 Bake in a preheated oven, 350°F/ 180°C, for 30 minutes or until set. Cut into slices and serve.

1 Lightly grease a 9 inch/23 cm deep cake pan and line the base.

2 Using a sharp knife, coarsely chop the arugula leaves.

3 Heat the oil in a skillet and fry the onion and garlic over low heat for 4–5 minutes or until softened.

Pasta Omelet

This is a superb way of using up any leftover pasta, such as penne, macaroni, or conchiglie.

NUTRITIONAL INFORMATION

Calories	460	Sugars	.........3g
Protein	........16g	Fat	..........34g
Carbohydrate	...23g	Saturates	.......6g

 10 mins   15–20 mins

SERVES 2

INGREDIENTS

4 tbsp olive oil

1 small onion, chopped

1 fennel bulb, thinly sliced

4 oz/115 g potato, diced

1 garlic clove, chopped

4 eggs

1 tbsp chopped fresh flat leaf parsley

pinch of chili powder

3½ oz/100 g cooked short pasta

2 tbsp stuffed green olives, halved

salt and pepper

fresh marjoram sprigs, to garnish

tomato salad, to serve

1 Heat half of the oil in a heavy skillet over low heat. Add the onion, fennel, and potato and cook, stirring occasionally, for 8-10 minutes until the potato is just tender.

2 Stir in the garlic and cook for 1 minute. Remove the skillet from the heat, transfer the vegetables to a plate, and set aside.

3 Beat the eggs until they are frothy. Stir in the parsley and season with salt, pepper, and a pinch of chili powder.

4 Heat 1 tbsp of the remaining oil in a clean skillet. Add half of the egg mixture to the skillet, then add the cooked vegetables, pasta, and half of the olives. Pour in the remaining egg mixture and cook until the sides begin to set.

5 Lift up the edges of the omelet with a spatula to allow the uncooked egg to spread underneath. Cook, shaking the skillet occasionally, until the underside is a light golden brown color.

6 Slide the omelet out of the skillet onto a plate. Wipe the pan with paper towels and heat the remaining oil. Invert the omelet into the pan and cook until the other side is a golden brown color.

7 Slide the omelet onto a warmed serving dish and garnish with the remaining olives and the sprigs of marjoram. Cut the omelet into wedges and serve with a tomato salad.

Three Cheese Bake

Serve this dish while the cheese is still hot and melted, because cooked cheese turns very rubbery if it is allowed to cool down.

NUTRITIONAL INFORMATION

Calories	710	Sugars	.........6g
Protein	........34g	Fat	..........30g
Carbohydrate	...80g	Saturates	......16g

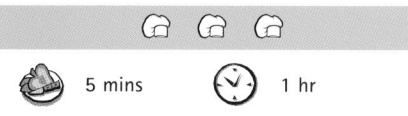

🧈 5 mins   🕐 1 hr

SERVES 4

INGREDIENTS

butter, for greasing

3½ cups dried penne pasta

2 eggs, beaten

1½ cups ricotta cheese

4 fresh basil sprigs

1 cup grated mozzarella or
   halloumi cheese

scant 1 cup freshly grated
   Parmesan cheese

salt and pepper

fresh basil leaves, to garnish (optional)

selection of cooked vegetables, to serve

3 Beat the eggs into the ricotta cheese and season to taste.

4 Spoon half of the pasta into the bottom of the prepared dish and cover with half of the basil leaves.

5 Spoon over half of the ricotta cheese mixture. Sprinkle over the mozzarella or halloumi cheese and top with the remaining basil leaves. Cover with the remaining pasta and then spoon over the remaining ricotta cheese mixture. Lightly sprinkle the freshly grated Parmesan cheese over the top.

6 Bake in a preheated oven, 375°F/ 190°C, for 30–40 minutes until golden brown and the cheese topping is hot and bubbling. Garnish with fresh basil leaves, if liked, and serve immediately with a selection of cooked vegetables.

1 Lightly grease a large casserole with a little butter.

2 Bring a pan of lightly salted water to a boil. Add the pasta, bring back to a boil, and cook for 8–10 minutes until just tender, but still firm to the bite. Drain the pasta, set aside, and keep warm.

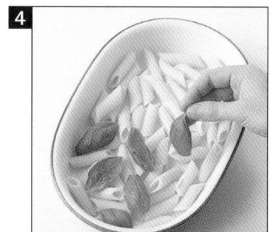

Traditional Cannelloni

You can buy ready made dried pasta tubes. However, if using fresh pasta (see page 6), you must cut out squares and roll them yourself.

NUTRITIONAL INFORMATION

Calories 342	Sugars 6g
Protein 15g	Fat 15g
Carbohydrate . . .38g	Saturates 8g

 50 mins   🕐 30 mins

SERVES 4

INGREDIENTS

20 tubes dried cannelloni (about 7 oz/ 200 g) or 20 square sheets of fresh pasta (about 12 oz/350 g)

generous 1 cup ricotta cheese

150 g/5½ oz frozen spinach, thawed

½ small red bell pepper, deseeded and diced

2 scallions, chopped

butter, for greasing

⅔ cup hot vegetable or stock

1 quantity Tomato Sauce (see page 7), made with 2 tbsp chopped fresh basil instead of parsley

⅓ cup freshly grated Parmesan or romano cheese

salt and pepper

1 If necessary, pre-cook dried cannelloni. Bring a large pan of water to a boil, add the pasta, bring back to a boil, and cook for 3–4 minutes. Cook in batches if this is easier.

2 Combine the ricotta, spinach, bell pepper, and scallions in a bowl and season to taste with salt and pepper.

3 Lightly grease a casserole, large enough to contain all of the pasta tubes in a single layer, with a little butter. Spoon the ricotta mixture into the pasta tubes and place them into the prepared casserole. If you are using fresh sheets of pasta, spread the ricotta mixture along one side of each fresh pasta square and roll up to form a tube.

4 Combine the stock and tomato sauce and pour it over the pasta tubes.

5 Sprinkle the Parmesan or romano cheese over the cannelloni and bake in a preheated oven, 375°F/190°C, for 20–25 minutes or until the pasta is cooked through and the topping is golden and bubbling. Serve immediately.

VARIATION

If you would prefer a creamier version, omit the stock and the Tomato Sauce and replace with Béchamel Sauce (see page 6).

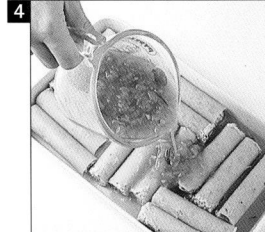

Paglia e Fieno

The name of this traditional dish—"straw and hay"—
refers to the colors of the pasta when mixed together.

NUTRITIONAL INFORMATION

Calories 699	Sugars 7g	
Protein 26g	Fat 39g	
Carbohydrate . . .65g	Saturates 23g	

10 mins   10 mins

SERVES 4

INGREDIENTS

4 tbsp butter

1 lb/450 g fresh peas, shelled

scant 1 cup heavy cream

1 lb/450 g mixed fresh green and white spaghetti or tagliatelle

⅔ cup freshly grated Parmesan cheese, plus extra to serve

pinch of freshly grated nutmeg

salt and pepper

1 Melt the butter in a large pan. Add the peas and cook, over low heat, for 2–3 minutes.

2 Pour ⅔ cup of the cream into the pan, bring to a boil, and then simmer for 1–1½ minutes or until slightly thickened. Remove the pan from the heat.

3 Meanwhile, bring a large pan of lightly salted water to a boil. Add the spaghetti or tagliatelle, bring back to a boil, and cook for 2–3 minutes or until just tender, but still firm to the bite. Remove the pan from the heat, drain the pasta thoroughly, and return to the pan.

4 Add the peas and cream sauce to the pasta. Return the pan to the heat and add the remaining cream and the Parmesan cheese and season to taste with salt, pepper, and grated nutmeg.

5 Using 2 forks, gently toss the pasta to coat with the peas and cream sauce, while heating through.

6 Transfer the pasta to a warmed serving dish and serve immediately, with extra Parmesan cheese.

VARIATION

Cook 5 oz/140 g sliced button or oyster mushrooms in 4 tablespoons butter over low heat for 4–5 minutes. Stir into the peas and cream sauce just before adding to the pasta in step 4.

Green Tagliatelle with Garlic

A rich pasta dish for garlic lovers everywhere. It is quick and easy to prepare and full of flavor.

NUTRITIONAL INFORMATION

Calories	474	Sugars	........3g
Protein	........16g	Fat	..........24g
Carbohydrate	...52g	Saturates	.......9g

 20 mins 15 mins

SERVES 4

INGREDIENTS

2 tbsp walnut oil

1 bunch of scallions, sliced

2 garlic cloves, thinly sliced

3¼ cups sliced mushrooms

1 lb/450 g fresh green and white tagliatelle

8 oz/225 g frozen spinach, thawed and drained

½ cup full-fat soft cheese with garlic and herbs

4 tbsp light cream

½ cup chopped, unsalted pistachio nuts

2 tbsp shredded fresh basil

salt and pepper

Italian bread, to serve

fresh basil sprigs, to garnish

3 Meanwhile, bring a large pan of lightly salted water to a boil. Add the tagliatelle, bring back to a boil, and cook for 3–5 minutes or until tender, but still firm to the bite. Drain the tagliatelle thoroughly and return to the pan.

4 Add the spinach to the skillet and heat through for 1–2 minutes. Add the cheese and heat until slightly melted. Stir in the cream and cook, without allowing the mixture to come to a boil, until warmed through.

5 Pour the sauce over the pasta, season to taste with salt and pepper, and mix well. Heat through gently, stirring constantly, for 2–3 minutes.

6 Transfer the pasta to a warmed serving dish and sprinkle with the pistachios and shredded basil. Garnish with the fresh basil sprigs and serve immediately with focaccia, ciabatta, or other Italian bread of your choice.

1 Heat the walnut oil in a large skillet. Add the scallions and garlic and cook for 1 minute until just softened.

2 Add the mushrooms to the skillet, stir well, cover, and cook over low heat for about 5 minutes until just softened, but not browned.

Patriotic Pasta

The ingredients of this dish have the same
bright colors as the Italian flag—hence its name.

NUTRITIONAL INFORMATION

Calories	325	Sugars 5g
Protein	.........8g	Fat 13g
Carbohydrate	...48g	Saturates 2g

 5 mins 15 mins

SERVES 4

INGREDIENTS

1 lb/450 g dried farfalle

3 tbsp olive oil

1 lb/450 g cherry tomatoes

3 oz/85 g arugula

salt and pepper

romano cheese, to garnish

1 Bring a large pan of lightly salted water to a boil. Add the farfalle, bring back to a boil, and cook for 8–10 minutes or until tender, but still firm to the bite. Drain the farfalle thoroughly and return to the pan.

2 Cut the cherry tomatoes in half and trim the arugula.

3 Heat the olive oil in a large, heavy pan. Add the tomatoes to the pan and cook for 1 minute.

4 Add the farfalle and the arugula to the pan and stir gently over low heat until thoroughly mixed and warmed through—the arugula should just have wilted. Season to taste with salt and pepper.

5 Meanwhile, using a vegetable peeler, shave thin slices of romano cheese.

6 Transfer the farfalle and vegetables to a warmed serving dish. Garnish with the romano cheese shavings and serve the pasta immediately.

COOK'S TIP
Romano cheese is a hard sheep's-milk cheese which resembles Parmesan and is often used for grating over a variety of dishes. It has a sharp flavor and is used only in small quantities.

Pasta & Vegetable Sauce

The different shapes and textures of the vegetables make a mouthwatering presentation in this light and summery dish.

NUTRITIONAL INFORMATION

Calories	389	Sugars	........4g
Protein	........16g	Fat	..........20g
Carbohydrate	...38g	Saturates	......11g

10 mins | 30 mins

SERVES 4

INGREDIENTS

2 cups dried gemelli or other
   pasta shapes

1 broccoli head, cut into florets

2 zucchini, sliced

8 oz/225 g asparagus spears

4 oz/115 g snow peas

1 cup frozen peas

2 tbsp butter

3 tbsp vegetable stock

4 tbsp heavy cream

freshly grated nutmeg

2 tbsp chopped fresh parsley

2 tbsp freshly grated Parmesan cheese

salt and pepper

1 Bring a large pan of lightly salted water to a boil. Add the pasta, bring back to a boil, and cook for 8–10 minutes or until tender, but still firm to the bite. Drain the pasta, return to the pan, cover, and keep warm.

2 Steam the broccoli, zucchini, asparagus spears, and snow peas over a pan of boiling salted water until they are just beginning to soften. Remove from the heat and refresh in cold water. Drain and set aside.

3 Bring a small pan of lightly salted water to a boil. Add the frozen peas and cook for 3 minutes. Drain the peas, refresh in cold water, and then drain again. Set aside with the other vegetables.

4 Put the butter and vegetable stock in a pan over medium heat. Add all of the vegetables, reserving a few of the asparagus spears, and toss carefully with a wooden spoon until they have heated through, taking care not to break them up.

5 Stir in the cream and heat through without bringing to a boil. Season to taste with salt, pepper, and nutmeg.

6 Transfer the pasta to a warmed serving dish and stir in the chopped parsley. Spoon over the vegetable sauce and sprinkle over the Parmesan cheese. Arrange the reserved asparagus spears in a pattern on top and serve.

Mushroom & Cheese Risotto

Make this creamy risotto with Italian arborio rice and freshly grated Parmesan cheese for the best results.

NUTRITIONAL INFORMATION

Calories	358	Sugars	........3g
Protein	........11g	Fat	..........14g
Carbohydrate	...50g	Saturates	.......5g

 20 mins 40 mins

SERVES 4

I N G R E D I E N T S

2 tbsp olive or vegetable oil

2 cups risotto rice

2 garlic cloves, crushed

1 onion, chopped

2 celery stalks, chopped

1 red or green bell pepper, deseeded and chopped

3¼ cups sliced mushrooms

1 tbsp chopped fresh oregano or 1 tsp dried oregano

4 cups vegetable stock

2 oz/55 g sun-dried tomatoes in olive oil, drained and chopped (optional)

⅔ cup finely grated Parmesan cheese

salt and pepper

TO GARNISH

fresh flat leaf parsley sprigs

fresh bay leaves

1 Heat the oil in a wok or large skillet. Add the rice and cook, stirring constantly, for 5 minutes.

2 Add the garlic, onion, celery, and bell pepper and cook, stirring constantly, for 5 minutes. Add the mushrooms and cook for 3–4 minutes.

3 Stir in the oregano and stock. Heat until just boiling, then reduce the heat, cover, and simmer gently for about 20 minutes or until the rice is tender and creamy.

4 Add the sun-dried tomatoes, if using, and season to taste with salt and pepper. Stir in half of the grated Parmesan cheese. Top with the remaining cheese, garnish with flat leaf parsley and bay leaves, and serve.

Bread Dough Base

Traditionally, pizza bases are made from bread dough;
this recipe will give you a base similar to an Italian pizza.

NUTRITIONAL INFORMATION

Calories	182	Sugars	.........2g
Protein	.........5g	Fat	...........3g
Carbohydrate	...36g	Saturates	.....0.5g

1½ hrs   0 mins

SERVES 4

I N G R E D I E N T S

15 g/½ oz fresh yeast or 1 tsp dried or
  active dry yeast

6 tbsp lukewarm water

½ tsp sugar

1 tbsp olive oil

1½ cups all-purpose flour, plus extra
  for dusting

1 tsp salt

1 Combine the fresh yeast with the water and sugar in a bowl. If using dried yeast, sprinkle it over the surface of the water and whisk in until dissolved.

2 Set aside in a warm place for 10–15 minutes until frothy on the surface. Stir in the olive oil.

3 Sift the flour and salt into a large bowl. If using easy-blend yeast, stir it in. Make a well in the center and pour in the yeast liquid, or water and oil (without the sugar for easy-blend yeast).

4 Using either floured hands or a wooden spoon, mix together to form a dough. Turn out onto a floured counter and knead for about 5 minutes or until smooth and elastic.

5 Place the dough in a large greased plastic bag and set aside in a warm place for about 1 hour or until doubled in size. Airing cupboards are often the best places for this process, as the temperature remains constant.

6 Turn out onto a lightly floured work surface and punch down the dough. This releases any air bubbles which would make the pizza uneven. Knead 4 or 5 times. The dough is now ready to use.

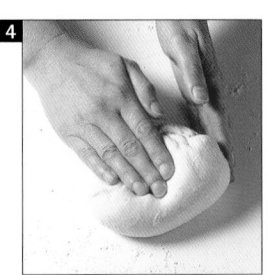

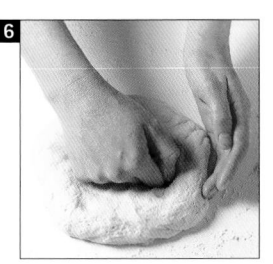

Giardiniera Pizza

As the name implies, this colorful pizza should be topped with fresh vegetables from the garden, especially in the summer months.

 15 mins   20 mins

SERVES 4

I N G R E D I E N T S

6 spinach leaves

Bread Dough Base (see page 838) or
 1 x 10 inch/25 cm pizza base

Basic Tomato Sauce (see page 7)

1 tomato, sliced

1 celery stalk, thinly sliced

½ green bell pepper, deseeded and
 thinly sliced

1 baby zucchini, sliced

1 oz/25 g asparagus tips

2½ tbsp corn, thawed if frozen

4 tbsp peas, thawed if frozen

4 scallions, trimmed and chopped

1 tbsp chopped fresh mixed herbs

½ cup grated mozzarella cheese

2 tbsp freshly grated Parmesan cheese

1 artichoke heart

olive oil, for drizzling

salt and pepper

1 Remove any tough stalks from the spinach and wash the leaves in cold water. Pat dry with paper towels.

2 Roll out or press the pizza base, using a rolling pin or your hands, into a 10 inch/25 cm circle on a lightly floured counter. Place the round on a large greased cookie sheet or pizza pan and push up the edge a little. Spread with the tomato sauce.

3 Arrange the spinach leaves on the sauce, followed by the tomato slices. Top with the remaining vegetables and the fresh mixed herbs.

4 Combine the cheeses and sprinkle over the pizza. Place the artichoke heart in the center. Drizzle the pizza with a little olive oil and season to taste.

5 Bake in a preheated oven, 400°F/200°C, for 18–20 minutes or until the edges are crisp and golden brown. Serve immediately.

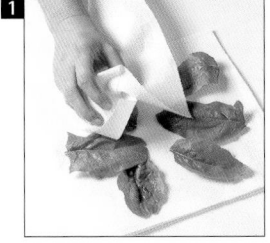

Mushroom & Walnut Pizza

Exotic mushrooms make a delicious pizza topping when mixed with walnuts and Roquefort cheese.

NUTRITIONAL INFORMATION

Calories ....499 Sugars 9g
Protein ....13g Fat 32g
Carbohydrate ...42g Saturates 11g

 10 mins   25 mins

SERVES 4

INGREDIENTS

Bread Dough Base (see page 838) or
 1 x 10 inch/25 cm pizza base

Basic Tomato Sauce (see page 7)

½ cup soft cheese

1 tbsp chopped fresh mixed herbs, such as
 parsley, oregano and basil

8 oz/225 g exotic mushrooms, such as
 oyster, shiitake or ceps, or 4 oz/115 g
 each exotic and white mushrooms

2 tbsp olive oil, plus extra for drizzling

¼ tsp fennel seeds

4 tbsp coarsely chopped walnuts

1½ oz/40 g blue cheese

salt and pepper

fresh flat leaf parsley sprig, to garnish

1 Roll out or press the pizza base, using a rolling pin or your hands, into a 10 inch/25 cm circle on a lightly floured counter. Place on a large greased cookie sheet or pizza pan and push up the edge a little with your fingers to form a rim.

2 Carefully spread the tomato sauce almost to the edge of the pizza base. Dot with the soft cheese and chopped fresh herbs.

3 Wipe and slice the mushrooms. Heat the oil in a large skillet or wok and stir-fry the mushrooms and fennel seeds for 2–3 minutes. Spread over the pizza with the walnuts.

4 Crumble the blue cheese over the pizza, drizzle with a little olive oil, and season with salt and pepper to taste.

5 Bake in a preheated oven, 400°F/200°C, for 18–20 minutes or until the edge is crisp and golden. Serve immediately, garnished with a sprig of flat leaf parsley.

Florentine Pizza

A pizza adaptation of Eggs Florentine—sliced hard-cooked eggs on freshly cooked spinach, with a crunchy almond topping.

NUTRITIONAL INFORMATION

Calories	474	Sugars	.........7g
Protein	........19g	Fat	..........26g
Carbohydrate	...43g	Saturates	.....7.5g

 20 mins   20 mins

SERVES 4

INGREDIENTS

Bread Dough Base (see page 838) or
   1 x 10 inch/25 cm pizza base

3 tbsp olive oil, plus extra for drizzling

2 tbsp freshly grated Parmesan cheese

Basic Tomato Sauce (see page 7)

6 oz/175 g spinach

1 small red onion, thinly sliced

¼ tsp freshly grated nutmeg

2 hard-cooked eggs

¼ cup fresh white bread crumbs

½ cup grated Jarlsberg, Cheddar, or Swiss
   cheese, grated

2 tbsp sliced almonds

salt and pepper

1 Roll out or press the dough, using a rolling pin or your hands, into a 10 inch/25 cm circle on a lightly floured counter. Brush with the olive oil and sprinkle with the Parmesan. Place on a large greased cookie sheet or pizza pan and push up the edge slightly. Spread the tomato sauce almost to the edge.

2 Remove the stalks from the spinach and wash the leaves thoroughly in plenty of cold water. Drain well and pat off the excess water with paper towels.

3 Heat the remaining oil and cook the onion for 5 minutes until softened. Add the spinach and cook until just wilted. Drain off any excess liquid. Arrange on the pizza and sprinkle over the nutmeg.

4 Shell and slice the eggs. Arrange the slices of egg on top of the spinach.

5 Combine the bread crumbs, cheese, and almonds and sprinkle over. Drizzle with a little olive oil and season to taste.

6 Bake in a preheated oven, 400°F/ 200°C, for 18–20 minutes or until the edge is crisp and golden. Serve the pizza immediately.

Bell Pepper & Onion Pizza

The vibrant colors of the bell peppers and red onion make this a delightful pizza. Served cut into fingers, it is ideal for a party or buffet.

NUTRITIONAL INFORMATION

Calories	380	Sugars	........19g
Protein	.........7g	Fat	..........17g
Carbohydrate	...53g	Saturates	.......2g

 25 mins   25 mins

SERVES 8

INGREDIENTS

Bread Dough Base (see page 838)

2 tbsp olive oil, plus extra for drizzling

½ red bell pepper deseeded and thinly sliced

½ green bell pepper, deseeded and thinly sliced

½ yellow bell pepper, deseeded and thinly sliced

1 small red onion, thinly sliced

1 garlic clove, crushed

Basic Tomato Sauce (see page 7)

3 tbsp raisins

4 tbsp pine nuts

1 tbsp chopped fresh thyme

salt and pepper

1 Roll out or press the dough, using a rolling pin or your hands, on a lightly floured counter to fit a 12 x 7 inch/ 30 x 18 cm greased jelly roll pan. Place the dough in the pan and push up the edges slightly.

2 Cover with plastic wrap and set the dough aside in a warm place for about 10 minutes to rise slightly.

3 Heat the oil in a large skillet. Add the bell peppers, onion, and garlic and cook gently for 5 minutes until they have softened. Set aside to cool.

4 Spread the tomato sauce over the base of the pizza almost to the edge.

5 Sprinkle over the raisins and top with the cooled bell pepper mixture. Add the pine nuts and thyme. Drizzle with a little olive oil and season to taste with salt and pepper.

6 Bake in a preheated oven, 400°F/ 200°C, for 18–20 minutes, or until the edges are crisp and golden. Cut into fingers and serve immediately.

Macaroni & Corn Crêpes

These vegetable crêpes can be filled with your favorite vegetables—
try shredded parsnips with 1 tablespoon of mustard.

NUTRITIONAL INFORMATION

Calories 702	Sugars 4g	
Protein 13g	Fat 50g	
Carbohydrate . . .55g	Saturates 23g	

 15 mins   40 mins

SERVES 4

INGREDIENTS

2 corn cobs

4 tbsp butter

4 oz/115 g red bell peppers, deseeded and finely diced

2½ cups dried short-cut macaroni

⅔ cup heavy cream

¼ cup all-purpose flour

4 egg yolks

4 tbsp olive oil

salt and pepper

TO SERVE

oyster mushrooms

fried leeks

1 Bring a pan of water to the boil, add the corn cobs, and cook for about 8 minutes. Drain thoroughly and refresh under cold running water for 3 minutes. Carefully cut away the kernels onto paper towels and set aside to dry.

2 Melt 2 tablespoons of the butter in a skillet. Add the bell peppers and cook over low heat for 4 minutes. Drain and pat dry with paper towels.

3 Bring a large pan of lightly salted water to a boil. Add the macaroni, bring back to a boil, and cook for about 12 minutes or until tender, but still firm to the bite. Drain the macaroni thoroughly and set aside to cool in cold water until required.

4 Beat the cream with the flour, a pinch of salt, and the egg yolks in a bowl until smooth. Add the corn and bell peppers. Drain the macaroni and then toss into the corn and cream mixture. Season with pepper to taste.

5 Heat the remaining butter with the oil in a large skillet. Drop spoonfuls of the mixture into the pan and press down until the mixture forms flat crêpes. Cook until golden on both sides, and all the mixture is used up. Serve immediately with oyster mushrooms and sautéed leeks.

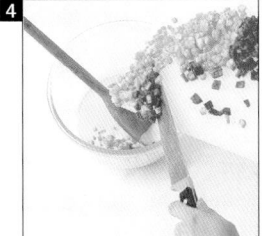

Vermicelli & Vegetable Pie

Lightly cooked vermicelli is pressed into a quiche pan and baked with a creamy mushroom filling to make an attractive, as well as tasty, dish.

NUTRITIONAL INFORMATION

Calories	528	Sugars	.........6g
Protein	........15g	Fat	..........32g
Carbohydrate	...47g	Saturates	......17g

15 mins   1 hr

SERVES 4

INGREDIENTS

6 tbsp butter, plus extra for greasing

8 oz/225 g dried vermicelli or spaghetti

1 tbsp olive oil

1 onion, chopped

5 oz/140 g white mushrooms

1 green bell pepper, deseeded and sliced into thin rings

⅔ cup milk

3 eggs, lightly beaten

2 tbsp heavy cream

1 tsp dried oregano

freshly grated nutmeg

3 tbsp freshly grated Parmesan cheese

salt and pepper

tomato and basil salad, to serve (optional)

1 Generously grease a 8 inch/20 cm loose-bottomed quiche pan with a little butter.

2 Bring a large pan of lightly salted water to a boil. Add the vermicelli and olive oil, bring back to a boil, and cook for 8–10 minutes until tender, but still firm to the bite. Drain, return to the pan, add 2 tablespoons of the butter, and shake the pan to coat the pasta.

3 Press the pasta onto the bottom and around the sides of the quiche pan to make a pie shell.

4 Melt the remaining butter in a skillet over medium heat. Add the onion and fry over low heat, stirring occasionally, until it is softened.

5 Add the mushrooms and bell pepper rings and cook, stirring constantly, for 2–3 minutes. Spoon the onion, mushroom and bell pepper mixture into the pie shell and press it evenly into the base.

6 Beat together the milk, eggs, and cream, stir in the oregano, and season to taste with nutmeg and pepper. Carefully pour this mixture over the vegetables and then sprinkle with the Parmesan cheese.

7 Bake the pie in a preheated oven, 350°F/180°C, for 40–45 minutes or until the filling has set.

8 Carefully slide the pie out of the pan and serve warm with a tomato and basil salad, if wished.

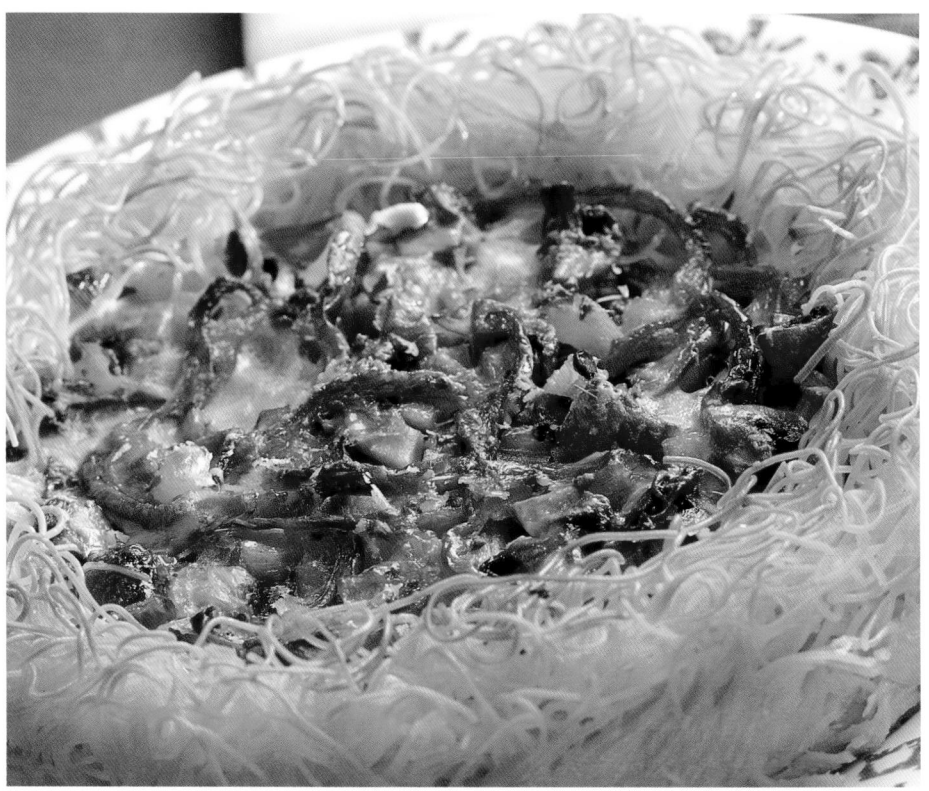

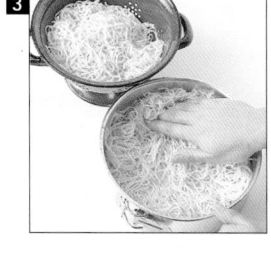

Feta & Spinach Omelet

This quick chunky omelet has pieces of potato cooked into the egg mixture and is then filled with feta cheese and spinach.

NUTRITIONAL INFORMATION

Calories	564	Sugars	.........6g
Protein	........30g	Fat	..........39g
Carbohydrate	...25g	Saturates	......19g

 20 mins   25–30 mins

SERVES 4

I N G R E D I E N T S

6 tbsp butter

3 lb/1.3 kg waxy potatoes, diced

3 garlic cloves, crushed

1 tsp paprika

2 tomatoes, peeled, deseeded, and diced

12 eggs

pepper

F I L L I N G

8 oz/225 g baby spinach

1 tsp fennel seeds

4½ oz/125 g feta cheese, diced
   (drained weight)

4 tbsp plain yogurt

1 Heat 1 tablespoon of the butter in a skillet and cook the potatoes over low heat, stirring, for 7–10 minutes until golden. Transfer to a bowl.

2 Add the garlic, paprika, and tomatoes to the skillet and cook for a further 2 minutes.

3 Whisk the eggs together and season with pepper. Pour the eggs into the potatoes and mix well.

4 Cook the spinach in boiling water for 1 minute until just wilted. Drain and refresh under cold running water. Pat dry with paper towels. Stir in the fennel seeds, feta cheese, and yogurt.

5 Heat a quarter of the remaining butter in a 6 inch/15 cm omelet pan. Ladle a quarter of the egg and potato mixture into the pan. Cook, turning once, for 2 minutes, until set.

6 Transfer the omelet to a serving plate. Spoon a quarter of the spinach mixture onto half of the omelet, then fold the omelet in half over the filling. Repeat to make 4 omelets.

VARIATION
Use any other cheese, such as blue cheese, instead of the feta, and blanched broccoli in place of the baby spinach, if you prefer.

Creamy Stuffed Mushrooms

These oven-baked mushrooms are covered with a creamy potato and mushroom filling topped with melted cheese.

NUTRITIONAL INFORMATION

Calories	.214	Sugars	.1g
Protein	.5g	Fat	.17g
Carbohydrate	.11g	Saturates	.11g

 40 mins   40 mins

SERVES 4

INGREDIENTS

½ cup dried porcini

8 oz/225 g mealy potatoes, diced

2 tbsp butter, melted

4 tbsp heavy cream

2 tbsp chopped fresh chives

8 large open-capped mushrooms

4 tbsp grated Emmenthal cheese

⅔ cup vegetable stock

salt and pepper

fresh chives, to garnish

1 Place the dried porcini in a small bowl. Add sufficient boiling water to cover and set aside to soak for 20 minutes.

2 Meanwhile, cook the potatoes in a medium pan of lightly salted boiling water for 10 minutes until cooked through and tender. Drain well and mash thoroughly until smooth.

3 Drain the soaked mushrooms and then chop them finely. Mix them into the mashed potato.

4 Thoroughly blend the butter, cream, and chives together and pour the mixture into the mushroom and potato mixture, mixing well. Season to taste with salt and pepper.

5 Remove the stems from the open-capped mushrooms. Chop the stems and stir them into the potato mixture. Spoon the mixture into the open-capped mushrooms and sprinkle the grated cheese over the top.

6 Arrange the filled mushrooms in a shallow casserole and pour in the vegetable stock.

7 Cover the dish and cook in a preheated oven, 425°F/220°C, for 20 minutes. Remove the lid and cook for 5 minutes until golden.

8 Garnish the mushrooms with fresh chives and serve at once.

VARIATION

Use fresh mushrooms instead of the dried ones, if preferred, and stir a mixture of chopped nuts into the mushroom stuffing mixture for extra crunch.

Potato-Filled Nan Breads

This is a filling Indian sandwich. Spicy potatoes fill the nan breads, which are served with a cool cucumber raita and lime pickle.

NUTRITIONAL INFORMATION

Calories	244	Sugars	........7g
Protein	.........8g	Fat	..........8g
Carbohydrate	...37g	Saturates	......1g

 10 mins   25 mins

SERVES 4

INGREDIENTS

8 oz/225 g waxy potatoes, scrubbed
  and diced

1 tbsp vegetable oil

1 onion, chopped

2 garlic cloves, crushed

1 tsp ground cumin

1 tsp ground coriander

½ tsp chili powder

1 tbsp tomato paste

3 tbsp vegetable stock

3 oz/85 g baby spinach, shredded

4 small or 2 large nan breads

lime pickle, to serve

RAITA

⅔ cup low-fat plain yogurt

4 tbsp diced cucumber

1 tbsp chopped fresh mint

1 Cook the diced potatoes in a pan of boiling water for 10 minutes. Drain thoroughly.

2 Heat the vegetable oil in a separate pan and cook the onion and garlic over low heat, stirring frequently, for 3 minutes. Add the spices and cook for a further 2 minutes.

3 Stir in the potatoes, tomato paste, vegetable stock, and spinach. Cook for 5 minutes until the potatoes are tender.

4 Warm the nan breads in a preheated oven, 300°F, for about 2 minutes.

5 To make the raita, combine the yogurt, cucumber, and mint in a small bowl.

6 Remove the nan breads from the oven. Using a sharp knife, cut a pocket in the side of each bread. Spoon the spicy potato mixture into each pocket.

7 Serve the filled nan breads immediately, accompanied by the raita and lime pickle.

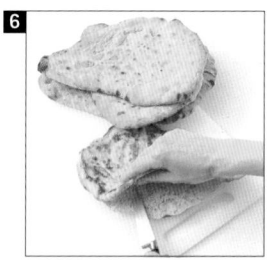

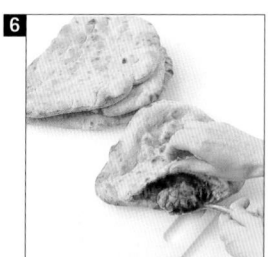

COOK'S TIP

To give the raita a much stronger flavor, make it in advance and chill in the refrigerator until ready to serve.

Potato-Topped Vegetables

This is a very colorful and nutritious dish, packed full of crunchy vegetables in a tasty white wine sauce.

NUTRITIONAL INFORMATION

Calories	.413	Sugars	.11g
Protein	.19g	Fat	.18g
Carbohydrate	.41g	Saturates	.11g

🖐 🖐

🥔 20 mins   🕐 1¼ hrs

SERVES 4

INGREDIENTS

1 carrot, diced

6 oz/175 g cauliflower florets

6 oz/175 g broccoli florets

1 fennel bulb, sliced

3 oz/85 g green beans, halved

2 tbsp butter

2½ tbsp all-purpose flour

⅔ cup vegetable stock

⅔ cup dry white wine

⅔ cup milk

6 oz/175 g crimini mushrooms, quartered

2 tbsp chopped fresh sage

TOPPING

2 lb/900 g mealy potatoes, diced

2 tbsp butter

4 tbsp plain yogurt

scant 1 cup freshly grated
    Parmesan cheese

1 tsp fennel seeds

salt and pepper

1 Cook the carrot, cauliflower, broccoli, fennel, and beans in a large pan of boiling water for 10 minutes until just tender. Drain the vegetables thoroughly and set aside.

2 Melt the butter in a pan. Stir in the flour and cook for 1 minute. Remove from the heat and stir in the stock, wine, and milk. Return to the heat and bring to a boil, stirring until thickened. Stir in the reserved vegetables, mushrooms, and sage.

3 Meanwhile, make the topping. Cook the potatoes in boiling water for 10–15 minutes. Drain thoroughly and mash with the butter, yogurt, and half the grated cheese. Stir in the fennel seeds. Season to taste.

4 Spoon the vegetable mixture into a 4 cup pie dish. Spoon the mashed potato over the top and sprinkle with the remaining cheese. Cook in a preheated oven, 375°F/190°C, for 30–35 minutes or until golden. Serve hot.

Three Cheese Soufflé

This soufflé is very simple to make, yet it has a delicious flavor and melts in your mouth. Choose three alternative cheeses, if preferred.

NUTRITIONAL INFORMATION

Calories 447   Sugars 1g
Protein ....22g   Fat 23g
Carbohydrate ...41g   Saturates 11g

🍽 10 mins   🕐 55 mins

SERVES 4

INGREDIENTS

2 tbsp butter

2 tsp all-purpose flour

2 lb/900 g mealy potatoes

8 eggs, separated

4 tbsp grated Swiss cheese

4 tbsp crumbled blue cheese

4 tbsp grated sharp Cheddar

salt and pepper

1 Butter a 10 cup soufflé dish and dust with the flour. Set aside.

2 Cook the potatoes in a pan of boiling water until tender. Mash until very smooth and then transfer to a mixing bowl to cool.

3 Beat the egg yolks into the potato and stir in the Swiss cheese, blue cheese, and Cheddar, mixing well. Season to taste with salt and pepper.

4 Whisk the egg whites until standing in peaks, then gently fold them into the potato mixture with a metal spoon until fully incorporated.

5 Spoon the potato mixture into the prepared soufflé dish.

6 Cook in a preheated oven, 425°F/ 220°C, for 35–40 minutes until risen and set. Serve immediately.

 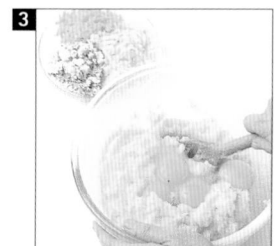 

COOK'S TIP

Insert a fine skewer into the center of the soufflé; it should come out clean when the soufflé is fully cooked through.

Nutty Harvest Loaf

This attractive and nutritious loaf is also utterly delicious.
Served with a fresh tomato sauce, it can be eaten hot or cold with salad.

NUTRITIONAL INFORMATION

Calories ....554 Sugars 12g
Protein ....16g Fat 37g
Carbohydrate ...43g Saturates 16g

20 mins   1½ hrs

SERVES 4

INGREDIENTS

2 tbsp butter, plus extra
   for greasing

1 lb/450 g mealy potatoes, diced

1 onion, chopped

2 garlic cloves, crushed

1 cup unsalted peanuts

1½ cups fresh white bread crumbs

1 egg, beaten

2 tbsp chopped fresh cilantro

⅔ cup vegetable stock

generous 1 cup sliced mushrooms

2 oz sun-dried tomatoes in oil
   drained and sliced

salt and pepper

SAUCE

⅔ cup crème fraîche

2 tsp tomato paste

2 tsp honey

2 tbsp chopped fresh cilantro

1 Grease a 1 lb/450 g loaf pan. Cook the potatoes in a pan of boiling water for 10 minutes until cooked through. Drain well, mash, and set aside.

2 Melt half of the butter in a skillet. Add the onion and garlic and cook gently for 2–3 minutes until soft. Finely chop the nuts or process them in a food processor for 30 seconds with the bread crumbs.

3 Mix the chopped nuts and bread crumbs into the potatoes with the egg, cilantro, and vegetable stock. Stir in the onion and garlic and mix well.

4 Melt the remaining butter in the skillet, add the sliced mushrooms, and cook for 2–3 minutes.

5 Press half of the potato mixture into the base of the prepared loaf pan. Spoon the mushrooms on top and sprinkle with the sun-dried tomatoes. Spoon the remaining potato mixture on top and smooth the surface. Cover with foil and bake in a preheated oven, 375°F/190°C, for 1 hour or until firm to the touch.

6 Meanwhile, mix the sauce ingredients together. Cut the nutty harvest loaf into slices and serve with the sauce.

Vegetable Cake

This is a savory version of a cheesecake with a layer of fried potatoes as a delicious base. Use frozen mixed vegetables for the topping, if you like.

NUTRITIONAL INFORMATION

Calories	502	Sugars	.........8g
Protein	........16g	Fat	..........31g
Carbohydrate	...41g	Saturates	......14g

 20 mins 45 mins

SERVES 4

I N G R E D I E N T S

B A S E

2 tbsp vegetable oil, plus extra
for brushing

2 lb 12 oz/1.25 kg waxy potatoes, sliced

T O P P I N G

1 tbsp vegetable oil

1 leek, chopped

1 zucchini, grated

1 red bell pepper, deseeded and diced

1 green bell pepper, deseeded and diced

1 carrot, grated

2 tsp chopped parsley

1 cup full-fat soft cheese

4 tbsp grated sharp cheese

2 eggs, beaten

salt and pepper

shredded cooked leek, to garnish

salad, to serve

1 Brush an 8 inch/20 cm springform cake pan with oil.

2 To make the base, heat the oil in a skillet. Cook the potato slices until softened and browned. Drain on paper towels and place in the bottom of the prepared pan.

3 To make the topping, heat the oil in a separate skillet. Add the leek and cook over low heat, stirring frequently, for 3–4 minutes until softened.

4 Add the zucchini, bell peppers, carrot, and parsley to the skillet and cook over low heat for 5–7 minutes or until the vegetables have softened.

5 Meanwhile, beat the cheeses and eggs together in a bowl. Stir in the vegetables and season to taste with salt and pepper. Spoon the mixture evenly over the potato base.

6 Cook in a preheated oven, 375°F/ 190°C, for 20–25 minutes until the cake is set.

7 Remove the vegetable cake from the pan, transfer to a warm serving plate, garnish with shredded leek, and serve with a crisp salad.

Pan Potato Cake

This tasty meal is made with sliced potatoes, beancurd, and vegetables cooked in the skillet from which it is served.

NUTRITIONAL INFORMATION

Calories	452	Sugars	.........6g
Protein	........17g	Fat	..........28g
Carbohydrate	...35g	Saturates	......13g

 15 mins   30 mins

SERVES 4

INGREDIENTS

1 lb 8 oz/675 g waxy potatoes, unpeeled and sliced

1 carrot, diced

8 oz/225 g small broccoli florets

5 tbsp butter

2 tbsp vegetable oil

1 red onion, quartered

2 garlic cloves, crushed

6 oz/175 g firm beancurd, diced

2 tbsp chopped fresh sage

¾ cup grated sharp cheese

1 Cook the sliced potatoes in a large pan of boiling water for 10 minutes. Drain thoroughly.

2 Meanwhile, cook the carrot and broccoli florets in a separate pan of boiling water for 5 minutes. Remove with a slotted spoon.

3 Heat the butter and oil in a 9 inch/ 23 cm skillet. Add the onion and garlic and fry over low heat for 2–3 minutes. Add half of the potato slices, covering the base of the skillet.

4 Cover the potato slices with the carrot, broccoli, and bean curd. Sprinkle with half of the sage and cover with the remaining potato slices. Sprinkle the grated cheese over the top.

5 Cook over medium heat for 8–10 minutes. Then place the skillet under a preheated broiler for 2–3 minutes, or until the cheese melts and browns.

6 Garnish with the remaining sage and serve immediately, straight from the skillet.

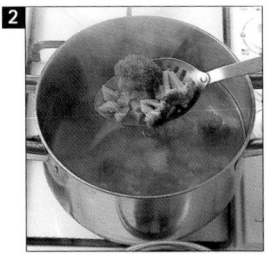  

COOK'S TIP

Make sure that the mixture fills the whole width of your skillet to enable the layers to remain intact.

Spicy Potato & Nut Terrine

This delicious baked terrine has a base of mashed potato flavored with nuts, cheese, herbs, and spices.

NUTRITIONAL INFORMATION

Calories	1100	Sugars	........13g
Protein	........34g	Fat	..........93g
Carbohydrate	...31g	Saturates	......22g

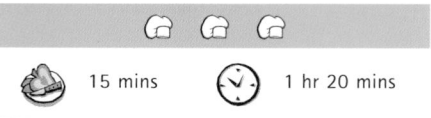

🥔 15 mins   🕐 1 hr 20 mins

SERVES 4

I N G R E D I E N T S

2 tbsp butter, plus extra for greasing

8 oz/225 g mealy potatoes, diced

2 cups shelled pecan nuts

2 cups unsalted cashew nuts

1 onion, finely chopped

2 garlic cloves, crushed

4 oz/115 g open-cap mushrooms, diced

2 tbsp chopped fresh mixed herbs

1 tsp paprika

1 tsp ground cumin

1 tsp ground coriander

4 eggs, beaten

½ cup full-fat soft cheese

⅔ cup freshly grated Parmesan cheese

salt and pepper

S A U C E

3 large tomatoes, peeled, deseeded, and chopped

2 tbsp tomato paste

5 tbsp red wine

1 tbsp red wine vinegar

pinch of superfine sugar

1 Lightly grease a 2 lb/900 g loaf pan with a little butter and line it with baking parchment.

2 Cook the potatoes in a large pan of lightly salted boiling water for 10 minutes or until cooked through. Drain and mash thoroughly.

3 Finely chop the pecan and cashew nuts or process in a food processor. Mix the nuts with the onion, garlic, and mushrooms. Melt the butter in a skillet and cook the nut mixture for 5–7 minutes. Add the herbs and spices. Stir in the eggs, cheeses, and potatoes and season to taste with salt and pepper.

4 Spoon the mixture into the prepared loaf pan, pressing it down quite firmly. Cook in a preheated oven, 375°F/190°C, for 1 hour or until set.

5 To make the sauce, mix the tomatoes, tomato paste, wine, wine vinegar, and sugar in a pan and bring to a boil, stirring constantly. Cook for 10 minutes, or until the tomatoes have reduced. Press the sauce through a strainer or process in a food processor for 30 seconds. Turn the terrine out of the pan onto a serving plate and cut into slices. Serve with the tomato sauce.

Layered Pies

These individual pies of layered potato, eggplant, and zucchini baked in a tomato sauce can be made in advance, so are good for entertaining.

NUTRITIONAL INFORMATION

Calories 427	Sugars 8g	
Protein 22g	Fat 21g	
Carbohydrate ...41g	Saturates 8g	

40 mins   1 hr 20 mins

SERVES 4

INGREDIENTS

3 large waxy potatoes, thinly sliced

1 small eggplant, thinly sliced

1 zucchini, sliced

3 tbsp vegetable oil

1 onion, diced

1 green bell pepper, deseeded and diced

1 tsp cumin seeds

2 tbsp chopped fresh basil

7 oz/200 g canned chopped tomatoes

6 oz/175 g mozzarella cheese, sliced

8 oz/225 g beancurd, sliced

1 cup fresh white bread crumbs

2 tbsp grated Parmesan cheese

salt and pepper

fresh basil leaves, to garnish

3 Meanwhile, heat 2 tablespoons of the oil in a skillet. Add the onion and cook over low heat, stirring occasionally, for 2–3 minutes until softened. Add the bell pepper, cumin seeds, basil, and canned tomatoes. Season to taste with salt and pepper and simmer for 30 minutes.

4 Rinse the eggplant slices thoroughly under cold running water and pat dry with paper towels. Heat the remaining oil in a large skillet. Add the eggplant slices and cook over medium heat for 3–5 minutes, turning to brown both sides. Drain and set aside.

5 Arrange half of the potato slices in the base of 4 small loose-based tart pans. Cover with half of the zucchini slices, half of the eggplant slices, and half of the mozzarella slices. Lay the beancurd on top and spoon over the tomato sauce. Repeat the layers of vegetables and cheese in the same order.

6 Combine the bread crumbs and Parmesan and sprinkle over the top. Cook in a preheated oven, 375°F/190°C, for 25–30 minutes or until golden. Garnish with fresh basil leaves and serve the pies immediately.

1 Cook the sliced potatoes in a pan of boiling water for 5 minutes. Drain and set aside.

2 Put the eggplant slices on a plate, sprinkle with salt, and set aside for 20 minutes. Meanwhile, blanch the zucchini in a pan of boiling water for 2-3 minutes. Drain and set aside.

Vegetable-Stuffed Paratas

This bread can be quite rich and is usually made for special occasions. It can be eaten on its own or with a vegetable curry.

NUTRITIONAL INFORMATION

Calories 391	Sugars 2g	
Protein 6g	Fat 24g	
Carbohydrate . . .40g	Saturates 2.5g	

25 mins   30–35 mins

SERVES 4

I N G R E D I E N T S

DOUGH

1¾ cups whole-wheat flour
  (ata or chapati flour)

½ tsp salt

scant 1 cup water

3½ oz/100 g vegetable ghee

2 tbsp ghee, for frying

FILLING

1½ lb/675 g potatoes

½ tsp turmeric

1 tsp garam masala

1 tsp finely chopped fresh ginger root

1 tbsp fresh cilantro leaves

3 green chiles, finely chopped

1 tsp salt

1 To make the paratas, mix the flour, salt, water, and ghee in a bowl to form a dough.

2 Divide the dough into 6–8 equal portions. Roll each portion out on to a floured counter. Brush the middle of the dough portions with ½ teaspoon of ghee. Fold the dough portions in half and roll into a pipelike shape, then flatten with the palms of your hands and roll around a finger to form a coil. Roll out again, using flour to dust when necessary, to form a round about 7 inches/18 cm in diameter.

3 Place the potatoes in a pan of boiling water and cook until soft enough to be mashed.

4 Blend the turmeric, garam masala, ginger, cilantro leaves, chiles, and salt together in a bowl.

5 Add the spice mixture to the mashed potato and mix well. Spread about 1 tablespoon of the spicy potato mixture on each dough portion and cover with another rolled-out piece of dough. Seal the edges well.

6 Heat 2 teaspoons of ghee in a heavy-based skillet. Place the paratas gently in the pan, in batches, and cook, turning and moving them about gently with a flat spoon, until golden.

7 Remove the paratas from the skillet and serve immediately.

Spinach Frittata

This Italian dish may be made with many flavorings. Spinach is used as the main ingredient in this recipe for color and flavor.

NUTRITIONAL INFORMATION

Calories 307	Sugars 4g	
Protein 15g	Fat 25g	
Carbohydrate 6g	Saturates 8g	

20 mins   20 mins

SERVES 4

INGREDIENTS

1 lb/450 g spinach

2 tsp water

4 eggs, beaten

2 tbsp light cream

2 garlic cloves, crushed

⅓ cup canned corn, drained

1 celery stalk, chopped

1 fresh red chile, chopped

2 tomatoes, deseeded and diced

2 tbsp olive oil

2 tbsp butter

4 tbsp pecan halves

2 tbsp grated romano cheese

1 oz/25 g Fontina cheese, cubed

a pinch of paprika

COOK'S TIP

Be careful not to burn the underside of the frittata during the initial cooking stage—this is why it is important to use a heavy skillet. Add a little extra oil to the pan when you turn the frittata over, if required.

1 Cook the spinach in 2 teaspoons of water in a covered pan for 5 minutes. Drain thoroughly and pat dry on absorbent paper towels.

2 Beat the eggs in a bowl and stir in the spinach, light cream, garlic, corn, celery, chile, and tomatoes until the ingredients are well mixed.

3 Heat the olive oil and butter in an 8 inch/20 cm heavy skillet over medium heat.

4 Spoon the egg mixture into the skillet and sprinkle with the pecan halves, romano and Fontina cheeses, and paprika. Cook, without stirring, over medium heat for 5–7 minutes or until the underside of the frittata is brown.

5 Put a large plate over the pan and invert to turn out the frittata. Slide it back into the skillet and cook the other side for a further 2–3 minutes. Serve the frittata straight from the skillet or transfer to a serving plate.

Italian Vegetable Tart

A rich tomato pastry base topped with a mouthwatering selection of vegetables and cheese makes a tart that's tasty as well as attractive.

NUTRITIONAL INFORMATION

Calories 438	Sugars 8g
Protein 9g	Fat 28g
Carbohydrate . . .40g	Saturates 15g

 1¾ hrs   40 mins

SERVES 4

I N G R E D I E N T S

1 eggplant, sliced

2 tbsp salt

4 tbsp olive oil

1 garlic clove, crushed

1 large yellow bell pepper, deseeded and sliced

1¼ cups Basic Tomato Sauce (see page 7)

4 oz/115 g sun-dried tomatoes in oil, drained and halved if necessary

6 oz/175 g mozzarella cheese, drained and thinly sliced

P A S T R Y

2 cups all-purpose flour, plus extra for dusting

pinch of celery salt

½ cup butter or margarine, plus extra for greasing

2 tbsp tomato paste

2–3 tbsp milk

1 To make the dough, sift the flour and celery salt into a bowl and rub in the butter or margarine until the mixture resembles fine bread crumbs.

2 Combine the tomato paste and milk and stir into the mixture to form a firm dough. Knead gently until smooth. Wrap and chill for 30 minutes.

3 Grease an 11 inch/28 cm loose-bottomed quiche pan. Roll out the dough on a lightly floured surface and use to line the pan. Trim and prick all over with a fork. Chill for 30 minutes.

4 Meanwhile, layer the eggplant in a dish, sprinkling with the salt. Set aside for 30 minutes.

5 Bake the pie shell in a preheated oven, 400°F/200°C, for about 20–25 minutes until cooked and lightly golden. Set aside. Increase the oven temperature to 450°F/230°C.

6 Rinse the eggplant thoroughly under cold running water and pat dry with paper towels. Heat 3 tablespoons of the oil in a heavy skillet and cook the garlic, eggplant, and bell pepper for 5–6 minutes until just softened. Drain on paper towels.

7 Spread the pie shell with the tomato sauce and arrange the cooked vegetables, sun-dried tomatoes, and mozzarella on top. Brush with the remaining olive oil and bake for 5 minutes until the cheese is just melting. Remove from the oven and serve immediately.

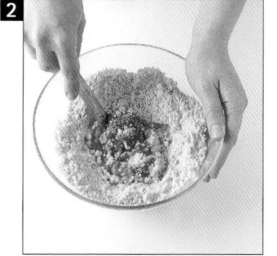  

Vegetables & Beancurd

This is a simple, clean-tasting dish of green vegetables, beancurd, and pasta, lightly tossed in olive oil.

NUTRITIONAL INFORMATION

Calories 400	Sugars 5g
Protein 19g	Fat 17g
Carbohydrate . . .46g	Saturates 5g

 25 mins 20 mins

SERVES 4

I N G R E D I E N T S

8 oz/225 g asparagus

4 oz/115 g snow peas

8 oz/225 g green beans

1 leek

8 oz/225 g shelled small fava beans

10½ oz/300 g dried fusilli

2 tbsp olive oil

2 tbsp butter or margarine

1 garlic clove, crushed

8 oz/225 g beancurd, cut into 1 inch/
 2.5 cm cubes

½ cup pitted green olives in
 brine, drained

salt and pepper

freshly grated Parmesan cheese, to serve

1 Cut the asparagus into 2 inch/5 cm lengths. Thinly slice the snow peas diagonally and slice the green beans into 1 inch/2.5 cm pieces. Thinly slice the leek.

2 Bring a large pan of water to a boil and add the asparagus, green beans, and fava beans. Bring back to a boil and cook for 4 minutes. Drain well, rinse in cold water, and drain again. Set aside.

3 Bring a large pan of lightly salted water to a boil. Add the pasta, bring back to a boil, and cook for 8–10 minutes until tender, but still firm to the bite. Drain well. Toss in 1 tablespoon of the oil and season to taste.

4 Meanwhile, heat the remaining oil and the butter or margarine in a wok or large skillet and gently cook the leek, garlic, and beancurd for 1–2 minutes until the vegetables have just softened.

5 Stir in the snow peas and cook for 1 further minute.

6 Add the blanched vegetables and olives to the skillet and heat through for 1 minute. Carefully stir in the pasta and adjust the seasoning if necessary. Cook for 1 minute and pile into a warmed serving dish. Serve immediately sprinkled with Parmesan.

Nutty Rice Burgers

Serve these burgers in toasted sesame seed rolls. If you wish, add a slice of cheese to top the burger at the end of cooking.

NUTRITIONAL INFORMATION

Calories 517	Sugars 5g
Protein 16g	Fat 26g
Carbohydrate . . .59g	Saturates 6g

 1¼ hrs   30 mins

SERVES 4

I N G R E D I E N T S

1 tbsp sunflower oil

1 small onion, finely chopped

1⅓ cups finely chopped mushrooms

2 cups cooked brown rice

1¾ cups bread crumbs

¾ cup chopped walnuts

1 egg, lightly beaten

2 tbsp brown fruity sauce

dash of Tabasco sauce

salt and pepper

vegetable oil

6 individual cheese slices (optional)

T O   S E R V E

onion slices

tomato slices

6 sesame seed rolls

1 Heat the oil in a large pan and cook the onions for 3–4 minutes until they just begin to soften. Add the mushrooms and cook for a further 2 minutes.

2 Remove the pan from the heat. Transfer to a bowl and stir the cooked rice, bread crumbs, walnuts, egg, brown fruity sauce, and a dash of Tabasco sauce into the vegetables. Season to taste with salt and pepper and mix well.

3 Shape the mixture into 6 burgers, pressing the mixture together with your fingers. Set aside to chill in the refrigerator for at least 30 minutes.

4 Grill the burgers on an oiled rack over medium coals for 5–6 minutes on each side, turning once and frequently basting with oil. Alternatively, cook under a preheated broiler.

5 If liked, top the burgers with a slice of cheese 2 minutes before the end of the cooking time. Grill or broil the onion and tomato slices for 3–4 minutes until they are just beginning to color.

6 Toast the sesame seed rolls at the side of the barbecue or under the broiler. Serve the burgers in the rolls, with the onions and tomatoes.

Vegetable Crêpes

Crêpes are ideal for filling with your favorite ingredients. In this recipe they are packed with a deliciously spicy vegetable filling.

NUTRITIONAL INFORMATION

Calories	509	Sugars	. . . . .10g
Protein	. . . . .17g	Fat	. . . . .34g
Carbohydrate	. . .36g	Saturates	. . . . . . .9g

 15 mins 45 mins

SERVES 4

INGREDIENTS

CREPES

generous ¾ cup all-purpose flour

pinch of salt

1 egg, lightly beaten

1¼ cups milk

vegetable oil, for frying

FILLING

2 tbsp vegetable oil

1 leek, shredded

½ tsp chili powder

½ tsp ground cumin

2 oz/55 g snow peas

3½ oz/100 g white mushrooms,

1 red bell pepper, deseeded and sliced

4 tbsp cashew nuts, chopped

SAUCE

2 tbsp margarine

3 tbsp all-purpose flour

⅔ cup vegetable stock

⅔ cup milk

1 tsp Dijon mustard

¾ cup grated Cheddar cheese

2 tbsp chopped fresh cilantro

1 For the crêpes, sift the flour and salt into a bowl. Beat in the egg and milk to make a batter.

2 For the filling, heat the oil and cook the leek for 2–3 minutes. Add the remaining ingredients and cook, stirring constantly, for 5 minutes.

3 For the sauce, melt the margarine and add the flour. Cook, stirring, for 1 minute. Remove from the heat, stir in the stock and milk, and return to the heat. Bring to a boil, stirring until thickened.

Stir in the mustard, half the cheese, and the cilantro and cook for 1 minute.

4 Heat 1 tablespoon of oil in a small skillet. Pour off the oil and add about 2½ tablespoons of the batter. Tilt to cover the base. Cook for 2 minutes, turn, and cook the other side for 1 minute. Repeat with the remaining batter. Spoon a little of the filling along the center of each crêpe and roll up. Place in a flameproof dish and pour the sauce on top. Top with cheese and heat under a hot broiler for 3–5 minutes or until the cheese melts.

Eggplant Rolls

Thin slices of eggplant are fried in olive oil and garlic, and then topped with pesto sauce and finely grated mozzarella cheese.

NUTRITIONAL INFORMATION

Calories	278	Sugars	.........2g
Protein	.........4g	Fat	..........28g
Carbohydrate	....2g	Saturates	.......7g

15-20 mins   20 mins

SERVES 4

INGREDIENTS

2 eggplants, thinly sliced lengthwise

5 tbsp olive oil, plus extra
  for brushing

1 garlic clove, crushed

4 tbsp pesto

1½ cups grated mozzarella cheese

fresh basil leaves, torn into pieces

salt and pepper

fresh basil leaves, to garnish

1 Place the eggplant slices in slices in a colander or on a plate and sprinkle liberally with salt. Set aside for 10–15 minutes to extract the bitter juices. Turn the slices over and repeat. Rinse thoroughly under cold running water and drain on paper towels.

2 Heat the olive oil in a large skillet and add the garlic. Add the eggplant slices, a few at a time, and fry lightly on both sides over medium heat. Drain them on paper towels.

3 Spread the pesto on 1 side of the eggplant slices. Top with the grated mozzarella and sprinkle with the torn basil leaves. Season to taste with salt and pepper. Roll up the slices and secure with wooden toothpicks.

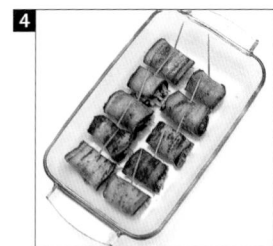

4 Lightly brush a casserole with a little olive oil and arrange the eggplant rolls in it. Place in a preheated oven, 350°F/180°C, and bake for 8–10 minutes.

5 Transfer the eggplant rolls to a warmed serving plate. Sprinkle with fresh basil leaves and serve immediately.

COOK'S TIP
Most eggplants produced commercially these days do not have bitter juices that must be removed before cooking. Nevertheless, salting is a good idea if the eggplants are to be fried, because it prevents them from absorbing too much oil.

Mushroom Tarts

Different varieties of mushrooms are becoming more widely available in supermarkets, so use this recipe to make the most of them.

NUTRITIONAL INFORMATION

Calories ....494 Sugars 2g
Protein ....9g Fat 35g
Carbohydrate ...38g Saturates 18g

15 mins   20 mins

SERVES 4

INGREDIENTS

1 lb 2 oz/500 g phyllo pastry, thawed if frozen

½ cup butter, melted

1 tbsp hazelnut oil

4 tbsp pine nuts

12 oz/350 g mixed mushrooms, such as white, crimini, oyster, and shiitake

2 tsp chopped fresh parsley

8 oz/225 g soft goat cheese

salt and pepper

fresh parsley sprigs to garnish

lettuce, tomatoes, cucumber, and scallions, to serve

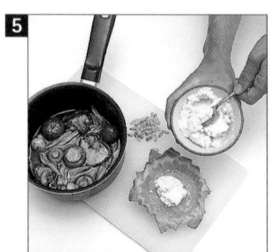

1 Cut the sheets of phyllo pastry into 4 inch/10 cm squares and line 4 individual tart pans, brushing each layer with melted butter. Line the pans with baking parchment and baking beans. Bake in a preheated oven, 400°F/200°C, for 6–8 minutes until golden.

2 Remove the tarts from the oven and carefully take out the foil or baking parchment and baking beans. Reduce the oven temperature to 350°F/180°C.

3 Put any remaining butter into a large pan with the hazelnut oil and fry the pine nuts until golden brown. Remove from the pan and drain on paper towels.

4 Add the mushrooms to the pan and cook gently, stirring frequently, for about 4–5 minutes. Add the parsley and season to taste with salt and pepper.

5 Spoon one-quarter of the goat cheese into the base of each cooked phyllo tart. Divide the mushrooms equally among them and sprinkle the pine nuts evenly over the top.

6 Return the tarts to the oven for about 5 minutes to heat through and then serve them, garnished with sprigs of parsley. Serve with lettuce, tomatoes, cucumber, and scallions.

Almond & Sesame Roast

Toasted almonds are combined with sesame seeds, rice, and vegetables in this tasty roast. Serve it with a delicious onion and mushroom sauce.

NUTRITIONAL INFORMATION

Calories . . . . .612 Sugars 7g
Protein . . . . .22g Fat 46g
Carbohydrate . . .29g Saturates 13g

 30–40 mins   35 mins

SERVES 4

INGREDIENTS

2 tbsp sesame or olive oil

1 small onion, finely chopped

½ cup risotto rice

1¼ cups vegetable stock

1 large carrot, grated

1 large leek, finely chopped

2 tsp sesame seeds, toasted

¾ cup chopped almonds, toasted

½ cup ground almonds

¾ cup grated sharp Cheddar cheese

2 eggs, beaten

1 tsp dried mixed herbs

butter, for greasing

salt and pepper

fresh flat leaf parsley sprigs, to garnish

fresh vegetables, to serve

SAUCE

2 tbsp butter

1 small onion, finely chopped

1½ cups finely chopped mushrooms

4 tbsp all-purpose flour

1¼ cups vegetable stock

1 Heat the oil in a large skillet and cook the onion gently for 2–3 minutes. Add the rice and cook gently for 5–6 minutes, stirring frequently.

2 Add the stock, bring to a boil, lower the heat, and simmer for 15 minutes or until the rice is tender. Add a little extra water if necessary. Remove from the heat and transfer to a large mixing bowl.

3 Add the carrot, leek, sesame seeds, almonds, cheese, beaten eggs, and herbs. Mix well and season with salt and pepper to taste. Transfer the mixture to a greased 1 lb 2 oz/500 g loaf pan, smoothing the surface. Bake in a preheated oven, 350°F/180°C, for 1 hour until set and firm. Let stand in the pan for 10 minutes.

4 To make the sauce, melt the butter in a small pan and cook the onion until dark golden brown. Add the mushrooms and cook for 2 minutes. Stir in the flour, cook gently for 1 minute, then gradually add the stock. Bring to a boil, stirring constantly, until thickened and blended. Season to taste with salt and pepper.

5 Turn out the nut roast, slice, and serve, garnished with parsley sprigs, with fresh vegetables, accompanied by the onion and mushroom sauce.

Nut & Vegetable Stir-Fry

In this colorful stir-fry, vegetables are cooked in a wonderfully aromatic sauce which combines peanuts, chili, coconut, coriander, and turmeric.

NUTRITIONAL INFORMATION

Calories 446   Sugars 17g
Protein . . . . .14g   Fat 25g
Carbohydrate . . .42g   Saturates 5g

10 mins   15 mins

SERVES 4

I N G R E D I E N T S

1 cup unsalted roasted peanuts

2 tsp hot chili sauce

¾ cup coconut milk

2 tbsp soy sauce

1 tbsp ground coriander

pinch of ground turmeric

1 tbsp molasses sugar

3 tbsp sesame oil

3-4 shallots, thinly sliced

1 garlic clove, thinly sliced

1–2 fresh red chiles, deseeded and finely chopped

1 large carrot, cut into fine strips

1 yellow bell pepper, deseeded and sliced

1 red bell pepper, deseeded and sliced

1 zucchini, cut into fine strips

4 oz/115 g sugar-snap peas, trimmed

3 inch/7.5 cm piece of cucumber, cut into strips

9 oz/250 g oyster mushrooms,

9 oz/250 g canned chestnuts, drained

2 tsp grated fresh ginger root

finely grated rind and juice of 1 lime

1 tbsp chopped fresh cilantro

salt and pepper

lime slices, to garnish

1 To make the peanut sauce, grind the peanuts in a blender or chop very finely. Put into a small pan with the hot chili sauce, coconut milk, soy sauce, ground coriander, ground turmeric, and molasses sugar. Set over low heat and simmer gently for 3–4 minutes. Keep warm and set aside until required.

2 Heat the sesame oil in a wok or large, heavy skillet. Add the shallots, garlic, and chiles and stir-fry over medium heat for 2 minutes.

3 Add the carrot, bell peppers, zucchini, and sugar-snap peas to the wok or pan and stir-fry for 2 more minutes.

4 Add the cucumber, mushrooms, chestnuts, ginger, lime rind and juice, and fresh cilantro and stir-fry briskly for about 5 minutes or until the vegetables are crisp, yet still crunchy. Season to taste with salt and pepper.

5 Divide the stir-fry among 4 warmed serving plates and garnish with slices of lime. Transfer the peanut sauce to a serving bowl and serve immediately with the vegetables.

Creamy Baked Fennel

Fennel tastes fabulous in this creamy sauce, flavored with caraway seeds. A crunchy bread crumb topping gives an interesting texture.

NUTRITIONAL INFORMATION

Calories . . . . . . .292 Sugars 5g
Protein . . . . .10g Fat 23g
Carbohydrate . . .12g Saturates 14g

🧈 10 mins 🕐 45 mins

SERVES 4

INGREDIENTS

2 tbsp lemon juice

2 fennel bulbs, thinly sliced

4 tbsp butter, plus extra for greasing

½ cup low-fat soft cheese

⅔ cup light cream

⅔ cup milk

1 egg, lightly beaten

2 tsp caraway seeds

1 cup fresh white bread crumbs

salt and pepper

fresh parsley sprigs, to garnish

1 Bring a pan of water to a boil and add the lemon juice and fennel. Cook for 2–3 minutes to blanch, drain well, and place in a greased casserole.

2 Beat the soft cheese in a bowl until smooth. Add the cream, milk, and beaten egg, and beat until combined. Season to taste with salt and pepper and pour the mixture over the fennel.

3 Melt 1 tablespoon of the butter in a small skillet and fry the caraway seeds over low heat, stirring constantly, for 1–2 minutes until they release their aroma. Sprinkle them over the fennel.

4 Melt the remaining butter in a skillet. Add the bread crumbs and fry over low heat, stirring frequently, until lightly browned. Sprinkle them evenly over the top of the fennel.

5 Place in a preheated oven, 350°F/180°C, and bake for 25–30 minutes or until the fennel is tender. Serve immediately, garnished with sprigs of fresh parsley.

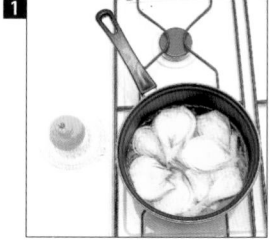

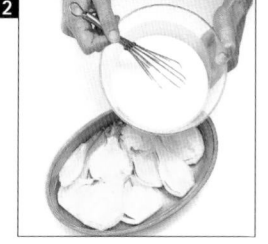

Feta Cheese Patties

Grated carrots, zucchini, and feta cheese are combined with cumin seeds, poppy seeds, curry powder, and chopped fresh parsley.

NUTRITIONAL INFORMATION

Calories 217   Sugars 6g
Protein . . . . .6g   Fat 16g
Carbohydrate . . .12g   Saturates 7g

 15 mins   20 mins

SERVES 4

INGREDIENTS

2 large carrots

1 large zucchini

1 small onion

2 oz /55 g feta cheese

4 tbsp all-purpose flour

¼ tsp cumin seeds

½ tsp poppy seeds

1 tsp medium curry powder

1 tbsp chopped fresh parsley

1 egg, beaten

2 tbsp butter

2 tbsp vegetable oil

salt and pepper

fresh herb sprigs, to garnish

1 Grate the carrots, zucchini, onion, and feta cheese coarsely, either by hand or process in a food processor.

2 Combine the flour, cumin seeds, poppy seeds, curry powder, and parsley in a large bowl. Season to taste with salt and pepper.

3 Add the carrot mixture to the seasoned flour, tossing well to combine. Stir in the beaten egg.

4 Heat the butter and oil in a large, heavy skillet. Place heaped tablespoonfuls of the carrot mixture in the skillet, flattening them slightly with the back of the spoon. Cook over low heat for about 2 minutes on each side until crisp and golden brown. Drain on paper towels and keep warm. Cook more patties in the same way until all the mixture is used.

5 Serve immediately, garnished with sprigs of fresh herbs.

Filled Baked Potatoes

Cook these potatoes conventionally, wrap them in foil, and keep them warm at the edge of the barbecue, ready to fill with inspired mixtures.

NUTRITIONAL INFORMATION

Calories	564	Sugars	........14g
Protein	........21g	Fat	..........29g
Carbohydrate	...58g	Saturates	......18g

 15 mins   1 hr 5 mins

SERVES 4

I N G R E D I E N T S

4 large or 8 medium baked potatoes

paprika or chili powder, or chopped fresh
  herbs, to garnish

M E X I C A N   R E L I S H

8 oz/225 g can corn, drained

½ red bell pepper, deseeded and chopped

2 inch/5 cm piece of cucumber,
  finely chopped

½ tsp chili powder

salt and pepper

C H E E S E   &   C H I V E S

½ cup full-fat soft cheese

½ cup plain yogurt

4 oz/115 g blue cheese, cut into cubes

1 celery stalk, finely chopped

2 tsp chopped fresh chives

celery salt and pepper

S P I C Y   M U S H R O O M S

2 tbsp butter or margarine

8 oz/225 g white mushrooms

⅔ cup plain yogurt

1 tbsp tomato paste

2 tsp mild curry powder

salt and pepper

1 Scrub the potatoes and prick them with a fork. Bake in a preheated oven, 400°F/200°C, for about 1 hour until they are just tender.

2 To make the Mexican relish, put half the corn into a bowl. Process the remainder in a blender or food processor for 10–15 seconds. Alternatively, chop and mash roughly by hand. Add the puréed corn to the corn kernels with the bell pepper, cucumber, and chili powder. Season to taste with salt and pepper.

3 To make the cheese & chives filling, combine the soft cheese and yogurt until smooth. Add the blue cheese, celery, and chives. Season to taste with celery salt and pepper.

4 To make the spicy mushrooms, melt the butter or margarine in a small skillet. Add the mushrooms and cook gently for 3–4 minutes. Remove from the heat and stir in the yogurt, tomato paste, and curry powder. Season to taste with salt and pepper.

5 Wrap the cooked potatoes in foil and keep warm at the edge of the barbecue. Serve the fillings sprinkled with paprika or chili powder or herbs.

Cheeseburgers in Buns

Ground soy and seasonings combine to make these tasty vegetarian burgers, which are topped with cheese.

NUTRITIONAL INFORMATION

Calories 551	Sugars 4g
Protein 29g	Fat 24g
Carbohydrate . . .57g	Saturates 5g

1¼ hrs   10 mins

SERVES 4

INGREDIENTS

5½ oz/150 g dehydrated ground soy

1¼ cups vegetable stock

1 small onion, finely chopped

1 cup all-purpose flour

1 egg, beaten

1 tbsp chopped fresh herbs

1 tbsp mushroom ketchup or soy sauce

2 tbsp vegetable oil

4 burger buns

4 cheese slices

salt and pepper

BARBECUE SAUCE

2 tbsp tomato ketchup

3 tbsp sweet relish

1 tbsp Worcestershire sauce

2 tsp Dijon mustard

1 tbsp white wine vinegar

2 tbsp fruity brown sauce

TO GARNISH

dill pickles

tomato slices

TO SERVE

lettuce, cucumber, and scallion salad

1 Put the ground soy into a large bowl. Pour in the vegetable stock and set aside to soak for about 15 minutes until it has been absorbed.

2 Meanwhile, make the barbecue sauce. Combine the tomato ketchup, relish, Worcestershire sauce, and mustard. Stir in the vinegar and fruity brown sauce, then cover, and chill until required.

3 Add the onion, flour, beaten egg, and chopped herbs to the soy and mix thoroughly. Stir in the mushroom ketchup or soy sauce and season to taste with salt and pepper, stirring to mix again.

4 Form the mixture into 8 burgers. Cover and chill until ready to cook.

5 Brush the burgers with oil and grill over hot coals, turning once. Allow about 5 minutes on each side. Alternatively, cook under a preheated broiler.

6 Split the buns and top with a burger. Lay a cheese slice on top and garnish with barbecue sauce, dill pickle, and tomato slices. Serve with a salad made with lettuce, scallions, and sliced cucumber.

Marinated Brochettes

These beancurd and mushroom brochettes are marinated in a lemon, garlic, and herb mixture so that they soak up a delicious flavor.

NUTRITIONAL INFORMATION

Calories .... 192 Sugars 0.5g
Protein .... 11g Fat 16g
Carbohydrate .... 1g Saturates 2g

2¼ hrs   6 mins

SERVES 4

INGREDIENTS

1 lemon

1 garlic clove, crushed

4 tbsp olive oil

4 tbsp white wine vinegar

1 tbsp chopped fresh herbs, such as rosemary, parsley, and thyme

10½ oz/300 g smoked tofu

12 oz/350 g mushrooms

salt and pepper

fresh herbs, to garnish

TO SERVE

mixed salad greens

cherry tomatoes, halved

1 Finely grate the rind from the lemon and squeeze out the juice.

2 Add the garlic, olive oil, vinegar, and chopped herbs and mix well. Season to taste with salt and pepper.

3 Slice the beancurd into large chunks with a sharp knife. Thread the pieces onto metal or wooden skewers, alternating them with the mushrooms.

4 Place the brochettes in a shallow, nonmetallic dish and pour over the marinade. Cover with plastic wrap and chill in the refrigerator for 1–2 hours, turning the brochettes in the marinade occasionally.

5 Remove the brochettes from the dish, reserving the marinade. Cook on a medium hot barbecue, brushing them frequently with the marinade and turning often, for about 6 minutes until cooked through and golden brown. Alternatively, cook under a preheated broiler, turning them frequently and brushing with the reserved marinade.

6 Transfer to warmed serving plates, garnish with fresh herbs, and serve immediately with mixed salad greens and cherry tomatoes.

Grape Leaf Packets

A wonderful combination of soft cheese, chopped dates, ground almonds, and lightly fried nuts is encased in grape leaves.

NUTRITIONAL INFORMATION

Calories	459	Sugars	.........8g
Protein	........12g	Fat	..........42g
Carbohydrate	....9g	Saturates	......20g

 25 mins   15 mins

SERVES 4

I N G R E D I E N T S

1¼ cups full-fat soft cheese

½ cup ground almonds

2 tbsp chopped pitted dates

2 tbsp butter

4 tbsp sliced almonds

12–16 grape leaves

salt and pepper

grilled baby corn, to serve

T O   G A R N I S H

fresh rosemary sprigs

tomato wedges

1 Beat the soft cheese in a large bowl until smooth. Add the ground almonds and chopped dates and mix together thoroughly. Season to taste with salt and pepper.

2 Melt the butter in a small skillet. Add the sliced almonds and cook over a very low heat, stirring constantly, for 2–3 minutes, until golden brown. Remove from the heat and set aside to cool for a few minutes.

3 Mix the sliced almonds into the soft cheese mixture, stirring well to combine thoroughly.

4 Soak the grape leaves in water, if specified on the packet. Drain them, lay them out on a counter and spoon an equal amount of the soft cheese mixture onto each. Fold over the leaves to enclose the filling.

5 Wrap the grape leaf packets in foil, 1 or 2 per foil package. Place over the barbecue to heat through for about 8–10 minutes, turning once. Serve with grilled baby corn and garnish with sprigs of rosemary and tomato wedges.

Turkish Kabobs

A spicy garbanzo bean sauce is served with colorful, grilled vegetable kabobs—perfect for a lunch on a warm summer's day.

NUTRITIONAL INFORMATION

Calories 303	Sugars 13g
Protein 13g	Fat 15g
Carbohydrate . . .30g	Saturates 2g

 15 mins   15 mins

SERVES 4

I N G R E D I E N T S

S A U C E

4 tbsp olive oil

3 garlic cloves, crushed

1 small onion, finely chopped

15 oz/425 g can garbanzo beans, rinsed and drained

1¼ cups natural yogurt

1 tsp ground cumin

½ tsp chili powder

lemon juice

salt and pepper

K A B O B S

1 eggplant

1 red bell pepper, seeded

1 green bell pepper, seeded

4 plum tomatoes

1 lemon, cut into wedges

8 small bay leaves

olive oil, for brushing

1 To make the sauce, heat the olive oil in a small skillet. Add the garlic and chopped onion and cook over medium heat, stirring occasionally, for about 5 minutes, until the onion is softened and has turned golden brown.

2 Put the garbanzo beans and yogurt into a blender or food processor and add the cumin, chili powder, and onion mixture. Process for about 15 seconds until smooth. Alternatively, mash the garbanzo beans with a potato masher and stir in the yogurt, ground cumin, chili powder, and onion mixture.

3 Scrape the puréed mixture into a bowl and season to taste with lemon juice, salt, and pepper. Cover with plastic wrap and chill in the refrigerator until ready to serve.

4 To prepare the kabobs, cut the vegetables into large chunks and thread them onto 4 skewers, placing a bay leaf and lemon wedge at both ends of each kabob.

5 Brush the kabobs with olive oil and cook them on the barbecue, turning frequently, for 5–8 minutes. Alternatively, cook under a preheated broiler. Heat the garbanzo sauce and serve with the kabobs.

 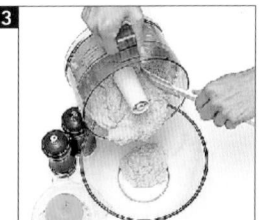 

Barbecued Bean Pot

Cook this tasty vegetable and Quorn casserole conventionally, then keep it piping hot over the barbecue.

NUTRITIONAL INFORMATION

Calories	.381	Sugars	17g
Protein	21g	Fat	19g
Carbohydrate	34g	Saturates	3g

10 mins   1 hr

SERVES 4

INGREDIENTS

¼ cup butter or margarine

1 large onion, chopped

2 garlic cloves, crushed

2 carrots, sliced

2 celery stalks, sliced

1 tbsp paprika

2 tsp ground cumin

14 oz/400 g can chopped tomatoes

15 oz/425 g can mixed beans, rinsed and drained

⅔ cup vegetable stock

1 tbsp molasses sugar or molasses

12 oz/350 g Quorn or soy cubes

salt and pepper

crusty French bread, to serve

VARIATION

If you prefer, cook the casserole in a preheated oven, 375°F/190°C from step 3, but keep the dish covered. Instead of mixed beans you could use just one type of canned beans.

1 Melt the butter or margarine in a large flameproof casserole and cook the onion and garlic over medium heat, stirring occasionally, for about 5 minutes, until golden brown.

2 Add the carrots and celery and cook, stirring occasionally, for a further 2 minutes, then stir in the paprika and ground cumin.

3 Add the tomatoes and beans. Pour in the stock and add the sugar or molasses. Bring to a boil, then reduce the heat and simmer, uncovered, stirring occasionally, for 30 minutes.

4 Add the Quorn or soy cubes to the casserole, cover, and cook, stirring occasionally, for a further 20 minutes.

5 Season to taste with salt and pepper, then transfer the casserole to the barbecue, setting it to one side to keep hot.

6 Ladle onto plates and serve with crusty French bread.

Stuffed Mushrooms

Use large open-cap mushrooms for this recipe for their flavor and suitability for filling.

NUTRITIONAL INFORMATION

Calories 273	Sugars 5g	
Protein 13g	Fat 18g	
Carbohydrate ...15g	Saturates 5g	

15 mins | 25 mins

SERVES 4

INGREDIENTS

8 open-cap mushrooms

1 tbsp olive oil

1 small leek, chopped

1 celery stalk, chopped

3½ oz/100 g firm beancurd, diced

1 zucchini, chopped

1 carrot, chopped

scant 2 cups whole-wheat bread crumbs

2 tbsp chopped fresh basil

1 tbsp tomato paste

2 tbsp pine nuts

¾ cup grated Cheddar cheese

⅔ cup vegetable stock

salt and pepper

salad, to serve

1 Remove the stems from the mushrooms and chop finely. Reserve the caps.

2 Heat the olive oil in a large, heavy skillet over medium heat. Add the chopped mushroom stems, leek, celery, beancurd, zucchini, and carrot and cook, stirring constantly, for 3–4 minutes.

3 Stir in the bread crumbs, chopped basil, tomato paste, and pine nuts. Season with salt and pepper to taste and mix thoroughly.

4 Spoon the mixture into the mushroom caps and top with the grated cheese.

5 Place the mushrooms in a shallow casserole and pour the vegetable stock around them.

6 Cook in a preheated oven, 425°F/220°C, for 20 minutes or until cooked through and the cheese has melted. Remove the mushrooms from the casserole and serve immediately with a salad.

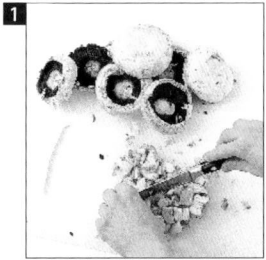

Vegetable Burgers & Fries

These spicy vegetable burgers are delicious, especially in a warm bun or roll and served with light French fries.

NUTRITIONAL INFORMATION

Calories 461	Sugars 4g	
Protein 18g	Fat 17g	
Carbohydrate . . .64g	Saturates 2g	

 45 mins 1 hr

SERVES 4

INGREDIENTS

VEGETABLE BURGERS

3½ oz/100 g spinach

2 tbsp olive oil

1 leek, chopped

2 garlic cloves, crushed

1⅓ cups chopped mushrooms

10½ oz/300 g firm beancurd, chopped

1 tsp chili powder

1 tsp curry powder

1 tbsp chopped fresh cilantro

1½ cups fresh whole-wheat bread crumbs

TO SERVE

burger bap or roll

salad greens

FRENCH FRIES

2 large potatoes

2 tbsp all-purpose flour

1 tsp chili powder

2 tbsp olive oil

1 To make the burgers, cook the spinach in a little boiling water for 2 minutes. Drain thoroughly and pat dry with paper towels.

2 Heat 1 tablespoon of the oil in a skillet and sauté the leek and garlic for 2–3 minutes. Add the remaining ingredients, except the bread crumbs, and cook for 5–7 minutes until the vegetables have softened. Toss in the spinach and cook for 1 minute.

3 Transfer the mixture to a food processor and process for 30 seconds until almost smooth. Transfer to a bowl, stir in the bread crumbs, mixing well, and set aside until cool enough to handle. Using floured hands, form the mixture into 4 equal-size burgers. Chill for 30 minutes.

4 To make the French fries, cut the potatoes into thin wedges and cook in a pan of boiling water for 10 minutes. Drain thoroughly and toss in the flour and chili powder. Lay the fries on a cookie sheet and sprinkle with the oil. Cook in a preheated oven, 400°F/200°C, for 30 minutes or until golden.

5 Meanwhile, heat the remaining oil in a skillet and cook the burgers for 8–10 minutes, turning once. Place in a bap, add some salad greens, and serve with the fries.

Garlic Mushroom Pizza

This pizza dough is flavored with garlic and herbs and topped with mixed mushrooms and melting cheese for a really delicious pizza.

NUTRITIONAL INFORMATION

Calories . . . . .541 Sugars 5g
Protein . . . . .16g Fat 15g
Carbohydrate . . .91g Saturates 6g

 45 mins   30 mins

SERVES 4

I N G R E D I E N T S

D O U G H

4 cups white bread flour, plus extra
   for dusting

2 tsp active dry yeast

2 garlic cloves, crushed

2 tbsp chopped fresh thyme

2 tbsp olive oil, plus extra for brushing

1¼ cups lukewarm water

T O P P I N G

2 tbsp butter or margarine

4¾ cups sliced mixed mushrooms

2 garlic cloves, crushed

2 tbsp chopped fresh parsley, plus extra
   to garnish

2 tbsp tomato paste

6 tbsp sieved tomatoes

¾ cup grated mozzarella cheese

salt and pepper

1 Put the flour, yeast, garlic, and thyme in a bowl. Make a well in the center and gradually stir in the oil and water. Bring together to form a soft dough.

2 Turn the dough onto a floured counter and knead for 5 minutes or until smooth. Roll into a 14 inch/35 cm round. Brush a cookie sheet with a little oil and place the dough base on it. Set aside in a warm place for 20 minutes or until the dough puffs up.

3 Meanwhile, make the topping. Melt the margarine or butter in a skillet and cook the mushrooms, garlic, and parsley over low heat for 5 minutes.

4 Combine the tomato paste and sieved tomatoes and spoon onto the pizza base, leaving a ½ inch/1 cm edge of dough. Spoon the mushroom mixture on top. Season to taste with salt and pepper and sprinkle the cheese on top.

5 Cook the pizza in a preheated oven, 375°F/190°C, for 20–25 minutes or until the base is crisp and the cheese has melted. Garnish with chopped parsley and serve the pizza immediately.

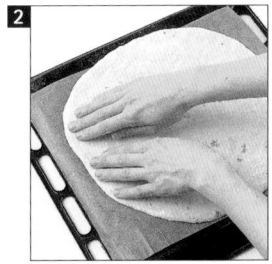

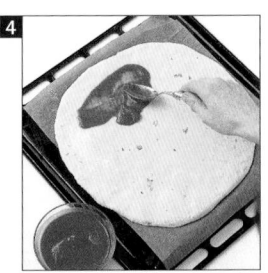

Cress & Cheese Tartlets

These tasty and attractive individual tartlets are great
served hot at lunchtime or cool for picnic food.

NUTRITIONAL INFORMATION

Calories	.410	Sugars	.4g
Protein	15g	Fat	29g
Carbohydrate	.24g	Saturates	.19g

 20 mins   25 mins

SERVES 4

INGREDIENTS

generous ¾ cup all-purpose flour, plus extra
 for dusting

pinch of salt

6 tbsp butter or margarine

2–3 tbsp cold water

2 bunches of watercress

2 garlic cloves, crushed

1 shallot, chopped

1¼ cups grated Cheddar cheese

4 tbsp plain yogurt

½ tsp paprika

1 Sift the flour into a mixing bowl and
add the salt. Rub 2 tablespoons of the
butter or margarine into the flour until the
mixture resembles bread crumbs. Stir in
enough of the cold water to make a
smooth dough.

VARIATION
Use spinach instead of the
watercress, making sure it is well
drained before mixing with the
remaining filling ingredients.

2 Roll the dough out on a lightly
floured counter and use to line
4 x 4 inch/10 cm tartlet pans. Prick the
bottoms with a fork and set aside to chill
in the refrigerator.

3 Heat the remaining butter or
margarine in a skillet. Discard the
stems from the watercress. Add the leaves
to the pan with the garlic and shallot and
cook for 1–2 minutes until wilted.

4 Remove the pan from the heat and
stir in the grated Cheddar cheese,
yogurt, and paprika.

5 Spoon the mixture into the tartlet
shells and cook in a preheated oven,
350°F/180°C, for 20 minutes or until the
filling is just firm. Turn out the tartlets and
serve immediately, if serving hot, or place
on a wire rack to cool, if serving cold.

Stuffed Vegetable Snacks

In this recipe, eggplants are filled with a spicy bulgur and vegetable stuffing for a delicious light meal.

NUTRITIONAL INFORMATION

Calories	360	Sugars	17g
Protein	9g	Fat	16g
Carbohydrate	50g	Saturates	2g

40 mins   30 mins

SERVES 4

INGREDIENTS

4 medium eggplants

1 cup bulgur

1¼ cups boiling water

3 tbsp olive oil

2 garlic cloves, crushed

2 tbsp pine nuts

½ tsp ground turmeric

1 tsp chili powder

2 celery stalks, chopped

4 scallions, chopped

1 carrot, grated

¾ cup chopped white mushrooms

2 tbsp raisins

2 tbsp chopped fresh cilantro

salt

salad greens, to serve

1 Cut the eggplants in half lengthwise and scoop out the flesh with a teaspoon without piercing the "shells." Chop the flesh and set aside. Rub the insides of the eggplants with a little salt and set aside for 20 minutes.

2 Meanwhile, put the bulgur in a large bowl and pour the boiling water over it. Set aside for about 20 minutes or until the bulgur has softened and completely absorbed the water.

3 Heat the oil in a heavy skillet. Add the garlic, pine nuts, turmeric, chili powder, celery, scallions, carrot, mushrooms, and raisins and cook over low heat, stirring occasionally, for about 2–3 minutes.

4 Stir in the reserved eggplant flesh and cook for a further 2–3 minutes. Add the chopped cilantro, mixing well.

5 Remove the skillet from the heat and stir in the bulgur. Rinse the eggplant shells under cold water and pat dry with paper towels.

6 Spoon the bulgur filling into the eggplants and place in a roasting pan. Pour in a little boiling water and cook in a preheated oven, 350°F/180°C, for about 15–20 minutes until piping hot. Remove from the oven, transfer to a warmed serving plate, and serve immediately with salad greens.

Lentil Croquettes

These mildly spiced croquettes are an ideal light
lunch served with a crisp salad and a tahini dip.

NUTRITIONAL INFORMATION

Calories 409	Sugars 5g	
Protein 19g	Fat 17g	
Carbohydrate ...48g	Saturates 2g	

🕝 🕝

🍲 1¼ hrs   🕐 1 hr

SERVES 4

I N G R E D I E N T S

1 cup split red lentils

1 green bell pepper, deseeded and
finely chopped

1 red onion, finely chopped

2 garlic cloves, crushed

1 tsp garam masala

½ tsp chili powder

1 tsp ground cumin

2 tsp lemon juice

2 tbsp chopped unsalted peanuts

2½ cups water

1 egg, beaten

3 tbsp all-purpose flour

1 tsp ground turmeric

1 tsp chili powder

4 tbsp vegetable oil

salt and pepper

salad greens and herbs, to serve

1 Put the lentils in a large pan with the
bell pepper, onion, garlic, garam
masala, chili powder, ground cumin, lemon
juice, and peanuts. Add the water and
bring to a boil. Reduce the heat and
simmer gently, stirring occasionally, for
about 30 minutes or until all the liquid has
been absorbed.

2 Remove the mixture from the heat
and set aside to cool slightly. Beat in
the egg and season to taste with salt and
pepper. Set aside to cool completely.

3 With floured hands, form the mixture
into 8 rectangles or ovals.

4 Combine the flour, turmeric, and chili
powder on a small plate. Roll the
croquettes in the spiced flour mixture to
coat thoroughly.

5 Heat the oil in a large skillet. Add the
croquettes, in batches, and fry,
turning once, for about 10 minutes until
crisp on both sides. Transfer to warmed
serving plates and serve the croquettes
immediately with crisp salad greens and
fresh herbs.

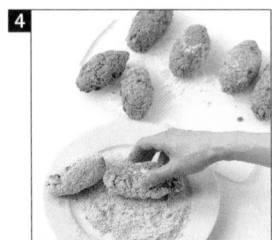

Brown Rice Gratin

This dish is extremely versatile and could be made with any vegetables that you have at hand and basmati rice instead of brown.

NUTRITIONAL INFORMATION

Calories . . . . .321 Sugars 6g
Protein . . . . .10g Fat 18g
Carbohydrate . . .32g Saturates 9g

 15 mins   1 hr

SERVES 4

I N G R E D I E N T S

½ cup brown rice

2 tbsp butter or margarine, plus extra for greasing

1 red onion, chopped

2 garlic cloves, crushed

1 carrot, cut into thin batons

1 zucchini, sliced

¾ cup baby corn cobs, halved lengthwise

2 tbsp sunflower seeds

3 tbsp chopped fresh mixed herbs

1 cup grated mozzarella cheese

2 tbsp whole-wheat bread crumbs

salt and pepper

1 Cook the rice in a pan of lightly salted boiling water for 20 minutes until tender. Drain well.

2 Lightly grease a 3¾ cup casserole with butter.

3 Melt the butter in a skillet. Cook the onion over low heat, stirring constantly, for 2 minutes or until soft.

4 Add the garlic, carrot, zucchini, and baby corn cobs and cook, stirring constantly, for a further 5 minutes until the vegetables are softened.

5 Combine the drained rice with the sunflower seeds and mixed herbs and stir into the skillet. Stir in half of the mozzarella cheese and season with salt and pepper to taste.

6 Spoon the mixture into the prepared casserole and top with the bread crumbs and remaining cheese. Cook in a preheated oven, 350°F/180°C, for about 25–30 minutes or until the cheese has begun to turn golden. Serve immediately.

Green Lentil Pan-Fry

The green lentils used in this recipe require soaking, but are worth it for the flavor. If time is short, use red split lentils that don't need soaking.

NUTRITIONAL INFORMATION

Calories	490	Sugars	........12g
Protein	........26g	Fat	..........18g
Carbohydrates	...61g	Saturates	.......8g

 30 mins   45 mins

SERVES 4

INGREDIENTS

¾ cup green lentils

4 tbsp butter or
   vegetarian margarine

2 garlic cloves, crushed

2 tbsp olive oil

1 tbsp apple vinegar

1 red onion, cut into 8 pieces

½ cup baby corn cobs, halved lengthwise

1 yellow bell pepper, deseeded and cut
   into strips

1 red bell pepper, deseeded and cut
   into strips

2 oz/55 g green beans, halved

½ cup vegetable stock

2 tbsp honey

salt and pepper

crusty bread, to serve

1 Soak the lentils in a large saucepan of cold water for 25 minutes. Bring to a boil, reduce the heat, and simmer for 20 minutes. Drain thoroughly.

2 Add 1 tablespoon of the butter or vegetarian margarine, 1 garlic clove, 1 tablespoon of oil, and the vinegar to the lentils and mix well.

3 Heat the remaining butter or margarine and oil in a skillet and stir-fry the remaining garlic, the onion, corn cobs, bell peppers, and green beans for 3–4 minutes.

4 Add the vegetable stock and bring to a boil. Simmer for about 10 minutes or until the liquid has evaporated.

5 Add the honey and season to taste. Stir in the lentil mixture and cook for 1 minute. Spoon onto warmed serving plates and serve with crusty bread.

VARIATION

This pan-fry is very versatile— you can use a mixture of your favorite vegetables, if you prefer. Try zucchini, carrots, or snow peas.

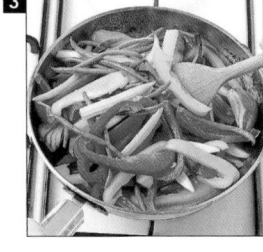

Cashew Nut Paella

Paella traditionally contains chicken and fish, but this recipe is packed with vegetables and nuts for a truly delicious and simple vegetarian dish.

NUTRITIONAL INFORMATION

Calories ....406 Sugars 8g
Protein ....10g Fat 22g
Carbohydrate ...44g Saturates 6g

 15 mins ⏱ 35 mins

SERVES 4

INGREDIENTS

2 tbsp olive oil

1 tbsp butter

1 red onion, chopped

⅔ cup risotto rice

1 tsp ground turmeric

1 tsp ground cumin

½ tsp chili powder

3 garlic cloves, crushed

1 fresh green chile, deseeded and sliced

1 green bell pepper, deseeded and diced

1 red bell pepper, deseeded and diced

¾ cup baby corn cobs,
    halved lengthwise

2 tbsp pitted black olives

1 large tomato, deseeded and diced

2 cups vegetable stock

¾ cup unsalted cashew nuts

½ cup frozen peas

2 tbsp chopped fresh parsley

pinch of cayenne pepper

salt and pepper

fresh herbs, to garnish

1 Heat the olive oil and butter in a large skillet or paella pan until the butter has melted.

2 Add the onion and cook over medium heat, stirring constantly, for about 2–3 minutes until softened.

3 Stir in the rice, turmeric, cumin, chili powder, garlic, sliced chile, green and red bell peppers, corn cobs, olives, and tomato and cook over medium heat, stirring occasionally, for 1–2 minutes.

4 Pour in the stock and bring the mixture to a boil. Reduce the heat and cook gently, stirring constantly, for 20 minutes.

5 Add the cashew nuts and peas and cook, stirring occasionally, for a further 5 minutes. Season to taste with salt and pepper and sprinkle with parsley and cayenne pepper. Transfer to warm serving plates, garnish with fresh herbs, and serve immediately.

Lentil & Rice Casserole

This is a really hearty dish, perfect for cold days when a filling hot dish is just what you need to keep the winter out.

NUTRITIONAL INFORMATION

Calories 312	Sugars 9g
Protein 20g	Fat 2g
Carbohydrate . . .51g	Saturates 0.4g

 15 mins 40 mins

SERVES 4

INGREDIENTS

1 cup split red lentils

generous ¼ cup long grain rice

5 cups vegetable stock

1 leek, cut into chunks

3 garlic cloves, crushed

14 oz/400 g can chopped tomatoes

1 tsp ground cumin

1 tsp chili powder

1 tsp garam masala

1 red bell pepper, deseeded and sliced

3½ oz/100 g small broccoli florets

8 baby corn cobs, halved lengthwise

2 oz/55 g green beans, halved

1 tbsp shredded fresh basil

salt and pepper

fresh basil sprigs, to garnish

VARIATION
You can vary the rice
in this recipe—use brown
or wild rice, if you prefer.

1 Place the lentils, rice, and vegetable stock in a large flameproof casserole and cook over low heat, stirring occasionally, for 20 minutes.

2 Add the leek, garlic, tomatoes and their can juice, ground cumin, chili powder, garam masala, sliced bell pepper, broccoli, corn cobs, and green beans to the casserole.

3 Bring the mixture to a boil, reduce the heat, cover, and simmer for a further 10–15 minutes or until all the vegetables are tender.

4 Add the shredded basil and season with salt and pepper to taste.

5 Garnish with fresh basil sprigs and serve immediately.

Vegetable Chop Suey

Make sure that the vegetables are all cut into pieces of a similar size in this recipe, so that they cook within the same amount of time.

NUTRITIONAL INFORMATION

Calories 155	Sugars 6g
Protein 4g	Fat 12g
Carbohydrate 9g	Saturates 2g

5 mins   5 mins

SERVES 4

INGREDIENTS

1 yellow bell pepper, deseeded

1 red bell pepper, deseeded

1 carrot

1 zucchini

1 fennel bulb

1 onion

2 oz/55 g snow peas

2 tbsp peanut oil

3 garlic cloves, crushed

1 tsp grated fresh ginger root

2 cups bean sprouts

2 tsp brown sugar

2 tbsp light soy sauce

½ cup vegetable stock

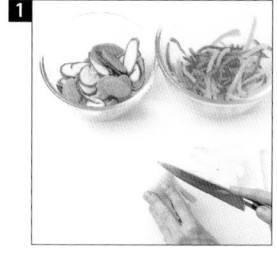
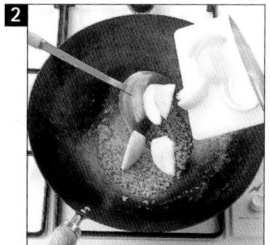
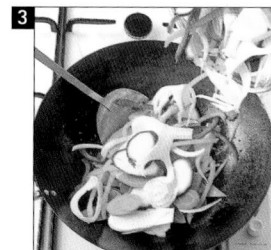

1 Cut the bell peppers, carrot, zucchini, and fennel into thin slices. Cut the onion into quarters and then cut each quarter in half. Slice the snow peas on the diagonal to create maximum surface area.

2 Heat the oil in a preheated wok, add the garlic and ginger, and stir-fry for 30 seconds. Add the onion and stir-fry for a further 30 seconds.

3 Add the bell peppers, carrot, zucchini, fennel, and snow peas to the wok and stir-fry for 2 minutes.

4 Add the bean sprouts to the wok and stir in the sugar, soy sauce, and stock. Reduce the heat to low and simmer for 1–2 minutes until the vegetables are tender and coated in the sauce.

5 Transfer the vegetables and sauce to a serving dish and serve immediately.

VARIATION

Use any combination of colorful vegetables that you have at hand to make this versatile dish.

Cauliflower & Broccoli Tart

This really is a tasty tart, the pie shell for which may be made in advance and frozen until required.

NUTRITIONAL INFORMATION

Calories 252	Sugars 3g	
Protein 7g	Fat 16g	
Carbohydrate ...22g	Saturates 5g	

15 mins   50 mins

SERVES 4

INGREDIENTS

PASTRY

1½ cups all-purpose flour, plus extra for dusting

pinch of salt

½ tsp paprika

1 tsp dried thyme

6 tbsp margarine

3 tbsp water

FILLING

3½ oz/100 g cauliflower florets

3½ oz/100 g broccoli florets

1 onion, cut into 8 wedges

2 tbsp butter or margarine

1 tbsp all-purpose flour

6 tbsp vegetable stock

½ cup milk

¾ cup grated Cheddar cheese

salt and pepper

paprika, to garnish

1 To make the dough, sift the flour and salt into a bowl. Add the paprika and thyme and rub in the margarine. Stir in the water and bind to form a dough.

2 Roll out on a floured counter and line a 7 inch/18 cm loose-bottomed quiche pan. Prick the base and line with baking parchment. Fill with baking beans and bake in a preheated oven, 375°F/190°C, for 15 minutes. Remove the parchment and beans and return the pie shell to the oven for 5 minutes.

3 To make the filling, cook the vegetables in a pan of lightly salted boiling water for 10–12 minutes until tender. Drain and reserve.

4 Melt the butter in a pan. Add the flour and cook, stirring constantly, for 1 minute. Remove from the heat, stir in the stock and milk, and return to the heat. Bring to a boil, stirring constantly, and add ½ cup of the cheese. Season to taste with salt and pepper.

5 Spoon the cauliflower, broccoli, and onion into the pie shell. Pour over the sauce and sprinkle with the remaining grated cheese. Return the pie to the oven for 10 minutes until the cheese is golden and bubbling. Garnish with paprika and serve immediately.

Macaroni Cheese & Tomato

This is a really simple, family dish which is inexpensive and easy to prepare and cook. Serve with a salad or fresh green vegetables.

NUTRITIONAL INFORMATION

Calories	592	Sugars	.........6g
Protein	........28g	Fat	..........29g
Carbohydrate	...57g	Saturates	......17g

 15 mins   35–40 mins

SERVES 4

INGREDIENTS

2 cups dried elbow-macaroni

1½ cups grated Cheddar cheese

generous 1 cup grated Parmesan cheese

1 tbsp butter or margarine, plus extra
for greasing

4 tbsp fresh white bread crumbs

1 tbsp chopped fresh basil

TOMATO SAUCE

1 tbsp olive oil

1 shallot, finely chopped

2 garlic cloves, crushed

1 lb 2 oz/500 g canned chopped tomatoes

1 tbsp chopped fresh basil

salt and pepper

1 To make the tomato sauce, heat the oil in a heavy pan. Add the shallots and garlic and cook, stirring constantly, for 1 minute. Add the tomatoes and basil and season with salt and pepper to taste. Cook over medium heat, stirring constantly, for 10 minutes.

2 Meanwhile, bring a large pan of lightly salted water to a boil. Add the macaroni, bring back to a boil, and cook for 8 minutes or until tender, but still firm to the bite. Drain well.

3 Combine the grated Cheddar and Parmesan in a bowl. Grease a deep, casserole. Spoon one-third of the tomato sauce into the bottom of the dish, cover with one-third of the macaroni, and then top with one-third of the mixed cheeses. Season to taste with salt and pepper. Repeat these layers twice, ending with a layer of grated cheese.

4 Combine the bread crumbs and basil and sprinkle evenly over the top. Dot the topping with the butter or margarine and cook in a preheated oven, 375°F/190°C, for 25 minutes or until the the topping is golden brown and bubbling. Serve immediately.

Winter Vegetable Casserole

This hearty supper dish is best served with plenty of warm crusty bread to mop up the delicious juices.

NUTRITIONAL INFORMATION

Calories	211	Sugars	.........6g
Protein	........11g	Fat	...........6g
Carbohydrate	...26g	Saturates	.....0.8g

10 mins   40 mins

SERVES 4

INGREDIENTS

1 tbsp olive oil

1 red onion, halved and sliced

3 garlic cloves, crushed

8 oz/225 g spinach

1 fennel bulb, cut into 8 wedges

1 red bell pepper, deseeded and diced

1 tbsp all-purpose flour

2 cups vegetable stock

6 tbsp dry white wine

14 oz/400 g can garbanzo beans, drained

1 bay leaf

1 tsp ground coriander

½ tsp paprika

salt and pepper

fennel fronds, to garnish

COOK'S TIP
Use other canned mixed beans instead of the garbanzo beans, if you prefer.

1 Heat the olive oil in a large flameproof casserole. Add the onion and garlic and cook over low heat, stirring frequently, for 1 minute. Add the spinach and cook, stirring occasionally, for 4 minutes or until wilted.

2 Add the fennel and red bell pepper and cook, stirring, for 2 minutes.

3 Stir in the flour and cook, stirring constantly, for 1 minute.

4 Add the stock, wine, garbanzo beans, bay leaf, ground coriander, and paprika, cover, and simmer for 30 minutes. Season to taste with salt and pepper, garnish with fennel fronds, and serve immediately straight from the casserole.

Sweet & Sour Beancurd

Sweet-and-sour sauce was one of the first Chinese sauces introduced to Western diets, and remains one of the most popular.

NUTRITIONAL INFORMATION

Calories 205   Sugars 12g
Protein ....11g   Fat 11g
Carbohydrate ...17g   Saturates 1g

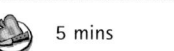   5 mins   10 mins

SERVES 4

INGREDIENTS

2 celery stalks

1 carrot

1 green bell pepper, deseeded

3 oz/85 g snow peas

2 tbsp vegetable oil

2 garlic cloves, crushed

8 baby corn cobs

2 cups bean sprouts

1 lb/450 g firm beancurd, cubed

rice or noodles, to serve

SAUCE

2 tbsp brown sugar

2 tbsp wine vinegar

1 cup vegetable stock

1 tsp tomato paste

1 tbsp cornstarch

1 Using a sharp knife, thinly slice the celery, cut the carrot into thin strips, dice the bell pepper, and cut the snow peas in half diagonally.

2 Heat the vegetable oil in a preheated wok until it is almost smoking. Reduce the heat slightly, add the crushed garlic, celery, carrot, bell pepper, snow peas, and baby corn cobs, and stir-fry for 3–4 minutes.

3 Add the bean sprouts and beancurd to the wok and cook for 2 minutes, stirring frequently.

4 To make the sauce, combine the sugar, wine vinegar, stock, tomato paste, and cornstarch, stirring well to mix. Stir into the wok, bring to a boil, and cook, stirring constantly, until the sauce thickens and clears. Continue to cook for 1 minute. Serve with rice or noodles.

COOK'S TIP

Be careful not to break up the beancurd cubes when stirring.

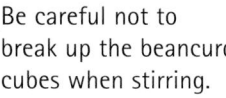

  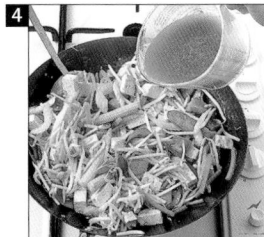

Potato & Lemon Casserole

This is based on a Moroccan dish in which potatoes are spiced with coriander and cumin and cooked in a lemon sauce.

NUTRITIONAL INFORMATION

Calories	338	Sugars	.........8g
Protein	.........5g	Fat	..........23g
Carbohydrate	...29g	Saturates	.......2g

 15 mins 35 mins

SERVES 4

I N G R E D I E N T S

scant ½ cup olive oil

2 red onions, cut into 8 wedges

3 garlic cloves, crushed

2 tsp ground cumin

2 tsp ground coriander

pinch of cayenne pepper

1 carrot, thickly sliced

2 small turnips, quartered

1 zucchini, sliced

1 lb 2 oz/500 g potatoes, thickly sliced

juice and rind of 2 large lemons

1¼ cups vegetable stock

2 tbsp chopped fresh cilantro

salt and pepper

COOK'S TIP

Check the vegetables while they are cooking, because they may begin to stick to the pan. Add a little more boiling water or stock if necessary.

1 Heat the olive oil in a flameproof casserole. Add the onion and sauté over medium heat, stirring frequently, for 3 minutes.

2 Add the garlic and cook for 30 seconds. Stir in the cumin, ground coriander, and cayenne and cook, stirring constantly, for 1 minute.

3 Add the carrot, turnips, zucchini, and potatoes and stir to coat in the oil.

4 Add the lemon juice and rind and the vegetable stock. Season to taste with salt and pepper. Cover and cook over medium heat, stirring occasionally, for 20–30 minutes until tender.

5 Remove the lid, sprinkle in the chopped fresh cilantro and stir well. Serve immediately.

Vegetable Cannelloni

This dish is made with prepared cannelloni tubes, but may also be made by rolling ready-bought lasagna sheets.

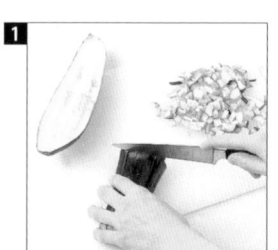

NUTRITIONAL INFORMATION

Calories 594   Sugars 12g
Protein ....13g   Fat 38g
Carbohydrate ...52g   Saturates 7g

 10 mins   45 mins

SERVES 4

INGREDIENTS

1 eggplant

½ cup olive oil

8 oz/225 g spinach

2 garlic cloves, crushed

1 tsp ground cumin

1¼ cups chopped mushrooms

12 cannelloni tubes

salt and pepper

TOMATO SAUCE

1 tbsp olive oil

1 onion, chopped

2 garlic cloves, crushed

2 x 14 oz/400 g cans chopped tomatoes

1 tsp superfine sugar

2 tbsp chopped fresh basil

2 oz/55 g sliced mozzarella

1 Cut the eggplant into small dice. Heat the oil in a skillet. Add the eggplant and cook over moderate heat, stirring frequently, for 2–3 minutes.

2 Add the spinach, garlic, cumin, and mushrooms and reduce the heat. Season to taste with salt and pepper and cook, stirring constantly, for 2–3 minutes. Spoon the mixture into the cannelloni tubes and arrange in a casserole in a single layer.

3 To make the sauce, heat the olive oil in a pan and cook the onion and garlic for 1 minute. Add the tomatoes, sugar, and basil and bring to a boil. Reduce the heat and simmer gently for about 5 minutes. Spoon the sauce over the cannelloni tubes.

4 Arrange the sliced mozzarella on top of the sauce and cook in a preheated oven, 375°F/190°C, for about 30 minutes or until the cheese is bubbling and golden brown. Serve immediately.

Cauliflower Bake

The red of the tomatoes is a great contrast to the cauliflower and herbs, making this dish appealing to both the eye and the palate.

NUTRITIONAL INFORMATION

Calories	305	Sugars	.........9g
Protein	........15g	Fat	..........14g
Carbohydrate	...31g	Saturates	.......6g

10 mins 40 mins

SERVES 4

INGREDIENTS

1 lb 2 oz/500 g cauliflower, broken into florets

1 lb 5 oz/600 g potatoes, cubed

4 oz/115 g cherry tomatoes

SAUCE

2 tbsp butter or margarine

1 leek, sliced

1 garlic clove, crushed

3 tbsp all-purpose flour

1¼ cups milk

¾ cup grated mixed cheese, such as Cheddar, Parmesan, and Swiss

½ tsp paprika

2 tbsp chopped fresh flat leaf parsley

salt and pepper

chopped fresh parsley, to garnish

1 Cook the cauliflower in a pan of boiling water for 10 minutes. Drain well and reserve. Meanwhile, cook the potatoes in another pan of boiling water for 10 minutes, drain and reserve.

2 To make the sauce, melt the butter or margarine in a pan and sauté the leek and garlic for 1 minute. Stir in the flour and cook, stirring constantly, for 1 minute. Remove the pan from the heat and gradually stir in the milk, ½ cup of the grated cheese, the paprika, and flat leaf parsley. Return the pan to the heat and bring to a boil, stirring constantly. Season with salt and pepper to taste.

3 Spoon the cauliflower into a deep casserole. Add the cherry tomatoes and top with the potatoes. Pour the sauce over the potatoes and sprinkle on the remaining cheese.

4 Cook in a preheated oven, 350°F/ 180°C, for 20 minutes or until the vegetables are cooked through and the cheese is golden brown and bubbling. Garnish and serve immediately.

VARIATION

This dish could be made with broccoli instead of the cauliflower as an alternative.

Artichoke & Cheese Tart

Artichoke hearts are delicious to eat and are delicate in flavor and appearance. They are ideal for cooking in a cheese-flavored pie shell.

NUTRITIONAL INFORMATION

Calories . . . . . . .276 Sugars 3g
Protein . . . . .10g Fat 19g
Carbohydrate . . .18g Saturates 10g

🥘 15 mins   🕐 30 mins

SERVES 8

I N G R E D I E N T S

1½ cups all-purpose whole-wheat flour, plus extra for dusting

2 garlic cloves, crushed

6 tbsp butter or margarine

3 tbsp water

salt and pepper

FILLING

2 tbsp olive oil

1 red onion, halved and sliced

10 canned or fresh artichoke hearts

scant 1 cup grated Cheddar cheese

½ cup crumbled Gorgonzola cheese

2 eggs, beaten

1 tbsp chopped fresh rosemary

⅔ cup milk

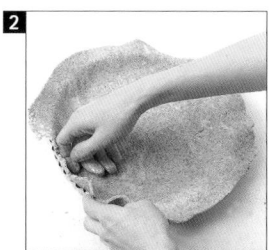  

1 To make the dough, sift the flour into a mixing bowl, add a pinch of salt and the garlic. Rub in the butter or margarine with the fingertips until the mixture resembles bread crumbs. Stir in the water and bring the mixture together to form a dough.

2 Roll out the dough on a lightly floured counter to fit an 8 inch/20 cm quiche pan. Prick the dough with a fork.

3 Heat the oil in a skillet. Add the onion and cook over medium heat, stirring occasionally, for 3 minutes. Add the artichoke hearts and cook, stirring frequently, for a further 2 minutes.

4 Combine the Cheddar, Gorgonzola, beaten eggs, rosemary, and milk in a large bowl. Remove the artichoke and onion mixture from the pan with a draining spoon and transfer to the cheese mixture, stirring gently. Season to taste with salt and pepper.

5 Spoon the artichoke and cheese mixture into the pie shell and cook in a preheated oven, 400°F200°C, for 25 minutes or until cooked and set. Serve the tart hot or cold.

Summertime Tagliatelle

This is a really fresh-tasting dish, made with zucchini and cream, which is ideal with a crisp white wine and some crusty bread.

NUTRITIONAL INFORMATION

Calories	502	Sugars	.........5g
Protein	........16g	Fat	..........30g
Carbohydrate	...44g	Saturates	.......9g

10 mins | 20 mins

SERVES 4

INGREDIENTS

1 lb 7 oz/650 g zucchini

6 tbsp olive oil

3 garlic cloves, crushed

3 tbsp chopped fresh basil

2 fresh red chiles, deseeded and sliced

juice of 1 large lemon

5 tbsp light cream

4 tbsp grated Parmesan cheese

8 oz/225 g dried tagliatelle

salt and pepper

crusty bread, to serve

1 Using a swivel vegetable peeler, slice the zucchini into thin ribbons.

2 Heat the oil in a skillet and cook the garlic for 30 seconds.

3 Add the zucchini ribbons and cook over low heat, stirring constantly, for 5–7 minutes. Stir in the basil, chiles, lemon juice, cream, and Parmesan cheese and season with salt and pepper to taste. Keep warm over very low heat.

4 Meanwhile, bring a large pan of lightly salted water to a boil. Add the pasta, bring back to a boil, and cook for 8–10 minutes until tender, but still firm to the bite. Drain thoroughly and put the pasta in a warm serving bowl.

5 Pile the zucchini mixture on top of the pasta. Serve immediately with crusty bread.

COOK'S TIP

Lime juice could be used instead of the lemon. As limes are usually smaller, squeeze the juice from 2 fruits.

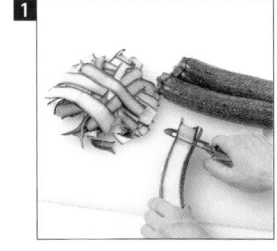

Spinach & Nut Pasta

Use any pasta shapes that you have for this recipe—fusilli were used here. Multicolored pasta is visually the most attractive to use.

NUTRITIONAL INFORMATION

Calories	603	Sugars	.........5g
Protein	........12g	Fat	..........41g
Carbohydrate	...46g	Saturates	.......6g

5 mins   15 mins

SERVES 4

INGREDIENTS

2 cups dried pasta shapes

½ cup olive oil

2 garlic cloves, crushed

1 onion, quartered and sliced

3 large flat mushrooms, sliced

8 oz/225 g spinach

2 tbsp pine nuts

5 tbsp dry white wine

salt and pepper

Parmesan shavings, to garnish

1 Bring a large pan of lightly salted water to a boil. Add the pasta, bring back to a boil, and cook for 8–10 minutes until tender, but still firm to the bite. Drain well.

2 Meanwhile, heat the oil in a large pan. Add the garlic and onion and cook over low heat, stirring occasionally, for 1 minute.

3 Add the sliced mushrooms to the pan and cook over medium heat, stirring occasionally, for 2 minutes.

4 Lower the heat, add the spinach, and cook, stirring occasionally, for about 4–5 minutes or until the spinach has just wilted.

5 Stir in the pine nuts and wine, season to taste with salt and pepper, and cook for 1 minute.

6 Transfer the pasta to a warm serving bowl and toss the sauce into it, mixing well. Garnish with shavings of Parmesan cheese and serve immediately.

COOK'S TIP

Grate a little nutmeg over the dish for extra flavor, because this spice has a particular affinity for spinach.

Cantonese Garden Vegetables

This dish tastes as fresh as it looks. Try to get hold of baby vegetables because they look and taste so much better in this dish.

NUTRITIONAL INFORMATION

Calories	130	Sugars	.........8g
Protein	.........6g	Fat	...........8g
Carbohydrate	....8g	Saturates	.......1g

 5 mins   10 mins

SERVES 4

INGREDIENTS

2 tbsp peanut oil

1 tsp Chinese five-spice powder

3 oz/85 g baby carrots, halved

2 celery stalks, sliced

2 baby leeks, sliced

2 oz/55 g snow peas

4 baby zucchini, halved lengthwise

8 baby corn cobs

8 oz/225 g firm marinated beancurd, cubed

4 tbsp fresh orange juice

1 tbsp honey

cooked rice or noodles, to serve

TO GARNISH

celery leaves

orange rind

VARIATION

Lemon juice would be just as delicious as the orange juice in this recipe, but use 3 tablespoons instead of 4 tablespoons.

1 Heat the peanut oil in a preheated wok or large, heavy skillet until almost smoking.

2 Add the Chinese five-spice powder, carrots, celery, leeks, snow peas, zucchini, and corn cobs and stir-fry for 3–4 minutes.

3 Add the beancurd to the wok or skillet and cook for a further 2 minutes, constantly stirring gently so the beancurd does not break up into smaller pieces.

4 Stir the fresh orange juice and honey into the wok or skillet, reduce the heat, and cook for 1–2 minutes.

5 Transfer the stir-fry to a serving dish, garnish with celery leaves and orange rind, and serve with rice or noodles.

Pear & Walnut Pasta

This is quite an unusual combination of ingredients in a savory dish, but is absolutely wonderful tossed into a fine pasta, such as spaghetti.

NUTRITIONAL INFORMATION

Calories	508	Sugars	.........9g
Protein	........15g	Fat	..........27g
Carbohydrate	...50g	Saturates	......11g

 10 mins   20 mins

SERVES 4

I N G R E D I E N T S

8 oz/225 g dried spaghetti

2 small ripe pears, peeled and sliced

⅔ cup vegetable stock

6 tbsp dry white wine

2 tbsp butter

1 tbsp olive oil

1 red onion, quartered and sliced

1 garlic clove, crushed

½ cup walnut halves

2 tbsp chopped fresh oregano

1 tbsp lemon juice

3 oz/85 g dolcelatte cheese

salt and pepper

fresh oregano sprigs, to garnish

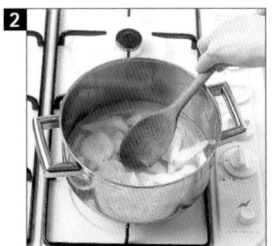

1 Bring a large pan of lightly salted water to a boil. Add the pasta, bring back to a boil, and cook for 8–10 minutes until tender, but still firm to the bite. Drain thoroughly, set aside, and keep warm until required.

2 Meanwhile, place the pears in a pan and pour in the stock and wine. Poach the pears over low heat for about 10 minutes until tender. Remove the pears with a draining spoon and reserve the cooking liquid. Set the pears aside.

3 Heat the butter and oil in a pan until the butter melts. Add the onion and garlic and cook over low heat, stirring frequently, for 2–3 minutes.

4 Stir in the walnut halves, chopped oregano, and lemon juice. Stir in the reserved pears with 4 tablespoons of the poaching liquid.

5 Crumble the dolcelatte cheese into the pan and cook over low heat, stirring occasionally, for 1–2 minutes or until the cheese is just beginning to melt. Season with salt and pepper to taste.

6 Add the pasta and toss in the sauce, using 2 forks. Transfer to a serving dish, garnish with oregano, and serve.

Vegetable Galette

This is a simply scrumptious dish of eggplants and zucchini layered with a quick tomato sauce and melted cheese.

NUTRITIONAL INFORMATION

Calories	.412	Sugars	.12g
Protein	.13g	Fat	.34g
Carbohydrate	.13g	Saturates	.11g

 40 mins   1¼ hrs

SERVES 4

INGREDIENTS

2 large eggplants, sliced

4 zucchini, sliced

2 x 14 oz/400 g cans chopped tomatoes, drained

2 tbsp tomato paste

2 garlic cloves, crushed

4 tbsp olive oil

1 tsp superfine sugar

2 tbsp chopped fresh basil

olive oil, for frying

8 oz/225 g mozzarella cheese, sliced

salt and pepper

fresh basil leaves, to garnish

1 Put the eggplant slices in a colander and sprinkle generously with salt. Set aside for 30 minutes, then rinse well under cold running water, and drain. Thinly slice the zucchini.

2 Meanwhile, put the tomatoes, tomato paste, garlic, olive oil, sugar, and chopped basil into a pan and simmer for 20 minutes or until reduced by half. Season to taste with salt and pepper.

3 Heat 2 tablespoons of olive oil in a large skillet and cook the eggplant

slices for 2–3 minutes until just beginning to brown. Remove from the skillet.

4 Add a further 2 tablespoons of oil to the skillet and cook the zucchini slices until browned.

5 Lay half of the eggplant slices in the bottom of a casserole. Cover with half

of the tomato sauce and then add a layer of zucchini. Top with half of the mozzarella slices.

6 Repeat the layers and bake in a preheated oven, 350°F/180°C, for 45–50 minutes or until the vegetables are tender. Garnish with basil leaves and serve immediately.

Spinach Crêpes

Serve these crêpes as a light lunch or supper dish, with a tomato and basil salad for a dramatic color contrast.

NUTRITIONAL INFORMATION

Calories	663	Sugars 9g
Protein	. . . . .32g	Fat 48g
Carbohydrate	. . .28g	Saturates 18g

 25 mins   25 mins

SERVES 4

INGREDIENTS

⅔ cup whole-wheat flour

1 egg

⅔ cup plain yogurt

3 tbsp water

1 tbsp vegetable oil, plus extra for brushing

7 oz/200 g frozen leaf spinach, thawed and puréed

pinch of grated nutmeg

salt and pepper

TO GARNISH

lemon wedges

fresh cilantro sprigs

FILLING

1 tbsp vegetable oil

3 scallions, thinly sliced

1 cup ricotta cheese

4 tbsp plain yogurt

¾ cup grated Swiss cheese

1 egg, lightly beaten

1 cup unsalted cashew nuts

2 tbsp chopped fresh parsley

pinch of cayenne pepper

1 Sift the flour and salt into a bowl and tip in any bran in the strainer. Whisk the egg with the yogurt, water, and oil. Gradually pour it onto the flour, beating constantly. Stir in the spinach and season with pepper and nutmeg to taste.

2 To make the filling, heat the oil in a pan and cook the scallions until translucent. Remove with a draining spoon and drain on paper towels. Beat the ricotta with the yogurt and half the Swiss cheese. Beat in the egg and stir in the cashew nuts and parsley. Season with salt and cayenne to taste.

3 Lightly brush a small, heavy skillet with oil and heat. Pour in 3–4 tablespoons of the crêpe batter and tilt the skillet so that it covers the base.

Cook for about 3 minutes until bubbles appear in the center. Turn and cook the other side for about 2 minutes until lightly browned. Slide the crêpe onto a warmed plate, cover with foil, and keep warm while you cook the remainder. The batter should make 8–12 crêpes.

4 Spread a little filling over each crêpe and fold in half, and then half again, envelope style. Spoon the remaining filling into the opening.

5 Grease a shallow, casserole and arrange the crêpes in a single layer. Sprinkle with the remaining cheese and cook in a preheated oven, 350°F/180°C, for about 15 minutes. Serve hot, garnished with lemon wedges and cilantro sprigs.

  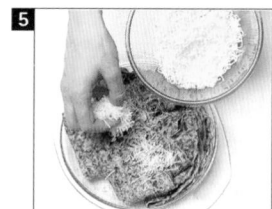

Red Curry with Cashews

This is a wonderfully quick dish to prepare. If you don't have time to prepare the curry paste, it can be bought ready-made.

NUTRITIONAL INFORMATION

Calories	274	Sugars	.........5g
Protein	........10g	Fat	..........10g
Carbohydrate	...38g	Saturates	.......3g

25 mins   15 mins

SERVES 4

INGREDIENTS

generous 1 cup coconut milk

1 kaffir lime leaf

¼ tsp light soy sauce

4 baby corn cobs, halved lengthwise

4 oz/115 g broccoli florets

4 oz/115 g green beans, cut into 2 inch/
   5 cm/ pieces

4 tbsp cashew nuts

15 fresh basil leaves

1 tbsp chopped fresh cilantro

1 tbsp chopped roasted peanuts, to garnish

RED CURRY PASTE

7 fresh red chiles, halved, deseeded,
   and blanched

2 tsp cumin seeds

2 tsp coriander seeds

1 inch/2.5 cm piece of galangal, chopped

½ lemongrass stem, chopped

1 tsp salt

grated rind of 1 lime

4 garlic cloves, chopped

3 shallots, chopped

2 kaffir lime leaves, shredded

1 tbsp vegetable oil

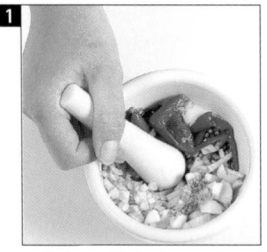  

1 To make the curry paste, grind all the ingredients in a large mortar with a pestle or in a grinder. Alternatively, process briefly in a food processor. (The quantity of red curry paste is more than required for this recipe. Store for up to 3 weeks in a sealed jar in the refrigerator.)

2 Put a wok or large, heavy-based skillet over high heat, add 3 tablespoons of the red curry paste, and stir until it gives off its aroma. Reduce the heat to medium.

3 Add the coconut milk, kaffir lime leaf, light soy sauce, baby corn cobs, broccoli florets, green beans, and cashew nuts. Bring to a boil and simmer for about 10 minutes until the vegetables are cooked, but still firm and crunchy.

4 Remove and discard the lime leaf and stir in the basil leaves and cilantro. Transfer to a warmed serving dish, garnish with peanuts, and serve immediately.

Cheese Potato Patties

Make these tasty potato patties for a quick and simple supper dish.
Serve them with scrambled eggs if you're very hungry.

NUTRITIONAL INFORMATION

Calories 766   Sugars 7g
Protein ....22g   Fat 50g
Carbohydrate ...60g   Saturates 20g

25 mins   35 mins

SERVES 4

I N G R E D I E N T S

2 lb 4 oz/1 kg potatoes

4 tbsp milk

4 tbsp butter or margarine

2 leeks, finely chopped

1 onion, finely chopped

1½ cups grated sharp Cheddar cheese

1 tbsp chopped fresh parsley or chives

1 egg, beaten

2 tbsp water

1½ cups fresh white or
    brown bread crumbs

vegetable oil, for frying

salt and pepper

fresh flat leaf parsley sprigs, to garnish

mixed salad greens, to serve

1 Put the potatoes in a large pan, add cold water to cover and a pinch of salt. Bring to a boil and simmer over medium heat for 20–25 minutes until tender. Drain and mash them with the milk and the butter or margarine.

2 Cook the leeks and onion in a small pan of lightly salted boiling water for about 10 minutes until tender. Drain well.

3 Combine the leeks and onion with the mashed potato, cheese, and parsley or chives in a large bowl. Season to taste with salt and pepper.

4 Beat the egg with the water in a shallow bowl. Sprinkle the bread crumbs into a separate shallow bowl. Shape the potato mixture into 12 even-size patties, brushing each with the egg mixture, then coating all over with the bread crumbs. Shake off any excess.

5 Heat the oil in a large skillet. Add the potato patties, in batches if necessary, and fry over low heat for about 2–3 minutes on each side until light golden brown. Transfer to warmed serving plates, garnish with flat leaf parsley, and serve with mixed salad greens.

Winter Vegetable Pot Pie

Seasonal fresh vegetables are casseroled with lentils, then topped with a ring of fresh cheese biscuits to make this tasty pot pie.

NUTRITIONAL INFORMATION

Calories ....734 Sugars 22g
Protein ....27g Fat 30g
Carbohydrate ...96g Saturates 16g

 20 mins   40 mins

SERVES 4

I N G R E D I E N T S

1 tbsp olive oil

1 garlic clove, crushed

8 small onions, halved

2 celery stalks, sliced

8 oz/225 g rutabaga, chopped

2 carrots, sliced

½ small cauliflower, broken into florets

3¼ cups sliced mushrooms

14 oz/400 g can chopped tomatoes

¼ cup red lentils

2 tbsp cornstarch

3–4 tbsp water

1¼ cups vegetable stock

2 tsp Tabasco sauce

2 tsp chopped fresh oregano

fresh oregano sprigs, to garnish

P O T   P I E   T O P P I N G

2 cups self-rising flour

4 tbsp butter

1 cup grated sharp Cheddar cheese

2 tsp chopped fresh oregano

1 egg, lightly beaten

⅔ cup milk

salt

1 Heat the oil and cook the garlic and onions for 5 minutes. Add the celery, rutabaga, carrots, and cauliflower and cook for 2–3 minutes. Add the mushrooms, tomatoes, and lentils. Mix the cornstarch and water and stir into the pan with the stock, Tabasco, and oregano.

2 Transfer to a casserole, cover, and bake in a preheated oven, 350°F/180°C, for 20 minutes.

3 To make the topping, sift the flour with a pinch of salt into a bowl. Rub in the butter, then stir in most of the cheese and the chopped herbs. Beat the egg with the milk and add enough to the dry ingredients to make a soft dough. Knead lightly, roll out to ½ inch/1 cm thick and cut into 2 inch/5 cm rounds.

4 Remove the casserole from the oven and increase the temperature to 400°F/200°C. Arrange the biscuits around the edge of the casserole, brush with the remaining egg and milk, and sprinkle with the reserved cheese. Cook for a further 10–12 minutes. Garnish and serve.

Spinach Crêpe Layer

Nutty-tasting buckwheat crêpes are combined with a
cheese and spinach mixture and baked with a crispy topping.

NUTRITIONAL INFORMATION

Calories 467	Sugars 10g	
Protein 29g	Fat 26g	
Carbohydrate ...31g	Saturates 7g	

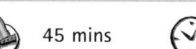

🥔 45 mins   🕐 1 hr 5 mins

SERVES 4

I N G R E D I E N T S

1 cup buckwheat flour

1 egg, beaten

1 tbsp walnut oil

1¼ cups milk

2 tsp vegetable oil

F I L L I N G

2 lb 4 oz/1 kg young spinach leaves

2 tbsp water

2 tsp walnut oil

1 bunch of scallions, white and green
parts, chopped

1 egg, beaten

1 egg yolk

1 cup cottage cheese

½ tsp grated nutmeg

4 tbsp grated sharp Cheddar cheese

1 tbsp walnut pieces

salt and pepper

1 Sift the flour into a bowl and add any
husks that remain in the strainer.

2 Make a well in the center and add the
egg and walnut oil. Gradually whisk
in the milk to make a smooth batter. Set
aside for 30 minutes.

3 To make the filling, wash the spinach
and pack into a pan with just the
water clinging to its leaves. Cover tightly
and cook on high heat for 5–6 minutes
until soft.

4 Drain well and set aside to cool. Heat
the walnut oil and cook the scallions
for 2–3 minutes until just soft. Drain on
paper towels and set aside.

5 Whisk the batter. Brush a small crêpe
pan with oil, heat until hot, and pour
in enough batter just to cover the bottom.
Cook for 1–2 minutes until set, flip over,
and cook for 1 minute until golden on the
underside. Turn onto a warmed plate.

Repeat to make 8–10 crêpes, layering them
with baking parchment.

6 Chop the spinach and pat dry with
paper towels. Combine with the
scallions, beaten egg, egg yolk, cottage
cheese, and nutmeg and season to taste
with salt and pepper.

7 Layer the crêpes and spinach mixture
on a cookie sheet lined with baking
paper, finishing with a crêpe. Sprinkle with
Cheddar cheese and bake in a preheated
oven, 375°F/190°C, for 20–25 minutes
until firm and golden. Sprinkle with the
walnuts and serve immediately.

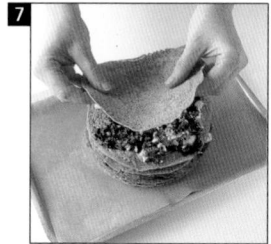

Indian-Style Omelet

Omelets are very versatile: they go with almost anything and you can also serve them at any time of the day.

NUTRITIONAL INFORMATION

Calories	132	Sugars	.........1g
Protein	.........7g	Fat	...........11g
Carbohydrate	....2g	Saturates	.......2g

 10 mins   20 mins

SERVES 4

INGREDIENTS

1 small onion, very finely chopped

2 fresh green chiles, deseeded and finely chopped

2 tbsp finely chopped fresh cilantro leaves

4 eggs

1 tsp salt

2 tbsp vegetable oil

fresh basil sprigs, to garnish

toasted bread or crisp salad greens, to serve

1 Place the onion, chiles, and cilantro in a large mixing bowl and combine.

2 Whisk the eggs in a separate bowl. Stir the onion mixture into the eggs. Add the salt and whisk again.

3 Heat 1 tablespoon of the oil in a large, heavy skillet over medium heat. Place a ladleful of the omelet batter in the pan. Cook the omelet, turning once and pressing down with a flat spoon to make sure that the egg is cooked right through, until the omelet is just firm and golden brown in color.

4 Repeat the same process with the remaining batter. Set the omelets aside, as you make them, and keep warm while you make the remaining batches.

5 Serve the omelets hot, garnished with fresh basil sprigs and accompanied by toasted bread. Alternatively, simply serve the omelets with a crisp salad greens for a light lunch.

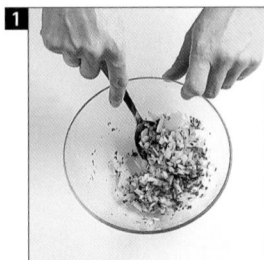

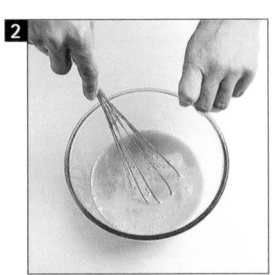

COOK'S TIP

Whether intensively farmed or organically produced, eggs are susceptible to bacteria. Never use cracked or dirty eggs and store them in the refrigerator, for up to 2 weeks, pointed end downward. Bring them to room temperature about 30 minutes before using.

Rice with Fruit & Nuts

Here is a tasty and filling rice dish that is nice and spicy and includes fruits for a refreshing flavor and toasted nuts for a crunchy texture.

NUTRITIONAL INFORMATION

Calories . . . . . . .423 Sugars 19g
Protein . . . . .10g Fat 17g
Carbohydrate . . .62g Saturates 2g

20 mins   1 hr

SERVES 6

INGREDIENTS

4 tbsp vegetable ghee or vegetable oil

1 large onion, chopped

2 garlic cloves, crushed

1 inch/2.5 cm piece of fresh ginger root chopped

1 tsp chili powder

1 tsp cumin seeds

1 tbsp mild or medium curry powder or paste

1½ cups brown rice

3¾ cups boiling vegetable stock

14 oz/400 g can chopped tomatoes

1½ cups ready-to-eat dried apricots or peaches, cut into slivers

1 red bell pepper, deseeded and diced

¾ cup frozen peas

1–2 small, slightly green bananas

½–¾ cup toasted nuts, such as almonds, cashews, and hazelnuts or pine nuts

salt and pepper

fresh cilantro sprigs, to garnish

1 Heat the ghee or oil in a large pan. Add the onion and cook over low heat for 3 minutes. Stir in the garlic, ginger, spices, and rice and cook gently, stirring constantly, for 2 minutes until the rice is coated in the spiced oil.

2 Pour in the boiling stock, add the chopped tomatoes, and season with salt and pepper to taste. Bring to a boil, then reduce the heat, cover, and simmer gently for 40 minutes or until the rice is almost cooked and most of the liquid has been absorbed.

3 Add the slivered apricots or peaches, diced red bell pepper, and peas. Cover and continue cooking for 10 minutes. Remove from the heat and set aside for 5 minutes without uncovering.

4 Peel and slice the bananas. Uncover the rice mixture and fork through to mix the ingredients and fluff up the rice. Add the toasted nuts and sliced bananas and toss lightly. Transfer to a warmed serving platter and garnish with fresh cilantro sprigs. Serve immediately.

Savory Pie

This tasty pie combines a delicious filling of lentils and red bell peppers in a crisp whole-wheat crust.

NUTRITIONAL INFORMATION

Calories	287	Sugars	.........5g
Protein	........10g	Fat	...........5g
Carbohydrate	...35g	Saturates	.......3g

 45 mins   🕐 50 mins

SERVES 8

INGREDIENTS

PIE DOUGH

2 cups plain whole-wheat flour

7 tbsp margarine, cut into small pieces

4 tbsp water

FILLING

¾ cup red lentils, rinsed

1¼ cups vegetable stock

1 tbsp margarine

1 onion, chopped

2 red bell peppers, deseeded and diced

1 tsp yeast extract

1 tbsp tomato paste

3 tbsp chopped fresh parsley

pepper

1 To make the pie dough, place the flour in a mixing bowl and rub in the margarine. Stir in the water and bring together to form a dough. Wrap and chill in the refrigerator for 30 minutes.

2 Meanwhile, make the filling. Put the lentils in a pan with the stock, bring to a boil, and simmer for 10 minutes until tender. Mash to a purée.

3 Melt the margarine in a small pan and cook the onion and bell peppers, stirring frequently, until just soft. Stir in the lentil purée, yeast extract, tomato paste, and parsley. Season with pepper.

4 On a lightly floured counter, roll out the dough and line a 9½ inch/24 cm loose-bottomed quiche pan. Prick the base with a fork and spoon the lentil mixture into the pie shell.

5 Bake in a preheated oven, 400°F/200°C, for 30 minutes, until the filling is firm.

VARIATION

Add corn to the pie in step 3 for a colorful and tasty change.

Spiced Spinach & Lentils

This interesting combination of lentils and spiced vegetables is delicious served with parathas, chapatis, or nan bread and yogurt.

NUTRITIONAL INFORMATION

Calories	362	Sugars	.........9g
Protein	........20g	Fat	..........13g
Carbohydrate	...44g	Saturates	.......2g

15 mins   30 mins

SERVES 4

INGREDIENTS

1 cup split red lentils

3 cups water

1 onion

1 eggplant

1 red bell pepper, deseeded

2 zucchini

4 oz/115 g mushrooms

8 oz/225g leaf spinach

4 tbsp vegetable ghee or vegetable oil

1 fresh green chile, deseeded and chopped

1 tsp ground cumin

1 tsp ground coriander

1 inch/2.5 cm piece of fresh ginger root, chopped

⅔ cup vegetable stock

salt

fresh cilantro sprigs, to garnish

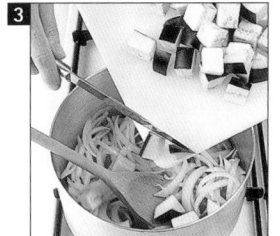

1 Place the lentils in a pan with the water. Cover and simmer for 15 minutes until soft, but still whole.

2 Meanwhile, quarter and slice the onion. Cut the eggplant and red bell pepper into ½ inch/1 cm pieces. Cut the zucchini into ½ inch/1 cm thick slices. Slice the mushrooms. Discard any coarse spinach stalks and wash the leaves well.

3 Heat the ghee or oil in a large pan, add the onion and red bell pepper, and cook gently for 3 minutes, stirring frequently. Stir in the eggplant, mushrooms, chile, spices, and ginger and cook gently for 1 minute. Add the spinach and stock and season with salt to taste. Stir until the spinach leaves wilt. Cover and simmer for about 10 minutes or until the vegetables are just tender.

4 Make a border of the lentils on a warm serving plate and spoon the vegetable mixture into the center. (The lentils may be stirred into the vegetable mixture, instead of being used as a border, if wished.) Garnish with cilantro sprigs and serve immediately.

COOK'S TIP

Wash the spinach thoroughly in several changes of cold water as it can be gritty. Drain well and shake off excess water from the leaves before adding it to the pan.

Fried Rice with Spicy Beans

This rice is really colorful and crunchy with the addition of corn and red kidney beans.

NUTRITIONAL INFORMATION

Calories	363	Sugars	.........3g
Protein	........10g	Fat	...........11g
Carbohydrate	...61g	Saturates	.......2g

 10 mins   25 mins

SERVES 4

I N G R E D I E N T S

3 tbsp sunflower oil

1 onion, finely chopped

generous 1 cup long grain rice

1 green bell pepper, deseeded and diced

1 tsp chili powder

2½ cups boiling water

¾ cup canned corn

8 oz/225 g canned red kidney beans, drained and rinsed

2 tbsp chopped fresh cilantro, plus extra for garnish (optional)

1 Heat the sunflower oil in a large preheated wok.

2 Add the onion and stir-fry over medium heat for about 2 minutes or until softened.

COOK'S TIP

For perfect fried rice, the raw rice should ideally be soaked in a bowl of water for a short time before cooking to remove excess starch. Short grain Asian rice can be substituted for the long grain rice.

3 Lower the heat, add the rice, green bell pepper and chili powder, and stir-fry for 1 minute.

4 Pour in the boiling water. Bring back to a boil, then reduce the heat, and simmer for 15 minutes.

5 Stir in the corn, kidney beans, and cilantro and heat through, stirring occasionally.

6 Transfer to a warmed serving bowl and serve hot, sprinkled with extra cilantro, if wished.

Brazil Nut & Mushroom Pie

The white mushrooms give this wholesome vegan pie a wonderful aromatic flavor. The pie can be frozen uncooked and baked from frozen.

NUTRITIONAL INFORMATION

Calories	530	Sugars	........4g
Protein	........12g	Fat	..........38g
Carbohydrate	...38g	Saturates	.......8g

 1 hr 50 mins

SERVES 6

I N G R E D I E N T S

PASTRY

2 cups whole-wheat flour

7 tbsp margarine, cut into small pieces

4 tbsp water

soy milk, to glaze

FILLING

2 tbsp margarine

1 onion, chopped

1 garlic clove, finely chopped

generous ⅓ cup sliced white mushrooms

1 tbsp all-purpose flour

⅔ cup vegetable stock

1½ cups Brazil nuts

1 tbsp tomato paste

1½ cups fresh whole-wheat bread crumbs

2 tbsp chopped fresh parsley

½ tsp pepper

1 To make the dough, place the flour in a mixing bowl and rub in the margarine with your fingertips until the mixture resembles fine bread crumbs. Stir in the water and bring together to form a smooth dough. Knead lightly, then wrap, and chill in the refrigerator for 30 minutes.

2 To make the filling, melt half of the margarine in a pan. Add the onion, garlic, and mushrooms and cook over medium heat, stirring occasionally, for 5 minutes, until softened.

3 Add the flour and cook for 1 minute, stirring constantly. Gradually add the stock, stirring until the sauce is smooth and beginning to thicken.

4 Chop the Brazil nuts. Stir the tomato paste, nuts, bread crumbs, parsley, and pepper into the pan. Remove from the heat and set aside to cool slightly.

5 On a lightly floured counter, roll out two-thirds of the pastry and use to line an 8 inch/20 cm loose-bottomed quiche pan or pie dish. Spread the filling in the pie shell. Brush the edges of the dough with soy milk. Roll out the remaining dough to fit the top of the pie. Seal the edges, make a slit in the top of the dough, and brush lightly with soy milk to glaze.

6 Bake in a preheated oven, 400°F/ 200°C, for 30–40 minutes, until golden brown. Serve immediately.

Vegetarian Sausages

The delicious cheese flavor will make these sausages a hit with vegetarians who need not feel left out when it comes to a barbecue.

NUTRITIONAL INFORMATION

Calories	.213	Sugars	.4g
Protein	.8g	Fat	.12g
Carbohydrate	.19g	Saturates	.4g

50 mins   25 mins

MAKES 8

INGREDIENTS

1 tbsp sunflower oil

1 small onion, finely chopped

¾ cup finely chopped mushrooms

½ red bell pepper, deseeded and finely chopped

14 oz/400 g can cannellini beans, rinsed and drained

2¾ cups fresh bread crumbs

scant 1 cup grated Cheddar cheese

1 tsp dried mixed herbs

1 egg yolk

seasoned all-purpose flour

vegetable oil, to baste

TO SERVE

hot dog rolls

slices of fried onion

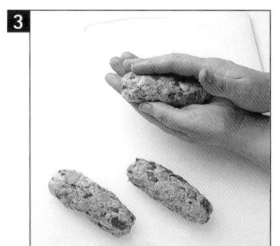

1 Heat the oil in a pan. Cook the onion, mushrooms, and red bell pepper over low heat for 5 minutes or until softened.

2 Mash the beans in a bowl with a potato masher. Add the onion, mushroom mixture, bread crumbs, cheese, herbs, and egg yolk and mix together well.

3 Press the mixture together with your fingers and shape into 8 sausages.

Roll each sausage in the seasoned flour to coat evenly. Set aside to chill in the refrigerator for at least 30 minutes.

4 Grill the sausages on a sheet of oiled foil set over medium coals for about 15–20 minutes, turning and basting

frequently with oil, until golden. Alternatively, cook under a preheated broiler, basting frequently with the oil.

5 Split a hot dog roll and insert a layer of fried onions. Place the sausage in the roll and serve immediately.

Broccoli with Fluffy Eggs

Broccoli or cauliflower florets in a mustard sauce are topped with an egg yolk set in whisked egg white and finished off with grated cheese.

NUTRITIONAL INFORMATION

Calories	733	Sugars	........11g
Protein	........43g	Fat	..........53g
Carbohydrate	...23g	Saturates	......25g

 10 mins 15 mins

SERVES 1

INGREDIENTS

6 oz/175 g broccoli or
　cauliflower florets

1 tbsp butter or margarine

2 tbsp all-purpose flour

⅔ cup milk

1 tbsp coarse grain mustard

dash of lemon juice

¾ cup grated sharp
　Cheddar cheese

1 extra large egg, separated

salt and pepper

paprika, to garnish

1 Cook the broccoli or cauliflower in lightly salted boiling water for about 3–4 minutes until tender, but still crisp.

2 Meanwhile, melt the butter or margarine in a small pan. Stir in the flour and cook, stirring constantly, for 1 minute. Gradually add the milk and bring to a boil, stirring constantly until thickened. Season to taste with salt and pepper. Stir in the mustard and lemon juice and simmer for 1–2 minutes.

3 Remove the sauce from the heat and stir in two-thirds of the grated cheese until melted.

4 Drain the broccoli or cauliflower very thoroughly and place on an ovenproof plate or dish. Pour the cheese sauce over it.

5 Whisk the egg white until very stiff and season lightly. Pile the egg white on top of the broccoli or cauliflower and make a well in the center.

6 Gently drop the egg yolk into the well in the egg white and sprinkle with the remaining cheese. Place under a preheated moderate broiler for 3–4 minutes until the meringue is lightly browned and the cheese has melted. Serve immediately, sprinkled with paprika.

Thai-Spiced Mushrooms

An unusual dish that makes a good vegetarian entrée.
Serve the mushrooms with a colorful fresh salad.

NUTRITIONAL INFORMATION

Calories	147	Sugars	........2g
Protein	.........6g	Fat	..........12g
Carbohydrate	....4g	Saturates	.......1g

 10 mins   10 mins

SERVES 4

INGREDIENTS

8 large, flat mushrooms

3 tbsp sunflower oil

2 tbsp light soy sauce

1 garlic clove, crushed

¾ inch/2 cm piece of fresh galangal or
ginger root, grated

1 tbsp Thai green curry paste

8 baby corn cobs, sliced

3 scallions, chopped

2 cups bean sprouts

3½ oz/100 g firm beancurd, diced

2 tsp sesame seeds, toasted

TO SERVE

chopped cucumber

sliced red bell pepper

COOK'S TIP

Galangal and ginger can be frozen
for several weeks, either peeled
and finely chopped ready to add to
dishes, or in whole pieces. Thaw the
piece or grate finely from frozen.

1 Remove the stems from the mushrooms and set aside. Place the caps on a cookie sheet. Mix 2 tablespoons of the sunflower oil with 1 tablespoon of the light soy sauce and brush all over the mushroom caps.

2 Cook the mushroom caps under a preheated broiler until golden and tender, turning them over once.

3 Meanwhile, chop the mushroom stems finely. Heat the remaining oil in a heavy skillet or wok and stir-fry the stems with the garlic and galangal or ginger for 1 minute.

4 Stir in the curry paste, baby corn, and scallions and stir-fry for 1 minute. Add the bean sprouts and stir-fry for a further minute.

5 Add the beancurd and remaining soy sauce, then toss lightly to heat through. Spoon the mixture into the mushroom caps.

6 Sprinkle with the sesame seeds. Serve immediately with chopped cucumber and sliced red bell pepper.

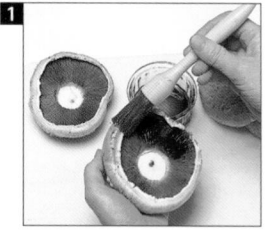

Asian Vegetables

Serve this colorful mixture with a pile of golden, crispy noodles as a vegetarian entrée or on its own to accompany meat dishes.

NUTRITIONAL INFORMATION

Calories	148	Sugars	.........7g
Protein	.........8g	Fat	...........7g
Carbohydrate	...14g	Saturates	.......1g

 2 mins   8 mins

SERVES 4

I N G R E D I E N T S

1 eggplant

salt

2 tbsp vegetable oil

3 garlic cloves, crushed

4 scallions, chopped

1 small red bell pepper, deseeded and thinly sliced

4 baby corn cobs, halved lengthwise

3 oz/85 g snow peas

7 oz/200 g Chinese mustard greens, coarsely shredded

14½ oz/425 g canned Chinese straw mushrooms, drained

2 cups bean sprouts

2 tbsp rice wine

2 tbsp yellow bean sauce

2 tbsp dark soy sauce

1 tsp chili sauce

1 tsp sugar

½ cup chicken or vegetable stock

1 tsp cornstarch

2 tsp water

1 Trim the eggplant and cut into 2 inch/5 cm long batons. Place in a colander, sprinkle with salt, and set aside to drain for 30 minutes. Rinse in cold water and dry with paper towels.

2 Heat the oil in a skillet or wok and stir-fry the garlic, scallions, and bell pepper over high heat for 1 minute. Stir in the eggplant pieces and stir-fry for a further minute or until softened.

3 Stir in the baby corn cobs and snow peas and stir-fry for about 1 minute. Add the mustard greens, mushrooms, and bean sprouts and stir-fry for 30 seconds.

4 Combine the rice wine, yellow bean sauce, soy sauce, chili sauce, and sugar and add to the pan with the stock. Bring to a boil, stirring constantly.

5 Blend the cornstarch with the water to form a smooth paste. Stir quickly into the skillet or wok and cook for a further minute. Serve immediately.

Spiced Cashew Nut Curry

This unusual vegetarian dish is best served as a side dish with other curries and with rice to soak up the wonderfully rich, spiced juices.

NUTRITIONAL INFORMATION

Calories ....455 Sugars 6g
Protein ....13g Fat 39g
Carbohydrate ...16g Saturates 11g

8¼ hrs   25 mins

SERVES 4

INGREDIENTS

2¼ cups unsalted cashew nuts

1 tsp coriander seeds

1 tsp cumin seeds

2 cardamom pods, crushed

1 tbsp sunflower oil

1 onion, thinly sliced

1 garlic clove, crushed

1 small fresh green chile, deseeded and chopped

1 cinnamon stick

½ tsp ground turmeric

4 tbsp coconut cream

1¼ cups hot vegetable stock

3 kaffir lime leaves, finely shredded

salt and pepper

boiled jasmine rice, to serve

1 Soak the cashew nuts in cold water overnight. Drain thoroughly. Crush the coriander seeds, cumin seeds, and cardamom pods with a pestle and mortar.

2 Heat the oil and stir-fry the onion and garlic for 2–3 minutes to soften, but not brown. Add the chile, crushed spices, cinnamon stick, and turmeric and stir-fry for a further minute.

3 Add the coconut cream and the hot stock to the pan. Bring to a boil, then add the cashew nuts and lime leaves.

4 Cover the pan, lower the heat, and simmer for about 20 minutes. Serve hot, accompanied by jasmine rice.

COOK'S TIP

All spices give the best flavor when freshly crushed, but if you prefer, you can use ground spices instead of crushing them yourself in a mortar with a pestle.

Yellow Curry

Potatoes are not highly regarded in Thai cooking because rice is the traditional staple. This dish is a tasty exception.

NUTRITIONAL INFORMATION

Calories 160	Sugars 4g	
Protein 3g	Fat 10g	
Carbohydrate . . .15g	Saturates 1g	

 5 mins   15 mins

SERVES 4

INGREDIENTS

2 garlic cloves, finely chopped

1¼ inch/3 cm piece of galangal, finely chopped

1 lemongrass stalk, finely chopped

1 tsp coriander seeds

3 tbsp vegetable oil

2 tsp Thai red curry paste

½ tsp ground turmeric

scant 1 cup coconut milk

9 oz/250 g potatoes, cubed

scant ½ cup vegetable stock

7 oz/200 g young spinach leaves

1 small onion, thinly sliced into rings

1 Place the garlic, galangal, lemongrass, and coriander seeds in a mortar and pound continuously with a pestle until a smooth paste forms.

2 Heat 2 tablespoons of the oil in a skillet or wok. Stir in the garlic paste and stir-fry for 30 seconds. Stir in the curry paste and turmeric, then add the coconut milk, and bring the mixture to a boil.

3 Add the potatoes and stock. Return to a boil, then lower the heat, and simmer, uncovered, for 10–12 minutes, until the potatoes are almost tender.

4 Stir in the spinach and simmer until the leaves are wilted.

5 Cook the onion in the remaining oil until crisp and golden brown. Place on top of the curry just before serving.

COOK'S TIP
Choose a firm, waxy potato for this dish, one that will keep its shape during cooking, in preference to a mealy variety that will break up easily once cooked.

Sweet Potato Patties

Enticing little tasty mouthfuls of sweet potato, served hot and sizzling from the skillet with a delicious fresh tomato sauce.

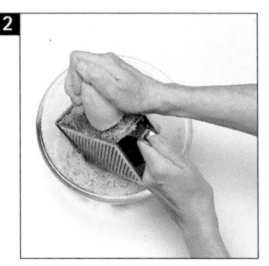

NUTRITIONAL INFORMATION

Calories	349	Sugars	.........9g
Protein	.........4g	Fat	..........24g
Carbohydrate	...32g	Saturates	.......3g

 15 mins   15 mins

SERVES 4

INGREDIENTS

1 lb 2 oz/500 g sweet potatoes

2 garlic cloves, crushed

1 small fresh green chile, chopped

2 fresh cilantro sprigs, chopped

1 tbsp dark soy sauce

all-purpose flour, for shaping

vegetable oil, for frying

sesame seeds, for sprinkling

SOY-TOMATO SAUCE

2 tsp vegetable oil

1 garlic clove, finely chopped

1½ tsp finely chopped fresh
   ginger root

3 tomatoes, peeled and chopped

2 tbsp dark soy sauce

1 tbsp lime juice

2 tbsp chopped fresh cilantro

1 To make the soy-tomato sauce, heat the oil in a wok and stir-fry the garlic and ginger for about 1 minute. Add the tomatoes and stir-fry for a further 2 minutes. Remove from the heat and stir in the soy sauce, lime juice, and chopped cilantro. Set aside and keep warm.

2 Peel the sweet potatoes and grate finely (you can do this quickly with a food processor). Place the garlic, chile, and cilantro in a mortar and crush to a smooth paste with a pestle. Stir in the soy sauce and mix with the sweet potatoes.

3 Divide the mixture into 12 equal portions. Dip into flour and pat into a flat, round patty shape.

4 Heat a shallow layer of oil in a wide skillet. Cook the sweet potato patties in batches over high heat until golden, turning once.

5 Drain on paper towels and sprinkle with sesame seeds. Serve hot, with a spoonful of the soy-tomato sauce.

COOK'S TIP

Although deeper in color than light soy sauce, dark soy sauce is not so strongly flavored and is sweeter.

Thai-Style Omelet

In Thailand, egg dishes such as this one are eaten as part of an entrée or as a snack, depending on the time of day.

NUTRITIONAL INFORMATION

Calories	304	Sugars 7g
Protein	. . . . .11g	Fat 24g
Carbohydrate	. . . .11g	Saturates 4g

 10 mins   10 mins

SERVES 4

I N G R E D I E N T S

3 tbsp vegetable oil

1 garlic clove, finely chopped

1 small onion, finely chopped

1 small eggplant, diced

½ small green bell pepper, deseeded
   and chopped

1 tomato, diced

1 large dried Chinese black mushroom,
   soaked, drained, and sliced

1 tbsp light soy sauce

½ tsp sugar

¼ tsp ground black pepper

2 large eggs

salad greens, tomato wedges, and
   cucumber slices, to garnish

1 Heat half the oil in a pan and cook the garlic over high heat for 30 seconds. Add the onion and eggplant and stir-fry until golden.

2 Add the green bell pepper and stir-fry for a further minute. Stir in the tomato, mushroom, soy sauce, sugar, and black pepper. Remove from the pan and keep hot.

3 Beat the eggs lightly. Heat the remaining oil, swirling to coat the pan. Pour in the eggs and swirl to set around the pan. When the egg is set, spoon the filling into the center. Fold in the sides of the omelet to make a neat, square package.

4 Slide the omelet carefully onto a warmed dish and garnish with salad greens, tomato wedges, and cucumber slices. Serve hot.

COOK'S TIP
If you heat the pan thoroughly before adding the oil, and heat the oil before adding the ingredients, you should not have a problem with ingredients sticking to the pan.

Desserts

For many people, a meal seems incomplete without a dessert, yet it can be difficult to find recipes that do not involve masses of sugar, lashings of cream, and mountains of chocolate. People with a sweet tooth, but a sensible eye on a healthy diet, need look no farther than this chapter. Fruit is an obvious ingredient, but there are many more possibilities—and much more exciting choices—than simple fruit salads. Rice desserts have come a long way from the nursery, especially when given a professional Asian touch, and this chapter also includes many other traditional and family favorites—with a healthy twist.

Green Fruit Salad

This delightfully refreshing fruit salad is the perfect finale for a Chinese meal. It has a lovely light syrup made with fresh mint and honey.

NUTRITIONAL INFORMATION

Calories	157	Sugars	........34g
Protein	.........1g	Fat	..........0.2g
Carbohydrate	...34g	Saturates	.......0g

30 mins   15 mins

SERVES 4

INGREDIENTS

1 small Charentais or honeydew melon

2 green apples

2 kiwi fruit

4 oz/115 g seedless white grapes

fresh mint sprigs, to decorate

SYRUP

1 orange

⅔ cup white wine

⅔ cup water

4 tbsp honey

fresh mint sprigs

COOK'S TIP
Single-flower honey has a better, more individual flavor than blended honey. Acacia honey is typically Chinese, but you could also try clove, lemon blossom, lime flower, or orange blossom.

1 To make the syrup, pare the rind from the orange using a potato peeler.

2 Put the orange rind in a pan with the white wine, water, and honey. Bring to a boil, then simmer gently for 10 minutes.

3 Remove the syrup from the heat. Add the mint sprigs and set aside to cool.

4 To prepare the fruit, first slice the melon in half and scoop out the seeds. Use a melon baller or a teaspoon to make melon balls.

5 Core and chop the apples. Peel and slice the kiwi fruit.

6 Strain the cooled syrup into a serving bowl, removing and reserving the orange rind, and discarding the mint sprigs.

7 Add the apple, grapes, kiwi fruit, and melon to the serving bowl. Stir through gently to mix.

8 Serve the fruit salad, decorated with sprigs of fresh mint and some of the reserved orange rind.

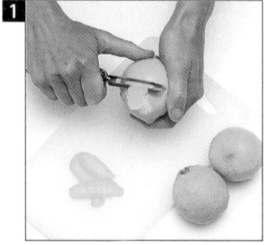 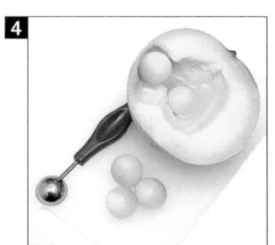 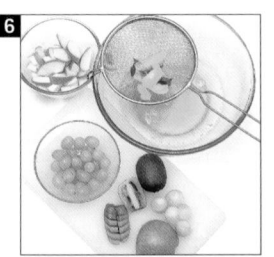

Orange & Grapefruit Salad

Sliced citrus fruits with a delicious almond and honey dressing make an unusual and refreshing dessert.

NUTRITIONAL INFORMATION

Calories 217   Sugars 33g
Protein . . . . .4g   Fat 9g
Carbohydrate . . .33g   Saturates 1g

2¼ hrs   3 mins

SERVES 4

I N G R E D I E N T S

2 grapefruit, ruby or plain

4 oranges

pared rind and juice of 1 lime

4 tbsp honey

2 tbsp warm water

1 fresh mint sprig, roughly chopped

½ cup chopped walnuts

1 Using a sharp knife, slice the top and bottom from the grapefruits, then slice away the rest of the skin and pith.

2 Cut between each segment of the grapefruit and remove the fleshy part only, discarding the membranes.

3 Using a sharp knife, slice the top and bottom from the oranges, then slice away the rest of the skin and pith.

4 Cut between each segment of the oranges to remove the fleshy part, discarding the membranes. Add the orange segments to the grapefruit.

5 Place the lime rind, 2 tablespoons of lime juice, the honey, and the warm water in a small bowl. Whisk with a fork to mix the dressing.

6 Pour the dressing over the segmented fruit, add the chopped mint, and mix well. Set aside to chill in the refrigerator for 2 hours for the flavors to mingle.

7 Place the chopped walnuts on a cookie sheet. Toast lightly under a preheated medium broiler for 2–3 minutes or until browned.

8 Sprinkle the toasted walnuts over the fruit and serve.

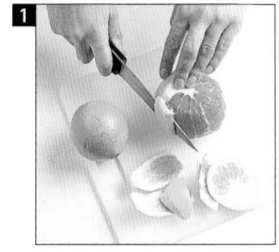

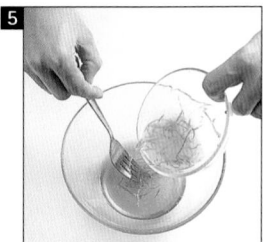

Citrus Meringue Crush

This is an excellent way to use up leftover meringue shells and is very simple to prepare. Serve with a spoonful of tangy fruit sauce.

NUTRITIONAL INFORMATION

Calories . . . . . . .165 Sugars 32g
Protein . . . . .5g Fat 1g
Carbohydrate . . .37g Saturates 0.4g

2 hrs   10 mins

SERVES 4

INGREDIENTS

8 ready-made meringue nests

1¼ cups low-fat plain yogurt

½ tsp finely grated orange rind

½ tsp finely grated lemon rind

½ tsp finely grated lime rind

2 tbsp orange liqueur or unsweetened
  orange juice

TO DECORATE

sliced kumquat

grated lime rind

SAUCE

2 oz/55 g kumquats

½ cup unsweetened orange juice

2 tbsp lemon juice

2 tbsp lime juice

2 tbsp water

2–3 tsp superfine sugar

1 tsp cornstarch mixed with
  1 tbsp water

1 Place the meringues in a plastic bag and using a rolling pin, crush into small pieces. Place in a mixing bowl. Stir in the yogurt, grated citrus rinds, and the liqueur or juice. Spoon the mixture into 4 mini-bowls and freeze for 1½–2 hours until firm.

2 Thinly slice the kumquats and place them in a small pan with the fruit juices and water. Bring gently to a boil and then simmer over low heat for 3–4 minutes until the kumquats soften.

3 Sweeten with sugar to taste, stir in the cornstarch mixture, and cook, stirring, until thickened. Pour into a small bowl, cover the surface with plastic wrap, and set aside to cool—the plastic wrap will help prevent a skin from forming. Chill in the refrigerator until required.

4 To serve, dip the meringue bowls in hot water for 5 seconds or until they loosen and turn onto serving plates. Spoon over a little sauce, decorate with slices of kumquat and lime rind, and serve.

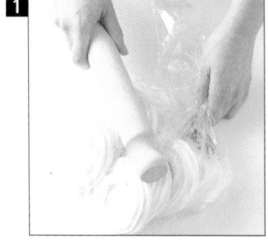

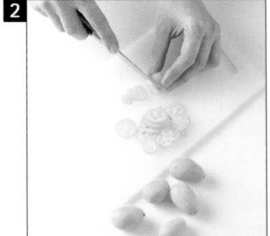

Fruit & Fiber Layers

A good, hearty dessert, guaranteed to fill you up.
Use your own favorite dried fruits in the compote.

NUTRITIONAL INFORMATION

Calories 348   Sugars 61g
Protein . . . . .10g   Fat 2g
Carbohydrate . . .77g   Saturates 1g

 2 hrs   15 mins

SERVES 4

I N G R E D I E N T S

½ cup no-need-to-soak dried apricots

½ cup no-need-to-soak prunes

½ cup no-need-to-soak dried peaches

2 cups dried apple

½ cup dried cherries

2 cups unsweetened apple juice

6 cardamom pods

6 cloves

1 cinnamon stick, broken

1¼ cups low-fat plain yogurt

1 cup crunchy oat cereal

apricot slices, to decorate

1 Place the apricots, prunes, peaches, apples, and cherries in a pan and pour in the apple juice. Add the cardamom pods, cloves, and cinnamon stick, bring to a boil, and simmer for 10–15 minutes until the fruits are plump and tender.

2 Remove the pan from the heat and set aside to cool completely, then transfer the mixture to a bowl and chill in the refrigerator for 1 hour. Remove and discard the spices from the fruits.

3 Spoon the compote into 4 dessert glasses, layering it alternately with yogurt and oat cereal, finishing with the oat cereal on top.

4 Decorate each dessert with slices of apricot and serve immediately.

COOK'S TIP

Check the ingredients labels of dried fruit because several types have added sugar or are rolled in sugar and this will affect the sweetness—and nutritional value— of the dish that you use them in.

Apples in Red Wine

This simple combination of apples and raspberries cooked in red wine is a colorful and tempting dessert.

NUTRITIONAL INFORMATION

Calories 221	Sugars 39g
Protein 2g	Fat 4g
Carbohydrate . . .39g	Saturates 1g

🍎 5 mins   🕐 20 mins

SERVES 4

I N G R E D I E N T S

4 dessert apples

2 tbsp lemon juice

3 tbsp low-fat spread

¼ cup molasses sugar

1 small orange

1 cinnamon stick, broken

⅔ cup red wine

1⅓ cups raspberries, hulled and thawed
   if frozen

fresh mint sprigs, to decorate

1 Peel and core the apples, then cut them into thick wedges. Place the apples in a bowl and toss thoroughly in the lemon juice to prevent the fruit from turning brown.

2 In a skillet, gently melt the low-fat spread over low heat, add the sugar, and stir to form a paste.

3 Stir the apple wedges into the skillet and cook, stirring, for 2 minutes until well coated in the sugar paste.

4 Using a vegetable peeler, pare off a few strips of orange rind. Add the orange rind to the skillet with the cinnamon pieces. Squeeze the juice from the orange and pour into the skillet with the red wine. Bring to a boil, then simmer for 10 minutes, stirring constantly.

5 Add the raspberries and cook for 5 minutes until the apples are tender.

6 Discard the orange rind and cinnamon pieces. Transfer the apple and raspberry mixture to a serving plate with the wine sauce. Decorate with a sprig of fresh mint and serve hot.

VARIATION

For other fruity combinations, cook the apples with blackberries, black currants or red currants. You may need to add more sugar if you use currants because they are not so sweet as raspberries.

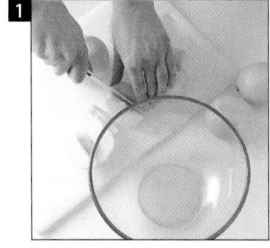  

Baked Pears with Cinnamon

This simple, healthy recipe is easy to prepare and cook, but is deliciously warming. For a treat, serve hot on a pool of low-fat custard.

NUTRITIONAL INFORMATION

Calories 207   Sugars 35g
Protein . . . . .3g   Fat 6g
Carbohydrate . . .37g   Saturates 2g

10 mins   25 mins

SERVES 4

I N G R E D I E N T S

4 ripe pears

2 tbsp lemon juice

¼ cup molasses sugar

1 tsp ground cinnamon

¼ cup low-fat spread

finely shredded lemon rind, to decorate

low-fat custard, to serve

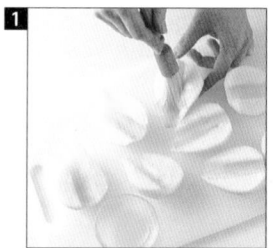

1 Core and peel the pears, then slice them in half lengthwise, and brush them all over with the lemon juice to prevent them from discoloring. Place the pears, cored side down, in a small nonstick roasting pan.

2 Place the sugar, cinnamon, and low-fat spread in a small pan and heat gently, stirring constantly, until the sugar has dissolved. Keep the heat very low to stop too much water evaporating from the low-fat spread as it gets hot. Spoon the mixture over the pears.

3 Bake the pears in a preheated oven, 400°F/200°C, for 20–25 minutes or until they are tender and golden, occasionally spooning the sugar mixture over the fruit during the cooking time.

4 To serve, heat the low-fat custard in a small pan over low heat or in a bowl in the microwave until it is piping hot and spoon a little over the surface of each of 4 warm dessert plates. Then arrange 2 pear halves on each plate.

5 Decorate the pears with a little finely shredded lemon rind and serve immediately.

VARIATION

For alternative flavors, replace the cinnamon with ground ginger and serve the pears sprinkled with chopped preserved ginger in syrup. Alternatively, use ground allspice and spoon over some warmed dark rum to serve.

Creamy Fruit Parfait

On the tiny Greek island of Kythera, this luscious combination of summer fruits and yogurt is served at tavernas as well as in homes.

NUTRITIONAL INFORMATION

Calories 261	Sugars 17g
Protein 10g	Fat 18g
Carbohydrate . . .17g	Saturates 7g

 15 mins   0 mins

SERVES 4–6

INGREDIENTS

1⅓ cups cherries

2 large peaches

2 large apricots

3 cups Strained Plain Yogurt (see page 432), or plain thick yogurt

½ cup walnut halves

2 tbsp flower-scented honey

fresh red currants or berries, to decorate (optional)

1 To prepare the fruit, use a cherry or olive pitter to remove the cherry pits. Cut each cherry in half. Cut the peaches and apricots in half lengthwise and remove the pits, then finely chop the flesh of all the fruit.

2 Place the finely chopped cherries, peaches, and apricots in a bowl and gently stir together.

3 Spoon one-third of the yogurt into an attractive glass serving bowl. Top with half the fruit mixture.

4 Repeat with another layer of yogurt and fruit and, finally, top with the remaining yogurt.

5 Place the walnuts in a small food processor and pulse until chopped, but not finely ground. Sprinkle the walnuts over the top layer of the yogurt.

6 Drizzle the honey over the nuts and yogurt. Cover the bowl with plastic wrap and chill in the refrigerator for at least 1 hour. Decorate the bowl with a small bunch of red currants, if using, just before serving.

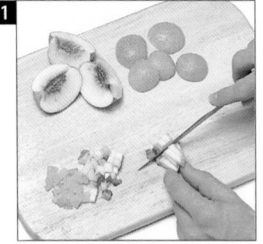

VARIATIONS

Vary the fruit to whatever is best in the market. Berries, figs, seedless grapes, and melons are also delicious in this simple family-style dessert.

Almond Rice Custard

This traditional Turkish dessert is simply an almond milk thickened with ground rice. Serve with the traditional decoration of strawberries.

NUTRITIONAL INFORMATION

Calories	220	Sugars	........20g
Protein	.........9g	Fat	..........10g
Carbohydrate	...24g	Saturates	.......2g

50 mins   30 mins

SERVES 6

INGREDIENTS

¾ cup whole blanched almonds

4 cups milk

¼ cup rice flour

pinch of salt

¼ cup sugar

½ tsp almond extract or 1 tbsp almond-flavor liqueur

toasted sliced almonds, to decorate

TO SERVE (OPTIONAL)

3 cups fresh strawberries, sliced, sprinkled with 2 tbsp sugar, and chilled

1 Put the almonds in a food processor and process until a thick paste forms. Bring 1 cup of the milk to a boil. Gradually pour into the almond paste, with the machine running, until the mixture is smooth. Set aside for about 10 minutes.

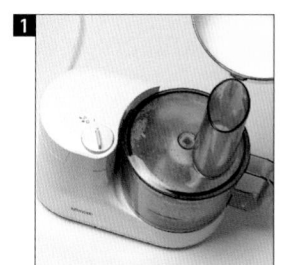

2 Combine the rice flour, salt, and sugar in a large bowl, then stir in about 4–5 tablespoons of the milk to form a smooth paste.

3 Bring the remaining milk to a boil in a heavy pan. Pour the hot milk into the rice flour paste and stir constantly, then return the mixture to the pan, and bring to a boil. Reduce the heat and simmer for about 10 minutes until smooth and thickened. Remove from the heat.

4 Strain the almond milk through a very fine strainer into the simmering rice custard, pressing through the almonds with the back of a spoon. Return to the heat and simmer for a further 7–10 minutes or until the mixture becomes thick.

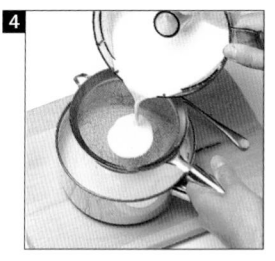

5 Remove from the heat and stir in the almond extract. Cool slightly, stirring, then pour into individual bowls. Sprinkle with the almonds and serve with the strawberries, if wished. Chill to serve later, if preferred.

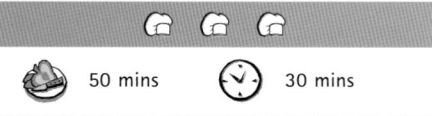

Black Rice Dessert

This sticky black rice is like congée, the traditional rice porridge eaten all over Southeast Asia for breakfast or as a base for other dishes.

NUTRITIONAL INFORMATION

Calories	300	Sugars	........33g
Protein	.........4g	Fat	...........5g
Carbohydrate	...62g	Saturates	.......4g

 25 mins    30 mins

SERVES 6–8

I N G R E D I E N T S

1½ cups black glutinous rice

3¾ cups boiling water

1 vanilla bean, split, black seeds removed and reserved

1 cup brown sugar

2 oz/55 g packet coconut powder

1⅔ cups canned thick coconut milk

2 ripe mangoes

6 passion fruit

TO DECORATE

shredded fresh coconut (optional)

fresh mint leaves

1 Put the rice in a large heavy pan and pour in the boiling water. Add the vanilla bean and seeds to the pan. Return to a boil, stirring once or twice. Reduce the heat to low and simmer, covered, for about 25 minutes until the rice is tender and the liquid almost absorbed; do not uncover during cooking.

2 Remove from the heat and stir in the sugar, coconut powder, and half the coconut milk. Stir until the sugar is dissolved. Cover and set aside for 10 minutes. If the rice becomes too thick, add a little more of the coconut milk or a little milk or water.

3 Cut each mango lengthwise along each side of the large pit to remove the flesh. Peel the mangoes, thinly slice, and arrange on a serving plate.

4 Cut the passion fruit crosswise in half and scoop out the pulp and juice. Spoon them over the mango slices.

5 Spoon the warm dessert into wide shallow bowls and decorate with shredded coconut and mint leaves. Drizzle some of the remaining coconut milk around the edges, if wished. Serve with the mango salad.

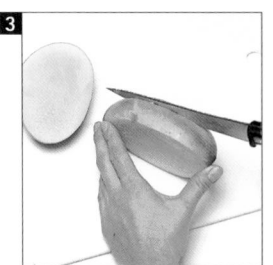

Orange-Scented Rice

This delicious creamy dessert is flavored with fresh oranges, orange-flavored liqueur, and two kinds of ginger.

NUTRITIONAL INFORMATION

Calories 412	Sugars 64g
Protein 7g	Fat 6g
Carbohydrate . . .82g	Saturates 4g

2 hrs   45 mins

SERVES 6

I N G R E D I E N T S

1¼ cups round grain rice

1 cup freshly squeezed
   orange juice

pinch of salt

1¼ cups milk

1 vanilla bean, split

2 inch/5 cm piece of fresh ginger root,
   gently bruised

1 cup sugar

¼ cup heavy cream

4 tbsp orange-flavored liqueur

2 tbsp butter

4–6 seedless oranges

2 pieces of preserved ginger, sliced thinly,
   plus 2 tbsp ginger syrup from the jar

ground ginger, for dusting

1 Put the rice in a pan with the orange juice and salt. Bring to a boil, skimming off any foam. Reduce the heat and simmer for about 10 minutes, stirring occasionally, until the juice is absorbed.

2 Gradually stir in the milk, add the vanilla bean and root ginger, and simmer for 30 minutes, stirring frequently, until the milk is absorbed and the rice is very tender. Remove from the heat. Remove the vanilla bean and ginger root.

3 Stir in half the sugar, half the cream, the orange liqueur, and butter until the sugar is dissolved and the butter is melted. Set aside to cool, then stir in the remaining cream, and pour into a bowl. Cover and set aside at room temperature.

4 Pare the rind from the oranges and reserve. Working over a bowl to catch the juices, remove the pith from all the oranges. Cut out the segments and drop into the bowl. Stir in the preserved ginger and syrup. Chill in the refrigerator.

5 Cut the pared orange rind into thin strips and blanch for 1 minute. Drain and rinse. Bring 1 cup water to a boil with the remaining sugar. Add the rind strips and simmer gently until the syrup is reduced by half. Set aside to cool.

6 Serve the rice with the chilled oranges and top with the caramelized orange rind strips.

Lebanese Almond Rice

This delicate rice cream is flavored with almonds and rosewater.
If pomegranates are in season, decorate with the gorgeous pink seeds.

NUTRITIONAL INFORMATION

Calories	199	Sugars	........17g
Protein	.........7g	Fat	...........9g
Carbohydrate	...23g	Saturates	.......2g

🍮 2½ hrs   🕐 10 mins

SERVES 6

INGREDIENTS

6 tbsp rice flour

pinch of salt

3 cups milk

¼ cup superfine sugar

¾ cup ground almonds

1 tbsp rosewater

TO DECORATE

2 tbsp chopped pistachios or toasted
sliced almonds

pomegranate seeds (optional)

washed rose petals (optional)

1 Put the rice flour in a bowl, stir in the salt, and make a well in the center.

2 Pour about ¼ cup of the milk into the well and whisk thoroughly to form a smooth paste.

3 Bring the remaining milk to a boil in a heavy pan. Whisk in the rice flour paste and the sugar and cook, stirring constantly, until the mixture thickens and bubbles. Reduce the heat and simmer gently for 5 minutes.

4 Whisk in the ground almonds until the mixture is smooth and thickened, then remove from the heat to cool slightly. Stir in the rosewater and cool completely, stirring occasionally.

5 Divide the mixture among 6 glasses or pour into a serving bowl. Chill for at least 2 hours before serving.

6 To serve, sprinkle with the pistachios or almonds, pomegranate seeds, and rose petals, if wished.

COOK'S TIP

For a smoother texture, this can be made without the ground almonds. Stir 2 tablespoons of cornstarch into the ground rice and use a little more of the milk to make the paste. Proceed as directed, omitting the ground almonds.

 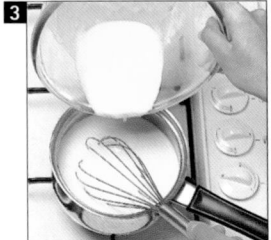 

Mini Orange Rice Cakes

These mini rice cakes, fragrant with orange or sometimes lemon rind, are found in many of the bakeries and coffee shops in Florence.

NUTRITIONAL INFORMATION

Calories 97   Sugars 9g
Protein . . . . .3g   Fat 3g
Carbohydrate . . .15g   Saturates 2g

 1½ hrs   20 mins

MAKES ABOUT 16

I N G R E D I E N T S

3 cups milk

pinch of salt

1 vanilla bean, split, seeds removed, and reserved

scant 1 cup risotto rice

½ cup sugar

2 tbsp butter

grated rind of 2 oranges

2 eggs, separated

2 tbsp orange-flavored liqueur or rum

1 tbsp freshly squeezed orange juice

confectioners' sugar, for dusting

1 orange, chopped, to decorate

1 Bring the milk to a boil in a large pan over medium-high heat. Add the salt and vanilla bean and seeds, and sprinkle in the rice. Return to a boil, stirring once or twice. Reduce the heat and simmer, stirring frequently, for about 10 minutes.

2 Add the sugar and butter and simmer for about 10 minutes, stirring frequently, until the mixture is thick and creamy. Pour into a bowl and stir in the orange rind. Remove the vanilla bean. Cool to room temperature, stirring occasionally.

3 Beat the egg yolks with the liqueur and orange juice, then beat into the cooled rice mixture.

4 Beat the egg whites until they hold their peaks almost stiff, but not too dry. Stir a spoonful into the rice mixture to lighten it, then gently fold in the remaining whites.

5 Spoon the mixture into ¼ cup muffin pan cups, lined with paper liners, filling to the brim. Bake in a preheated oven, 375°F/190°C, for about 20 minutes until golden and cooked through. Place on a wire rack to cool for 2 minutes, then remove the liners. Set aside to cool completely.

6 Decorate with chopped orange and dust with confectioners' sugar just before serving.

Italian Lemon Rice Cake

This lemony cake should have a crisp crust with a soft moist center. Soaking the currants in rum brings out their fruitiness.

NUTRITIONAL INFORMATION

Calories 283   Sugars 24g
Protein ....7g   Fat 10g
Carbohydrate ...41g   Saturates 6g

1¼ hrs   1¼ hrs

SERVES 8–10

INGREDIENTS

4 cups milk

pinch of salt

1¾ cups risotto or round grain rice

1 vanilla bean, split

¼ cup currants

¼ cup rum or water

2 tsp melted butter, for greasing

cornmeal or polenta, for dusting

¾ cup sugar

grated rind of 1 large lemon

4 tbsp butter, diced

3 eggs

2–3 tbsp lemon juice (optional)

confectioners' sugar

TO SERVE

¾ cup mascarpone cheese

2 tbsp rum

2 tbsp whipping cream

1 Bring the milk to a boil. Sprinkle in the salt and rice and bring back to a boil. Add the vanilla bean and seeds. Lower the heat and simmer, stirring occasionally, for 30 minutes.

2 Meanwhile, bring the currants and rum to a boil, then set aside.

3 Brush the base and side of a 10 inch/25 cm loose-bottomed cake pan with butter. Dust with about 2–3 tablespoons of cornmeal and shake out any excess.

4 Remove the rice from the heat and remove the vanilla bean. Stir in all but 1 tablespoon of sugar, with the lemon rind and butter, until the sugar is dissolved. Place in ice water to cool. Stir in the soaked currants and remaining rum.

5 Beat the eggs, with an electric mixer, for about 2 minutes until light and foamy. Gradually beat in about half the rice mixture, then stir in the rest. If using, stir in the lemon juice.

6 Pour into the prepared pan and smooth the top. Sprinkle with the reserved sugar and bake in a preheated oven, 325°F/160°C, for about 40 minutes until risen and golden and slightly firm. Cool in the pan on a wire rack.

7 Turn out and dust with confectioners' sugar. Transfer the cake to a serving plate. Whisk the mascarpone with the rum and cream and serve with the cake.

Spicy Carrot-Rice Loaf

Rice flour gives this delicious loaf a tender crumb while the cooked rice adds a chewy texture. Use any kind of cooked rice.

NUTRITIONAL INFORMATION

Calories	330	Sugars	........27g
Protein	.........5g	Fat	..........12g
Carbohydrate	...53g	Saturates	.......7g

 1½ hrs   1–1¼ hrs

SERVES 8–10

I N G R E D I E N T S

½ cup butter, melted and cooled, plus extra for greasing

2 cups all-purpose flour, plus extra for dusting

⅓ cup rice flour

2 tsp baking powder

½ tsp baking soda

½ tsp salt

1 tsp ground cinnamon

½ tsp freshly ground nutmeg

½ tsp ground ginger

⅓ cup cooked risotto or long grain white rice

½ cup chopped pecan nuts

⅔ cup golden raisins or raisins

3 eggs

1 cup sugar

½ cup brown sugar

2 carrots, grated

confectioners' sugar, for dusting

1 Lightly grease a 9 x 5 inch/ 23 x 12.5 cm loaf pan. Line with nonstick baking parchment and grease with a little butter. Dust lightly with flour.

2 Sift the flour, rice flour, baking powder, baking soda, salt, and spices into a bowl. Add the rice, nuts, and golden raisins or raisins and toss well to coat. Make a well in the center of the dry ingredients and set aside.

3 Using an electric mixer, beat the eggs for about 2 minutes until light and foaming. Add the sugars and continue beating for a further 2 minutes. Beat in the melted butter, then stir in the grated carrots until blended.

4 Pour the egg and carrot mixture into the well and, using a fork, stir until a soft batter forms. Do not over mix; the batter should be slightly lumpy.

5 Pour into the prepared pan and smooth the top. Bake in a preheated oven, 350°F/180°C, for about 1–1¼ hours until risen and golden. Cover the loaf with foil if it colors too quickly.

6 Cool the loaf in the pan on a wire rack for about 10 minutes. Carefully turn out and set aside to cool completely. Dust with a little confectioners' sugar and cut into thin slices to serve.

Aztec Oranges

Simplicity itself, this refreshing orange dessert is hard to beat and is the perfect follow-up to a hearty, spiced entrée dish.

NUTRITIONAL INFORMATION

Calories 98	Sugars 20g	
Protein 2g	Fat 0g	
Carbohydrate ...20g	Saturates 0g	

🧊 45 mins 🕐 0 mins

SERVES 4–6

INGREDIENTS

6 oranges

1 lime

2 tbsp tequila

2 tbsp orange-flavored liqueur

brown sugar, to taste

fine lime rind strips, to decorate (see Cook's Tip)

1 Using a sharp knife, cut a slice off the top and bottom of the oranges, then remove the peel and pith, cutting downward and taking care to retain the shape of the oranges.

2 Holding the oranges on their side, cut them horizontally into slices.

3 Place the oranges in a bowl. Cut the lime in half and squeeze over the oranges. Sprinkle with the tequila and liqueur, then sprinkle with sugar to taste.

4 Cover with plastic wrap and chill in the refrigerator until ready to serve, then transfer to a serving dish, and garnish with lime strips.

COOK'S TIP

To make the decoration, finely pare the rind from a lime using a vegetable peeler, then cut into thin strips. Blanch in boiling water for 2 minutes. Drain and rinse under cold running water. Drain again and pat dry with paper towels.

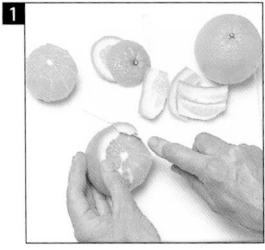

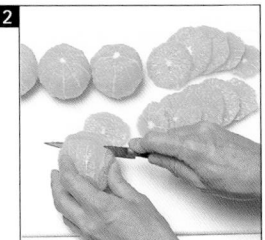

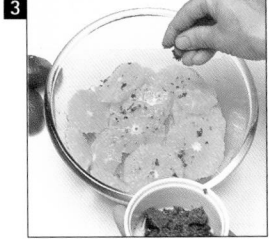

Pineapple Compote

For a more elaborate dish, accompany the pineapple with a scoop of good-quality pineapple sorbet.

NUTRITIONAL INFORMATION

Calories	87	Sugars	........19g
Protein	.........1g	Fat	...........0g
Carbohydrate	...19g	Saturates	.......0g

🐻

🍲 45 mins 🕐 0 mins

SERVES 4–6

INGREDIENTS

1 ripe pineapple

sugar

juice of 1 lemon

2–3 tbsp tequila or a few drops of vanilla extract

several fresh mint sprigs, leaves removed and cut into thin strips

fresh mint sprig, to decorate

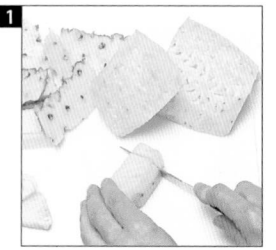  

1 Using a sharp knife, cut off the top and bottom of the pineapple. Place upright on a board, then slice off the skin, cutting downward. Cut in half, remove the core, then cut the flesh into slices. Cut the fruit into chunks.

2 Put the pineapple in a bowl and sprinkle with the sugar, lemon juice, tequila, or vanilla extract.

3 Toss the pineapple to coat well, then chill until ready to serve.

4 To serve, arrange on a serving plate and sprinkle with the mint strips. Decorate the dish with a mint sprig.

COOK'S TIP

Make sure you slice off the "eyes" when removing the skin from the pineapple.

Oranges & Strawberries

Ideal as a summery dessert, this dish can also be served as a fresh fruit dish with brunch. The oranges enhance the delicate flavor of the berries.

NUTRITIONAL INFORMATION

Calories	84	Sugars	. . . . .20g
Protein	. . . . .2g	Fat	. . . . .0g
Carbohydrate	. . .20g	Saturates	. . . . . . .0g

 45 mins   0 mins

SERVES 4

I N G R E D I E N T S

3 sweet oranges

2 cups strawberries

grated rind and juice of 1 lime

1–2 tbsp superfine sugar

fresh mint sprig, to decorate

1 Using a sharp knife, cut a slice off the top and bottom of the oranges, then remove the peel and all the pith, cutting downward and taking care to retain the shape of the oranges.

2 Using a small sharp knife, cut down between the membranes of the oranges to remove the segments. Discard the membranes.

3 Hull the strawberries, pulling the leaves off with a pinching action. Cut into slices, along the length of the strawberries.

4 Put the oranges and strawberries in a bowl, then sprinkle with the lime rind, lime juice, and sugar. Chill in the refrigerator until ready to serve.

5 To serve, transfer to a serving bowl and decorate the dish with a mint sprig.

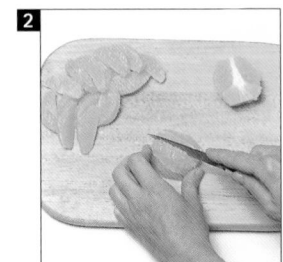

VARIATION

An optional hint of orange-flavored liqueur is delicious on this—reduce or omit the sugar. You can replace the oranges with mangoes, and the strawberries with blackberries, for a dramatically colored dessert.

Icy Fruit Blizzard

Keep a store of prepared fruit in the freezer, then whirl it up into this refreshing dessert, which is as light and healthy as it is satisfying.

NUTRITIONAL INFORMATION

Calories	178	Sugars	........43g
Protein	.........2g	Fat	...........1g
Carbohydrate	...43g	Saturates	.......0g

2¼ hrs · 0 mins

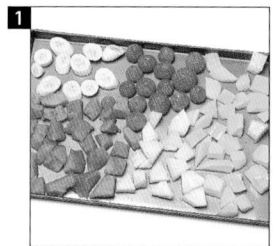  

SERVES 4

I N G R E D I E N T S

1 pineapple

1 large piece of deseeded watermelon, peeled and cut into small pieces

2 cups strawberries or other berries, hulled and whole or sliced

1 mango, peach, or nectarine, peeled and sliced

1 banana, peeled and sliced

orange juice

superfine sugar

1 Cover 2 nonstick cookie sheets or ordinary cookie sheets with a sheet of plastic wrap. Arrange the fruit on top and freeze for at least 2 hours or until firm and icy.

2 Place 1 type of fruit in a food processor and process until it is broken up into small pieces.

3 Add a little orange juice and sugar, to taste, and continue to process until it forms a granular mixture. Repeat with the remaining fruit. Arrange in chilled bowls and serve immediately.

Cottage Cheese Hearts

These look very attractive when they are made in the French coeur à la crème china molds, but small ramekins could be used instead.

NUTRITIONAL INFORMATION

Calories	114	Sugars	. . . . .19g
Protein	. . . . .9g	Fat	. . . . .1g
Carbohydrate	. . .19g	Saturates	. . . . .0.4g

1¼ hrs   0 mins

SERVES 4

INGREDIENTS

scant ¾ cup low-fat cottage cheese

⅔ cup low-fat plain yogurt

1 egg white

2 tbsp superfine sugar

1–2 tsp vanilla extract

rose-scented geranium leaves, to decorate (optional)

SAUCE

2 cups strawberries

4 tbsp unsweetened orange juice

2–3 tsp confectioners' sugar

1 Line 4 heart-shaped molds with clean cheesecloth. Place a strainer over a mixing bowl and using the back of a metal spoon, press through the cottage cheese. Mix in the yogurt.

2 Whisk the egg white until stiff. Fold into the cheese mixture with the superfine sugar and vanilla extract.

3 Spoon the cheese mixture into the molds and smooth the tops. Place on a wire rack over a tray and set aside to chill in the refrigerator for about 1 hour until firm and drained.

4 Meanwhile, make the sauce. Wash the strawberries under cold running water. Reserving a few strawberries for decoration, hull, and chop the remainder.

5 Place the strawberries in a blender or food processor with the orange juice and process until smooth. Alternatively, push through a strainer to purée. Mix with the confectioners' sugar to taste. Scrape into a bowl, cover, and set aside to chill in the refrigerator until required.

6 Remove the cheese hearts from the molds and transfer to serving plates.

7 Remove the cheesecloth, decorate with strawberries and geranium leaves, if using, and serve with the sauce.

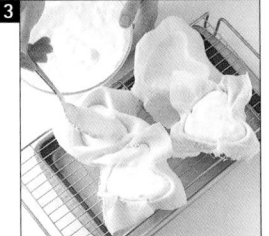

Carrot & Ginger Cake

This melt-in-your-mouth version of a favorite cake has a fraction of the fat of the traditional cake.

NUTRITIONAL INFORMATION

Calories 249   Sugars 28g
Protein . . . . .7g   Fat 6g
Carbohydrate . . .46g   Saturates 1g

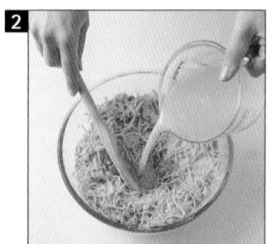
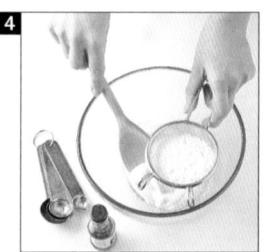

15 mins   1¼ hrs

SERVES 10

I N G R E D I E N T S

butter, for greasing

2 cups all-purpose flour

1 tsp baking powder

1 tsp baking soda

2 tsp ground ginger

½ tsp salt

¾ cup molasses sugar

1⅔ cups grated carrots

2 pieces chopped preserved ginger

1 tbsp grated fresh ginger root

generous ⅓ cup seedless raisins

2 eggs, beaten

3 tbsp corn oil

juice of 1 orange

F R O S T I N G

1 cup low-fat soft cheese

4 tbsp confectioners' sugar

1 tsp vanilla extract

T O   D E C O R A T E

grated carrot

finely chopped preserved ginger

ground ginger

1 Preheat the oven to 350°F/180°C. Grease and line an 8 inch/20 cm round cake pan with baking parchment.

2 Sift the flour, baking powder, baking soda, ground ginger, and salt into a bowl. Stir in the sugar, carrots, preserved ginger, fresh ginger root, and raisins. Beat together the eggs, oil. and orange juice, then pour into the bowl. Mix the ingredients together well.

3 Spoon the mixture into the pan and bake in the oven for 1–1¼ hours until firm to the touch or until a toothpick inserted into the center of the cake comes out clean.

4 To make the frosting, place the soft cheese in a bowl and beat to soften. Sift in the confectioners' sugar and add the vanilla extract. Mix well.

5 Remove the cake from the pan and smooth the frosting over the top. Decorate the cake and serve.

Chocolate Cheese Pots

These super-light desserts are just the thing if you have a craving for chocolate. Serve them on their own or with a selection of fruits.

NUTRITIONAL INFORMATION

Calories	.117	Sugars	.17g
Protein	.9g	Fat	.1g
Carbohydrate	.18g	Saturates	.1g

40 mins   0 mins

SERVES 4

INGREDIENTS

1¼ cup ricotta cheese

⅔ cup low-fat plain yogurt

2 tbsp confectioners' sugar

4 tsp low-fat drinking chocolate powder

4 tsp unsweetened cocoa

1 tsp vanilla extract

2 tbsp dark rum, optional

2 egg whites

4 chocolate cake decorations

TO SERVE

pieces of kiwi fruit, orange, and banana

strawberries and raspberries

1 Combine the ricotta cheese and low-fat yogurt in a bowl. Sift in the confectioners' sugar, drinking chocolate, and unsweetened cocoa and mix well. Add the vanilla extract and rum, if using.

2 In a clean bowl, whisk the egg whites until stiff. Using a metal spoon, gently fold the egg whites into the chocolate mixture.

3 Spoon the yogurt and chocolate mixture into 4 small china dessert pots and set aside in the refrigerator to chill for about 30 minutes.

4 Decorate each chocolate cheese pot with a chocolate cake decoration and serve with an assortment of fresh fruit, such as pieces of kiwi fruit, orange, banana, strawberries and raspberries.

COOK'S TIP

This chocolate mixture can also be used as a cheesecake filling. Make the base out of crushed amaretti cookies and egg white, and set the filling with 2 teaspoons of powdered gelatin dissolved in 2 tablespoons of boiling water.

Strawberry Meringues

The combination of aromatic strawberries and rosewater with crisp caramelized sugar meringues makes this a truly irresistible dessert.

NUTRITIONAL INFORMATION

Calories	145	Sugars 35g
Protein	.........3g	Fat 0.3g
Carbohydrate	...35g	Saturates 0.1g

🥄 1 hr   🕐 3½ hrs

SERVES 4

INGREDIENTS

3 egg whites

pinch of salt

¾ cup molasses sugar, crushed

2 cups strawberries, hulled

2 tsp rose water

⅔ cup ricotta cheese

extra strawberries, to serve (optional)

TO DECORATE

rose-scented geranium leaves

rose petals

1 In a large grease-free bowl, whisk the egg whites with the salt until very stiff and dry. Gradually whisk in the sugar, a spoonful at a time, until the mixture is stiff again.

2 Line a cookie sheet with baking parchment and drop 12 spoonfuls of the meringue mixture onto it. Bake in a preheated oven, 250°F/120°C, for 3–3½ hours until completely dried out and crisp. Set aside to cool.

3 Reserve ½ cup of the strawberries. Place the remaining strawberries in a blender or food processor and blend for a few seconds until smooth.

4 Alternatively, mash the strawberries with a fork and press through a strainer to form a purée. Stir in the rosewater. Chill until required.

5 To serve, slice the reserved strawberries lengthwise. Sandwich the meringues together with ricotta and sliced strawberries.

6 Spoon the strawberry rose purée onto six serving plates and top with a meringue.

7 Decorate with rose petals and rose-scented geranium leaves, and serve with extra strawberries, if using.

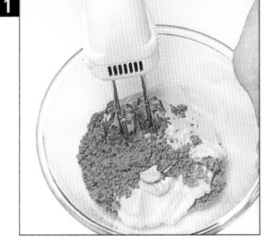

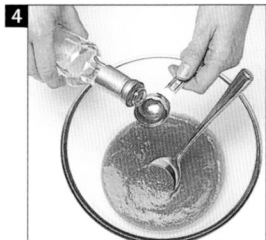

Pears with Maple Cream

These spicy cinnamon pears are accompanied by a delicious melt-in-your-mouth maple and ricotta cream—you won't believe it's low in fat!

NUTRITIONAL INFORMATION

Calories 190	Sugars 28g	
Protein 6g	Fat 7g	
Carbohydrate ...28g	Saturates 4g	

10 mins   25 mins

SERVES 4

INGREDIENTS

1 lemon

4 firm pears

1¼ cups hard cider or unsweetened apple juice

1 cinnamon stick, broken in half

fresh mint leaves to decorate

MAPLE RICOTTA CREAM

½ cup low-fat ricotta cheese

½ cup farmer's cheese

½ tsp ground cinnamon

½ tsp grated lemon rind

1 tbsp maple syrup

lemon rind, to decorate

1 Using a vegetable peeler, remove the rind from the lemon and place in a nonstick skillet. Squeeze the lemon and pour into a shallow bowl.

2 Peel the pears, then halve, and core them. Toss them in the lemon juice to prevent discoloration. Place in the skillet and pour over the remaining lemon juice.

3 Add the hard cider or apple juice and cinnamon stick halves. Gently bring to a boil, lower the heat so the liquid just simmers, and cook the pears for 10 minutes. Remove the pears using a slotted spoon. Reserve the cooking liquid. Place the pears in a warmed heatproof serving dish, cover with foil, and put in a warming drawer or low oven.

4 Return the skillet to the heat, bring to a boil, then simmer for 8–10 minutes until reduced by half. Spoon the mixture over the pears.

5 To make the maple ricotta cream, combine all the ingredients. Decorate the cream with lemon rind, and the pears with mint leaves, and serve together.

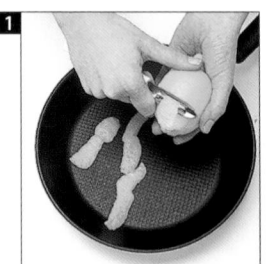

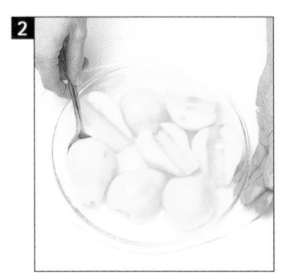

COOK'S TIP

Red Anjou and Packham's pears are suitable for this recipe. Pears ripen quickly and can bruise easily. It's best to buy them just before you plan to cook them.

Chocolate & Pineapple Cake

Decorated with thick yogurt and canned pineapple, this is a low-fat cake, but it is by no means lacking in flavor.

NUTRITIONAL INFORMATION

Calories ....199 Sugars 19g
Protein ....5g Fat 9g
Carbohydrate ...28g Saturates 3g

10 mins   25 mins

SERVES 9

INGREDIENTS

⅔ cup low-fat spread, plus extra for greasing

scant ¾ cup superfine sugar

generous ¾ cup self-rising flour, sifted

3 tbsp unsweetened cocoa, sifted

1½ tsp baking powder

2 eggs

8 oz/225 g can pineapple pieces in natural juice

½ cup low-fat thick plain yogurt

about 1 tbsp confectioners' sugar

grated chocolate, to decorate

1 Lightly grease an 8 inch/20 cm square cake pan with a little low-fat spread.

2 Place the low-fat spread, superfine sugar, flour, unsweetened cocoa, baking powder, and eggs in a large mixing bowl. Beat with a wooden spoon or electric hand whisk until smooth.

3 Pour the cake mixture into the prepared pan and level the surface. Bake in a preheated oven, 325°F/190°C, for 20–25 minutes or until springy to the touch. Set aside to cool slightly in the pan before transferring to a wire rack to cool completely.

4 Drain the pineapple, chop the pineapple pieces, and drain again. Reserve a little pineapple for decoration, then stir the remainder into the yogurt, and sweeten to taste with confectioners' sugar.

5 Spread the pineapple and yogurt mixture over the cake and decorate with the reserved pineapple pieces. Sprinkle with the grated chocolate.

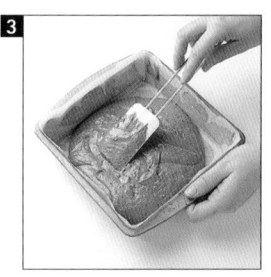

Summer Fruit Salad

A mixture of soft summer fruits in an orange-flavored syrup with a dash of port. Serve with low-fat yogurt.

NUTRITIONAL INFORMATION

Calories 110   Sugars 26g
Protein . . . . .1g   Fat 0.1g
Carbohydrate . . .26g   Saturates 0g

 5 mins   10 mins

SERVES 6

INGREDIENTS

6 tbsp superfine sugar

5 tbsp water

grated rind and juice of 1 small orange

2¼ cups red currants, stripped from their stalks

2 tsp arrowroot

2 tbsp port

1 cup blackberries

1 cup blueberries

1 cup strawberries

1⅓ cups raspberries

low-fat yogurt, to serve

1 Put the sugar, water, and grated orange rind into a heavy pan and heat gently, stirring until the sugar has completely dissolved.

COOK'S TIP

Although this salad is really best made with fresh fruits in season, you can achieve an acceptable result with frozen equivalents, with perhaps the exception of strawberries. You can buy frozen fruits of the forest, which would be ideal, in most supermarkets.

2 Add the red currants and orange juice, bring to a boil, and simmer gently for 2–3 minutes.

3 Strain the fruit, reserving the syrup, and put into a bowl.

4 Blend the arrowroot with a little water. Return the syrup to the pan, add the arrowroot, and bring to a boil, stirring constantly until thickened.

5 Add the port and mix together well. Then pour the syrup over the red currants in the bowl.

6 Add the blackberries, blueberries, strawberries, and raspberries. Mix the fruit together and set aside to cool until required. Serve in individual glass dishes with low-fat yogurt.

Fruity Muffins

The perfect choice for people on a low-fat diet,
these little cakes contain no butter, just a little corn oil.

NUTRITIONAL INFORMATION

Calories	162	Sugars	........11g
Protein	.........4g	Fat	...........4g
Carbohydrate	...28g	Saturates	......1g

 10 mins   30 mins

MAKES 10

I N G R E D I E N T S

2 cups self-rising whole-wheat flour

2 tsp baking powder

2 tbsp molasses sugar

3½ oz/100 g no-need-to-soak dried
  apricots, finely chopped

1 medium banana, mashed with 1 tbsp
  orange juice

1 tsp finely grated orange rind

1¼ cups skim milk

1 egg, beaten

3 tbsp corn oil

2 tbsp rolled oats

fruit spread, honey, or maple syrup,
  to serve

1 Place 10 paper muffin cases in a deep patty pan. Sift the flour and baking powder into a mixing bowl, adding any husks that remain in the strainer. Stir in the sugar and chopped apricots.

2 Make a well in the center and add the banana, orange rind, milk, beaten egg, and oil. Mix together well to form a thick batter. Divide the batter evenly among the 10 paper cases.

3 Sprinkle with a few rolled oats and bake in a preheated oven, 400°F/ 200°C, for 25–30 minutes until well risen and firm to the touch or until a toothpick inserted into the center comes out clean.

4 Transfer the muffins to a wire rack to cool slightly. Serve the muffins while still warm with a little fruit spread, honey, or maple syrup.

VARIATION

If you like dried figs, they
make a deliciously crunchy
alternative to the apricots; they
also go very well with the flavor
of orange. Other no-need-to-soak
dried fruits, chopped finely,
can be used as well.

Almond Trifles

Amaretti cookies made with ground almonds have a high fat content. Use cookies made from apricot kernels for a lower fat content.

NUTRITIONAL INFORMATION

Calories 241   Sugars 23g
Protein . . . . .9g   Fat 6g
Carbohydrate . . .35g   Saturates 2g

  1¼ hrs   0 mins

SERVES 4

INGREDIENTS

8 amaretti cookies

4 tbsp brandy or Amaretto liqueur

1⅓ cups raspberries

1¼ cups low-fat custard

1¼ cups low-fat plain thick yogurt

1 tsp almond extract

2 tbsp sliced almonds, toasted

1 tsp unsweetened cocoa

1 Place the cookies in a mixing bowl and using the end of a rolling pin, carefully crush them into small pieces.

2 Divide the crushed cookies among 4 serving glasses. Sprinkle over the brandy or liqueur and set aside for about 30 minutes to soften.

3 Top with a layer of raspberries, reserving a few for decoration, and spoon over enough custard just to cover.

4 Combine the yogurt with the almond extract and spoon the mixture over the custard, smoothing the surface. Chill in the refrigerator for about 30 minutes.

5 Before serving, sprinkle with the toasted almonds and dust with unsweetened cocoa.

6 Decorate the trifles with the reserved raspberries and serve immediately.

VARIATION

Try this trifle with assorted summer fruits. If they are a frozen mix, use them frozen and allow them to thaw so that the juices soak into the cookie base—it will taste delicious.

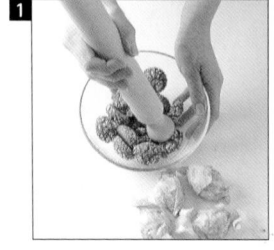

Spun Sugar Pears

Whole pears are poached in a Madeira syrup in the microwave, then served with a delicate spun sugar surround.

NUTRITIONAL INFORMATION

Calories 166	Sugars 41g	
Protein 0.3g	Fat 0g	
Carbohydrate ...41g	Saturates 0g	

🧊 20 mins   🕐 35 mins

SERVES 4

INGREDIENTS

⅔ cup water

⅔ cup sweet Madeira wine

scant ⅔ cup superfine sugar

2 tbsp lime juice

4 ripe pears, peeled, stalks left on

fresh mint sprigs, to decorate

SPUN SUGAR

scant ⅔ cup superfine sugar

3 tbsp water

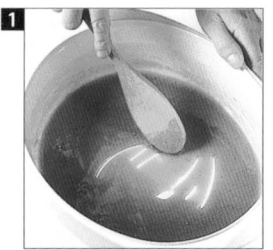 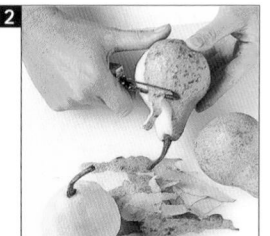 

1 Combine the water, Madeira, sugar, and lime juice in a large bowl. Cover and cook on HIGH power for 3 minutes. Stir well until the sugar dissolves.

2 Peel the pears and cut a thin slice from the base of each, so that they stand upright.

3 Add the pears to the bowl, spooning the wine syrup over them. Cover and cook on HIGH power for about 10 minutes, turning the pears over every few minutes, until they are tender. The cooking time may vary slightly depending on the ripeness of the pears. Set aside to cool, covered, in the syrup.

4 Remove the cooled pears from the syrup and set aside on serving plates. Cook the syrup, uncovered, on HIGH power for about 15 minutes until reduced by half and thickened slightly. Set aside for 5 minutes. Spoon the syrup over the pears.

5 To make the spun sugar, combine the sugar and water in a bowl. Cook, uncovered, on HIGH power for

1½ minutes. Stir until the sugar has dissolved completely. Continue to cook on HIGH power for about 5–6 minutes more until the sugar has caramelized.

6 Wait for the caramel bubbles to subside and set aside for 2 minutes. Dip a teaspoon in the caramel and spin sugar around each pear in a circular motion. Serve decorated with mint.

Rich Fruit Cake

Serve this moist, fruit-laden cake for a special occasion.
It would also make an excellent Thanksgiving cake.

NUTRITIONAL INFORMATION

Calories 772	Sugars 137g	
Protein 14g	Fat 5g	
Carbohydrate ..179g	Saturates 1g	

35 mins   1¾ hrs

SERVES 4

INGREDIENTS

butter or margarine, for greasing

6 oz/175 g unsweetened stoned dates

½ cup no-need-to-soak dried prunes

scant 1 cup unsweetened orange juice

2 tbsp molasses

1 tsp finely grated lemon rind

1 tsp finely grated orange rind

2 cups self-rising whole-wheat flour

1 tsp apple spice

scant 1 cup seedless raisins

scant 1 cup golden raisins

½ cup currants

1 cup dried cranberries

3 large eggs, separated

TO DECORATE

1 tbsp apricot jelly, softened

confectioners' sugar, to dust

generous 1 cup sugarpaste

strips of orange rind

strips of lemon rind

1 Grease and line a deep 8 inch/20 cm round cake pan. Chop the dates and prunes and place in a pan. Pour over the orange juice and simmer for 10 minutes. Remove the pan from the heat and beat the fruit mixture until puréed. Add the molasses and lemon and orange rinds. Set aside to cool.

2 Sift the flour and spice into a bowl, adding any husks from the strainer. Add the dried fruits. When the date and prune mixture is cool, whisk in the egg yolks. In a clean bowl, whisk the egg whites until stiff. Spoon the fruit mixture into the dry ingredients and mix together.

3 Gently fold in the egg whites. Transfer to the prepared pan and bake in a preheated oven, 325°F/170°C, for 1½ hours. Set aside to cool.

4 Remove the cake from the pan and brush the top with jelly. Dust the counter with confectioners' sugar and roll out the sugarpaste thinly. Lay it over the top of the cake and trim the edges. Decorate with orange and lemon rind.

Summer Fruit Clafoutis

Serve this mouthwatering French-style fruit-in-batter dessert hot or cold with low-fat yogurt.

NUTRITIONAL INFORMATION

Calories	228	Sugars	........26g
Protein	.........9g	Fat	...........2g
Carbohydrate	...42g	Saturates	......1g

🍓 🍓 🍓

🍲 1¾ hrs   🕐 50 mins

SERVES 4

I N G R E D I E N T S

1 lb 2 oz/500 g prepared fresh assorted soft fruits, such as blackberries, raspberries, strawberries, blueberries, cherries, gooseberries, red currants, black currants

4 tbsp soft fruit liqueur such as crème de cassis, kirsch, or framboise

4 tbsp nonfat dry milk

1 cup all-purpose flour

pinch of salt

¼ cup superfine sugar

2 eggs, beaten

1¼ cups skim milk

1 tsp vanilla extract

2 tsp superfine sugar, for dusting

TO SERVE

assorted soft fruits

low-fat yogurt

1 Place the assorted fruits in a mixing bowl and spoon over the fruit liqueur. Cover and chill for 1 hour for the fruit to macerate.

2 In a large bowl, combine the nonfat dry milk, flour, salt, and sugar. Make a well in the center and gradually whisk in the eggs, milk, and vanilla extract, using a balloon whisk, until smooth. Transfer to a pitcher and set aside for 30 minutes.

3 Line the base of a 9 inch/23 cm round ovenproof dish with baking parchment and spoon in all the fruits and their juices.

4 Whisk the batter again and pour it over the fruits, stand the dish on a cookie sheet, and bake in a preheated oven, 400°F/200°C, for 50 minutes until firm, risen, and golden brown.

5 Dust with superfine sugar. Serve immediately with extra fruits and low-fat plain yogurt.

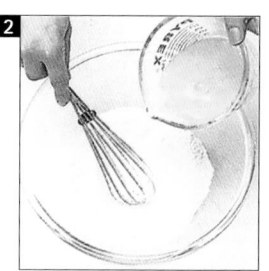

Beancurd Cake

This cake has a rich, creamy texture just like cheesecake, but contains no dairy produce. Crushed graham crackers make an easy pie shell.

NUTRITIONAL INFORMATION

Calories ....282 Sugars 17g
Protein ....9g Fat 15g
Carbohydrate ...29g Saturates 4g

10 mins   45 mins

SERVES 4

INGREDIENTS

¼ cup margarine, melted, plus extra for greasing

4 oz/115 g low-fat graham crackers, crushed

⅓ cup pitted dates, chopped

4 tbsp lemon juice

rind of 1 lemon

3 tbsp water

12 oz/350g firm beancurd

⅔ cup apple juice

1 banana, mashed

1 tsp vanilla extract

1 mango, peeled and chopped

1 Lightly grease a 7 inch/18 cm round loose-bottomed cake pan.

2 Mix together the graham cracker crumbs and melted margarine in a bowl. Press the mixture into the base of the prepared pan.

3 Put the chopped dates, lemon juice, lemon rind, and water into a pan and bring to a boil.

4 Simmer for 5 minutes until the dates are soft, then mash them coarsely.

5 Place the mixture in a blender or food processor with the beancurd, apple juice, mashed banana, and vanilla extract and process to a thick, smooth purée. Pour the purée into the prepared cracker crumb base and smooth the surface.

6 Bake in a preheated oven, 350°F/ 180°C, for 30–40 minutes until lightly golden. Set aside to cool in the pan, then chill before serving.

7 Place the chopped mango in a blender and process until smooth. Scrape into a bowl. Serve it as a sauce with the chilled cheesecake.

Fruit Loaf with Apple Spread

This sweet, fruity loaf is ideal served with coffee for a healthy snack.
The fruit spread can be made quickly while the cake is in the oven.

NUTRITIONAL INFORMATION

Calories 733   Sugars 110g
Protein . . . . .12g   Fat 5g
Carbohydrate . . .171g   Saturates 1g

1¼ hrs   2 hrs

SERVES 4

I N G R E D I E N T S

1¾ cups rolled oats

scant ½ cup molasses sugar

1 tsp ground cinnamon

scant 1 cup golden raisins

generous 1 cup seedless raisins

2 tbsp malt extract

1¼ cups unsweetened apple juice

1½ cups self-rising whole-wheat flour

1½ tsp baking powder

strawberries and apple wedges, to serve

F R U I T   S P R E A D

2 cups strawberries, washed and hulled

2 dessert apples, cored, chopped, and
    mixed with 1 tbsp lemon juice to prevent
    them from browning

1¼ cups unsweetened apple juice

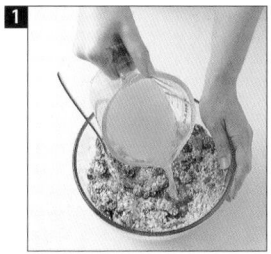

1 Grease and line a 2 lb/900 g loaf
   pan and set aside. Place the oats,
sugar, cinnamon, golden raisins, raisins,
and malt extract in a mixing bowl. Pour in
the apple juice, stir well, and set aside to
soak for 30 minutes.

2 Sift in the flour and baking powder,
   adding any husks that remain in the
strainer, and fold in using a metal spoon.

Spoon the mixture into the prepared pan
and bake in a preheated oven,
350°F/180°C, for 1½ hours until firm or
until a toothpick inserted into the center
comes out clean.

3 Remove the pan from the oven and
   place on a wire rack to cool for about
10 minutes, then turn the loaf out onto the
rack and set aside to cool completely.

4 Meanwhile, make the fruit spread.
   Place the strawberries and apples in a
pan and pour in the apple juice. Bring to a
boil, cover, and simmer for 30 minutes.
Beat the sauce well and spoon into a
clean, warmed jar. Set aside to cool, then
seal, and label.

5 Serve the loaf with the fruit spread
   and strawberries, and apple wedges.

Warm Currants in Cassis

Crème de cassis is a black currant liqueur which comes from France and is an excellent flavoring for fruit dishes.

NUTRITIONAL INFORMATION

Calories	202	Sugars	........35g
Protein	.........2g	Fat	...........6g
Carbohydrate	...35g	Saturates	......4g

10 mins   10 mins

SERVES 4

INGREDIENTS

3 cups black currants

2 cups red currants

4 tbsp superfine sugar

grated rind and juice of 1 orange

2 tsp arrowroot

2 tbsp crème de cassis

whipped cream or low-fat yogurt, to serve

1 Using a fork, strip the black currants and red currants from their stalks and put in a pan.

2 Add the superfine sugar and orange rind and juice and heat gently, stirring, until the sugar has dissolved. Bring to a boil and simmer gently for 5 minutes.

3 Strain the currants and place in a bowl, then return the juice to the pan.

4 Blend the arrowroot with a little water and mix into the juice in the pan. Boil the mixture until thickened.

5 Set aside to cool slightly, then stir in the cassis.

6 Serve in individual dishes with whipped cream or yogurt.

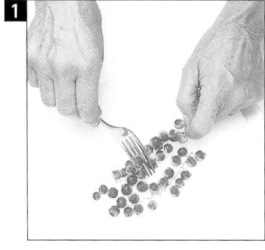

Winter Desserts

An interesting alternative to the familiar and ever-popular summer dessert that uses dried fruits and a tasty malt loaf.

NUTRITIONAL INFORMATION

Calories	....	.447
Protein	....	.9g
Carbohydrate	...	.80g

Sugars	....	.68g
Fat	....	.11g
Saturates	......	.5g

12 hrs   15 mins

SERVES 4

I N G R E D I E N T S

11½ oz/325 g fruit malt loaf

scant ¾ cup no-need-to-soak dried apricots, coarsely chopped

6 cups coarsely chopped dried apple

generous 1¾ cups orange juice

1 tsp grated orange rind, plus extra to decorate

2 tbsp orange liqueur

low-fat crème fraîche or low-fat natural yogurt, to serve

1 Cut the malt loaf into ½ inch/5 mm thick slices.

2 Place the apricots, apple, and orange juice in a pan. Bring to a boil, then simmer for 10 minutes. Remove the fruit, using a slotted spoon, and reserve the liquid. Place the fruit in a dish and set aside to cool. Stir in the orange rind and orange liqueur.

3 Line 4 x ¾ cup bowls or ramekin dishes with baking parchment.

4 Cut 4 circles from the malt loaf slices to fit the tops of the molds and cut the remaining slices to line them.

5 Soak the malt loaf slices in the reserved fruit syrup, then arrange around the base and sides of the molds. Trim away any crusts which overhang the edges. Fill the centers with the chopped fruit, pressing down well, and place the malt loaf circles on top.

6 Cover with baking parchment and weigh each bowl down with an 8 oz/225 g weight or a food can. Chill in the refrigerator overnight.

7 Remove the weight and baking parchment. Carefully turn the puddings out onto 4 serving plates. Remove the lining paper.

8 Decorate with orange rind and serve with crème fraîche or yogurt.

Red Fruits with Frothy Sauce

A colorful combination of soft fruits, served with a marshmallow sauce, is an ideal dessert when summer fruits are in season.

NUTRITIONAL INFORMATION

Calories 219   Sugars 55g
Protein . . . . .2g   Fat 0.3g
Carbohydrate . . .55g   Saturates 0g

1¼ hrs   20 mins

SERVES 4

INGREDIENTS

2 cups red currants, trimmed, thawed
 if frozen

2 cups cranberries

⅓ cup molasses sugar

scant 1 cup unsweetened apple juice

1 cinnamon stick, broken

2⅔ cup small strawberries, hulled
 and halved

SAUCE

1⅓ cups raspberries, thawed if frozen

2 tbsp fruit cordial

3½ oz/100 g marshmallows

1 Place the red currants, cranberries, and sugar in a pan. Pour in the apple juice and add the cinnamon stick. Bring the mixture to a boil and simmer gently for 10 minutes until the fruit is soft.

2 Stir the strawberries into the fruit mixture and mix well. Transfer the mixture to a bowl, cover with plastic wrap, and set aside to chill in the refrigerator for about 1 hour. Remove and discard the cinnamon stick.

3 Just before serving, make the sauce. Put the raspberries and fruit cordial in a small pan, bring to a boil, and simmer for 2–3 minutes until the fruit just begins to soften. Stir the marshmallows into the raspberry mixture and heat through, stirring constantly, until the marshmallows begin to melt.

4 Transfer the fruit salad to serving bowls. Spoon over the raspberry and marshmallow sauce and serve.

COOK'S TIP

This sauce is delicious poured over low-fat ice cream. For an extra-colorful sauce, replace the raspberries with an assortment of summer berries.

Fruity Potato Cake

Sweet potatoes mix beautifully with fruit and brown sugar in this unusual cake. Add a few drops of rum or brandy if you like.

NUTRITIONAL INFORMATION

Calories	275	Sugars	........44g
Protein	.........6g	Fat	...........5g
Carbohydrate	...55g	Saturates	......2g

 15 mins   1½ hrs

SERVES 6

I N G R E D I E N T S

1 tbsp butter, melted, plus extra
   for greasing

1½ lb/675 g sweet potatoes, diced

½ cup raw sugar

3 eggs

3 tbsp skim milk

1 tbsp lemon juice

grated rind of 1 lemon

1 tsp caraway seeds

1 cup chopped dried fruits, such as apple,
   pear or mango

2 tsp baking powder

1 Lightly grease a 7 inch/18 cm square cake pan.

2 Bring a large pan of water to a boil. Add the sweet potatoes, bring back to a boil and cook, for 10 minutes or until soft. Drain and mash until smooth.

3 Transfer the mashed sweet potatoes to a mixing bowl while still hot and add the butter and sugar, mixing thoroughly to dissolve.

4 Beat in the eggs, skim milk, lemon juice and rind, caraway seeds, and chopped dried fruit. Add the baking powder and mix well.

5 Pour the mixture into the prepared cake pan and smooth the top. Cook in a preheated oven, 325°F/160°C, for about 1-1¼ hours or until cooked through and a

toothpick inserted into the center comes out clean.

6 Remove the cake from the pan and transfer to a wire rack to cool. Cut into thick slices to serve or wrap in plastic wrap and store in the freezer. (To serve, thaw and warm through.)

Paper-Thin Fruit Pies

The extra-crisp pie shells, filled with slices of fruit and glazed with apricot jelly, are best served hot with low-fat custard.

NUTRITIONAL INFORMATION

Calories 158	Sugars 12g	
Protein 2g	Fat 10g	
Carbohydrate ...14g	Saturates 2g	

20 mins   15 mins

SERVES 4

INGREDIENTS

1 medium dessert apple

1 medium ripe pear

2 tbsp lemon juice

¼ cup low-fat spread

4 rectangular sheets of phyllo pastry, thawed if frozen

2 tbsp low-sugar apricot jelly

1 tbsp unsweetened orange juice

1 tbsp finely chopped pistachio nuts, shelled

2 tsp confectioners' sugar, for dusting

low-fat custard, to serve

1 Core and thinly slice the apple and pear and immediately toss them in the lemon juice to prevent them from turning brown. Gently melt the low-fat spread in a pan over low heat.

2 Cut the sheets of dough into 4 and cover with a clean, damp dish cloth. Brush 4 nonstick muffin pans, measuring 4 inches/10 cm in diameter, with a little of the low-fat spread.

3 Working on each pie separately, brush 4 sheets of dough with low-fat spread. Press a small sheet of dough into the base of 1 pan. Arrange the other sheets of dough on top at slightly different angles. Repeat with the other sheets of dough to make another 3 pies.

4 Arrange the apple and pear slices alternately in the center of each pie shell and lightly crimp the edges of the dough of each pie.

5 Stir the jelly and orange juice together until smooth and brush over the fruit. Bake in a preheated oven, 400°F/200°C, for 12–15 minutes. Sprinkle with the pistachio nuts, dust lightly with confectioners' sugar, and serve hot with low-fat custard.

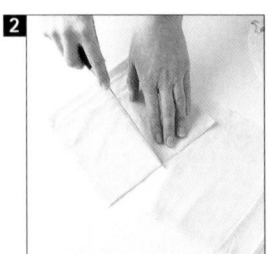

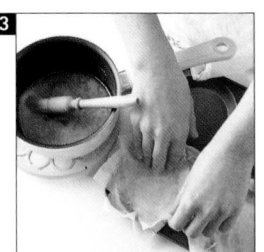

VARIATION

Other combinations of fruit are equally delicious. Try peach and apricot, raspberry and apple, or pineapple and mango.

Lace Crêpes with Fruit

These super-light crêpes melt in your mouth. They are filled with a gingered fruit salad of melon, grapes, and lychees.

NUTRITIONAL INFORMATION

Calories 176	Sugars 22g	
Protein 3g	Fat 2g	
Carbohydrate . . .36g	Saturates 0.2g	

🥄 10 mins   🕐 5 mins

SERVES 4

INGREDIENTS

3 egg whites

4 tbsp cornstarch

3 tbsp cold water

1 tsp vegetable oil

FRUIT FILLING

12 oz/350g fresh lychees

¼ ogen or charentais melon

6 oz/175 g seedless green grapes

½ inch/1 cm piece of fresh ginger root

2 pieces of preserved ginger in syrup

2 tbsp ginger wine or dry sherry

1 To make the fruit filling, peel the lychees and remove the pits. Place the lychees in a bowl. Scoop out the seeds from the melon and remove the skin. Cut the melon flesh into small pieces and place in the bowl.

2 Wash and dry the grapes, remove the stalks, and add to the bowl. Peel the ginger and cut into thin shreds or grate finely. Drain the preserved ginger pieces, reserving the syrup, and chop the ginger pieces finely.

3 Stir the root and preserved ginger into the bowl with the ginger wine or sherry and the preserved ginger syrup. Cover with plastic wrap and set aside.

4 Meanwhile, prepare the crêpes. In a small pitcher, combine the egg whites, cornstarch, and cold water, stirring until very smooth.

5 Brush a small nonstick crêpe pan with oil and heat until hot. Drizzle the surface of the pan with a quarter of the cornstarch mixture to give a lacy effect. Cook for a few seconds until set, then

carefully lift out, and transfer to absorbent paper towels to drain. Set aside and keep warm. Repeat with the remaining mixture to make 4 crêpes in total.

6 To serve, place a crêpe on each of 4 serving plates and top with the fruit filling. Fold over the crêpes and serve hot.

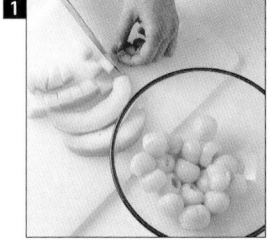

Crispy-Topped Fruit Bake

The sugar lumps give a lovely crunchy texture to this easy-to-make blackberry and apple dessert.

NUTRITIONAL INFORMATION

Calories	227	Sugars	........30g
Protein	.........5g	Fat	...........1g
Carbohydrate	...53g	Saturates	.....0.2g

🍰 🍰

🍧 15 mins   🕐 1 hr

SERVES 10

INGREDIENTS

butter or margarine, for greasing

12 oz/350 g cooking apples

3 tbsp lemon juice

2½ cups self-rising whole-wheat flour

½ tsp baking powder

1 tsp ground cinnamon, plus extra
   for dusting

¾ cup prepared blackberries, thawed
   if frozen, plus extra to decorate

¾ cup molasses sugar

1 egg, beaten

scant 1 cup low-fat plain yogurt

2 oz/55 g white or brown sugar lumps,
   lightly crushed

sliced dessert apple, to decorate

1 Grease and line a 2 lb/900 g loaf pan with a little butter or margarine. Core, peel, and finely dice the apples. Place them in a pan with the lemon juice, bring to a boil, cover, and simmer for about 10 minutes until soft and pulpy. Beat well and set aside to cool.

2 Sift the flour, baking powder, and cinnamon into a bowl, adding any husks that remain in the strainer. Stir in ½ cup of the blackberries and the sugar.

3 Make a well in the center of the ingredients and add the egg, yogurt, and cooled apple purée. Mix well to incorporate thoroughly. Spoon the mixture into the prepared loaf pan and smooth the top.

4 Sprinkle with the remaining blackberries, pressing them down into the cake mixture, and top with the crushed sugar lumps. Bake in a preheated oven, 375°F/190°C, for 40–45 minutes. Remove from the oven and set aside in the pan to cool.

5 Remove the cake from the pan and peel away the lining paper. Serve dusted with cinnamon and decorated with extra blackberries and apple slices.

VARIATION

Try replacing the
blackberries with blueberries.
Use the canned or frozen variety
if fresh blueberries are unavailable.

Italian Bread Dessert

This deliciously rich dessert is cooked with cream and apples and is delicately flavored with orange.

NUTRITIONAL INFORMATION

Calories 387	Sugars 31g
Protein 8g	Fat 20g
Carbohydrate . . .45g	Saturates 12g

 45 mins   25 mins

SERVES 4

I N G R E D I E N T S

1 tbsp butter

2 small dessert apples, peeled, cored and sliced into rings

½ cup granulated sugar

2 tbsp white wine

4 thick slices of bread (about 4 oz/115 g) crusts removed (day-old baguette is ideal)

1¼ cups light cream

2 eggs, beaten

pared rind of 1 orange, cut into short thin sticks

1 Lightly grease a 5 cup deep casserole with the butter.

2 Arrange the apple rings in the bottom of the dish. Sprinkle half of the sugar over the apples.

3 Pour the wine over the apples. Add the bread slices, pushing them down with your hands to flatten them slightly.

4 Mix the cream with the eggs, the remaining sugar, and the orange rind and pour the mixture over the bread. Set aside to soak for 30 minutes.

5 Bake the pudding in a preheated oven, 350°F/180°C, for 25 minutes until golden and set. Remove from the oven, set aside to cool slightly, and serve warm.

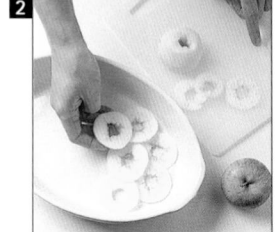

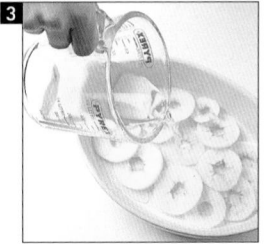

Cream Custards

Individual pan-cooked cream custards are flavored
with nutmeg and topped with caramelized orange strips.

NUTRITIONAL INFORMATION

Calories	406	Sugars	38g
Protein	8g	Fat	26g
Carbohydrate	38g	Saturates	15g

2¼ hrs   25 mins

SERVES 4

INGREDIENTS

2 cups light cream

generous ½ cup superfine sugar

1 orange

2 tsp grated nutmeg

3 large eggs, beaten

1 tbsp honey

1 tsp ground cinnamon

1 Place the cream and sugar in a large nonstick pan and heat gently, stirring, until the sugar caramelizes.

2 Finely grate half of the orange rind and stir it into the pan with the nutmeg.

3 Add the eggs and cook over low heat for 10–15 minutes, stirring constantly until thickened.

4 Strain the custard through a fine strainer into 4 shallow serving dishes. Set aside to chill in the refrigerator for 2 hours.

5 Meanwhile, pare the remaining orange rind with a vegetable peeler and cut it into thin batons.

6 Place the honey and cinnamon in a pan with 2 tablespoons of water and heat gently. Add the orange rind and cook for 2–3 minutes, stirring constantly, until the mixture has caramelized.

7 Pour the mixture into a bowl and separate out the orange strips. Set aside to cool until set.

8 Once the custards have set, decorate them with the caramelized orange rind, and serve.

COOK'S TIP

The cream custards will keep for 1–2 days in the refrigerator. Decorate with the caramelized orange rind just before serving.

German Noodle Dessert

This rich and satisfying dessert is a traditional Jewish recipe that will quickly become popular with all the family.

NUTRITIONAL INFORMATION

Calories	719	Sugars	........28g
Protein	........20g	Fat	..........45g
Carbohydrate	...62g	Saturates	.....25g

 10 mins   45 mins

SERVES 4

INGREDIENTS

4 tbsp butter, plus extra for greasing

6 oz/175 g ribbon egg noodles

½ cup cream cheese

1 cup cottage cheese

scant ½ cup superfine sugar

2 eggs, lightly beaten

½ cup sour cream

1 tsp vanilla extract

pinch of ground cinnamon

1 tsp grated lemon rind

¼ cup flaked almonds

generous ⅓ cup dry white bread crumbs

confectioners' sugar, for dusting

1 Lightly grease an oval casserole with a little butter. Bring a large pan of water to a boil. Add the noodles, bring back to a boil, and cook over medium heat for 10 minutes until tender, but still firm to the bite. Drain and set aside.

2 Beat the cream cheese with the cottage cheese and superfine sugar in a mixing bowl until the mixture is smooth. Add the beaten eggs, a little at a time, beating thoroughly after each addition.

3 Stir in the sour cream, vanilla extract, cinnamon, and lemon rind and fold in the noodles. Transfer the mixture to the prepared casserole and smooth the surface.

4 Melt the butter in a small skillet over low heat. Add the almonds and cook gently, stirring constantly, for about 1–1½ minutes until they are lightly colored. Remove the skillet from the heat and stir the bread crumbs into the almonds.

5 Sprinkle the almond and bread crumb mixture evenly over the top of the pudding and bake in a preheated oven, 350°F/180°C, for about 35–40 minutes until just set. Dust the top with a little sifted confectioners' sugar and serve immediately.

VARIATION

Although not authentic, you could add 3 tablespoons of raisins with the lemon rind in step 3, if desired.

Peaches & Mascarpone

If you prepare these in advance, all you have to do is pop the peaches on the barbecue grill when you are ready to serve them.

NUTRITIONAL INFORMATION

Calories	301	Sugars	.......24g
Protein	.........6g	Fat	.........20g
Carbohydrate	...24g	Saturates	.......9g

 10 mins 10 mins

SERVES 4

INGREDIENTS

4 peaches

¾ cup mascarpone cheese

⅓ cup pecans or walnuts, chopped

1 tsp sunflower oil

4 tbsp maple syrup

1 Cut the peaches in half and remove the pits. If you are preparing this recipe in advance, press the peach halves together again and wrap them in plastic wrap until required.

2 Combine the mascarpone and pecans or walnuts in a small bowl. Set aside to chill in the refrigerator until required.

3 To serve, brush the peaches with a little oil and place on a rack set over medium hot coals. Grill for 5–10 minutes, turning once, until hot.

4 Transfer the peaches to a serving dish and top with the mascarpone cheese mixture.

5 Drizzle the maple syrup over the peaches and mascarpone filling and serve immediately.

VARIATION
You can use nectarines instead of peaches for this recipe. Remember to choose ripe but firm fruit which won't go soft and mushy when it is grilled. Prepare the nectarines in the same way as the peaches and grill or 5–10 minutes.

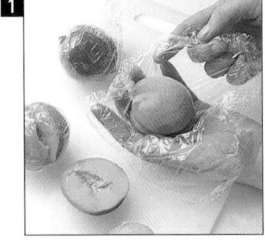

Orange & Almond Cake

This light and tangy citrus cake from Sicily is better eaten as a dessert than as a cake. It is especially good served at the end of a large meal.

NUTRITIONAL INFORMATION

Calories	399	Sugars	........20g
Protein	.........8g	Fat	..........31g
Carbohydrate	...23g	Saturates	......13g

 30 mins

 40 mins

SERVES 8

INGREDIENTS

4 eggs, separated

scant ⅔ cup superfine sugar, plus 2 tsp for the cream

finely grated rind and juice of 2 oranges

finely grated rind and juice of 1 lemon

1 cup ground almonds

4 tbsp self-rising flour

scant 1 cup whipping cream

1 tsp ground cinnamon

4 tbsp sliced almonds, toasted

confectioners' sugar, for dusting

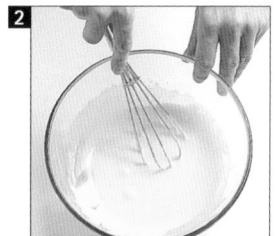

1 Grease and line the base of a 7 inch/18 cm round deep cake pan.

2 Blend the egg yolks with the sugar until the mixture is thick and creamy. Whisk half of the orange rind and all of the lemon rind into the egg yolks.

3 Combine the orange and lemon juice with the ground almonds and stir into the egg yolks. Fold in the flour. Whisk the egg whites until stiff and gently fold in.

4 Pour the mixture into the pan and smooth the surface. Bake in a preheated oven, 350°F/180°C, for 35–40 minutes or until golden and springy to the touch. Set aside to cool in the pan for 10 minutes and then turn out onto a rack to cool completely.

5 Whip the cream to form soft peaks. Stir in the remaining orange rind, cinnamon, and sugar.

6 Cover the cake with the almonds, dust with confectioners' sugar, and serve with the cream.

VARIATION

To serve with a syrup, boil the juice and finely grated rind of 2 oranges, scant ½ cup superfine sugar, and 2 tablespoons water for 5–6 minutes. Stir in 1 tablespoon orange liqueur just before serving.

Raspberry Shortcake

For this lovely summery dessert, two crisp rounds of shortbread are sandwiched together with fresh raspberries and lightly whipped cream.

NUTRITIONAL INFORMATION

Calories	496	Sugars	........14g
Protein	.........4g	Fat	..........41g
Carbohydrate	...30g	Saturates	......26g

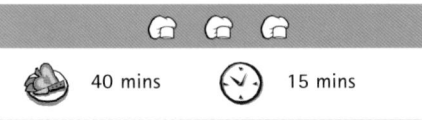

40 mins   15 mins

SERVES 8

INGREDIENTS

7 tbsp butter, cut into cubes, plus
   extra for greasing

1½ cups self-rising flour

scant ½ cup superfine sugar

1 egg yolk

1 tbsp rose water

2½ cups whipping cream, lightly whipped

1⅓ cups raspberries, plus a few extra
   for decoration

TO DECORATE

confectioners' sugar

mint leaves

1 Lightly grease 2 cookie sheets with a little butter.

2 To make the shortcake, sift the self-rising flour into a bowl. Add the butter and rub it into the flour with your fingertips until the mixture resembles fine bread crumbs.

3 Stir the sugar, egg yolk, and rose water into the mixture and bring together with your fingers to form a soft dough. Divide the dough in half.

4 Roll out each piece of dough to an 8 inch/20 cm round on a lightly floured counter. Carefully lift each of them with the rolling pin onto the prepared cookie sheets. Gently crimp the edges of the dough with your finger.

5 Bake in a preheated oven, 375°F/190°C, for 15 minutes until lightly golden. Transfer the shortcakes to a wire rack and set aside to cool completely.

6 Mix the whipped cream with the raspberries and spoon the mixture on top of 1 of the shortcakes, spreading it out evenly. Top with the other shortcake round, dust with a little confectioners' sugar, and decorate with the extra raspberries and mint leaves.

COOK'S TIP

The shortcake can be made a few days in advance and stored in an airtight container until required.

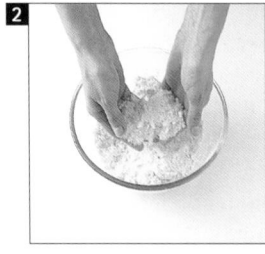

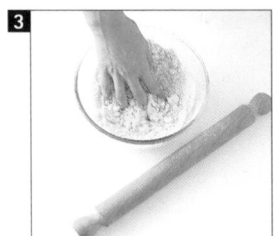

Sweet Potato Bread

This is a great-tasting loaf, colored light orange by the sweet potato.
Added sweetness from the honey is offset by the tangy orange rind.

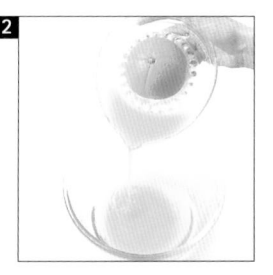

NUTRITIONAL INFORMATION

Calories	267	Sugars	.........7g
Protein	.........4g	Fat	...........9g
Carbohydrate	...45g	Saturates	.......4g

 1½ hrs   1¼ hrs

SERVES 8

INGREDIENTS

5 tbsp butter, plus extra for greasing

8 oz/225 g sweet potatoes, diced

⅔ cup lukewarm water

2 tbsp honey

2 tbsp vegetable oil

3 tbsp orange juice

scant ½ cup semolina

2 cups white bread flour

1 envelope (2½ tsp) active dry yeast

1 tsp ground cinnamon

grated rind of 1 orange

1 Lightly grease a 1½ lb/675 g loaf pan. Cook the sweet potatoes in a pan of boiling water for about 10 minutes or until soft. Drain thoroughly and mash until smooth.

2 Meanwhile, mix the water, honey, oil, and orange juice together in a large mixing bowl.

3 Add the mashed sweet potatoes, semolina, three-quarters of the flour, the yeast, ground cinnamon, and grated orange rind and mix thoroughly to form a dough. Set aside for about 10 minutes.

4 Dice the butter and knead it into the dough with the remaining flour. Knead for about 5 minutes until smooth.

5 Place the dough in the prepared loaf pan. Cover and set aside in a warm place for 1 hour or until doubled in size.

6 Cook the loaf in a preheated oven, 375°F/190°C, for 45–60 minutes, or until the base sounds hollow when tapped. Serve the bread warm, cut into slices.

Potato Muffins

Using potatoes in sweet dishes may seem an odd idea, but, in fact, they add a lightness and lift to all kinds of baked goods.

NUTRITIONAL INFORMATION

Calories	100	Sugars	11g
Protein	3g	Fat	2g
Carbohydrate	19g	Saturates	1g

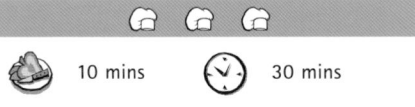

10 mins 🕐 30 mins

MAKES 12

INGREDIENTS

butter, for greasing

⅔ cup self-rising flour, plus extra for dusting

6 oz/175 g mealy potatoes, diced

2 tbsp brown sugar

1 tsp baking powder

scant 1 cup raisins

4 eggs, separated

1 Lightly grease and flour 12 muffin pans. Cook the diced potatoes in a pan of boiling water for 10 minutes or until tender. Drain thoroughly and mash until smooth.

2 Transfer the mashed potatoes to a mixing bowl and add the flour, sugar, baking powder, raisins, and egg yolks. Stir well to mix thoroughly.

3 In a clean bowl, whisk the egg whites until they are standing in peaks. Using a metal spoon, gently fold them into the potato mixture until fully incorporated.

4 Divide the mixture among the prepared pans.

5 Cook in a preheated oven, 400°F/200°C, for 10 minutes. Reduce the oven temperature to 325°F/160°C and cook the muffins for 7–10 minutes, or until risen.

6 Remove the muffins from the pans and serve warm.

COOK'S TIP
Instead of spreading the muffins with plain butter, serve them with cinnamon butter made by blending 5 tablespoons butter with a large pinch of ground cinnamon.

Fruit & Nut Loaf

This loaf is like a fruit bread which may be served warm or cold, perhaps spread with a little margarine or butter or topped with jelly.

NUTRITIONAL INFORMATION

Calories 531	Sugars 53g
Protein 12g	Fat 14g
Carbohydrate . . .96g	Saturates 2g

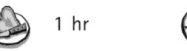

1 hr   40 mins

SERVES 4

INGREDIENTS

2 cups white bread flour, plus extra for dusting

½ tsp salt

1 tbsp margarine, plus extra for greasing

2 tbsp brown sugar

⅔ cup golden raisins

¼ cup no-need to soak dried apricots, chopped

½ cup chopped hazelnuts

2 tsp active dry yeast

6 tbsp orange juice

6 tbsp low-fat plain yogurt

2 tbsp strained apricot jelly

1 Sift the flour and salt into a bowl. Rub in the margarine and stir in the sugar, raisins, apricots, nuts, and yeast.

2 Warm the orange juice in a pan but do not allow it to boil.

3 Stir the warm orange juice into the flour mixture with the plain yogurt and then bring the mixture together to form a dough.

4 Knead the dough on a lightly floured counter for 5 minutes until smooth and elastic. Shape into a round and place on a lightly greased cookie sheet. Cover with a clean dish cloth and set aside to rise in a warm place until doubled in size.

5 Cook the loaf in a preheated oven, 425°F/220°C, for 35–40 minutes until cooked through. Transfer to a cooling rack and brush the cake with the apricot jelly. Let the cake cool before serving.

COOK'S TIP

To test whether yeast bread or cake is done, tap the loaf from underneath. If it sounds hollow, the bread or cake is ready.

Tropical Fruit Fool

Fruit fools are always popular, and this light, tangy version will be no exception. You can use your favorite fruits in this recipe.

NUTRITIONAL INFORMATION

Calories	149	Sugars	25g
Protein	6g	Fat	0.4g
Carbohydrate	32g	Saturates	0.2g

35 mins   0 mins

SERVES 4

INGREDIENTS

1 medium ripe mango

2 kiwi fruit

1 medium banana

2 tbsp lime juice

½ tsp finely grated lime rind, plus extra to decorate

2 egg whites

15 oz/425 g can low-fat custard

½ tsp vanilla extract

2 passion fruit

1 Peel the mango, then slice either side of the smooth, flat central pit. Roughly chop the flesh and process the fruit in a food processor or blender until smooth. Alternatively, mash with a fork.

2 Peel the kiwi fruit, chop the flesh into small pieces, and place in a bowl. Peel and chop the banana, and add to the bowl. Toss all of the fruit in the lime juice and rind and mix well.

3 In a grease-free bowl, whisk the egg whites until stiff and then gently fold in the custard and vanilla extract until thoroughly mixed.

4 In 4 tall glasses, alternately layer the chopped fruit, mango purée, and custard mixture, finishing with the custard on top. Set aside to chill in the refrigerator for 20 minutes.

5 Halve the passion fruits, scoop out the seeds, and spoon the passion fruit over the fruit fools. Decorate each serving with the extra lime rind and serve.

VARIATION
Other tropical fruits to try include papaya purée, with chopped pineapple and dates or pomegranate seeds to decorate.

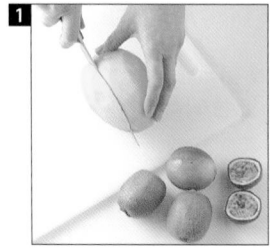

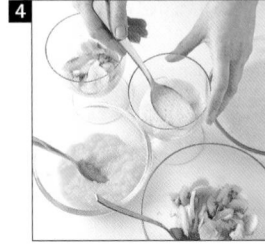

Mixed Fruit Brûlées

Traditionally a rich mixture made with cream, this fruit-based version
is just as tempting using low-fat smetana and yogurt as a topping.

NUTRITIONAL INFORMATION

Calories ....165 Sugars 21g
Protein ....5g Fat 7g
Carbohydrate ...21g Saturates 5g

 5 mins   5 mins

SERVES 4

I N G R E D I E N T S

1 lb/450 g prepared assorted summer
fruits, such as strawberries, raspberries,
black currants, red currants, and cherries,
thawed if frozen

⅔ cup smetana

⅔ cup low-fat plain yogurt

1 tsp vanilla extract

4 tbsp raw sugar

1 Divide the prepared strawberries, raspberries, black currants, red currants and cherries evenly among 4 small heatproof ramekin dishes.

2 Combine the smetana, yogurt, and vanilla extract.

3 Spoon the mixture over the fruit, to cover it completely.

4 Top each serving with 1 tablespoon raw sugar and place the desserts under a preheated broiler for 2–3 minutes until the sugar melts and begins to caramelize. Set aside for a couple of minutes before serving.

COOK'S TIP

Look out for half-fat creams, in light and heavy varieties. They are good substitutes for occasional use. Alternatively, in this recipe, double the quantity of yogurt for a lower-fat version.

Orchard Fruits Bristol

An elegant fruit salad of poached pears and apples, oranges, and strawberries in a wine and caramel syrup topped with crumbled caramel.

NUTRITIONAL INFORMATION

Calories	395	Sugars	.......94g
Protein	.........3g	Fat	..........0.5g
Carbohydrate	...94g	Saturates	......0g

30 mins   20 mins

SERVES 4

INGREDIENTS

4 oranges

generous ¾ cup granulated sugar

4 tbsp water

⅔ cup white wine

4 firm pears

4 dessert apples

1 cup strawberries

1 Pare the rind thinly from 1 orange and cut into narrow strips. Cook in the minimum of boiling water for 3–4 minutes until tender. Drain and reserve the cooking liquid. Squeeze the juice from this and 1 other orange.

2 Lay a sheet of nonstick baking parchment on a cookie sheet or board.

3 Heat the sugar gently in a pan until it melts, then continue without stirring until it turns a pale golden brown. Pour half the caramel quickly onto the parchment and set aside to set.

4 Add the water and squeezed orange juice immediately to the caramel left in the pan with ⅔ cup of the reserved cooking liquid. Heat until it melts, then add the wine, and remove the pan from the heat.

5 Peel, core, and slice the pears and apples thickly (you can leave the apple skins on, if you prefer) and add to the caramel syrup. Bring gently to a boil and simmer for 3–4 minutes until just beginning to soften—they should still be firm in the center. Transfer the pears and apples to a bowl.

6 Cut away the peel and pith from the remaining oranges and either ease out the segments or cut into slices, discarding any pits. Add to the other fruits. Hull the strawberries and halve, quarter, or slice thickly, depending on the size, and add to the other fruits.

7 Add the orange strands to the syrup and bring back to a boil for 1 minute, then pour over the fruits. Set aside until cold, then break up the caramel and sprinkle it over the fruit. Cover and chill until ready to serve.

COOK'S TIP

The caramel will begin to melt when added to the fruit, so do this as near to serving as possible.

Giggle Cake

It's a mystery how this cake got its name—
perhaps it's because it's easy to make and fun to eat.

25 mins   1¼ hrs

SERVES 8

INGREDIENTS

12 oz/350g mixed dried fruit

generous ½ cup butter or margarine, plus
    extra for greasing

¾ cup brown sugar

2 cups self-rising flour

pinch of salt

2 eggs, beaten

8 oz/225 g can chopped pineapple, drained

¾ cup candied cherries, halved

1 Put the mixed dried fruit into a large bowl and cover with boiling water. Set aside to soak for 10–15 minutes, then drain well.

2 Put the butter or margarine and sugar into a large pan and heat gently until melted. Add the drained mixed dried fruit and cook over low heat, stirring frequently, for 4–5 minutes. Remove from the heat and transfer to a mixing bowl. Set aside to cool.

3 Sift together the flour and salt into the dried fruit mixture and stir well. Add the eggs, mixing until the ingredients are thoroughly incorporated.

4 Add the pineapples and cherries to the cake mixture and stir to combine.

Transfer to a greased and lined 2 lb/ 1 kg loaf pan and level the surface.

5 Bake in a preheated oven, 350°F/ 180°C, for about 1 hour. Test the cake with a fine toothpick; if it comes out clean, the cake is cooked. If not, return to the oven for a few more minutes. Transfer the cake to a wire rack to cool completely before serving.

VARIATION

If you wish, add 1 teaspoon ground apple spice to the cake mixture, sifting it in with the flour. Bake the cake in a 7 inch/18 cm round cake pan if you don't have a loaf pan of the right size. Remember to grease and line it first.

Eve's Dessert

This is a popular family dessert with soft apples
on the bottom and a light buttery sponge cake topping.

NUTRITIONAL INFORMATION

Calories	365	Sugars	........40g
Protein	.........5g	Fat	..........14g
Carbohydrate	...58g	Saturates	.......7g

15 mins   45 mins

SERVES 4

I N G R E D I E N T S

6 tbsp butter, plus extra for greasing

1lb/450 g cooking apples, peeled, cored
  and sliced

½ cup granulated sugar

1 tbsp lemon juice

scant ½ cup golden raisins

scant ½ cup superfine sugar

1 egg, beaten

1⅓ cups self-rising flour

3 tbsp milk

¼ cup sliced almonds

custard or heavy cream, to serve

COOK'S TIP

To increase the almond
flavor of this pudding, add
¼ cup ground almonds
with the flour in step 4.

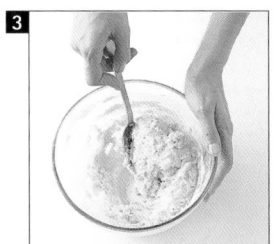

1 Grease a 3¾ cup casserole with a little butter.

2 Mix the apples with the granulated sugar, lemon juice, and golden raisins. Spoon the mixture into the casserole.

3 In a bowl, cream the butter and superfine sugar together until pale. Add the beaten egg, a little at a time.

4 Carefully fold in the self-rising flour and stir in the milk to give a soft, pourable consistency.

5 Spread the mixture over the apples and sprinkle with the sliced almonds.

6 Bake in a preheated oven, 350°F/ 180°C, for 40–45 minutes until the sponge cake topping is golden brown.

7 Serve the pudding piping hot, accompanied by homemade custard or heavy cream.

Plum Pot Pie

This is another popular dessert which can be adapted
to suit almost all types of fruit if plums are not available.

NUTRITIONAL INFORMATION

Calories 430   Sugars 46g
Protein ....7g   Fat 12g
Carbohydrate ...79g   Saturates 7g

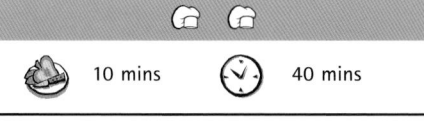

🍲 10 mins   🕐 40 mins

SERVES 6

INGREDIENTS

butter, for greasing

2 lb 4 oz/1 kg plums, pitted
   and sliced

½ cup superfine sugar

1 tbsp lemon juice

2¼ cups all-purpose flour

2 tsp baking powder

½ cup granulated sugar

1 egg, beaten

⅔ cup buttermilk

6 tbsp butter, melted and cooled

heavy cream, to serve

1 Lightly grease an 8¾ cup casserole with butter.

2 In a large bowl, combine the plums, superfine sugar, lemon juice, and ¼ cup of the all-purpose flour.

3 Spoon the coated plums into the bottom of the prepared casserole, spreading them out evenly.

4 Sift the remaining flour, together with the baking powder, into a large bowl and add the granulated sugar. Stir well to combine.

5 Add the beaten egg, buttermilk, and cooled melted butter. Mix everything gently together to form a soft dough.

6 Place spoonfuls of the dough on top of the fruit mixture until it is almost completely covered.

7 Bake the pot pie in a preheated oven, 375°F/190°C, for 35–40 minutes until the topping is golden brown and the plums are bubbling.

8 Serve the pot pie piping hot, with heavy cream.

COOK'S TIP
If you cannot find buttermilk,
try using sour cream.

Banana & Cranberry Loaf

The addition of chopped nuts, candied peel, fresh orange juice, and dried cranberries makes this a rich, moist tea bread.

NUTRITIONAL INFORMATION

Calories	388	Sugars	........40g
Protein	.........5g	Fat	..........17g
Carbohydrate	...57g	Saturates	.......2g

 45 mins   1 hr

SERVES 8

INGREDIENTS

butter, for greasing

1½ cups self-rising flour

½ tsp baking powder

⅔ cup soft brown sugar

2 bananas, mashed

⅓ cup chopped candied peel

¼ cup chopped mixed nuts

½ cup dried cranberries

5–6 tbsp orange juice

2 eggs, beaten

⅔ cup sunflower oil

¾ cup confectioners' sugar, sifted

grated rind of 1 orange

1 Grease a 2 lb/900 g loaf pan and line the base with baking parchment.

2 Sift the flour and baking powder into a mixing bowl. Stir in the brown sugar, bananas, chopped candied peel, nuts, and dried cranberries.

3 Stir the orange juice, eggs, and sunflower oil together until well combined. Add the mixture to the dry ingredients and mix until thoroughly blended. Spoon the mixture into the prepared loaf pan and smooth the top.

4 Bake in a preheated oven, 350°F/ 180°C, for about 1 hour until firm to the touch or until a toothpick inserted into the center of the loaf comes out clean.

5 Turn out the loaf and set aside to cool on a wire rack.

6 Mix the confectioners' sugar with a little water and drizzle the frosting over the loaf. Sprinkle the orange rind over the top. Let the frosting set before slicing.

COOK'S TIP

This tea bread will keep for a couple of days. Wrap it carefully and store in a cool, dry place.

Tropical Fruit Bread

The flavors in this bread will bring a touch of sunshine
to your dining room, whatever the time of year.

NUTRITIONAL INFORMATION

Calories	228	Sugars	........10g
Protein	.........6g	Fat	..........7g
Carbohydrate	...37g	Saturates	.......5g

1¼ hrs   30 mins

SERVES 4

INGREDIENTS

2 tbsp butter, cut into small pieces, plus
    extra for greasing

3 cups white bread flour

½ cup bran

½ tsp salt

½ tsp ground ginger

1 envelope active dry yeast

2 tbsp soft brown sugar

generous 1 cup lukewarm water

⅓ cup candied pineapple, finely chopped

2 tbsp finely chopped dried mango

⅔ cup dry shredded coconut, toasted

1 egg, lightly beaten

2 tbsp coconut shreds

1 Grease a cookie sheet. Sift the flour into a large mixing bowl. Stir in the bran, salt, ginger, yeast, and sugar. Rub in the butter with your fingers, then add the water, and mix to form a dough.

2 On a lightly floured counter, knead the dough for 5–8 minutes until smooth. Alternatively, use an electric mixer with a dough hook. Place the dough in a greased bowl, cover, and let rise in a warm place for 30 minutes until doubled in size.

3 Knead the pineapple, mango, and dry shredded coconut into the dough. Shape into a round and place on the cookie sheet. Score the top with the back of a knife. Cover and set aside for a further 30 minutes in a warm place.

4 Brush the loaf with the beaten egg and sprinkle with the coconut shreds. Bake in a preheated oven, 425°F/ 220°C, for about 30 minutes or until golden brown.

5 Set the bread aside to cool on a wire rack before serving.

COOK'S TIP
To test the bread after the second rising, gently poke the dough with your finger—it should spring back if it has risen enough.

Olive Oil, Fruit & Nut Cake

It is worth using a good quality olive oil for this cake because this will determine its flavor. The cake will keep well in an airtight container.

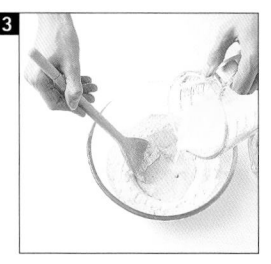

NUTRITIONAL INFORMATION

Calories 309   Sugars 17g
Protein ....4g   Fat 17g
Carbohydrate ...38g   Saturates 3g

 10 mins    45 mins

SERVES 8

INGREDIENTS

butter, for greasing

2 cups self-rising flour

¼ cup superfine sugar

½ cup milk

¼ cup orange juice

⅔ cup olive oil

¾ cup mixed dried fruit

¼ cup pine nuts

1 Grease a 7 inch/18 cm cake pan and line with baking parchment.

2 Sift the flour into a mixing bowl and stir in the superfine sugar.

3 Make a well in the center of the dry ingredients and pour in the milk and orange juice. Stir the mixture with a wooden spoon, gradually beating in the flour and sugar.

4 Pour in the olive oil, stirring well so that all of the ingredients are thoroughly mixed.

5 Stir the mixed dried fruit and pine nuts into the mixture and spoon into the prepared pan. Gently smooth the top with a spatula.

6 Bake the cake in a preheated oven, 350°F/180°C, for about 45 minutes, until it is golden brown and just firm to the touch.

7 Let the cake cool in the pan for a few minutes before transferring to a wire rack to cool completely.

8 Serve the cake warm or cold and cut into slices.

COOK'S TIP

Pine nuts are best known as the flavoring ingredient in the classic Italian pesto, but here they give a delicate, slightly resinous flavor to this cake.

Crunchy Fruit Cake

Polenta adds texture to this fruit cake, as well as a golden yellow color. It also acts as a flour, binding the ingredients together.

NUTRITIONAL INFORMATION

Calories 328	Sugars 33g	
Protein 59g	Fat 15g	
Carbohydrate ...47g	Saturates 7g	

5–10 mins   1 hr

MAKES 1 LOAF

INGREDIENTS

scant ½ cup butter, softened, plus extra for greasing

½ cup superfine sugar

2 eggs, beaten

7 tbsp self-rising flour, sifted

1 tsp baking powder

¾ cup polenta

1⅔ cups mixed dried fruit

¼ cup pine nuts

grated rind of 1 lemon

4 tbsp lemon juice

2 tbsp milk

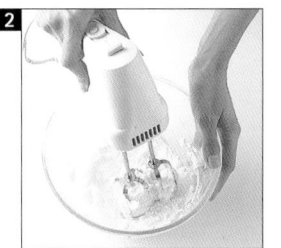  

1 Grease a 7 inch/18 cm cake pan with a little butter and line the base with baking parchment.

2 In a bowl, whisk together the butter and sugar until light and fluffy.

3 Whisk in the beaten eggs, a little at a time, whisking thoroughly after each addition.

4 Gently fold the flour, baking powder, and polenta into the mixture until totally incorporated.

5 Stir in the mixed dried fruit, pine nuts, grated lemon rind, lemon juice, and milk.

6 Spoon the mixture into the prepared pan and level the surface.

7 Bake in a preheated oven, 350°F/ 180°C, for about 1 hour or until a toothpick inserted into the center of the cake comes out clean.

8 Let the cake cool in the pan before turning out.

VARIATION
To give a crumblier light fruit cake, omit the polenta and use 1¼ cups self-rising flour instead.

Apple Cake with Hard Cider

This can be warmed through and served with cream for a dessert or eaten as a cake at snacktimes or with a morning cup of coffee.

NUTRITIONAL INFORMATION

Calories	263	Sugars	........22g
Protein	.........4g	Fat	...........9g
Carbohydrate	...43g	Saturates	.......5g

 1 hr 5 mins   40 mins

SERVES 8

INGREDIENTS

6 tbsp butter, cut into small pieces, plus extra for greasing

2 cups self-rising flour

1 tsp baking powder

scant ½ cup superfine sugar

4 cups chopped dried apple

⅔ cup raisins

⅔ cup hard cider

1 egg, beaten

1 cup raspberries

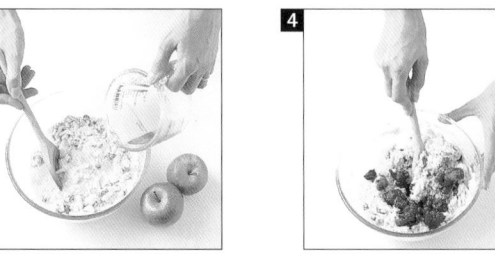

1 Grease an 8 inch/20 cm cake pan and line with baking parchment.

2 Sift the flour and baking powder into a mixing bowl and rub in the butter with your fingertips until the mixture resembles fine bread crumbs.

3 Stir in the superfine sugar, chopped dried apple, and raisins.

4 Pour in the hard cider and egg and mix together until thoroughly blended. Stir in the raspberries very gently so they do not break up.

5 Pour the mixture into the prepared cake pan.

6 Bake in a preheated oven, 375°F/190°C, for about 40 minutes until risen and lightly golden.

7 Set the cake aside to cool in the pan, then turn out onto a wire rack. Set aside until completely cold before serving.

VARIATION

If you don't want to use hard cider or you are making the cake for children, replace it with clear apple juice.

Oat & Raisin Cookies

These oaty, fruity cookies couldn't be easier to make and are delicious served with a creamy rum and raisin ice cream.

NUTRITIONAL INFORMATION

Calories	227	Sugars	........22g
Protein	.........4g	Fat	...........7g
Carbohydrate	...39g	Saturates	.......3g

 50 mins   15 mins

SERVES 4

I N G R E D I E N T S

4 tbsp butter, plus extra for greasing

⅔ cup superfine sugar

1 egg, beaten

½ cup all-purpose flour

½ tsp salt

½ tsp baking powder

1¾ cups rolled oats

scant 1 cup raisins

2 tbsp sesame seeds

1 Lightly grease 2 cookie sheets with a little butter.

2 In a large mixing bowl, cream together the butter and sugar until light and fluffy.

3 Gradually add the beaten egg, beating well after each addition, until thoroughly combined.

4 Sift the flour, salt, and baking powder into the creamed mixture. Mix gently to combine. Add the rolled oats, raisins, and sesame seeds and mix together until thoroughly combined.

5 Place spoonfuls of the mixture, spaced well apart on the prepared cookie sheets to allow room to expand during cooking, and flatten them slightly with the back of a spoon.

6 Bake the cookies in a preheated oven, 350°F/180°C, for 15 minutes.

7 Let the cookies cool slightly on the cookie sheets.

8 Carefully transfer the cookies to a wire rack and set aside to cool completely before serving.

COOK'S TIP
To enjoy these cookies at their best, store them in an airtight container.

Chocolate Mousse

This is a light and fluffy mousse with a subtle hint of orange.
It is wickedly delicious served with a fresh fruit sauce.

NUTRITIONAL INFORMATION

Calories	164	Sugars	........24g
Protein	.........5g	Fat	...........5g
Carbohydrate	...25g	Saturates	.......3g

 2¼ hrs   5 mins

SERVES 8

INGREDIENTS

3½ oz/100 g semisweet chocolate, melted

1¼ cups plain yogurt

⅔ cup Quark

4 tbsp superfine sugar

1 tbsp orange juice

1 tbsp brandy

1½ tsp gelatin, or gelozone
   (vegetarian gelatin)

9 tbsp cold water

2 large egg whites

TO DECORATE

roughly grated bittersweet and
   white chocolate

orange rind

1 Put the melted chocolate, yogurt, Quark, sugar, orange juice, and brandy in a food processor or blender and process for 30 seconds. Transfer the mixture to a large bowl.

2 Sprinkle the gelatin or gelozone over the water and stir until dissolved.

3 In a pan, bring the gelatin or gelozone and water to a boil for 2 minutes. Cool slightly, then thoroughly stir into the chocolate mixture.

4 Whisk the egg whites until stiff peaks form and fold into the chocolate mixture using a metal spoon.

5 Line a 1 lb 2 oz/500 g loaf pan with plastic wrap. Spoon the mousse into the pan. Chill in the refrigerator for 2 hours until set. Turn the mousse out onto a serving plate, decorate with grated chocolate and orange rind. and serve.

COOK'S TIP

For a quick fruit sauce, process a can of mandarin segments in natural juice in a food processor and press through a strainer. Stir in 1 tablespoon honey and serve with the mousse.

Berry Cheesecake

Use a mixture of berries, such as blueberries, blackberries, raspberries, and strawberries, for a really fruity cheesecake.

NUTRITIONAL INFORMATION

Calories 478	Sugars 28g	
Protein 10g	Fat 32g	
Carbohydrate ...40g	Saturates 15g	

2¼ hrs   5 mins

SERVES 8

INGREDIENTS

BASE

6 tbsp margarine

6 oz/175 g oatmeal cookies

⅔ cup dry shredded coconut

TOPPING

1½ tsp gelatin

generous ½ cup cold water

½ cup evaporated milk

1 egg

6 tbsp brown sugar

2 cups soft cream cheese

3 cups mixed berries

2 tbsp honey

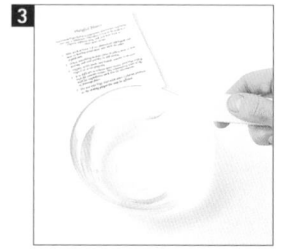  

1 Melt the margarine in a pan. Put the cookies into a food processor and process until crushed, or crush finely with a rolling pin. Stir the crumbs into the margarine with the coconut.

2 Press the mixture evenly into a base-lined 8 inch/20 cm springform pan and set aside to chill in the refrigerator.

3 To make the topping, sprinkle the gelatin over the water and stir to dissolve. Bring to a boil and boil for 2 minutes. Set aside to cool slightly.

4 Beat the milk with the egg, sugar, and cream cheese until smooth. Stir in ½ cup of the berries. Add the gelatin in a thin stream, stirring constantly.

5 Spoon the mixture onto the cookie base and return to the refrigerator to chill for 2 hours or until set.

6 Remove the cheesecake from the pan and transfer to a serving plate. Arrange the remaining berries on top of the cheesecake and drizzle the honey over the top. Serve.

Steamed Coffee Sponge

This sponge dessert is very light and is delicious served with a coffee or chocolate sauce.

NUTRITIONAL INFORMATION

Calories 343	Sugars 21g	
Protein 9g	Fat 12g	
Carbohydrate ...54g	Saturates 4g	

10 mins 1–1¼ hrs

SERVES 4

INGREDIENTS

2 tbsp margarine

2 tbsp brown sugar

2 eggs

5½ tbsp all-purpose flour

¾ tsp baking powder

6 tbsp milk

1 tsp coffee extract

sauce

1¼ cups milk

1 tbsp brown sugar

1 tsp unsweetened cocoa

2 tbsp cornstarch

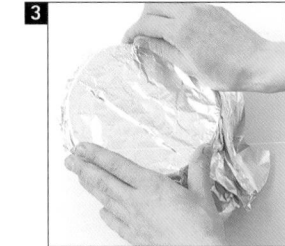

1 Lightly grease a 2½ cup heatproof bowl. Cream the margarine and sugar until the mixture is light and fluffy, then beat in the eggs.

2 Gradually stir in the flour and baking powder, then stir in the milk and coffee essence to make a smooth batter.

3 Spoon the mixture into the bowl and cover with a pleated piece of baking parchment and then a pleated piece of foil, securing around the bowl with tightly tied string.

4 Place in a steamer or large pan half full of boiling water. Cover and steam for 1–1¼ hours or until cooked through.

5 To make the sauce, put the milk, sugar, and unsweetened cocoa in a pan and heat until the sugar dissolves. Blend the cornstarch with 4 tablespoons of water to a paste and stir into the pan.

Bring the sauce to the boil, stirring until thickened. Cook for 1 minute.

6 Turn the pudding out o to a warmed serving plate and spoon the sauce over the top. Serve immediately.

Fruit Brûlée

This is a cheat's brûlée, in that yogurt is used to cover a base of fruit, before being sprinkled with sugar and broiled.

NUTRITIONAL INFORMATION

Calories 311   Sugars 48g
Protein . . . . .7g   Fat 11g
Carbohydrate . . .48g   Saturates 7g

 1¼ hrs   15 mins

SERVES 4

I N G R E D I E N T S

4 plums, pitted and sliced

2 cooking apples, peeled and sliced

1 tsp ground ginger

2½ cups strained plain yogurt

2 tbsp confectioners' sugar, sifted

1 tsp almond extract

⅓ cup raw sugar

1 Put the plums and apples in a pan with 2 tablespoons of water and cook for 7–10 minutes, until tender, but not mushy. Set aside to cool, then stir in the ground ginger.

2 Using a draining spoon, spoon the mixture into the base of a shallow, heatproof serving dish.

3 Combine the yogurt, confectioners' sugar, and almond extract and spoon onto the fruit to cover.

4 Sprinkle the raw sugar over the top of the yogurt and cook under a hot broiler for 3–4 minutes or until the sugar has melted and formed a crust.

5 Set aside to chill in the refrigerator for 1 hour before serving.

Pear Cake

This is a really moist cake, deliciously flavored with chopped pears and cinnamon and drizzled with honey.

NUTRITIONAL INFORMATION

Calories 119	Sugars 16g	
Protein 2g	Fat 0.3g	
Carbohydrate . . .29g	Saturates 0g	

1 hr   1½ hrs

SERVES 12

INGREDIENTS

margarine, for greasing

4 pears, peeled and cored

2 tbsp water

1¾ cups all-purpose flour

2 tsp baking powder

scant ½ cup brown sugar

4 tbsp milk

2 tbsp honey, plus extra for drizzling

2 tsp ground cinnamon

2 egg whites

1 Grease and line the base of an 8 inch/20 cm cake pan.

2 Put 1 pear in a food processor with the water and process until almost smooth. Transfer to a mixing bowl.

3 Sift in the flour and baking powder. Beat in the sugar, milk, honey, and cinnamon and mix well.

4 Chop all but 1 of the remaining pears and add to the mixture.

5 Whisk the egg whites until peaks form and gently fold into the mixture until fully blended.

6 Slice the remaining pear and arrange it in a fan pattern on the bottom of the prepared pan.

7 Spoon the cake mixture into the pan and cook in a preheated oven, 300°F/150°C, for 1¼–1½ hours or until cooked through and golden.

8 Remove the cake from the oven and set aside to cool in the pan for 10 minutes. Turn the cake out onto a wire cooling rack and drizzle with honey. Set aside to cool completely, then cut into slices to serve.

COOK'S TIP

To test if the cake is cooked through, insert a toothpick into the center—if it comes out clean, the cake is cooked. If not, return the cake to the oven and test at frequent intervals.

Mixed Fruit Crust

In this crusty dessert, tropical fruits are flavored with ginger and coconut, for something a little different and very tasty.

NUTRITIONAL INFORMATION

Calories	602	Sugars	........51g
Protein	.........6g	Fat	..........29g
Carbohydrate	...84g	Saturates	......11g

10 mins   50 mins

SERVES 4

INGREDIENTS

2 mangoes, sliced

1 papaya, seeded and sliced

8 oz/225 g fresh pineapple, cubed

1½ tsp ground ginger

7 tbsp margarine

scant ½ cup light brown sugar

1½ cups all-purpose flour

⅔ cup dry shredded coconut, plus extra
   to decorate

1 Place the fruit in a pan with ½ teaspoon of the ground ginger, 2 tablespoons of the margarine, and 4 tablespoons of the sugar. Cook over low heat for 10 minutes until the fruit softens. Spoon the fruit into the bottom of a shallow casserole.

2 Combine the flour and remaining ginger. Rub in the remaining margarine until the mixture resembles fine bread crumbs. Stir in the remaining sugar and the coconut and spoon over the fruit to cover completely.

3 Cook the crumble in a preheated oven, 350°F/180°C, for about 40 minutes or until the top is crisp. Decorate with a sprinkling of dry shredded coconut and serve immediately.

Banana & Mango Tart

Bananas and mangoes are a great combination of colors and flavors, especially when topped with toasted coconut chips.

NUTRITIONAL INFORMATION

Calories	235	Sugars 17g
Protein	.........4g	Fat 10g
Carbohydrate	...35g	Saturates 5g

1¼ hrs   5 mins

SERVES 8

INGREDIENTS

8 inch/20 cm ready-made pie shell

FILLING

2 small ripe bananas

1 mango, sliced

3½ tbsp cornstarch

6 tbsp raw sugar

1¼ cups soy milk

⅔ cup coconut milk

1 tsp vanilla extract

toasted coconut chips, to decorate

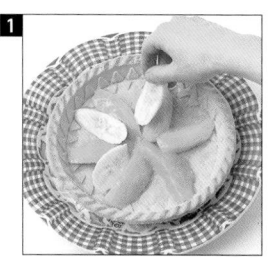

COOK'S TIP

Coconut chips are available in some supermarkets and most health food shops. They are worth using as they look more attractive and are not so sweet as dry shredded coconut.

1 Slice the bananas and arrange half of them in the pie shell with half of the mango pieces.

2 Put the cornstarch and sugar in a pan and mix together. Gradually, whisk in the soy milk and coconut milk until combined. Simmer over low heat, whisking constantly, for 2–3 minutes until the mixture thickens.

3 Stir in the vanilla extract, then spoon the mixture over the fruit.

4 Top with the remaining fruit and toasted coconut chips. Chill in the refrigerator for 1 hour before serving.

Chocolate Cheesecake

This cheesecake takes a little time to prepare and cook, but is well worth the effort. It is quite rich and is good served with a little fresh fruit.

NUTRITIONAL INFORMATION

Calories 471   Sugars 20g
Protein . . . . .10g   Fat 33g
Carbohydrate . . .28g   Saturates 5g

1¼ hrs   1–1¼ hrs

SERVES 12

INGREDIENTS

generous ¾ cup all-purpose flour

scant 1 cup ground almonds

scant 1 cup molasses sugar

scant ¾ cup margarine

1 lb 8 oz/675 g firm beancurd

¾ cup vegetable oil

½ cup orange juice

¾ cup brandy

6 tbsp unsweetened cocoa, plus extra
   to decorate

2 tsp almond extract

TO DECORATE

confectioners' sugar

ground cherries (physalis)

1 Put the flour, ground almonds, and 1 tablespoon of the sugar in a bowl and mix well. Rub the margarine into the mixture to form a dough.

2 Lightly grease and line the bottom of a 9 inch/23 cm springform pan. Press the dough into the bottom of the pan to cover, pushing the dough right up to the edge of the pan.

3 Roughly chop the beancurd and put in a food processor with the vegetable oil, orange juice, brandy, unsweetened cocoa, almond extract, and remaining sugar and process until smooth and creamy. Pour over the base in the pan and cook in a preheated oven, 325°F/160°C, for about 1–1¼ hours or until set.

4 Let cool in the pan for 5 minutes, then remove from the pan, and chill in the refrigerator. Dust with confectioners' sugar and unsweetened cocoa. Decorate with ground cherries and serve.

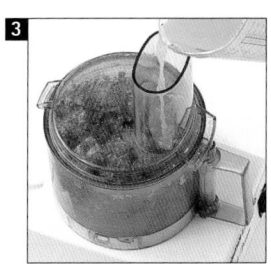

COOK'S TIP

Ground cherries make an attractive decoration for many desserts. Peel open the papery husks to expose the bright orange fruits.

Date & Apricot Tart

There is no need to add any extra sugar to this filling because the dried fruit is naturally sweet.

NUTRITIONAL INFORMATION

Calories ....359 Sugars 34g
Protein ....7g Fat 15g
Carbohydrate ...53g Saturates 2g

45 mins   50 mins

SERVES 8

INGREDIENTS

2 cups plain whole-wheat flour, plus extra for dusting

½ cup mixed nuts, ground

7 tbsp margarine, cut into small pieces

4 tbsp water

1 cup dried apricots, chopped

1⅓ cups chopped pitted dates

scant 1 cup apple juice

1 tsp ground cinnamon

grated rind of 1 lemon

custard, to serve (optional)

1 Place the flour and ground nuts in a mixing bowl and rub in the margarine with your fingertips until the mixture resembles bread crumbs. Stir in the water and bring together to form a dough. Wrap the dough in plastic wrap and chill in the refrigerator for 30 minutes.

2 Meanwhile, place the apricots and dates in a pan, with the apple juice, cinnamon, and lemon rind. Bring to a boil, cover, and simmer over low heat for about 15 minutes until the fruit softens. Mash to a purée.

3 Reserve a small ball of pastry for making lattice strips. On a lightly floured counter, roll out the rest of the dough to form a round and use to line a 9 inch/23 cm loose-based quiche pan.

4 Spread the fruit filling evenly over the base of the pie shell. Roll out the reserved pastry and cut into strips ½ inch/ 1 cm wide. Cut the strips to fit the tart and twist them across the top of the fruit to form a decorative lattice pattern. Moisten the edges of the strips with a little water and seal them firmly around the rim of the tart.

5 Bake in a preheated oven, 400°F/ 200°C, for 25–30 minutes until golden brown. Cut into slices and serve immediately with custard, if using.

Fruity Queen of Desserts

A delicious version of a classic British dessert, made here with fresh bananas and apricot jelly.

NUTRITIONAL INFORMATION

Calories 406   Sugars 60g
Protein . . . . .13g   Fat 7g
Carbohydrate . . .77g   Saturates 3g

 30 mins   1 hr

SERVES 4

INGREDIENTS

2 cups fresh white bread crumbs

2½ cups milk

3 eggs

½ tsp vanilla extract

4 tbsp superfine sugar

2 bananas

1 tbsp lemon juice

3 tbsp apricot jelly

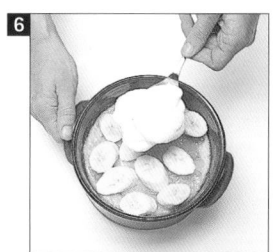

1 Sprinkle the bread crumbs evenly into a 4 cup casserole. Heat the milk until just lukewarm, then pour it over the bread crumbs.

2 Separate 2 of the eggs and beat the yolks with the remaining whole egg. Add to the casserole with the vanilla extract and half the sugar, stirring well to mix. Set aside for 10 minutes.

3 Bake in a preheated oven, 350°F/ 180°C, for 40 minutes until set. Remove the dish from the oven.

4 Slice the bananas and sprinkle with the lemon juice. Spoon the apricot jelly onto the pudding and spread out to cover the surface. Arrange the banana slices on top of the apricot jelly.

5 Whisk the egg whites until stiff, then add the remaining sugar. Continue whisking until the meringue is very stiff and glossy.

6 Pile the meringue on top of the pudding, return to the oven, and cook for a further 10–15 minutes until the meringue is just set and golden brown. Serve immediately.

COOK'S TIP

The meringue will have a soft, marshmallow-like texture, unlike a hard meringue which is cooked slowly for 2–3 hours, until dry. Always use a grease-free bowl and whisk for beating egg whites.

Rice & Banana Brûlée

Take a can of creamed rice, flavor it with orange rind, preserved ginger, raisins, and sliced bananas and top with a brown sugar glaze.

NUTRITIONAL INFORMATION

Calories ....509 Sugars 98g
Protein ....9g Fat 6g
Carbohydrate ...112g Saturates 4g

 50 mins   2–3 mins

SERVES 2

INGREDIENTS

14 oz/400 g can creamed rice

grated rind of ½ orange

2 pieces of preserved ginger, finely chopped

2 tsp ginger syrup from the jar

⅓ cup raisins

1–2 bananas

1–2 tsp lemon juice

4–5 tbsp raw sugar

1 Empty the can of creamed rice into a bowl and stir in the grated orange rind, ginger, ginger syrup, and raisins.

2 Cut the bananas diagonally into slices, toss in the lemon juice to prevent them from discoloring, drain, and divide between 2 individual flameproof dishes.

3 Spoon the rice mixture in an even layer over the bananas so that the dishes are almost full.

4 Sprinkle an even layer of sugar over the rice in each dish.

5 Place the dishes under a preheated moderate broiler and heat until the sugar melts, taking care the sugar does not burn.

6 Set aside to cool until the caramel sets, then chill in the refrigerator until ready to serve. Tap the caramel with the back of a spoon to break it.

COOK'S TIP

Canned creamed rice is very versatile and is delicious heated with orange segments and grated apples added. Try it served cold with grated chocolate and mixed chopped nuts stirred through it.

Almond Sherbet

It is best to use whole almonds rather than ready-ground almonds for this dish because they give it a better texture.

NUTRITIONAL INFORMATION

Calories 836	Sugars 33g	
Protein 29g	Fat 65g	
Carbohydrate ...36g	Saturates 7g	

 3¾ hrs 0 mins

SERVES 2

INGREDIENTS

2 cups shelled almonds

2 tbsp sugar

1¼ cups milk

1¼ cups water

1 Put the almonds in a bowl, cover with water, and set aside to soak for at least 3 hours or preferably overnight.

2 Using a sharp knife, chop the almonds into small pieces. Grind to a fine paste in a food processor or in a mortar with a pestle.

3 Add the sugar to the almond paste and grind once again to form a very fine paste.

4 Add the milk and water and mix thoroughly, preferably in a blender or food processor.

5 Transfer the almond sherbet to a large serving dish.

6 Chill the almond sherbet in the refrigerator for about 30 minutes. Stir it well just before serving.

Lime Cheesecakes

These cheesecakes are flavored with lime and mint, and set on a base of crushed graham crackers mixed with chocolate.

NUTRITIONAL INFORMATION

Calories	696	Sugars	.......44g
Protein	........18g	Fat	..........40g
Carbohydrate	...70g	Saturates	......22g

🥔 3 hrs 🕐 5 mins

SERVES 2

INGREDIENTS

BASE

2 tbsp butter, plus extra for greasing

1 oz/25 g bittersweet chocolate

1½ cups crushed graham crackers

FILLING

finely grated rind of 1 lime

⅓ cup strained cottage cheese

⅓ cup low-fat soft cheese

1 fresh mint sprig, very finely
   chopped (optional)

1 tsp gelatin

1 tbsp lime juice

1 egg yolk

3 tbsp superfine sugar

TO DECORATE

whipped cream

kiwi fruit slices

fresh mint sprigs

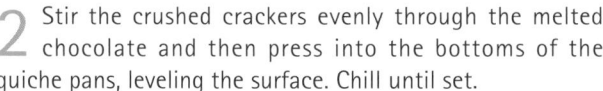

1 Grease 2 fluted, loose-bottomed 4½ inch/11 cm quiche pans thoroughly. To make the base, melt the butter and chocolate in a heatproof bowl over a pan of gently simmering water or melt in a microwave set on HIGH power for about 1 minute. Stir until smooth.

2 Stir the crushed crackers evenly through the melted chocolate and then press into the bottoms of the quiche pans, leveling the surface. Chill until set.

3 To make the filling, put the grated lime rind and cheeses into a bowl and beat until smooth and evenly blended, then beat in the mint, if using.

4 Dissolve the gelatin in the lime juice in a heatproof bowl over a pan of simmering water or in a microwave oven set on HIGH power for about 30 seconds.

5 Beat the egg yolk and sugar together until creamy and fold into the cheese mixture, followed by the dissolved gelatin. Pour over the base and chill until set.

6 To serve, remove the cheesecakes carefully from the quiche pans. Decorate with whipped cream, slices of kiwi fruit, and mint sprigs.

Baked Semolina Dessert

Succulent plums simmered in orange juice and spices complement this rich and creamy semolina dessert perfectly.

NUTRITIONAL INFORMATION

Calories ....304 Sugars 32g
Protein ....9g Fat 12g
Carbohydrate ...43g Saturates 4g

5 mins   45 mins

SERVES 4

I N G R E D I E N T S

2 tbsp butter or margarine

2½ cups milk

finely pared rind and juice of 1 orange

⅓ cup semolina

pinch of grated nutmeg

2 tbsp superfine sugar

1 egg, beaten

TO SERVE

small piece of butter

grated nutmeg

SPICED PLUMS

8 oz/225 g plums, halved and pitted

⅔ cup orange juice

2 tbsp superfine sugar

½ tsp ground apple spice

1 Grease a 4 cup casserole with a little of the butter or margarine. Put the milk, the remaining butter or margarine, and the orange rind in a pan. Sprinkle in the semolina and bring to a boil over low heat, stirring constantly. Simmer gently for about 2–3 minutes. Remove the pan from the heat.

2 Add the nutmeg, orange juice, and sugar, stirring well. Add the egg and stir to mix.

3 Transfer the mixture to the prepared casserole and bake in a preheated oven, 375°F/190°C, for about 30 minutes until lightly browned.

4 To make the spiced plums, put the plums, orange juice, sugar, and spice into a pan and simmer gently for about 10 minutes until the plums are just tender.

Remove the pan from the heat and set aside to cool slightly.

5 Top the dessert with a piece of butter and a sprinkling of grated nutmeg, and serve with the spiced plums.

Fruity Crêpe Bundles

This unusual crêpe is filled with a sweet cream flavored with ginger, nuts, and apricots and served with a raspberry and orange sauce.

NUTRITIONAL INFORMATION

Calories	610	Sugars	. . . . .60g
Protein	. . . . .19g	Fat	. . . . .20g
Carbohydrate	. . .94g	Saturates	. . . . . . .5g

 15 mins   35 mins

SERVES 2

INGREDIENTS

BATTER

½ cup all-purpose flour

pinch of salt

¼ tsp ground cinnamon

1 egg

generous ½ cup milk

white vegetable shortening, for cooking

FILLING

1½ tsp all-purpose flour, sifted

1½ tsp cornstarch

1 tbsp superfine sugar

1 egg

⅔ cup milk

4 tbsp chopped nuts

scant ¼ cup ready-to-eat dried apricots, chopped

1 piece of preserved or candied ginger, finely chopped

SAUCE

3 tbsp raspberry preserve

4½ tsp orange juice

finely grated rind of ¼ orange

1 To make the batter, sift the flour, salt, and cinnamon into a bowl and make a well in the center. Add the egg and milk and gradually beat in until smooth.

2 Melt a little shortening in a medium skillet. Pour in half the batter. Cook for 2 minutes until golden, then turn and cook the other side for about 1 minute until browned. Set aside and make a second crêpe.

3 For the filling, beat the flour with the cornstarch, sugar, and egg. Gently heat the milk in a pan, then beat 2 tablespoons of it into the flour mixture. Transfer to the pan and cook gently, stirring constantly until thick. Remove from the heat, cover with baking parchment to prevent a skin from forming, and set aside to cool.

4 Beat the nuts, apricots, and ginger into the cooled mixture and put a heaping tablespoonful in the center of each crêpe. Gather and squeeze the edges together to make a bundle. Place in a casserole and bake in a preheated oven, 350°F/180°C, for 15–20 minutes until hot and golden, but not too brown.

5 To make the sauce, melt the preserve gently with the orange juice, then strain. Return to a clean pan with the orange rind and heat through. Serve with the crêpes.

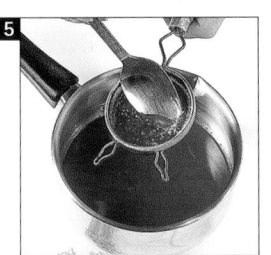

Carrot Dessert

This makes an impressive dinner-party dessert. It is best served warm with cream and can be made well in advance because it freezes well.

NUTRITIONAL INFORMATION

Calories 509	Sugars 54g	
Protein 8g	Fat 30g	
Carbohydrate ...55g	Saturates 19g	

 10 mins   1 hr

SERVES 6

I N G R E D I E N T S

3 lb 5 oz/1.5 kg carrots

⅔ cup ghee

2½ cups milk

¾ cup evaporated milk

10 whole cardamoms, peeled and crushed

8–10 tbsp sugar

TO DECORATE

4 tbsp chopped pistachio nuts

2 leaves varq (silver leaf), optional

1 Grate the carrots. Heat the ghee in a large, heavy pan over medium heat. Add the grated carrots and cook, stirring constantly, for about 15–20 minutes or until the moisture from the carrots has evaporated and the carrots have darkened in color.

2 Add the milk, evaporated milk, crushed cardamoms, and sugar and cook, stirring constantly, for a further 30–35 minutes until the mixture is a rich brownish-red color.

3 Transfer the carrot mixture to a large shallow serving dish. Decorate with the pistachio nuts and varq, if using, and serve immediately.

COOK'S TIP

Pure ghee is best for this dessert because it will taste better. However, if you are trying to limit your fat intake, you can use vegetable ghee instead.

Crêpes with Apples

The sharpness of the apples contrasts with the sweetness of the butterscotch sauce in this mouthwatering crêpe recipe.

NUTRITIONAL INFORMATION

Calories	543	Sugars	........55g
Protein	.........8g	Fat	..........24g
Carbohydrate	...78g	Saturates	......14g

15 mins　　45 mins

SERVES 4

INGREDIENTS

generous 1 cup all-purpose flour

pinch of salt

1 tsp finely grated lemon rind

1 egg

1¼ cups milk

1–2 tbsp vegetable oil, plus extra for greasing

pared lemon rind, to garnish

FILLING

8 oz/225 g cooking apples, peeled, cored and sliced

2 tbsp golden raisins

SAUCE

6 tbsp butter

3 tbsp light corn syrup

⅓ cup molasses sugar

1 tbsp rum or brandy (optional)

1 tbsp lemon juice

1 Sift the flour and salt into a bowl. Add the lemon rind, egg, and milk and whisk to make a smooth batter.

2 Heat a little oil in a heavy skillet. Make 8 thin crêpes, using extra oil as required. Stack the cooked crêpes, layering them with kitchen paper or baking parchment and keep warm.

3 To make the filling, cook the apples with the golden raisins in a little water over a low heat until soft. Divide the mixture evenly among the crêpes and roll up or fold into triangles. Brush a casserole with a little oil and arrange the crêpes in it. Bake in a preheated oven, 325°F/160°C, for about 15 minutes until warmed through.

4 To make the sauce, melt the butter, syrup, and sugar together in a pan, stirring well. Add the rum or brandy, if using, and the lemon juice. Do not let the mixture boil.

5 Serve the crêpes on warm plates, with a little sauce poured over, and garnished with lemon rind.

Sweet Potato Dessert

This unusual milky dessert is very easy to make and is equally delicious whether it is eaten hot or cold.

NUTRITIONAL INFORMATION

Calories 234   Sugars 23g
Protein ....5g   Fat 3g
Carbohydrate ...51g   Saturates 1g

15 mins   20 mins

SERVES 4

INGREDIENTS

2 lb 4 oz/1 kg sweet potatoes

3¾ cups milk

scant 1 cup sugar

chopped almonds, to decorate

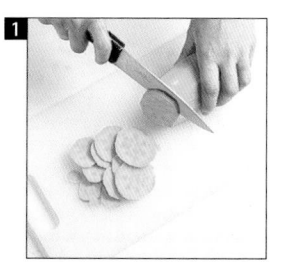
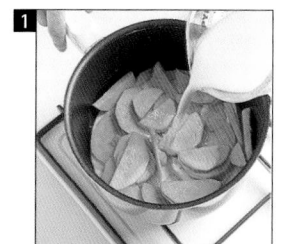

1 Using a sharp knife, peel the sweet potatoes. Rinse them and then cut them into slices. Place in a large pan. Cover with 2½ cups of the milk and cook over low heat until the sweet potato is soft enough to be mashed.

2 Remove the sweet potatoes from the heat and mash thoroughly until completely smooth. Add the sugar and the remaining milk and stir gently until completely blended together.

3 Return the pan to the heat and simmer the mixture until it starts to thicken (it should reach the consistency of a creamy soup).

4 Transfer to a serving dish. Decorate with almonds and serve immediately.

COOK'S TIP

Sweet potatoes are longer than ordinary potatoes and have a pinkish or yellowish skin with yellow or white flesh. As their name suggests, they taste slightly sweet.

Spiced Fruit Garland

There is nothing like the delicious smell of yeast cooking for creating a warm atmosphere. It must be something to do with the anticipation.

NUTRITIONAL INFORMATION

Calories	327	Sugars	........28g
Protein	.........6g	Fat	...........11g
Carbohydrate	...55g	Saturates	.......5g

  1½ hrs   30 mins

SERVES 12

INGREDIENTS

3½ cups white bread flour, plus extra for dusting

½ tsp salt

4 tbsp butter

4 tbsp superfine sugar

1 envelope active dry yeast

⅔ cup lukewarm milk

1 egg, beaten

vegetable oil, for brushing

FILLING

1½ cups mixed dried fruit

2 tbsp candied cherries, chopped

½ cup ground almonds

4 tbsp molasses sugar

1 tsp ground cinnamon

½ tsp ground nutmeg

2 tbsp butter, melted

TO DECORATE

¼ cup confectioners' sugar

candied cherries

chopped nuts

angelica

1 Sift the flour and salt into a large bowl. Rub in the butter and stir in the sugar and yeast. Make a well in the center and add the milk and egg. Draw in the flour gradually, mixing well to make a smooth dough.

2 Knead the dough on a lightly floured counter for about 8–10 minutes. Place in a lightly oiled bowl, cover, and set aside in a warm place to rise until doubled in size.

3 Knead lightly for 1 minute and then roll out into a 16 x 9 inch/40 x 23 cm rectangle. Combine all the filling ingredients and spread over the rectangle, leaving a ¾ in/2 cm border around the edge. From the long edge, roll the rectangle into a cylinder, pressing the edge to seal it. Form the roll into a circle, sealing the ends together.

4 Lift the ring onto a greased cookie sheet and cut it into 12 slices, without cutting right through. Twist each slice so that a cut surface lies uppermost. Set aside in a warm place for 30–40 minutes to rise.

5 Bake in a preheated oven, 400°F/200°C, for 25–30 minutes. Cool on a wire rack. Mix the confectioners' sugar with a little water to make a thin candied frosting and drizzle over. Arrange the cherries on top and sprinkle with the chopped nuts and angelica.

Ground Almonds in Milk

Traditionally served at breakfast in India, this almond-based dish is said to sharpen the mind. However, it can be served as a delicious dessert.

NUTRITIONAL INFORMATION

Calories	314	Sugars	. . . . .18g
Protein	. . . . .8g	Fat	. . . . .21g
Carbohydrate	. . .23g	Saturates	. . . . . . .3g

 5 mins   10 mins

SERVES 4

I N G R E D I E N T S

2 tbsp vegetable or pure ghee

4 tbsp all-purpose flour

scant 1 cup ground almonds

1¼ cups milk

4 tbsp sugar

fresh mint leaves, to decorate

1 Place the ghee in a small, heavy pan and melt over a gentle heat, stirring constantly so that it doesn't burn.

2 Reduce the heat and add the flour, constantly stirring vigorously to remove any lumps. Stir in the almonds.

3 Gradually stir in the milk and sugar. Bring to a boil, stirring constantly. Continue cooking, stirring constantly, for 3–5 minutes or until the mixture is smooth and reaches the consistency of a creamy soup.

4 Transfer to a serving dish, decorate with fresh mint leaves, and serve hot.

Apricot Slices

These vegan slices are ideal for children's lunches.
They are full of flavor and made with healthy ingredients.

NUTRITIONAL INFORMATION

Calories	198	Sugars	........13g
Protein	.........4g	Fat	...........9g
Carbohydrate	...25g	Saturates	.......2g

50 mins   1 hr

MAKES 12

I N G R E D I E N T S

PASTRY

7 tbsp margarine, cut into
   small pieces, plus extra for greasing

2 cups whole-wheat flour

½ cup finely ground mixed nuts

4 tbsp water

soy milk, to glaze

FILLING

1 cup dried apricots

grated rind of 1 orange

1½ cups apple juice

1 tsp ground cinnamon

generous ⅓ cup raisins

1 Lightly grease a 9 inch/23 cm square cake pan. To make the dough, place the flour and nuts in a mixing bowl and rub in the margarine with your fingers until the mixture resembles bread crumbs. Stir in the water and bring together to form a dough. Wrap and set aside to chill in the refrigerator for 30 minutes.

2 To make the filling, place the apricots, orange rind, and apple juice in a pan and bring to a boil. Simmer for 30 minutes until the apricots are mushy. Cool slightly, then process in a food processor or blender to a purée. Alternatively, press the mixture through a fine strainer. Stir in the cinnamon and raisins.

3 Divide the dough in half, roll out 1 half, and use to line the base of the pan. Spread the apricot purée over the top and brush the edges of the dough with water. Roll out the rest of the dough to fit over the top of the apricot purée. Press down and seal the edges.

4 Prick the top of the dough with a fork and brush with soy milk. Bake in a preheated oven, 400°F/200°C, for 20–25 minutes until the pastry is golden. Set aside to cool slightly before cutting into 12 bars. Serve the slices either warm or cold.

COOK'S TIP

These slices will keep in an
airtight container for 3–4 days.

Mangoes in Syrup

A simple, fresh-tasting fruit dessert to round off a
rich meal perfectly. Serve the mango lightly chilled.

NUTRITIONAL INFORMATION

Calories 117   Sugars 30g
Protein . . . . .1g   Fat 0g
Carbohydrate . . .30g   Saturates 0g

 1 hr   5 mins

SERVES 4

I N G R E D I E N T S

2 large, ripe mangoes

1 lime

1 lemongrass stem, chopped

3 tbsp superfine sugar

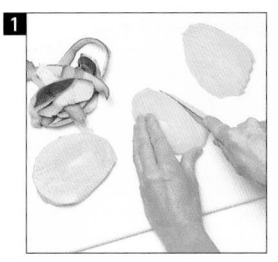
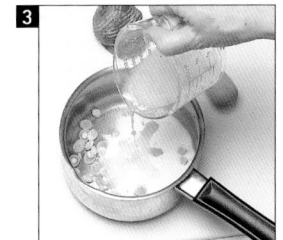

1 Peel the mangoes, then cut away the flesh from either side of the the large pits. Slice the flesh into long, thin slices and arrange them in a large, chilled serving dish.

2 Remove a few shreds of the rind from the lime and reserve for decoration, then cut the lime in half and squeeze out the juice.

3 Place the lime juice in a small pan with the lemongrass and sugar. Heat gently, without boiling, until the sugar is completely dissolved. Remove from the heat and set aside to cool completely.

4 Strain the cooled syrup into a pitcher and pour evenly over the mango slices. Sprinkle with the lime rind strips, cover, and chill before serving.

COOK'S TIP
To serve this dessert on a hot day, particularly if it is to stand for a while, place the dish on a bed of crushed ice to keep the fruit and syrup chilled.

Rose Ice

A delicately perfumed sweet granita ice, which is coarser than many ice creams. This looks very pretty on a glass dish sprinkled with rose petals.

NUTRITIONAL INFORMATION

Calories	76	Sugars	. . . . .9g
Protein	. . . . .2g	Fat	. . . . .4g
Carbohydrate	. . . .9g	Saturates	. . . . . . .3g

 3 hrs 10 mins

SERVES 4

INGREDIENTS

1⅔ cups water

2 tbsp coconut cream

4 tbsp sweetened condensed milk

2 tsp rosewater

a few drops pink food coloring (optional)

pink rose petals, to decorate

1 Place the water in a small pan and add the coconut cream. Heat the mixture gently without boiling, stirring.

2 Remove from the heat and let cool. Stir in the condensed milk, rosewater, and food coloring, if using.

3 Pour into a freezer container and freeze for 1–1½ hours until slushy.

4 Remove from the freezer and break up the ice crystals with a fork. Return to the freezer and freeze until firm.

5 Spoon the ice roughly into a pile on a serving dish and sprinkle with rose petals to serve.

COOK'S TIP

To prevent the ice from thawing too quickly at the table, nestle the base of the serving dish in another dish filled with crushed ice.

Mango & Lime Sherbet

A refreshing sherbet is the perfect way to round off a spicy Thai meal, and mangoes make a deliciously smooth-textured, velvety sherbet.

NUTRITIONAL INFORMATION

Calories 158	Sugars 34g
Protein 1g	Fat 3g
Carbohydrate ...34g	Saturates 2g

4 hrs   4 mins

SERVES 4

INGREDIENTS

6 tbsp superfine sugar

scant ½ cup water

rind of 3 limes, finely grated

2 tbsp coconut cream

2 large, ripe mangoes

generous ½ cup lime juice

curls of fresh coconut, toasted, to decorate

1 Place the sugar, water, and lime rind in a small pan and heat gently, stirring constantly, until the sugar dissolves. Boil rapidly for 2 minutes to reduce slightly, then remove from the heat and strain into a bowl or pitcher. Stir in the coconut cream and set aside to cool.

2 Halve the mangoes, remove the pits, and peel thinly. Chop the flesh coarsely and place in a food processor with the lime juice. Process to a smooth purée and transfer to a small bowl.

3 Pour the cooled syrup into the mango purée, mixing evenly. Tip into a freezer container and freeze for 1 hour, or until slushy in texture. (Alternatively, use an electric ice-cream maker.)

4 Remove the container from the freezer and beat with an electric mixer to break up the ice crystals.

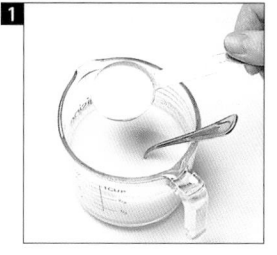

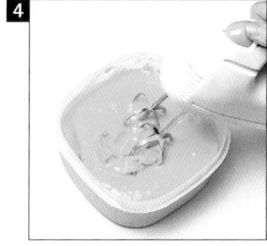

Refreeze for a further hour, then remove from the freezer, and beat the contents again until smooth.

5 Cover the container, return to the freezer, and freeze until firm. To serve, remove from the freezer and leave at room temperature for about 15 minutes to soften slightly before scooping. Sprinkle with toasted coconut to serve.

COOK'S TIP

If you prefer, canned mangoes in syrup can be used to make the sherbet. Omit the sugar and water, and steep the lime rind in the canned syrup instead.

Lychee & Ginger Sherbet

A refreshing palate-cleanser after a rich meal, this sherbet couldn't be easier to make, and can be served with a fruit salad.

NUTRITIONAL INFORMATION

Calories . . . . . . .159 Sugars 40g
Protein . . . . .2g Fat 0g
Carbohydrate . . .40g Saturates 0g

4 hrs   0 mins

SERVES 4

I N G R E D I E N T S

2 x 14 oz/400 g cans lychees in syrup

finely grated rind of 1 lime

2 tbsp lime juice

3 tbsp preserved ginger syrup

2 egg whites

T O   D E C O R A T E

starfruit slices

slivers of preserved ginger

1 Drain the lychees, reserving the syrup. Place the fruits in a blender or food processor with the lime rind, juice, and preserved ginger syrup and process until completely smooth. Transfer to a mixing bowl.

2 Mix the purée thoroughly with the reserved syrup, then pour into a freezerproof container, and freeze for about 1–1½ hours until slushy in texture. (Alternatively, use an ice-cream maker.)

3 Remove from the freezer and whisk to break up the ice crystals. Whisk the egg whites in a clean, dry bowl until stiff, then quickly and lightly fold them into the iced lychee mixture.

4 Return to the freezer and freeze until firm. Remove from the freezer 15 minutes before serving to soften slightly. Serve the sherbet in scoops, with slices of starfruit and ginger to decorate.

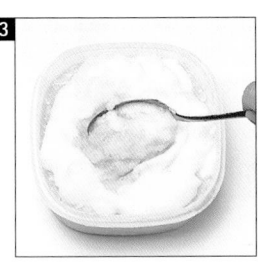

COOK'S TIP

It is not recommended that raw egg whites are served to young children, pregnant women, the elderly, or anyone weakened by chronic illness. The egg whites may be left out of this recipe, but you will need to whisk the sorbet a second time.

Pineapple with Lime

Thai pineapples are sweet and fragrant, and this local fruit appears regularly as a dessert, usually served very simply.

NUTRITIONAL INFORMATION

Calories	93	Sugars 23g
Protein	.........1g	Fat 0g
Carbohydrate	...23g	Saturates 0g

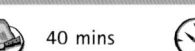

40 mins   1 min

SERVES 4

INGREDIENTS

1 pineapple

2 cardamom pods

4 tbsp water

1 strip of lime rind, thinly pared

1 tbsp brown sugar

3 tbsp lime juice

fresh mint sprigs and whipped cream, to decorate

1 Using a sharp knife, cut the top and base from the pineapple, then cut away the peel and remove all the "eyes" from the flesh. Cut into quarters and remove the core. Slice the pineapple flesh lengthwise.

2 Crush the cardamom pods in a mortar with a pestle and place in a small pan with the lime rind and water. Heat gently until the mixture is boiling, then simmer for 30 seconds.

3 Remove the pan from the heat and stir in the sugar until it has dissolved, then cover, and set aside to steep for 5 minutes.

4 Add the lime juice, stir well to mix, then strain the syrup over the pineapple. Chill for 30 minutes.

5 Arrange the pineapple on a serving dish, spoon the syrup over it, and serve decorated with fresh mint sprigs and whipped cream.

COOK'S TIP

To remove the "eyes" from pineapple, cut off the peel, then use a small sharp knife to cut a V-shaped channel down the pineapple, cutting diagonally through the lines of brown "eyes" in the flesh, to make spiraling cuts around the fruit.

Mung Bean Custards

Mung beans give this sweet custard an unusual texture, and it's a real treat served with a generous spoonful of crème fraîche.

NUTRITIONAL INFORMATION

Calories	163	Sugars	........19g
Protein	.........8g	Fat	...........3g
Carbohydrate	...29g	Saturates	.......1g

 40 mins 50–60 mins

SERVES 6

INGREDIENTS

⅔ cup dried mung beans

2 eggs, beaten

¾ cup coconut milk

½ cup superfine sugar

1 tbsp ground rice

1 tsp ground cinnamon

butter, for greasing

TO DECORATE

ground cinnamon

crème fraîche or whipped cream

finely grated lime rind

sliced starfruit

pomegranate seeds

1 Place the beans in a pan with enough water to cover. Bring to a boil, then lower the heat, and simmer for about 30–40 minutes until the beans are very tender. Drain well.

2 Mash the beans, then press through a strainer to make a smooth purée. Place the bean purée, eggs, coconut milk, sugar, rice flour, and cinnamon in a large bowl and beat well until mixed.

3 Grease and base-line 4 x ⅔ cup molds or ramekin dishes and pour in the mixture. Place on a cookie sheet and bake in a preheated oven, 350°F/180°C, for 20–25 minutes or until just set.

4 Cool the custards in the molds or ramekins, then run a knife around the edges to loosen, and turn out onto a serving plate. Sprinkle with cinnamon. Top with crème fraîche or whipped cream and sprinkle with lime rind. Serve with starfruit and pomegranate seeds.

COOK'S TIP

To save time, use canned mung beans. Omit Step 1, drain the beans thoroughly, and continue with step 2.

Bananas in Coconut Milk

An unusual dessert which is equally good served hot or cold.
This is a classic Thai combination of fruits and vegetables.

NUTRITIONAL INFORMATION

Calories 157	Sugars 36g
Protein 2g	Fat 1g
Carbohydrate ...38g	Saturates 0g

 10 mins   3–5 mins

SERVES 4

INGREDIENTS

4 large bananas

1½ cups coconut milk

2 tbsp superfine sugar

pinch of salt

½ tsp orange-flower water

1 tbsp shredded fresh mint

2 tbsp mung beans, cooked

fresh mint sprigs, to decorate

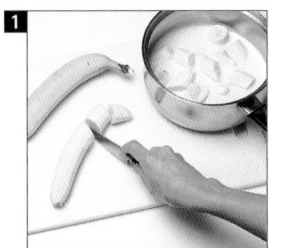

1 Peel the bananas and cut them into short chunks. Place in a large, heavy pan with the coconut milk, superfine sugar, and salt. Heat gently until boiling, then simmer for 1 minute. Remove the pan from the heat.

2 Sprinkle the orange-flower water over, stir in the mint, and spoon into a serving dish.

3 Place the mung beans in a heavy skillet and cook over high heat until turning crisp and golden, shaking the pan occasionally. Remove, cool slightly, and crush lightly in a mortar with a pestle.

4 Sprinkle the toasted beans over the bananas and serve warm or cold, decorated with fresh mint sprigs.

COOK'S TIP
If you prefer, the mung beans could be replaced with sliced, toasted almonds or hazelnuts.

Thai Rice Dessert

This Thai-style version of rice dessert is mildly spiced and creamy, with a rich custard topping. It's excellent served warm or cold.

NUTRITIONAL INFORMATION

Calories 351   Sugars 16g
Protein . . . . .7g   Fat 21g
Carbohydrate . . .37g   Saturates 16g

 10 mins   1–1¼ hrs

SERVES 4

INGREDIENTS

½ cup short grain rice

2 tbsp palm sugar

1 cardamom pod, split

1¼ cups coconut milk

⅔ cup water

3 eggs

scant 1 cup coconut cream

1½ tbsp superfine sugar

sweetened coconut flakes, to decorate

fresh fruit, to serve

1 Place the rice and palm sugar in a pan. Crush the seeds from the cardamom pod in a mortar with a pestle and add to the pan. Stir in the coconut milk and water.

2 Bring to a boil, stirring to dissolve the sugar. Lower the heat and simmer, uncovered, stirring occasionally, for about 20 minutes until the rice is tender and most of the liquid is absorbed.

3 Spoon the rice into 4 individual ovenproof dishes and spread evenly. Place the dishes in a wide roasting pan with water to come about halfway up the sides.

4 Beat the eggs with the coconut cream and superfine sugar and spoon over the rice. Cover with foil and bake in a preheated oven, 350°F/180°C, for about 45–50 minutes until the custard sets.

5 Serve the rice desserts warm or cold, with fresh fruit and decorated with coconut flakes.

COOK'S TIP

Cardamom is quite a powerful spice, so if you find it too strong, it can be left out altogether or replaced with a little ground cinnamon.

Balinese Banana Crêpes

These little stacks of rich banana crêpes, drizzled with fragrant lime juice, are quite irresistible any time of day.

NUTRITIONAL INFORMATION

Calories	225	Sugars	........11g
Protein	.........9g	Fat	...........7g
Carbohydrate	...34g	Saturates	.......2g

1¼ hrs   20 mins

SERVES 6

I N G R E D I E N T S

1½ cups all-purpose flour

pinch of salt

4 eggs, beaten

2 large, ripe bananas, peeled and mashed

1¼ cups coconut milk

vegetable oil, for frying

TO DECORATE

sliced banana

6 tbsp lime juice

confectioners' sugar

coconut cream

1 Place the flour, salt, eggs, bananas, and coconut milk in a blender or food processor and process to a smooth batter. Alternatively, if you don't have a food processor, sift the flour and salt into a bowl and make a well in the center, then add the remaining ingredients, and beat well until smooth.

2 Chill the batter for 1 hour. Remove from the refrigerator and beat briefly again. Heat a small amount of oil in a small skillet until very hot.

3 Drop tablespoonfuls of batter into the pan. Cook until the crêpes are golden underneath.

4 Turn over and cook the other side until golden brown. Cook in batches until all the batter is used up, making about 36 crêpes. Remove and drain on paper towels.

5 Serve the crêpes in a stack, decorated with sliced bananas, sprinkled with lime juice and sugar, and topped with coconut cream.

COOK'S TIP
These little crêpes are best eaten hot and freshly cooked, so keep them hot in a low oven while the others are cooking.

Coconut Crêpes

These pretty, lacy-thin crêpes, which are often colored a delicate pale-pink or tinted green, are sold by Thai street vendors.

NUTRITIONAL INFORMATION

Calories 218	Sugars 8g
Protein 6g	Fat 7g
Carbohydrate . . .31g	Saturates 2g

10 mins   20 mins

SERVES 4

INGREDIENTS

⅔ cup rice flour

3 tbsp superfine sugar

pinch of salt

2 eggs

2½ cups coconut milk

4 tbsp dry shredded coconut

vegetable oil, for frying

2 tbsp palm sugar, to decorate

fresh mango or banana, to serve

1 Place the rice flour, sugar, and salt in a bowl and add the eggs and coconut milk, whisking until a smooth batter forms. Alternatively, place all the ingredients in a blender and process to a smooth batter. Beat in half the coconut.

2 Heat a small amount of oil in a wide, heavy skillet. Pour in a little batter, swirling the skillet to cover the surface thinly and evenly. Cook until pale golden underneath.

3 Turn or toss the crêpe and cook the other side until light golden brown.

4 Turn out the crêpe and keep hot while using the remaining batter to make a total of 8 crêpes.

5 Serve the crêpes folded or loosely rolled, with slices of mango or banana and sprinkled with palm sugar and the remaining coconut, toasted.

COOK'S TIP
Rice flour gives the crêpes a light, smooth texture, but if it's not available, use ordinary all-purpose flour instead.

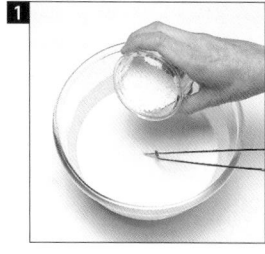  

Grilled Baked Apples

When they are wrapped in kitchen foil, apples bake to perfection on the barbecue and make a delightful finale to any meal.

NUTRITIONAL INFORMATION

Calories	294	Sugars	........30g
Protein	.........3g	Fat	..........18g
Carbohydrate	...31g	Saturates	.......7g

🍧 15 mins   🕐 25–30 mins

SERVES 4

I N G R E D I E N T S

4 medium cooking apples

4 tbsp chopped walnuts

4 tbsp ground almonds

2 tbsp molasses sugar

1 oz/25 g cherries, chopped

2 tbsp chopped preserved ginger

1 tbsp amaretto (optional)

2 tbsp butter

light cream or plain yogurt, to serve

1 Core the apples and using a knife, score each around the middle to prevent the skins from splitting while they are grilling.

2 To make the filling, combine the walnuts, almonds, sugar, cherries, ginger, and amaretto liqueur, if using, in a small bowl.

3 Spoon the filling mixture into each apple, pushing it down into the hollowed-out core. Mound a little of the filling mixture on top of each apple.

4 Place each apple on a large square of double thickness kitchen foil and generously dot all over with the butter. Wrap up the foil so that the apple is completely enclosed.

5 Grill the foil packets over hot coals for 25–30 minutes or until the apples are tender.

6 Transfer the apples to warm, individual serving plates. Serve immediately with lashings of light cream or thick plain yogurt.

COOK'S TIP

If the coals are dying down, place the kitchen foil packets directly on them, raking them up around the apples. Grill for 25–30 minutes and serve with the cream or yogurt.

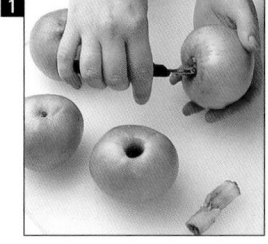

Baked Bananas

The orange-flavored cream can be prepared in advance, but do not make up the banana packets until just before you need to cook them.

NUTRITIONAL INFORMATION

Calories	380	Sugars	........40g
Protein	.........2g	Fat	..........18g
Carbohydrate	...43g	Saturates	.....11g

 30 mins   10 mins

SERVES 4

INGREDIENTS

4 bananas

2 passion fruit

4 tbsp orange juice

4 tbsp orange-flavored liqueur

ORANGE-FLAVORED CREAM

⅔ cup heavy cream

3 tbsp confectioners' sugar

2 tbsp orange-flavored liqueur

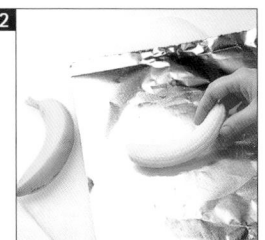

1 To make the orange-flavored cream, pour the heavy cream into a mixing bowl and sprinkle with the confectioners' sugar. Whisk the mixture until it is standing in soft peaks. Carefully fold in the orange-flavored liqueur and chill in the refrigerator until required.

2 Peel the bananas and place each 1 on a sheet of kitchen foil.

VARIATION

Leave the bananas in their skins for a really quick dessert. Split the banana skins and pop in 1–2 squares of chocolate. Wrap the bananas in kitchen foil and bake for 10 minutes or until the chocolate has just melted.

3 Cut the passion fruit in half and squeeze the juice of each half over each banana. Spoon over the orange juice and liqueur.

4 Fold the kitchen foil over the top of the bananas so that they are completely enclosed.

5 Place the packets on a cookie sheet and bake the bananas in a preheated

oven, 350°F/180°C, for about 10 minutes or until they are just tender (test by inserting a toothpick).

6 Transfer the foil packets to warm, individual serving plates. Open out the foil packets at the table and then serve immediately with the chilled orange-flavored cream.

Piña Colada Pineapple

The flavors of pineapple and coconut blend as well together on the barbecue as they do in the well-known cocktail.

NUTRITIONAL INFORMATION

Calories . . . . .231 Sugars 22g
Protein . . . . .1g Fat 15g
Carbohydrate . . .22g Saturates 11g

 15 mins   25 mins

SERVES 4

INGREDIENTS

1 small pineapple

2 tbsp sweet butter

2 tbsp molasses sugar

½ cup grated fresh coconut

2 tbsp coconut-flavored liqueur or rum

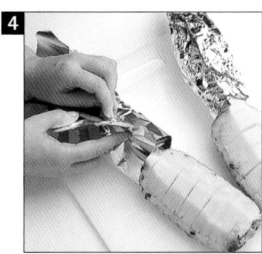

1 Using a very sharp knife, cut the pineapple into quarters and then remove the tough core from the center, leaving the leaves attached.

2 Carefully cut the pineapple flesh away from the skin. Remove any "eyes" with small sharp knife. Make horizontal cuts across the flesh of the pineapple quarters.

3 Place the butter in a pan and heat gently until melted, stirring constantly. Brush the melted butter over the pineapple and sprinkle with the sugar.

4 Cover the pineapple leaves with kitchen foil in order to prevent them from burning and transfer the pineapple quarters to a rack set over hot coals.

5 Grill the pineapple for about 10 minutes.

6 Sprinkle the coconut over the pineapple and grill, cut side up, for a further 5–10 minutes or until the pineapple is piping hot.

7 Transfer the pineapple to serving plates and remove the foil from the leaves. Spoon a little coconut-flavoured liqueur or rum over the pineapple and serve immediately.

COOK'S TIP

Fresh coconut has the best flavor for this dish. If you prefer, however, you can use dry shredded coconut.

Exotic Fruit Crêpes

These crêpes are filled with an exotic array of tropical fruits. Decorate lavishly with tropical flowers or mint sprigs.

NUTRITIONAL INFORMATION

Calories 382	Sugars 24g
Protein 7g	Fat 17g
Carbohydrate . . .53g	Saturates 3g

40 mins   35 mins

SERVES 4

INGREDIENTS

BATTER

generous 1 cup all-purpose flour

pinch of salt

1 egg

1 egg yolk

1¼ cups coconut milk

4 tsp vegetable oil, plus extra for frying

FILLING

1 banana

1 papaya

juice of 1 lime

2 passion fruit

1 mango, peeled, pitted, and sliced

4 lychees, pitted and halved

1–2 tbsp honey

flowers or fresh mint sprigs, to decorate

1 Sift the flour and salt into a bowl. Make a well in the center and add the egg, egg yolk, and a little of the coconut milk. Gradually draw the flour into the egg mixture, beating well and gradually adding the remaining coconut milk to make a smooth batter. Stir in the oil. Cover and chill for 30 minutes.

2 Peel and slice the banana and place in a bowl. Peel and slice the papaya, discarding the seeds. Add to the banana with the lime juice and mix well. Cut the passion fruit in half and scoop out the flesh and seeds into the fruit bowl. Stir in the mango, lychees, and honey.

3 Heat a little oil in a 6 inch/15 cm skillet. Pour in just enough of the crêpe batter to cover the bottom of the pan and tilt so that it spreads thinly and evenly. Cook until the crêpe is just set and the underside is lightly browned, turn, and briefly cook the other side. Remove from the skillet and keep warm. Repeat with the remaining batter to make a total of 8 crêpes.

4 To serve, place a little of the prepared fruit filling along the center of each crepe and then roll it into a cone shape. Lay, seam side down, on warmed serving plates, decorate with flowers or mint sprigs, and serve.

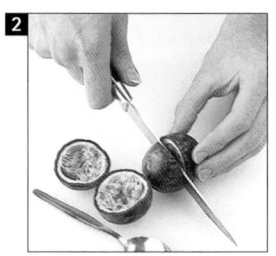

Sticky Sesame Bananas

These tasty morsels are a real treat. Pieces of banana are
dipped in caramel and then sprinkled with a few sesame seeds.

NUTRITIONAL INFORMATION

Calories 215   Sugars 38g
Protein . . . . .6g   Fat 3g
Carbohydrate . . .41g   Saturates 1g

🧊 10 mins   🕐 20 mins

SERVES 4

I N G R E D I E N T S

4 ripe medium bananas

3 tbsp lemon juice

generous 1 cup superfine sugar

4 tbsp cold water

2 tbsp sesame seeds

⅔ cup low-fat plain yogurt

1 tbsp confectioners' sugar

1 tsp vanilla extract

TO DECORATE

shredded lemon rind

shredded lime rind

1 Peel the bananas and cut into 2 inch/
5 cm pieces. Place the banana pieces
in a bowl, spoon over the lemon juice, and
stir well to coat—this will help prevent the
bananas from discoloring.

2 Place the sugar and water in a small
pan and heat gently, stirring
constantly, until the sugar dissolves. Bring
to a boil and cook for 5–6 minutes until
the mixture turns golden brown.

3 Meanwhile, drain the bananas and
blot with paper towels to dry. Line a
cookie sheet or board with baking
parchment and arrange the bananas, well
spaced apart, on top.

4 When the caramel is ready, drizzle it
over the bananas, working quickly
because the caramel sets almost instantly.
Sprinkle the sesame seeds over the
caramelized bananas and set aside to cool
for 10 minutes.

5 Combine the yogurt, confectioners'
sugar, and vanilla extract.

6 Peel the bananas away from the
baking parchment and arrange on
serving plates.

7 Serve the yogurt as a dip, decorated
with the shredded lemon and
lime rind.

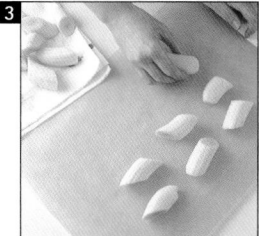

Balsamic Strawberries

Generations of Italian cooks have known that the unlikely combination of freshly ground black pepper and ripe, juicy strawberries is fantastic.

NUTRITIONAL INFORMATION

Calories 132	Sugars 5g
Protein 1g	Fat 12g
Carbohydrate 5g	Saturates 7g

 4¼ hrs   0 mins

SERVES 4–6

I N G R E D I E N T S

1 lb/450 g fresh strawberries

2–3 tbsp balsamic vinegar

fresh mint leaves, torn, plus extra to decorate (optional)

½–¾ cup mascarpone cheese

pepper

1 Wipe the strawberries with a damp cloth, rather than rinsing them, so they do not become soggy. Using a paring knife, cut off the green stalks at the top and use the tip of the knife to remove the core or hull.

2 Cut each strawberry in half lengthwise or into quarters if large. Transfer to a bowl.

COOK'S TIP

This is most enjoyable when it is made with the best-quality balsamic vinegar, one that has aged slowly and has turned thick and syrupy. Unfortunately, the genuine mixture is always expensive. Less expensive versions are artificially sweetened and colored with caramel.

3 Add the balsamic vinegar, allowing ½ tablespoon per person. Add several twists of ground black pepper, then gently stir together. Cover with plastic wrap and chill for up to 4 hours.

4 Just before serving, stir in torn mint leaves to taste. Spoon the mascarpone into bowls and spoon the berries on top. Decorate with a few mint leaves, if wished. Sprinkle with extra pepper to taste.

Figs with Orange Cream

Luscious, sweet fresh figs are served with a delicate sauce, flavored with a hint of orange.

NUTRITIONAL INFORMATION

Calories	20	Sugars	........13g
Protein	.........3g	Fat	..........18g
Carbohydrate	...14g	Saturates	.......9g

24 hrs   3–5 mins

SERVES 4

INGREDIENTS

8 large fresh figs

4 large fresh fig leaves, if available, rinsed and dried

CREME FRAICHE (OPTIONAL)

2 tbsp buttermilk

1¼ cups heavy cream

ORANGE-BLOSSOM CREAM

½ cup crème fraîche, homemade or bought

about 4 tbsp orange-blossom water

1 tsp orange-blossom honey

finely grated rind of ½ orange

2 tbsp sliced almonds, to decorate (optional)

1 If you are making the crème fraîche, begin at least a day ahead. Put the buttermilk in a preserving jar or a jar with a screw top. Add the cream, close securely, and shake to blend. Set aside at room room temperature for 6–8 hours until set, then chill for at least 8 hours, and up to 4 days. It will develop a slight tangy flavor. Lightly beat before using.

2 To toast the almonds for the decoration, place in a dry skillet over medium heat and stir until lightly browned. Take care that they do not burn. Immediately tip the almonds out of the pan. Set aside.

3 To make the orange-blossom cream, put the crème fraîche in a small bowl and stir in the orange-blossom water with the orange-blossom honey, and orange rind. Taste and add a little extra orange-blossom water if necessary.

4 To serve, cut the stems off the figs, but do not peel them. Stand the figs upright with the pointed end upward. Cut each into quarters without cutting all the way through, so you can open them out into attractive "flowers."

5 If you are using fig leaves, place 1 in the center of each serving plate. Arrange 2 figs on top of each leaf, and spoon a small amount of the orange-flavored cream alongside them. Sprinkle the cream with the toasted sliced almonds, if desired, just before serving.

Poached Peaches

Soaking the peaches overnight is an old Turkish tip to prevent the fruit from becoming too soft and falling apart while they are being poached.

NUTRITIONAL INFORMATION

Calories	372	Sugars	........34g
Protein	.........3g	Fat	..........20g
Carbohydrate	...34g	Saturates	......12g

 24 hrs   10 mins

SERVES 4–6

INGREDIENTS

8–12 ripe peaches

1 large lime

2 cups fruity, dry white wine

1 tbsp black peppercorns, lightly crushed

3 inch/7.5 cm cinnamon stick, halved

finely pared rind of 1 unwaxed lemon

½ cup superfine sugar

fresh mint sprigs, to decorate

AMARETTO-MASCARPONE CREAM

2 tbsp Amaretto liqueur

generous 1 cup mascarpone cheese

3 Meanwhile, make the amaretto-mascarpone cream. Stir the amaretto into the mascarpone until thoroughly incorporated, cover, and chill.

4 Place the wine, peppercorns, cinnamon, lemon rind, and sugar in a pan over medium-high heat and stir until the sugar dissolves.

5 Boil the syrup for 2 minutes. Reduce to a simmer. Remove the peaches from the refrigerator, add them to the syrup, and poach for 2 minutes or until tender—they should not be falling apart.

6 Using a draining spoon, transfer the peaches to a bowl. Bring the syrup to a boil and continue boiling until thickened and reduced to about ½ cup. Pour the syrup into a heatproof bowl and set aside to cool. When cool, pour over the peaches. Cover and chill until required. To serve, decorate with mint.

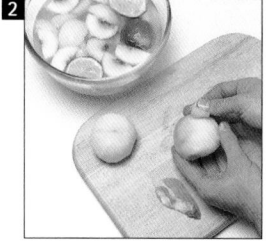  

1 Fill a large bowl with ice water. Bring a large pan of water to a boil. Add the peaches and cook for 1 minute. Using a draining spoon, immediately transfer the peaches to the ice water to stop the cooking process.

2 Squeeze the juice from the lime into a bowl of water. Peel the peaches, then quarter each, and remove the pit. Drop the fruit into the lime water as it is prepared. Cover and chill in the refrigerator for 24 hours.

Lemon & Nut Rice Dessert

Rice is transformed into a creamy, family-style dessert. At the height of summer, serve well chilled with a mixture of summer berries.

NUTRITIONAL INFORMATION

Calories	332	Sugars	........22g
Protein	........11g	Fat	..........10g
Carbohydrate	...52g	Saturates	.......3g

1½ hrs   25 mins

SERVES 4

INGREDIENTS

1 tsp cornstarch

3¾ cups milk, plus an extra 2 tbsp

generous ½ cup short grain rice

about 2 tbsp sugar or 1 tbsp honey

finely grated rind of 1 large lemon

freshly squeezed lemon juice

½ cup shelled pistachio nuts

1 Place the cornstarch in a small bowl and stir in 2 tablespoons of the milk, stirring until there are no lumps. Rinse a pan with cold water.

2 Place the remaining milk and the cornstarch mixture in a pan over medium–high heat and heat, stirring occasionally, until small bubbles form all around the edge. Do not boil.

3 Stir in the rice, lower the heat, and continue stirring for 20 minutes or until all but about 2 tablespoons of the excess liquid has evaporated and the rice grains are tender.

4 Remove from the heat and pour into a heatproof bowl. Stir in sugar to taste. Stir in the lemon rind, then stir in lemon juice to taste. Set the bowl aside to cool completely.

5 Tightly cover the top of the cool rice with a sheet of plastic wrap and chill in the refrigerator for at least 1 hour—the colder the rice is, the better it tastes with fresh fruit.

6 Meanwhile, finely chop the pistachio nuts. To serve, spoon the rice pudding into individual bowls and sprinkle with the chopped nuts.

COOK'S TIP
It is important to rinse the pan in step 1 to prevent the milk from scorching on the sides or base.

Orange & Bitters Sherbet

Made from a distinctive Italian drink and freshly squeezed orange juice, this smooth, pale-pink sherbet is a cooling dessert with a refreshing tang.

NUTRITIONAL INFORMATION

Calories	212	Sugars	.......52g
Protein	.........2g	Fat	...........0g
Carbohydrate	...52g	Saturates	.......0g

 3 hrs   3–5 mins

SERVES 4–6

INGREDIENTS

3–4 large oranges

generous 1 cup superfine sugar

2½ cups water

3 tbsp red Italian bitters, such as Campari

2 extra large egg whites

TO DECORATE

fresh mint leaves

candied citrus peel (optional)

1 Working over a bowl to catch any juice, pare the rind from 3 of the oranges, without removing the bitter white pith. If some of the pith does come off with the rind, use the knife to scrape it off.

2 Put the sugar and water in a pan and stir over low heat until dissolved. Increase the heat and boil for 2 minutes, without stirring. Using a wet pastry brush, brush any crystals down the side of the pan, if necessary.

3 Remove the pan from the heat and pour into a heatproof nonmetallic bowl. Add the orange rind and set aside to steep while the mixture cools to room temperature.

4 Roll the pared oranges back and forth on the counter, pressing down firmly. Cut them in half and squeeze ½ cup juice. If you need more juice, squeeze the remaining orange.

5 When the syrup is cool, stir in the orange juice and bitters. Strain into a container, cover, and chill for at least 30 minutes.

6 Put the mixture in an ice-cream maker and churn for about 15 minutes. Alternatively, follow the instructions on page 1001. Whisk the egg whites in a clean, grease-free bowl until stiff peaks form.

7 Add the egg whites to the ice-cream maker and continue churning for 5 minutes or according to the manufacturer's instructions. Transfer to a shallow, freezerproof container, cover, and freeze for up to 2 months.

8 About 15 minutes before serving, place the ice cream in the refrigerator to soften. Scoop into bowls and serve decorated with mint leaves and candied citrus peel, if wished.

Lemon Granita

Soft and granular, this iced dessert has a sharp, zingy flavor, which is refreshing and ideal for rounding off any rich meal.

NUTRITIONAL INFORMATION

Calories 78	Sugars 20g
Protein 1g	Fat 0g
Carbohydrate ...20g	Saturates 0g

 4 hrs   5 mins

SERVES 4–6

I N G R E D I E N T S

4 large unwaxed lemons

½ cup superfine sugar

3 cups water

fresh mint sprigs, to decorate (optional)

1 Pare 6 strips of rind from 1 of the lemons, then finely grate the remaining rind from the remaining lemons, being very careful not to remove any bitter white pith.

2 Roll the lemons back and forth on the counter, pressing down firmly. Cut each in half and squeeze ½ cup juice. Add the grated rind to the juice. Set aside.

3 Put the pared strips of lemon rind, sugar, and water in a pan and stir over low heat to dissolve the sugar. Increase the heat and boil for 4 minutes, without stirring. Use a wet pastry brush to brush down any spatters on the side of the pan. Remove from the heat, pour into a nonmetallic bowl, and set aside to cool.

4 Remove the strips of rind from the syrup. Stir in the grated rind and juice. Transfer to a shallow metal container, cover, and freeze for up to 3 months.

  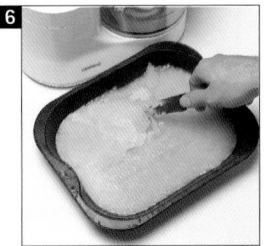

5 Chill serving bowls 30 minutes before serving. To serve, invert the container onto a cutting board. Rinse a cloth in very hot water, wring it out, then rub on the bottom of the container for 15 seconds. Give the container a shake and the mixture should fall out.

6 Break up the granita with a knife and transfer to a food processor. Process until it becomes granular. Serve in the chilled bowls (or in scooped-out lemons). Decorate with mint sprigs, if wished.

VARIATION

Lemon-scented herbs add a unique and unexpected flavor. Add 4 small lemon balm sprigs or 2 lemon thyme sprigs to the syrup in Step 3. Remove and discard with the pared rind in Step 4. Or stir ½ tablespoon finely chopped lemon thyme into the mixture in Step 4.

Espresso Granita

Enjoy this crunchy granita as a cooling mid-morning snack or as a light dessert at the end of an al fresco supper.

NUTRITIONAL INFORMATION

Calories	133	Sugars	........35g
Protein	.........0g	Fat	...........0g
Carbohydrate	...35g	Saturates	.......0g

4 hrs   5 mins

SERVES 4–6

I N G R E D I E N T S

1 cup superfine sugar

2½ cups water

½ tsp vanilla extract

2½ cups very strong espresso coffee, chilled

fresh mint, to decorate

1 Put the sugar in a pan with the water and stir over low heat to dissolve the sugar. Increase the heat and boil for 4 minutes, without stirring. Use a wet pastry brush to brush down any spatters on the side of the pan.

2 Remove the pan from the heat and pour the syrup into a heat-proof nonmetallic bowl. Sit the bowl in the kitchen sink filled with ice water to speed up the cooling process. Stir in the vanilla extract and coffee and leave until completely cool.

3 Transfer to a shallow metal container, cover, and freeze for up to 3 months.

4 Before serving, chill individual serving bowls in the refrigerator.

5 To serve, invert the container onto a cutting board. Rinse a cloth in very hot water, wring it out, then rub on the bottom of the container for 15 seconds. Give the container a sharp shake and the mixture should fall out.

6 Break up the granita with a knife and transfer to a food processor. Process until it becomes grainy and crunchy. Serve in the chilled bowls, decorated with mint.

COOK'S TIP

A very dark, fruit-flavored espresso is the only choice for this Italian speciality. Otherwise the flavor will be marred by the freezing.

Ricotta-Lemon Cheesecake

Italian bakers pride themselves on their baked ricotta cheesecakes, studded with fruit soaked in spirits.

NUTRITIONAL INFORMATION

Calories	188	Sugars	21g
Protein	6g	Fat	8g
Carbohydrate	23g	Saturates	4g

 3¾ hrs   30–40 mins

SERVES 6–8

INGREDIENTS

generous ⅓ cup golden raisins

3 tbsp Marsala or grappa

butter, for greasing

2 tbsp semolina, plus extra for dusting

1½ cups ricotta cheese, drained

3 large egg yolks, beaten

½ cup superfine sugar

3 tbsp lemon juice

2 tbsp candied orange peel, finely chopped

finely grated rind of 2 large lemons

TO DECORATE

confectioners' sugar

fresh mint sprigs

red currants or berries (optional)

1 Soak the golden raisins in the Marsala or grappa in a small bowl for about 30 minutes or until the liquid has been absorbed and the fruit is swollen.

2 Cut out a circle of baking parchment to fit the bottom of a loose-based 8 inch/20 cm round cake pan that is about 2 inches/5 cm deep. Grease the side and base of the pan and line the base. Lightly dust with semolina and tip out the excess.

3 Using a wooden spoon, press the ricotta cheese though a nylon strainer into a bowl. Beat in the egg yolks, sugar, semolina, and lemon juice and continue beating until blended.

4 Fold in the golden raisins, orange peel and lemon rind. Pour into the prepared pan and smooth the surface.

5 Bake the cheesecake in the center of a preheated oven, 350°F/180°C, for 30–40 minutes until firm when you press the top and coming away slightly from the side of the pan.

6 Turn off the oven and open the door. Let the cheesecake cool in the turned-off oven for 2–3 hours. To serve, remove from the pan and transfer to a plate. Sift over a layer of confectioners' sugar from at least 12 inches/30 cm above the cheesecake to dust the top and sides lightly. Decorate with mint and red currants, if wished.

index